Health Economics

Health Economics

By Frank A. Sloan and Chee-Ruey Hsieh

The MIT Press
Cambridge, Massachusetts • London, England

MIT Press books may be purchased at special quantity discounts for business or sales promotional use. For information, please email special_sales@mitpress.mit.edu or write to Special Sales Department, The MIT Press, 55 Hayward Street, Cambridge, MA 02142.

This book was set in Melior and MetaPlus by Toppan Best-set Premedia Limited. Printed and bound in the United States of America.

Library of Congress Cataloging-in-Publication Data

Sloan, Frank A.
Health economics / Frank A. Sloan and Chee-Ruey Hsieh.
p. cm.
Includes bibliographical references and index.
ISBN 978-0-262-01676-6 (hardcover : alk. paper)
1. Medical economics. I. Hsieh, Chee-Ruey. II. Title.
RA410.S55 2012
338.4′73621—dc23
2011032823

10 9 8 7 6 5 4 3 2 1

Brief Table of Contents

Contents

PREFACE

Health economics is a growing research field. The number of textbooks in this field has increased as well. Although there are many choices, it is difficult to find a textbook that exactly fits the needs of a particular class of students—who themselves are highly diverse. Health economics is a field within the more general field of applied microeconomics. But unlike other microeconomic applications, such as public economics, labor economics, and industrial organization, health economics is widely taught outside economics departments, such as in schools of public health (e.g., in hospital administration programs), public policy, business, nursing, pharmacy, and medicine. Moreover, the number of university-based programs in global health has exploded in recent years.

In these programs taught outside economics departments, the demand for health economics stems much more from an inherent interest in health care than from a primary interest in economics. Yet an understanding of economics as applied to health care can be very important to the development of such students' careers and for understanding the workings of health care markets more generally. One of our students recently told us that before taking a course in health economics she had believed, as she was told, that pharmaceutical companies were "bad" for not developing drugs needed by people in low-income countries. After taking the course, she better understood the constraints under which such companies operate, the incentives they face, and proposed public policy solutions for encouraging research and development of drugs for diseases that are highly prevalent in low-income countries—material addressed in this book.

Students have access to lengthy descriptions of health systems from other sources. What is needed—and what we set ourselves to provide—is a book combining economic concepts with empirical evidence to enhance the reader's understanding of how health care institutions and markets function.

This book's goal is to present theoretical and empirical findings as they pertain to decisions individuals make about their health and health care and choices the suppliers of health care services make. It is also intended to serve as a guide for government decision making about resource allocation and policy in the health sector. The theoretical and empirical approaches discussed in this book draw heavily on the more general field of applied microeconomics. At the same time, no analysis of health economics is complete without a description and analysis of important institutional features of health sectors in countries around the world. These institutional features encompass both financing and the provision of personal health care services.

This book makes at least three innovative contributions. First, reflecting the increased interest in global health, we take a global view in the sense that our analysis is not country-specific (i.e., largely focused on the United States) but applies to countries all over the world. Where other books might offer a chapter on international health systems, this book presents far more on global health, yet simultaneously has a substantial amount of empirical evidence on health care services and markets in the United States. Having authors from two distinct parts of the world has helped with the global perspective, for the issues addressed in this book often apply to every country. For example, individuals in every country make similar important decisions about their careers, including whether or not to become a physician, how to select a physician specialty, and the choice of practice location and type of practice. Similarly, pharmaceutical manufacturers in many countries face the same decisions about whether or not to invest in new products and how to set the price and promote these new products.

Second, while health economics has been, in our view appropriately, regarded as a topic in applied microeconomics, this book also takes a macroeconomic perspective. One chapter describes how the health sector operates from the perspective of the macroeconomy. Thus, the book is organized sequentially in a way that has been widely used in economics, beginning with the individual and firm level, then shifting to the market level, and finally moving to a macroeconomic level that views the economy as a whole and considers the role of health and health care within the macroeconomy.

Quality of care has traditionally been viewed as the exclusive domain of medical experts. In the last decade or so, experts from other disciplines have become actively involved in research on health care quality. Economists have joined in such analysis, too. After all, enterprises in all sectors make decisions about levels of quality to offer, just as we all do as consumers. Further, consumer ignorance about quality is a source of market power. We economists are interested in ways to make markets, including health care markets, more transparent. Chapter 7 deals specifically with health care quality.

This book includes three chapters on health systems (chapters 11–13), providing an analysis brand new to this field. In addition, chapter 16 provides an overview of the link between health and economic sectors, also a new contribution. This chapter should interest public policy makers and health industry leaders, as well as college and university students.

Third, this book takes a comprehensive view in the sense that it includes detailed discussions of health and health behaviors as well as health care, nurses as well as physicians, nonlabor inputs in the production of health (i.e., pharmaceuticals) as well as labor-intensive hospitals and physicians' services, and macro- as well as microanalysis.

The book's comprehensiveness can be seen in three other dimensions: space, time, and methods. On the space dimension, this book takes a global perspective. We discuss the role of the consumer in the health sector not only by focusing on demand for personal health care services (chapter 3) but also by focusing on the demand for health behavior (chapter 2) and health insurance (chapter 4). Similarly, our discussion of the supply side of the health care market draws in all major players, including physicians (chapters 5 and 7), hospitals (chapters 6 and 7, which mainly focus on quality of care), nurses (chapter 8), pharmaceutical manufacturers (chapter 9), and private insurers (chapter 10). The discussion of health care systems extends to all possible systems in the world (chapters 11–13).

In addition to the positive economics, which aims to explain why behaviors are observed (what is), we also include two chapters (chapters 14 and 15) on normative economics, methodologies used for making recommendations about policies that should be adopted (what ought to be). We then extend our analysis to the macroeconomics of the health sector (chapter 16) and the future development of the field of health economics (chapter 17).

With regard to the time dimension, we include discussions of some classics in health economics, but we also introduce some of the newest material in the field. Examples of classics are Arrow (1963), Newhouse (1970), Grossman (1972), Pauly and Redisch (1973), Rothschild and Stiglitz (1976), and Manning, Newhouse, Duan, et al. (1987). Although these works were published well before student readers' births and even most professors' births, they raised important issues in the health economics field that have greatly influenced other work and remain highly relevant today. Also, Sloan's long-standing interest in the supply of health care is reflected in the chapters on the supply, organization, and financing of personal health care services.

With regard to analytic methods, we have made a substantial effort to close the gaps among conceptual analysis, empirical evidence, and the institutional features of the health sector. You as readers will be the judges how successful we have been in this respect.

Much of the conceptual analysis reviews and extends material economics majors will have learned in other economics courses. Empirical research is often regarded by students as a bitter pill. "Why do I have to learn the details of studies?" The answer is that you will not need to know the details of specific studies later in life. However, having analytic skills, being able to critically evaluate empirical material, summarize it in capsule form, and draw policy recommendations (private and public) from it, is very important for later life.

Students and professors in economics department often perceive the complex institutional features of the health sector as barriers to entry into this field. By contrast, the theoretical reasoning of economics often is a barrier to students who do not major in economics. This book attempts to reduce these important barriers to entry. It explains some of the complex institutions and provides references for readers who want to learn more. The book presents a theoretical background for non-economics majors that is also designed to serve as a review for majors. One role of applied economics courses is to reinforce concepts introduced in theory courses.

Given the broad potential readership, the book is designed for use by students in undergraduate economic programs, as well by students in various undergraduate and graduate professional programs who have taken few or no prior courses in economics. The book contains many graphs and tables; the use of calculus is minimized.

Overall, this book is designed for a one-semester course in health economics with no economics prerequisites. However, if it is supplemented by readings from other sources, it will be more appropriate for a year-long course. One way to divide the course is on the basis of the traditional paradigm of demand and supply. The book is a bit imbalanced in favor of supply, but there are many more journal articles on demand, especially on demand globally.

For students with an economics background, this book should enhance an understanding of how economic analysis can be applied to various settings in the real world. In the United States, which is a large and extreme case, the health sector now occupies one-sixth of gross domestic product. Other high-income countries are also experiencing substantial relative growth in their health sectors, though at a lower percentage of GDP. Middle-income and some low-income countries have this to look forward to. Professors can use this book to teach applications of economic concepts rather than dwell on minute details of the US health care system or the systems in other countries.

For students in other fields of concentration, this book can be used in various settings to introduce economics concepts as they apply to health and health care and to read up-to-date summaries of research findings and issues in health economics without spending substantial effort on learning the basic tools of economic analysis or having to skip learning some highly relevant concepts altogether.

Reflecting that health economics began in the United States more than half a century ago, much of the material in this book is based on US studies. However, in recent years an increasing share of health economics studies has come from other countries. As communications technology has improved, global awareness of issues particular to middle- and low-income countries has increased, as has research on health care issues specific to these countries. Although constrained by what remains a relative lack of studies using data from these countries, this book incorporates much of the health economics research from low- and middle-income countries that currently exists. We hope that publication of this book with its explanations and methodological approaches will help promote health economics research in many understudied countries.

References

Arrow, K. J. 1963. Uncertainty and the Welfare Economics of Medical Care. *American Economic Review* 53 (5): 941–973.

Grossman, M. 1972. *The Demand for Health: A Theoretical and Empirical Investigation.* New York: Columbia University Press.

Manning, W. G., J. P. Newhouse, N. Duan, et al. 1987. Health Insurance and the Demand for Medical Care: Evidence from a Randomized Experiment. *American Economic Review* 77 (3): 251–277.

Newhouse, J. P. 1970. Toward a Theory of Nonprofit Institutions: An Economic Model of a Hospital. *American Economic Review* 60 (1): 64–74.

Pauly, M., and M. Redisch. 1973. Not-for-Profit Hospital as a Physicians' Cooperative. *American Economic Review* 63 (1): 87–99.

Rothschild, M., and J. Stiglitz. 1976. Equilibrium in Competitive Insurance Markets: An Essay on the Economics of Imperfect Information. *Quarterly Journal of Economics* 90 (4): 629–649.

Acknowledgments

We thank Zhiyu (Felix) Feng, now a PhD student at Duke University, for help in formulating many of the problems at the end of the chapters. We thank Ming-Hsein Wu, Economics Institute Academia Sinica, for his excellent assistance in processing the data and preparing the figures and tables for this book. We thank Linda Tally, Duke University Department of Economics, and Megan Buckner, Duke University Center for Health Policy, for research and editorial assistance, and Kerri Lavallee, a student at Cornell University who worked at Duke University during the summer of 2010, for help with the references. John Covell, economics editor at the MIT Press, provided advice and encouragement from the original conception of this book to the finish.

Last but not least, we thank our wives for making every day worthwhile.

Frank A. Sloan
Chee-Ruey Hsieh

INTRODUCTION AND OVERVIEW

Health economics is a growing field within the discipline of economics. Health economics deals with issues related to the financing and delivery of health services and the role of such services and other personal decisions in contributing to personal health.

Unlike the opening of department stores and car dealerships, there is no grand opening for a new field in a discipline such as economics. As an academic field of inquiry, there was virtually no health economics research before 1945, and relatively little after that date until the 1960s (Phelps 1995; Fuchs 1996). During the early 1960s, two Nobel laureates published papers that had an important impact on the development of health economics as a field. One was the seminal paper by Kenneth Arrow emphasizing the role of uncertainty in determining key institutional features of the health sector (Arrow 1963). The other was Gary Becker's treatise on human capital, which provided the theoretical foundation for economists to analyze the role of health care in the production of health (Becker 1964). Since the early 1960s, health economics has enjoyed several decades of remarkable growth, and the future of this field looks extremely bright as well (Fuchs 2000).

This chapter introduces some key economic concepts and describes the content of the book.

1.1 Health Economics as a Field of Inquiry

The Importance of Health Economics

Everyone is affected by health and personal health care services in important ways. Your health affects your enjoyment of life, your ability to contribute to your family's well-being and to be a productive member of the workforce, and, earlier in life, your ability to be productive in school. Most people receive at least one personal health care service annually. By midlife, and certainly later in life, the consumption of personal health services tends to be much higher than for younger adults. When employed, you probably will pay taxes that finance health insurance and personal health care services. Given the importance of the health sector in many countries, many of you will eventually find employment in an organization involved in health care provision or financing, or be involved with health care as an attorney, a business leader, or a government official.

The impact of health economics is felt not only within the discipline of economics but also outside the field. Health economists are as likely to be cited in scholarly journals and other publications outside the economics literature, such as in medical, public health, and public policy books and journals, as they are in economics publications. Fuchs (2000) attributed this phenomenon to the "two-hat" nature of health economics. On the one hand, health economics is a behavioral science: high-quality research in this field advances the discipline of economics in general and, more broadly, all the social science disciplines. On the other hand, health economics provides valuable insights into and empirical evidence on important health policy issues and health services research, a general field in which experts in clinical practice and public health are engaged.

Judged by their participation in the public policy arena and the media, health economists have had an important presence. Of course, our advice has been disregarded more often than it has been followed. Practical political considerations often weigh much more heavily in actual public policy decisions than they do in economists' policy recommendations. Also, new public policy directions are much more likely to be undertaken when there is a crisis. At other times, inertia prevents the adoption of even sound new ideas.

Health economists investigate positive issues—empirical relationships among variables as they are—more frequently than they do normative issues, or policy recommendations about how resources *should* be allocated and distributed. Examples of research on positive issues are inquiries into the response of demand to changes in the price of personal health care services, individuals' choices among several health insurance plans, the decision to start or stop smoking, the decisions pharmaceutical manufacturers make about investments in research and development, determinants of physicians' fees, and hospitals' price and output decisions.

People, firms, and health care organizations are motivated by incentives. Not all incentives that affect decisions are financial, but many are. To achieve socially desirable outcomes, incentives must be structured appropriately. In most markets in most economies, prices provide inducements for those levels of outputs of goods and services to be supplied that are most desired, given the resources available to the party making the decision. Governments are largely on the sidelines, policing abuses and imposing taxes to raise revenue, but in general, governments do not play an active role in resource allocation in most markets. As explained below, however, government intervention is more common in health care than in most sectors.

THE GROWTH OF HEALTH ECONOMICS

There is no common metric to measure the growth of a research field. Two alternative measures are among those that can be used to gauge the tremendous expansion of the field of health economics in the past several decades. First, the number of PhDs awarded annually in health economics has increased rapidly over time. For example, in the United States, the number of dissertations on health economics increased elevenfold from 1965 to 1994. By contrast, the number of dissertations in all fields of economics increased only 2.5 times during the same period (Fuchs 1996). A similar pattern is evident from lists of doctoral dissertations in economics published in the *Journal of Economic Literature,* which reveals a high rate of growth of health economics in terms of the number of dissertations completed during 1991–2008 (fig. 1.1).

Second, by a number of metrics, the supply of health economists and of health economics, measured in terms of books and papers published, public testimony, editorials, and other media reports, has increased. Growth in the supply of PhDs in health economics has enabled many professional schools, government agencies, and research institutes to add health economists to their staffs, which in turn has increased the capacity for health economics research and policy development. The share of National Bureau of Economic Research (NBER) working papers devoted to health economics has grown from 1.2 percent in 1986 to 12 percent in 2008 (fig. 1.1). The number of professional journals devoted to health economics has also increased. The first professional journal in the field, the *Journal of Health Economics*, began in 1982. By 2006 there were seven journals specializing in health economics (table 1.1). Particularly in view of the growth of both real expenditures on personal health care services worldwide and the growing number and size of public health programs, it seems reasonable to expect these trends to continue.

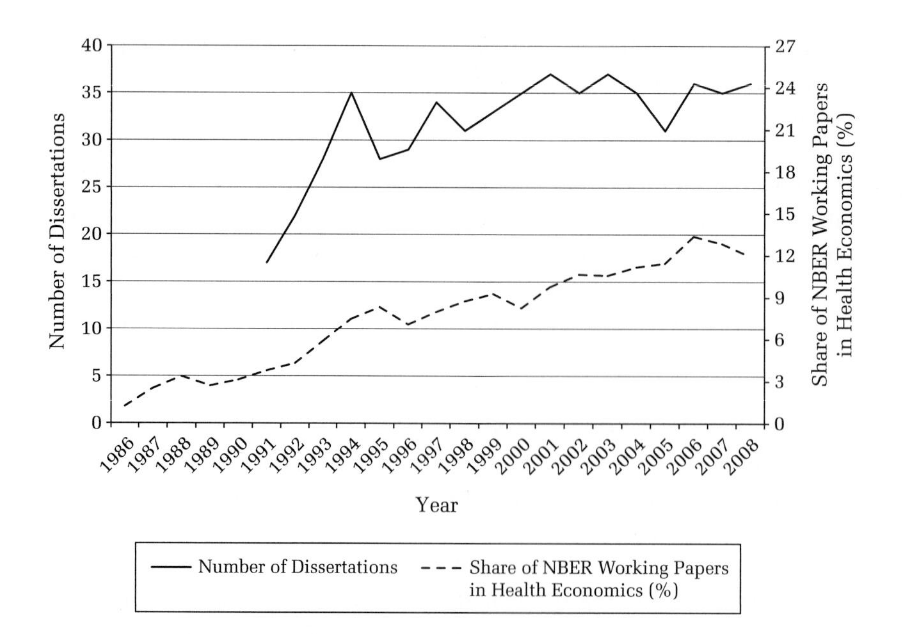

Figure 1.1
Trends in Health Economics Research.
Sources: Counts from the *Journal of Economic Literature*, 1991–2008, and National Bureau of Economic Research Working Papers, 1986–2008.

Table 1.1
Professional Journals in the Field of Health Economics

Name of Journal	Founding Year	Articles Published in 2009
Journal of Health Economics	1982	91
Health Economics	1992	107
Journal of Mental Health Policy and Economics	1998	16
European Journal of Health Economics	2001	43
International Journal of Health Care Finance and Economics	2001	24
Applied Health Economics and Health Policy	2002	22
Health Economics, Policy and Law	2006	24
Total		327

1.2 FACTORS ACCOUNTING FOR THE GROWTH OF HEALTH ECONOMICS

Two external factors account for the dramatic growth of health economics as a field: (1) global health and longevity gains and (2) the expansion of health sectors throughout the world.

IMPROVEMENTS IN HEALTH AND LONGEVITY

Because of their effect on individuals' productivity and enjoyment of life, improvements in health and longevity are closely related to overall improvements in well-being. One study argues that between 1950 and 2000, improvements in health in the United States were as valuable as all other sources of economic growth combined (Nordhaus 2005). Medical care was unquestionably far more productive in the year 2000 than it was a century earlier. However, medical care delivery and technological advances in diagnostic and therapeutic procedures are not the only source of health improvements over the past century. Health behaviors and environmental factors, including improvements in sanitation and shifts in the occupational structure and those attributable to urbanization, have certainly played a role.

Health and longevity have improved dramatically in most countries around the world, especially in the middle-income and the most affluent countries. Oeppen and Vaupel (2002) documented secular trends in longevity in countries with the highest longevity. In these countries, female life expectancy at birth increased by 40 years in the 160 years preceding the start of the twenty-first century. This increase amounts to a rise in longevity of three months *per year* over an extended time period, 1840–2000. More recently, gains in life expectancy have also been observed in less affluent countries. For example, the longevity gain between 1960 and 2005 in the United States was 7.9 years. By contrast, the gain in life expectancy at birth in China was 35.5 years during the same period (fig. 1.2).

More specifically, 149 out of 156 countries worldwide experienced substantial longevity gains during 1960–2005 (fig. 1.3). Most countries experienced longevity gains in the range of 5 to 10 years. Eight countries, including China, Indonesia, and Vietnam, realized a gain of more than 25 years in life expectancy at birth during the 45-year period. Overall, the relationship between the magnitude of longevity gains and income level is an inverse U shape. Middle-income countries tended to experience greater gains than did low- and high-income countries (table 1.2).

Even though many countries have experienced improvements in population health and longevity, appreciable disparities remain. A widely used if imperfect measure of a country's economic well-being is the gross domestic product (GDP) per capita of population. Underlying the comparison of per capita GDP and longevity is the notion that higher income leads to better health. Of course, causality runs in the opposite direction as well: better health leads to higher income. Although

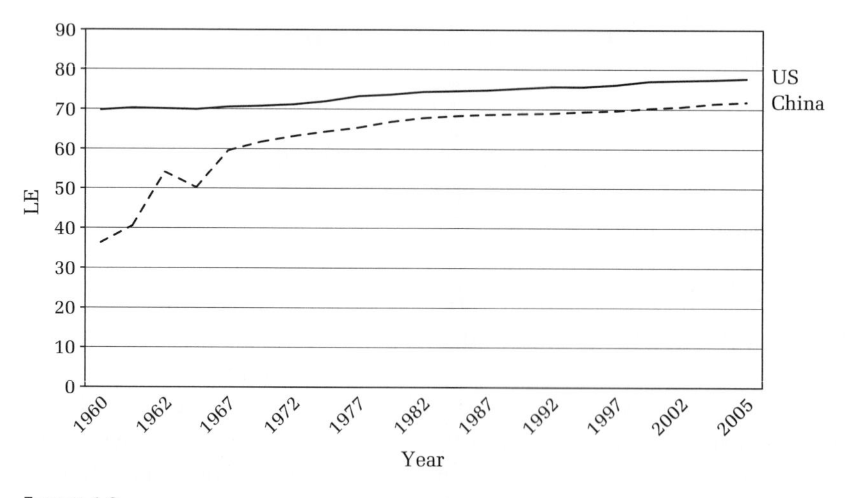

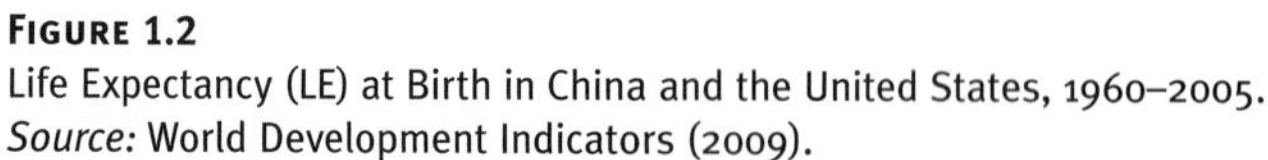

Figure 1.2
Life Expectancy (LE) at Birth in China and the United States, 1960–2005.
Source: World Development Indicators (2009).

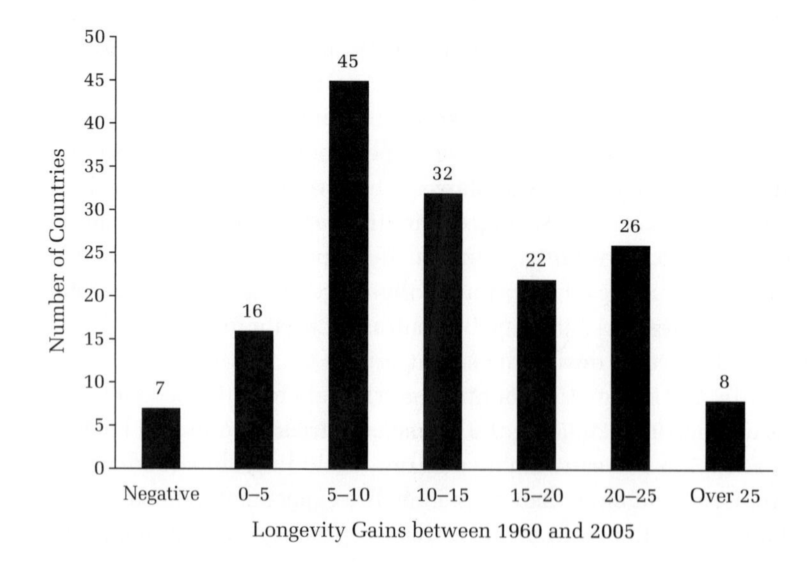

Figure 1.3
Global Distribution of Longevity Gains.
Note: We exclude countries with missing data on longevity gains. The figure includes data from 156 countries.
Source: World Bank Group, World Development Indicators (2007).

Table 1.2
Global Distribution of Longevity Gains between 1960 and 2005 by Income Level of Country

	Longevity Gains between 1960 and 2005			
Income Group	Mean	Standard Deviation	Minimum	Maximum
High-income countries	12.25	6.11	5.56	27.86
High middle-income countries	13.50	7.20	0.14	24.86
Other middle-income countries	16.32	8.25	1.06	35.51
Low-income countries	11.46	7.05	0.78	24.41
All countries	13.37	7.36	0.14	35.51

Note: Data on 149 countries are included in this table. High-income countries are those with a per capita GDP greater than the 75th percentile of world income distribution. High middle-income countries have a per capita GDP between the 75th percentile and the 50the percentile. Other middle-income countries are those with a per capita GDP in the 25th to 50th percentile range of the world's income distribution. Low-income countries have a per capita GDP less than the 25th percentile of the world income distribution.
Sources: World Bank Group, World Development Indicators (2007).

we draw a conceptual distinction here, in practice, the relationship truly works in both directions.

Countries with higher national income as reflected in their per capita GDP tend to have a higher life expectancy at birth (fig 1.4). The relationship is nonlinear in that the slope depicting the relationship between per capita GDP and life expectancy is much higher at levels below about $4,000 per capita GDP than at levels above this. Purchasing power parity (PPP) is a measure used to compare the equivalent purchasing power of a dollar in various countries and is a more accurate measure for this purpose than are exchange rates of countries' currencies.

The circles in figure 1.4 represent a country's population size. Thus, the circles are relatively large for China, India, and the United States. When the circle for a country is above the curve depicting the average relationship between longevity and per capita GDP, the country's life expectancy is above average, given the country's per capita GDP, and conversely. Thus, in 2000, Japan, Italy, Spain, and Mexico had a higher life expectancy than one would expect based on each country's output per person. Conversely, the United States, and especially Russia and the Union of South Africa, were below average. China and India were about at the average for their per capita GDPs.

The poor performance of South Africa can be attributed in part to large differences in income between the country's black majority and white minority. Inequality in health within countries is by no means unique to South Africa but typifies several European countries (see, e.g., Mackenbach, Stirbu, Roskam, et al.

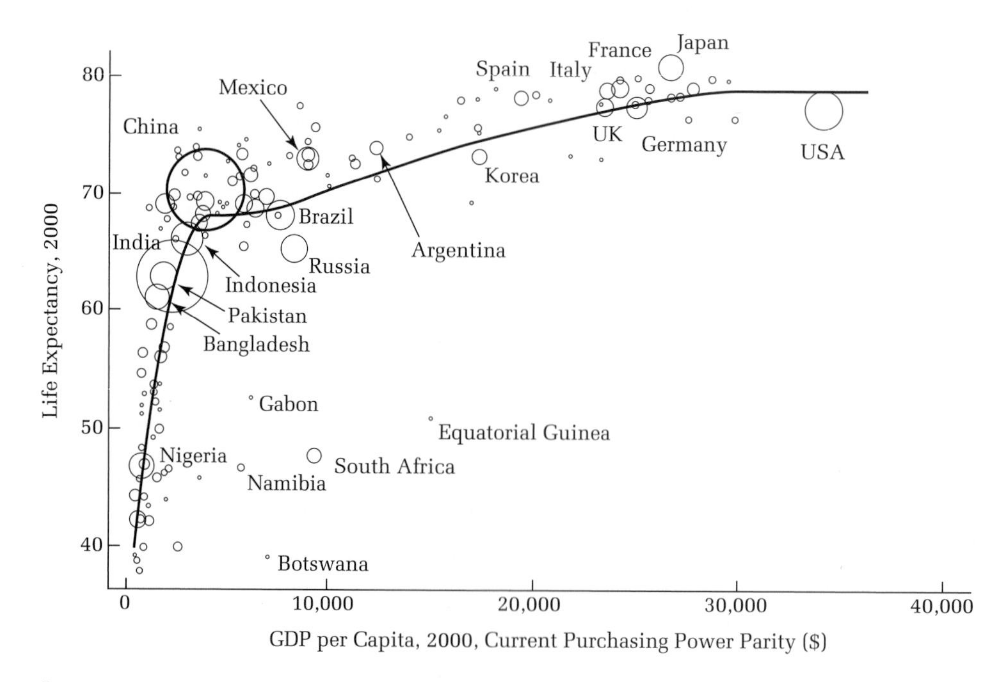

FIGURE 1.4
Relationship between Life Expectancy at Birth and Gross Domestic Product per Capita.
Sources: Deaton (2003) and Cutler, Deaton, and Lleras-Muney (2006).

2008) and the United States as well. Huge disparities in health among countries globally are a major concern, as are disparities within countries.

Several factors underlie the relationship between per capita GDP and longevity. Among these are improvements in sanitation, better nutrition, and greater availability of medical care (Cutler, Deaton, and Lleras-Muney 2006). In sum, two stylized facts are the major global improvements in population health and longevity, coupled with substantial variation in population health within and among countries. These stylized facts raise several important issues for health economists to explore. For example, to what extent does the provision of personal health services contribute to improved population health? And how much do the organization and financing of health services contribute to variation in productivity of personal health care services, measured in terms of various population health indicators?

EXPANSION OF HEALTH SECTORS

The most widely used quantitative indicator of a country's national output is its GDP, which measures the market value of all final goods and services produced in a country in a given year. In essence, GDP is a measure of the size of the economic

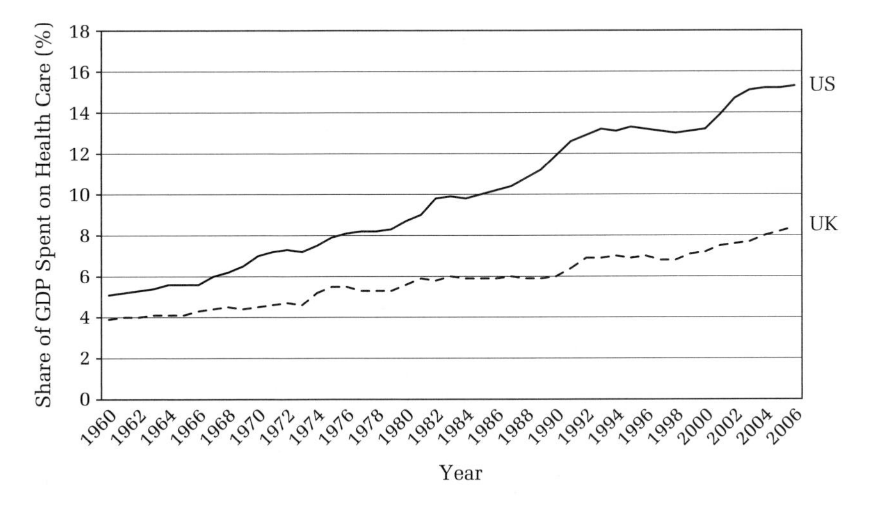

FIGURE 1.5
Total Expenditures on Health Care as Percent of Gross Domestic Product, 1960–2006.
Source: OECD, *Health Data* (2008).

pie. A country's national output can be allocated to various activities, such as housing, food, transportation, health care, education, and national defense. Thus, the share of GDP allocated to health care is a measure of the size of a country's health sector relative to its national output.

During the past several decades, many countries have experienced major expansions in the size of their health sectors, as measured by the share of GDP spent on health care. In the United States, the share of GDP allocated to health care tripled over 4.5 decades, from 5.1 percent in 1960 to 15.3 percent in 2006. During the same period, this share increased from 3.9 percent to 8.4 percent in the United Kingdom (fig. 1.5). Although different countries experienced a similar positive trend in health care spending, there are substantial variations among countries. In 2006, the share of GDP allocated to health care ranged from 1.9 percent to 17.7 percent for 175 countries globally (table 1.3).

A country's share of GDP allocated to health care is positively associated with its income level, suggesting that health care is a "normal good" (the term used in economics to mean that consumption of the good rises with increases in income). People are willing to pay more relative to other consumption goods to be in good health when they become more affluent (Hall and Jones 2007). Consequently, economic growth is an important determinant of health sector size. In addition to income, several other factors, among them technological change in medicine, population aging, and the implementation of health insurance, have contributed to the growth in real health care spending, where "real" refers to spending relative to the prices of all goods and services.

TABLE 1.3
Global Distribution of GDP Share Spent on Health Care by Income Level of Country

	Share of GDP Spent on Health Care in 2006 (%)			
Income Group	Mean	Standard Deviation	Minimum	Maximum
High-income countries	7.84	2.78	2.20	15.30
High middle-income countries	6.34	2.17	2.10	14.40
Other Middle-income countries	5.74	2.15	2.00	13.30
Low-income countries	5.60	2.10	2.20	17.70
All countries	6.38	2.46	2.00	15.30

Note: A total of 168 countries are included in this table. See table 1.2 for a description of income categories.
Sources: World Bank Group, World Development Indicators (2009).

As the health sector has expanded, there has been growing public concern about both efficiency and equity in health services delivery. *Efficiency* refers to how society uses its given resources to maximize the welfare of its members; *equity* refers to how society distributes its goods and services among its members. Concerns about efficiency and equity in any sector raise some major questions: Which, how, and for whom will health services be produced? That is, which health services are to be produced, and in what quantities? How, utilizing which technologies, are health services to be produced? Who will use those health services that are produced? In particular, technological change in medicine often increases the gap between what medicine can do and what it is economically feasible to do (Fuchs 2000).

1.3 IMPORTANT INSTITUTIONAL FEATURES OF HEALTH CARE

While the health care sectors of countries have unique features, there are also many similarities. Following are some of the similarities. First, the sectors' outputs are consumed by individuals. These outputs tend to rival in consumption. This means, for example, if one of us receives an x-ray, that same x-ray cannot be consumed by someone else. By contrast, some goods, such as national defense and public health, are *public goods*. These goods are not rival in that consumption of the safety from a strong national defense or public health policy by one individual does not reduce the potential for others to consume the goods. The health sector encompasses some public goods, in particular those deriving from biomedical research and public health programs. However, in terms of dollar value, personal health care services dominate. Second, as with the vast majority of other goods and services, decision making about the use of personal health care services is highly decentralized. Each day, hundreds of millions of individuals around the world make decisions about the use of health services.

Third, suppliers of health services respond to financial and nonfinancial incentives as do suppliers of other goods and services. Just because a country's health system is government-run does not mean that individual suppliers are not responsive to incentives. Physicians paid a fixed salary by the government are likely to take account of the fact that an extra hour of work is not likely to result in higher compensation in deciding whether or not they will stay late to serve those patients in the waiting room after official closing time.

Given these similarities, many aspects of health economics are amenable to study using the same methods that microeconomists use to study behaviors in other markets. Health economics is a subfield of applied microeconomics. Students of health economics are helped by courses in labor economics, public economics, industrial organization, and econometrics, and conversely, the study of health economics can be helpful for students in the other applied microeconomic fields.

On the other hand, health care also has more unique features, more than we can consider here. These features are not necessarily unique to health care, but taken in combination, they do account for ways in which health care services are financed and delivered. Three important features are health insurance, externalities, and asymmetric information.

HEALTH INSURANCE

The use of personal health care services is to some extent random because the onset of illness is random. As a result, risk-averse individuals, presumably most persons, seek to reduce expenditure risk by obtaining health insurance. Because health insurance reduces personal expenditure risk, owing to the stochastic nature of illness, risk-averse people are better off with insurance. Both public and private insurance provide protection against expenditure risk.

While insurance improves a person's well-being by providing protection against loss in the event of illness, by lowering the price individuals pay out of pocket for personal health care services, consumption decisions are distorted. When there are no externalities, a topic to be discussed below, consumption of any good or service is optimal when use is at the level at which the marginal value of such services to consumers equals the marginal cost of supplying the good or service. However, health insurance lowers the out-of-pocket price, which in turn increases the quantity of personal health services demanded—a phenomenon called *moral hazard*. Given the reduced price to consumers and the resulting increase in the quantity of services demanded, use may increase to a level at which marginal cost is far above the marginal value of such services to consumers. If so, there is a misallocation of resources in that the value consumers place on the service is less than the cost of producing another unit of the service.

To see this, imagine that medical care is provided to consumers at a zero out-of-pocket price. Then consumers will use medical care up to the point at which the last unit of service consumed has a zero value. But the cost of producing that last unit of service is likely to be far more than zero. Having output at a level at which the marginal valuation to consumers is less than the marginal cost represents a misallocation of scarce resources. Consumer well-being from available scarce resources could be increased by decreasing the output of the service.

Various ways of reducing moral hazard are employed by both government and private organizations. One alternative is to limit the supply of health resources. Another is to monitor the utilization of personal health care services, disallowing insurance coverage for services considered to be of low marginal value. Still another is to increase cost sharing, that is, the share of the payment to the provider that the insured consumer bears. While increased cost sharing increases expenditure risk, it reduces moral hazard. Some have argued that individuals in the United States are overinsured in that at the prevailing rates of insurance coverage, the societal loss in well-being attributable to moral hazard exceeds the gains in well-being that the coverage provides in terms of expenditure risk protection (see, e.g., Feldstein 1973), but there is no consensus on this issue.

Another problem, largely limited to private health insurance markets, is *adverse selection*. Adverse selection may arise when consumers know more about their own health risks, and hence their future use of personal health care services, than insurers do. Suppose you were just told by a doctor that you have cancer. Or even without going to a doctor, you feel pain in your chest when walking up a couple of flights of steps. Your first thoughts are likely to be about your health and your own longevity. But your second thought is likely to be about your health insurance coverage. If you can, you would like to purchase a comprehensive insurance policy covering large health care expenses. By contrast, if you are a jogger and a nonsmoker, you may figure that you will remain healthy, and be more interested in purchasing jogging shoes, memberships in health clubs, and bicycles than in purchasing comprehensive health insurance policies.

Adverse selection can lead consumers who are healthier to eschew high-cost, complete health insurance coverage or eschew coverage altogether, leaving the market to individuals at higher risk for adverse health outcomes. In theory, adverse selection can lead to the unraveling of insurance markets (Rothschild and Stiglitz 1976). Not knowing each insured's health risk, insurers frequently do not charge sufficiently different premiums to high- versus low-risk individuals. Thus, for any premium that allows the insurer to break even, insurance is an attractive purchase for the high- but not the low-risk individuals. Thus, fewer low-risk persons demand insurance.

To break even on the remaining persons it covers, the insurer must raise premiums. But at the higher premium, some people who bought insurance before decide against buying insurance. These are the lower-risk of the higher-risk persons who purchased insurance last year. Again, with the sicker pool of insureds, the insurer finds that its premium income is insufficient. So it raises premiums again. The healthier persons in this group drop out of the insurance market. This process of unraveling continues until only a very few high-risk individuals remain in the market. All the rest of the population is made worse off because they have lost a mechanism for reducing expenditure risk at premiums that are appropriate for the health expenditures they are likely to incur.

There are several approaches for dealing with adverse selection. One is to eliminate a choice of insurance plans entirely, which occurs when government provides a single insurance plan. Lack of choice, however, may be welfare reducing in its own right in that less risk-averse persons would purchase less comprehensive policies than would more risk-averse individuals if choices were available.

Another option is to develop and implement improved methods of predicting each individual's future use of personal health care services. In this way, the information asymmetry between buyers and sellers of insurance is reduced. This is called *risk adjustment*.

Externalities and Government Intervention in Health Care Services Provision

For the vast majority of goods and services, including many personal health services, the benefit from consumption accrues exclusively to the individual consuming the good or service and his or her family. However, for an important subset of health care services, the benefits of consumption extend beyond the household. These *externalities* in consumption have important implications for how health care is financed and produced.

When making private decisions, consumers may not consider the effects of their consumption decisions on others. This may be true in deciding whether or not to obtain a vaccination to prevent an infectious disease—*pure health externalities* for which consumption by person A has a direct potential effect on whether or not person B contracts the disease. If you obtain a vaccination before you travel, you not only protect yourself against the disease, you protect the passengers who sit next to you on a bus, train, or airplane as well. Particularly since the passengers are likely to be strangers, you will probably not consider the effect on these strangers when you decide whether or not to get the shot. However, from society's vantage point, the benefit to strangers is consequential. If people consider only benefits to themselves, their consumption of personal health care services that have health externalities will be suboptimal, that is, too low. Health externalities provide the rationale for a wide variety of public health programs, ranging from malaria eradication to the provision of flu vaccines to adults and several different types of immunizations to children.

A second type is a *financial externality.* When person C smokes and subsequently contracts lung cancer, which is not contagious, because of risk pooling in the form of health insurance, person D may end up paying for person C's treatment for this cancer. To make smokers take account of financial externalities, governments may impose an excise tax on cigarettes.

A third type of externality is more subtle and falls in the category of consumption externalities. In most countries, there is a broad consensus that each person should have access to at least minimal levels of personal health care services, just as there is a widespread consensus that young children should be able to consume milk. If person E sees person F collapse on the street, for purely altruistic reasons person E may feel better if person F has immediate access to an ambulance and emergency care. The ambulance service and emergency care are *merit wants*—goods or services that generate externalities in consumption only because people think that in a just society, people should be able to consume the good or service. For this reason, to continue our example, the government may supply ambulance services or emergency care for all or for persons with low income at a price well below the cost of production. Absent government intervention, output levels of merit wants may be too low and access of the poor to such goods and services too limited.

Still another type of externality relates to *public goods.* As briefly described above, a good is public if it is nonrival in consumption. That is, consumption by person G does not exclude consumption by person H of that same good or service. For example, if G receives a physician visit, that same visit cannot be provided to H. But the use of scientific findings in treating G in no way limits H's benefit from these same findings. The public good feature of biomedical research provides the rationale for public subsidies and sometimes the public provision of such research (research conducted in government laboratories). It also provides the rationale for granting patent protection to firms engaged in such research as an alternative to government subsidy.

If there are no externalities and the good or service is rival in consumption, consumer information is good, and there are no scale economies in production, an important conclusion of economics is that competitive forces lead to provision of the good or service at socially optimal output levels. Further, under competition, socially optimal levels of quality are provided at the level at which consumers' marginal willingness to pay for additional quality equals the marginal cost of supplying it. However, in markets in which competition does not prevail but rather suppliers are able to exercise market power, price may greatly exceed marginal cost, and as a result, output will be below its socially optimal level. Among the remedies for market power is *antitrust policy.*

Many countries have limited the role of competition by implementing the public provision of services or by leaving the market in private hands but limiting private sellers' ability to set product prices by, for example, implementing price controls or fixing prices for the health care goods and services that government purchases. Under such circumstances, competitive forces cannot operate to produce socially desirable outcomes. Government intervention may be justified when the preconditions required for competitive forces to yield socially desirable outcomes do not prevail, for example when consumer information is poor, there are barriers to entry, or there are economies of scale in production.

Asymmetric Information between Consumers and Suppliers of Health Care and the Institutional Responses

Asymmetric information is present when one party to a transaction has information pertinent to the transaction that another party does not possess. For example, a company executive is likely to have information on an imminent company announcement about the profit it earned last quarter. This announcement is likely to be followed by changes in demand for the company's stock, an increase if the news is good and a decrease if the news is bad. Absent rules or regulations to prohibit this, the executive might buy or sell his stock in the company depending on the nature of the news to be announced. In this example, the executive has information relevant to a stock transaction that traders on the outside do not have. Adverse selection in insurance markets is another example. Here the insurance purchaser has private information that the insurer does not have.

A key attribute of health care is that the supplier of health care services often, if not typically, possesses information about a disease or its treatment that the patient does not have. Such asymmetric information is a potentially important source of market power for physicians.

A prerequisite for competition to prevail in a market is that consumers have good information. Health care consumers may lack sufficient information to make informed choices. One response of an uninformed consumer is to seek the advice of a physician. In fact, one of the fundamental services physicians supply to their patients is conveying information. Ideally, physicians would provide unbiased information to their patients. But a difficulty arises under conditions of asymmetric knowledge, for physicians may exploit the information asymmetry.

Society has designed a wide variety of ways to deal with the information asymmetry. *Professional norms* are designed to combat any tendency physicians might have to take advantage of their superior information. Medical school graduates take the Hippocratic oath, in which the oath taker promises to act in his or her patients' interests. While acting in patients' interest is an ideal, in practice, professional norms operate imperfectly because the strong financial motives to supply profitable services may lead some physicians to take advantage of patients by exploiting the information asymmetry. Furthermore, what is in the patient's interest may not be very clear given uncertainties in patients' diagnoses and in the effects of various therapies. Not only is the effect of therapy often uncertain, there is often substantial heterogeneity in the effects of treatments. Owing to genetic and other factors, the same drug has different effects in different individuals. A surgical procedure likewise can differ in effectiveness, and the underlying probability of adverse effects of surgery is likely to differ among individuals as well, both because patients differ and because surgeons differ in their ability to perform the procedure.

Aside from implementing professional norms, which largely rely on the self-regulation of behavior, countries have implemented public and quasi-public regulations to cope with asymmetric information, as well as private institutional arrangements. Professional and institutional licensure and certification fall in the former category. Physicians must be licensed before they can practice medicine. Institutional licensure includes licensure of hospitals. Laws allow for the formation of private nonprofit hospitals, organizations that are not organized for the purpose of maximizing profits for shareholders (Sloan 2000).

In recent years, increasing emphasis has been placed on educating health care consumers about their options. This has taken the form of direct-to-consumer advertising of prescription drugs (Berndt and Donohue 2008) and report cards on the performance of hospitals (Gowrisankaran 2008). Even though information provision also has potential pitfalls—for example, direct-to-consumer advertising may give the seller more market power—such advertising may also help consumers know more about their treatment options.

Physicians become knowledgeable about the efficacy of treatments by reading articles in professional journals, enrolling in continuing medical education programs, listening to sales representatives of pharmaceutical manufacturers, and discussing treatments with colleagues. Given the rapid rate of technological change, evidence on efficacy is always changing. Thus, physicians, other health professionals, and health care administrators use various approaches to acquire knowledge about recent technological developments.

1.4 Government Intervention in Health Care Markets

The World Health Organization (WHO) at one time ranked countries' health systems in terms of their performance. These rankings reflected the performance of the public sector of the countries in health care as well as other factors. The WHO

TABLE 1.4
Ranking of Performance of Health Care Systems, 2000

Top 10	Rank 30–39	Bottom 10
France	Canada	Angola
Italy	Finland	Zambia
San Marino	Australia	Lesotho
Andorra	Chile	Mozambique
Malta	Denmark	Malawi
Singapore	Dominica	Liberia
Spain	Costa Rica	Nigeria
Oman	United States of America	Democratic Republic of Congo
Austria	Slovenia	Central African Republic
Japan	Cuba	Myanmar

Source: World Health Organization (http://www.photius.com/healthranks.html, accessed July 27, 2010).

indicates that it no longer produces a ranking table because of the complexity of the task.

Although individual rankings can be debated, it is noteworthy that France, Italy, Spain, Austria, and Japan were in the top ten of the WHO's ranking in 2000. The United States ranked thirty-seventh, which was about the same ranking as Canada, Finland, Australia, Slovenia, and Cuba. In the bottom ten, ranked 181–190, were low-income countries, mainly in Africa.

Government's Roles in Achieving an Equitable Distribution of Resources

Governments throughout the world have been more active in health care than in most other sectors of their economies. High levels of government activity in health care have created substantial demand for policy analysis by health economists.

A major reason for government intervention is redistributive. The underlying notion is that in just societies, people should have minimal access to certain goods, irrespective of their ability to pay. Historically, such goods were provided by private philanthropy, but apparently in insufficient amounts, providing a rationale for government intervention. Absent government intervention, market forces may lead to a situation in which less affluent populations and populations disadvantaged for other reasons, such as geographic remoteness of locations at which health services are delivered relative to where persons work and live, may have inadequate access to personal health care services. Governments have a choice whether or not to transfer resources to disadvantaged populations in the form of income or in kind transfers.

Economists typically prefer income transfers, leaving it to the recipients of the transfers to allocate the subsidies in a way that maximizes well-being from the household's perspective (Currie and Gahvari 2008). However, for merit wants, societies clearly prefer to redistribute in kind out of a concern that households will underconsume the very goods and services to which societies attach the highest priority. Income transfers may be allocated to other goods and services instead of physician visits and other types of personal health care services.

Countries differ in how in-kind transfers are made. Many countries mainly rely on direct provision through public clinics and hospitals. Some high-income countries, including the UK, Denmark, Norway, and New Zealand, as well as low-income countries, such as those in sub-Saharan Africa, rely on direct government provision of personal health care services. Governments subsidize the production of personal health care services in the form of free clinics and hospitals.

In countries with limited resources, there may be few government-sponsored facilities, and the few that exist may be geographically remote from much of the country's population. Because of the high cost, many persons may obtain care only after their diseases have reached an advanced stage, if they receive care at all. Facilities receive budgetary allocations from the government on a regular basis. The limiting factors are the facilities' budgets and physical plant. Higher-income persons may obtain care from private providers who are not subsidized by the government.

Some countries have single-payer government financing, combined with private provision. Health insurance is provided as social insurance. In these countries, insurance coverage is universal or nearly so and provided without regard to a person's ability to pay. Examples of countries with single-payer systems are Canada and Taiwan. In Germany, which has had a social insurance system for health care since the late nineteenth century, coverage of employees below a certain monthly salary is mandated by law. Although such health insurance is provided by private sick funds, coverage attributes are subject to strict government oversight and regulation. For persons not employed, there is welfare-based insurance coverage similar to Medicaid in the United States.

A third alternative is the private provision of insurance, as is common in the United States. However, even in the United States, about half of expenditures on personal health services are financed by public funds.

THE EQUITY-EFFICIENCY QUANDARY AND GOVERNMENT'S ROLE

While there is a broad consensus that some redistribution of resources is appropriate, there is no consensus on either the proper amount of redistribution or how this should be accomplished. Also, in seeking to redistribute resources, there has been an unfortunate tendency on the part of some to view public policies as almost entirely redistributional and to ignore the effects of public policies on health care resource allocation.

Public policies can also have important potential effects on incentives individuals face as health care consumers, as household decision makers more generally, and as suppliers of health care. Before defining the economic concept of *efficiency* more precisely, we supply a few examples to help set the stage.

To ensure that poor families have access to personal health care services, from the standpoint of equity, it may be desirable to provide such families with a government-paid health insurance policy. However, if one has to be poor to receive this benefit, the cost to a family of engaging in work for pay can become prohibitively high. Not only is the publicly financed health insurance policy potentially lost but the family faces the prospect of paying for health insurance privately, clearly a disincentive to engage in market work.

There is a widespread misperception among some that the government can cut fees to physicians by a given percentage without there being any effect on the supply of physicians' services, or cut prices of pharmaceutical products by this amount or more without having an effect on pharmaceutical research and development. But as fees decrease, physicians may reduce the time they supply to the market, and, for private funds to be allocated to investments in research and development, pharmaceutical manufacturers must be able to count on a return that covers their cost of capital.

The social insurance model of health insurance provision has advantages in helping countries achieve a fairer distribution of income; moreover, the provision of such insurance improves individuals' well-being by reducing out-of-pocket expenditure risk as well. However, when public insurance is subsidized by compulsory payments, such as through a payroll tax, such taxes may distort decisions people make in allocating time to market work versus time spent in other pursuits.

Efficiency has two meanings in economics. One is the usual meaning, which is referred to as *technical efficiency* (Leibenstein 1966). If a unit of output can be produced with two units of labor and three units of capital, producing the unit with more inputs, for example with three units of labor and four units of capital, would be technically inefficient. Technical efficiency issues have been raised in the context of health care just as they have been raised elsewhere. For example, an issue in a health care context is whether or not for-profit hospitals are more technically efficient than hospitals run by the government or private nonprofit organizations.

The other type of efficiency, which is used more often in economics than technical efficiency, is *allocative efficiency*. The three examples above of the equity-efficiency trade-off refer to allocative efficiency. Allocative efficiency describes a situation in which scarce resources are allocated in a way that maximizes social well-being given society's resource endowment. In the production process, this is done so that the ratios of each input's marginal product to its piece are equal in all inputs.

Households are endowed with a fixed amount of time to allocate among various market and nonmarket (e.g., time spent in leisure activities, helping children with homework) uses. Households value both leisure time and the consumption of goods and services. By spending less time on leisure activities and correspondingly more time on market work, households gain more resources to allocate to consumption. If, however, the return from work is reduced because in the case of a physician, the fee is reduced, or for other families, public health insurance is withdrawn when household income increases or a payroll tax decreases the return from work, public policies distort incentives to engage in market work.

Both because redistributive effects of public policies are more readily understood by the public and because they are often easier to quantify than are allocative distortions, the redistributive aspects of public policies often receive greater public notice. On the other hand, economists have a strong theoretical framework for evaluating economic efficiency, much more so than for assessing the adequacy of a particular income distribution. For this reason, economists tend to emphasize the efficiency aspects of public policies. Assessing equity and the equity-efficiency trade-offs involves making value judgments and adopting assessment approaches, which economists tend to feel rather uncomfortable doing.

Much of economic analysis *and* this book is concerned with efficiency rather than equity issues. Lack of emphasis does not reflect a belief that equity concerns are unimportant, just that we economists do not believe we have as much to say about them. Although it is feasible to do this, technical efficiency is better judged by experts in specific technologies, such as engineers, than by economists.

Government's Role in Correcting Market Failures

In the presence of externalities, asymmetric information, and supply-side imperfections, such as barriers to entry, private markets in general and competition in particular cannot achieve a socially optimal allocation of resources. In economic jargon, absent some type of government intervention, *markets fail* to achieve a social optimum. While government may cause distortions, a common allegation in political discourse, it may also correct distortions that occur absent government intervention. Externalities may be corrected by tax and government transfer policies or by regulations that require private parties to undertake various precautions, for example that a child be vaccinated before enrolling in school or that a manufacturer eliminate or reduce pollutants arising from the manufacturing process. Incompetent or unethical physicians may be eliminated from the market by requiring that physicians have licenses. Antitrust policy may be a counterweight to private attempts to monopolize a market.

1.5 THE BOOK'S FOUR PARTS: A ROAD MAP

STRUCTURE OF THE BOOK

The structure of this book is similar to the paradigm of economic analysis, beginning with consumers on the demand side and then shifting to firms on the supply side of the market. After analyzing decisions at the individual and firm level in the second through tenth chapters, we devote three chapters to market-level analysis, which incorporates the simultaneous responses of participants on both demand and supply sides of the market. While most of the book deals with positive economics, that is, modeling the responses of market participants to the various incentives they face, two chapters deal expressly with normative issues, in particular decisions by governments about which services to cover based on comparisons of the benefits and costs of specific technologies.

This analysis is followed by chapters on the relationship of investments in health and health care to economic growth, and on the frontiers of health economics. A road map to the four parts of the book is shown graphically in figure 1.6.

Part I analyzes three types of decisions commonly made by individuals: (1) decisions about their demand for health and other consumption behaviors that

Decision Analysis at Individual and Firm Levels		
Demand Side (Part I)	**Supply Side (Part II)**	
Demand for health and health behavior (2)	Physician firms (5)	Quality (7)
	Hospitals (6)	
Demand for health care (3)	Nurses (8)	
Demand for health insurance (4)	Pharmaceutical firms (9)	
	Private insurer firms (10)	

System Analysis at Market Level (Part III)
Cash system and private system (11)
Semipublic system (12)
Public system (13)

Performance of Health Care Sector: Positive and Normative Aspects (Part IV)
Cost-Effectiveness analysis (14)
Cost-Benefit analysis (15)
The link between health and economic sector (16)
Frontiers of health economics (17)

FIGURE 1.6
Health Economics Road Map as Presented in This Book.
Note: Numbers in parentheses refer to chapters of this book.

affect health, (2) decisions about the amounts and types of personal health care services demanded, (3) individuals' demand for health insurance coverage.

Part II assesses the decision making of each major participant on the supply side of health care markets—physicians, nurses, hospitals, and pharmaceutical manufacturers. An important feature of health care is the key roles played by private and public insurers in decisions made at the level of individual decision makers. Hence, we consider both demand and supply of private insurance, as well as decision making by public insurers and the choices societies make in setting up their public health insurance plans.

Countries make important choices about how personal health care services are financed and about the types of organizations that supply those services, the topic of Part III. One important choice about financing involves whether the country will rely on public financing of personal health care services or allow or encourage private insurance markets. Another important choice is whether or not the country is to rely on government provision of services, privately provided services by not-for-profit or for-profit organizations, or some combination of public and private provision. These are not easy choices; Part III describes the pros and cons of the alternatives. Our goal is to provide a framework for analyzing specific types of health care systems. To accommodate students' needs for specific information about particular countries, we provide links to specific websites.

Finally, Part IV provides a direct link between health economics and public policy, starting with descriptions of economic approaches for program evaluation—how the costs and benefits of various investments in health should be quantified. This subject should be particularly interesting to students in public policy, pharmacy, and medicine since demands for evaluations of specific health care technologies occur most frequently in these contexts. Another important public policy issue relates to the size of the health care sector. Is there a particular size of a health sector that is "too large"? Too large often is interpreted as meaning that beyond some point, further spending on personal health care services is largely wasteful. There is an alternative argument that expenditures on such services contribute to a country's economic growth, and furthermore, as countries become more affluent, they demand higher levels of health and health care services for this reason. A chapter in Part IV is devoted to this set of issues. The last chapter summarizes the book by focusing on five major controversies in health economics, all of which have important consequences for public policy and future health economics research.

A brief description of the contents of each chapter follows.

PART I DEMAND FOR HEALTH, HEALTH CARE SERVICES, AND INSURANCE

Part I focuses on the demand side of the market for personal health care services. Demand decisions may be divided into decisions individuals make before becoming ill (ex ante) and those made after becoming ill (ex post). Ex ante decisions involve choices about health behaviors, the use of preventive services, and insurance purchases. Health behaviors and the use of preventive care affect the probability of becoming ill. In economics, problems are solved by backward induction. Hence, in making decisions about prevention, the individual takes account of the consequences of taking or not taking care of him- or herself.

Although markets for private health insurance are small or nonexistent in some countries, it is still important to understand why people demand insurance, even if you live in one of these countries. Publicly provided insurance also fulfills the basic goal of insurance coverage, to protect people against the risk of high out-of-pocket expenditures on personal health services.

People consume personal health care services and engage in healthy behaviors because they are better off when they are in good health. However, being in good health is generally not individuals' only objective in life. The consumption of other goods and services is also of value. Some of these goods are productive in making people healthy, such as eating nutritious foods. The consumption of others may yield enjoyment, such as the consumption of tobacco products, but detract from health. In general, the consumption of personal health care services means fewer personal resources are available for consuming other goods and services.

Chapter 2 focuses on the personal demand for health and the consumption of personal health services and health behaviors as *derived demands*. An individual "produces" his or her own health, employing combinations of personal health services and health behaviors. The relationship between these inputs and health outcomes is given by a health production function. Given the product technology and prices of input and such exogenous factors as the person's genetic makeup, revealed as one ages, individuals make decisions about their health and the levels of the health inputs they "employ." Typically, the relationship between inputs and health outcomes for an individual is uncertain. Decision analysts have developed decision trees, which are a useful tool for analyzing decisions made under conditions of uncertainty. Decision trees describe production function relationships. Utilities the decision maker attaches to various outcomes are elicited as an integral part of the decision-making process. Inputs, such as how often to visit a physician and whether or not to get a flu shot, take a drug, or smoke, and output choices — expected levels of future health, are made to maximize the individual's expected utility.

The expected utility maximization framework of decision making has been the traditional approach that economists use to analyze decisions made under conditions of uncertainty. This traditional framework has been challenged, and a new subfield, *behavioral economics*, has emerged. We discuss the behavioral economics critique and empirical evidence the critics cite in support of these arguments.

Chapter 3 describes the theory of and empirical evidence on the relationship between the quantity of health services demanded and the out-of-pocket price of such services. We discuss methods researchers have used to study the demand for personal health care and the findings of these studies. In particular, we focus on empirical evidence on the effects of such variables as out-of-pocket money prices and *time prices*—time allocated for consuming a unit of a good or service—on the demand for personal health services.

In chapter 3, the individual's health insurance coverage, either by a private or by a public insurance plan, is taken as given. Relying on the concept of expected utility maximization, chapter 4 presents the economic framework for analyzing an individual's demand for insurance and empirical evidence on factors affecting individuals' demand for health insurance coverage. As with other goods and services, an individual's demand for private insurance partly depends on its price. The price of insurance is not shown on a sticker as is the price of many other goods, such as shirts and ties and automobiles. A major objective of chapter 4 is to explain the concept of price of insurance. We show how using an expected utility framework, people can be better off with than without insurance.

In the presence of asymmetric information, in this case consumers knowing more than insurance companies about their future health and hence their potential use of personal health care services, certain types of insurance may become unavailable. Insurers do not have information on the individual's health care consumption intentions initially and thus do not charge those persons who expect to be sick a premium sufficiently high to cover the high expected use of services. Selection is adverse in that insurers do not charge a sufficiently high premium and therefore lose money on those insured individuals who expect to be high users.

Part II Supply of Health Care Services and Insurance

The major suppliers of personal health care services are physicians, nurses, hospitals, and pharmaceutical manufacturers. In addition, in some countries, private insurers offer coverage of personal health care services. Part II analyzes the behavior of these suppliers.

The physician is the captain of the health care team. Reflecting public law and regulation, physicians are the only providers of some health care services, such as surgery. Moreover, physicians provide medical advice to their patients and often direct the activities of nonphysician providers of health care services. Chapter 5 is about the market for physicians and physicians' services.

The supply of physicians' services depends on career decisions that physicians make, as well as decisions they make about their practices, including pricing, hours of work, the mix of services they provide, and the types of patients they accept for care. Physicians make several important decisions about their careers: (1) whether or not to become a physician, (2) the choice of specialty, (3) geographic location, and (4) type of practice (independent solo, group, or salaried practice).

Important issues about physicians' career choices discussed in chapter 5 are: (1) How important are financial incentives in the choice of medicine as a career, choice specialty, and practice location? (2) How do physicians select practice types, and in turn, how do the incentives associated with each affect physician incentives? These questions are important in every country.

In contrast to many but not all other sectors in the economy,[1] the physician is an agent for the patient. Particularly since the physician is in a position to recommend care that he or she subsequently provides and may profit from by providing, some health economists and health policy researchers from other disciplines have expressed doubt that many aspects of the physicians' services market can be properly understood by applying analytic methods common in other fields of microeconomics, in which consumers can be assumed to be sufficiently knowledgeable about the goods being consumed (box 1.1).

A major learning objective of chapter 5 is to understand the role of agency and the model developed to reflect asymmetric information between patients and their physicians. We describe alternative models of behavior, consider stylized facts of the physicians' services markets that the alternatives can explain that more traditional models cannot explain, provide a critique of these alternative models, and summarize empirical tests and the findings of studies that have evaluated these models empirically.

Worldwide, hospitals incorporate the latest in medical technology in a country and tend to care for the most seriously ill persons. An important distinguishing characteristic of hospitals is that relatively few are organized on a for-profit basis. Rather, private not-for-profit and public ownership forms are dominant. By contrast, an important article by Kenneth Arrow (1963) explains existing widespread institutional arrangements in health care markets as second-best alternatives. For example, the first-best option would be to insure health. However, absent the feasibility of this, consumers require other protections, which, for example, nonprofit ownership of hospitals presumably provides. Whether or not not-for-profit hospitals indeed perform better than their for-profit counterparts is an empirical question, examined in this book in chapter 6.

Several interesting and important questions follow from the observation that in contrast to other sectors and parts of the health care sector, such as pharmaceutical manufacturers, for-profit hospital organizations are in the minority. Why are the other forms dominant in the hospital sector? Are for-profit hospitals more or less efficient than hospitals organized as private nonprofit or public entities? Do for-profit hospitals provide lower or higher quality of care?

In all countries, physicians are an important part of the production process in hospitals. However, physicians in some countries, mostly notably in the United States, typically are not employed by the hospitals in which they work. Rather, they work in hospitals as self-employed agents and, in important ways, rather than report to hospital officials, the hospital officials report to them. We describe a model in which physicians run the hospitals to serve their own collective interest.

1. Lawyers, real estate, and financial planners are agents in their respective markets.

Box 1.1
Two Classic Studies in Health Economics

An issue that arose during the early years of the field of health economics and persists to some extent today is whether or not health and health care services are fundamentally different from other goods and services, requiring fundamentally different analysis, or whether health and health care services are fundamentally the same but with some important nuances and subject to analysis with standard economic tools—with the tools evolving and improving over time.

In other words, is health care basically "a wolf in sheep's clothing" or "a sheep in wolf's clothing?" If a wolf in sheep's clothing, relationships may not look that different, but they are fundamentally different. The implication is that economists should be very cautious about applying the methods, especially the theoretical methods, that they learned in graduate school and on the job to study health issues. If a sheep in wolf's clothing, things may seem basically different in this field, but they are the same as in other sectors after accounting for a few nuances.

Whether or not health care is really different has important public policy implications. The stated rationale for licensure of physicians is to protect patients from incompetent and self-serving physicians. More than six decades ago, a landmark economic study of incomes in various professions, including dentistry and medicine, Milton Friedman's and Simon Kuznets's *Income from Professional Practice* (1945), questioned whether licensure served the public interest or instead the collective financial interest of those with licenses. In addition to assembling data on national income in the 1930s, Kuznets had assembled data on income in various occupations, completing a draft in 1936. Friedman picked up the project, completing it as his PhD dissertation in 1945. The importance of this study for health economics was its focus on barriers to entry to occupations imposed by licensure and the resulting effect of increasing physicians' incomes above the level that would prevail under competition. Both these economists subsequently were awarded Nobel Prizes in Economics.

In 1958, Reuben Kessel published an article in the first issue of the *Journal of Law & Economics* on price discrimination by physicians, a common practice in the United States before health insurance coverage became widespread. He argued against the conventional wisdom, which was that multipart pricing of physicians' services was an act of charity. Rather, he argued that price discrimination reflects the exercise of market power by physicians. In both Friedman and Kuznets' book and Kessel's article, the implication was that the motive for institutional arrangements in the markets of physicians' services was financial gain rather than consumer protection.

At least as much as other types of personal health care services, hospital care is covered by health insurance. As a result, patients are largely insulated from the rising costs and prices of hospital care. To the extent they do not perform the role of watchdog over cost containment, countries have adopted various forms of public regulation to achieve hospital cost containment. These hospital cost-containment approaches and empirical evidence on their effectiveness are discussed in chapter 6.

The track record of regulatory approaches in curbing inflation in health care cost has been mixed. Hence, there has been increased interest in relying on market-oriented forces to achieve socially desirable outcomes. Chapter 6 evaluates the empirical evidence on the effects of competition among hospitals.

Within a product market, the quality of most goods and services tends to vary markedly. Heterogeneity in quality is a fact of life in markets for automobiles, hotels, restaurants, and clothes. In most markets, one takes for granted that people who wish to purchase higher quality will pay more for the product. Market forces eliminate products that do not offer good value for the money. At most, the role of government is to ensure accurate product labeling.

Largely because of asymmetric information between suppliers and consumers of health care and because quality can mean the difference between life and death, ensuring that the quality of health care services is above some minimum level has been seen as a matter of public interest and a rationale for government involvement in health care markets. After decades of public intervention, however, it is increasingly evident that the quality of health care is not always as high as is often alleged. Errors frequently occur in physicians' offices, clinics, and hospitals, with frequent serious adverse consequences for patients. Chapter 7 deals with quality of care: how it is defined and measured in a health care context, including indicators of adverse outcomes patients experience while in the hospital, and regulatory mechanisms, including self-regulation, that have been implemented with the ostensible goal of quality assurance.

In the United States in particular, but in some other high-income countries as well, medical malpractice litigation is widespread, being justified in part as a quality assurance mechanism. Since many readers are likely to be unfamiliar with tort law, the general category of law under which medical malpractice falls, chapter 7 presents some background information on tort liability and its conceptual role as a quality assurance mechanism.

Nurses are the most numerous health professionals and have important roles in providing various personal health services, in particular hospital, nursing home, and home health care. Chapter 8 begins with an overview of labor markets for nurses worldwide, including a discussion of economic concepts of surplus and shortage and the role of monopsony power in markets for nurses. A buyer or an employer of an input has *monopsony* power if the amount of the input that the buyer or employer purchases influences the price it pays for that input. For example, if a hospital employs more nurses, does it have to pay a higher hourly wage to the nurses it hires? In a competitive labor market, the number of nurses hired would not influence the wage rate.

An important public policy issue relates to whether or not higher nurse-to-patient ratios improve the quality of hospital care and long-term care services, and the advantages and disadvantages of government requirements that health care organizations maintain minimum ratios of nurses to patients. Chapter 8 discusses empirical evidence on this issue and its implications for public policy.

Technological changes embodied in new pharmaceutical products have been an important cause of improvements in health in countries at all levels of economic development. Pharmaceutical manufacturers as profit-maximizing firms with long time horizons decide on investments in new products; once products are developed, there are issues of pricing in various countries, and product promotion. Some manufacturers concentrate on producing generic products that are exact copies of existing pharmaceutical products for which patent protection has been exhausted. Chapter 9 focuses on the microeconomic decisions of pharmaceutical firms in which firms develop strategies to respond to rivals' decisions and to anticipated actions by governments, including policies related to drug approval, drug formularies, and patent protection. Under some circumstances, the market may not provide a sufficient incentive for a sufficient supply response, for example for rare diseases, for diseases highly prevalent in low-income countries, or when there are externalities not captured by the individual user. Various public policies to encourage pharmaceutical innovation when the market provides an insufficient incentive are described in chapter 9.

Chapter 10 focuses on the supply of private health insurance. The chapter explains how premiums are set and why insurance cycles exist. Despite widespread moral hazard and adverse selection, two impediments to well-functioning insurance markets, insurance is generally available in countries that substantially rely on private financing of personal health care services. How do insurers structure benefits to cope with these problems? Health insurance is often employer-provided. What is the rationale for employer provision? Who pays for employer-provided coverage? This question leads to a discussion of the economics of fringe benefits. In all countries, insurance is subject to various forms of government regulation. What is the rationale, what forms does such regulation take, and what are the economic effects of regulation?

Part III Market Structure in the Health Care Sector

Part III analyzes resource allocation arising from the interaction of three parties in health care markets, patients, providers, and payers, using a microeconomic methodology to investigate how price and quantity are determined under various market structures. Based on the share of revenue from government sources and the share of supply operated by the public sector, a country's health care markets fall into four categories: (1) a cash system—out-of-pocket payment by users of services is the major source of financing in the health care market; (2) a private system—private health insurers are a major payer in the market; (3) a quasi-public (social insurance) system; and (4) a public system, which affords both the public provision of services *and* public financing.

Chapter 11 begins with the rationale for this classification system and alternative approaches to classifying health care systems around the world. A common characteristic of cash and private systems is dependence on the private sector for financing personal health care services. Both cash and private systems are described and assessed in chapter 11. Health care systems in India and China, both of which impose substantial cost sharing on patients, are described as examples of cash systems. The United States is the best example of a private system. Important to the US system are such concepts as capitation, managed care, selective contracting (which restricts the insured person's choice of provider as a means for the payer to gain bargaining power), and managed competition.

Government rather than private insurers is the dominant or only payer in countries with quasi-public health care systems, the subject of chapter 12. Governments in their role as payers face several important decisions. First, how should payment be structured? That is, what is the unit of payment (e.g., for hospitals, the patient day, the patient admission, fixed total budget)? There is a substantial amount of empirical evidence on this question. Second, should public payment be payment in full, or is there a role for patient supplementation of fees, including co-payments and reference pricing for drugs? Governments in effect set separate prices for providers and patients. Third, which services should be covered—brand-name pharmaceuticals or generics, devices such as implantable cardiac defibrillators? Chapter 12 reviews existing empirical evidence on the effects of these choices on the price, quantity, and quality of health care. We illustrate quasi-public systems with some country-specific examples, including Canada, China, Germany, Japan, South Korea, Taiwan, and the United States (Medicare and Medicaid).

Countries in still another group have health systems with both public supply and financing. Chapter 13 addresses the issues arising with this type of system. What is the economic rationale for such systems, and how do they compare to others in terms of both efficiency and equity? In these systems, government also has important choices. First, how much money should be allocated to health care in the aggregate? Second, how should these resources be allocated: by geography, by demographic group, such as for children or the elderly, or by type of care—preventive, curative, and palliative? Third, how should providers, such as physicians, be paid? Fourth, should private supplementation of government payment be permitted, and if so, under what circumstances should supplementation be permitted or encouraged? The chapter also provides examples of public provision in practice, such as the National Health Service in the UK.

Part IV Performance of the Health Care Sector: Positive and Normative Aspects

A number of questions will have been raised in the chapters preceding Part IV but not answered adequately. For example, how much should the government allocate to the health care sector? How should a social insurance program decide whether or not to adopt a new technology? What is the contribution of personal health services to economic growth and overall population health and longevity? Should there be a single tier, or should government seek to maintain some minimum level of health care for all and allow differences to exist? To what extent can market mechanisms achieve social objectives, and to what extent is government intervention or direct provision desirable?

Whether or not a new technology should be adopted depends on both its costs and benefits. Several countries now use forms of cost-benefit analysis in deciding whether or not to cover a new technology. Such analysis can also be used to decide on the level of reimbursement for the technology.

Especially in view of the rising cost of health care, countries are increasingly interested in knowing whether particular health technologies are worth their cost. Optimal resource allocation requires that only those technologies for which benefit exceeds cost should be adopted. This, of course, is easier said than done. Economists and other researchers have developed methods for assessing the value of technologies in relationship to their cost. The three major methodologies are cost-benefit, cost-effectiveness, and cost-utility analysis. In cost-benefit analysis, an approach first developed to assess the value of public expenditures, ranging from expenditures on parks and water projects to weapons, benefit is measured in monetary terms. Benefit may be measured from demand curves for the item, such as for a park, but demand curves are not available for all goods and services or there is a judgment that demand curves would not accurately reveal consumer valuations. Then other methods are used to elicit valuations from consumers or potential consumers. Some critics of cost-benefit analysis, mainly noneconomists, are suspicious of placing value on such intangibles as the value of a life year, which is often done in cost-benefit analysis.

Chapter 14 discusses how costs should be measured in cost-benefit or cost-effectiveness analysis. Cost measurement depends in large part on the perspective of the analyst. The perspective of the government will differ from that of a private payer. Not all relevant costs are explicit, such as the value of time spent in receipt of services, and we discuss alternative ways of valuing such inputs. A major task of chapter 14 is to describe cost-effectiveness analysis and how it has been implemented in health care in practice.

The difference between cost-effectiveness analysis and cost-benefit analysis is that in the former, benefit is measured as a nonpecuniary value, whereas in benefit-cost analysis, the metric of benefit is cast in pecuniary terms. Benefit measurement is quite complex. In a sector in which outputs have prices that result from the workings of competitive market forces, the market price is an adequate measure of benefit. However, given market imperfections, in particular, because personal health care services are covered by insurance, price is not an adequate indicator of value or benefit. Thus, value must be imputed.

As described in chapter 15, the value of a life year can be inferred from market data. For example, the higher hourly wage paid to workers who bear an additional risk of death on the job (e.g., workers who wash windows of tall buildings versus workers with desk jobs) reflects workers' marginal willingness to pay to avoid the additional risk of death. Estimates of the added compensation from assuming additional personal job-related risk are used as estimates of value of life in benefit-cost analysis. Similarly, market values of safety devices, such as devices that detect radon, are assumed to reflect individuals' willingness to pay to reduce the probability of death.

An alternative approach uses estimates of maximum willingness to pay to avoid risk, derived from willingness-to-pay ("contingent valuation") surveys. People are asked how much they would be willing to pay at most to avoid specific risks. As described in the chapter, each approach has its pluses and minuses.

In many countries, especially those with a relatively high per capita income, population health and longevity increased substantially over the twentieth century. In others, trends in health indicators are far less favorable. Improved health may have important benefits in terms of improving market productivity as well as being of value in its own right. In public discussions aimed at a lay audience, countries are compared based on their citizens' life expectancy and per capita spending on health care. In chapter 16, which focuses on the contribution of personal health services to longevity, population health, and economic growth, we argue that although these comparisons are easy to understand, they can also be misleading. In particular, they imply that countries with higher per capita spending on health care have inefficient health care systems. Many factors affect population and health and longevity. Spending on personal health care services is only one of several potential determinants of health and longevity. Several recent rigorous studies quantify the effects of personal health services in the aggregate and particular health services on national output or health and longevity. Chapter 16 analyzes the interaction between the health and economic sectors, viewing the health sector's role in the national economy, for example, as an employer (but not only as an employer). How the health care system is structured has important implications for other macroeconomic outcomes, such as precautionary saving, labor market outcomes (e.g., job lock in the United States), and deadweight losses associated with higher rates of taxation, which may in turn discourage the entry of business enterprises in a country.

The final chapter, chapter 17, concludes our book by providing our final thoughts on five health economic controversies: (1) Are people and institutions really rational and forward-looking in decision making, as economists generally assume? (2) How do people and institutions obtain information relevant to their decisions? To what extent does asymmetric information actually affect the performance of health care markets, including markets for private health insurance? (3) How does the way that health care providers are paid and how they compete affect the performance of providers, and social welfare more generally? (4) How does the regulatory process affect the behavior of regulated health care firms? (5) How do physicians really make clinical decisions, and how do these clinical decisions affect the substantial geographic variation in expenditures within and between countries?

1.6 Conclusion

Health economics has grown as a field for various reasons that this chapter has identified. Various institutional features of the health sector provide a fertile field for intellectual innovation.

Key Concepts

- incentive
- health insurance
- moral hazard
- adverse selection
- externality
- merit want
- public good
- asymmetric information
- professional norm
- efficiency
- equity
- technical (or *X*-) efficiency
- allocative efficiency
- market failure

Review and Discussion Questions

1.1 Explain the term "moral hazard" in your own words. Moral hazard pertains not only to health insurance. Explain how moral hazard may operate in markets for homeowners' insurance (insurance against loss incurred by homeowners on their own home and property) and in automobile liability insurance.

1.2 Define adverse selection. Give three examples of adverse selection in markets other than for health insurance and explain the rationale for each choice.

1.3 How might adverse selection arise in the market for used cars? What is likely to be the effect of adverse selection in the used car market if it were to arise?

1.4 How do professional norms apply to your life as a student?

1.5 Explain the distinction between economic efficiency and equity. Is there always a trade-off between efficiency and equity as economists use these terms? Give examples of instances of (1) a trade-off and (2) no trade-off between efficiency and equity. What is a pure externality?

1.6 Compare treatments for infective and chronic diseases and explain which one is more likely to create health externalities to society and which one is more likely to impose financial externalities to society. Is there any different implication for government intervention to control for infective and chronic diseases from the viewpoint of externalities?

1.7 Explain the term "asymmetric information" between physicians and their patients. Please give two examples of how physicians could use the advantage of asymmetric information to earn more profits or raise the price of their services.

1.8 Using hospital care as an example, explain the distinction between technical efficiency and allocative efficiency.

EXERCISES

1.1 Suppose the government in a middle-income country announced its policy goal to implement a universal health insurance program within five years. Would implementation of this policy increase the demand for health economics research in this country? List at least three factors to justify your answer no matter whether your answer is "yes," "no," or "maybe."

1.2 Health economics has enjoyed several decades of remarkable growth, but will this growth continue? Using your country as an example, list at least three reasons to support your answer.

Online Supplemental Material

Encyclopedia of Health Economics

http://www.dictionaryofeconomics.com/article?id=pde2008_H000031 (*The New Palgrave Dictionary of Economics Online*)

http://en.wikipedia.org/wiki/Health_economics

Health Economics Education

http://www.economicsnetwork.ac.uk/health

Health Economics Information Resources

http://www.nlm.nih.gov/nichsr/edu/healthecon/

http://www.herc.research.va.gov/home/default.asp

http://www.york.ac.uk/res/herc

Supplemental Readings

Arrow, K. J. 1963. Uncertainty and the Welfare Economics of Medical Care. *American Economic Review* 53 (5): 941–973.

Mackenbach, J. P., U. Stirbu, A. J. R. Roskam, et al. 2008. Socioeconomic Inequalities in Health in 22 European Countries. *New England Journal of Medicine* 358 (23): 2468–2481.

Nordhaus, W. D. 2005. Irving Fisher and the Contribution of Improved Longevity to Living Standards. *American Journal of Economics and Sociology* 64 (26): 367–392.

Oeppen, J., and J. W. Vaupel. 2002. Broken Limits to Life Expectancy. *Science* 296 (5570): 1029–1031.

References

Arrow, K. J. 1963. Uncertainty and the Welfare Economics of Medical Care. *American Economic Review* 53 (5): 941–973.

Becker, G. S. 1964. *Human Capital.* New York: National Bureau of Economic Research.

Berndt, E. R., and J. M. Donohue. 2008. Direct-to-Consumer Advertising in Health Care: An Overview of Economic Issues. In *Incentives and Choice in Health Care*, ed. F. A. Sloan and H. Kasper, 131–162. Cambridge, MA: MIT Press.

Currie, J., and F. Gahvari. 2008. Transfers in Cash and In-Kind: Theory Meets the Data. *Journal of Economic Literature* 46 (2): 333–383.

Cutler, D., A. Deaton, and A. Lleras-Muney. 2006. The Determinants of Mortality. *Journal of Economic Perspectives* 20 (3): 97–120.

Deaton, A. 2003. *Health and National Income.* Center for Health & Wellbeing Research Program in Development Studies, Princeton University, Princeton, NJ.

Feldstein, M. S. 1973. The Welfare Loss of Excess Health Insurance. *Journal of Political Economy* 81(2): 251–280.

Friedman, M., and S. Kuznets. 1945. *Income from Independent Professional Practice.* New York: National Bureau of Economic Research.

Fuchs, V. R. 1996. Economics, Values, and Health Care Reform. *American Economic Review* 86 (1): 1–24.

Fuchs, V. R. 2000. The Future of Health Economics. *Journal of Health Economics* 19 (2): 141–157.

Gowrisankaran, G. 2008. Competition, Information Provision, and Hospital Quality. In *Incentives and Choice in Health Care,* ed. F. A. Sloan and H. Kasper, 319–352. Cambridge, MA: MIT Press.

Hall, R. E., and C. I. Jones. 2007. The Value of Life and the Rise in Health Spending. *Quarterly Journal of Economics* 122 (1): 39–72.

Kessel, R. A. 1958. Price Discrimination in Medicine. *Journal of Law & Economics* 1 (1): 20–53.

Leibenstein, H. 1966. Allocative vs. X-Efficiency. *American Economic Review* 56 (3): 392–416.

Mackenbach, J. P., U. Stirbu, A.-J. Roskam, et al. 2008. Socioeconomic Inequalities in Health in 22 European Countries. *New England Journal of Medicine* 358 (23): 2468–2481.

Nordhaus, W. D. 2005. Irving Fisher and the Contribution of Improved Longevity to Living Standards. *American Journal of Economics and Sociology* 64 (26): 367–392.

Oeppen, J., and J. W. Vaupel. 2002. Broken Limits to Life Expectancy. *Science* 296 (5570): 1029–1031.

Organisation for Economic Co-operation and Development. 2008. OECD Health Data. http://www.oecd.org/document/56.

Phelps, C. E. 1995. Perspectives in Health Economics. *Health Economics* 4 (5): 335–353.

Rothschild, M., and J. Stiglitz. 1976. Equilibrium in Competitive Insurance Markets: An Essay on the Economics of Imperfect Information. *Quarterly Journal of Economics* 90 (4): 629–649.

Sloan, F. A. 2000. Not-for-Profit Ownership and Hospital Behavior. In *Handbook of Health Economics,* ed. A. J. Culyer and J. P. Newhouse, 1141–1174. Amsterdam: Elsevier Science.

World Bank Group. 2007. World Development Indicators. http://data.worldbank.org/indicator.

World Bank Group. 2009. World Development Indicators. http://data.worldbank.org/indicator.

World Health Organization (WHO). 2000. Ranking of Performance of Health Care Systems. http://www.who.int/whr/2000/media_centre/press_release/en.

PART

Demand for Health, Health Care, and Insurance

Chapter 2

Health and Health Behaviors

Being in good health is a necessary but not a sufficient condition for living a productive and long life. Productivity applies to both work and nonwork activities. Although much of health economics is about supply and demand for personal health care services, the use of health services is derived from the fundamental objective of health promotion. Health services and health behaviors are conceptualized as inputs in the production function, with health being the output.

Even though health is undoubtedly important to people, we all care about more than just being in good health. We value other possessions, such as our houses, cars, cell phones, companionship, and feelings of self-worth. The consumption of some goods, such as tobacco products, yields current pleasure but is likely to have adverse health effects later in life. Thus, such consumption is a "good" for the individual while the individual is consuming it but can be a "bad" in the long run. The consumption of some personal health services is unpleasant in the short run—going to the physician or dentist involves both time and often inconvenience—and the receipt of some services can be unpleasant and even painful, but there may be benefits in the long run.

Thus, for example, in deciding whether or not to undergo a medical screening procedure such as mammography (a procedure to detect breast cancer) or a colonoscopy (a procedure to detect colon cancer), a person is concerned not only about promoting current health but about future health as well. Maintaining a normal weight may make one more attractive currently as well as more physically fit, but maintaining normal weight today may also prevent the development of diabetes later in life. Thus, eating a slice of apple pie today may yield utility for several reasons in the current period, but the decision will also depend, to a lesser or greater degree, on the implications of eating the pie today for one's future health.

In economics, decisions made by individuals or households are analyzed as if a decision maker were maximizing his or her utility subject to constraints that limit how much utility can be achieved. On any given day, an individual may realize benefits in terms of being healthy at the time, engaging in some "unhealthy" activities, such as smoking and excess alcohol consumption or eating a slice of apple pie with ice cream (rather than just an apple a day, which may indeed yield future health benefits), and living in an attractive and comfortable dwelling. Such consumption is limited by family income, prices paid by family members for goods and services consumed, the time available for market work and other activities, and other factors. The utility household members derive from consumption reflects individual wants or preferences.

This chapter begins with conceptual discussions of rationality and forward-looking behavior, health production functions, the demand for health services, and health behaviors as derived demands. We then describe decision trees and the process of backward induction and apply the concepts to the decision about whether or not to engage in preventive care. These tools are useful for analyzing any problem in which the outcomes of decisions are uncertain. Future outcomes are unknown when these choices are made. Next we discuss a general framework used in many economic studies about consumer choices in relation to specific health behaviors, followed by a discussion of empirical findings on several consumer choices—food consumption and physical exercise, cigarette and alcohol consumption, and the use of preventive care.

The traditional economic framework commonly used in microeconomics to assess impacts on household decisions of various changes that are outside the control of households has been challenged by a new economic subfield, *behavioral economics*. We discuss the behavioral economics critique of traditional "neoclassical" economics and empirical evidence the critics cite to advance their arguments. The critique raises several fundamental questions, such as, Are people forward-looking or myopic? Are choices people make rational or irrational (i.e., influenced by cues, such as seeing someone else enjoying a cigarette)? And on discounting, do short-term discount rates differ from long-run rates? Some argue that short-term rates are higher than long-term rates. A higher rate means that one is more present-oriented than if the discount rate is comparatively low. The final section summarizes the chapter's key points.

2.1 RATIONALITY AND OTHER ECONOMIC ASSUMPTIONS

A major feature of health and health care is that the decisions one makes today affect health not only currently but in the future as well (box 2.1). Economics generally

Box 2.1
Long-Run Effects of Current Health Decisions: Child Health and Adult Outcomes

Decisions one makes about one's own health today have important effects on outcomes decades later. There is some statistical evidence that nutrition in utero affects one's health as an adult (Barker 1997). Some of this research is based on animal studies, for which it is possible to deprive the fetus of food and observe subsequent outcomes, such as mortality. In other work, people in Holland exposed to famine conditions prenatally during World War II in 1944–1945 were compared with people born a year earlier and a year later in terms of their glucose tolerance as adults (glucose intolerance leads to an increased risk of diabetes). The authors found that food deprivation of the fetus was linked to higher adult glucose intolerance (Ravelli, van der Meulen, Michels, et al. 1998).

Smith (2009) tested whether child health affects various nonhealth outcomes in adults, including educational attainment, family income and wealth, and individuals' earnings and labor supply. To establish a causal link between child health and adult outcomes, it is necessary to control for other factors that affect adult outcomes and are correlated with child health. Many factors could be measured from the data, but the author could not be sure that all relevant factors could be measured. Thus, he compared adult outcomes of siblings from the same household who had different levels of child health. These comparisons allowed him to account for unmeasured family and neighborhood background effects that, if not accounted for, may have led to biased estimates of the effect of child health on adult outcomes. Smith found that, except for educational attainment, poor child health has a large effect on adult outcomes. Some of the financial impact of poor childhood health is reduced financial resources in the early adulthood. Another part of the financial impact is due to a decreased adult labor supply, which in turn reduces individual earnings and family income.

assumes that people are rational and forward-looking. By "rational," economists mean that in weighing choices, individuals use all relevant information available to them and weigh the benefits and costs of specific choices based on this information. Rationality does not require that a person be omniscient, able to accurately predict the outcomes of each choice. Various events are likely to occur subsequently that may have important effects on outcomes. For example, the decision whether or not to attend college is largely made several years in advance, particularly since it is necessary to take college preparatory courses. The decision to attend college typically reflects comparisons for future earnings, nonpecuniary (nonmonetary) returns, the cost of attending college, and other factors. However, after the decision is made, ill health, war, or unemployment of a parent may affect whether or not the planned decision is actually realized. Rationality does not require that the individual be able to forecast all events that may intervene. In fact, these events are uncertain; for example, actual entry into college will depend on actual realizations of these events.

By "forward-looking," economists mean that individuals consider not only the present costs and benefits of choices but future ones as well. For example, in deciding whether or not to have a knee replacement, the individual will consider current benefits, such as a reduction in pain and improved mobility, and also future ones, such as the length of time to re-replacement. Artificial joints, like natural joints, depreciate over time.

Economists assume that from today's vantage point, a dollar of benefit or cost today is worth more than a dollar of benefit accrued or spent tomorrow. The trade-off between today and tomorrow reflects an individual's time preference. Let r be the rate of the individual's time preference. Then a dollar received tomorrow is worth only $\$1/(1 + r)$ today $(1 > r \geq 0)$. A person may be forward-looking but impatient. Then he or she has a high r, and conversely for a more patient person.

Although decisions one makes about one's health today have implications for one's health tomorrow, another major distinguishing feature of health and health care is that decisions are often if not typically made under uncertainty. People eat delicious deserts, consume alcohol, smoke cigarettes, go to a physician for an annual physical examination, and follow a physician's advice, all without knowing how these choices will actually affect personal health and well-being. The vast majority of people who smoke cigarettes do not get lung cancer or have a heart attack. Smoking only increases the probability of experiencing these adverse health outcomes. It is possible to know averages, but there is substantial variation about the averages for several reasons, including genetic and environmental factors and interactions among the various health behaviors. As an example of an interaction, not only does smoking make it more difficult to jog, but the mean probability of getting lung cancer possibly differs between jogging and nonjogging smokers in ways that are not even fully understood by medical experts.

Economists' assumptions may seem implausible, and admittedly they often are. In the context of health and health care, an objection to the rationality assumption is that if people use the best information they have, this may not be good enough. After all, one reason for visiting a physician is to obtain information about the prevention, diagnosis, and treatment of disease. There is asymmetric information between the physician and the patient. If the physician acts in the patient's best interest—that is, in economic terminology, if the physician is a perfect agent for the principal, in this case the patient—the well-informed physician-patient team can make a decision as a fully informed patient would. However, if the physician has interests of his or her own, the rationality assumption may not hold.

Economists typically defend their assumptions in the following way. Assumptions are made to make economic models more tractable and to yield predictions which then can be tested empirically. The assumptions are a building block, a means to an end, not an end in itself. However, in recent years, even economists have begun to challenge their traditional assumptions, and a new field, behavioral economics, is gaining in popularity. We will have more to say about behavioral economics below.

2.2 HEALTH PRODUCTION FUNCTIONS

THE CONCEPT

A production function relates inputs to outputs. It is a technical relationship, for example, describing the relationship between the dose of drug administered to a patient and the resulting health outcome. Production functions are used in economic analysis, but estimating relationships between inputs and outputs is largely the task of scientists, engineers, and other analysts, although economists also estimate production functions.

A production function is expressed as:

$$Output_{ij} = f_i\,(Input1_{ij}, Input2_{ij}; Z_{ij}) \tag{2.1}$$

In equation 2.1, $Output_{ij}$ is the quantity of output i produced in a given period by the jth individual, and $Input1_i$ and $Input2_i$ are two input quantities used by person j to produce output $Output_{ij}$. The function f reflects a specific technology translating inputs into outputs. In a health context, we can take as an example a person who has been diagnosed with high blood pressure (hypertension). $Input1_{ij}$ is the number of meals person j eats in a time period, say a year, during which the person adheres to a salt-free diet, and $Input2_{ij}$ is the number of days during the year in which j takes antihypertensive medication. The variable Z_j represents individual j's genetic makeup, which does not vary over time. The semicolon in front of this term indicates that Z_j is exogenous to the decision maker, that is, outside the decision maker's control. By contrast, the *inputs* are decision variables assumed to be endogenous—within the decision maker's control. The $Output_{ij}$ could be the number of days during the year on which the person has a blood pressure reading within the generally accepted normal range.

$Output_{ij}$, $Input1_{ij}$, and $Input2_{ij}$ represent flows—rates of output per unit of time, such as days during the year on which the person has a normal blood pressure reading, number of days on which person j takes medication for hypertension, and so on. Blood pressure is a concern not because it is that important in its own right but rather because persons with uncontrolled blood pressure are subject to a higher probability of acquiring specific chronic diseases, such as heart attacks and heart failure, stroke, kidney failure, or death. Therefore, for example, in a more complex model, $Output_{ij}$ for person j in various years may be inputs and the presence of heart disease or mortality may be outputs.

HEALTH STOCKS AND FLOWS

There is an important distinction between *stocks* and *flows*. A stock represents a quantity at a specific point in time. A flow represents a rate between two time periods. For example, on January 1 of a year, households have a specific amount of wealth, which is a stock. This stock generates a flow of income per day, month, or year. The numbers of cars a manufacturer has in its inventory is a stock, but the number of cars produced per hour is a flow. Likewise, a family possesses a certain number of automobiles on a date, a stock. This stock generates a specific amount of transportation services per day, month, or year.

In this sense, personal health on a given day represents a stock of capital. The corresponding flow is a healthy day or a day during which a person can perform his or her usual activities. The number of days in a month one has high blood pressure is a flow, as is the number of days in a month a person jogs. However, we know that consistently high blood pressure and many days of inactivity can adversely affect heart health, which is a stock.

2.3 THE DEMAND FOR HEALTH: HEALTH AS A CAPITAL STOCK

EVOLUTION OF A PERSON'S HEALTH OVER TIME

As first conceptualized by Michael Grossman (1972), a person's general state of health corresponds to the person's health capital.[1] The stock of health capital yields a flow of healthy days per unit of time.[2] Since we consider health in the aggregate rather than a particular aspect of health, we drop subscript i, and for simplicity, we also suppress subscript j, although we continue to describe the health of one individual. However, since the individual's health varies over time, we include a subscript for t, which may be a year or a shorter or longer time period.

The relationship between a person's health stock (H_T) and his or her health flow(h_t) per unit of time t is given by

$$h_t = f(H_t). \tag{2.2}$$

The relationship between h_t and H_t is positive. A higher health stock in period t yields a higher flow of healthy days.

Healthy days and other goods and services are valued by consumers. The number of healthy days and the consumption of other goods and services are linked. If the person loses time from work because of an illness, earnings fall. And since there is no savings in Grossman's model, when family income falls, so does the consumption of other goods and services. People invest in their own health by utilizing personal health care services. Although other health inputs, including

1. *Although this article is old, it is one of the most widely cited articles in all of health economics. According to the* Web of Science, *a popular database for literature in all fields, Grossman (1972) was cited sixty-three times during 2008 alone (flow). According to Google Scholar, this paper was cited 2,143 times from its publication to April 2010 (stock).*

2. *The goal of this discussion of the Grossman model is to introduce the reader to the fundamental concepts of health capital and the demand for health. We present as few equations as possible. For a somewhat more technical but nevertheless very readable presentation of the model that contains more equations, see Gilleskie (2008).*

Box 2.2
Humans Depreciate, Too!

Physical capital includes a plant, durable equipment, and endowments of resources, such as mineral deposits and arable land. Intangible capital includes intellectual property. Human capital consists of skills and knowledge from schooling, on-the-job training, and self-improvement. Health capital consists of cognitive function, physical function, and mental or emotional health.

It seems straightforward that machines depreciate. Intellectual property depreciates since ideas and inventions become old and are replaced by newer ones. Cognitive skills depreciate. There is a distinction between fluid intelligence, measured by processing speed on tasks, and crystallized intelligence, measured, for example, by one's vocabulary. Fluid intelligence rises initially after birth, peaks at about age 14, and declines subsequently. Crystallized intelligence continues to rise throughout adulthood but at a decreasing rate until about age 65, when health shocks, such as strokes and the onset of dementia, begin to take their toll. Increased mental exercise improves crystallized intelligence and leads to a lower subsequent decline. Physical function peaks in early adulthood and declines at an increasing rate with age. For example, accumulation of plaque in blood vessels often begins in early adulthood. Chest pain, heart attacks, and strokes tend to occur much later in life (see McFadden 2009 for a discussion of these points). Mortality rates increase with age. In 2007 in the United States, the probability at age 20 of dying within a year was 0.0013 for males and 0.0005 for females. The probability at age 50 was 0.0055 for males, 0.0034 for females; at 65, 0.0167 for males, 0.0107 for females; and at age 85, 0.1059 for males, 0.0785 for females (see Social Security Online 2007). Clearly, the depreciation rate, as measured by mortality, increases markedly with age. However, for some aspects of human capital, the relationship between age and the depreciation rate is not monotonic, particularly at earlier ages.

health behaviors, such as smoking and exercising, also affect H_t, to keep the analysis tractable, we ignore this complication for now. Health services use is a flow; in Grossman's framework, the use of health services represents a gross health investment by an individual. Gross investment is distinguished from net investment in that the latter incorporates depreciation of the health stock occurring during a period t. Net investment is gross investment less depreciation. In this context, a person's health deteriorates or depreciates each period at a depreciation rate of δ, just as any item of plant or equipment depreciates. Knees wear out just as car engines do (box 2.2).

The depreciation rate is assumed to be fixed at some value that is outside the decision maker's control, that is, it is exogenous to the decision maker. The depreciation rate not only varies among individuals but for a given individual varies over time; for now, consider only one individual (suppressing the subscript j) and let the depreciation rate be time invariant. The depreciation rate parameter δ is not affected by the person's health care decisions. Let the person's rate of gross investment in health be I_t, where t is a time period, such as a year. The individual's health stock evolves over time according to

$$H_t = I_{t-1} + (1 - \delta)H_{t-1}. \tag{2.3}$$

Equation 2.3 states that a person's health at time t equals the amount the person invested in health in time $t-1$ plus that part of the previous period's health stock that did not depreciate between periods $t-1$ and t. The function g(·) for gross investment is

$$I_{t-1} = g(m_{t-1}, T^H{}_{t-1}), \tag{2.4}$$

where m_{t-1} represents the amount of medical care utilized in a period (here in $t-1$) and T^H is the amount of time the person spends obtaining medical care. This includes the time spent getting to the doctor, waiting for the doctor, and following the regimen prescribed by the doctor, such as taking prescribed medicines.

Gross investment, I_t, can never be negative, but H_t is larger or smaller than H_{t-1}, depending on the amount of gross investment in period $t-1$ and the depreciation rate. Low gross investment or a high depreciation rate can lead to a decline in health.

Demand for Health and for Medical Care

The health production function (equations 2.1 and 2.2) depicts a technical relationship between health, the output, and medical services and health behaviors, the inputs. A production function does not describe decisions, only the technical possibility of translating inputs into outputs. Demand for medical care is derived from the person's demand for health.

In the general literature on investment, the optimal capital stock is the amount at which the cost of capital equals the marginal efficiency of capital (MEC) (fig. 2.1). The MEC reflects the percentage increase in output made possible by adding another unit of capital, all expressed as value (dollar) terms. To help understand the concept of MEC, suppose an investment of $100 yields additional output valued at $3 per year. Then the MEC would be the increase in the value of annual output per $100 of investment, or 0.03. The MEC schedule has a negative slope since the decision maker is assumed to rank its potential investments from highest to lowest in terms of their expected return (per dollar of investment). The cost of capital represents the amount per time period, such as a year, investors require to supply $100 of capital funds to the borrower. The borrower will not want to pay more than 3 percent per period for funds that yield 3 percent. Thus, the equilibrium capital stock the firm will want to hold is at the level of capital at which the rate of return or MEC equals the cost of capital. In figure 2.1, the capital stock is on the x-axis

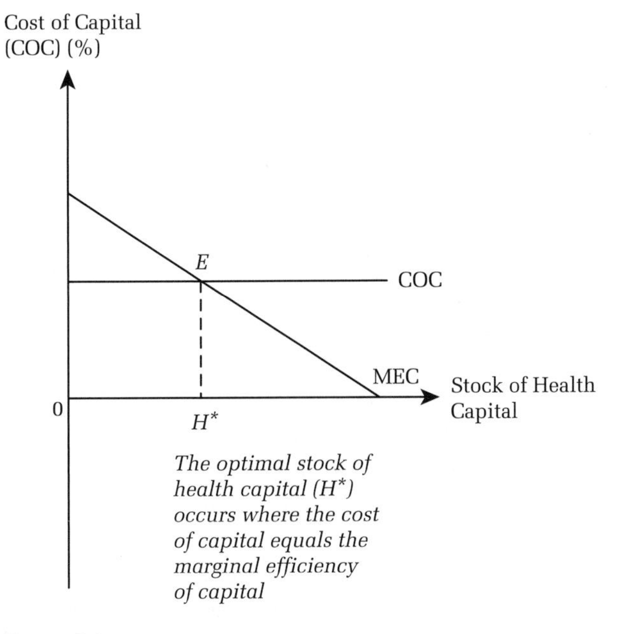

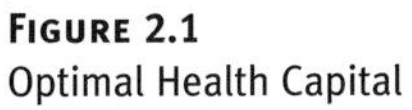
FIGURE 2.1
Optimal Health Capital

and the cost of capital and the MEC are on the *y*-axis. Investment moves the capital stock to the right along the *x*-axis. The ultimate decision is about how much capital to hold. Investment is the way of achieving this end.

When an asset depreciates or appreciates over time, the cost of capital equals the *sum* of (1) the cost of obtaining a dollar of capital for a period, say a year, at a rate i, (2) the depreciation rate on the capital stock at δ, and (3) the appreciation rate of a unit of capital at a. A dollar of capital can come from borrowing (issuing debt) from issuing stock in one's company, or from internal funds. Roughly speaking, the cost of debt capital is the interest rate; the cost of issuing equity depends on dividends to be paid and the cost of diluting ownership and control in the company when issuing stock; and the opportunity cost is the cost of internal funds when the investment is financed by internal funds. All of these costs are in i. Depreciation is also the cost of holding an investment good for a period. For example, if one operates a rental car business, the cost of capital is higher if the rate of depreciation on cars in the fleet is higher, holding other factors constant. Finally, the appreciation rate on the investment good is an offsetting factor. For example, a car may depreciate but, if car prices are rising, the latter is an offset to the former.

Before turning to health and medical care, it is useful to discuss an example from another context to illustrate the general principle. Suppose you owned a car rental business. The decision is how many cars to own for rental purposes. You can borrow funds at a 5 percent interest rate, the cars depreciate at a rate of 25 percent per year, and the general annual rate of inflation in car prices is 3 percent. Then the cost of capital is 27 percent. You stop adding to your fleet of cars at the point at which the rate of return on rental cars declines to 27 percent. Once you decide how many cars you wish to own, you buy or sell cars to achieve the optimal number of cars in your fleet.

The rate of return on cars reflects the revenue obtained from each car for the year, expenses on maintenance and upkeep, and labor and other costs of renting out the cars. If the rental price increases, the rate of return increases. If the wage of your mechanics increases, the rate of return decreases. If crime in the neighborhood increases, necessitating hiring more guards for the company's parking lot, the rate of return decreases. One reason that the MEC curve is downward sloping is that the demand curve for rental cars facing the firm is downward sloping. Perhaps there are diseconomies of scale in car rentals as well, especially at a single location.

The cost of capital as applied to health decisions is both similar to and different from the cost as it applies to a company's investment decisions. Clearly, an individual does not issue stock for the purpose of making investments in his or her personal health. However, the person may draw on personal savings or borrow money from a bank to finance a stay in the hospital. Health capital depreciates. Knees can become arthritic. Replacements for natural knees also depreciate over time, and eventually may be replaced. Likewise, there is appreciation in medical prices. If the price of a knee replacement is expected to double, a person who would benefit from having this procedure may decide to obtain it sooner. In a health context, you as an investor can only buy, not sell, health assets. Capital stock is reduced through depreciation, which occurs over time.

The cost-of-capital schedule may be horizontal or positively sloped. If the latter, this means that the cost of capital rises with the amount of capital goods purchased. For simplicity, we draw the cost of capital with a zero slope.

The MEC of health depends on how a unit of investment affects the health stock, the variable cost of maintaining the stock (analogously, painting a house periodically to keep up its appearance), the productivity of investments in health capital, and the value the individual attaches to a one-unit change in health. Value depends on the individual's preferences. People differ in how much they value health, just as they differ in how much they value housing, transportation, and other goods and services. There are likely to be important differences in the productivity of health investments among individuals as well. For example, people may differ in their understanding of the physician's advice for postoperative care.

The MEC (for marginal efficiency of investment a concept from macroeconomics and the theory of investment in particular) is the rate of return on a unit of capital. In evaluating capital projects, one expects a decision maker to rank order

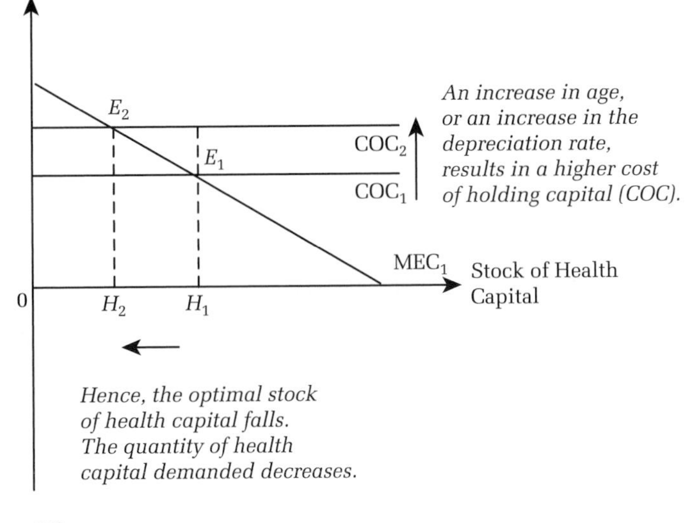

FIGURE 2.2
Optimal Health Capital and Changes in the Depreciation Rate

projects in terms of their (prospective) rates of return—from highest to lowest rates of return. Thus, the MEC schedule has a negative slope.

The optimal capital stock for the company, or in our context the optimal amount of health capital an individual desires to hold in a specific time period, is determined by where the cost of capital and the MEC are equal. Intuitively, if the cost of capital is 5 percent and the MEC is 8 percent, the company can increase its profits if it adds to its capital stock, and conversely if the MEC is only 3 percent. Investment, in our context, the consumption of personal health care services, and the time associated with such consumption are means toward an end—having the optimal amount of health capital.

Shifts in the cost of capital and MEC schedules change the optimal capital stock for an individual. First let's consider an increase in the cost of capital stemming from an increase in the person's depreciation rate (fig. 2.2). Suppose the individual is unexpectedly diagnosed with cancer, or we are comparing an elderly individual with a high depreciation rate with a student in her early twenties with a low depreciation rate. A high depreciation rate, holding other factors constant, implies a lower desired health care stock.

Now, consider shifts in the MEC schedule. An increase in input productivity (e.g., in the effect of an extra visit to a physician for consultation on personal health) raises rates of return and hence shifts the MEC schedule to the right. For example, consider the knee replacement. A better device—one that lasts longer or works

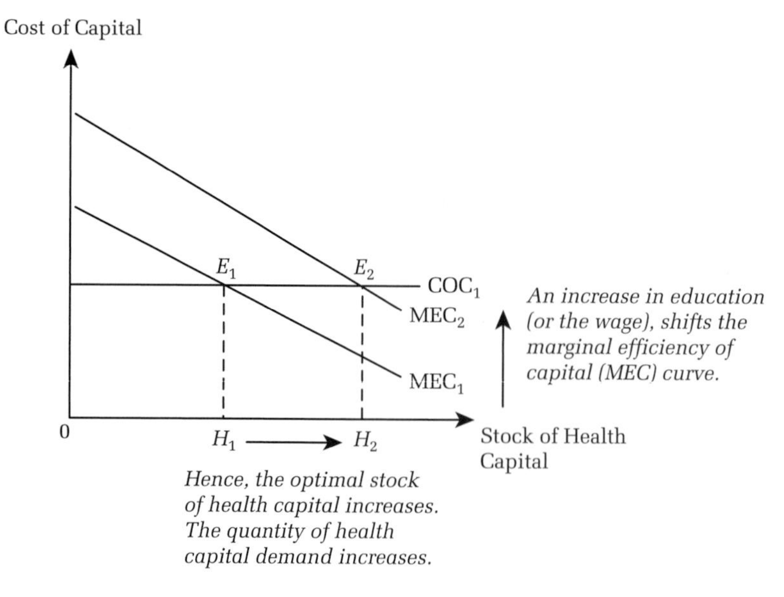

FIGURE 2.3
Optimal Health Capital from Changes in the Marginal Efficiency of Capital

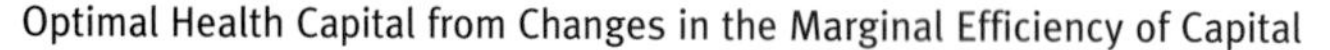

better—has a higher rate of return. Thus, the MEC shifts upward for this reason, and the health stock and investment, including in artificial knees, rise. Conversely, an increase in the price of an input used to produce a unit of capital, such as the artificial knee, shifts the MEC schedule to the left (fig. 2.3). Since capital is "made" by investment, the amount of investment per period declines as well. Conceptually, an increase in the value the individual places on being in good health relative to the value he or she places on flows from the other composite good also shifts the MEC schedule upward, resulting in more gross investment in health.

Another factor shifting the MEC schedule rightward is an increase in the returns on investments in health capital. The health flow may become more highly valued either because of an increase in utility of a healthy day or, with the caveat noted below, because of an increase in the return from market work—the person's wage, since more healthy time allows higher earnings to accrue from market work.

PREDICTIONS OF THE GROSSMAN MODEL

The Grossman investment model offers several predictions about the effects of changes that are exogenous to households on health capital and health investment.

A REDUCTION IN THE PRICE OF MEDICAL CARE

Consider the effect of a reduction in the price of medical care. The individual consumer cannot influence the price of medical care. He or she is a "price taker" in this market. The price reduction has two effects. It will lead to the substitution of medical care for other health inputs, such as self-care or the purchase and use of over-the-counter medicines. And it shifts the MEC to the right, which leads the person to want to hold more health capital and demand more medical care for this reason as well. Thus, the model predicts that a decrease in price leads to the greater use of medical care and improved personal health.

An Increase in the Individual's Wage Rate

An increase in the person's wage has two effects on medical care use and health capital. The higher wage increases the opportunity cost of time, in this sense making it more expensive to visit a physician. For this reason, an increase in wage affects health investment and health capital in the same way as an increase in the price of medical care does. But in addition, an increase in wage raises the return on a healthy day since the individual can earn more in a day when she is able to work. The latter effect tends to increase demand for health capital and health investment. Thus, a change in the individual's wage rate has an ambiguous effect on a person's medical care use and health capital.

An Increase in the Individual's Age

Now consider the effects of a person's age on medical care use and health (box 2.3). In the Grossman model, the rate of depreciation (δ) of the health stock increases with age. This is a plausible assumption. For example, agility decreases with age at a higher rate than at lower ages. An increase in δ reduces the amount of health capital the individual desires to "hold," which, other factors held constant, reduces demand for medical care. But an increase in δ also decreases H directly (see equation 2.2). Thus, even though the desired health stock is lower, absent some increased investment, H may be below its optimal level. This leads to increased demand for medical care. Although the individual's optimal H decreases with age, older persons use more medical care, a pattern observed in empirical studies. Death occurs in the Grossman model when the individual's health stock declines below a minimum level, H_d, say below H_2 in figure 2.2.

An Increase in the Individual's Educational Attainment

On average, persons who have completed more years of schooling are in better health (box 2.4). By contrast, the pattern of medical care use by educational attainment is less clear. Grossman (1972) argued that education increases the productivity of investments in health. A more educated person is more likely to be sensitive to signs and symptoms of illness and to visit a doctor sooner in cases for which medical care is likely to be productive. If treatment is initiated earlier, it may be more productive in improving health. Also, more highly educated individuals may be better in understanding the physician's diagnosis and recommended treatments. For these reasons, we would expect the MEC schedule to shift to the right when the person

Box 2.3
Relationship between Health Care Expenditure Per Person and Age

Spending on personal health care services increases with age in all countries for which we have the information. Data on health care spending by age for 1992 and 2000 in France provide an example (fig. 2.4). Mean individual health care expenditures per person increased with age in both years, but more so in 2000 than in 1992. The increase with age is explained by the Grossman model. The change in the rate of increase with age between 1992 and 2000 is not.

In France, there was little change in the relationship between age and health care spending for physicians' services between the two years. However, spending on pharmaceuticals and on hospitals rose much more markedly with age in 2000 than in 1992. Dormont, Grignon, and Huber (2006) attribute most of the change in the age-health spending relationship to the technological advances that occurred in the intervening years. For example, persons with a heart attack were more likely to undergo complex cardiac procedures in 2000 than in 1992.

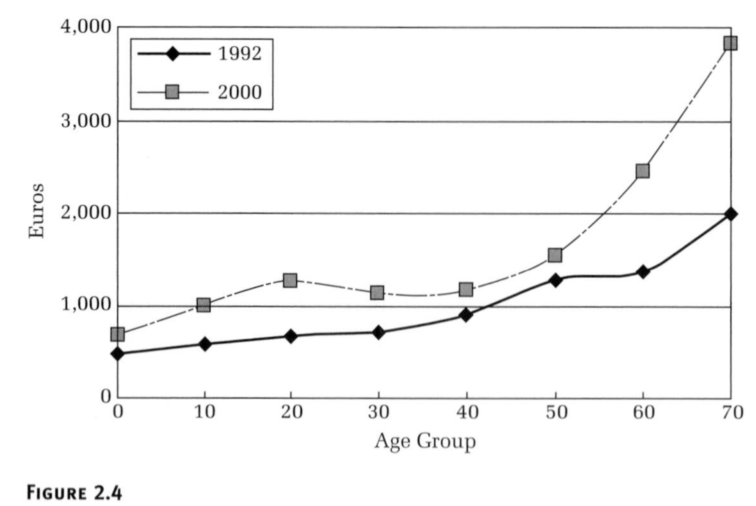

FIGURE 2.4
Mean Individual Health Care Expenditures by Age Group, Years 1992 and 2000.
Source: Dormont, Grignon, and Huber (2006).

Box 2.4
Effects of Educational Attainment on Adult Health

In the Grossman model, education improves individuals' efficiency in producing health. This means that persons with higher educational attainment are better at evaluating their health and seeking medical attention when it is appropriate to do so. They may also be better in understanding the physician's advice and instructions. By being more efficient in health production, they demand higher levels of health. Thus, the model offers an explicit prediction that higher educational attainment causes higher levels of health stock, and the model is ambiguous about whether or not health care utilization is higher or lower.

Economists have been very interested in ascertaining empirically whether higher educational attainment leads to better health in adulthood. While the question is easily understood, demonstrating a causal effect empirically is actually quite difficult. Several problems must be overcome. First, the causal relationship can run both ways, from education to health and from health to education. More specifically, healthier youths may be more likely to stay in school. Thus, unless the researcher accounts for child, adolescent, and young adult health, as well as educational attainment, the measured effect of education on adult health may be overstated. Second, educational attainment may be correlated with other factors that affect both educational attainment and health, and it is important to account for these other factors in empirical analysis. For example, persons who are more patient, that is, have lower rates of time preference (see this chapter's discussion of discounting), may demand both more education and more health. Persons who are more motivated to pursue a professional career and want to become business executives or high-level government officials may decide to stay in school longer and be more careful about their health. Having more highly educated parents may be helpful for completing one's homework, but such parents, being more efficient in health production, may also help their children learn good health habits.

Finding data on all of these possible correlates of educational attainment is indeed an arduous task. One way around this set of problems is to find variables causing changes in educational attainment that are not correlated with these other factors that may have independent effects on adult health. For example, Albuoy and Lequien (2009), using longitudinal data (data that follow individuals over time) from France, focused on two reforms, which raised minimum school attendance to age 14 and then from 14 to age 16. Changes in mandatory schooling attendance laws are plausibly unrelated to the personal and family characteristics possibly affecting adult health described above but are likely to have increased the mean number of years of schooling completed. The authors found empirical evidence that these reforms increased education levels, but although subsequent declines in mortality were observed, none of the declines were statistically significant. Thus, on the basis of this study's findings alone, one cannot properly conclude that education improves health. The article includes a comprehensive literature review; many previous studies did not show a

Box 2.4
(continued)

causal effect. Failure to find a relationship does not mean that Grossman's framework is wrong. Rather, it means that some rigorous empirical tests do not lend support to his hypothesis.

By using a cohort data set of education reform in Taiwan, another similar study found evidence that there is a causal relationship between parental education and child health (Chou, Liu, Grossman, et al. 2010). In 1968, Taiwan extended the compulsory education system from six years (primary school) to nine years (junior high school). Chou and her colleagues found that this reform led to a significant increase in years of schooling for individuals born after 1956, which in turn lowered the incidence of low birth weight and mortality of infants born in the period 1978–1999. This result suggests that an increase in parents' schooling causes better infant health.

has completed more years of schooling. More highly educated persons should be healthier for this reason, but the effect of education on medical care use is less clear since health inputs may be more productive for more highly educated persons. Hence, less medical care is needed to produce a given level of health. Education also affects the wage rate, but Grossman accounted for the wage effect separately.

2.4 Measuring Health Capital

Ideally, there would be a single metric of health capital, such as the market value of a building for physical capital, and measurement could be performed by simply placing one's finger on a button, and the "health capital meter" would provide a numerical value of the person's health stock. Unlike physical capital, there is no accepted unitary measure of health capital. Moreover, there is no market price for good health, although health definitely has value. It is just hard to measure. Although difficult, in recent years there have been many attempts at quantification of the value of changes in health. There is no single commonly accepted measure of health status, but there are several widely used proxies.

Mortality

The most objective single health status measure is mortality. In the Grossman model, death occurs when health capital falls below a certain threshold. An advantage of mortality as a measure of health capital is that there is no interrater variability in mortality as there is in assessing other dimensions of health, certainly psychological states but even physiological dimensions. For example, on a disability scale of 0 to 10, where 10 is totally disabled, one rater may rate inability to climb three flights of stairs as a 6. Another person may consider this a 9. Patients are often asked to rate their pain on a scale from 0 to 10. There is interpersonal variability in rating the same level of pain as well.

Mortality-based measures include life expectancy, measured at birth or later in the life course. Life expectancy measures median years of survival of the persons in a given cohort. The median is calculated at the 50th percentile of personal longevity.

Although mortality-based measures may be adequate for countries with low life expectancies, in countries in which longevity has increased markedly, so has the burden of chronic disease. Thus, researchers have characterized health in terms of measures that reflect the quantity as well as the quality of life. Grossman measured the flow from the stock of health as the number of healthy days in a year minus the number of days during which the person was ill or the number of days the person spent in bed. However, people often experience health losses that do not involve being in bed, or even being "sick" in the usual sense of the word. For example, some people may have frequent headaches or stiffness in the neck or leg and continue to work or attend school. Or they might have a mental condition such as being depressed. A depressed person might go to work and conduct household activities, but not feel good about it.

Quality-of-Life Rating Scales

To account for such sources of variation in health, researchers have used two conceptually different approaches. In one approach, used in some disciplines other than economics, such as psychology, quality of life is measured by a rating scale. A survey respondent is read a description of a case (e.g., about a person with a specific disease), and the respondent is asked to rate the case on a scale, for example a 10-point scale ranging from 0 for dead to 10 for asymptomatic (Patrick and Erickson 1993; Kaplan 1995). The responses are then used as a measure of quality of life for a person with this diagnosis or condition. Suppose the mean response for a particular ailment (e.g., serious migraine headaches) is 6.7 and persons with the ailment have a mean life expectancy of 20 years. The quality-adjusted life-years interval for persons in this category is 20×0.67 or 13.4 years. In health care jargon, quality-adjusted life years are called QALYs. By contrast, a person with an amputated leg with the same life expectancy might hypothetically have $20 \times 0.43 = 8.6$ QALYs remaining. QALYs do have the virtue of describing health in a single metric, and this measure is widely used for this reason. Given the complexity of the human body, the health of each of us could conceivably be described in each of hundreds of metrics.

Economists have been critical of the use of rating scales to measure quality of life. In particular, economics focuses on choices people make subject to constraints, such as an income constraint. Consuming a good or a service means giving up something else. With the rating scale, survey respondents could rate all illnesses and conditions as low or high life quality. One's answer to one question has no direct bearing on one's answer to another.

QUALITY OF LIFE DERIVED FROM TRADE-OFF QUESTIONS

We are about to introduce this book's first application of decision making under uncertainty. Before proceeding, we describe an important concept. Suppose there are two alternative outcomes, X_1 and X_2. These are two different values of the same measure, which are realized at a future date. X_1 and X_2 may be prices of a share of stock, test scores, or the number of apples that grow on a tree. Let Θ be the probability that the value will be X_1 and $(1 - \Theta)$ be the probability that the value will be X_2. Then the *expected value* of X is

$$E(X) = \Theta X_1 + (1 - \Theta)X_2. \quad (2.5)$$

The probabilities Θ and $(1 - \Theta)$ weigh the likelihood of each outcome occurring, where the weights sum to 1.0.

One method for deriving a measure of QALY is to use responses to *standard gamble* questions. People are read a description of life with a certain disease. Then they are asked the following trade-off question (actually a series of questions, but our description describes the underlying concept). Suppose you had this disease and there was a surgical operation that would either (1) cure you of the disease completely, and you would be in perfect health, *or* (2) kill you during the operation painlessly and quickly. At what probability of death would you be indifferent between having the operation or not? The respondent is asked to assume that the operation would be completely covered by health insurance. For this reason, there would be no monetary cost to the respondent of undergoing the procedure. In this application, being in perfect health is set at a value of 1.0. Being dead is valued at 0.0. Thus, the maximum probability of death the respondent would accept to undergo the operation reveals the decrement to health due to having the disease.

To see the standard gamble works, using subscripts to depict states of the world, let U_a be the person's utility when perfectly healthy, U_d be the utility when dead, U_b be the person's utility with the disease, and Θ^* be the probability of dying painlessly and quickly during the operation that makes the person indifferent between undergoing the operation or not. Then

$$U_b = (1 - \Theta^*)U_a + \Theta^* U_d. \quad (2.6)$$

Set U_a to 1.0 and U_d to 0.0. If the person answering the standard gamble question gives us Θ^*, then we can determine the utility of being in the state with the disease U_b. For example, if Θ^* is 0.2, the utility of being in the state with the disease is 0.8. Values of U_b can be computed for a variety of disease states or for general measures of health capital. In this example, the Θ* values are weights. Using the standard gamble questions, the weights are elicited from survey respondents. The weights in this case reveal the relative utilities of being in the alternative health states.

Responding to a question about having an operation to cure one of chronic obstructive pulmonary disease (COPD), a medical term for chronic bronchitis and emphysema, lung diseases often caused by smoking, respondents gave a mean value of Θ* of 0.423 and a median value of 0.325 (Khwaja, Sloan, and Wang 2009), implying values of U_b of 0.577 (= 1.0 – 0.423) and 0.675, respectively. The U_b's can be interpreted as QALYs. Interestingly, as reported by Khwaja, Sloan, and Wang, the mean value of quality of life with COPD obtained from current smokers was higher than the mean values obtained from former and never smokers, implying that smokers derive less utility loss from getting COPD than nonsmokers do, which may be one reason why they smoke.[3] To develop an index for a country as a whole, one would need to ask similar questions about a host of diseases and conditions and survey persons from across the country.

2.5 Adding Uncertainty: Decision Trees, Backward Induction, and Decision Making under Uncertainty

Grossman's model was pathbreaking at the time his paper was published and is still considered an outstanding contribution. However, Grossman did not incorporate uncertainty into his model (see, e.g., Gilleskie 2008). Most decisions one makes about one's health involve a high degree of uncertainty about the effects of decisions. Thus, in analyzing decisions people make about their health and health care, it is important to consider uncertainty. But as in general happens, adding realism comes at the cost of added complexity.

The formal theory used by economists to evaluate decisions under uncertainty was originally developed by John von Neumann, a mathematician, and Oskar Morgenstern, an economist, in the late 1940s (see von Neumann and Morgenstern 1944). The underlying premise of this framework is that when outcomes from a decision are uncertain, people select the alternative that has the highest expected utility. We will have much more to say about their concept when we discuss individual demand for private health insurance in chapter 4.

In the context of our standard gamble example, those persons who believe that the actual probability of dying during the operation is less than Θ* will undergo the operation. Those who believe that the actual probability exceeds Θ* will reject the operation and live the rest of their life with their disease (for example, COPD). If the probability is less than Θ*, a person's expected utility is higher if she has the operation, and conversely if the probability is greater than Θ*. The

3. An alternative interpretation is that the smokers knew they had a higher probability of getting COPD and they rationalized an unpleasant situation that they were likely to confront by minimizing its adverse consequences.

probability Θ^* may be expected to vary among individuals. Those who attach a lower utility to being in a state of health with the disease will have a higher Θ^*, and conversely.

The standard gamble question depicts a problem of decision making under uncertainty. People who decide to undergo the procedure to cure their disease do not know in advance whether they will actually survive the operation or not. Ex ante, the probabilities of dying or being completely cured are between 0 and 1. Ex post, or after the operation, the probability of death is either 0 or 1. In other words, the effects of inputs on outputs are uncertain.

The example of having an operation to cure COPD is completely hypothetical. No such operation actually exists. Furthermore, although it is a useful analytic device, few persons undergo surgical procedures in which the probability of dying during the operation is as high as 0.2 or 0.4. Such a risk would only be undertaken, as a general rule, after all possible therapeutic alternatives had been exhausted.

A Realistic Application: A Pediatrician's Decision about Ordering a Throat Culture

There are many realistic applications in which patients and their physicians make clinical decisions under conditions of uncertainty. As a case in point, consider whether or not a pediatrician should obtain a specimen for culture from children who visit the pediatrician's office with sore throats.[4] There are three alternatives: give antibiotics to all children with sore throats, test all children for a throat infection and give antibiotics to all children who test positive, and give antibiotics to none of the children with sore throats.

To focus on the issue at hand, how people make decisions when the decision criterion is an expected value, we assume that the physician always acts in the best interest of the patient, and both the physician and the patient (or in this case the patient's parent) are rational—that is, they consider the full range of benefits and costs in making a decision.

Costs in this context are the costs of the culture, of the antibiotics, and of not treating a strep throat. An untreated case of streptococcal infection may lead to rheumatic heart disease, which may in turn lead to disability, premature death, or cardiac surgery to repair a damaged heart valve resulting from rheumatic fever. Thus, days with strep throat represent a health flow, and inputs or health investments are the throat cultures and antibiotics (and implicitly physician time). Assume for now that antibiotics always cure strep throat, and there are no errors in the throat culture results.

The option to be selected is the one with the minimum cost. Cost incorporates both the costs of resources expended in diagnosis and treatment *and* the monetary equivalent of the utility loss from illness. By casting utility loss as a cost, we do not explicitly consider utilities in this application. Rather, utility is present but in the background as a factor determining cost.

4. This example is taken by Keeler (1995). This chapter in a book on cost-effectiveness and cost-benefit analysis provides several applications of decision analysis.

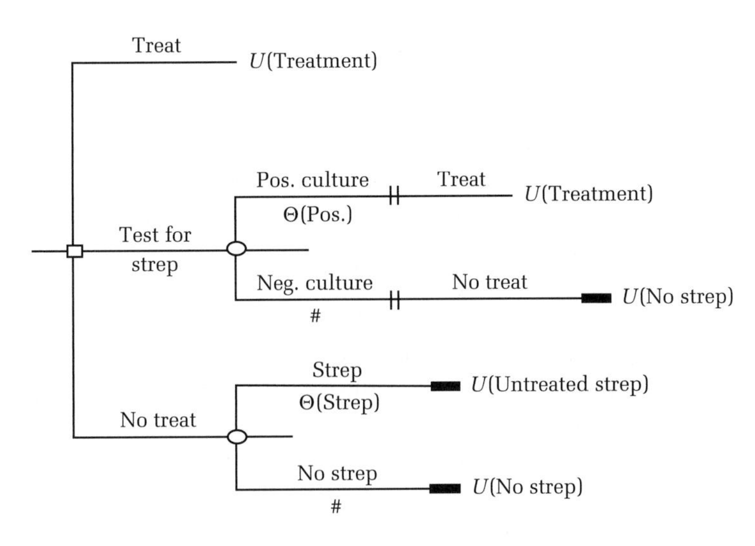

FIGURE 2.5
Decision Tree for Managing a Sore Throat.
Source: Keeler (1995).

By convention, in drawing the decision trees used in decision analysis, squares represent choice nodes. Circles represent states of nature with associated probabilities of outcomes that are beyond the decision maker's control. Throat cultures and antibiotic treatment have associated prices. The cost of an untreated streptococcal infection must be computed in terms of the loss in utility from a decrease in health capital attributable to rheumatic fever, which reflects both the loss of health capital and the utility loss associated with a unit of loss of health capital (fig. 2.5).

Now let us consider each of the alternatives. One option is always to treat a sore throat ("treat," top of fig. 2.5). The total cost is the sum of the cost of the antibiotic C_a and the cost of antibiotic resistance C_{ar} (also part of health capital, i.e., it makes a negative contribution to health capital), which occurs with a probability Θ_{ar}. The cost of antibiotic resistance depends partly on the availability of alternative antibiotics that may be effective against the bacteria causing infection in the future. If new antibiotics are anticipated, there is less reason for physicians to be cautious about prescribing currently available drugs because of a concern about drug resistance. The decision maker believes that the probability of strep is a certain value Θ_s, and the probability the child does not have strep is $(1 - \Theta_s)$. If the child does not have strep, the total cost is the cost of the throat culture. (There is no utility loss when there is no streptococcal infection.) The expected cost is $(1 - \Theta_s)C_c$ when the child has no strep versus $\Theta_s(C_c + C_a)$ if the culture reveals the presence of strep.

The third option is not to culture or treat with an antibiotic ("no treat," bottom of fig. 2.5). Then the expected cost is $\Theta_s C_{rf}$, where C_{rf} is the cost of having rheumatic fever, measured in terms of the utility loss from decreased health capital and the treatment cost needed to restore health capital to its level prior to the onset of rheumatic fever.

To select the option with the lowest cost, the decision maker computes expected costs by taking into account the probabilities of various outcomes and the costs to be incurred in the future. The optimal decision depends on the probabilities Θ_{ar} and Θ_s, and the costs are C_{ar}, C_c, C_a, and C_{rf}. Changes in the probabilities and costs could dramatically change the optimal decision and hence the demand for cultures, antibiotics, and cures for damaged heart valves. If, for example, every child with a sore throat had streptococcal infection ($\Theta_s = 1$), there would be no reason to test for strep, and similarly, if the probability of strep was nearly zero and the costs of untreated strep were low, there would be no need to test for strep.

For various reasons, these parameters may differ among countries. If antibiotics are cheap and substitute antibiotics are readily available to handle drug resistance, the demand for throat cultures may fall.

The pecuniary value of a unit of health capital may vary among countries and among persons within a country (see, e.g., Murphy and Topel 2006; Hall and Jones 2007; chapter 16, this book). The cost of a throat culture may vary because of differences in the prices of cultures, whether or not cultures are subsidized by health insurance or available at a free clinic, and the distances a parent and child must travel to reach a facility at which cultures are administered.

Errors in Diagnostic Tests

In the above example, the culture results are never wrong. More realistically, tests are not perfect. Neither are treatments. For example, drugs and surgery vary in their effectiveness. Perhaps at some time in the future, advances in knowledge about genetics will make it possible to perfectly match patients and therapeutic approaches (e.g., various drugs within a drug class) perfectly, but the state of current knowledge falls far short of this ideal.

In table 2.1, of the 200 persons with no strep (as determined later after the initial culture was performed), the culture was positive in 20 percent (40/200) of children, suggesting strep, a false positive. On the other hand, of the 100 cases in

Table 2.1
Hypothetical Data on Children with Sore Throats

	Child Had		
Test Results	Strep	No Strep	Total
Strep (positive)	90	40	130
Strep (negative)	10	160	170
Total	100	200	300

which the child actually had strep, the test yielded negative results 10 percent of the time, which are false negatives. A false positive result may have led to a treatment that was not warranted and a false negative result may have led to no recommendation for treatment when treatment was warranted. In total, 16.7 percent of tests yielded erroneous findings.

The existence of false positive and false negative test results may affect the optimal testing and treatment strategy. If the initial probability of having the disease is high, then a negative culture is likely to be a false negative. To the extent that this is so, the optimal strategy may be to administer the antibiotic without the culture. Conversely, if the initial probability of having the disease is low, then a positive test result is likely to be a false positive, in which case the optimal strategy may be to forgo both the test and the treatment, but this will also depend on the cost of untreated disease. The probability of disease in table 2.1 is somewhere in the middle, in which case testing and treatment are likely to be the optimal strategy.

The decision tree and associated probabilities at first glance seem distant from the production function given by equation 2.1. But there is a definite relationship between the two. Suppose that the input is a physician visit in which sore throats are diagnosed and treated, and the output is measured in terms of cures. The marginal product of the visit will depend on both the accuracy of the culture and the effectiveness of the antibiotic in treating streptococcal infection. False negatives and false positives will lower the productivity of the visit. Cures in turn will affect health according to equation 2.2.

2.6 Consumer Choices about Health Behaviors: A General Framework

Unhealthy Behaviors

Above, we specified medical care and patient time associated with the receipt of medical care as components of health investment. It is a simple matter to add patient time allocated to activities that enhance health, such as time spent on physical exercise. However, not all time is spent on activities that improve health. Not only is time spent on activities that have no effect on health, but people often engage in health-reducing behaviors as well. Such activities as smoking, excessive alcohol and illicit drug use, driving at high speeds, and skydiving are often if not generally bad for one's health.

In an economic framework, a person engages in health-decreasing activities because the outputs of such activities, such as getting intoxicated, experiencing thrills from taking risks, or impressing a member of the opposite gender, yield utility in their own right. Thus, for example, a person may smoke for enjoyment even though the person knows that smoking is bad for his or her health in the long run. These are choices for which there is long-run pain for short-term gain. There are also activities with long-term gain for short-term pain, such as jogging, for some if not for all of us, or getting a colonoscopy. Getting a colonoscopy involves short-term inconvenience (taking bad-tasting medication to clear one's intestines the day before the procedure, with associated cramps, fasting, and loss of time from other activities) and out-of-pocket cost, but in the long run, screening for colon cancer may avert serious colon cancer, morbidity, disability, and death.

THE CONCEPT OF PRESENT VALUE

As an example of how initiating a habit harmful to one's health can be viewed in an economic framework, we consider the decision to start and stop smoking. Smoking is both common and harmful to health. Because the benefits and costs of smoking do not all accrue simultaneously (some of the costs occur years after a person starts smoking), as a first step, we introduce the concept of present value (PV) of an asset.

Suppose one possesses a bond that pays \$1 a year for T years. At the end of T, the lender repays the purchase price of the bond. Then PV is the following:

$$PV = 1/(1+i) + 1/(1+i)^2 + 1/(1+i)^3 + 1/(1+i)^4 \ldots + 1/(1+i)^T + \text{purchase price}/(1+i)^T. \quad (2.7)$$

Other factors being the same, PV is lower for higher values of i, the discount rate, and conversely. With a higher value of i, returns accruing in the distant future receive relatively less weight in present value than do returns accruing earlier. Conversely, costs incurred far in the future have less of an influence on PV when i is high. Many if not most health behaviors involve a trade-off between taking a precaution now in return for an improvement in health later. Smoking involves lack of precaution now, with adverse health effects, when they occur, often appearing many decades after a person initiates the habit.

FUNDAMENTAL UNDERLYING ASSUMPTIONS

ASSUMPTIONS: RATIONAL, FORWARD-LOOKING, AND TIME CONSISTENCY DESCRIBED

In an economic framework, economists typically assume that people are (1) *rational*, that is, that they take into account all available information in making decisions; (2) *forward-looking*, considering future benefits and costs as well as those accruing currently; and (3) *time consistent*, that is, they apply the same discount rate throughout the time horizon of the decision and over which the consequences of the decision are expected to occur.

To understand what being rational, forward-looking, and time consistent is not, consider the alternatives. An irrational person may be *impulsive*, making spur-of-the-moment decisions based on cues. Or the person may be *boundedly rational*, that is, not able to fully evaluate the pros and cons of alternative options because the person is limited cognitively. Persons who do not take account of future benefits and costs in weighing options are *myopic*.

Time-inconsistent individuals apply a higher discount rate i in the short run than they do in longer run. If benefits from the decision are realized first, such as enjoying a cigarette after a good meal, followed in time by costs, such as adverse health effects from being a smoker, a higher discount rate would tend to make future costs less important when discounted to the present. Since the discount rate for the decision of whether or not to smoke today is high relative to the discount rate between tomorrow and the day after tomorrow and between the day after tomorrow and the day after that, the time-inconsistent individual reasons, "I'll stop smoking tomorrow." (Tomorrow, the discount rate will be lower than today.) Thus, the future costs of smoking will loom larger in the decision whether or not to smoke tomorrow than it does in the decision about whether to smoke today. Similarly, a time-inconsistent individual would eat the apple pie with ice cream for dessert today, reasoning that he will start dieting tomorrow. Today, the benefit of dieting, the benefit of a trim waistline, is discounted at a high rate and hence not worth as much as when the decision is made tomorrow. Of course, tomorrow never comes. When offered apple pie tomorrow, the decision is like today's. A time-inconsistent individual might well be attracted by a furniture store's advertisement that buyers can buy furniture now, with payments to begin only next year.

In deciding whether or not to order a desert at a restaurant, a patron may reason that he will start dieting tomorrow to justify ordering the desert today. Like a rational economic agent, the patron is forward-looking in contemplating the downstream consequences of a current action. Following this reasoning, the patron knows he will enjoy the desert now and the consequences of the desert, weight gain and possible deleterious effects on health and appearance, will occur later. In deciding whether or not to consume the desert today, the person implicitly compares the benefit, the enjoyment of eating the desert now with the consequence, not being able to fit into his clothes tomorrow. In thinking about dieting tomorrow, the person thinks that the comparison tomorrow will involve a benefit from the desert to be derived if the desert is consumed tomorrow versus a cost, which is not being able to fit in one's clothes the day after tomorrow. Of course, if the person eats the desert on both evenings, it is possible that the clothes purchased tomorrow will not fit the next day, necessitating another purchase of even larger clothes.

More formally, on evening 0, the individual derives a benefit from the desert of B_0. This benefit is compared with a cost of $C_1/(1 + i_0)$. Cost has a subscript of 1 since the weight gain becomes apparent only tomorrow. If the former exceeds the later, he consumes the desert. On the second evening, the comparison is between the benefit, still B_0, and the cost, still C, but the C is now divided by $(1 + i_1)$, where $i_1 < i_0$. In other words, in the longer run, the patron is less present-oriented than in the short run. The problem is that the long run never arrives because although the patron knows better, he lacks self-control. These are called time-inconsistent preferences in that the discount rate between the first and the second day is not the same as between the second and the third day, or between the third and the fourth day, and so on.

To deal with lack of self-control, forward-looking agents may employ precommitment devices. For example, one may forgo going to the restaurant altogether to avoid being tempted to order a caloric desert. Or when shopping, a person may not buy ice cream in the grocery store because he knows if it is available at home in the refrigerator, he will eat it as a midnight snack. The same goes for cigarettes or liquor in the home. For very obese persons, bariatric surgery, which reduces the effective size of the stomach, may be an effective self-control device.

Ex Ante Expectations and Decisions, Ex Post Realizations, and Revising Expectations from Learning

Analytically, a person makes a decision by working backward, starting at the end of the person's time horizon and working backward to the decision point. The economic term for this thought process is *backward induction*. People are assumed to make as sound a decision as possible given events that have already transpired.

Suppose there are T time periods. Then in this model of backward induction, a person considers what the optimal decision is in period T. The logic is then repeated for one period earlier, $T - 1$. The net result is an efficient string of choices leading back to the initial period, period 0. In period 0, the person makes decisions based on what he or she expects the future to hold. Over time, what was once a prediction becomes a reality—an outcome is either realized or it is not, and individuals may make midcourse corrections to accommodate new information that accumulates over time.

For example, to illustrate the difference between ex ante and ex post, the learning process, and midcourse corrections that result from learning, suppose a family is planning a picnic and chooses among three alternative days on which to have the picnic. On day 0, the family makes subjective judgments about the probabilities that it will rain on days 1, 2, and 3, and it decides to plan the picnic for day 1. On day 0, the probabilities of rain on day 1 are between 0 and 1. On day 1 itself, the probability of rain is either 0 or 1. It either rains or it does not rain. Based on whether or not it rains on day 1, the family may postpone the picnic from day 1 to day 2 or 3, or based on the experience of having seen a heavy rain on day 1, they may revise the probabilities of rain on days 2 and 3 upward and decide to postpone the picnic to another season. Given the experience with day 1, the parents have learned something (perhaps not much) about the probability of rain at this time of year and have revised their estimates of the probability of rain in the near term accordingly.

In the context of the smoking decision, although the probability of developing a persistent cough or a more serious chronic illness such as COPD is increased by smoking, not everyone who smokes develops a persistent cough or COPD. Some smokers may decide to quit smoking once they learn that smoking makes them cough. Others who do not cough when they smoke may reason that smoking may be harmful to others but not to themselves, and these people may be more likely to continue to smoke. In essence, the smokers learn over time about *their own* health risks of smoking; this risk varies among smokers because of genetics and other factors.

Is the Economic Framework of Health Behavior Decision Making Plausible?

The economic framework of decision making just described will certainly give those who remember their teenage years, or who have been parents of teenagers recently, pause. One's first reaction is likely to be, teenagers do not think this way! They do not think ahead to the consequences of their current actions. Many would say much the same about the behavior of adults as well.

Mainstream economists have several responses to these concerns. First, laws permitting adults to engage in potentially harmful health behaviors ordinarily assume that adults can make informed intertemporal choices. The alternative is to ask government to engage in loco parentis. Second, to the extent that adults, including young adults, have difficulty forming probabilities and thinking about utilities in alternative states of the world, states they have not personally experienced, there is a role for public health education strategies, such as tobacco control programs, to provide this information. Third, people engage in health behaviors that are often contrary to their continuing to be in good health because they are physically addicted. The answer to this objection is that the decision depicted above occurs *before* becoming addicted, and also, physical addiction can be represented in an economic framework as the (dis)utility of quitting. Fourth, economists argue that one should not judge a model by its assumptions but on the basis of empirical tests of its predictions. There is empirical evidence that people quit smoking after receiving bad news about their health (Sloan, Smith, and Taylor 2003). Many of the health messages are quite serious and attributable to smoking, such as a heart attack, stroke, or the onset of COPD. People update their subjective beliefs about longevity following adverse health events (Smith, Taylor, Sloan, et al. 2001). Information updating can be rational and part of an economic model of health decision making. If models based on alternative assumptions, for example myopia and time inconsistency, biased beliefs about the outcomes stemming from various health behaviors, let them compete with the traditional economic frameworks. If they provide better explanatory power, they are worth using.

ECONOMIC EVIDENCE ON HEALTH BEHAVIORS AND PUBLIC POLICY IMPLICATIONS

There is a large literature on demand for medical care services. We leave a discussion of empirical evidence from this literature to the next chapter. We discuss empirical evidence on health behaviors, including those that have potential adverse effects on health, here.

Economic models of decision making offer predictions of the effect of price changes on demand, and the economic analysis of health behaviors is no exception. Economists view empirical evidence that people respond to changes in prices of products that are potentially harmful to health as evidence that their framework has predictive value. When the price of a good, such as a pack of cigarettes, rises, the expected utility of becoming a smoker falls. Economic studies show that the demand for cigarettes and alcoholic behaviors respond to price changes (see, e.g., Chaloupka and Warner 2000; Cook and Moore 2000).

Economists distinguish between the *extensive margin* and the *intensive margin*. The extensive margin refers to whether or not *any* amount of the good or service is consumed. The intensive margin refers to consumption, conditional on at least one unit being consumed. The decision to smoke, a decision at the extensive margin, is negatively correlated with the price of cigarettes, with an associated elasticity of about –0.48 (see Cawley 2008). This suggests that raising the excise tax on cigarettes is an effective policy instrument for reducing rates of smoking. Price appears to be a factor in boys starting to smoke but not girls (Gilleskie and Strumpf 2005). The decision to be a current alcohol drinker has a price elasticity of –0.55, and the prevalence of beer drinking among youths has a price elasticity of –0.2 (Cawley 2008). On the intensive margin, for example the number of cigarettes smoked by smokers per day, higher prices of cigarettes have a greater deterrent effect on heavy smoking (11+ cigarettes daily) than on lighter smoking (6–10 cigarettes daily), but higher prices have important effects on both.

Gertler, Shah, and Bertozzi (2005) reported the results of a survey of over 1,000 prostitutes in Mexico. Unlike tobacco and alcohol, participation in commercial sex involves negotiation between the consumer and the seller. The authors found, for example, that prostitutes charged 23 percent more for unprotected sex, a measure of quality of commercial sex services. This suggests that markets for this type of activity are not that different from markets for other goods and services. This finding also illustrates trade-offs between some other objective and good health. If the consumers of this service were mainly concerned about staying in good health, the price of prostitution services would be higher, not lower, for protected sex.

Some substance abuse treatment programs use financial incentives to reinforce therapy. The incentives can take the form of vouchers that clients receive if they are compliant with therapy. One study estimated that vouchers increased compliance with therapy by an average of 30 percent (Cawley 2008). Again, the subsidies raise the relative return of not using the addictive good.

The assumption of rationality does not require that consumers have perfect information. As consumers learn more, their behaviors often change. One type of information relates to scientific findings, such as those embodied in the US Surgeon General's report on the harms of smoking in 1964. There is some evidence that the report led to an immediate reduction in smoking rates (see Cawley 2008), although whether or not the response was due to the report has been disputed since there was adverse publicity about the harms of smoking before the report appeared (Sloan, Smith, and Taylor 2002).

The Surgeon General's report and journal articles about the adverse effects of smoking provide consumers with general information. Nearly everyone is able to tell a story about someone who smoked for decades and lived a long and healthy life. The effects of smoking indeed vary from individual to individual, and a person has no way of knowing in advance whether or not he or she will develop a smoking-related illness.

2.7 FRONTIER ISSUES: THE BEHAVIORAL ECONOMICS CRITIQUE—THEORY AND EVIDENCE

Formal economic models of rational choice are attractive analytically, but they have many critics, even within the economics profession, and certainly among scholars in other disciplines. Each of us can tell stories that seem quite inconsistent with rational, forward-looking, and time-consistent decision making.

For example, teenagers think they are invulnerable. They can smoke and quit any time they wish.[5] Why would a buyer in autumn be lured to purchase a product by an advertisement offering no money down on the product and no interest payments until next year, although the seller may more than make up from its seeming generosity by charging higher interest after January 1 of the following year? A car dealer raises the hoods on its new cars for passersby to see. Why would a person buy a new car because he saw a bunch of hoods raised, presumably a subliminal greeting? As for health behaviors, why would seeing a comic-looking camel induce one to smoke Camels or young people running along a beach and laughing to drink beer? It would seem that the camel (e.g., "Joe Camel" in old Camel cigarette advertisements, now banned by US law) would not reveal much information about the quality of the smoke or even about the quality of Camel cigarettes. Beer consumption should reduce one's ability to run on the beach, although perhaps it encourages one to laugh.

Economists specializing in the field of behavioral economics are borrowing concepts from the field of psychology to answer these questions. The use of addictive substances is particularly interesting because their use and abuse seem to violate standard assumptions of economic models, but other health behaviors are pertinent as well.[6]

5. An interesting economics article seeks to explain the phenomenon of "accidental addiction." See Orphanides and Zervos (1995).

6. Decades ago, the Nobel Laureate in Economics, Herbert Simon, questioned the standard assumption of economics that people make rational decisions, arguing people are partly rational because of limits in processing information relevant to some of the decisions they make. Some decisions are reached on an emotional or irrational basis. He coined the term "bounded rationality." More recently, cognitive psychologists Tversky and Kahneman (1981) went even further than Simon, demonstrating that people do not make rational decisions even for simple problems. For their work, Kahneman was awarded the Nobel Prize in Economics. Tversky had died earlier, and Nobel Prizes are awarded only to living persons. All three scholars would question whether people have the cognitive capacity to make the rational choice of whether or not to begin and conditional on beginning to quit smoking using the framework depicted in equation 2.8, appendix 2A.

Cawley (2008), in a review of the literature on addictive behaviors, distinguished among three alternative models of addictive behavior: perfectly rational, imperfectly rational, and irrational. The best-known model that deals with addictive behavior and that is based on the assumption of rationality is Gary Becker and Kevin Murphy's (1988) rational addiction model. In their framework, addiction is a choice of a rational utility-maximizing individual with stable preferences. Three important features characterize addictive behavior: (1) *Tolerance.* Higher levels of past consumption of an addictive good make a specific level of current consumption less satisfying. (2) *Withdrawal.* Addicted individuals feel worse when they stop consuming the good. (3) *Reinforcement.* Persons who consume more of the addictive good derive higher satisfaction from consuming an extra unit; the higher marginal return from consuming more leads to even higher levels of consumption of the addictive good.

The Becker-Murphy model explains that even persons who consume addictive goods can be forward-looking and use available information to compare future benefits with the adverse consequences of their present actions. In fact, a major motivation for the model was to show how the consumption of addictive goods can be incorporated into a standard economic framework.

Because of reinforcement, the model predicts that the way to successful cessation is to quit "cold turkey." Gradual quitting does not work in this model because the addict will always derive a lot of satisfaction from smoking a cigarette. Thus, the path to successful quitting requires that the habit be broken, reducing marginal utility from smoking a cigarette.

Alternatively, individuals are imperfectly rational about the consumption of addictive goods. They are imperfectly rational in the sense that, while accounting for the future consequences of present actions, they may (1) have time-inconsistent preferences, (2) misperceive the probability of harm following from their current behavior, (3) have cognitive difficulties in forming probabilities or learning from the experiences of others, or (4) have imperfect information about their own probability of getting addicted.

Imperfect information about the probability of becoming addicted mainly applies to younger persons. Orphanides and Zervos (1995) and Wang (2007) developed models in which individuals have imperfect information about their own propensities to become addicted. Youths experiment with addictive goods and get addicted "unexpectedly." These models can explain such empirical failures of the perfectly rational addiction model as "randomness of addiction," "unhappy addicts," and "failed attempts to quit smoking." Fudenberg and Levine (2006) constructed a simple "dual-self" model that provides a unified explanation for phenomena unexplained by the perfectly rational addiction model, including time inconsistency/hyperbolic discounting.

In the dual-self model, people may know what is best for them, but they realize that in certain situations, when in the other self, they may not act in their long-run self interest. Therefore, people employ self-control mechanisms. An argument against the use of excise taxes is their regressivity. Such taxes impose a relatively higher burden on the poor than on the non-poor. However, the price elasticity of demand for cigarettes is higher for the poor than for others (Gruber, Sen, and Stabile 2003). Using a framework of imperfect rationality, Gruber and Köszegi (2004) argued that excise taxes act as an aid to self-control, in that they help people control their ability to abstain from smoking cigarettes. When the benefit of promoting self-control is considered, excise taxes are much less regressive than is typically alleged.

In the irrational model, decisions are mainly influenced by emotions experienced when consumption decisions are made (Loewenstein 2001). Emotional reactions to risky situations often diverge from objective assessments of risks, and when a divergence occurs between effect and choices based on objective evaluation of risk versus benefit, emotional reactions tend to dominate. The consumption of addictive goods may result from visceral urges provoked by external cues, which lead to impulsive behaviors, which do not occur absent the external cues (Loewenstein 1999).

More formally, the decision maker's brain switches between "hot" and "cold" states (Bernheim and Rangel 2004). The decision maker consumes harmful addictive goods while in the hot state and makes rational choices while in the cold state. This framework is consistent with several stylized facts about addiction, such as the high likelihood of a relapse following quit attempts. Acting on emotions and impulses may explain how Joe Camel advertisements or raised automobile hoods increase the consumption of these products.

2.8 Summary and Conclusions

Analysis of decisions people make about their health is important for several reasons. Demand for personal health services, the subject of the next chapter, is a demand derived from demand for health. Health investments undertaken today have important implications for personal health at a later date, and these decisions are made under conditions of uncertainty. The subject provides an opportunity to review (or learn for the first time) the distinction between capital stock and investment flows and the determinants of optimal capital stock from the vantage point of the company owner, or in our case the individual decision maker. We describe how changes in age, wages, and educational attainment affect demand for health capital. Each one of these topics is an important subject in its own right. There are dozens of books and journal articles on each topic, or even more. We have merely scratched the surface in this chapter. Hopefully, some readers will continue their study of this important area.

Health behaviors are highly germane to us all. The topic of health behaviors provides a fruitful context for investigating and assessing alternative models of personal decision making, including whether or not people are rational, forward-looking, and time consistent when making important personal decisions—a very controversial set of questions that is by no means yet resolved.

Many of the concepts introduced in this chapter have very broad applicability. For example, decisions such as the physician's decision to test or not to test for streptococcal infection applies in a very wide variety of contexts, not just personal health and personal decision making. Firms evaluate various options on a daily basis, employing the same framework, at least implicitly. Government agencies are often advised by outside groups to use such techniques, whether they actually use them or not.

Key Concepts

- health production function
- health capital
- cost of capital
- stock
- flow
- marginal efficiency of capital
- mortality
- quality-adjusted life years
- standard gamble
- decision tree
- present value
- rational
- forward-looking
- time consistent
- time preference
- myopic
- behavioral economics
- extensive margin
- intensive margin
- rational addiction model
- imperfectly rational

Review and Discussion Questions

2.1 Economics often uses the household as the decision-making unit. What precisely is meant by a "household" as the term is used in economics? What do you see as the key advantages and disadvantages of analyzing the household as the decision-making unit in the context of health economics decision making?

2.2 Economists often assume that people are rational and forward-looking in their decisions. What is really meant by the terms "rational" and "forward-looking"? Give concrete examples of a decision in which people are likely to be rational and forward-looking and one in which this assumption seems less tenable. What empirical tests would you use to determine whether people are rational and forward-looking in a particular context or not?

2.3 In this chapter, as in economics literature, we refer to health as a form of *capital* and term it as *human capital*. List at least two similarities and differences between *physical capital* and *human capital*. By treating health as a form of capital, what are the costs and benefits (returns) of holding health capital?

2.4 What is meant by the term "behavioral economics"? Give three examples in which concepts from behavioral economics have been applied. In what ways did behavioral economics provide insights that standard neoclassical economics would not have provided?

EXERCISES

2.1 A patient with arthritis of the knee is planning to have a knee replacement. He has applied for a loan for this surgery; the loan has an annual interest rate of 6 percent. The artificial knee can function for 10 years before it needs to be replaced. Fees for knee replacement surgery are expected to grow at 5 percent annually.

a. Why is an artificial knee a form of health capital?

b. Assume the artificial knee depreciates at a constant rate every year until the time of replacement, which is 10 years hence. What is the cost of this capital?

c. Suppose that instead of a loan, the patient plans to pay the surgery from his or her own savings. Assume that the bank's interest rate on savings deposits equals its rate on loans. Does this change your answer to (b)? Why or why not?

d. Draw the COC (cost of capital) line on a graph, with health capital on the x-axis and the COC rate on the y-axis. What is the slope of the COC schedule? Explain why it looks the way it does.

2.2. Suppose a hospital has 500 beds. It faces a demand curve $x = 1{,}200 - 2p$, where p is the price of a bed day and x is the number of patient days of care demanded. The fixed cost of adding a new bed is $150 and the total *housekeeping* cost is given by $C = (B/3.5)^2$, where B is the total number of beds.

a. Suppose the hospital's market price is fixed at \$250/bed day. What is the net marginal revenue to this hospital from an increase of one additional bed?

b. With p fixed at 250, graph the net marginal revenue curve, with the number of beds on the x-axis and dollars on the y-axis. Explain its shape.

c. Suppose the hospital is restricted from increasing its capacity for now, but it can set the price for each bed day. What is the optimal price level for the hospital if the hospital's objective is to maximize profits? Will the hospital fully use its current capacity in this case?

d. Now suppose the hospital is considering building a branch in another town. There is no existing hospital in that town. The cost of each new bed and house-keeping are the same as above, but the hospital's demand curve in this other town is $x = 800 - 1.2p$. What is its profit-maximizing price per bed day? How many beds should the new hospital have?

2.3 Assume the health production function is $h = 365 - 1/H$, where h is the number of healthy days a person has in each year and H is the person's health capital. Assume this person earns a wage of \$100/day, and the marginal cost of health investment $\pi = 25$ and is constant over time. The annual interest rate is 5 percent, and health capital depreciates at a rate of 15 percent per annum.

a. What does the MEC for this person's health capital look like? Draw the MEC curve on a graph, with health capital on the x-axis and the rate of return on the y-axis. Explain the shape of this MEC curve.

b. What is the cost of health capital in this problem?

c. Find the optimal level of health this person demands under the above conditions.

d. Suppose the person acquires a *chronic disease* and his health depreciation rate rises to 35 percent annually. How does this change your answer to part (c)?

e. Suppose instead of having a chronic disease the person experiences a recession and his wage falls to \$50/day. Assume the change in the price of time inputs accounts for 20 percent of the total change in cost of a unit of health investment. Show graphically how this change affects the MEC curve. What is the person's optimal health demand now?

f. Now focus on the role of human capital in this model. Suppose a person's edu-cational attainment increases. How does the MEC curve shift in this case? How does this shift affect the person's investment in health capital?

2.4 A person with osteoarthritis of the knee (a common condition in middle-aged and elderly individuals) plans to have a knee replacement. Assume he has a quasi-linear utility function ($U(\cdot)$) over wage w and his health H. That is, $U(w,H) = w + 10^4 \ln H$. Suppose with an artificial knee, the person can enjoy 20 additional healthy days annually during the next 10 years, during which he can earn a wage of $150/day. The annual interest rate is 2 percent.

a. What is the increase in the person's wage income if the person decides to get his knee replaced?

b. What is the net present value of the monetary return on knee replacement surgery?

Now suppose that in addition to the above conditions, the person also has a current health capital of 500 units. In the next decade, the additional health capital attributable to the artificial knee is given in the following table:

Year	1	2	3	4	5	6	7	8	9	10
Health Capital	50	49	48	46	43	39	34	28	21	12

The patient discounts his utility from health capital at a 10 percent annual rate. That is, he is indifferent between receiving 100 units of health capital this year and receiving 110 units next year.

c. What is the present value of his utility gain from having knee replacement surgery?

d. If the total cost (including both the monetary loss from paying the surgical fee and the disutility from undergoing the surgery and recovering) is 30,000, should the person undergo the surgical procedure?

2.5 Suppose a person is asked a standard gamble question about three kinds of diseases. For each disease, the person decides to undergo surgery if the expected utility from the operation exceeds or is equal to the patient's utility if he or she does not undergo surgery and continues having the disease. The person's expected utility is therefore $(1 - \Theta)U_a + \Theta U_d$, where U_a is the utility if the operation is successful, U_d is the utility if it fails, and Θ is the probability of failure. The patient assigns the following probabilities of surgical failure to the diseases:

Disease	A	B	C
Θ	0.25	0.4	0.01

a. Assume $U_a = 1$ and $U_d = 0$. Then what is the utility of having each of the diseases if the person is indifferent between having and not having the operation?

b. If the diseases are liver cancer, glaucoma, and dental caries, which one is most likely to be denoted as A above?

Viscusi and Evans (1990) took a similar approach to analyzing the loss in utility from being healthy to becoming sick. In the experiment they discussed in their paper, workers were randomly assigned to label four different chemicals: asbestos, TNT, sodium bicarbonate, and chloroacetophenone. The first two chemicals are quite dangerous and could cause death if they exploded. The third is rather harmless, and the fourth will only cause some tearing if proper treatment is not received. The authors asked the workers how much money they would have to receive in compensation if they were reassigned to label another chemical.

We will now apply the standard gamble concept to this problem. Assume the workers' utility function is $U(w) = \ln w$, where w is the hourly wage received from the labeling work and $U(\text{death}) = 0$.

c. The probability of TNT exploding is Θ_{TNT}, and if it explodes, the worker cannot survive. Also suppose the wage of labeling sodium bicarbonate is w_S per hour. What is the minimum wage a worker must receive if he were reassigned to label TNT as a function of Θ_{TNT} and w_S?

d. Which labeling work must have a higher wage, asbestos or chloroacetophenone?

e. What is the wage function for chloroacetophenone? Use w_S as the benchmark again. Which value(s) do you need to be able to solve this problem?

f. One major implication of Viscusi and Evans's research is that people may have different utility functions when healthy than when sick. Suppose the utility function is $V(w) = 0.5\ln w$ if the worker is sick but alive. How does this change your answer to part (e)?

2.6 Consider the following scenario, which is slightly different from the throat culture example in the chapter. A parent makes a decision about her child's care when the child is suspected to be infected by streptococci. The parent has three choices: ask the physician to give her child an antibiotic without performing the culture, perform the culture and give the child antibiotics only if the result is positive, or do nothing. If the child receives an antibiotic without being infected, she will develop a resistance to antibiotics (i.e., antibiotics will not kill infections that the child may get in the future) with probability Θ_{ar} and cost C_{ar} for further treatment. If she is infected and receives the antibiotic, she will be cured immediately without any side effects. If she is infected but not treated, the infection will develop into a rheumatic heart disease, which will cost C_{rf} as a result. The probability of being infected before the treatment, which is known by the parent, is Θ_s. The cost of antibiotics is C_a and the cost of a culture is C_c. The values for these probabilities and costs are given below:

Θ_s	Θ_{ar}	C_a	C_c	C_{ar}	C_{rf}
0.5	0.2	10	8.5	30	1,000

a. Draw the decision tree for the parent. Be sure to calculate the utility and cost of each possible outcome at the end of each branch.

b. What is the expected cost to the parent if she decides to give her child antibiotics without having the test performed?

c. If the parent's object is to minimize expected cost, what is her optimal decision?

d. What if the probability of infection fell from 0.5 to 0.2? Would this change your answer to part (c)?

ONLINE SUPPLEMENTAL MATERIAL

ADDICTION

http://www.dictionaryofeconomics.com/article?id=pde2008_A000252&edition=current&q=smoking%20behavior&topicid=&result_number=5

BEHAVIORAL ECONOMICS

http://en.wikipedia.org/wiki/Behavioral_economics

http://www.dictionaryofeconomics.com/article?id=pde2008_B000176&edition=current&q=behavioral%20economics&topicid=&result_number=4 (Rationality, bounded)

QUALITY-ADJUSTED LIFE YEARS

http://en.wikipedia.org/wiki/Quality-adjusted_life_year

WHO FRAMEWORK CONVENTION ON TOBACCO CONTROL

http://www.who.int/fctc/en/

SUPPLEMENTAL READINGS

Cawley, J. 2008. Reefer Madness, Frank the Tank, or Pretty Woman: To What Extent Do Addictive Behaviors Respond to Incentives? In *Incentives and Choice in Health Care*, ed. F. A. Sloan and H. Kasper, 163–193. Cambridge: MIT Press.

Viscusi, W. K., and W. N. Evans. 1990. Utility-Functions That Depend on Health-Status: Estimates and Economic Implications. *American Economic Review* 80 (3): 353–374.

APPENDIX 2A: APPLICATION TO DECISION TO START AND STOP SMOKING

To illustrate how health behaviors fit into an economic framework when the outcomes of the behaviors are uncertain, we model the decision of a person to start smoking and to quit smoking at a later date if he or she begins to experience adverse health consequences of smoking. The decision to start smoking is based on a comparison of the expected utility if the person smokes compared to the expected utility if the person does not smoke. Expected utility reflects (1) utilities in each period associated with each outcome of the decision, (2) beliefs about the probabilities of various outcomes at the time the smoking decision is made, (3) decision rules to be used in the future conditional on observing specific types of information, and (4) the person's subjective rate of discount r.

Suppose that there are three periods in one's life: youth (period 0), young adulthood (period 1), and mature adulthood (period 2). In period 0, the person decides whether or not to begin smoking. In period 1, the smoker decides whether or not to quit. If the smoker does not quit before entering period 2, it is too late to change his or her mind. The person is in the hands of his or her genes and past smoking behavior. No one starts smoking after period 0.

When the person begins smoking in period 0, the person does not know how smoking will affect his or her personal health. In fact, in period 0, there are no adverse health events to signal whether or not the person's genetic heritage is such that smoking will adversely affect health. Even the youth's parents are likely to be too young to have experienced major health shocks from smoking yet. However, the person is assumed to know the probability that he or she will experience a signal of worsening health in period 1; an example of a period 1 signal is periodic coughing spells. Some smokers who experience periodic coughing spells in period 1 develop COPD in period 2, but many coughers, in the fact the majority of such persons, do not get COPD. For smokers who continue to smoke into period 2, the probability of receiving bad news, that is, of getting COPD, depends on whether or

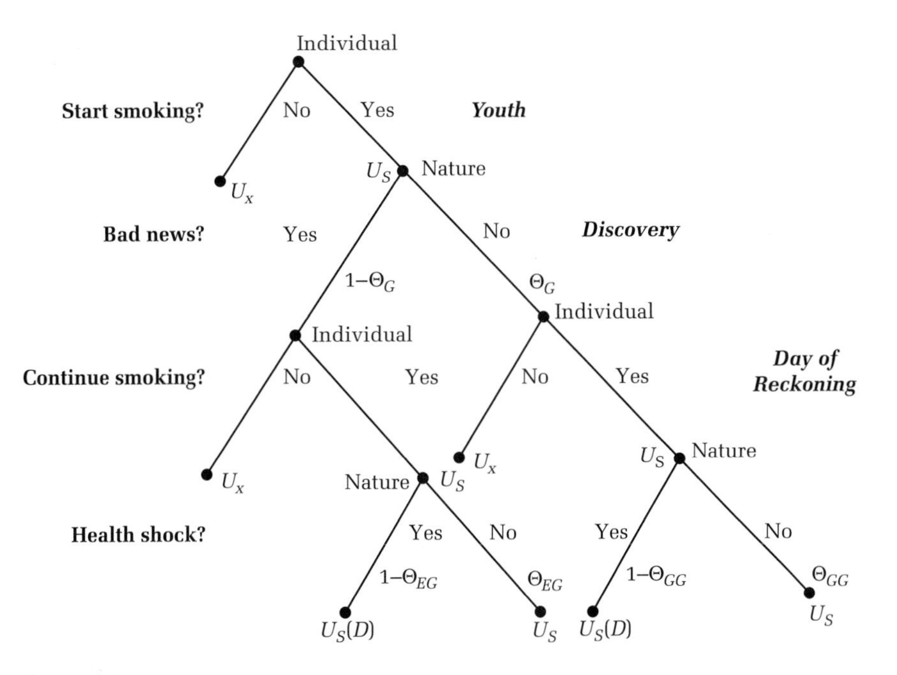

FIGURE 2.6
Game Tree: Decision to Start Smoking
Source: Reprinted by permission of the publisher from *The Smoking Puzzle: Information, Risk Perception, and Choice*, by Frank A. Sloan, V. Kerry Smith, and Donald H. Taylor Jr. (Cambridge, MA: Harvard University Press), 31. Copyright (c) 2003 by the President and Fellows of Harvard College.

not the smoker received an adverse health signal in period 1. If the person receives bad news in period 1, he or she has a greater likelihood of receiving *additional* bad news in period 2—that is, the probability that COPD will develop—than if the person does not receive bad news in period 1. But even if the news in period 1 is good, there is still a chance that the person will receive bad news in period 2.

The decision to initiate smoking can be depicted by a "game tree" (fig. 2.6). Typically the games in game theory involve two players. Here the game is between the individual and nature, which is the other player. Nature reveals good or bad news, which the individual uses to decide whether or not to make midcourse corrections, such as whether or not to quit smoking.

We now describe the four elements of the game tree: (1) utilities, (2) beliefs the individual has at the time the smoking decision is made about receiving good or bad news, (3) the decision rule guiding midcourse corrections in period 1, and (4) the person's subjective rate of discount.

The utility of smoking is U_S. Smoking yields various benefits to the smoker, including enjoyment of the taste, relief of stress, having something to do with one's hands, and impressing one's peers. Thus, when the person does not experience harm from smoking, he or she enjoys the utility of smoking U_S in each period with $U_S > 0$. Let U_0 be the utility of never smoking. To simplify the analysis, we set this utility to zero ($U_0 = 0$). $U_S > U_0$.

For persons who start smoking in period 0 and stop in period 1, we assign a utility of U_X, where U_X <0. This utility is negative because (1) there is a cost to breaking the smoking habit and (2) persons who quit may experience some permanent harm to health, although less that that for continuing smokers on average. We assume that if the person quits in period 1, he or she experiences the same health in period 2 as a person who never smokes. In period 2, if the smoker gets COPD, he or she is permanently disabled with a utility of U_{SD}, where $U_{SD} < U_X < 0$.

In period 1, nature determines whether the person receives good (G) or bad news (B) about the person's health. G news could be no smoking-related symptoms and B news could be a smoking-related symptom such as becoming tired after walking several blocks, a symptom the person did not observe in period 1. Based on the signal received, the person can quit smoking with a net utility cost of U_X, which is negative. Otherwise, the person continues to smoke with utility at U_S. In period 2, nature reveals to the person whether the person will remain healthy with utility U_S or suffer a smoking-related disease, such as COPD, with associated utility of U_{SD}.

In period 0, the person has subjective beliefs about receiving good or bad news in periods 1 and in period 2, conditional on having received good or bad news in period 1. Θ_B is the probability of receiving bad news in period 1; Θ_G, the probability of good news in period 1, that is, of receiving no signal of adverse health in period 1 is $(1 - \Theta_B) = \Theta_G$. Since in period 0 the individual has not yet received news that will first come in period 1, she also forms probabilities in period 0 of the type of news she will receive in periods 1 and 2 if she decides to start smoking. Further, let Θ_{BB} be the probability that a smoker receives bad news in period 2, given that she received bad news in period 1; if the cough does not get any worse or goes away by period 2, goods news follows bad news. The probability of good news in period 2 conditional on bad news in period 1 is Θ_{BG}. The probability of bad news following bad news is higher than the probability of good news following bad news, that is, $\Theta_{BB} > \Theta_{BG}$. Just because a smoker did not receive bad news in period 1 does not rule out the possibility that a smoker will develop COPD in period 2. For such persons, the period 2 probability is Θ_{GB}. Finally, there is the probability that smokers are indeed immune to the harms of smoking Θ_{GG}.

The third building block of the game tree is the person's decision rule about whether or not to quit smoking, based on the new information received. In this highly simplified model, the only decision available to the person once smoking has been initiated in period 0 is whether or not to quit in period 1. The decision to continue smoking or alternatively to quit is based on utilities in periods 1 and 2, probabilities of receiving good or bad news given the information about the person's health available in period 1, and the person's discount rate.

Fourth, discount rates are expected to vary among individuals. Persons with higher discount rates are more likely to begin smoking in period 0 since the benefits of smoking accrue to the individual before the costs from this activity do. Since the focus here is not on discounting, we assume that individuals are time consistent with a single rate of discount (r).

To summarize, ex post, that is, during period 2, one will learn for sure whether or not one is immune to the health harms of smoking. But ex ante, that is when the initiation decision is made during youth, all the decision maker knows are the probabilities for periods 1 and 2. In period 1, the smoker decides whether or not to quit or not, with quitting only being an option in period 1. Afterward, the smoker continues as a nonsmoker. (In this scenario, the adage "it is never too late to quit" does not apply. After period 1, it is too late.) In period 2, either the smoker gets COPD and becomes disabled for life (death does not add any new insights to this framework) or remains healthy for life.[7]

In period 0, the expected utility for youths who are thinking about starting smoking is (Sloan, Smith, and Taylor 2003):

$$U_S + \Theta_G \max\{\Theta_{GG}U_S + (1 - \Theta_{GG})U_{SD})/(1 + r)^2 + U_S/(1 + r),\ U_X/(1 + r)\}$$
$$+ \{(1 - \Theta_G)\max(\Theta_{BG}U_S + (1 - \Theta_{BG})U_{SD})/(1 + r)^2 + U_S/(1 + r),\ U_X/(1 + r))\}. \quad (2.8)$$

If the value of equation 2.8 is positive, the youth starts smoking, and conversely, if the value is negative, the youth does not smoke and enjoys zero expected utility.

We now examine equation 2.8 term by term. In period 0, the person's utility from smoking is U_S. In period 1, the person receives good or bad news in the form of smoking-related symptoms. In period 0, the decision maker thinks that these probabilities as Θ_G and $(1 - \Theta_G)$, respectively. The second term, which begins with Θ_G, pertains to the period 1 decision in which the person receives good news in period 1—no smoking-related symptoms, and the third term, which begins with $(1 - \Theta_G)$, pertains to the period 1 decision in which the person receives bad news in period 1.

Now suppose the person obtains good news. Then she decides whether or not to quit. If the person continues to smoke, she obtains utility U_S in period 1, since it is too late to quit in period 2, realizes utility U_S if she remains in good health *or* U_{SD} if she experiences a smoking-related disease in period 2. Alternatively, if she quits in period 1, the utility in period 1 is U_X. The decision maker bases the decision on whether or not to quit in period 1 on whether utility from the vantage point of period 1 is higher if the person continues to smoke or not, which is what the max term implies.

7. The expected utility is the sum of utilities in each state (e.g., utility in good and in bad health), weighted by the probability that the state occurs. For example, if the probability of being in good health is 0.9, the probability of being in bad health is 0.1, and if the utilities in good and in bad health are 90 and 30, respectively, the expected utility is 84.

If the person receives bad news in period 2, except for the differences in the probabilities of utilities in period 2, the problem is the same as when good news is received. The probability of a bad outcome in period 2 is higher than when there is good news in period 1. Thus, the probability of quitting in period 2 is higher in this case.

Figure 2.6 and equation 2.8 illustrate how the composite of assumptions reduce the decision of whether or not to start smoking to appearing if all is known by the beginning smoker. In fact, by treating the decision as a sequence of first steps at each period, we allow the person to revise the perceived probabilities of good and bad news. The person may also update his or her beliefs about the probabilities based on receiving general information about the harms of smoking or observing, for example, a relative who smoked develop a chronically disabling condition.

In this framework, there is no explicit role for medical care. At the cost of added complexity, one could allow for the possibility that medical care is productive in treating any smoking-related disease that may occur in period 2, thereby linking a health behavior to medical care use. Medical care could reduce U_{SD} but at the cost of reduced consumption of other goods (to the extent that medical care is not covered by health insurance), which would reduce utility.

This analysis offers several important implications. First, people who are more optimistic about receiving good news later in the life course will be more likely to start smoking. Second, persons with a higher rate of time preference, a higher r, are more likely to start smoking since the cost of smoking mainly occurs later in the life course—in this stylized example, only later. Third, persons who attach a lower cost to quitting or who derive more pleasure from cigarette consumption or impressing their peers would be more likely to initiate the smoking habit.

REFERENCES

Albuoy, V., and L. Lequien. 2009. Does Compulsory Education Lower Mortality? *Journal of Health Economics* 28 (1): 155–168.

Barker, D. J. P. 1997. Maternal Nutrition, Fetal Nutrition, and Disease in Later Life. *Nutrition* (Burbank) 13 (9): 807–813.

Becker, G. S., and K. M. Murphy. 1988. A Theory of Rational Addiction. *Journal of Political Economy* 96 (4): 675–700.

Bernheim, D., and A. Rangel. 2004. Addiction and Cue-Triggered Decision Processes. *American Economic Review* 94 (5): 1558–1590.

Cawley, J. 2008. Reefer Madness, Frank the Tank, or Pretty Woman: To What Extent Do Addictive Behaviors Respond to Incentives? In *Incentives and Choice in Health Care*, ed. F. A. Sloan and H. Kasper, 163–193. Cambridge, MA: MIT Press.

Chaloupka, F. J., and K. E. Warner. 2000. The Economics of Smoking. In *Handbook of Health Economics*, ed. A. J. Culyer and J. P. Newhouse, 1B:1539–1612. Amsterdam: Elsevier Science.

Chou, S. Y., J. T. Liu, M. Grossman, et al. 2010. Parental Education and Child Health: Evidence from a Natural Experiment in Taiwan. *American Economic Journal: Applied Economics* 2 (1): 33–61.

Cook, P. J., and M. J. Moore. 2000. Alcohol. In *Handbook of Health Economics*, ed. A. J. Culyer and J. P. Newhouse, 1B:1629–1666. Amsterdam: Elsevier Science.

Dormont, B., M. Grignon, and H. Huber. 2006. Aging and Changes in Medical Practices: Reassessing the Influence of Demography. *Health Economics* 15:947–963.

Fudenberg, D., and D. K. Levine. 2006. *A Dual-Self Model of Impulse Control.* Cambridge, MA: Harvard University, Institute of Economic Research.

Gertler, P., M. Shah, and S. M. Bertozzi. 2005. Risky Business: The Market for Unprotected Commercial Sex. *Journal of Political Economy* 113 (3): 518–550.

Gilleskie, D. 2008. Health Capital: Theory and Empirical Evidence. In *Incentives and Choice in Health Care*, ed. F. A. Sloan and H. Kasper, 51–83. Cambridge, MA: MIT Press.

Gilleskie, D. B., and K. S. Strumpf. 2005. The Behavioral Dynamics of Youth Smoking. *Journal of Human Resources* 40 (4): 822–866.

Grossman, M. 1972. On the Concept of Health Capital and the Demand for Health. *Journal of Political Economy* 80 (2): 223–255.

Gruber, J., and B. Köszegi. 2004. Tax Incidence When Individuals Are Time-Inconsistent: The Case of Cigarette Excise Taxes. *Journal of Public Economics* 88 (9–10): 1959–1987.

Gruber, J., A. Sen, and M. Stabile. 2003. Estimating Price Elasticities When There Is Smuggling: The Sensitivity of Smoking to Price in Canada. *Journal of Health Economics* 22 (5): 821–842.

Hall, R. E., and C. I. Jones. 2007. The Value of Life and the Rise in Health Spending. *Quarterly Journal of Economics* 122 (1): 39–72.

Kaplan, R. M. 1995. Utility Assessment for Estimating Quality: Adjusted Life Years. In *Valuing Health Care*, ed. F. A. Sloan, 31–60. New York: Cambridge University Press.

Keeler, E. B. 1995. Decision Trees and Markov Models in Cost-Effectiveness Research. In *Valuing Health Care*, ed. F. A. Sloan, 185–206. New York: Cambridge University Press.

Khwaja, A., F. A. Sloan, and Y. Wang. 2009. Do Smokers Value Their Health and Longevity Less? *Journal of Law & Economics* 51 (1): 171–196.

Loewenstein, G. 1999. A Visceral Account of Addiction. In *Getting Hooked: Rationality and Addiction*, ed. J. Elster and O.-J. Skolg, 235–265. New York: Cambridge University Press.

Loewenstein, G. 2001. The Creative Destruction of Decision Research. *Journal of Consumer Research: An Interdisciplinary Quarterly* 28 (3): 499–505.

McFadden, D. 2009. Human Capital Accumulation and Depreciation. *Review of Agricultural Economics* 30 (3): 379–385.

Murphy, K. M., and R. H. Topel. 2006. The Value of Health and Longevity. *Journal of Political Economy* 114 (5): 871–903.

Orphanides, A., and D. Zervos. 1995. Rational Addiction with Learning and Regret. *Journal of Political Economy* 103 (4): 739–758.

Patrick, D. L., and P. Erickson. 1993. *Health Status and Health Policy: Quality of Life in Health Care Evaluation and Resource Allocation.* New York: Oxford University Press.

Ravelli, A. C. J., J. H. P. van der Meulen, R. P. J. Michels, et al. 1998. Glucose Tolerance in Adults after Prenatal Exposure to Famine. *Lancet* 351 (9097): 173–177.

Sloan, F. A., V. K. Smith, and D. H. Taylor Jr. 2002. Information, Addiction, and "Bad Choices": Lessons from a Century of Cigarettes. *Economics Letters* 77 (2): 147–155.

Sloan, F. A., V. K. Smith, and D. H. Taylor Jr. 2003. *The Smoking Puzzle: Information, Risk Perception, and Choice.* Cambridge, MA: Harvard University Press.

Smith, J. P. 2009. The Impact of Childhood Health and Adult Labor Market Outcomes. *Review of Economics and Statistics* 91 (3): 478–489.

Smith, V. K., D. H. Taylor Jr., F. A. Sloan, et al. 2001. Do Smokers Respond to Health Shocks? *Review of Economics and Statistics* 83 (4): 675–687.

Social Security Online. 2007. Period Life Table, 2007. http://www.ssa.gov/OACT/STATS/table4c6.html (accessed October 6, 2009).

Tversky, A., and D. Kahneman. 1981. The Framing of Decisions and the Psychology of Choice. *Science* 211 (4481): 453–458.

Viscusi, W. K., and W. N. Evans. 1990. Utility-Functions That Depend on Health-Status: Estimates and Economic Implications. *American Economic Review* 80 (3): 353–374.

von Neumann, J., and O. Morgenstern. 1944. *Theory of Games and Economic Behavior.* Princeton, NJ: Princeton University Press.

Wang, R. 2007. The Optimal Consumption and the Quitting of Harmful Addictive Goods. *B. E. Journal of Economic Analysis & Policy* 7 (1).

DEMAND FOR HEALTH CARE SERVICES

This chapter focuses on demand for health care services, including preventive, diagnostic, and therapeutic services. Examples of preventive services are vaccinations, counseling about proper diet and physical exercise, and routine dental examinations, including teeth cleaning. A drug that lowers blood pressure or cholesterol may prevent a heart attack or a stroke. The use of glucose monitoring equipment may prevent the onset of complications of diabetes. Diagnostic tests, such as mammography and colonoscopy (tests to detect cancerous or precancerous tumors of the breast and colon, respectively), are in a sense preventive as well in that these tests may detect polyps and very small tumors before they grow into larger malignant tumors. Various tests for detecting heart disease, such as electrocardiography, which measures the electrical activity of the heart, also fall in this category. Therapeutic services treat disease, by means of either drugs, or medical devices (such as a pacemaker for cardiac disease), or radiation, or a surgical procedure.

A person's demand for personal health care services is a derived demand, with the final product being good health. Personal health care services are an input in the health production function, as are good diet, exercise, and adequate sleep.

Economists study demand for several reasons. First, individuals are frequently insured for many health services. Demand curves for health services are downward sloping, as are demand curves for other goods and services. Insurance coverage lowers the price of health services to individuals, leading to increases in the quantity of such services demanded. Private and public health insurers need to know how responsive the quantity demanded is to price reductions that occur when there is health insurance coverage. Private insurers need to know what premium to charge. Public insurers need to forecast budgetary outlays when they extend coverage to a new health service or for projections to determine the future financial status of the program. The change in quantity demanded for a change in the price of care paid out of pocket by insured persons is called *moral hazard*. There is nothing immoral about moral hazard, although, as discussed in this chapter, the existence of moral hazard is important from the vantage point of social welfare.

A second reason for studying demand is to assess differences in the use of services among various groups, defined on the basis of household income, urban versus rural residential status, or race and ethnicity. While moral hazard is important in terms of how it affects the allocation of scarce resources, how health services are allocated is important for equity reasons. In a market economy, the distribution of goods and services is most often left to the actions of market forces. Patterns of buying trucks and tennis shoes are not a public concern. However, consumption patterns of personal health care services are a legitimate public concern. For one, there are health externalities in the consumption of some services, such as vaccinations. Such externalities arise because the health of person B is potentially affected by the consumption of the service by person A. When person A fails to be vaccinated for influenza, person B may be more likely to become infected with this disease. But the distribution of health services is also a public matter for reasons of social justice. There are externalities in consumption simply because person A does not receive adequate care, even if the failure to receive such care does not make person B more likely to become ill. Person B is made better off by person A's consumption of the service simply because he feels good when A is receiving what she needs. Goods that have this property are termed "merit wants." There is a public interest in child nutrition not because malnutrition is infectious but, in part, because of a consensus that all children should have access to adequate diets. Another reason is that undernourished children may receive less education as children and be in poorer health as adults, an issue discussed in the previous chapter.

Third, forecasts of demand are needed for many long-term decisions, just as forecasts of future traffic flows are needed for planning the size of a bridge. Public policy makers need to consider future demand when making investments in medical school capacity or hospitals. Similarly, long-term forecasts of health care expenditures are needed for projecting revenue inflows needed to be allocated currently to cover future expenditure outflows.

Businesses involved in health services provision have a vital interest in demand, both for purposes of deciding on prices, quantity, and quality levels and also for gauging the profitability of investments in new products. Private insurers need to know about demand to structure plan benefits and pricing and set premiums.

This chapter focuses on the responsiveness of quantity demanded to the price paid by the consumer-patient out of pocket. This topic encompasses the influence of prices on demand and interrelationships in demand among various types of personal health services. For example, if the price of a preventive service is reduced, what is the impact on the quantity of therapeutic services demanded? For example, if the price of blood pressure medication is reduced, can one expect savings in the use of therapeutic services devoted to the care of persons who have sustained heart attacks?

3.1 Basic Economic Concepts of Demand

Economists measure the percent change in quantity demanded for a percent change in price as a price elasticity. Elasticities are convenient for expressing the responsiveness of quantity demanded to price changes. Let Δx_i be the change in quantity of good i demanded for a given change in price Δp_i. Then the *own-price elasticity* is the percentage change in quantity, $\Delta x_i/x_i$, divided by the percentage change in price, $\Delta p_i/p_i$:

$$(\Delta x_i/x_i)/(\Delta p_i/p_i) = (\Delta x_i/\Delta p_i) \cdot (p_i/x_i). \tag{3.1}$$

With a linear demand curve, the own-price elasticity depends on the values of p and x at which the elasticity is evaluated. Often, the elasticity is evaluated at the mean values of p_i and x_i. A demand curve can be obtained by fitting a regression line to the data.

Alternatively, the price elasticity can be derived using the concept of arc elasticity. To see how an arc elasticity is calculated, suppose we have data on two quantity-price combinations, (x_1,p_1) and (x_2,p_2). Then the arc elasticity is given by

$$\begin{aligned}&((x_1 - x_2)/(x_1 + x_2)/2/(p_1 - p_2)/(p_1 + p_2)/2) \\ &\quad = ((x_1 - x_2)(p_1 + p_2))/((p_1 - p_2)(x_1 + x_2)).\end{aligned} \tag{3.2}$$

The own-price elasticity is “elastic” or “inelastic” depending on whether the elasticity of demand is less than –1 or greater than –1. The elasticity ε_i must be negative because $\Delta x_i/\Delta p_i$ is negative. If the elasticity is less than –1, then a 1 percent decrease (increase) in price leads to a more than 1 percent increase (decrease) in quantity demanded. Since expenditure is the product of price and quantity, if quantity rises by more than price falls, then expenditures rise when demand is elastic, and conversely for inelastic demand.

In assessing the elasticity of demand, it is important to consider whose demand one is measuring. A *person's* demand for a good may be inelastic but the demand curve facing a single *firm* may at the same time be highly elastic or even infinitely elastic. Think of the demand for gasoline. An individual's demand for gasoline may be fairly inelastic, especially in the short run. After all, a vehicle consumes a certain amount of gasoline per mile. And one lives a certain distance from one's place of employment. And there is a cost to trading in an automobile. For various reasons, it may pay to keep one's car for a time even if the price of gasoline has risen considerably. While one can save some gasoline by driving at more constant speeds and by keeping the tires properly inflated, fundamentally it is hard to change the gasoline mileage on a given car. However, in the longer run, one can more easily trade cars and insulate houses in response to a dramatic increase in the price of gasoline or home heating oil. When the price of gasoline rises, people begin to think about trading in their "gas guzzlers" for more economical cars, but actually doing this takes time.

Similarly, an individual's demand curve for physicians' services may be fairly inelastic in the short run. When we are ill, we often seek care from our regular physician. There is a value to maintaining continuity of care. But in the longer run, if the physician raises his or her fees by a large amount, an individual, especially one without health insurance, may select another physician.

Changes in prices not only affect demand for the good or service whose price has changed (own-price changes), with the quantity response to such price changes expressed as own-price elasticities, but changes in the price of a good or service may also affect demand for other goods and services. Goods or services may be substitutes, complements, or neither substitutes nor complements. Two goods or services are substitutes if a fall (rise) in the price of one good or service leads to a fall (rise) in the quantity demanded of the other good or service. Two goods or services are complements if a fall (rise) in the price of one good or service leads to a rise (fall) in the quantity demanded of the other good or service.

In elasticity terms, define $\varepsilon_{ij} = (\Delta x_i/\Delta p_j) \times (p_j/x_i)$. If ε_{ij} is positive, good i and good j are substitutes; if ε_{ij} is negative, the two goods are complements; or if ε_{ij} is zero, there is no relationship in demand between the two goods, that is, demands for the two goods are independent.

Air travel and car highway travel are substitutes. The use of drugs for high blood pressure and inpatient hospital days for treating heart attack may be substitutes. If the price of such drugs decreases and their use increases, the demand for hospital care may decrease. In technical terms, the cross price elasticity is negative in the case of complements and positive in the case of substitutes.

Several decades ago, economists asked whether ambulatory care, or care delivered in physicians' offices, and hospital care were substitutes or complements. If the two services are substitutes, offering health insurance for hospital care but not for physicians' services would decrease demand for services in physicians' offices. Conversely, if they are complements, people would not visit physicians. These persons would therefore not be referred to hospitals for treatment. Thus, this

Box 3.1
Are Visits to Physicians and the Use of Over-the-Counter Medications Substitutes? The Case of the Common Cold

Ii and Ohkusa (2002) used data from a household survey from Japan to assess whether people with a common cold would increase their use of over-the-counter (OTC) medications if the coinsurance rate on spending on physicians' services, the fraction of total expenditure that insured persons must pay out of pocket, were increased by 10 percent. In Japan, both physicians' services and prescribed medications but not OTC medications are covered by public health insurance. In Japan, physicians dispense prescribed medications.

They found that the price elasticity of demand for medical services ranged from –0.23 to –0.36, which implies that a 10 percent increase in the coinsurance rate would decrease demand for such services from 2.3 percent to 3.6 percent. The 10 percent increase in the coinsurance rate would increase demand for OTC drugs to treat common colds, implying that physicians' services–prescribed medicines and OTC drugs are substitutes. The authors further reported that the savings in expenditures on physicians and prescribed drugs would be far higher than the increase in spending on OTC drugs.

Although physicians' services and OTC drugs are substitutes in the context of a common cold, whether or not two services or goods are substitutes or complements more generally is an empirical question. For example, one result of the RAND Health Insurance Experiment described below is that physicians' services and hospital care are complements. Complementarity likely arises in this latter context because it generally takes a physician's referral to be admitted to a hospital. People who do not see physicians may be admitted to a hospital on an emergency basis, but they are much less likely to be admitted in nonemergency situations.

imbalance in insurance coverage would cause hospital use to be lower than it would be if both services in physicians' offices and hospitals had similar rates of coverage. Over-the-counter (OTC) drugs typically are not covered by insurance, while physician visits are. People with insurance coverage for physicians' services would plausibly substitute physician visits for OTC medicines when they have a cold. Or would they? (See box 3.1.)

3.2 DEMAND IN THE CONTEXT OF HEALTH INSURANCE COVERAGE

Health insurance is designed to reduce the price of health care services at the point of service, that is, when personal health care services are consumed. Health insurance can take many forms.

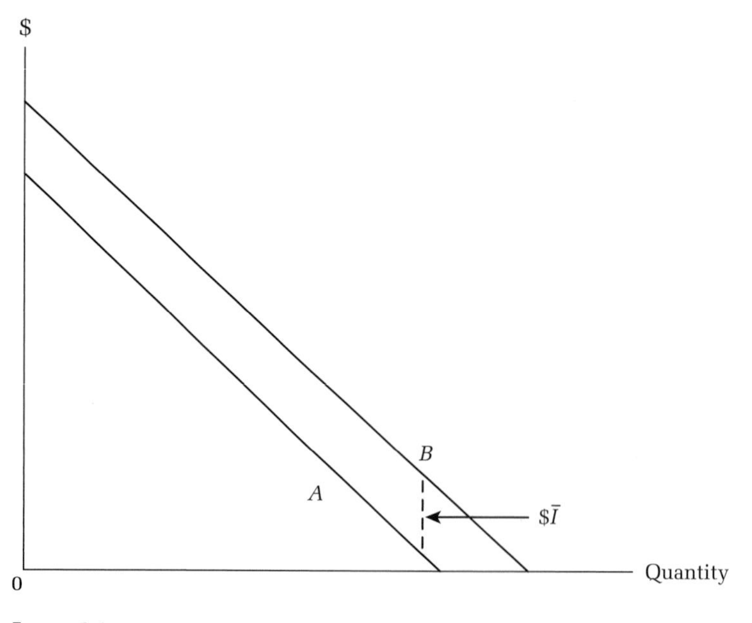

FIGURE 3.1
Effect of an Indemnity in the Amount of $\$I$ on the Consumer's Demand Curve

One form is a *fixed dollar subsidy*. The insurance policy specifies a fixed dollar amount that the insurer will pay for a particular type of service. This form of subsidy is often called an "indemnity" in the insurance industry. The insurance policy might pay $\$\bar{I}$ for an office visit and $\$\bar{\bar{I}}$ for a particular kind of surgery. In figure 3.1, where the indemnity is set at $\$I$, the effect of introducing coverage paying $\$I$ per unit of service is to cause a parallel shift in the demand curve by the amount $\$I$. The shift is parallel and outward (to the right) for this reason. If a patient were willing to pay \$3 for a unit of service without insurance, with insurance offering an indemnity of $\$I$, the same individual is now willing to pay $\$3 + \$I$ since the insured person is assured that he or she will be paid $\$I$ back after the insurer receives documentation that the services were rendered. If the willingness to pay is \$9 for a unit without insurance, the same individual is now willing to pay $\$9 + \$I$, and so on. The basic underlying willingness to pay out of the consumer's own pocket has not changed.

Although, as seen below, indemnities have certain advantages, they suffer from one major disadvantage from the vantage point of the individual with such insurance coverage. The amount of the subsidy does not change as the price of the service changes. Thus, if one obtains care from a high-priced doctor as opposed to a lower-priced one, the subsidy is the same. This places individuals with such health insurance coverage at substantial risk of high out-of-pocket expenditures in the event of an illness, particularly a serious one, for which a high-priced doctor, such as a leading specialist in a medical field, may be more productive than a lower-quality one.

On the other hand, while indemnities rank poorly in terms of expenditure risk protection (i.e., poor in terms of protecting ill persons' income net of spending on the personal health care services they receive), indemnities have an economic-efficiency-enhancing aspect. This form of subsidy produces less of a distortion in demand than do other types of subsidies. Suppose that high- and low-priced physicians are of equal quality. Then efficiency would dictate a consumer choice of the lower-priced physician. But complete health insurance insulates consumers from the price difference. However, with a fixed dollar subsidy, the difference in price accrues to the consumer, thus giving the consumer an incentive to search out the lower-priced physician.

An alternative to a fixed dollar subsidy is an *ad valorem subsidy*. The term *ad valorem* comes from the Latin and means "according to the value." An ad valorem subsidy increases with increases in the price of the subsidized good or service. A simple insurance contract employing an ad valorem subsidy would pay a specific percentage of the price, say, 80 percent. In this case, the insurance policy pays 80 percent and the insured individual pays 20 percent of the charge. Ad valorem subsidies cause the postinsurance demand curve to rotate around the point at which the demand curve touches the *x*- or quantity axis (fig. 3.2).

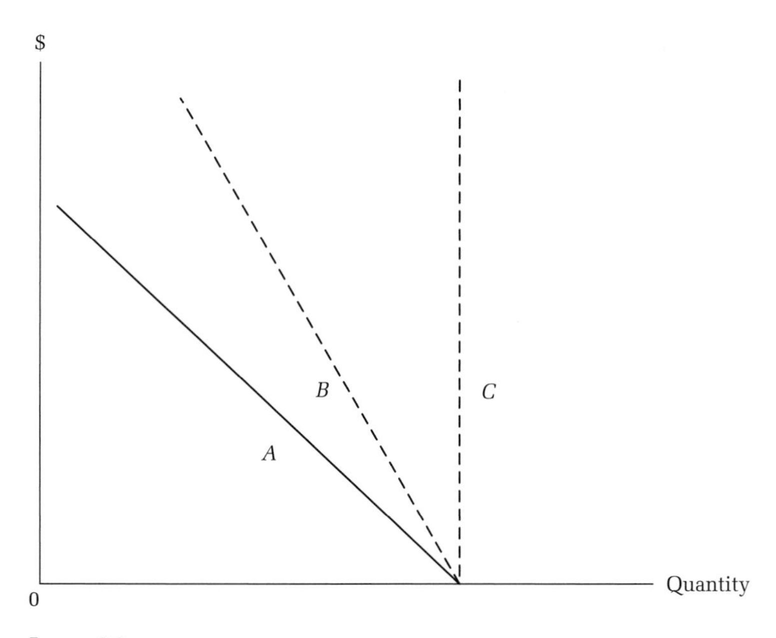

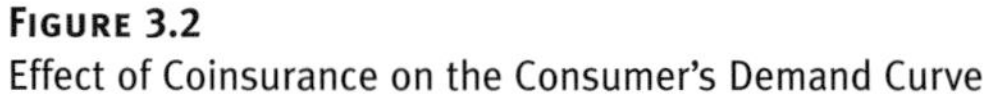
Figure 3.2
Effect of Coinsurance on the Consumer's Demand Curve

We leave it as an exercise for you to demonstrate why this is so. The fraction of the bill that the patient pays is called *coinsurance*. In the 80/20 case, 0.2 is the coinsurance rate. Coinsurance is much less commonly used at present than in the past. In figure 3.2, demand curve A is the consumer's demand curve without health insurance and demand curve B is the demand curve with a coinsurance rate of about 0.5. Demand curve C shows the demand of a consumer with insurance that pays the entire bill—that is, the coinsurance rate is zero ("free" care).

Many insurance contracts contain *deductibles* or minimum amounts of expenditure that the insured person must bear before the insurer subsidizes care. There are two main justifications for deductibles. First, having a deductible means that the insurer will not pay for many services the individual with such insurance receives. There is a savings in administrative expense to the insurer by having to write fewer checks. Another reason is that over the range covered by the deductible, insurance will not affect demand for care (fig. 3.3).

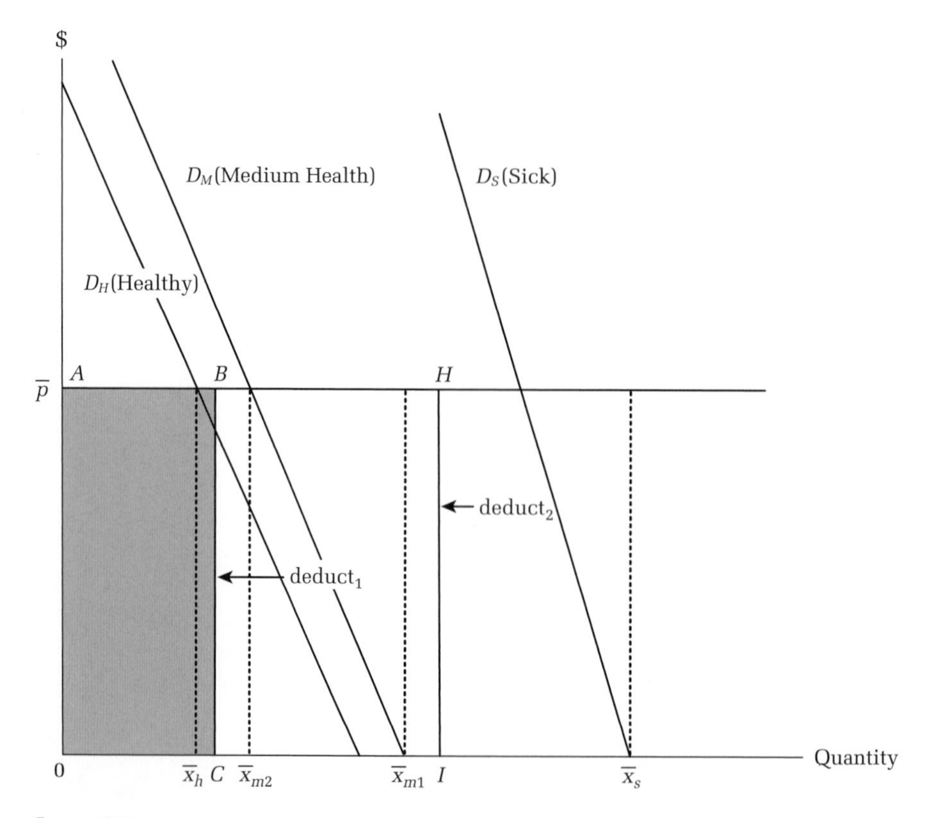

FIGURE 3.3
Effect of a Deductible on the Consumer's Demand Curve

Let the deductible in figure 3.3 be the rectangle *ABC*0. The deductible is shown as the shaded area of a rectangle. With a deductible of this amount and a price of $\bar{p}$, the healthy (*h*) consumer will consume $0\bar{x}_h$, the same amount he or she would consume without insurance. However, with this deductible, consumers in medium (*m*) health and those who are sick (*s*) will consume $0\bar{x}_{m1}$ and $0\bar{x}_s$, respectively. At the margin, individuals in the latter two groups face a zero price of care.

We consider the effects of a higher deductible below. However, if the deductible is increased to *AHI*0, then the person in medium health consumes $0\bar{x}_{m2}$ units of medical services. The quantity demanded by the other two groups is unchanged.

Still another feature of insurance contracts is the *co-pay*. In contrast to deductibles, which apply to total expenditures on health services, a co-pay is imposed for each unit of service. In a sense, it is the opposite of an indemnity. A co-pay is a deductible per unit of service, in contrast to the usual meaning of a deductible, which applies to a certain amount of expenditure that must be incurred by the insured individual before coverage applies.

In figure 3.4, the insured individual pays $*y* per unit of service while the insurer pays the rest. For example, the insurance contract may specify that the insured person must pay $*y* for each monthly prescription, with the insurer paying the rest. In this case, insurance has no effect on the demand curve up to the amount of the co-pay. Thereafter, if insurance pays the rest, the person will be indifferent whether the price of the drug charged the insurance plan is slightly above or much above the co-pay (fig. 3.4). Thus, the demand curve is completely inelastic above the co-pay amount (pivots at *B*).

Table 3.1 provides a summary of alternative forms of health insurance and their impacts on demand curves for personal health care services. In practice, an insurance policy can be a mix of different forms of health insurance. For example, in the past, a typical health insurance policy in the United States was a policy with deductible plus coinsurance for the expenditure above the threshold of the deductible amount. More recently, co-pays have become more common, with correspondingly greater reliance on managed care to control use of services (see chapter 11).

The cost-sharing provisions of the health insurance plans Duke University offered its employees in a recent year, an example of health insurance plans provided by large employers in the United States, are described in box 3.2. The features of Duke University's plans are illustrative. There is variation among health plans provided by US employers. The major provisions of Medicare, public health insurance for the elderly, disabled, and persons with end-stage kidney disease in the United States, and Taiwan's public single-payer insurance plan are described in boxes 3.3 and 3.4, respectively.

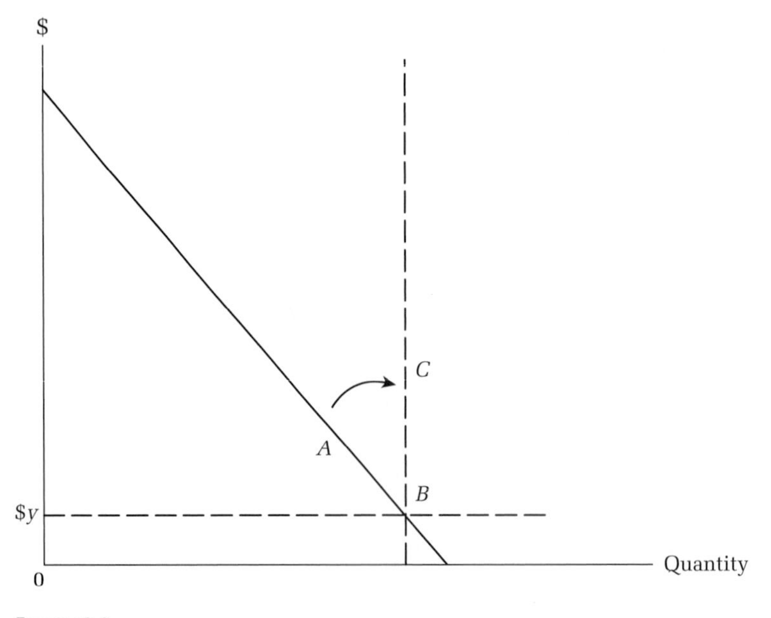

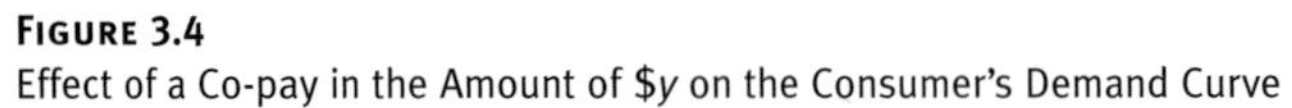

FIGURE 3.4
Effect of a Co-pay in the Amount of $y on the Consumer's Demand Curve

TABLE 3.1
Alternative Forms of Health Insurance and Their Impacts on the Demand Curve

Type of Insurance	Definition	Effect on Demand Curve
Fixed dollar subsidy (indemnity)	The insurance policy pays a fixed dollar amount for a particular type of service.	Pure income effect: a parallel shift occurs in the demand curve, without changing the relative price of health care.
Ad valorem subsidy (coinsurance)	The insurance pays a specific percentage of the price.	Change in the relative price of health care: the demand curve rotates outward (becomes less elastic).
Deductible	The insured person bears the full cost of health care before a threshold amount (e.g., US$1,000) and the insurance pays the rest of health care cost beyond the threshold amount.	No effect on the demand curve before the threshold amount; the demand curve become a vertical curve beyond the threshold amount.
Co-pay	The insured person pays a fixed dollar per unit service and the insurer pays the rest.	No effect on demand curve below the co-pay amount; the demand curve becomes inelastic (a vertical curve) above the co-pay amount.

Box 3.2
Cost Sharing and Benefit Structure of Duke University Health Plans in 2009

The Duke University Health System is a large private US employer. As of 2009, it employed about 25,000 persons. Although private employers differ in their offerings, Duke provides an example of the type of health plan coverage offered by large employers in the United States. The offering is more generous than would typically be the case for small US employers.

For 2010, Duke offered employees an alternative of coverage under four health plans—three health maintenance organizations (HMOs) and a preferred provider organization (PPO). The HMOs provided coverage only if the insured individual obtained care from a provider within the plan's network of providers. The PPO, by contrast, covered care from providers within and without the plan's provider network. However, in a PPO, if care is obtained outside the network, the insured's out-of-pocket payment is higher. The HMOs differed in whether they subjected the enrollee to an annual deductible or not. The HMO with the lower out-of-pocket premium ("basic HMO") had a $500 deductible per person and a $1,500 deductible per family. When the Duke employee had family coverage, the operative deductible was the one that was satisfied first. The basic HMO and the PPO had coinsurance rates, but the coinsurance amount was subject to a maximum stop loss. The other HMOs did not impose coinsurance. Plans had co-pays, which varied per unit of service. For example, co-pays for a visit to a primary care physician varied from $15 to $20. Those for specialist visits varied from $45 to $60 per visit. All plans covered a large number of types of service, including visits to physicians, various diagnostic tests, inpatient care, and ambulatory hospital care. There was a co-pay for a hospital admission that ranged from $450 to $700, depending on the plan. Pharmaceuticals were covered, but with substantial cost sharing unless the mail-order program was used. The maximum lifetime payment was $2 million for each plan. The monthly premium for an individual plan, which the employee paid through payroll deduction, ranged from $23 to $99 per month. The corresponding premiums for family coverage ranged from $225 to $444 per month. In addition, the employer made monthly contributions to premiums.

Source: Duke Human Resources.

Box 3.3
Cost Sharing and Benefit Structure of US Medicare

US Medicare covers persons over age 65, those with end-stage kidney disease, and persons whom Medicare accepts as disabled. It consists of four parts: hospital insurance—Part A, which covers inpatient care in hospitals, skilled nursing facility care, hospice care, and home health care; medical insurance—Part B, which covers physicians' services and outpatient care and some preventive care services; Advantage Plans—Part C, which provide health care coverage by health maintenance

Box 3.3
(continued)

organizations (HMOs) or preferred provider organizations (PPOs) as alternatives to conventional fee-for-service Parts A, B, and D; and prescription drug coverage—Part D, which provides coverage for prescription drugs.

Part A is provided at no out-of-pocket cost to persons who qualify for Medicare. Part A covers the entire cost of inpatient stays above a deductible. Skilled nursing facility care is provided for up to 100 days following a three-day minimum stay in an inpatient hospital.

Part B charged a monthly premium of $96.40 in 2009; individuals with an adjusted gross income of more than $85,000 or married persons with adjusted gross incomes of more than $170,000 paid higher monthly premiums than this. Part B also imposed an annual deductible. Medicare imposed a 20 percent coinsurance on Medicare-approved Part B expenses above the deductible. Patient cost sharing was often paid by private Medicare supplemental insurance plans (Medigap plans).

Medicare Advantage Plans were required to at least cover all types of services covered by Parts A and B. Such plans may offer additional coverage, such as for vision, hearing, dental, or health and wellness programs, as well as prescription drugs. Some Medicare Advantage Plans have provider networks, which restricts the beneficiary's choice of provider. Each plan could charge different out-of-pocket costs, usually co-payments, but also coinsurance and deductibles. Out-of-pocket premiums vary by plan.

Unless obtained through an Advantage Plan, Medicare coverage for prescription drugs could be obtained through Part D. Such plans assess a monthly premium. Enrolled persons pay an annual deductible, co-payments, and coinsurance. Most Medicare drug plans have a coverage gap (termed the "donut hole"). After the beneficiary has spent a certain amount on Medicare-covered prescription drugs, he or she must pay all medication costs out of pocket up to a limit. Coverage for drug expenditures begins above this limit.

Box 3.4
Cost Sharing and Benefit Structure of Taiwan's Universal Health Insurance Plan

The universal health insurance program in Taiwan, termed NHI, for national health insurance, is financed by payroll taxes, with large government subsidies from general revenue. The NHI provides comprehensive coverage, including outpatient visits for Chinese and Western medicine, dental services, hospital stays, emergency services, prescription drugs, and rehabilitation services.

To deal with moral hazard, NHI has implemented demand-side cost sharing for outpatient visits, hospital inpatient care, and prescription drugs. For outpatient visits, the fixed co-pay per visit in 2009 ranged from New Taiwan dollars NT$50 to NT$360 (in December 2008, the exchange rate was NT$32.85 to US$1), depending on the type

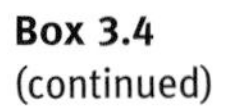

Box 3.4
(continued)

of provider and the accreditation level of the hospital. The coinsurance rate for hospital inpatient services was 10 percent for stays under 30 days. There was no drug co-pay if the drug expenditure per visit was under NT$100. The drug co-pay was NT$20 when the drug expenditure per visit ranged from NT$100 to NT$200. The co-pay increased by NT$20 for each NT$100 increase in the amount of expenditure on drugs per visit. The maximum co-pay was NT$200. Overall, co-pays for prescription drugs were low, ranging from NT$20 to $200, depending on the amount of drug expenditures per outpatient visit.

To protect households from high out-of-pocket expenditures, there was an out-of-pocket expenditure ceiling for hospital inpatient services; the ceiling was NT$19,000 per admission and NT$31,000 per year. In addition, there was a co-payment exemption for specific groups of persons, including persons with payer-defined catastrophic illness, low-income persons, veterans, and persons living in remote areas.

3.3 THE CONCEPT OF TIME PRICE

Up to now, we have not taken account of the fact that the out-of-pocket price one pays for care is not the only price the consumer of personal health care services faces. To visit a physician, one has to take time from one's usual pursuits to travel to the physician's office or clinic, then wait for the physician in the waiting room and spend time in an examining room, only to repeat the travel time on the way home. Further, there are the out-of-pocket expenses of gasoline, tolls, transit fare, and other expenses. In many cases, a parent, spouse, or caregiver accompanies the patient, which may add an appreciable amount to the full price of a visit to a physician. We limit the analysis to money and time cost of the physician visit here to simplify the discussion.

Consider the *full price* of an office visit, p_f:

$$p_f = cp + wt, \tag{3.3}$$

where c = coinsurance rate, p = the physician's fee, w = the value of the person's (patient's) time per unit of time, and t = total patient time consumed by a visit. The variable w is the value of the person's time spent doing other activities, for example forgone earnings or the value of time spent in parenting. For some individuals, especially those with an insurance policy with a low c, wt could be a more important determinant of the full price than p is.

The concept of time prices offers a useful framework for explaining several stylized facts observed in countries throughout the world. First, in many countries, "free" care is provided in public clinics. The term "free" is placed in quotation

Box 3.5
Time Prices and Demand for Care

Time consumed in the receipt of personal health services takes several forms: travel time, time spent waiting at the physician's office, time spent during the visit, and time spent on visit follow-up, such as time devoted to purchasing drugs prescribed during the visit. A barrier to the use of care, especially in lower-income countries, is distance to the provider. Greater distance imposes costs on users, in the form of both the time spent in travel per se and the out-of-pocket costs incurred in paying for transport.

A few empirical studies have investigated the role of distance from providers. A study of demand for medical care in rural Kenya (Mwabu, Ainsworth, and Nyamete 1993) reported that both distance from health care facilities and user fees were more of a deterrent to the use of care for women than for men. Elasticities of use with respect to distance were between –0.1 and –0.3.

A study of choice of health care provider in Nigeria (Ichoku and Leibbrandt 2003) found that given the decision to visit a health care provider, the probability of visiting a particular facility decreased by about 0.1 for each additional kilometer that the person lived from that facility. The same study found that waiting time in the clinic did not have a statistically significant effect on choice of that facility. An earlier study of demand for health care in Nigeria (Akin, Guilkey, and Denton 1995) found that the longer it took to travel to a facility, the more likely the individual was to select that facility for care. The authors cautioned that this time cost variable was obviously proxying for something other than time cost, or some other factor may have explained this implausible finding.

In a study of the utilization of public health centers in Portugal (Lourenco and Ferreira 2005), the researchers failed to find a relationship between total time spent at the center and demand for care at the center. However, total time reflects time spent with health care providers in part, and such time may be considered to be a "good," in contrast to other forms of time cost, which plausibly are "bads."

marks because typically patients have long waiting times in such facilities, sometimes much longer waits than in private physicians' offices. Patients differ in their w's and hence in the importance of wt as a fraction of p_f. For this reason, one would expect sorting, with people with a low w selecting sources of care with a higher t, such as care at public outpatient clinics, and persons with a higher w selecting sources of care with a low t even if the p is higher, such as care at private physicians' offices.

Second, as c is reduced, all persons have an incentive to select care with low t's. At the limit, where $c = 0$, people will not be concerned about fees at all. They will select sources of care with the lowest wt, care sites near their homes or workplaces and those with low waiting times. The demand for free public clinics may be expected to fall. Thus, the public provision of complete insurance ($c = 0$ or nearly 0) should lead to a decline in the number of free public clinics.

Third, reductions in c will reduce the elasticity of demand with respect to fees (money prices). At $c = 0$, this elasticity will be zero. Box 3.5 describes some empirical evidence on the impact of time prices on demand for personal health care services.

3.4 Empirical Studies of Demand

Data Used in Demand Studies

Observational Data

Many empirical studies of demand for personal health care services have been conducted since about 1970. While economists have emphasized the roles of price and income as determinants of demand, many other studies have focused on other demand determinants, including psychological, sociological, and cultural factors, as well as public policies that may affect the utilization of and expenditures on care. A later section in this chapter provides a brief review of the evidence on demand determinants other than price and income, but as a text on health economics, our emphasis is on the roles of prices and income.

The vast majority of studies are based on *observational data*. These data are not obtained from randomized controlled trials, to be described later. They are called observational because persons are not randomly assigned to treatment and control groups. Rather, data on individuals' characteristics and activities are simply recorded as reported to interviewers or as written in clinic (medical) records or administrative records.

Surveys record many characteristics of the respondent and may include questions on the respondent's health insurance and income. Clinic records are likely to have medical information that cannot easily be obtained from household surveys. Yet the number of clinics from which the samples are drawn is often small (frequently only one clinic), and there is a risk that evidence from a clinic or a few clinics may not generalize to individuals selected from a larger pool. Administrative data often come from public or private insurers in the form of claims data. Claims data often have detailed information on patient diagnoses and the procedures performed. And claims databases can be quite large in terms of the number of individuals included. However, they may lack information on characteristics of the individual that are often obtainable from household surveys.

Although the pros and cons of various types of observational data differ, they share one common disadvantage for analysis of the effects of price on the utilization of and expenditures on personal health care services. People who expect to use more health services in the future may select health plans offering more generous insurance coverage than persons who do not expect high rates of use in the future. Or if there is no law compelling individuals to have health insurance coverage or it is not provided by the government, young, healthy persons may decide to forgo health insurance altogether. The phenomenon of basing one's choice of insurance on one's expected future use of covered services is called *adverse selection* (see chapter 1).

Adverse selection is not unique to insurance. Suppose that one wanted to compare the effectiveness of drug A with that of drug B in the treatment of a specific disease. If the researcher used observational data, she would assemble information on persons with the disease who used drug A or drug B, perhaps from clinic and insurance files. The researcher would compare the health outcomes of persons taking drug A versus drug B. A serious methodological deficiency of this approach is that doctors are likely to prescribe drug A for those patients for whom drug A is more appropriate, and similarly for drug B. Thus, a comparison of drugs A and B would reflect not only the relative effectiveness of the drugs but also characteristics of the patients treated with each of the drugs. For example, if drug A has more undesirable side effects but is truly more effective, the drug might be consumed disproportionately by patients with more serious forms of the disease. Because these patients are sicker, they will have poorer health outcomes with or without use of the drug than will users of drug B. If patient health could be measured fully and accurately, there would be no adverse selection problem. However, in practice, full and accurate measurement generally is not possible.

RANDOMIZED CONTROLLED TRIALS

For this reason, regulatory authorities require that studies of drug effectiveness and safety be based on information obtained from randomized controlled trials (RCTs) rather than on observational data. The latter type of data is used for postmarketing surveillance, for example, to document adverse side effects from the drug after it has been widely marketed. RCTs are conducted over a shorter time period and on much smaller samples than become available after a drug has been marketed globally and for several years.

In an RCT, a drug company or medical device manufacturer (e.g., a manufacturer of artificial joints or of cardiac pacemakers), desiring to gain regulatory approval to market a new drug or medical device, advertises for volunteers among persons with the disease treated by the drug. Volunteers are then randomly assigned to one of the study drug treatments. In the best of these studies, double-blind experiments, neither the patient nor the physician knows to which drug group the patient has been randomly assigned. Random assignment, particularly with double blinding, eliminates the effect of physician decision making about the choice of drug that is likely to be systematically related to patient health in ways that the physicians but not the researcher can observe. Once the influence of drug selection related to patient health factors not observable to the researcher has been eliminated, the observed differences in outcome can be attributed to the effects of the drug itself.

RCTs are very common in studies of drug outcomes but are extremely rare in social science research. One reason is that RCTs are expensive in general and in the social sciences tend to be even more expensive than in medical research. Second, double blinding is not possible in social science research. When a double-blind protocol is used in a drug RCT, not only does the patient not know whether he or she is in the treatment or control group, the physician prescribing the drug does not know this either.

While people can be randomly assigned to insurance plans, there is no way of concealing the plan to which people are assigned. One cannot coat a health insurance plan in the same way one can coat a pill (to disguise the fact that the pill contains an inert substance or is a generic drug already on the market) used in the control group to make it look identical to a pill being evaluated by the RCT.

But in spite of these disadvantages, an RCT to measure the effects of insurance has the advantage of avoiding the adverse selection problem described above. A study participant has the option of not participating in the RCT at all, but, given participation, the person has no choice of insurance plan. Of course, a participant cannot be forced to stay in the RCT. Attrition is a problem in RCTs of all types for this reason, and social experiments are no exception (Philipson and Hedges 1998). Because RCTs are so expensive and eliciting participation and attrition are likely to be more consequential in studies of longer duration, RCTs are generally conducted for only a short time period. The RCT described in the next section, which lasted for three to five years, is on the lengthy side among RCTs. Also, given the expense of administering RCTs, sample sizes are kept at a level likely to allow statistically significant findings but may not be sufficiently large to detect rare outcomes, such as from a drug. Also, the sample sizes may be insufficient to yield reliable estimates for population subgroups, such as racial or ethnic minorities or elderly persons.

NATURAL EXPERIMENTS

There is another type of experiment that is much less costly than most RCTs. This is a *natural experiment.* These experiments take advantage of a change in the features of a health insurance plan. For example, in the 1990s, government health authorities in Belgium increased co-payment rates for three types of physicians' services—office visits to general practitioners (GPs), home visits by GPs, and visits to specialist physicians (Cockx and Brasseur 2003). Since the insurance was not voluntarily purchased but provided by the government, the change was totally outside the individual person's or the person's physician's control.

The change was *exogenous* to the persons affected by the change. Thus, any change in use could be attributed to the change in co-payments, with one proviso.

Some other factor, say a recession or a natural disaster, could have affected use of services, and this other factor might have coincided with the change in the co-payment. For this reason, the authors used a control group that consisted of Belgians for whom the co-payment did not change. The latter group would have also been affected by these other factors but not by the change in co-payments.

The researchers computed the mean difference in quantity post versus pre for persons in the treatment group T (Δx_{iT}), minus the mean difference in quantity for the same post period for the control group C (Δx_{iC}). The change in price for the treatment group was Δcp_{jT}. For the control group, Δcp_{jC} was zero since the change in the co-payment did not apply to these individuals. The difference in difference between treatment and control groups is called a difference-in-difference estimator.

Using this approach, Cockx and Brasseur (2003) found price elasticities of –0.13 for men and –0.03 for women. These price elasticities are low, but not atypical for price elasticities of demand for personal health care services. The –0.13 elasticity for men implies that a 1 percent increase in price would reduce the quantity of services demanded by 0.13 percent.

A prior study for the same country by van de Voorde, van Doorslaer, and Schokkaert (2001) but using a longer time period and a different methodology found price elasticities of demand for GP office visits in the –0.16 to –0.12 range. Elasticities for GP home visits ranged from –0.39 to –0.28 and for visits to specialists were –0.10.

THE RAND HEALTH INSURANCE EXPERIMENT

THE RESEARCH ISSUES

Many studies of demand for personal health care services have been conducted using observational data. However, one RCT of effects of insurance coverage on demand for personal health services, though now about three decades old, even today, is the most widely cited study of demand for personal health services by far. This RCT study is called the Health Insurance Experiment (HIE) and was conducted by economists, physicians, and others at the RAND Corporation during the 1970s. We continue to discuss the study more than three decades after it was completed because the HIE remains the classic study of demand for personal health care services.

The HIE addressed these specific research issues. First, how does cost sharing affect demand for personal health services? Is the demand response to increased cost sharing different for poor than for non-poor persons? One might expect poor individuals to be more responsive to changes in the out-of-pocket (money) price than non-poor individuals. One reason is that the money price is a higher proportion of the full price of a unit of services for poor than for non-poor individuals.

For this reason, increasing cost sharing would have a greater impact on consumption of services by the poor.

Second, how does cost sharing affect demand for particular services (e.g., hospital, mental, and dental services)? One might expect that cost sharing would have a greater impact on demand for services that people regard as discretionary or that can easily be postponed, such as physical examinations, than on demand for emergency care, such as to fix a broken bone.

Third, does consumption of personal health care services improve personal health? The presumption for many decades was that receipt of more medical care leads to better health, but this proposition has been increasingly questioned in the last three decades or so. In particular, some medical care may be highly productive, but other types may not be. Or some people may be consuming care at a margin (a considerable amount of care) at which additional units of care are no longer productive in terms of improving health. The HIE began a very active line of research, called *health outcomes research*, which has involved evaluation of various preventive, diagnostic, and therapeutic services using observational data.

Fourth, does insurance paid on a capitation basis result in lower health care expenditures than insurance that pays on a fee-for-service basis? Under pure capitation, health insurance plans pay health care providers a fixed amount per person per year, and for this premium, the insured person is entitled to all care deemed medically necessary at zero or a very low out-of-pocket price to the policyholders. The provision of additional services does not result in additional payment to health care providers as it does under fee-for-service arrangements. In fact, the provider incurs additional cost per additional unit of service and no additional revenue. Since the marginal cost of providing an additional service is positive—that is, time and other inputs, such as medical supplies, are consumed in supplying additional units of service—providers lose money when they supply additional services. For this reason, providers may ration care. By rationing, we mean supplying fewer services than the consumer demands at a given price. A plausible hypothesis is that the utilization of personal health care services is lower when people are covered by capitated insurance plans than under insurance that pays providers on a fee-for-service basis.

HIE Study Design

The HIE enrolled about 2,000 nonelderly families from six different areas in the United States for a period of three to five years (Newhouse and the Insurance Experiment Group 1993). Persons older than age 62 were excluded. Families were randomly assigned to one of fourteen fee-for-service insurance plans differing in (1) coinsurance or cost-sharing rates and (2) maximum expenditures (MDE). An MDE is a limit on total out-of-pocket expenditures for medical services incurred in a year, often called a *stop loss*. If, for example, the stop loss is $1,000, this means that insured individuals can expect to pay no more than $1,000 per year out of pocket. Every dollar of expenditure above the stop loss is fully covered by the insurance plan. The difference between gross and net (i.e., out-of-pocket) expenditure rises with increases in the coinsurance rate. If the coinsurance rate is 0, the difference is $1,000. If, however, the coinsurance rate is 0.25, the difference is $4,000, which means that the insured individual is subject to some cost sharing until gross expenditure reaches a $4,000 threshold.

At the time of enrollment in the HIE, families exchanged their own health insurance policies for an HIE policy. The match between study participants and their existing insurance policies and the HIE policies they received in return was random.

Participation in RCTs is not random, however. As in all RCTs, individuals' participation in the HIE was entirely voluntary. To induce people to participate, participants in the HIE received sufficient compensation up front so that they could not be financially worse off than with their existing policy even if they reached the maximum out-of-pocket level of expenditures (hold harmless clause). One of the HIE plans covered all care for free, that is, at no cost to the family. At the other extreme, people paid 95 percent of expenses out of pocket up to the stop loss, which was set at 10 percent of the family's income.

Thus, under the latter HIE plan, if the person was a member of a household with $20,000 in annual income, the stop loss would have been $2,000 per year. The person would pay 95 percent of the medical expenditures until the gross expenditure (expenditure before insurance was paid) reached $2,105.26 per year. Additional expenditure was covered in full. The HIE included this plan type to measure the effect of only providing insurance coverage for large expenditures on demand for care.

There were also intermediate levels of cost sharing, 25 percent and 50 percent. There was also an individual deductible plan, which imposed an up-front deductible for $150 for outpatient care but provided complete coverage for hospital inpatient care. The purpose of the individual deductible plan was to gauge whether inpatient and outpatient (ambulatory) care are substitutes or complements. If compared to the free care plan, hospital utilization was lower under the individual deductible plan, this would indicate that ambulatory and inpatient care are complements. Conversely, if hospital utilization was higher under this plan, this would suggest that the types of care are substitutes.

In addition, some persons were randomly assigned to a single capitation plan in Seattle, Washington. Since out-of-pocket payments incurred by families were negligible under this plan, a comparison of use in the free plan versus the capitation plan provided evidence on the effects of capitation on demand for care.

HIE RESULTS

Table 3.2 summarizes estimates of the impact of cost sharing on use of hospital inpatient and ambulatory care. Ambulatory care is care provided to persons that

TABLE 3.2
Annual Use of Medical Services Per Capita, by Plan

Plan	Likelihood of Any Use (%)	Outpatient Expenditures (1991 $)	Face-to-Face Visits (n)	Share of Enrollees with One or More Admissions (%)	Total Expenditures (1991 $)	Total Admissions	Inpatient Expenditures (1991 $)
Free	86.8	446	4.55	10.3	982	0.128	536
25%	78.7	341	3.33	8.4	831	0.105	489
50%	77.2	294	3.03	7.2	884	0.092	590
95%	67.7	266	2.73	7.9	679	0.099	413
Individual deductible	72.3	308	3.02	9.6	797	0.115	489

Source: Newhouse and the Insurance Experiment Group (1993, 41). Used with permission of the RAND Corporation.

does not involve an overnight stay in a hospital or other health care facility. Increased cost sharing caused families to use less care. The likelihood or probability of use of any service during the year varied from 86.8 percent for families assigned to the free plan to 67.7 percent for persons assigned to the 95 percent plan.

Considering these four plans, total expenditures (paid by the families and the insurance plan to which they were assigned) per enrollee on care varied from $982 to $679 per year (nominal US dollars).[1] Comparing the individual deductible plan with the free plan, both of which offered free hospital care, rates of at least one admission per year were 9.6 percent for enrolled families with the individual deductible and 10.3 percent for those on the free plan. Also, outpatient expenditures and the number of face-to-face visits per year were lower for enrolled families with the individual deductible than for those on the free plan. Thus, imposing a deductible on outpatient care resulted in lower use of both outpatient and inpatient care, implying that outpatient and inpatient care are complements, not substitutes.

While conducting an RCT trial in the social sciences, though not unique to the HIE, is highly unusual, another innovation was to measure the impact of cost sharing on health. As just seen, imposing a cost-sharing provision reduced the use of services. But does the lower rates of use result in people becoming less healthy?

Results from the HIE imply that for the vast majority of persons, the 94 percent of persons who did not have low income and were not in poor health, there was little or no measurable effect on health outcomes for any of the cost-sharing plans compared to free care, with a couple of exceptions.

1. The US Consumer Price Index for all goods and services has more than doubled since the RAND HIE study was conducted. The US Consumer Price Index for medical care services has more than tripled during this period.

Persons covered by the free care plan were more likely to keep their eyeglass prescriptions up to date and to have somewhat better oral health. For a subgroup of low-income persons initially in poor health, especially those with high blood pressure, imposing cost sharing did adversely affect health. This result implies that providing free care for particular services and subpopulations may be desirable, but that providing free care to everyone does not result in a measurable improvement in health for the population as a whole.

The result is highly provocative, especially since countries around the world are allocating ever larger shares of their national product to personal health care services. While the HIE finding on health outcomes is correct given the study design, some design elements may be responsible for this result. For one, persons older than 62 were not included in the HIE study. Health tends to depreciate at an increasing rate during the sixties and later in the life course. Second, a three- to five-year follow-up period, understandable since the HIE was so expensive to conduct, may have been insufficiently long to allow the HIE researchers to document a relationship between health services use and health. The HIE researchers hypothesized that discretionary health care services may be more price-elastic than nondiscretionary services. The HIE examined the impact of cost sharing versus free care on overall visits to emergency rooms, and emergency room visits by diagnosis. The diagnoses were categorized as more urgent and less urgent by a panel of emergency room physicians (table 3.3).

If we focus now on the category "visits with any of the above diagnoses" for "more urgent" versus "less urgent" diagnoses, there was a 23 percent difference in emergency room visits per 10,000 persons for the more urgent diagnoses between the plans that imposed some cost sharing and the free plan, with those with cost sharing having a lower rate of emergency room visits. By contrast, for less urgent diagnoses, the difference was 47 percent. These results imply that (1) imposing cost sharing leads to lower utilization of the emergency room and (2) the reduction is greater for less urgent—presumably more discretionary—diagnoses than for more urgent diagnoses. In a few cases (chest pain/acute heart disease, surgical abdominal disease, head injury, and acute alcohol/drug reaction), the cost-sharing group had higher utilization. These diagnoses in particular may require care as soon as it can be obtained, and thus demand may be particularly nonresponsive to cost sharing for these diagnoses. Also, for some of the individual diagnoses, the sample sizes were undoubtedly quite small, and thus mean rates of use were highly subject to random variation. That cost sharing provided a greater deterrent to more discretionary use of emergency rooms than to less discretionary uses is a finding favorable to requiring cost sharing in health insurance plans.

Physician researchers on the HIE team classified health conditions into one of four categories based on their judgments about the effectiveness of personal health care services in improving the health of persons with the conditions. The categories were (1) highly effective, (2) quite effective, (3) less effective, and (4)

TABLE 3.3
Response to Plans, by Diagnosis[a]

Diagnosis	Annual ER Visits per 10,000 Persons: Cost-Sharing Plans (25%, 50%, 95%, Individual Deductible)	Free Plan	Visits on Cost-Sharing Plans as a Proportion of Visits on Free Plan
More urgent diagnosis			
Fracture/dislocation	134	168	0.8
Miscellaneous serious trauma[b]	57	67	0.85
Asthma	30	83	0.36
Otitis media	40	78	0.51
Chest pain/acute heart disease	59	57	1.04
Cellulitis/abscess/wound infection	36	39	0.92
Surgical abdominal disease[c]	42	38	1.11
Head injury	36	33	1.09
Urinary tract infection	22	43	0.51
Acute eye injury/infection	34	34	1.01
Obstetric	29	31	0.94
Allergic reaction	26	26	1.00
Acute alcohol/drug reaction	27	20	1.35
Burn, second degree/complicated	19	22	0.86
Visits with any of the above diagnoses	991	1,280	0.77[d]
Less urgent diagnosis			
Abrasion/contusion	228	403	0.54
Sprain	164	249	0.63
Upper respiratory infection	92	190	0.51
Influenza/viral syndrome	40	61	0.65
Gastroenteritis/diarrhea	36	67	0.62
Abdominal pain (no other diagnosis)	34	65	0.53
Back/neck pain	32	67	0.45
Arthritis/bursitis	30	63	0.45
Headache	8	59	0.11
Acute bronchitis	14	36	0.42
Burn, first degree	7	28	0.28
Visits involving only the above diagnoses	663	1,185	0.53[d]

Notes: a. Equal partial weights were used to count visits involving multiple diagnoses. For example, if a visit resulted in three diagnoses, each diagnosis was credited with one-third of a visit. b. Includes foreign bodies, ingestions, ligamentous ruptures, and internal, neurovascular, and crush injuries. c. Includes cholecystitis, gastrointestinal bleeding, appendicitis, intestinal obstruction, and peptic ulcer disease. d. $p < 0.01$ for the difference between cost-sharing plans and the free plan, and for the difference between visits involving more urgent diagnoses and visits involving only less urgent diagnoses.
Source: Newhouse and the Insurance Experiment Group (1993, 155–156). Used with permission of the RAND Corporation.

TABLE 3.4
Predicted Percentages of Adults and Children with an Episode of Care, by Medical Effectiveness Categories and Plan

	Adults (n = 3,643)			Children (n = 1,830)		
Medical Care Effectiveness Category	Free Plan (%)	Cost Sharing (%)	Cost Sharing as % of Free Plan	Free Plan (%)	Cost Sharing (%)	Cost Sharing as % of Free Plan
Highly effective						
Acute	28.4	19.0	67[a]	32.0	23.1	72[a]
Acute chronic	16.8	13.3	79[a]	19.4	16.1	83
Chronic	12.6	10.7	85	4.7	2.4	52[a]
Quite effective	23.2	17.6	76[a]	22.4	17.6	79[a]
Less effective	25.0	18.6	74[a]	12.9	9.7	76
Rarely effective	10.5	7.4	70[a]	5.1	3.4	67
Rarely effective but self-care effective	38.8	29.2	75[a]	35.6	23.9	67[a]

Note: a. Effect of cost sharing significant at $p < 0.05$.
Source: Newhouse and the Insurance Experiment Group (1993, 166). Used with permission of the RAND Corporation.

rarely effective, as well as a fifth category, rarely effective, but self-care by the patient is effective (table 3.4).

"Effectiveness" in relation to medical care is a complex concept. A person may visit a physician with a common cold or the flu, for example, to obtain reassurance that the cold is nothing worse or to obtain immediate symptomatic relief, even though in time the cold or the flu would run its course without the visit. For adults, cost sharing has the most effect on the use of highly effective acute care services and the least effect on the use of highly effective chronic care services. The use of rarely effective care services is decreased by cost sharing at almost the same rate as is the use of highly effective acute care services. For children, the largest decrease in use as a result of cost sharing is for highly effective chronic care services and the smallest decrease is for the use of acute and acute chronic highly effective care services. These results imply that rather than cost sharing eliminating ineffective services, there is a mixed pattern—both effective and ineffective services are eliminated by cost sharing. But in the end, as noted above, imposing cost sharing did not have a negative effect on overall health for the vast majority of persons enrolled in the HIE.

A substantial proportion of dental care services can be postponed and are elective. For example, a middle-aged person perhaps could use a new crown on a tooth. But replacing the existing crown can wait, and perhaps the existing one is satisfactory, if not as good as it once was. Although routine cleaning is probably good for preventing major dental problems, it is often easy for people to postpone such preventive care. These examples are different from obtaining medical care for

TABLE 3.5
Use of Dental Service by Dental Insurance Plan

	Year 1 of Dental Coverage			Year 2 of Dental Coverage		
Dental Insurance Plan	Probability (%)	Visits (*n*)	Expenses Per Enrollee ($)	Probability (%)	Visits (*n*)	Expenses Per Enrollee ($)
Free	68.7	2.50	509	66.8	1.93	349
25%	53.6	1.73	300	52.6	1.51	254
50%	54.1	1.80	293	53.0	1.50	237
95%	47.1	1.39	197	48.3	1.44	240
Individual deductible	48.9	1.70	324	48.1	1.33	212

Note: Expenses in 1991 US$.
Source: Newhouse and the Insurance Experiment Group (1993, 54). Used with permission of the RAND Corporation.

a serious acute illness, such as pneumonia, or postponing surgery for a cancer a doctor just discovered.

The HIE covered dental expenditures with the same types of plans offered by hospital inpatient and ambulatory medical services. The results for dental visits and expenditures revealed a much greater response in the first year than in the second year of the experiment (table 3.5). Not shown in the table is the greater response to cost sharing in the final year of the HIE than in the next to final year.

Why the utilization and expenditure response would be greater in both the first and the last year than in the intervening years is readily explained. We return to the example of the crown and the middle-aged person. The dentist had been telling the person for a while that he ought to get his crown replaced, but the dentist's fee for the replacement was a deterrent since the man did not have insurance coverage for dental care. (Until about the 1990s, having insurance coverage for hospital and ambulatory medical care was much more common than was coverage for dental services.) Now that the man is enrolled in an HIE dental plan with not much cost sharing, he decides it is time to listen to his dentist and replace the crown. In the last year of the HIE, he realizes he will soon be without coverage. So he decides to have all the dental care he is likely to need in the future done in the final year of the HIE.

Table 3.5 shows that the probability of any use of the dentist is not much different between the first and the second year of the HIE. Thus, the effect of cost sharing on timing of the use of services is greatest for persons who see the dentist at least once during the year, not on the probability of seeing a dentist one or more times during the year. However, cost sharing in both years does affect whether or not people make at least one visit during the year to the dentist.

An implication of the findings for dental services is that cost sharing is clearly a deterrent to the use of such services. If the government were to offer universal coverage of such services, it should expect an initial surge in demand for such care.

EFFECTS OF DEDUCTIBLES

Many health insurance plans are structured to have a deductible, a minimum amount that the insured person must spend on covered services before the insurance policy pays anything. In addition to assessing the effects of coinsurance on demand for care, the HIE also assessed the effects of deductibles. The HIE researchers initially hypothesized that raising deductibles from a near zero level would have very little effect on demand, raising deductibles from a moderately sized deductible would have much larger deterrent effect on demand, and raising deductibles that were already high would have little effect on demand (Newhouse and the Insurance Experiment Group 1993, 139).

The reason a change from a very low deductible would have very little effect is that low deductibles are likely to be satisfied with virtually any use of services. For example, if a $5 deductible were increased to $6, this would have little effect if a physician visit were priced at $50. Anyone who visited the doctor only once would have satisfied either deductible.

Now suppose the deductible were set at $5,000. Then at the margins relevant for most people, it would be as if they had no insurance coverage at all. Raising the deductible to $5,010 would have no effect. However, suppose the deductible were $750. Then raising the deductible to, say, $775 might have an effect on demand for personal health care services if many persons incur annual expenditures on such care in this range.

In fact, the HIE researchers found that both small and medium-sized deductibles affected demand. However, the effect tapered off, so that after a certain point, increasing the deductible did not decrease demand further.

COST SHARING: GREATER EFFECT ON DEMAND FOR LOW-INCOME THAN HIGH-INCOME FAMILIES?

One of the important goals of the HIE was to compare the effect of cost sharing by level of family income. The HIE researchers' expectation when designing the study was that cost sharing would have a greater effect on lower-income than on higher-income households. The reasoning was that lower-income families would postpone or forgo care to the extent possible if they had to bear the cost themselves. On the other hand, more affluent families would not be as likely to postpone or forgo care.

However, the researchers found that cost sharing's effects did not vary according to the family's place in the distribution of income (table 3.6). The researchers divided the distribution of income into thirds (terciles) and found little variation

TABLE 3.6
Annual Expenditures and Use by Income Tercile

	Income Ranges		
Plan	Lowest Tercile	Middle Tercile	Highest Tercile
Probability of any use			
Free	82.8	87.4	90.1
25%	71.8	80.1	84.8
50%	64.7	76.2	82.3
95%	61.7	68.9	73.8
Individual deductible	65.3	73.9	79.1
Probability of any inpatient use			
Free	10.63	10.14	10.35
25%	10.03	8.44	7.97
50%	9.08	8.06	7.77
95%	8.77	7.38	7.07
Individual deductible	9.26	9.44	9.88
Expenses (1991$)			
Free	1,093	965	1,060
25%	891	771	817
50%	800	721	773
95%	762	648	691
Individual deductible	798	778	878

Source: Newhouse and the Insurance Experiment Group (1993, 46). Used with permission of the RAND Corporation.

in price elasticities by income tercile. We leave it as an exercise to compute price elasticities by tercile.

INCOME EFFECTS ON DEMAND FOR CARE

The discussion to this point has focused on the effects of changes in price to the patient on demand for care. Gauging the effect of family income on demand is also of substantial interest to health policy makers and to others. The effect of income on demand, as measured by the HIE, is complex. The demand for many if not most goods rises with income; such goods are called "normal goods" for this reason. But in addition, persons with higher income are likely to have a higher opportunity cost of time. For this reason, the consumption of goods and services requiring time on the part of consumers, such as personal health care services, may decline with increases in income. Personal health services themselves differ in terms of time required from patients. Taking a prescription drug requires little patient time. By contrast, spending time as a patient in a hospital can require quite a bit of patient and family time. More affluent families may hire a person to watch over the patient at the hospital, such as a nurse's aide. Less affluent families may depend on a family member for this purpose.

Still another consideration is that in some countries, notably the United States, public insurance for persons under the age of 65 is available only to persons with low income and few assets. When this is so, the money price of services declines with income. To the extent that physicians and other health providers charge lower prices to low-income persons who lack health insurance (see Kessel 1958 for an analysis of this phenomenon in the United States in the 1950s), low-income persons' demand should be expected to be higher than it would be in the absence of such price discrimination.

Income elasticities may be calculated in essentially the same way as arc price elasticities. The part of the formula relating to quantity remains the same. However, two income points replace the two price points in the arc elasticity formula described above.

Before turning to the HIE results, we need to discuss one important design feature of the HIE that has an important effect on income elasticities of demand in one important respect. The HIE set a stop loss at 10 percent of annual family income. At this level, a single hospitalization would be likely to trigger the stop loss provision. Thus, families with high expenditures on personal health care services were likely in effect to have had full coverage for services, largely independent of their incomes. This factor may have reduced income elasticity estimates derived from the HIE.

Table 3.6 can be used to calculate income elasticities of demand for care. Holding the type of plan constant, one can compute income elasticities along any of the rows in the table. For example, among those randomized to the free care plan, 82.8 percent, 87.4 percent, and 90.1 percent, respectively, on average used at least one unit of care during the year. However, for hospital admissions, the relationship between income and utilization is U-shaped: 10.6 percent of those in the lowest income tercile were admitted at least once in the year, but only 10.1 percent of those in the middle tercile were admitted. But among persons in the highest tercile of family income, 10.4 percent were admitted to hospitals at least once in a year. Similarly, expenditures exhibit a U-shaped pattern by income tercile, being highest for the lowest income tercile, lowest for the middle, and second highest for the highest income tercile.

This pattern plausibly reflects two factors. First, the HIE researchers did not control for factors other than family income, such as health status. It is likely that the health of income earners in households in the lowest tercile was poorer than in the other terciles. Hence, spending on health care services among families in the lowest tercile could have been increased relative to the other terciles as a result of poor health. Second, the HIE plans' stop loss provision was plausibly somewhat more likely to have been applied for persons with low family income. This feature of the HIE reduced differences in utilization and expenditures below the differences that would have occurred if no stop loss provision had been in place.

The fact that the percentage of any use of personal health care services in a year rose by tercile reflects the fact that hospital care is much more expensive than physicians' services. Thus, the effect of the stop loss was less for physicians' services than for hospital services, and variations in the any use percentages were driven by variations in use of physicians' services.

Effects of Capitation on Use of Services

While the vast majority of persons in the world with health insurance have insurance that pays providers on a fee-for-service basis, some plans pay a group of providers a fixed amount per enrollee.

From the standpoint of out-of-pocket payments imposed on patients, capitated plans most closely resemble a free plan. Although capitation plans often impose a co-payment per visit, co-payments tend to be low. After the co-payment is paid, insurance covers the rest.

While comparisons of use are available from many sources, they are based on observational data. One might expect that healthier persons would subject themselves to rationing under a capitated insurance plan since they expect to use few services during the year. If so, lower utilization under fee-for-service arrangements than under capitation may reflect differences in the health of enrollees in the two types of plans rather than reflect differences in the plans' payment methods.

The HIE provides empirical evidence on the effects of capitation versus fee-for-service plans on the use of and expenditures on personal health care services. The HIE randomly assigned 1,149 persons who had been enrolled in fee-for-service plans during the previous year to a capitated plan in Seattle in the US state of Washington. In addition, 733 persons who had been enrolled in the same capitated plan in the previous year were selected as controls. The latter were controls in the sense that they had selected the capitated plan on their own, presumably because they believed they would be better off in doing so. Thus, by comparing use and expenditures of the randomly assigned enrollees who selected capitation voluntarily, the researchers could measure whether those who selected the plan voluntarily had different use and expenditure patterns from those who were randomly assigned to the plan. Further, by comparing results between those randomly assigned to capitation with the results for the fee-for-service plans to which all enrollees were randomly assigned, the HIE researchers could estimate the differences in use and expenditures between capitated and fee-for-service insurance plans.

Utilization patterns for the capitated control group (those enrolled in the capitated plan before the HIE) and the capitated experimental group (those who were randomly assigned to capitation by the HIE) were quite similar (table 3.7).

TABLE 3.7
Probability of Using Any Hospital or Medical Service and Annual Expenditure Per Enrollee (1991$)

Plan	Enrollees Using Any Hospital or Ambulatory Service in Year (%)	Enrollees with One or More Hospitalizations in Year (%)	Annual Expenditure Per Enrollee in Year (1991$)
Capitated experimental	86.8	7.1	600
Capitated control	91.0	6.4	641
Fee for service			
Free	85.3	11.1	833
25%	76.1	8.8	848
95%	68.4	8.5	628
Individual deductible	73.9	7.9	565

Source: Newhouse and the Insurance Experiment Group (1993, 272). Used with permission of the RAND Corporation.

Although the percentage of enrollees using any covered services during the year and expenditures per year were slightly higher for the control group than for the experimental group, the percentage of persons in the control group admitted to a hospital at least once during the year was lower than for the experimental group. Thus, there is no evidence that healthier persons selected capitation over fee-for-service plans as would have been the case if utilization and expenditures were consistently higher in the control group than in the experimental group.

However, many researchers and policy makers have questioned whether this conclusion is generalizable and holds today. The general consensus is that healthier persons are more likely to select capitated plans. For one, maintaining an existing relationship with one's existing fee-for-service physician is more important if one is in the midst of a health crisis. Also, being able to select a physician who really specializes in the disease or condition you have is much more important when you have a serious chronic condition.

More striking are the differences between the capitated groups and the various fee-for-service groups. The estimates for the fee-for-service groups are similar to but not exactly the same as those reported above, for a (not important) methodological reason. Because cost sharing is similar, the most direct comparison is between the capitated experimental group and the free fee-for-service plans. Expenditures were 28 percent lower for the experimental group than for the free fee-for-service plan. The difference between expenditures between the capitated control and the free fee-for-service groups was 23 percent. Expenditures for the two capitated groups were similar to those for the 95 percent fee-for-service plan. Thus, doctors policing utilization and with patients having no financial incentive for health care

TABLE 3.8
Number of Admissions and Face-to-Face Visits Per Year, by Plan

Plan	Admissions Per 100 Enrollees	Hospital Days Per 100 Enrollees	Face-to-Face Visits	Preventive Visits
Capitated experimental	8.4	49	4.3	0.55
Capitated control	8.3	38	4.7	0.6
Fee-for-service				
Free	13.8	83	4.2	0.41
25%	10.0	87	3.5	0.32
95%	10.5	46	2.9	0.29
Individual deductible	8.8	28	3.3	0.27

Source: Newhouse and the Insurance Experiment Group (1993, 273). Used with permission of the RAND Corporation.

cost control was equivalent to no policing by doctors and patients paying virtually all of the bill up to a stop loss.

There were 40 percent fewer hospital admissions and hospital days among persons enrolled in the two capitated groups than among persons enrolled in the free fee-for-service plan (table 3.8). The number of face-to-face visits with physicians was roughly similar among the three plans. The number of preventive visits per year was higher in the two capitated groups, plausibly reflecting the incentive that providers face under capitation to keep their enrollees healthy and thus out of the hospital, the most costly site of care.

OTHER EMPIRICAL EVIDENCE ON THE EFFECT OF PRICE ON THE QUANTITY DEMANDED

The use of and expenditures on prescription drugs have both been increasing. As a result, in the United States, private health insurance plans have implemented various forms of cost sharing. Using data from thirty US employers with fifty-two health plans, Goldman, Joyce, Escarce, et al. (2004) found that the demand for prescription drugs used intermittently, such as antihistamines and some pain killers, was more sensitive to co-payment changes than was the demand for drugs used on an ongoing basis by persons with a chronic illness. Price elasticities for individual prescription drugs ranged from –0.44 to –0.08.

One approach to both cost containment and quality assurance is based on the use of a drug formulary. A formulary is a list of drugs, those that were covered by public or private insurance plans, or in the case of hospitals, drugs stocked by the hospital for use at the facility. Hospitals were the first to adopt formularies on a widespread basis. The hospital formulary stocked drugs recommended by physicians on the medical staff. The motives were to reduce the number of types of drugs that the hospital held in inventory and to stock those drugs that medical staff members believed to be effective.

Some private insurance plans in the United States have implemented a three-tier formulary to encourage physicians to prescribe less expensive drugs. The lowest co-pay is charged for generic drugs, that is, for chemical formulas no longer under patent. The middle-level co-pay is charged for branded (patented) drugs. The highest-level co-pay is charged for branded drugs not in the formulary. Having a preferred drug list, that is, drugs in the first two tiers, is potentially beneficial to health plans in that by concentrating its purchasing on fewer drug products, it gains market power to negotiate favorable prices from pharmaceutical manufacturers. Yet by having drugs in the third tier, the insurer allows some insurance coverage for drugs that may offer some added potential benefit to some patients by being more effective treatment for some individuals or avoiding adverse side effects that some patients may have with the less expensive drugs.

Some studies have investigated the effects of three-tier cost sharing on demand for pharmaceuticals. For example, Huskamp, Frank, McGuigan, et al. (2005) evaluated a natural experiment, which occurred when the health plan for a large US employer implemented a three-tier co-pay plan for its pharmaceutical benefit. The authors concluded that the plan increased out-of-pocket payments by the employees enrolled in the plan, but it also increased the plan's bargaining power with pharmaceutical manufacturers, resulting in lower prices for drugs paid for by the plan.

EMPIRICAL EVIDENCE ON THE EFFECTS OF HEALTH INSURANCE ON DEMAND IN A LOW-INCOME COUNTRY

In Vietnam, individuals are covered by one of three types of health insurance or they are not insured. The three types of insurance are (1) a compulsory plan, (2) voluntarily purchased health insurance, and (3) a health insurance program for the poor. The compulsory plan covers currently employed and retired civil servants, employees of state enterprises, employees of private enterprises with more than ten employees, employees of foreign-owned organizations, the disabled, "people of merit" (e.g., mothers, widows, and orphans of veterans), invalids of the armed services, and elderly persons aged 90+. No family members are covered by the compulsory plan. Coinsurance varies for some high-technology diagnostic services from 20 percent to 50 percent. Compared to persons with no insurance, the compulsory plan increased the probability of hospital admission by 117 percent (Sepehri, Simpson, and Sarma 2006). For enrollees in the voluntary plan and the plan for the poor, the probabilities of admission were 53 percent and 185 percent higher than for the uninsured, respectively. Mean lengths of stay by insurance type were 18 percent, 2 percent, and 39 percent higher for the compulsory, voluntary, and plan for the poor relative to the uninsured group, respectively. The percent differences are larger than anything observed for hospital utilization from the HIE.

The authors of the Vietnam study did control for other demographic and health factors, but the large differences suggest there may be still some other unmeasured differences that account for some of the differences. Bias due to omitted factors would not occur in an RCT such as the HIE.

3.5 WELFARE ANALYSIS

Economists perform welfare analysis to determine whether or not a particular change increases or decreases societal well-being, or "welfare." Since a demand curve for a good or service reflects individuals' maximum willingness to pay at different levels of quantity, demand curves are used in welfare analysis.

A demand curve can be viewed from two perspectives. In one, the demand curve gives the quantity demanded conditional on the price of the good or service. From this perspective, the consumer is given a price and then responds with a quantity he or she is willing to purchase at that price. Then the price can be varied and another quantity elicited. From a second perspective, the demand curve gives the maximum amount the person is willing to pay per unit, conditional on purchasing a specific number of units. Graphically, using the first perspective, one starts with a value on the y-axis, which is then associated with a quantity on the x-axis. Using the second, one starts with a quantity on the x-axis and elicits a value from the consumer on the y-axis.

The second perspective is used by economists in welfare analysis, a methodology that compares the social benefits versus the costs of a particular policy change. Here the change involves a change in provision of a health insurance plan, such as an increase in the plan's deductible.

We start with the concept of *consumer surplus*. The demand curve represents the maximum the individual is willing to pay for a specific quantity of the good or service. In figure 3.5a, the consumer demands nine units at a $0 price. For eight units, she is willing to pay somewhat more per unit. At the market price of $0A$, she demands five units. The consumer is willing to pay most for the first unit, somewhat less for the second unit, and so on. At price $\bar{p}$, she pays an amount $0ABC$. However, she values the five units more than $0ABC$, which is what she pays. The value is given by the area $0DBC$. $0DBC$ is the sum of $0ABC$ and the triangle ADB. The triangle is called consumer surplus, which represents the value the consumer attaches to the purchase over the amount she actually pays, which is $0ABC$. The shaded rectangles give approximately actual amounts of consumer surplus for each unit purchased. However, it simplifies the analysis by approximating this series of rectangles by a triangle.

Now suppose that the price per unit falls from $\bar{p}$ to zero. Then the consumer will purchase units until the value of the marginal unit is zero. This occurs after

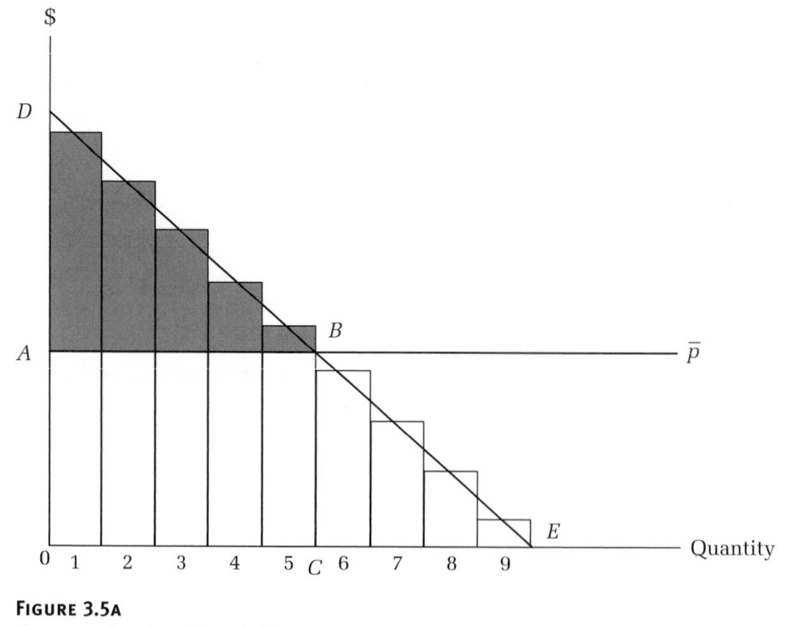

FIGURE 3.5A
Consumer Surplus: Discrete Case

nine units are purchased in figure 3.5a. From the individual consumer's vantage point, paying a zero price is advantageous. Who from the standpoint of a private individual could not be in favor of this? However, from society's standpoint, this is overconsumption unless the marginal cost of producing nine units is zero, which is highly unlikely. Suppose instead the marginal cost equals $\bar{p}$, which would occur under perfectly functioning competitive markets. Then for each unit after five, the consumer is not willing to pay as much as $\bar{p}$ = marginal cost (MC), and more value is used up in resources to produce the nine units than the consumer, here a representative of all consumers, is willing to pay for them.

Setting price at zero results in a welfare loss of *BEF* in figure 3.5b. With a zero price, there is a welfare loss of *BFE*. Providers are paid 0*AFE* by insurers. Although people pay nothing for the services they receive at the point of service, insurers must collect the 0*AFE* that they pay the providers. So consumers pay this as a premium, or as taxpayers if the insurance plan is provided by governments. Thus, in sum, the representative consumer is willing to pay up to 0*DBE* for $\bar{x}$. services and pays 0*AFE* in premiums. So the consumer enjoys the consumer surplus of *ADB* but incurs a welfare loss of *BFE*. From what we have said thus far, the consumer is better off without health insurance. If she has no insurance, she pays a price $\bar{p}$ and enjoys the consumer surplus of *ABD*. However, if she has complete insurance, that is, she receives "free" care at the point of service, the benefit *ADB* is offset at least in part by the welfare loss, *BEF*. The area *BEF* may more than offset the consumer surplus *ADB*.

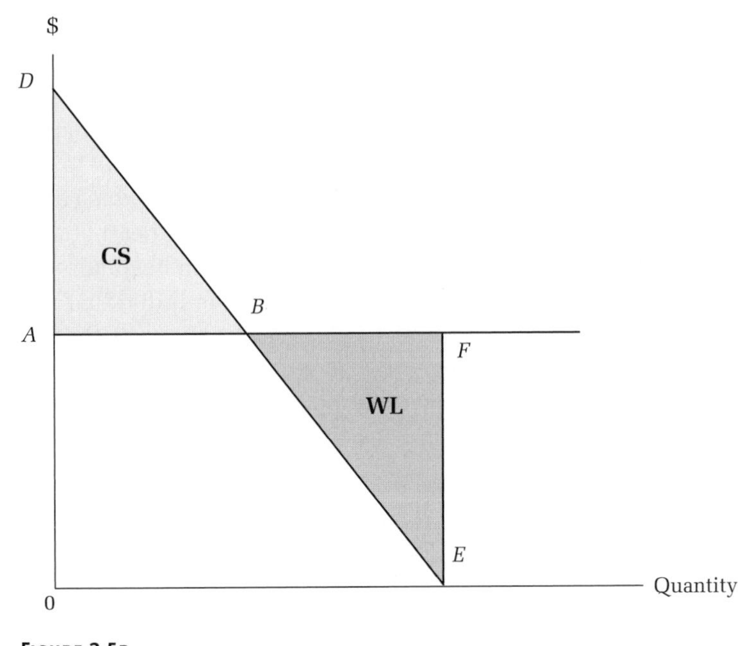

FIGURE 3.5B

Consumer Surplus (CS) and Welfare Loss (WL): Continuous Case

Economists use demand curves to value the benefit of a particular public project, or we could use demand curves to value whether or not the provisions of a particular national health insurance plan are socially optimal. The consumer surplus is a measure of social benefit to consumers under some restrictive assumptions. First, one must trust that consumers are knowledgeable about the benefits to themselves when they make purchasing decisions. Especially, outside of the economics profession, there is widespread skepticism that consumers are able to assess the benefits, and for this reason, other measures of benefit are used. Second, there can be no externalities in receipt of the service. If, for example, the service is a vaccination against a communicable disease, summing over individual consumer demand curves will underestimate social benefit. Third, one must assume that the income effects of price changes are small.

This assumption is not totally realistic since a product price decrease increases the consumer's real income. However, for decreases in price of most products, the increase in real income is small unless many product prices fall together. In public policy deliberations, the quantity demanded is often taken at the level of observed consumption, which under complete insurance may be a mean quantity per consumer where the demand curve intersects the quantity axis. Such consumption levels are sometimes considered to be the level of "need," which is compared to a measure of supply to determine whether there is a surplus or a shortage of a given type of health care personnel. But the quantity at which the demand curve intersects the quantity axis may be far higher than the level of use that is socially optimal.

Newhouse and Sinaiko (2008) have pointed out an important limitation of the welfare analysis just described, namely that demand for particular personal health care services may be interrelated, which at a minimum greatly adds to the complexity of welfare analysis. Suppose, for example, taking a drug to reduce high blood pressure on a regular basis reduces the probability of having a heart attack. Then taking the drug should affect the demand for curative care from hospitals and physicians. It is necessary to consider these effects as well. If the individual has health insurance coverage for hospital and physicians' services, it is unlikely that this person's demand for the blood pressure medication will fully reflect the benefit of reduced use of hospital and physician care at some later date.

3.6 Other Determinants of Demand for Personal Health Care Services

Although economists, as we have done in this chapter, tend to emphasize the roles of the price of personal health care services and income as determinants of the demand for care, there are clearly many other important demand determinants. As discussed in chapter 2, health services are an input into the production of health. Except perhaps for hypochondriacs or persons who find visiting the doctor entertaining, the vast majority of people seek care to improve their personal health. The final output is health. The flow from the health stock, healthy days or their equivalent, is an argument in individuals' utility functions. People are at a higher level of utility when their health is good, holding other factors constant.

In chapter 2, we showed how a person's age can be incorporated into a standard economic framework. A person's health stock tends to depreciate with age, and higher rates of depreciation lead to more investment in health. In an effort to restore good health, people demand knee replacements, plastic surgery to remove lines in the face that grow more numerous with age, drugs to decrease levels of blood glucose for persons who develop diabetes, the prevalence of which increases with age, and so on.

Likewise, economics can at least partially explain differences in the use of health care services by a person's educational attainment. More educated persons may be more efficient in health production (see Grossman 1972a, 1972b) because they are better able to detect signs and symptoms of illnesses earlier, better able to understand physicians' recommendations, or more efficient in searching among physicians to select a physician for a particular condition they might have. Furthermore, education may affect time preference, the trade-off of costs and future returns from an investment (Fuchs 1982; Becker and Mulligan 1997).

Economists can incorporate such demand factors in their models, but they cannot eliminate the possibility that such variables as age and educational attainment operate through other causal pathways than implied by economic theory. In an economic framework, many of these demand determinants other than price and income appear as preference differences in the person's utility function. In economics, we say that individuals maximize utility, and we write down a general utility function. However, with very few exceptions, economics does not provide explanations of how preferences are formed. For example, different cultures have different views of illness and death or of privacy, which may affect the use of personal health services. Economics must take these preferences as given. We economists have no theory as to why an individual may get more extra utility from another unit of transportation, for example, than from another unit of health.

Other demand factors are biologically determined. Economics cannot explain individual differences in genetic makeup or how these genetic factors affect health and the derived demand for personal health services.

Further, in a larger model, health behaviors and the use of personal health services are jointly determined. For example, a person with mild diabetes might be able to control his or her disease with moderate exercise and a healthy diet. Some persons may have a distaste for exercising, preferring to take pills for diabetes. Since the pills require a prescription, this type of person may be more likely to visit a doctor.

In sum, economics is very useful for explaining how price and income affect demand for health services. Through models such as Grossman's (1972a, 1972b), an economic framework can provide a partial explanation for the roles of such variables as educational attainment and age as demand determinants. But other disciplines have other explanations that are equally plausible. Economics can explain a lot, but there is a lot we economists cannot explain. To gain a fuller understanding of the determinants of demand for health care services and health, it is important to work with scholars in several disciplines.

3.7 SUMMARY AND CONCLUSIONS

In combination with the previous chapter, this chapter has provided an economic framework for studying price and income determinants of demand for personal health services. We have also described alternative sources of data for testing hypotheses about demand relationships and estimating responsiveness of the quantity demanded to price and income changes. The difference between observational data and data from RCTs is an important one; the issues that lead one to conduct an RCT have many other applications than just studies of demand for personal health services. This chapter has devoted considerable attention to the RAND

Corporation's HIE study. Although this study is now old, it remains the landmark study of demand for health services. Given the considerable expense of the study, it is highly unlikely that it will be repeated any time in the future.

While the HIE continues to be regarded as a pathbreaking study, no study is without limitations. In the case of the HIE, major limitations are that it only focused on the demand side of the market—quantity and price depend on both supply and demand, and, except possibly for the comparisons of fee-for-service and capitation methods of payment, it did not investigate how providers respond to various incentives or disincentives to supply additional services. Having a stop loss set at 10 percent of personal income and excluding persons over age 62 also limits the inferences that can be drawn from the HIE findings.

The HIE study shows that the amounts people pay out of pocket for health services does affect demand. Lowering the out-of-pocket price results in a welfare loss even though, as described in chapter 4, out-of-pocket price reductions also result in a welfare gain that is partially offsetting or could more than offset the welfare loss described in this chapter.

In the HIE, individuals were assigned health insurance plans randomly as part of the experiment. In the real world, whether or not a person is covered by health insurance at all may be a matter of personal choice, as the provisions of the plan conditional on deciding to be insured may be. For this reason, choice of health plan, health services' utilization, and even health may be jointly determined, or at least determined as a sequence of closely related choices. Chapter 4's analysis of demand for private insurance thus follows directly from the discussions of demand for health and demand for personal health services in chapters 2 and 3.

KEY CONCEPTS

- Moral hazard
- income elasticity
- complements
- coinsurance
- co-pay
- fixed dollar subsidy
- time price
- observational data
- the RAND Health Insurance Experiment
- welfare loss
- price elasticity
- substitutes
- indemnity
- deductible
- stop loss
- ad valorem subsidy
- randomized controlled trial
- natural experiments
- consumer surplus

Review and Discussion Questions

3.1 Give examples to illustrate how the following can be substitutes or complements:

- physician and hospital services;
- physician services and prescription drugs;
- dentist and dental hygienist services;
- optometrist and ophthalmologist services;
- office manager and physician.

3.2 Prior to 1970, private health insurers in the United States usually treated maternity care differently from other medical expenses; maternity care was either excluded entirely from coverage or subject to a flat lump-sum cash ("indemnity," in insurance jargon) benefit. Why do you think this was so? (Please give a reason other than discrimination against women, which might have been a reason as well but does not illustrate the economic principle we are looking for.) During the 1970s, twenty-three US states mandated that treatment related to pregnancy be covered by insurers in the same way as any other types of treatment were, and in 1978, such coverage became uniform throughout the United States. Would mandated maternity benefits make working in a salaried position more or less attractive to women? Would it make women of childbearing age more or less attractive to employees? Would it increase or decrease the number of births performed by cesarean section (surgical removal of the baby from the mother's uterus, a more expensive method of delivery than a normal delivery)? Who do you think bore the expense of implementing this mandate—consumers in the form of higher product prices, firms' owners in the form of lower profits, or employees in the form of lower pay? Explain your answer.

3.3 Does the welfare loss from overconsumption of medical care in the presence of health insurance coverage imply that consumers will not demand health insurance? Why or why not?

Exercises

3.1 Suppose a demand curve has the form $x = 100 - 10p$. What is the quantity consumed at $p = 5$? What is the elasticity of demand at $p = 5$? Suppose the demand curve is a demand curve facing the firm, such as a physician's office. At what level of p is marginal revenue zero? Why may the demand curve for the firm have a negative slope? When marginal revenue is zero, what is the price elasticity at this level of p? Would giving the patient a \$5 subsidy per visit tend to increase or decrease the elasticity of demand? Justify your answers.

3.2 Suppose that the price of a unit of medical care is \$100 and the person's insurance policy covers up to \$100,000 in expenditures incurred on behalf of the insured individual per year. Show graphically how the maximum payment limit affects the quantity demanded. Assume a zero co-pay up to the limit.

3.3 An individual has preferences for an aggregate consumption commodity (x) and health (H) represented by a utility function $U(x, H) = \alpha \ln(x) + \beta \ln(H)$. The price of the aggregate commodity (x) is p_x and the price of medical care (m) is p_m. The input of medical care (m) produces health (H) via a health production relationship that can be represented by the function $g(m) = \ln(m)$; that is, $H = \ln(m)$.

a. Compute the optimal demand for medical care (m), the aggregate consumption commodity (x) and health (H) as functions of prices (p_x, p_m), income (y), and the parameters of the model (α, β). You may assume a standard budget constraint.

b. Calculate the price elasticity of demand for medical care.

3.4 Explain the difference between a "stop loss" and a "deductible." Let the demand curve for an individual be $x_m = 30 - p_m$. Suppose all doctors charge \$10 per unit of care consumed. Let there be a deductible of \$100 and a stop loss of \$200. Let the coinsurance rate be 0.5. What is the effect of such insurance on the demand for medical care?

3.5

a. Show the effect graphically of a deductible on the demand for medical care.

Assume no insurance coverage initially. Then assume there is an insurance policy with a \$500 deductible. The price of medical care is \$50 per unit. After the deductible is satisfied, the health insurance plan pays for 75 percent of expenses.

b. Now assume the policy does not have a deductible but pays 100 percent of expenses up to a stop loss of \$2,000. Show this graphically.

3.6 The following questions are based on table 3.2:

a. Compute arc elasticities for free to 25%, 25% to 50%, and 50% to 95% plans for face-to-face visits. What do these results imply about the price elasticities of face-to-visits that is relevant to public policy? Compute arc elasticities for expenses overall. Again, what are the implications for public policy?

b. How does mean predicted expenditure compare in the free versus the 95% plan?

c. Cost sharing for outpatient services (individual deductible plan) produces a different pattern than does cost sharing for all services. Explain.

d. The admission rate for the individual deductible plan lies roughly midway between the free plan and the family coinsurance plan rates. Explain.

3.7

a. How are the income terciles in table 3.6 defined?

b. How do probability of any use, probability of admission, and expenses change with increases in income? What accounts for the differences in patterns across the three categories?

c. How does cost sharing affect expenses in each of the three income groups? Describe with elasticities. Based on your calculation, please answer the question on whether the demand response to increased cost sharing is different between the poor person and the non-poor person. Are your results obtained from table 3.6 consistent with theoretical prediction?

3.8 Suppose that doctors were to increase direct advertisement to the public about their services (with no other changes in the economic environment). What would you expect to happen to the demand for medical care (in the short run)? Explain graphically. Do not write more than five lines. What might you expect to happen in the long run (e.g., over 5 to 10 years)? Do not write more than five lines for this part as well.

3.9 Explain which of the following types of insurance coverage would most likely cause the most major problems resulting from moral hazard. (If you do not know some of the medical terms, check out Google.com.)

a. indemnity payments of $10,000 for each eye or limb lost or indemnity payments of $50 for each day spent in the nursing home;

b. arthroscopic surgery for knee injuries or amputation of the foot;

c. family counseling or electroconvulsive therapy;

d. decongestants or antibiotics.

3.10 Bill's new insurance policy contains a prescription plan that provides all drugs through a local pharmacy with a $2 co-payment. Under the old insurance plan, Bill had to pay for his own medication and purchased nine inhalers at $17 apiece to help control his asthma. With the new plan, Bill purchases fifteen inhalers, keeping some of the spares in his glove compartment and desk, since he only has to pay a $2 co-payment for each one. How much are the six additional inhalers worth to Bill? How much do they cost him? How much do they cost the insurance company? Is Bill better off or worse off under the new plan?

3.11 Use the equation for time price given by equation 3.3 in the text to answer the following questions.

a. Would you expect the elasticity of demand with respect to c to be higher or lower for a business executive than for a day laborer? Explain your answer.

b. Who would be more likely to use a "free clinic" (free in the sense that the money price of services = 0)? Why?

3.12 Suppose the county in which you live provides flu shots at pharmacies in the county for $5. Facing a budgetary crisis, the county raises the price of flu shots to $10. After two flu seasons, the county observes that the percentage of the population getting flu shots decreased from 50 percent to 40 percent. Calculate the implied arc elasticity of demand. What is potentially wrong with this calculation, and what additional data would you need to collect to fix it?

3.13 Assume there are two drugs designed to treat high blood pressure, drug A and drug B. Blood pressure readings from patients taking drug A are consistently higher than those of patients taking drug B. Does this mean that drug B is more effective than drug A? Why or why not? Describe how a randomized controlled trial could be set up to settle this issue.

ONLINE SUPPLEMENTAL MATERIAL

CAREER GUIDE TO THE HEALTH CARE INDUSTRY

http://www.bls.gov/oco/cg/cgs035.htm

RAND HEALTH INSURANCE EXPERIMENT

http://www.rand.org/health/projects/hie.html

RANDOMIZED CONTROLLED TRIALS

http://www.bmj.com/content/316/7126/201.full

http://www.ajronline.org/cgi/content/full/183/6/1539

MEDICAL EXPENDITURE PANEL SURVEY

http://www.ahrq.gov/data/mepsix.htm

SUPPLEMENTAL READINGS

Goldman, D. P., G. F. Joyce, J. J. Escarce, et al. 2004. Pharmacy Benefits and the Use of Drugs by the Chronically Ill. *Journal of the American Medical Association* 291 (19): 2344–2350.

Huskamp, H. A., R. G. Frank, K. S. McGuigan, et al. 2005. The Impact of a Three-Tier Formulary on Demand Response for Prescription Drugs. *Journal of Economics & Management Strategy* 14 (3): 729–753.

Newhouse, J. P., and A. D. Sinaiko. 2008. What We Know and Don't Know About the Effects of Cost Sharing on the Demand for Medical Care—And So What? In *Incentives and Choice in Health Care*, ed. F. A. Sloan and H. Kasper, 85–102. Cambridge, MA: MIT Press.

REFERENCES

Akin, J. S., D. K. Guilkey, and E. H. Denton. 1995. Quality of Service and Demand for Health Care in Nigeria: A Multinomial Probit Estimation. *Social Science & Medicine* 40 (11): 1527–1537.

Becker, G. S., and C. B. Mulligan. 1997. The Endogenous Determination of Time Preference. *Quarterly Journal of Economics* 112 (3): 729–758.

Cockx, B., and C. Brasseur. 2003. The Demand for Physician Services: Evidence from a Natural Experiment. *Journal of Health Economics* 22 (6): 881–913.

Fuchs, V. 1982. Time Preference and Health: An Exploratory Study. In *Economic Aspects of Health*, ed. V. R. Fuchs. Chicago: University of Chicago Press.

Goldman, D. P., G. F. Joyce, J. J. Escarce, et al. 2004. Pharmacy Benefits and the Use of Drugs by the Chronically Ill. *Journal of the American Medical Association* 291 (19): 2344–2350.

Grossman, M. 1972a. *The Demand for Health: A Theoretical and Empirical Investigation*. New York: Columbia University Press.

Grossman, M. 1972b. On the Concept of Health Capital and the Demand for Health. *Journal of Political Economy* 80 (2): 223–255.

Huskamp, H. A., R. G. Frank, K. A. McGuigan, et al. 2005. The Impact of a Three-Tier Formulary on Demand Response for Prescription Drugs. *Journal of Economics & Management Strategy* 14 (3): 729–753.

Ichoku, H. E., and M. Leibbrandt. 2003. Demand for Healthcare Services in Nigeria: A Multivariate Nested Logit Model. *African Development Review—Revue Africaine de Developpement* 15 (2–3): 396–424.

Ii, M., and Y. Ohkusa. 2002. Should the Coinsurance Rate Be Increased in the Case of the Common Cold? An Analysis Based on an Original Survey. *Journal of the Japanese and International Economies* 16:353–371.

Kessel, R. 1958. Price Discrimination in Medicine. *Journal of Law & Economics* 1 (1): 20–53.

Lourenco, O. D., and P. L. Ferreira. 2005. Utilization of Public Health Centres in Portugal: Effect of Time Costs and Other Determinants. Finite Mixture Models Applied to Truncated Samples. *Health Economics* 14 (9): 939–953.

Mwabu, G., M. Ainsworth, and A. Nyamete. 1993. Quality of Medical Care and Choice of Medical Treatment in Kenya: An Empirical Analysis. *Journal of Human Resources* 28 (4): 838–862.

Newhouse, J. P., and the Insurance Experiment Group. 1993. *Free for All? Lessons from the RAND Health Insurance Experiment*. Cambridge, MA: Harvard University Press.

Newhouse, J. P., and A. D. Sinaiko. 2008. What We Know and Don't Know about the Effects of Cost Sharing on the Demand for Medical Care—And So What? In *Incentives and Choice in Health Care*, ed. F. A. Sloan and H. Kasper, 85–102. Cambridge, MA: MIT Press.

Philipson, T., and L. V. Hedges. 1998. Subject Evaluation in Social Experiments. *Econometrica* 66 (2): 381–408.

Sepehri, A., W. Simpson, and S. Sarma. 2006. The Influence of Health Insurance on Hospital Admission and Length of Stay: The Case of Vietnam. *Social Science & Medicine* 63 (7): 1757–1770.

Van de Voorde, C., E. van Doorslaer, and E. Schokkaert. 2001. Effects of Cost Sharing on Physician Utilization under Favourable Conditions for Supplier-Induced Demand. *Health Economics* 10 (5): 457–471.

DEMAND FOR PRIVATE HEALTH INSURANCE

While most countries, especially high- and middle-income countries, offer some public health insurance coverage, private health insurance is also marketed in most of these countries. The same underlying concepts apply to both public and private health insurance in that both protect covered persons against the risk of incurring out-of-pocket expenditures for personal health services ("expenditure risk"). In this chapter, we focus on the demand side of private insurance market, leaving the topics of supply of private health insurance to chapters 10 and 11 and public health insurance to chapter 12.

The fundamental reason people demand insurance is that they are risk averse. This chapter starts with the concepts of expected utility and risk aversion. We show how risk aversion causes individuals to demand insurance and why risk-averse individuals are willing to pay more than their expected losses for insurance. Since there are administrative costs to running an insurance company, a necessary condition for the existence of an insurance market is that people be willing to pay more than their insurance policy's expected loss.

While the provision of insurance can improve the well-being of members of society, it is possible for people to have too much coverage, that is, to be overinsured. Overinsurance arises when the welfare loss due to moral hazard, discussed in chapter 3, exceeds the welfare gain arising from insurance's expenditure risk protection feature.

Initially, we assume there is only one insurer offering one insurance plan. Of course, realistically, there are likely to be many insurers with many plans in a market. With many insurance products available to an individual, healthy individuals may tend to buy lower-cost policies offering less coverage, such as plans with higher deductibles, coinsurance, or co-pays, since they do not expect to become ill. By contrast, persons in poor health may demand more complete coverage. Adverse selection in health insurance markets arises when individuals select insurance policies based in part on their individual health when the health of the individual is not fully reflected in premium differences. A possible consequence of adverse selection in private insurance markets is that certain types of insurance coverage, especially relatively complete coverage, become unavailable. Although having cost sharing reduces moral hazard and the welfare loss associated with it, at least some persons, those who are very risk averse, are made worse off when complete insurance is unavailable.

This chapter begins with a discussion of the relationship among health, health insurance, and the use of personal health care services. Here, unlike in the previous chapter, the major choice being made is the selection of a health insurance policy by an individual. Expected use of services during the policy year potentially plays a role in such choices. Willingness to pay for an insurance policy depends in part on the extent to which the person is tolerant or intolerant of bearing risk; the latter type of person is said to be risk averse. Using a minimal number of assumptions, we show how individuals decide on their willingness to pay the insurer for risk bearing. When insurers rather than individual risk-averse consumers bear risk, there is a welfare gain to such individuals. This gain, however, may be offset in part or in full by the welfare loss from moral hazard, which we described in the last chapter. The model we describe offers several predictions about how various factors affect demand for private insurance.

The two major threats to the existence of private insurance markets are adverse selection and moral hazard. We discuss why adverse selection may arise in insurance markets and what insurers can do about it, as well as the effects adverse selection may have on the functioning of insurance markets. We then describe the results of empirical studies of adverse selection in various types of insurance markets. Overall, although there is some evidence of adverse selection, which certainly played out in the story about the Harvard University health plan we describe below, there is also evidence against adverse selection in some insurance markets. Since the empirical evidence on adverse selection is mixed, the presence or absence of adverse selection should be assessed on an insurance market–specific basis.

4.1 RELATIONSHIPS AMONG HEALTH, HEALTH INSURANCE, AND THE USE OF PERSONAL HEALTH CARE SERVICES

The demand for personal health services and the demand for health insurance are closely linked. First, provisions of the health insurance policy, such as deductibles, co-pays, and stop losses, influence the quantity and types of services demanded.

Second, the person's expectation of the quantity and types of services to be used in the period to be covered by the insurance policy may influence the person's choice of health insurance plan. Two persons with the same demographic characteristics and even with the same health history may nevertheless expect vastly different utilization of personal health services during the next policy year. The insurer may be at a disadvantage in knowing these differences when the health insurance premium is set. If so, there is asymmetric information between potential buyers and sellers of insurance. Those buyers who expect to incur expenditures during the policy year in excess of the premium will want to purchase the insurance policy. Those with expected expenditures below the premium may want to reject the policy and look elsewhere or perhaps not purchase insurance at all.

Many decisions, such as which college or university to attend, career choice, and choice of spouse, have uncertain outcomes. In chapter 2, we described uncertainties in future health that lead to uncertainties about the future use of personal health services.

The uncertainty driving the demand for health insurance arises from the random nature of health and illness. In the absence of some institutional factors to be described below, if one knew with certainty what one would pay for personal health care services next year, there would be no demand for health insurance. Conditional on being alive, we can quite be sure that we will eat two or three meals a day and brush our teeth twice daily next year. We do not buy insurance coverage for next year's food expenditures or toothpaste because future expenditures on these items are reasonably certain. Yet we may or may not be involved in a motor vehicle accident, and our homes may or may not be destroyed by fire. For this reason, there is a demand for automobile insurance and homeowners' coverage.

Health per se is uninsurable. Although there are income replacement insurance policies, usually known as disability insurance, in general, one cannot purchase an insurance policy on one's own health (Arrow 1963). Health care providers are compensated based on the care they give rather than on the outcomes of such care, with very rare exceptions such as are discussed in box 4.1. For example, there is no market that would compensate persons if they were unable to walk or if their heart or lung capacity dropped below a certain threshold. However, markets for health insurance supply insurance policies that cover services in the event one breaks a leg or if a heart attack or chronic obstructive pulmonary disease (COPD) damages one's heart or lungs.

Why is health uninsurable (with rare exceptions such as those described in box 4.1)? In a hypothetical world in which hospitals and physicians did not exist, there might still be a private market to protect individuals against loss due to illness. People would likely seek protection from income loss due to illness and premature death and for other losses such as expenditures on a caregiver should they become unable to care for themselves.

Box 4.1
Optimal and Second-Best Health Insurance

As originally pointed out by Kenneth Arrow (1963), one of the first economists to receive the Nobel Prize in Economics, the first-best solution for coping with uncertainty in health care would be to have health insurance that paid for health to be restored to its original state, that is, the state of health before the illness or injury occurred. Such insurance is not marketed in large part because health care providers are not paid in proportion to the share of original health restored.

There is one case in which payment on the basis of health improvements is made. Leonard (2003) reported on methods of paying traditional healers in Africa. Such healers are often paid based on the health outcomes they achieve. Traditional healers can enforce outcome-contingent payment because patients believe that healers are agents of higher powers, As a result, healers can enforce and verify outcomes of treatment of gall illness or injury conditions. Healers have a reputation of poisoning or cursing patients with whom they are displeased. Thus, if a patient does not pay the healer for the value added in health attributable to the healer's effort, the healer may revoke the health improvement or invoke a curse. Since payment is outcome-contingent, the healer has an incentive to exert effort up to the point at which the marginal benefit from extending extra effort equals the marginal cost to the health of doing so. Patients may also have an incentive to exert effort in their treatment, and there may be complementarities between healer and patient efforts.

Of course, the marginal product of healer effort has not been demonstrated empirically. We need not assume that the marginal product is zero or even negative, especially when combined with patient effort to improve health outcomes. There is no conceptual reason that empirical analysis of outcomes in the context of healers could not be conducted. If it is possible to elicit cooperation from healers in research projects, this seems like a worthwhile undertaking.

4.2 INSURANCE CONCEPTS AND TERMINOLOGY

It is difficult to analyze the decisions of participants in health care markets without considering health insurance. Although widespread, insurance is a specialized subject with its own terminology and concepts. For this reason, we begin our analysis of demand for health insurance coverage with a description of some fundamental terms and concepts.

FIRST-PARTY AND THIRD-PARTY INSURANCE

Insurance may be categorized in several ways. One important distinction is between first-party and third-party insurance. First-party insurance protects policyholders against losses occurring as the result of accident, injury, illness, or some other adverse event to the policyholder him- or herself. Health, disability, and life insurance, and the kind of motor vehicle insurance that covers losses incurred by one's own motor vehicle ("collision insurance" in the United States), are examples of first-party insurance.

Third-party insurance protects policyholders against the loss incurred by others when the loss is attributable to an action or inaction on the part of the policyholder for which the policyholder is held responsible. For example, homeowners may insure against injuries to others that occur on the policyholders' premises. Suppose during a snowfall, the policyholder-homeowner forgets to clear the walkway and a visitor falls and breaks a bone. The homeowner may be held responsible for this injury since he or she failed to take adequate precautions, namely, to clear the walkway or post a sign that the walkway was slippery; the homeowner may thus be held responsible for covering the cost of the accident. Similarly, motor vehicle operators purchase insurance to cover the losses to others caused by an accident. Physicians purchase insurance to cover the losses to others from medical injuries attributable to an inaction or action of physicians. This is medical malpractice insurance (see chapter 7).

PECUNIARY AND NONPECUNIARY LOSS

Health insurance covers a range of expenditures associated with the receipt of personal health care services, but it does not include payment for nonpecuniary loss. Such loss includes loss attributed to pain and suffering or loss of consortium (e.g., loss of the companionship of a spouse), or loss of a chance at life. Although becoming sick or injured can be highly unpleasant and painful, and lead to a loss in utility, there is generally no private first-party insurance protection against such loss from pain and suffering. A possible reason is that people may feign or exaggerate pain in order to collect from the insurance company, which is a form of moral hazard.

However, such nonpecuniary loss is generally covered by third-party insurance. A possible reason is that in a third-party context, the injurer has an incentive to question claims of the injured party that the latter incurred nonpecuniary loss as a result of an accident or surgery, and demands for payment for nonpecuniary loss are potentially subject to review by a court of law. By contrast, there is no such review of first-party insurance claims.

THE PRICE OF INSURANCE

Like all goods and services, demand for insurance depends on its "own" price. In the context of insurance, it is necessary to consider two prices. The first is the premium on the health insurance policy. The second is the loading factor on the policy.

The premium is the sum of two parts, the actuarially fair premium and the loading factor. The actuarially fair premium is the amount that an insurer expects to pay for covered expenditures incurred by the policyholder during the policy year. The policy year represents the time period for which the premium, and hence coverage, applies. The loading factor consists of costs associated with the business of insurance, such as the cost of marketing health insurance, claims processing, and other costs, plus a profit, all expressed on a per policy basis. For example, if the insurer expects to pay $800 for the person's medical expenditures if the person becomes ill, which has a probability of 0.4, and to pay out nothing for medical expenditures if the person remains healthy, the expected value (a concept described in chapter 2) of insurer payments on behalf of the policyholder is $320.

However, the insurer incurs costs per insured individual in excess of $320 for several reasons. First, it incurs expenses marketing the company's products to potential customers and enrolling customers in its plans. Second, there are costs of claims processing. Third, the insurer must pay suppliers of capital. Capital funds may be in the form of equity (retained earnings, sale of stock in the company) or debt capital (sale of bonds, bank loans). Capital has an associated cost even if capital funds come from retained earnings, in which case use of the funds incurs opportunity costs. If the retained earnings were not used in the business of insurance, they could potentially have been used in another business pursuit.

Thus, if the insurer charged a premium of only $320, it would operate at a loss. The loading factor on an insurance policy is the price of insurance. The loading factor may be high, even as a proportion of the expected value of insurer payments to physicians, hospitals, and other health care providers for covered services.

Holding all other factors constant, including the individual's expectation of his or her future loss, as this price rises, the quantity of health insurance demanded falls. Policies offering full coverage have higher premiums than those with substantial cost sharing, but the loading may not be correspondingly higher.

The theory of demand for insurance explains the following phenomenon. Why do people purchase insurance at all? Why do they not self-insure? Why pay a price for purchased insurance when insurance can be obtained free of the loading by self-insuring? Why would one ever pay a load on an insurance policy? Why not simply save an amount equal to the actuarially fair premium and forgo purchasing health insurance, which is a rationale for precautionary saving?

The theory of the demand for insurance explains why people are willing to pay a load that is at least as great as required by insurers to supply health insurance. People are willing to pay a load because they are risk averse. Most persons are risk averse (see, e.g., Barsky, Juster, Kimball, et al. 1997). This is the conclusion. We now describe the basis for this conclusion.

4.3 DIMINISHING MARGINAL UTILITY OF WEALTH AND THE DEMAND FOR INSURANCE

UTILITY OF WEALTH

People desire income and wealth because it enables them to consume goods and services. Thus, since consumption yields utility, so does income and wealth. In the single-period model we use here, income and wealth are equivalent. Utility is never observed; rather, it is hypothesized to underlie the consumption choices people make.

Consider three possible relationships between utility and wealth ($U(W)$) in figure 4.1. In all three, utility rises with consumption, but it rises at different rates per unit increase in wealth. That is, the marginal utility of wealth ($\Delta U/\Delta W$) is always positive. However, the slope of the marginal utility of wealth differs among the three curves.

Curve A shows a positive marginal utility of wealth, but the marginal utility of wealth decreases as wealth increases. When there is a positive but diminishing marginal utility, we mean that the individual prefers more wealth to less wealth,

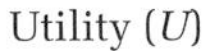

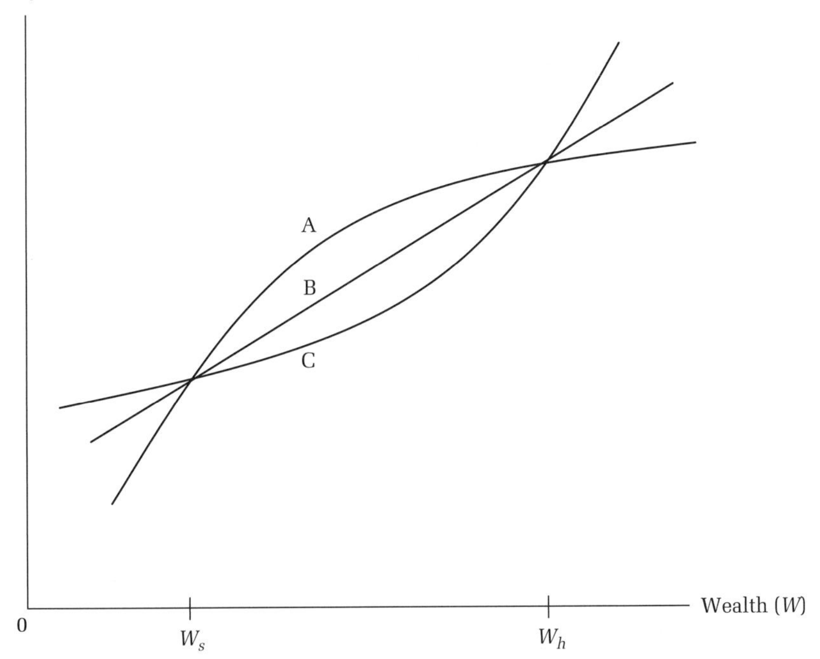

FIGURE 4.1
Possible Relationships between Wealth and the Utility of Wealth

irrespective of how much wealth the individual has. However, the extra or marginal utility the individual obtains from possessing an extra unit of wealth declines with each additional unit of wealth obtained. Thus, the marginal utility of wealth is lower at W_h than at W_s. The notion that people have diminishing marginal utility of wealth provides a justification for progressive taxation of income or wealth. If a rich person values a dollar less at the margin than a poor person does, transferring a dollar from the rich to the poor increases society's well-being. Persons with the utility function depicted by curve A in figure 4.1 are said to be *risk averse*.

Alternatively, $U(W)$ may be linear (curve B). Then marginal utility, although positive, is a constant value; the marginal utility of wealth does not change as wealth changes. Such persons are said to be *risk neutral*.

In the third category (curve C), the marginal utility of wealth increases with increasing wealth. Under this condition, the marginal utility of W_h exceeds marginal utility at W_s. Such persons are called *risk lovers*. To the extent that people are risk neutral, a case can be made for proportional rather than progressive taxation. If risk lovers are in the majority, there is a case for regressive taxation.

The curves in figure 4.1 could be drawn if we were to elicit from an individual the number of utils, a theoretical measure of happiness the person derives from each level of wealth. These curves themselves show utility derived from specific amount of wealth *obtained with certainty*. Although incorporated in an analysis of decision making under uncertainty below, these curves give utility for hypothetical, certain levels of wealth. Utils are a theoretical concept. No one has ever seen a util. Thus, rather than ask people about their utils, analysts infer utility in more indirect ways.

EXPECTED UTILITY

Many outcomes, including future health status, are uncertain. Uncertainty is everywhere, and since health and longevity are so important to human beings, uncertainty about future health and personal health expenditures is among the most important uncertainties people face.

The concepts described in this section were formalized more than 60 years ago by John von Neumann and Oskar Morgenstern (1944). The concept of expected utility maximization remains the workhorse of economic analysis of decisions made under uncertainty. If there were no uncertainty, expected loss would be L (the loss conditional on a loss occurring) and the probability of a loss occurring, Θ, would be one. There would be no market for insurance.

Expected utility is distinct from expected loss. Imagine that at a given point in time, such as a year, an individual can have either wealth W_h if he or she is healthy *or* wealth W_s if he or she is sick. $W_h > W_s$, and expected loss $(EL) = (1 - \Theta)0 - \Theta L = -\Theta(W_h - W_s)$. Individuals derive a level of utility from having W_h available for consumption, $U(W_h)$, and a level of utility to having W_s, $U(W_s)$, where $U(W_h) > U(W_s)$. At this level of generality, without knowing the parameters of the

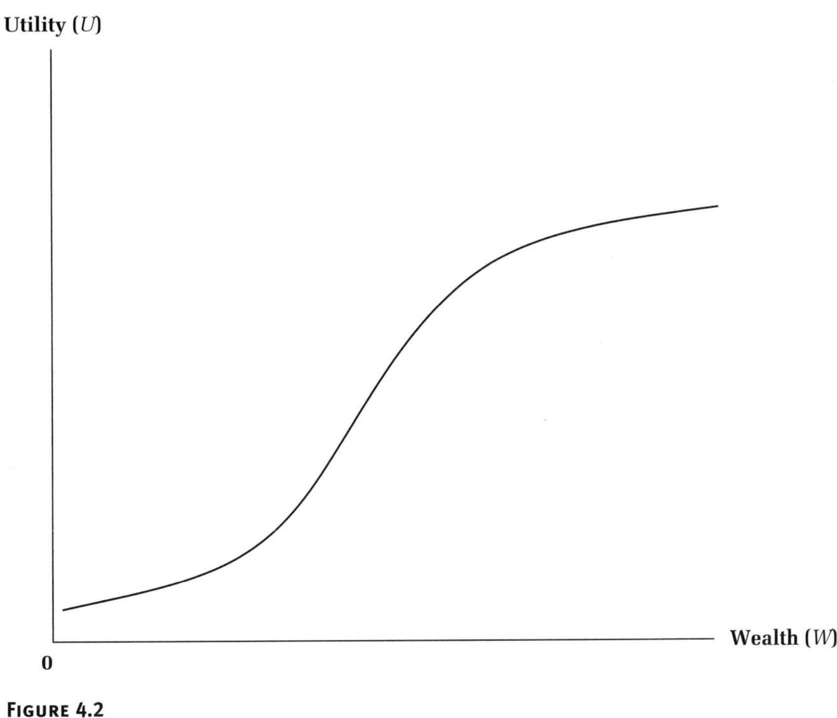

FIGURE 4.2

Utility of a Person Who Is Both a Risk-Loving and a Risk-Averse Individual

utility function, which would tell us how much more utility accrues to the individual in the healthy than in the sick state (then plugging in values of W, we would know values of U), we do not know how much higher $U(W_h)$ is than $U(W_s)$, only that the utility is higher. In this simple model, the only way that health affects utility is through its effect on personal wealth. We do not allow utility to be a direct function of health here.

As we will show more formally below, ordinarily only risk-averse individuals, that, individuals with the A-type utility of wealth curve (fig. 4.1), demand insurance. Risk lovers (curve C individuals) gamble and do not demand insurance. A risk-neutral individual would not be willing to pay any more than the actuarial value of the loss for insurance.

It is possible for a utility function to be both convex and concave with respect to the wealth axis (fig. 4.2). People may be risk lovers when very poor, but at higher levels of wealth may demand insurance. Friedman and Savage (1948) explained the coexistence of gambling and insurance on this basis. They observed that poor people often engage in actuarially unfair gambles, that is, they pay more than the expected value of prizes (a concept explained more fully below), while more affluent persons often buy insurance against potential income loss.

Having reviewed these concepts and remarks about utility of wealth functions, we now turn to a more formal explanation of the model of demand for insurance.

4.4 Model of Demand for Insurance

The Basic Model

We assume:

1. A representative individual maximizes his or her expected utility.
2. If the person becomes ill, he or she incurs a fixed loss, L.
3. The probability of loss Θ is fixed.
4. The individual chooses between two courses of action: (1) buy insurance, and thereby incur a relatively small but certain loss in the form of an insurance premium, or (2) self-insure and pay no premium, but face a low probability of a large loss if the person becomes ill and a large probability of no loss.
5. The marginal utility of wealth (or income) is decreasing in wealth (income); that is, the person is risk averse.
6. Only wealth, not health, affects the marginal utility of wealth. This means that, holding wealth constant, the individual enjoys an extra dollar of wealth and the added consumption from this wealth the same, irrespective of whether the individual is in the healthy state or the sick state. Alternatively, one can think of the marginal utility of wealth and consumption being different in different health states. Suppose an individual became sick. Would the individual derive more or less utility from watching a big-screen television set, traveling to a mountain resort, or receiving care from a private duty nurse? Clearly, we are unable to logically deduce whether or not the marginal utility of consumption would rise or fall with diminished health.

If the person remains well, $L = 0$ and wealth $= W_h$. However, if he or she becomes ill, the loss is L, and the person is left with W_s. $W_s = W_h - L$. Ex ante, it is expected loss (EL), not loss per se (L), that is relevant to the individual in deciding whether or not to purchase an insurance policy. $EL < L$. $W_h - EL = W_w$. W_w thus reflects the weighted average EL.

While the utility function ($U(W)$) shows utility as a function of wealth, this utility function only applies for certain wealth. If wealth is uncertain because the individual faces the possibility of a loss, owing, for example, to an illness, the relevant concept is expected utility rather than utility. When the individual faces the loss L with probability Θ, his or her expected utility (EU) is not $U(W_w)$ but rather a weighted average of the utilities when well and when sick.

The expected utility of wealth is given by

$$EU(W) = (1 - \Theta)U(W_h) + \Theta U(W_s). \tag{4.1}$$

$EU(W)$ is not $U(W_w)$ but, if the person is risk averse, is something less than $U(W_w)$. Let W_w' be the wealth for which $EU(W)$ equals $U(W_w)$—the utility from the gamble equals the utility from a certain level of wealth. Then let $U(W_w)'$ be the level of utility when W_w' is certain. Then the individual could give an insurance company up to $(W_w - W_w')$ in a premium *above* the expected loss on the insurance policy and still be as well off as if he or she did not buy insurance and faced the prospect of an uncertain W_h or W_s. Ex post, that is, after the year is over, the person never attains this level of wealth without insurance, but rather has W_h or W_s, depending on whether the person stayed healthy or not. W_w is a weighted average of mutually exclusive outcomes.

Graphically, $U(W_s)$ is at point A in figure 4.3 and $U(W_h)$ is at point B. The cord connecting points A and B represents the locus of expected values of $U(W_s)$ and $U(W_h)$. As Θ increases, the expected value moves along the cord to the left, and conversely for reductions in Θ.

We digress for a moment to show that the cord connecting U when healthy and when sick is linear. We take as given that there are only two outcomes, being healthy and becoming sick. Then the expected utility is a weighted average of utility when healthy. Recall that $EU = (1 - \Theta)U(W_h) + \Theta U(W_s)$. Now suppose that the probability of becoming sick rises from Θ to Θ_δ. The EU becomes $EU' = (1 - \Theta_\delta)U(W_h) + \Theta_\delta U(W_s)$. $EU' < EU$. If $(\Theta_\delta/\Theta) = 0.9$, $EU' = 0.9EU$. Expected loss and expected utility vary as Θ varies.

Now consider how much utility the person derives from W_w, which is W_h minus the expected loss from health expenditures incurred by the individual. If the insurer set the premium of the insurance policy at its actuarial value, W_w is the level of wealth the person would have left over after paying this premium. But note that W_w corresponds to utility levels at points C and D. Utility at D is higher than at C. Point D is the utility this risk-averse individual would obtain if the wealth level W_w were certain. However, without full insurance, W_w is an expected value, not a certain value. Thus, the risk-averse individual prefers certainty to the chance that he or she will end up with W_w. The utility difference between a certain and an uncertain wealth of W_w is the vertical distance between points D and C.

Since utility is higher at D than it is at C, an insurer can charge a premium in excess of the actuarial value of the loss, and the risk-averse person will still be better off or at least not worse off than with an uncertain level of wealth with the expected value W_w. EC in figure 4.3 represents the maximum amount above the actuarial value of the loss that the person would be willing to pay to have a certain

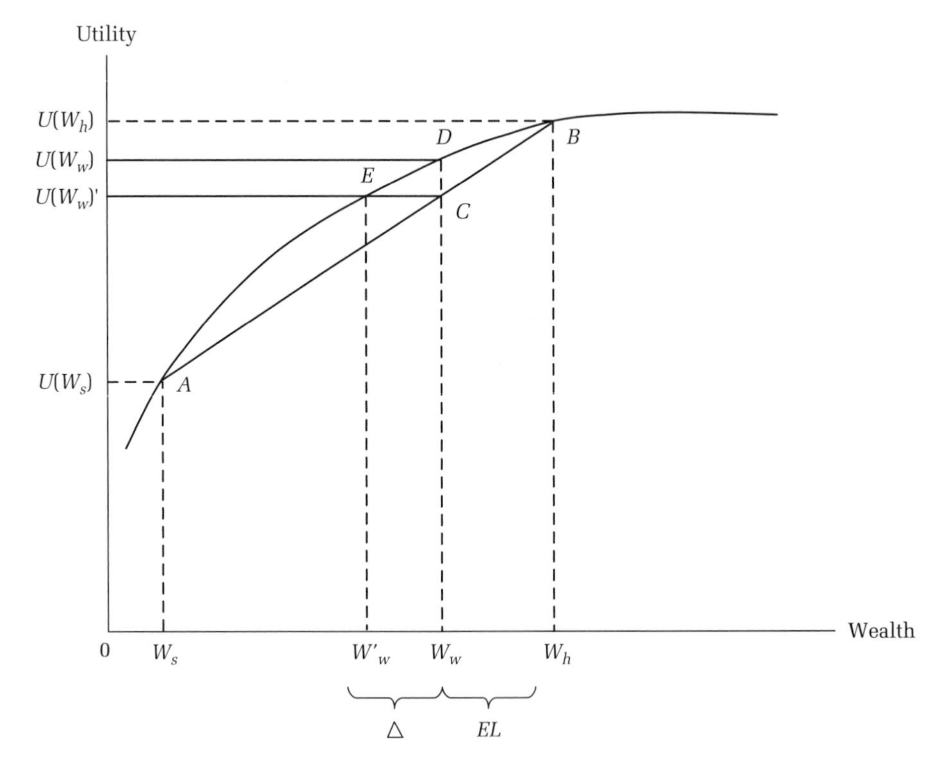

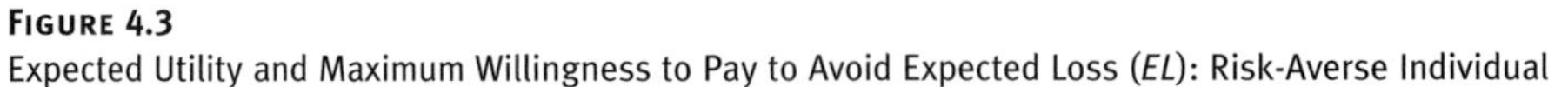

FIGURE 4.3
Expected Utility and Maximum Willingness to Pay to Avoid Expected Loss (*EL*): Risk-Averse Individual

rather than an uncertain level of wealth. The utility of wealth at *E* is equal to the expected utility of wealth at *C*. If the insurer extracts less money than *EC* from the individual, the individual's utility exceeds the value at *E*, and wealth is greater than $W_{W'}$.

EFFECTS OF SHIFTS IN THE UTILITY FUNCTION, CHANGES IN Θ, AND CHANGES IN *L* ON THE DECISION TO PURCHASE INSURANCE

SHIFTS IN THE UTILITY FUNCTION

Now suppose that the utility of wealth in the healthy state increases. The person now values W_h more than previously and the utility of W_s stays the same. Then the slope of the cord connecting the two utilities increases (becomes steeper), and the cord becomes closer to the utility function. Or the person now values W_h less than before, and the distance between the cord and the utility function become farther apart.

To generalize, the distance between the utility function depends on the extent to which marginal utility decreases as wealth increases. A greater distance between the utility function and the cord implies that the individual is willing to pay a greater premium in excess of *EL*. A greater distance implies a higher willingness to pay for insurance, that is, a higher demand for insurance.

If marginal utility does not vary with wealth, that is, if it is a constant value, the cord and the utility function coincide. The person is *risk neutral*, and the maximum amount the person is willing to pay for insurance above *EL* is zero. Under these circumstances, an insurance market cannot exist. Insurers would not be willing to supply insurance at a zero loading. Thus, a prerequisite for the existence of an insurance market is a diminishing marginal utility of wealth (or income).

Change in Probability of Incurring a Loss (Becoming Sick)

When Θ, the probability of incurring a loss because of illness, decreases, the actuarially fair premium decreases. There is a corresponding upward movement along the cord in figure 4.3. (The reverse occurs for increases in Θ.)

Suppose that Θ becomes so small that the point on the cord is almost at point *B*. Then the distance between the cord and the utility curve becomes very small. When this distance is small, it is easily shown that the line (parallel to the wealth axis) from the point on the cord to the utility curve becomes very small as well. When this line is short, willingness to pay a premium much above the actuarially fair premium is low as well. In other words, demand for insurance is low.

Likewise, for points on the cord near *A*, the probability of incurring a loss is nearly 1.0. There is not much demand for insurance when losses are nearly certain to occur, either.

To generalize, holding other factors constant, demand for insurance is highest when Θ is in the midrange and lowest when Θ is nearly 0.0 or 1.0.

Change in the Magnitude of the Loss Conditional on Incurring a Loss (Becoming Sick)

Because of health care cost inflation, which has occurred in many countries, the potential loss conditional on becoming sick has increased, especially in those countries without comprehensive public health insurance systems.

An increase in *L* means that W_s moves to the left. Thus the cord from *A* to *B* lies below the cord shown at figure 4.3 except at point *B*, which is the same as in the figure. A lower cord implies a greater horizontal distance between the cord and the utility curve. A greater distance implies that demand for insurance is higher than for a lower *L*. The inference is that an increase in *L*, holding other factors constant, boosts demand for insurance.

The Risk-Lover Case

Thus far we have seen that risk-averse individuals may be better off with insurance and risk-neutral persons do not demand insurance. Now consider the third case,

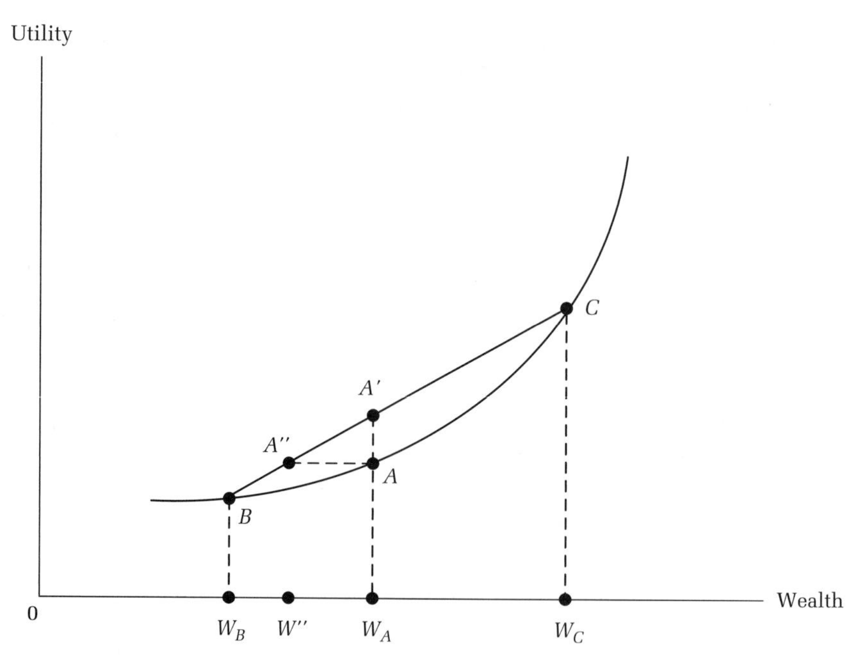

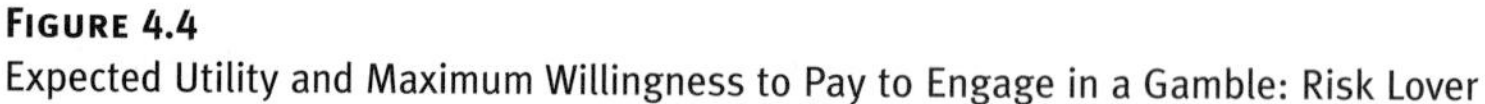

FIGURE 4.4
Expected Utility and Maximum Willingness to Pay to Engage in a Gamble: Risk Lover

in which the marginal utility of wealth is increasing (not decreasing or constant). Persons with an increasing marginal utility of wealth do not insure but rather engage in gambling. An increasing marginal utility of wealth means that the person values receiving an extra dollar more when wealthy than when poor.

Now let the person's initial wealth be W_A (fig. 4.4). The probability of winning is $\Theta_{w.}$ Then the expected gain is EG, where $EG = \Theta_w G$ and G (= $W_C - W_A$) is the amount the gambler wins if he or she wins. A risk lover is willing to pay more than EG for the opportunity to gamble. The person in figure 4.4 has higher utility when W_A is uncertain (point A') than when wealth is certain (point A). So the person has a maximum willingness to pay for a gamble, which is $W_A - W_{A.}''$ This loading factor is a substantial share of the price of the gamble, which is $W_A - W_B$.

IMPLICATIONS OF THEORY: DETERMINANTS OF DEMAND FOR INSURANCE

The above framework yields several predictions about who will demand insurance and under which circumstances insurance will be demanded. First, let's consider the price of insurance. Risk-neutral persons and risk lovers do not demand insurance. Willingness to pay for insurance among risk-averse individuals depends on the extent to which the marginal utility of wealth declines with increases in wealth. Increases in the loading should lead to decreased demand for insurance. The first persons to drop out of the insurance market when premiums increase are the relatively less risk-averse individuals.

Second, demand for insurance depends on the size of the loss incurred by the household when people become sick. Hospital care tends to be expensive. By contrast, a follow-up office visit (a revisit) is typically *relatively* less expensive. With higher loss, holding the degree of risk aversion constant, the cord becomes more distant from the utility function.

For this reason, we expect higher demand for insurance for services with a high associated loss than for services with a lower associated loss. In the United States, private hospital insurance coverage grew widespread before private insurance for physicians' services became widespread.

Third, to the extent that the marginal utility of wealth declines with increased wealth, one would expect relatively less affluent persons to have a greater demand for insurance than more affluent persons. A $1,000 loss to a millionaire generates a lower loss in utility than the same loss occurring to an individual with an annual income of $10,000.

However, in reality, more affluent persons are more likely to be covered by insurance. As discussed below, this fact does not contradict the expected income hypothesis; rather this empirical pattern reflects various policy and institutional factors.

Fourth, demand for insurance reflects variance of loss. Probabilities of loss near 1 or near 0 have a low variance. The variance is highest at the middle of the 0–1 interval, that is, at $\Theta = 0.5$.

Finally, as indicated above, the expected utility model assumes that demand for care is not responsive to price. Rather, L is assumed to be fixed. But, more realistically, the quantity of care demanded is generally responsive to changes in its price. Thus, the demand for insurance coverage for services whose demand is relatively price inelastic is relatively high.

Recall from the previous chapter that the welfare loss from insurance coverage depends on the price elasticity of demand for the service. The welfare loss is higher when the price elasticity of demand is higher. When the price elasticity is higher, the expected loss is higher, leading to a higher premium. Even if the individual does not consume more services when insurance is complete, in setting the premium of the insurance policy, the insurer assumes that the quantity demanded will be greater when the price to the user is lower. So the premium will be higher.

The decision to purchase insurance is made before illness strikes. Ex ante, the consumer is unlikely to want to pay for all the services that people with complete coverage use.

THE PREMIUM OF A HEALTH INSURANCE POLICY

Let R be the health insurance premium of a health insurance policy. Then

$$R = (1 + L_d)(1 - c)pxEL, \tag{4.2}$$

where R is the premium, L_d is the loading, c is the coinsurance rate specified in the insurance policy, p is the price of medical care, and x is the number of units of medical care. $px = EL$, where EL is expected loss. For example, if the loading is 0.4 and c is 0.2, the premium is 1.4 times 0.8 times EL.

As explained more fully in chapter 10, the loading is much lower for insuring groups, especially large groups organized by a large employer, than for insuring individuals, and lower for larger than for small insuring groups. The loading reflects administration and marketing cost, the cost of claims processing, a hedge against adverse selection, and profit.

4.5 EMPIRICAL ISSUES

WHY DO THE PROBABILITY AND MAGNITUDE OF THE LOSS VARY?

The probability of loss is first and foremost a function of a person's health history. If one has had cancer or a heart attack in the past, the probability of getting another bout of cancer or a heart attack tends to be higher. Of course, there is inter-year variability, and poor health in the recent past is not a perfect predictor of health in the following year. Insurance coverage, income, and access to health care providers also affect the loss probability. The above model of demand for insurance assumes that insurance has no impact on either p or EL. But the empirical evidence suggests otherwise.

Demographic characteristics, such as age and gender, are positively associated with service use. A healthy 85-year-old has a higher probability of suffering a major health shock than does a healthy 35-year-old. Moreover, recommendations for preventive care and screening vary by age. Females tend to use more medical care than males, for example, during the childbearing years. However, these expenditures are largely predictable—that is, Θ is near 0.0 or 1.0—and hence, based on the above model (and disregarding institutional factors discussed below), one would expect less demand for insurance coverage for such services.

The size of the expected loss reflects medical care prices and the person's health. A serious illness is generally more costly to treat than a less serious one. As indicated above, type of care is also a factor. A unit of inpatient hospital care tends to be more costly than a unit of physicians' services in an ambulatory setting. There are regional differences within a large country and inter-country differences in physicians' practice patterns. Thus, for example, there is geographic variation in how a specific form of cancer is treated. Thus, *EL* will differ for this reason as well.

WHY INCOME AFFECTS DEMAND FOR INSURANCE

Income elasticities of demand for private health insurance are consistently positive (see, e.g., Marquis, Buntin, Escarce, et al. 2004). Although higher income shifts the demand curve for private insurance outward and to the right, underlying the overall positive relationship are factors that lead to decreased as well as increased demand for insurance.

As emphasized above, only risk-averse individuals demand insurance. And higher degrees of risk aversion should lead to higher demand for insurance. The marginal utility of wealth and income is thought to be higher for the poor than for the affluent. For this reason, more affluent individuals should demand less, not more, insurance. Most of the other factors affecting demand for insurance, however, support a positive relationship between wealth or income and demand for insurance.

Demand for insurance reflects the person's expected loss (*EL*). To the extent that personal health care services are a normal good, one expects the use of such services to rise with income. However, the demand for hospital care does not monotonically rise with income since poor persons tend to be relatively heavy consumers of hospital care (see chapter 3). But other services, particularly elective services, are likely to be positively related to a person's income. As *EL* increases, so does the demand for insurance, particularly if the individual's subjective belief about his or her future loss is not reflected in the insurer's premium, which is the phenomenon of adverse selection.

The role of income as a factor shifting the demand curve for personal health care services is made more complicated by the role of time prices. The time price is part of the full price of care (see chapter 3). More affluent persons are likely to have higher time prices. For this reason, higher-income persons would demand less care. But on the other hand, since the opportunity cost of time is higher, the cost of time lost from work due to illness is also higher (Blau and Gilleskie 2008). For this reason, people with higher time prices would demand more care, especially care that would reduce the probability that the illness worsens.

Two factors add to the complexity of income's role in the demand for insurance. First, lower-income persons are more likely to be eligible for public insurance. In the United States, this public insurance is called Medicaid. In Germany, there is a similar program to Medicaid (see chapter 12). In addition, statutory insurance is compulsory only for individuals below a certain level of annual compensation. After this level is reached, the individual may opt out of statutory insurance and purchase private insurance instead. For this reason alone, the demand for private health insurance would rise with income.

Further, in the United States, employer contributions to an employee's health insurance are not counted as personal income. Since personal income tax rates rise with income, what is in effect a public subsidy of private health insurance purchases rises with income. Thus, in establishments in which compensation tends to be high, there is an incentive for employees to want to receive compensation in the form of such fringe benefits as health insurance. Thus, we would expect employers to offer more complete insurance coverage when compensation levels are higher. US law requires that the same health insurance plan be offered by an employer to all employees irrespective of the amount the employee is paid. Yet when the median worker is paid more, it is more likely that the employer will offer more generous benefits to all of its employees (Goldstein and Pauly 1976).

The loading factor is much lower for private group insurance than it is for individual coverage. Holding other factors constant, persons with high incomes are more likely to be employed than are those with low incomes. Thus, higher-income persons are more likely to have health insurance, and more complete health insurance, than are lower-income persons for this reason as well.

4.6 Health Insurance and Welfare: The Deadweight Loss of Excess Insurance Revisited

Any politician who claimed that his or her constituents were overinsured would almost surely lose the next election. Yet some economists have made the case that people sometimes have too much insurance. While surprising at first glance, the argument that people are sometimes overinsured has both theoretical and empirical support. There is a welfare gain to risk-averse individuals from having insurance. Above, we defined the maximum premium that a risk-averse person is willing to pay for a given amount of insurance. If the person has to pay this maximum amount for insurance, then there is no welfare gain from expenditure risk reduction. But if he or she pays anything less than this maximum amount, there is a welfare gain. Assuming that one can find a functional form that well approximates the utility function in figure 4.3, and that the amount spent on premiums is less than the maximum willingness to pay, one can calculate the welfare gain from the provision of health insurance. The calculations themselves are a bit complex, but the underlying concept is quite straightforward.

Offsetting this welfare gain is the welfare loss arising from moral hazard (see chapter 3). If demand curves for personal health care services were totally unresponsive to the price paid by the policyholder out of pocket, there would be no welfare loss, but empirical evidence, as discussed in the previous chapter, conclusively demonstrates that the quantity of personal health care services demanded is somewhat price responsive.

The welfare loss from moral hazard depends on the area of a triangle whose base varies directly with the change in quantity demanded when price to the consumer falls. People are overinsured if the welfare loss arising from moral hazard is larger than the welfare gain from expenditure risk reduction. More than three decades ago, based on his calculations of welfare loss versus welfare gain, Martin Feldstein (1973) concluded that the empirical evidence showed that people in the United States had too much health insurance.

Manning, Newhouse, Duan, et al. (1987) analyzed the welfare loss of moving from the 95 percent family plan with a $1,000 stop loss (in the RAND Health Insurance Experiment; see chapter 3) to a free plan. The authors concluded that the welfare loss from increased moral hazard in the free plan from the switch would amount to $37–$60 billion, compared to the annual health expenditure in 1984 in the United States of around $200 billion. They acknowledged that it would be appropriate to deduct some amount for the welfare gain from additional expenditure risk protection in the free plan, but given the $1,000 cap, the added risk protection would be small.

Although this type of study is compelling, being based both on economic theory and empirical evidence, the conclusion holds only under the assumptions that economists typically make in such an analysis. For example, to the extent that there are externalities in consumption, that is, that person A is made worse off if a seemingly deserving person B does not obtain care, one cannot simply sum areas of triangles lying above individual demand curves, as we did in chapter 3.

This externality provides another rationale for insurance provision. Others may argue that having health insurance is something akin to a constitutional right every member of a society has. If so, there is not much economic analysis can say about whether the amount of health people in a country possess is too little, too much, or just right.

4.7 ROLE OF TAX SUBSIDIES IN DEMAND FOR HEALTH INSURANCE

In the United States, health insurance provided as a fringe benefit is not subject to any form of taxation, either the Social Security or Medicare payroll taxes on earnings or the personal income tax. Thus, if one has a marginal tax rate of 40 percent, for example, then, compared to a dollar of wage compensation, a dollar of compensation in the form of health insurance benefits is worth $1.67. The relative advantage of receiving compensation as a health insurance benefit increases with increases in the person's marginal tax rate.

Since the marginal tax rate on personal income rises with income, the benefit is worth relatively more to higher earners. For this reason alone, it is not surprising that in the United States, the fraction of persons with health insurance coverage rises with the level of wealth. Decreasing risk aversion with increased income is a reason that demand for health insurance should be lower among the affluent, but this effect may be more offset by such factors as the tax subsidy of health insurance premiums.

This tax subsidy also serves to limit employee awareness of increasing health insurance premiums. There have been proposals to limit the amount of health insurance benefit subject to this tax exclusion ("tax cap"), but none of these proposals have been enacted into law by the US Congress. Another type of proposal would be to exchange the tax exclusion for a refundable tax credit when the taxpayer purchases a qualified health insurance policy. A tax credit is a subsidy fixed in monetary terms. It is subtracted from the taxpayer's total tax obligation. If the tax payer, for example, owed $10,000 in taxes and the tax credit was $1,000, this person would pay $9,000. The refundable feature means that if subtracting led to a negative amount, that amount would be paid to the taxpayer as a tax refund.

Suppose the tax payer owed $0 in taxes. Then a $1,000 tax credit would result in a tax refund of $1,000.

The advantage of a refundable tax credit is that, unlike the tax exclusion, the tax credit does not increase with the taxpayer's income but rather is a fixed amount. Also, since the tax credit is fixed and does not depend on the insurance premium, people have a financial incentive to shop for efficient plans and pay for expensive add-on features in full. Under the current system in the United States, more expensive insurance plans are subsidized in that the taxpayer pays only (1 – the taxpayer's marginal tax rate) for each dollar of additional expense.

Even though the advantages of a tax cap or a tax credit are well understood in the United States, there is political opposition to implementing a tax cap on the grounds that it represents an increase in taxes, which it does to higher-income taxpayers and to taxpayers located in geographic areas that have relatively high prices of health care services; thus the objection is on normative rather than on positive grounds. Refundable tax credits are sometimes opposed because it is argued that individuals in poorer health may require a higher refundable tax credit since they may be expected to pay more for health insurance on average. Currently, if persons in poor health are employed or if they have access to an employer-based health insurance plan through a family member who is employed, they are not surcharged for being in poorer health. However, if refundable tax credits were adopted, employer-based insurance coverage would probably become less common, and individuals would more often obtain health insurance outside their employment. It is under such circumstances that insurers may impose premium surcharges on individuals in poorer health.

The importance of the tax subsidy as a determinant of demand for health insurance depends on the price elasticity of such demand. Most estimates of the price elasticity are between –0.2 and –1.0, although estimates above –1.0 have been reported. Even an elasticity as low as –0.2 implies that the tax subsidy has an important distortionary effect on demand for insurance.[1]

4.8 Adverse Selection

How Adverse Selection May Arise in Health Insurance Markets

In most markets, more choice is preferred to less. In private health insurance markets, individuals have choices: (1) when they seek to obtain health insurance on their own, as they do for individual health insurance in the United States; (2) when they purchase private supplemental health insurance that covers health expenditures not covered by a public health insurer, as with Medicare in the United States; (3) when they choose between a traditional fee-for-service Medicare plan and Medicare operated by a health maintenance organization; and (4) when they purchase private insurance rather than completely rely on the public National Health Service (NHS) in the UK or when individuals select a sickness fund that operates under Germany's statutory health insurance program.

When health insurance is employer-based, as is much health insurance in the United States, employees often have a choice of several health insurance plans sponsored by the employer. Plans may differ, for example, in what they cover and how much cost sharing they require.

A compelling argument can be made that competition among health insurers and choices of plans offered by each insurer and by employers allows for satisfaction of diverse preferences and provides a mechanism whereby the market can weed out inefficient insurers—those insurers that are slow claims processors or that make frequent errors in claims processing, are affiliated with providers that consumers do not prefer, mistreat providers so that providers do not want to deal with them, or offer a structure of covered benefits that is unappealing to many consumers.

People do indeed have diverse preferences, including differences in risk preferences.[2] A more risk-averse individual may be expected to demand health insurance policies with smaller amounts of cost sharing. Younger families may be expected to be more interested in having insurance with generous maternity benefits. Older individuals may be more interested in coverage for long-term care (e.g., home health services, nursing home services).

As long as insurers can anticipate use of services during the term of the insurance contract as well as insured persons can, insurers should be able to accurately predict the health expenditures of their policyholders in advance of the policy year. Thus, for example, an insurer would expect an older person to use more and perhaps more complex services during a policy year than a younger person would.

1. See, for example, Pauly (1986), Sloan and Adamache (1986), Gruber and Lettau (2004), and Marquis, Bunton, Escarce, et al. (2004).

2. Risk preferences represent only one type of preference. Other types include time preference, differences in the marginal utility of current consumption, and preferences for the consumption of particular goods and services.

The insured's age is easily observed by the insurer, and the law permitting, the insurer can adjust premiums to reflect such age-related differences in health services use.

However, under some circumstances, the individual may know more about his or her health than do insurers. Suppose an individual has been experiencing chest pains when climbing several flights of steps. The individual expects she may have heart disease but has not visited a doctor for this concern yet. She figures that she will be using a lot of services during the coming year in diagnosing and treating this disease. The insurer knows nothing about this and does not adjust the premium accordingly but instead charges a premium appropriate for the average person in the individual's age and gender category and geographic area.

Faced with premiums charged by each insurer/policy, the individual selects a policy with little cost sharing, since this will mean lower out-of-pocket payments for medical services during the coming year. The insurer will lose money on this person but it does not know this in advance. More generally, what we have just described is adverse selection in health insurance markets. One could perhaps argue that the insurer could require that the insured undergo a thorough health examination before the insurance policy is issued. However, unless the patient self-reports his or her symptoms, the physician may have to administer many types of tests involving several organ systems in order to detect underlying illness.

Consider how costly it would be to screen for heart disease if the persons being screened reveal no information on their symptoms. Some persons may show what seem to be abnormalities on tests but these results may be normal for the person and do not signify underlying diseases. These are false positives (see chapter 2). Very many persons would have to undergo screening to find a few true positives.

Where this is lawful, private insurers can and do adopt practices to combat adverse selection. One approach is to exclude preexisting illnesses in the insurance contract. Such measures can vary in stringency. For example, an insurer could refuse to pay for services related to a condition that it argues would have been known previously by the insured. However, some insured individuals would legitimately have health shocks during the policy year that they did not know about or suspect would occur in advance of purchasing the health insurance policy. Some people do indeed experience heart attacks or discover that they have cancer unexpectedly, and they have a legitimate desire for expenditure risk protection from such events. Even persons with a prior illness may be surprised as well as unhappy about a reoccurrence.

Alternatively, an insurer could insert a clause that provides a reduced premium in the second year for persons who use the plan sparingly in the first year.[3] But then the insurer would have to charge a higher premium to all newly insured individuals in the first year as it learns the health risks of the newly insured individuals.

3. One of us has a dental insurance policy that includes a provision of this type. Both adverse selection and moral hazard are particularly problematic for dental insurance. On moral hazard in this context, see chapter 3.

In some jurisdictions, most recently in the United States as part of national health reform legislation enacted in 2010, the law prevents the insurer from inserting preexisting condition clauses into insurance contracts. The argument for these statutory prohibitions is that such clauses are unfair to persons with adverse health histories.

In addition, some jurisdictions prevent insurers from using a person's health history as a basis for setting premiums. In some areas with such statutes, the insurer is allowed to vary premiums on a limited basis, such as by age, gender, and geographic location (region, urban versus rural, etc.). These are called *community rating* laws. The term community rating applies because premiums are set equally for broad classes of individuals.

At least at first glance, the rationale for a community rating law may seem strange to some. Should not people be asked to pay more for insurance if their expected losses are relatively high? A rationale for community rating is that we do not pick our parents, and thus our genetic makeup is given to each of us. If one has genes that predispose one to get certain diseases, there should be no financial penalty for this. But even if community rating can be justified on equity grounds, it can adversely affect the workings of a competitive private health insurance market.

Under competition, people would pay the expected value of their health care expenditures under the insurance contract. But under community rating, people pay more or less than these expected values, depending on their health. In fact, under community rating, adverse selection can occur without asymmetric information between insured individuals and insurers. The insurer may know that the insured is sick and how sick the insured is, but the insurer cannot use this information in setting the premiums that insured individuals pay.

In the United States, most private health insurance is part of the fringe benefit package from the individual's employer. At the time of open enrollment, employees, especially those persons employed by large organizations, can choose among health insurance plans with differing characteristics. Among the characteristics are the amount of cost sharing and the health care providers included in the plan. Residents of a particular geographic location may prefer a particular plan because the doctors that work near the employee's home are affiliated with a particular plan.

To the extent that the employee selects a plan based on where she lives or based on her risk preferences, there is no problem of adverse selection. However, if she knows she is sick, she may select a plan with more complete coverage. Then there is an adverse selection problem. The insurer will anticipate that the relatively ill will predominantly select certain plans, and adjust the premiums for such plans accordingly. The insurer in this case and certainly the employer are likely to have detailed records on the employee's use of services in the past, but it is considered unethical and generally illegal to take use this information for premium setting.

The insurer can use this information in the aggregate to set the premium for a certain plan, but for a particular plan, there can be no variations in premiums among employees of a particular organization. And if the insurer offers insurance coverage to several organizations, it can vary premiums among employers.

Adverse selection in insurance markets can result in some types of plans not being offered in the marketplace at all. For example, risk-averse individuals may prefer nearly complete coverage, but when there is adverse selection, such policies may not be available in the marketplace.

Adverse Selection and Unraveling in Insurance Markets

Adverse selection is not unique to private health insurance markets. It exists in other insurance markets as well. A very well-known exposition of adverse selection and its effects is a theoretical article by Michael Rothschild and Joseph Stiglitz (1976). In this section, we apply some of the basic arguments in this famous article, using the market for health insurance as a case in point. Rothschild and Stiglitz's analysis applied to all types of privately purchased insurance.

Assume initially:

- All people are identical. Each person requires $800 of care if he or she becomes ill.
- If the person becomes ill and receives treatment, he or she survives.
- There is no moral hazard. For example, people do not change their consumption of personal health care services because they have health insurance.
- There are two insurance policies in the market, one offering a maximum payment of $600 for medical treatment and the other offering complete insurance—$800 worth of coverage.
- The premium *difference* of the two policies is $60 per year or $5 per month, reflecting differences in expected loss between the two policies plus an additional load reflecting the added cost of administering the higher limit policy.
- The additional load represents the minimal added cost of providing the more complete coverage.
- The choice between two policies is made by the individual based on the individual's risk aversion.
- The load on the insurance policies is efficient—that is, the amounts that would prevail in a perfectly competitive insurance market.

Given these assumptions, a person buys more complete coverage if willingness to pay for the extra coverage is greater than or equal to the marginal cost of supplying it ($MC = EL + \text{load}$). The expected loss (EL) is independent of the person's degree of risk aversion. Thus, even if the insurer had all possible information about

FIGURE 4.5
Adverse Selection: Only One Health Type of Person

people it insures, it would not charge different premiums except to reflect the limits on coverage ($600 versus $800 maximum payment in the event of an illness).

In deciding between the policy with the lower maximum or the higher maximum payment limit, the question for the consumer is only whether or not the extra $60 is worth it, given his or her own risk preferences. Those who are more risk averse may find the $800 limit policy more attractive, but this depends on precisely how risk averse the person is.

If the world were as simple as depicted above, Rothschild and Stiglitz's (1976) contribution would lie in describing the complexity of insurance markets with asymmetric information and the adverse effects of such asymmetric information.

Above, there was only one type of person with a probability Θ of an illness occurring during the year (fig. 4.5). There could be many such persons. The important point is that there is no difference in expected loss, only in the degree of risk aversion

Now assume that there are two types of persons, one person having a higher probability of becoming ill: the one with the lower probability having a probability Θ_L and the one with a higher probability having a probability Θ_H of becoming ill (fig. 4.6). The *L*-type consumer might have a different genetic makeup as reflected in a different family history of disease than does the *H*-type. But the insurer does not know which type of genetic makeup each person has. The insurer does not know the difference between Θ_L and Θ_H but rather assumes that the individuals are equally likely to become ill, and just uses the probability Θ in calculating the premiums it charges for the two plans.

Assume that there are an equal number of *L*-type and *H*-type persons. Hence, $\Theta = (\Theta_L + \Theta_H)/2$. The insurer charges both individuals the same $60 difference in premium.

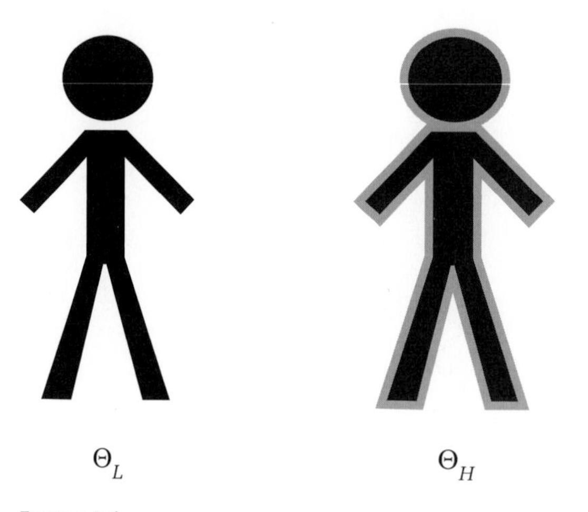

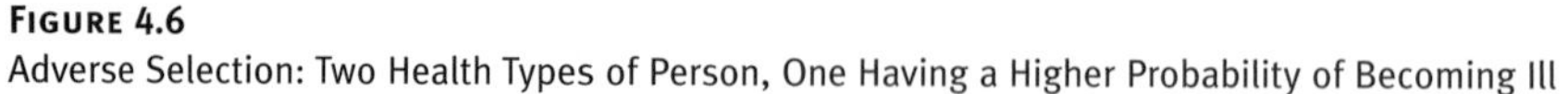
FIGURE 4.6
Adverse Selection: Two Health Types of Person, One Having a Higher Probability of Becoming Ill

Under these circumstances, the person with the adverse family history picks the $800 coverage policy. The *L*-type person picks the more limited $600 coverage policy (fig. 4.7). During the year covered by the policies, the insurer notices that it is making money on the $600 policy and losing money on the $800 policy. For this reason, the next year the insurer sets the premium *difference* between the two types of policies at $80 (fig. 4.8).

To continue, we need a finer distinction among types of individuals based on their true probabilities of becoming ill. Assume that there is further heterogeneity in the high-probability category, there being two types, *HL* and *HH*, with *HH* having a higher probability of becoming ill than *HL*.

Now *HH* picks the $800 plan, but given the higher premium difference, *HL*-type persons opt for the $600 plan. Next year the premium must rise even more. *HH*-type people continue to opt for the $800 plan. Again the premium difference rises until there are few if any policyholders in the high-option plan.

Since policyholders are assumed to be equally risk averse, the choice of insurance policy is always made on the basis of policyholder's expected loss and the premium difference. But after rounds of premium increases and increasingly higher-risk persons selecting the high-option plan, the high-option plan eventually becomes unavailable in the market. There is virtually no one left to choose it.

One could conclude from this that it is just tough luck for the high-option plan. After all, the market for automobiles priced at over $100,000 (US$) is thin. On the other hand, many people would conclude that a high-option health insurance plan is not really the equivalent of a $110,000 automobile. Not having complete health insurance available will penalize highly risk-averse individuals who absent the unraveling process would want such insurance.

FIGURE 4.7
Adverse Selection: Individual Choices When the Premium Difference Is $60
Left: Expecting a lower than average loss, the individual with a lower probability of becoming ill (p_L) picks the policy with the $600 limit. *Right:* Expecting a higher than average loss, the high-risk individual with the higher probability of becoming ill (p_H) picks the policy with the $800 limit. The insurer charges both individuals the $60 difference in premium for the two policies. The individuals make their choice on the basis of their risk aversion and expected loss.

To continue the above example, some individuals who would have been willing to pay for the more complete coverage are priced out of such coverage. In the end, they purchase $600 coverage when they would have preferred the $800 coverage if it were available at (their) EL + load.

In the real world, insurance policies differ in many ways, not just in dollar limits on coverage. Some policies offer additional benefits (e.g., cover more visits a year, cover more drugs). Some policies, as in the example, have a higher ceiling on dollar outlays per year or per life. Some policies have lower co-pays than others. Some policies offer lower deductibles than others. Some policies offer more choice of physicians (i.e., cover the services of more physicians).

But the general conclusion is the same. Under adverse selection, some types of high-option coverage may become unavailable in the marketplace because of a process analogous to the health insurance example described above.

Insurer observes an \$80 difference in cost of issuing the two policies because *EL* for the higher-risk person is almost (less load) \$80 higher than for insuring the low-risk person. Thus, the insurer raises the difference in the premium for the two plans paid by the policyholder to \$80 per year.

Chooses *low* coverage

Θ_L

Chooses *low* coverage

Θ_{HL}

Chooses *high* coverage

Θ_{HH}

FIGURE 4.8
Adverse Selection: Individual Choices When the Premium Difference Is \$80
The insurer observes an \$80 difference in the cost of issuing the two policies because the expected loss, *EL*, for the higher-risk person is almost (less load) \$80 more than for insuring the low-risk person. Thus, the insurer raises the difference in the premium for the two plans paid by the policyholder to \$80 per year.

ADVERSE SELECTION AND UNRAVELING: THE CASE OF HARVARD UNIVERSITY

Cutler and Reber (1998) described how unraveling occurred in Harvard University's health insurance benefit offering. One case study alone does not establish that adverse selection and unraveling are empirically important phenomena in the United States and in other countries with private health insurance markets. But the Harvard experience serves to illustrate the concepts.

As background for this case study, we start with a brief description of the history of health insurance in the United States. Before the 1930s, there was essentially no private health insurance market. People paid for personal health care services out of pocket. During the depths of the Great Depression of the 1930s, there are stories of patients who were farmers paying for a doctor's visit with chickens in lieu of cash, which such patients often did not have.

Some of the insurance plans that evolved in the 1930s paid health care providers on the basis of the provider's accounting cost, with the patient paying next to nothing out of pocket. Other plans paid a fixed dollar payment per unit of service such as for a doctor's visit, with the patient generally paying out of pocket the difference between what the insurer paid and the physician's fee. Still other plans paid a percentage of the doctor's usual fee (often 80 percent) after a deductible was exceeded (say, $100).

During World War II, when employers faced a shortage of workers owing in part to the large number of men who enlisted in the armed forces and wage controls imposed by the government, employers increasingly began to offer health insurance coverage through the workplace as a way to attract employees. Further, as noted above, the US government did not tax employer-provided health insurance. Employer outlays for such insurance were considered a cost of the employer doing business; nor were such outlays subject to individual personal income taxation.

This generous tax policy undoubtedly contributed to the growth of employer-based group health insurance in the United States. For many employees, the tax benefit was worth more than the load included in health insurance premiums. Under such circumstances, employees would want as many goods and services covered by insurance as possible, including services that the individual was sure he or she would use in the forthcoming year.

Particularly given the generous tax policy, health insurance plans became ever more generous. In general, employers at first offered only one plan to all employees. US law required that the provision be the same for all employees, irrespective of their level of compensation. When employers started to offer more than one plan, employers tended to subsidize the more expensive plans more, with the result that high-option plans cost the employee about the same in terms of the amount deducted on a regular basis from the paycheck as did lower-option plans. There was a definite financial incentive for employees to select higher-option health insurance plans when they were given this choice.

Employer outlays for health insurance continued to increase in the US. Up to a point, both employers and employees were satisfied with this situation, even if a large part or all of the added outlays resulted in lower take-home pay for employees (Pauly 1997).

As employer outlays for employees' personal health care services continued to rise and reached a certain point, employers began to question the wisdom of their practices. Harvard University, a large employer in the Boston area, was no exception.

Harvard University experienced the same types of problems as did many employers in the United States. Harvard offered several health insurance plans and subsidized the more costly ones. Then in 1995, Harvard changed to making a fixed dollar contribution to each plan it offered, with the employees paying the difference if they selected a higher, more costly option plan.

The most generous plan was a preferred provider plan (PPO) offered by Massachusetts Blue Cross-Blue Shield. The PPO option offered coverage of care provided by "preferred providers," those providers with contracts with the plan, as well as "non-preferred providers," who did not have contracts with the plan. Patients paid more out of pocket if they obtained services from the latter type of provider.

The theory underlying the change to a fixed dollar subsidy made a lot of sense. Now, given employee free choice but being responsible dollar for dollar for the difference between the lowest-cost option and the one they chose, employees would become price-conscious shoppers. They would realize that high-option plans with associated high amounts of moral hazard (and welfare loss from moral hazard) might not be for them, and such persons would opt for plans with lower premiums.

However, the Achilles' heel of a program of this sort was adverse selection. Having free choice of provider is logically more attractive to persons with serious chronic illnesses. After all, if you knew you had cancer, you would be interested in being treated by the best among the cancer specialists, and such specialists may not be affiliated with a particular health plan. (Health maintenance organizations, or HMOs, generally only cover care provided by physicians in their provider networks. PPOs, by contrast, provide partial coverage for care provided outside their networks, but they provide more coverage if care is obtained from a member of the PPO's physician or hospital network. Chapter 11 provides further discussion of HMOs and managed care more generally.) For lesser conditions, obtaining care from the best physician may not make much difference to the outcome.

What happened after 1995 followed the pattern of the above health insurance example. Out-of-(employee)-pocket premiums for the Blue Cross-Blue Shield PPO plan kept rising and employee enrollment in the plan kept falling, to the point that Harvard stopped offering the plan to employees as an option.

Were employees made worse off as a result? The answer is probably "yes." Clearly, the sick employees who could no longer take advantage of Harvard's cross subsidy of the higher-cost health plans were made worse off, but others were made worse off as well. Among these were employees who lived in parts of the Boston area far from the locations in which providers with contracts with the plans that continued to be offered had their offices and clinics. Also, risk-averse persons who would be willing to pay for the type of insurance offered by the PPO if the premium reflected only their expect loss plus an efficient load were made worse off.

Cutler and Reber (1998) performed a welfare calculation of the net benefit of switching from a system in which a proportion of the cost of each plan was subsidized, with the result that higher-cost plans were subsidized more, to a fixed dollar contribution per health plan that required the Harvard employee to pay the difference if the employee selected a higher-cost plan. They estimated savings of 5–8 percent of baseline spending by Harvard University on the health benefits it offered employees.

These savings came at least in part from introducing a system in which employees had a greater incentive to be conscious about the costs of their health care. As a result, the Harvard health plans monitored provider behavior more carefully, installed new information systems, and denied payments for certain (presumably low-benefit) procedures. At the same time, there was a welfare loss from risk-averse employees not being able to enroll in the PPO, which amounted to 2–4 percent of baseline cost. Some risk-averse employees were no longer able to join the PPO, which they would have preferred.

Overall, the efficiency gains offset the welfare loss, implying that the switch to fixed dollar per employee contributions was worthwhile for Harvard University to undertake. Cutler and Reber estimated that the savings to Harvard (5–8 percent of baseline spending) were greater than the welfare loss from adverse selection (2–4 percent of baseline spending).

Cutler and Reber made another important but somewhat subtle point about their welfare analysis. As a result of increased competitive pressures—after the change in policy, employees had a financial incentive to select less expensive health plans—Harvard's health plans bargained more aggressively with health care providers in the Boston area and obtained contracts offering the providers lower pay. Unless the quantity and quality of services were adversely affected by these actions, the savings from obtaining lower pay from providers amounted to a transfer payment from hospitals and doctors to the plan, Harvard, and its employees, not an efficiency gain. Consumers gained and providers lost.

EMPIRICAL EVIDENCE ON ADVERSE SELECTION IN PRIVATE HEALTH INSURANCE MARKETS

Theory and one case study do not demonstrate that adverse selection in health insurance markets is generally an important phenomenon in the real world. To see whether or not adverse selection is important in the real world, it is necessary to turn to the empirical evidence. Cutler and Zeckhauser (2000, 617–621) provided a comprehensive table of studies offering empirical evidence on adverse selection in health insurance. With one exception, the vast majority of studies listed are based on data from the United States. Of the thirty-two studies listed in their review, only five did not find empirical evidence of adverse selection in plan choices. However, a quite rigorous, more recent study using data on single employed individuals who responded to the National Medical Expenditure Survey, a national survey of utilization of and expenditures on personal health services in the United States, by Cardon and Hendel (2001) did not find evidence of adverse selection.

The one non-US article reviewed by Cutler and Zeckhauser is a study by van de Ven and van Vliet (1995) from the Netherlands. That study used survey and claims data from the largest Dutch insurer, Zilveren Kreis. In the Netherlands since almost 1975, in an attempt to deal with adverse selection, there has been increasing differentiation of premiums for individual health insurance. Premiums differ by age, gender, family size, health status at time of enrollment, and health habits (smoking, drinking, exercise), and there is a bonus system reflecting the person's past claims. Persons with no claims experience a reduction in premiums (van de Ven, van Vliet, Schut, et al. 2000). Sophisticated methods have been developed for estimating premium subsidies so that persons in poor health can pay for risk-rated insurance policies (Stam, van Vliet, and van de Ven 2010). We discuss risk adjustment later in this chapter.

We review three additional studies of the experience outside the United States here, both of which find empirical evidence for adverse selection. Savage and Wright (2003) studied demand for private insurance for hospital care in Australia, a country with a public hospital system but with private hospitals that offer shorter queues—that is, a shorter time to admission to the hospital—as well as higher amenity care, such as nicer hospital rooms. Savage and Wright found some evidence that persons with adverse health conditions are more likely to demand private insurance for hospital care. However, since the study did not indicate the extent to which premiums for such coverage or the underwriting policies of insurers (i.e., willingness to insure particular types of persons) varied by health status, it is unclear whether adverse selection was truly present in this market.

Sapelli and Vial (2003) evaluated the extent of adverse selection in the Chilean health insurance market. As in Australia, there is a public as well as a private system. Sapelli and Vial concluded that the public system obtains patients who are less healthy on characteristics observable by the insurers (and researchers). By contrast, on nonobservable health variables, which can potentially lead to adverse selection, they found empirical support only for adverse selection for hospitalizations. The authors concluded that private insurers in Chile do not in general face adverse selection.

Wang, Zhang, Yip, et al. (2006) examined adverse selection in the context of a subsidized private insurance plan in a poor rural area of China. Although the subsidized plan achieved a 71 percent rate of enrollment, a substantial share of the population eligible for the plan, persons in worse health were more likely to enroll.

To combat adverse selection, the plan set the household as the enrollment unit. Presumably one member of the household would be in especially poor health, and the utilization experience of the entire household would be more nearly representative of utilization by families overall. However, nearly a third of households enrolled only some household members. Adverse selection was likely among these partially enrolled households.

These more recent studies and ones we do not describe here indicate that adverse selection *may* exist in any context in which health insurance is voluntarily purchased. Whether or not adverse selection exists in any particular situation is highly context-specific. One needs to analyze each case separately. Insurers can adopt subtle practices to protect themselves against adverse selection. We discuss these subtle practices further below.

Finally, two recent US studies did not find evidence of adverse selection in health insurance markets. One analyzed choices made in the Medigap health insurance market (box 4.2) and the other studied decisions about whether or not to obtain private insurance for long-term care services, nursing home, hospice, and care provided to disabled persons in the home (box 4.3).

Box 4.2

Advantageous Selection in Markets for Private Health Insurance: Evidence from the US Medigap Insurance Market

Conventional asymmetric information models, such as the one by Rothschild and Stiglitz (1976), assume one-dimensional private information and predict a positive correlation between insurance coverage and ex post realization of loss. In the Rothschild-Stiglitz framework, the private information is about the probability of experiencing a loss during the period covered by the insurance policy. But individuals may have private information about other motivations for purchasing insurance, and these motivations may lead to people one would not normally expect on the basis of probability of loss to purchase complete insurance coverage. In fact, private information about these other motivations may lead to advantageous as opposed to adverse selection.

Fang, Keane, and Silverman (2008) examined sources of advantageous selection in the US Medigap insurance market. Medigap is private health insurance that covers services not covered by Medicare, as well as cost-sharing obligations Medicare imposes on beneficiaries. The advantage of studying Medigap is that insurance policies are standardized by the US government, making features of individual Medigap policies easy to compare.

The authors regressed total medical expenditure in a year on a binary variable (have Medigap = 1, do not have Medigap = 0) and other explanatory variables. They found that when not controlling for the individual beneficiary's health status, those

Box 4.2
(continued)

with Medigap incurred annual expenditures on personal health care services that were about $4,000 lower than did those without Medigap. However, controlling for health status, beneficiaries with Medigap incurred annual expenditures $1,900 higher than those who did not have Medigap coverage. This latter result implies advantageous, not adverse, selection. The authors investigated sources of advantageous selection. One key hypothesis was that persons who purchase Medigap insurance are more risk averse than others. This would make sense, given the analysis of risk aversion presented in the text of this chapter. However, the higher expenditures associated with having a Medigap policy were only slightly changed once the authors included an explanatory variable for the individual's risk preferences.

Another possibility the authors investigated was whether Medigap policyholders differed in cognitive ability. Cognitive ability may act as a source of advantageous selection via its effect on individuals' information about health risks. Cognitively able individuals may be more knowledgeable about potential health risks, and therefore may be more likely to purchase Medigap. The authors found that among the factors explaining why Medicare beneficiaries purchase Medigap policy, cognitive ability is particularly important.

Clearly, the existence of adverse selection in insurance markets is not a foregone conclusion. There may be differences in the extent of adverse versus advantageous selection even among various health insurance markets.

Box 4.3
Selection in the Market for Private Long-Term Care Insurance in the United States

Finkelstein and McGarry (2006), studying the private long-term care insurance market in the United States, documented the importance of multidimensional heterogeneity among potential purchasers of insurance, which was also described in box 4.1. Using longitudinal data on individuals who were age 70 and older at baseline, the authors found a statistically insignificant correlation between long-term care coverage in 1995 and the use of nursing home care during 1995–2000, even after controlling for insurers' assessments of a person's risk type. The evidence could be consistent with "no asymmetric information" or "multidimensional information."

The survey they used asked in 1995, "What do you think are the chances that you will move to a nursing home in the next 5 years?" Persons giving a higher probability in response to this question were more likely to have been in a nursing home after the survey through 2000, but they were also more likely to have purchased long-term care coverage. Although health can to some extent be observed by the insurer, the response to a question about the person's beliefs about entering a nursing home in the foreseeable future can only be known to the person. The person in applying for an insurance policy will have to answer questions about his or her health truthfully

Box 4.3
(continued)

and completely, but as a practical matter, it is difficult for an insurer to obtain information about an individual's aversion to being in a nursing home or lack thereof. After controlling for objective measures of the person's health, what is left in the question about the probability of entering a nursing home in the next five years is information about individual preferences, which is private. Further, they found that while risk-averse persons were more likely to have private long-term care insurance, they were actually less likely to enter a nursing home during 1995–2000.

The bottom line is that observing health characteristics is not enough to know whether or not a person will be a high utilizer in the future. In this application, risk aversion affects demand for insurance, as the theory would lead us to have expected, but this does not translate into high rates of utilization of long-term care.

This important study provides even more evidence that the presence or absence of adverse selection must be examined on a case-by-case basis. Generalization to all private insurance markets is itself a risky proposition.

4.9 "Risk Adjustment" and Adverse and Preferred Risk Selection

In a country with a single-payer system that offers no choice of health plan and applies to everyone, adverse selection is not an issue (see chapter 12). However, in countries in which choice of health plan is a matter of individual choice, adverse selection may exist even if having health insurance coverage is mandatory and health insurance premiums are subsidized. For example, in Germany, persons with earnings below a certain threshold must be covered by a statutory health insurance plan (sickness fund). However, they are free to choose among plans, and different plans charge different contribution percentages, or shares of employee compensation that the employer and employee must pay in equal amounts to the health plan.

In the United States, under Medicare, beneficiaries can select standard fee-for-service Medicare, the beneficiary's default choice, or they can enroll in a Medicare HMO if an HMO plan is offered in the beneficiary's geographic area. Medicare provides a per enrollee subsidy if the beneficiary enrolls in a Medicare-qualified HMO. This subsidy is based on beneficiary demographic characteristics and location, but it is not based on beneficiary health status.

Not surprisingly, given the heterogeneity in health among persons with the same broadly defined demographic characteristics, HMOs that enroll US Medicare beneficiaries are eager to attract individuals who are relatively healthy. Here the health plans rather than the beneficiaries are the main actors, and the phenomenon is *preferred risk selection* (also called advantageous risk selection). With preferred risk selection, insurers employ subtle techniques to attract persons who are likely to be less costly to insure. Insurers can influence who wants to join their plans by locating their facilities in geographic areas where beneficiaries are likely to be healthier, not retaining the best physicians in fields in which treatment is costly, not affiliating with major university hospitals that offer highly specialized care, and other approaches to "cream skimming."

To counter the incentives HMOs have to "cream skim," that is, to market themselves to and enroll the lowest utilizers of personal health care services, a public health insurance program might do well to risk adjust its per enrollee subsidy so that the subsidy reflects health status as well as demographic characteristics and beneficiary place of residence.

Glazer and McGuire (2000) described how US Medicare and other governments that subsidize health insurance plans can do a better job based on health data on individuals that are available to health plans. Various approaches for risk classification have been developed that can also be of use, but no single method is foolproof (Frank, Glazer, and McGuire 2000; Robinson 2008).

Ideally, it would be possible for a government agency to require that persons eligible for its program stick a finger in a meter that would accurately record all aspects of the person's health. However, no such meter has been developed, and it is therefore necessary to deal with imperfect substitutes, such as claims data submitted by health care providers to insurers, which contain information on the insured person's diagnoses and services rendered during the patient encounter. No single method of risk adjustment is foolproof (Iezonni 1997).

4.10 Summary and Conclusions

In the end, how one views the adverse selection problem depends on how one views the appropriate structure of health care financing and delivery more generally. In contexts in which people are not given a choice of health plans, such as in single-payer systems, adverse selection is not an issue. On the other hand, if one views the role of government in a quite limited way, such as mainly providing a safety net for the poor, with others being asked to fend for themselves in the private, adverse selection is not much of an issue either.

In the long run, absent government intervention to preclude it, insurers can develop effective methods to combat adverse selection. For one, they can refuse to renew insured individuals who prove to be costly in any policy year. Insurers can ask for medical records prior to enrolling an individual. An issue for societies to decide, however, is whether or not active attempts by private insurers to skim the market conforms to the society's social norms. A middle course is to improve risk adjustment from time to time and "grin and bear" adverse selection in the interim.

To the extent that it exists in health insurance markets, the adverse selection issue is not unique to such markets. For example, why do almost new cars sell for much less than brand-new cars? George Akerlof (1970) reasoned that new cars are of two types, good cars and "lemons." While the two types look alike, the owner knows from experience that his or her car is repair-prone. Hence, those "pre-owned" cars that are put up for sale are disproportionately lemons. Although prospective buyers may not be able to detect a lemon by inspecting it, they are only willing to purchase such cars if they are able to do so at a discounted price.

When it exists, insurers can combat adverse selection in various ways, including refusing to renew the health insurance policies of persons who used substantial amounts of personal health services during a year, refusing to cover preexisting conditions, and applying blanket refusals to accept persons with certain health characteristics or other characteristics judged by insurers to be positively correlated with adverse selection. However, these practices may be viewed by society as inherently unfair. Statutes outlawing such practices have often been enacted for this reason. However, when the law is too strict, insurers may not be willing to supply health insurance.

Another option when adverse selection is perceived to be quantitatively important is to eliminate insurance choices by statute. But this approach has disadvantages as well, in particular not recognizing diversity of preferences among individuals. Moreover, a dose of choice and competition in insurance markets may be a good thing. Competition ferrets out those sellers who do not provide a product that buyers want or who are inefficient suppliers.

Group health insurance provided through employment is still another option. Since people select employers for several reasons, health insurance being only one, employer provision of health insurance is a potential solution to adverse selection. But over time, again to satisfy diverse preferences among employees, employers have offered several plan options. This opens the door to adverse selection, especially when coupled with a policy of fixed dollar contributions, as Harvard University decided to do.

In the end, there is no simple answer. Economists can only offer options with trade-offs.

Key Concepts

- risk averse
- risk neutral
- risk lover
- risk protection
- demand for health insurance
- first-party insurance

- third-party insurance
- nonpecuniary loss
- expected utility
- marginal utility of wealth
- adverse selection
- risk selection
- pecuniary loss
- uncertainty
- expected loss
- asymmetric information
- risk adjustment

REVIEW AND DISCUSSION QUESTIONS

4.1 How can a person benefit from having health insurance coverage if the premiums paid exceed the cost of the medical care received? How can an insurance company benefit if the medical care it provides costs more than the premiums paid in?

4.2 Explain the terms "welfare gain of health insurance" and "welfare loss of health insurance" in your own words. What is meant by the statement that people are overinsured?

4.3 What is the "price" of health insurance?

4.4 Explain why diminishing marginal utility of wealth is a prerequisite for the existence of a health insurance market.

4.5 Explain the term "adverse selection" in your own words. Adverse selection does not only pertain to health insurance. Explain how adverse selection may operate in markets for homeowners' insurance and in automobile liability insurance. Explain how adverse selection might work in the market for used cars.

4.6 What is meant by the statement that "income elasticity of demand for private health insurance is positive"? List at least three potential channels underlying the observation that personal income is positively associated with the probability that an individual has health insurance coverage. What do you expect would occur if the US government were to completely remove the tax subsidy on health insurance? Explain your answer.

EXERCISES

4.1 Suppose a person is diagnosed with lung cancer. Describe four types of pecuniary losses and two types of nonpecuniary losses that are likely to arise.

4.2 The following table displays uncertainties in John's monthly income:

State	Probability (Θ)	Income (Y)	Utility (U)
Sick	0.4	2,500	U(2,500)
Healthy	0.6	4,900	U(4,900)

a. What is John's expected income (expected value of income)?

b. Let John's utility function be $U = Y^{0.5}$, where Y is John's monthly income. Calculate John's expected utility of income (expected value of utility of income).

c. Compare the utility of John's expected income and the expected utility of his income. Is John risk averse or not (refer to John's utility function given above)? Explain your answer by a graph, with income on the horizontal axis and utility on the vertical axis.

d. Calculate the maximum amount that John is willing to pay to avoid the risk of income loss resulting from becoming sick.

4.3 Based on the same information reported in the above table, calculate the maximum amount that John is willing to pay to avoid the risk of income loss resulting from becoming sick if the probability of becoming sick increases from 0.4 to 0.5. Is John more likely to buy health insurance than he would under conditions specified in exercise 2? Justify your answer by comparing your results for this question with what you obtained in exercise 2.

4.4 Similarly, based on the same information supplied in the above table, calculate the maximum amount that John is willing to pay to avoid the risk of income loss resulting from becoming sick if the amount of income loss increases from 2,400 to 4,000, that is, John receives only 900 when sick. Is John more likely to buy health insurance than under conditions of exercise 2? Why is this so?

4.5 Assume that the individual is a risk lover. The individual can purchase a gamble with a 0.01 probability of winning $10,000. Assume the person has an annual income of $10,000. What is the actuarial value of the gamble? Show graphically why the person would rather gamble than not, and explain your answer.

4.6 In each of the following pairs, which situation would pose a potentially larger adverse selection problem? Explain your answers.

a. A policy covering accidents for all children attending summer camps or a policy covering accidents for college students traveling abroad.

b. Inclusion of HIV/AIDS treatment in a standard benefit package offered to teachers or an optional rider providing HIV/AIDS coverage for an additional premium.

c. Basic medical services insurance package offered to students entering college or basic medical services package offered to professors seeking early retirement.

d. Optional mental health coverage offered to employees of ABC Inc. or optional mental health coverage offered to children of ABC Inc. employees.

4.7 Considering each of the following pairs, in which of the two is purchase of health insurance more likely. Explain your answers.

a. the rich versus the poor;

b. hospital care versus a physician office visit;

c. a probability of getting sick of 0.95 versus a 0.5 probability of getting sick;

d. a tax subsidy (the premium of health insurance is not subject to any form of taxation) versus a tax credit.

Online Supplemental Material

Economic Research Initiative on the Uninsured (ERIU)

http://www.rwjf-eriu.org/index.html

Supplemental Readings

Fang, H., M. Keane, and D. Silverman. 2008. Sources of Advantageous Selection: Evidence from the Medigap Insurance Market. *Journal of Political Economy* 116 (2): 303–350.

Finkelstein, A., and K. McGarry. 2006. Multiple Dimensions of Private Information: Evidence from the Long-Term Care Insurance Market. *American Economic Review* 96 (4): 938–958.

Pauly, M. V. 2008. Adverse Selection and Moral Hazard: Implications for Health Insurance Markets. In *Incentives and Choice in Health Care*, ed. F. Sloan and H. Kasper, 103–130. Cambridge, MA: MIT Press.

References

Akerlof, G. 1970. The Market for Lemons: Qualitative Uncertainty and the Market Mechanism. *Quarterly Journal of Economics* 84 (3): 488–500.

Arrow, K. J. 1963. Uncertainty and the Welfare Economics of Medical Care. *American Economic Review* 53 (5): 941–973.

Barsky, R. B., F. T. Juster, M. S. Kimball, et al. 1997. Preference Parameters and Behavioral Heterogeneity: An Experimental Approach in the Health and Retirement Study. *Quarterly Journal of Economics* 112 (2): 537–579.

Blau, D. M., and D. B. Gilleskie. 2008. The Role of Retiree Health Insurance in the Employment Behavior of Older Men. *International Economic Review* 49 (2): 475–514.

Cardon, J. H., and I. Hendel. 2001. Asymmetric Information in Health Insurance: Evidence from the National Medical Expenditure Survey. *RAND Journal of Economics* 32 (3): 408–427.

Cutler, D. M., and S. J. Reber. 1998. Paying for Health Insurance: The Trade-off between Competition and Adverse Selection. *Quarterly Journal of Economics* 113 (2): 433–466.

Cutler, D. M., and R. J. Zeckhauser. 2000. The Anatomy of Health Insurance. In *Handbook of Health Economics*, ed. A. J. Culyer and J. P. Newhouse, 1A:617–621. Amsterdam: Elsevier Science.

Fang, H., M. Keane, and D. Silverman. 2008. Sources of Advantageous Selection: Evidence from the Medigap Insurance Market. *Journal of Political Economy* 116 (2): 303–350.

Feldstein, M. S. 1973. The Welfare Loss of Excess Health Insurance. *Journal of Political Economy* 81 (2): 251–280.

Finkelstein, A., and K. McGarry. 2006. Multiple Dimensions of Private Information: Evidence from the Long-Term Care Insurance Market. *American Economic Review* 96 (4): 938–958.

Frank, R. G., J. Glazer, and T. G. McGuire. 2000. Measuring Adverse Selection in Managed Health Care. *Journal of Health Economics* 19 (6): 829–854.

Friedman, M., and L. J. Savage. 1948. The Utility Analysis of Choices Involving Risk. *Journal of Political Economy* 56 (4): 279–304.

Glazer, J., and T. G. McGuire. 2000. Optimal Risk Adjustment in Markets with Adverse Selection: An Application to Managed Care. *American Economic Review* 90 (4): 1055–1071.

Goldstein, G. S., and M. V. Pauly. 1976. Group Health Insurance as a Local Public Good. In *The Role of Health Insurance in the Health Services Sector*, ed. R. N. Rosett, 73–114. Sagamore Beach, MA: Watson Publishing International.

Gruber, J., and M. Lettau. 2004. How Elastic Is the Firm's Demand for Health Insurance? *Journal of Public Economics* 88 (7–8): 1273–1293.

Iezonni, L. I. 1997. The Risks of Risk Adjustment. *Journal of the American Medical Association* 278 (19): 1600–1607.

Leonard, K. L. 2003. African Traditional Healers and Outcome-Contingent Contracts in Health Care. *Journal of Development Economics* 71 (1): 1–22.

Manning, W. G., J. P. Newhouse, N. Duan, et al. 1987. Health Insurance and the Demand for Medical Care: Evidence from a Randomized Experiment. *American Economic Review* 77 (3): 251–277.

Marquis, M. S., M. B. Buntin, J. J. Escarce, et al. 2004. Subsidies and the Demand for Individual Health Insurance in California. *Health Services Research* 39 (5): 1547–1570.

Pauly, M. V. 1986. Taxation, Health-Insurance, and Market Failure in the Medical Economy. *Journal of Economic Literature* 24 (2): 629–675.

Pauly, M. V. 1997. *Health Benefits at Work: An Economic and Political Analysis of Employment-Based Health Insurance.* Ann Arbor: University of Michigan Press.

Pauly, M. V. 2008. Adverse Selection and Moral Hazard Implications for Health Insurance Markets. In *Incentives and Choice in Health Care*, ed. F. Sloan and H. Kasper, 103–130. Cambridge, MA: MIT Press.

Robinson, J. W. 2008. Regression Tree Boosting to Adjust Health Care Cost Predictions for Diagnostic Mix. *Health Services Research* 43 (2): 755–772.

Rothschild, M., and J. Stiglitz. 1976. Equilibrium in Competitive Insurance Markets: An Essay on the Economics of Imperfect Information. *Quarterly Journal of Economics* 90 (4): 629–649.

Sapelli, C., and B. Vial. 2003. Self-Selection and Moral Hazard in Chilean Health Insurance. *Journal of Health Economics* 22 (3): 459–476.

Savage, E., and D. J. Wright. 2003. Moral Hazard and Adverse Selection in Australian Private Hospitals: 1989–1990. *Journal of Health Economics* 22 (3): 331–359.

Sloan, F. A., and K. W. Adamache. 1986. Taxation and the Growth of Nonwage Compensation. *Public Finance Quarterly* 14 (2): 115–137.

Stam, P. J. A., R. C. J. A. van Vliet, and W. P. M. M. van de Ven. 2010. A Limited-Sample Benchmark Approach to Assess and Improve the Performance of Risk Equalization Models. *Journal of Health Economics* 29 (3): 426–437.

Van de Ven, W. P. M. M., R. C. J. A. van Vliet, F. T. Schut, et al. 2000. Access to Coverage for High-Risks in a Competitive Individual Health Insurance Market: Via Premium Rate Restrictions or Risk-Adjusted Premium Subsidies? *Journal of Health Economics* 19 (3): 311–339.

Van de Ven, W. P. M. M., and R. J. A. van Vliet. 1995. Consumer Information Surplus and Adverse Selection in Competitive Health Insurance Markets: An Empirical Study. *Journal of Health Economics* 14 (2): 149–169.

von Neumann, J., and O. Morgenstern. 1944. *Theory of Games and Economic Behavior.* Princeton, NJ: Princeton University Press.

Wang, H., L. Zhang, W. Yip, et al. 2006. Adverse Selection in a Voluntary Rural Mutual Health Care Health Insurance Scheme in China. *Social Science & Medicine* 63 (5): 1236–1245.

PART II

Supply of Health Care Services and Insurance

CHAPTER 5

THE MARKET FOR PHYSICIANS' SERVICES

Physicians are the captains of the health care team. Physicians provide three distinct types of services. First, they provide advice to their patients about disease prevention, diagnosis, and treatment, including referrals to other sources of personal health care services and prescriptions for drugs that could not be purchased by the patient without a physician's recommendation. Second, physicians themselves perform preventive, diagnostic, and therapeutic services. Third, physicians certify the presence of illness and disability to other parties. Certification of a disability is typically required before a person can receive compensation for a disability or coverage for particular services under a health insurance policy. Although there are partial substitutes for physicians, for some tasks, the only substitutes are other physicians.

Economists often make a conceptual distinction between the "long run" and the "short run." In the short run, at least one factor of production is fixed. In a model in which capital and labor are the two factors of production, in the short run, capital is assumed to be fixed but labor varies. In the long run, both capital and labor vary. In the context of physician supply, short-run decisions relate to physician decisions about pricing, hours of work, and the number of patients seen per unit of time, as well as the mix of patients seen, where the term "mix" reflects the composition of patients according to insurer type in countries with multipayer systems, as well as composition with respect to types of medical problems for which patients are seen.

Long-run decisions include decisions about entry and exit from practices of various types. These decisions involve choices about medical school capacities, the career decisions of students—the decision to become a physician, specialty choice, and practice location, including choice of country of practice and choice of geographic location within a country—and the choice of practice type, such as whether to work for the government or to be in private practice, and if so, whether to practice alone or in a group. All of these can be seen as long-run decisions. The choice of practice type and location are somewhat shorter-run "long-run" decisions than are occupational choices and choice of specialty.

In economic models, an assumption is typically made that economic agents are forward-looking. Thus, for example, in much the same way that expectations about the future influence health behaviors (see chapter 2), knowledge that physicians' fees will be fixed at a low level by price controls is expected to influence students' career decisions. Forecasts of growth in demand for care are likely to influence decisions medical schools make about the number of students they admit. Thus, the short and long run are inextricably linked. However, the vast majority of medical schools are run by governments or private nonprofit organizations. Casual empiricism suggests that medical school capacity often responds to anticipated demand, but there are no formal economic models of medical school decision making. There are models that forecast future demand for physicians. The remainder of this chapter is organized around long- and short-run decisions in the market for physicians' services.

5.1 MEDICAL SCHOOL CAPACITY AND CONCEPTS OF PHYSICIAN SHORTAGE AND SURPLUS

Policy discussions of impending shortages and surpluses of physicians are closely linked to decisions about medical school capacity. Starting a new medical school typically involves years of planning. Given the length of the medical education process, it takes years after a student is first admitted to medical school until the supply of practicing physicians is affected. Because the lag between decisions about capacity and the effect on supply is so long, medical school planners need to be forward-looking and face many uncertainties in their planning activities.

Outside economics, surplus and shortage are typically measured relative to a measure of "need" (see chapter 8 for a discussion of these concepts in the context of professional nurses). To an economist, "need" is not a useful concept. We know, for example, that two people who are identical in terms of their health are likely to use health care services at highly different rates for various reasons, including personal preferences and wealth.

In the framework used by economists, prices adjust until markets clear, that is, until market forces lead to a price at which the quantity demanded is equal to the quantity supplied. If the price is below the market-clearing price, there is excess

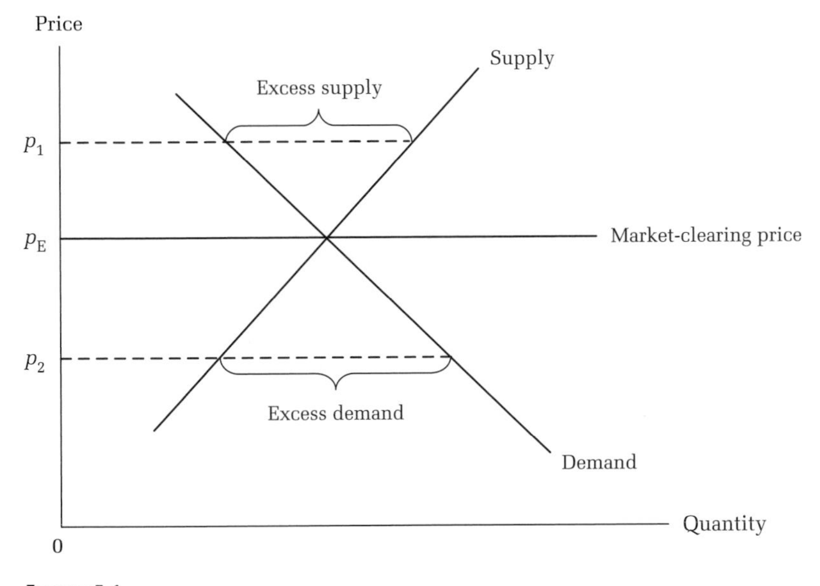

FIGURE 5.1
The Economic Concept of Shortage (Excess Demand) and Surplus (Excess Supply)

demand or a "shortage," and if price is above the market-clearing price, there is excess supply or a "surplus" (fig. 5.1).

Before dismissing the noneconomic concept of shortage and surplus entirely, let us consider the rationale for this concept. First, medical education is expensive, and the expense is borne to a considerable extent by the public at large. If physician fees dropped to a certain level, some physicians might decide to become taxi drivers. This might be acceptable if the cost of medical education were fully borne by the medical student, but it is much less so when public subsidies finance medical education, the much more usual case. Second, in a perfectly competitive market, consumers are fully knowledgeable about the products they consume.

But in this context, there is the issue of asymmetric information we have already described—physicians knowing more about medical technology than their patients do. There is a widespread concern, particularly among noneconomists, that when facing a surplus, physicians may *induce demand* for their services. For example, when one revisit may be appropriate, a physician who is paid on a fee-for-service basis might recommend more than one revisit because it is in the physician's financial interest to do this. And the unknowing patient would conform to this recommendation by keeping the appointment.

Even if physicians do not generate extra demand, more physicians are likely to make medical care more accessible. With more physicians, patient travel time is likely to decrease as physicians locate in more remote areas, waiting time to an appointment may fall, and physicians may spend more time with each patient. Lower travel time reduces the full price of care (see chapter 3) and hence increases the quantity of physicians' services demanded. Higher quality, perhaps in the form of longer visits, may be expected to increase demand and spending on physicians' services as well. Of course, whether the higher expenditures result from physicians providing more highly beneficial care to patients or reflect higher utilization rates with low marginal benefit to patients makes a big difference.

Partly because of reservations about the applicability of the conventional supply-demand model to medicine, various commissions charged with making recommendations about the future need for physicians forecast need based on projections of future population and its demographic composition. More sophisticated analyses project frequencies of various types of diseases the future population is likely to have. Forecasted need is then compared to forecasted supply, which reflects the number of medical school graduates, net inflows into or outflows of graduates from the country, and projected rates of retirement from practice, as well as losses to activities other than the practice of medicine (e.g., research, teaching, administration, careers outside medicine).

The predictions from these projection models have often proved to be quite inaccurate. In the United States, in the 1980s, a high-level commission predicted there would be a surplus of physicians in that country by the year 2000. By any measure, this surplus never materialized, and more recent predictions are for an emerging physician shortage in the United States (Cooper 2004).

Whatever number of students medical schools accept, the number of applicants tends to be far greater than the number of acceptances. Particularly in view of the public expense, medical schools desire the admission process to be selective. As explained by Friedman and Kuznets (1945), the motive for limiting medical school capacity may be to boost physician incomes. They attributed high physician incomes to such entry barriers. This view seems to fit the United States better during years in which medical school capacity was very limited—after about 1910 following the Flexner Report, which led to the closing of many US medical schools, to about 1970 than in more recent years.

5.2 PHYSICIAN SUPPLY IN THE LONG RUN

CHOICE OF MEDICINE AS A CAREER

Without denying the importance of nonmonetary incentives, economists have tended to focus on responses to monetary incentives as motivators of occupational choice. But economists recognize that nonmonetary factors are important as well. For example, in the context of career choice, economics is clear that if aspects of a job are undesirable, pay must be increased to compensate the employee for the undesirable factor. These are "compensating wage differentials."[1]

Before presenting the empirical evidence, it is useful to think about career choices in conceptual terms. We start with the notion that for each individual i and each career alternative j, there is a stream of anticipated future earnings (Y_{ij}) and nonmonetary attributes of the occupation (A_j). Among the nonmonetary attributes are the occupation's prestige, its intellectual content, the types of people one interacts with, the flexibility of the work schedule, the risk of injury, and job-related stress.

Values of Y_{ij} vary not only by j but also by i because people have different earnings potential in different types of work. There are innate differences among people in physical and mental abilities and in their personalities. Further, individuals differ in the utility that they attach to earnings and the nonmonetary attributes of the job.

Let $U_i = U_i(Y_{ij}, A_j)$. (5.1)

People derive utility from consumer goods and services that they can purchase from their earnings and from the nonmonetary attributes of each occupation.

Y_{ij} and A_j are substitutes. A higher level of anticipated earnings can compensate an individual for accepting work in an occupation with a lower A_j. Since the value of adding an additional unit of A_j (the marginal utility of a unit of A_j) differs among individuals, people will require different compensating earnings differentials to make them equally well off if they select an occupation with a lower A. Suppose, for example, that some people place a high value on having a flexible work schedule, and work flexibility can be thought of as an index varying from "very inflexible" to "very flexible," while others attach little importance to such flexibility. If the career generally demands an inflexible work schedule, holding other factors constant, the person who values a flexible schedule will require a higher earnings differential to offset the utility loss from having to work irregular hours or hours during which the person faces other demands on the person's time, such as for child care. As another example, some people may be attracted to a career in which there is a lot of interaction with other people. Others might want to work alone. For the latter type, a substantial amount of interpersonal interaction with patients is a "bad." For sociable persons, such interpersonal contact is a "good." Bads are offset by higher earnings, and conversely for goods.

Now suppose that the career options are medicine or becoming a college professor. College professors have flexible work hours while physicians often do not. Then for the individual who values flexible hours, anticipated earnings will need to be higher in medicine than in college teaching for the person to be attracted to a medical career. Depending on the nonmonetary attribute and the individual's

1. See, for example, Nicholson (2008) for a discussion of compensating wage differentials in the context of medicine.

utility function, that is, how much the individual values (or dislikes) a unit increase in the attribute, the compensating earnings differential could be positive or negative.

Following this reasoning, one can imagine that some persons are attracted to medicine at a very low level of anticipated earnings, which may be far below the level of earnings in the other occupations the person is considering. These are individuals who place a very high value on the nonmonetary attributes of being a physician—possibly the prestige or the satisfaction gained from helping patients. Other individuals are less strongly motivated by the nonmonetary attributes and are more motivated by money, which can be used to purchase goods and services. For these persons, to be attracted to a medical career, anticipated physician earnings can be lower for those who attach greater value to such nonmonetary attributes of a medical career.

This heterogeneity in preferences explains why the supply curve for a given occupation is likely to be positively sloped. When the pay level is relatively low, people who place a high value on such nonmonetary attributes of the work are attracted to the occupation. But to attract others, pay must rise (fig. 5.2).

Earnings in an occupation are determined by both the demand for and the supply of persons to the occupation. The demand curve for any input, including an hour of a person's time devoted to work in an occupation, reflects both (1) the contribution of a unit of the input to additional output—the input's marginal product (MP)—and (2) the contribution of additional output to additional revenue or marginal revenue (MR). Thus, the employer's maximum willingness to pay for a given quantity of the input is the product of MP and MR, or the marginal revenue product (MRP). An increase in MP, for example from a technological change that makes physicians more productive (e.g., a medical information system), shifts the demand curve for physicians outward. Equilibrium earnings are determined at the intersection of the supply and demand curves. As shown in figure 5.2, for equilibrium earnings E^*, the corresponding employment is L^*.

The equalizing earnings differential between the two occupations depends on where the MRP (or value of the marginal product, which is the product of MP and the product price if the product market is competitive) crosses the supply curve for each occupation. Characteristics of jobs that are unattractive to potential entrants shift the supply curve to the left, and good ones shift it to the right. Of course, there is heterogeneity among individuals in valuations attached to specific characteristics associated with occupation. One may think of the supply curve as the amount needed to bribe person to enter the occupation—the more that is considered "bad" about the occupation, the higher the bribe must be (fig. 5.3).

The theory of equalizing earnings differentials, or equalizing after accounting for nonmonetary characteristics of jobs, assumes free entry into occupations. In fact, of course, entry into medical school is not free. In the United States in recent decades, there have been two to four times more applicants than are accepted by medical schools.

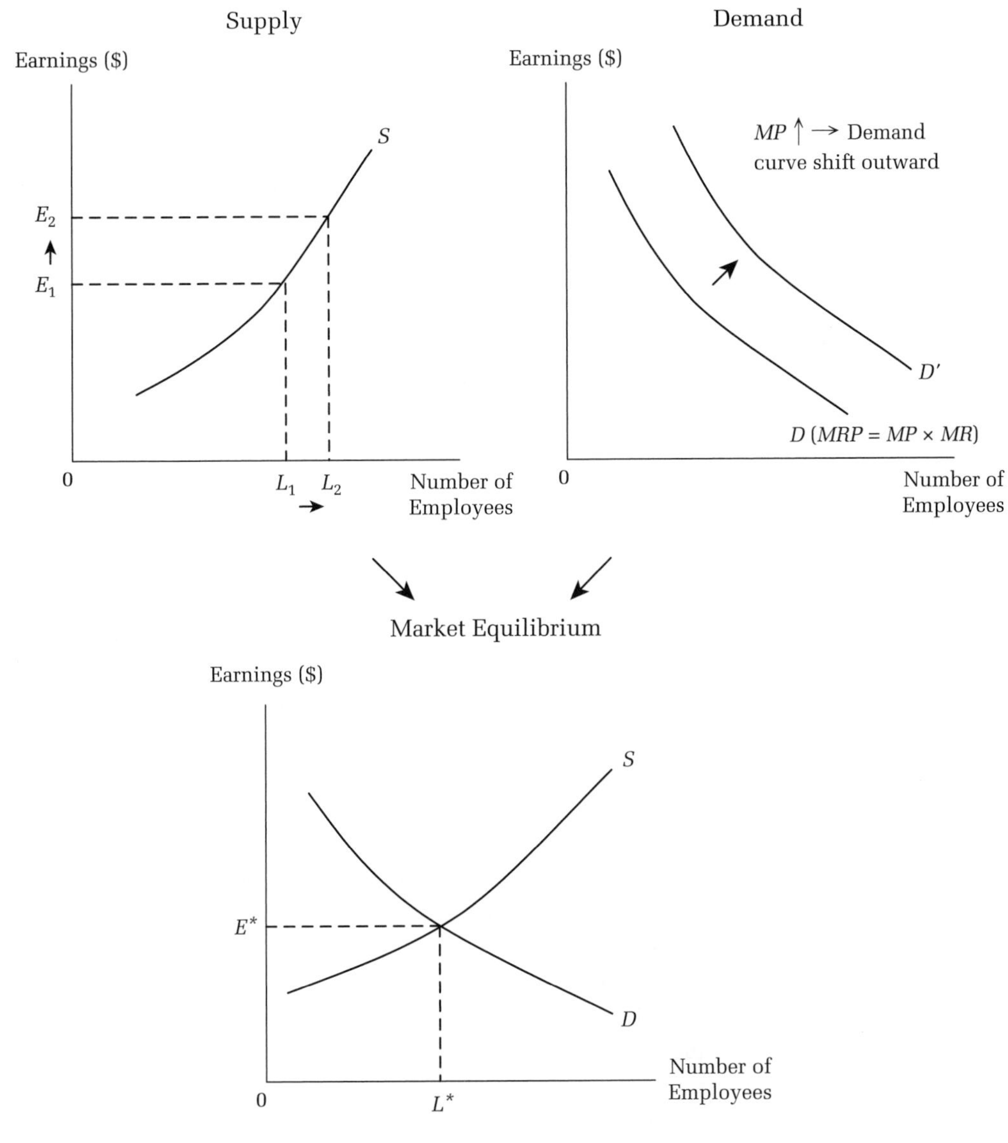

FIGURE 5.2
The Determinant of Equilibrium Earnings in an Occupation

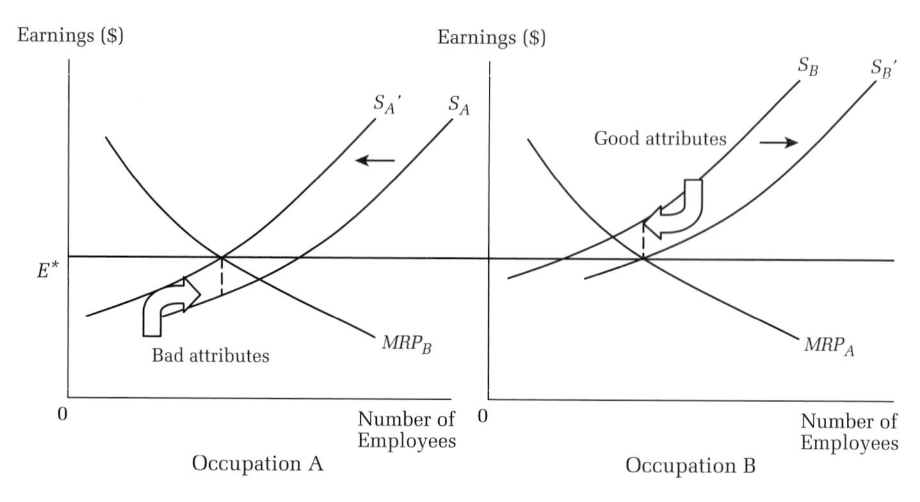

FIGURE 5.3
The Equalizing Earnings Differential between the Two Occupations

In a study using US time series data for the years 1934–1966, Sloan (1971) found that the number of applicants to medical school in the United States was positively related to physician earnings but negatively related to medical school tuition—tuition being the price of medical education. In every year, the number of applicants far exceeded the number of places in first-year classes of medical schools;[2] the number of applicants increased in years in which the probability of acceptance increased. He also reported that students with A averages in colleges were less responsive to monetary incentives than were those with B averages, perhaps because a greater proportion of the A students selected medicine to pursue an academic career rather than to enter private medical practice. To our knowledge, there are no more recent studies of this issue.

Physicians make several important decisions about their careers: (1) whether or not to become a physician, (2) choice of specialty, (3) geographic location, and (4) type of practice (e.g., independent solo, group, or salaried practice). Several pertinent questions are the following: (1) How important are financial incentives in the choice of medicine as a career, choice specialty, and practice location? (2) How do physicians select practice types, and in turn, how do the incentives associated with each affect physician incentives? These questions are important in every country.

2. See Nicholson (2008, 215) for data on the numbers of applicants to US medical schools and the size of first-year classes from 1960 to 2005.

PHYSICIAN CHOICE OF SPECIALTY

In contrast to the choice of medicine as a career, there are numerous studies of choice of physician specialty by medical students. Many studies focus on the role of changes in the internal rate of return or present value of earnings streams in various specialties on specialty choice. For this reason, we begin with a description of these concepts.

CONCEPT OF PRESENT VALUE

Let PV_j be the present value of returns net of the cost of an investment in training in occupation j and i be the market rate of interest, R_{jt} be earnings in year t, C_{jt} be the cost associated with the investment in training for occupation j in year t, n be the number of periods (years) in which the person expects to be active in the occupation j, and S_{jn} the value of the sale of the asset at year n, for example, the sale of a physician practice, a subsidy provided to the person at retirement.[3] Then

$$PV_j = (R_{j1} - C_{j1})/(1 + i) + (R_{j2} - C_{j2})/(1 + i)^2 + (R_{j3} - C_{j3})/(1 + i)^3 \ldots + (R_{jn} - C_{jn})/(1 + i)^n + S_{jn}/(1+i)^n \quad (5.2)$$

The investor undertakes the project if PV_j is positive or zero. If PV_j is negative, the project is not undertaken. If the investment is a building or research on a new drug (see chapter 9), there is conceptually no limit to the number of investment projects that can be undertaken. However, for investments in human capital, the investor can generally select only one investment. For example, the person chooses to become either an engineer, or a lawyer, or a physician. Thus, the decision maker takes the PV_j of each alternative occupation into consideration in making the choice.

In a competitive capital market and one in which the risk of default on the loan does not differ among individuals, the value of i is fixed at some constant value. Holding other factors constant, if the interest rate rises, PV_j falls, and conversely for a decrease in the interest rate.

In markets for human capital, the assumption of competitive capital markets and uniform default risk is unlikely to hold, for several reasons. Most important, a substantial amount of investment in human capital comes from family savings and the earnings of family members. There is likely to be substantial heterogeneity in the value households attach to a dollar of funds allocated to educational investments. In particular, for capital-starved households, the value attached to such funds may be substantial and is likely to increase with the amount invested. In economic terminology, the marginal cost of funds is the cost of raising a dollar of funds as a function of the amount of funds raised. For example, if the person raises $\$x$ for a investment, the cost of raising the last dollar may be C. The cost of raising $\$x + 1$ may be C', where $C' > C$ (fig. 5.4). Scholarships and grants for education lower the cost of capital for education, shifting a positively sloped marginal cost of funds to the right.

3. This framework is described in detail in Becker (1964).

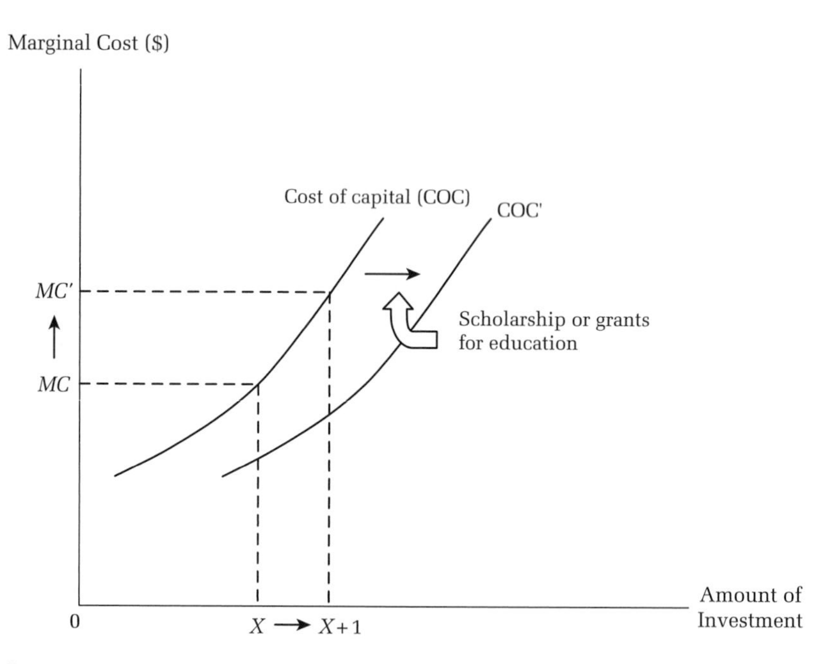

FIGURE 5.4
The Relationship between the Marginal Costs of Funds and the Amount of Investment

CONCEPT OF INTERNAL RATE OF RETURN

The internal rate of return on an investment is the internal rate r, which makes the present value of the right-hand side of equation 5.2 zero.

$$0 = (R_{j1} - C_{j1})/(1 + i) + (R_{j2} - C_{j2})/(1 + i)^2 + (R_{j3} - C_{j3})/(1 + i)^3 \ldots + (R_{jn} - C_{jn})/(1 + \mathrm{i})^n + S_{jn}, \quad (5.3)$$

where n shows the time horizon relevant for the project (n = number of periods).

If the value of r which satisfies equation 5.3 is greater than or equal to the marginal cost of funds or i—the assumption here being that the marginal cost of funds does not vary with the size of the investment—the project is undertaken. If this r is less than the marginal cost of funds, the project is not undertaken. For careers, a person can accept only one "project." The choice of projects is mutually exclusive.

An application of these concepts is Weeks, Wallace, Wallace, et al. (1994), who computed costs and returns in alternative careers, including medicine, as well as returns to specialization within the medical field in the United States for the year 1990.[4] The authors compared returns and costs in several occupations: business, law, medicine, and dentistry. Within medicine, the authors computed profitability of investments in primary care specialties, such as pediatrics, general or

4. See Nicholson (2008) for a review of studies of returns on medical education in the United States

family medicine, and general internal medicine, and in procedure-oriented specialties, such as radiology and general surgery.

For cost, the authors measured tuition and fees in each year the person was engaged in the educational process, length of training, and the opportunity cost of being in school. If the person was not in school, it was assumed that the individual would have earned the amount equivalent to that of a high school graduate who was employed on a full-time basis. For returns, the authors generally used median earnings in the occupation or specialty by age group.

As is usual in this type of study, the authors used cross-sectional earnings data. The underlying assumption is relative earnings by age in an occupation or specialty will remain unchanged in decades to come. Hours of work per week differ by occupation and among the physician specialties.[5] For physician specialties, the study accounted for length of residency programs assuming completion without interruption. The authors wanted to control for grade point averages in occupations at entry, but data were not available. The rationale for adjusting for grades is that entry into some types of professional training is much more competitive than it is for others. To the extent that physicians earned higher grades before entry into medical school than did others who entered training for other careers, earnings differentials between medicine and other occupations may be overstated since persons who become physicians may have greater motivation to work and greater ability, which would have resulted in relatively high earnings if they had entered the other occupations as well as medicine. To the extent that this is so, observed differences in earnings between medicine and earnings in other occupations may be overstated.

The authors used different interest rates to discount future earnings of alternatively 0.05, 0.07, and 0.10. These rates are higher than long-term real interest rates on riskless securities, which are about 3 percent. A rationale for using a rate higher than for riskless securities is that the earnings stream is likely to be risky. Earnings in many occupations are subject to considerable variation. Weeks and coauthors begin their calculations after the person graduates from high school. Thus, year 1 is the first year of college. The first year of medical school in the United States is year 5.

The internal rates of return on investments in selected occupations or specialties were as follows: business, 0.29, law, 0.25; dentistry, 0.21; procedure-based medicine, 0.21; and primary care medicine, 0.15. Thus, although the rate of return of 0.15 for primary care was far above interest rates that have prevailed in the United States in most of the past century, it was much lower than the 0.21 for procedure-based medicine. Even procedure-based medicine returns were lower than returns for business and law.[6] A principal difference between medicine and business and law is that the length of training is much shorter in business and law on average than in medicine. And even though policy makers have stressed the importance of attracting more trained personnel into the primary care medical

5. To eliminate this source of variation in earnings, the authors adjusted earnings for differences in hours of work by occupation/specialty. Particularly since it is not possible to account for the many other differences among the occupations and the specialties, it is questionable whether the hours-of-work adjustment should have been made.

6. Procedure-based specialties include radiology, diagnostic cardiology, and surgical specialties. In such fields, the main focus is on performing procedures rather than on providing medical advice to patients and maintaining the health of patients over the longer term. Physicians in procedure-oriented specialties tend to earn more than their colleagues in primary care specialties.

TABLE 5.1
Estimation of the Internal Rate of Return and Net Present Value for the US Professional Education in 1990

Occupation	Hours-Adjusted Internal Rate of Return (%)	Hours-Adjusted Net Present Value (US$)
Primary care medicine	15.91	4.41
Procedure-based medicine	20.88	10.39
Dentistry	20.73	6.72
Business	28.96	6.68
Law	25.35	9.53

Note: The net present value is discounted at 5 percent.
Source: Weeks, Wallace, Wallace, et al. (1994, table 3).

fields, returns on education in procedure-based fields remained appreciably higher (table 5.1).

As an alternative to the rate of return calculations, Weeks and coauthors showed the results of their present value calculations by occupation/specialty. Ranked in terms of highest present value to lowest using an interest rate of 0.05, the ranking was as follows: procedure-based specialty medicine, law, dentistry, business, and primary care medicine. Using an interest rate of 0.10, the relative ranking of present value between dentistry and business reversed. However, procedure-based medicine remained at the top and primary care medicine at the bottom. Overall, investments in professional education yielded substantial financial rewards (table 5.1).

The relatively brief training periods in law and business increases rates of return in these occupations. Given the assumed interest rates in the present value calculations, all of which are far below the estimated rates of returns, the present value estimates are far less sensitive to lengthy training periods than are the rates of return calculations. Weeks and Wallace (2002), using 1997 data, updated the earlier analysis (which was based on 1990 data), finding that primary care physicians remained at the bottom in terms of rate of return on their education. However, among the professional groups studied, primary care medicine realized the largest percentage gain in net present value of all the groups. Primary care remained at the bottom despite policy initiatives implemented to encourage entry into primary care during the 1990s.

The higher earnings in procedure-based than in primary care fields of medicine are not unique to United States. For example, Lin, Kao, Tang. et al. (2005) documented a similar pattern in Taiwan, a country with public national health insurance. In Taiwan, the national health insurance program controls the amount and rate of remuneration of physicians (see chapter 12).

Nicholson (2008) summarizes rates of return from physician specialty training. The returns on training in some procedure-oriented specialties, such as anesthesiology and radiology, exceed 1.0, which is equivalent to a 100 percent return on a dollar invested in training in these specialties. These high rates of return occur from a combination of much higher earnings in these fields than in family practice and the relatively short residency training periods in these fields. At least in the United States in the latter part of the twentieth century, there were definite financial incentives for physicians to specialize in certain fields.

Based on an analysis of students' earnings expectations, Nicholson (2005) reported that medical students underestimate physicians' earnings. The median student underestimated physician earnings by 15 percent between 1974 and 1998, and the median absolute value of the estimation errors (considering both under- and overestimates of earnings) was 26 percent of actual earnings. Although students' assessments were relatively inaccurate and downward biased, accuracy improved by 35 percent between the first and fourth years of medical school. Specialty choice is likely to be made during the third and fourth years of medical school.

To the extent that earnings differ appreciably among physician specialties, do earnings differences systematically affect choice of specialty? As discussed more fully in Nicholson (2008), some studies find that rates of return on specialty training have virtually no impact on specialty choices, while at least one study finds a substantial effect. A difference is that the studies showing no effect used data on actual patterns of entry, while the study with the large effect used students' desired specialty choices as the dependent variable. The difference between the two is that limits on openings in specialty training programs can constrain students' actual choices. One would expect that admission to specialty training would be especially tough in those fields for which the rate of return is relatively high, unless, of course, specialty boards, which control entry, allow the number of positions to increase when admission becomes increasing tough to gain. In fact, such boards appear not to increase slots sufficiently to meaningfully decrease the difficulty of entry. One study estimated that about half of the differential in earnings between primary care and non-primary care physicians is due to entry barriers in latter (Bhattacharya 2005).

While economists, starting with Friedman and Kuznets (1945), have maintained that entry barriers in medicine are motivated by the collective financial self-interest of the medical profession, physicians point to justifications for high financial returns on medical education and to high returns in some specialties that are not financially motivated. For example, one reason advanced for limiting capacity in residency programs (hospital-affiliated specialty training programs for medical school graduates desiring to enter a specialty) is that residents in a specialty should perform a minimum number of procedures during their training in order to become proficient in these procedures; without limits on program size, there may not be a sufficient number of patients to provide adequate training opportunities. A related issue is that if there are too many practicing physicians in a particular specialty, the volume per specialist may be insufficient for the specialist to maintain his or her skills, and quality of care would suffer as a result. Limits on specialty training capacity plausibly reflect both financial and nonfinancial motives.

PHYSICIAN GEOGRAPHIC LOCATION DECISIONS

A major public policy issue in virtually all countries concerns the maldistribution of physicians geographically. In large cities, there are often many physicians. By contrast, there are few physicians relative to population in many rural areas, even though the population is far smaller there. There are substantial differences in physician availability in large cities as well, with physicians being less plentiful in areas of the city where predominantly low-income families reside.[7]

A simple economic model of the spatial distribution of firms predicts that physicians in a given specialty will tend to locate so as to equalize their patient loads. Assuming constant demand per person, if there are twice as many physicians in one location than in another, there will be twice as many physicians in the specialty in the former than in the latter location (Newhouse, Williams, Bennett, et al. 1982). Below a certain population threshold, there will be no specialists of a given type in a community. The threshold depends on the total number of specialists in the market.

Suppose, for example, there are 100 physicians to be allocated to various geographic locations in a country. The population size is 100,500. Further, the 100,500 people are distributed in three locations, one with a population of 80,000, another with a population of 20,000, and a third with a population of 500. Assuming that physicians will locate to equalize the physician-to-population ratios in the three locations, the largest town will get 80 physicians, the second largest 20, and the third town, no physicians. Now suppose the number of physician increases to 210. In equilibrium, there will be slightly fewer than 500 patients per doctor. The smallest community will now get a doctor. Thus, there is a case for increasing the country's total physician supply in order for the smallest communities to have their own physicians.

However, increasing aggregate supply is an inefficient approach to solving a maldistribution problem. First, for the least populous community to obtain one physician, it is necessary for physician supply in the two larger communities to more than double.

The above framework assumes that physicians are indifferent about where they locate. Yet in reality, communities vary in their nonfinancial attributes (e.g., quality of schools, libraries, recreational opportunities), and physicians and their families are likely to prefer some communities to others for this reason. Given

7. See, for example, empirical evidence on the distribution of general practitioners in Munich, Germany, described by Shannon and Cutchin (1994).

heterogeneity in preferences of persons who enter the medical profession, one option is to select medical students who are likely to prefer a particular geographic location. For example, students who have families in rural areas may prefer to live there, holding other factors constant. Or to the extent that physicians like to locate near large bodies of water or in the mountains, it may be desirable to attract students who have lived in areas far from water and mountains under the presumption that many such persons like living in such areas.

Second, the above framework assumes that per capita demand for physicians' services is constant. However, per capita demand is higher among persons with health insurance coverage and high incomes. Thus, if the small community in the above example is also relatively poor, it may not attract a physician even if the aggregate supply rose to 210.

Third, the above framework does not explicitly consider the possibility that physicians will locate strategically. If population density differs within a market, a physician may locate so as to be near a population cluster and hence, attract disproportionately large amounts of patients within the cluster. For example, a physician would locate in between two population clusters rather than outside one.

Rosenthal, Zaslavsky, and Newhouse (2005) studied geographic location patterns of physicians in the United States between 1979 and 1999, a period during which aggregate physician supply in this country nearly doubled. For most specialties studied, there was a diffusion of physicians to smaller communities as aggregate supply increased. However, in specialties with relatively few physicians, the smallest communities still lacked a physician in 1999.

The authors cautioned that physician-to-population ratios may not be fully accurate measures of individuals' access to a physician. Gauged in terms of travel time to a physician in a particular specialty, access in nonmetropolitan areas adjacent to major metropolitan areas was higher than in nonmetropolitan areas distant from large cities.

THE ECONOMICS OF PHYSICIAN GROUP PRACTICE

Another set of choices physicians face is the type of organization in which they will practice. In some countries, many physicians practice in groups that are independent of other organizations, such as hospitals. In the United States, market changes are leading greater numbers of physicians to select employed practice, such as hospital employment. However, independent practice remains the predominant practice arrangement. Group practice offers a number of potential advantages.

ECONOMIES OF SCALE AND SCOPE

First, being in a group may allow the physician to exploit economies of scale and scope. *Economies of scale* are realized when unit cost decreases as output increases.

Often such economies arise because the initial investment of capital is spread over a larger output as output increases. Examples are medical equipment, such as a CT scanner or a computer system for medical records or patient billing. Another source of economies of scale is that larger firms may have more market power in markets for inputs they purchase.

Economies of scope exist when the provision of one type of output makes it possible for another type of output to be produced more efficiently. Suppose, for example, that a radiologist practices with a general surgeon. There may be efficiencies in the diagnosis and treatment of cancer if a rapid and accurate diagnosis can be followed by a timely surgical procedure. With technological change in communication, however, some sources of economies of scope may have lessened. For example, a radiologist in India may interpret a scan obtained in the United States, while the surgeon sleeps, and the interpretation may be available for the surgeon the next day.

Referrals

Second, a motive for young physicians to join a group practice is to build practice volume by gaining referrals. There may be gains from trade between more established physicians wanting to reduce practice volume and newer physicians wanting to build it. By practicing together, the referring physician can share in the patient revenue from the referred patients that would be likely to occur if the practices were separate. A young physician may gain from a revenue-sharing arrangement initially, but as he or she gains experience with the practice, this physician may be expected to subsidize other, less experienced colleagues. Some physicians join groups to be able to practice medicine rather than spend a lot of time in business management. Income pooling with other physicians in the practice provides a form of insurance against the risk of reductions in income in a particular year.

Coverage of Patients

Third, many physicians select group over solo practice because this arrangement offers coverage of patient emergencies during nights and weekends. Coverage is particularly useful in such fields as obstetrics. Babies want to be delivered nights, weekends, and holidays, as well as during normal business hours.

Reduction in Earnings Fluctuations

Fourth, group practice tends to result in reduced fluctuations in earnings, a situation likely to be preferred by risk-averse physicians. Physicians in groups may be paid in several ways. One option is salaried practice. In this case, the group receives fee-for-service revenue, but employed physicians receive a fixed salary. Within a time period, such as a year, there are no fluctuations in salaried physician earnings. While this may appeal to risk-averse physicians, salaried physician practitioners do not have a direct financial incentive to be concerned about either practice cost or revenue. For this reason, practice cost may be higher and volume of service lower than it would be if the physician faced financial incentives to be efficient and to exert effort. Another option for group practices is expense sharing. According to this arrangement, physicians share practice expenses, but each physician receives his or her billed revenue. Particularly if by incurring additional expense, the physician can generate more revenue, there is an incentive to incur additional expense. Without any monitoring of individual physician behavior, each physician has an incentive to incur extra expenses, especially when the group size is large.

To see this, suppose that 100 physicians in a group share expenses. Then, assuming equal expense sharing, the cost to an individual physician of adding a dollar in practice expense is only $0.01.[8] For this reason, expense-sharing practices are likely to have some type of monitoring of individual physicians to oversee individual physician use of practice resources.

More typically, physicians in groups share revenue as well as expense. The practice's tax on individual physician revenue may vary from $(N-1)/N$, where N is the number of physicians in the group, to other arrangements in which revenue shares vary with various factors, such as the amount of revenue generated by the individual physician.

Even in a two-physician equal revenue- and expense-sharing practice, marginal revenue from seeing patients is cut in half. This plausibly reduces individual physician effort. Fortunately, with as few as two partners, observing the other partner's effort should not be that difficult. Nor should it be as difficult to agree to mutually beneficial levels of effort. With a much larger group, however, monitoring the effort of individual physicians and agreeing on rules regarding levels of individual physician effort are likely to be more difficult to achieve. But a larger group offers the individual physician more risk protection from negative shocks to revenue.

EMPIRICAL EVIDENCE

In a study of group practices in the United States, Gaynor and Gertler (1995) hypothesized that (1) more financially risk-averse physicians join groups and (2) physician groups place more emphasis on reducing financial risk to individual group members ("risk spreading") and correspondingly less emphasis on providing financial incentives for individual physician effort. Using data from a large cross section of physician practices of varying sizes and compensation arrangements, Gaynor and Gertler found that compensation arrangements with greater revenue sharing significantly reduced individual physician effort. When physicians were not rewarded for extra effort at the margin, they saw fewer patients. This mattered especially when the number of physician group members was large. At the limit, revenue and expense sharing reduces individual physician incentives to the point at which the individual physician member gains virtually no additional income from seeing an additional patient, as occurs in salaried practice. Physicians in

8. *See, for example, Newhouse (1973).*

Gaynor and Gertler's sample with a greater taste for steady income selected salary compensation. The choice of a large versus a small group practice, a partnership, or solo practice involved a trade-off between risk protection in a large revenue- and expense-sharing practice and efficiency in a smaller practice. When, in addition, economies of scale and scope are also considered, the trade-offs become more complicated. Other research from Canada shows that physicians have higher output when they are organized on a fee-for-service basis than on a salaried basis (Ferrall, Gregory, and Tholl 1998).

5.3 Physicians' Short-Run Decisions

Overview

Now we assume that the physicians are in place, and we describe the market for physicians' services, conditional on choices of occupation, specialty, location, and practice mode having been made. This separation is made for analytic convenience. In practice, people make personal choices with long-run implications. Thus, physicians forecast prices and outputs and profits (incomes) in various settings well or not so well and make specialty, location, and practice type choices accordingly.

The market for physicians' services is often cited as a case in which standard economic analysis does not apply (box 5.1). Policy decisions often are based on a premise of failure in the market for physicians' services (box 5.2).

Some public policy makers and some scholars reach this conclusion for several reasons. First, there is the impression that people do not know much about medical care and the production of health. For this reason, the assumption of perfect information, which underlies the perfect competition framework, is questioned.

Second, higher-income individuals sometimes pay higher fees than those with lower incomes, seemingly for the same quality of service. Unless the price differences are positively related to quality differences, this may be an indication of price discrimination (Kessel 1958). Under perfect competition, sellers do not possess the market power to price discriminate.

Third, not only is there variability in physicians' fees within small geographic areas but fees tend to be *higher* in areas with higher ratios of physicians to population. It is argued that if competitive forces operated, fees would generally be lower, not higher, in such areas.

Fourth, a point related to the second, expenditures on physicians' services appear to be higher and expenditures per physician not that much lower or lower at all in areas with higher numbers of physicians per capita population (Schwartz, Williams, Newhouse, et al. 1988). If so, medical organizations have no real financial motive to lobby for barriers to entry to protect their incomes.

Box 5.1
Is the Market for Physicians' Services Really Unique?

The tripartite role described in this chapter's introduction is not unique to physicians. An automobile mechanic, for example, might determine the need for a repair and then offer to perform the repair. Mechanics may certify that an automobile is in good condition. Similarly, lawyers perform at least two of the roles, as do insurance adjusters. Lawyers may assess the merits of a potential client's legal claim and then, conditional on the client agreeing to this, represent the client's legal interests. An insurance adjuster may assess the damage caused by a storm to a house and estimate the amount of money needed to repair the damage. As with physicians and lawyers, the underlying assumptions are that the adjuster is competent and trustworthy and that the estimate includes the materials and labor needed to restore the house to its condition before the storm occurred.

In all of these markets, consumers know less than the professionals do. The patient knows less about medicine than the physician does, the automobile owner knows less about transmissions than the mechanic, the client knows less about law than the lawyer, and the homeowner knows less about the cost of materials and labor than the insurance adjuster.

How can one be sure that the physician or other professional or business is sufficiently trustworthy? One approach is to rely on competitive forces. For example, following an instance of poor performance, such as lost luggage on a flight, the consumer may use another airline the next time. For many physician encounters, reliance on competitive forces may suffice. Suppose, for example, the physician seems distracted during a routine physical examination. The patient who had no illness detectible may select another physician subsequently without incurring major harm. For some products, such as automobiles, there are reliable sources of written information on frequency of repair, or for airlines on frequencies of late flights or lost baggage. Consumers can rely on this information as an accurate description of the product's quality, and, based on quality and price, consumers can make informed product choices.

The competitive approach faces two challenges in the context of medical care. First, performance failures can sometimes result in serious harm. Of course, the same may be said for automobiles and airplanes that crash, but in some industries the consequences of performance failures (e.g., the failure of a few pages in a textbook to be printed) are plausibly less. Second, there are problems in rating the quality of individual physicians based on their performance records. A heart surgeon may experience a high death rate in performing heart surgery not because the surgeon is incompetent but because he or she operates on patients with difficult conditions who are at higher risk from surgery. Also, in contrast to automobile frequency-of-repair records, which may be based on hundreds of thousands of cars, the caseload of an individual physician may be too low to provide a reliable basis for evaluating the physician's failure rate. Safety records are evaluated not on a pilot-specific basis but rather on the performance of all the airline's pilots.

Box 5.2
Policy Responses to Perceived Physician Market Failure

If reliance on competitive forces is misplaced, then what are the alternatives? One alternative is to rely on *professional norms*. Professional norms are rules of behavior widely accepted by the profession. These rules may be enforced, but they are sufficiently inculcated that members of the profession generally abide by the rules even if they are not enforced.

On graduating from medical school, physicians are asked to take the Hippocratic oath, which states they will put their patients' interest first. However, professional norms do not guarantee that quality will be maintained. After all, a physician may have a good attitude but not be competent. Physicians may not be most up-to-date about technical advances in their fields.

Other forms of self-regulation and external regulation allegedly designed to safeguard quality of care include medical school accreditation, licensure, and certification in a physician specialty. High-quality medical education may lead to high quality of care, but again, there is no guarantee. For one, a physician is likely to practice for forty years or so after graduation, and there can be substantial technological change (and some forgetting) over this period. Economists tend to be suspicious of licensure since the licensure process can be used to bar entry into the profession. In contrast to licensure, which is required for a physician to practice, certification indicates that the physician has certain educational preparation and has passed certain tests. A noncertified physician can still practice medicine or even perform services common to a specific specialty. But even certification does not ensure quality. In practice, few physicians are ever decertified.

Other quality assurance mechanisms in health care in the United States employ peer review at the level of the medical staff of a hospital (discussed in chapter 7) and by insurers. With hospital peer review, physicians on the medical staff determine who can have and retain privileges to practice at the hospital. In some rare cases, poor performance by a physician may lead to exclusion from the insurer's network of physicians.

No method of quality assurance is foolproof. The method on which the vast majority of countries rely is to require that the physicians satisfy certain educational requirements and take an examination prior to becoming licensed. Worldwide, the capacity of accredited medical schools places an upper limit on physician supply. Many physicians emigrate from the country from which they receive their basic medical education. Thus, the supply in any country will depend on whether it experiences net inflows or outflows of physicians.

Fifth, when the prices of physicians' services are set administratively, either by a government agency or by a private insurer, the quantity of physicians' services sometimes increases after the price is reduced. In "normal" markets, one might expect quantity decreases following a reduction in an administrative price.

A normal competitive market is characterized by many buyers and sellers; each buyer and seller is a price taker. No individual participant in a competitive market is able to affect price. Equilibrium price and quantity are determined at the intersection of industry supply and demand curves. In the sense that there are many buyers and sellers, the market for physicians' services resembles a perfectly competitive market.

In the market for an agricultural product such as oranges, which is a perfectly competitive product market, orange growers plant, fertilize, and harvest based on an anticipated price of oranges over which growers have no control. Similarly, food wholesalers, retailers, and ultimately consumers of oranges as individuals have no control over product prices. Rather, price is determined by the impersonal forces of supply and demand for oranges. If there is one quality level, then there is one price. If, by contrast, there are several qualities, there are different prices reflecting the different qualities. Price differentials reflect both the marginal cost of producing additional quality as well as consumer willingness to pay for products of different qualities. If, for example, orange growers employ extra fertilizer to obtain larger oranges, the growers must be able to recover the extra cost of the fertilizer in the prices they obtain from selling the oranges in order for them to invest in the fertilizer. Similarly, people need to be willing to pay more for larger oranges.

In sum, "normal" markets provide a variety of quality levels. There is nothing in quality variation per se that necessarily impedes the workings of a competitive market. We observe differences in quality of hotels, restaurants, clothing, toys, and many other goods and services.

In some settings, physicians are price takers, but this occurs when health insurers set prices that physicians who care for patients with the insurers' coverage are often obliged to accept as payment in full. When physicians are price takers, the quantity of service often increases in response to administered price decreases.

In other settings, patients pay physicians directly on a fee-for-service basis. In such situations, the physician is often a price setter, not a price taker. Especially when physicians set prices for services, there is often substantial price dispersion for the same service in a given geographic area. Prices of physicians' services are often higher in areas in which there are more physicians. Normally, in a competitive market, one would expect that an increase in supply would lead to lower prices.

Some of these stylized facts that seem to be inconsistent with a competitive market can be easily reconciled with economic theory. Other facts are less easily reconciled. We first see how far we can go in reconciling stylized facts of the physicians' services market with standard economic models when (1) physicians' fees are set by market forces and (2) physicians' fees are set by a public or private administrative organization. While individual physicians are price takers if the product market is perfectly competitive, they are also price takers when their fees are set by a government agency or a private insurer.

RECONCILING STYLIZED FACTS OF THE PHYSICIANS' SERVICES MARKET WITH STANDARD ECONOMIC MODELS

WHY THE DEMAND CURVE FACING THE INDIVIDUAL PHYSICIAN MAY BE DOWNWARD SLOPING

As noted above, price differences can exist under perfect competition. But the differences reflect differences in quality, and whether physicians who charge higher prices are really better physicians is questionable. It seems necessary to look at other explanations for price differences within geographic areas, such as within cities.

To the extent that the market for physicians' services is *monopolistically competitive* rather than *perfectly competitive*, differences in prices for the same services, such as within a city, are readily explained. In monopolistically competitive markets, each seller faces its own product demand curve. Price differentials among sellers in a market can persist in the long term.

In a perfectly competitive market, the demand curve facing the individual seller is flat. If the seller charges a price above the market-clearing price, the seller loses all customers. For example, a grower cannot sell an orange for any amount above the market-clearing price for oranges. There may be differences in prices, but this price variation is easily explained. For example, prices tend to be higher when oranges are sold at greater distance from where they are grown. If a seller has a large supply of oranges on hand, the seller may fear that the oranges may spoil sitting on the shelves and offer oranges for sale at a lower price than otherwise for this reason.

In a market in which perfect competition does not prevail, the demand curve facing the individual seller is downward sloping. The quantity demanded rises as price falls. In such markets, rather than supply the quantity at which marginal cost equals price, the quantity is set where the marginal cost equals the marginal revenue (fig. 5.5a). The price of all goods or services sold depends on the quantity supplied; the seller takes this into account in deciding how much quantity to supply.

Why might the physician's demand curve be downward sloping rather than perfectly horizontal? First, search among doctors is costly for patients. If the patient is satisfied with a doctor, the cost of further searching may not be worthwhile. Thus, a patient may not leave his or her physician even if the physician's price is slightly above another's (but see box 5.3).

A second reason to expect that physicians face downward-sloping demand curves is that people may be willing to pay more for the convenience of visiting a physician who is geographically closer to the patient. Thus, if a physician who is

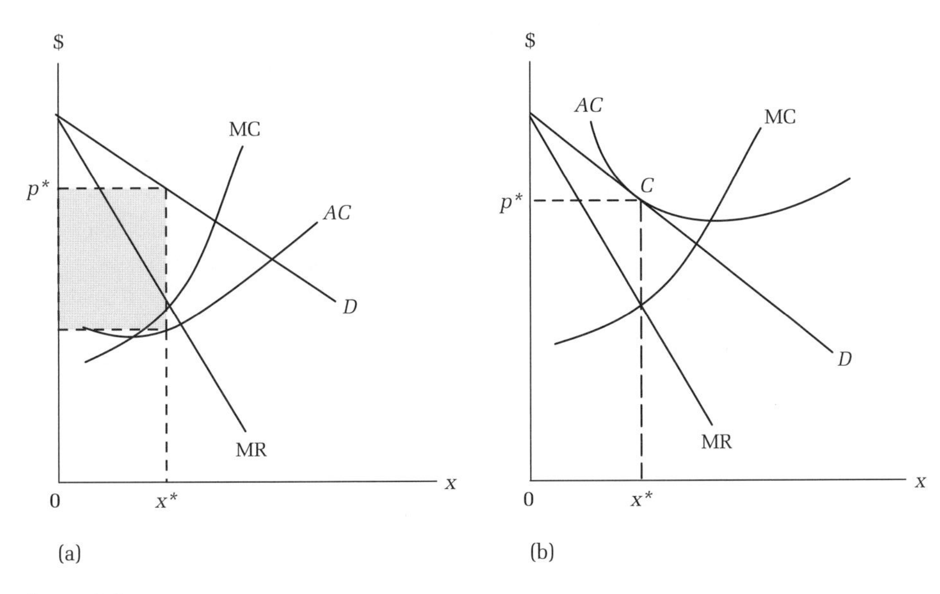

FIGURE 5.5
Equilibrium in Pure Monopoly and Monopolistic Competition

10 miles away cuts his or her fee, a patient might be disinclined to switch from a physician who is located much closer. On the other hand, to attract patients from distant as opposed to nearby locations, the physician may have to offer services at a lower price.

Under *monopolistic competition*, there are no important barriers to entry, and each seller's demand curve is negatively sloped. Thus, as more (monopolistically competitive) sellers enter the area, the demand curve shifts in until each seller earns zero profits. The zero profit equilibrium is shown in figure 5.5b, at point *C*.

WHY ARE PHYSICIANS' FEES OFTEN HIGHER IN MARKETS WITH MORE PHYSICIANS?

The monopolistic competition model can explain why price dispersion may exist in a particular geographic area as well as among areas, but the model is not directly useful for explaining why physicians' fees are higher in areas with more physicians relative to population.

PRACTICE INPUT PRICE DIFFERENCES

One explanation for such fee differentials is that the costs of some inputs in the production of physicians' services are higher in areas in which physicians tend to be numerous. Since office space tends to be more costly in central cities than in the suburbs than in rural areas, some patients who work or live downtown or for whom downtown locations are geographically accessible may be willing to pay

Box 5.3
Search, Experience, and Credence Goods

Economists distinguish among *search*, *experience*, and *credence goods*. Physicians' services are sometimes experience goods and sometimes credence goods, but rarely search goods.

For a *search good*, it is possible to learn a lot about the good's characteristics before purchasing it. Suppose one is considering the purchase of an automobile. There are numerous ratings of the car's performance, durability, appearance, and other dimensions of quality. Especially with the Internet, it is possible to compare the prices of alternative dealers. While one may learn something from a test drive of the automobile, much information about specific automobiles can be gleaned from other information sources.

By contrast, to assess an *experience good*, the consumer must first consume a unit of the good. For example, before seeing a physician for the first time, a person does not know whether or not the physician is a good match for him or her. Once a consumer has found a good match and the physician learns a lot about you and your health, changing to another physician and repeating the exercise may be quite costly. It seems unlikely that many patients would switch doctors just because the price of another doctor was slightly lower than one's regular doctor. The presence of health insurance will also diminish the consumer's incentive to change physicians. If a large part or all of the price difference is covered by health insurance, people should be much less responsive to price differences among doctors.

With an experience good, consumers are fairly knowledgeable about the seller after consuming it. There are some goods and services for which consumers are not well equipped to gauge quality, *credence goods*. Advice is likely to be part of the service sought. Consumers do now know which quality of the good or service that they need. These are credence goods. Consuming the good requires faith. Clearly, attending church, synagogue, a mosque, or a temple requires an element of faith. But so do some rarely performed types of medical care. In such cases, it is hard to ask others about their experiences. Further, even if the person you asked has had a favorable experience, this may not be the case for you because of differences in genetic makeup or some other factor. With credence goods, goods for which attributes are difficult or impossible for consumers to evaluate, there is a concern that consumers are vulnerable to self-serving behaviors on the part of suppliers. In the context of medicine, it is often difficult for patients to evaluate what the physician is doing or not doing. It is certainly difficult for a patient undergoing surgery to know what is going on. Nor is it possible for insurers and others outside the operating room to know precisely what happened there. The market may not provide sufficient incentives to deter such fraudulent behavior (Dulleck and Kerschbamer 2006).

more to visit a physician who is located downtown. Particularly in large cities, geographic location could be an important source of price variation. This could be a reason that fees tend to be higher in the center of New York City (Manhattan) than in the suburbs, although the physician-to-population ratio is much higher in Manhattan.

THE PAULY-SATTERTHWAITE MODEL

Differences in office space cost may explain some price dispersion, but often dispersion in physicians' fees within cities is far greater than can be explained on the basis of space cost alone. Pauly and Satterthwaite (1981) and earlier work by Satterthwaite (1979) suggest another reason.

They argued that patient search cost is higher in large cities than in smaller cities or in nonmetropolitan areas. Higher search cost in turn is expected to make the demand curves facing individual physicians less elastic, surely less than infinitely elastic. Demand is less elastic because if the physician were to raise prices, patients would have less information and would face higher search costs in learning about the prices of other physicians in the area. Holding other factors constant, price is higher when the demand curve facing the individual seller is less elastic.[9]

Indeed, there is something to be learned from asking other people about their doctors. Pauly and Satterthwaite described the search process as follows. Suppose one were a new to a city and were a guest at a party. The guest would ask someone who has lived in the city for some time, "Do you know anything about Dr. Johnson? Is he a good doctor?" If there are only one or two doctors in the town, the person would certainly be likely to know something about Dr. Johnson. But in a large city, it would often be necessary to ask many persons at the party about Dr. Johnson before finding someone who actually knew something about him. In this sense, search cost is higher in large cities, resulting in more inelastic physician demand curves and higher prices.

There are other questions that the newcomer could ask, and the answers to these questions would not vary by city size. For example, one could ask the person about his or her doctor or whether the person knows of a doctor he or she would recommend. If the line of questioning proceeded in this way, there would be no difference in search cost between a large and a small city. The Pauly-Satterthwaite explanation is interesting, but it does not fully resolve the issue of why physicians' fees are often higher in cities in which relatively many doctors practice relative to the city's population.

THE QUALITY-AMENITIES MODEL

In another framework, as more physicians enter a market, qualitative changes in the product occur. For example, waiting time in the physician's office may decrease and physicians may spend more time with patients on average. Travel time to a physician from work or home may decrease.

9. We do not explain how price is set by a seller with market power in its product market here. We suggest consulting a textbook on microeconomics for an explanation.

Nearly everywhere in the world, patients spend time in a waiting room before being seen by a physician. While they can be distressing to patients, such waits have an economic explanation, however.

If a physician were to maintain a zero wait time in the office, there would be times during which patients would be unavailable to be seen by physicians. Some patients may arrive late and others may forget they had an appointment. With many patients in the physician's waiting room, it is less likely that the physician will be unoccupied because no patient is available. When physicians are more numerous relative to the number of potential patients in the market, physicians are more likely to wait, and conversely. An increase in quality should lead to an increase in price, both in perfectly competitive markets and in those with monopolistic elements.

When there are more physicians in a market, there is a greater heterogeneity of practice styles, including some "boutique practices." Such practices offer more professional time for patients and shorter waits, among other differences. But such boutique practices tend to charge higher prices (Boardman, Dowd, Eisenberg, et al. 1983).

The astute reader will see a definite parallel between the quality-amenity model and our depiction of the market for oranges above, a market we said was perfectly competitive. If in fact we could explain physician fee variation by variation in characteristics and this variation were not responsible for increased search cost, it would be appropriate to characterize the physicians' services market as competitive.

SUMMING UP

We now take stock of how well the standard models do in accounting for the stylized facts of the physicians' services market when price is set by market forces.

On the first, consumer ignorance, in the standard models, obtaining information is costly to consumers, more so for some types of services than for others. It is easier to find out whether an obstetrician is a good doctor by asking others than whether a brain surgeon is good because relatively few people undergo brain surgery. In general, economists do not test the assumptions of their models but rather test the models' predictions. Hence, economists have little evidence to add directly to the debate as to whether or not consumer ignorance is truly widespread in markets for physicians' services.

On the second fact, economists explain that higher-income persons may purchase a higher quality of services, where quality includes but is not limited to such product attributes as waiting time and length of visit with the physician. However, we cannot know for sure whether or not quality differences fully explain the price differences observed with a market, the third stylized fact. On the fourth point, qualitative changes occur when physician density increases, and it is conceptually possible that these changes may explain some of difference in expenditures on physicians' services among geographic areas, but there is insufficient evidence to conclude that such changes explain all or even the major part of the difference.

RECONCILING STYLIZED FACTS OF THE PHYSICIANS' SERVICES MARKET WITH STANDARD ECONOMIC MODELS: FEES SET ADMINISTRATIVELY

QUANTITY INCREASES WITH ADMINISTERED PRICE DECREASES

In many countries, especially those with government-provided health insurance, individual physicians, practicing alone or in groups, have no or at most only very limited power to set prices. When there is public health insurance, price tends to be set by the government (see chapters 12 and 13). Also, large private insurers often dictate prices to individual physicians, who can either accept the price schedule presented to them or refuse to accept payment and patients from this payment source. The physician's decision is then how much quantity of which types of services to provide to persons covered by the insurance plan.

BACKWARD-BENDING SUPPLY CURVE OF PHYSICIANS

Initially assume that the physician produces one type of service and there is one insurer, which sets the product price. Under these assumptions, and because physician time is the major input in medical practice, we can analyze the physician's response to price in terms of a model of labor supply. The concept of a supply curve is introduced here since it applies only when the firm is a price taker. If the firm sets its product price, economists generally assume that the firm's decisions are guided by profit maximization rather than by utility maximization, the motivation assumed here.

In the usual model of labor supply, the individual decides how much labor to supply given the wage, which is exogenous to the individual. Here, since the physician's wage rate is substantially determined by the administered price, we use wage and price interchangeably.

A reason for the negative relationship between prices and quantities provided—that is, quantity increases when the administered price is reduced—may be that the physician labor supply curve is backward bending or negatively-sloped throughout. The concept of a backward-bending labor supply curve comes from microeconomic theory.

Rewrite equation 5.1 as follows:

$$U_i = U_i(Y_i, l_i). \tag{5.4}$$

According to equation 5.4, individual i's utility is a function of income or goods and leisure (l_i). As the hours of work increase, leisure hours decline and utility falls.

$$Y_i = (T - l_i)w + Y_o. \tag{5.5}$$

The person's income depends on the number of hours he or she works $(T - l_i)$, where T is the total amount of time available to the individual to allocate between market work and leisure, and Y_{oi} is the other income the individual receives which is unrelated to work hours, such as from investments or public subsidies. In this framework, the individual's decision problem is to find that level of l_i that maximizes utility subject to the constraint given by equation 5.5.

A decrease in the price of a physician's service leads to a decrease in physician hourly compensation, w. The trade-off between goods and leisure is given by the wage. Suppose that the physician has no other source of income and has a maximum of 80 hours per week to devote to work (T = 80). (The rest of the 88 hours in the week is presumably devoted to various personal activities, including eating and sleeping.) If the physician works 80 hours weekly, weekly earnings are $80w$, where w is the hourly wage. An increase in the wage raises maximum weekly earnings, and conversely for a decrease in the wage.

In figure 5.6, before the reduction in the price, the physician has l_A hours of leisure and can consume G_A units of goods and services. After the price decrease, the new equilibrium is l_B hours of leisure and G_B consumption units. Since l_A

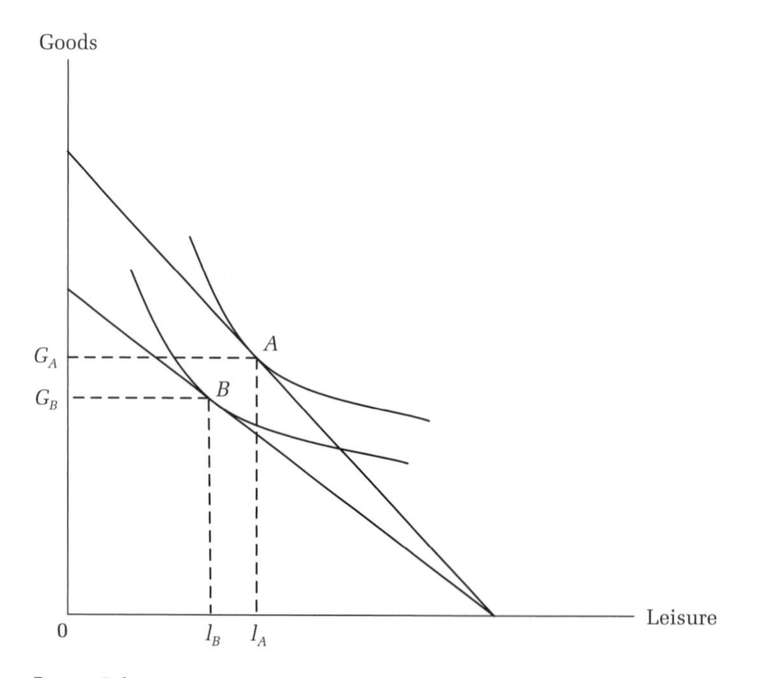

FIGURE 5.6
The Physician Work-Leisure Decision

exceeds l_B, this implies that the person works more hours at B than at A. Consumption is lower at B than at A.

Underlying the change in leisure and consumption are two effects: a *substitution effect* and an *income effect*. At a lower wage, according to the substitution effect, the reduced wage reduces the price of leisure, and for this reason, the physician works fewer hours per week. He "buys" more leisure. However, assuming that leisure is a normal good—more of it is consumed at higher income levels—the lower wage induces the physician to work longer hours since the physician is poorer following the reduction in wage. If the income effect dominates the substitution effect, as shown in figure 5.6, a reduction in the administered price leading to a lower wage increases work hours. As work hours increase, the quantity of service provided increases.[10]

Thus, according to standard economic theory, a reduction in an administered price could lead to an increase in hours of work and hence in output. However, does empirical research on physician work hours support a negative relationship between the physician wage and work hours? Actually, the empirical research conducted to date supports either a zero or a positive effect, not a negative effect of the physician wage on physician labor supply (Sloan and Steinwald 1975; Noether 1986; Rizzo and Blumenthal 1994; Showalter and Thurston 1997; Baltagi, Bratberg, and Holmås 2005). In sum, at least to date, there is no empirical support for the strong income effects that would lead physicians to provide more care following an administrative price cut.

OTHER EMPIRICAL EVIDENCE ON THE EFFECTS OF ADMINISTERED PRICE REDUCTIONS ON VOLUME OF PHYSICIAN SERVICES

There has been some empirical research on the effects of administered price changes on the quantity of services supplied. In a study of procedures "overpriced" by the US Medicare program (thought to be priced well above marginal cost) for which Medicare reduced prices in 1990,[11] Nguyen and Derrick (1997) found no statistically significant effect on volume of services following the price reductions overall, but for the 20 percent of physicians who experienced the greatest price reduction, the authors found that a 1 percent reduction in the administered price led to a 0.4 percent increase in volume of the procedure provided. Yip (1998) studied overpriced Medicare procedures in New York and in the state of Washington in the United States and found that cuts in administered prices did lead to volume increases.

SUMMING UP

The concept of the backward-bending supply curve is useful for explaining physician supply responses to administered price reductions. While the theoretical concept is clear, the empirical evidence is not. Some studies show that administered price reductions increase volume of service, but many studies do not show this.

10. We have presented sufficient material here to introduce students to the concept of labor supply or to serve as a review for students who have had been exposed to the concept in a course on microeconomics. We include a problem on income and substitution effects at the end of this chapter. For students who have not seen the concept before and want to learn about it in greater depth, we suggest consulting a textbook on microeconomics or on labor economics.

11. For a more detailed description of these programs, see chapter 12.

RECONCILING STYLIZED FACTS OF THE PHYSICIANS' SERVICES MARKET: OTHER MODELS

TARGET INCOME AND SUPPLIER-INDUCED DEMAND

Standard economic theory takes one only so far in explaining the important stylized facts of the physicians' services market. A substantial number of health economists and probably the majority of researchers from other disciplines who study the physicians' services market maintain that standard economic models are inappropriate in this application. But if standard economic models do not do the job of explaining physician behavior, are the alternative frameworks really any better?

According to the target income (TI) hypothesis, physicians set price and output to achieve an income target (Y_{Ti}). Setting aside practice cost (expenses incurred by the physician for nonphysician inputs, such as for receptionist pay, office rent, and utilities) to simplify the discussion and adding cost leads to no additional insights. Let $Y_{Ti} = p_i \times x_i$, where p_i and x_i are the price and quantity set by physician *i*. According to the TI hypothesis, if physicians become more numerous relative to the population and hence x_i decreases, physicians raise p_i to achieve Y_{Ti}. This presumably can explain the observed fact that prices are often higher in areas with greater physician density (see, e.g., Fuchs 1978).

The TI hypothesis possibly can explain the positive relationship between the price of physicians' services in markets in which physicians have price-setting power and the existence of a relatively high physician-to-population ratio. However, the TI hypothesis suffers from two major flaws. First, it is not clear how the income target Y_{Ti} is set. There are many possibilities, probably too many. For example, a physician with more children might have a higher Y_{Ti}. A physician living in an affluent neighborhood might have a higher Y_{Ti}, as would a physician desiring to purchase an expensive sports car.

Second, there is an infinite number of combinations of p_i and x_i that can satisfy the target. Presumably, although not in the model, if leisure is valued by the physician, he or she would want to work as little as possible. Then why not set x_i at 1, letting price of a single unit of service be sufficiently high to achieve the target? In sum, the TI hypothesis does not make for a very satisfying theory of physician behavior.

An alternative to the target income hypothesis is the physician-induced demand hypothesis (PID), originally proposed by Evans (1974). In standard economic theory, demand curves are stable. Perhaps they can be shifted outward by an advertising campaign, but at a minimum, shifting demand is costly. According to the PID hypothesis, information between physicians and patients is so asymmetric that a physician can shift out the demand curve for his or her services when it is in the physician's self-interest to do so. Shifting involves recommending a service such as a revisit or a surgical procedure whether or not the recommended care is of potential benefit to the patient. The key feature is that under PID, demand is shifted in the physician's interest not in the consumer's. The only reason a consumer would accept this situation is asymmetric information between doctors and their patients.

In a standard economic framework, the patient visits the doctor to obtain information and assumes the doctor will make recommendations that the patient would make if the patient were as knowledgeable as the doctor. A monopolist can select price-quantity combinations along a stable demand curve to maximize profits.

With PID, however, the physician presumably has this power (unless the payment system requires that the physician be a price taker), but in addition, patients do not learn from any source how to distinguish between beneficial and nonbeneficial or even harmful care, and therefore the physician can set the demand curve wherever he or she desires.

There is a potential constraint on demand inducement, namely, professional ethics. Because of professional norms or some other reason, a physician may feel guilty about shifting demand for financial gain, but being ethical is a normal good. If demand is pushed too low by an influx of physicians and demand per physician and income falls dramatically, ethics may be less of an impediment to demand inducement than if physician income is considerably higher.

In the work-leisure analysis described above, there are two arguments in the physician's utility function: consumption and leisure. In the PID hypothesis, there are three arguments, consumption, leisure, and the physician's ethics (Evans 1974; McGuire and Pauly 1991). Shifting demand outward is good for consumption in that there is additional income to purchase more goods and services, but it is bad for leisure since the physician needs to work harder if he or she shifts out demand. Also, ethical considerations militate against demand shifting. However, if consumption is low, demand shifting is more likely. In the PID hypothesis, the quantity of services provided by each physician may increase following an administered price decrease.

Interestingly, to the extent that PID characterizes physicians' services markets, it is not limited to those cases in which physicians are paid on a fee-for-service basis. Under capitation, physicians may have a financial incentive to deliver less service than a well-informed patient would want to obtain. PID can exacerbate this problem. A physician could deliver even less care under capitation with PID than in the absence of PID.

Thus, depending on the method of physician payment, PID leads to either too much or too little care being provided. Further, the demand curves that are used in welfare analysis (see chapters 3 and 4) have no meaning under PID. By definition, if the patients' demand curves are easily shifted because patients lack the knowledge about the care they would benefit from, it is inappropriate to use demand curves as a measure of patient willingness to pay for care.

The PID model is less of a conceptual straw man than is the target income hypothesis. In an important paper, McGuire and Pauly (1991) showed in a theoretical analysis that the TI is just an extreme case of the operation of income effects. At any income above the TI, a decrease in price does not affect physician supply. However, if price is reduced just a dollar below the target, physicians increase supply to reach the income target as they would in the backward-bending supply curve analysis described above. But, as noted above, the empirical evidence does not support strong income effects on physician labor supply.

Empirical Findings on TI and PID

Economic theory is important for providing a framework for analysis. However, empirical research is needed to gauge actual relationships among variables. We now turn to a brief review of empirical research on the PID hypothesis.

In assessing these results, several key points should be kept in mind. First, the fundamental question is not whether or not PID *ever* exists. There can be little doubt that some PID exists, especially for credence-type medical services. Rather, the issue concerns the empirical importance of PID. How widespread is PID? And to the extent that it is widespread, which public policies are likely to be most successful in countering it?

Several studies have been conducted by Jonathan Gruber and colleagues, using data from the United States. This research overall provides mixed evidence on the empirical importance of PID. Gruber, Kim, and Mayzlin (1999) focused on the choice of cesarean versus normal deliveries. The fee for cesarean sections tends to be higher than that for normal deliveries, and there is a concern that high cesarean rates in the United States may reflect financial incentives facing individual physicians. In this study, the authors examined whether changes in the relative fees for cesarean sections and normal (vaginal) deliveries paid by Medicaid, the US public program financing care of the poor, affect the relative frequency with which cesarean sections and normal deliveries are performed. As explained more fully below, physicians are price takers if they participate in the Medicaid program. That is, if they accept Medicaid patients for care, they must accept Medicaid's fee as payment in full. Physicians are free not to accept such patients.

Using the theory of the firm generally used by economists, there are no income effects. Thus, if the relative fee of cesarean sections falls, one would expect more normal deliveries. By contrast, under PID, one would expect a fall in the price of cesarean sections to lead to an increase in cesareans as physicians induce demand for such services to achieve and increase in income. The authors found that a decrease in the relative price of cesarean sections relative to normal deliveries led to a decrease in the relative number of cesarean sections performed, evidence against the PID. Mitchell, Hadley, and Gaskin (2002) reported similar results for physician responses to changes in the relative prices of ophthalmologic services paid under the US Medicare program.

Gruber and Owings (1996) assessed whether or not the declining fertility rate, a 13.5 percent decrease in the US national fertility rate between 1970 and 1982, a change that is not under obstetrician-gynecologists' control but one that would be expected to reduced their incomes, led to an increase in cesarean section deliveries (which are higher priced than normal deliveries), as the PID hypothesis would predict. The authors reported that cesarean sections rose as a consequence of the fertility rate decrease, evidence favorable to PID. A 10 percent decline in the birth rate led to a 3 percent increase in the cesarean section rate.

Early studies of PID (e.g., Fuchs 1978) interpreted evidence of a positive relationship between quantity of physicians' services provided and physician availability (the physician-to-population ratio) as evidence in support of PID. However, this positive association is evidence for both PID and standard economic models. In the latter, more physicians would be expected to enter a market in which there was more demand. Also, as physicians become more numerous, they are likely to be more accessible to patients; for example, they might locate their offices closer to where patients work and live, and demand would increase for this reason.

Dranove and Wehner (1994) argued that the birth rate is not likely to respond to changes in the availability of physicians who perform obstetric deliveries. Yet they found that the birth rate is higher in areas with more physicians who deliver babies. This study should remind us to take a cautious view of studies inferring PID from a positive correlation between quantity and physician supply. It is much more likely that obstetricians locate in areas where there is a high demand for obstetric care per obstetrician than it is that a greater supply of obstetricians leads to more pregnancies. It is critical to identify the mechanism according to which quantity increases with increased supply. Some recent studies have found some direct evidence of a quantity-setting effect consistent with PID, Chalkley and Tilley (2005) for dentists in the UK and Lien, Ma, and McGuire (2004) among substance abuse counselors in the United States. Yet Carlsen and Grytten (1998), using data on physician visits and the provision of laboratory services in Norway, found no empirical evidence of inducement.

The bottom line is that the empirical evidence on PID is mixed. TI is so conceptually flawed that it has not been assessed empirically. A first empirical step in such an analysis would be to evaluate how income targets are set by physicians. PID may exist some of the time and in certain countries, depending on how the health care system is structured and financed and the extent to which consumers of personal health care services possess adequate knowledge of quality, appropriateness of services, and prices.

PUBLIC POLICY IMPLICATIONS IF PID IS SUPPORTED BY EMPIRICAL EVIDENCE

The public policy implications appropriate for a world in which PID is a dominant force are rather bleak. One popular approach—adopted, for example, by the Medicare program in the United States and by statutory health insurance in Germany—is for the government to set an expenditure target for spending on physicians' services. After the target is reached, a percentage increase in quantity is offset by an equivalent percentage reduction in price. Thus, while individual physicians may induce demand, in the aggregate, the programs are protected against inducement. While this type of policy may "work" from the standpoint of cost containment, individual patients may be adversely affected by unneeded treatments or shortages of care in instances in which PID does not operate (but rather the availability of certain beneficial types of care is adversely affected). Also, if the policy is practiced over a period of years, prices will become very low. To the extent to which price falls well below the marginal cost of supplying the service, will physicians continue to supply it?

One solution for PID is thought to be capitation. In response to a concern about capitation, Ireland switched to this type of system for payment for general practitioner services provided to lower-income persons (Madden, Nolan, and Nolan 2005). However, under PID, capitation leads to *underprovision* of care. Capitation provides incentives that encourage physicians to limit medical expenditures. There is empirical evidence that these incentives work to limit expenditures (Gaynor, Rebitzer, and Taylor 2004), but quality of care is about the same in capitated as in fee-for-service plans (Miller and Luft 2002).

McGuire (2008) described a fee structure that may be optimal even in situations in which the PID model is valid. We do not discuss his proposal here, but suggest to readers that the proposal and the background he provided are well worth reading not only for the proposal but also as a review and extension of the models presented in this chapter.

5.4 PRICE DISCRIMINATION

BACKGROUND

With the spread of health insurance, price discrimination of the kind described by Kessel (1958) based on pricing practices prevailing in the 1950s, charging higher prices for high-than for low-income patients, has become much less common than it once was. However, another type of price discrimination has arisen in countries with multiple insurers, such as the United States.

In the United States, private health insurers tend to make higher payments for physicians' services than does Medicare, and Medicare pays more than Medicaid. Since the mid-1990s, insurers in the United States have increasingly required that physicians adhere to the fee schedules established by the insurers. That is, although there may be deductibles and co-pays, physicians can accept the fee determined by the insurer as payment in full. *Balance billing,* or charging the patient more than the scheduled amount, either is limited to a percentage above the scheduled amount or is completely prohibited. Before the mid-1990s, physicians had greater latitude in setting their own fees. Often, patients received a bill from the physician and collected reimbursement directly from the insurer. The insurer paid patients for care received using the cost-sharing approaches described in chapter 3.

Medicaid was implemented in the mid-1960s with the objective of improving the access of low-income persons to "mainstream" medicine. However, fees paid to physicians for providing services to persons covered by Medicaid have tended to be far below those paid by other insurers. Further, Medicaid requires that its payment be payment in full. There can be no balance billing. As a consequence, many US physicians refuse to accept Medicaid-insured persons.

Physicians' decisions to accept Medicaid can be analyzed assuming that physicians are profit-maximizing, price-discriminating monopolists. To price discriminate, there must be two distinct product markets, each with its own demand curve. To obtain higher profit from price discrimination, there must be differences in the price elasticities of demand between the two markets. There can be no resale of product from the low-priced to the higher-priced market, which clearly applies in the case of personal services.

THEORY

To see how price discrimination works in the context of physicians' services, we assume that the physician faces two demand curves. In one market, the physician can set his or her fee. Insurance affects the position and shape of this demand curve, but the only constraint on physician fee setting in this market is market forces. In the other market, the physician is a price taker. If the physician accepts a patient for care who has this type of insurance coverage, the physician must accept the insurer's payment as payment in full. Physicians are free to accept or reject patients on a patient-specific basis. That is, the physician may decide to accept up to a certain number of patients of this type and reject the others. Medicaid has paid physicians on this basis since its inception (Sloan, Mitchell, and Cromwell 1978).

The demand curve in the first market is D_P (fig. 5.7). The demand curve in the first market is downward sloping. Marginal revenue (the addition to total revenue when another unit of service is sold) associated with D_P is MR_P. While the physician is a price setter in the first (non-Medicaid) market, the physician is a price taker from Medicaid. We assume that, in the Medicaid market, the physician can sell as many services as he or she wishes at the price set by the Medicaid program. In other words, the price elasticity of demand in this market is infinite. The requirement that the elasticities of demand differ between the two markets is thus satisfied. In addition, there is an administrative cost per unit of output. The administrative cost represents the cost of collecting payment from Medicaid ($\hat{g}$) and from non-Medicaid sources ($\breve{g}$). For example, if there are delays in payment and the physician has to remind the insurer or Medicaid that he has not been paid, his

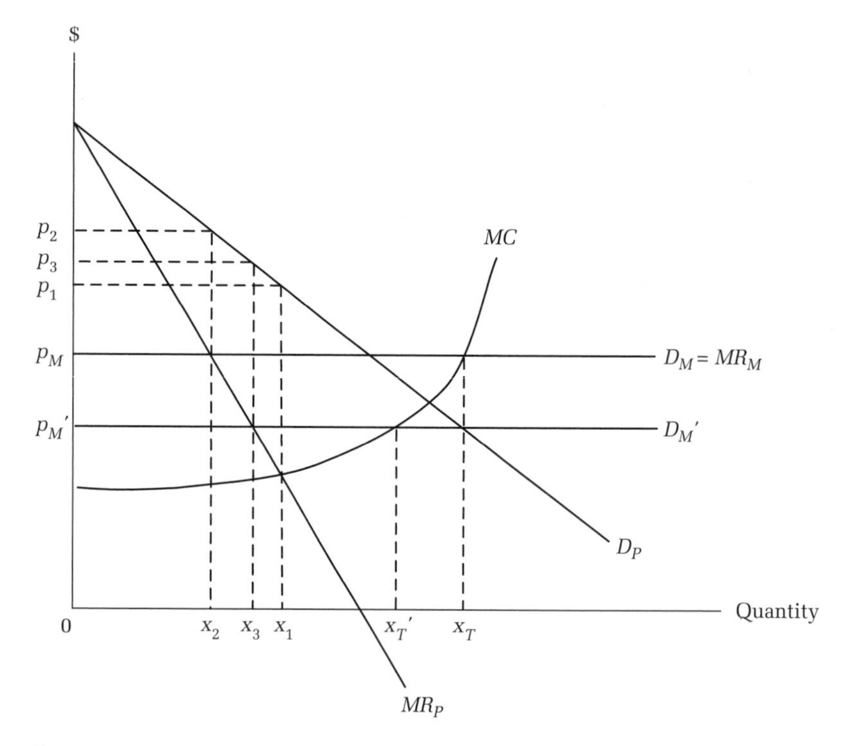

FIGURE 5.7
The Physician as Price Setter and Price Taker

administrative cost rises. Since the administrative cost differs by payer, we subtract the per unit administrative cost from the prices in the two markets.

Other than for administration, a common cost function for the physician firm applies to both markets. Costs include the imputed value of physician time and cost of nonphysician labor and capital inputs.

The marginal cost curve (the change in total cost per unit change in volume of service) for the practice is MC. Since the total cost of treatment in both markets is assumed to be identical in the two markets, MC is also identical in both markets. Marginal cost equals marginal revenue net of $\breve{g}$ in this market at (x_1, p_1), which gives the output in the first market and the associated price to patients in this market.

In the second market, in which the physician is a price taker, the demand curve is infinitely elastic. $p_M - \hat{g} = MR_M$. M stands for Medicaid. The demand curve is flat and net of the per unit administrative cost equal to marginal revenue for two reasons. The physician has no control over price in this market, and it is further assumed that, for all practical purposes, there is an infinite number of patients in this market that the physician can accept.

In this model, the physician is assumed to first accept for care those patients who are most profitable; the physician accepts patients in decreasing order of profitability. According to this rule, the physician starts with patients in the first market, accepting these patients up to (x_2, p_2), which is determined by $MR_M = MR_P$. From this point, the physician accepts patients in the second market until the physician reaches quantity x_T. The number of units accepted from the price-taking market is $x_T - x_2$. The rest of the units come from the first market.

Now suppose the price in the second market falls to p'_M. Then total output falls to x'_T. Output to the first market rises to x_3, which is determined by $D_M' = MR_p$. Since output in the first market rises, price falls in this market from p_2 to p_3. Output to the second market falls from $x_T - x_2$ to $x'_T - x_3$. The model's main implication is that patients covered by the public program represented by the second market lose some access to physicians after the price cut. Total physician output falls, but the change in output is due to the decrease in output allocated to persons in the second market. Persons in the first market benefit from a reduction in price, and output to this market increases.

The next step is to assess the effects of changes in variables that are exogenous to the physician on the physician's decision variables: output to both markets and price in the price-setting market. We distinguish between two cases. In case 1, the physician serves only the non-Medicaid market. In case 2, the physician serves both markets (fig. 5.8). (For the mathematical expressions underlying the predicted effects of changes in exogenous variables, see Sloan, Mitchell, and Cromwell [1978].)

The model predicts unambiguously that an outward shift in the non-Medicaid (price-setting) demand curve will raise output in the non-Medicaid market. If the physician did not accept Medicaid patients before the shift (case 1), the physician will not accept such patients following the shift. If the physician serves only the non-Medicaid market, the outward shift in non-Medicaid demand will have no effect on output to Medicaid patients. Rather, the physician will increase output to non-Medicaid patients.

An increase in demand in the non-Medicaid market may be caused by an increase in the population age or an increase in the per capita income of persons not on Medicaid. An increase in a non-Medicaid fee schedule would have the same effect qualitatively as an increase in demand in the non-Medicaid market due to a change in population size or a change in the demographic composition of the population, such as population aging.

If the shift is sufficiently large, and the physician was treating Medicaid patients before the shift, the physician may decide to close the practice to Medicaid patients. The physician will consider a dollar decrease in per unit administrative cost fully equivalent to a dollar increase in price.

An increase in a factor affecting practice cost, such as an increase in the wage rates of nonphysician personnel employed by the physician, would raise marginal

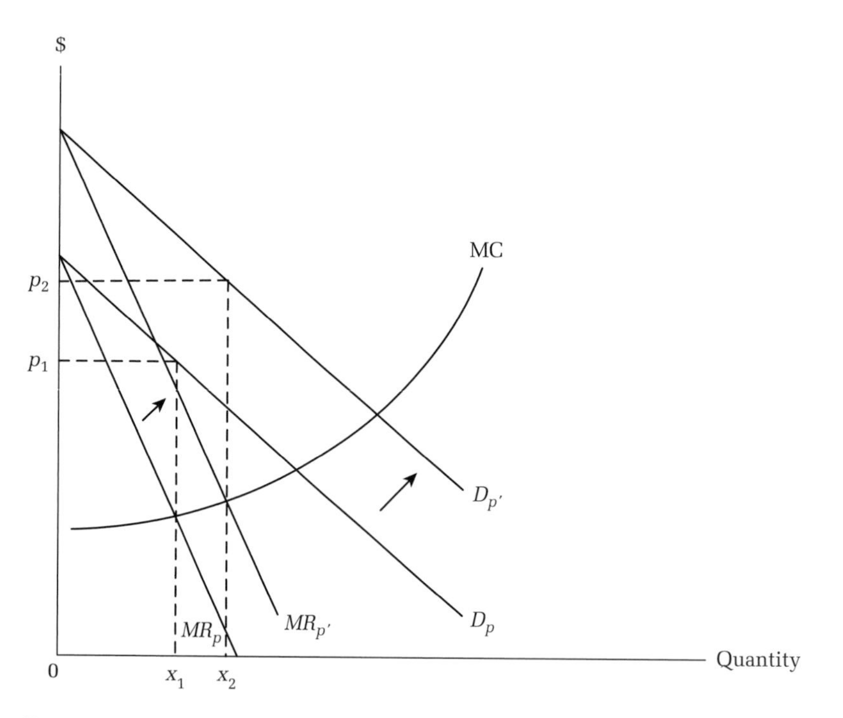

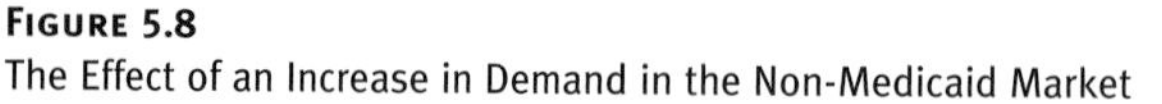

FIGURE 5.8
The Effect of an Increase in Demand in the Non-Medicaid Market

cost. If the physician was participating in both markets before the change, the physician would be expected to reduce output to Medicaid patients first. Output to the Medicaid market would be reduced until marginal revenue from Medicaid patients equaled marginal cost, which is assumed to fall with decreases in output, such as decreasing from $x_T - x_2$ to $x_T' - x_2$, as shown in figure 5.9. Output to the non-Medicaid market would not be affected as long as the physician was accepting Medicaid patients, such as x_2 in figure 5.9. But once the physician became a nonparticipant in Medicaid, output in the non-Medicaid market would fall until marginal revenue in the non-Medicaid market equaled marginal cost.

EMPIRICAL EVIDENCE

Economists have conducted much empirical analysis of physician decision-making based on this two-market model or variants of it. Overall, these studies documented a strong relationship between Medicaid fees relative to other payers and physician participation in Medicaid (see Sloan, Mitchell, and Cromwell 1978; Hadley 1979; Held and Holahan 1985; Mitchell 1991; Adams 1994). Decreases in fees paid for providing services to Medicaid patients reduce physician willingness to accept

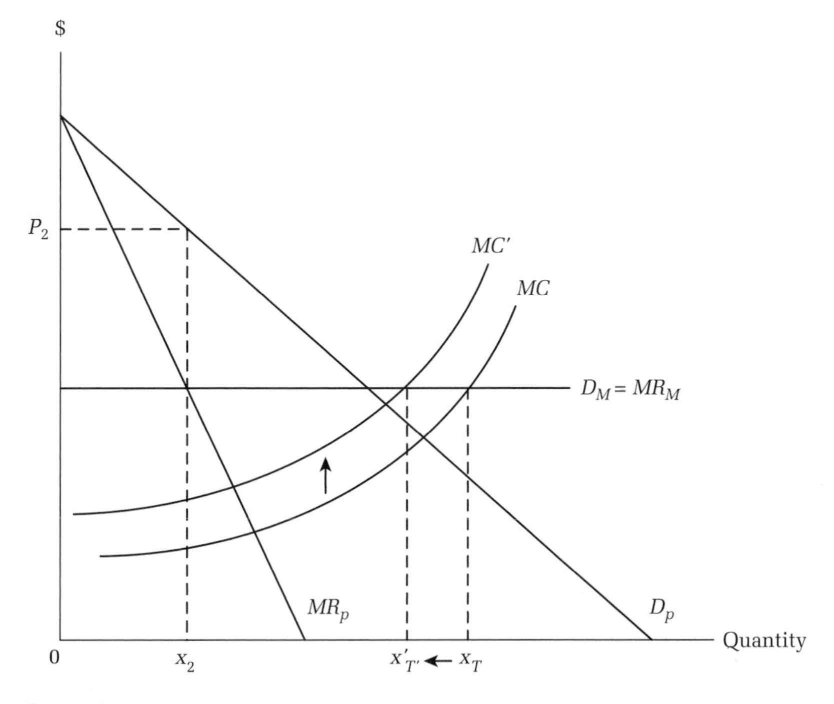

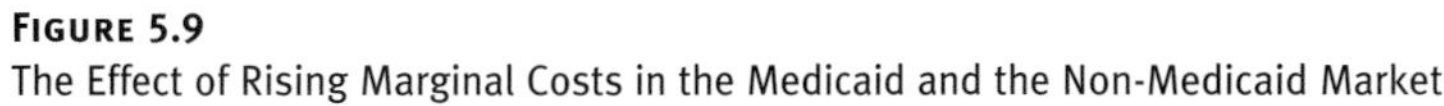
Figure 5.9
The Effect of Rising Marginal Costs in the Medicaid and the Non-Medicaid Market

Medicaid patients, and conversely for increases in such fees (Sloan, Mitchell, and Cromwell 1978; Baker and Royalty 2000; Cunningham and Hadley 2008). Publicly employed physicians see fewer Medicaid patients when Medicaid fees increase (Baker and Royalty 2000), but this is presumably because Medicaid patients' access to private physicians has increased. Studies using data on Medicaid-covered individuals in general provide support for the framework. For example, in one study, when Medicaid fees increased, Medicaid recipients were more likely to have a usual source of medical care and were more likely to visit a physician (Shen and Zuckerman 2005).

The lesson for Medicaid programs is that they compete for physician time. Medicaid fees and ease of collection are important determinants of physician willingness to accept Medicaid patients for care.

We have described what economists call third-degree price discrimination here. There is also first-degree price discrimination, which involves charging each consumer the price that represents the consumer's maximum willingness to pay for the good or service. Physicians can price discriminate over quantities for the same consumer as well as across consumers.

5.5 Summary and Conclusions

Economists distinguish between the short and the long run. This chapter has been organized around this conceptual distinction. Our analysis of long-run decisions included choice of occupation, such as a career in medicine; choice of physician specialty; choice of geographic location; and choice of practice mode. Since this book is about health economics, we focused on financial incentives and their role in career choices. While money affects students' choices, clearly other incentives matter as well. The economic analysis of long-run decisions physician make has been predominantly of US data. In the United States, there are definite financial returns to specialization. One remarkable finding is that although there has been a lot of public rhetoric emphasizing the importance of primary care, there is substantial financial incentive not to enter primary care fields, and this differential has persisted over time. The framework for analyzing geographic location of physicians assumes that market pressures cause physicians to locate in smaller communities when physicians become more numerous in the aggregate. This assumes that physicians cannot generate demand for their own services. If they can, physicians could continue to locate in large cities without experiencing a decline in their earnings. Group practice offers several advantages, including diversification against the risk of reduced earnings, since incomes within the group are pooled. Yet such pooling may dilute financial incentives that individual physician members of the group face to devote effort to seeing patients and to practicing efficiently.

The short-run decisions involve choices about price and output, the quality of such output, and physician hours of work. The major question is whether or not standard economic models adequately describe markets for physicians' services. Our clear bias as authors is first to examine standard economic models to be sure they do not provide adequate explanations of the stylized facts. In fact, they do describe some features of these markets. Others who start with a bias that standard economic models may not be relevant in this context are attracted to the nonstandard models, especially the physician-induced demand model. The fact that more doctors leads to higher rates of utilization of physicians' services can be explained by standard models. The anomalies of pricing are less adequately explained by such models. We conclude that the empirical evidence supporting PID is not strong, but the evidence on the other side is insufficiently strong to rule it out either. Empirical evidence for the two-market model described at the end of this chapter is stronger than the evidence for PID on balance. This two-market model is based on a standard economic framework of price discrimination. Empirical evidence in support of this model, if anything, supports the relevance of a standard economic framework.

The debate in the health economics community about the adequacy of standard economic approaches for analyzing the physicians' services market continues, albeit at a reduced level, and we cannot resolve this debate here. Economists have debated the issue since the late 1960s and early 1970s, and the controversy is not fully settled yet.

Key Concepts

- physician supply
- financial incentives
- internal rate of return
- present value
- economies of scale
- economies of scope
- monopolistic competition
- credence goods
- search goods
- experience goods
- backward-bending supply curve
- substitution effect
- income effect
- target income
- physician-induced demand
- asymmetric information
- price discrimination

Review and Discussion Questions

5.1 List three factors that are plausible influences on physicians' marginal revenue product and explain your answers.

5.2 In this chapter, we noted there is some empirical evidence that beginning medical students systematically underestimate physicians' earnings. What might explain why prospective medical students and beginning medical students tend to underestimate earnings in this occupation?

5.3 The physician (supplier)-induced demand model has been proposed as a framework for explaining important features of physicians' services markets. Answer the following questions about physician-induced demand:

a. What is meant by physician-induced demand?

b. Specifically which stylized facts about physicians' services markets does PID attempt to explain?

c. What empirical evidence has been used to support the PID hypothesis?

d. What would be the consequences of an increase in physician supply on the price of physician services, the quantity of physician visits, and total physician expenditures according to the PID hypothesis? How would these predictions differ from those of a conventional economic model of physician behavior?

5.4 Explain the distinction between perfectly competitive and monopolistically competitive markets. Which type of market structure provides a better description of the market for physicians' services? Justify your answer.

5.5 Define "search," "experience," and "credence" goods. Which label best applies to each of the following? Discuss each case and justify your answers.

a. notebook computer;

b. physician office visit;

c. applying for admission to medical school;

d. surgical treatment;

e. prescription drugs.

5.6 If the internal rate of return on legal education were twice that of the internal rate of return on medical education, how would you determine whether or not this is an equilibrium differential? Be sure to explain the distinction between the difference in compensation that represents an equilibrium differential from one that does not.

5.7 As reported in Gaynor and Gertler's paper, more than 60 percent of US physicians practice in some type of group setting.

a. List the pros and cons of group practices as compared to solo practice. That is, what benefits can physicians receive if they join the group practice, and what costs do physicians or society as a whole need to pay for group practices?

b. Which of the following doctors are more likely to join group practices, other things being equal? Explain your answers.

i. risk-averse versus risk-neutral physicians;

ii. young versus mature physicians;

iii. male versus female physicians.

5.8 The Pauly-Satterthwaite model was developed to explain why physicians' fees tend to be higher in markets with more physicians relative to the population.

a. Using graphs, show why physicians' fees may be higher in geographic areas in which physicians are relatively numerous.

b. What is the argument that search costs are higher in market areas with more doctors (according to the model)? How would the existence of other organizations, such as governments and private health insurers, as participants in the market for physicians' services affect the analysis?

5.9 Suppose you are contemplating a career as a physician, and you hear the following news from your country. Explain whether the following news is "good news" or "bad news" for your decision to choose medicine as a career. Good news means that the event increases your financial incentive to become a physician, and vice versa for bad news. Discuss each case separately, and justify your answers. Identify uncertainties that add ambiguity to the analysis.

a. The share of gross domestic product spent on health care has increased substantially over time and is expected to increase in the future.

b. Payment reform will lead to a switch from fee-for-service payments to a capitation plan.

c. The government announces it will build a new medical school in your state.

d. The government announces it will implement national health insurance that will provide comprehensive benefits to every citizen.

EXERCISES

5.1 The following two tables are mean physician net income by physician age after expenses and before taxes (in thousands of dollars), by year and by specialty.

Table A: Physician Age and Earnings ($ thous.)

	1973	1974	1975	1977	1978	1979	1981	1982	1983
Physician age									
Less than 36 years	32.8	40.6	43.7	49.6	49.0	64.3	62.5	73.3	77.0
36–45 years	51.9	57.1	62.9	69.9	70.1	87.5	98.1	100.2	110.2
46–55 years	55.0	58.9	62.3	67.7	76.2	87.1	110.8	116.5	133.6
56–65 years	48.3	49.3	54.1	58.7	65.3	75.9	95.6	99.5	103.1
66 or more years	31.9	34.0	35.0	36.8	44.4	54.9	68.3	64.3	71.9

Table B: Physician Specialty and Earnings ($ thous.)

	Specialty									
	All Physicians*	GP/FP	Int. Med.	Surg.	Ped.	Ob./Gyn.	Rad.	Psych.	Anesth.	Path.
Physician age										
Less than 36 years	77.0	57.9	68.0	108.8	44.7	78.9	100.3	64.9	126.9	90.3
36–45 years	110.2	68.2	95.1	146.3	81.2	118.7	150.1	81.7	146.1	109.9
46–55 years	133.6	77.8	125.4	183.8	81.2	139.4	161.6	90.4	161.3	134.1
56–65 years	103.1	76.4	98.3	120.0	73.6	129.0	171.5	79.0	119.8	141.3
66 or more years	71.9	50.0	75.0	94.8	59.4	89.5	—	62.1		

Notes: *Includes physicians in specialties not listed separately. Abbreviations: GP/FP, general practitioner/family practitioner; Int. Med., internal medicine; Surg., surgery; Ped., pediatrics; Ob./Gyn., obstetrics/gynecology; Rad., radiology; Psych., psychiatry; Anesth., anesthesiology; and Path., pathology.

a. Based on data reported in these two tables, please compute the present value of a medical education, assuming a 3 percent real discount rate.

b. Based on the same data, please compute the internal rate of return on medical education.

5.2 Suppose a country has a total of three cities: city A has a population of 550,000, and cities B and C have populations of 200,000 and 10,000, respectively. Say there are 60 physicians in the country. Assume that per capita demand for medical care is the same in the three cities, and the cities are equally desirable places in which to practice medicine and live.

a. How will the physicians be allocated among the three cities if physicians' earnings are to be equalized among the cities?

b. Suppose physician supply increased by a third in the country. How would this affect the allocation of physicians among the cities?

5.3 Suppose the country's national health insurance authority cuts the price it pays physicians for performing a procedure. Use a goods-leisure analysis (goods or income on one axis and leisure on the other) to answer the following questions:

a. A backward-bending supply curve of labor can be derived from the indifference curve analysis of goods and leisure. Explain using graphs (one for the indifference curve analysis and the other for the supply of labor function corresponding to the indifference curve analysis).

b. Isolate income and substitution effects from a decrease in the wage rate. (*Note*: In isolating the income and substitution effect, the practice is to draw a line parallel to the new price line and tangent to the indifference curve where the person was *before* the price change.)

c. Now assume that Medicare is the only payer. Medicare decreases the unit price of a service from $34 to $24. Show how the goods-leisure analysis is useful for addressing this question. (You will need to translate price per unit of service into work hours. Just make an assumption and state what it is.)

5.4 Analyze the effects of the following changes on the physician's decision to participate in the Medicaid program and on the number of visits provided to Medicaid and privately insured patients.

a. A cut in the fee Medicaid pays physicians for a visit (and Medicaid requires physicians who accept this payment to accept it as payment in full). How would the cut affect the number of visits provided to Medicaid patients? Use a graph. Show the point at which the doctor will not provide care to Medicaid patients at all.

b. A $10 increase in the amount a private insurer pays per visit. Show the effect of the price change on the provision of care to Medicaid and private patients.

c. A 15 percent increase in the wage rates of nonphysician personnel employed in the practice. (You need to assume a fraction of practice expense that goes to the wages of nonphysician personnel.) How will this wage change affect physician participation in Medicaid? Show graphically.

5.5 In 1988, there was a Medicare fee reduction in the United States. Medicare cut the payment for open heart surgery by 2–15 percent. Answer the following questions:

a. For thoracic surgeons, who perform open heart surgery, what is the income effect of this fee cut?

b. What is the substitution effect induced by this fee cut, again for thoracic surgeons?

c. What happens when the income effect dominates the substitution effect? Does an insurer realize savings from a fee cut when the income effect dominates the substitution effect? Explain your answer. Suppose you were director of your country's national health insurance program. What public policies would you implement if you knew that the income effect dominates the substitution effect?

Online Supplemental Material

Geographic Distribution of Physicians

http://www.ncbi.nlm.nih.gov/pmc/articles/PMC1361233

Physician Supply

http://online.wsj.com/article/SB10001424052702304506904575180331528424238.html

Physician Income

http://economix.blogs.nytimes.com/2009/07/17/what-is-a-just-physician-income

Supplemental Readings

Dulleck, U., and R. Kerschbamer. 2006. On Doctors, Mechanics, and Computer Specialists: The Economics of Credence Goods. *Journal of Economic Literature* 44 (1): 5–42.

Nicholson, S. 2008. Medical Career Choices and Rates of Return. In *Incentives and Choice in Health Care*, ed. F. A. Sloan and. H. Kasper, 195–226. Cambridge, MA: MIT Press.

Rosenthal, M. B., A. Zaslavsky, and J. P. Newhouse. 2005. The Geographic Distribution of Physicians Revisited. *Health Services Research* 40 (6): 1931–1952.

Williams, T. E., B. Satiani, A. Thomas, et al. 2009. The Impending Shortage and the Estimated Cost of Training the Future. *Annals of Surgery* 250 (4): 590–597.

References

Adams, E. K. 1994. Effect of Increased Medicaid Fees on Physician Participation and Enrollee Service Utilization in Tennessee, 1985–1988. *Inquiry* 31 (2): 173–187.

Baker, L. C., and A. B. Royalty. 2000. Medicaid Policy, Physician Behavior, and Health Care for the Low-Income Population. *Journal of Human Resources* 35 (3): 480–502.

Baltagi, B. H., E. Bratberg, and T. H. Holmås. 2005. A Panel Data Study of Physicians' Labor Supply: The Case of Norway. *Health Economics* 14 (10): 1035–1045.

Becker, G. S. 1964. *Human Capital*. New York: National Bureau of Economic Research.

Bhattacharya, J. 2005. Specialty Selection and Lifetime Returns to Specialization within Medicine. *Journal of Human Resources* 40 (1): 115–143.

Boardman, A. E., B. Dowd, J. M. Eisenberg, et al. 1983. A Model of Physicians' Practice Attributes Determination. *Journal of Health Economics* 2 (3): 259–268.

Carlsen, F., and J. Grytten. 1998. More Physicians: Improved Availability or Induced Demand? *Health Economics* 7 (6): 495–508.

Chalkley, M., and C. Tilley. 2005. The Existence and Nature of Physician Agency: Evidence of Stinting from the British National Health Service. *Journal of Economics & Management Strategy* 14 (3): 647–664.

Cooper, R. A. 2004. Weighing the Evidence for Expanding Physician Supply. *Annals of Internal Medicine* 141 (9): 705–714.

Cunningham, P. J., and J. Hadley. 2008. Effects of Changes in Incomes and Practice Circumstances on Physicians' Decisions to Treat Charity and Medicaid Patients. *Milbank Memorial Fund Quarterly: Health and Society* 86 (1): 91–123.

Dranove, D., and P. Wehner. 1994. Physician-Induced Demand for Childbirths. *Journal of Health Economics* 13 (1): 61–73.

Dulleck, U., and R. Kerschbamer. 2006. On Doctors, Mechanics, and Computer Specialists: The Economics of Credence Goods. *Journal of Economic Literature* 44 (1): 5–42.

Evans, R. G. 1974. Supplier-Induced Demand. In *The Economics of Health and Medical Care*, ed. M. Perlman, 162–173. London: Macmillan.

Ferrall, C., A. W. Gregory, and W. G. Tholl. 1998. Endogenous Work Hours and Practice Patterns of Canadian Physicians. *Canadian Journal of Economics—Revue Canadienne d'Economique* 31 (1): 1–27.

Friedman, M., and S. Kuznets. 1945. *Income from Independent Professional Practice*. New York: National Bureau of Economic Research.

Fuchs, V. R. 1978. The Supply of Surgeons and the Demand for Operations. *Journal of Human Resources* 13 (Supplement): 35–56.

Gaynor, M., and P. Gertler. 1995. Moral Hazard and Risk Spreading in Partnerships. *RAND Journal of Economics* 26 (4): 591.

Gaynor, M., J. B. Rebitzer, and L. J. Taylor. 2004. Physician Incentives in Health Maintenance Organizations. *Journal of Political Economy* 112 (4): 915–931.

Gruber, J., J. Kim, and D. Mayzlin. 1999. Physician Fees and Procedure Intensity: The Case of Cesarean Delivery. *Journal of Health Economics* 18 (4): 473–490.

Gruber, J., and M. Owings. 1996. Physician Financial Incentives and Cesarean Section Delivery. *RAND Journal of Economics* 27 (1): 99–123.

Hadley, J. 1979. Physician Participation in Medicaid: Evidence from California. *Health Services Research* 14 (4): 266–280.

Held, P. J., and J. Holahan. 1985. Containing Medicaid Costs in an Era of Growing Physician Supply. *Health Care Financing Review* 7 (1): 49–60.

Kessel, R. 1958. Price Discrimination in Medicine. *Journal of Law & Economics* 1 (1): 20–53.

Lien, H. M., C. T. A. Ma, and T. G. McGuire. 2004. Provider-Client Interactions and Quantity of Health Care Use. *Journal of Health Economics* 23 (6): 1261–1283.

Lin, H.-C., S. Kao, C.-H. Tang, et al. 2005. Using a Population-Based Database to Explore the Inter-Specialty Differences in Physician Practice Incomes in Taiwan. *Health Policy* (Amsterdam) 73 (3): 253–262.

Madden, D., A. Nolan, and B. Nolan. 2005. GP Reimbursement and Visiting Behaviour in Ireland. *Health Economics* 14 (10): 1047–1060.

McGuire, T. G. 2008. Physician Fees and Behavior: Implications for Structuring a Fee Schedule. In *Incentives and Choice in Health Care*, ed. F. A. Sloan and H. Kasper, 263–288. Cambridge, MA: MIT Press.

McGuire, T. G., and M. V. Pauly. 1991. Physician Response to Fee Changes with Multiple Payers. *Journal of Health Economics* 10 (4): 385–410.

Miller, R. H., and H. S. Luft. 2002. HMO Plan Performance Update: An Analysis of the Literature, 1997–2001. *Health Affairs* 21 (4): 63–86.

Mitchell, J. 1991. Physician Participation in Medicaid Revisited. *Medical Care* 29 (7): 645–653.

Mitchell, J., J. Hadley, and D. J. Gaskin. 2002. Spillover Effects of Medicare Fee Reductions: Evidence from Ophthalmology. *International Journal of Health Care Finance and Economics* 2 (3): 171–188.

Newhouse, J. P. 1973. Economics of Group Practice. *Journal of Human Resources* 8 (1): 37–56.

Newhouse, J. P., A. P. Williams, B. W. Bennett, et al. 1982. Where Have All the Doctors Gone? *Journal of the American Medical Association* 247 (17): 2392–2396.

Nguyen, N. X., and F. W. Derrick. 1997. Physician Behavioral Response to a Medicare Price Reduction. *Health Services Research* 32 (3): 283–299.

Nicholson, S. 2005. How Much Do Medical Students Know about Physician Income? *Journal of Human Resources* 40 (1): 100–114.

Nicholson, S. 2008. Medical Career Choices and Rates of Return. In *Incentives and Choice in Health Care*, ed. F. A. Sloan and H. Kasper, 195–226. Cambridge, MA: MIT Press.

Noether, M. 1986. The Growing Supply of Physicians: Has the Market Become More Competitive? *Journal of Labor Economics* 4 (4): 503–537.

Pauly, M. V., and M. A. Satterthwaite. 1981. The Pricing of Primary Care Physicians' Services: A Test of the Role of Consumer Information. *Bell Journal of Economics* 12 (2): 488–506.

Rizzo, J. A., and D. Blumenthal. 1994. Physician Labor Supply: Do Income Effects Matter? *Journal of Health Economics* 13 (4): 433–453.

Rosenthal, M. B., A. Zaslavsky, and J. P. Newhouse. 2005. The Geographic Distribution of Physicians Revisited. *Health Services Research* 40 (6): 1931–1952.

Satterthwaite, M. A. 1979. Consumer Information, Equilibrium Industry Price, and the Number of Sellers. *Bell Journal of Economics* 10 (2): 483–502.

Schwartz, W. B., A. P. Williams, J. P. Newhouse, et al. 1988. Are We Training Too Many Medical Subspecialists? *Journal of the American Medical Association* 259 (2): 233–239.

Shannon, G. W., and M. P. Cutchin. 1994. General Practitioner Distribution and Population Dynamics: Munich, 1950–1990. *Social Science & Medicine* 39 (1): 23–38.

Shen, Y.-C., and S. Zuckerman. 2005. The Effect of Medicaid Payment Generosity on Access and Use among Beneficiaries. *Health Services Research* 40 (3): 723–744.

Showalter, M. H., and N. K. Thurston. 1997. Taxes and Labor Supply of High-Income Physicians. *Journal of Public Economics* 66 (1): 73–97.

Sloan, F. A. 1971. The Demand for Higher Education: The Case of Medical School Applicants. *Journal of Human Resources* 6 (4): 466–489.

Sloan, F. A., J. Mitchell, and J. Cromwell. 1978. Physician Participation in State Medicaid Programs. *Journal of Human Resources* 13 (Supplement): 211–245.

Sloan, F. A., and B. Steinwald. 1975. The Role of Health Insurance in the Physicians' Services Market. *Inquiry* 12 (4): 275–299.

Weeks, W. B., and A. E. Wallace. 2002. The More Things Change: Revisiting a Comparison of Educational Costs and Incomes of Physicians and Other Professionals. *Academic Medicine* 77 (4): 312–319.

Weeks, W. B., A. E. Wallace, M. M. Wallace, et al. 1994. A Comparison of the Educational Costs and Incomes of Physicians and Other Professionals. *New England Journal of Medicine* 330 (18): 1280–1286.

Yip, W. C. 1998. Physician Response to Medicare Fee Reductions: Changes in the Volume of Coronary Artery Bypass Graft (CABG) Surgeries in the Medicare and Private Sectors. *Journal of Health Economics* 17 (6): 675–699.

CHAPTER 6

HOSPITALS

Worldwide, hospitals incorporate the latest in medical technology in a country and tend to care for the most acutely ill persons. Patients seek hospital care either because they have an acute illness, such as pneumonia, or because they are experiencing particularly serious adverse consequences of a chronic illness, such as a heart attack among persons with heart disease.

This was not always so. In the nineteenth century, in such countries as the United States and the United Kingdom, hospitals tended to be almshouses, caring for the poor, while more affluent persons received care at home. Given very inadequate infectious disease control in hospitals, patients ran the risk of acquiring diseases during their hospital stays that they did not have on admission. During the first half of the twentieth century, infection control in hospitals improved appreciably. Especially in high-income countries, hospitals made most of their strides in technology adoption during the latter half of the twentieth century, but at the same time, more sophisticated technology and more intensive care in hospitals led to increases in hospital costs.

During much of the latter part of the twentieth century and on into the twenty-first century, governments and private insurers in high-income countries have devoted much effort to hospital cost containment. One reason why care in many hospitals is so expensive is that hospital care tends to be very labor-intensive. More often than not, labor in hospitals is not a substitute for capital. Rather, technological change is embodied in plant and equipment, for example in surgical suites and medical imaging equipment. A considerable amount of labor is needed to operate the technology. Thus, capital and labor in hospitals are often complements.

The hospital occupies a central place in health systems in all countries. This chapter describes important theories of hospital behavior and why the private not-for-profit ownership form is dominant in many countries. We present empirical evidence on differences in hospital performance by ownership. One special feature of hospitals involves the relationship between the medical staff and the hospital, and this relationship is evolving, as described in the chapter. A major policy decision in every country is how to pay hospitals for services rendered. We discuss alternative payment arrangements, the role of public regulation in this sector, and reliance on competition as opposed to hospital regulation as a method for achieving socially desirable outcomes.

6.1 CONTEXT

Aside from the technological sophistication of many hospitals, important among the distinguishing characteristics of hospitals is that relatively few hospitals are organized on a for-profit basis. This is in contrast to physicians' practices, pharmaceutical companies, and nursing homes, which are most often organized on a for-profit basis. Rather, private not-for-profit and public ownership forms are most numerous, with the relative shares of not-for-profit and public forms varying substantially among countries. A not-for-profit or public hospital may be expected to make decisions about the mix and amount of services it provides and pricing based on considerations other than pure profit seeking. Profits cannot be distributed to shareholders, or more generally "residual claimants," as occurs with for-profit organizations. Residual claimants are parties that receive the balance remaining after labor and capital inputs have been paid. This limitation on the distribution of profits has been termed a "nondistribution constraint" (Hansmann 1996). Rather than distribute profits, such funds may be allocated to other uses, for example, to providing a higher level of quality than the market demands.

The dominance of organizational forms other than the for-profit form leads to several questions, addressed in this chapter. First, how do hospital not-for-profits differ from their for-profit counterparts, and what is the economic rationale for this form of organization? Second, how does ownership form affect hospital performance? This latter question is important in sectors other than health care. Countries make various decisions about ownership in a variety of sectors of the economy, such as whether or not to nationalize telephone or airline companies or keep them private. Third, who is the residual claimant—the party to whom profits and losses accrue after all revenue has been received and all inputs in the production process have been paid—when the hospital is not-for-profit: physicians at the hospital? Hospital administrators? Trustees? And why does the identity of the residual claimant matter? Private hospitals may have three types of managers: administrators employed by the hospital, the medical staff, and hospital trustees. Rather than report to hospital trustees, public hospital administrators may report to public officials within a municipality's department of health.

Hospitals are not the only type of organization in which for-profit entities are a minority. Libraries, museums, and houses of worship are other examples. Our discussion of not-for-profitness and its effects is applicable to such types of organizations as well—with some differences in detail reflecting differences in product markets and attributes.

In some countries, such as the United States, physicians who practice at hospitals (the "medical staff") are generally not employed by hospitals but rather are affiliated with independent physicians' practices. There are medical staff organizations in hospitals, which set operating rules for the provision of medical care within hospitals, but medical staff organizations typically do not become involved in financial transactions. In many other countries, for example Germany, the medical staff is employed by the hospital. Other physicians are in independent practice but do not treat patients within the walls of the hospital.

The separate organizational forms of physicians and hospitals are not unique to the hospital sector. For example, independent farmers form purchasing cooperatives. These cooperatives serve the collective interests of individual independent farmers by allowing them to purchase supplies such as seed and fertilizer at lower prices than they could if they purchased individually rather than collectively.

Increasing hospital costs, which have far outpaced inflation and the growth of gross domestic product, have led governments to adopt several alternative approaches to regulating hospitals, including imposing controls over hospital entry into a market and controls over hospital prices and budgets. Again, although regulation is common in the hospital sector worldwide, such regulation is not unique to hospitals. For example, private transportation companies (e.g., taxis, buses) are often subject to regulation. Antitrust enforcement has become increasingly common in such countries as the United States. However, such enforcement is clearly not unique to the hospital sector in that country.

6.2 Alternative Models of Hospital Behavior

The Profit-Maximizing Hospital: The Base Case

Even though most hospitals are not-for-profit, the for-profit ownership form is the most common in most other sectors, and for-profit decision making provides a useful framework for comparing the other frameworks presented below. We assume that health care delivery in the country is essentially private. The models described in this chapter are most applicable to high-income countries. Furthermore, since the authors have been based in the United States, the models are mostly directly applicable to US hospitals, but they offer useful frameworks for other countries as well, although with some modifications to reflect institutional practices in these countries. Chapter 13 describes health care systems in which the provision of services is public.

Initially we make these assumptions: First, the hospital decides on the quantity of services it will provide during a given period, say a day.[1] A measure of quantity is the number of patients hospitalized at the facility in a day.

The hospital faces a downward-sloping demand curve for its services. As explained earlier, having a downward-sloping demand curve means that the organization has the power to set price. The hospital's product market is not perfectly competitive. In most hospital markets, there are few sellers, if for no other reason than residents are likely to prefer nearby hospitals to those at greater differences, which in and of itself confers some market power on individual hospitals. Another factor affecting the competitiveness of individual hospitals is the market power of purchasers of hospital services. Where insurers or governments have market power, individual hospitals have less market power, and conversely. If the market for hospital services were competitive or if a government agency had the power to dictate the prices hospitals charge, the demand curve facing the organization would be horizontal.

With a downward-sloping demand curve, there is a one-to-one relationship between quantity of output x and p, the price the organization charges for the single product it sells. $p = p(x)$.

Let profit be π. Then

$$\pi = p(x)x - C(x),$$

where $C(x)$ is the total cost of producing output at quantity x.

$$\frac{dC}{dx}$$

is the first derivative of total cost with respect to x.

$$\frac{dC}{dx}$$

is the firm's marginal cost. Total revenue $R(x)$ is $p(x)x$. Marginal revenue is

$$\frac{dR}{dx} = \frac{dp}{dx}x + p(x).$$

1. *We will use calculus in this chapter; we suppress a subscript for the individual hospital.*

Profit is maximized at

$$\frac{d\pi}{dx} = 0. \text{ That is, } \frac{dp}{dx} \cdot x + p(x) - \frac{dC}{dx} = 0.$$

Quantity is set at the quantity at which marginal revenue equals marginal cost. Once optimal quantity x^* has been determined, optimal price p^* is read from the demand curve. The optimal values are shown graphically in chapter 5, figure 5.5a.

In the previous chapter in the monopolistic competition model, marginal revenue was shown to equal marginal cost at the point at which profit was zero. Monopolistic competition is more realistic in the physician than in the hospital market since physicians are often numerous in a market. By contrast, there are typically few hospitals—often only one. Figure 5.5b depicts optimal price-quantity combinations under monopolistic competition. In this model, profit is zero in equilibrium. This is shown with the average cost curve tangent to the average revenue curve. By contrast, in the simple monopoly case, the firm is likely to earn a profit shown by the rectangle (see fig. 5.5a).

Now consider a case in which the firm has control over both the quantity and the quality of the product it provides. Let the quality level be y. Then the problem for the firm is to set quantity, quality, and hence price, which rises with increases in quality but falls with increases in quantity. Total cost C is positively related to both x and y.

$$\text{Profit } \pi = p(x,y)x - C(x,y). \tag{6.1}$$

Finding the optimal levels of x and y that maximize π involves setting x^* at the quantity at which marginal revenue equals marginal cost and y^* at the quality at which marginal revenue from changes in y equals the marginal cost of changing y.

$$\frac{dp}{dx} x + p(x,y) - \frac{dC}{dx} \text{ and } \frac{dp}{dy} \cdot x + p(x,y) = \frac{dC}{dy} \tag{6.2}$$

Intuitively, the firm finds the quantity-quality combination that yields the largest *difference* between revenue and cost.

An important implication of this model is that firms will provide different levels of quality. Quality will be higher when the price increase associated with an increase in quality is higher, that is,

$$\frac{dp}{dy}$$

is higher and/or the added cost of producing higher quality is lower, that is,

$$\frac{dC}{dy},$$

although positive, is relatively low.

A Model of a Private Not-for-Profit Hospital

The Model's Basics

The above model is for firms that have profit maximization as an organizational objective. Other models have been developed to depict hospital behavior when the hospital is not organized on a for-profit basis.

In an oft-cited model of a not-for-profit hospital developed by Joseph Newhouse (1970), hospitals are not interested in profit for its own sake. Rather, the hospital is interested in maximizing utility (U), which depends on the amount of quantity and quality of care the hospital provides. Let $U = U(x,y)$. The hospital maximizes utility subject to a constraint.

To derive the constraint, consider the hospital's demand and average cost curve in figure 6.1. The demand curve relates price to quantity of hospital care demanded; the average cost is a function of quantity as well. Both demand and average cost curves are defined for a given quality level. When quality changes, the

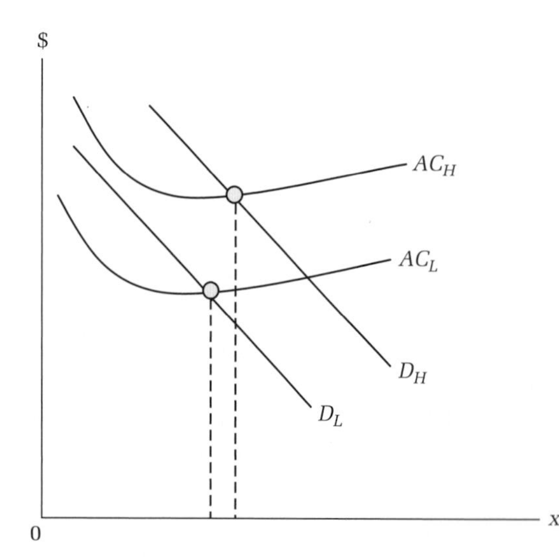

FIGURE 6.1
Hospital Demand and Cost Curves for Hospitals with High (H) and Low (L) Quality
Figure 6.1 shows intersections when quality is allowed to vary from L to H, not optimal quantity (x), when the hospital is the profit maximizer.

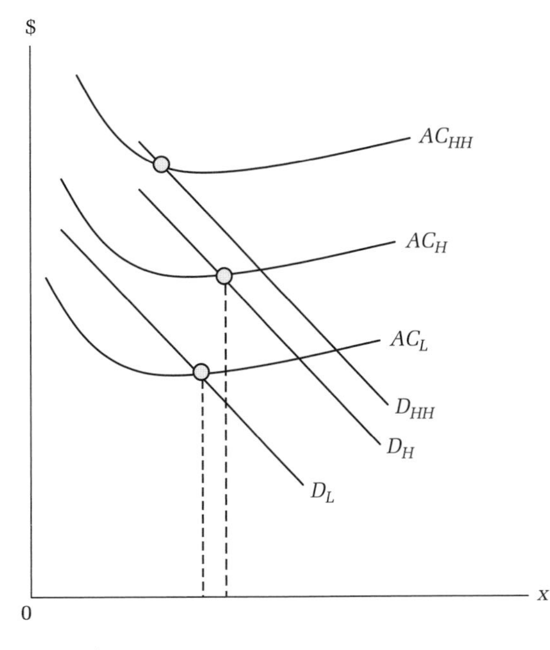

FIGURE 6.2
Hospital Demand and Cost Curves for Hospitals with High (*H*), Low (*L*), and Very High (*HH*) Quality. Intersections when quality is allowed to vary from *L* to *H* to *HH*. Note that the intersections move from left to right to left.

demand and cost curves must shift, the former, however, only if patients are willing to pay a higher price for a higher-quality level. If not, the demand curve does not shift. The demand curve shifts outward (rightward) as quality is increased. But the average cost curve ($C/x = AC$) also increases with increases in hospital quality.

The demand curve relates average price to quantity. Let R be the hospital's total revenue. Then average revenue or price is R/x. Thus, where the demand and average cost curves intersect, $R = C$, such as at the intersection of D_L and AC_L and D_H and AC_H, profit is zero. Since demand and average cost curves are defined for a single quality level, when quality changes, so do the intersections of the two curves. An increase in quality leads to an intersection at a higher level of x if for a given increase in quality, the demand curve shifts by more than the average cost curve, as seen when quality increases from a low level (L) to a high level (H), and conversely if the average cost curve shifts more than the demand curve, as when quality increases from H to HH (fig. 6.2).

A curve connecting the points of intersection of demand and average cost curves defines the hospital's production possibility curve (fig. 6.3). In the model, a not-for-profit hospital earns zero profit. The points along the production possibility curve represent points on which the hospital can operate. Points inside the production possibility curve are also feasible, but they do not yield zero hospital profit.

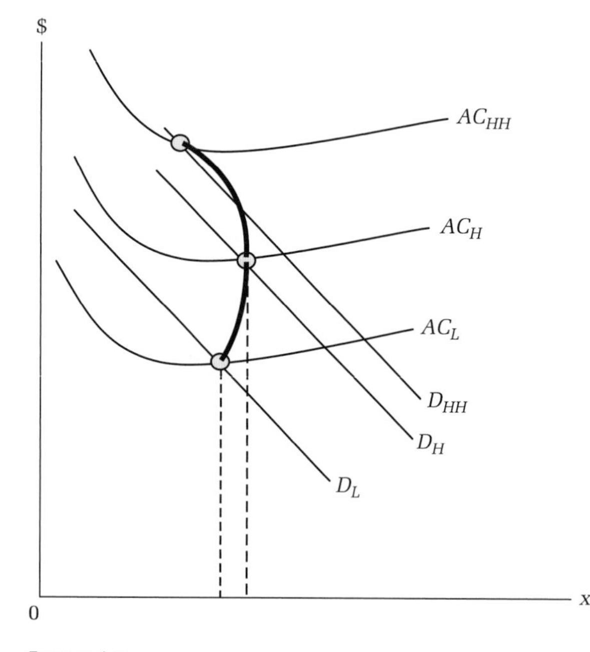

FIGURE 6.3
Hospital Quantity-Quality Frontier.
Intersections when quality is allowed to vary from *L* to *H*. to *HH*. The heavy black curve is the locus of intersections of *AC* and *D*. This is the production frontier or the production possibility curve.

The production possibility curve is positively sloped at low levels of quality but negatively sloped at higher levels of quality (fig. 6.4). There is an intuitive explanation for this pattern. At low levels of quality, a given increase in quality is highly valued by patients, resulting in relatively large outward shifts in demand relative to smaller upward shifts in average cost. At some level of quality, the two shifts are equal, and for higher levels of quality increase than this, the demand curve shifts out less than the average cost curve shifts up. Then the intersections move to the left, that is, to lower levels of quantity than if average cost had shifted less than the demand curve shifted.

Thus far, the hospital's levels of quality, quantity, price, and average cost are indeterminate. There are infinite combinations of these variables. To see how the hospital selects optimal levels of these variables, we recall that the hospital has a utility function, U, which depends on the same variables as does the production possibility curve, x and y. Utility is maximized at the point of tangency of the slope of the U and the production possibility curve (fig. 6.4). Since the slope of the hospital utility function is negative, depicting various combinations of x and y yielding the same utility, the tangency occurs mostly on the negatively sloped portion of the production possibility curve.

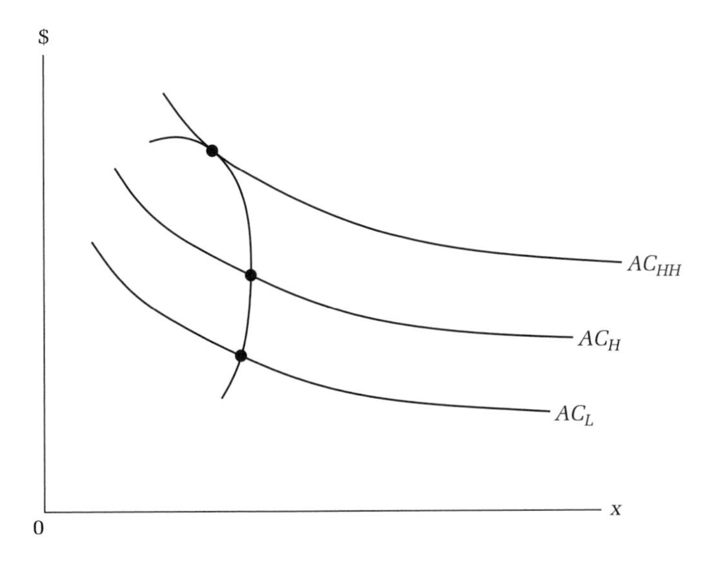

FIGURE 6.4
The Hospital's Optimum Quantity and Quality.
Intersections when quality is allowed to vary from *L* to *H* to *HH*. The graph shows the optimal quantity-quality combinations for the hospital.

Hospital utility functions are likely to differ among hospitals. Some hospitals may place a higher value on providing a high quantity of hospital care. Others may be more oriented toward providing high quality at the sacrifice of some quantity.

How is the hospital's utility defined? A first step is to identify who maximizes utility, that is, who makes choices on the hospital's behalf. Newhouse allows for several hospital "bosses" (our term), including hospital administrators, medical staff, and trustees. There is only one U, and the relative importance of each group in forming the hospital's U may be expected to differ among hospitals, as do relative preferences for x and y. For this reason, exactly which combination of x and y will be chosen by the hospital cannot be determined from the model. However, it is possible to assess the effects of certain changes that are beyond the hospital's control (exogenous changes) on the hospital's production possibility curves.

Thus far, we have been silent about what Newhouse meant by quality of hospital care. In the Newhouse model, quality is equated with money. A hospital with an average cost of $100 per patient day is half as good as one with a $200 average cost. Presumably the $200 hospital employs twice the level of inputs than the $100 per hospital day hospital does and in this sense is twice as good. This is admittedly a crude measure of quality. We defer our discussion of how quality of care is measured in the real world to chapter 7.

Effects of Exogenous Changes in Wage Rates, Population Size, Fraction of Persons with Health Insurance Coverage, and Subsidies of Hospitals

Exogenous changes, a general concept, here refer to changes beyond the hospital's control. Endogenous changes are ones the hospital makes in response to changes in various exogenous factors.

Important among the exogenous changes are the following: an increase in the wage rate of the hospital's employees, an increase in the population in the hospital's market area with health insurance coverage, and implementation of a fixed dollar subsidy per x by the city administration. We assume here that hospitals are price takers in markets for their labor. This means that hospitals must respond to wage increases offered by other potential employers of their labor. We also assume that the hospital has no influence over the public subsidies it receives. It is plausible that a change in the population with health insurance is exogenous to an individual hospital.

We leave it as exercises for readers to figure out how the production possibility curve will shift in response to each change. A fixed dollar subsidy per x will allow the hospital to charge patients a price that is less than average cost.

The Pauly-Redisch Model of the Not-for-Profit Hospital as a Physicians' Cooperative

Another well-known model of hospital behavior but one that emphasizes a completely different aspect of hospital behavior is by Pauly and Redisch (1973). This model, too, has stood the test of time.

In the United States, up to now, physicians who practice in hospitals most frequently do so as independent agents.[2] Although employment arrangements for physicians are becoming more common, most physicians who practice at a hospital are not employees of the hospital. Some but not the majority of physicians have contractual relationships with hospitals. Contracts have been most common among specialists whose presence is critical to hospital operations, including emergency room physicians, anesthesiologists, radiologists, and pathologists.

There is a medical staff organization at each hospital that is under the physicians' control. The hospital administration and his or her staff are responsible for employing hospital personnel such as nurses and laboratory technicians, purchasing medical supplies, and providing hospital plant and equipment and the maintenance thereof.

The medical staff organization grants individual physicians "staff privileges," which allow physicians to practice at the hospital. Physicians admit their patients to hospitals where they provide care for their patients. The medical staff organization sets many if not most of the clinical policies at the hospital, for example, which physicians are allowed to perform surgical procedures at the hospital, and limits on the types of surgical procedures that individual physicians can

2. In some countries, such as France, physicians who work in private hospitals are paid on a fee-for-service basis for the services they provide. However, the medical staff of public hospitals is salaried (Burstall and Wallerstein 1994, 377).

perform. Staff members who are employees of the hospital or self-employed but with a contractual arrangement with the hospital work with physicians who are not employees.

Hospital trustees serve on the board of the hospital. They meet periodically to review hospital operations and finances. Trustee approval is generally required to approve major changes in hospital policy or for major investments in hospital plant and equipment. At least historically, hospital trustees have had an oversight role, but they have often been fairly passive decision makers, relying for many of their decisions on the recommendations of the hospital administration and medical staff. In the United States, trustees may be specialized in health care, but more often they bring other experiences to the hospital board, such as business experience. Some hospital boards expect trustees to be actively involved in raising funds for the hospital. Since not-for-profit and public hospitals do not have shareholders, shareholders do not elect board members. Many board members are appointed by existing trustees or hospital executives, which potentially raises concerns about the independence of such board members, whether hospital performance is adequately scrutinized, and the power of boards constituted in this way. If boards are not powerful, this enhances the relative power of other hospital stakeholders, including the physicians who practice there.

The medical staff organization has the formal responsibility of evaluating physician competence before a physician is allowed to join the hospital medical staff. The organization is formally responsible for oversight of quality of care at the hospital. A stated rationale for medical staff organizations is quality assurance. However, by limiting entry, medical staffs may also have an anticompetitive effect on the market for hospital care. The Pauly-Redisch model focuses on such possible anticompetitive effects.

All medical staffs scrutinize physician credentials prior to admitting a physician to membership. However, membership on some medical staffs is closed. That is, the medical staff bars additional physicians from being included on the hospital's medical staff. The medical staff would not state that the entry barrier reflects self-serving anticompetitive motives. Rather, the rationale is likely to be cast in terms of lack of operating room capacity or lack of hospital capacity to allow additional physicians to admit their patients to the hospital more generally.

While hospitals' organizational structure in principle is designed to safeguard quality of patient care, from another vantage point the structure may bear a similarity to a cartel designed to maximize profits for the residual claimants, the group of individuals who receive the profit if a profit is made. Not-for-profit hospitals do not formally distribute profits to shareholders. This does not mean that profits are not earned; nor does it mean that profits are not distributed in some implicit form, for example, in the form of equipment that physicians use in their practices and for services for which they can bill separately, free and reserved parking for medical staff, hospital personnel who provide follow-up for surgical patients in the hospital, allowing the surgeon to see other patients in his or her hospital office, and travel to resort areas for meetings.

In their seminal paper, Mark Pauly and Michael Redisch (1973) noted the similarity between hospitals' medical staff organizations and other cooperatives, including workers' cooperatives, that existed in some socialist countries, such as the former Yugoslavia, or farmers' cooperatives in capitalist countries.

A cooperative may form for various reasons. For example, a farmers' cooperative may form to enable farmer members to realize economies in purchasing of seed and fertilizer or to own farm equipment jointly. The farmer members remain independent entrepreneurs. Any profit the cooperative earns is shared by the members. In some respects, the farmers' cooperative resembles the physician group practice described in chapter 5.

The Pauly-Redisch model relies on several assumptions. First, although the patient who is hospitalized receives two bills, one from the hospital and the other from the patient's physician, a widespread common practice in the United States, the patient cares only about the *total* price of the hospital stay, not the separate charges of the hospital and the physician. For this reason, demand as measured by the number of hospital stays demanded depends on the total price per hospital stay. A hospital stay typically spans several days. In this model, length of stay is assumed to be fixed.

Second, the Pauly-Redisch model takes the term "not-for-profit" literally. The hospital earns zero profit.[3] Any profit earned as a result of running the hospital accrues to the physician members of the medical staff.

Let p be the total price of the hospital stay and x be the total number of stays demanded. Then $p = p(x)$. Price p includes payment to the hospital and to the doctor. Let p_h be the price the hospital charges. The hospital must break even. That is, revenue or $p_h x = wL + cK$, where w is the wage rate paid hospital employees, L is the number of persons employed other than physicians, c is the price of capital, and K is the units of capital employed.

Total revenue is distributed between the hospital and the hospital's physicians (medical staff). Then $px = p_h x + Y_M M$, where Y_M is the mean income per physician on the medical staff and M is the number of medical staff members at the hospital. The product $Y_M M$ may be rewritten as $Y_M M = (p - p_h)x$. Then $Y_M = ((p - p_h)x)/M$. Substituting $wL - cK$ for $p_h x$ yields $Y_M = (px - wL - cK)/M$.

Quantity x is produced by three inputs, physicians working at the hospital, nonphysican labor, and capital. The quantity $x = x(M,L,K)$. Since $p = p(x)$, when x increases, p falls. Thus, adding more hospital inputs M, L, and K increases x and causes the price to fall.

3. *As noted above, in the United States, private not-for-profit hospitals generally earn profits.*

Input levels M, L, and K, which determine hospital output levels, are set to maximize income per doctor at the hospital. The collective decision of the hospital's doctors is thus to maximize Y_M, where $Y_M = (px - wL - cK)/M$. The total collective income of the doctors on the hospital's medical staff is the product of income per doctor and the number of doctors on the medical staff. Mathematically this is done by taking the first derivatives of Y_M and setting them to zero. These are termed the first-order conditions.

For non-physician labor, Y_M is maximized when this condition is satisfied:

$$\frac{\partial Y}{\partial L} M = \frac{p \cdot \frac{\partial x}{\partial L} + x \cdot \frac{\partial p}{\partial x} \cdot \frac{\partial x}{\partial L} - w}{M} = 0. \tag{6.3}$$

This equation can be rewritten as

$$\frac{\partial x}{\partial L}\left(p + x \cdot \frac{\partial p}{\partial x}\right) = w.$$

The first term on the left side is the marginal product of labor. The term in parentheses is the hospital's marginal revenue. The product of marginal product of labor and marginal revenue is the marginal revenue product of labor. Equation 6.3 indicates that the hospital hires labor until the marginal revenue product (MRP_L) equals the wage rate. This equilibrium condition for the optimal amount of labor for the hospital to employ (L^*) is shown in figure 6.5.

The same analysis applies for capital, but then K is substituted for L and c is substituted for w. For capital, maximizing income per physician requires setting K to K^*, where the marginal revenue product of capital is equal to the rental cost of capital c.

The condition for the optimal medical staff size M^* is more complicated.

$$\frac{\partial Y_M}{\partial M} = \frac{p \cdot \frac{\partial x}{\partial M} + x \frac{\partial p}{\partial x} \cdot \frac{\partial x}{\partial M}}{M} - \frac{p \cdot x - cK - wL}{M^2} = 0 \tag{6.4}$$

Multiply the equation by M and move the second term to the right side of the equation. This fraction, the first term, equals Y_M, the second term, which is income per doctor or, equivalently, the average revenue product of physicians at the hospital. The left side of the equation is the marginal revenue product of physicians (MRP_M). Thus, M^*, the optimal number of physicians on the medical staff of the hospital, is set at the point at which the average revenue product equals the marginal revenue product of physicians.

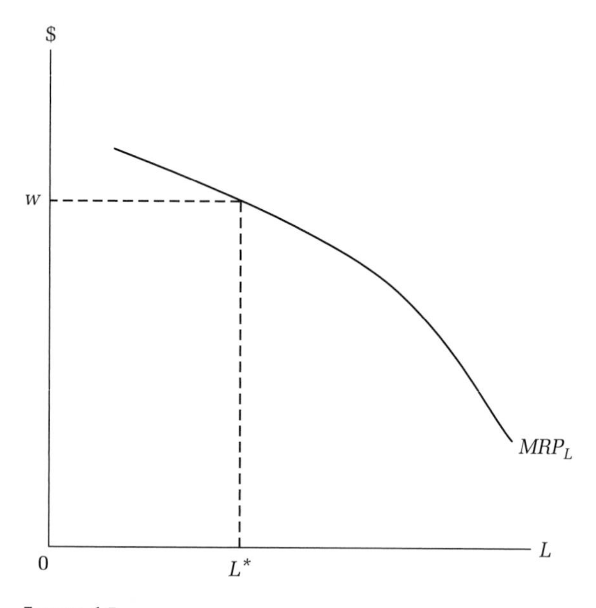

FIGURE 6.5
The Hospital's Choice of Labor Input

The equilibrium is shown graphically in figure 6.6. The MRP_M curve is negatively sloped. The other curve is the average net income of physicians on the medical staff, Y_M. Average net income initially rises with increases in hospital medical staff size M, reaches a maximum, and then decreases as additional physicians are added. Income per doctor is maximized at the quantity of medical staff members where the marginal revenue product of physicians equals average net income, which is the optimal medical staff size (M^*) from the collective financial vantage point of physicians on the hospital's medical staff. This is a private optimum, not a social optimum.

Thus far, we have assumed that the hospital medical staff can attract the number of physicians that is consistent with maximizing income per doctor on the hospital's medical staff. That is, once it decides how many doctors it wants, the doctors can be attracted and paid Y_M.

This assumption may be realistic for some communities, particularly in very large cities, but not for others, such as smaller communities. If the supply curve of physicians were infinitely elastic, like S_M (fig. 6.7), then there would be more physicians available to the hospital than M^*. If so, the hospital's medical staff would have to turn down applications for membership on the medical staff. In such a case, membership is "closed," and no applicants even if qualified on medical grounds would be able to join.

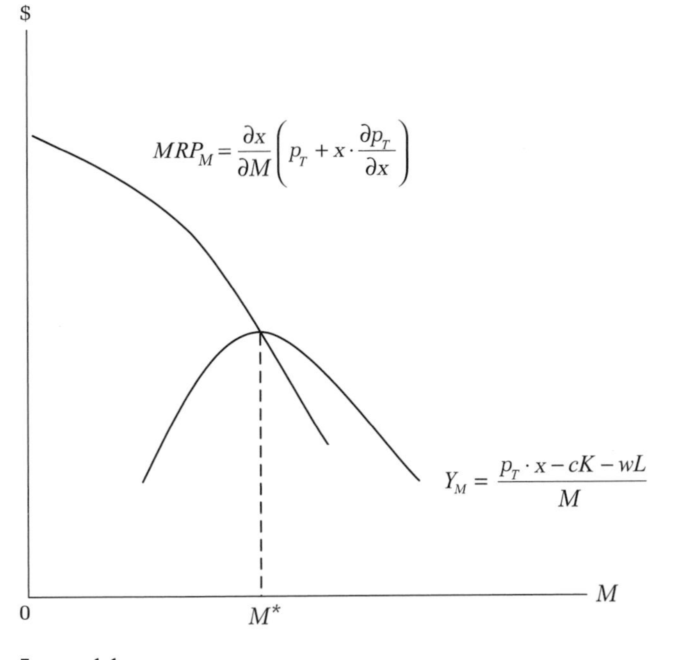

FIGURE 6.6
Number of Physicians on the Hospital's Medical Staff

But in many communities, hospitals face positively sloped supply-of-physicians curves (fig. 6.8). The slope is positive because physicians are heterogeneous with respect to their preferences for specific locations. For example, physicians and their families may place different emphasis on living near their relatives, being in a community with good schools, living near the beach or near the mountains, and so on. At a low income per physician, a hospital will attract those physicians with ties to the location, perhaps because they were born and raised in the location. To attract additional physicians, income will have to rise. At some income, physicians with preferences for locating near a beach or practicing in a major teaching hospital may be willing to locate in a mountainous community and practice at a nonteaching hospital. The notion of compensating wage or income differentials developed in the previous chapter applies here as well.

Figure 6.8 shows two alternative supply-of-physicians curves for individual hospitals, S_L and S_H. The reason that S_L lies upward and to the left of S_H is that it is located in an area that is generally less attractive to physicians than the area for which S_H is the relevant supply curve. Suppose, for example, that the crime rate is much higher in one city than in another. Then, holding other factors

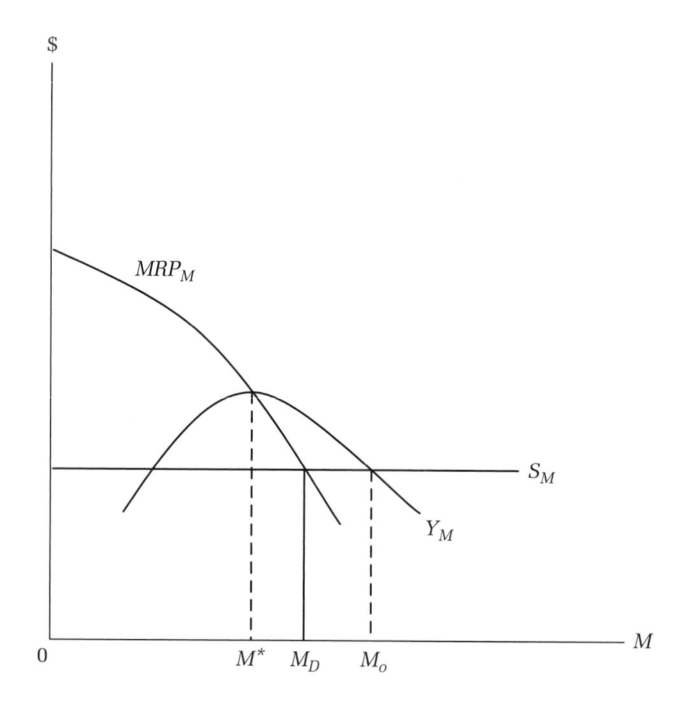

FIGURE 6.7

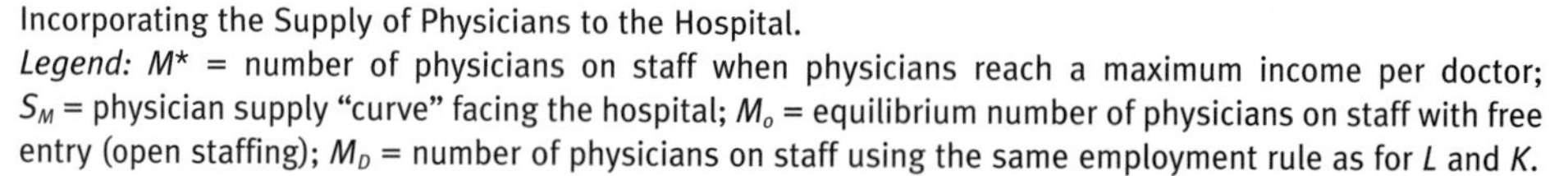
Incorporating the Supply of Physicians to the Hospital.
Legend: M^* = number of physicians on staff when physicians reach a maximum income per doctor; S_M = physician supply "curve" facing the hospital; M_o = equilibrium number of physicians on staff with free entry (open staffing); M_D = number of physicians on staff using the same employment rule as for L and K.

constant, physicians will require to be paid more to offset the undesirability of living and working in a high-crime area.

Recall that M^* is the number of physicians on the medical staff at the point at which the marginal revenue product of physicians equals the average net income of physicians. Suppose that the supply curve intersects the average revenue product curve to the left of M^*, a situation depicted by the intersection of S_L with the average revenue product curve in figure 6.8. Then the hospital will not be able to attract as many physicians as it desires.

There are two implications. First, such hospitals will maintain an open medical staff, welcoming all qualified physicians who wish to practice there. Second, the hospital may complain to public policy makers that the area faces a physician shortage. Governments might respond by implementing incentives for physicians to practice in the community.

The goal of attracting more physicians to the area can be accomplished in several ways. For example, the government may subsidize the educational expenses of persons who agree to practice in a "shortage area" for a few years after entering

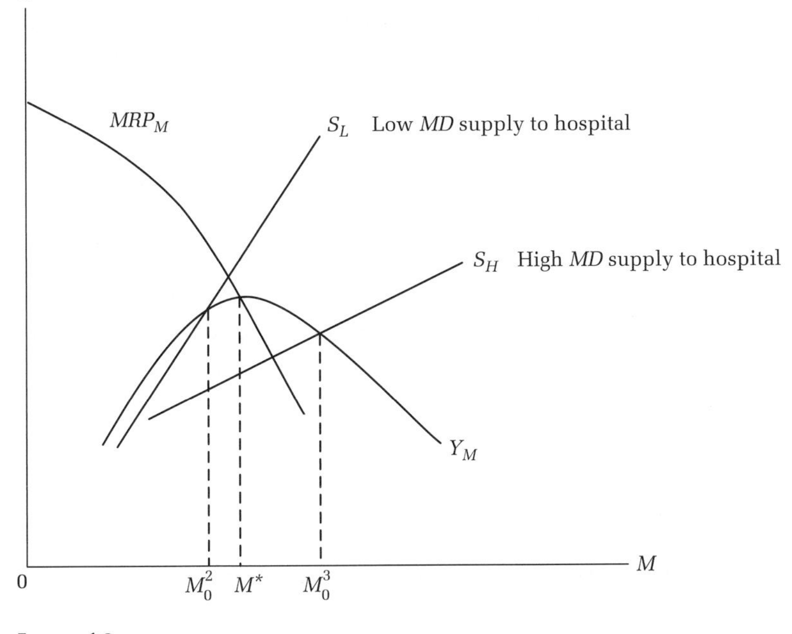

FIGURE 6.8
Alternative Physician Supply Scenarios

the practice of medicine. Or the community may be able to convince the governmental authority to open a medical school nearby. This medical school would attract individuals who had roots in the area and would be willing to practice in the community upon graduation.

A different picture emerges if the relevant physician supply curve is S_H. Then the physician supply curve intersects the average revenue curve to the right of M^*. In this situation, more physicians will be available than the hospital's medical staff desires. In this situation, the medical staff will restrict entry. The medical staff will be "closed." That is, not all qualified physicians who apply will be admitted to the medical staff.

Up to now, we have assumed that there is full agreement among the residual claimants, the physicians on the hospital's medical staff, about the optimal levels of each input, L, K, and M. Not only is there full agreement, at least after the input decisions have been reached, but every member of the medical staff works in the collective interest of the medical staff as a whole.

However, human nature may differ from the ideal, which is that decision makers always serve the collective interest. In practice, individual physicians may find it financially advantageous to use resources to their own individual advantage. For example, if a nurse monitors the health of patients more than is expected by the collective, the nurse may effectively substitute for the physician's time. Or a physician may use the hospital's office staff for personal use. Because of individual pursuit of self-interest, the collective may break down. This may be a particularly serious problem for large hospitals where there are many physicians on the medical staff, making the actions of individual physicians harder to monitor. Also, if there are more physicians, the actions of one "bad apple" have less of a deleterious effect on the performance of the organization as a whole. This serves as a disincentive for monitoring.

In practice, hospital medical staffs in the United States do implement various rules and employ monitoring systems to guard against individualistic behavior. However, rule making and monitoring require resources, and these resources add to the cost of hospital care.

PHYSICIAN-HOSPITAL ORGANIZATIONS

A recent development in the United States has been the growth in the number of physician-hospital organizations, or PHOs. These organizations are more formal combinations of medical staff and hospitals than the arrangements described above. One of the major activities of PHOs is joint marketing of their product to insurers. Rather than have insurers negotiate contracts separately with the hospital and each physician, the PHOs negotiate with each insurer as a single bargaining unit. The negotiations encompass not only physicians' services performed in the hospital but physicians' services performed in physicians' private offices as well. Conceptually, PHOs can be efficiency-enhancing and hence in the public interest, or alternatively they may detract from economic efficiency (Cuellar and Gertler 2006).

The argument for PHOs goes as follows. In an environment in which health care providers compete for health care contracts from health insurers, PHOs may facilitate the use of financial incentives to members of the PHO to lower cost and improve quality of care, especially since care for an episode of illness or for a chronic disease typically spans both inpatient and ambulatory care settings, including physicians' offices. The greater scale of PHOs than hospitals and physicians' offices working administratively separately makes it feasible to adopt large-scale management information systems that can be use to track patients' care and outcomes—thereby, for example, avoiding the waste of duplicate testing. The PHO may be better positioned to monitor quality of care in ambulatory care settings than other organizations. PHOs may allow for better sharing of expensive equipment and facilities than is possible under the more separate arrangement described by the Pauly-Redisch model.

On the other hand, PHOs also may increase the bargaining power of hospitals-physicians vis-à-vis individual health insurers. In the United States, unlike in some countries, such as Germany, where statutory insurers negotiate jointly, negotiations are conducted separately with each insurer. The default in the absence of a PHO is negotiation between individual physicians and individual insurers and individual hospitals and individual insurers. Physicians have more bargaining power if they conduct collective negotiations than if they bargain individually.

Many geographic markets are insufficiently large to support more than one PHO. While hospitals are often monopolists in their market areas, physicians typically are not. The PHO may allow the physicians in a market to leverage bargaining power through the hospital's monopoly position. In one empirical investigation, Cuellar and Gertler (2006) found that integration in the form of PHOs has little impact on efficiency, but markets with PHOs do have higher prices, especially markets in which the PHO operates in less competitive health care markets.

SUMMING UP

We have described three organizational forms of hospitals: for-profit; private not-for-profit; and a private not-for-profit form in which physicians on the hospital medical staff are the residual claimants. A profit-maximizing hospital does not provide zero quality or even the minimum quality allowed for by public regulations but rather that quality level at which it maximizes profits. The hospital takes account of consumers' valuations of quality and picks that quality level at which consumers' marginal valuation of quality (the amount that consumers are willing to pay for an extra unit of quality, e.g., a reduction in the minimum nurse response time of a minute) equals the marginal cost of raising quality, such as the extra cost of achieving a minute in response time, by, for example, hiring additional nurses or improving information technology, which leads to better communication with patients.

In Newhouse's private not-profit hospital model, consumers' valuations of quality are reflected in the position of the hospital's demand curve for care. Intersections of demand curves or, equivalently, average revenue curves and average cost curves determine the feasible set of attainable quantity-quality combinations that the hospital can achieve. The ultimate choice of the quantity-quality combination depends on the preferences of the hospital decision makers. If the decision makers place an emphasis on accepting large numbers of persons in the community for care, then quantity will be weighted more heavily in the final quantity-quality decision. Conversely, if the decision makers are oriented toward prestige, they might select a combination involving relatively higher quality and lower quantity. The key point is that quantity-quality in the Newhouse model depends on decision makers' preferences at least in part. By contrast, a profit maximizer's quantity and quality decisions are totally driven by impersonal market forces. If the government is the insurer, then it is the government's demand curve that matters.

In the Pauly-Redisch framework, the hospital breaks even, but input levels are set to maximize profit per physician on the hospital's medical staff. The Pauly-Redisch model is silent about the quality of hospital care. However, at the cost of adding complexity, quality could be included as a decision variable. Output would then have quality and quantity dimensions, and the hospital production function would reflect this.

We have not explicitly presented a model for public hospitals, the third major ownership form. The for-profit and the physicians' cooperative models provide inappropriate frameworks for public hospitals. However, the Newhouse model encompasses public as well as private not-for-profit hospitals. Public hospital decision makers may be expected to place greater weight on promoting access to hospitals, especially for low-income persons. Also, private not-for-profit hospitals need to break even or nearly so. Public hospitals may have a higher allocable deficit per patient stay, with the loss being made up by a public subsidy. Public hospitals break even, but a large part of revenue comes from the public sponsor of the hospital.

6.3 HOSPITAL OWNERSHIP AND PERFORMANCE

WHY ARE FOR-PROFIT HOSPITALS A MINORITY?

Whether the hospital is organized as a for-profit organization or as some other form affects both the hospital decision-making process and actual decisions. But why are only a minority of hospitals organized as for-profit organizations? Countries differ appreciably in the relative shares of public and private not-profit hospitals. Generally, the public sector dominates in low- and middle-income countries,[4] but the private not-for-profit sector tends to be larger in many high-income countries.[5]

One might attribute the preponderance of private not-for-profit and government hospitals to historical factors, but this type of explanation is not very satisfying. One puzzling fact is that personal health care services other than hospital care are often provided by for-profit organizations. Physicians in many countries practice as for-profit organizations. With few exceptions (e.g., public vaccine manufacturers), pharmaceutical and medical device manufacturers are for-profit. We put this puzzle aside for a moment to consider answers economists have given to the question of why alternatives to the for-profit organizational form are dominant in hospital sectors.

FIDUCIARY RELATIONSHIPS AND COMPLEX OUTPUT

In a seminal article on distinctive features of health care, Kenneth Arrow (1963) argued that the not-for-profit form is a response to a market failure in the health care sector. Ideally, people would be able to purchase insurance, which would cover the cost of restoring an individual's health to the level that prevailed before a health shock, such as a heart attack, occurred. People are able to buy such insurance for other hazards. For example, insurance covers the cost of restoring a

4. For example, for Costa Rica, see Arocena and García-Prado (2006); for Uganda, see Ssengooba, Atuyambe, McPake, et al. (2002).

5. For example, in Germany in 1994, a slight majority of hospital beds were under public ownership; see Hoffmeyer and McCarthy (1994, 451). For South Korea and Asian countries of the Pacific Rim, see Noh, Lee, Yun, et al. (2006); for Norway, see Magnussen, Hagen, and Kaarboe (2007).

damaged automobile to its state before the collision or the injury victim is given cash, which is equivalent in value to the automobile prior to the collision. Health insurers are not in a position to guarantee that they will restore the insured individual to the state existing before an accident or illness occurred. Rather, personal health care services are covered without any guarantee that the person's health will be as good as new after therapy. For this reason, it is important that people can trust health care providers to act in the best interests of their patients. At the very least, providers can focus on doing their best, and not be sidetracked by considerations of financial self-interest. Consumers may view organizations that do not place profit making as their primary objective as more trustworthy than those that view profit maximization as their overriding organizational objective.

The importance of trust is made even more important given the complex output of hospitals. Often when a patient is admitted to a hospital, neither the underlying diagnosis nor the appropriate course of therapy is known. Given the rapid pace at which decisions are often made and the fact that patients may often not be well positioned to make fully informed decisions under these circumstances, it is important that patients can trust that hospital personnel are making those decisions that patients would make if they were fully informed and able to make decisions, and that hospital personnel do not place cost saving ahead of concern for what is best for the patient. A profit-seeking hospital, by contrast, may have a greater incentive to cut corners or promote therapeutic alternatives that are more profitable to the hospital but not necessarily better for the patient.

In an important sense, hospital care is an experience good (see chapter 5). However, while for the consumption of restaurant services, a patron who is not satisfied with the taste of the food at a restaurant may not return, a hospitalized patient who experiences a serious adverse outcome in a hospital may die, thus precluding future options.

NONCONTRACTIBLE QUALITY

Many aspects of quality are easily observed by the parties involved in a transaction. Patrons of a restaurant can monitor the appearance of the food, its tastiness, variety, and whether or not it is served at the appropriate temperature. However, the bacterial count of the food is not readily observable and perhaps may only be observable if and after the patron suffers from food poisoning. Without minimizing the aggravation of food poisoning, we note that at least such adverse outcomes are observable soon after the meal is over.

Similarly, some aspects of hospital care are readily observable: the attractiveness of the rooms, the food, whether or not staff members come quickly when called by patients, and the attitudes of hospital personnel. Because these product attributes are observable to patients and their families as consumers, these aspects of quality are contractible.

However, many aspects are not nearly as readily observable by patients, for example, the accuracy with which radiographs are interpreted or the quality of laboratory personnel. Some medical errors may be immediately apparent, but others may only become evident sometime after the hospitalization, such as whether or not all cancer cells were removed during cancer surgery.

Profit-seeking organizations may be more easily tempted to skimp on the cost of care and the quality of inputs, which are not as easily monitored by patients, than organizations set up according to a different objective. Hart, Shleifer, and Vishny (1997), who did not apply their conceptual analysis specifically to hospitals but rather to a range of institutions, suggested, for example, that a for-profit prison might skimp on input quality since the patrons, the prisoners, are not well positioned to seek an alternative provider of prison services.[6] Quality can be contractible only when either its provision can be enforced contractually or unsatisfied customers can switch to a competitor that provides quality at the level the customer demands without suffering undue harm. For the same reason that, with a few exceptions, prisons are not-for-profit, and most hospitals are not organized on this basis either.

PUBLIC GOODS

For private goods, consumption by one individual reduces the amount that another individual can consume of the same good. By contrast, with a public good, an individual can consume the good without diminishing its use by others.[7] In economic terminology, consumption of the good is not *rival*.

Most hospital care falls in the category of a rival or private good. After one patient "consumes" a given surgical procedure, another patient cannot consume it. However, some hospital outputs are public goods. For example, hospitals generally maintain some excess capacity to be used in a large-scale medical emergency, such as an accident involving several motor vehicles. Hospitals may be involved in public health campaigns of various types. Unless explicitly compensated for this, a for-profit hospital would generally be unwilling to provide public goods. Of course, even a for-profit hospital might engage in some public good provision as a type of advertising. If the for-profit hospital can convince potential patients that it is community-oriented, not a crass profit seeker, this could be good for its business.

IMPLICIT SUBSIDIES

In the Newhouse model, hospitals typically provide more quality than a profit-maximizing hospital would provide. In essence, such higher quality is cross-subsidized by the hospital forgoing profits it could have realized if it had not provided so much quality. Cross subsidies involve transferring funds from one profitable activity to another less profitable or unprofitable activity. Some hospital services or some types of patients have traditionally been unprofitable or relatively less

6. We explain this model in detail in chapter 13.

7. See chapter 1 for a discussion of public goods.

profitable, for example, obstetric care in contrast to cardiac care. An argument against the for-profit form is that some of these subsidized activities are highly socially worthwhile but will only be provided if they can be cross-subsidized (Weisbrod 1988). The argument is that society desires that certain activities take place, although there is no willingness to make explicit payments to provide financial support for them.

Economists have sometimes countered this argument, which contends that the existence of implicit subsidies allows hospitals to support hospital decision makers' pet projects but ones that are not really favored by the citizenry more generally.

Explicit Subsidies

Even if tax law permitted deductions for charitable giving to for-profit organizations, it seems unlikely that donors would be predisposed to make donations, which would have the effect of enriching shareholders. By contrast, not-for-profit organizations do not have shareholders. Thus, to the extent that society wishes that the preferences of voluntary contributors be honored, it makes sense to have recipient organizations, such as hospitals, be not-for-profit.

Cartels

The Pauly-Redisch model of the hospital describes the private not-for-profit hospital as a physicians' cooperative. The more pejorative term cartel may also apply to such an organization. The private not-for-profit form possibly facilitates cartelizing in two ways. First, there is no competition with shareholders for the residual (profit). Second, the physicians can enjoy the benefits of favorable tax treatment that are provided to such organizations.

Low Profits

Finally, the share of hospitals under for-profit ownership may be low because profits are insufficient for such hospitals to enter the market. And given the absence of for-profit hospitals, other types of hospitals fill the gap. In the United States, however, hospitals have been profitable, particularly in certain years (American Hospital Association 2002).

Empirical Evidence on Hospital Ownership and Performance

Allegations against For-Profit Hospitals

In the United States in particular, where publicly traded for-profit hospital companies have gained a foothold, for-profit hospitals have come under attack. The critics of for-profit hospitals have voiced several concerns, including lack of community benefit, cream skimming, diversion, and exploitation (Hyman 1998). Lack of community benefit refers to the claim that for-profit hospitals do not produce their share of public goods, such as provision of charity care to indigent patients, or medical education or biomedical or clinical research, for which they do not receive an explicit public subsidy. "Cream skimming" refers to an allegation that for-profit hospitals locate in geographic areas in which mainly relatively affluent persons live (Norton and Staiger 1994), have a focus on profitable services, and eschew providing services that are not profitable or caring for patients who ex ante (i.e., before the patient is admitted) appear to be unprofitable to the hospital. Diversion implies that for-profit hospitals allocate too much to administration, marketing, and taxes—spending that could have been more productively allocated to providing patient care (Woolhandler and Himmelstein 1997). Exploitation can be construed to mean that for-profit hospitals charge higher prices, channel demand to their facilities, including facilities that treat patients after they are discharged from the hospital, and may even induce demand. It has also been alleged that for-profit hospitals upcode diagnoses with the express purpose of obtaining higher payments from the government (Silverman and Skinner 2004).

Upcoding diagnoses means that hospitals figure out the algorithms used by insurers for purposes of determining payment. There is often some discretion in how a patient's diagnoses are coded. The hospital knows that if it uses certain codes or presents the codes in a certain rank order, it will receive higher payment. It is not that hospitals falsely state the diagnoses that led to the patient's admission to a hospital. Rather, it knows that some codes pay more than others, and it can use these codes or order of codes to obtain a higher payment. For example, a patient may have two or more diagnoses. Listing one before the others may yield a higher payment than if the others are listed first.

As with many important controversies, there is another side. The most common arguments relate to efficiency and standardization. Since for-profit hospitals have well-defined residual claimants, in a closely held, non-publicly traded hospital company, the owners may be physicians or other entrepreneurs who started the hospital. For publicly traded hospital companies, the owners are mainly shareholders with no direct role in provision of hospital services. Owner-shareholders presumably have a stake in having a profitable company and are not tolerant of inefficiency. The residual claimants in the case of hospitals not operated on a for-profit basis are not nearly as well defined, except perhaps in the Pauly-Redisch framework. Officially, a not-for-profit hospital is affiliated with a religious organization or a community in which it is located. But perhaps a religious organization or a community will have less incentive to monitor efficiency. Likewise, for public hospitals, the ultimate residual claimant is the taxpayer, but taxpayers have much to worry about other than the efficiency of hospitals run by the governments to which they pay taxes.

Another aspect of efficiency relates to scale economies. It is asserted that being part of a chain of hospitals is a source of scale economies. There may be scale economies in data management, for example, but the scale economies have not yet been documented empirically.

Standardization means that for hospitals in a chain, various features are the same. When a consumer goes to a fast-food restaurant or a hotel that is part of a chain, he or she is likely to have some idea about the quality and type of service to expect in advance of actually consuming the service. Such familiarity facilitates consumer search and is efficiency enhancing. On the other hand, standardization may limit the responsiveness of hospitals in the chain to variations in the preferences of local populations.

There is now a vast empirical literature on the relative performance of hospitals by ownership form. We start with a discussion of one study of the issue to illustrate how such studies are done. Then we review the findings of a much larger number of studies on the issue.

Empirical Analysis of the Effects of Ownership on Hospital Performance

In "Hospital Ownership and Cost and Quality of Care: Is There a Dime's Worth of Difference?" Sloan, Picone, Taylor, et al. (2001) investigated how for-profit hospitals in the United States compare on cost and quality. That for-profit hospitals would differ in quality from their private not-for-profit counterparts is suggested theoretically by the Newhouse model. The empirical analysis of Sloan et al. was limited to data on persons over age 65 enrolled in Medicare, the public insurance program covering persons over age 65 in the United States, who were admitted to hospitals with a primary diagnosis of hip fracture, stroke, coronary heart disease, or congestive heart failure—common diagnoses among elderly persons who are admitted to hospitals. The outcome measures studied were: survival, changes in functional and cognitive status, and changes in living arrangements (e.g., admission to a nursing home). Survival was measured at one month, six months, and one year following admission to the hospital. Presumably, if hospital quality is better, the probability of survival will be higher, holding many other factors constant.

Functional status refers to the person's ability to physically and mentally perform various activities of daily living, such as bathing, shopping, and doing one's laundry. Cognitive status refers to the person's ability to reason and think through problems. The conditions for which the patients were admitted often have long-run adverse effects on functional and cognitive status. Stroke is associated with dementia. Through pathways that have not been well documented, elderly persons with hip fractures not only often have more limited physical function as a permanent condition following hip fractures but often suffer cognitive decline as well. The quality of care received in the first few days of a hospital stay may affect the patient's functional and cognitive status in the long run.

The question the authors addressed is whether or not the decline in function and cognition is less if the patient is admitted to one of the hospital ownership types than to the others. Persons who are more functionally or cognitively impaired may not be able to live alone, and thus move to living with children or to a nursing home or other facility in which assistance with tasks of daily life is provided. In effect, an elderly person's living arrangement is another proxy for functional and cognitive status, which is good to have, since there may be measurement errors in any single scale, and it is important to know how robust findings are to changes in use of a particular scale.

The authors also measured payments Medicare made on behalf of the patient starting with the day the patient was admitted to the hospital through six months following the admission date. The six-month period included the Medicare payments for the hospital stay and payments by Medicare after the patient was discharged from the hospital. Post-discharge payments included payments for physicians' services, nursing home stays, home health care, visits to hospital outpatient clinics, readmissions to hospitals, and hospice care.

Although Medicare paid hospitals a fixed amount per case for a particular diagnosis, hospitals may be able to secure higher payment by manipulating the diagnosis codes or transferring the patient to a facility that is paid on some other basis, such as a nursing home for posthospital care to which payment is per day. A profit-seeking hospital may be more inclined to discharge a patient from the hospital early, which would not have adversely affected the payment for the stay but would have increased payments made to the hospital if the hospital owned the facility to which the patient was transferred. For each patient in their sample, the authors tracked all payments made by Medicare on behalf of the patient from the day the patient was admitted to the hospital to six months after the admission date.

The authors found no difference in the probabilities of patient survival according to the ownership of the hospital to which the person was initially admitted following a health shock. With a few exceptions, they did not find statistically significant differences in the other health outcome measures either.

However, Medicare spent much more if the person had been admitted to a for-profit hospital for one of the conditions included in the study. The authors concluded that "for-profit hospitals were more expensive to Medicare, especially in terms of payments other than for the index hospitalizations.[8] The higher cash flow to for-profits plausibly reflects their greater incentive to maximize reimbursements from payers by various means including formal and informal contractual relationships with suppliers of health care services" (Sloan, Picone, Taylor, et al. 2001, 18). By "formal and informal contractual relationships," the authors mean owning or other affiliating with a provider other than a hospital—a nursing home, a hospice, or a home health agency. Services rendered by the latter types of providers are covered by Medicare, especially following a hospital stay.

8. The index hospitalization was the hospital stay for which the person was entered into the analysis sample.

REVIEWS OF THE LITERATURE ON THE EFFECTS OF OWNERSHIP ON HOSPITAL PERFORMANCE

There are two systematic reviews of the evidence in the literature on studies of adverse health outcomes following hospitalization. Devereaux, Choi, Lachetti, et al. (2002) concluded that the evidence overall shows that for-profit hospitals have a slightly worse record on patients surviving treatment at their facilities relative to private not-for-profit facilities. On the other hand, Eggleston, Shen, Lau, et al. (2008), based on a summary of a far larger number of empirical studies, emphasized differences in methodologies among studies as a major source of the differences in findings. Judging from the display of information in their study, even when researchers found a statistically significant difference in survival probability by ownership type, the difference was very small.

In contrast to quality or outcomes as endpoints, there is little debate among experts over the relatively costliness of for-profit hospitals. Despite the arguments of advocates of for-profit hospitals, there is no evidence that potential efficiency gains have been realized. Of course, one can always argue that such hospitals are better in satisfying the wants of patients. But the argument that they provide a better match with patient preferences has not been rigorously demonstrated, either.

Our discussion of hospital ownership thus far has implicitly assumed that all hospitals with a particular form of ownership act alike. There is empirical evidence that private not-for-profit hospitals behave differently, more like for-profits, when they face competition from for-profits (see, e.g., Duggan 2002). Other literature relates changes in behavior to changes in ownership and observes that hospitals learn from experience. In one study (Picone, Chou, and Sloan 2002), hospitals converting to for-profit status cut costs following conversion, which was followed by an increase in patient mortality and an increase in cost attributable to an increase in hospital input levels.

6.4 REGULATION OF HOSPITALS

CONTEXT

One of the major health policy lessons from the twentieth century is that an infusion of funds into the health sector without simultaneously implementing cost controls will inevitably lead to high rates of increased spending on health care services. For example, in 1966 the United States implemented Medicare, public insurance for the elderly and severely disabled, and Medicaid, public insurance for the indigent, without simultaneously introducing cost controls (Finkelstein 2007). By 1972, public policy makers were already surprised by the rapid rise in spending on these public programs, far greater than had been anticipated by the actuaries who estimated program cost prior to implementation of the programs. Since the most complete coverage was for hospital care, increased spending was most evident in this sector. By the late 1960s and early 1970s, US states and the federal government began to implement hospital cost-containment programs (Sloan 1980).

By contrast, Taiwan implemented national health insurance in 1995 with little or no subsequent increase in spending. The key difference between the two countries is that Taiwan, which had the advantage of benefiting from other countries' experiences, coupled the increase in coverage with implementation of strict controls over hospital revenues (see chapter 12).

The following discussion assumes that hospitals are independent entities and hence subject to external regulation and payment. However, as explained in detail in chapter 13, in some countries, hospitals are run by the government and are not independent entities. In the United States, many hospitals are government-owned; they receive public funds from the entity that owns the hospital as well as from higher levels of government. This has led to unintended consequences, as described in box 6.1. We defer further discussion of public hospitals to chapter 13.

Box 6.1

Intergovernmental Transfers, Fiscal Shenanigans, and Hospital Patient Mortality

Intergovernmental transfers, that is, transfers from a higher level of government, such as a national government, to a lower level of government, such as a state, county, or municipality, are quite common. There are at least three justifications for such transfers of funds. First, there may be widespread interest in promoting a particular activity at a more local level. Second, there may be a motive to redistribute money from more affluent areas to areas in which people are less affluent. Third, higher levels of government may be more efficient in collecting tax revenue. However, there is widespread concern that transfers of public funds from a higher level to a lower level of government may substitute for, or in economic terminology "crowd out," spending by the lower level of government.

In the United States, as described more fully in other chapters, Medicaid is a federal-state program that focuses on financing care for individuals living in low-income households. The federal government sets broad standards for Medicaid, such as standards for eligibility, while each state develops more detailed standards and program characteristics on its own that are consistent with the federal standards.

One mechanism for funding hospitals under Medicaid is the Disproportionate Share (DSH) Program. The purpose of this program is to provide funding to hospitals that care for large numbers of indigent persons. DSH, like Medicaid more generally, is financed by a federal-state matching formula.

Baicker and Staiger (2005) investigated the extent to which states could use the DSH federal-state matching formula to their advantage. Government hospitals operating in cities and counties have historically provided substantial amounts of care to indigent persons. Some funding for these facilities is raised locally, but a substantial amount of funding comes from intergovernmental transfers, such as from state to local governments. States are required by Medicaid to match federal contributions to DSH. But rather than have the DSH funds represent an additional source of funding for these hospitals, states have effectively used funds they would otherwise have spent on local government hospitals for matching purposes.

Box 6.1
(continued)

To illustrate, suppose a state made a $25 million annual contribution to a local hospital. After DSH was implemented, the state labeled the $25 million a match. Therefore, in the extreme, the hospital could receive a $25 million contribution from the federal government without the state spending any extra funds (assuming a 50-50 match, which is the match for many states). The authors found that this type of practice was widespread following implementation of DSH. These are the "fiscal shenanigans."

Given this result, Baicker and Staiger asked a second question. Were patient outcomes at hospitals improved as a result of the DSH program? Of course, to the extent that there were fiscal shenanigans, outcomes should have improved less than they otherwise would have improved. A program structured like DSH would be expected to improve patient outcomes for at least two reasons. First, indigent persons are likely to be relatively sensitive to changes in hospital quality. Second, quality should improve not only for these patients but for more affluent patients as well since the increase in DSH funds, net of the shenanigans, is likely to be used to improve facilities and upgrade staffing, which in turn should lead to improved quality, on average. The authors measured changes in mortality for two types of patients, infants and persons admitted to hospitals for heart attacks. In both cases, DSH led to better outcomes. These results are plausible since despite the crowding out of funds, DSH did lead to some increased funding of hospital services for large numbers of indigent persons.

Retrospective Cost Reimbursement

In many countries, hospitals are paid on a *retrospective cost* basis. For example, when first implemented, Medicare, like some other major private health insurers in the United States, paid hospitals on this cost basis. What this means is if a hospital incurred a dollar of expense and Medicare accounted for, say, 35 percent of that hospital's patient load, the hospital would be entitled to a payment of $0.35. If the expense were $2.00, the hospital would be entitled to a payment of $0.70 from Medicare. The system was retrospective in that hospitals were paid for their expenses after the expenses were incurred. During the year, hospitals would receive payments based on a cost projection. However, after the year, hospital accountants would finalize data on expenses incurred, and a final settlement would be made based on this number. A hospital that wasted its resources would be entitled to a higher payment from insurers like Medicare. Hospitals therefore had little incentive to be efficient. Higher costs generated higher revenue for the hospital.

If the vast majority of a hospital's patients have insurance and the payment by the insurers for care provided by the hospital is not fixed, that is, it is paid based on actual costs incurred after they are incurred (retrospective cost reimbursement), the stage is set for a "medical arms race." The arms race, non-price competition rather than competition based on price, works as follows.

When people have nearly complete insurance coverage for hospital care, the demand for such care is very inelastic. Both industry demand and hospital demand are inelastic. From the vantage point of the hospital, incurring higher cost leads to higher revenue. The hospital wants to attract patients. But to do this, it needs to attract patient referrals from the physicians in the community. The hospital has no financial incentive to say no to a demand by physicians that it acquire some new expensive equipment that the physician wants for his or her hospital practice. In fact, the hospital knows that the insurers will cover the acquisition and operating cost of such equipment. Hence, the hospital has every incentive to say yes to physician demands. If the hospital refuses to go along with the physician's demand, the physician may admit his or her patients to another hospital in the community. Since the physician's threat is more credible if there are other hospitals in the community, the medical arms race is worse when there are several hospital competitors. In communities in which a single hospital has a monopoly, the hospital can reason that the physician has no other option but to admit patients to its facility. The patients may not care about hospital costs and prices, but they will care if they are likely to travel to another community for care.

Normally, increased competition would lower cost and the difference between price and the cost of producing a good or service ("price-cost margins"). But with cost-based reimbursement and nearly complete insurance coverage (meaning that the patient pays little or nothing out of pocket for care), increased competition has the opposite result. As cost rises, quality may rise. But even if it does, it may be much higher than is socially optimal. A higher than socially optimal level of quality arises when the marginal willingness to pay for one unit increase in quality is less than its marginal cost. Furthermore, hospitals have an incentive to acquire plant and equipment that may be underutilized. Under retrospective cost-based reimbursement, if only ten patients use an item of equipment during the year, the cost of the equipment (debt service, depreciation, rental if the hospital rents rather than owns the equipment) would be allocated among the insurers in the same way as if 1,000 patients had utilized it.

The astute reader is likely to ask, if the system was so flawed, why have so many insurers around the world, both private and public, implemented it at one time or other, and why is the system for paying hospitals commonplace in many countries, even today?

Retrospective cost reimbursement makes sense when output and the process of producing the output are difficult to specify in advance. Imagine the task of developing new aircraft for combat missions. Especially when a country is at war, the aircraft is badly needed for combat. Manufacturers would not agree to develop the aircraft for a fixed price since it is not at all clear how difficult it will be to develop new aircraft that fulfills the government's requirements or, if the government is in a hurry to obtain the aircraft, how costly it will be to accelerate development and manufacturing processes. So rather than offer fixed price contracts, the government offers cost-based contracts. The manufacturer's cost is subject to external audit and has to be reasonable in the view of government accountants. But if audit standards are met and developing the aircraft costs more than anticipated, the government is willing to cover the cost overrun.

For example, the government may not cover cocktail parties or trips to an exotic island for staff or even for customers, if the business purpose were not clear. But it may well cover cost overruns due to a project being more complex than anticipated even if rigorous measures of the added complexity are not presented.

Similarly, governments provide research grants on a retrospective cost basis to universities and other research entities. Research outcomes are often highly uncertain, and research output is often difficult to quantify even after the fact. Hence, there is a strong case for cost-based reimbursement in some situations. Universities and other research entities generally like retrospective cost reimbursement, and if anything, would lobby against proposals to abolish it.

Advocates of retrospective cost reimbursement of hospital care argued that hospitalized patients are very heterogeneous, even those patients admitted with the same primary diagnosis. There has been some concern that paying a fixed price for the care of a patient with a specific diagnosis may be unfair to hospitals that happen to treat patients with relatively severe forms of the disease. The care of such patients may require relatively sophisticated technology and high levels of nursing care. There is a concern that, if these additional costs are not covered, hospitals will refuse to accept those patients who require extra care.

In countries with pluralistic financing systems, methods of payment tend to be pluralistic as well (see chapter 11). In the United States historically, some health insurers paid hospitals on a retrospective cost basis. Other insurers paid based on hospital prices (charges). These insurers paid a percentage of hospital charges or a fixed dollar amount per covered service (e.g., $X for an appendectomy, called an "indemnity"), with the patient paying the difference between the fixed dollar amount and the hospital's charge out of pocket. When the insurer paid on the basis of a percentage of hospital charges, the hospital could know that the insurer's payments would rise if the hospital raised its costs and prices or just its prices. In this important sense, charge-based reimbursement strongly resembles cost-based reimbursement.

Regulatory Responses

Most countries in the world with substantial health insurance coverage for hospital care and with cost-based reimbursement of hospitals have implemented some form of regulation to temper the rise in spending on hospital care. As a result, cost-based reimbursement of hospitals without controls has become a rarity.

The major forms of hospital cost-containment controls consist of entry regulation and price and revenue regulation. Arguments for regulation are (1) moral hazard exists in the presence of health insurance and (2) some government intervention is needed to counter the perverse incentives of the cost-based reimbursement system. Regulation primarily arises in countries in which hospitals are mainly private. In a country in which hospitals are public, such as in the UK (see chapter 13), public entities have exclusive responsibility for decision making.

ENTRY REGULATION

Entry regulation applies to the entry of new hospitals as well as the expansion of services at existing hospitals.[9] The concept has been applied in sectors other than health care. For example, routes of bus lines and airlines may be regulated, as may the entry of new bus and airline companies. Similarly, the entry of liquor stores and bars is often subject to government regulation. A major argument for entry regulation is that "excess competition" is not in the public interest. Excess competition includes the medical arms race, but it may also apply in industries in which price wars lead to insolvencies. While excess competition of this sort may be undesirable, particularly in such sectors as insurance (Munch and Smallwood 1980), there is also a risk that entry regulation provides a de facto franchise for incumbents in an industry. In fact, the major advocates for such regulation are often incumbents.

In some countries, such as Canada and Germany, entry regulation in the health field is combined with capital budgeting. Capital and operating funds are available only if the regulatory agency approves the project. In the United States, the two functions are separate. In the US states with such regulation, hospital capital projects meeting the criteria for regulation must be approved by a public agency before construction can begin. Building a hospital or acquiring equipment without approval is illegal. The applicant for regulatory approval of a capital project presents its plans for financing the project. However, applicants obtain financing from banks, bond issues, and internal funds. Governments have no capital budgets for hospital plant and equipment purchases.

In principle, there is a strong case that entry regulation can combat hospitals' incentives under retrospective reimbursement to acquire plants and equipment. To gain regulatory approval, a hospital must present detailed plans and projections of use and show that the investment is needed. Going ahead with investments that are not approved can be an outright violation of the law, or place payments to hospitals from government health insurance plans in jeopardy.

In the United States, entry regulation takes the form of state certificate of need (CON) laws. For many years, states were required under federal law to enact CON laws. However, the federal law is no longer in effect, and several states have consequently dropped their CON laws. State CON laws cover several types of health

9. For a much more detailed review of the US experience with hospital regulation, see Salkever (2000).

care services, including hospitals, but they exclude physicians' private offices. Under cost-based reimbursement, as we have seen, there is an incentive to build various forms of hospital capacity with the knowledge that health insurers will foot the bill even if the capacity is not demanded and is underutilized.

Central to these laws is the notion that the need for facilities can be defined for a particular geographic area. "Need" is not a word in the vocabulary of economics. Economists distinguish between "need" and "demand." To economists, it seems unlikely that a fixed number of facilities is "required" for a given population. There are substitutes for hospital care, including ambulatory care. This means that as hospitals raise their prices, purchasers will find other sources of care when it is feasible to do so.

Historically, CON agencies in the United States have specified specific standards to which CON applicants must adhere, notably, that bed construction not result in a community with more than four beds per 1,000 population. But critics of CON ask what would happen if a community had 3.5 or 4.5 beds per 1,000 population? Presumably the marginal benefit of beds declines as beds are added, but it seems more reasonable to assume that marginal benefit declines in a smooth fashion rather than only at a specific bed ratio. Further, it is likely that communities differ in the extent to which they derive benefits from adding hospital capacity, and not only because of differences in the demographic composition of the community, a factor the CON review process generally considers. Under complete or nearly complete health insurance coupled with cost-based reimbursement, there may well be overinvestment in hospital capacity. But basing allocations of hospital capacity on fixed predetermined ratios does not ensure socially optimal levels of investment either.

In recent years in the United States, CON's programmatic emphasis has been expanded to include access to care and to quality of care. The argument for a role for public regulation to safeguard access is that a free market results in an inequitable distribution of capacity. In particular, hospitals will want to locate in parts of the city where middle-income and high-income persons live and will not want to locate in impoverished neighborhoods. CON programs can prevent hospitals from locating or relocating in more affluent areas. Also, CON can impose requirements that hospitals provide minimum amounts of care to the poor or to persons without health insurance as a prerequisite for obtaining a certificate. However, the extent to which such provisions are enforced after the facility is built is unknown.

As for quality, there is a vast literature on the relationship between the quantity of services provided by a hospital and health outcomes. Under cost-based reimbursement and similar payment systems, there is likely to be a proliferation of hospitals offering a particular type of service, in particular a particular surgical procedure, such as open heart surgery. Hospitals, and surgeons at these facilities, that undertake low numbers of specialized sophisticated procedures are not likely to have the good health outcomes that their counterparts with a higher volume have. As in other areas, practice makes perfect. Further, there are important fixed costs in running programs for some complex procedures. For example, for open heart surgery, not only is the equipment expensive but a certain number of specialized personal must be available at all times. In a low-volume program, equipment and staff are likely to be idle much of the time.

The empirical evidence on the effectiveness of CON programs in the United States in constraining the growth in hospital cost has been mixed, with some studies suggesting that CON has actually increased spending on hospital care. Before turning to the evidence, it is useful to consider why entry regulation may not have the intended cost-constraining effect.

First and most important, in the United States, the agency that approves capital expenditures does not have a budget for capital expenditures. Thus, the agency stands to face political opposition from the hospital and its allies when a CON application is declined. Yet in approving a hospital's application, the agency does not bear any direct cost consequences from its decision.

Second, the CON applicant has a major stake in the outcome of its application. By contrast, individual citizens have little interest and stake in the outcome of the review. Although having a hospital nearby may be personally advantageous someday, most citizen voters are not admitted to hospitals most of the time. The issue of patient travel time or more generally access to hospitals is likely not to be a very salient political issue. Opposition to a given application is not likely to come from the members of the public at large but rather from potential competitors of the applicant. CON programs favor the status quo. CON may confer a de facto franchise on existing hospitals.

Third, entry regulation does not apply across the board but only to certain types of facilities, including hospitals. Thus, for example, a CON program may deny a hospital a CON for an expensive piece of imaging equipment. Yet this barrier can be circumvented by acquiring the same equipment for use in physicians' offices, which are exempt from CON regulation.

Salkever and Bice (1976) performed the earliest empirical analysis of the effects of entry regulation on hospital investment and capital stock. These authors found that CON constrained the growth of hospital beds in US states with CON, but actually increased hospital investment in plant assets per hospital bed. Salkever and Bice argued that CON programs had a ratio of beds to population to serve as a benchmark and thus could turn down applicants for hospital beds if building the beds would lead to a ratio in excess of four beds per 1,000. But the CON programs did not have explicit criteria for judging other types of investments in hospital capacity, such as for specialized hospital equipment, say, the number of CT scanners per capita population in the hospital's market or "catchment" area. Thus, when they lacked fixed criteria, the CON panels had more difficulty saying no to a hospital application. Consequently, when CON limited hospital bed construction, the funds were channeled into other types of hospital investments. These results were confirmed by subsequent empirical analysis (Sloan and Steinwald 1975; Sloan 1980, 1983), which found that CON regulation did not reduce capital expenditures on hospitals or decrease other indicators of hospital spending.

Many US states have been reluctant to discontinue their CON programs even after federal law permitted them to do so. Many states did drop CON. The concern among the states that retained CON has been that removing CON would lead to a surge in health care spending, including spending on hospital care. If CON programs had really been effective in constraining spending, this would be a legitimate concern. However, the empirical evidence does not support the view that CON has been effective in cost containment. Conover and Sloan (1998) investigated whether or not states that dropped CON experienced a surge in health care spending subsequently. Based on their empirical analysis, they concluded that concerns about a surge are unfounded.

Much less is known about CON's impacts on access to and the quality of hospital care than about its effect on hospital cost and spending on hospital care. In the CON application process, some weight may be given to the potential effects on access of underserved populations, including the uninsured. However, how important are these considerations in the *actual* approval process, and what mechanisms do states employ to ensure promises are kept? It is often asserted by program officials and advocates for CON that access is an important consideration in CON approval of projects, but systematically assembled empirical evidence is lacking.

Custer, Ketsche, Sherman, et al. (2006, 274) studied data on individual hospitals to analyze the relationship between CON and the share of inpatients classified as "self-pay," that is, those who have no health insurance coverage and therefore pay for care out of pocket. The authors did not find that CON programs increased the share of such persons admitted to hospitals. A related but conceptually distinct issue pertains to the geographic distribution of hospital inpatient and outpatient facilities. In particular, does CON improve the geographic distribution of such facilities, such as addressing an imbalance in distribution of hospital facilities relative to population between large cities and rural areas? Up to now, there have been no empirical studies of this issue.

There is solid empirical evidence that health outcomes are better in hospital facilities that have higher volume for several services, in particular cardiac services. Birkmeyer, Siewers, Finlayson, et al. (2002) showed that very high-volume facilities achieved substantial, and statistically significant, surgical mortality reductions for coronary artery bypass grafts (CABG) (–20 percent), aortic valve replacements (–24 percent), and mitral valve replacements (–23 percent).

Moreover, studies have examined the impact of CON on outcomes following CABG surgery. One study focused on the determinants of surgical mortality for CABG procedures performed during 1994–1999 in the United States

(Vaughan-Sarrazin, Hannan, Gormley, et al. 2002). Mortality adjusted for differences in case mix severity by hospital was 22 percent higher in eighteen states that had no CON regulation of open-heart surgery units during this period compared to twenty-six states that maintained such regulation during the entire period. Mean patient volume per center was 84 percent higher in states with CON regulation than in those without, supporting the idea that CON led to improvements in outcomes by regionalizing facilities. While this study controlled extensively for various patient characteristics, it did not control for other factors that may have affected health outcomes. Moreover, the use of cross-sectional data limited the authors' ability to reach conclusions about cause and effect, as it is conceivable that states without CON regulation of open heart surgery (coronary artery bypass graft, CABG) had worse surgical outcomes for reasons unrelated to CON.

A different study compared the outcomes of persons undergoing CABG from three years prior to the US state of Pennsylvania's elimination of CON to three years after (Robinson, Nash, Moxey, et al. 2001). Despite a 25 percent increase in the number of open heart surgery programs after CON was lifted, the authors found no statistically significant difference in the number of CABG operations performed statewide or any difference in the mortality experience of hospitals that were approved under CON to perform CABG compared to those that implemented CABG surgery programs following CON's removal.

A strength of this study is its longitudinal comparison focusing on the impact of lifting CON. The disadvantage is that it is a case study of a single US state, one that happened to also have a statewide public performance monitoring system that included hospital reporting of CABG outcomes. In the absence of this reporting system, the results may have been very different.

Nevertheless, despite the limitations of past research on CON programs' impact on quality of care, it appears that CON programs have a favorable impact on the outcomes of hospitalized patients admitted with some primary diagnoses. But other approaches may also have a favorable impact on quality without having the negative feature of conferring de facto franchises on incumbents, which CON programs have.

Price-Revenue Regulation and Prospective Payment

Entry regulation is designed to limit a medical arms race that may occur under retrospective cost reimbursement of hospitals. Entry regulation is in effect a bandage that seeks to counter the adverse effects of retrospective cost reimbursement without changing the payment system itself. A more direct policy option is to change the payment system itself. This can be done by specifying terms of hospital payment before rather than after care is delivered. Payment systems that specify payment terms in advance are called *prospective payment* systems.

A necessary condition for paying hospitals prospectively is having a definition of the product to be paid for. Under retrospective cost reimbursement, the insurer pays for costs incurred by the hospital in caring for the persons it insures. No measure of product or output is needed. The insurer merely reimburses for expenses incurred on behalf of persons while they are hospitalized. The difficulty of arriving at a consensus about how hospital output should be measured has been an impediment to the adoption of hospital prospective payment.

Hospital output can be measured in several ways. The most detailed unit of output is the individual service, such as administration of a drug (e.g., aspirin or a fluid administered intravenously), room and board for a day, minutes the patient spent in the operating room, and so on. Slightly more aggregated is a patient day, which bundles all services performed during a 24-hour period. At the next level is the hospital stay, which combines the days the person spent in the hospital during a stay.

Alternatively, the hospital may be paid on a *capitation* basis. When paid on a capitation basis, the hospital is under contract with a health insurer and is paid a fixed dollar amount per year for each person in the plan, whether or not the person receives care at the hospital.

Still another approach is for the hospital to be paid a fixed amount per year for operating its facility, called a *global budget*. This amount, set in advance of the year to which it applies, is designed to cover all care delivered by the hospital during the year. This *total budget* approach is used in Canada (see chapter 12).

Price and revenue regulation is a very broad category. About the only common feature such regulatory programs have is that payment is set in advance of service provision. The category encompasses price controls in which hospital prices for each service are frozen and subject to annual updates according to a specific formula, prospective payment using the day or the stay as the unit of output, capitation plans, and total hospital budgeting.

Hospitals face substantially different incentives under prospective payment. Under retrospective cost reimbursement, by raising costs, hospitals generate more revenue. By contrast, under prospective payment, hospitals gain by reducing cost since payment tends to be invariant with respect to a hospital's cost.

Each prospective payment method has advantages and disadvantages. Systems that use individual services as the unit of output have the advantage of making payment highly individualized so that payment can reflect the complexity of a specific patient's condition and treatment. However, there are important disadvantages that probably outweigh this advantage. In particular, individual services may be mispriced. If the price is set too low, there is an incentive for underprovision. Conversely, if the price is set too high, well above the marginal cost of delivering the service, hospitals have an incentive to overprovide the service.

In the United States, the Nixon administration's Economic Stabilization Program (ESP), implemented for a while in the early 1970s, began as a price freeze (Salkever 2000). All price freezes "work" in the very short run in that inflation is contained. However, in the longer run, important distortions emerge since the normal market process of price increases and decreases does not exist. For example, if a price is held below its market-clearing level, product shortages can and almost surely do ensue. After a brief period during which all prices were frozen, ESP substituted a system of controlled prices for the price freeze. Price controls, which predominated in certain sectors of the US economy, including health care in general and hospitals in particular, allowed for exceptions to help deal with shortages as they arose. When controls were lifted, a major bout of hospital cost inflation ensued. Overall, the experience with price controls in the United States during the 1970s, as well as during World War II, is not worthy of repeating.

Alternatively, some prospective payment systems pay hospitals on a per diem (day) basis. Payment is for all services provided during the day. While far simpler to administer than a piece-rate system, per diem payment gives hospitals an incentive to increase length of patient stay. Typically, substantial resources are devoted to diagnosis and treatment during the first few days of a stay. As the patient remains in the hospital, the intensity of care is likely to decline. Thus, average cost often declines as the patient's length of stay increases. If the payment is fixed and average cost declines with longer stays, hospitals can profit by extending patient stays.

The hospital admission or case has been used as the unit of output for payment, most notably by Medicare's prospective payment system (PPS) in the United States. PPS replaced retrospective cost reimbursement that Medicare had used as the basis for paying hospitals previously. With the case as output, in addition to being conscious of the costs incurred in the provision of care, which applies to all prospective payment systems, hospitals have an incentive to reduce length of stay, thereby increasing profit per case since the payment it receives does not decline as length of stay declines. However, patients may be discharged from hospitals both "quicker and sicker," although the empirical evidence indicates overall that the Medicare PPS system resulted in quicker discharges but not sicker patients following discharge. A disadvantage of using the case instead of the patient day as the unit of output is that payment may not track severity of disease as well as a per diem system does. Thus, with per case payment, the hospital is generally placed at a disadvantage in accepting patients with relatively severe conditions among those with the same diagnosis for care.

Capitated systems have not proved to be popular to date with hospitals or with the public more generally. From the hospital's vantage point, under capitation, the organization is asked to accept a risk that the persons for whom the hospital receives a capitated payment may prove to be less healthy than anticipated.

In addition, the hospital is being asked to undertake a risk-bearing role as an insurer does. The hospital may not have a sufficiently large patient base to adequately diversify away the risk of individual patient variation in the use of hospital care.

Global budgeting has been applied in Canada (Rozek and Mulhern 1994).[10] For example, when universal hospital insurance (Medicare) was first implemented in Ontario, Canada, the Ministry of Health engaged in an extensive line-by-line review of each hospital's budget. Based on these data, the Ministry set up global budgets for each hospital. The global budgets, administered by the Ministry of Health, cover the hospital's operating costs and equipment depreciation; other capital costs and graduate medical education are funded through other methods. In addition to Ministry allocations, hospitals receive approximately 20 percent of total hospital operating funds from sources other than those of the Ministry (e.g., from the workers' compensation program, payments for care provided to people living outside Ontario, differential room charges, and income from endowments and parking lot fees). The starting point for a hospital's budget is the previous year's funding level. The funding level is increased each year to account for four different areas of designated increases: inflation, growth, new and expanded services, and life support. The increases in the global budget to account for inflation and growth are set by formula, while the other two are subject to negotiations between each individual hospital and the Ministry.

The purpose of the inflation adjustment is to increase hospital budgets to compensate hospitals for increases in the prices they pay for hospital inputs they purchase. The growth payments are meant to pay hospitals for the increased costs resulting from increases in the volume of services they provide, such as increases in outpatient visits or in patient days, using existing equipment and facilities. If a hospital wants to add a new program or expand an old one, it must receive permission to do so from both the Ministry of Health and the local planning agency. The capital costs to support a new program come from fund-raising and appropriations from the Ministry; the operating costs associated with a program can be included in the budget only with Ministry approval. Many high-technology services, such as diagnostic imaging and laboratory services, are available only in hospitals. Thus, control over the hospital's budget is the primary tool used to limit the growth of such services. A small number of programs, mainly in teaching hospitals, are designated life support programs, such as hemodialysis and cardiac surgery. The increase in the costs associated with these programs is funded through the life-support program.

While global budgets give government substantial control over hospital spending, they have important disadvantages. First, inequities among hospitals develop over time. Hospitals with high initial budgets, due for example to inefficiency not accounted for in setting up initial budgets, tend to maintain relatively high budgets over time. Second, the growth payments reward hospitals that do not

10. The discussion of global budgeting in Canada draws on Lave, Jacobs, and Markel (1992).

reduce length of stay and otherwise maintain outputs at inefficiently high levels. In two provinces, there is evidence of bed blockers (Rozek and Mulhern 1994, 282). Bed blockers are patients who have been hospitalized for a long time but for whom the marginal cost to the hospital per extra day in the hospital is low. By having bed blockers, hospitals can maintain volume while reducing the average cost of patients in the hospital. Such cost containment runs completely counter to efficiency enhancement. Third, there is no adjustment of changes in case mix either at the hospital level or in the hospital's catchment area. One could say these are just details in implementation. But when there are larger numbers of hospitals in a particular jurisdiction, as a practical matter, it would be very difficult to customize individual hospital budgets to reflect each hospital's situation and maintain incentives for efficiency. The Canadian province of Ontario has addressed these deficiencies in large part by deviating from pure global budgeting and adopting some features of US payment systems of hospitals.

There is a large body of empirical research on the performance of rate and revenue regulation in the hospital sector. The vast majority of empirical studies are for the United States. Thus, our brief overview of empirical findings focuses on evidence from the United States.

The Nixon administration's ESP lasted only three years. Overall, based on the "war stories" of ESP, this approach is unlikely to be implemented any time soon, except perhaps during a major war or other national crisis. However, the empirical findings are mixed. Studies assessing the ESP experience include Ginsburg (1978), Sloan (1981, 1983), Lanning, Morrisey, and Ohsfeldt (1991), and Antel, Ohsfeldt, and Becker (1995).

Prospective payment programs implemented by a few US states (other than Maryland, which used individual services as outputs) used either the per diem or the case as the unit of output. As Salkever (2000) emphasized, empirical findings on the effect of these programs on hospital cost have varied over time. Early studies (e.g., Sloan 1980, 1983; Coelen and Sullivan 1981) generally found that these programs reduced hospital costs below what they would have been in the absence of these programs. However, later studies (e.g., Antel, Ohsfeldt, and Becker 1995) failed to find an effect on cost. One reason for the change may be the growth of competitive forces in the hospital sector, described below, as well as the introduction of Medicare PPS. Over time, states have dropped rate-setting programs, which is consistent with the empirical evidence of a diminishing effect of such programs on hospital.

Medicare PPS applies only to Medicare, not to all sources of hospital payment as did the state rate-setting programs. Antel, Ohsfeldt, and Becker (1995), using state-year data for 1968–1990, found that if anything, PPS increased cost per hospital admission. However, other studies (Coulam and Gaumer 1991; Gold, Chu, Felt, et al. 1993) found that PPS reduced hospital costs. Based on his assessment of the findings overall, Salkever (2000) concluded that PPS did reduce hospital cost. At a minimum, PPS changed the psychology of hospital managers. No longer was there a reward for inefficiency.

6.5 AN ALTERNATIVE TO REGULATING HOSPITALS: INCREASING COMPETITION AMONG HOSPITALS

DESCRIPTION

While the medical arms race represents a form of competition, it is a different form from what economists typically mean by competition. First, in the medical arms race, competition is not based on differences in competitors' prices. Prices are irrelevant to the physician's decision about the hospital to which his or her patient is admitted. Second, generally when competition prevails in product market, the consumer makes informed choices based on comparisons of prices and product attributes.

The physician has tended to dominant in deciding whether and to which hospital the patient is admitted. In an important sense, if there is a consumer of hospital services, it has been the patient's physician. Private or public insurers have had no voice in this decision. In fact, in the United States, there were laws preventing insurers from influencing choice of hospital. Insurer influence on choice of hospital was considered to be interference in the practice of medicine. Given that insurers had to pay for care the patient received at any facility of the physician's and the hospital's choosing, insurers were placed at a substantial disadvantage in negotiating contracts with individual hospitals. A hospital could essentially force the insurer to pay virtually any cost or price the hospital demanded.

Since the early 1980s, statutory changes have resulted in a major change in the way that hospital care is purchased in the United States. The result has been an increase in hospital competition, but competition in the sense that economists use the term. The new system relies on competition among health insurance plans. Plans compete on the basis of premiums, benefit structure, and the hospitals and physicians affiliated with each plan.

The statutory change has involved enactment of "selective contracting" laws. Under such laws, insurers can contract with fewer than all hospitals and physicians in a geographic area. With the power of walking away from a hospital that demands too high a payment, insurers have been granted substantially greater bargaining power vis-à-vis hospitals. An inefficient hospital now faces the threat of losing important contracts and hence large numbers of patients. Now, in contrast to the situation that prevailed under retrospective cost reimbursement and similar payment systems, the hospital has a much clearer incentive to be efficient.

A second major development, which also occurred in the United States in the 1980s, was the implementation of the Medicare PPS system. In contrast to private health insurers, Medicare does not have the power to exclude hospitals from its network. But PPS pays a fixed amount per hospital stay, and the amount is independent of an individual hospital's costs. Thus, an inefficient hospital potentially would provide care to Medicare beneficiaries at a loss.

Whereas before, with more hospitals in a market area, a medical arms race might have been likely to ensue, under the new, more competitive regime, more hospitals mean lower costs and prices, holding other factors constant. In fact, if a hospital has a monopoly in its market area, it would be relatively well positioned to negotiate with individual insurers. If an insurer wants to do business in the area, it has to deal with the monopolist hospital. However, under selective contracting, when there is competition among hospitals, insurers can exclude a hospital with which it cannot arrive at an agreement on prices.

Empirical Evidence on the Effects of Competition under the New Regime

We can view competition among hospitals in the post-PPS era in two ways: direct observation of change, and empirical analysis of the effects of PPS and other changes that accompanied PPS.

Prior to the 1980s, there was little competition among US hospitals. Many hospitals were (and many are) nonprofits in the community they served. Hospital marketing departments, if they existed, were small. Hospitals saw themselves to a greater or lesser extent as public utilities.

Since the 1980s, hospitals have increasingly had to bargain with insurers over terms of payment. Many have greatly expanded their capacity to deliver care on an ambulatory basis. Hospitals now frequently advertise for patients. The advertisement in figure 6.9 is an example of a major teaching hospital aiming to attract patients with a specialized condition (disease of a heart valve) from a geographic area far larger than the city where it is located. Patients with Medicare and some private insurance plans may be covered by insurance if they travel to a distant hospital for care. However, many patients would be restricted by their insurance policies to use hospitals in their networks.

Although the new system has attractive features, empirical analysis was needed to rigorously demonstrate its effects.

Robinson and Luft (1985) assessed the effect of the medical arms race on hospital costs in the 1970s and early 1980s. They computed the number of competitors faced by each hospital in the United States. A 15-mile radius from a hospital was considered sufficiently close for another hospital to be in competition with the hospital in question. Controlling for a large number of other factors, they found that hospitals with more competitors had higher costs per admission. Similarly, other studies found that hospitals with more competitors had higher ratios

A super subspecialist

Duke cardiothoracic surgeon Donald Glower, MD, and colleagues help patients look forward to healthier lives.

Talk about your unique specialty.
I am what you would call a super-subspecialist because of what I do with heart valves. My work focuses upon minimally invasive valve surgery, which didn't even exist 20 years ago. It's a very narrow niche—not many people do this. Minimally invasive valve surgery simply minimizes the cuts and allows us to get into the body and disturb a lot less tissue than with other types of procedures, so the recovery is typically much quicker and less painful.

You've been a surgeon for 30 years. You must have learned a lot about the concerns of a patient facing heart surgery.
Yes, and that's why I think it's important to have a lot of interaction with patients before surgery. This can be a very scary situation for most people. Giving people some hope is important, and I enjoy this aspect of my work.

How does Duke stand out in the field of cardiothoracic surgery?
Duke is a world leader in minimally invasive valve surgery, heart and lung transplantation, and endovascular therapy for cardiovascular disease. The Duke faculty are great to work with and it really is true that here at Duke, you can come up with almost any idea and you'll find someone at Duke who wants to collaborate with you. It's very exciting—lots of bright people on the leading edge. And Duke is rapidly adaptable. If you have a good idea, lots of people can get behind you and support you. By golly, if it makes sense, the research happens.

Why would a patient travel a great distance to come to Duke?
Duke is an exciting place with lots of bright people focused on developing new ways to help patients. Whatever problem might arise, there are expert physicians who would love to help solve the problem. There's a lot of good quality care available elsewhere, but patients who come to us are looking for something unusual—something not available just anywhere. We have world experts who are able to deal with the most complex needs.

Dr. Glower and colleagues are committed to excellence in the treatment of heart disease, lung disease, aneurysms of the great vessels, and disorders of the esophagus.

FIGURE 6.9
Hospital Advertises for Patients Needing Specialized Care
Source: Copyright 2010 Duke University Health System

of hospital employees to patients, a higher probability of having cardiac facilities at the hospital, and more special services, such as mammography and cobalt therapy (for cancer) (Luft, Robinson, Garnick, et al. 1986; Robinson, Garnick, and McPhee 1987; Robinson 1988). Subsequently, Zwanziger and Melnick (1988) focused on the change in the relationship among costs, technology diffusion, and the number of competitors after the change in payment practices introduced by Medicare in 1983, as well as the selective contracting law's implementation in California in 1982, and found that the positive relationship between the number of competitors of a hospital and measures of hospital cost evident in 1983 had disappeared by 1985.

Keeler, Melnick, and Zwanziger (1999), using data from the period after PPS was implemented, 1986–1994, reached the same conclusion. Over this period, the relationship between concentration of hospitals in a market and hospital prices steadily changed, with the relationship between hospital prices and competition in local markets being stronger toward the end than at the beginning of their observational period.

Keeler and co-authors measured competition within a local market in this study and many others measured by the *Herfindahl-Hirschman Index* (HHI),

$$\text{HHI} = \Sigma s_i^2, \tag{6.5}$$

where s_i is the fraction of total hospital discharges in the market that hospital i has. In other studies, output has been defined as patient days rather than discharges.

The summation in equation 6.5 includes all hospitals in the hospital's market area. If the hospital is a monopolist, that is, has all discharges in the market, the HHI is 1. If there are four hospitals with unequal number of discharges, the HHI is $0.15^2 + 0.35^2 + 0.27^2 + 0.23^2 = 0.27$, for example. As the number of hospitals in a market rises, the HHI approaches zero in value. The key assumption underlying the use of the HHI as a measure of competition is that sellers find it easier to collude in price-setting when the HHI is higher.

The conclusion that the medical arms race was important before 1983 has been challenged by Dranove, Shanley, and Simon (1992), who argued that the Robinson-Luft analysis was misspecified and the results could be attributed to confounding. By confounding, researchers mean that other variates not included in the model but should have been included and are systematically related to explanatory variables included in the model leads to biased parameter estimates on the included explanatory variables.

Although empirical evidence in support of the medical arms race hypothesis has been challenged, retrospective cost-based reimbursement clearly gave hospitals an incentive to compete by offering a broader and rich range of services. Whether or not the incentive per se has contributed to hospital cost inflation is another matter.

EMPIRICAL EVIDENCE ON THE EFFECTS OF INCREASED COMPETITION ON HOSPITAL QUALITY

A major issue with competition among hospitals is whether or not increased competition leads hospitals to reduce quality or increase it. The conventional wisdom among health professionals decades ago was that competition reduced quality. This thinking relied on the view that only health professionals could judge what was good for patients, and patients and other non-health professionals were incapable of determining the care they needed. Consumer preferences were regarded as unimportant and not to receive weight in health decisions. Against this background, there were bans on advertising by health professionals and other professionals, such as lawyers. It was unprofessional to discuss fees. Competition among hospitals such as occurs in other sectors was viewed as unseemly.

In the era in which many say that the medical arms race ruled in the United States, the general conclusion was that competition increased quality. Yet under the new regime, as hospitals compete for contracts in a competitive market, might there be a tendency for hospitals to cut quality, especially noncontractible quality? Several studies of US markets have addressed this issue.

A well-cited study using data on persons hospitalized for heart attacks from the US Medicare program by Kessler and McClellan (2000), entitled "Is Hospital Competition Socially Wasteful?," focused on the effect of hospital competition on quality of care using mortality following hospitalization as the outcome measure of quality. The authors' measure of hospital competition was the HHI in the hospital's market area. The HHI is likely to be endogenous to a hospital's quality since its market share, which is part of the calculation of the HHI, is likely to depend on the hospital's quality level. Hospitals with poor quality should attract fewer patients, holding other factors constant.

Kessler and McClellan accounted for endogeneity of the HHI by estimating equations to predict each patient's choice of hospital based on the distance from place of residence to alternative hospitals in the market as an important explanatory variable.[11] Given the emergency nature of a heart attack, people will consider relative distances a major factor in choice of hospital. It seems unlikely that a person would base the choice of housing location on the quality of nearby hospitals, especially if the person does not have a chronic condition that may lead to a hospital admission on an emergency basis. If the latter assumption is acceptable, Kessler and McClellan's technique allows examining the concentration of hospital output without considering that some hospitals may offer better cardiac care and attract patients for this reason.

Kessler and McClellan's key finding was that before 1991 in the United States, increased competition among hospitals in a market reduced quality despite the medical arms race, but after 1991, increased competition in a market area increased quality. They attributed the change to the changed Medicare payment policy implemented in 1980s and to the growth of HMOs during 1990s. Although much of the

11. These studies require a measure of competition among hospitals and the usual measure of choice is the HHI. The use of the HHI has been subject to several critiques. One is theoretical. The ideal measure would gauge the elasticity of the individual hospital's demand curve. The HHI is not such a measure. This is a somewhat subtle point and thus merits some discussion here. The elasticity of demand measured in chapter 3 using data from the RAND Health Insurance Experiment and other data sources is an industry demand curve. The industry demand curve is the (vertical) sum of demand curves of individual consumers in a market. By contrast, the relevant demand curve for an analysis of competition among sellers in a market is the individual seller's demand curve, in this context, the individual hospital's demand curve. It is quite possible that the industry demand curve is quite inelastic, that is, the quantity demanded is quite unresponsive to price, and the individual seller's demand curve is virtually flat (horizontal). With a flat demand curve, if the seller raises its price a tiny bit above the market-clearing price, the seller stands to lose all sales. For example, the demand for gasoline is much less elastic than is the demand curve for an individual gas station. The same presumably goes for hospitals. In the case of hospitals, the high elasticity of demand faced by the individual hospital is not because patients tend to choose hospitals based on small differences in price. Rather, it is the insurers that cover the patients that do this. And under selective contracting, insurers can channel patients to hospitals in their networks. Another problem with the HHI is that there is, as noted above, substantial evidence that quality of care increases with the number of procedures that a hospital performs. The HHI considers market shares, not levels of output.

growth in HMO enrollment involved persons not enrolled in Medicare but rather in other health insurance plans, they argued there was a spillover from the private insurance market to Medicare. If higher quality were offered to privately insured patients, as a practical matter, it would be offered to Medicare beneficiaries as well.

Gowrisankaran and Town (2003) used data on hospitalized patients with all different types of payment sources in Los Angeles, California. The patients were admitted either for pneumonia or for a heart attack. In this study, increased competition for Medicare patients decreased quality, but increased competition for privately insured patients who were enrolled in HMOs increased quality. The results for Medicare contradict the findings of Kessler and McClellan (2000). One reason why increased competition could lower quality is that the price paid by the insurer is less than the marginal cost that the hospital incurs in treating patients. But as Gaynor (2006, 38) notes, the treatment of heart attacks is thought to be highly profitable, even when the payment source is Medicare.

The results of the Gowrisankaran and Town study point to the danger of generalizing from a single study. The question of whether or not increased competition leads to higher or lower quality is still unsettled empirically. And whether it does or does not is likely to depend on particulars, such as whether the hospital possesses market power to set prices for its services or the price is set high externally, such as by an insurer-purchaser, relative to the marginal cost to the hospital of providing the service.

6.6 SUMMARY AND CONCLUSIONS

One distinguishing feature of hospitals is that the vast majority are organized as not-for-profit enterprises. This chapter has explored possible reasons for the predominance of not-for-profit hospitals and has described economic models relevant to not-for-profit hospitals' behavior. Still another possibility that we did not explore is that not-for-profit hospitals maximize profits and use these profits to subsidize unprofitable activities.

Relationships between physicians and hospitals differ among countries. In this chapter, we have emphasized US hospitals, where hospitals and medical staffs are most often organized as separate entities, although hospitals have appropriately been called "the doctor's workshop." In many other countries, physicians either practice in hospital settings or as ambulatory care physicians. When a person is hospitalized, the person obtains care from a physician other than the one the person sees on an ambulatory basis. The separation of hospital-based from ambulatory care physicians virtually eliminates the possibility of the cartel-like arrangement in the Pauly-Redisch model of the physicians' cooperative or in a physician-hospital organization.

Competition among hospitals is generally on a non-price basis to the extent that it exists at all. In the United States, price competition among hospitals is growing and replacing the regulatory approaches that were implemented as solutions to high rates of hospital cost inflation in the 1960s and 1970s.

In theory, price competition has attractive features. Whether or not societies are better off with a competitive hospital sector remains to be seen. Price competition among hospitals appears to have been successful in controlling the growth of hospital costs. However, empirical evidence on the quality of care under conditions of price competition is mixed.

Quality measure and quality assurance are both complex issues in the health care field. The next chapter analyses issues of quality of care in both hospital and ambulatory care.

KEY CONCEPTS

- not-for-profit hospital
- physician-hospital organizations
- noncontractible quality
- price regulation
- non-price competition
- medical arms race
- global budgets
- Herfindahl-Hirschman Index (HHI)
- residual claimant
- physicians' cooperative model
- entry regulation
- price competition
- retrospective cost reimbursement
- prospective payment
- selective contracting

REVIEW AND DISCUSSION QUESTIONS

6.1 Who are decision makers in hospitals? Do the hospital's decision makers differ in the Newhouse model and the Pauly-Redisch model? If so, explain how they differ.

6.2 Suppose a for-profit hospital makes its decisions by adopting the rule of profit maximizing and another not-for-profit hospital follows the decision rule described by the Newhouse model. Which hospital is likely to be more efficient? How can hospital efficiency be measured?

6.3 What is meant by the term "physicians' cooperative"? Give three examples of cooperatives in markets other than for physicians' services and explain the motivation for forming such cooperatives.

6.4 In the Pauly-Redisch model, physicians on the medical staff are the residual claimants.

a. What is meant by the term "residual claimant"—in general and in this context?

b. What is meant by closed versus open staffing of hospitals? Describe the circumstances under which staffing is closed and open, using a graph.

c. In what sense might closed staffing be a good thing from the standpoint of doctors? From the standpoint of consumer welfare? In what sense might closed staffing be disadvantageous to consumers?

6.5 Describe at least three arguments in the economic literature to justify the fact that not-for-profit hospitals, both private and public, tend to be more numerous than for-profit hospitals in many health care systems around the world.

6.6 What is the theoretical relationship between hospital ownership and hospital performance? Do private not-for-profit hospitals enjoy any advantage that might increase their measured efficiency relative to that of for-profit hospitals? What do the Newhouse and the physicians' cooperative models imply about the efficiency of private not-for-profit hospitals relative to that of for-profit hospitals?

6.7 Overall, what does the empirical evidence show about the relative performance of for-profit and private not-for-profit hospitals?

6.8 What is meant by the expression "medical arms race"? What are preconditions for such a race to occur? What are the consequences of hospital competition induced by a medical arms race?

6.9 Explain the distinction between retrospective cost-based reimbursement and a prospective payment system (PPS), such as the one operated by the Medicare program in the United States. Why do health care payers generally prefer PPS to cost-based reimbursement but providers often prefer cost-based reimbursement to PPS?

EXERCISES

6.1 Hospitals are thought to be subject to economies and diseconomies of scale and scope. What is meant by economies/diseconomies of scale and scope? What are sources of scale economies/diseconomies and scope economies/diseconomies in hospital settings? List and discuss up to three each for scale and scope economies.

6.2 Assume the hospital is a monopolist with a demand function given by $p = 404 - 2x$, where p is price of hospital care and x is the quantity of hospital care, and a cost function given by $C = 300 + 4x + 8x^2$, where C is total cost. Compute marginal cost and average cost. In addition, calculate the hospital's profit-maximizing output, price, revenue, and profit.

6.3 Now assume that the hospital is a monopolist with a demand function that incorporates quality of care as well as quantity. Quality enters into both the demand and cost functions according to $p = 100 - 3x + 4\sqrt{y}$ and $C = 4x^2 + 10x + y$, where p is the price of hospital care, x is the quantity of hospital care, y is the quality of hospital care, and C is total cost. Compute the hospital's profit-maximizing output, quality, price, revenue, and profit.

6.4 Suppose that a hospital has a production function of the type $\text{Ln}x = \gamma + \alpha \ln S + \beta \ln B$, where x is the quantity of output, S is the level of hospital services (e.g., radiographs, laboratory tests, patient physical therapy sessions), and B is number of hospital beds; γ, α, and β are parameters. The hospital buys S at price p_S and B at price p_B.

a. Compute the hospital's marginal product and its average product.

b. If regulators force the hospital to decrease the amount of B by 10 percent, what must the hospital do to maintain quantity x?

c. If the hospital maintains quantity x, what will be the effect of the regulation on total hospital expenditures? Explain your answer.

6.5 As described in the chapter, in Newhouse's model, the hospital maximizes utility, which depends on levels of quantity and quality of care, subject to a break-even constraint (price equals average cost). Use this model to analyze the effects of the following exogenous changes in the hospital's production possibility curve—that is, the hospital quantity-quality frontier (as shown in fig. 6.3)—and the hospital's optimal choices of quantity and quality of care (as shown in fig. 6.4).

a. an increase in the wage rate paid to the hospital's employees;

b. an increase in the number of persons with health insurance coverage in the hospital's market area;

c. implementation of a fixed dollar subsidy per unit of hospital care by the city government.

6.6 Based on the Pauly-Redisch model, analyze the effects of the following exogenous changes on the optimal number of physicians on a hospital's medical staff (as shown in fig. 6.6).

a. an increase in the wage rate of the hospital's employees;

b. an increase in the number of persons with health insurance coverage in the hospital's market area;

c. implementation of a fixed dollar subsidy per unit of hospital care by the city government.

6.7 In some settings, physicians are employed on a fixed salary basis by the hospital. In others, physicians function as independent entrepreneurs and bill for care they deliver to hospitalized patients separately from the hospital's bill for its services. Describe three differences that you would expect to arise under these distinct employment/compensation arrangements for physicians.

6.8 Suppose there are two hospitals in town, Adam Hospital and Brown Hospital. Both hospitals face similar demand and cost functions. Thus, using the terminology of the Newhouse model, both hospitals have a similar production possibility curve. However, utility functions differ between these two hospitals. The boss of Adam Hospital focuses on increasing access to health care in the community and hence places a higher value on providing a high quantity of hospital care. By contrast, the boss of Brown Hospital focuses on increasing the quality of health care in the community and hence places a higher value on adopting the new medical technology.

a. Show graphically how these two hospitals make choices of optimal quantity and quality (given their different objective functions). Which hospital is more likely to become a large hospital (in terms of hospital beds)? Explain your answer.

b. Assume that the local government imposes an entry restriction to limit expansion of hospital beds in the community. Specifically, the government requires a certificate of need if a hospital adds more than 100 new beds. Which hospital is more likely to be affected by such entry regulation, and why is this so?

c. Assume that the local government adopts a regulation to restrict adoption of new medical technology. Specifically, the government prohibits small hospitals (e.g., those hospitals with 250 beds or fewer) from adopting new and expensive medical technology. Which hospital is more likely to be affected by this entry regulation? Explain your answer.

6.9 Assume there is only one hospital in a small town. This hospital faces a demand function given by $p = 304 - 2x$, where p is the price of hospital care and

x is the quantity of hospital care, and a cost function given by $C = 500 + 4x + 8x^2$, where C is total cost.

a. Suppose the local government imposes price regulation on hospitals that freezes the price of hospital care at 250. Show the effects of this price ceiling on the hospital's quantity of care and its revenue and profit. Be sure to indicate what the values of quantity, revenue, and profit would be in the absence of such regulation.

b. If the local government were to further lower the maximum price that the hospital can charge to patients to 240, compute the effect of this new price ceiling on the hospital's quantity of care and its revenue and profit, compared to the older, higher price ceiling. Will this hospital remain in the market or will it exit? Explain your answer.

6.10 Suppose Town A and Town B each have four hospitals. The following table gives the bed size and output of each hospital.

Hospitals	Town A Size (No. of Beds)	Town A Output (Annual No. of Patient Discharges)	Town B Size (No. of Beds)	Town B Output (Annual No. of Patient Discharges)
A	250	8,000	100	2,200
B	250	7,300	50	1,100
C	250	6,400	500	16,000
D	250	5,400	350	10,000

Based on the above information, what is the Herfindahl-Hirschman Index (HHI) for each town? Which market (Town A or Town B) is more concentrated? Does your answer depend on how you measure hospital market shares?

ONLINE SUPPLEMENTAL MATERIAL

NOT-FOR-PROFIT OWNERSHIP

http://econpapers.repec.org/bookchap/eeeheachp/1-21.htm

HOSPITALS IN THE NEWS (A FREE COLLECTION OF ARTICLES ABOUT HOSPITALS PUBLISHED IN THE *New York Times*)

http://topics.nytimes.com/top/news/health/diseasesconditionsandhealthtopics/hospitals/index.html

Hospital Payment Systems in Europe

http://www.euro.who.int/en/home/projects/observatory/publications/euro-observer/hospital-payment-systems-in-europe

Hospital Quality Initiatives

https://www.cms.gov/HospitalQualityInits

http://www.aha.org/aha_app/issues/HQA/index.jsp

Hospital Associations

http://www.fah.org/fahCMS/home.aspx

http://www.cha.ca

http://www.aha.org

Healthcare Cost and Utilization Project

http://www.ahrq.gov/data/hcup

Supplemental Reading

Cuellar, A. E., and P. J. Gertler. 2006. Strategic Integration of Hospitals and Physicians. *Journal of Health Economics* 25 (1): 1–28.

Duggan, M. 2004. Does Contracting Out Increase the Efficiency of Government Programs? Evidence from Medicaid HMOs. *Journal of Public Economics* 88 (12): 2549–2572.

Eggleston, K., Y. C. Shen, J. Lau, et al. 2008. Hospital Ownership and Quality of Care: What Explains the Different Results in the Literature? *Health Economics* 17 (12): 1345–1362.

Finkelstein, A. 2007. The Aggregate Effects of Health Insurance: Evidence from the Introduction of Medicare. *Quarterly Journal of Economics* 122 (1): 1–37.

References

American Hospital Association. 2002. *Trends in Hospital Financing: TrendWatch Chartbook 2002*, 41–48. Washington, DC: American Hospital Association, the Lewin Group.

Antel, J. J., R. L. Ohsfeldt, and E. R. Becker. 1995. State Regulation and Hospital Costs. *Review of Economics and Statistics* 77 (3): 416–422.

Arocena, P., and A. García-Prado. 2006. Accounting for Quality in the Measurement of Hospital Performance: Evidence from Costa Rica. *Health Economics* 16 (7): 667–685.

Arrow, K. J. 1963. Uncertainty and the Welfare Economics of Medical Care. *American Economic Review* 53 (5):941–973.

Baicker, K., and D. Staiger. 2005. Fiscal Shenanigans, Targeted Federal Health Care Funds, and Patient Mortality. *Quarterly Journal of Economics* 120 (1): 345–386.

Birkmeyer, J. D., A. E. Siewers, E. V. Finlayson, et al. 2002. Hospital Volume and Surgical Mortality in the United States. *New England Journal of Medicine* 346 (15): 1128–1137.

Burstall, M., and K. Wallerstein. 1994. The Health Care System in France. In *Financing Health Care*, ed. U. K. Hoffmeyer and T. R. McCarthy. Dordrecht: Kluwer Academic.

Coelen, C., and D. Sullivan. 1981. An Analysis of the Effects of Prospective Reimbursement Programs on Hospital Expenditures. *Health Care Financing Review* 2 (3): 1–40.

Conover, C. J., and F. A. Sloan. 1998. Does Removing Certificate-of-Need Regulations Lead to a Surge in Health Care Spending? *Journal of Health Politics, Policy and Law* 23 (3): 455–481.

Coulam, R. F., and G. L. Gaumer. 1991. Medicare's Prospective Payment System: A Critical Appraisal. *Health Care Financing Review: Annual Supplement* 13 (Supplement): 45–77.

Cuellar, A. E., and P. J. Gertler. 2006. Strategic Integration of Hospitals and Physicians. *Journal of Health Economics* 25 (1): 1–28.

Custer, W. S., P. Ketsche, B. Sherman, et al. 2006. Report of Data Analyses to the Georgia Commission on the Efficacy of the CON Program, Georgia State University, Atlanta.

Devereaux, P. J., P. T. L. Choi, C. Lachetti, et al. 2002. A Systematic Review and Meta-analysis of Studies Comparing Mortality Rates of Private For-Profit and Private Not-For-Profit Hospitals. *Canadian Medical Association Journal* 166 (11): 1399–1406.

Dranove, D., M. Shanley, and C. Simon. 1992. Is Hospital Competition Wasteful? *RAND Journal of Economics* 23 (2): 247–262.

Duggan, M. 2002. Hospital Market Structure and the Behavior of Not-For-Profit Hospitals. *RAND Journal of Economics* 33 (3): 433–446.

Duggan, M. 2004. Does Contracting Out Increase the Efficiency of Government Programs? Evidence from Medicaid HMOs. *Journal of Public Economics* 88 (12): 2549–2572.

Eggleston, K., Y. C. Shen, J. Lau, et al. 2008. Hospital Ownership and Quality of Care: What Explains the Different Results in the Literature? *Health Economics* 17 (12): 1345–1362.

Finkelstein, A. 2007. The Aggregate Effects of Health Insurance: Evidence from the Introduction of Medicare. *Quarterly Journal of Economics* 122 (1): 1–37.

Gaynor, M. 2006. Competition and Quality in Health Care Markets. *Foundations and Trends in Microeconomics* 2 (6): 441–508.

Ginsburg, P. B. 1978. Impact of the Economic Stabilization Program on Hospitals: An Analysis with Aggregate Data. In *Hospital Cost Containment: Selected Notes for Future Policy*, ed. M. Zubkoff, I. Raskin and R. Hanft, 293–323. New York: Milbank Memorial Fund.

Gold, M., K. Chu, S. Felt, et al. 1993. Effects of Selected Cost-Containment Efforts: 1971–1993. *Health Care Financing Review* 14 (3): 183–225.

Gowrisankaran, G., and R. Town 2003. Competition, Payers, and Hospital Quality. *Health Services Research* 38 (6p1): 1403–1422.

Hansmann, H. 1996. The Changing Roles of Public, Private, and Nonprofit Enterprise in Education, Health Care, and Other Human Services. In *Individual and Social Responsibility*, ed. V. R. Fuchs, 245–276. Chicago: University of Chicago Press.

Hart, O., A. Shleifer, and R. W. Vishny. 1997. The Proper Scope of Government: Theory and an Application to Prisons. *Quarterly Journal of Economics* 112 (4): 1127–1161.

Hoffmeyer, U., and T. R. McCarthy. 1994. The Health Care System in Germany. In *Financing Health Care*, ed. U. Hoffmeyer and T. R. McCarthy, 1: 419–512. Dordrecht: Kluwer Academic.

Hyman, D. A. 1998. Hospital Conversions: Fact, Fantasy, and Regulatory Follies. *Journal of Corporation Law* 23 (4): 741–778.

Keeler, E. B., G. Melnick, and J. Zwanziger. 1999. The Changing Effects of Competition on Non-Profit and For-Profit Hospital Pricing Behavior. *Journal of Health Economics* 18 (1): 69–86.

Kessler, D. P., and M. B. McClellan. 2000. Is Hospital Competition Socially Wasteful? *Quarterly Journal of Economics* 115 (2): 577–615.

Lanning, J. A., M. A. Morrisey, and R. L. Ohsfeldt. 1991. Endogenous Hospital Regulation and Its Effects on Hospital and Non-Hospital Expenditures. *Journal of Regulatory Economics* 3 (2): 137–154.

Lave, J. R., P. Jacobs, and F. Markel. 1992. Transitional Funding: Changing Ontario's Global Budgeting System. *Health Care Financing Review* 13 (3): 77–84.

Luft, H. S., J. C. Robinson, D. W. Garnick, et al. 1986. The Role of Specialized Clinical Services in Competition among Hospitals. *Inquiry* 23 (1): 83–94.

Magnussen, J., T. P. Hagen, and O. M. Kaarboe. 2007. Centralized or Decentralized? A Case Study of Norwegian Hospital Reform. *Social Science & Medicine* 64 (10): 2129–2137.

Munch, P., and D. E. Smallwood. 1980. Solvency Regulation in the Property-Liability Insurance Industry: Empirical Evidence. *Bell Journal of Economics* 11 (1): 261–282.

Newhouse, J. P. 1970. Toward a Theory of Nonprofit Institutions: An Economic Model of a Hospital. *American Economic Review* 60 (1): 64–74.

Noh, M., Y. Lee, S.-C. Yun, et al. 2006. Determinants of Hospital Closure in South Korea: Use of a Hierarchical Generalized Linear Model. *Social Science & Medicine* 63 (9): 2320–2329.

Norton, E. C., and D. O. Staiger. 1994. How Hospital Ownership Affects Access to Care for the Uninsured. *RAND Journal of Economics* 25 (1): 171–185.

Pauly, M., and M. Redisch. 1973. Not-for-Profit Hospital as a Physicians' Cooperative. *American Economic Review* 63 (1): 87–99.

Picone, G., S.-Y. Chou, and F. Sloan. 2002. Are For-Profit Hospital Conversions Harmful to Patients and to Medicare? *RAND Journal of Economics* 33 (3): 507–523.

Robinson, J. C. 1988. Hospital Quality Competition and the Economics of Imperfect Information. *Milbank Quarterly* 66 (3): 465–481.

Robinson, J. C., D. W. Garnick, and S. J. McPhee. 1987. Market and Regulatory Influences on the Availability of Coronary Angioplasty and Bypass Surgery in U.S. Hospitals. *New England Journal of Medicine* 317 (2): 85–90.

Robinson, J. C., and H. S. Luft. 1985. The Impact of Hospital Market Structure on Patient Volume, Average Length of Stay, and the Cost of Care. *Health Economics* 4 (4): 333–356.

Robinson, J. L., D. B. Nash, E. Moxey, et al. 2001. Certificate of Need and the Quality of Cardiac Surgery. *American Journal of Medical Quality* 16 (5): 155–160.

Rozek, R., and C. Mulhern. 1994. The Health Care System in Canada. In *Financing Health Care*, ed. U. Hoffmeyer and T. R. McCarthy, 255–344. Dordrecht: Kluwer Academic.

Salkever, D. S. 2000. Regulation of Prices and Investment in Hospitals in the United States. In *Handbook of Health Economics*, ed. J. P. Newhouse and A. J. Culyer, 1B:1490–1535. Amsterdam: Elsevier Science.

Salkever, D. S., and T. W. Bice. 1976. The Impact of Certificate-of-Need Controls on Hospital Investment. *Milbank Memorial Fund Quarterly: Health and Society* 54 (2): 185–214.

Silverman, E., and J. Skinner. 2004. Medicare Upcoding and Hospital Ownership. *Health Economics* 23 (2): 369–389.

Sloan, F. A. 1980. Internal Organization of Hospitals: A Descriptive Study. *Health Services Research* 15 (3): 203–230.

Sloan, F. A. 1981. Regulation and the Rising Cost of Hospital Care. *Review of Economics and Statistics* 63 (4): 479–487.

Sloan, F. A. 1983. Rate Regulation as a Strategy for Hospital Cost Control: Evidence from the Last Decade. *Milbank Memorial Fund Quarterly: Health and Society* 61 (2):195–221.

Sloan, F. A., G. A. Picone, D. H. Taylor, et al. 2001. Hospital Ownership and Cost and Quality of Care: Is There a Dime's Worth of Difference? *Journal of Health Economics* 20 (1): 1–21.

Sloan, F. A., and B. Steinwald. 1975. The Role of Health Insurance in the Physicians' Services Market. *Inquiry* 12 (4): 275–299.

Ssengooba, F., L. Atuyambe, B. McPake, et al. 2002. What Could Be Achieved with Greater Public Hospital Autonomy? Comparison of Public and PNFP Hospitals in Uganda. *Public Administration and Development* 22 (5): 415–428.

Vaughan-Sarrazin, M. S., E. L. Hannan, C. J. Gormley, et al. 2002. Mortality in Medicare Beneficiaries Following Coronary Artery Bypass Graft Surgery in States With and Without Certificate of Need Regulation. *Journal of the American Medical Association* 288 (15): 1859–1866.

Weisbrod, B. A. 1988. *The Nonprofit Economy*. Cambridge, MA: Harvard University Press.

Woolhandler, S., and D. U. Himmelstein. 1997. Costs of Care and Administration at For-Profit and Other Hospitals in the United States. *New England Journal of Medicine* 336 (11): 769–774.

Zwanziger, J., and G. A. Melnick. 1988. The Effects of Hospital Competition and the Medicare PPS Program on Hospital Cost Behavior in California. *Journal of Health Economics* 7 (4): 301–320.

QUALITY OF CARE AND MEDICAL MALPRACTICE

At first glance, it must seem unusual that a health economics textbook would devote considerable attention to quality of care. A popular but inaccurate view of economics is that the discipline deals only with cost and money. Accordingly, it would be legitimate to think that health economics deals with health care cost containment and the cost-effectiveness of specific health care technologies. After all, as explained in chapter 14, cost-effectiveness is a ratio of cost to some health outcome resulting from the use of the health care technology. Yet as we have seen in previous chapters, health care quality issues keep coming up. Since quality reflects the use of scarce resources and people are willing to pay varying extra amounts more for it, quality is very much an economic issue.

This chapter focuses on health care quality—how it is measured, the levels of quality that are currently delivered, how well the market works in delivering socially optimal levels of quality (and what economists mean by "socially optimal quality"), public policies that are appropriate when markets fail to deliver socially optimal quality levels, and the pluses and minuses of public policies designed to promote quality. There are some minuses!

7.1 MARKETS AND MARKET FAILURE

Quality differs in markets for almost an endless list of goods and services. Some individuals are willing to pay more for a higher-quality good or service; such higher quality is supplied if the additional amount consumers are willing to pay for such extra quality is equal to or greater than the marginal cost of providing the extra quality. Higher quality may reflect a combination of better materials being used to manufacture a product, more investment in design to achieve a more attractive product, and more resources being devoted to identifying product defects before the product is sold. In addition, higher quality includes a greater redundancy of inputs in the production process, which allows the firm to accommodate stochastic variation in demand for its product, greater product variety, more consumer assistance in production selection at the point of sale, faster delivery, and more lenient product exchange and return policies.

Governments do not regulate the quality of T-shirts or picture frames. Presumably the quality of the T-shirts and picture frames that markets provide is adequate to satisfy consumer wants. If it is not, presumably other T-shirt and picture frame suppliers will take their places in the marketplace. Externalities are not generally an important feature of either T-shirts or picture frames. While onlookers may become upset by the language or image on a T-shirt, the adverse reaction most directly adversely affects the wearer of the T-shirt. Further, we can safely assume that consumers are good at judging the types of products they want. If people want T-shirts with elaborate designs and in loud colors, the market will presumably provide such products.

A key rationale for government intervention in regulating quality is asymmetric information between buyers and sellers of the product. But public regulation may be warranted even when information is not asymmetric. Even when full information is available to consumers, some argue that consumers and sellers make bad decisions and thus require the benefit of public regulation to constrain or channel choices (see Breyer 1982). For example, consumers may borrow more money than is prudent, and banks may be too willing to lend to such consumers. These practices may lead to defaults, which, when widespread, can have an adverse effect on the economy overall. This type of externality has provided a rationale for government intervention in credit markets.

Individuals do not always have full information for making decisions. For one, markets may fail when parties to a transaction provide misleading or false information to others or fail to mention facts that these other parties may regard as pertinent to making a specific choice. Consumers of medical care may not be well positioned to evaluate the characteristics of alternative products, and they certainly are not as well positioned as the seller of the product, which reflects asymmetric information. For such goods, an element of trust on the part of the purchaser is required. Such goods are called *credence goods*.

At least some types of medical care, such as emergency room visits, complex surgery, and hospital stays for some conditions, logically fall in the category of credence goods.[1] Since consumption of credence goods is inherently based on trust, it seems unlikely that we would observe advertisements for B-quality hospital care in the way that we observe advertisements for low-priced hotel rooms. Hospitals

1. See box 5.2 in chapter 5 for a definition of credence goods.

might claim that their care is of the highest quality, but they would be reluctant to assert that their care is A quality, and their competitor across the street offers B-quality care. These claims are sometimes made in direct-to-consumer advertisements of pharmaceutical products (Berndt and Donohue 2008), but only two countries allow such advertisements, the United States and New Zealand.

The localized nature of hospital and physicians' services has limited the amount of rating of quality by national organizations. The same applies to other services as well. For example, *Consumer Reports* rates the quality of cell phone service in some large US cities, but service in the vast majority of locations is not rated. Hotel chains that are national or international receive quality ratings, but the presumption is that the quality of these facilities does not vary meaningfully in different geographic locations.

The quality of goods is often rated. One can obtain data comparing fuel consumption, speed, agility, and other characteristics of automobiles under controlled conditions. Frequency-of-repair records of various motor vehicles are not subject to controlled conditions. Different automobiles are often driven differently. Minivans seem unlikely to be run in drag races as some sports cars often are, or, if drag races are unseemly, minivans are unlikely to be seen racing around mountain curves as in television advertisements for some sports cars. Yet owners of sports cars may be more cautious about having regular oil changes than minivan owners are. These types of comparisons are likely to be more useful within a category of motor vehicle rather than across categories.

Because quality comparisons are commonplace, automobile manufacturers must consider the marginal cost versus marginal return of increased investments in quality lest they market their products at uncompetitive prices and lose market share. The Big Three automobile producers in the United States have learned this lesson the hard way by losing substantial market share. This has driven them to substantially improve the quality of their products in recent years. For automobiles, market forces provide a strong incentive for manufacturers to make cost-quality trade-offs. Cars with favorable frequency-of-repair records command much higher prices as both new and used cars than do cars with unfavorable records.

In the health care sector, quality varies, but the relationship between product quality and price appears to be much weaker than that for many goods and services. The localized nature of these markets is only one reason for the difference. Other reasons include the large number of low-volume providers—some inefficiently small, the complexity of the products, and the important role of professional norms. Reliance on such norms means that patients are to trust their physicians and physicians are to be worthy of such trust and are not to exploit such trust for their own personal gain. Frequency-of-repair records of motor vehicles have their counterpart in rates of adverse health outcomes that result from the receipt of medical care.

Injuries that occur as a result of receipt of medical care are called *iatrogenic injuries*. While we are often willing to overlook differences in consumer behavior, such as fast driving or poor maintenance, when comparing frequency of automobile repair, health care providers rightly warn that comparisons of rates of adverse health outcomes arising from the receipt of medical care may be misleading because patients differ in severity of illness in ways that are difficult to measure. Thus, for example, if patient outcomes are compared to gauge hospital quality, some hospitals accept relatively sick patients for treatment, and if the comparisons fail to account for these differences, the reported differences in patient outcomes will yield misleading inferences about quality differences. In such cases, quality differences are likely to be overstated. A hospital with a high rate of adverse outcomes may actually be better than one with fewer such outcomes.

Hospitals fearing that a high adverse outcome rate may adversely reflect their reputation consequently may seek to admit patients for care who will make them look good, and severely ill patients may be denied access. Car dealers, in contrast to doctors and hospitals, would not be likely to query potential customers about their driving records and habits. If they did, they would almost certainly lose market share to car dealers that did not make such inquiries. In contrast to hospitals, few would blame a car dealer with a service department if its customers had a high rate of accidents (unless the accidents could be directly attributed to a failure of the car dealer to take precautions, such as to check whether or not the bolts on the wheels were tightened after a tire rotation). Few would blame the dealer even if the new cars it sold had an unfavorable repair record. But hospitals stand to be blamed for poor outcomes, if the outcomes become widely known. Few journalists are likely to adjust the rates of adverse hospital outcomes for differences in the hospital's patient case mix.

However, if patients (or even their doctors, when making a patient referral to another doctor) are unable to judge the quality of care of particular hospitals and doctors, these health care providers have little to gain financially from reducing rates of adverse outcomes. Even though there are nonfinancial reasons for providers to be concerned about quality (e.g., ethics, professional norms), the financial incentive to improve quality seems to be less than it should be, although admittedly, quality is difficult to measure in the context of health care.

Health care executives often seem to view various investments in quality as costly and unprofitable, which is consistent with the view that adequate financial incentives for quality promotion are lacking at present. Also, many hospitals are still operated as free-standing independent organizations, and physicians' practices are generally much smaller than hospitals. Thus, the high fixed cost of investments in quality, such as investments in computerizing patient records, can be an important impediment to undertaking such investments. In the absence of adequate market incentives, the role of ensuring quality falls to public regulation and civil litigation.

7.2 CHARACTERISTICS OF HEALTH CARE QUALITY

HOW ECONOMISTS VIEW QUALITY

In most markets, firms produce heterogeneous goods with various attributes, and quality is one of the important attributes that distinguish one good from the other. If markets function well, goods with different quality levels would be sold at different prices. Since producing a high-quality good is relatively costly to firms, firms charge a higher price for a high-quality good. Thus, for most goods, high quality means a high cost or a high price. Quality then is a one-dimensional concept and can be simply measured by "money," either by cost or price. This is the concept employed in many economic literatures, including the Newhouse hospital model described in chapter 6.

In the context of health care, however, quality is a multi-dimensional concept that incorporates the ability, effort, and time that physicians spend in making a diagnosis and providing treatment, as well as various attributes of the delivery of health services, such as attentiveness, care, and diligence. Some types of quality are contractible, among them the number of meals patients receive daily while hospitalized, the size of hospital rooms, and the presence of a nurse at a nursing station 24 hours a day. However, other elements of quality are "noncontractible," such as the quality with which radiographs are interpreted or the probability that a physician washes his or her hands after examining a patient (McGuire 2000). Noncontractible quality means that the aspect cannot be used as a basis for payment because it is difficult to incorporate time, attentiveness, care, or diligence in a payment system. Noncontractible quality is of value to the consumer, but the consumer is not well positioned to measure it. Since such quality, like contractible quality, is costly to produce and the consumer cannot really know whether it is provided or not, there is a temptation not to provide it, particularly because added payment for added resource use may not be forthcoming.

When markets do not provide socially optimal levels of quality, other mechanisms can arise to compensate for this form of market failure. Globally, at least four approaches have been used to improve the quality of health care (table 7.1).

The first approach relies on professional norms, which involve self-regulation by professionals. The second approach relies on government to implement various form of regulation to ensure quality. The third approach is to rely on competitive forces to achieve socially optimal quality, or at least to move in this direction. Various policies may be needed to push competitive forces in the right direction. The final approach involves the use of tort law, which creates the threat of a lawsuit initiated by injured patients to provide an incentive for physicians to eschew low-quality (suboptimal level) of care. Later sections of this chapter analyze each of these four mechanisms in detail.

TABLE 7.1
Incentive Mechanisms for Ensuring Health Care Quality

Channel	Who Initiates Action
Professional norms	Providers
Regulation	Governments
Market competition	Patients
Tort law	Injured persons

Box 7.1
Staffing Net of Absences: A Structural Measure of Quality of Care

One major problem plaguing many low-income countries, but not unique to them, is health worker absenteeism. Chaudhury, Hammer, Kremer, et al. (2006) reviewed empirical evidence on absenteeism from several countries: Bangladesh, India, Indonesia, Peru, and Uganda. On average, 35 percent of health workers were absent when observed by the researchers in these countries. Absenteeism rates varied from 25 percent in Peru to 40 percent in India and Indonesia. Physicians were relatively more likely to be absent than were other health workers, probably because they were working in private practice during the hours the public clinics were open. Absenteeism was higher in lower-income countries than in those with relatively high incomes. In a study using data from rural Tanzania (Klemick, Leonard, and Masatu 2009), persons were less likely to select clinics for care if the facility had relatively high rates of absenteeism, but this result was not statistically significant at conventional levels.

How the Quality of Personal Health Care Services Is Measured

The quality of health care services can be measured by structure, process, or outcome (Donabedian 1985). Measures of *structure* describe input use, for example, the number of full-time-equivalent nurses per hospital bed, or whether or not the hospital offers particular types of services, such as cardiac surgery, the availability of drugs at a facility, and descriptors of infrastructure (Mariko 2003). Measures of staffing may reflect employee absences (box 7.1).

Process refers to how care is delivered. For example, how long does it take after a person arrives at a hospital emergency department complaining of chest pain to be examined by a physician? When patients are discharged from the hospital, with what frequency are they given prescriptions for medications appropriate to their conditions? In what percentage of cases are persons in high-risk groups vaccinated for illnesses that could cause them substantial harm? Are the appropriate diagnostic tests ordered, given the patient's signs and symptoms (box 7.2)?

Box 7.2
Measures of Process Quality of Care

Das, Hammer, and Leonard (2008) documented the quality of medical advice in low-income countries, primarily from studies conducted in Tanzania, India, Indonesia, and Peru. Measures of quality of advice are process measures in that they describe how care is delivered using measures that are hypothesized to be systematically related to the quality of care. They measured process quality in two ways, through medical vignettes and direct observation of the doctor-patient interaction. A medical vignette describes a clinical scenario. Symptoms are first described to a physician. Physicians are then asked about the follow-up questions they would ask and the diagnostic and therapeutic procedures they would perform. Physicians who ask the appropriate questions and mention the appropriate procedures are judged to be more competent. The other approach is direct observation of what physicians actually do with actual patients, without or with surveys of patients about the physician-patient interaction as the patients leave the clinic.

The study reached quite pessimistic conclusions. Quality of care was observed to be quite low in low-income countries. Low competence of physicians was compounded by low effort. Physicians were more knowledgeable than was evident from the care they actually provided. The poor were placed at a particular disadvantage because of poor quality of medical advice. Leonard, Masatu, and Vialou (2007) describe the process of quality analysis in one country, Tanzania, in greater detail.

Some databases track this type of detail on process quality. This allows researchers to uncover the extent to which the care for each patient aligns with medically appropriate measures and to use this information to evaluate hospitals according to the care they provide.

There is some evidence that process-of-care measures are related to other quality measures, such as a hospital's general reputation. For example, Chen, Radford, Wang, et al. (1999) reported that hospitals rated as the best in the United States by *U.S. News and World Report*'s influential list of "America's Best Hospitals" performed better than average on most process measures in treating patients hospitalized for heart attacks. But even these outstanding hospitals were not perfect, providing a prescription for beta-blockers, a drug recommended for all persons who have experienced a heart attack, to only 75.0 percent of such patients at the time of discharge from the hospital.

Outcome measures gauge effects of care. For example, among persons hospitalized for heart attacks, what percentage of persons admitted to a specific hospital with a primary diagnosis of a heart attack are alive a year following hospital admission (box 7.3)? What percentage of patients develop a hospital-acquired infection (e.g., pneumonia) during a stay at the hospital? How frequent are adverse health outcomes due to prescribing the wrong medication? How often is there a surgical

Box 7.3
Outcomes-Based Measures of Quality of Care

Björkman and Svensson (2009) describe a randomized field experiment that entailed community-based monitoring of public primary health providers in Uganda. The experiment was based on the presumption that the quality of care in low-income countries, such as Uganda, is poor because monitoring of health care providers tends to be lacking. The rationale for the monitoring intervention was that although individual patients can perceive problems with quality of care, they generally do not have knowledge about outcomes for the clinic or community as a whole. For this reason, and because monitoring a public facility is a public good (other patients benefit from an individual patient's monitoring effort), there will suboptimal levels of monitoring if monitoring is not organized at the community level.

In this experiment, local nongovernmental organizations (NGOs) helped organize grassroots efforts at the community level that provided monitoring of clinic services. Communities with and without this intervention were selected at random.

The study used various process indicators of quality, but in addition, outcome-based measures of quality of care were included in the evaluation of effects of the intervention. In particular, the authors documented a statistically significant reduction in low-birth-weight infants and a 33 percent reduction in under-age-five mortality in the treatment communities.

procedure on the wrong body part because, e.g., of a misinterpreted X-ray? What is the mean improvement in physical functioning following knee replacement surgery?

At first glance, it would always seem preferable to use outcome measures to gauge an organization's quality. And in an ideal world, such measures would be preferable. Patients value good outcomes, which are reflected in higher patient utility. If patients and their physicians possess accurate measures of outcomes and if they are valid and reliable indicators of quality, there would be less reason to know much about structure and process.

But outcome measures also have limitations. First, outcomes data are often unavailable, and other types of measures of quality are used for this reason. Second, adverse outcomes occur for reasons other than poor medical care. There is substantial heterogeneity in patients' conditions on admission to a hospital or at the time of a visit to a doctor's office. For example, some patients have advanced cancer. Others have cancer in a very early stage. In comparing outcomes among providers, it is important to adjust for these differences. Such "risk adjustments," although feasible, can be quite complex in their own right.

Third, outcomes measured at a subsequent point in time may be truly attributable to other factors. For example, the mortality rate one year following admission to a hospital for a heart attack reflects not only the quality of care provided by the hospital and the patient's condition at admission but also important intervening events that may have occurred after the patient was discharged from the hospital.

Fourth, outcome measures have a random component. Some adverse events occur for reasons that cannot be anticipated in advance. For example, a patient may have an adverse reaction to a drug for reasons that are unknown to physicians, irrespective of how competent they are.

For these reasons, outcome measures are inherently noisy. The task for the researcher or quality-of-care evaluator is to extract the quality signal out of the noise.

It is conceptually possible but impractical to measure *every* relevant aspect of quality. For example, whether or not a physician routinely reports test findings to patients is a measure of process quality, but there are many such measures that could be monitored.

7.3 ADVERSE EVENTS AND NEGLIGENT INJURIES

THE ISSUES

If quality is higher than the level at which marginal social cost equals marginal social benefit, quality is too high. However, recent publicity about the frequency of iatrogenic injuries (those caused by an action or inaction during the course of diagnosis or treatment) suggests the opposite. Care is not of the quality level it should be.

The causes of the observed rates of iatrogenic injury are not entirely clear. But the message is, "getting medical care may be harmful to your health." Although the estimates are US-specific, it seems unlikely that the United States is unique among countries in this regard. A study conducted in New Zealand used a similar research methodology (Bismark, Brennan, Paterson, et al. 2006) and reached similar conclusions as the prestigious Institute of Medicine (IOM 2000) did in a well-publicized US report, *To Err Is Human*. The IOM concluded that 98,000 deaths occur in US hospitals annually as a result of avoidable, medical errors—more deaths than from motor vehicle accidents, AIDS, and breast cancer.

HOW THE ESTIMATES OF ADVERSE OUTCOMES WERE GENERATED

Since the mid-1970s, three major studies of the epidemiology of medical injuries among patients hospitalized in the United States have been conducted (table 7.2, see section 7.8).[2] These studies involved assembling information on process of care and health outcomes from patients' medical records. Once the data were assembled, medical experts made judgments about whether the adverse outcomes could have been prevented if care recommended by expert panels had been followed.

2. These studies were conducted in the US states of California, New York, Colorado, and Utah.

For each medical record, physician reviewers who participated in the epidemiologic assessments of medical errors graded the confidence that an adverse event occurred on a scale from 0 to 6 (Brennan, Leape, Laird, et al. 1991). If the confidence level exceeded 1, a judgment was made whether or not there was negligence. Then, raters also noted the confidence level in this judgment. There were two physician reviewers for each record, and the physicians conducted their reviews independently. When there was disagreement between the reviewers, this was noted by a medical records analyst and resolved by an independent review by a supervisory physician.

THE QUALITY OF THE ESTIMATES

To Err Is Human, which summarized the results of the previous studies, received substantial publicity in the United States, and to a lesser extent throughout the world. On the one hand, one can argue that the number of iatrogenic injuries is high, even if the report's point estimates are wrong. However, the estimates of deaths per annum resulting from hospitals' medical errors are indeed less precise than the IOM's message implied. For one, medical accidents, unlike motor vehicle and workplace accidents, are not discrete events. Many persons enter the hospital in a frail condition and hence are particularly vulnerable to medical errors. But even if the error had not occurred, many persons admitted to a hospital do not have a long life expectancy. For this reason, life years lost would be a much more precise characterization of the harm attributable to errors.

Negative outcomes do occur, and with an appropriate level of informed consent; patients know or should know about these before agreeing to undergo or to forgo a procedure. To determine whether or not an error has occurred, it is necessary to parse the adverse event into a part that reflects an error (and hence substandard care) and a part that represents an unfortunate mishap but at the same time an appropriate level of care.

Another methodological issue is inter-rater variability in assessments of quality. Quality assessment, especially at the level of a overall judgment as to whether or not the quality of care given to a particular patient was adequate or not, is not totally objective but rather is subject to individual interpretation. Despite safeguards undertaken by the study investigators, including training of medical records reviewers, what is poor quality to one reviewer may be seen as adequate quality by another. There are just too many permutations and combinations of situations for any training process to result in fully consistent measurements of quality.

Concluding that these medical assessments are a "gold standard" of quality measurement would be to give them too much credit. Nevertheless, the epidemiologic studies of medical injury were pathbreaking, particularly at the time they were conducted. Furthermore, the studies required substantial resources and patience to conduct at the high standard at which these studies were conducted.

In many cases, the underlying quality-of-care issue is not that complex, however. The most common adverse event in one of the three studies was adverse reactions to drugs (19 percent), followed by wound infections (14 percent). Documenting adverse reactions to drugs or wound infections should not require appreciable technical and specialized skills, but whether or not the care that preceded the adverse outcome was truly substandard often involves a greater amount of subjectivity.

Identifying other alleged errors is likely to require more specialized expertise. The reviewers identified errors in management in 58 percent of the adverse events, with nearly half of these attributed to negligence. Failure to diagnose was also common, as were adverse events in the emergency room (Leape, Brennan, Laird, et al. 1991).

Reviewers examined medical records from one hospital admission that individual persons had. With this limited amount of information, the reviewers could not have known about outcomes that became evident months or even years after the hospitalization evaluated in the study occurred. At the time of discharge from the hospital, there may have been no adverse outcomes. Many major injuries, such as birth injuries, are latent for years, and the fact that an injury had occurred becomes evident only gradually. Of course, this would lead to an underestimate of the amount of iatrogenic injury.

DO OBSERVED RATES OF MEDICAL ERRORS AND ADVERSE OUTCOMES REPRESENT A MARKET FAILURE JUSTIFYING GOVERNMENT OR OTHER INTERVENTION?

Despite some technical limitations of these studies, they made an important contribution in demonstrating that iatrogenic injury is an important public health issue. Whether or not observed rates of medical errors and adverse outcomes represent a market failure, thus justifying some form of external intervention, is a complex issue. At one level, the solution would seem to be improved information with the appropriate amount of risk adjustment for variation in patient severity of illness. If potential consumers were to become knowledgeable of relatively high error rates in advance of being admitted for treatment, some would argue that this would be a sufficient safeguard. If so, the next question is why such consumers have not been adequately informed to date.

The reason may be as simple as that information is a public good. Individual consumers are not well positioned to gather the requisite data for themselves and make the appropriate risk adjustments. *Consumer Reports*, for example, publishes comparisons of quality of quite a number of goods and services. *Consumer Reports* derives most of its revenue from subscription and store sales of the magazine, although it does accept donations. Car magazines provide detailed comparisons of automobile quality, often head-to-head comparisons of cars in the same category.

The publishers of car magazines are for-profit businesses that derive their revenue from magazine sales and advertisements.

In the case of health care, one would expect that private organizations would arise to provide such information, possibly with private or public subsidies. The high cost of assembling this information may cause market failure and provide a rationale for government involvement in a market-perfecting activity. What makes this type of information provision costly is that especially for some important but rare outcomes, to achieve statistical reliability it may be necessary to assemble large amounts of data, in addition to the necessity of risk adjustment. This is in contrast to automobiles, for which monitoring gas mileage and braking may require testing only one vehicle.

7.4 SUPPLY-SIDE QUALITY-OF-CARE SAFEGUARDS AND GOVERNMENT OVERSIGHT AND REGULATION

OVERVIEW

Historically, there has been widespread skepticism, including among health professionals, that consumers are sufficiently well equipped to adequately gauge quality of care. The underlying assumption until late in the twentieth century was that health care providers know about and can adequately assess quality. Or the presumption was that all doctors and hospitals are good.

Prior to the regulation of pharmaceuticals, there were many accounts of salespeople marketing cures for all types of ailments to an unsuspecting public. Before the twentieth century, becoming a physician did not take much formal education. In the United States, proprietary medical schools often provided medical education. To the extent that there are medical errors today, they undoubtedly pale in comparison to the rates of errors in the nineteenth century and earlier. However, except for anecdotal accounts of individual cases in which errors occurred, errors were not measured.

PROFESSIONAL NORMS

The policy "cure" for bad quality of medical care decades ago was not to rely on the judgments of consumers but to regulate the supply side through a combination of professional norms, self-regulation by medical professionals, and government regulation. "Professional norms" specify how a professional is supposed to act, as reflected, for example, in the Hippocratic oath, written in 400 B.C.

Professional norms are enforced first and foremost by the professional him- or herself. But other members of the profession are asked to look over their shoulders for unprofessional behavior of their peers. If professional norms have been deemed to have been seriously violated, a health professional may be subject to formal sanctions. In less extreme cases, however, enforcement involves informal sanctions. In recent times, medical school admissions committees assess applicants' reasons for wanting to become physicians and the likelihood that they will comply with professional norms.

Peer Review

The main rationale stated for medical staff organization of hospitals is to safeguard the quality of the hospital's care (see chapter 6). Medical staffs do this by reviewing credentials, other qualifications, and experience prior to admitting a physician to the medical staff. Subsequently, once the physician is admitted to the medical staff, the organization is responsible for overseeing the quality of care provided by the physician at the hospital. Peer review in ambulatory settings often occurs informally.

One rationale for hospital peer review by medical staff, although a comparatively recent one, is that some internal mechanism for quality monitoring is needed if hospitals are really to compete with each other. But there are risks to such peer review. In particular, medical staff peer reviewers are likely to be competitors of the individual physicians they review. Banning a physician in part or in full may allow peer reviewers to improve their own competitive position (Blumstein and Sloan 1988). Physicians denied hospital privileges have often sought legal remedies on the grounds that the medical staff's decision was modified by a desire to reduce competition. Also, to what extent peer reviewers systematically modified monitor medical errors is unknown. The Pauly-Redisch model (see chapter 6) suggests that medical staff operate the hospital in their own collective financial interest, which is clearly a reason for hospital medical staff organization in addition to quality assurance. The model does not prove that the cartelization process it describes actually exists. To know this, one would need to conduct empirical analysis in a number of hospital settings, which has not been done to date.

Licensure

The oldest quality safeguard is licensure by governments. However, licensure is at best a weak safeguard of quality. Unless a physician moves to another jurisdiction, licensure is a once-and-for-all process, although many jurisdictions impose continuing medical education requirements as a condition for continued licensure. Unlike driver's licenses, which require periodic reexaminations, physicians are typically licensed for life. Hospitals and other medical facilities are also licensed by governments, but less is known about how such licensure actually works in practice.

Economists have long been suspicious of the professional licensure process. In health care, providers have for too long insisted to the public that "we are all good." While there may be an interest in quality assurance, professionals have a financial incentive to limit supply (see, e.g., Friedman and Kuznets 1945).

Delicensure is rare and done in response to very major lapses and major misconduct. In one US state, Florida, even physicians with very high and persistent medical malpractice rates were investigated by the licensing board only very rarely (Sloan, Mergenhagen, Burfield, et al. 1989). State licensure boards in the United States have changed, largely in response to political pressures that they serve the public interest (Ameringer 1999).

Certification

Certification differs from licensure in that the certifying body indicates only that the medical professional or facility has satisfied certain requirements and, unlike licensure, imposes no absolute barrier to entry. Rather, consumers are to observe whether or not the provider is credentialed and by whom in making his or her purchasing decision. Given that there is no absolute barrier to entry, the anticompetitive effects of certification seem less than for licensure (see, e.g., Friedman 1962). Moreover, certification, if done properly, may even be pro-competitive in informing consumers about providers' qualifications. In the United States, physicians may be certified through twenty-four different specialty boards. Not all of these boards require recertification, and those that do typically require it only every 7 to 10 years, which may be too infrequent in specialties subject to rapid technological change.

7.5 Mandatory Error Reporting

Description

To a far greater extent than the purely supply-side quality assurance mechanisms, in particular reliance on professional norms, peer review by medical staffs of hospitals, and licensure laws, mandatory error reporting requires suppliers to provide information to a public authority on their adverse outcome or error rates, which is published and used by consumers in making decisions about choice of provider.

Mandatory reporting of adverse outcomes is frequently proposed as a patient safety initiative. The reports of adverse outcomes can be used by government regulatory agencies to identify where errors are occurring (Marchev, Rosenthal, and Booth 2003). If reporting systems provide timely and complete information to regulators, this should, at least in principle, improve the agencies' role as monitors.

From 1986 to 1992, the US Medicare program reported risk-adjusted hospital mortality rates[3] for Medicare beneficiaries admitted to hospitals. One study found that hospitals for which there was an adverse report did not experience much change in demand (Mennemeyer, Morrisey, and Howard 1997). Although the results were statistically significant at conventional levels, when the reported mor-

3. See chapter 6 for a discussion of risk adjustment.

tality rate doubled, the patient volume at the hospital decreased by only one patient per week.

We can speculate as to the reasons for the small demand response. One reason may be that consumers do not value these differences in quality, but this explanation seems implausible. Another is that the elderly are not well positioned to make detailed comparisons among hospitals. Some elderly persons are frail and suffer from cognitive limitations. On the other hand, elderly persons are likely to know many other persons, including friends and relatives, who are admitted to hospitals, and hospital issues are frequently discussed. However, at the other extreme, the elderly may be quite knowledgeable and aware of the deficiencies of such report cards—that some variations among hospitals reflect random noise, severity of patient illness at admission that has been inadequately accounted for, and there may be appreciable within-hospital quality differences. This extreme position is probably not correct either. In any case, facing political pressure, for a time, Medicare dropped its report cards. Some state governments in the United States began publishing them subsequently.

Peterson, DeLong, Jollis, et al. (1998), who analyzed the New York experience with providing information on patient outcomes, found that the rate of cardiac surgery in New York increased following the introduction of report cards; fewer New York residents underwent bypass surgery out-of-state. Taken at face value, this result suggests that patients value this form of quality monitoring.

Dranove, Kessler, McClellan, et al. (2003), who analyzed the experience of cardiac surgery report cards in New York and Pennsylvania, reported that patients who before surgery had attributes associated with a higher probability of surviving the surgical procedure were more likely to be selected for treatment following publication of the report cards. They attributed such favorable selection for treatment to public disclosure of hospital-specific mortality rates—just as the critics of public disclosure had feared.

Dranove and coauthors compared effects pre– and post–mandatory reporting and used as a control group for the same time periods neighboring states that did not implement mandatory reporting. This is called a "difference-in-difference" approach. One difference is post versus pre in the treatment group (New York and Pennsylvania hospitals) and the other is the difference for the same two periods in the control group (hospitals in the neighboring states). Use of the control group allowed the authors to account for *other* changes that occurred during the time period during which report cards were implemented but that were not related to report cards. For example, technological progress common to all of the states may have resulted in changes in the types of patients getting treatment and their health outcomes. Dranove and coauthors found that, following the implementation of report cards, persons undergoing coronary artery bypass surgery had incurred $300 less in health expenditures *before* they received surgery than did persons in the control states. The lower expenditures suggest that the persons in the post–report card implementation group in New York and Pennsylvania were relatively healthy at the time they were admitted to the hospital. Also, mean expenditure prior to surgery did not change in the same time interval as it did in the control states.

This evidence suggests that report cards led New York and Pennsylvania hospitals to select disproportionate numbers of persons who would be likely to survive their heart attacks and surgery in the post–report card period. Thus, access of the relatively sick to such services may have deteriorated—a form of "gaming" to report cards that may not be in the public interest. We should not view such gaming as entirely bad since hospitals in the past may have been performing cardiac surgery on some persons who were at high risk and may have been better off with less aggressive therapy.[4]

Jin and Leslie (2003) studied the effects of introducing hygiene quality grade cards in a non–health care setting—at restaurants in Los Angeles in 1998. The authors found that grade cards caused restaurant health inspection scores to increase, consumer demand to become sensitive to changes in restaurants' hygiene quality, and the number of food-borne illness hospitalizations to decrease.

Although the finding is interesting, there are important differences between hospitals and restaurants. Consumers are relatively well positioned to make informed choices among restaurants. Hygiene ratings are posted in a prominent place in the restaurant. Hence, a patron who is unsatisfied with the rating can walk out before being served. The frail and very elderly do not constitute such an important share of the business of restaurants as they do of hospitals and nursing homes. And a favorable selection of restaurant patrons is not the issue it is for hospitals. In contrast to a cardiac surgeon, restaurants would have considerable difficulty in gauging the risk of patrons getting food-borne illnesses when they entered the restaurant.

IMPLICATIONS

Each quality assurance mechanism is deficient in some respect. None will do the job of ensuring patient safety by itself. More information is not necessarily better than less information if the data are not properly adjusted for patient case mix (severity). This can be done with methods that currently exist, but data assembly and adjustment can become very expensive. When the stakeholders—physicians and hospitals—do not like the results, one can expect vigorous political opposition to release of data on patient outcomes.

While the idea of providing information to consumers has its pitfalls, so does supply-side regulation of quality. The temptation is great for suppliers to pursue financial self-interest as well as or even instead of quality assurance. A knowledgeable public is at least a partial safeguard. Without pressure from market forces, satisfying consumer wants for high-quality care seems unlikely. On the other hand, quality provision consumes resources. When patients are fully insured, the same type of welfare loss we have described for quantity (see chapters 3 and 4) can occur

4. Other findings from the Dranove, Kessler, McClellan, et al. (2003) study also support the conclusion that report cards led to a smaller fraction of patients undergoing cardiac surgery within a day of their admission to the hospital for a heart attack, implying that report cards might cause some hospitals to withhold immediate treatment because of the risk of poor report card scores. Following the introduction of report cards, there was increased use of less expensive substitute technologies such as coronary angioplasties, again suggesting an increased use of bypass surgery among low-risk heart patients. Thus, the results obtained by Dranove and co-workers suggest that what changed following the introduction of report cards was the case mix of persons undergoing such surgery, not the quality of care provided to patients.

in the quality dimension. In the end, attainment of socially optimal levels of quality will require some out-of-pocket outlays by consumers, either in the form of higher health insurance premiums if persons want to have access to higher-quality (and more expensive) providers through the health plan's network or cost sharing at the point of service.

7.6 TORT LAW AS A MECHANISM FOR IMPROVING PATIENT SAFETY AND HEALTH CARE QUALITY

WHY OTHER QUALITY ASSURANCE MECHANISMS MAY FAIL

Medical malpractice is only one of several quality assurance mechanisms but the most controversial one by far. While medical malpractice has received the most publicity in the United States, it has become a public policy issue in high-income countries around the world, mainly because of the rise in medical malpractice insurance premiums (Organisation for Economic Co-operation and Development 2007).

The trial bar, lawyers representing plaintiffs in medical malpractice cases, has argued, with considerable justification, that there would be no role for tort liability if the other quality assurance mechanisms functioned well. However, absent effective private mechanisms and government intervention, tort liability with contingency fees gives injury victims, irrespective of their financial status, a way to address grievances while simultaneously helping to prevent injuries for someone else. Based on the resolution of the legal dispute, a warning is issued about the consequences of failure to exercise due care. This is a contentious issue with lawyers for the defense.

Physicians' compensation is not based on the health outcomes of their patients (see chapter 5). However, lawyers paid on a contingency fee basis do receive outcome-based compensation. If the plaintiff wins, they earn a percentage of the award. If, however, the case is resolved without the plaintiff receiving compensation, the lawyer receives nothing.

Before describing tort law in general and medical malpractice in particular, it is useful to consider why the other quality assurance mechanisms might fail to accomplish their stated purposed. There are several reasons.

First, public bureaucracies may be beholden to special interests or simply unresponsive, given the internal incentives of staff or understaffing. For one, some public employees may desire positions in regulated industries where pay is often higher than in government. Persons interested in being employed by firms they regulate may not want to be touch on a future employer.

More generally, the capture theory of public regulation implies that regulation is often used to protect existing sellers rather than to pursue the stated goals of regulation (Sage 2003). For example, medical licensure may be captured by those with licenses who rather than discipline those who repeatedly make medical errors use licensure to restrict entry.

Second, given the complexity of medical care, it is difficult for public agencies or private credentialing organizations to oversee all aspects of care that may potentially affect quality. Third, imposing *and* enforcing minimum standards runs the risk of denying care to persons in areas in which care is generally inaccessible. Finally, individual health care providers lack an incentive to honestly disclose indicators of quality, in large part because their competitors may not be as truthful and so may gain a competitive advantage. This is an important rationale for public disclosure requirements.

A basic difference between tort law and the other quality assurance mechanisms is that with tort law, the injury victim, not the government or a health care provider, initiates the action. The injury victim and patients more generally have a direct stake in ensuring that quality care is provided. However, as we shall see, medical malpractice, like the other quality assurance mechanisms, is far from perfect.

THE ABCs OF TORT LAW

TORT LAW DEFINED

In contrast to criminal law, which is enforced by government agencies, civil law relies on enforcement by private parties under rules promulgated by the public sector. One branch of civil law is tort law. A tort occurs when someone deliberately or through carelessness causes harm to another person or property. In common law, a tort is a civil or private wrong for which the law provides a remedy in the form of monetary payments and other remedies for the injured party or parties—the victims of wrongdoing. Under tort law, enforcement is performed by injury victims rather than by public officials, thus possibly overcoming the reluctance, or the lack of resources, of public officials to observe and act upon observed departures from regulatory rules.

By contrast, under criminal law, public officials prosecute parties accused of breaking the law. Criminal law is more effective than tort law when law breakers are likely to be "judgment proof," that is, unable to pay for the damage they caused. With few exceptions, criminal law is not applied in the context of injuries related to medical care (see box 7.4 for exceptions).

Tort law applies to civil wrongs arising from extracontractual liability, that is, for wrongs other than those arising from a breach of contractual obligations. Tort law has several goals, among the most important of which are (1) to deter misconduct and hence injury and (2) to compensate injury victims. There are also other objectives, such as meting out justice and providing a safety valve for airing

Box 7.4
Medical Malpractice Criminal Law

While in most countries, medical malpractice lawsuits are brought as civil actions, there are exceptions in which medical malpractice cases are prosecuted as criminal actions. In civil cases, the plaintiff is the private party who alleges an injury. By contrast, in criminal cases, rather than be brought by a plaintiff, who is typically represented by an attorney, the case is brought and pursued by a public prosecutor. This means that rather than seek representation by an attorney, an employee of the state must be convinced that the case is worth bringing. Another substantial difference between civil and criminal penalties is that the latter may include not only monetary penalties in the form of fines but incarceration as well.

In both Japan and Taiwan, physicians potentially face both civil and criminal liability in medical malpractice lawsuits (Yang, Tsai, and Chiu 2009). In Taiwan, criminal lawsuits are the more common of the two. Injured patients and their families can seek legal counsel and file a civil lawsuit or can go to prosecutors to seek an indictment under criminal law. Most do the latter because it is both more convenient and less expensive. Prosecutors are obligated under Taiwan's Criminal Code to investigate allegations brought to their attention. Convicted physicians face up to five years' imprisonment if convicted of a wrongful death charge. Cases involving physical injuries are considered to be lesser crimes and are subject to less severe penalties, including probation.[5]

victims' grievances. These latter objectives are important to maintaining a civil society. However, the deterrence is most directly pertinent for promoting the public's health.

The Socially Optimal Injury Rate

An insight of economics is that optimal deterrence does not require that the injury rate be zero. Rather, the socially optimal rate of injuries would be zero only if the cost of averting injuries were zero. Conceptually, the goal of injury prevention is to minimize the total cost of injuries consisting of (1) the costs resulting from the injury and (2) the costs of averting it. Costs resulting from an injury include, but are not limited to, expenditures on medical care and rehabilitative services; the costs associated with reduced longevity; increased disability, pain, and suffering; and property losses. The costs of averting injuries range from investments in the goods or services themselves and in redundancy (backup systems to be used in the event of failure) to the time and effort involved in monitoring.

More specifically, let e be a potential injurer's expenditure on accident prevention during a specific time period, $\Theta(e)$ be the probability of an accident occurring, like e defined for a specific time period, and $D(e)$ be total loss incurred by the accident victim(s) should an accident occur. As a potential injurer (e.g., a

5. *See Yang, Tsai, and Chiu (2009) and references at the end of this article.*

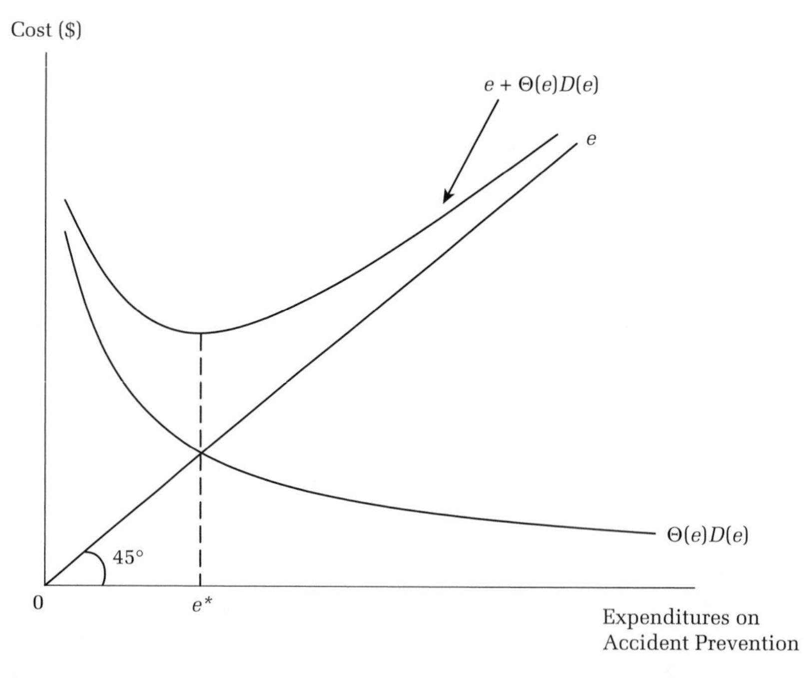

FIGURE 7.1
Total Cost of Injury Prevention and Expected Accident Cost (Social Cost) and Optimal Care

medical provider) spends more resources to avoid injury, the probability of an accident (Θ) and the total loss associated with the accident (D) decline.

Then the social objective is to find the e that minimizes total social cost.

$$e + \Theta(e)D(e). \tag{7.1}$$

In figure 7.1, e is a 45-degree line from the origin since effort on accident prevention is measured by monetary expenditure, which is equal to the dollar value expressed on the vertical line. The expected loss $\Theta(e)D(e)$ declines as e increases, but at a decreasing rate of decline. The sum $e + \Theta(e)D(e)$ declines up to the point where the curve for the expected loss intersects with the 45-degree line and increases with further units of e. For this reason, e^* is considered to be the socially optimal investment in prevention because the total social cost is the minimum at this point.

In other words, the total social cost of injuries is minimized by investing in injury prevention up to the point at which the marginal cost of injury prevention equals the marginal benefit of such investments, which is the value of reductions in injury cost (Calabresi 1970). Investing an infinite amount in injury prevention would only be optimal if the costs resulting from the injury were infinite, which is implausible. In addition, allocating infinite amounts to injury prevention would leave no resources to satisfy other wants. In promoting socially appropriate deterrence, the task of tort is to provide signals to private decision makers about how much they should invest in injury-prevention activities.

Now suppose potential injurers faced no potential loss from the injuries they might cause. Then from a private standpoint, and assuming that accidents cause no damage to oneself, the optimal level of e would be zero. Potential injurers would allocate much less than the socially optimal amounts to injury prevention.

THE NEGLIGENCE RULE: ONLY ONE OF SEVERAL ALTERNATIVE LIABILITY RULES

Under a rule of *strict liability*, the injurer bears the loss if it is determined that the injurer *caused* the loss. Alternatively, under a *negligence* liability rule, the injurer, not the injury victim, bears the loss if it can be determined that (1) a loss occurred, (2) the injurer in fact caused the loss, and (3) the loss occurred because of the injurer's failure to exercise due care, where the ideal is that due care is set at the socially optimal level of care defined in the conceptual terms (e^*) above. The third step is key, but rather than specify a socially optimal level of care, courts use the concept of "standard of care." The standard of care has traditionally been defined as the care level prevailing in the area in which the injury occurred, but this definition is shifting at least in some places to a criterion of whether the defendant deviated from "reasonable" conduct.

In sum, to prevail in a tort lawsuit under a negligence rule, the plaintiff must prove that the defendant owed a duty of care to the plaintiff, the defendant breached this duty by failing to adhere to the standard of care expected, and this breach of duty caused an injury to the plaintiff.

Alternatively, returning to figure 7.1, if the potential injurer faced a *strict liability* rule, he or she would be responsible for any losses that the injurer causes. Under this rule, the potential injurer would select the optimal amount of care e^* since investment minimizes his or her expected loss.

Still another alternative is that potential injurers operate under a *negligence* rule. Under these circumstances, there is an additional condition to causation for payment, namely, that the injurer did not adhere to a due care standard when the accident occurred. Then if the due care standard is set at e^* or higher, the injurer pays nothing. If, however, e is less than e^*, the injury pays the accident victim's loss. Thus, for e equal to or greater than e^*, the injurer's cost equals e. For e less than e^*, the injurer's cost is $e + \Theta(e)D(e)$. The potential injurer's cost is thus lowest at e^* (fig. 7.2).

Under both negligence and strict liability rules, socially optimal amounts are allocated to prevention. There is likely to be more litigation under strict liability, however. The legal cost of proving both causation and failure to set injury precaution at e^* or higher is likely to be higher under negligence because proving that the injurer failed to exercise due care can be very costly.

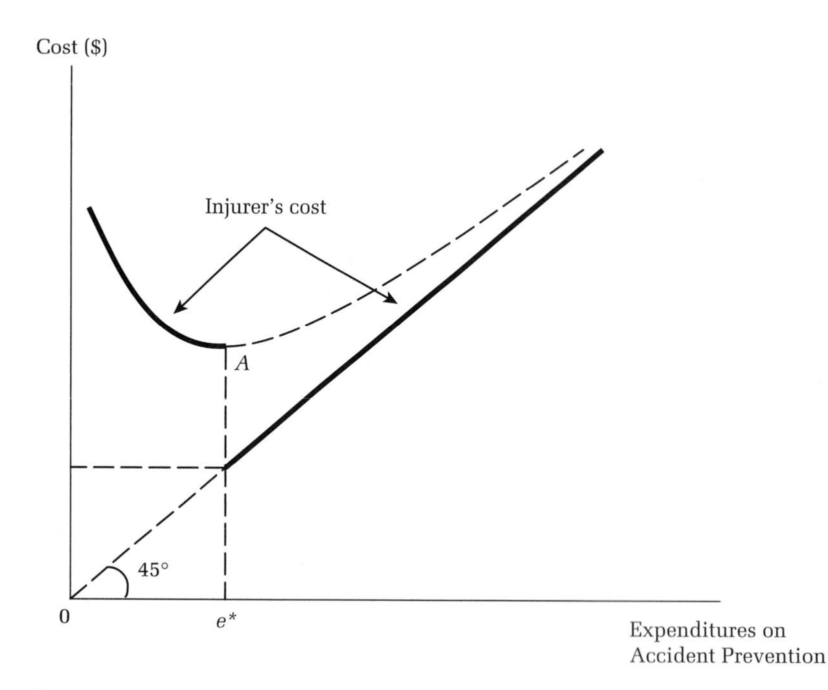

FIGURE 7.2
Potential Injurer's Choice of Care under a Negligence Rule

The rationale for strict liability is that one party is better positioned to implement measures to avoid the injury. For example, the manufacturer of lawn mowers can prevent injuries by installing barriers between the blade and the lawn-mower users. This precaution is designed to prevent even a careless lawn-mower user from injuring him- or herself. Under a negligence rule, the defense could argue that the user was careless and this led to the accident, but determining whether or not the user had indeed been careless or as an amateur was just unaware may involve substantial litigation cost.

CONTRACTS VERSUS TORTS

An alternative to imposing liability on health care providers would be to achieve injury prevention by contract. This is not feasible in some contexts. For example, it is not feasible for individual drivers of motor vehicles to contract with drivers they have never met to establish mechanisms specified in contracts for accident prevention.

Contracting might work as an alternative to medical liability, however. Individuals would purchase insurance from an enterprise, such as a managed care organization (MCO; see chapter 11). The enterprise would then contract with specific hospitals and physicians to supply care at a particular level of quality. To ensure quality, these hospitals and physicians could implement specific patient safety programs agreed upon with the MCO in advance. The insurance contract could also provide a schedule of indemnity payments to compensate insured individuals if an iatrogenic injury occurred.

According to the Coase theorem (Coase 1960), if all parties are fully informed about risk and if contracting is costless, then the allocation of resources to loss prevention, which is what exercising due care is about, will be the same, whether or not losses reside with the injury victim or with the injurer. Whether or not the injurer or the injury victim bears the loss, there is an incentive for potential injurers to take safety precautions.

However, even if we accept Coase's premise, if consumers in general or patients in particular misperceive risks, or if contracting is costly, then loss prevention may be insufficient (Spence 1977; Shavell 1980). Indeed, the risks of adverse outcomes may be misperceived (i.e., perceived to be less than they really are) or consumers or their agents (e.g., MCOs) may not be well positioned to monitor the quality of care received. If so, absent some type of intervention in the market, such as imposing liability, fines, surcharges, or some other penalty on potential injurers, the rate of risky procedures will be too high, and the amount of care undertaken per procedure may be too low compared to the socially optimal level.

At first glance, it may seem obvious that consumers misperceive risks and are not well positioned to monitor quality. However, the issue is more complex than this, and in the end, the accuracy of risk perceptions and the extent of quality monitoring are empirical issues. Health care consumers may be knowledgeable about some risks, such as the risk of adverse outcomes in the case of routine pregnancies, but highly uninformed about care for a very rare condition (Pauly 2001). Markets may often be adequate in conveying differences in quality, though perhaps not as frequently as one would like. But even when markets fail, there are quality assurance mechanisms in addition to tort.

If *no liability* is imposed, such as under a no-fault system (see chapter 10), each party to an accident bears his or her own loss. Potential injurers have nothing to lose in the event of an accident as injurers but they bear the full loss if they are injury victims. In the context of medical malpractice, patients, not providers, are the victims. But in other contexts, such as motor vehicle liability, each driver can be either an injurer or a victim.

Under no liability, potential injury victims invest in precaution up to the point at which the marginal cost of precaution equals the marginal benefit measured in terms of averted losses, which is at the socially optimal care level. Under the negligence rule, by contrast, the injurer compensates the victim only if he or she fails to exercise due care, which by assumption is set at the socially optimal precaution level. At the same time, potential injury victims expect that others (potential injurers) will exercise due care and thus not have to pay the victim in the event an accident occurs. Given this assumption, the optimal care level for injury victims is at the due care standard. Under the negligence rule, accidents would occur (at the socially optimal level), but no one would ever be negligent. This theoretical prediction, of course, runs counter to the facts.

When the Negligence Rule Leads Private Parties to Select a Socially Optimal Precaution Level

The above theoretical results about effects of the negligence rule apply only under very restrictive assumptions. Among the most important assumptions are the following: (1) due care standards, when applicable, and damages are set appropriately—the former to reflect the socially optimal care level and the latter as an accurate measure of losses incurred; and (2) claims for damages are filed whenever, but only when injuries are truly caused by an action or an inaction of an injurer under strict liability and whenever there is causation and the due care standard is breached under the negligence rule.

In reality, fewer than the appropriate number of medical malpractice claims are filed because of the transactions costs of obtaining payment for losses incurred. Moreover, insofar as under the negligence rule, it is necessary to demonstrate both causation and damages, one would expect to observe more claims under strict liability than under the negligence rule.

Tort Liability under Attack

Since about the 1970s, especially in the United States, tort liability in general, not just medical malpractice, has been under attack from critics, who cite the costly and capricious nature of tort liability and its impact in higher prices and decreased availability of those goods and services particularly likely to be involved in litigation. Criticisms have not been applied equally to all areas of tort. The least criticism has been directed toward routine personal injury torts, such as slip and fall cases and automobile accidents. In the middle are cases that are brought by individual plaintiffs, as opposed to class action suits. This category includes medical malpractice suits. The third category, the most controversial one, includes mass torts cases in which many plaintiffs join together in suing a large entity such as a publicly held corporation (e.g., over silicone breast implants, cigarettes, or pharmaceutical products such as Vioxx).

Much of the criticism is emotionally charged, based on anecdotes, and often devoid of analytic content and replete with factual errors (see, e.g., Haltom and McCann 2004; Baker 2005). Concerns are raised more frequently during times of rising insurance premiums, but the major concern among scholars of tort law is the actual performance of tort in attaining the above objectives.

However, critics, including scholars, have raised some fundamental issues, which merit careful scrutiny. There is now a large body of empirical evidence on the performance of tort liability as it has been applied in several contexts. Most pertinent to this book are concerns about deterrence.

Most important, as discussed more fully below, there is no evidence that the threat of tort deters medical injury, although such evidence exists for other applications of tort law, such as for dram shop liability and to a lesser extent for motor vehicle liability (Sloan, Stout, Whetten-Goldstein, et al. 2000; White 2004).

Why the threat of a civil lawsuit is effective under some circumstances and not under others is not entirely clear. One reason, not the only one, may be that the underlying technology of injury prevention is easier in some areas than in others. Having a bartender order a taxicab for a patron who has consumed too many beers is a simpler technology than preventing a mishap in transplanting an organ or even in preventing a mix-up in distributing medications in a hospital since so many hands are involved in this activity.

The above-stated rationale for tort assumes that the legal system is efficient and accurate in adjudicating claims. At some point, inefficiencies and inaccuracies would tip the balance against the use of tort liability. Inefficiencies and inaccuracies have been alleged by the critics of tort liability in general and of medical malpractice liability in particular, who point to the long time it takes to resolve tort claims, the substantial cost of claims resolution, and errors in determining liability and setting damages. Based on the statements of the critics, this hardly seems like an efficient and accurate system. However, advocates for tort view it as an effective private mechanism for meting out justice, especially when other systems, such as self-regulation by business and professional organizations and public regulation, fail to achieve their stated purposes. Defenders of tort liability further argue that individualized justice is expensive to achieve and hence is inherently expensive.

7.7 Medical Malpractice

Overview

While most has been written about medical malpractice in the United States, it exists in countries throughout the world (OECD 2007). Many of the complaints about medical malpractice one hears in the United States are also heard in other countries.

Medical malpractice involves a number of parties, each with its own objectives and constraints. For analytic purposes, we consider four distinct but interrelated markets. The first market is for medical care, where consumers are patients and physicians are suppliers of care. Second, there is the legal market, where both injury victims and physicians as defendants demand legal services, supplied by lawyers and the courts. Third is the market for medical malpractice insurance. In this market, the consumers are physicians and other health professionals and the suppliers are medical malpractice insurers. Finally, there is the market for government activity, in which the law-as-market view posits that legislation and government activity is a good demanded and supplied much like other goods. We describe the first two markets here.

Medical Care Market

Individuals may select physicians, a hospital, and other health care providers based on perceived quality, distance, and other factors. Conceptually, providers take account of downstream liability cost in setting their professional care standards. Ideally, providers could be sure they could escape liability by exercising the standard of due care set at the socially optimal care level. At least three impediments stand in the way.

First, courts are likely not to set the care standard at socially optimal levels or they may be inconsistent in the standards they set. Realistically, medical care is so multifaceted there is no way courts could set consistent standards for every medical situation, although setting consistent standards for situations that frequently lead to lawsuits would be helpful.

Second, as explained below, the number of lawsuits against health care providers falls far short of the number of medical errors that are committed by these individuals and organizations. This is not unique to medical malpractice. Citations of drivers who exceed the speed limit are far rarer than the number of drivers who exceed such speed limits. Underclaiming or too few citations can lead to excessively careless behavior.

Third, the vast majority of physicians have complete insurance for their medical malpractice losses (Danzon 1985). Consequently, physicians do not bear a financial cost for the negligent injuries they cause. Nor, in contrast to motor vehicle liability insurance, are medical malpractice premiums experience-rated (Sloan 1990; OECD 2007). Although complete non-experience-rated insurance may be expected to blunt any deterrent effect that imposing medical liability might otherwise have, being sued does exact a price in terms of psychological distress and possibly loss of reputation as well. Furthermore, the time and earnings losses associated with being involved as a defendant in a lawsuit are not covered by medical malpractice insurance.

A distinction is often made between "positive" and "negative" defensive medicine in discussions of medical malpractice. *Positive defensive medicine* refers to increases in the cost of personal health care services attributable to the threat of being sued. Confronted with the threat of suits, physicians may order more tests, perform more surgical procedures, and undertake other medical interventions than they might in the absence of this type of threat.

Negative defensive medicine applies to a physician's withdrawal of care as a result of retirement, location change, or the dropping of procedures that often lead to lawsuits, such as those associated with obstetric care. That the threat of liability may affect the activity level that potentially exposes an agent to litigation is not unique to medical malpractice. For example, the cost of products liability may cause the manufacturer of a product to raise its price. Following the price increase, the quantity demanded falls, and eventually the manufacturer goes out of business.

For an economist, a test or procedure or other intervention becomes "defensive" when, in the view of an informed decision maker, ex ante, the marginal benefit is less than its marginal cost. Using this definition, to the extent that the threat of medical malpractice litigation increases the provision of care for which marginal benefit exceeds marginal cost, then such litigation serves its desired purpose, and conversely.

Several other definitions have been used in the field. For example, the US Office of Technology Assessment, US Congress (1994, 13), defined defensive medicine as the following way:

> Defensive medicine occurs when doctors order tests, procedures, or visits, or avoid high-risk patients or procedures, primarily (but not necessarily solely) to reduce their exposure to malpractice liability. When physicians do extra tests or procedures primarily to reduce malpractice liability, they are practicing positive defensive medicine. When they avoid certain patients or procedures, they are practicing negative defensive medicine.

The first definition, from the economics and law tradition, uses the concept of optimal care as the level of care that would maximize consumer well-being, given available scarce resources. This optimal level of care calls on health professionals' assistance to serve as the patient's agent to the extent that patients are not able to select optimal care on their own. The goal of tort liability is to encourage socially optimal choices. The US Office of Technology Assessment definition, based on a view shared by the vast majority of health professionals, begins with a very different premise. Medical liability has little or nothing to do with optimal care. Instead, the threat of being sued is an unnecessary disruption, and changes in resource allocation attributable to the threat are inherently wasteful.

Ideally, medical malpractice would lead to the provision of optimal levels of care.[6] But there may be under- or overdeterrence (the latter called "defensive medicine"). If the threat of liability is excessive or imposed arbitrarily, overdeterrence could result. Overdeterrence occurs when quality is supplied at a level above the socially optimal level. For example, physicians may overprescribe diagnostic tests and therapeutic procedures. The threat of lawsuits may also cause physicians to avoid certain types of procedures and locations. Again, we cannot generalize that such responses are desirable or undesirable. If a physician is not competent in performing a procedure because, for example, he or she performs few of them, then the threat is a positive outcome. On the other hand, if the threat truly

6. *See, for example, Shavell (1980).*

drives competent physicians from care that is demanded, the threat may be counterproductive.

LEGAL MARKET

In the legal market, individuals who have experienced iatrogenic injuries and who may have been passive in their role as patients become active participants as plaintiffs. In the vast majority of claims, as with other personal injuries, lawyers are paid on a contingency fee basis, which typically amounts to 33–40 percent of total compensation to plaintiffs (Sloan, Githens, Clayton, et al. 1993).

In the event the plaintiff drops the case or the plaintiff loses at verdict, the plaintiff's attorney receives no compensation. For this reason, attorneys have a strong incentive to accept only those cases that are likely to result in compensation greater than or equal to the legal cost they incur, including a return on their own time. Medical malpractice litigation can be quite complex in that technical details are often involved, at least relative to other legal disputes, as for example automobile accidents, for which causation may be more easily determined and for which a police report exists. There is empirical evidence that attorneys specializing in medical malpractice litigation obtain higher levels of compensation for their clients (Sloan, Githens, Clayton, et al. 1993).

Critics of the legal market in the context of medical malpractice allege that (1) lawyers frequently encourage persons with adverse outcomes from the receipt of medical care and who have nonmeritorious claims to file lawsuits, (2) liability laws unduly favor plaintiffs, and (3) plaintiffs are overcompensated for their losses. There are concerns that jury decisions are unduly swayed by the severity and circumstances of the plaintiff 's injury, but these criticisms are rebutted with empirical evidence from other studies (see, e.g., Vidmar 1998, 2004).

Researchers have conducted much empirical analysis on medical malpractice, particularly in the United States.[7] The results of empirical analysis fail to find that injury victims are overcompensated for their losses when they sue for medical malpractice (Sloan, Githens, Clayton, et al. 1993). Although plaintiffs in medical malpractice cases lose most often at trial (Sieg 2000), this does not mean that medical cases as a group are frivolous, although perhaps some are. Rather, plaintiff attorneys sometimes go to trial rather than drop a case for strategic reasons. If plaintiffs' lawyers never went to trial, they would lose bargaining power in settlement negotiations. The vast majority of medical malpractice lawsuits are either dropped or settled without much court involvement.

Viewed from a societal perspective, the primary role of the medical liability system must be quality assurance. When quality of care is high, the risk of iatrogenic injury decreases. Thus, the failure to regulate quality and therefore deter injury is a major deficiency of medical malpractice as it exists today. We turn to empirical evidence on medical malpractice as an injury deterrent in the following section.

7. There is theoretical and empirical evidence on why injury victims file claims (Hickson, Clayton, Entman, et al. 1994; Hickson, Clayton, Githens, et al. 1992; Hickson, Federspiel, Pichert, et al. 2002; Sloan and Hsieh 1995; Farber and White 1991; Nalebuff 1987; Nalebuff and Scharfstein 1987; May and Stengel 1990); variation in injuries relative to claims frequency (Weiler, Hiatt, Newhouse, et al. 1993; Mills, Boyden, and Rubsamen 1977), the determinants of award sizes (e.g., Danzon and Lillard 1983; Sloan and Hsieh 1990), comparisons of injury cost with compensation (Sloan, Githens, Clayton, et al. 1993), awards obtained with the use of a specialist lawyer (Sloan, Githens, Clayton, et al. 1993), outcomes in medical no-fault versus tort cases (Bovbjerg and Sloan 1998), and the effects of contingency fees on legal outcomes and on jury behavior in tort litigation (Vidmar 1995, 2003).

7.8 DOES THE THREAT OF MEDICAL MALPRACTICE SUITS DETER IATROGENIC INJURIES?

One series of influential studies has documented the frequency of medical error rates in hospitals. Three major studies of the epidemiology of medical injuries among patients hospitalized in the United States have been conducted since the mid-1970s (table 7.2). The earliest study was based on reviews of 20,864 patient records in California in 1974 (Mills, Boyden, and Rubsamen 1977). Building on the methods of the California study, the Harvard Medical Practice study reviewed records of 31,429 patients hospitalized in the state of New York during 1984, and reviewed litigation records (Weiler, Hiatt, Newhouse, et al. 1993). More recently, Colorado and Utah used the New York methodology in reviews of medical records of persons hospitalized in Colorado and Utah (Thomas, Studdert, Burstein, et al. 2000; Mello and Brennan 2002). Rates of injury due to receipt or nonreceipt of medical care were highest in the California study and lowest in the studies conducted 18 years later in Colorado and Utah (table 7.2). However, the share of injuries attributed to negligence was highest in Utah.

In the Harvard study, the best known of the three, two physician reviewers, working independently, rated their confidence that an adverse event attributable to the receipt or nonreceipt of medical care occurred, based on reviews of each medical record on a scale from 0 to 6 (Brennan, Leape, Laird, et al. 1991). Similarly, the reviewers assessed negligence. When there was disagreement among the reviewers, this was noted by a medical records analyst and resolved on independent review by a supervisory physician. This was an "implicit review," meaning that it was up to the physician to make an assessment of negligence without following explicit specialty-specific criteria.

The study reports there were 7.6 times as many negligent injuries as there were claims; only 2 percent of negligent adverse events resulted in medical

TABLE 7.2
Epidemiological Surveys of Medical Injuries among Patients Hospitalized in the United States

Year	Location	Sample Size	Injury rate (%)	Injuries caused by negligence (%)
1974	California State	23 hospitals 20,864 patients	4.7	17
1984	New York State	51 hospitals 31,429 patients	3.7	28
1992	Colorado and Utah	10,000 patients, Colorado; 5,000 patients, Utah	2.9	27 Colorado 33 Utah

Sources: Danzon (1991); Studdert, Thomas, Burstin, et al. (2000).

malpractice claims. Thus, only a small fraction of cases that could have resulted in medical malpractice lawsuits were in fact filed. But also troubling was the high frequency of "invalid" claims, those not matching the study's determination of liability from raters' evaluations of the medical records, which outnumbered valid claims by a ratio of three to one (Studdert, Mello, and Brennan 2004). From these studies, it is evident that errors occur in both directions: not enough valid claims were filed and too many invalid claims were filed.

A recent study placed medical malpractice in the United States in a more favorable light. Peters (2007) synthesized the findings of a dozen empirical studies on the relationship between malpractice settlement rates and quality of care. He found that both the likelihood of a settlement payment and the amount paid in settlement were closely related to the quality of the underlying claim of medical malpractice. In fact, all studies except the Harvard study found a correlation between settlement rate and case quality. Peters found that the number of categories claims used in the study made a material difference. The studies that divided the claims into three categories, such as negligent, not negligent, and uncertain, showed a stronger link between negligence and settlement outcome than the studies using two categories, such as negligent or not negligent. In addition, Peters found that only 10–20 percent of claimants with low-odds of winning claims received a settlement. This figure corresponds to a normal rate of disagreement when independent observers rate performance.

A second group of studies provides empirical evidence on medical malpractice's role in deterring iatrogenic injuries. Although medical malpractice, like tort liability more generally, has many goals, at the top of the list is injury deterrence. Whether or not the threat of tort liability actually deters is fundamentally an empirical question and cannot be decided based on theoretical arguments alone or on the basis of casual empirical observations. Overall, the quantitative evidence on this issue is conflicting and does not support the notion that the threat of medical malpractice litigation reduces medical errors or improves medical quality in general.

Empirical analysis of this issue has used two approaches. One approach is to examine providers within a government jurisdiction, more specifically a US state, and determine whether or not injury rates or practice patterns consistent with higher quality of care occur in areas within the jurisdiction in which the threat of medical malpractice lawsuits is higher. The other approach is to examine the effects of changes in tort law affecting the probability of being sued and examine whether or not these changes affect the rates of adverse outcomes.

The first approach was implemented in a study of adverse outcomes in the forty-nine New York hospitals conducted for the Harvard study described above (Weiler, Hiatt, Newhouse, et al. 1993). The threat of a malpractice claim was measured as the fraction of negligent injuries (as determined by the researchers' assessments of medical records at the hospital) that actually resulted in a medical malpractice claim. Dependent variables for the equation measuring the threat of lawsuits on outcomes were the fraction of hospitalizations that resulted in injuries, and the fraction of all injuries that were attributable to negligence. The authors failed to obtain statistically significant results, implying no effect of variations in the threat on outcomes at these forty-nine hospitals.

A research study using the second approach resulted in a highly cited paper on the topic of defensive medicine by Kessler and McClellan (1996). Although the focus of the study is on defensive medicine, it is also useful as an outcomes study because tort reforms that reduced the threat of lawsuits should have increased the rates of adverse outcomes to the extent that tort liability was an injury deterrent. Empirical details are provided in box 7.5.

Box 7.5
Empirical Analysis of Defensive Medicine: The Kessler-McClellan Study

Kessler and McClellan (1996) used longitudinal data on all elderly (aged 65+) Medicare beneficiaries who were hospitalized for a new acute myocardial infarction (AMI) or newly diagnosed ischemic heart disease (IHD) in 1984, 1987, and 1990. The key explanatory variables were tort law reforms implemented in the state in which the beneficiary was admitted for treatment. The authors assessed the effect of the statutory changes on total hospital Medicare payments during the year after the admission for the AMI or IHD to measure the effect of the statutory changes on intensity of treatment. If the changes succeeded in reducing the extent of defensive medicine, one should see reductions in treatment intensity or cost attributable to these changes. Kessler and McClellan also studied the impact of the tort reforms on patient outcomes because if higher cost resulted in better health outcomes, this would not be considered to be defensive medicine. Rather, it would be seen as good care.

Using Kessler and McClellan's methodology, defensive medicine is reduced if the reforms reduced treatment intensity but did not adversely affect patient outcomes. Their outcomes measured mortality within one year of admission for the treatment for AMI or IHD and whether the patient experienced a subsequent AMI or heart failure, judged by admission for either condition in the year following the index event. Kessler and McClellan combined reforms into two variables: "direct" and "indirect." Direct reforms include caps on damage awards, the abolition of punitive damages, no mandatory prejudgment interest, and collateral source rule reform.[8]

Punitive damages are obligations of the defendant to pay amounts over and above the amount needed to compensate the plaintiff for losses incurred. Incurred losses include pecuniary losses, such as for medical care and lost wages, and nonpecuniary loss, such as losses due to pain and suffering. The goal of punitive damages is to punish the defendant by more than the amount of loss needed to restore the plaintiff to his or her previous condition. Prejudgment interest refers to interest payments the defendant might otherwise be compelled to make on losses unpaid to the plaintiff

8. Punitive damages maybe awarded when the defendant's action is found to have deliberatively harmed the patient or represented conduct not befitting a professional. A few states have abolished punitive damages in medical malpractice cases even though punitive damages are rarely paid in the context of medical malpractice. Prejudgment interest refers to interest payments on the loss between the date of injury or the date a lawsuit is filed and the date the verdict is reached. Limits on prejudgment interest have the effect of reducing such interest payments.

Box 7.5
(continued)

from the time of the injury to the date on which the case is resolved, whether or not the defendant is found to be liable for the injury.

The general rule in countries that use the common law system, such as the US and the UK, is that the payments plaintiffs receive for a loss from their insurers are not deducted from the amounts they receive in a medical malpractice verdict. When the rule is modified, such amounts are deducted from the medical malpractice payment award.

Indirect reforms included other reforms that may affect pressures from tort on care provision but affect awards only indirectly, such as limitations on the plaintiff's attorney's contingency fees, which may make it more difficult for injury victims to file medical malpractice claims. Indirect reforms are limits on contingency fees, mandatory periodic payments, JSL reform, and the availability of a patient compensation fund. The study controls for the effects of other factors by including explanatory variables for state and year.

Under the contingency fee system, the lawyer for the plaintiff is paid only if he or she wins the case, and conditional on winning, the lawyer receives a certain predetermined share of the payment to the plaintiff, in the United States, generally 33–40 percent. Some tort reforms place an upper limit on this percentage.

In general, payment is made to the plaintiff in a lump sum. Some critics of medical malpractice argue that the percentages going to plaintiffs' lawyers are too high. Caps on contingency fees represent such limits. Since the plaintiff's attorney still incurs the cost of his or her side of the case, but with limits on contingency fees, the attorney may receive a lower payment. In this way, such limits reduce the incentive lawyers have to represent medical malpractice plaintiffs.

Kessler and McClellan found that in states adopting direct reforms, compared to states without reforms, Medicare payments for hospital care during the first year declined 5–9 percent. Similarly, in states with indirect reforms, Medicare payments declined 1.8 percent. Mortality was almost entirely unchanged in reform and nonreform states.

Kessler and McClellan concluded that liability reforms reduced defensive medicine practices, given their results showing that reforms reduced the cost of care while not adversely affecting outcomes. For those concerned with defensive medicine, the results are generally good news. However, if the issue of interest is the deterrent effect of tort liability, the lack of an effect of relaxing the threat of liability on health outcomes is not favorable news.

A follow-up study by Sloan and Shadle (2009), which in addition to examining hospitalizations for heart disease examined the effects of the same tort reforms on the cost of hospitalizations for breast cancer, stroke, and diabetes, found no effect of the tort reforms Kessler and McClellan examined on Medicare payments for hospitals, and with one exception found no effects of the reforms on health outcomes either. This lack of findings on hospitalizations for a broader range of diagnoses raises a question whether or not Kessler and McClellan's findings, which were only for heart disease, generalize. However, the Sloan and Shadle results do support an important inference from the Kessler and McClellan study, namely, that relaxing the threat of lawsuits would not lead to worse health outcomes, as opponents of tort reform argue it would.

Several studies have assessed the effect of the threat of medical malpractice lawsuits on the probability that a cesarean section may be performed rather than a vaginal delivery. These studies are useful as birth injuries are a frequent allegation in medical malpractice suits, more frequent than allegations of failure to perform a cardiac procedure (Sloan, Githens, Clayton, et al. 1993). The results of these studies have been mixed. Using data from Florida, Sloan, Entman, Reilly, et al. (1997) reported that malpractice pressures had no effect on the method of obstetric delivery (cesarean versus vaginal delivery). However, an earlier study using data from New York State had found an effect (Localio, Lawthers, Bengtson, et al. 1993). Dubay, Kaestner, and Waidmann (1999) used data from birth certificates from 1990 through 1992 to assess the impact of medical malpractice risk on cesarean rates and infant health. They found that a $10,000 reduction in malpractice premiums could result in a 1.4–2.4 percent decline in the cesarean section rate for some mothers, except those of the highest socioeconomic status. The authors concluded that caps on total damages could reduce the number of cesarean sections by 3 percent and total obstetric charges by 0.27 percent.

More recently, studies by Kim (2007), Currie and McLeod (2008), and Yang, Mello, Subramanian, et al. (2009) examined the impacts of tort reforms on the use and mix of obstetric services and on health outcomes. Kim used various measures of the risk of being sued and found that cesarean section rates and most other measures of physician behavior employed in the study (e.g., the use of forceps, vacuum extraction) were not affected by variation in the risk of being sued. Currie and McLeod (2008) found that reform of the joint and several liability (JSL) rule reduced complications of labor and procedure use, while caps on noneconomic damages increased them. JSL reform made it more difficult for a plaintiff to successfully sue the physician's hospital. To the extent that the hospital is a less dependable source of payment in the event of a payment for a claim resulting from care provided at the hospital, physicians have an added incentive to be careful. On the other hand, noneconomic damage caps reduce the amount that the physician can expect to pay in the event he or she loses a lawsuit. Thus, there is a reduction in the physician's incentive to undertake precautions to avoid a medical mishap. Yang and coauthors (2009), using medical malpractice insurance premiums and tort reforms as measures of the threat of liability, found that an increased threat of liability influenced the choice of delivery method (cesarean section versus vaginal delivery). However, the effect sizes are not large.

When these studies are viewed as a group, it is difficult to find evidence of a consistent link between the threat of tort liability and a reduction in medical error rates. There is some evidence for positive defensive medicine. However, the case that positive defensive medicine is a *major* factor driving up spending on personal health services, as is often alleged, is weak at best.

7.9 SUMMARY AND CONCLUSIONS

Much of health policy has focused on the quality of care. Many health care institutional arrangements reflect the motive to preserve and enhance quality. Historically, there has been a widespread suspicion that consumers of health care are not well positioned to judge the quality of care they receive, and this has led to substantial emphasis on supply-side approaches to quality assurance. Each perhaps has positive attributes, but each has its potential flaws as well. A general strategy of replacing demand-side with supply-side monitoring of quality is fraught with complexity and adverse side effects. In particular, it seems reasonable to expect that while most health professionals have an interest in providing a high quality of care, they are also likely to have other motives. Thus, professional norms and licensure, while well-intentioned, can be used to boost the profits of suppliers. Professional norms can reduce the flow of consumer information, thus conferring market power on individual sellers. Licensure can be used as a barrier to entry, conferring a de facto franchise on existing licensed professionals or at least using the licensure process to bar entry of those who follow undesirable commercial (read: competitive) approaches. Similarly, hospital peer review can be used both to improve the quality of hospital care and to bar the entry of physician competitors to the hospital.

Medical malpractice has important flaws, which this chapter has documented. On the other hand, widespread opposition to medical malpractice stems in part from the fact that it empowers consumers to lodge complaints against providers.

Public policies that improve the flow of information to consumers, who in turn will be in a better position to make allocative choices, are promising. Even these policies, however, have some potential shortcomings, which we have identified. In particular, if providers are to be graded, they can improve their quality or they can select patients who because of their relatively light conditions help improve the providers' grades. This raises challenges for the information reports—how to classify patients according to their medical conditions prior to treatment and how to deal with small samples per provider, which decreases the reliability of the reports. Clearly, there are many situations in which insurers as purchasers of health care need to act in the interests of the persons they insure. In the end, demand-side quality assurance offers substantial promise. We have some way to go before this promise is fully realized, however.

KEY CONCEPTS

- health care quality
- iatrogenic injury
- structure
- process
- outcome
- professional norms
- peer review
- licensure
- report cards
- medical malpractice
- contingent fees
- tort law
- due care
- strict liability rule
- negligence liability rule
- the Coase theorem
- defensive medicine

REVIEW AND DISCUSSION QUESTIONS

7.1 List five health care quality assurance mechanisms in your country. Assess the advantages and disadvantages of each.

7.2 Describe the system of tort liability as it applies to medical injuries as it currently exists in your country. Assess the strengths and weaknesses of the system to the extent that these can be determined, given the body of empirical evidence currently available.

7.3 Discuss how to analyze the following statement: "There are too many medical malpractice lawsuits." Try to represent the points of view on both sides of the argument.

7.4 A common statement is that "determination of medical liability by the courts is random, like a lottery." If this is true, how would it affect a health professional's optimal investment in injury prevention?

7.5 Discuss key elements of a health care contract that might serve as an alternative to tort. Be sure to indicate how the contract would substitute for tort. What are major advantages and disadvantages of the contract that you design?

7.6

a. Based on empirical evidence (from any country), how effective is the threat of a medical malpractice lawsuit in deterring medical injuries?

b. What could be done to make medical malpractice liability a more effective deterrent?

c. Specifically, what is the role of experience-rated medical malpractice insurance premiums? Why is experience rating not more widespread in this line of insurance than it is?

7.7 Explain the term "defensive medicine" in your own words. What are the consequences of practicing defensive medicine for health care costs and for patient care outcomes?

7.8 Assess the advantages and disadvantages of using report cards as an approach to improving the quality of health care. Is more information necessarily better than no information? Why or why not?

EXERCISES

7.1 Suppose a physician receives a fixed payment ($\hat{p}$) for providing health care services to a patient and there is a probability of the patient incurring iatrogenic injury (Θ) that causes monetary loss to the patient ($\hat{L}$). Assume that the patient's monetary loss is fixed once the injury has occurred. However, the probability of injury depends on the physician's level of care (e, for effort). That is, $\Theta = \Theta(e)$. The probability of injury decreases as the level of physician care increases (i.e., $\Theta(e) < 0$). In addition, the effort involved in increasing the level of care is costly to the physician in terms of time, stress, and nonphysician inputs the physician employs in his or her practice. Thus, the physician faces a cost function C, which also depends on the level of care. $C = C(e)$. $C'(e) > 0$; cost increases with the level of care. Using this information, answer the following questions.

a. Assume that the physician's sole objective in practicing medicine is to maximize profit, list the physician's objective (profit) function under the following liability regimes: (i) no liability, (ii) strict liability, and (iii) negligence liability.

b. With the level of care (e) on the horizontal axis and the profit ($) on the vertical axis, show graphically how the physician determines the optimal level of care under each of the three alternative liability regimes.

c. Use a graph similar to figure 7.1 to show how to decide what the socially optimal level of care is.

d. If the court has sufficient information to set the compensation ($\hat{D}$) equal to the injury victim's monetary loss ($\hat{L}$), which liability rules can ensure that the physician's optimal care level and the socially optimal care level coincide? Explain your answer.

e. Using a graph, explain the distinction between strict liability and the negligence rule. Under what condition do we expect that these liability rules will achieve the same level of optimal care?

7.2 Suppose a patient who was injured because of a medical error (e.g., an adverse drug reaction) is thinking about whether or not to file a medical malpractice claim against his doctor. Suppose he is a "rational" decision maker in the sense that he decides whether or not to file a claim based on his prediction of returns versus costs if he files. Let Θ represent the probability of eventually receiving compensation if he files, V be the size of payment conditional on receiving any compensation, and C be cost of filing and pursuing a claim.

a. What is the expected value (payoff) of the claim to the injury victim at filing?

b. Suppose patient A lives in a country where lawyers are paid on a contingency fee basis and patient B lives in another country where contingency fees are prohibited and lawyers are paid by the hour for their legal work. Suppose both the probability of receiving compensation and the size of payment conditional on receiving some payment are the same for patients A and B. Which person is more likely to file a medical malpractice claim? Explain your answer. (*Hint:* Pay attention to incentives faced by both patients and their lawyers.)

c. Suppose both patients C and D live in the United States, where lawyers are paid contingency fees, and the cases are comparable in the sense that the probabilities of receiving compensation are the same. However, patient C lives in a state where there is no cap on medical malpractice awards, while patient D lives in a state where there is a cap. Under these circumstances, which patient is more likely to file a medical malpractice claim? Why?

7.3 In recent years, many organizations around the world have published rankings of both universities and hospitals. For example, the *U.S. News and World Report* has regularly published "The Top 10 Best Universities in the US" and "the Top 10 Best Hospitals in the US" for many years.

a. What are likely to be differences between the hospital ranking and the university ranking in terms of their information content? Which one is likely to provide more valid and reliable information for potential users? Why is this so?

b. Would you expect there to be any difference between private and public agencies in performing rankings of hospitals? Suppose both a private firm and a public agency were to publish a "10 Best Hospitals" list for the city where you live. Which organization's ranking would be more valuable to probable hospital patients? Justify your answer.

c. List the pros and cons of hospital rankings from the viewpoint of the consumer.

d. How would you expect hospitals to respond to published hospital rankings? Is there any evidence to support your argument?

7.4 Conduct a field survey in the community in which you live (either your own survey or by searching websites) on price variations between low- and high-quality goods for each of the following six products: (1) digital camera, (2) college or university tuition, (3) physician fees for a routine outpatient visit, (4) charge for a hospital day, (5) a midday meal at a full-service restaurant, and (6) monthly rent for a three-bedroom apartment. Among these six products, for which is the correlation between price and quality likely to be the highest? The lowest? Explain why correlations for some products should be strong and for others weak or even nearly zero.

7.5 In table 7.1, we list four incentive mechanisms (professional norms, regulation, market competition, and tort law) for ensuring high levels of health care quality.

a. Among these four mechanisms, which one seems to play a relatively more important role in your country? Explain your answer.

b. Do the four mechanisms listed in table 7.1 also ensure high quality levels for higher education (university)? Why or why not?

c. Medical malpractice claims (i.e., patients suing their physicians and/or hospitals) are fairly common in many countries. Is it common for students to sue their university professors for a suboptimal quality of teaching? Can you conceive of tort law being used as mechanism for ensuring a high quality of higher education? Why or why not?

Online Supplemental Material

Hospital Rankings

http://health.usnews.com/best-hospitals/rankings

http://www.hospitalcompare.hhs.gov/hospital-search.aspx?AspxAutoDetectCookieSupport=1

Health Care Quality Indicators

http://www.oecd.org/document/34/0,3746,en_2649_37407_37088930_1_1_1_37407,00.html

Medical Malpractice in the News

http://topics.nytimes.com/topics/news/health/diseasesconditionsandhealthtopics/malpractice/index.html

TO ERR IS HUMAN

http://www.iom.edu/~/media/Files/Report%20Files/1999/To-Err-is-Human/To%20Err%20is%20Human%201999%20%20report%20brief.pdf

LIBRARY OF CONGRESS: MEDICAL MALPRACTICE LIABILITY

Germany:

http://www.loc.gov/law/help/medical-malpractice-liability/germany.php

Canada:

http://www.loc.gov/law/help/medical-malpractice-liability/canada.php

UK:

http://www.loc.gov/law/help/medical-malpractice-liability/uk.php

India:

http://www.loc.gov/law/help/medical-malpractice-liability/india.php

MEDICAL MALPRACTICE CLAIMS

http://www.npdb-hipdb.hrsa.gov/resources/publicData.jsp

MY OWN NETWORK—AGENCY FOR HEALTHCARE RESEARCH AND QUALITY

http://monahrq.ahrq.gov

SAFETY NET MONITORING

http://www.ahrq.gov/data/safetynet

PHYSICIAN INSURERS

http://www.piaa.us

SUPPLEMENTAL READING

Currie, J., and W. B. McLeod. 2008. First Do No Harm? Tort Reform and Birth Outcomes. *Quarterly Journal of Economics* 123 (2): 795–830.

Dranove, D., D. Kessler, M. McClellan, et al. 2003. Is More Information Better? The Effects of "Report Cards" on Health Care Providers. *Journal of Political Economy* 111 (3): 555–588.

Jin, G. Z., and P. Leslie. 2003. The Effect of Information on Product Quality: Evidence from Restaurant Hygiene Grade Cards. *Quarterly Journal of Economics* 118 (2): 409–451.

Leonard, K., M. C. Masatu, and A. Vialou. 2007. Getting Doctors to Do Their Best: The Role of Ability and Motivation in Health Care Quality. *Journal of Human Resources* 42 (3): 682–700.

Sloan, F. A., and J. H. Shadle. 2009. Is There Empirical Evidence for "Defensive Medicine"? A Reassessment. *Journal of Health Economics* 28 (2): 481–491.

References

Ameringer, C. F. 1999. *State Medical Boards and the Politics of Public Protection.* Baltimore, MD: Johns Hopkins University Press.

Baker, T. 2005. Reconsidering the Harvard Medical Practice Study Conclusions about the Validity of Medical Malpractice Claims. *Journal of Law, Medicine & Ethics* 33 (3): 501–514.

Berndt, E. R., and J. M. Donohue. 2008. Direct-to-Consumer Advertising in Health Care: An Overview of Economic Issues. In *Incentives and Choice in Health Care*, ed. F. A. Sloan and H. Kasper, 131–162. Cambridge, MA: MIT Press.

Bismark, M. M., T. A. Brennan, R. J. Paterson, et al. 2006. Relationship between Complaints and Quality of Care in New Zealand: A Descriptive Analysis of Complainants and Non-Complainants Following Adverse Events. *Quality & Safety in Health Care* 15 (1): 17–22.

Björkman, M., and J. Svensson. 2009. Power to the People: Evidence from a Randomized Field Experiment on Community-Based Monitoring in Uganda. *Quarterly Journal of Economics* 124 (2): 735–769.

Blumstein, J. F., and F. A. Sloan. 1988. Antitrust and Hospital Peer Review. *Law and Contemporary Problems* 51 (2): 7–92.

Bovbjerg, R. R., and F. A. Sloan. 1998. No-Fault for Medical Injury: Theory and Evidence. *University of Cincinnati Law Review* 67 (2).

Brennan, T. A., L. L. Leape, N. M. Laird, et al. 1991. Incidence of Adverse Events and Negligence in Hospitalized Patients: Results of the Harvard Medical Practice Study I. *New England Journal of Medicine* 324 (6): 370–376.

Breyer, F. 1982. Rational Purchase of Medical Care and Differential Insurance Coverage for Diagnostic Services. *Journal of Health Economics* 1 (2): 147–156.

Calabresi, G. 1970. *The Cost of Accidents.* New Haven, CT: Yale University Press.

Chaudhury, N., J. Hammer, M. Kremer, et al. 2006. Missing in Action: Teacher and Health Worker Absence in Developing Countries. *Journal of Economic Perspectives* 20 (1): 91–116.

Chen, J., M. J. Radford, Y. Wang, et al. 1999. Do "America's Best Hospitals" Perform Better for Acute Myocardial Infarction? *New England Journal of Medicine* 340 (4): 286–292.

Coase, R. 1960. The Problem of Social Cost. *Journal of Law & Economics* 3 (1): 1–44.

Currie, J., and W. B. McLeod. 2008. First Do No Harm? Tort Reform and Birth Outcomes. *Quarterly Journal of Economics* 123 (2):795–830.

Danzon, P., and L. A. Lillard. 1983. Settlement Out of Court: The Disposition of Medical Malpractice Claims. *Journal of Legal Studies* 12:345–377.

Danzon, P. M. 1985. Liability and Liability Insurance for Medical Malpractice. *Journal of Health Economics* 4 (4): 309–331.

Danzon, P. M. 1991. Liability for Medical Malpractice. *Journal of Economic Perspectives* 5 (3): 51–69.

Das, J., J. Hammer, and K. Leonard. 2008. The Quality of Medical Advice in Low-Income Countries. *Journal of Economic Perspectives* 22 (2): 93–114.

Donabedian, A. 1985. Twenty Years of Research on the Quality of Medical Care: 1964–1984. *Evaluation & the Health Professions* 8 (3): 243–265.

Dranove, D., D. Kessler, M. McClellan, et al. 2003. Is More Information Better? The Effects of "Report Cards" on Health Care Providers. *Journal of Political Economy* 111 (3): 555–588.

Dubay, L., R. Kaestner, and T. Waidmann. 1999. The Impact of Malpractice Fears on Cesarean Section Rates. *Journal of Health Economics* 18 (4): 491–522.

Farber, H. S., and M. J. White. 1991. Medical Malpractice: An Empirical Examination of the Litigation Process. *RAND Journal of Economics* 22:199–217.

Friedman, M. 1962. *Capitalism and Freedom*. Chicago: University of Chicago Press.

Friedman, M., and S. Kuznets. 1945. *Income from Independent Professional Practice*. New York: National Bureau of Economic Research.

Haltom, W., and M. McCann. 2004. *Distorting the Law*. Chicago: University of Chicago Press.

Hickson, G. B., E. W. Clayton, S. S. Entman, et al. 1994. Obstetricians' Prior Malpractice Experience and Patients' Satisfaction with Care. *Journal of the American Medical Association* 272 (20): 1583–1587.

Hickson, G. B., E. W. Clayton, P. B. Githens, et al. 1992. Factors That Prompted Families to File Medical Malpractice Claims Following Perinatal Injuries. *Journal of the American Medical Association* 267 (10): 1359–1363.

Hickson, G. B., C. F. Federspiel, J. W. Pichert, et al. 2002. Patient Complaints and Malpractice Risk. *Journal of the American Medical Association* 287 (22): 2951–2957.

Institute of Medicine (IOM). 2000. *To Err Is Human: Building a Safer Health System*. Washington, DC: National Academies Press.

Jin, G. Z., and P. Leslie. 2003. The Effect of Information on Product Quality: Evidence from Restaurant Hygiene Grade Cards. *Quarterly Journal of Economics* 118 (2): 409–451.

Kessler, D., and M. McClellan. 1996. Do Doctors Practice Defensive Medicine? *Quarterly Journal of Economics* 111 (2): 353–390.

Kim, B. 2007. The Impact of Malpractice Risk on the Use of Obstetrics Procedures. *Journal of Legal Studies* 36:S79–S119.

Klemick, H., K. L. Leonard, and M. C. Masatu. 2009. Defining Access to Health Care: Evidence on the Importance of Quality and Distance in Rural Tanzania. *American Journal of Agricultural Economics* 91 (2): 347–358.

Leape, L. L., T. A. Brennan, N. Laird, et al. 1991. The Nature of Adverse Events in Hospitalized Patients: Results of the Harvard Medical Practice Study II. *New England Journal of Medicine* 324 (6): 377–384.

Leonard, K. L., M. C. Masatu, and A. Vialou. 2007. Getting Doctors to Do Their Best: The Roles of Ability and Motivation in Health Care Quality. *Journal of Human Resources* 42 (3): 682–700.

Localio, A. R., A. G. Lawthers, J. M. Bengtson, et al. 1993. Relationship between Malpractice Claims and Cesarean Delivery. *Journal of the American Medical Association* 269 (3): 366–373.

Marchev, M., J. Rosenthal, and M. Booth. 2003. *How States Report Medical Errors to the Public: Issues and Barriers*. Portland, ME: National Academy for State Health Policy.

Mariko, M. 2003. Quality of Care and the Demand for Health Services in Barmako, Mali: The Specific Roles of Structural, Process, and Outcome Components. *Social Science & Medicine* 56:1183–1196.

May, M. L., and D. B. Stengel. 1990. Who Sues Their Doctors? *Law & Society Review* 24 (1): 105–120.

McGuire, T. G. 2000. Physician Agency. In *Handbook for Health Economics*, ed. J. P. Newhouse and A. J. Culyer, 462–528. Amsterdam: Elsevier Science.

Mello, M. M., and T. A. Brennan. 2002. Deterrence of Medical Errors: Theory and Evidence for Malpractice Reform. *Texas Law Review* 80 (7): 1595–1637.

Mennemeyer, S. T., M. A. Morrisey and L. Z. Howard. 1997. Death and Reputation: How Consumers Acted upon HCFA Mortality Information. *Inquiry* 34:117–128.

Mills, D. H., J. S. Boyden, and D. S. Rubsamen. 1977. *Report on the Medical Insurance Feasibility Study*. San Francisco: Sponsored by the California Medical Association and California Hospital Association.

Nalebuff, B. 1987. Credible Pretrial Negotiation. *RAND Journal of Economics* 18:198–210.

Nalebuff, B., and D. Scharfstein. 1987. Testing in Models of Asymmetric Information. *Review of Economics and Statistics* 54:265–277.

Organisation for Economic Co-operation and Development (OECD). 2007. *Health Update.* Paris: OECD Publishing.

Pauly, M. V. 2001. Making Sense of a Complex System: Empirical Studies of Employment-Based Health Insurance. *International Journal of Health Care Finance and Economics* 1 (3/4): 333–339.

Peters, P. G. 2007. Doctors & Juries. *Michigan Law Review* 105 (7): 1453–1495.

Peterson, E. D., E. R. DeLong, J. G. Jollis, et al. 1998. The Effects of New York's Bypass Surgery Provider Profiling on Access to Care and Patient Outcomes in the Elderly. *Journal of the American College of Cardiology* 32 (4): 993–999.

Sage, W. M. 2003. Managed Care's Crimea: Medical Necessity, Therapeutic Benefit, and the Goals of Administrative Process in Health Insurance. *Duke Law Journal* 53 (2): 597–651.

Shavell, S. 1980. Strict Liability versus Negligence. *Journal of Legal Studies* 9 (1): 1–25.

Sieg, H. 2000. Estimating a Bargaining Model with Asymmetric Information: Evidence from Medical Malpractice Disputes. *Journal of Political Economy* 108 (5): 1006–1021.

Sloan, F. A. 1990. Experience Rating: Does It Make Sense for Medical Malpractice Insurance? *American Economic Review* 80 (2): 128–133.

Sloan, F. A., S. S. Entman, B. Reilly, et al. 1997. Tort Liability and Obstetricians' Care Levels. *International Review of Law and Economics* 17 (2): 245–260.

Sloan, F. A., P. B. Githens, E. W. Clayton, et al. 1993. *Suing for Medical Malpractice.* Chicago: University of Chicago Press.

Sloan, F., and C. Hsieh. 1990. Variability in Medical Malpractice Payments. *Law & Society Review* 24:601–650.

Sloan, F. A., and C. R. Hsieh. 1995. Injury, Liability, and the Decision to File a Medical Malpractice Claim. *Law & Society Review* 29 (3): 413–435.

Sloan, F. A., P. M. Mergenhagen, W. B. Burfield, et al. 1989. Medical Malpractice Experience of Physicians: Predictable or Haphazard? *Journal of the American Medical Association* 262 (23): 3291–3297.

Sloan, F. A., and J. H. Shadle. 2009. Is There Empirical Evidence for "Defensive Medicine"? A Reassessment. *Journal of Health Economics* 28 (2): 481–491.

Sloan, F. A., E. M. Stout, K. Whetten-Goldstein, et al. 2000. *Drinkers, Drivers, and Bartenders.* Chicago: University of Chicago Press.

Spence, M. 1977. Consumer Misperceptions, Product Failure and Producer Liability. *Review of Economic Studies* 44 (3): 561–572.

Studdert, D. M., M. M. Mello, and T. A. Brennan. 2004. Medical Malpractice. *New England Journal of Medicine* 350 (3): 283–292.

Studdert, D. M., E. J. Thomas, H. R. Burstin, et al. 2000. Negligent Care and Malpractice Claiming Behavior in Utah and Colorado. *Medical Care* 38 (3): 250–260.

Thomas, E. J., H. R. Studdert, H. R. Burstein, et al. 2000. Incidence and Types of Adverse Events and Negligent Care in Utah and Colorado. *Medical Care* 38 (3): 261–271.

U.S. Office of Technology Assessment, U. S. Congress. 1994. *Identifying Health Technologies That Work.* Washington, DC: Diane Publishing Co.

Vidmar, N. 1995. *Medical Malpractice and the American Jury: Confronting the Myths about Jury Incompetence, Deep Pockets, and Outrageous Damage Awards.* Ann Arbor: University of Michigan Press.

Vidmar, N. 1998. The Performance of the American Civil Jury: An Empirical Perspective. *Arizona Law Review* 40 (4): 849–899.

Vidmar, N. 2003. The American Civil Jury for Ausländer (Foreigners). *Duke Journal of Comparative & International Law* 13 (3): 95–120.

Vidmar, N. 2004. Experimental Simulations and Tort Reform: Avoidance, Error and Overreaching in Sunstein et al.'s Punitive Damages. *Emory Law Journal* 53 (3): 1359–1404.

Weiler, P. C., H. Hiatt, J. P. Newhouse, W. Johnson, T. A. Brennan, and L. Leape. 1993. *A Measure of Malpractice: Medical Injury, Malpractice Litigation, and Patient Compensation.* Cambridge, MA: Harvard University Press.

White, M. J. 2004. Asbestos and the Future of Mass Torts. *Journal of Economic Perspectives* 18 (2): 183–204.

Yang, C. M., S. H. Tsai, and W. T. Chiu. 2009. How Risky Is Caring for Emergency Patients at Risk of Malpractice Litigation: A Population-Based Epidemiological Study of Taiwan's Experiences. *BMC Health Services Research* 9: 168–173.

Yang, Y. T., M. M. Mello, S. V. Subramanian, et al. 2009. Relationship between Malpractice Litigation Pressure and Rates of Cesarean Section and Vaginal Birth after Cesarean Section. *Medical Care* 47 (2): 234–242.

NURSES IN HOSPITAL AND LONG-TERM CARE SERVICE

Health care is a major source of employment of labor at virtually all skill levels, with the skill mix differing substantially among countries. Some health care workers have relatively minimal amounts of training specific to health care. Others acquire skills on the job. Still others acquire formal education in health care, which is later supplemented with on-the-job training and experience. Dominant among the latter are professional nurses, both in numbers and in responsibility for provision of health care on an ongoing basis. This chapter focuses on professional nurses.

Nurses are the largest group of health care professionals. Nurses assume important roles in the provision of various personal health services, in particular hospital-based, nursing home, and home health care. We begin this chapter with an overview of labor markets for nurses worldwide. We then describe two concepts: (1) economic concepts of surplus and shortage, terms that mean something different from their common meanings when used by economists, and (2) the role of monopsony power in markets for nurses.

We then discuss the role of nurses in the production of hospital and long-term care services. Professional nurses provide much if not most direct care in hospitals. Professional nurses also often serve in supervisory roles in long-term care settings.

One important health policy issue concerns the quality of care in hospitals and nursing homes. Quality of care and approaches for improving it are increasingly important to policy makers, especially in high-income countries. In this chapter, we provide empirical evidence on the question of whether or not higher nurse-to-patient ratios improve the quality of hospital and long-term care services, and we look at the advantages and disadvantages of government requirements that health care organizations maintain minimum ratios of nurses to patients.

8.1 LABOR MARKETS FOR NURSES WORLDWIDE

Nurse labor is one of the primary inputs in the production of personal health care services. The labor supply decisions of nurses have important effects on access, quality, and cost of the health care provided to patients. For example, when nurses are scarce relative to patients in a hospital, the quality of care may suffer because nurses can pay less attention to each individual patient and patients are more likely to have to wait for nurses to provide any care at all. Although the relationship between nurse staffing and quality of care is an intuitively plausible one, only recently have studies actually quantified the relationship empirically.

Nurses' compensation accounts for a large portion of hospital labor costs globally. Because of societal pressures to maintain and improve quality of care and simultaneous pressures on health care budgets, labor supply decisions of nurses have become a major policy concern for health care policy makers in many countries. Health care administrators have spent much time worrying about how to attract nurses to their organizations while at the same time preserving their organizations' financial strength.

Professional nurses are employed in private and public hospitals, long-term care institutions, clinics, and other health facilities; some nurses are self-employed. A common metric used in making geographic comparisons of the distribution of nurses is the number of nurses per 1,000 population, hereafter referred to as *nurse density*.

There are substantial differences in nurse density across countries (table 8.1). Based on data from 175 countries for years around the year 2000, the global mean of nurse density is 3.56, with a range from 0.11 to 15.20 per 1,000 population. In table 8.1, we further group the countries into four groups according to their gross domestic product (GDP) per capita in constant 2000 US dollars. Nurse density increased with a country's income level. In low-income countries, there were 1.03 nurses per 1,000 population. This ratio was 7.03 in high-income countries.

Despite the positive relationship between income and nurse density, there was still substantial variation among countries with similar income levels. For example, nurse density ranged from 0.80 to 15.20 in high-income countries. According to another data source, which documents density for member countries of the Organisation for Economic Co-operation and Development (OECD), the number of nurses per 1,000 population ranged from 1.7 in Turkey and Korea to 14.8 in Ireland (table 8.2).

Several factors account for variation in the number of nurses relative to population among countries. Three plausible factors are GDP per capita, per capita

TABLE 8.1
Global Distribution of Nurses by Income Level of Country

Income Group	Number of Countries within the Group	Nurses Per 1,000 population			
		Mean	Standard Deviation	Minimum	Maximum
High-income countries	43	7.03	3.92	0.80	15.20
High middle-income countries	44	3.38	2.41	0.45	9.71
Middle-income countries	44	2.87	2.74	0.14	11.63
Low-income countries	44	1.03	1.39	0.11	6.14
All countries	175	3.56	3.49	0.11	15.20

Note: High-income countries are countries with a GDP per capita greater than the 75th percentile of world income distribution. High middle-income countries are those with GDP per capita in the range between 75th percentile and the 50th percentile of world income distribution. Middle-income countries are those countries with GDP per capita in the range of 25th percentile to 50th percentile of world income distribution. Low-income countries are those with GDP per capita less than 25th percentile of world income distribution.
Sources: Data for income are from the World Bank Group, World Development Indicators (2007). Data for nurse density are from the World Health Organization, World Health Report (2006). The description statistics for each income groups are calculated by authors.

expenditures on personal health care services, and physician density. On the first, the simple correlation between a country's nurse density and its GDP per capita is 0.71 (table 8.3), confirming that nurse density increases with income. In addition, the parameter estimate from a regression of nurse density on GDP per capita yields an estimated elasticity of nurse density with respect to income of 0.53. This elasticity estimate implies that, on average, a 10 percent increase in GDP per capita leads to a 5.3 percent increase in the country's nurse density. A clear implication is that a reason for low nurse density in some countries is that the countries are at a low level of economic development.

Second, countries that spend more on personal health care services per person may well buy more *caring* (or subjective components of personal health care services, which are nevertheless important to people) but relatively little additional *curing* (or physiological health).[1] Since nursing is a "caring" profession, part of nurses' responsibility is to reduce pain and suffering and mitigate the inconveniences associated with the receipt of personal health care services, it is plausible to expect that countries spending more on health care would have a higher nurse density. Based on data from 175 countries, the simple correlation between nurse density and share of GDP allocated to personal health care services is 0.37, indicating that nurse density increases with a country's commitment of resources to personal health care services (table 8.3).

1. *See, for example, Newhouse (1976).*

TABLE 8.2
Profiles of Active Nurses in OECD Countries

County	Nurses, 2003*	Avg. Annual Growth Rate of Active Nurses, 1990–2003*	Ratios of Active Nurses to Active Physicians, 2003	% Female Particip. in Nurse Workforce, 2000
Australia	10.2	–1.0	4.2	92.1
Austria	9.4	2.0	2.8	88.4
Belgium	5.8	N/A	1.4	90.9
Canada	9.8	–1.0	4.7	95.2
Czech Republic	9.4	0.9	2.7	N/A
Denmark	10.3[a]	N/A	3.6	93.5
Finland	9.3	3.4	3.6	94.7
France	7.3	2.2	2.1	87.2
Germany	9.7	N/A	2.9	86.4
Greece	3.9[c]	N/A	0.9	91.0
Hungary	5.1	1.0	1.6	N/A
Iceland	13.7	0.7	3.8	N/A
Ireland	14.8	2.1	5.7	91.0
Italy	5.4	N/A	1.3	72.7
Japan	7.8[a]	2.4	3.9	96.6
Korea	1.7	N/A	1.1	99.8
Luxembourg	10.6[a]	N/A	4.1	N/A
Mexico	2.1	1.7	1.4	95.0
Netherlands	12.8[2]	N/A	3.9	88.1
New Zealand	9.1	–0.2	4.1	90.2
Norway	10.4[b]	N/A	3.5	92.2
Poland	4.9	–0.7	2.0	N/A
Portugal	4.2	3.2	1.3	N/A
Slovak Republic	6.5	N/A	2.1	97.3
Spain	7.5	N/A	2.3	80.7
Sweden	10.2[a]	0.9	3.1	92.5
Switzerland	10.7[3]	N/A	3.1	87.6
Turkey	1.7	1.9	1.2	N/A
United Kingdom	9.1	1.1	4.1	90.4
United States	7.9[a]	0.8	3.4	94.6
Median	9.1	N/A	3.1	91.0

Notes: *per 1,000 population; a. 2002. b. 2001. c. 2000. N/A, data not available.
Sources: Organisation for Economic Co-operation and Development (2005), Health at a Glance: OECD Indicators, p. 41.

TABLE 8.3
Determinants of the International Variations in Nurse Density

Variables	Simple Correlation Coefficient with Nurse Density	Elasticity (Based on Regression Coefficient)
GDP per capita	0.71	0.53
Share of GDP spent on health care	0.37	1.17
Number of physicians per 1,000 population	0.72	0.62

Sources: Data for income are from 2007 World Development Indicators, Data for nurse density, share of GDP spent on health care and physician density are from the World Health Organization, World Health Report (2006). Simple correlation coefficient and elasticity are calculated by authors.

Using a parameter estimate from a regression of nurse density on this share, the estimated elasticity of nurse density with respect to the share of GDP allocated to personal health care services is 1.17, indicating that a 10 percent increase in GDP share spent on health care leads to an 11.7 percent increase in nurse density.

However, the above relationship does not hold if the analysis is limited to high-income countries. An OECD study (OECD 2004) reported no statistically significant relationship between nurse density and health expenditures as a percentage of GDP. This lack of a relationship in this analysis may reflect a relatively small sample size as well as heterogeneity in nurse remuneration levels among high-income countries.

Third, the correlation between nurse density and physician density is 0.72 (table 8.3). The parameter estimate from a regression of nurse density on physician density yields an estimated elasticity of nurse density with respect to physician density of 0.62, indicating that a 10 percent increase in physician density leads to a 6.2 percent increase in nurse density on average. This suggests that specific health care technologies adopted in a country may be simultaneously physician- and nurse-using.

If variation in physician density alone accounted for most of the variation in nurse density among countries, then one would expect to observe small differences in the ratio of active nurses to active physicians among countries. However, in fact, there is appreciable intercountry variation in ratios of active nurses to physicians (table 8.2). Some countries, such as Ireland and Canada, employ about five nurses per physician, while other countries, such as Korea and Turkey, employ only about one nurse per physician.

Furthermore, international differences in nurse density may reflect differences in quality of health care that may not be readily measured at the country level. At the individual hospital level (discussed more fully below), several studies have documented that patient outcomes are better when nurse staffing is higher. However, it may be inappropriate to infer that a relationship at the level of a hospital or nursing home extends to a country as well.

Although countries differ in nurse density, there are many similarities in labor markets for nurses among countries, at least among high-income countries. First, the number of nurses per 1,000 population increased during 1990–2003 in most high-income countries except Australia, Canada, New Zealand, and Poland (table 8.2). The mean annual growth of active nurses per 1,000 population ranged from 0.7 percent in Iceland to 3.4 percent in Finland between 1990 and 2003. The increase in number of nurses probably reflects a strong growth in demand for personal health care services, resulting in part from technological advances and to some extent from population aging. However, just because nurse supply has grown does not necessarily mean that it has grown sufficiently. Whether or not the growth in the supply of nurses has kept up with the increase in demand for personal health care services is an important policy question to be examined in greater detail below.

Second, the labor market for nurses has several distinctive characteristics that apply to many high-income as well as lower-income countries. Among these, the most important is that nursing has predominantly been a female profession, over 90 percent female in fifteen OECD countries. In South Korea, nearly 100 percent of nurses are women.

An important consequence of this extraordinarily high share of female nurses is that, at least until quite recently, most nurses have not been the primary earners in their households, and nonwage factors are likely to be important determinants of labor supply. Despite its importance to patients and to health care, nursing has long been perceived as a "vocation" rather than a "profession" in many societies (Heyes 2005). Furthermore, high proportions of registered nurses in many countries are dissatisfied with their jobs (Aiken, Clarke, Sloane, et al. 2001). Among many job attributes, Shields and Ward (2001) found evidence that dissatisfaction with promotion and training opportunities has a stronger impact on intentions to quit nursing jobs than does workload or pay. Nursing is often very stressful with a very flat career path, relatively low earnings growth, and often limited opportunities for professional advancement (Steinbrook 2002).

Third, there is a widespread perception of excess demand for nurses in several countries, although in a few countries the perception is one of excess supply. Excess demand for nurses is not a new phenomenon. Many countries, such as the United States and United Kingdom, have experienced recurring periods of excess demand for nurses since at least the end of World War II (Shields 2004). Also, excess demand is not limited to countries with relatively low nurse density but exists in other countries as well, such as Australia, Canada, Germany, and Norway (OECD 2004).

In common parlance, conditions of excess demand are termed "shortages" and those of excess supply are termed "surpluses." In economics, such shortages and surpluses are temporary unless there is a restraint on wage changes, which keep the labor market from clearing, that is, reaching an equilibrium in which the quantity supplied equals the quantity demanded.

However, the market-clearing process may be impeded by constantly shifting demand and supply curves. A situation of persistent excess demand may arise from a trend in which growth in the supply of nurses fails to match an increased demand for nurses. During the past four decades, many countries experienced a sustained growth in demand for personal health care services, which in turn increased the *derived* demand for nursing services.

By contrast, several factors have restrained the growth in the supply of nurses. Women now have more career options than previously. For example, while medicine once was dominated by males, many females now enter medical school, and a career in medicine competes with nursing. In other markets, such as the market for gasoline, price increases lead to market clearing. In markets for nurses, however, markets often seem to fail to clear, and if they do, it is only with a substantial lag.

Why markets for nursing do not seem to clear is an important public policy issue. Consumers are willing to pay for such care and would be better off if these wants were satisfied.

8.2 SUPPLY OF NURSES: TOO MANY OR TOO FEW?

ECONOMIC CONCEPTS OF SURPLUS AND SHORTAGE

Although there is widespread agreement in many countries that a shortage of nurses exists, concepts of shortages and how to measure them differ. Noneconomists, including many health policy analysts, tend to use two different approaches to define shortage. The first is a need-based approach that identifies the number of nurses *required* to perform certain tasks according to the professional judgment. There is a shortage if the number of nurses needed exceeds the current employment of full-time-equivalent nurses. A second approach uses a ratio technique that compares the current nurse/population ratio to the future nurse/population ratio and defines as a shortage a projected future ratio less than the existing one (Lane and Gohmann 1995).

Economists define a shortage quite differently. A shortage exists when the quantity of nurses demanded exceeds the quantity of nurses supplied *at the current market wage* (fig. 8.1).[2] In the standard supply-and-demand framework of economics, the quantity of nurses demanded declines with increases in the real nurses' wage and the quantity supplied increases with increases in the real wage. The intersection of a demand curve (D_1) and a supply curve (S_1) determines the equilibrium market wage at w_1 and employment level at N_1.

2. Similarly, a surplus exists when the quantity demanded for nurses is less than the quantity supplied of nurses at the current market wage.

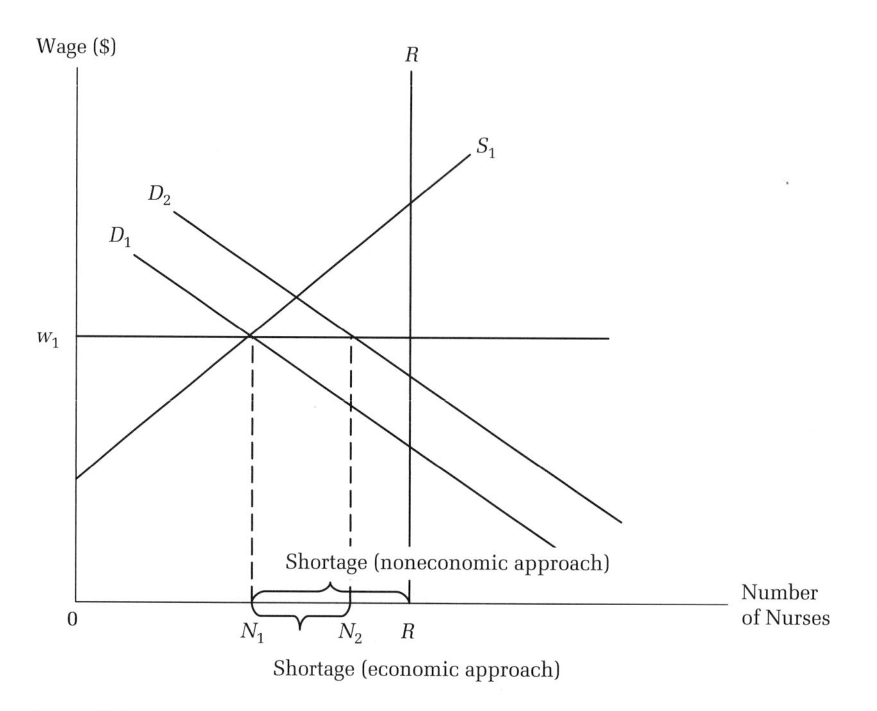

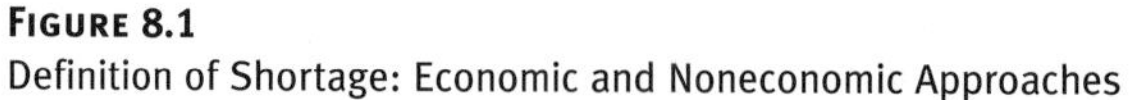

FIGURE 8.1
Definition of Shortage: Economic and Noneconomic Approaches

Assume that there is an exogenous shift—an outward shift in demand from D_1 to D_2 for nurses—owing to a factor external to the market for nurses, such as higher per capita income. Assuming that the market wage is fixed at its current level (w_1) for some reason, such as public regulation or union contract, then the quantity of nurses demanded is N_2 while the quantity of nurses supplied remains at N_1 since the market wage level remains constant. Therefore, there is an excess demand for nurses at the existing market wage, and the magnitude of the shortage is the horizontal distance between N_2 and N_1, $(N_2 - N_1)$.

Assume the vertical line *RR* indicates the ideal level of required nurse staffing using clinical or medical criteria. The number of nurses required to satisfy this professional standard is *R*, and the quantity of nursing labor supplied at the current market wage is N_1. Therefore, the shortage of nurses as measured by this noneconomic approach is $R - N_1$. This example illustrates why there are differences in the estimated magnitude of shortages, depending on whether the economic approach or a noneconomic approach is utilized.

Furthermore, different approaches for measuring shortage or surplus may lead to different conclusions about whether a surplus or a shortage of nurses exists. For example, if we assume that there is a further exogenous increase in the supply

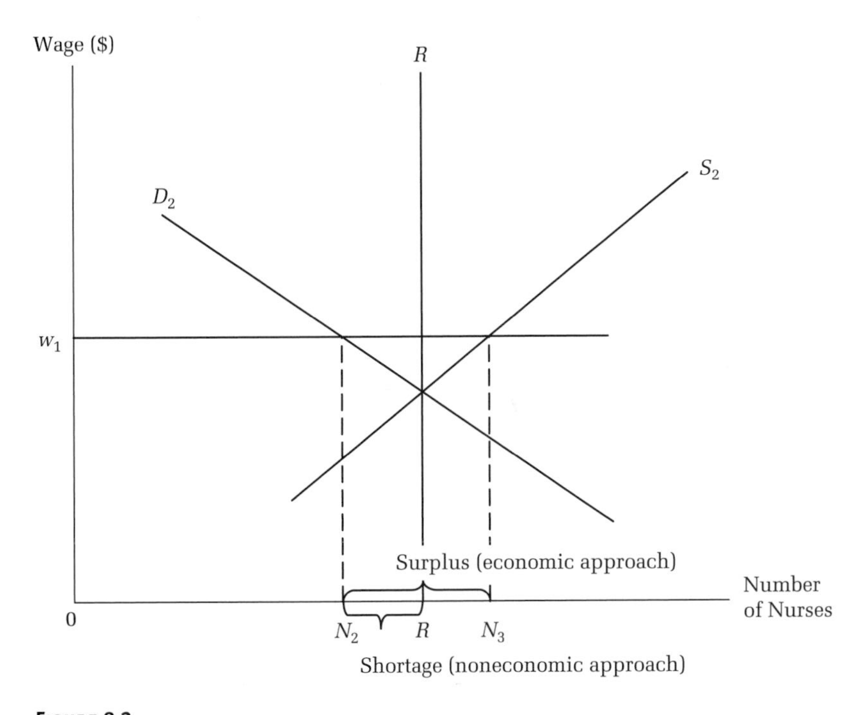

FIGURE 8.2
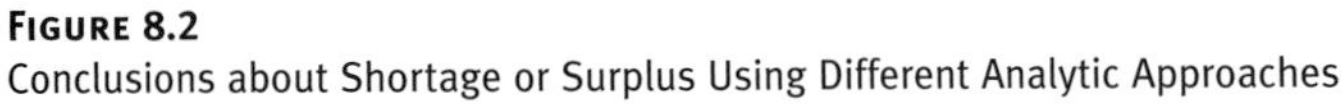
Conclusions about Shortage or Surplus Using Different Analytic Approaches

of nurses resulting from a change in government policy on recruiting nurses from overseas, then the supply curve of nurses become S_2 (fig. 8.2). In this case, the quantity of nurses supplied becomes N_3 while the quantity of nurses demanded remains at N_2 when the market wage is fixed at w_1. Thus, there is an excess supply (surplus) of nurses according to the economic approach. The surplus of nurses is equal to $N_3 - N_2$. However, according to the noneconomic approach, there is a shortage of nurses because the number of nurses needed (determined by the *RR* line) exceeds the quantity of nurses demanded at the current wage level (N_2). The shortage of nurses is $R - N_2$.

Lane and Gohmann (1995) showed how different approaches to defining shortages lead to different conclusions about whether or not a shortage or surplus exists. They used US data from 1991 to estimate parameters of equations for the demand for and supply of nurses. Using their parameter estimates, they defined a county as a shortage area if the quantity demanded exceeded the quantity supplied by more than 10 percent. Among the 1,880 counties in their analysis, the empirical model designated 423 US counties as shortage areas. By contrast, the noneconomic approach used by the US Office of Shortage Designations placed 565 counties in this category. The two approaches agreed on the shortage status of only 133 counties.

Different approaches for identifying shortages not only lead to different conclusions as to when and where shortages exist, the different approaches also result in different recommended policies for remedying a shortage. The noneconomic approach focuses on identifying a fixed need without considering market mechanisms that generally lead to market clearing. Thus, the only policy option implied by the noneconomic approach is to shift the supply curve to eliminate a shortage.

By contrast, the economic approach implies consideration of a range of market mechanisms, including changes in technology, substitution possibilities reflecting the relative availability of factors of production, and the wage adjustment process. The economic approach consequently provides policy makers with more options for eliminating a shortage, and for the working of market mechanisms that complement public policies (Lane and Gohmann 1995).

Even if we accept the economic approach as a useful guide to policy making, a question still remains as to why there are persistent shortages of nurses in many countries. A persistent nursing shortage requires two necessary conditions (fig. 8.1): (1) the quantity demanded is greater than the quantity supplied, and (2) wage rigidity, so that market wages do not adjust instantaneously to an excess demand for the factor of production, in this context, nurses. We explain the persistence of nursing shortage from the perspective of these two necessary conditions.

The demand for nurses is a derived demand, derived from a product demand—the demand for acute health care and long-term care services. During the past three decades, many countries have experienced rapid growth in demand for health care, which reflects increased health insurance coverage, rising personal incomes, population aging, technological change, and other factors (see, e.g., Newhouse 1992). In particular, the average annual growth rate in real health care expenditures has exceeded the average annual growth rate in real GDP for some time. As a result, the demand for nurses has increased steadily. By contrast, growth in the supply of nurses has not matched the rapid increase in the demand for nurses in many countries. Many countries thus appear to be suffering from nurse shortages. Although each country may have some specific policies that affect the supply of nurses, there are some common factors among countries that contribute to the slower increase in the supply of nurses.

Although the increase in the supply of nurses lags behind the increase in demand for nurses, the shortage would not occur if market wages could adjust instantaneously. Therefore, an important question to be asked in addressing the persistent shortage of nurses is why markets fail to clear. If wage rates adjust in response to the market disequilibrium between demand and supply, then the shortage (or surplus) of nurses will be eliminated as wages rise (or fall). In this case, a shortage is only a temporary phenomenon. However, if there is a failure of wages to adjust rapidly, then the market disequilibrium will prevail in the long run. Therefore, it is important to ask why there is a failure of wage adjustment in the labor market for nurses. There are two major explanations: (1) public regulation of nurses' pay and (2) monopsony power in labor market for nurses.

ROLE OF PUBLIC REGULATION

Many countries rely on the public sector to finance *and* deliver health care services (see chapters 11–13). With government substantially involved in the financing and provision of services, the government often finds it advantageous to regulate prices of health care services, and most health care workers are government employees. Government wages may not be responsive to market forces, or there may be a lag in wage adjustment (Shields 2004).

Box 8.1
Unintended Consequences of Pay Regulation in Labor Markets for Nurses

The economic literature has shown that the net advantages of different jobs will tend to be equal if there is a wage competition in labor markets. As a result, a higher pay or a wage premium is necessary to compensate for a more risky job. Similarly, a job located in an area with higher cost of living receives a higher pay. The pay regulation of the public sector restricts the wage adjustment across heterogeneous geographic labor markets and hence undermines the equality of net advantages across different jobs, which in turn can have harmful unintended consequences. In this box, we review two recent studies that show the evidence of unintended consequences arising from pay regulation in the labor market for nurses.

In the UK, pay for nurses and physicians in NHS hospitals is regulated to a precise national scale that is almost uniform across the country and allows only minor differences in pay between different areas. Since the private sector does not regulate the wage and the supply of labor is determined by the relative pay offered in different jobs, the little spatial variation in nurses' pay affects the competitiveness of pay for nurses between local labor markets, which in turn affects recruitment and retention. Elliott and colleagues empirically measured the competitiveness of pay for nurses by calculating the difference between standardized spatial wage differentials (SSWDs) estimated for nurses and comparator occupations, hereafter referred as the SSWD gap (Elliot, Ma, Scott, et al. 2007). The authors first showed that there are substantial variations in SSWDs between different areas. They then estimated the effect of the SSWD gap on the ability of the NHS to attract and retain nurses, as measured by vacancy rates for qualified nurses. The estimated coefficient is significantly negative, indicating that NHS nursing vacancies are lower if NHS nurses have higher wages than persons in the comparator occupations. For every 10 percent increase in the gap between the relative pay of nurses and that of their comparators, vacancy rates in the NHS decrease by 0.18 to 1.71 percentage points, depending on the comparator group chosen.

Another recent study further empirically examined the effect of the wage gap between nurses and other occupations on hospital outcomes. Propper and Van Reenen

Box 8.1
(continued)

measured the above-mentioned wage gap by wage level outside of the regulated sector, hereafter referred to as outside wage (Propper, and van Reenen 2010). The authors argued that nurses supply less labor (including lower participation rates, fewer qualified staff offering themselves for work, and higher rates of vacancies and turnover) when better outside opportunities are available locally, as measured by higher wages in the outside labor market relative to the wage inside the hospital. Thus, areas with higher outside wages would be at a disadvantage in recruiting, retaining, and motivating higher-quality workers. Consequently, higher outside wages lead to poorer outcomes of hospitalized patients. Their empirical study lends support this view, finding that a 10 percent increase in the outside wage is associated with a 4–8 percent increase in mortality within 30 days of emergency admission for patients with acute myocardial infarction. They also found that the negative association between firm performance and the outside wage is unique to the regulated sector (hospitals) because they did not find the same relationships in other 43 service sectors in which their pay was not regulated. This result suggests that the negative effect of outside wages on hospital performance is not simply due to fewer staff or general UK labor market conditions. Rather, there is evidence that this effect arises from the fact that hospitals in high-outside-wage areas tend to rely disproportionately on temporary agency staff, which in turn is associated with poorer health outcomes.

An important policy implication from these two studies is that a uniform increase in wage rates for nurses is not an effective approach for easing a shortage of nurses and improving quality of health care. Rather, a more effective approach for reducing nursing shortages in the NHS is to introduce policies leading to a greater responsiveness of nurses' pay to local labor market conditions, that is, paying more to reduce excess demand gaps for nurses.

Under dual public financing and provision, the government may operate under a fixed budget constraint (fig. 8.3). Given a fixed budget, the public health care system can employ more nurses if the wages of nurses are set at lower levels, and vice versa. Thus, the budget constraint can be expressed as a rectangular hyperbola with the vertical axis representing the wage rates and the horizontal axis the number of nurses employed, shown as the B curve in figure 8.3. Although the B curve represents a potential long-run trade-off, at a point in time, public employers are generally restrained from reducing employment by work rules, such as those pertaining to seniority. The downward-sloping (D) and upward-sloping (S) curves represent the demand and supply of nurses, respectively. The horizontal line (w_g) represents the wage level of nurses, which is set by the government. Persistent nurse shortages exist because w_g is lower than the equilibrium market wage (w^*). When nurses are offered w_g, the quantity supplied of nurses is N_s, which is determined by the intersection of w_g and the supply curve. However, at w_g, the quantity

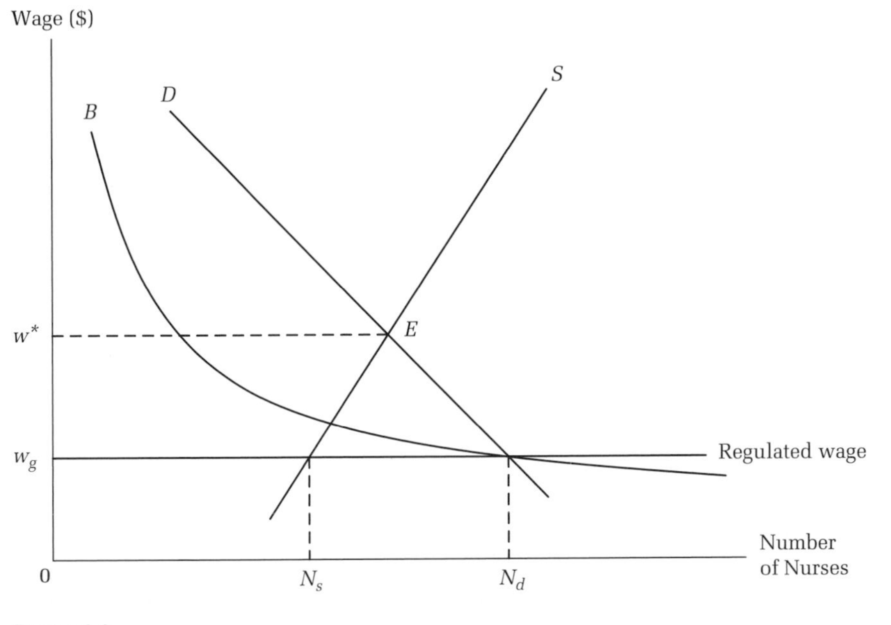

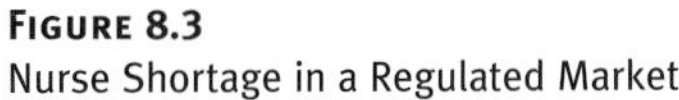
FIGURE 8.3
Nurse Shortage in a Regulated Market

of nurses demanded is N_d, which is determined by the intersection of w_g, the demand curve, and the budget constraint. Since the quantity demanded exceeds the quantity supplied at w_g, there is a shortage of nurses, the horizontal distance between N_d and N_s.

Governments have several options for eliminating a shortage. First, the regulatory agency can increase the wage, perhaps to a higher wage but one still below the market-clearing wage. The higher wage in turn increases the quantity of nurses supplied through these two channels: (1) increased hours of work per nurse already employed and (2) an increase in labor force participation and employment of persons trained in nursing. Also, the increase in wage level may induce a substitution of other inputs for nurses, such as a reduction in the skill mix of nursing personnel or the use of relatively more nurse-saving capital.

For example, the use of disposable supplies may save nurse time. By configuring hospital space in certain ways, it becomes easier to view activities on the hospital floor, and hence it may be possible to employ nurses more efficiently. As a result, the quantity of nurses demanded decreases.

Changes in quantity supplied and demanded working together reduce the gap between demand and supply. Therefore, an increase in the government-determined wage and the budget share can potentially reduce the magnitude of nurse shortages. However, the phenomenon of a nurse shortage still exists as long as the wage rate offered by public employers is below the market equilibrium wage, and the budget constraint cannot sustain the employment level under the market equilibrium wage.

Second, nurse shortages can be mitigated or eliminated by policies that shift the supply curve outward. In the short run, a shift of labor supply curve can be achieved by recruiting more nurses from overseas. Many high-income countries have adopted this strategy for solving their nursing shortages. But this approach just shifts nurse shortages from high-income countries to other countries unless the other countries have nonemployed nurses. In the long run, a shift in the labor supply curve may be achieved by increasing nursing school enrollments.

Box 8.2
International Nurse Migration

Many countries have relied on recruiting nurses from foreign countries as a strategy for solving the problem of a nursing shortage. This strategy has accelerated international nurse migration. As a result, nurses from other countries, hereafter referred as foreign nurses, are likely to play an increasingly large role in providing nursing care in several developed countries. As shown in figure 8.4, the major host countries of international nurse migration include Canada, Germany, Ireland, New Zealand, the United States, and the UK. In these countries, the share of foreign nurses ranges from 3 percent in Germany to 21 percent in New Zealand. In terms of total number employed, the United States is the largest host country of foreign nurses, although its share of foreign nurses is only about 5 percent. According to the World Health Organization's 2006 World Health Report, nearly 100,000 foreign nurses are employed in the United States. Furthermore, the relative importance of foreign nurses has increased rapidly in the United States if we count the share of foreign nurses from employment growth. Between 1983 and 2003, foreign nurses accounted for nearly one-third of the total growth of nurse employment in the US nurse labor market (Buerhaus, Staiger, and Auerbach 2004).

The major source countries of foreign nurses are India, Nigeria, Philippines, South Africa, and Zimbabwe, which are middle- and low-income countries. In addition, the nurse density per 1,000 population in these source countries ranges from 0.45 to 4.72, which in general is significantly lower than the nurse density in host countries (Aiken, Buchan, Sochlaski, et al. 2004). Thus, it is important to explore further the consequences of international nurse migration.

There are two important consequences of international nurse migration. On the one hand, international nurse migration imposes a negative externality on the source countries in the sense that host countries' use of international recruitment to fill their vacancies may exacerbate nursing shortages in the source countries. For example, Zimbabwe, a country whose nurse density is only about 1.29 per 1,000 population, lost 32 percent of its nurses to employment in the UK between 1999 and 2001 (Kingma 2007). On the other hand, migrant nurses send money home to their families, and

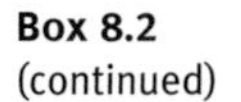

such remittances have significantly contributed to the decline in the poverty rate in several low-income countries, such as Uganda. Furthermore, remittances from foreign nurses and other migrants constitute a significant portion of the GDP in several source countries, and the importance of remittances to the national economy may even exceed foreign direct investment. For example, total recorded remittances (from foreign nurses and other migrants) account for about 10 percent of GDP in the Philippines (Kingma 2007).

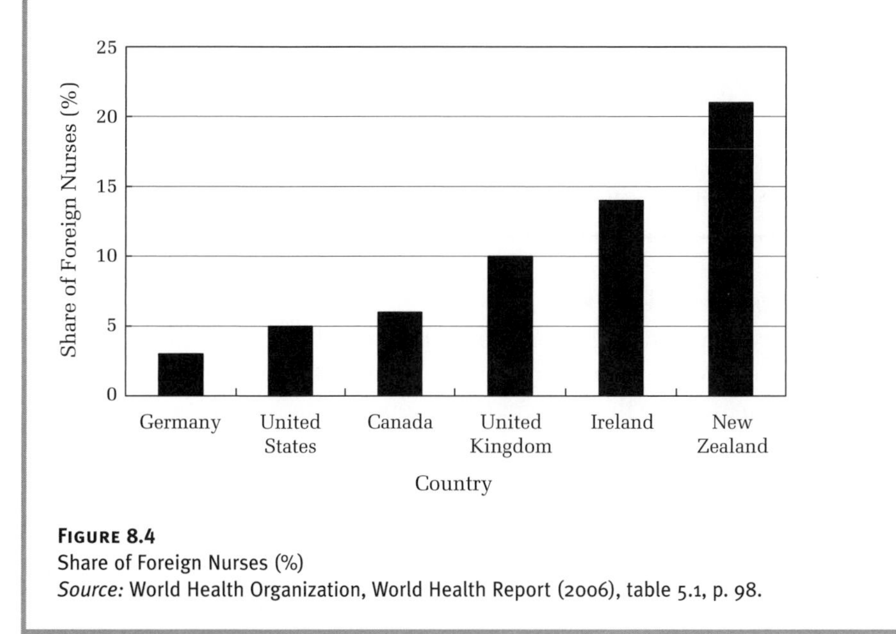

Figure 8.4
Share of Foreign Nurses (%)
Source: World Health Organization, World Health Report (2006), table 5.1, p. 98.

Both of these approaches have shortcomings. The approach of increasing wages substantially may be infeasible because of seniority rules. Public systems in particular are likely to have rules protecting the jobs of currently employed persons. Increasing wages appreciably will lead to wages far greater than the minimum levels of compensation many nurses in the workforce require for supplying the labor they supply. Thus, there is an increase in economic rents. And shifting supply, particularly through increases in the capacity of nursing schools, will take time for a meaningful increase in the supply of active nurses to be realized. A more feasible approach is a mixed strategy that combines both wage adjustment and supply-shifting approaches. For example, wages may be increased somewhat and more funds allocated to the employer's budget, in effect shifting the budget constraint curve (B) outward. Meanwhile, some combinations of supply-side policies, such as recruiting more nurses from overseas and increasing nursing school enrollments, may shift the supply curve outward.

The curves in figure 8.3 are drawn to illustrate general propositions. The theory makes no statement about the actual positions or shapes of these curves.

There are important empirical questions, the answers to which should guide public policy. First, how responsive is the nurse labor supply to changes in the wage rate? If the supply curve is quite inelastic, offering a higher wage will not elicit much added supply. Second, to the extent that supply increases, does the increased supply primarily come from increased hours of work, from higher rates of labor force participation of nurses not currently employed, or from persons not currently trained as nurses and nurses from other countries? Third, what is the relative effect of changing wages versus shifting the supply curve in reducing nursing shortages? If the labor supply decisions of nurses are responsive to wage changes, then the adjustment in the wage is an effective approach for coping with nurse shortages. Otherwise, shifting the labor supply curve becomes a more effective policy option to address the issue of nurse shortages. We examine the evidence on these empirical questions below.

Role of Monopsony Power

An alternative explanation for a persistent shortage of nurses is monopsony in nurse labor markets. Monopsony occurs when there is a single buyer in an input market, which is parallel to the concept of monopoly when there is a single seller in a product market. Buyers may possess monopsony power in an input market if (1) they are a single buyer and (2) the mobility of the input is restricted to that market.

Hospitals in single-hospital markets may be monopsonists if they are the only buyers of a specialized type of personnel and if the personnel are not in a position to consider alternative sources of employment outside the local market because commuting or moving is costly. Because both conditions are often satisfied in the context of nurses, especially with regard to hospital employment, the labor market for nurses is often offered as an example of monopsony (Hirsch and Schumacher 1995; Boal and Ransom 1997).

Even if many hospitals are monopsonists in the market for nurses, this certainly cannot be true of many other hospitals, particularly the many hospitals located in metropolitan areas, unless they are involved in collusive wage agreements among the competing hospitals; such collusive arrangements would have to be established on a market-by-market basis. The existence of collusion in wage setting in one geographic market does not necessarily imply it exists in other geographic markets.

Alternatively, rather than there being a single buyer of a specialized input such as professional nurses, employers may compete with one another to some extent. In markets with few buyers, the labor market for nurses may be appropriately described as "oligopsonistic" rather than monopsonistic, which is parallel to the concept of oligopoly in a product market (Bhaskar, Manning, and To 2002). Both oligopsony and monopsony describe a market in which employers have the ability or market power to set the wage rate.

By contrast, the employer does not possess any market power to influence market wage rates determined in a perfectly competitive labor market; the employer is a "wage taker" rather than a "wage setter." When a wage taker, the individual employer must accept the wage rate determined by market forces, and there is only one single market wage rate for a given quality of worker.

The monopsony case is simpler than the oligopsony case since with the latter one must consider strategic interactions among employers, and the results of any conceptual analysis are likely to be weaker. Thus, we focus on monopsony here. The bottom line for monopsony is that both the wage rate and employment levels are lower than would prevail under perfect competition.

In figure 8.5, the downward-sloping curve represents the marginal revenue product (MRP) of nurses, which also represents the demand for labor. The MRP is the product of the marginal product of the input, in this case nurses, and marginal revenue. For example, if adding a nurse will allow the hospital to accept four additional patients for treatment, the MRP is four times the marginal revenue,

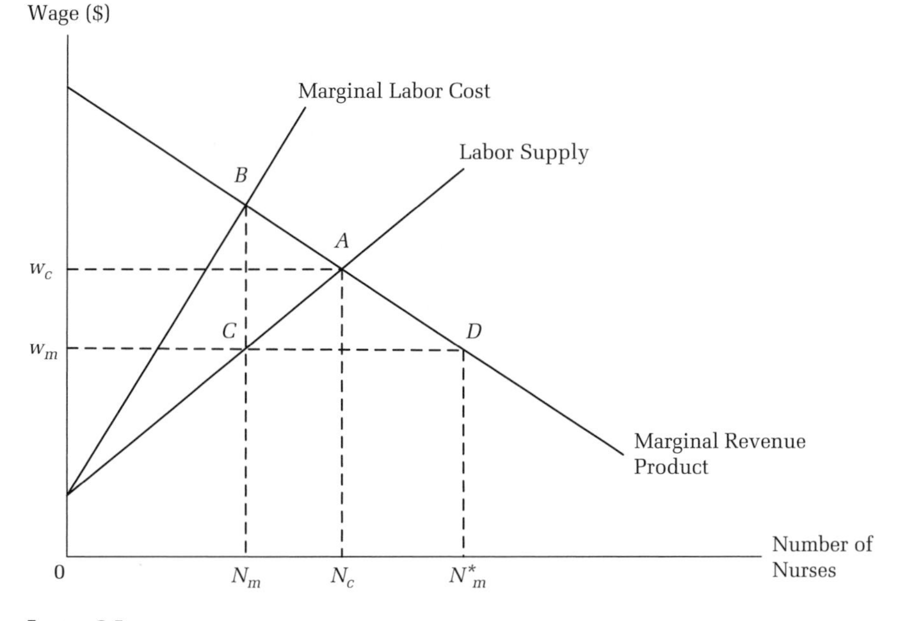

FIGURE 8.5
Nurse Shortage under Monopsony

which, since marginal revenue is less than the product price, is less than the hospital's price of care.

The lower upward-sloping curve is the labor supply curve, indicating that more workers are drawn into employment as the wage rises. The single employer realizes that to attract more nurses, it has to offer a higher wage rate. The analysis makes the fairly realistic assumption that it is not possible for employers to wage discriminate among employees, that is, to offer a higher wage to a newly employed worker than to an existing worker.

For this reason, an increase in the wage rate must be paid not only to new employees but to existing ones as well. Suppose the hospital has 100 employees and the wage is $20 per hour. To attract another employee, the hospital raises the wage to $21. However, it cannot simply pay the new employees $1 extra. Rather, it must pay $121 extra per hour—$100 more to its existing workers and $21 to the new worker, which is the marginal labor cost (MLC).

An important implication is that the MLC curve lies above the upward-sloping labor supply curve (fig. 8.5). The MLC curve, not the supply curve, is the relevant curve the employer uses in determining how many workers it wants to employ. In making this decision, a firm pursuing profit maximization determines its optimal employment level at the point where MRP equals MLC, shown as point *B* in figure 8.3, and optimal employment is l_m.

At this employment level, the monopsonist determines the wage level from the labor supply curve, point *C* in figure 8.5, with a corresponding wage level of w_m. At this wage, the firm's demand for labor is l_m^*, which is determined by an MRP corresponding to wage level w_m (point *D*). Therefore, a "shortage" of labor exists, as measured by the difference $l_m^* - l_m$, in the sense that the firm desires to hire additional workers at the monoposonistic wage (w_m), but it cannot do so while simultaneously maximizing profit. This is because the firm needs to raise wage rates to attract more workers beyond l_m, and a higher wage above w_m would decrease its profitability. However, the firm may post the difference $l_m^* - l_m$ as the number of job openings it has. It will constantly be looking for workers for positions it cannot fill.

Policy makers, however, may be misled into thinking that the difference represents true excess demand, and implement policies designed to close the gap. Even if they do not act on this information, the existence of vacancies may be interpreted as a shortage, and this shortage may be reported to international agencies such as the OECD.

A key assumption underlying the monopsony model is limited mobility of labor, which may occur for three possible reasons. First, the workers may not have perfect information about alternative possible jobs. Second, it is costly for workers to move between employers, especially when they are geographically dispersed. Third, workers may have heterogeneous preferences for different jobs (Bhaskar,

Manning, and To 2002). If mobility of labor were free, workers would switch jobs if employers continued to offer wages below the competitive levels. But with limited mobility of labor, the employer reasons that it is unlikely that the worker will leave, which confers market power to set a wage below the level that would prevail in a competitive market. In a competitive labor market, the equilibrium wage is w_c, which is set at the intersection of the labor supply curve and the MRP curve, and the corresponding employment level is l_c (fig. 8.5).

This result has two important implications. First, under competition, employers can hire all the workers they want at the going wage. Thus, there is no excess demand or shortage in the economic sense in the labor market. Second, the wage paid to employees is equal to their MRP. Both outcomes suggest that the later market equilibrium is efficient.

By contrast, in a monopsonistic market, the equilibrium is not efficient for these reasons. First, vacancies persist under monopsony. Second, employment under monopsony (l_m) is less than that which prevails in a competitive market (l_c). Third, the equilibrium wage level under monopsony (w_m) is less than the workers' MRP, as shown by the vertical distance between points *B* and *C*. The gap between MRP and wage under the monopsony is:

$$E = (MRP - w)/w = 1/\varepsilon, \quad (8.1)$$

where ε is the elasticity of the supply of labor to the employer with respect to the wage. *E* measures the departure of wages paid to employees from their MRP in percentage terms. In the economics literature, *E* is often interpreted as a measure of "exploitation," or more precisely as the amount of exploitation that employees are exploited (Boal and Ransom 1997).

Also, *E* is often used to measure the employer's market power. According to equation 8.1, the departure of wage from the MRP is inversely related to the elasticity of labor supply, indicating that the more inelastic labor supply is to the employer, the wider is the gap between the MRP and the wage. In a perfectly competitive market, *E* is zero since the elasticity of labor supply approaches infinity and hence the employer does not possess any market power. The value of *E* is relatively large if the elasticity of labor supply is small, indicating that employers facing relatively inelastic labor supply curves possess relatively much market power.

The monopsony model is attractive, at least theoretically, for describing important stylized facts about nurse labor markets. Particularly in countries with public health care systems, the government is the buyer of services of specialized health personnel. However, the monopsony framework is based on an assumption of profit maximization, and it is a stretch to apply this model to public employers. While the model seems more applicable to private employers, it is important to recall that many health care employers, especially hospitals, are organized on a private not-for-profit basis.

Such organizations may have many different goals. It is conceptually possible that such an organization may have such nonpecuniary objectives as teaching, research, or providing care to the poor (see chapter 6). However, to serve these objectives, it may want to behave as a profit maximizer would in input markets. In this sense, the monopsony model could still be applicable. In the end, whether or not health sector employers are monopsonists or oligopsonists cannot be decided on the basis of theory alone. Rather, this is an empirical question. We return to this issue below.

8.3 EMPIRICAL ESTIMATES OF NURSES' RESPONSE TO A WAGE CHANGE

There are two approaches to test empirically whether the labor market for nurses is a monopsony. The first approach is to estimate the elasticity of labor supply of nurses to an *individual* hospital. In general, the elasticity of labor supply to an individual firm will differ substantially from the elasticity of labor supply to the market as a whole. In fact, in a competitive labor market, the individual firm faces an infinitely elastic labor supply curve even if the curve for the market as a whole is upward sloping. However, under monopsony, the two supply curves are the same. As shown in equation 8.1, the difference of the wage from the corresponding MRP is inversely related to the elasticity of labor supply. Thus, the wage elasticity of labor supply yields an estimate of the extent of measuring monopsony power. In addition, estimating the wage elasticity of labor supply provides an empirical basis for understanding the extent to which nurse labor supply responds to wage changes, which in turn provides useful evidence for evaluating whether increasing nurse pay is an effective policy instrument for easing shortages of nurses, as economists define them (Shields 2004).

The second approach for gauging monopsony power and its extent is to examine the relationship among hospital wages, employment, and market structure. The rationale for this approach is that the presence of an upward-sloping labor supply curve is a necessary but not a sufficient condition for the existence of monopsony power. Thus, estimating the wage elasticity of nurse labor supply is insufficient to demonstrate evidence of a monopsonistic outcome. Rather, the determinants of wage and employment outcomes must be directly tested (Hirsch and Schumacher 1995, 2005).

The monopsony model predicts that nurses' wages decline as hospital concentration increases. While strictly speaking, a monoponist is a single purchaser of a specialized factor of production, having fewer employers in a market may facilitate collusive arrangements among employers that compete for the same types of labor.

Several studies have estimated the effects of wage on the labor supply of nurses since 1970.[3] These studies apply diverse econometric and other statistical methods to data from various countries. Most use cross-sectional data at the level of the US state, the hospital, or the individual nurse, while only a few studies have employed individual-level panel data on nurses.

The wage elasticity estimates for the nurse labor supply from previous studies fall within a wide range, from –0.39 to 2.8, but most estimates fall within a narrower range, from 0.1 to 1.5 (Antonazzo, Scott, Skatun, et al. 2003; Shields 2004). This is still an enormous range, with estimates around 0.1, implying that supply is inelastic, to estimates in excess of one, implying a considerable supply response to wage changes.

There are four important questions to be addressed in estimating the labor supply of nurses. First, does an increased wage provide an incentive for nurses to increase the number of hours they work? In theory, the effects of changing the wage rate on number of hours worked are twofold, which can be described by a substitution effect and an income effect. The substitution effect describes the incentive that workers have to work more as the wage rises. The wage represents the opportunity cost (price) of leisure (not working), and leisure becomes more expensive when wages increase. But assuming that more leisure is demanded when income increases, workers also have an incentive to work less when wages increase. The income effect indicates the extent to which an increase in the wage leads to a reduction in the number of hours worked because the demand for leisure increases as the rising wage increases the nurses' incomes. The two effects operate in opposite directions, a wage increase leading to more hours according to the substitution effect and fewer hours according to the income effect.

At a low wage, the income effect may not be sufficiently strong to dominate the substitution effect. Therefore, the increase in wage often leads to an increase in the number of hours worked, which suggests that the labor supply curve is upward sloping (fig. 8.6). However, as wage rates rise, the negative income effect on work hours may become sufficiently large to outweigh the positive substitution effect on work hours. The number of hours worked may consequently decrease as the wage rises, which leads to a backward-bending labor supply curve.

Only a few empirical studies provide evidence of a backward-bending labor supply, that is, where the wage elasticity of the labor supply is negative (Bognanno, Hixson, and Jeffers 1974; Link 1992). The majority of such studies find that the wage elasticity of the labor supply is positive, suggesting that the nurse's labor supply is upward sloping.

The second question concerns the relative effectiveness of the wage increase on labor force participation and on the number-of-hours decision for those who work. In practice, some qualified nurses may decide not to go to work because the

3. Antonazzo, Scott, Skatun, et al. (2003) and Shields (2004) provide detailed reviews on these studies.

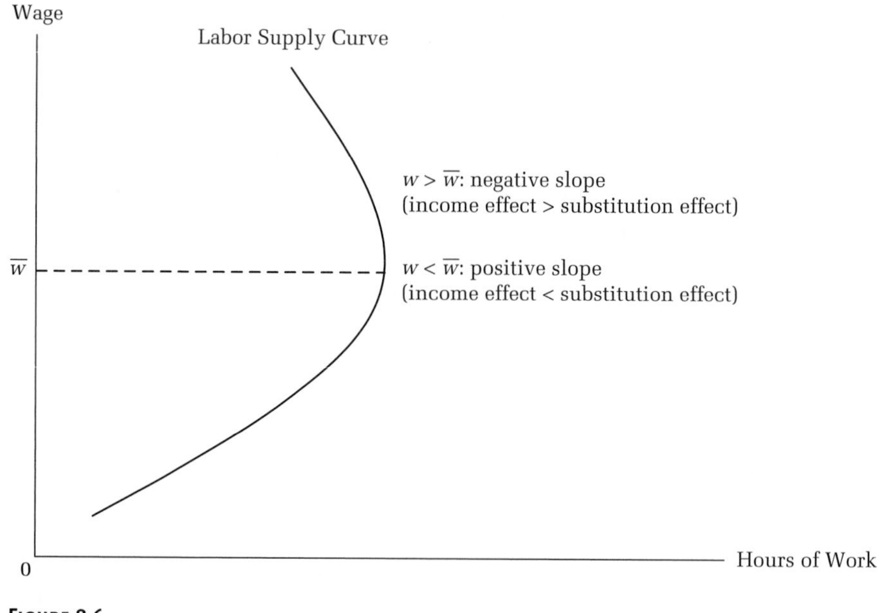

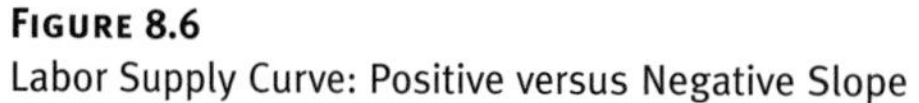

FIGURE 8.6
Labor Supply Curve: Positive versus Negative Slope

prevailing market wage is below their reservation wage. The reservation wage represents the minimum wage required to elicit a unit of labor from the supplier of labor. This minimum wage reflects the person's productivity in nonmarket work (work in the household, e.g., child care, help with children's homework, cooking, cleaning, paying bills, and purely leisure time). For a person to supply a unit of labor, the market wage must be at least as high as the reservation wage.

In this case, an increase in wage leads to an increase in the nurses' labor supply at both the extensive and intensive margins. The extensive margin involves the decision to participate in a market transaction at all. In this application, this is the decision to participate in the nurse labor market. The intensive margin involves the decision of how much to transact, in this application, the amount of labor to supply, conditional on supplying at least one unit of labor to the market. An increased wage may encourage some nurses who previously had not sought work to do so—the decision at the extensive margin. But it also may encourage more hours of work by those who participate—the decision at the intensive margin. Whether or not the participation effect exceeds the hours-of-work effect or the converse cannot be decided theoretically but rather is an empirical question.

Some empirical studies assess only the determinants of nurse labor force participation, while others focus only on hours-of-work responses to wage changes and other factors. Sloan and Richupan (1975) used 1960 US Census data to assess both. They found that the number of hours worked is more responsive to wage changes than is labor force participation. They reported that a 1.0 percent increase in nurses' wage rates increased their labor force participation by 1.8 percent and increased the number of hours worked by 2.8 percent.

By contrast, a study conducted with 1980 data from the UK by Phillips (1995) suggests that labor force participation is more responsive to wage changes than is the number of hours worked. He found that a 1.0 percent wage increase led to an increase in labor force participation of 1.4 percent but led to an increase in hours worked of only 0.15 percent. Even though the two studies addressed both participation and work hours, the results come from two different countries and two distinct time periods. Work patterns of women were different in 1980 than in 1960, a period before women's rights in the workplace were emphasized.

The third empirical question is whether or not labor supply is more responsive to wage changes in the long run than in the short run. Theoretically, one would expect the mobility of nurses across markets and the adjustment of working hours to likely be higher in the long run than in the short run. Thus, the magnitude of employer market power is likely to be lower in the long run than in the short run.

Empirical research by Sullivan (1989) provides empirical evidence in support of this premise. His results indicate that the wage elasticity of the labor supply of nurses over a one-year period is 1.26 and over a three-year period is 3.86. These results thus indicate that hospitals have very substantial monopsony power in the labor market for nurses and that the monopsony power in the short run (1/1.26 = 0.79) is substantially larger than in the long run (1/3.86 = 0.26). This inference applies only to markets with a single employer or at most a few who can collude. Establishing such evidence from aggregate supply curves is not a sufficient condition for monopsony but rather a first step.

Finally, we consider methodological issues of the various studies. Three emphasized here are issues related to (1) the samples used in the empirical analysis, (2) establishing that wage rates truly affect supply, and the observed relationship is not driven by effects of supply on wages, and (3) measurement errors in wage rates from survey data (Antonazzo, Scott, Skatun, et al. 2003).

Some of these problems have been overcome by using better data or appropriate econometric techniques. For example, to handle the problem of reverse causality, that is, wage rates affecting supply *and* supply affecting wage rates, Staiger, Spetz, and Phibbs (1999) took advantage of data from a natural experiment.[4] In 1991, the US Veterans Administration, which operates hospitals throughout the United States, changed its method for setting nurses' wages from paying nurses based on a national scale to paying nurses according to a system that set wage levels referenced to data from local wage surveys. Thus, in some areas wages fell and in others they rose, but the change in wages was independent of changes in nurse supply.

Staiger, Spetz, and Phibbs estimated a short-run elasticity of labor supply to an individual hospital of 0.1, the lowest supply elasticity estimate in the literature.

4. On natural experiments, see chapter 3.

This suggests that other estimates that do not explicitly account for reverse causality may be overestimates of the true relationship.

Askildsen, Baltagi, and Holmås (2003) addressed the same issue by using longitudinal data obtained on nearly 20,000 Norwegian nurses observed over a six-year period (1993–1998). They obtained a labor supply elasticity of 0.21, almost the same as Staiger, Spetz, and Phibbs did.

As emphasized above, estimating the labor supply elasticity is only one step in ascertaining whether or not a market for nurses is monopsonistic. If there is more than one buyer of labor, there is an issue of whether or not they collude in setting wages. Since direct evidence of collusion is difficult for us as outsiders to this market to observe, economists study factors that would facilitate such collusion.

At the top of the list is a concentration of labor purchasers. Some early studies found a statistically significant effect of market concentration on nurses' wages. For example, Link and Landon (1976) observed that wages are lower when there are fewer hospitals in a geographic area or, in economic terminology, when hospital markets are more concentrated. Unfortunately, market concentration is associated with other factors, such as population density, which are also likely to be associated with wages. In a rural community, there is likely to be only one hospital employer, but in a city with a million residents, there are likely to be many. Thus, a result that wages are lower in markets with a highly concentrated hospital sector may only mean that concentration is negatively correlated with population density, and it is density, not concentration, that affects wages. In the end, it may really take some direct empirical evidence of coordination among hospital employers in a large city to establish the existence of monopsony there (Adamache and Sloan 1982; Boal and Ransom 1997).

Hirsch and Schumacher (1995) tested the presence of monopsony power by examining relative nursing versus non-nursing wage rates across markets that they argued were more and less likely to be monopsonistic. By measuring nursing wages relative to non-nursing wages within the same labor market, this study controlled for differences in cost of living and other area-specific factors.

In theory, the monopsony model predicts that the relative nursing/non-nursing wage is lower in labor markets that are small and with a limited number of employers. Based on data from the 1985–1993 US Current Population Surveys, however, Hirsch and Schumacher found no evidence to support this prediction.

Ten years later, Hirsch and Schumacher (2005) presented a new method for obtaining evidence on monopsony in nurse labor markets. They used the fraction of new recruits from nonemployment (unemployment or outside the labor force) as a new measure of monopsonistic power. Conceptually, mobility of labor reduces the ability of individual employers to set wages. Thus, they predicted that the lower the proportion of new hires coming from employment with other firms (i.e., the higher the fraction of new recruits from nonemployment), the lower are expected wages, other things being equal. This relationship was not supported empirically, however, implying that monopsony power is lacking in this sector.

8.4 Nonwage Determinants of the Nurse Labor Supply

Nurses' decisions to supply labor to the market are plausibly motivated by a number of factors in addition to wages. For one, nursing is a profession for which intrinsic rewards are important, such as being able to function in the workplace as a decision maker (see, e.g., Shields 2004; Heyes 2005).

Although unlike in other social sciences, the focus of economic analysis has been on the effects of financial incentives, particularly in recent years there has been some theoretical research on nonfinancial incentives as well. In this research there is a distinction between intrinsic motivation, the desire to perform a task for its own sake, and extrinsic motivation, in which explicit rewards, including pay, promotion, and recognition (e.g., medals for outstanding performance) or penalties to elicit willingness to perform tasks (see, e.g., Golden and Sloan 2008). This body of theoretical research, which is based on a substantial amount of experimental and field research by noneconomists, indicates that extrinsic motivation may crowd out effort that would have been forthcoming in the absence of extrinsic motivators.

For example, offering compensation for a task may suggest to the worker that he or she either is not motivated to perform the task, absent the incentive, or faces a high cost of performing it. In the former case, offering an incentive makes the worker think that the boss does not trust his or her motivation to do the task without a bribe. In the latter case, the boss knows that the task is arduous and tries to bribe the worker to undertake it. Absent an explicit incentive, the worker may think that the task is easy. With the bribe, the worker becomes suspicious that he or she is being unduly influenced.

In health care, societies have traditionally relied on professionalism, intrinsic motivation, to achieve desirable outcomes. This has been thought to provide a motivation for health professionals to perform in the interests of patients. There is a risk that offering explicit rewards for good acts will crowd out intrinsic motivation.

While much of the economic literature focuses on wage as a motivator, Heyes (2005) presents a simple model suggesting that increasing the wage may actually decrease the proportion of employed nurses who view nursing as a vocation, and hence the overall performance of nurses in patient care may decline. Heyes (2005) models how the nurse views this work as a dichotomous variable. A nurse who does not place an emphasis on the professional aspect of nursing will work if and only if the market wage exceeds her reservation wage. By contrast, nurses who view nursing as a professional career will choose to work if and only if the market wage plus a premium (a nonpecuniary benefit or intrinsic reward) is greater than their reservation wage. At a given market wage, individuals who view nursing as a profession are more likely to choose this field as a career, other factors being equal. Therefore, the proportion of employed nurses who have a professional orientation to nursing decreases as market wages increase.

This conclusion is the opposite of the *efficient wage hypothesis*, which maintains that higher wages boost job performance (Summers 1988). A key assumption in Heyes's model that leads to this difference in conclusions is that more highly productive nurses tend to have lower reservation wages. Thus, an important implication of his model is that there is an efficiency loss arising from the employment of the wrong type of nurses if the policy makers try to raise nursing wages to reduce an excess demand for nurses.

Utility from being a professional in nursing is a nonwage attribute of the nursing profession that may affect nurse labor supply. Conversely, data from the British National Health Service (NHS) in the UK and from Norway indicate that job dissatisfaction is a major factor in nurses' decisions to quit (Shields and Ward 2001; Holmås 2002). Sources of dissatisfaction may relate to extrinsic as well as intrinsic factors. In the Norwegian study, nurses working at hospitals with a high occupancy rate or a relatively large number of hospital beds per nurse were more likely to quit their jobs.

Having discussed determinants of nurse supply, we now turn to the demand side. As previously discussed, the demand for nurses reflects their MRP. Included in MRP is the marginal product of the nurse. Although in a traditional setting, the product might be considered an output such as a hospital day, in health care, the trend has been to consider more refined measures of output (see chapter 7).

8.5 Nurses in the Production of Hospital Services

Do Higher Nurse-to-Patient Ratios Improve the Quality of Hospital Care?

Nurses provide an important input in the production of personal health care services, of which hospital inpatient care is an excellent but by no means the only example. Nurses monitor changes inpatient status, which can lead to early detection and prompt intervention that improves individuals' long-term health and saves patients' lives. When staffing levels are lean, nurse workloads tend to increase, which in turn may decrease the effectiveness of nurse surveillance in hospitals. A widely held notion is that inadequate nursing staffing is a major impediment to the provision of high-quality hospital care (Aiken, Clarke, Sloane, et al. 2002). The high variability of nurse staffing levels in hospitals, which includes low staffing on the left tail of the distribution of hospitals by nurse staffing levels, has raised a serious policy concern about whether or not hospital nurse staffing levels are adequate to provide safe and effective care. Furthermore, hospitals around the world have faced dramatic changes in their operating environments since about the 1990s for various reasons, including the diffusion of managed care in the United States and the reforms of the hospital payment system in many other countries, including the United States (Gaynor and Haas-Wilson 1999).

Insofar as spending on nursing personnel amounts to approximately 30 percent of hospital budgets on average, many hospitals have reduced nurse staffing as one of their strategies to respond to a tightening in the market environment (Mark, Harless, McCue, et al. 2004). This trend, in combination with the persistent shortages of nurses, has led to studies being conducted to examine the relationship between nurse staffing and the quality of hospital care empirically.

Overall, empirical support for the view that richer nurse staffing leads to better patient care is mixed. Recent studies in the medical literature have tended to be more supportive of a relationship between staffing and quality than those in the economics literature have.

The existing literature can be divided into (1) cross-hospital studies, (2) within-hospital comparisons, and (3) longitudinal studies. The cross-hospital studies conduct cross-sectional analyses by comparing different hospitals at a point in time. For example, in a study published in a major medical journal, Aiken, Clarke, Sloane, et al. (2002) used data from 168 communities in the US state of Pennsylvania to examine the impact of nurse staffing levels on patient outcomes. Aiken and coauthors measured nurse staffing by the mean patient load per nurse. Patient outcomes were 30-day mortality (the percentage of patients who died within 30 days of the date they were admitted to the hospital) and "failure to rescue" (the percentage of cases in which patients died who would not have died had they received appropriate care). The authors found that hospitals with higher nurse-to-patient ratios had lower probabilities of adverse patient outcomes occurring, after controlling for the patient and hospital characteristics.

Similarly, in another medical article reporting results from data on 799 hospitals in eleven US states, Needleman, Buerhaus, Mattke, et al. (2002) examined the relationship between time spent per patient by nurses on patient outcomes, fourteen types of outcomes (including shorter length of stay; lower rates of urinary tract infection, upper gastrointestinal bleeding, pneumonia, shock or cardiac arrest; and failure to rescue) occurring during hospitalization. They reported that more time spent by professional nurses with patients led to better patient outcomes in general, but they found no relationship between time spent by professional nurses and the probability of *in-hospital* death.

Although these cross-hospital studies imply that richer nurse staffing generally leads to better outcomes of care in hospital settings, they are subject to criticism on the grounds that it may not be nurse staffing per se that leads to improved outcomes but rather the effect of some third omitted factor. For example, an institution may have other types of staffing that produce better outcomes or may have stronger nursing leadership that advocates both for more nurse employees and for hospital-wide processes leading to higher quality of care at the facility. In economic jargon, failure to include such third factors leads to "omitted variables bias," that is, to an overstatement (in this case; see Mark, Harless, McCue, et al. 2004; Evans and Kim 2006) or an understatement of a variable's true effect. Such a third variable may be medical technology.

Box 8.3
Correlation versus Causation

The debates in the literature regarding the effect of nurse staffing on the quality of health care provided do not align with whether there is a positive relationship between nurse staffing and health outcomes. Rather, the debates focus on whether this positive relationship is a causal relation or just a correlation. The causation argument states that an increase in the level of nurse staffing causes an improvement in health outcomes. However, the correlation argument states that there are common third variables that are important determinants of both nurse staffing and quality of health care. One or more third variables affect both nurse staffing and health outcomes in the same direction. Thus, there is an observed positive relationship between nurse staffing and quality of health care. These two arguments can be illustrated by the following graph:

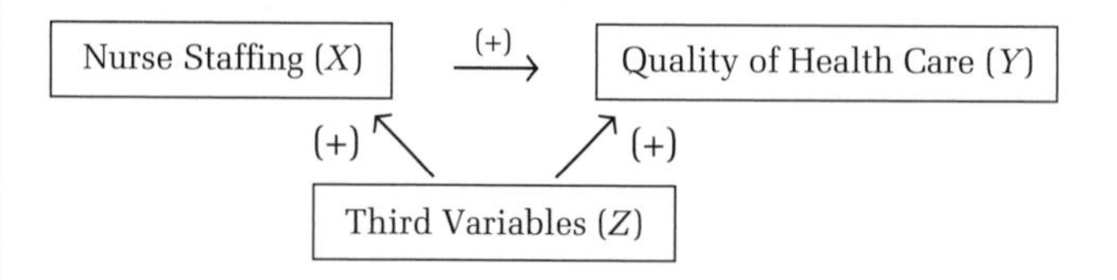

The causation hypothesis emphasizes that the positive relationship between nurse staffing and quality of health care comes from the direct causal relation, that is, X causes Y. The third-variable hypothesis emphasizes that any observed positive relationship results from an indirect correlation—that is, one or more third variables, such as Z, affects X and Y in the same direction simultaneously.

In this chapter, we have mentioned that a potential third variable that affects both nurse staffing and quality of health care in the same direction is medical technology. Whether the causation hypothesis or the third-variable hypothesis provides a better explanation of the positive relationship between nurse staffing and quality of health care is an empirical issue and requires a more rigorous study.

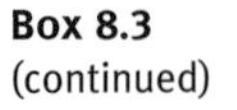

Box 8.3
(continued)

The debate on causation and third-variable hypotheses is not unique in the positive relationship between nurse staffing and quality of health care. There are many similar cases. For example, there is also a debate over the explanation for the observed positive correlation between schooling and health: one explanation argues that there is a causal relationship that runs from increases in schooling to increases in health; while the other argues that differences in one or more third variables (Z), such as time preference, affect both schooling and health in the same direction (Grossman 2000). Another example is the observed positive correlation between schooling and earnings. In this case, the potential third variable is ability, which affects both schooling and earning in the same direction. In chapter 16 of this book we discuss another similar case, the observed positive correlation between population health and national income. In this case, the potential third variables that affect population health and national income in the same direction include the quality of social institutions and the governing ability of the government.

The debates over causation or third-variable hypotheses have important policy implications. More specifically, they directly affect the effectiveness of government policy to promote a policy such as the legislation on minimum nurse-to-patient ratios, if the government accepts the causation hypothesis that an increase in say staffing will lead to an increase in health. However, the effectiveness of such a policy will decline or even completely vanish if there is no such causal relationship between staffing and health. For example, the return on the minimum-nurse-staffing policy will be higher if there is a causal relationship between nurse staffing and quality of health care. If, however, the third-variable hypothesis is relevant, then increasing the level of nurse staffing will not effectively accomplish the goal of improved health outcomes.

Since hospitals differ in many ways other than nurse staffing, gauging the effects of changing levels of staffing at the same hospital is an attractive approach. For example, Bell and Redelmeier (2001) used data from Canada to compare patient outcomes within the same hospitals for patients admitted to hospitals on weekends and on weekdays. In practice, the level of nurse staffing in hospitals, even relative to the number of patients in the hospital, is often lower on weekends than on weekdays. Thus, to the extent that nurse-to-patient ratios affect patient outcomes, one would expect that in-hospital mortality rates among patients admitted to hospitals on weekends might be higher than among patients admitted at other times. Based on observations from more than three million admissions and controlling for other factors (differences in age, sex, and coexisting disorders), the authors found that weekend admissions are associated with significantly higher in-hospital mortality rates than are weekday admissions among patients with three diseases, ruptured abdominal aortic aneurysm, acute epiglottitis, and pulmonary embolism, conditions for which outcomes are thought to be relatively responsive to nurse staffing levels.

However, a weakness of this study is that the types of patients admitted on weekends may be more likely to be admitted on an emergency basis even if the diagnosis is the same (Evans and Kim 2006). Patients admitted on weekends may differ from others in ways not observable to the researcher. Probably the major reason that patients are admitted on weekdays rather than on weekends is that their physicians prefer a weekday admission. But another reason is that in light of reduced staffing on weekends, there is a higher risk to patients should a major complication arise. For these reasons, patients admitted to hospitals at different times do not make up random samples. Rather, patients are admitted on weekends because it is difficult for them to receive adequate care at home—for example, patients who experience difficulty breathing. It is possible that the observed differences in patient outcomes arising from different timing of hospital admissions attributed by researchers to differences in nurse staffing are really attributable to differences in illness severity that are not recorded in the data.

Recent studies have employed longitudinal data to examine the relationship between nurse staffing and the quality of hospital care. The advantage of longitudinal data is that researchers have enough information to control for hospital heterogeneity and changes in hospital quality over time. For example, using data obtained from 422 hospitals in the United States during 1990–1995 and a sophisticated econometric method applied to longitudinal data on these hospitals, Mark, Harless, McCue, et al. (2004) found that increasing nurse staffing reduces in-hospital mortality. However, the marginal effect of increased nurse staffing on mortality decreases as the level of nurse staffing rises, indicating there are diminishing returns to adding nursing staff.

The diminishing marginal effect suggests that adding more professional nurses to a less well-staffed facility leads to a greater improvement in quality of hospital care than at a well-staffed facility. This finding is confirmed by another similar study of the impact of managed care penetration on the relationship between nurse staffing and the quality of hospital care (Mark, Harless, and McCue 2005). But more important, this study found that the relationship between nurse staffing and the quality of hospital care depends on the level of managed care penetration in the hospital's market area. In markets with a higher penetration of managed care, higher nurse staffing is associated with lower mortality. However, this relationship does not hold for hospitals in market areas with a lower penetration of managed care. A plausible explanation for this result is that the expansion of managed care forces the hospital to reduce slack resources and hence makes the effect of increasing nurse staffing on the mortality rate more readily discernible.

Although longitudinal studies offer several advantages for controlling for the effect of factors not included in the analysis, there is still another methodological issue, namely, that hospitals with adverse outcomes may adjust their nurse staffing levels in an effort to reduce them. In economic terminology, staffing may be endogenous to outcomes at the facility.

To deal with feedbacks from outcomes to staffing, Evans and Kim (2006) defined a measure of nurse staffing that should not reflect outcomes at the hospital. They took advantage of the fact that the number of nurses present at a hospital on a given day tends to be determined one or two weeks in advance. Thus, on a given day, the nurse-to-patient ratio is influenced only by the patient census at the hospital. Richness of staffing at any given point in time fluctuates with the number of hospital admissions, which is generally beyond the control of the hospitals. With a fixed staffing level, the effective staffing level decreases as the number of hospital admissions increases, and vice versa. Other things being equal, an unanticipated increase in hospital admissions may reduce the nurse-to-patient ratio below the ratio desired by the hospital. The authors used these unanticipated fluctuations in staffing to identify a relationship between staffing and outcomes.

Based on a census of hospital discharges from the US state of California over the 1996–2000 period, Evans and Kim (2006) estimated the impact of effective hospital staffing levels on patient outcomes, measured by length of stay, in-hospital mortality, and hospital readmission rates. Although the patterns in their data displayed considerable day-to-day variation in staff-to-patient ratios, they did not generally find a statistically significant impact of staffing on outcome. Thus, a person who happens to be admitted to the hospital on a busy day should not have a special concern about the care he or she will receive.

Public Policy Responses

The potential impact of nurse-to-patient ratios on quality of hospital care commands more than academic interest. In the United States, evidence indicating that nursing staffing affects the quality of hospital care has been cited in policy debates about whether government should enact a law to require that hospitals maintain minimum ratios of nurses to patients. In 1999, California enacted a law regulating minimum nurse-to-patient ratios for its hospitals, which went into effect in January 2004. The minimum nurse-to-patient ratios set by government regulation range from one to one in surgery operating rooms to one to eight in newborn nurseries (Evans and Kim 2006). Similar regulation has been imposed on hospitals by the state of Victoria, Australia (OECD 2004).

Although governments' role in requiring minimum nurse-to-patient ratios has been motivated by the goal of improving patient outcomes, there are costs and benefits of such mandates. On the cost side, the major impact of mandatory minimum staffing ratios is that hospitals below the minimum levels face an increase in their wage bills. The cost impact is likely to be especially large in areas in which nurse labor markets are tight. Especially in such situations, a substantial increase in wages may be needed to induce sufficient increases in nurse labor supply, given the above-mentioned evidence that nurses are very unresponsive to wage changes. One study estimates that hospitals in California would incur US$400 million annually to achieve the legislated minimum nurse-to-patient ratios (Evans and Kim 2006).

A recent study found evidence that the minimum-nursing-staff legislation raises the wages of nurses in California (Mark, Harless, and Spetz 2009). Compared to nurses employed in metropolitan areas outside California, this study found that nurses in California metropolitan areas experienced a higher growth rate in real wages by more than 12 percent during the period 2000–2006.

Furthermore, regulation of minimum nurse-to-patient ratios restricts the substitution of health care inputs in the production of hospital care, which in turn may have an adverse impact on hospital productivity. The implicit assumption behind the regulation is that only additional nurses can improve patient outcomes, but hospitals employ many types of personnel that also may be productive in this respect.

In figure 8.7, hospitals could employ two types of labor inputs to produce a given quantity of output: (1) nurses and (2) other personnel. The line *EN* represents the isocost line, indicating that hospitals can employ different combinations of nurses and other personnel with a given budget. The curves x_2 and x_1 represent

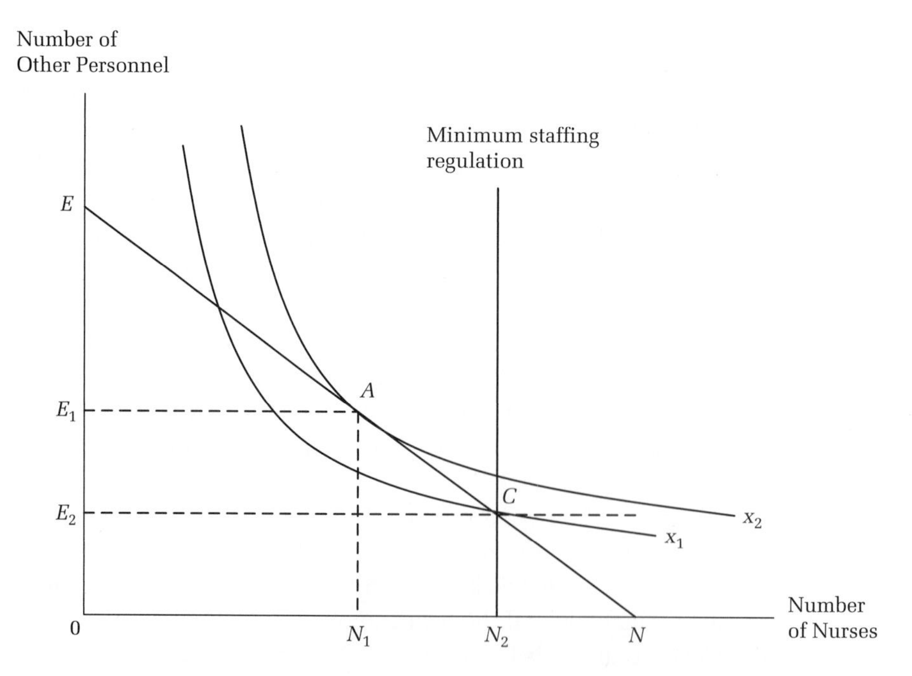

FIGURE 8.7
Optimal Mix of Hospital Labor Inputs

isoquants, indicating that hospitals can produce the same output with different combinations of two labor inputs.

The optimal input mix of personnel is at point *A*, given factor prices of the two inputs. "Optimal" means that the hospital can produce a given output (in this case, x_2) with a minimum cost. At this optimal choice (point *A*), the hospital employs nurses by N_1 and other personnel by E_1.

However, the minimum-staffing regulation requires that the hospital employ nurses at N_2, which in turn forces the hospital to operate at point *C* under a given budget. At point *C*, the hospital cannot produce as much output for a given wage bill (the isocost curve). In this sense, the law introduces inefficiency in the allocation of resources. This suggests that there is an opportunity cost of regulation that discourages innovation in the development of other types of health professionals by hospitals. In addition, the minimum-staffing regulation restricts innovation in the amounts and combinations of input use, such as labor and capital.

The analysis does not end here. On the benefit side, there are two potential effects of the legislated minimum nurse-to-patient ratios. First, patients may benefit from a better quality of hospital care. But the existing literature has produced no consensus on the magnitude of effect of nurse staffing levels on patient outcomes. Studies published in medical journals (e.g., Aiken, Clarke, Sloane, et al. 2002) have concluded that increased staffing improves quality of care, while some economic research reaches the opposite conclusion (Evans and Kim 2006), namely that increases in staffing have no statistically significant effect on patient outcomes.

Second, richer staffing reduces the workload per nurse, thus increasing nurses' job satisfaction (Aiken, Clarke, Sloane, et al. 2002) by, for example, decreasing "burnout" (emotional exhaustion due to job stress) and decreasing quit rates (Shields and Ward 2001). Nurse staffing in hospitals generally is subject to high turnover rates (Frijters, Shields, and Price 2007). A reduction in nurse turnover arising from the mandating legislation on minimum nurse-to-patient ratios may provide a benefit to hospitals in this regard, that is, savings from reducing the administrative burdens and job training. However, whether or not cost savings arising from reduced nursing staff turnover are sufficiently large to compensate for the increased costs of higher staffing levels is unclear. If the benefits of increasing nurse staffing to hospitals are high, there is a question about why there is not higher staffing absent these laws.

Of course, whatever the overall benefits and costs, benefits and costs are borne by different parties. Nurses clearly benefit from increased demand for their services. To the extent that patient care is improved, patients benefit, particularly if the cost of the improvement is borne by others. The costs of such legislation are mainly borne by insurance premium payers and taxpayers, and perhaps by hospitals in terms of direct costs of hospital personnel and costs of efficiency loss—costs not forward-shiftable to others. In the end, it is the "owners" (perhaps ill-defined;

see chapter 6) who are the residual claimants and ultimately bear the burden of the added cost that cannot be shifted. As was discussed in chapter 6, identifying who the residual claimants are is difficult in this context.

8.6 Nurses in the Production of Nursing Home Services

Overview

In the health field, a distinction is made between acute care and long-term care. By *acute care*, insiders in the field mean hospital and physician services, even though many, if not most, of such services are provided to individuals with chronic conditions on an ongoing basis. But any single spell of illness is typically only of short duration.

By contrast, *long-term care* refers to care delivered over a long time horizon. For example, while a person may be in a hospital for a week for a hip replacement, the person might be in a nursing facility for rehabilitation and later for residential care for months and even years.

Long-term care includes care in nursing homes, home health visits (care provided in the home by health care professionals), hospice care (care provided for terminally ill patients in a variety of settings), and "informal" care provided by families on an unpaid basis. By far the largest component of paid long-term care is nursing home care. Thus, we limit our discussion of long-term care to nursing homes.

Nursing homes (residential care facilities) are major employers of nurses, professional nurses, and in even greater numbers nursing personnel with substantially less educational preparation than professional nurses receive. For various reasons, including population aging, the demand for long-term residential care is increasing rapidly around the world, especially in high-income countries. Many elderly enter a nursing home when they are no longer able to live independently. In high-income countries, nursing home residents account for 5–10 percent of the population aged 65 and older. From a lifetime perspective, a man who reaches age 65 and lives in the United States has a one in three chance of being admitted to a nursing home prior to death. For women, this probability exceeds 50 percent (Norton 2000).

Nursing homes provide long-term care using a mix of professional nursing staff and nonprofessional staff. Nursing staff includes professional nurses, also called registered nurses (RNs), licensed practical nurses (LPNs), and nurses' aides (NAs), who provide most direct care to patients, such as helping residents with activities of daily living, including eating, dressing, bathing, toileting, and walking.

RNs usually provide in-house training for the nursing aide staff. They also deal with medical emergencies, sometimes until a physician can be consulted.

In the United States in 1987, on average, there were 51.2 full-time-equivalent nursing staff per 100 residents in nursing homes. By type of nurse, there were 5.6 RNs and 9.4 LPNs, with the rest (70 percent) being NAs (Cohen and Spector 1996).

These categories of nurses differ appreciably in terms of education and training and are imperfect substitutes for each other. Thus, both the number of nursing staff and the mix at a nursing home may affect the quality of care provided at the home.

In this section, we examine three important questions concerning nurse staffing and quality of care in nursing homes: (1) What are the major economic factors accounting for variation in nurse-to-resident ratios ("intensity") and mix of nurse staffing in nursing homes? (2) What is the relationship between nurse staffing and patient outcomes in nursing homes? (3) What is the rationale for the government regulation of staffing levels and mix in nursing homes? For example, an Institute of Medicine (part of the US National Academy of Sciences) report recommended a minimum standard of 24-hour staffing of nursing homes in the United States (Davis, Wunderlich, and Sloan 1996).

Effects of Economic Factors on Nurse Staffing and Mix

In this subsection, we consider three "economic" factors affecting nurse staffing levels and mix of staff in nursing homes: ownership type, wage rates, and methods of payment for nursing home care. In the United States, these three factors are well-studied determinants of nurse staff intensity in nursing homes.

Unlike hospitals (see chapter 6), the nursing home market in the United States is dominated by for-profit firms. For example, about two-thirds of the nursing homes were for-profit in 1995 (Norton 2000). However, as with hospital care, nursing home care inputs are "noncontractible" (see chapter 7) in the sense that it is nearly impossible to specify the type and level of care provision under all possible contingencies. Also, the output of nursing home care is difficult to observe by nursing home residents because they are often frail and disabled. The health and physical function of elderly in such facilities are expected to decline even if high-quality care is provided. Thus, the fact that health and function decline with time spent in a nursing home cannot necessarily be attributed to the level of care a nursing home provides.

Particularly because many nursing home residents do not have close relatives and friends who visit them very regularly, persons who make the decision to place an elderly person in a nursing home may not have good knowledge about how the home operates. Thus, because quality is difficult for residents to monitor and often there are no relatives and friends to monitor, asymmetric information between the nursing home and consumers is likely to exist (Chou 2002). A profit-seeking nursing home has an incentive to engage in cost cutting since it reasons that the effects of the cost reductions will not be observed by consumers. The incentive to cut cost may be weaker for the nonprofit firms because of the nondistribution constraint (see chapter 6).

For this reason, private nonprofit nursing homes may provide better quality of care than for-profit firms when asymmetric information is present. Chou found empirical evidence of a statistically significant difference in quality of care between for-profit and nonprofit homes when residents had no spouse and no child visiting within one month of admission. The difference in quality among ownership forms of nursing homes vanished when the residents had family members to monitor the quality of care, indicating that for-profit nursing homes are prone to compromise services that are difficult to observe.

Although Chou's study did not directly examine the relationship between ownership of nursing homes and decisions about levels of nursing staffing but rather on outcome indicators such as presence of bedsores, her empirical evidence suggests that a reason for the difference in outcomes between for-profit and not-for-profit homes may be differences in nursing staffing patterns. In fact, an earlier US study by Cohen and Spector (1996) reported that nonprofit homes have lower LPN staffing intensity and higher RN staffing compared to for-profit homes, that is, a higher skill mix of nursing staff.

Given the dominance of for-profit firms in the nursing home market, the decision on the optimal number and optimal mix of nursing staff is expected to be influenced by various incentives, such as the wage level of nursing staff, as well as reimbursement used by health insurers and the level of reimbursement. In the short run, with capital fixed, a profit-maximizing home chooses the cost-minimizing combination of labor and materials (e.g., restraints on the residents to keep them from wandering or drugs to induce them to sleep) to produce a given amount of nursing home care. Nursing homes can choose either labor-intensive or materials-intensive methods to produce long-term care. Substitution between inputs depends on relative input prices.

Profit-seeking nursing firms more frequently adopt a materials-intensive method in markets in which wages of nursing staff are relatively high. Even if such nursing homes had price-setting power, they would have an incentive to minimize cost (see, e.g., Cawley, Grabowski, and Hirth 2006). However, a second factor reinforces such behavior. In the vast majority of high-income countries, including the United States, the government is the primary payer for nursing home care, and for such care, the government, not the nursing home, is the price setter.[5] A low and fixed output price places extra pressure on nursing homes to adopt input substitution in response to rising wages.

There are many examples of input substitution in nursing home care. For example, incontinence can be managed by a labor-intensive approach, including regularly scheduled toileting and bladder rehabilitation, or by a materials-intensive

5. For example, in the United States, through Medicaid and Medicare, the public sector paid 64 percent of total expenditures spent on nursing home care in 2002 (Kumar, Norton, and Encinosa 2006).

approach through urethral catheterization. Similarly, monitoring and controlling residents' behavior can be managed by a labor-intensive approach, such as personal monitoring, or by a materials-intensive approach, such as administering psychoactive drugs. A reliance on materials-intensive inputs can increase the risk of morbidity and mortality (Cawley, Grabowski, and Hirth 2006).[6]

Although most governments have adopted fixed-priced systems in recent years, previously, many used cost-based reimbursement. To the extent that nursing homes were paid on the basis of the costs they incurred, it should come as no surprise that cost-based reimbursement gave nursing homes an incentive to boost input use, including specifically nurse staffing. A study published in the 1990s reported empirical evidence consistent with this (Cohen and Spector 1996).

EFFECTS OF NURSE STAFFING LEVELS AND MIX ON PATIENT OUTCOMES

Research on the topic of the relationship between input levels and mix on patient outcomes in nursing homes predates similar research in a hospital setting (Davis, Wunderlich, and Sloan 1996). Compared to hospitals, the nursing home production function is much less complex, and nurses are more dominant. This simplifies the task of assessing nurses' contribution to quality care in nursing home settings.

We review two recent studies on this subject here. Schnelle, Simmons, Harrington, et al. (2004) compared quality of care at nursing homes with high versus low staffing levels and found that highest-staffed nursing homes provided better quality of care on thirteen of sixteen care processes. "Care process" refers to types of services provided to patients, especially under certain circumstances—for example, for patients who cannot move and are bedridden, the procedures to prevent bedsores. However, as with hospitals (although to a lesser extent), factors other than nurse staffing may affect care processes, and some of these factors may be systematically related to nurse staffing and mix.

In the second study, using data from 658 nursing homes and 2,663 residents of these homes in the United States, Cohen and Spector (1996) found that higher staffing improved patient outcomes, measured by mortality. Their results imply that a 10 percent increase in the RN-to-patient ratio decreases mortality by 1 percent. They reported no statistically significant effect of RN staffing intensity on the functional status of patients.[7]

IMPLICATIONS FOR PUBLIC POLICY

As in hospital care, the evidence on the positive relationship between the intensity of nursing staff and the quality of long-term care has given rise to a policy debate about the need to impose minimum staffing laws on nursing home. The rationale for government regulation of this industry stems in part from the fact that government is the major payer of long-term care. In addition, the presence of asymmetric information between nursing homes and their residents provides an incentive that for-profit homes take advantage of their residents to make a profit. This provides

6. Using longitudinal data from 1991 to 2000 on nearly every nursing home in the United States, the authors empirically assessed the impact of increases in local wages for nursing home workers on nursing staff intensity, materials intensity, and the quality of care in nursing homes. They found that higher wages led to a lower intensity of nursing staff for both nurses' aides and professional nurses. However, the results are not statistically significant. A plausible explanation for this result is that the existence of a minimum staffing requirement imposed by government regulation limits nursing home responses to wage changes. Although higher wages did not affect nursing staff intensity, the authors found that higher wages did lead to increasingly materials-intensive care provision. Specifically, they found that an increase of 10 percent in wages for nursing home workers yielded a 2.63 percent increase in the share of residents who were on psychoactive drugs. Furthermore, higher wages were associated with lower quality of nursing home care, as measured by the percentage of residents with bowel and bladder incontinence as well as bedfast. They reported that a 10 percent increase in wages was associated with a 3.2–3.6 percent increase in the share of residents who were incontinent and an 8.6 percent increase in the share of residents who were bedfast.

7. Earlier evidence on the effects of RN staffing in nursing homes on outcomes led an Institute of Medicine committee to conclude that higher RN staffing in nursing homes does improve outcomes. However, evidence published subsequently is mixed, giving reason for more caution about the relationship (see Davis, Wunderlich, and Sloan 1996). This Institute of Medicine study concluded that there is weaker support for a relationship in hospitals than in nursing homes.

a rationale for government regulation through which minimum quality standards serve a role in protecting consumers.

While the policy content of government regulation of nursing homes varies among countries, the major focus of such regulation is on residents' safety and health outcomes. For example, in the United States, Congress passed the Omnibus Budget Reconciliation Act (OBRA) in 1987 (effective October 1990) to regulate the quality of care in the nursing home industry. OBRA contains: (1) minimum quality standards, (2) a survey and inspection process, and (3) an enforcement system. The minimum quality standards require all nursing homes to have at least eight hours of RN coverage per day and LPN coverage 24 hours a day. OBRA introduced standard enforcement procedures and severe penalties to deter nursing homes from violating these minimum quality standards (Kumar, Norton, and Encinosa 2006).

Using data from the National Long-Term Care Survey, a household survey of US elderly persons, Kumar, Norton, and Encinosa (2006) examined the impact of OBRA on the quality of nursing home care as measured by residents' outcomes. The results indicate that the overall effect of government regulation depends on the nursing home's profitability, as proxied by the size of nursing home.

Kumar and colleagues reported that regulation decreases quality in less profitable (smaller) nursing homes. But the effect of government regulation on quality of care is positive in the more profitable (larger) nursing homes. The reason why larger nursing homes tend to be more profitable is that they can take advantage of economies of scale. Even a small nursing home needs to maintain certain administrative staff. For small homes, moreover, quality regulation forces homes to shift resources from unregulated areas to those areas subject to regulation. This may result in a decrease in overall quality, considering both dimensions monitored by regulation as well as some that are not.

In addition, the results show that the effect of regulation was higher during the transition period (from March 31, 1990, to April 1, 1991) than during the post-transition period (from April 1, 1991, to April 1, 1993). Initially, nursing homes may have expected that the government would enforce its regulations. Later, it became apparent that some of the regulations would not be enforced.

Overall, the empirical evidence reported by Kumar, Norton, and Encinosa (2006) has two important policy implications for government regulation of minimum quality standards in the nursing home industry. First, the extent to which nursing homes comply with the regulation requirements depends on their size. Small nursing homes may face tighter financial constraints and be unable to adjust their nursing staff according to the minimum quality standards. Second, the effects of government regulation depend on whether the threat of law enforcement is credible. During the early period after the regulation became effective, the perceived threat for not complying with the regulatory requirements may have provided an incentive for providers to increase quality of care. However, nursing homes subsequently learned that the threat of law enforcement is not credible.

8.7 SUMMARY AND CONCLUSIONS

In this chapter, we have investigated several important issues in labor markets for nurses and the role of nursing staff in the production of hospital and nursing home care. These are our major findings.

First, overall, the empirical literature indicates that nurse labor supply is quite unresponsive to wage changes. The most precise estimates of wage elasticity for the nurse labor supply range between 0.1 and 0.2, suggesting that (1) the nurse labor supply curve is upward sloping, (2) if other conditions hold, hospitals have substantial market power to set wages for nurses, and (3) if other conditions hold, the alleged nurse shortage is just that—it is alleged, not real.

Second, in many high-income countries, there is widespread concern that the supply of nurses is inadequate. A persistent shortfall in nurse supply may also be an effect of public regulation

Given the preconditions that must be satisfied for monopsony to exist, it seems unlikely that the model is appropriate in large cities unless one can demonstrate that some collusive arrangement exists. For this reason, it is not surprising that there is no strong empirical evidence supporting monopsony in markets for nurses. The low responsiveness of supply to wages is a necessary but not a sufficient condition for monopsony to exist. A more compelling explanation for persistent excess demand for nurses is the continuing outward shifts in demand, coupled with lags in the supply response.

Third, given the importance of nursing staff in the production of hospital and nursing home care, quite a number of studies, diverse methodologically and in terms of the data used, have addressed the question of whether higher nurse-to-patient ratios improve quality of care. Overall, the evidence is mixed, with some cross-sectional and within-hospital studies lending empirical support for a relationship but other studies, based on longitudinal data and using more advanced econometric techniques to control for various biases, finding at most limited empirical support for a *causal* link between nurse staffing and quality.

Finally, arguments that there is a relationship between nurse-to-patient ratios and quality of care, with some empirical support, especially from studies published in medical journals, have raised policy concerns about whether public intervention in the form of minimum staffing laws is needed. If such laws can be justified at all, they may make more sense for nursing homes than for hospitals. However, even here there is no clear empirical evidence to support public regulation of quality. For nursing homes, the problem may be that governments have budgeted too little for enforcement. Thus, in reality, even with laws on the books, nursing homes that do not comply with the mandated standards may be able to continue this practice without threats of meaningful sanctions. Lack of regulation is not only a matter of inadequate resources for enforcement. In addition, regulatory agencies face a dilemma. If they are too tough on the firms they regulate, this may cause some to exit, which in turn would lead to access barriers for elderly and disabled persons to nursing home care.

KEY CONCEPTS

- surplus
- shortage
- parameter estimate
- equilibrium
- market-clearing wage
- derived demand
- monopsony
- oligopsony
- wage taker
- wage setter
- marginal labor cost (MLC)
- nonpecuniary objective

REVIEW AND DISCUSSION QUESTIONS

8.1 List three similarities in labor markets for nurses in high-income countries.

8.2 Describe economists' definition of shortage. Is there any alternative definition of shortage used by other professionals? Match policy solutions to ease the problem of shortage according to the definition of shortage that is used.

8.3 Based on economists' definition of shortage, what are the two necessary conditions that lead to a persistent nursing shortage?

8.4 What is a monopsony? Under what circumstances is a monopsony likely to arise? What is the empirical evidence that hospitals possess monopsony power in the market for professional nurses (including empirical tests of the monopsony hypothesis)? If hospitals possess such power, what are the implications for public policy?

8.5 What are the alternative hypotheses that you have learned in this chapter to explain the phenomenon of "nursing shortage"? What is the strength of the empirical evidence to support these hypotheses? What are the plausible explanations for the failure of wage adjustment in the labor market for nurses?

8.6 What practical difference does it make if nursing is viewed as a vocation rather than as a profession? If nursing is primarily viewed as a vocation, is increasing the nurses' wage likely to be an effective policy to ease a nurse shortage? Under such circumstances, what are the potential impacts of such policy on the quality of care? How would your policies as an employer differ if nursing is widely viewed as a profession?

8.7 What are the extensive and intensive margins in the nurse labor supply? Conceptually, would you expect that the extensive margin in the nurse labor supply is more responsive to wage change in modern society (such as in the 2000s) than in a more traditional society in which women are viewed as "secondary" workers in families (such as in the 1950s)? Explain your answer.

8.8 What is the substitution effect of a wage increase? What is the income effect? What does the labor supply curve looks like if the income effect exceeds the substitution effect? For which of the following occupations is it more likely that the income effect of a wage change exceeds the substitution effect? Justify your answers.

- Physician
- Dentist
- Professional nurse
- Nurses' aide
- Medical secretary

8.9 Do you expect that quality of care is significantly different between for-profit and not-for-profit nursing homes? Which type of nursing home would provide better quality of care to residents? Why?

8.10 What are the costs and benefits of government regulation of minimum nurse-to-patient ratios for hospitals? Who pays the costs and who receives the benefits of such regulation?

8.11 What is the economic rationale of government regulation of minimum nurse staffing for hospitals and nursing homes? Do you agree that such regulation is more justifiable for nursing homes than for hospitals? Why or why not?

EXERCISES

8.1 The Good Works General Hospital has a local monopoly in the sale of hospital services in its market area. Its product demand curve is $p = 30 - 0.4x$, where p is the price of a hospital day and x is the number of hospital days per year at Good Works. Given this demand curve, derive the equation for marginal revenue (MR).

Good Works is the only employer of professional nurses in its market area. It faces a supply of nurse labor of $w = 5 + 0.9E$, where w is the nurse hourly wage and E is the full-time-equivalent of nurses employed by Good Works. What is the marginal factor cost of nurse labor? Assume each nurse can monitor four patient rooms per hour (with one patient per room) and Good Works is a profit maximizer. Then how many professional nurses should Good Works employ? At what hourly wage? What price should Good Works charge for a hospital day?

8.2

a. Suppose that the supply function changed to $w = 10 + 0.9E$. What would be the new values of the hourly wage, the product price, and nurse employment?

b. Assuming the original supply function of nurses, what would be the new values of the hourly wage, the product price, and nurse employment if nurses were able to monitor only two rooms per hour?

8.3 Consider the community (city or town) in which you live. Are local hospitals likely to be monopsonists? Why or why not?

8.4 For which of the following occupations is Good Works General Hospital likely to possess monopsony power? Discuss each occupation and justify your answers.

- Receptionist
- Hospital administrator
- X-ray technician
- Professional nurse
- Nurses' aide

What do you think are the three most important nonwage determinants of nurse labor supply? Justify each answer. For each, how is the supply of nurse labor curve expected to change for a given change in the nonwage attribute?

8.5 Following the concept of full price in exercise 11 of chapter 3, let Y represent full income, where Y = wage income + nonwage income.

a. Would you expect the elasticity of labor supply with respect to wage to be higher or lower for a nurse with a higher share of nonwage income than for a nurse with a lower share of nonwage income? Explain your answer.

b. Based on your answer to (a), would you expect the elasticity of labor supply with respect to wage to be higher or lower for a "female profession" (such as nursing) compared to a "male profession" (such as pilot), other things being equal? Explain your answer.

8.6 Suppose $H = 0.5w - 5$ is Mary's labor supply curve, where H is hours of work per week and w is the wage rate per hour. What is the "reservation wage" for Mary that she would like to go to work (participate in the labor market)? What is the wage elasticity of labor supply at $w = 100$? Would Mary like to spend more hours on work if the wage rate increased to 150 per hour? Can you explain why?

8.7 Suppose the aggregate demand curve for a nurse in an island city is $N^d = 300 - 5w$, where w is the hourly wage rate for nurses and N^d is the number of nurses demanded in this city. The supply of nurses is $N^s = 5w - 100$, where N^s is number of nurses supplied to market. In addition, the city government publicly announces that the city needs to hire 125 nurses in order to provide good-quality hospital care to its citizens. Meanwhile, the city government regulates the wage rate for nurses at $w = 30$.

Answer the following questions:

a. Use both economic and need-based approaches to calculate the nursing shortage under the current regulated wage rate. Do these two approaches yield the same estimates on the number of nursing shortage?

b. If the city government decides to recruit nurses from overseas and this policy shifts the supply of nurse to $N^{s'} = 5w - 50$, does this policy solve the problem of nursing shortage or just mitigate the extent of nursing shortage? Does your answer differ according to different definitions of "shortage"? Explain your answer.

c. If the city government further announces raising the wage rate for nurses from 30 to 40 and the policy that allows recruiting nurses from overseas remains valid, does the city government solve the problem of nursing shortage or create a new problem? Does your answer differ according to different definitions of "shortage"? Explain your answer.

8.8 Suppose a for-profit nursing home can produce long-term care services (x) using two inputs: labor (such as nurses, l) and material (such as psychoactive drugs, M). Thus, the production function of the nursing home can be described as $x = f(l, M)$. In addition, w represents the market price of labor input (wage) and p represents the market price of material inputs. Thus, the cost function of the nursing home can be described by $C = w \times l + p \times M$. Answer the following questions:

a. Use a graph to explain how the nursing home decides the optimal uses of labor and material inputs.

b. Suppose the government imposes a regulation on minimum nursing staffing and this minimum nursing staffing level exceeds the level the nursing home decides is optimal. Use a graph to explain the effect of government regulation on the nursing home's input choices. Does regulation increase the cost of nursing home care if the nursing home wants to keep its output constant? What other choices can the nursing home make if the nursing home wants to keep cost constant in response to the government regulation? Consider another case in which the government does not impose any regulation on nursing home input use but the market wage of nurses increases substantially owing to an unanticipated policy shock, such as a government requirement that employers provide health insurance coverage to employees. Use a graph to explain the effect of the higher wage on the optimal use of inputs by the nursing home, and discuss the potential consequences of such a change on the mix of inputs and on the quality of nursing home care provided.

Online Supplemental Material

International Nurse Migration

http://www.intlnursemigration.org/sections/research/publications.shtml

Nursing Labor Market

http://www.rcn.org.uk/__data/assets/pdf_file/0004/347953/003862.pdf

http://www.cna-nurses.ca/CNA/documents/pdf/publications/International_Nursing_Labour_Market_e.pdf

http://www.rwjf.org/pr/product.jsp?id=19813.

The World Health Report

http://www.who.int/whr/2006/en

Supplemental Readings

Aiken, L. H., S. P. Clarke, and D. M. Sloane. 2002. Hospital Staffing, Organization, and Quality of Care: Cross-national Findings. *International Journal for Quality in Health Care* 14 (1): 5–13.

Cawley, J., D. C. Grabowski, and R. Hirth. 2006. Factor Substitution in Nursing Homes. *Journal of Health Economics* 25 (2): 234–247.

Chou, S. Y. 2002. Asymmetric Information, Ownership and Quality of Care: An Empirical Analysis of Nursing Homes. *Journal of Health Economics* 21 (2): 293–311.

Mark, B., D. F. Harless, and J. Spetz. 2009. California's Minimum-Nurse-Staffing Legislation and Nurses' Wages. *Health Affairs* 28 (2): W326–W334.

REFERENCES

Adamache, K. W., and F. A. Sloan. 1982. Unions and Hospitals: Some Unresolved Issues. *Journal of Health Economics* 1 (1): 81–108.

Aiken, L. H., J. Buchan, J. Sochlaski, et al. 2004. Trends in International Nurse Migration. *Health Affairs* 23 (3): 69–77.

Aiken, L. H., S. P. Clarke, D. M. Sloane, et al. 2001. Nurses' Reports on Hospital Care in Five Countries. *Health Affairs* 20 (3): 43–53.

Aiken, L. H., S. P. Clarke, D. M. Sloane, et al. 2002. Hospital Nurse Staffing and Patient Mortality, Nurse Burnout, and Job Dissatisfaction. *Journal of the American Medical Association* 288 (16): 1987–1993.

Antonazzo, E., A. Scott, D. Skatun, et al. 2003. The Labour Market for Nursing: A Review of the Labour Supply Literature. *Health Economics* 12 (6): 465–478.

Askildsen, J. E., B. H. Baltagi, and T. H. Holmås. 2003. Wage Policy in the Health Care Sector: A Panel Data Analysis of Nurses' Labour Supply. *Health Economics* 12 (9): 705–719.

Bell, C. M., and D. A. Redelmeier. 2001. Mortality among Patients Admitted to Hospitals on Weekends as Compared with Weekdays. *New England Journal of Medicine* 345 (9): 663–668.

Bhaskar, V., A. Manning, and T. To. 2002. Oligopsony and Monopsonistic Competition in Labor Markets. *Journal of Economic Perspectives* 16 (2): 155.

Boal, W. M., and M. R. Ransom. 1997. Monopsony in the Labor Market. *Journal of Economic Literature* 35 (1): 86–112.

Bognanno, M. F., J. S. Hixson, and J. R. Jeffers. 1974. The Short-Run Supply of Nurse's Time. *Journal of Human Resources* 9 (1): 80–94.

Buerhaus, P. I., D. O. Staiger, and D. I. Auerbach. 2004. New Signs of a Strengthening U.S. Nurse Labor Market? *Health Affairs Web Exclusive* W4:526–533.

Cawley, J., D. C. Grabowski, and R. A. Hirth. 2006. Factor Substitution in Nursing Homes. *Journal of Health Economics* 25 (2): 234–247.

Chou, S.-Y. 2002. Asymmetric Information, Ownership and Quality of Care: An Empirical Analysis of Nursing Homes. *Journal of Health Economics* 21 (2): 293–311.

Cohen, J. W., and W. D. Spector. 1996. The Effect of Medicaid Reimbursement on Quality of Care in Nursing Homes. *Journal of Health Economics* 15 (1): 23–48.

Davis, C., G. Wunderlich, and F. A. Sloan. 1996. *Nursing Staff in Hospitals and Nursing Homes: Is It Adequate?* Washington, DC: National Academy Press.

Elliot, R. F., A. H. Y. Ma, A. Scott, et al. 2007. Geographically Differentiated Pay in the Labor Market for Nurses. *Journal of Health Economics* 26:190–212.

Evans, W. N., and B. Kim. 2006. Patient Outcomes When Hospitals Experience a Surge in Admissions. *Journal of Health Economics* 25 (2): 365–388.

Frijters, P., M. A. Shields, and S. W. Price. 2007. Investigating the Quitting Decision of Nurses: Panel Data Evidence from the British National Health Service. *Health Economics* 16 (1): 57–73.

Gaynor, M., and D. Haas-Wilson. 1999. Change, Consolidation, and Competition in Health Care Markets. *Journal of Economic Perspectives* 13 (1): 141–164.

Golden, B. R., and F. A. Sloan. 2008. Physician Pay for Performance: Alternative Perspectives. In *Incentives and Choice in Health Care*, ed. F. A. Sloan and H. Kasper, 289–317. Cambridge, MA: MIT Press.

Grossman, B. 2000. Group Work with Children and Adolescents: Prevention and Intervention in School and Community Systems. *Journal of Sociology and Social Welfare* 27 (4): 203–205.

Heyes, A. 2005. The Economics of Vocation or "Why Is a Badly Paid Nurse a Good Nurse"? *Journal of Health Economics* 24 (3): 561–569.

Hirsch, B. T., and E. J. Schumacher. 1995. Monopsony Power and Relative Wages in the Labor Market for Nurses. *Journal of Health Economics* 14 (4): 443–476.

Hirsch, B. T., and E. J. Schumacher. 2005. Classic or New Monopsony? Searching for Evidence in Nursing Labor Markets. *Journal of Health Economics* 24 (5): 969–989.

Holmås, T. H. 2002. Keeping Nurses at Work: A Duration Analysis. *Journal of Health Economics* 11 (6): 493–503.

Kingma, M. 2007. Nurses on the Move: A Global Overview. *Health Services Research* 42 (3): 1281–1298.

Kumar, V., E. C. Norton, and W. E. Encinosa. 2006. OBRA 1987 and the Quality of Nursing Home Care. *International Journal of Health Care Finance and Economics* 6 (1): 49–81.

Lane, J., and S. Gohmann. 1995. Shortage or Surplus: Economic and Noneconomic Approaches to the Analysis of Nursing Labor Markets. *Southern Economic Journal* 61 (3): 644–653.

Link, C. R. 1992. Labor Supply Behavior of Registered Nurses: Female Labor Supply in the Future? *Research in Labor Economics* 13 (1): 287–320.

Link, C. R., and J. H. Landon. 1976. Market Structure, Nonpecuniary Factors and Professional Salaries: Registered Nurses. *Journal of Economics and Business* 28 (2): 151–155.

Mark, B., D. F. Harless, and J. Spetz. 2009. California's Minimum-Nurse-Staffing Legislation and Nurses' Wages. *Health Affairs* 28 (2): w326–w334.

Mark, B. A., D. W. Harless, M. McCue, et al. 2004. A Longitudinal Examination of Hospital Registered Nurse Staffing and Quality of Care. *Health Services Research* 39 (2): 279–300.

Mark, B. A., D. W. Harless, and M. McCue. 2005. The Impact of HMO Penetration on the Relationship between Nurse Staffing and Quality. *Health Economics* 14 (7): 737–753.

Needleman, J., P. Buerhaus, S. Mattke, et al. 2002. Nurse-Staffing Levels and the Quality of Care in Hospitals. *New England Journal of Medicine* 346 (22): 1715–1722.

Newhouse, J. P. 1976. *Income and Medical Care Expenditure across Countries*. New York: RAND Corp.

Newhouse, J. P. 1992. Medical Care Costs: How Much Welfare Loss? *Journal of Economic Perspectives* 6 (3): 3–21.

Norton, E. C. 2000. Long-Term Care. In *Handbook of Health Economics*, ed. A. J. Culyer and J. P. Newhouse, 1B:955–994. Amsterdam: Elsevier Science.

Organisation for Economic Co-Operation and Development (OECD). 2005. *Towards a High-Performing Health System*. Paris: OECD Publishing.

Phillips, V. L. 1995. Nurses' Labor Supply: Participation, Hours of Work, and Discontinuities in the Supply Function. *Journal of Health Economics* 14 (5): 567–582.

Propper, C., and J. Van Reenen. 2010. Can Pay Regulation Kill? Panel Data Evidence on the Effect of Labor Markets on Hospital Performance. *Journal of Political Economy* 118 (2): 222–273.

Schnelle, J. F., S. F. Simmons, C. Harrington, et al. 2004. Relationship of Nursing Home Staffing to Quality of Care. *Health Services Research* 39 (2): 225–250.

Shields, M. A. 2004. Addressing Nurse Shortages: What Can Policy Makers Learn from the Econometric Evidence on Nurse Labour Supply? *Economic Journal* 114 (499): F464–F498.

Shields, M. A., and M. Ward. 2001. Improving Nurse Retention in the National Health Service in England: The Impact of Job Satisfaction on Intentions to Quit. *Journal of Health Economics* 20 (5): 677–701.

Sloan, F. A., and S. Richupan. 1975. Short-Run Supply Responses of Professional Nurses: A Microanalysis. *Journal of Human Resources* 10 (2): 241–257.

Staiger, D., J. Spetz, and C. Phibbs. 1999. Is There Monopsony in the Labor Market? Evidence from a Natural Experiment. National Bureau of Economic Research Working Paper No. 7258. Cambridge, MA: National Bureau of Economic Research.

Steinbrook, R. 2002. Nursing in the Crossfire. *New England Journal of Medicine* 346 (22): 1757–1766.

Sullivan, D. 1989. Monopsony Power in the Market for Nurses. *Journal of Law & Economics* 32 (2): S135–S178.

Summers, L. H. 1988. Relative Wages, Efficiency Wages, and Keynesian Unemployment. *American Economic Review* 78 (2): 383–388.

World Bank Group. 2007. World Development Indicators. http://data.worldbank.org/indicator, accessed 7/18/2011.

World Health Organization (WHO). 2006. World Health Report 2006. http://www.who.int/whr/2006/en, accessed 7/18/2011.

PHARMACEUTICAL MANUFACTURERS

Pharmaceutical manufacturers, profit-maximizing firms with long time horizons, decide on investments in new products. Among these new products, prescription drugs are of particular interest since they are major inputs in the production of good health. In addition, new prescription drugs are a major source of advances in health care technologies, which in turn often result in extending the capability of medicine to prevent and treat diseases and improve the quality of life. Once products are developed, there are issues of pricing and product promotion in countries in which the products become available. Some manufacturers concentrate on producing generics, which are chemically equivalent to branded products but are only sold after the patent on the branded drug expires. A patent gives the branded product a monopoly status until the patent expires.

This chapter focuses on the microeconomic decisions of pharmaceutical firms, including research and development (R&D) investment, pricing new products, competition between branded and generic products, advertising, and international pricing. The firms' strategies reflect the actual and anticipated decisions of rivals and of governments.

Governments make decisions about drug approval, drug formularies, and patent protection. Unlike the vast majority of goods and services, pharmaceuticals are subject to entry regulation, similar in a sense to certificate of need regulation of hospitals described in chapter 6 in that government approval is needed before a drug can be marketed. Having a patent affects the entry of competitors, but does not give a firm the right to sell the patented product. Drug formularies are lists of drugs that are covered by a public or a private insurance plan. Exclusion from a formulary may mean that use of the drug is not subsidized at all or is only partially subsidized by the insurance plan.

When a drug is not covered by a patent, competitors are free to enter the market for the product. Price competition is likely to result in an appreciable reduction in profit from the sale of the drug. As a result of these public policy decisions and others, the market may not provide a sufficient incentive to elicit company investment in the R&D needed to develop a new pharmaceutical product. Market size may be insufficient for various reasons. For example, the diseases treated by the product may be rare, or the diseases may be highly prevalent in low-income countries but the ability or willingness to pay for the product is insufficient, or there may be important health and financial externalities not captured by the individual user of the drug and government intervention to take account of these externalities in use is lacking. We also discuss various policies to encourage pharmaceutical innovation when the market alone provides an inadequate incentive for pharmaceutical R&D.

9.1 COMPANIES' DECISIONS ABOUT INVESTMENTS IN R&D

BASIC FACTS OF THE PHARMACEUTICAL R&D PROCESS

The pharmaceutical R&D process consists of two distinct stages, discovery and development. The discovery stage includes basic science research and the application of "upstream" basic research to search for new compounds with which to develop new drugs. The development stage refers to "downstream" market-oriented R&D, including preclinical testing and three phases of clinical trials to demonstrate the safety and efficacy of the specific compound. Safety criteria are met if the probability of an adverse health effect from taking the drug is below some minimum threshold. Efficacy means that the drug generally works to produce the health outcome the manufacturer states that it does.

The drug development process is lengthy, risky, and costly (table 9.1). On average, the three phases of clinical testing of a new drug take about six years in total. Following clinical testing, a New Drug Application (NDA) is submitted to the regulatory agency. In the United States, the mean time required for a decision to be reached on an NDA is about two years. In addition, the discovery stage also takes about six years. Adding all these steps together, the total amount of time required for developing new pharmaceutical products, from basic research to approval to market launch, is about 14 years on average in the United States.

Since there are many regulatory hurdles in the R&D process, many trials fail to pass these hurdles and hence can be abandoned at any time. As a result, there are higher failure rates in the drug discovery and development process than in developing products in many other sectors. For example, only 40 percent of drugs

Table 9.1
Basic Facts of the Drug Development Process

Stages	Contents	Mean Cost (in millions of 2000 dollars)	Mean Phase Length (months)	Probability of Success (%)	
				Conditional	Unconditional
Preclinical testing	Laboratory and animal testing	—	72	—	—
Investigational New Drug Application	Requesting the authorization to begin human testing	—	—	40	—
Clinical testing					
Phase I	20–80 volunteers, safety and dosage	15.2	21.6	75	30
Phase II	100–300 patients, safety, dosing and efficacy	23.5	25.7	48	14
Phase III	Large-scale randomized trial of clinical effectiveness and side effects	86.3	30.5	64	9
New Drug Application	Application for commercial marketing of the new drug	—	24	90	8

Sources: DiMasi, Hansen, and Grabowski (2003) and Philipson and Sun (2008).

for which an Investigational New Drug Application (INDA) is filed progress to Phase I testing and only 75 percent of drugs for which a first phase of clinical test is initiated progress to Phase II testing (table 9.1). Combining the conditional probabilities of success (at the probability of success at a stage, given success in the prior stage) at each stage together, the overall probability of success, which refers the unconditional probability of reaching a given stage, is extremely low. Only 8 percent of drugs for which an INDA is filed eventually receive approval from the Food and Drug Administration (FDA) for marketing.

The cost of R&D in the pharmaceutical industry reflects the high cost of drug discovery and development while the drug is under development, the lengthy time period generally required to develop a new pharmaceutical product, and the low probability that a specific attempt to develop a particular drug will actually result in a marketable product (Danzon, Nicholson, and Pereira 2005). The mean out-of-pocket R&D cost to a pharmaceutical manufacturer for Phase I to III trials in the 1990s ranged from $15.2 to $86.3 million (in 2000 US dollars) (table 9.1). Pharmaceutical R&D takes on average 12 to 15 years to successfully develop a new drug. For a considerable time period, the pharmaceutical company incurs investment cost without receiving any revenue from the sale of the drug. There is an "opportunity cost" to R&D funds tied up over such a lengthy time horizon.

THE OPTIMAL INVESTMENT DECISION FROM A PHARMACEUTICAL COMPANY'S VANTAGE POINT

Given that pharmaceutical R&D is a complicated, lengthy, and risky process, firms face a two-step decision process. In the first step, the firm decides whether or not to devote resources to a specific R&D project. In the second step, the firm decides on the optimal price at which to sell the newly invented good. This price determines the profit flow at each date and hence the rate of return on the investment.

The problem is solved by backward induction. First, the optimal price is derived under the assumption that the R&D investment has already taken place. Optimal pricing in part reflects a government's patent policies. Second, results from the first stage are used in calculating whether or not the investment should be undertaken, which is based on a comparison of *anticipated* marginal returns and the marginal cost of capital. Firms expend the resources if the marginal return is greater than or equal to the marginal cost of capital, and reject the project otherwise.

Marginal returns can be represented by a marginal efficiency of investment (MEI) schedule. The MEI schedule shows projects ranked by their internal rates of return (see chapter 5).[1] The ranking is in decreasing order of projects' internal rates of return (fig. 9.1). The MEI declines as the firm invests more in a given period

1. In chapter 2, we describe the marginal efficiency of capital (MEC) and here the marginal efficiency of investment. With the MEC, capital is on the horizontal axis. With the MEI, investment is on this axis. As discussed in chapter 2, investment is a flow while capital is a stock. Net investment is the difference between gross investment and depreciation. Depreciation equals the capital stock times the depreciation rate. In chapter 2, we depict human health as a capital stock. This chapter focuses on pharmaceutical manufacturers' decisions to invest in R&D.

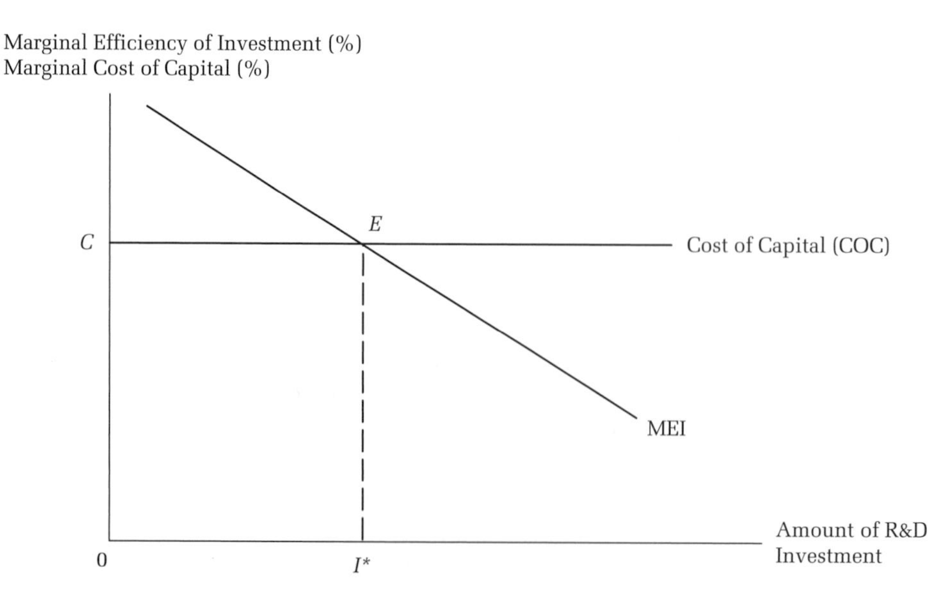

FIGURE 9.1
Determination of Optimal Level of R&D Investment

since projects are undertaken in decreasing order of their anticipated rates of return, starting with the project with the highest rate of return. The shape and position of the MEI curve reflects demand curves for final products as well as the marginal cost of manufacturing, packaging, and distributing the products once the investments have been completed.

The marginal cost of capital (COC) schedule shows the marginal cost of capital as investment activity expands in any period. The COC can have a zero or a positive slope. A positive slope indicates that the firm must pay a higher price for capital if it invests more. For simplicity, the COC curve is shown with a zero slope in figure 9.1, which is appropriate if the COC does not vary with the amount the firm invests. The position of the COC curve depends in part on creditors' assessments of the risk that the creditors will receive payment for principal and interest, that is, the borrower's bankruptcy risk, as well as conditions in the capital markets more generally.

Optimal R&D investment by a pharmaceutical company is shown where the MEI and COC curves intersect, at point E, and the amount of investment chosen by the firm is I^*. Here, anticipated marginal returns from investment in R&D, as reflected in the internal rate of return, and the marginal cost of funds for such investment are equal; at this level of investment, the firm achieves the maximum expected profit from its R&D investment.

INCENTIVES FOR PHARMACEUTICAL INNOVATION

Based on the above framework (illustrated in fig. 9.1), we further assess the effects of specific government policies or exogenous factors affecting incentives for pharmaceutical innovation. In this section, we analyze three types of incentives that aim to promote investment in pharmaceutical R&D: (1) pull incentives, (2) push incentives, and (3) combinations of pull and push incentives.

PULL INCENTIVES

Pull incentives affect demand for the final product resulting from the investment in R&D and hence shift the MEI curve outward. Other factors being equal, the new MEI curve (MEI′) intersects the COC curve at point E_1 (fig. 9.2); the firm's optimal R&D investment now becomes I^d. The increase in R&D investment, as measured by the difference between I^d and I^*, represents the amount of new R&D investment induced by an exogenous change that shifts the MEI curve outward. Such shifts occur, for example, in response to an increase in market size, reflecting in part governments' decisions to cover the new product under their public insurance systems, coverage decisions by private insurers, and an increase in the willingness of such insurers to pay a higher price for the new product than it previously did. The MEI shifts for other reasons as well, such as increases in population size, increases in the number of types of persons especially likely to use the new product, as well as growth in personal

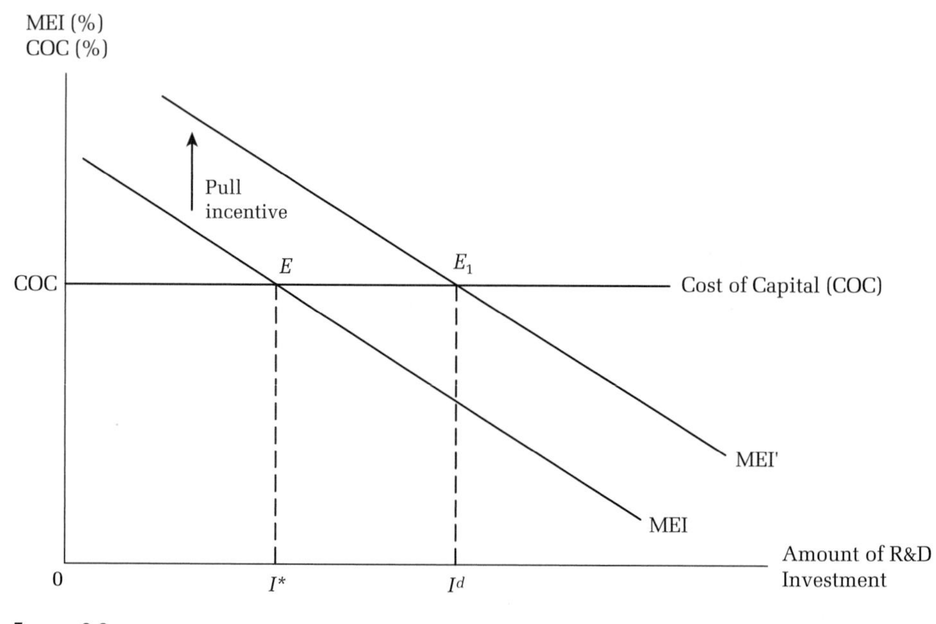

FIGURE 9.2
The Effect of a Pull Incentive on R&D Investment

income, which affects individuals' willingness (and ability) to pay for the new product.

PUSH INCENTIVES

Push incentives are designed to reduce the cost of investing in new product development. Push incentives can affect the marginal cost of funds to the firm for investments in R&D. For example, governments could grant pharmaceutical companies access to tax-exempt debt, which would reduce the interest rate the companies have to pay on their loans. The COC curve then shifts downward to COC′ if there is an exogenous change that leads to a decrease in the user cost of capital for R&D investment (fig. 9.3). Other factors being equal, the new COC curve (COC′) intersects the MEI curve at point E_2, with I^c being the firm's new optimal level of R&D investment. The increase in R&D investment, as measured by the difference between I^c and I^*, represents the new R&D investment induced by push incentives. Macroeconomic policies affecting market rates of interest also affect the COC.

In addition to the effective interest rate subsidy, or more generally, any monetary policy that lowers the real rate of interest, push incentives also include government grants for basic research, a more generous depreciation policy, and an investment tax credit. These policies affect the cash flow associated with the investment, which in turn affects the MEI. Thus, a new public program of cash grants,

Box 9.1
Pull Incentives and Pharmaceutical Innovation

Several studies have documented the empirical relationship between pull incentives and pharmaceutical innovation from various settings. Here we illustrate with two examples. First, using data from the United States, Finkelstein (2004) investigated whether an increase in market size resulting from changes in health policies affects R&D investment behavior in the vaccine industry. In 1991, the US Centers for Disease Control recommended that all infants be vaccinated against hepatitis B. In 1993, Medicare provided insurance coverage for influenza vaccinations administered to its beneficiaries. These two policies increased the potential market size for vaccines, which in turn, in combination with the adoption of a no-fault compensation system for injuries attributable to the use of certain childhood vaccines in 1986, substantially increased the expected return from developing new vaccines for infectious diseases. By comparing changes in the number of new vaccine clinical trials between treatment diseases (affected by the policies) and control diseases (not affected by the policies), she found evidence linking the policy changes to rates of innovation in vaccine markets. Her estimates indicate that a $1 increase in annual expected market revenue from a vaccine leads to a six-cent increase in vaccine R&D investment.

Second, Acemoglu and Linn (2004) measured changes in market size from demographic trends in the United States. During a recent 30-year period, demographic trends led to a decline in the market for drugs mostly consumed by the young (ages 0–30). By contrast, markets for drugs mostly consumed by the middle-aged increased. More specifically, Acemoglu and Linn's measure of potential market size for each drug category involved a combination of the number of consumers and their incomes. The authors found that the change in potential market size has a significant positive impact on pharmaceutical innovation, as measured by the number of new drugs entering the US market. A 1 percent increase in potential market size leads to about a 4 percent increase in the entry of new drugs, in the form of either new nongeneric drugs or new molecular entities.

although a push policy, would shift the MEI curve outward, as would an increase in the patent period or the price of the new product, both pull policies.

An example of a push incentive to promote pharmaceutical innovation is public investment in basic research. Such research may lead to new insights that provide scientific direction for the drug development process that occurs later. A characteristic of basic research is its public-good nature. For this reason, private firms do not have incentives to invest in such research. Rather, as with the financing of other public goods, such as national defense, the financing of basic scientific research is highly dependent on public funding.

Despite its public-good nature, basic research is not free from the firm's standpoint (Gambardella 1995). The dissemination of scientific knowledge from

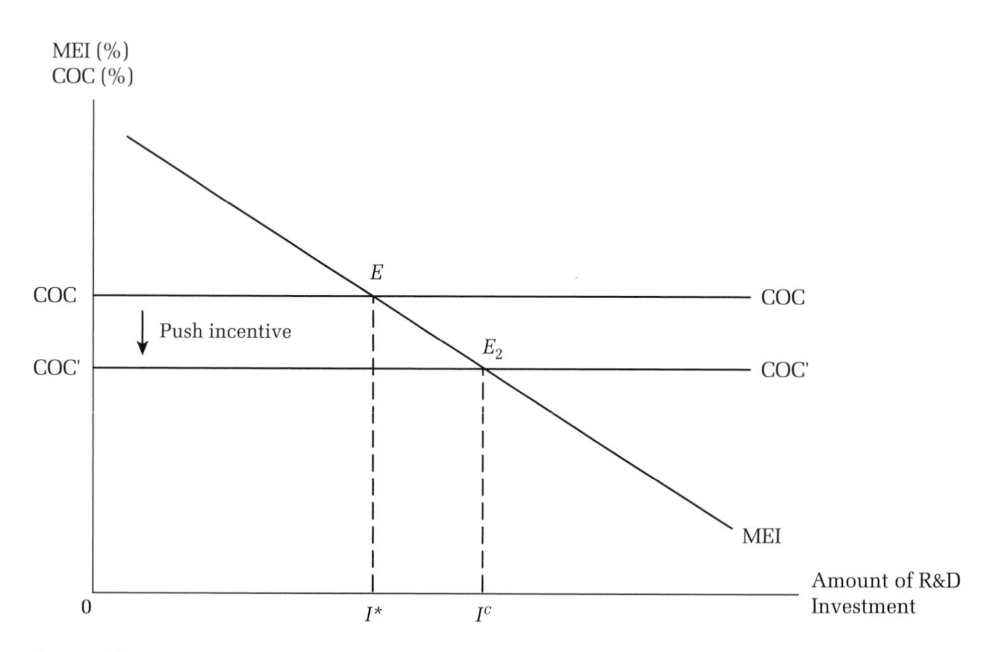

FIGURE 9.3

The Effect of a Push Incentive That Reduces the Market Rate of Interest a Firm Pays on Its Loans on R&D Investment

public to private sectors can be quite costly and time-consuming. Firms must invest in knowledge capital so that they can access and absorb basic research findings (Cockburn and Henderson 1998). The form of investment in knowledge capital includes some in-house basic research and maintaining an extensive connection between pharmaceutical company scientists and publicly funded researchers through collaborative efforts in publishing scientific papers.

Cockburn and Henderson found that the number of co-authorships of scientific papers is positively related to a firm's private research productivity as measured by the number of important patents. Since private research mainly focuses on downstream market-oriented R&D for developing new drugs, Cockburn and Henderson's empirical results suggest that upstream basic research and downstream market-oriented R&D are complements rather than substitutes in the pharmaceutical R&D process.

Specifically, public investment in basic research stimulates companies' investments in R&D in three ways, by providing (1) fundamental biological and chemical knowledge of drugs, (2) medical knowledge for the design of human clinical trials required by regulatory agencies as proof of drug safety and efficacy, and (3) insights into potential new indications for drugs after they have been approved. Based on detailed case histories of the development of twenty-one important drugs introduced between 1965 and 1992, Cockburn and Henderson found that two-thirds of these drugs were developed with at least some government financial support. This evidence suggests that increased public investment in basic research decreases the cost of acquiring knowledge capital for pharmaceutical innovation, which in turn provides an incentive for increasing spending on downstream R&D investment by private enterprises.

COMBINATIONS OF PULL AND PUSH INCENTIVES

The relative effectiveness of pull versus push incentives cannot be deduced from theory alone but rather must be established by examining the empirical evidence. That is, in theory, the effect of push incentives ($I^c - I^*$ in fig. 9.3) is not necessarily less than the effect of pull incentives ($I^d - I^*$ in fig. 9.2).

Kremer and Glennerster (2004) argued that pull incentives tend to be more promising. With pull incentives, the reward is for results; with push incentives, by contrast, the rewards are more frequently based on promises. For example, an applicant for a government grant, a push incentive, can make various claims about the uniqueness of an approach, but once awarded the grant, there is no direct incentive to deliver on the promise except the threat that nonperformance will result in fewer grants in the future. Unfortunately, conclusive empirical evidence comparing pull versus push incentives is lacking.

A combination of pull and push incentives may stimulate more added investment than when only one type is applied alone (fig. 9.4). For this reason, rather

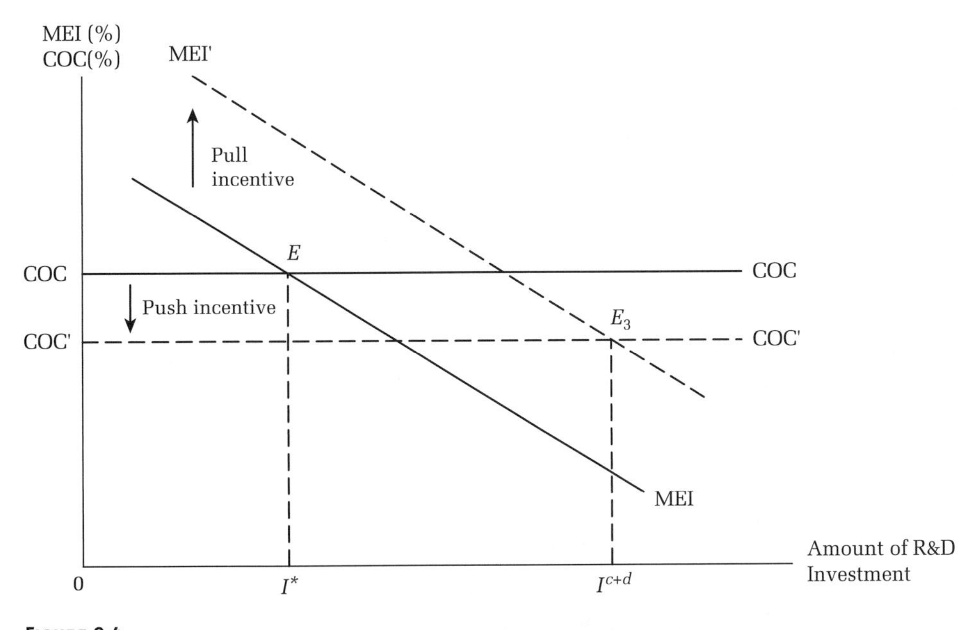

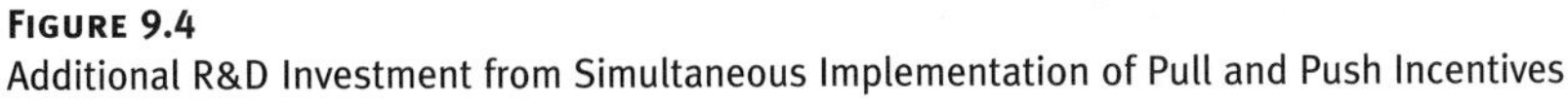
FIGURE 9.4
Additional R&D Investment from Simultaneous Implementation of Pull and Push Incentives

than choose between the two, a government may be well advised to include a mix of pull and push policies in its pharmaceutical R&D investment stimulus package. Depending on the precise mix of policies implemented, this approach could shift the MEI curve outward and shift the COC curve downward at the same time, leading, for example, to a new optimal investment decision at E_3, with I^{c+d} being the firm's new optimal R&D investment. In this example, the new R&D investment induced by adopting both pull and push incentives simultaneously exceeds the new investment induced by pull or push incentives alone.

The 1983 US Orphan Drug Act is a well-known example of the use of both pull and push incentives by a government to promote pharmaceutical innovation. The rationale for the act was to stimulate R&D investment in drugs with relatively small potential market sizes (i.e., to treat rare diseases). The act provides a tax credit of up to 50 percent of certain clinical testing expenses incurred by pharmaceutical firms to generate required data for marketing approval. In addition, the act provides seven years of marketing exclusivity, which is a pull incentive that increases the expected market revenue from developing drugs to treat rare diseases.

Following implementation of the Orphan Drug Act, the mean annual number of new drugs brought to market for treating rare diseases increased appreciably. During the decade prior to enactment of the act, only one orphan product was developed by the pharmaceutical industry per year. Between 1983 and 1994, the FDA designated about 600 pharmaceuticals as orphan products, which allowed firms to obtain tax credits for clinical testing expenses. During the same period, the FDA also approved 111 orphan drugs for marketing, which allowed firms to obtain the protection of marketing exclusivity for seven years.

Disincentives for Pharmaceutical Innovation

Certain government policies provide disincentives for pharmaceutical innovation. For example, if country's drug coverages and payment policies become more uncertain, firms may add a risk premium in calculating their optimal investment decisions as a consequence. The risk premium adds to the cost of capital; the COC curve shifts upward, and hence the intersection of the COC and MEI curves occurs at a higher point on the MEI curve, and the firm's optimal R&D investment falls. Or the national agency responsible for approving new drug products for sale in a country can lengthen or add complexity to its drug approval process. This in turn delays the time at which positive cash flow from the new product can be anticipated and lowers the expected rate of return on investments in pharmaceutical R&D. The probability that a new drug will ever appear on the market is reflected in the MEI. If government regulatory agencies become more stringent in approving drugs, this too affects private investment in R&D.

A widely discussed disincentive for pharmaceutical R&D is price regulation. By definition, price regulation means that the government sets a regulated price below the market price that firms would set in the absence of such regulation. By reducing prices of regulated products, such regulation decreases firms' expected returns from R&D investments; in other words, it shifts the MEI curve inward, which in turn decreases the pharmaceutical firm's optimal R&D investment. Furthermore, the decrease in returns from investing in R&D decreases the firm's profit margin, thereby reducing the internal funds available to the firm for investments of all types.

The cost of capital from internal funds may be lower than that from external funds, such as debt and equity (the latter from issuing new stock in the company). To the extent that this is so, public policies that have the effect of reducing firm profitability can reduce retained earnings and lower investments in R&D.

When the cost of internal funds is lower than the cost of external funds, the slope of the COC is positive. Showing this in the framework of figure 9.1 would require that we draw the COC with a positive slope. Price regulation would then shift the COC curve upward and to the left, leading firms to invest less in R&D than before price constraints were imposed. Combining these two effects, it is apparent that price regulation provides a disincentive for pharmaceutical innovation.

Several studies have documented an empirical relationship between price regulation and investment in pharmaceutical R&D. Using a panel data set with data on fourteen large pharmaceutical firms in the world for the period 1994–1997, Vernon (2005) estimated the effects of expected profitability and cash flow on R&D investment intensity, as measured by the ratio of R&D expenditures to total sales.

His empirical analysis yielded three important findings. First, both pharmaceutical profit expectations and lagged cash flows had significant positive impacts on the amount firms invest in R&D. Lagged cash flow is the amount of revenue over cost accruing to the company in the previous period. Second, the mean pre-tax pharmaceutical profit margin in a nonregulated (the US) market was approximately four to five times as large as that in regulated (non-US) markets. Third, simulations revealed that R&D investment would decline by 23–33 percent if the United States adopted pharmaceutical price regulation.

Giaccotto, Santerre, and Vernon (2005) used US industry-level data for the years 1952–2001 to estimate the relationship between real drug prices and R&D investment. They found that real drug prices (drug prices relative to the consumer price index for all goods and services) had a significant positive impact on R&D investment. The elasticity estimate of about 0.6 implies that a 10 percent increase in real drug prices leads to a 6 percent increase in pharmaceutical R&D investment.

In addition to the direct effect on a firm's R&D investment behavior, price regulation adversely affects incentives for pharmaceutical innovation indirectly through its impact on market competition. Several studies have shown that drug price regulation leads to a downward-sloping price curve over the drug's life cycle—prices fall as more time from the date of drug introduction elapses (Danzon and Chao 2000b; Ekelund and Persson 2003). Regulatory pressure on prices over the product life cycle may provide a disincentive for the pharmaceutical firm to develop new products with important therapeutic gains. Pharmaceutical firms based in countries with substantial regulation of pharmaceutical prices tend to focus on quick but minor innovations, such as introducing line extension through a stream of minor new products (e.g., new dosage forms) in order to obtain a higher price on the new products.

Grabowski and Wang (2006) used global new chemical entities (NCEs) and first-in-class NCEs to measure the importance of pharmaceutical innovation. They defined global NCEs as those introduced in at least four of the G7 countries (Canada, France, Germany, Italy, Japan, the UK, and the United States), the world's largest pharmaceutical markets. They defined first-in-class NCEs as the first NCE in a therapeutic class.

They found that global NCEs accounted for over half of all NCE launches in the United States during 1982–2003, and first-in-class NCEs accounted for about a fifth of all NCE launches in the United States during the same period (table 9.2). By contrast, the shares of global NCEs and first-in-class NCEs were only about 10 percent and 3 percent, respectively, in Italy and Japan, implying that pharmaceutical innovation is retarded in countries with price regulation.

Table 9.2
Output of Pharmaceutical Innovation by Country, 1982–2003

	Number of New Chemical Entities (NCEs)			Share in Total NCEs (%)	
Country	All NCEs	Global NCEs	First-in-Class NCEs	Global NCEs	First-in-Class NCEs
European countries					
France	53	20	5	37.7	9.4
Germany	95	48	10	50.5	10.5
Italy	43	5	1	11.6	2.3
Switzerland	83	56	19	67.5	22.9
UK	70	50	13	71.4	18.6
Other countries					
Japan	205	24	8	11.7	3.9
United States	272	147	54	54.0	19.9
Rest of world	20	4	2	20.0	10.0
Total	912	385	116	42.2	12.7

Source: Grabowski and Wang (2006).

Furthermore, price regulation reduces incentives for innovation through its impact on the launch delay of new drugs. Based on a sample of NCE launches between 1994 and 1998 in 85 major markets, Danzon, Wang, and Wang (2005) found that the expected price of a new product in a country significantly affects the timing and occurrence of a launch in that country. Countries with lower expected prices tend to have fewer launches and longer launch delays. Such delays and fewer launches of new drugs or no launch reduce expected revenues that the firm can recoup from its R&D investment, thus lowering its incentive to invest in pharmaceutical R&D.

9.2 PRICING OF NEW DRUGS

RATIONALE FOR PATENTS AND PUBLIC POLICY TRADE-OFFS

A patent is an exclusive right to use of knowledge of a new chemical structure, which in turn allows pharmaceutical manufacturers to have a monopoly on their new products for a fixed period of time to allow them to recoup their investments from the monopoly profit. The outcome of pharmaceutical R&D is knowledge about a new chemical structure. Once the new drug is marketed and available to potential competitors as well as patients, it is a relatively easy matter for a competitor to learn the chemical structure and develop a copy. A low cost of imitation implies a low cost of entry into the market for the product. Competition from imitators reduces the product's price. Thus, an innovator could not generally recoup the cost of R&D investment without patent protection.

Compared to the high R&D cost per new NCE, the estimated cost of bringing imitative products (generic drugs) to the market is less than 1 percent of the R&D investment outlay incurred by the initial NCE developer (Reiffen and Ward 2005). The generic imitator does not need to undertake many of the same safety and efficacy tests as the innovator to gain regulatory agency approval. Under the current regulation in many countries, the primary requirement for generic manufacturers is that they demonstrate the bioequivalence of a drug to the innovator's product.

The very large difference in the fixed cost of bringing a new product to market between innovators and imitators implies that patents are an important incentive for pharmaceutical R&D (fig.9.5). As emphasized above, the cost of developing new pharmaceutical products is substantial. Once these products are developed, receive government approval, and are marketed, the high R&D expenditures become a fixed or sunk cost. The substantial high fixed cost leads to a decline in average unit cost per unit of output (AC) as firms increase the quantity of output. Compared to the high fixed cost, the marginal cost of producing, packaging, and distributing an additional batch of product tends to be quite low, much less than the AC. The marginal cost curve (MC) is a flat line and lies below a negatively sloped AC curve.

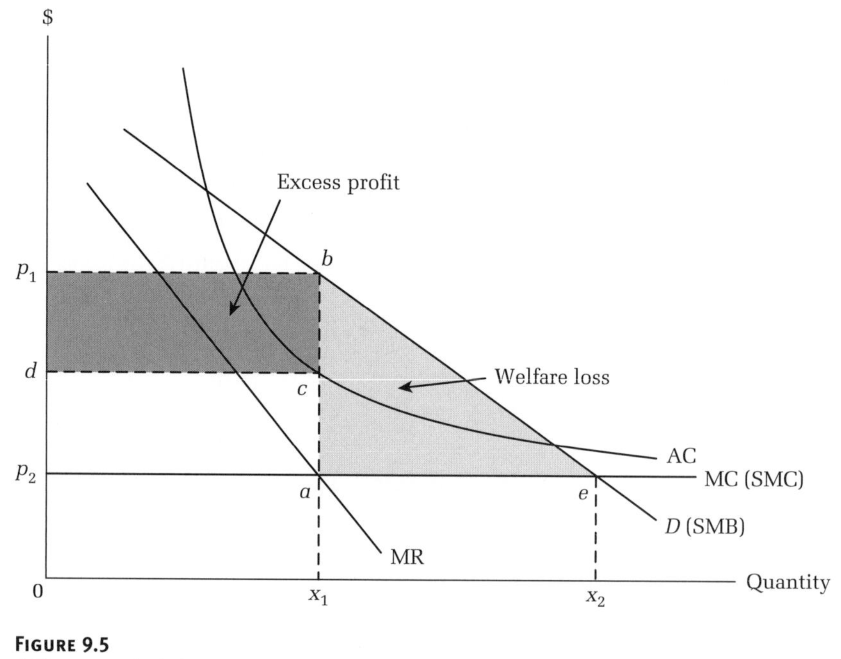

Figure 9.5
A Pharmaceutical Firm's Cost Structure and Pricing

Let *D* be the demand curve. Marginal revenue corresponding to the *D* curve is represented by MR curve. Under the patent system, innovators possess market power to set product price. To pursue maximum profit, the innovator sets its optimal quantity of output at the output level where marginal revenue equals marginal cost, which is x_1. The innovator then prices the new drug at p_1. Since p_1 exceeds average unit cost at x_1, the innovator earns a profit per unit of output, the vertical distance between points *b* and *c*. The profit that accrues to the innovator is the area of the rectangle p_1bcd.

This pharmaceutical research firm recoups its R&D cost from this profit, which creates the incentive for innovation. Monopoly pricing achieves dynamic efficiency—which means that there are adequate financial incentives for firms to undertake those R&D investments for products for which patient willingness to pay in the aggregate exceeds the full cost of bringing the products to market, including the cost of R&D investments.

However, monopoly pricing limits the use of the drug below the socially optimal rate of use and hence creates a loss in social welfare. At the monopoly price, there are consumers with a willingness to pay (as shown by market demand curve *D*) in excess of the marginal cost of producing the good. Thus, there is a welfare loss, equal to the area of triangle *abe*.

At a given point in time, pharmaceutical technology is fixed. The optimal allocation of resources in the short-run, or the output level consistent with static efficiency, is at the output at which marginal social benefit (SMB) from consuming the drug equals the marginal social cost (SMC) of producing, packaging, and distributing the drug. In the absence of externalities, static efficiency can be achieved by competition which drives the price of new drugs down to marginal cost, p_2, where social marginal benefit (*D* curve) and social marginal cost (MC curve) are equal. However, since p_2 is below the average unit cost corresponding to quantity of output x_2, this competitive price does not allow firms to recoup their R&D investment outlays.

The above analysis suggests that the cost structure of innovative firms, in combination with the patent protection that provides a legal barrier preventing entry by imitative firms, creates a time inconsistency problem in pricing new pharmaceutical products. There is a trade-off between static efficiency (in the short run) and dynamic efficiency (in the long run). On the one hand, patents allow firms to charge prices for new drugs at monopoly levels, which provides an incentive for innovative firms to develop new products. On the other hand, if competitively set prices are the ideal and the relevant reference point, there is a welfare loss from monopoly pricing. Thus, there is a trade-off between preserving incentives for innovation, on the one hand, and reducing the welfare loss by removing barriers to generic competition on the other.

During the period of patent protection, only one firm produces the drug based on a specific set of chemical ingredients. However, while such patent protection is a source of market power, it is incorrect to infer that the patent holder necessarily possesses monopoly power in its market. The reason is that, in general, a particular disease (e.g., diabetes, depression) can be treated by various drugs that, although differing in precise chemical composition, have similar therapeutic properties.

For example, several drugs are designed to lower blood glucose levels of persons diagnosed with diabetes. There are also several antidepressants. An antidepressant on patent competes with other patented antidepressants and many other generic antidepressants whose patents have expired. A patent is for a specific combination of chemicals embodied in a product. Drugs in the same therapeutic category, say, antidepressants, but with different chemical compositions compete with one another.

Because of differences in chemical composition and genetic differences among patients, there may be a better match between drug and patients for some drugs in a therapeutic category than for others. Match is measured in terms of therapeutic effectiveness (did the patient get better?) and lack of adverse side effects (did the patient suffer adverse outcomes attributable to use of the drug, e.g., dry mouth for some antidepressants?). Or several drugs within the therapeutic category may match well and others not so well. Since the interactions between patients and drugs vary appreciably among patients, it can be a major task for a physician to find a good match between the patient and the drug. Price is one factor, but the quality of the match is also a major determinant of drug choice.

Most branded drugs face some competition. Using a sample consisting of 148 new branded drugs introduced into the US market, Lu and Comanor (1998) found that all but 13 had at least one competitor within the same therapeutic category; the mean number of competitors was 1.86. These findings imply that the market structure of branded drugs with patent protection more closely resembles a differentiated oligopoly than a pure monopoly.

An oligopolist has few competitors, which are easily identified by all sellers in a market. Oligopolists' strategies are interdependent. Relevant strategies include pricing and advertising. It does make a difference to an individual oligopolist's product demand, for example, if competitors follow its price decrease or keep the price as it was.

While there are many competitors in a competitive market, such as farmers growing tomatoes, there are few pharmaceutical manufacturers that have a branded product in a particular therapeutic category. In setting prices, an oligopolist takes account of price changes its oligopolist competitors might make if the oligopolist were to change its price. By contrast, an individual tomato farmer has no control over price. The farmer's only choices (a nontrivial number) are how many tomatoes to grow, of which variety, and perhaps how much to invest in tomato growing, how often to water the plants, how much fertilizer to use, how to scare away the birds and insects, how much scaring to engage in, and so on. The farmer's strategy is based on anticipated outcomes for the market as a whole, not on the behavior of particular (other) farmers.

Pricing New Drugs: Empirical Evidence

A new drug's price is largely determined by demand conditions in the market. Such demand conditions include patients' valuations of the new drug and whether or not the new drug is covered by health insurance (see fig. 9.5). Only a few countries, such as the United States and Germany, allow pharmaceutical firms to set the prices of their new products. Thus, the empirical evidence on pricing new drugs comes from these two countries. In most countries, the government sets the prices of pharmaceutical products.

Lu and Comanor (1998) reported that the launch price of new drugs in the United States primarily reflects consumers' marginal valuations of the new drugs, not their marginal production cost. More specifically, pharmaceutical manufacturers adopt a "skimming strategy" to extract high prices from consumers willing to pay a lot for a new drug that represents a major therapeutic advance over existing competitive products. Manufacturers initially set the price of the new innovative drug two or three times higher than the price of the existing product. When competitors follow with innovative but similar new products of their own, the originators gradually reduce their price as these competitors enter into the market.

For example, consider the market for antidepressants. About two decades ago, manufacturers introduced antidepressant drugs called selective serotonin reuptake inhibitors (SSRIs). Before the introduction of the first SSRI, which was Eli Lilly Company's Prozac, other drugs, such as tricylics, were prescribed for depression; although effective, they had certain adverse side effects, such as causing dry mouth.

The SSRIs were a major therapeutic advance. However, over time, following Prozac, other companies introduced SSRIs, among them Zoloft and Paxil, which are not chemically identical to Prozac but are sufficiently similar to Prozac to be classified as SSRIs. While the older drugs competed with Prozac before the other SSRIs were introduced, the other SSRIs are closer substitutes for Prozac than the older drugs are.

By contrast, pharmaceutical companies often adopt a penetration strategy in pricing their new products that have little or no therapeutic advantages over existing products by setting launch prices at or below those of their substitutes. However, Lu and Comanor found that the mean real price increased substantially over time, presumably after the drugs became the drug of choice for a group of users. In the market for SSRIs, Prozac represented a major therapeutic advance. Zoloft and Paxil, while not identical to Prozac chemically and therefore possibly more effective and with fewer adverse side effects for some patients than Prozac (and vice versa), did not represent major therapeutic breakthroughs when they were introduced. Once an SSRI seems to work for a patient, physicians are reluctant to prescribe another SSRI. To change, the patient needs to gradually reduce the dosage of the currently prescribed SSRI and then take the new SSRI for a while to gauge its benefit. In this sense, once on an SSRI, a patient is "hooked" (not in the same sense as one is hooked on an illicit drug, but sufficiently so as to make the demand elasticity for the SSRI the patient is using quite inelastic).

Lu and Comanor also found that launch prices of drugs used to treat acute conditions, for example, anti-infectives, were set higher than those indicated for chronic illnesses, even after accounting for the degree of therapeutic advance. This evidence reinforces the previous finding that the launch price of new drugs depends primarily on consumers' marginal valuation of the products. Marginal valuations are high for new anti-infectives since many patients may have developed resistance to existing products.

Based on the data obtained from Germany, Pavcnik (2002) also found empirical evidence that the price of brand-name drugs is responsive to the change of demand conditions. Prior to 1989, prescription drugs were covered by statutory health insurance in Germany. Patients paid only a fixed prescription fee. In 1989, Germany introduced a reference pricing policy that imposes a maximum reimbursement price for a given product. The patient bears the excess cost out of pocket if the market price of the pharmaceutical product exceeds the maximum reimbursement. Because the consumer bears the amount above the reference price in full, implementing reference pricing should shift the demand curve for prescription drugs inward (relative to a policy in which insurance pays more for higher-priced drugs). As a result of the change to reference pricing, the markup of price over marginal cost declines.

The empirical results are consistent with this prediction. Pavcnik (2002) found that the pricing behavior of pharmaceutical firms is very sensitive to potential patient out-of-pocket expenses. On average, price declines following the change in statutory health insurance reimbursement ranged from 10 to 26 percent. In addition, Pavcnik found that price declines were more pronounced for brand-name products than for generics.

9.3 Entry of Generic Drugs and Its Consequences

Competition between Generic and Brand-Name Drugs

When a patent on a brand-name drug expires, generic drugs enter the market, resulting in competition between generic and brand-name drugs. The entry of generics raises three important issues related to drug pricing. First, how do imitative firms price their generic products? Second, how does the innovative firm, the producer of the brand-name drug, respond to the entry of generics? Third, how does the price regulation affect the competition between generic and brand-name drugs?

Several empirical studies have studied the pricing behavior of firms with generic products. Caves, Whinston, and Hurwitz (1991) reported that the launch price of generic products in the United States ranges from 40 to 70 percent of the price of the brand-name drug before the patent expired. Subsequently, the price of generic products declines as more generic products enter the market.

For example, the authors found that the generic price fell to about 29 percent of its pre-patent expiration price ("base price") when there were 10 competitors in the market. As the number of competitors increased to twenty, the generic price was set at only about 17 percent of the base price.

Empirical results of recent studies are consistent with this finding, indicating that generic firms set lower prices when there are more competitors. The price of generic drugs at two years after entry declined to 54 percent of the original price level at the date of entry (table 9.3). Thus, based on both theory and empirical evidence, the long-run equilibrium price of a generic product approaches the product's marginal cost (see, e.g., Reiffen and Ward 2005).

Firms with branded products adopt an entirely different pricing strategy. Both Caves, Whinston, and Hurwitz (1991) and Grabowski and Vernon (1992) found that

TABLE 9.3
Effects of Generic Entry on the US Pharmaceutical Market

	At Date of Entry	One Year after Entry	Two Years after Entry
Average brand-name price index	1.00	1.05	1.09
Average generic price index	1.00	0.67	0.54
Average generic-to-brand price ratio	0.68	0.43	0.33
Average generic market share in physical units (proportion of total market)	0.20	0.64	0.73

Note: The drugs include ten major 1992–1993 drugs. Each value is an unweighted average of the values for all drugs in each category.
Source: Viscusi, Harrington, and Vernon (2005), table 24.1.

the prices of the original branded drug remained constant or even increased slightly after a generic's entry. Based on a sample of ten major drugs in the United States, table 9.3 shows that the mean price of brand-name drugs rose 9 percent two years after generic entry. The reason is that the market becomes segmented as the generic products enter the market. Price-sensitive consumers shift to generic products, and price-insensitive consumers continue using the brand-name drugs, even after patent expiration. The brand-loyal consumers may believe that the branded drug is better than the generic even though they are chemically identical, perhaps because the branded seller has better quality control. When the price elasticity for a product is lower, the price is higher.

With generic prices declining sharply and branded price rising slightly over time, the ratio of generic to brand-name prices should decrease over time. At date of generic drug entry, this ratio was 0.68. Two years after generic entry, this ratio declined to 0.33 (table 9.3).

However, the story does not end here. Hurwitz and Caves (1988) reported that the branded firm lost more market share after generic entry when the price difference between branded and generic drugs was higher. Generic firms on average gained about 20 percent of market share at entry. Two years after entry, generic market share increased to about 73 percent (table 9.3).

The above empirical findings come from the United States, where firms can freely set prices for their pharmaceutical products. Danzon and Chao (2000b) obtained evidence that price regulation undermines generic competition in regulated markets, such as in France, Italy, and Japan. In these three countries, there is little association between drug prices and the number of generic competitors. This implies that a fixed regulated price serves to protect a generic firm from the adverse effects of competition from other generic firms on its product prices. In other words, under drug price regulation, there is no direct market pressure to lower prices as additional generic firms enter the market.

In addition, several empirical studies have demonstrated that the prices of branded drugs tend to fall substantially over time in markets subject to price regulation. Thus, in a regulated market, the seller of a brand-name drug has no latitude in affecting price through any competitive strategy (Ekelund and Persson 2003).

Combining the above two stylized facts from regulated markets, the price difference between brand-name and generic drugs in a regulated market is small and remains almost constant over time. By contrast, in a market in which pharmaceutical manufacturers are price makers, the real price of branded drugs may rise over time and the price of generic drugs may decline sharply as more generic drugs enter the market. Thus, in a free market, the price difference between brand-name and generic drugs is large at one point in time and increases over time as compared to a regulated market.

For example, in the United States, the average generic-to-brand price ratio declines to about 0.3 over three years after the first generic entry (Saha, Grabowski, Birnbaum, et al. 2006). However, in a regulated market such as Taiwan, the average generic-to-brand price ratio is about 0.70–0.85 (Liu, Yang, and Hsieh 2009).

Factors Affecting Generic Competition

Four factors are important determinants of the extent of generic competition: (1) the cost of generic entry, (2) the expected profit from generic entry, (3) public policies allowing generic substitution, and (4) incentives for generic substitution among consumers, physicians, and pharmacists.

The cost of generic entry is the most important determinant of generic competition (Grabowski 2007). Before enactment of the Hatch-Waxman Act of 1984, a generic firm in the United States had to undertake many of the same safety and efficacy tests as the branded firm did to gain the government approval for marketing its product. The high cost of new clinical trials served to deter market entry of generic drugs. As a result, about two-thirds of brand-name drugs with large sales whose patents had expired had no generic competitors in the early 1980s.

The Hatch-Waxman Act established an Abbreviated New Drug Application (ANDA) for generic firms, which allows generic firms to rely on the safety and efficacy clinical trial data of the brand-name drug. Thus, the primary current requirement for generic firms to secure approval for generic entry is to demonstrate that their drugs are the bioequivalents of the branded products. This statute greatly reduced the cost of generic entry. Consequently, the entry of generics into the US market increased rapidly after 1984. The market share (based on drug quantities) of generic drugs rose from 19 percent in 1984 to 51 percent in 2002 (Grabowski 2007).

Since producers of generic drugs, like producers of brand-name drugs, are organized as for-profit enterprises, it is not surprising that generic entry is more likely in markets with larger expected revenues or higher profit margins. Several studies have shown that the number of generic entrants significantly depends on the profit margins earned by firms with branded products.

Specifically, generic firms are more likely to enter markets for chronic conditions with large sales. In addition, generic entry was positively related to the precompetition sales revenue received by the branded firm (Grabowski and Vernon 1992; Morton and Scott 1999; Morton 2000). Danzon and Chao (2000b) also found that low regulated prices for branded products at the time of patent expiration discourage market entry of generics in regulated markets.

The third factor affecting the extent of generic competition relates to whether or not institutional arrangements, embodied in law, public regulation, or custom, permit generic substitution. With generic substitution as practiced in the United States, the physician writes a prescription for a brand-name drug, such as Paxil. Unless the physician specifies otherwise, the pharmacist can substitute the generic drug equivalent if it is available.

In many Asian countries, such as China, Japan and Taiwan, physicians both prescribe *and* dispense drugs. Thus, they are in a position to profit directly from the sale of prescription drugs. This system, in combination with government regulation of the reimbursement price for prescription drugs, allows physicians to capture the profit margin, the difference between the selling price and the acquisition price from the wholesale market. Given this arrangement, physician prescription decisions do not reflect drug price differences but rather differences in drug profit margins. This in turn forces pharmaceutical manufacturers to compete in the wholesale market by cutting price below the selling price or the price that physicians receive from health insurance when they prescribe the drug. Manufacturers can induce physicians to switch prescriptions to their drugs by increasing the profit margin offered to dispensing physicians (Danzon and Chao 2000b; Iizuka 2007). Under this system, the only motivation for generic substitution is if generic firms offer higher profit margins to physicians than those for branded drugs. This is highly likely given that the entry (fixed) cost of generic drugs is far lower than for brand-name drugs. Liu, Yang, and Hsieh (2009) found evidence that obtaining a profit, the difference between the reimbursement amount and the acquisition price, has provided a major inducement for generic substitution in Taiwan.

In Western countries, by contrast, the separation of prescribing and dispensing drugs has long been accepted practice. Since physicians typically prescribe by brand rather than by chemical name, generic substitution is possible only if the law expressly allows pharmacists to substitute generics for branded counterparts. For example, in the United States, by the 1990s, all states had enacted substitution laws that authorized pharmacists to substitute generic equivalents unless the prescribing physician took specific steps to prohibit substitution, such as explicitly writing "dispense as written." By contrast, in other countries, such as France and Italy, generic substitution by pharmacists is not permitted (Danzon and Chao 2000b; Grabowski 2007).

Given that the prices of generic products are lower than those of their branded counterparts, health insurers have a strong incentive to encourage generic substitution when permissive substitution laws permit this. In the United States, for example, health insurers have designed explicit incentives to increase utilization of generic drugs. Many health insurers offer incentives to consumers to increase the utilization of generic drugs by using a three-tiered cost-sharing approach. Under such an arrangement, the insurer imposes co-payments per prescription on its insured patients, and the amount of the co-payment varies with the tier of formulary system (see chapter 3).

Health insurers also provide various incentives to influence physicians' prescribing behavior. Among these, the most powerful incentive to enhance physicians' willingness to comply with formularies is to provide physicians with financial incentives to avoid drug spending in excess of a certain amount. In addition, some insurers pay higher dispensing fees if pharmacists dispense generic drugs instead of their branded counterparts (Grabowski 2007). Health insurers, such as managed care organizations, by affecting physicians' incentives, can have a major influence on the growth in use of generic products. In particular, Saha, Grabowski, Birnbaum, et al. (2006) found empirical evidence that the growth of enrollments in managed care plans in the United States markedly increased the market share of generic products, after controlling for other influences on demand for and supply of generic products.

Consequences of Generic Competition

Given that the prices of generic products are lower than those of brand-name drugs, the use of generic products is generally cost saving. The amount of cost savings, however, depends on the price difference between branded and generic drugs. As seen above, this price differential is larger in unregulated pharmaceutical markets than in markets in which prices are regulated. Thus, in an unregulated market, generic competition generates significant cost savings to health insurers and hence is an effective policy tool for cost containment.

Another important consequence of generic competition is its impact on pharmaceutical innovation. Pricing new drugs by the criterion of static efficiency does not preserve incentives for pharmaceutical innovation, although it removes the welfare loss from monopoly pricing (see discussion of fig. 9.5 above). It is consequently very tempting for public decision makers in small countries to focus on static efficiency, that is, not providing adequate financial incentives for R&D, since they perceive that their policies will not affect the development of new products. Policy makers with short time horizons in larger countries may be similarly tempted. Therefore, a key policy challenge is how to achieve an appropriate balance between static efficiency, which reflects short-term benefits from greater price competition, and dynamic efficiency, which also reflects long-term benefits from appropriate incentives for innovation. Generic competition provides an approach for achieving such policy balance.

Generic competition in unregulated markets often leads to a large decline in sales of brand-name drugs within a very short period, which in turn reduces pharmaceutical R&D investment (Grabowski 2007). A decrease in the expected revenue of R&D output decreases the incentive to invest in pharmaceutical R&D. However, under the current patent system, generic entry is an expected outcome following patent expiration. Thus, the threat of generic competition consequently forces firms manufacturing branded products (those still under patent) to implement various strategic responses in advance of patent expiration, especially on their important products, such as investing in new products and maintaining a healthy pipeline of products under development. This suggests that market pressure arising from generic competition is a key incentive for pharmaceutical innovation. The decline in generic competition resulting from price regulation weakens incentives for such innovation.

In short, generic entry promotes market competition, which in turn may outweigh the effect of revenue loss and provide a positive incentive for pharmaceutical manufacturers to increase investment in R&D. Therefore, in an unregulated market, generic competition potentially can achieve a good balance between static and dynamic efficiency. By contrast, in a regulated market, price regulation undermines generic competition, which in turn reduces the favorable effects of generic competition on pharmaceutical innovation.

9.4 ADVERTISING

A key attribute of the pharmaceutical market is imperfect information about the effectiveness of particular drugs. Patients often lack sufficient information to know when specific drugs are appropriate for treatment. Therefore, physicians act as front-line professional agents, making consumption decisions on behalf of patients. Prescription drugs, in contrast to drugs purchased by consumers "over-the-counter," require a prescription from a physician, by definition.

However, even physicians may have difficulty in gauging the value of specific drugs in absolute terms and relative to their cost. One reason is that patients with a particular diagnosis tend to be heterogeneous, both with respect to the severity of their disease and in their genetic makeup. Especially because of genetic differences, drugs often work differently on different people, and the adverse side effects of drugs differ as well. People even differ on how willing they are to tolerate adverse side effects as a trade-off for a particular therapeutic gain.

Some people, for example, are very intolerant of the discomfort that may accompany taking a particular drug. Others are quite tolerant of discomfort, which they are willing to bear as a trade-off for getting better. Some may suffer little discomfort, while others face substantial discomfort from taking the same drug.

Another source of physician ignorance is the large number of new drugs introduced annually. It is difficult for individual physicians to keep up with therapeutic gains, adverse side effects, and prices of so many new drugs. Information on whether the quality of a new product exceeds the quality of an older one in its therapeutic class on average is often lacking. At least as of the 1990s, and we know of no objective evidence that the situation has markedly changed since then, there were few objective head-to-head comparisons of specific drugs (Sloan, Whetten-Goldstein, and Wilson 1997).

In a head-to-head comparison, effectiveness and adverse side effects of specific drugs are compared. By contrast, in a drug randomized, controlled trial (RCT), the drug is compared against either no drug treatment or an existing drug treatment, but not against the full set of pharmaceutical alternatives that a physician considers when making a choice of drug for a particular patient.

One reason for the lack of head-to-head comparisons is that such comparisons are often expensive to make, and public regulatory authorities do not typically require them. Long-term effects, either favorable or adverse, cannot be known from RCTs that precede regulatory approval. In addition, other applications of new drugs are often discovered following a drug's initial introduction. For example, a drug that helps prevent osteoporosis in women may be found to be useful in preventing breast cancer.

Over time, physicians gain knowledge about patterns of heterogeneity among individual patients, both beneficial and adverse effects. Some amount of individualized learning on the part of patients and their physicians occurs (Crawford and Shum 2005), but this learning process can be costly in terms of health and the use of health care resources.

In response to the lack of information on quality, pharmaceutical manufacturers rely on various forms of marketing and advertising to disseminate the quality information on specific drugs to physicians, such as sending sales representatives to visit physicians in their offices and provide them with oral explanations of the drug's beneficial effects as well as written promotional materials and free samples.

In two countries, the United States and New Zealand, pharmaceutical companies are allowed to advertise their products directly to consumers (Berndt and Donohue 2008). In general, however, physicians are the targets of drug advertising. The following section analyzes the pharmaceutical firm's incentive to spend resources on marketing, the composition of such marketing efforts, and their effects.

Companies' Incentives to Allocate Funds to Marketing

In many countries, prescription drugs are one of the most heavily promoted products. For example, in 1996, US pharmaceutical firms spent 14.2 percent of their sales revenue on product promotion (table 9.4). In 2003, they spent 17.1 percent.

TABLE 9.4
Advertising Intensity of Prescription Drugs and Its Composition: US Pharmaceutical Manufacturers

Promotion Expenditures and Promotion Expenditures by Expenditure Type	1996	2003
Promotion expenditure as % of sales	14.2	17.1
Composition of promotion expenditures (% of total promotion expenditures)		
Detailing	32.8	20.4
Retail value of free samples	53.5	63.4
Medical journal advertising	5.0	1.7
Direct-to-consumer advertising (DTCA)	8.6	14.5
DTCA advertising spending (in billions of US$)	0.84	3.55

Source: Berndt (2007), tables 9.1 and 9.2.

As a profit maximizer, a pharmaceutical manufacturer expends marketing resources up to the point at which the incremental net revenue from sales resulting from the additional advertising expense equals that expense. Based on this condition, a classic paper showed that in equilibrium, the ratio of the optimal advertising expenditure (A) to sales (S) satisfies the following relationship (Dorfman and Steiner 1954):

$$A/S = E_a[(p - MC)/p] = E_a/E_p, \tag{9.1}$$

where E_a is the advertising elasticity of demand, indicating the percentage change of the quantity demand in corresponding to a given percentage change in advertising expenditure; p is the product price; MC is the marginal cost; $(p - MC)/p$ is the price-cost margin, which is equal to $1/E_p$; and E_p is the absolute value of the price elasticity of demand.

Equation 9.1 implies that firms allocate a larger share of their resources to advertising when (1) the price-cost margin is higher, (2) the advertising elasticity of demand is higher, and (3) the price elasticity of demand is lower. This equation is useful for explaining why pharmaceutical manufacturers allocate a relatively large share of their resources to advertising.

First, as discussed above, by conferring market power on firms, patent protection enables firms to price their products much above marginal cost. This high price-cost margin mainly reflects a combination of a high fixed (R&D) cost and a low marginal (production and distribution) cost. Therefore, compared to other industries, the price-cost margin in the pharmaceutical industry is very high. This high price-cost margin gives pharmaceutical manufacturers a major incentive to allocate resources to advertising. Given the low marginal cost of output in this sector, pharmaceutical companies have a strong incentive to shift the demand curves for their products outward by advertising.

Second, drug advertising and detailing to physicians are important for informing physicians as drug prescribers about the availability of particular branded products and about their attributes (and scientific evidence on these attributes). Direct-to-consumer advertising is aimed at making the consumer aware of the product so that consumers can ask their physicians if the drug is appropriate for them (Berndt and Donohue 2008).

Third, expenditures on prescription drugs are often covered by health insurance, especially in high-income countries. An effect of health insurance coverage is to reduce the price elasticity of demand for prescription drugs. The price elasticity of demand for prescription drugs ranges from –0.1 to –0.2, indicating that a 10 percent increase in out-of-pocket payment leads to a decrease in the quantity of prescription drugs of only 1–2 percent (Berndt 2007). For this reason, growth in insurance coverage for prescribed drugs should greatly increase pharmaceutical company spending on advertising.

COMPOSITION OF PHARMACEUTICAL COMPANY MARKETING

The promotional efforts of pharmaceutical manufacturers have traditionally targeted physicians. Such efforts include advertising in medical journals, the provision of free samples to physicians, and detailing—one-on-one encounters between pharmaceutical sales representatives and individual physicians.

However, beginning in the 1990s, increased pressure for drug cost containment led pharmaceutical manufacturers to target consumers directly in drug promotion in the two countries that permit it. One motive for direct-to-consumer advertising (DTCA) is to encourage physicians to prescribe drugs that are on the list of drugs covered by the insurance plan, that is, on the plan's formulary. The other motive is a bit more indirect. If in response to DTCA, patients ask physicians sufficiently often about a drug not on the formulary, this will create pressure for its inclusion (Scherer 2000). Other reasons for the growth of DTCA include increased consumer empowerment, growth in insurance coverage of prescription drugs, and the baby boom cohort becoming older and experiencing identifiable symptoms treatable with prescription drugs (Berndt 2002).

The marketing practices of pharmaceuticals have changed in recent years with growth in DTCA and declines in such promotional expenses as on detailing (table 9.4). In 1996, drug manufacturers on average allocated about one-third of their promotional expenditures to detailing. By 2003, the share was about a fifth of promotional expenditures. Similarly, the share of promotional expenditure spent on medical journal advertising decreased from 5 percent in 1996 to slightly less than 2 percent by 2003. By contrast, the share of promotional expenditure spent on DTCA increased from nearly 9 percent in 1996 to nearly 15 percent in 2003.

DETAILING AND ITS EFFECTS

Except for the free sample provision to physicians, the largest component of marketing is detailing to physicians (table 9.4). *Detailing* mainly consists of marketing efforts to differentiate the detailer's product from its competitors' in product attributes other than price, such as evidence of drug efficacy, frequency of dosage per day, adverse interactions with other drugs, other adverse side effects, and indications for which the regulatory agency has granted approval of the drug. Detailing also seeks to promote brand loyalty among those prescribers already using the product. The quantity and quality of the new products affect the amount of detailing that firms conduct, which serves to emphasize the role of information provision in detailing.

Berndt, Bui, Reiley, et al. (1995) conducted an empirical analysis that revealed that both detailing to physicians and medical journal advertising raise both market demand and market share (relative to incumbents'). Also, DTCA has a positive impact on market demand, although the estimated elasticity is relatively small. The sum of those three marketing elasticities (E_a) is 0.76, indicating that a 10 percent increase in cumulative marketing information stock leads to a 7.6 percent increase in the market demand. Among the channels of marketing efforts they studied, Berndt and co-authors found that detailing to physicians is most effective, with an elasticity estimate of 0.55, which accounted for about 72 percent (0.55/0.76) of the overall effect of marketing on demand.

DIRECT-TO-CONSUMER ADVERTISING AND ITS EFFECTS

Although the importance of DTCA has increased, not every firm in the two countries that permit it has selected DTCA as a promotional strategy. Berndt (2007) reported that only 18 percent of the 391 major branded-drug companies marketing in the United States allocated any funds to DTCA, and expenditures on DTCA were highly concentrated on about twenty products. DTCA spending is targeted to specific therapeutic classes and drugs. DTCA intensity varies widely among therapeutic classes, from relatively low for antidepressants to relatively high for nasal sprays. Based on panel data obtained on 169 drugs and 21 therapeutic classes during 1996–1999, Iizuka (2004) found that DTCA spending is positively associated with potential market size and drug quality (measured by whether or not the drug is a major therapeutic advance over the existing drugs) but negatively associated with the vintage of drugs and the entry of generic drugs. Conceptually, the elasticity of sales with respect to advertising (E_a) is greater for higher-quality products and products with a larger potential market size. By contrast, advertising elasticities decline as drugs age and generic products enter the market. Hence, empirical findings are consistent with the equation 9.1's theoretical prediction that firms devote a relatively large share of their resources to advertising when the advertising elasticity is relatively high.

Overall, empirical research on DTCA indicates that the primary effect of DTCA spending is to increase aggregate market demand for products in a therapeutic category rather than to raise market shares of individual pharmaceutical products. Specifically, the empirical evidence shows that the advertising elasticity of DTCA spending is around 0.1, implying that a 10 percent increase in DTCA spending leads to a 1 percent increase in market demand. In addition, empirical research has found that DTCA has a significant positive effect on demand for prescription drugs by increasing the share of physician visits during which the drug is prescribed. By contrast, the same empirical research has shown that DTCA spending has no significant effect on the choice of medication (Berndt 2007).

In sum, the major impact of DTCA is to motivate individuals to visit their physicians. Once patients come to physicians' offices, prescription choice is still primarily determined by physicians. DTCA is effective in increasing market demand, but does not significantly influence brand choice and individual pharmaceuticals' market shares.

Given the evidence that DTCA leads to an increase in demand for prescription drugs, does DTCA improve patient welfare? Kravitz, Epstein, Feldman, et al. (2005) examined this issue using data from an RCT. This study yielded two important findings. First, DTCA mitigated undertreatment for patients visiting physicians with a major depressive disorder. Second, DTCA encouraged medically ambiguous and questionable utilization of antidepressant drugs for patients with adjustment disorders. Taken in combination, these results suggest that the expansion of market demand from DTCA may come from two sources: (1) reducing the undertreatment of serious illness and (2) increasing some overtreatment or possibly inappropriate treatment for patients with less severe symptoms. Thus, these findings, although limited to a single condition, suggest that the overall effect of DTCA on consumer welfare is ambiguous.

9.5 International Pricing

Cross-National Price Differentials

Cross-national differences in pharmaceutical prices have long been a source of controversy in the public policy arena. People in countries with relatively higher prices of drugs often argue that they are paying too much for these products. Studies have made cross-national drug price comparisons (Danzon and Chao 2000a; Furukawa 2007).

These studies show that not only does differential pricing for pharmaceuticals exist between high-income countries and low-income countries but there are appreciable differences in prices among high-income countries as well. For example,

Danzon and Chao (2000a) found that pharmaceutical prices on average in Germany were 25 percent higher than US prices, whereas prices in France were 32 percent lower on average, after accounting for variations in dosage and product mix across countries.

Price differences reflect influences from both the demand and the supply sides of the market. On the demand side, many countries regulate drug prices, emphasizing static over dynamic efficiency, for two reasons. First, a single country, especially a small one, can free ride on larger ones, paying only the marginal cost of drug production, packaging, and distribution and allowing others to pay the fixed R&D investment costs. Second, given the long lag time between R&D investment and the launch of a new product, it is easy to pay low prices in the short run and suffer the long-run consequences at a much later date (Danzon and Towse 2003).

Prices of branded products under patent tend to be lower in regulated markets, such as France and Italy, than in the major unregulated market, the United States (Danzon and Furukawa 2003). By contrast, market competition often forces the price of a generic product down to marginal cost in the unregulated market, while regulation undermines the generic competition. Thus, the prices of generic products in several regulated markets, such as Japan and Italy, are higher than in the United States.

On the other hand, even absent government regulation, pharmaceutical manufacturers as profit maximizers are motivated to engage in price discrimination across countries in order to increase their profits. There are two preconditions for price discrimination to occur: (1) markets must be separate with demand curves differing in their elasticities of demand, and (2) consumers must not be able to resell the product across markets.

The latter is automatically true of services, such as physician visits or hospital days, which cannot be resold. However, drugs are a good, not a service. Thus, resale across national boundaries is possible, but made more difficult by declaring resale illegal and enforcing the law. Elasticities of demand for pharmaceutical products are likely to differ because incomes differ among countries. Also health insurers have a major role in determining the price elasticity of demand for drugs. Assuming that these two conditions hold, an optimal pricing rule across markets satisfies the following condition:

$$(p^j - MC^j)/p^j = 1/E_p^j, \tag{9.2}$$

where p^j is the price in country j, MC^j represents the marginal cost; and E_p^j is the price elasticity of demand for pharmaceutical in country j. It is plausible that marginal cost is the same across countries. Thus, according to equation 9.2, firms set price differentials across countries that are inversely related to the demand elasticities for the product in these countries.

Several empirical studies have demonstrated that demand is more elastic in lower-income countries. Thus, price-discriminating firms tend to price their products lower in such countries and set a higher price in high-income countries.

THE CONSEQUENCES OF DIFFERENTIAL PRICING

Compared to uniform pricing of individual pharmaceutical products globally, differential pricing has had several important consequences. First, pharmaceutical manufacturers tend to sell more drugs with differential pricing than they would with uniform pricing. Under a uniform pricing rule, a profit-maximizing firm sets a price above the marginal cost, for example, p_1 in figure 9.6. This arrangement would price out many consumers in low-income countries who are willing to pay prices in excess of the marginal cost but not a price as high as p_1. Thus, the welfare of these consumers would increase if they could buy the product at a lower price, such as p_2 in figure 9.6. Pharmaceutical manufacturers would benefit from these additional sales as long as the lower price exceeded marginal cost and the markets could be separated. Hence, an important consequence of differential pricing across countries is increased access to pharmaceuticals for consumers in low-income countries, such as an increase in quantity of consumption from x_1 to x_2, as shown in figure 9.6. Based on a simulation by comparing the regimes of one price per

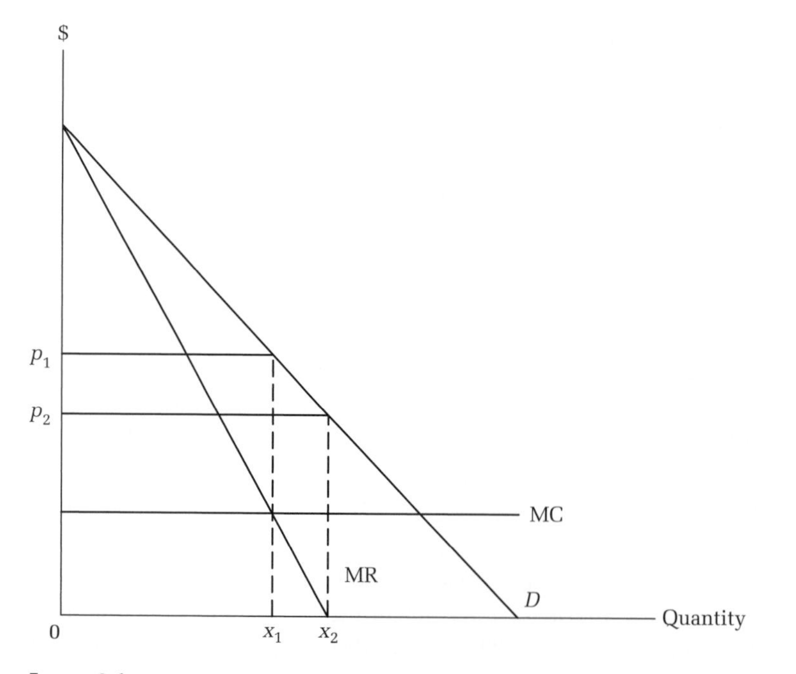

FIGURE 9.6
Uniform versus Differential Pricing

country and a single global price, Dumoulin (2001) found that differential pricing increases access to drugs by a factor of four to seven.

Second, although the differential pricing promotes consumer access to drugs, it also creates an incentive for parallel trade. Under parallel trade, a particular product is imported from one country by a second country and then exported to the first country and sold in the first country at a price below the price of the same product sold directly by the manufacturer in the first country. For example, suppose the price of a particular drug manufactured in the United States is lower in Canada than it is in the United States because the US pharmaceutical manufacturer exports the drug to Canada at a price lower than it sells the same product in the United States. Subsequently the drug is exported from Canada to the United States and sold in the United States at a price well below the price at which the drug is sold by the manufacturer in the United States.

The re-importation of the drug into the United States in turn puts downward pressure on the price of the drug in the United States, thus reducing the Canadian-US price differential that existed prior to reimportation. Pharmaceutical manufacturers clearly oppose this practice since it limits their ability to price discriminate.

Although the existence of parallel trade may increase the efficiency of the market in some sectors of the economy, there is no efficiency gain from parallel trade in the pharmaceutical market. The reason is that lower prices of pharmaceuticals in some countries do not stem from a comparative advantage in lower R&D investment cost or from higher productivity. Rather, the price differentials usually result from strict price regulation, lower product liability cost, lack of patent protection, or lower per capita income, factors that lead pharmaceutical manufacturers to set lower prices (Danzon and Towse 2003). Also, parallel trade may increase social costs through the extra costs paid for transportation, relabeling, and quality control. Despite these concerns, some countries permit the parallel trade of drugs. With parallel trade, the precondition of price discrimination that there is no resale of goods from low-priced to high-priced markets is violated. Overall, it seems likely that a threat of parallel trade would substantially limit cross-national differences in pharmaceutical prices.

Third, price differences across countries create an incentive for regulators to use drug prices in other countries as reference prices for regulating their domestic prices. This practice creates a negative externality to the extent that a lower price in low-income countries spills over to regulatory price setting in high-income countries. Many countries have formally adopted such "external referencing" in regulating drug prices, including Canada, Greece, Italy, Netherlands, and Taiwan. This external referencing erodes separation of markets, a precondition for price discrimination to occur across countries. In response to the threat of external referencing, pharmaceutical manufacturers tend to set a uniform price or narrow the range of price differentials across countries. For example, Danzon, Wang, and Wang

(2005) found that pharmaceutical manufacturers frequently have attempted to obtain a uniform launch price from member countries of the European Union, and there is a delay in launch or no launch at all in countries that do not permit this target price to be used.

Fourth, price differentials across countries create an illusion of inequity in allocating joint R&D investment costs, which in turn can become a source of friction in international relations. Some policy makers consider price differentials among countries resulting from price controls a barrier to free trade and hence attempt to use the threat of trade sanctions to force other countries to set drug prices higher (Reinhardt 2007). They often mistakenly assume that joint R&D costs should be allocated equally across all countries, at least among high-income countries. For this reason, lower prices prevailing in regulated markets often are interpreted as "cost shifting" from low-price to high-price countries or "unfair sharing" in allocating the R&D costs across countries. Therefore, the key to resolving controversies over price differentials across countries lies in finding a satisfactory solution for equitably sharing the costs of R&D investments among countries.

RAMSEY OPTIMAL PRICING

The central issue in the international pricing of pharmaceuticals involves allocation of the joint costs of R&D investments among countries. Although the first-best or fully efficient solution requires product pricing at marginal cost, this approach would provide a disincentive for companies to invest in new products. Danzon and Towse (2003) argued that Ramsey pricing, described below, provides a second-best solution for optimally allocating costs of investments in pharmaceutical R&D among countries. This second-best approach provides a balance between static efficiency in drug utilization and dynamic efficiency in drug innovation. In addition, this approach also satisfies concerns that the solution be an equitable one.

The following are two necessary conditions for achieving the second best solution:

$$p_j \geqq MC_j. \tag{9.3}$$

$$\Sigma(p_j - MC_j) \geqq F. \tag{9.4}$$

Inequality 9.3 states that price must be at least equal to marginal cost in each country. This condition ensures that the product will be supplied and the pricing will satisfy the static efficiency criterion that marginal benefit be greater than or equal to marginal cost. Inequality 9.4 states that the price-cost margins across countries are large enough when summed together to cover the global joint costs of R&D investment (F). This condition is a break-even condition for the firm and satisfies the dynamic efficiency criterion for investment in R&D.

Ramsey optimal pricing, named for its developer, Frank P. Ramsey (1927), has been widely used for many types of pricing decisions, such as government price regulation of public utilities. The pricing rule gives an equilibrium solution of pricing structure among countries or among markets within countries that maximizes social welfare subject to the two constraints in inequalities 9.3 and 9.4. The equilibrium pricing solution is the following:

$$(p_j - MC_j)/p_j = D/E_{jp}, \tag{9.5}$$

where D represents a profit constraint indicating that the rate of return must be at least equal to the cost of capital. Equation 9.5 indicates that the markup of price over marginal cost in country j is inversely proportional to the price elasticity of the demand for prescription drugs in country j. If the marginal cost is the same in all countries, the Ramsey optimal pricing solution suggests that prices should differ across countries in inverse relation to their demand elasticities.

The Ramsey optimal pricing rule in equation 9.5 is a second-best efficiency solution because it minimizes the welfare loss resulting from the deviation from the first-best outcome. It suggests prices be set at a low markup over marginal cost for more price-sensitive consumers, and vice versa.

The underlying rationale is that price-sensitive consumers would reduce their consumption by a larger proportion if the manufacturers were to charge a uniform price. Because consumers in low-income countries on average have more elastic demand, the Ramsey optimal pricing rule implies that prices should be lower in lower-income countries, and vice versa. This is also consistent with a widely accepted view of equity that cross-national drug prices should reflect cross-national differences in ability to pay (Reinhardt 2007).

Ramsey optimal pricing is very similar to the pricing rule adopted by a price-discriminating monopolist. Comparing price markups in equations 9.2 and 9.5, the only difference is the term for the profit constraint D. Thus, relative markups across countries are about the same under a profit-maximizing principle as under Ramsey pricing, but price levels may differ in absolute terms because the constrained profit may not be equal to the maximum profit. However, in the long run, entry and market competition may reduce the expected profits to normal levels at the margin. For this reason, price markups over marginal cost set by a profit-maximizing firm with some market power approximate Ramsey prices in the long run.

Empirical Evidence on Ramsey Pricing of Pharmaceuticals

Taking income as a proxy for the price elasticity of demand (elasticity falls with increases in income), Ramsey pricing predicts a positive relationship between the pharmaceutical price level and per capita income. Danzon and Furukawa (2003) tested this hypothesis by comparing mean price levels for pharmaceuticals in nine

TABLE 9.5
Pharmaceutical Price Indexes in Relation to Per Capita Income in Nine Countries

Country	GDP Per Capita (1999 US$)	GDP Index (US = 100)	Price Index[a] (US = 100)	Price to Income Index[b] (US = 100)
High-income countries				
United States	33,038	100	100	100
Canada	21,306	64	67	104
France	24,628	75	70	93
Germany	25,624	78	86	110
Italy	20,487	62	87	141
Japan	35,479	107	127	118
UK	24,874	75	94	125
Middle-income countries				
Chile	4,864	15	78	528
Mexico	4,976	15	80	529

Notes: a. Price indexes were calculated by molecule indication from a sample of 249 leading US molecules in 1999. b. Price index normalized by income = (Price index/GDP normalized to US) × 100.
Sources: Copyrighted and published by Project HOPE/*Health Affairs* as Exhibit 8 in Danzon and Furukawa (2003). The published article is archived and available online at www.healthaffairs.org.

countries: Canada, Chile, France, Germany, Italy, Japan, Mexico, the UK, and the United States. They used the "molecule-indication" as the unit of analysis and compared manufacturers' prices instead of retail prices in order to exclude the effect of wholesale pricing, retail markups, and taxes on cross-national price differences. They first calculated overall price indexes relative to US prices for the eight other countries. Foreign prices are lower (higher) than US prices if index values are less (greater) than 100. The authors computed price indexes ranging from 67 for Canada to 127 for Japan (table 9.5), which implies that Canada's prices are 33 percent lower than those in the United States and Japan's prices are 27 percent higher than US prices. They then normalized the overall price indexes by income. That is, the overall price index is divided by the ratio of GDP per capita to US GDP per capita (GDP normalized to US level).

Price indexes relative to GDP per capita population ranged from 93 to 141 among six high-income countries. By contrast, the value of the price indexes normalized by income was greater than 500 for two middle-income countries. This suggests that price differentials were correlated with income within the high-income countries (Canada, France, Germany, Italy, Japan, the UK, and the United States), but this relationship did not hold within the middle-income countries

(Chile and Mexico). Therefore, the prediction of Ramsey optimal pricing is only partially supported by the evidence obtained from high-income countries—drug price differentials among high-income countries being roughly proportional to income differentials. Cross-national price differentials among a wide range of countries with different income levels appear to deviate substantially from what might be expected from Ramsey pricing.

There are two plausible explanations for the weak relationship between per capita GDP and pharmaceutical prices. First, as discussed above, the threats of parallel trade and external referencing make the range of sustainable price differentials smaller than they would be absent these phenomena. Thus, manufacturers are reluctant to grant a relatively lower price to low- and middle-income countries. Many manufacturers prefer to choose the strategy of delaying the launch or not launching at all if the price is considered by manufacturers to be too low. Second, there is a highly unequal distribution of income in some low- and middle-income countries, which in turn creates market segments within countries. Hence, a small but high-income subgroup dominates potential pharmaceutical sales. With support from the market of the high-income subgroup, the pharmaceutical manufacturers tend to charge a higher price, one that is unaffordable to other segments of the population and incompatible with the mean per capita income of these countries (Danzon and Towse 2003).

The weak relationship between cross-national price differentials and global income differences implies there is a welfare loss for consumers in low-income countries. Consumers in low-income countries either face an unaffordable price or a delay in the launch of new drugs, or even no launch at all. Therefore, increasing price differentials among countries potentially could substantially improve access to drugs in such countries. However, a sustainable, broad-based differential pricing structure is possible only if high-income countries forgo the temptation to engage in parallel trade and external referencing.

9.6 Developing New Drugs: Rare Diseases and Diseases Prevalent in Low-Income Countries

Rewards as a Substitute for Patents: Overview

As mentioned above, firms' decision rule for deciding on R&D investment is based on profit maximization, not maximizing health gains; the allocation of resources to investments in R&D by pharmaceutical companies is guided by market demand (or ability to pay) rather than by health needs. In high-income countries, people are able and willing to pay more for good health than are those in middle- and low-income countries. For this reason, R&D expenditures are highly concentrated on prescription drugs that people in high-income countries demand.

By contrast, there is a substantial disparity between ability to pay and unrealized health benefits in lower-income countries. In such countries, not only is income low, but effective demand for disease prevention and therapy is also correspondingly low. Consequently, R&D investments on diseases that are highly prevalent in such countries, such as tropical diseases, are low or even negligible. For example, new molecular entities (NMEs) for the treatment of tropical diseases in humans accounted for less than 1 percent of all NMEs licensed worldwide during 1975–1997(Kremer and Glennerster 2004). This suggests that a market mechanism based on the patent system may not generate a sufficient incentive for pharmaceutical innovation in some areas. The cause of this market failure is a maldistribution of income.

There is another type of market failure that can lead to suboptimal vaccine R&D investment arising from external benefits in consumption. The social benefits of vaccines include not only internal benefits from disease prevention accruing to individuals who are vaccinated but also external benefits from preventing the spread of disease to others. Individuals' maximum willingness to pay for vaccines plausibly does not reflect those external benefits. Vaccines for major communicable diseases may have much larger social benefits than many drugs. Pharmaceutical companies tend to earn lower profits from vaccines than from drugs. Companies thus have a lesser incentive to discover and develop new vaccines because of the relatively low profit, although their potential value to population health may be very high.

As a result of low income in many countries and the external benefits of vaccines, researchers have investigated other mechanisms to stimulate pharmaceutical innovation when the patent system fails. One promising alternative is a system of rewards paid by the government or private foundations (hereinafter referred as sponsors) to pharmaceutical firms. Under the reward system, the property rights of the innovation are purchased by the sponsors in the form of rewards; sponsors in turn place the innovation in the public domain, making it available freely to competing manufacturers.

One of the practical issues faced by the reward system is how to decide on the size of the rewards. Theoretically, the problem is rather straightforward. One could compute the consumer surplus, assuming pricing at marginal cost and at the output at which the demand curve intersects the marginal cost curve. This simple reward system gives a company with a new drug a subsidy in the amount of consumer surplus from the sponsors as a reward to recoup its spending on R&D investment. The new pharmaceutical product in turn can be produced and sold in a competitive market by the innovator(s) at a competitive price.

Rewards have two advantages over patents. First, the sponsor can provide incentives for pharmaceutical R&D investment without granting the firms monopoly power over price and removing the legal barrier to entry to other firms. With rewards, new drugs can be sold at a price equal to marginal cost, which in turn reduces the welfare loss from patents, increases the accessibility of new drugs, and reduces the cost burden on health insurers. Second, sponsors can select the magnitude of research incentives by adjusting the level of rewards. For example, to the extent that there are consumption externalities, one would need to adjust for this since the consumer surplus as revealed by the market does not capture externalities. The maximum price would be the area of the adjusted (for externalities) consumer surplus divided by the socially optimal output (again accounting for externalities). Based on these two advantages, Shavell and Ypersele (2001) concluded that an optional rewards system, in which the firm can freely choose between rewards and patents, is superior to the patent system.

In practice, computing the maximum price or reward is more complex than this. For one, Garber, Jones, and Romer (2006) have cautioned that with insurance and moral hazard, the monopoly profit may exceed the relevant consumer surplus. The relevant surplus is calculated before insurance. Thus, it is conceivable that rewards to firms under the patent system are too high.

Also, the calculations involve new rather than existing products. Thus, many assumptions are required to obtain estimates of maximum prices or rewards. If rewards are set too low, incentives for innovation will be insufficient. However, there is also a risk that rewards may be set too high. If so, there will be too much investment in R&D (Comanor 2007).

The following subsections analyze three proposals that use the reward system to provide incentives to develop new drugs and vaccines for developing countries.

SPECIFIC PROPOSALS

ADVANCE PURCHASE COMMITMENTS

Kremer and Glennerster (2004) have proposed using an advance purchase commitment as an incentive to induce development of a malaria vaccine. The same approach is likely to be equally applicable as an incentive for promoting companies' investment in R&D on vaccines for other diseases highly prevalent in low-income countries or for pharmaceuticals designed for this purpose. This approach offers the innovator a subsidy of a fixed price per unit for a given number of units if the innovators develop a new vaccine that satisfies certain technical characteristics.

The rationale of this approach is to use the subsidy offered by the sponsors to close the gap between the high cost of investment in R&D for new vaccines and low ability to pay in low-income countries. Firms do not have an adequate incentive to invest in vaccine R&D because the sustainable market price (p) is insufficiently high to allow it to recoup the R&D cost (C). If the sponsor offers a subsidy in the amount of $C/quantity - p$ per unit up to a certain quantity, then the total revenue received by the innovator equals the revenue from the market plus the sponsor's subsidy, which together with the subsidy may be sufficient to cover the cost of the investment in R&D. In sum, advance purchase commitments increase expected revenues from investments in R&D without limiting the role of patents.

A principal difficulty with advance purchase commitments, however, concerns the sponsor's need to specify the desired and feasible technical characteristics of a vaccine that has not yet been developed. This difficulty in turn creates two distortions in incentives for R&D investment (Hollis 2007). First, firms lack incentives to develop new products exceeding technical specifications set by sponsors. Therefore, it provides no incentive for a firm to conduct incremental innovation that could improve the quality of a new product over time. Second, sponsors run the risk of exhausting the funds available for subsidy if the technical standard is set too low. There would be too many products to subsidize. By contrast, the firm would have no incentive to develop the new product if the technical standard were set too high. If the sponsor were to allow some flexibility in interpreting the technical standard, the system would leave a great deal of discretion to members of the technical committee. This discretion in turn would make the subsidy program become committee- rather than market-driven. The funds for the subsidy would not be used in a socially optimal way as a consequence.

Optional Rewards Based on Therapeutic Effect

Hollis (2007) proposed an optional rewards system under which the pharmaceutical firm could choose between the reward and the patent system and the firm would be paid for pharmaceutical innovation directly by sponsors based on the therapeutic effectiveness of drugs if the firm opted for the reward system. This system explicitly links the profitability of drug innovations to their therapeutic impacts rather than to consumers' ability to pay. This payment scheme closes the gap between the pursuit of profit and the pursuit of better health and hence provides an incentive to channel R&D resources into the development of drugs with large potential health impacts rather than products demanded by relatively affluent persons.

Compared to advance purchase commitments, the advantage of the optional rewards system is that sponsors do not need to specify technical specifications in advance. Rather, sponsors need only evaluate therapeutic effectiveness after the new drugs have received regulatory approval. Therefore, the success of the optional rewards system lies in the details of implementation, such as whether or not there are valid and reliable measures of treatment effects and whether or not the commitment of payment for innovative drugs is regarded as credible by the firms that do the investing.

Several countries have adopted various methods for comparing the costs of new drugs with their effects on health outcomes, a set of activities sometimes termed *economic evaluation*. Although the methods have shortcomings and many practical issues remain, the international experience suggests that the process of measuring therapeutic effect has proved workable, and to date, no country formally adopting economic evaluation has abandoned the policy. Although developing countries may have greater difficulty collecting data for measuring therapeutic effect than developed countries, there will inevitably be learning by doing. Some mistakes must be made for progress against some major diseases to be realized. Thus, the proposal for making rewards a function of both therapeutic impact and the number of persons affected is both a feasible and an efficient approach for inducing pharmaceutical innovation to combat diseases concentrated in low-income countries (box 9.2).

Box 9.2
The Health Impact Fund

Banerjee, Hollis, and Pogge (2010) extended the concept of optional rewards into a practical system, the Health Impact Fund (HIF). The primary goal of the HIF is to solve the dilemma arising from the trade-off between *static efficiency* (increasing access to new drugs) and *dynamic efficiency* (preserving incentive for innovation). The HIF offers innovative pharmaceutical firms a choice between exercising their usual patent rights through high prices *or* registering their product with the HIF. If a firm chooses option B, the plan would require the firm to sell its product worldwide at an administered price near the average cost of production and distribution, the break-even price ($p = AC$), as in figure 9.5. In exchange, the firm would receive a stream of payments from the HIF based on the assessed global health impact of its drug. In other words, the HIF is an optional pay-for-performance scheme for new pharmaceuticals. Thus, the key issues for the real operation of the HIF are where the "pay" (funds) comes from and how to measure the "performance" of a new drug.

According to Banerjee, Hollis, and Pogge (2010), funds for the HIF are to be provided by partner countries that agree to support it. They estimate that a reasonable starting level of funds would be US$6 billion per year. At this scale, the HIF could support the development of about two new drugs per year, sustaining a stock of about twenty medicines. Given the relatively large size of the funds, most countries are unable to institute the HIF single-handedly. Rather, international cooperation at the government level is an effective approach to set up the funds. They suggest that the founding partner states could begin the fund at a cost of 0.03 percent of their respective GDPs, given that a threshold participation of states represents about one-third of global income.

With regard to the measure of the performance, the HIF foresees offering firms a share of a fixed fund for each of 10 years, in proportion to the share of health impact of their registered product out of all registered products. For example, if all registered products were estimated to have saved twenty million "quality-adjusted life years (QALYs), a registered product that saved two million of those QALYs would receive 10 percent of the fund (2/20).

PRIORITY REVIEW VOUCHER

Ridley, Grabowski, and Moe (2006) proposed a reward system under which firms would receive a "priority review voucher" if they successfully developed new drugs for treating diseases concentrated in low-income countries. The voucher would transferable and would give a privilege to the bearer of the voucher to use the priority review process in a new drug application for another drug. Compared to the standard review process, the priority review process for NDAs in the United States increases the effective patent life (EPL) by one year. The market value of a one-year increase in EPL for a "blockbuster drug," defined by the authors as a drug with annual sales exceeding $1 billion in its fifth year on the market, is approximately US$300 million. Thus, the voucher would generate substantial rewards to innovators, particularly if a market for the priority review voucher were to evolve. Then innovators could sell the voucher to other pharmaceutical firms that have the potential to develop a blockbuster drug.

The rationale behind this incentive scheme is to use the market mechanism in high-income countries to solve market failure in countries with lower incomes. By linking incentives in two different markets, this system provides benefits not only for lower-income countries but also for high-income countries. The drug that consumers and health insurers in high-income countries value more would reach the market sooner if the voucher market functioned well. Furthermore, the advantage of the priority review voucher is that effective incentives for induced innovation would not be limited by the amount of funds available to sponsors. Rather, the sponsor would rely on a market implemented in high-income countries to create incentives for pharmaceutical innovation in lower-income countries. The size of the reward would be determined by the market, instead of on the basis of the judgment of committee members or a cost-effectiveness analysis conducted by an outside advisory group. Both administrative and reward costs to sponsors (and taxpayers) would low, allowing this incentive scheme to be applied to a wider range of diseases than the two aforementioned incentive systems.

9.7 SUMMARY AND CONCLUSIONS

This chapter has discussed several microeconomic decisions of pharmaceutical firms under the patent system, including R&D investment, pricing new products, competition between branded and generic products, advertising, and international pricing. We have also described how a reward system might be designed to foster pharmaceutical innovation when the patent system provides an insufficient incentive for such innovation.

First, our analysis has shown that optimal investment R&D decisions by pharmaceutical companies are made by investing up to the point at which marginal returns from investment equal the marginal cost of capital. Governments can use various incentive designs affecting marginal revenue or the marginal cost of R&D investment to promote pharmaceutical innovation.

Second, the pricing of new drugs involves a trade-off between static and dynamic efficiency. In a pharmaceutical market not subject to price regulation, profit-maximizing pharmaceutical manufacturers set the prices of new products above their marginal costs, which allows the manufacturers to recoup the cost of their investment in R&D. Empirical evidence shows that the prices of new drug products primarily reflect marginal value, not the marginal cost of producing, packaging, and distributing drugs to consumers.

Third, after patent protection of a branded drug expires, the innovator faces competition from firms marketing generic drugs. Sellers of generic drugs adopt competitive product pricing to deter entry of other generic firms. However, firms selling branded products do not adopt this strategy to deter entry of generic products. Instead, the price of branded drugs may even rise after generic entry, even at the cost of the firm's potentially losing substantial market share. Competition from generics has important effects on cost containment and pharmaceutical innovation. In an unregulated market, competition drives the price of generic products down, toward marginal cost. Thus, through generic competition, it is possible to achieve a good balance between static and dynamic efficiency. By contrast, in a regulated market, regulation undermines generic competition, which in turn has negative impacts on both the effectiveness of using generic substitution as a policy tool for achieving cost containment and incentives for innovation.

Fourth, pharmaceutical manufacturers have powerful incentives to spend resources on advertising. Such firms have spent a large share of promotion expenditure on detailing; in recent years, a small but increasing share of the promotion expenditure has been spent on direct-to-consumer advertising (DTCA). The empirical evidence shows that both detailing and DTCA have significant positive effects on market demand, suggesting that demand for pharmaceuticals is responsive to advertising.

Fifth, pharmaceutical manufacturers have strong incentives to sell their products at different prices in different countries. This practice is beneficial to firms' profitability, as well as increasing consumer access to drugs. However, the cross-national price differentials create an incentive for parallel trade and external referencing that serves to limit the size of price differentials that can be sustained. Cross-national price differentials of pharmaceuticals are relevant to a debated policy issue on how to share the global joint cost of R&D investments among countries.

A possible solution to this question is the concept of Ramsey optimal pricing, which implies that cross-national drug prices should reflect cross-national differences in ability to pay. The existing empirical evidence provides only weak support for this type of pattern, suggesting that the threat of parallel trade and external reference pricing narrow the range of sustainable price differentials across countries, which in turn reduces consumer access to drugs in low-income countries.

Finally, we discussed the theoretical rationale and practical feasibility of using a rewards system to develop new vaccines, drugs for rare disease, and diseases highly prevent in low-income countries. However, the specific proposals we have discussed are at present theoretical concepts rather than implemented payment schemes that have been subjected to rigorous empirical evaluation. By paying high prices in drugs prescribed for them, patents, especially in some high-income countries, will continue to do the heavy lifting in encouraging investments in R&D in the pharmaceutical sector for some time to come.

Key Concepts

- patent protection
- R&D investment
- static efficiency
- dynamic efficiency
- effective patent life
- generic competition
- drug advertising
- optimal investment decision
- pricing new drugs
- cost of capital
- marginal efficiency of investment
- push incentives
- pull incentives
- price regulation
- advertising elasticity of demand
- cross-national price differentials
- price discrimination
- second best
- Ramsey pricing
- advance purchase commitment
- optional rewards system
- priority review voucher

Review and Discussion Questions

9.1 List the pros and cons of the patent system from the viewpoint of society as a whole.

9.2 Explain the terms "static efficiency" and "dynamic efficiency" in your own words. These two terms pertain not only to the pharmaceutical market. Explain how static efficiency and dynamic efficiency may operate in markets for physicians' and hospital services. What about another context, such as the automobile market?

9.3 Before 2006, the US Medicare system did not provide insurance coverage for prescription drugs but did provide coverage for physician visits and inpatient care. Beginning in 2006, the US Medicare program expanded its coverage to include a prescription drug benefit. How do you think this expansion of Medicare coverage will affect pharmaceutical manufacturers' R&D investment decisions?

9.4 Following the same institutional background described in the above question, do you expect that the introduction of Medicare prescription drug benefit will have any effect on the price elasticity of demand for prescription drugs by the US elderly? Will US pharmaceutical manufactures increase advertising intensity in response to this policy change?

9.5 What is generic competition? List four factors that affect the degree of generic competition. What are the major institutional factors that promote or undermine generic competition in your country?

9.6 What is price discrimination? List two preconditions before the strategy of price discrimination could be adopted in practice. Do these two preconditions hold in the pharmaceutical market? Why or why not?

9.7 What is parallel trade? What is the effect of parallel trade on the price differentials of pharmaceutical products among countries if governments around the world do not ban parallel trade in the pharmaceutical market? Discuss the efficiency and equity implications of allowing parallel trade in pharmaceutical markets to flourish.

9.8 There is ample empirical evidence to show that on average, pharmaceutical prices in Canada are lower than those in the United States. Identify at least two important factors that cause price differentials between Canada and the United States. Do you think that the pharmaceutical manufacturers would lower the prices of pharmaceutical products in the United States if the Canadian government agreed to increase the reimbursement price of pharmaceutical products in Canada? Explain your answer.

9.9 Assume that you live in a country that imposes strict price regulation on pharmaceutical products (e.g., Italy). Compared to the "average" person in the United States, what are the benefits of drug consumption that you enjoy in your country? Do you think you should pay some "cost" to realize such benefits? If so, which costs should you pay?

9.10 The World Trade Organization's Agreement on Trade Related Aspects of Intellectual Property Rights (TRIPS) requires all member countries to grant and enforce 20-year patents on pharmaceutical innovations. Because most high-income countries already offered such protection, the main result of TRIPS has been to strengthen pharmaceutical patent rights in a group of low-income countries. Based on this chapter's analysis, make theoretical predictions about the effects of TRIPS on the following: (1) R&D investment by pharmaceutical manufactures in high-income countries, (2) the prices of pharmaceutical products in low-income countries, and (3) cross-national differences in pharmaceutical prices.

EXERCISES

9.1 Suppose that the demand function of a pharmaceutical firm is $p = 20 - 0.5x$, where p is the price of a prescription drug and x is the number of prescription drugs demanded by patients. For simplicity, assume that the pharmaceutical firm can produce an extra pill at a constant cost, and hence the marginal cost function is $MC = 4$.

a. Compute the optimal price and quantity for the pharmaceutical firm if the firm receives patent protection from the government.

b. Assuming that generic competition will drive down the price to marginal cost, compute the quantity of demanded for this product when the patent expires.

c. Based on your answer, calculate the welfare loss that the patent system imposes on this product.

9.2 Suppose that a pharmaceutical firm receives approval for marketing a drug in country A and country B. The demand functions for this drug in countries A and B are $p = 84 - 2x$ and $p = 124 - 3x$, respectively, where p is the price of a prescription drug and x is the quantity of the prescription drug demanded by patients. Assume that pharmaceutical markets in country A and country B are spatially separated and parallel trade is completely prohibited by the government. For simplicity, assume that there are no transportation costs and the marginal cost of producing an additional pill of drugs is constant at US$4, that is, $MC = 4$.

a. Determine the optimal price for this pharmaceutical product in country A and country B if the firm seeks to maximize profit.

b. Calculate the price elasticity of demand for drugs in country A and country B under such optimal pricing.

c. Compare the relationship between the optimal price and the price elasticity between countries A and B. Is your result consistent with Ramsey optimal pricing?

9.3 Use equation 9.1 to indicate which of the following prescription drugs are likely to receive relatively high advertising budgets from their parent pharmaceutical companies: Explain your answers.

- new branded drugs for treating chronic disease;
- new branded drugs for treating acute disease;
- off-patent branded drugs for treating chronic disease;
- generic drugs.

9.4 Use the framework in figure 9.5 to show how to determine the optimal size of government reward that can preserve the same incentive for innovation as the patent system now has. Do you expect that the price and consumption of a specific pharmaceutical product would differ from that under the patent system if the government used the amount of the reward that you calculate to purchase the property right to a successful new pharmaceutical product from its pharmaceutical manufacturer inventor and make it freely available to competing manufacturers? Explain your answer.

9.5 Some researchers argue that pharmacogenomics (PG), which is the science of using genomic markers to predict drug response, can substantially reduce expected drug development costs through increasing the probability of technical success, requiring shorter clinical development times, and requiring smaller clinical trials. Based on the analytic framework described by figure 9.1, what would you expect the impact of PG on R&D investment by pharmaceutical manufactures to be?

9.6 Suppose that a large pharmaceutical firm has the capacity to undertake six R&D investment projects, namely, projects A to E, and the expected marginal rates of return on these projects are 12, 10, 8, 6, 4, and 2 percent, respectively. Assume that the size of the company's investment does not affect its cost of capital and that the firm can finance the investment expenditure at an annual interest rate of 6 percent with a long-term bank loan.

a. Draw the COC (cost of capital) line and MEI (marginal efficiency of investment) lines on a graph with the number of R&D projects on the horizontal axis and the rates (COC, MEI) on the vertical axis. In how many R&D projects will the firm invest?

b. If the government wants to use the industrial policy to bolster the economy and introduces a tax credit policy designed to reduce the cost of capital from 6 percent to 4 percent, would a representative firm be likely to increase its investment in R&D? How many R&D projects would the firm undertake now?

c. If the government imposes price regulation on all pharmaceutical products and this price regulation reduces the expected rate of return by 2 percent for every product, how many R&D projects would the firm undertake now?

ONLINE SUPPLEMENTAL MATERIAL

PHARMACEUTICAL R&D

http://www.cbo.gov/ftpdocs/76xx/doc7615/10-02-DrugR-D.pdf

http://www.oneworldhealth.org

PHARMACEUTICAL PRICING

http://www.oecd-ilibrary.org/social-issues-migration-health/pharmaceutical-pricing-policies-in-a-global-market_9789264044159-en

THE HEALTH IMPACT FUND

http://www.yale.edu/macmillan/igh/

http://www.thelancet.com/journals/lancet/article/PIIS0140-6736(09)61296-4/fulltext?version=printerFriendly

WTO TRADE-RELATED ASPECTS OF INTELLECTUAL PROPERTY RIGHTS

http://www.wto.org/english/tratop_e/trips_e/trips_e.htm

SUPPLEMENTAL READINGS

Danzon, P. M., and M. F. Furukawa. 2003. Prices and Availability of Pharmaceuticals: Evidence from Nine Countries. *Health Affairs Web Exclusive* W3:521–536.

Hollis, A. 2007. Drugs for Neglected Diseases: New Incentives for Innovation. In *Pharmaceutical Innovation: Incentives, Competition, and Cost-Benefit Analysis in International Perspective*, ed. F. A. Sloan and C.-R. Hsieh, 75–90. New York: Cambridge University Press.

Philipson, T. J., and E. Sun. 2008. Is the Food and Drug Administration Safe and Effective? *Journal of Economic Perspectives* 22 (1): 85–102.

Reinhardt, U. 2007. The Pharmaceutical Sector in Health Care. In *Pharmaceutical Innovation: Incentives, Competition, and Cost-Benefit Analysis in International Perspective*, ed. F. A. Sloan and C.-R. Hsieh, 25–53. New York: Cambridge University Press.

Ridley, D. B., H. G. Grabowski, and J. Moe. 2006. Developing Drugs for Developing Countries. *Health Affairs* 25 (2): 313–324.

REFERENCES

Acemoglu, D., and J. Linn. 2004. Market Size in Innovation: Theory and Evidence from the Pharmaceutical Industry. *Quarterly Journal of Economics* 119 (3): 1049–1090.

Banerjee, A., A. Hollis, and T. Pogge. 2010. The Health Impact Fund: Incentives for Improving Access to Medicines. *Lancet* 375 (9709): 166–169.

Berndt, E. R. 2002. Pharmaceuticals in U.S. Health Care: Determinants of Quantity and Price. *Journal of Economic Perspectives* 16 (4): 45–66.

Berndt, E. R. 2007. The United States' Experience with Direct-to-Consumer Advertising of Prescription Drugs: What Have We Learned? In *Pharmaceutical Innovation: Incentives, Competition, and Cost-Benefit Analysis in International Perspective*, ed. F. A. Sloan and C.-R. Hsieh, 174–195. New York: Cambridge University Press.

Berndt, E. R., L. Bui, D. R. Reiley, et al. 1995. Information, Marketing, and Pricing in the U.S. Antiulcer Drug Market. *American Economic Review* 85 (2): 100–105.

Berndt, E. R., and J. M. Donohue. 2008. Direct-to-Consumer Advertising in Health Care: An Overview of Economic Issues. In *Incentives and Choice in Health Care*, ed. F. A. Sloan and H. Kasper, 131–162. Cambridge, MA: MIT Press.

Caves, R. E., M. D. Whinston, and M. A. Hurwitz. 1991. Patent Expiration, Entry, and Competition in the U.S. Pharmaceutical Industry. Brookings Papers on Economic Activity. *Microeconomics.* 1991:1–66.

Cockburn, I. M., and R. M. Henderson. 1998. Absorptive Capacity, Coauthoring Behavior, and the Organization of Research in Drug Discovery. *Journal of Industrial Economics* 46 (2): 157–182.

Comanor, W. 2007. The Economics of Research and Development in the Pharmaceutical Industry. In *Pharmaceutical Innovation: Incentives, Competition, and Cost-Benefit Analysis in International Perspective*, ed. F. A. Sloan and C.-R. Hsieh, 54–72. New York: Cambridge University Press.

Crawford, G. S., and M. Shum. 2005. Uncertainty and Learning in Pharmaceutical Demand. *Econometrica* 73 (4): 1137–1173.

Danzon, P. M., and L.-W. Chao. 2000a. Cross-National Price Differences for Pharmaceuticals: How Large, and Why? *Journal of Health Economics* 19 (2): 159–195.

Danzon, P. M., and L.-W. Chao. 2000b. Does Regulation Drive Out Competition in Pharmaceutical Markets? *Journal of Law & Economics* 43 (2): 311–357.

Danzon, P. M., and M. F. Furukawa. 2003. Prices and Availability of Pharmaceuticals: Evidence from Nine Countries. *Health Affairs Web Exclusive* W3:521–536.

Danzon, P. M., S. Nicholson, and N. S. Pereira. 2005. Productivity in Pharmaceutical-Biotechnology R&D: The Role of Experience and Alliances. *Journal of Health Economics* 24 (2): 317–339.

Danzon, P. M., and A. Towse. 2003. Differential Pricing for Pharmaceuticals: Reconciling Access, R&D and Patents. *International Journal of Health Care Finance and Economics* 3 (3): 183–205.

Danzon, P. M., Y. R. Wang, and L. Wang. 2005. The Impact of Price Regulation on the Launch Delay of New Drugs: Evidence from Twenty-Five Major Markets in the 1990s. *Health Economics* 14 (3): 269–292.

DiMasi, J. A., R. W. Hansen, and H. G. Grabowski. 2003. The Price of Innovation: New Estimates of Drug Development Costs. *Journal of Health Economics* 22 (2): 151–185.

Dorfman, R., and P. O. Steiner. 1954. Optimal Advertising and Optimal Quality. *American Economic Review* 44 (5): 826–836.

Dumoulin, J. 2001. Global Pricing Strategies for Innovative Essential Drugs. *International Journal of Biotechnology* 3 (3/4): 338–349.

Ekelund, M., and B. Persson. 2003. Pharmaceutical Pricing in a Regulated Market. *Review of Economics and Statistics* 85 (2): 298–306.

Finkelstein, A. 2004. Static and Dynamic Effects of Health Policy: Evidence from the Vaccine Industry. *Quarterly Journal of Economics* 119 (2): 527–564.

Furukawa, Y. 2007. The Protection of Intellectual Property Rights and Endogenous Growth: Is Stronger Always Better? *Journal of Economic Dynamics and Control* 31 (11): 3644–3670.

Gambardella, A. 1995. *Science and Innovation: The U.S. Pharmaceutical Industry During the 1980s.* New York: Cambridge University Press.

Garber, A. M., C. I. Jones, and P. M. Romer. 2006. Insurance and Incentives for Medical Innovation. National Bureau of Economic Research Working Paper No.12080. Cambridge, MA: National Bureau of Economic Research.

Giaccotto, C., R. E. Santerre, and J. A. Vernon. 2005. Drug Prices and Research and Development Investment Behavior in the Pharmaceutical Industry. *Journal of Law & Economics* 48 (1): 195–214.

Grabowski, H. G. 2007. Competition between Generic and Branded Drugs. In *Pharmaceutical Innovation: Incentives, Competition, and Cost-Benefit Analysis in International Perspective*, ed. F. A. Sloan and C.-R. Hsieh, 153–173. New York: Cambridge University Perspective.

Grabowski, H. G., and J. M. Vernon. 1992. Brand Loyalty, Entry, and Price Competition in Pharmaceuticals after the 1984 Drug Act. *Journal of Law & Economics* 35 (2): 331–350.

Grabowski, H. G., and Y. R. Wang. 2006. The Quantity and Quality of Worldwide New Drug Introductions, 1982–2003. *Health Affairs* 25 (2): 452–460.

Hollis, A. 2007. Drugs for Neglected Diseases: New Incentives for Innovation. In *Pharmaceutical Innovation: Incentives, Competition, and Cost-Benefit Analysis in International Perspective*, ed. F. A. Sloan and C.-R. Hsieh, 75–90. New York: Cambridge University Press.

Hurwitz, M. A., and R. E. Caves. 1988. Persuasion or Information: Promotion and the Shares of Brand Name and Generic Pharmaceuticals. *Journal of Law & Economics* 31 (2): 299–320.

Iizuka, T. 2004. What Explains the Use of Direct-to-Consumer Advertising of Prescription Drugs? *Journal of Industrial Economics* 52 (3): 349–379.

Iizuka, T. 2007. Experts' Agency Problems: Evidence from the Prescription Drug Market in Japan. *Rand Journal of Economics* 38 (3): 844–862.

Kravitz, R. L., R. M. Epstein, M. D. Feldman, et al. 2005. Influence of Patients' Requests for Direct-to-Consumer Advertised Antidepressants: A Randomized Controlled Trial. *Journal of the American Medical Association* 293 (16): 1995–2002.

Kremer, M., and R. Glennerster. 2004. *Strong Medicine: Creating Incentives for Pharmaceutical Research on Neglected Diseases.* Princeton, NJ: Princeton University Press.

Liu, Y. M., Y. H. K. Yang, and C. R. Hsieh. 2009. Financial Incentives and Physicians' Prescription Decisions on the Choice between Brand-Name and Generic Drugs: Evidence from Taiwan. *Journal of Health Economics* 28 (2): 341–349.

Lu, Z. J., and W. S. Comanor. 1998. Strategic Pricing of New Pharmaceuticals. *Review of Economics and Statistics* 80 (1): 108–118.

Morton, F., and M. Scott. 1999. Entry Decisions in the Generic Pharmaceutical Industry. *Rand Journal of Economics* 30 (3): 421–440.

Morton, F. M. S. 2000. Barriers to Entry, Brand Advertising, and Generic Entry in the US Pharmaceutical Industry. *International Journal of Industrial Organization* 18 (7): 1085–1104.

Pavcnik, N. 2002. Do Pharmaceutical Prices Respond to Potential Patient Out-of-Pocket Expenses? *Rand Journal of Economics* 33 (3): 469–487.

Philipson, T. J., and E. Sun. 2008. Is the Food and Drug Administration Safe and Effective? *Journal of Economic Perspectives* 22 (1): 85–102.

Ramsey, F. P. 1927. A Contribution to the Theory of Taxation. *Economic Journal* 37 (145): 47–61.

Reiffen, D., and M. R. Ward. 2005. Generic Drug Industry Dynamics. *Review of Economics and Statistics* 87 (1): 37–49.

Reinhardt, U. 2007. The Pharmaceutical Sector in Health Care. In *Pharmaceutical Innovation: Incentives, Competition, and Cost-Benefit Analysis in International Perspective*, ed. F. A. Sloan and C.-R. Hsieh, 25–53. New York: Cambridge University Press.

Ridley, D. B., H. G. Grabowski, and J. L. Moe. 2006. Developing Drugs for Developing Countries. *Health Affairs* 25 (2): 313–324.

Saha, A., H. Grabowski, H. Birnbaum, et al. 2006. Generic Competition in the US Pharmaceutical Industry. *International Journal of the Economics of Business* 13 (1): 15–38.

Scherer, F. M. 2000. The Pharmaceutical Industry. *Handbook of Health Economics* 1 (2): 1297–1336.

Shavell, S., and T. V. Ypersele. 2001. Rewards versus Intellectual Property Rights. *Journal of Law & Economics* 44 (2): 525–547.

Sloan, F. A., K. Whetten-Goldstein, and A. Wilson. 1997. Hospital Pharmacy Decisions, Cost Containment, and the Use of Cost-Effectiveness Analysis. *Social Science & Medicine* 45 (4): 523–533.

Vernon, J. A. 2005. Examining the Link between Price Regulation and Pharmaceutical R&D Investment. *Health Economics* 14 (1): 1–16.

Viscusi, W. K., J. E. Harrington, Jr., and J. M. Vernon. 2005. Table 24.1. *Economics of Regulation and Antitrust*. Cambridge, MA: MIT Press.

CHAPTER 10

The Supply of Private Health Insurance

Having discussed the demand for private health insurance in chapter 4, we now turn to the supply of such insurance. Many countries have a private health insurance sector. However, the importance of this sector varies greatly among countries.

This chapter deals with these important issues related to supply. How do insurers reduce individuals' out-of-pocket health care expenditure risk? How do investments affect insurers' risk of insolvency and the premiums they charge? Why do underwriting cycles—cycles in premiums and in the availability of insurance coverage—arise in markets for insurance? Compared to other lines of insurance, how important are underwriting cycles in health insurance markets? Why is so much private health insurance in such countries as the United States provided through employment? And among employer-based insurance plans, why do so many employers self-insure? Why do insurers and self-insuring groups purchase reinsurance, and what forms does reinsurance take? What are the advantages and disadvantages of private provision of health insurance? What is the rationale for public regulation of private health insurance, and what forms does such regulation take? More specifically, what are the effects of government requirements that employers offer particular benefits as part of their insurance plans and, more generally, requirements that employers provide health insurance? What is meant by community rating of insurance premiums? What is the rationale for this practice? What are its likely effects? Why is private health insurance unlikely to provide coverage to all residents of a country, and what types of public policies may achieve universal health insurance coverage in a system built on private health insurance? What is meant by managed care and selective contracting? How does managed care compare with traditional insurance in terms of cost and quality?

10.1 THE ABCs OF THE BUSINESS OF INSURANCE

FUNCTIONS OF INSURERS

Insurers perform several fundamental functions.

RISK BEARING

First and foremost, insurers perform a risk-bearing function. During a year, one individual with health insurance coverage may have a hysterectomy, another may experience a heart attack, and still others may not use any medical care at all or very little of it because they remain healthy. A single individual can "diversify away" some risk (eliminate some risk to him- or herself), such as investment risk (fluctuations in asset prices), by holding a well-balanced portfolio of equities, bonds, real estate, and other "alternative" investments (e.g., hedge funds). Thus, if values of shares on the stock market fall, the individual with a diversified asset portfolio can depend on the relative stability of the portfolio as a whole. People cannot diversify against all risk of fluctuations in their portfolios, but diversification certainly helps.

The same individual cannot diversify away expenditure risk stemming from major adverse health events to self. One's health, except for minor perturbations, is like holding one financial asset, not assets in a well-diversified portfolio. Yet by pooling *independent* risks, the risks of many individuals, insurers can diversify away losses accruing to individuals arising from adverse health events.

Many adverse events that individuals experience are likely to be independent of one another. When person A experiences a heart attack in a year, this has no impact on the probability that person B in another household will experience the same. (This is generally true of chronic but not acute infectious illnesses. In an epidemic, risks are correlated.)

If risks are completely independent, the risk per person in the pool of size n is $(1/n)$ multiplied by the variance in loss per insured. Thus, since n is in the denominator of this expression for risk, per person risk declines as n rises. However, if risks are correlated, the benefit of pooling is reduced in proportion to the extent of the correlation. There is not much to gain from pooling the risks of illness from an influenza epidemic that strikes many insured individuals in a locality at the same time, but in the twenty-first century, especially in high-income countries, such epidemics tend to be rare and account for a minor part of spending on personal health care services.

Similarly, there are opportunities for insurers that sell homeowner's insurance to diversify the risks of some mishaps, such as a fire in the kitchen or an old tree falling on a roof, but risk diversification becomes more problematic for insurers in the case of hurricanes or earthquakes, which are likely to affect many insured homes in a given locality or none at all.

Some risks faced by health insurers are not easily diversified away, e.g., increases in prices insurers pay for personal health care services. If health insurers expect medical care prices to rise by 3 percent during the year and in actuality such prices rise four times as much, insurers would incur a loss.

However, fortunately, nondiversifiable risk tends to be less important in health insurance markets than in some other lines of insurance, for two reasons. First, the period being insured is typically only one year. Not much unanticipated inflation, for example, can generally occur within a year. Second, health insurers often negotiate rates of payment to physicians and hospitals in advance. Thus, even if physicians and hospitals were to raise their prices, these price increases would not apply to the health insurers, which have negotiated fixed fees for the duration of their contracts.

Nondiversifiable risk is a substantial problem in some other lines of insurance, specifically those in which insurance claims arise from events occurring during a policy year but the losses payable under the terms of the insurance policy may actually be paid years later. Such is the case in lines of insurance with a long claims tail, such as medical malpractice insurance (see, e.g., Sloan and Chepke 2008). Medical malpractice claims are often paid many years after the injury that led to the claim occurred, or even years after the claim was filed. By contrast, health insurance claims are filed immediately or almost immediately after the covered service is actually rendered.

A tool insurers employ for dealing with nondiversifiable risk is to purchase reinsurance. Essentially, the insurer ("primary insurer") purchases insurance from another insurer to cover very large individual claims or to cover losses in the aggregate above some high dollar threshold.

MARKETING AND UNDERWRITING

To acquire customers, insurers engage in marketing and underwriting. While marketing serves to enlarge the pool of customers, underwriting entails assessing the probability that a potential customer will incur claims during a given year and setting the premium accordingly or, alternatively, deciding to reject the customer's application for insurance coverage. It would seem logical that insurers would accept all comers and charge a premium to cover expected loss plus a competitively determined loading factor. However, in some cases, insurers may have difficulty assessing the frequency of claims the insured individual is likely to incur ex ante and, rather than run the risk of seriously underpricing the insurance policy, may decide to refuse to provide coverage to that individual.

One concern insurers have is that a person with a preexisting condition may demand large amounts of health insurance coverage because he or she predicts that he or she will be a high user of services in the near future. Such asymmetric information—the consumer knows more about future utilization than the insurer does—is called *adverse selection*. Insurers often deal with adverse selection by

Box 10.1
What Are Health Insurance Exchanges?

Health insurance exchanges became a popular topic in the United States, following debate leading to passage of health insurance reform in the United States in 2010. In the United States, most private insurance is group-based, with the employer-based coverage being by far the predominant form of group health insurance coverage.

Compared to group coverage, individual health insurance coverage is quite expensive. One reason for this is the cost of marketing health insurance policies to individuals and enrolling them in such plans, and often the lack of competition among insurers offering individual coverage. Although there are typically many insurers marketing products to individuals, premium and quality comparisons among insurance products tends to be quite difficult. Consumer ignorance in turn confers market power on sellers of individual health insurance policies.

Health insurance exchanges, which are new organizational entities designed to create competitive insurance markets, serve several purposes (see, e.g., Kaiser Family Foundation 2009). First, they facilitate comparisons of plan characteristics by creating a classification system of plans. Characteristics of plans include cost-sharing provisions, such as deductibles, coinsurance rates, co-pays, and out-of-pocket limits, that a policyholder can expect to spend in a given year, as well as lists of services covered by each plan. Second, in addition to presenting information on plan characteristics, exchanges provide information on plan performance, such as the availability of wellness programs and disease management program, and consumer satisfaction with plan administration. Third, exchanges assist with enrollment and with the application of government subsidies for the purchase of insurance. Fourth, they can assist insured individuals in transitioning from one plan to another. Fifth, they can limit practices deemed undesirable that are subject to government regulation, such as denial of coverage due to a preexisting condition.

Exchanges are independent organizations that are governed by boards of directors. In the United States, they are to be implemented by 2014.

rejecting the person's insurance application. Such practices have led to considerable political pressure in the United States to require that insurers take all comers, that is, everyone who applies for coverage.

Another concern relates to the high cost of marketing individual insurance plans and enrolling individuals in these plans. To reduce such marketing costs and improve consumer information about particular individual health insurance products, recent health reform in the United States calls for insurance exchanges to be implemented in the future (box 10.1).

CLAIMS PROCESSING

Another function of insurers is to process claims. During the course of a year, a health insurer may process millions of health insurance claims. Health insurers are not unique in this regard. For example, motor vehicle insurers process many claims annually from accidents incurred by the persons they insure.

Loss Prevention

In addition, insurers engage in loss prevention to varying degrees. Such activities include negotiating contract terms, most important the prices of services paid to health care providers, and monitoring utilization to reduce payments for services with low marginal benefit to insured individuals. Absent loss prevention, individuals with complete or nearly complete insurance may demand services that offer little or no benefit. Some insurers operate disease management programs that seek to promote prevention and screening in order to reduce rates of adverse health outcomes of chronic disease and the associated expense in future years.

For example, a disease management program for diabetes would promote control of blood sugar (blood glucose) levels, blood pressure, and cholesterol levels and the use of various forms of screening, such as of the eyes and the lower extremities (legs, feet), since these practices are known to lower the rates of diabetic complications and hence lower spending on treating these complications in later years. Insurers have a greater incentive to offer disease management programs when turnover rates of the people they insure are low. A low turnover rate permits the insurer to capture the financial returns from disease prevention and screening.

Measuring the Financial Strength of Insurers: An Insurer's Income Statement and Balance Sheet

Income Statement

An insurance company's income statement records its revenue, expenses, and profits (or losses) for a particular period, its fiscal year. In the context of insurance, there are essentially two revenue streams—revenue from the sale of insurance and revenue from investments. Expenses consist of payments to policyholders (or to the parties to which policyholders have contractual obligations, e.g., the physicians from whom policyholders have received services), other expenses attributable to processing individual claims and writing checks, and expenses for marketing, managing investments, and general overhead. The difference between total revenue and total expenses is total profit, sometimes termed *surplus* in insurance jargon. The core of the insurance business is assuming (or *underwriting*) the risk of uncertain future events in exchange for a premium.

Underwriting profits are the difference between premiums and *paid losses* and other expenses associated with the sale of insurance in a fiscal year. Premium income is invested from the time it is received to the time that payments for loss and other expenses are made. For health insurance, the difference between the time premiums are received and the time payments are made to providers on behalf of insured individuals is relatively short.

BALANCE SHEET

A firm's balance sheet lists assets, liabilities, and equity, the latter being the difference between assets and liabilities. Because of government regulation of insurer solvency and insurers' own decisions to avoid bankruptcy, insurers are generally very conservative investors. For this reason, a large part of an insurer's asset portfolio is invested in fixed income (interest-bearing) securities.

Also important to an insurer's bottom line is its liabilities, which consist of its reserves on the insurance policies it issues. When an insurer issues an insurance policy, it incurs a dollar obligation that both prudence and law or regulation dictate must be backed by assets of corresponding size. Losses are incurred throughout the policy year, not on the date the premium is received (or day 1 of the policy year). With some exceptions, insurers do not know immediately that a loss has actually been incurred, although they are increasingly trying to keep abreast of losses as they are incurred.

There is a distinction between unearned and earned premiums. Premiums switch from "unearned" to "earned" as the policy year evolves. Earned refers to the part of the policy year that has passed. Since that part of the policy year has elapsed, for earned premiums, there is a loss—either a loss the insurer has knowledge of or does not have knowledge of. Corresponding to these are two types of loss, reserves incurred but not reported (IBNR) and case reserves.

As its name suggests, IBNR reserves are established to cover losses that have occurred but have not yet been reported to the insurer (e.g., a policyholder made a visit to physician but the claim has not yet been filed). Once the report is made and the insurer has determined the most likely loss from the specific claim, some part of IBNR reserves converts to a case reserve on that claim. The case reserve reflects the insurer's best estimate of the loss that will ultimately result from that claim. The case reserve or, equivalently, the anticipated loss on the claim is not set in stone; rather, it is adjusted up or down periodically as new information pertinent to the claim is revealed to the insurer.

INSURERS' CASH FLOW, INCOME FROM INVESTMENTS, AND PREMIUM SETTING

TIMING OF INSURERS' REVENUE AND EXPENSES

Insurers collect premiums in advance of paying losses. The time that elapses between the date premiums are collected and the date that losses are paid to policyholders differs appreciably by the line of insurance. The lag is short in such lines as health, homeowners', motor vehicle, and term life insurance. It is long in some lines of liability insurance, including medical malpractice insurance, and in whole life insurance.

Between the time premium income is received and losses are paid, the insurer invests premium income, which yields a second type of income flow to the insurer, investment income. A longer lag between premium collection and loss payout allows the insurer to make more money from investments.

Investment Income

Insurers derive income from both underwriting and investments. Investments can help the insurer diversify away risk to the extent that underwriting losses are uncorrelated with investment returns. For some risks, for example, losses from work-related injuries and illnesses covered by workers' compensation, claims for disability under workers' compensation policies may be higher during recessions when investment returns are depressed. This seems less likely for health insurance, although to our knowledge there are no formal studies of this issue.

Higher Investment Income Leads to Lower Premiums on the Underwriting Side of an Insurer's Business

Premiums are set based on forecasts of future losses from insurance written in a particular policy year, an adjustment for risk, the claims tail, and the anticipated returns to be earned on investments from the premium funds collected for the policy year, as well as market factors. Because it can earn investment return on premiums, the insurer can charge a premium that is below the anticipated loss on the insurance policy. Higher risk tends to result in higher premiums. A longer tail and higher *anticipated* investment returns tend to result in lower premiums, and conversely. When an insurer computes a premium for a future period, it does take into account expected returns from investing money it collects from premiums that it will retain until payments on losses are made. The potential return is positively related to the length of the time period that elapses from the date the claim is filed until payment is actually made.

Investment income varies for two reasons: (1) rates of return on investments per year differ, and (2) the length of the time that premium income can be held in investments differs. In a competitive insurance market, the competitive process drives premiums to a level at which the marginal insurer can earn its cost of capital (the return it must pay its suppliers of capital) but no more. Thus, if rates of return on investments rise, other factors held constant, a dollar of premium income becomes more valuable for what it will bring to the insurer in terms of investment income. Thus, the competitive process drives premiums down to a level that yields a competitive rate of return on a dollar of investment in the insurance company. Premiums are expected to vary inversely with interest rates. When interest rates fall, which reduces the yield from investments, premiums rise to restore a competitive return on investment, and conversely. The same principle applies to stock returns, but insurers tend to maintain asset portfolios that are not volatile, in part because of government regulation of insurer solvency. Also, in lines such as health insurance, the lag between premium collection and payment of losses is quite short, a few months on average, which makes premiums relative insensitive to interest rate changes.

Other factors held constant, including annual rates of return on investments, premiums will be lower relative to anticipated losses paid to policyholders (underwriting losses) and the longer the lag is between premium collection and loss payments, which for health insurance tends to be very short. One mistake some analysts of insurance markets frequently make is to attribute increased insurance premiums to poor investment returns. This is false reasoning. When considering returns on investments, insurance companies are forward—not backward—looking. Forecasting future returns is fraught with uncertainty. Interest rates reflect many factors, including inflationary expectations and monetary policies of central banks.

In a competitive insurance market, no one should be willing to pay a higher premium to a company just to allow the company to recover losses from errors it made in past investments. If one insurer is a poor manager of its investments, another insurer with sound investments can enter the market and successfully gain business from the poor insurer/investor. Insurance is inherently forward-looking, with respect to both expected losses from policyholders on the underwriting side and expected gains from investments on the investment side of its business.

REINSURANCE

Some premiums from a primary health insurer (the insurer that sells insurance to policyholders) may be ceded to a reinsurer. In this transaction, a primary insurer exchanges money (pays a premium) for a promise by the reinsurer to cover a specific expense, should the criteria for payment in the contract warrant this. Reinsurance is insurance for the primary insurer, or in the case of health insurance an employer often self-insures for the insurance provided to its employees but purchases reinsurance to cover unusually high losses. By reinsuring, the primary insurer reduces its liabilities and its risk of insolvency, but it sacrifices some revenue in return.

There are three common types of reinsurance contracts: quota share, aggregate stop-loss, and excess-of-loss reinsurance (see, e.g., Swartz 2006, 104–105). Under quota share reinsurance, the reinsurer is paid a share of the premium collected in exchange for assuming a share of the losses. Under aggregate stop-loss reinsurance, reinsurance covers amounts above a threshold of aggregate loss incurred by the insurer during a policy year. Excess-of-loss reinsurance covers amounts above a threshold of the loss incurred by an individual insured.

Reinsurance is typically sold in layers of coverage for a specified range of losses. For example, under an excess-of-loss arrangement, the primary insurer might cover the first $100,000 of loss incurred by a single policyholder in a year, with the first layer of reinsurance being for the next $100,000 of loss and another layer being for over $200,000 to $1 million, and so on.

UNDERWRITING CYCLES

Private insurance markets have been subject to boom-and-bust cycles, which are termed "insurance underwriting cycles" (Kipp, Cookson, and Mattie 2003; Grossman and Ginsburg 2004). These cycles are characterized by a period in which insurers make profits, followed by a period of almost equal length during which insurers incur losses. Following the period of losses, premiums rise by more than losses increased, restoring profitability.

Several factors seem to explain cycles. First, premiums are set in advance of the period during which losses are realized. Loss projection is an imprecise process. Second, when profitable, there is insurer entry. In seeking to gain a foothold, entrants often underprice insurance. This leads to price cuts by incumbent firms, which also underprice. Third, solvency regulation may be partly responsible for the cycles. Regulatory agencies require that insurers maintain a minimum surplus. This may lead to overpricing in anticipation of low investment yields. High prices in turn attract entrants. Substantial premium increases may lead to demand for public policy makers to "do something" about the rising price of insurance.

10.2 ARE INSURERS' PREMIUMS AND RETURNS EXCESSIVE?

Especially when insurance premiums rise, there is often a search for the "culprit." Often, in such situations, there are widespread complaints that "big" insurance companies earn excessive profits. Indeed, health care is costly, but such cost is also high for insurers. Unfortunately, there are no rigorous studies of whether or not premiums or returns accruing to private insurers are excessive or not. However, it is useful nevertheless to consider in general terms how one would conduct such an assessment.

In chapter 4, we stated that the premium equals the sum of the loading and the expected loss on an insurance policy. In this chapter, we have added a complication—namely, that premium income is typically collected before losses are paid. In the interim, insurers can earn investment income. As returns on investments rise and the length of the time elapsed between receipt of the premium and payment for losses increases, premiums fall in a competitive insurance market.

Premiums may be excessive if (1) losses are excessive and (2) returns are excessive relative to the risk borne by insurers. Losses may be excessive if insurers engage in suboptimal amounts of loss prevention or are not effective in negotiating prices with physicians and hospitals. Optimal loss prevention occurs at the margin at which a dollar of expenditure on loss prevention yields a dollar saving in losses. If the saving is more than a dollar, such expenditure is too low, and conversely.

Insurers may not be tough negotiators for at least two reasons. First, in the United States, historically hospital and physician associations established nonprofit insurance companies (Blue Cross and Blue Shield plans) and hospital officials and physicians were members of their boards of directors (Adamache and Sloan 1983; Pauly 1998). When formed, all Blue Cross Blue Shield plans were nonprofit. In the last few years, many Blue plans have converted to for-profit status, and this is no longer the case. Second, when there is only one hospital in a market area with which to negotiate, insurers may be ill positioned to obtain favorable terms from hospitals. This may be particularly true when insurers have to negotiate with a single physician-hospital organization (PHO) in a community (see chapter 6). Antitrust policy may be (and has been) used to ensure that negotiations are arm's length.

The issue of whether or not profits are excessive is more complex. Under competition, market forces drive returns down to the point at which the marginal rate of return on a company's investments equals the marginal cost of capital. Since investors must be compensated for risk bearing by receiving a higher rate of return on their investments, the cost of capital is correspondingly higher for riskier investments. In particular, the finance literature distinguishes between diversifiable and nondiversifiable risk. At the most basic level, insurers diversify the risk of loss by pooling uncorrelated risks of individual insureds. By pooling, what is a risk of loss to an individual is a much smaller risk to the pool. In any period, most insureds are fortunate not to incur losses. Others are not so fortunate and incur losses. If individual losses are uncorrelated, risk pooling diversifies away much of the "underwriting risk" (risk on the insurance line of business) of individual losses. Similarly, as already noted, insurers can diversify investment risk by holding a mix of different types of assets.

The insurer's cost of capital reflects (1) the rate of return on a risk-free asset, such as a short-term government bond (e.g., a 90-day US Treasury bill), and (2) a return to nondiversifiable risk. A major potential source of nondiversifiable risk to a health insurance is adverse selection. If people with certain characteristics such that they think they will be heavy users in the next year systematically select insurance plans with certain characteristics, for example, relatively complete coverage, then losses will be correlated. Or a breakthrough technology may be welcomed by insured patients because of the health benefit it confers, yet it may affect treatment patterns for many insureds with a particular condition.

Technological change is not as important a source of nondiversifiable risk for health insurance as it may be in other lines of insurance in which the claims tail is much longer. Health insurers can estimate the likely effect of an innovation on expenditures they will incur during the following policy year.

In the insurance industry, as in banking, there is a public policy concern about the effect of insolvency on the firm's customers, in this context, the insurer's policyholders (Munch and Smallwood 1980; Winter 1991; Born 2001). There is a public interest in protecting consumers from the risk of having paid a premium, becoming ill and using personal health services, and then learning that the insurer is insolvent. For this reason, there are laws and regulations designed to reduce insurance company bankruptcy risk. The total risk of an insurer's portfolio affects the likelihood that it will become insolvent. Bankruptcy risk is reduced when insurers hold additional retained earnings (surplus) as a precaution against shortfalls. Another safeguard is reinsurance. However, reinsurance is highly experience rated. An insurer that uses its reinsurance will typically pay higher reinsurance premiums in the future. Insurers may take precautions to avoid bankruptcy voluntarily. The rationale for solvency regulation of insurers, however, is that these voluntary efforts may be insufficient, and some public oversight of individual insurers is desirable.

10.3 Private versus Public Provision of Health Insurance Coverage

Individuals' willingness to pay amounts above the policyholder's expected loss—either from a premium that reflects more than expected loss or by investment returns that accrue from the time premiums are paid and the time losses are paid—allows a market for private insurance to exist. Despite widespread moral hazard and adverse selection, insurance generally is available. In many countries, most coverage is provided by public insurance, with private health insurance being an add-on or supplement to public coverage. As a supplement, private health insurance covers services not covered by the public plan or provides coverage for a quality level not supported by the public plan, such as a better hospital room. In most countries, insurance for nursing home stays and other long-term care services are not covered by public insurance. There may be private markets for such coverage in such cases.

Among Organisation for Economic Co-operation and Development (OECD) member countries, the United States is the only country in which a large share of the population mainly relies on private health insurance coverage. Only for persons over the age of 65 is there universal public coverage in the United States, under the Medicare program. And there is private supplemental health insurance coverage to cover cost sharing that Medicare imposes on beneficiaries, as well as services not covered by Medicare.

Most, but certainly not all, countries that are members of the OECD are high-income countries. Among OECD members in 2005, the share of total expenditure on health services financed by private health insurance was by far the highest for the United States—36.4 percent (table 10.1). The second to fourth highest private insurance shares were for the Netherlands (19.4percent), Canada (12.7 percent),

Table 10.1
Share of Health Care Expenditure by Source of Expenditure in Selected OECD Countries, 2005

Country	Public Expenditure on Health (%)	Private Health Insurance (%)	All Other Private Funds (%)	Out-of-Pocket Payment (%)
United States	45.1	36.4	5.4	13.1
Netherlands	64.8	19.4	8.1	7.7
Canada	70.2	12.7	2.6	14.5
France	79.9	12.7	0.7	6.7
Germany	77.0	9.2	0.8	13.0
Switzerland	59.6	8.9	0.9	30.6
Australia	67.0	7.4	7.4	18.2
Ireland	79.5	6.8	1.5	12.2
Spain	70.6	5.9	0.7	22.8
Belgium	69.4	4.8	5.6	20.2
Austria	76.5	4.7	2.6	16.2
New Zealand	77.4	4.7	1.1	16.8
Portugal	71.8	3.9	1.5	22.8
Korea	53.1	3.4	5.0	38.5
Mexico	45.5	3.3	0.0	51.2
Japan	82.7	2.5	0.5	14.3
Luxembourg	90.2	2.3	1.0	6.5
Finland	75.0	2.2	3.2	19.6
Denmark	79.2	1.5	4.4	14.9
Hungary	70.9	1.1	4.7	23.3
Italy	76.7	0.9	1.8	20.6
Poland	69.3	0.6	4.0	26.1
Czech Republic	88.6	0.2	0.3	10.9
Iceland	81.4	0.0	0.0	18.6
Norway	83.5	0.0	0.8	15.7

Note: Countries are ranked by decreasing size of private health insurance.
Source: OECD, OECD Health Data (2008).

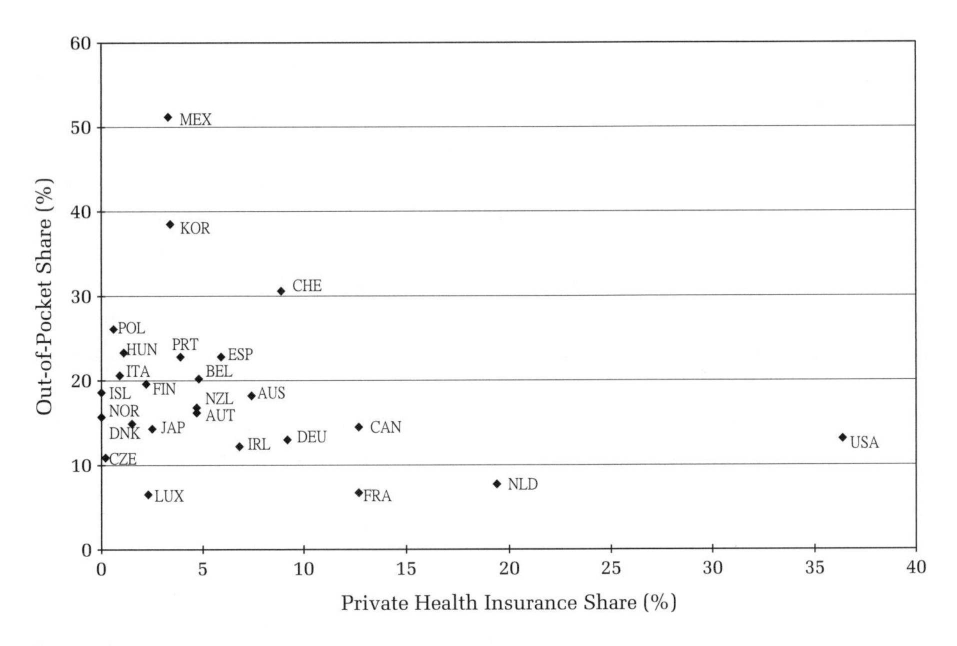

FIGURE 10.1
Shares of Health Expenditures Financed by Out-of-Pocket Payment versus Countries' Private Health Insurance Shares

and France (12.7 percent), with Germany and Switzerland close behind. Among OECD countries, Iceland, the Czech Republic, and Norway did not have private health insurance or insurance from other private funds.

Figure 10.1 shows the relationship between the share of health expenditures financed by out-of-pocket payment and by private health insurance. It suggests that the share of health expenditures financed by out-of-pocket payments is not necessarily highest where the private health insurance share is the highest. For example, in Mexico, consumers bore a greater than 50 percent out-of-pocket share of personal health expenditures in 2005, and private health insurance accounted for only 3 percent of health expenditures. In Switzerland, the out-of-pocket share was about 30 percent in that year, and private health insurance accounted for only 9 percent of health care expenditures in that country.

THE CASE FOR AND AGAINST RELYING ON PRIVATE HEALTH INSURANCE FOR PROVISION OF COVERAGE TO A POPULATION

Advocates of private health insurance systems make several arguments.[1] First and foremost, because private health insurers face a profit motive, they have a greater incentive to be responsive to policyholders than do managers of publicly financed systems. This type of responsiveness may take many forms. For example, if consumers are willing to pay for a new technology, private insurers should be willing

1. See also chapters 11 and 12.

to provide such additional coverage, although at a higher premium. Although they pay a higher premium, consumers are presumably better off by having access to a service that they value. By contrast, concerned with cost containment and being less responsive to consumers, and having monopsony power in health care markets (i.e., public insurers are in a position to dictate the prices they pay to hospitals, physicians, and other health care providers), public insurers may be less inclined to provide coverage for new technologies. This may serve as an important impediment to innovation. Also, in a public system, issues of what services to cover can become highly politicized. In the private sector, by contrast, coverage issues are private concerns. Private health insurers seem more likely to cover new technologies that they believe their customers will value.

There is an important difference between *static* and *dynamic efficiency* (see chapter 9). If potential innovators become convinced that their new products will not be purchased, or will be purchased reluctantly and with a lag at prices that do not cover their cost of research and development, they will be less likely to bring innovative products to market.

In a competitive insurance market, insurers know they must provide value for the premium dollar or lose market share to their competitors. For this reason, they may be expected to be tough in negotiating contracts with health care providers. Inefficiency in health care provision must result in higher premiums. If private health insurers tolerate inefficiency on the part of providers and their competitors are not equally tolerant of such inefficiency, insurers stand to lose market share.

Second, given that people have different preferences, not only for risk but also for the types of services they value and hence want to have included in a benefit package, private health insurers can offer products that reflect this heterogeneity in preferences. When benefit structure is decided collectively and publicly, as a practical matter, it becomes more difficult to allow for such heterogeneity.

Third, the provision of public and of private health insurance are not mutually exclusive. For example, in the United States, Medicaid and particularly Medicare have contracted with private health maintenance organizations for provision of care to some persons enrolled in the Medicare program.

Despite these advantages of private health insurance, it has many critics as well. What proponents of private insurance view as advantages, some opponents see as disadvantages.

There is an argument that private insurance is not superior to public insurance in satisfying consumer preferences. For one, most health insurance in the country with the largest private sector, the United States, is provided on a group basis. While the provisions of group health insurance plans may satisfy the median employee's preferences (see Goldstein and Pauly 1976), it is clearly difficult for group plans to satisfy individual employee preferences. Also, some differences in preferences may reflect adverse selection on the part of potential policyholders. Private health plans implement various restrictions to guard against adverse selection, including implementing preexisting condition clauses, which disallow coverage for services for conditions that existed at the time the person joined the health plan, or they fail to renew insurance policies if the person incurred considerable expense during the policy year, or premiums are raised to the extent that they are unaffordable to the policyholder.

As for private health insurance that supplements public health insurance coverage, there is the argument that private insurers free ride on the public plans. They potentially do this when they cover public plans' deductibles, coinsurance, and co-pays. Imposing cost sharing reduces the quantity of personal health services demanded (see chapter 3). Thus, eliminating or reducing cost sharing may be expected to increase outlays not only for the private supplemental plan but for the public plan as well.

The critics have additional arguments against the private provision of health insurance. Private health insurance is inefficient when measured in terms of administrative expense, which is much higher in the United States than in Canada, a country reliant on public health insurance (see, e.g., Woolhandler and Himmelstein 1991, 1997; Woolhandler, Campbell, and Himmelstein 2003). If such administrative cost could be eliminated or at least reduced, the savings could presumably be reallocated to the direct provision of personal health care services. Administrative expenses are incurred by both insurers and providers. Private insurers bear the costs of marketing and enrolling persons in their plans, particularly if no public coverage under the public insurance program is universal. Given high rates of turnover—many people switch private insurers annually—insurers constantly incur costs of enrollment.

In addition, by providing preventive services and actively managing chronic diseases, there are long-term savings in expenditures on personal health care services to be realized. Because of all the churning of enrollees, health insurers do not devote a socially optimal amount of resources to disease prevention and management. Given the large number of insurers, it is difficult to track persons through the system. This leads to uncoordinated care and unnecessary testing, since medical information systems are not integrated.

Private insurers engage in some marketing practices that are widely viewed as contrary to the public interest. For example, persons with prior adverse health experience may be refused coverage. This is often viewed as unfair in that at least some adverse health experience cannot be helped. After all, one does not select one's parents.

Insurers engage in the practice of "cream skimming" in the context of health insurance, enrolling the healthy and rejecting those who are not so healthy. Insurance contracts tend to be complex, making it difficult for consumers to compare contracts on premiums versus coverage provided by each insurance policy.

Finally, there is concern about the consolidation of health insurers in the United States and its implications for competition (Robinson 2004). In most states in 2002–2003, market concentration was at a level that would elicit concern by public agencies charged with antitrust monitoring and enforcement. Although market concentration is not a sufficient condition for exercise of market power, it facilitates the exercise of market power (Hyman and Kovacic 2004). As discussed more fully below, in the United States, private insurance tends to be employer-based. Although there are efficiencies in employer-based coverage, there are also inefficiencies. Perhaps most important, there is the phenomenon of "job lock" (Gruber and Madrian 1994; Madrian 1994). People who have a major illness in the family may be reluctant to change employers, even if they would be more productive in the alternative employment setting, because they may have to undergo a waiting period before benefits from the new employer take effect or otherwise. This introduces inefficiency into the operation of labor markets. There is an impediment to optimal matching of people to jobs in which they have a comparative advantage.

The case for and against private health insurance in the countries other than the United States are different from the United States in the sense that private health insurance in these other countries may tend to serve more as a political safety value, allowing more affluent citizens to obtain another tier of care, than as a vehicle for promoting efficiency in health services provision and for promoting technological change.

10.4 Employer-Based Private Health Insurance Coverage

Advantages of Employer-Based Coverage

In the United States, private health insurance coverage is primarily obtained through one's place of employment. Employer-based coverage is much more widespread than is individual private health insurance coverage for several reasons. First and foremost are the economies of scale in provision. It is much less expensive on a per-insured basis to provide insurance in large groups since marketing and enrollment costs per insured are substantially reduced in such settings, as is claims processing, to a perhaps lesser extent (table 10.2). Insofar as the risk falls as the number of persons in the insuring group increases, employers with fewer than 200 employees rarely self-insure (Swartz 2006, 68).

Second, insurance provided through the employer mitigates the problem of adverse selection (but at the same time makes insurance less responsive to individual preferences of employees within an employment group), particularly in large employer groups. Most employees select their employer for a number of reasons, including pay, working conditions, opportunities for career advancement, vacation, and fringe benefits, of which health insurance is only one. An important

TABLE 10.2
Loading Factors by Group Size (% of Premium)

Group Size	Loading Factor
Individual policy	60–80
Small groups (1–10 persons)	30–40
Moderate group (11–100)	20–30
Medium groups (100–200)	15–20
Large groups (201–1,000)	8–15
Very large groups (1,000+)	5–8
Mean for all plan (weighted average)	15–25

Source: Charles E. Phelps, *Health Economics*, 3rd ed., 43. © 2003. Reprinted by permission of Pearson Education, Inc., Upper Saddle River, New Jersey.

rationale for public insurance as well is to avoid adverse selection problems that may exist in private health insurance markets.

Third, in the United States, employer-provided self-insured (by the employer) private health insurance is subject to federal, not state, laws—more specifically the federal Employee Retirement Income Security Act of 1974 (ERISA). Thus, state insurance laws, such as those mandating that certain services be covered by all insurance policies sold in the state, do not apply to employer-based coverage. A mandated benefit might require inclusion of chiropractic services or home health care in the benefit package. To the extent that an insured person does not value or expect to use such services, the mandate effectively amounts to a premium increase. We return to the issue of health insurance regulation later in this chapter.

The provision of health insurance through employment is highly advantageous to employees and their families in the United States since contributions made on behalf of the employee by the employer are not subject to either state or federal corporate or personal income tax. For persons in high marginal personal income tax brackets, this tax subsidy is particularly advantageous. For such persons, it may be rational to demand that even routine health care services be included in the benefit package since the value of the tax subsidy is likely to exceed the loading factor, especially if the person works for a large employer.

Typically, larger employers in the United States self-insure for payments made on behalf of employees for health services, but pay insurers for administering the insurance plan. Such employers tend to be sufficiently large to permit an ample amount of risk diversification. However, since the vast majority of employers are in a business other than insurance, they prefer to have private health insurers who are specialists in the health insurance business process and pay claims and negotiate with individual physicians and hospitals over contract terms than to perform these functions themselves.

Who Really Pays for Employer-Based Health Insurance Coverage?

Health insurance is only one of several types of fringe benefits that employers provide. The most important other fringe benefit is retirement benefits. But employers also offer educational benefits, paid vacation time, and paid sick days.

Employers and others argue that employer-provided health insurance coverage places a heavy burden on employers, especially in recent years, in light of the substantial increase in per employee cost of such coverage. There are statements to the effect that there is more health insurance in an automobile produced in the United States than there is steel. As a result, advocates for manufacturers and some media pundits have argued that US manufacturers are placed at a competitive disadvantage versus their competitors in other countries with large public health insurance systems.

This raises a fundamental question. When health insurance is provided through employment, who pays? The employee? The employer? Or some combination of the two? About one matter there is no debate: in a country like the United States, in which there is a substantial tax subsidy of private health insurance premiums, the public pays for the tax subsidy in some way, certainly through higher tax rates on a narrower tax base than it otherwise would pay.

The matter of whether the employer or the employee pays for health insurance provided through employment is a controversial issue, pitting the economists' view against the view of the public at large, including employers.

To see the economist's argument, which is that the employee ultimately pays for health insurance through reduced compensation in other forms, we assume initially, as is plausible for most employees, that the employee values both health insurance benefits and earnings. The latter allows the employee to purchase goods and services other than health care (fig. 10.2). Because both other consumption and health insurance are "goods," the indifference curve for each worker has the negative slope it does.

The employer is indifferent between paying a dollar in health insurance benefits or a dollar in wage income. Thus, the isoprofit curve π_0 (constant level of profit) is linear with a negative slope of –1 since both other goods and services are denominated in dollars. If the health insurance benefit were to increase by $500, wage compensation would have to decline by $500 so that a constant level of profit was maintained. At point *M*, the slope of worker A's indifference curve and the slope of the isoprofit curve are tangent, and worker A chooses to be paid H_A in health insurance benefits and w_A in wage compensation. By contrast, worker B has a lower marginal valuation of health insurance as a fringe benefit and chooses to receive his entire compensation in the form of wages at w_B. Worker C is more productive than workers A and B. He generates an isoprofit of π_1. His wage-health insurance compensation package is located at point *N*.

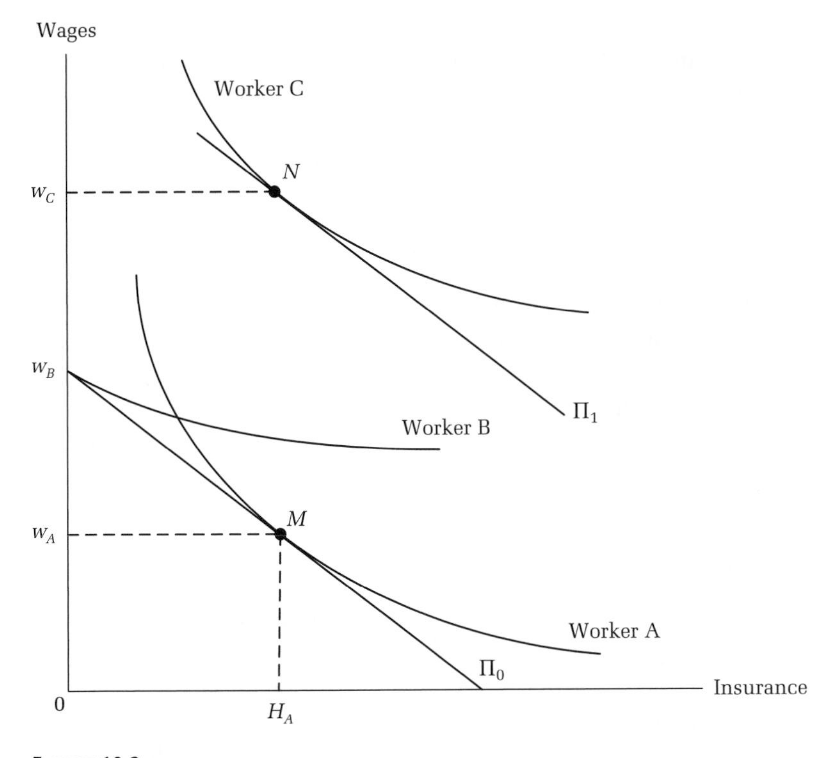

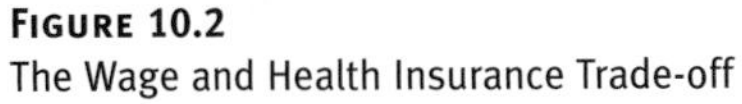
FIGURE 10.2
The Wage and Health Insurance Trade-off

Now, if the median employee is like worker B, then the employer pays a higher wage and does not offer health insurance. If the median employee is like worker A, the wage is lower and health insurance is provided. An important regulation governing the provision of private health insurance as a fringe benefit in the United States is that all full-time employees in a firm must be offered the same health insurance benefit. Thus, at present, no insurance may be provided if many of the employees are of type B, but insurance would be provided if employees are of type A. In reality, employees of a given firm are likely to have heterogeneous preferences for wage income versus fringe benefits, including health insurance.

One reason is that some employees have spouses who receive private health insurance in the family through his or her job. Insurers coordinate benefits. This means if one's spouse's insurance covers a physician visit, there is no benefit from having one's own policy cover it. We have little understanding of how the choice of plan offerings is done in practice. One study (Goldstein and Pauly 1976) developed a model to explain this choice.

From the underlying microeconomic theory, we would expect that in a competitive labor market, there would be a negative relationship between (1) the provision of an insurance benefit with employment, and the generosity of such benefits if provided, and (2) the wage rate the individual employee receives. However, empirical research has found a positive, not a negative, relationship between wage compensation and compensation in the form of health insurance benefits (Currie and Madrian 1999; Pauly 2001). A reason for the positive correlation is that employees who have health insurance through their place of employment have certain unmeasured characteristics that those employees who lack employer-based insurance do not have. Possibly employees who have health insurance are more motivated workers than those who lack insurance, or perhaps they have skills not explicitly measured in the empirical studies . For example, worker C in figure 10.2 may be more productive for these reasons than worker B is. But w_B is less than w_C, although the person has health insurance.

In other words, in empirical analysis, to gauge the impact of the provision of employer-based health insurance on wages paid employees, the researcher would like to compare compensation patterns between workers A and B, who are equally productive, but unless the researcher takes specific precautions, he or she will compare worker C with workers A and B, the former being on a higher isoprofit line than the latter. Unlike for health insurance (the Health Insurance Experiment; see chapter 3), there are no randomized controlled trials of employee compensation patterns. Rather, researchers desiring to assess the impact of the provision of employer-based health insurance on wages must use observational data (see chapter 3). These are data from firms that make various choices about the health insurance plans they offer their employees, not data emerging from the random assignment of health insurance plans to employers. Ideally, the researcher would be able to control for ability or productivity differences among individuals in the sample, but such differences, though observable to employers, are not easily observed by researchers.

An econometric solution is the use of instrumental variables. Assume that the dependent variable is the employee's earnings. Among the explanatory variables is whether or not the employee has employer-provided health insurance.[2] With the instrumental variables approach, the researcher selects a variable that is correlated with the endogenous explanatory variable but does not affect the dependent variable in the main equation—in this application, earnings. One such (instrumental) variable is whether or not the employee's *spouse* has health insurance through his or her place of employment. If the employee can secure health insurance through his or her spouse's place of employment, the employee may not be nearly as interested in obtaining health insurance from his or her own employer. Rather, other factors about the job held constant, he or she will prefer a job that offers a higher wage but no health insurance since he or she has coverage through the spouse's place of work. At the same time, the spouse's health insurance coverage is plausibly unrelated to the worker's ability or productivity (unless there is assortative mating—spouses who are productive in the marketplace may also have

2. An alternative explanatory variable is the generosity of the health insurance benefit, but this adds complexity to our discussion without adding much additional insight.

spouses who are productive in this respect); thus, unmeasured ability or productivity should not affect the person's wage.

Olson (2002), who used this instrumental variables approach, found that women whose husbands had employer-provided health insurance were less likely to be employed in jobs that provided health insurance as a fringe benefit. In particular, he found that the probability that a woman whose husband had health insurance through his job was 15.5 percentage points less likely to work at a job providing health insurance than women whose husbands did not obtain health insurance through their place of employment. Overall, wives with health insurance obtained through their own employers worked for a wage that was about 20 percent lower than what they would have received working at a job without such benefits.[3] This result implies that workers in the United States pay a considerable amount for receiving private health insurance through their employers.

10.5 GOVERNMENT REGULATION OF PRIVATE HEALTH INSURANCE

RATIONALE FOR GOVERNMENT REGULATION

Regulation is an important feature of insurance markets of all types. In all countries in which private health insurance policies are sold, insurance is subject to various forms of regulation. Four major justifications are (1) to prevent bankruptcies by maintaining insurers' solvency, (2) to keep premiums at nearly actuarially fair rates by preventing insurers from exercising market power in setting premiums, (3) to ensure the availability of coverage by implementing laws and regulations to ensure availability, and (4) to supply information to insurance purchasers to improve the performance of insurance markets and ensure fair play. Such regulation applies to insurance plans that are marketed to consumers, not to employer-based, self-insured health care plans.

Historically, the main role of insurance regulation was to ensure the solvency of insurers in advance of insurer bankruptcy and to mitigate the losses of policyholders in the event that bankruptcies occurred. Solvency regulation, the rationale for which has already been discussed, is less important in a line such as health insurance since the claims tail is lower than for other lines of insurance, such as medical malpractice insurance. If the claim is likely to be paid years after the premium is paid, insurer bankruptcy becomes a very important issue. Also, solvency regulation does not apply to self-insured employment-based insurance plans.

The purpose of insurance is to mitigate a policyholder's financial risk; thus, if and when an insurer goes bankrupt, in the end, the insured party has not really been relieved of any risk. Additionally, individual purchasers may have insufficient information, combined with too much complexity for consumers of insurance

3. For a more recent empirical application, see Lehrer and Pereira (2007).

to really know which insurers are less likely to become insolvent. Toward this end, regulators monitor whether premiums are adequate to cover expected loss, with a reasonable load to cover the cost of administering the plan, and whether or not insurers are taking unreasonable financial risks with their investments. Ex ante (or before bankruptcy occurs), government oversight involves seeing that premiums are adequate to cover anticipated losses and expenses and that the asset mix of reserves is not too risky.

Another task of regulators is to restructure insurers for which insolvency seems imminent. Ex post mitigation of loss includes government requirements that insurers contribute to a risk pool or guaranty fund, which compensates policyholders who otherwise would not receive payment for losses they incur as a result of insurer bankruptcy.

An important objective of premium regulation is to prevent insurers from exercising market power in setting premiums. In contrast to solvency regulation, which guards against premiums being set too low, under premium regulation, governments monitor whether premiums are too high in order to ensure the public access to insurance at quasi-competitive rates. Excessive prices in the market may result from lack of consumer knowledge and high consumer search costs, which limit competition. In addition, competition may theoretically be diminished because it is difficult for insurers to determine consumers' risk level, creating an informational advantage for existing insurers and creating a barrier to entry.

When insurance premium spikes occur, governments are pressured to act in various ways to reduce premiums or limit further rises in premiums. On the other hand, insurers facing competitive threats or attempting to increase their market share may actually set premiums too low relative to expected losses. There is an analogy to the fairy tale Goldilocks and the Three Bears: "This porridge is too hot. This porridge is too cold. This porridge is just right." In the long run, it seems likely that the porridge, or the insurance premiums, may be just right. However, in the shorter run, the porridge may be either too hot or too cold—excessive prices when too hot and inadequate prices when too cold.

Another goal of insurance regulation is to ensure that insurance is readily available to potential purchasers. Some types of insurance are seen as essential for individuals to have. Health insurance falls in this category.

Without government intervention, insurers may find it desirable to exclude some potential policyholders. Such exclusions may take various forms (Swartz 2006, 75–77). Insurers may outright refuse to issue a health insurance policy to some individuals. They may specialize in marketing to certain types of individuals who tend to be good health risks, such as persons who have left the armed services, persons engaged in a learned profession, or self-employed individuals. They may deny coverage to persons with specific preexisting health conditions. They may seek to attract relatively healthy individuals by subsidizing memberships in health clubs.

However, it may be in the public interest that such risks be covered. Such concerns have arisen in the context of automobile insurance as well as health insurance. Being able to drive may be essential to maintaining employment, and the availability of liability insurance is directly linked to being able to drive in states with compulsory motor vehicle liability insurance laws.

The astute reader will think, "Wait a minute! Earlier in this book, you complained about adverse selection, and now you are criticizing insurers for trying to do something about this." The astute reader has a point. Insurers attempt to weed out persons who are likely to be heavy users of health services from their insurance pools. This is a way of combating adverse selection. But at the same time, societies apparently view health insurance as a right; you do not get to pick your parents or your genes, and further, it is unseemly when people who face adverse circumstances, such as being in bad health, are denied insurance coverage.

A final rationale for insurance regulation is information provision and fair play. Information provision and government review of policy forms (a government reviews insurance contracts to be sure the language is understandable, clear, and accurate and conveys the key features of the contracts) are more important when the customer is not highly educated or is an infrequent purchaser of coverage. The motive of fair play sometimes leads to requirements that insurers sell insurance to high-risk customers at premiums below the actuarial value of the loss. This has occurred in motor vehicle liability insurance most prominently, which has been combined with withdrawal restrictions forcing insurers to remain in an unprofitable market for longer than they would voluntarily choose.

Insurance Mandates: A Form of Private Regulation of Private Health Insurance

Insurance mandates take two distinct forms. The most common is a legal requirement that insurers that market policies offer a specific benefit, such as maternity stays, mental health services, and chiropractic care. One rationale for such requirements is that people may be insufficiently well informed about the benefits to be derived from such services because they have not used such services previously. Or they tend to underestimate the probability that they will need such services in the future (Summers 1989). However, when the need arises, they will presumably be pleased that the services are covered. An unstated rationale for such mandates—and a very real reason that mandates exist—is that a professional group whose members supply the services benefits from insurance mandates in the form of increased demand and hence compensation.

The other form of mandate is a requirement that an employer provide health insurance to employees who satisfy some criteria specified by the law or a set of regulations formulated on the basis of the law, such as working more than a specific number of hours per week.

Advocates of insurance mandates make several arguments in support of these laws and regulations. First, on equity grounds, it is argued that every person should have access to health insurance as a right. Second, the lack of health insurance leads to payment shortfalls, which, if sufficiently large, could lead to bankruptcies of suppliers of personal health care services. Uninsured persons are treated in hospital emergency rooms, often at little or no out-of-pocket cost to the uninsured person. As a consequence, the prices of emergency room services paid by insured persons rise. This burden is ultimately paid by those persons who have insurance—a cost-shifting argument. If this is so, then why doesn't government provide health insurance in the first place?

Third, mandating private health insurance coverage as opposed to public provision of health insurance avoids the deadweight loss that would result from an increase in taxes to finance the public provision of health insurance. By *deadweight loss*, economists mean a loss attributable to a change in allocation of scarce resources from the allocation that would have occurred in the absence of some distortion. For example, moral hazard involves a deadweight loss (see chapter 3). In the context of health insurance mandates, the deadweight loss may take the form, for example, of reduced incentives to work when marginal personal income tax rates are raised.

Suppose that the government required employers to provide a health insurance policy valued at $1,000. This mandate would shift each employer's demand curve for labor downward by $1,000 (fig. 10.3), that is, from D_0 to D_1. However, at least some of the employees value the benefit. Thus, the aggregate supply curve of labor shifts downward from S_0 to S_1, but the downward shift in labor supply is not as great as the downward shift in employer demand. The supply curve of labor of those persons who do not value getting health insurance through the job does not change. Thus, the wage-employment equilibrium changes from (w_0, E_0) to (w_1, E_1) following implementation of the mandate. Both wage rates and employment fall as a result of a requirement that employers offer health insurance to all of their employees. If, however, the supply curve shifts downward by as much as the downward shift in demand, implying that the employees' valuation of the mandate equals the cost of the mandate, then the mandate causes a decrease in wage rates but no change in employment (fig. 10.4).

Mandated benefits represent a tax equal to the difference between the employers' cost of providing the benefit and the employees' valuation of the benefit, not the cost of providing the benefit (Summers 1989, 181). From a societal vantage point, there is a question about how employees' valuations should be measured. To the extent that employees "undervalue" a service with which they have had no prior experience or underestimate the probability of using the service, it is not at all clear that ex ante valuations are meaningful and useful for making welfare comparisons.

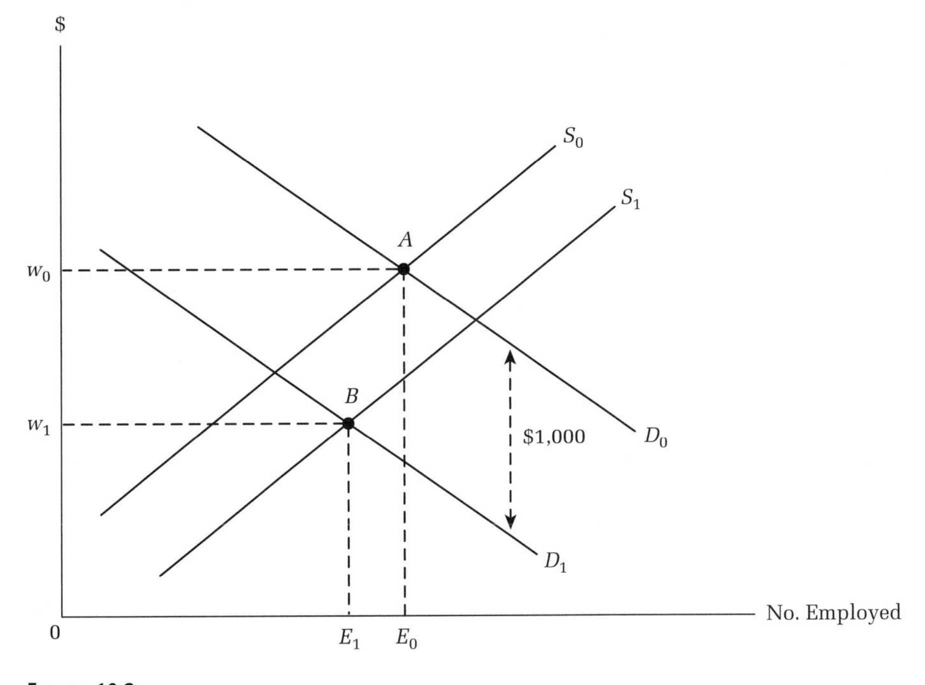

FIGURE 10.3
Case in Which the Cost of the Mandate Exceeds Employees' Valuation of Mandated Benefit

If, rather than mandating particular benefits, the government decided to provide coverage to all as a public benefit, the resulting welfare losses could be larger than with the mandate. Employers and employees who otherwise would have been unaffected by a mandate (nonemployed persons) would be subject to increased taxes.

Conceptually, the distortion could be minimized by imposing a head tax on everyone. A head tax is a tax of a fixed dollar amount per person. If one pays a specific sum just for breathing, distortions in economic activity are limited. On the other hand, head taxes raise questions of vertical equity (meaning that the rich should pay higher taxes than the poor) since the poor pay the same tax as the rich. By contrast, payroll or personal income taxes may be fairer, but they introduce distortions, such as in the worker's work-leisure decision.

Mandated benefits have deficiencies if one views the lack of coverage as reflecting individuals' underestimating the probability of event occurring. Persons who are not employed are unaffected by an employer benefit mandate. Thus, if the objective is that obstetric care be covered, with mandated employer-based insurance benefits, nonemployed women would not have such coverage. Another class of problems results from wage rigidities. For persons who earn the legal minimum

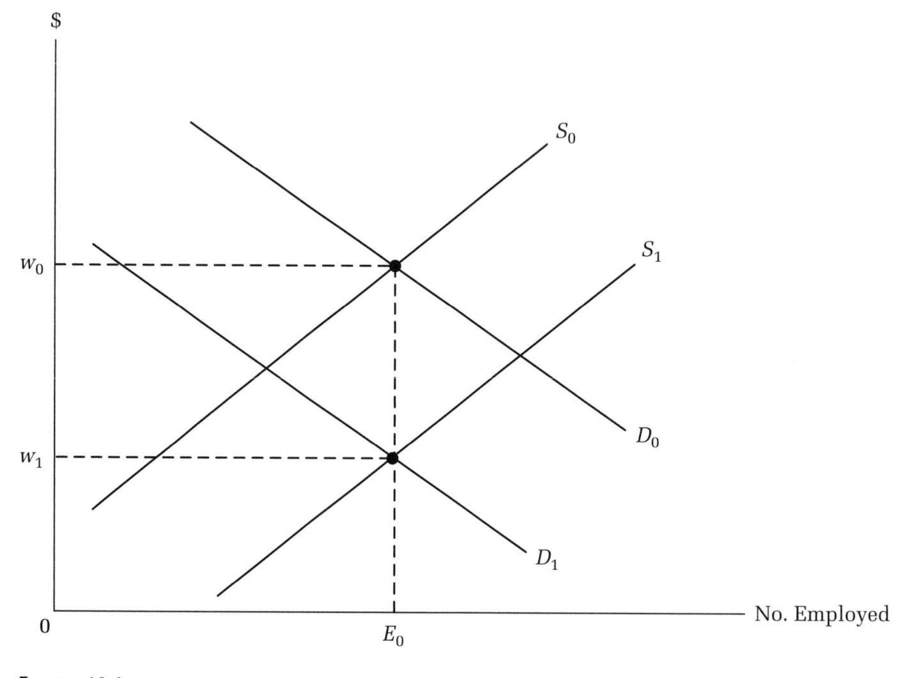

FIGURE 10.4
Case in Which the Cost of the Mandate Equals Employees' Valuation of Mandated Benefit

wage, mandated health insurance cannot result in a lower wage rate. Rather, the full effect of the mandate is on reduced employment.

The law generally requires that if an employer provides health insurance to its employees, the health insurance benefit must be the same for all employees. But the cost of providing the benefit plausibly differs markedly among employees. Older employees use much more health care on average than do younger employees. At younger ages, however, female employees are likely to use maternity benefits. If wages can perfectly adjust—for example, if older workers' wages fall relative to those for younger workers—the market will adjust for the mandate without important changes in the relative employment of older versus younger workers occurring. However, if wage rigidities prevent such adjustments from occurring, that is, if cuts in absolute wages are difficult to implement, then employers affected by the mandate will seek to hire disproportionate numbers of younger workers or part-time workers, who may be exempt from the mandate. This type of distortion would not occur under public provision of the services.

One reason why mandated benefits are so politically popular is that the cost of such benefits does not appear in public budgets. Thus, politicians can claim they have delivered new benefits to their constituents without actually having to raise taxes. Superficially, mandated benefits appear to be "free," but in reality they are not free. Even though the electorate is likely to pay for mandated benefits in terms of real wage reductions, perhaps not realized precisely at the time the mandate is implemented but gradually over time, the electorate may be insufficiently informed to recognize this.

Empirical studies have been conducted on the effects of mandated insurance benefits on wages and employment. There is a risk of overgeneralizing because there is likely to be variation in employee valuation of mandated benefits. Probably the best-known empirical study is by Gruber (1994), who studied the impact of mandated maturity benefits. The rationale for requiring that maternity benefits be an included insurance benefit relates to equal treatment of pregnant women and other employees. Before mandates were enacted by state governments in the United States and by the US government, health insurance benefits generally limited maternity benefits in two ways. Either there was no coverage for costs incurred during pregnancy or benefits were paid as a lump-sum benefit, independent of the cost the family actually incurred for prenatal care and obstetric deliveries.

The Gruber study used a time series of US state cross sections, which took advantage of (1) the fact that the mandate applied to some employees within a state that had a mandate, (2) variation among states in having or not having mandates, and (3) changes in state laws requiring maternity benefits over time. Gruber found that employees who were likely to benefit, primarily young adult women or spouses with family coverage in the age group in which pregnancies are most likely to occur, bore the cost of the mandate in terms of reduced wages. For this reason, there was very little change in employment.

Mandates can have important effects other than on wage compensation and employment levels. Schmidt (2007) studied whether mandates to include the cost of infertility treatments in the health insurance package affected fertility rates. She found that mandates significantly increased first birth rates among women over age 35.

Klick and Markowitz (2006) studied the impact of mandated mental health benefits on suicide rates. Suicides are often caused by mental illness. The authors found no effect of mandates on suicide rates. The effects of mandates seem to vary according to the benefits being mandated and also the details of implementation, such as the quantity of services covered required as part of a benefit package.

Community Rating

Views on the goals of health insurance differ both within and among countries. According to one view, demand for health insurance stems from a household's desire for health expenditure risk protection. The aggregate demand for health insurance then is the sum of individual households' demand for coverage. It follows that premiums should reflect the loss anticipated for the household unit during the policy year. As the health of family members and hence anticipated expenditures change, premiums should be adjusted accordingly. The sick should pay more for health insurance than the well do.

A contrasting view is that we are all in this boat together. Some people are more fortunate to be endowed with good health; others are less fortunate in this regard. While the healthy are lucky, they are unlucky in being obligated to subsidize their fellow citizens who are less healthy than they are. The theory that we are all in the boat together and hence all are obligated to bear part of the burden is called the *solidarity principle* (Zweifel and Breyer 1997).

With group employer-based insurance, the healthy implicitly subsidize the sick members of the group. Holding other factors constant, unhealthy or older employees are more costly to employers. To the extent that older workers are predominantly employed in certain job categories, it is feasible for employers to adjust wages downward to compensate for the higher anticipated health insurance outlays. In fact, there is empirical evidence that this does occur (see Pauly 1997, 90).

Even when employers do not self-insure, the insurance that they purchase is likely to be highly experience rated. That is, the premiums for year $t + 1$ reflect losses actually incurred by the group in year t. Self-insured groups are experience rated in that the self-insured entity bears the entire cost of the group (less the component that is borne by citizens at large, given the tax exclusion of health insurance benefits provided by employers).

In individual insurance markets, at least conceptually, matters might be different. Theoretically, if insurers had as much information as insured individuals do, there would be no cross subsidies. Every premium would be actuarially fair, that is, premiums would be set equal to expected loss, plus a competitively determined loading factor.

Recent empirical evidence for the United States implies that there are small differences in premiums among the healthy and sick in individual insurance markets, which implies that a considerable amount of risk pooling occurs. This may occur because insurers do not update premiums dollar for dollar for every dollar change in an individual insured's health expenditure (Marquis and Buntin 2006). On the other hand, there *are* some health-related differences in premiums, and many unhealthy individuals lack health insurance coverage of any type in the United States.

To protect persons in poor health within their jurisdictions, some US states have adopted the requirement that individual insurance premiums be community rated. Community rating means that premiums can reflect the experience of the community as a whole, with some differentials in premiums according to such factors as age and gender, but an individual's health expenditure history is not to be used as a factor in premium setting.

To the extent that premium differences based on health are reduced by community rating, one would expect an increase in demand for community-rated insurance relative to demand without such laws, and this shift has been observed (see, e.g., Buchanan and Marquis 1999), with higher percentages of unhealthy persons being insured and the healthy being uninsured. However, the empirical evidence indicates that any effect of community rating on the share of persons without health insurance is at most small (Sloan and Conover 1998).

MANAGED CARE DEFINED

Given the combination of high fees and little cost sharing at the point of delivery of services, along with the rising expenditures on personal health services that ensued, by the 1980s the stage was set for major changes in health insurance contracts. Although managed care as a concept was decades old, meaningful growth of managed care enrollments in the United States first occurred during the 1980s. Managed care plans have grown very rapidly and have become the dominant form of health insurance contract in the United States (Glied 2000).

Although there is no standard definition of managed care, three elements are important to any definition with the elements varying in importance by type of managed care plan (table 10.3). The first element is some management of utilization by the health plan. This may take the form of prior authorization by the insurer before a patient can be admitted to a hospital or undergo a major procedure, such as a surgical operation. In some health plans, restriction on choice of provider is accomplished through the use of gatekeeper physicians who must approve all referrals to specialists. Some managed care plans have used this gatekeeper arrangement to restrict the use of specialty services by holding primary care physicians

TABLE 10.3
Important Features of Traditional Health Insurance and Alternative Forms of Managed Health Care

		Managed Care		
Dimension	Indemnity Insurance	PPO	IPA/Network HMO	Group/Staff HMO
Role of insurer	Pay bills	Pay bills; form network	Pay bills; form network; monitor utilization	Provide care
Role of cost sharing	Incentives to control use of services	Incentives to use selected providers	Incentives to use selected providers	Incentives to use selected providers
Qualified providers	Almost all	Almost all (network)	Network	Network
Choice of providers	Patient	Patient	Gatekeeper (in network)	Gatekeeper (in network)
Payment of providers	Fee-for-service	Discounted FFS	Capitation	Salary
Limits on utilization	Demand side	Supply side (price)	Supply side (price, quantity)	Supply side (price, quantity)

Source: Cutler, McClellan, and Newhouse (2000), table 1.

(general or family physicians, general internists, pediatricians) financially responsible for referrals. *Financial responsibility* means that the physician has a financial disincentive to refer his or her patients to other physicians or to admit them to hospitals. Another form of utilization control is ex post utilization review. The service is provided but payment for the service may be subsequently denied if the insurer determines that the service was not clinically justified or simply not covered.

Second, managed care plans impose limits on the physicians, hospitals, and pharmaceutical products covered by the plan. For example, a physician who is a high utilizer of diagnostic tests and has a low threshold for admitting patients to the hospital may be excluded from a health plan. To be covered by the plan, the patient must go to providers on the insurer's list. If the patient sees a physician not on the list, coverage for the services provided by the physicians is denied.

Under a provider selection process called *selective contracting*, managed care plans can decide to include some providers in their networks and exclude others. In contrast, under the traditional health insurance system, insurers are required to deal with all licensed providers. To do otherwise would be considered to interfere with the practice of medicine.

By requiring or encouraging patients to use selected providers, managed care plans gain bargaining power to obtain a lower price from providers with whom they contract. By increasing patient flow, the selected providers in turn have the potential of increasing quality of care through a volume-outcome effect ("Practice (through higher volume) may make perfect"). Selective contracting with providers and provider networks is potentially a valuable tool for managed care plans to reduce cost and improve quality. Since about 2000, managed care plans in the United States have relaxed their policies of steering their plan enrollees to particular health care providers (Fang and Rizzo 2009, 2010). This may be a market response to the "managed care backlash" described below.

The third element is financial incentives. There are financial incentives for providers and patients. A major financial incentive for providers to limit utilization is provided by capitation payment. Under capitation, the provider receives a fixed payment per patient per time period, such as a month. The cost of any services provided is borne by the provider. Thus, in contrast to the fee-for-service system that prevails under traditional health insurance, in which providing more services is likely to mean higher profit, under capitation, the provision of more services reduces profit (see, e.g., Cutler, McClellan, and Newhouse 2000; Glied 2000; Baker and Phibbs 2002). Because providers, particularly physicians, bear the cost of extra services at the margin, capitation payment amounts to supply-side cost sharing; physicians share in the full financial risk of illness (Ellis and McGuire 1993).

Managed care plans have a strong incentive to search for low-priced providers. Under traditional health insurance, individual patients have little incentive to search for low-cost providers because they at most bear a small portion of the full cost of care. Rather, the insurer bears the expenditure risk (and presumably is well positioned to do this, given the pooling of uncorrelated expenditure risks of individuals). In addition, the search cost is likely to be higher for individual patients than for health plans. For individuals, the receipt of health care is typically a relatively rare event. For insurers, health care utilization is an everyday occurrence. Insurers' search costs are lower because they can take advantage of economies of scale in developing large information systems for searching. The benefits of searching for low-cost providers are higher in managed care plans because coverage tends to be complete. (There is relatively little patient cost sharing.) Thus, if the plan saves $1,000, for example, by identifying and recruiting a low-cost physician to the plan, much if not practically all of the saving will accrue to the health plan. Managed care plans can use the network as a tool to influence the patient flow to the selected provider. The inclusion or exclusion of providers in the network can alter market demand faced by the individual physicians, which in turn gives such plans an important instrument to influence physician behavior in terms of their choice of quantity and quality of health care services (McGuire 2000).

Managed care plans sometimes employ demand-side cost sharing to influence patient flows. As with traditional health insurance, demand-side cost sharing, in the form of co-payments or deductibles, is applied to control the use of health care services. In addition, managed care plans use demand-side cost sharing to encourage persons they insure to use services provided by providers within the plan's own network (Glied 2000), although to a lesser extent than traditional health insurers in the United States do. For example, some managed care plans employ differential cost sharing, which requires insured persons to pay a higher co-payment for using out-of-network services and imposes no or a lower co-payment for using services within the network. Multi-tiered pricing is also used to encourage the insured to use drugs on the plan's formulary and to use generic rather than branded drugs.

There are three types of managed care plans in the United States (table 10.3). First, some managed care plans fully integrate insurance, financing, and care provision functions. These are group and staff model health maintenance organization (HMOs). An HMO plan covers services on a capitated basis, which means that the provider or organization receives a fixed payment per enrollee for the provision of services over a fixed time period, such as a year. When the organization rather than the individual physician is paid the capitated payment, the most common approach, physicians may be employed on a salaried basis, which is in sharp contrast to traditional health insurance, in which insurance and service delivery are fully separated and the role of the insurer is limited to paying bills, while payment to providers is made on a fee-for-service basis (table 10.3).

A survey of primary care urban California physicians' experiences with financial incentives in managed care plans conducted in 1996 documented the widespread use of explicit incentives (40 percent reported being subject to such incentives) for physicians to limit care, such as financial rewards for limiting hospital admissions of their patients as well as limiting referrals to specialists (Grumbach, Osmond, Vranizan, et al. 1998). Such incentives may be employed in addition to or instead of compensation of a salaried basis. An empirical evaluation of the effects of physician incentives in HMOs concluded that medical expenditures of HMOs were 5 percent lower than they would have been in the absence of such incentives (Gaynor, Rebitzer, and Taylor 2004).

Other two types of managed care organizations are in between the traditional insurance model and the group/staff model. In one, through contractual arrangements, insured individuals' choice of providers is limited to a defined set of independent providers, independent practice associations (IPAs). In the other, preferred provider organizations (PPOs), insured individuals pay discounted fees if they receive care from providers in the PPOs' networks, but insured individuals receive some insurance benefits even if they see providers outside such networks. In essence, under this arrangement, a patient's choice of providers is unrestricted, but the plans provide incentives to use selected providers and monitor the care provided. A point-of-service (POS) plan is a program in which enrollees may receive care within the PPO network or go outside the network and receive indemnity insurance, which is a fixed dollar subsidy per unit of service, with the insured person paying the full difference between the physician's fee and the fixed dollar subsidy (see, e.g., Fang and Rizzo 2010).

THE EFFECT OF MANAGED CARE ON MARKET STRUCTURE AND PROVIDERS' AND PATIENTS' INCENTIVES

An important feature of managed care is selective contracting and network formation. Limiting coverage to a defined set of providers offers two advantages to managed care networks and to society more generally to the extent that competition among providers is welfare increasing. The first advantage is that selective contracting allows managed care organizations to exclude providers it judges to be inefficient or of low quality. Second, by limiting the number of providers in its network, the organization gains bargaining power in its negotiations with providers. The advantage to providers of being in the network is that they receive a guaranteed set of customers. On the other hand, for giving providers this additional business, the managed care organization typically demands and obtains discounted prices on covered services.

This process by which physicians who charge higher fees may be excluded from the network substantially increases the price elasticity of demand facing the individual provider or provider group. If the physicians charge slightly more than the managed care network demands, they may lose access to many potential patients, specifically those patients enrolled in the managed care plan in question. The selective contracting process thus introduces price competition into medical markets where this is lacking under traditional health insurance plans.

Negotiated discounted rates with a defined panel of providers may reduce the profitability of services and hence reduce rates of entry of new firms, although the providers may be compensated by increasing the flow of patients. Furthermore, managed care plans may encourage their enrollees to consume a different bundle of services than that consumed by patients with traditional health insurance, such as a shift from hospital inpatient to outpatient services or from curative care to preventive care (Baker and Brown 1999).

Using mammography provision as an example, Baker and Brown (1999) found that the growth of managed care led to consolidation of providers in this health care market. More specifically, they found that an increased managed care market share is associated with decreased numbers of mammography facilities and with increases in volume per facility for those facilities that remained in the market.

Selective contacting also alters consumer incentives. Under traditional health insurance, patients are free to choose their providers. But patients have little incentive to select low-cost providers because patients bear only a small portion of the full cost of care and may lack knowledge about which providers are low cost. Advertising bans limit dissemination of price information. Thus, to learn about prices, it is necessary to actually visit particular providers. As a consequence, competition among providers is mainly on a non-price basis. For example, hospitals tend to invest in new technologies and equipment to attract patients and their primary care physicians, described as a "medical arm race" in literature (see Dranove and Satterthwaite 2000; chapter 6, this book). More intense competition among hospitals historically has been associated with higher, not lower, cost (Dranove, Shanley, and White 1993).

By contrast, managed care plans are relatively well positioned to search for low-cost providers, and with selective contracting, they can limit plan enrollees' use of services to those providers they select. The focus of market competition consequently shifts from non-price aspects to price. Dranove, Shanley, and White (1993) described this as "payer-driven competition," in contrast to "patient-driven competition" under traditional health insurance.

Selective contracting can effectively operate only when there is a choice among providers. Thus, selective contracting is more likely to succeed in markets where there are many providers and their operation is not at full capacity. Dranove, Simon, and White (1998) found that managed care plans are more likely to use selective contracting in markets with more hospitals with lower occupancy rates.

Under patient-driven competition, there is a negative relationship between price, such as the prices of hospital services, and market concentration. Under payer-driven competition, the relation between price and market concentration becomes positive because the managed care plans are more likely to obtain a lower price as the market becomes less concentrated (Dranove and Satterthwaite 2000).

Using data from the 1980s from the US state of California, Dranove, Shanley, and White (1993) tested the price-concentration relationship, finding that prices of hospital services and market concentration (as measured by the Herfindahl-Hirschman Index) were significantly negatively related in 1983. By contrast, the price-concentration relationship became significantly positive in 1988. Taken together, these results suggest that a switch from patient-driven to payer-driven competition occurred in California following the change in the law in 1982 that permitted payers to use selective contracting.

Many managed care plans use capitation as their major payment to physicians. McGuire (2000, 2008) developed a conceptual framework for analyzing the effect of capitation on physician incentives. Physician revenue is

$$R + p_s x, \tag{10.1}$$

where R is a fixed amount representing capitation payments that is made independent of the services provided, x is the quantity of physician services, and p_s is the payment per unit of service. Thus, $p_s x$ represents variable revenue, which depends on the quantity of services the physician provides. The revenue function incorporates the element of supply-side cost sharing if p_s is less than marginal cost per unit of service. If the physician only has patients covered by a pure capitation contract, p_s equals zero. Payers can design incentives to elicit desired behavior from a provider by choosing the appropriate combination of fixed revenue (R) and fee for variable revenue portion (p_s).

Quality is essentially noncontractible in that it is difficult to use as a basis for payment. Noncontractible inputs include physician time, attentiveness, and diligence. Each potentially affects the outcomes of care, but these inputs cannot be directly monitored or set by the payer. The benefit the patient receives thus depends not only on the quantity of services but also on these hard to monitor qualitative aspects of care. The marginal benefit of quality is positive but declines, at least past some quality threshold. The provision of quality is costly to physicians, although not used as a basis for payment. The marginal cost of services is positively related to the quality level.

Patients value quality. Thus, although providing higher quality entails a cost to the physician, higher quality increases patient demand. In this way, physicians are rewarded for providing a higher quality of care by being able to attract more patients.

The physician chooses both quantity and quality (as measured by effort) of health care services to maximize profit. The distinction of quantity and quality in this model is that quantity is contractible but quality is not.

The optimal solution for the choice of quantity satisfies the condition that the marginal benefit received by the physician equals the marginal cost borne by the physician. At least in principle, it is possible to design a payment scheme, that is, a combination of R and p_s, to elicit socially optimal levels of quantity and quality from physicians.

MANAGED CARE AND HEALTH SYSTEM PERFORMANCE

OVERVIEW

Although managed care offers several attractive features in theory, in the end, what matters is how it works in practice. Performance has been measured by indicators of spending, price, quantity (utilization per capita), quality, and technology adoption. We first describe some individual studies and then report results from literature reviews that have been conducted on this subject.

EFFECTS OF MANAGED CARE ON SPENDING ON PERSONAL HEALTH CARE

Cutler and Sheiner (1998) used variation in managed care penetration across states between 1988 and 1993 in the United States as a laboratory for examining the impact of managed care, measured by population share of HMO enrollments, on the growth of aggregate expenditures on health care services. They concluded that increased managed care plan penetration decreases growth in such spending. States with higher managed care penetration experienced substantially lower expenditure growth during this period. The systemwide savings from managed care mainly came from a reduction in expenditures for hospital care, which in turn primarily came from reductions in patient length of hospital stay. A 10 percent increase in the managed care share decreased the growth of hospital spending by about 0.5 percent and total health care spending by about 0.4 percent, which implies that increased spending on physicians offset some of the savings in hospital spending.

Conceptually, managed care plans can reduce the growth of health care spending through four mechanisms. First, managed care organizations might reduce price through negotiating price reductions or searching for low-cost providers, using selective contracting as a negotiating tool. Second, such organizations might reduce the quantity of health services provided to patients through various forms of utilization review. Third, they might save money through offering lower quality at lower cost. Fourth, they might reduce the growth of health care spending by reducing the rate of technology adoption, because technology change in medicine has long been identified as a major driver of increasing spending in health care (Newhouse 1992). Given these four channels, how in fact do managed care organizations achieve their savings?

Cutler, McClellan, and Newhouse (2000) addressed this question by comparing prices paid and treatments received for a common set of conditions in different insurance plans. Their data came from two different sources: claims records from a large US firm offering both managed care policies and a traditional health insurance policy, and state data containing inpatient claims for all persons people admitted to hospitals in the US state of Massachusetts. Focusing on care for patients with heart disease, Cutler and coauthors measured the difference in spending on services between persons enrolled in managed care and those with traditional insurance plans; they decomposed the difference in spending into a pure price component and a quantity/quality component.

They found a statistically significant difference in the mean level of payment for heart attacks between managed care plans and traditional insurance plans. For example, average reimbursement by HMOs was only 61 percent that of the traditional insurance policies. Procedure use was about the same between the two types of health insurance plans. However, the amount paid by managed care plans for a common bundle of services was only 57 percent of the amount paid by traditional health plans, after accounting for differences in patient characteristics. Health outcomes did not depend on the type of insurance plan selected. Cutler and colleagues concluded that virtually all the difference in health care spending between managed care and traditional insurance plans came from lower unit prices rather than from a reduction in the quantity or quality of services received.[4] With regard to the impact of managed care on quality of care, the existing literature indicates there is little difference in the quality of care provided under managed care plans and traditional insurance plan (Glied 2000; Baker and McClellan 2001). The empirical evidence is inconsistent with the argument that managed care plans might save money by offering lower quality at lower cost. Rather, managed care provides care of comparable quality but at a lower cost.

However, simple comparisons of cost between the two types of plan ignore that managed care may affect the utilization of health care services persons enrolled in traditional insurance plans. These spillovers may occur through at least two mechanisms. First, where there are high levels of managed care penetration, the demand for certain types of services, such as hospital inpatient care, is likely to be low. This may lead to reductions in the capacity of such services, such as the number of hospital beds. Lower capacity in turn may make it more difficult for persons enrolled in traditional health insurance plans to be treated in these facilities. Managed care may reduce health cost growth by reducing rates of technology diffusion, which is recognized as a major source of health care expenditure growth.

Second, there will be spillovers in how patients are treated for specific conditions. It is difficult for physicians to maintain different approaches to care based on the treatment philosophies and policies of individual insurers. Thus, once managed care becomes an important force in a community, physicians may decide to adopt the managed care style of practice for all of their patients. There is empirical support that this type of spillover effect occurs (Baker and McClellan 2001; Chandra and Staiger 2007). The growth of managed care results in the systemwide provision of high-quality care at lower cost.

4. The gross price of personal health care services (price charged by the provider) has its own impact on medical care demand. An increased price leads to a reduction in the quantity of services demanded (see chapter 3). But it can also affect the choice of insurer (Dusansky and Koc 2006), and the nature of the insurance contract can also affect demand. To the extent that managed care plans are relatively effective negotiators with providers, one would expect the relative demand for such health plans to increase during periods of medical price inflation.

Although we have emphasized results from individual studies, the thrust of the literature is consistent with the findings from the studies just described. After reviewing many individual studies, Glied (2000) concluded that total health care spending in managed care plans tends to be about 10–15 percent lower than in other insurance plans, based on a review of seventy-nine studies published between 1997 and mid-2001. Differences in expenditures do not reflect lower rates of visits to physicians among persons enrolled in managed care plans. If anything, such utilization tends to be higher in such plans (Deb, Li, Trivedi, et al. 2006).

Not all empirical studies agree that managed care results in reduced expenditures on personal health services or in the composition of reductions, to the extent that they exist. For example, Shin and Moon (2007) concluded that HMO plans reduce members' out-of-pocket spending relative to that of members of other health insurance plans. But they found no difference between HMOs and other plans in what the plans themselves spent. A comparison of utilization between fee-for-service and managed care among pregnant women and during labor and delivery yielded mixed findings, including higher rates of use of ultrasound use during pregnancy in managed care plans but lower rates of cesarean sections among women enrolled in such plans (Turcotte, Robst, and Polachek 2006).

EFFECTS OF MANAGED CARE ON DIFFUSION OF TECHNOLOGY

Managed care affects the diffusion of new and expensive technologies in several ways. First, to the extent that managed care plans pay less per unit of service for intensive treatments that depend on use of new medical technology and equipment, the expected profitability from adopting a new technology declines, which in turn reduces the incentive for technology adoption.

Second, when prices paid providers fall, the price-cost margin of hospitals and other services is reduced, which in turn affects the overall financial position of providers of health care services. As a result, the availability of relatively low-cost internal funds to finance the adoption of new technology decreases, potentially forcing adopters of new technologies to use higher-cost external funds to finance the capital projects. This raises the expected cost of adopting new technology and hence decreases such investment (see chapter 9).

Third, the growth of managed care has shifted the nature of competition from patient-driven to payer-driven competition. Under patient-driven competition, hospitals tend to compete on a non-price basis, such as through offering new technology. The cost of adopting new technology is then financed by increased revenue, either charge-based (fee-for-service) or cost-based reimbursement (see chapter 6). By contrast, under payer-driven competition, hospitals compete by offering lower prices to managed care plans. Early adoption of new technologies has consequently become less relevant for attracting patients to individual hospitals.

All three factors work to decrease technology diffusion in areas in which managed care plans enroll a large share of the population. Several empirical studies provide support for this proposition. Using state data, Cutler and Sheiner (1998) found that increased HMO enrollment was associated with less rapid diffusion of a range of new technologies in hospitals, and this effect increased over time. In addition, they found that the growth of managed care changed the composition of technology leaders in health care markets: states with high managed care activity that were formerly technology leaders became only average in new technology acquisition. Baker (2001) reported that increases in HMO market share are associated with slower diffusion of magnetic resonance imaging (MRI), as well as declines in the use of MRI procedures. Baker and Phibbs (2002) reported that increases in managed care activity are associated with slower adoption of neonatal intensive care units.

More recently, Mas and Seinfeld (2008) examined the effects of managed care in general and HMO penetration in particular on the diffusion of thirteen technologies in the United States. These technologies included those used in diagnostic radiology (diagnostic radioisotope studies, ultrasonography, computed tomography, MRI, positron emission tomography), radiation therapy (X-ray therapy, therapeutic radioisotope treatment, radioactive implants, megavoltage irradiation, stereotactic radiosurgery), and cardiac technology (cardiac catheterization, open heart surgery, and angioplasty). Although the magnitude of effect of HMO enrollment on the presence of the technologies differed by technology, the effects were uniformly negative and statistically significant at conventional levels.

Although a less rapid diffusion of new technologies contributes to reduced long-term growth of health care expenditures, less rapid diffusion could have the unfortunate adverse side effect of reducing the rate of improvement in health outcomes. Thus, the welfare effect of slower technology diffusion cannot be deduced without further considering its impact on health outcomes.

Baker and Phibbs (2002) examined this issue by decomposing neonatal intensive care units (NICUs) into two types, high- and midlevel, and found that slower diffusion of NICUs attributable to the growth of managed care primarily reflected a slower adoption in less sophisticated midlevel units. Increases in the availability of midlevel NICUs were associated with increases in mortality for very low-birth-weight infants, but this relationship was reversed for high-level NICUs. This pattern of results suggests that the slower diffusion of technology may not necessarily produce a classical welfare trade-off between cost and outcomes. If reductions in the rate of technology diffusion are mainly attributable to changes in the adoption of technologies with low marginal benefits, these reductions may not adversely affect outcomes in a major way.

Miller and Luft (2002) concluded that HMOs and traditional health insurance plans offer comparable quality of care, but that HMOs have a somewhat lower use of hospitals and other expensive services. However, they cautioned that HMO enrollees reported worse results on several indicators of access to care and had lower levels of satisfaction with care received than did persons with traditional health insurance. Further, there was variability in quality within the HMO sector. Xu and Jensen (2007), studying the impact of HMO membership on functional status (ability to perform tasks of daily living) of the near elderly (persons near but below age 65), found that HMO members fared worse in that they experienced greater declines in functional status if they had chronic conditions. For the near elderly overall, however, there were no differences in functional status decline between persons enrolled in traditional fee-for-service insurance plans and those enrolled in HMOs.

Data from the RAND Health Insurance Experiment show a similar pattern as the Xu-Jensen study. In particular, per capita spending in a staff model HMO was 40 percent lower than in a fee-for-service plan in the same city. While the health effects of plan membership were generally similar between HMO and fee-for-service plans, low-income enrollees who began the experiment with health problems fared worse in the HMO than in the fee-for-service plan (Ware, Brook, Rogers, et al. 1986).

The averages thus obscure some difference in quality among individual plans. Gottfried and Sloan (2002) reviewed the evidence on the quality of care provided by HMOs versus that provided by non-HMOs in the treatment of specific conditions, including cardiovascular disease, cancer, geriatric problems, pregnancy, and pediatric disease. Like Miller and Luft, they described findings indicating that enrollees in HMO plans expressed dissatisfaction with some aspect of their experiences, but overall, on most indicators, the quality of care financed by HMOs was comparable to that the quality of care financed by non-HMOs.

Rizzo (2005) studied the impact of an individual's HMO membership on the probability of receipt of various types of preventive services. After all, HMO stands for "health maintenance organization." So at least the rhetoric is that these organizations strive to keep their members well. Rizzo evaluated the relationship with eight alternative measures of preventive care and found that preventive care was more likely to be used by HMO members than by members of traditional health insurance plans.

Finally, Aizer, Currie, and Moretti (2007) investigated whether managed care harms the health of infants when enrollment in managed care is mandatory. The US state of California's Medicaid program requires some pregnant women to be enrolled in managed care as a condition of coverage. The authors found that Medicaid managed care decreased the quality of prenatal care the women received and increased the rate of low-birth-weight infants, premature births, and infant deaths. At least in this case, health care providers responded to managed care incentives to reduce the costs of care by limiting services provided in a way that led to decreases in infant health. Perhaps there is a lesson here: that competition among managed care originations does not suffice to ensure quality when the persons served are vulnerable and do not have the exit option of leaving a plan with which they are dissatisfied for another plan. On the other hand, there is some empirical evidence that is more favorable to Medicaid managed care as contrasted with Medicaid coverage provided on a fee-for-service basis. Mitchell and Gaskin (2007) reported that caregivers of Medicaid children visiting fee-for-service providers encountered greater difficulty navigating the health care system. In particular, levels of comprehensive care plan assessment and primary care provider case management were seen to be better for Medicaid recipients seeking managed care than fee-for-service providers (Mitchell and Gaskin 2007).

The Backlash against Managed Care

Much of the empirical evidence is quite favorable to managed care plans in general and to HMOs in particular. Nevertheless, from about the mid-1990s through the early 2000s, there was a backlash against such plans. Although most consumers generally were satisfied with the overall quality of managed care, the US public developed a general concern about the quality of such care (Sloan and Hall 2002). Dissatisfaction appears to have stemmed from perceived restrictions on access to emergency room care, specialists, and other forms of care that may potentially be beneficial to individuals covered by such care. Physicians complained that they faced constraints on care decisions imposed by such plans.

In sum, curbing service use is painful, and much easier to talk about in general than when it actually applies to actual specific situations. The public does not like losing specific benefits, although traditional health insurance may impose a welfare loss on society more generally. No one represents the welfare loss. Consumers, by contrast, are good about representing the losses they incur as individuals. The backlash led to the enactment of managed care patient protection laws designed to reduce the ability of managed care organizations to constrain cost growth. Such laws included laws providing direct access to specialists without having to have prior authorization from a primary care physician gatekeeper, laws requiring minimum patient hospital stays for obstetric deliveries, "prudent layperson standards," which protect coverage for emergency room visits when in the judgment of a prudent layperson such care is warranted, and "any willing provider" laws, which require plans to accept providers who apply to be covered—a direct assault on the concept of selective contracting. Overall, the enactment of patient protection laws neither affected the utilization of services nor improved patient satisfaction with care (Sloan, Rattliff, and Hall 2005).

Private Health Insurance and Universal Health Insurance Coverage

A system based on private health insurance coverage, even if subsidized, as it is in the United States, will not lead to coverage of the entire population unless there are mandates for coverage and a public provision for disadvantaged groups in the population. The main reason why some public provision of insurance is needed is that not everyone is employed or is in a family with an employed individual.

One constant across countries is that people seem to like what they have. In a country in which most persons have private health insurance coverage, such as the United States, the most feasible proposals for universal health insurance coverage have been to extend private health insurance to previously uncovered individuals since this more closely resembles the status quo.

However, mandates that require employers to provide health insurance coverage to their employees may adversely affect employment, and the public provision of coverage to fill the gaps in coverage, will crowd out private insurance. If public insurance is available at less than actuarially fair premiums, employers and employees may find it optimal for employers to drop their private insurance benefit. Public health insurance plans charging actuarially fair premiums seems inconsistent with such programs' redistributional objectives. Understandably, the road from reliance on private health insurance to universal coverage is not well trod.

On the other hand, we need to be careful not to overemphasize the differences between private and public health insurance. Public provision in the form of social insurance (see chapter 12) does not eliminate the need for premium collection and basing premiums on forecasts of plan expenditures. In a self-funded public plan, younger persons would contribute more than their annual anticipated outlays in anticipation of higher outlays when they became older.

Public programs tend eschew such a self-funded approach in favor of pay-as-you-go (PAYGO) financing in which the young in a given year cross-subsidize elders. PAYGO financing is attractive in the short run, but in the long run, financing problems almost surely ensue. As the percentage of elderly persons rises, not only does the payment obligation rise, but the fraction of younger persons who subsidize the more costly public program falls. Fewer young persons have a larger aggregate burden to bear.

10.6 SUMMARY AND CONCLUSIONS

This chapter has discussed issues in the supply of health insurance markets and hence complements the discussion of demand in chapter 4 and of private health insurance systems in chapter 11. In chapter 4, we saw that risk-averse individuals are willing to pay more than the expected loss for protection against such loss. In this chapter, we have seen that by pooling individual risks, insurers can diversify away much of the risk of high loss from an adverse health event that people as uninsured individuals would face.

Insurers have two basic flows of income, one from underwriting and the other from investments. Changes in the length of time insurers have to use policyholders' money for investment purposes and in anticipated rates of return from investment affect premiums. We made a distinction between diversifiable and nondiversifiable risk and argued that nondiversifiable risk in particular affects the rate of return even an insurer in a competitive market needs to stay in business.

One source of nondiversifiable risk is adverse selection. Insurers combat adverse selection in various ways, including refusing to underwrite some risks or renew the insurance policies of persons who incur substantial medical expenditures during a policy year.

Health insurance is a subject in which the trade-off between allocative efficiency and equity is particularly evident. In an efficient market, people would have accurate beliefs about the probability that they will use medical services during the year and the amounts they will use conditional on any use. Premiums would reflect an accurate assessment of policyholders' expected loss during the policy year. Thus, after a person experienced a health shock, premiums would rise to reflect the change in health risk. Thus, sick people would pay more for health insurance. Since all parties would have good information, there would be no role for government provision or the review of information provided by insurers to policyholders. There would be free entry and exit of insurers. Thus, individual policyholders would face a bankruptcy risk, but, since the market had good information on solvency risk, presumably insurers with a higher bankruptcy risk would receive a lower premium than an insurer with a lower bankruptcy risk could. Thus, there would be no need for solvency regulation. Since the insurance market would be competitive, there would be no need for government oversight of premiums to offset private insurers' use of market power or to protect consumers from insurer insolvency. People would choose jobs based on their preferences for wages versus fringe benefits, of which health insurance is one. There would be no tax advantages to obtaining health insurance through one's job. If people decided to forgo health insurance, they would be exposed to large losses from high health expenditures, but this would be the luck of the draw by an informed consumer population.

Clearly, at every turn, equity considerations interfere with an idealized world in which economic efficiency is the dominant guide for public policy. To the extent that consumers lack relevant information about the probability that they will be ill, the prices of care, how to read insurance contracts, and the trade-offs between wages and fringe benefits, there is a fairly broad consensus that government should intervene. Likewise, there is widespread agreement that a person who is unlucky in having the genetic background that he or she has should not be asked to pay the full price for the difference between being unlucky and being lucky in one's genetic background. If insurers are able to exercise market power over either consumers or physicians and hospitals—that is, in situations in which economic efficiency is violated—government must be there as well.

We do not take a position about the weight that should be given to these distributional concerns. Rather we have endeavored to describe and analyze them from the standpoint of economics.

Key Concepts

- diversifiable risk
- premium setting
- reinsurance
- public health insurance
- mandated insurance benefits
- pay-as-you-go financing (PAYGO)
- independent practice association
- nondiversifiable risk
- underwriting
- private health insurance
- employer-based health insurance
- community rating
- health maintenance organization
- preferred provider organization

Review and Discussion Questions

10.1 List three advantages that employer-based private health insurance has over individually purchased private health insurance.

10.2 What are the major advantages and disadvantages of private health insurance compared to public health insurance?

10.3 Analyze the following statement: "The great importance of private health insurance sector is the major obstacle to implementing national (universal) health insurance in the United States."

10.4 In the context of private health insurance, what does the statement "this porridge is too hot" mean? What are some policy concerns if this porridge is really too hot? What kind of regulations can government adopt to ensure that "this porridge is just right"? Does the government run a risk that "this porridge will become too cold"? Explain your answers.

10.5 It is often argued that employer-based health insurance places a heavy burden on employers, and hence US manufacturers are placed at a competitive disadvantage in the global market. Is this argument valid? Why or why not?

10.6 Distinguish between demand-side and supply-side moral hazard. Why does each arise?

10.7 Explain the term "managed care" in your own words. List at least four dimensions that make managed care plans different from traditional health insurance.

10.8 The mainstream consensus in the literature is that total health care spending in managed care plans tends to be about 10–15 percent lower compared to traditional health insurance plans. Identify the potential channels that help managed care plans save costs. Based on the existing evidence, how does managed care achieve these savings

10.9 Specifically how does managed care alter physicians' incentives? How might managed care plans reduce supply-side moral hazard? Is there a risk that incentives physicians face under managed care may lead to too little care being provided? Why might care levels be too low? What are the criteria for determining whether optimal levels of care are being provided or not?

10.10 What is a preferred provider organization? How do incentives to patients and physicians differ from the incentives of an HMO?

10.11 What is meant by selective contracting? How is selective contracting useful in achieving health care cost containment?

10.12 Distinguish among the types of managed care plans in the United States.

10.13 How might there be spillover effects from managed care to traditional health insurance plans? How do such spillovers affect the measurement of the comparative cost of managed care and traditional fee-for-service health insurance plans?

10.14 Specifically why would one expect that the diffusion of new health care technologies might be slower under managed care plans than under traditional health insurance plans?

EXERCISES

10.1 Define the profit function of the private insurer in the line of health insurance. That is, what are the revenues and costs of the insurance firm? Based on your definition, please analyze the effects of the following exogenous changes on the insurer's profit:

a. an increase in interest rate;

b. an increase in the insurer's share price in the stock market;

c. a general increase in health care expenditures;

d. an increase in population size;

e. an increase in the country's unemployment rate;

f. a shift of the payment system from fee-for-service to capitation.

10.2 Suppose country A adopts a public health insurance plan that provides coverage for various types of personal health care services, with moderate demand-side cost sharing. Meanwhile, country A also allows private firms to offer health insurance for uncovered services and to pay for cost sharing of covered services. There are two types of private health insurance: (a) indemnity benefits that the insurance policy pays a fixed dollar amount for a particular type of service; (b) service benefits that the insurance policy pays a specific percentage of the out-of-pocket price. Answer each of the following questions:

a. What is meant by the statement that "private insurers 'free ride' on public plans"? Which type of private health insurance is more like to become the free rider, indemnity or service benefit plans? Explain your answer.

b. Which type of private health insurance (again, indemnity or service benefit) can provide better protection against the risk of financial loss when the insured is sick?

10.3 Explain the differences among the following three types of government intervention in the health insurance market: (1) public subsidy, (2) mandated insurance benefits, and (3) direct public provision. If the goal of government intervention is to achieve universal coverage, which strategy is the best (most efficient) in terms of minimizing the deadweight loss?

10.4 As mentioned in this chapter, some insurers operate disease management programs that seek to promote prevention and screening in order to reduce adverse health outcomes of chronic disease and the associated expense. Does the incentive for such loss prevention differ between private insurers and public insurers? Which type of insurer is more likely to adopt a loss prevention program? Explain your answer.

10.5 Compare differences between public health insurance and private health insurance along the following dimensions:

a. the decision to adopt new medical technologies;

b. premium setting;

c. administrative expense;

d. satisfying differences in consumer preferences (consumer preference heterogeneity);

e. providing preventive services.

Online Supplemental Material

Private Health Insurance

http://www.who.int/health_financing/private_health_in_dp_04_3.pdf

The History of Health Insurance in the United States

http://eh.net/encyclopedia/article/thomasson.insurance.health.us

Employment-Based Health Insurance

http://www.bepress.com/fhep/13/2/13/

http://www.investigatorawards.org/publications/policy_challenges/pdf/Chapter%203.pdf

Managed Care

http://www.themcic.com

Health Insurance Plans in America

http://www.ahip.org

http://www.bcbs.com

Supplemental Readings

Cutler, D. M., and R. J. Zeckhauser. 2000. The Anatomy of Health Insurance. In *Handbook of Health Economics*, ed. A. J. Culyer and J. P. Newhouse, 1A:617–621. Amsterdam: Elsevier Science.

Lehrer, S. F., and N. S. Pereira. 2007. Worker Sorting, Compensating Differentials and Health Insurance: Evidence from Displaced Workers. *Journal of Health Economics* 26 (5): 1034–1056.

Olson, C. A. 2002. Do Workers Accept Lower Wages in Exchange for Health Benefits? *Journal of Labor Economics* 20 (S2): S91–S114.

References

Adamache, K. W., and F. A. Sloan. 1983. Competition between Non-Profit and For-Profit Health Insurers. *Journal of Health Economics* 2 (3): 225–243.

Aizer, A., J. Currie, and E. Moretti. 2007. Does Managed Care Hurt Health? Evidence from Medicaid Mothers. *Review of Economics and Statistics* 89 (3): 385–399.

Baker, L. C. 2001. Managed Care and Technology Adoption in Health Care: Evidence from Magnetic Resonance Imaging. *Journal of Health Economics* 20 (3): 385–421.

Baker, L. C., and M. L. Brown. 1999. Managed Care, Consolidation among Health Care Providers, and Health Care: Evidence from Mammography. *RAND Journal of Economics* 30 (2): 351–374.

Baker, L. C., and M. B. McClellan. 2001. Managed Care, Health Care Quality, and Regulation. *Journal of Legal Studies* 30 (2): 715–741.

Baker, L. C., and C. S. Phibbs. 2002. Managed Care, Technology Adoption, and Health Care: The Adoption of Neonatal Intensive Care. *RAND Journal of Economics* 33 (3): 524–548.

Born, P. H. 2001. Insurer Profitability in Different Regulatory and Legal Environments. *Journal of Regulatory Economics* 19 (3): 211–237.

Buchanan, J. L., and M. S. Marquis. 1999. Who Gains and Who Loses with Community Rating for Small Business? *Inquiry—The Journal of Health Care Organization, Provision and Financing* 36 (1): 30–43.

Chandra, A., and D. O. Staiger. 2007. Productivity Spillovers in Health Care: Evidence from the Treatment of Heart Attacks. *Journal of Political Economy* 115 (1): 103–140.

Currie, J., and B. C. Madrian. 1999. Health, Health Insurance and the Labor Market. In *Handbook of Labor Economics*, ed. O. Ashenfelter and D. Card, 3:3309–3416. Amsterdam: Elsevier Science.

Cutler, D. M., M. McClellan, and J. P. Newhouse. 2000. How Does Managed Care Do It? *RAND Journal of Economics* 31 (3): 526–548.

Cutler, D. M., and L. Sheiner. 1998. Managed Care and the Growth of Medical Expenditures. In *Frontiers in Health Policy Research*, ed. A. M. Garber, 1. Cambridge, MA: MIT Press.

Cutler, D. M., and R. J. Zeckhauser. 2000. The Anatomy of Health Insurance. In *Handbook of Health Economics*, ed. A. J. Culyer and J. P. Newhouse, 1A:617–621. Amsterdam: Elsevier Science.

Deb, P. C., K. Li, P. K. Trivedi, et al. 2006. The Effect of Managed Care on Use of Health Care Services: Results from Two Contemporaneous Household Surveys. *Health Economics* 15 (7): 743–760.

Dranove, D., and M. A. Satterthwaite. 2000. The Industrial Organization of Health Care Markets. In *Handbook of Health Economics*, ed. J. P. Newhouse and A. J. Culyer, 1B:1093–1135. Amsterdam: Elsevier Science.

Dranove, D., M. Shanley, and W. D. White. 1993. Price and Concentration in Hospital Markets: The Switch from Patient-Driven to Payer-Driven Competition. *Journal of Law & Economics* 36 (1): 179–204.

Dranove, D., C. Simon, and W. D. White. 1998. The Determinants of Managed Care Penetration. *Journal of Health Economics* 17 (6): 729–745.

Dusansky, R., and C. Koc. 2006. Health Care, Insurance, and the Contract Choice Effect. *Economic Inquiry* 44 (1): 121–127.

Ellis, R. P., and T. G. McGuire. 1993. Supply-Side and Demand-Side Cost Sharing in Health Care. *Journal of Economic Perspectives* 7 (4): 135–151.

Fang, H., and J. A. Rizzo. 2009. Managed Care and Physicians' Perceptions of Drug Formulary Use. *American Journal of Managed Care* 16 (6): 395–400.

Fang, H., and J. A. Rizzo. 2010. Has the Influence of Managed Care Waned? Evidence from the Market for Physician Services. *International Journal of Health Care Finance and Economics* 10 (1): 85–103.

Gaynor, M., J. B. Rebitzer, and L. J. Taylor. 2004. Physician Incentives in Health Maintenance Organizations. *Journal of Political Economy* 112 (4): 915–931.

Glied, S. 2000. Managed Care. In *Handbook of Health Economics*, ed. J. P. Newhouse and A. J. Culyer, 1A:707–745. Amsterdam: Elsevier Science.

Goldstein, G. S., and M. V. Pauly. 1976. Group Health Insurance as a Local Public Good. In *The Role of Health Insurance in the Health Services Sector*, ed. R. N. Rosett, 73–114. Sagamore Beach, MA: Watson Publishing International.

Gottfried, J., and F. Sloan. 2002. The Quality of Managed Care: Evidence from the Medical Literature. *Law and Contemporary Problems* 65 (4): 103–138.

Grossman, J. M., and P. B. Ginsburg. 2004. As the Health Insurance Underwriting Cycle Turns: What Next? *Health Affairs* 23 (6): 91–101.

Gruber, J. 1994. The Incidence of Mandated Maternity Benefits. *American Economic Review* 84 (3): 622–641.

Gruber, J., and B. C. Madrian. 1994. Health Insurance and Job Mobility: The Effects of Public Policy on Job-Lock. *Industrial & Labor Relations Review* 48 (1): 86–102.

Grumbach, K., D. Osmond, K. Vranizan, et al. 1998. Primary Care Physicians' Experience of Financial Incentives in Managed-Care Systems. *New England Journal of Medicine* 339 (21): 1516–1521.

Hyman, D. A., and W. E. Kovacic. 2004. Monopoly, Monopsony, and Market Definition: An Antitrust Perspective on Market Concentration among Health insurers. *Health Affairs* 23 (6): 25–28.

Kaiser Family Foundation. 2009. Explaining Health Care Reform: What Are Health Insurance Exchanges? www.kff.org/healthreform/upload/7908.pdf (accessed March 10, 2011).

Kipp, R., J. P. Cookson, and L. L. Mattie. 2003. *Health Insurance Underwriting Cycle Effect on Health Plan Premiums and Profitability*, 44. Milliman USA.

Klick, J., and S. Markowitz. 2006. Are Mental Health Insurance Mandates Effective? Evidence from Suicides. *Health Economics* 15 (1): 83–97.

Lehrer, S. F., and N. S. Pereira. 2007. Worker Sorting, Compensating Differentials and Health Insurance: Evidence from Displaced Workers. *Journal of Health Economics* 26 (5): 1034–1056.

Madrian, B. C. 1994. Employment-Based Health Insurance and Job Mobility: Is There Evidence of Job-Lock? *Quarterly Journal of Economics* 109 (1): 27–54.

Marquis, M. S., and M. B. Buntin. 2006. How Much Risk Pooling Is There in the Individual Insurance Market? (Health Insurance). *Health Services Research* 41 (5): 1782–1800.

Mas, N., and J. Seinfeld. 2008. Is Managed Care Restraining the Adoption of Technology by Hospitals? *Journal of Health Economics* 27:1026–1045.

McGuire, T. G. 2000. Physician Agency. In *Handbook for Health Economics*, ed. J. P. Newhouse and A. J. Culyer, 462–528. Amsterdam: Elsevier Science.

McGuire, T. G. 2008. Physician Fees and Behavior: Implications for Structuring a Fee Schedule. In *Incentives and Choice in Health Care*, ed. F. A. Sloan and H. Kasper, 263–288. Cambridge, MA: MIT Press.

Miller, R. H., and H. S. Luft. 2002. HMO Plan Performance Update: An Analysis of the Literature, 1997–2001. *Health Affairs* 21 (4): 63–86.

Mitchell, J. M., and D. J. Gaskin. 2007. Caregivers' Ratings of Access: Do Children with Special Health Care Needs Fare Better under Fee-For Service or Partially Capitated Managed Care? *Medical Care* 45 (2): 146–153.

Munch, P., and D. E. Smallwood. 1980. Solvency Regulation in the Property-Liability Insurance Industry: Empirical Evidence. *Bell Journal of Economics* 11 (1): 261–282.

Newhouse, J. P. 1992. Medical Care Costs: How Much Welfare Loss? *Journal of Economic Perspectives* 6 (3): 3–21.

Olson, C. A. 2002. Do Workers Accept Lower Wages in Exchange for Health Benefits? *Journal of Labor Economics* 20 (S2): S91–S114.

Organisation for Economic Co-operation and Development. 2008. OECD Health Data 2008. http://www.oecd.org/document/56.

Pauly, M. V. 1997. *Health Benefits at Work: An Economic and Political Analysis of Employment-Based Health Insurance.* Ann Arbor, MI: University of Michigan Press.

Pauly, M. V. 1998. Managed Care, Market Power, and Monospony. *Health Services Research* 33 (5): 1439–1460.

Pauly, M. V. 2001. Making Sense of a Complex System: Empirical Studies of Employment-Based Health Insurance. *International Journal of Health Care Finance and Economics* 1 (3/4): 333–339.

Phelps, C. 2003. *Health Economics.* Boston: Addison Wesley.

Rizzo, J. A. 2005. Are HMOs Bad for Health Maintenance? *Health Economics* 14:1117–1131.

Robinson, J. C. 2004. Consolidation and the Transformation of Competition in Health Insurance. *Health Affairs* 23 (6): 11–24.

Schmidt, L. 2007. Effects of Infertility Insurance Mandates on Fertility. *Journal of Health Economics* 26 (3): 431–446.

Shin, J., and S. Moon. 2007. Do HMO Plans Reduce Health Care Expenditure in the Private Sector? *Economic Inquiry* 44 (1): 82–99.

Sloan, F. A., and L. Chepke. 2008. *Medical Malpractice.* Cambridge, MA: MIT Press.

Sloan, F. A., and C. J. Conover. 1998. Effects of State Reforms on Health Insurance Coverage of Adults. *Inquiry—The Journal of Health Care Organization, Provision and Financing* 35 (3): 280–293.

Sloan, F. A., and M. A. Hall. 2002. Market Failures and the Evolution of State Regulation of Managed Care. *Law and Contemporary Problems* 65 (4): 169–206.

Sloan, F. A., J. R. Rattliff, and M. A. Hall. 2005. Impacts of Managed Care Patient Protection Laws on Health Services Utilization and Patient Satisfaction with Care. *Health Services Research* 49 (3): 647–667.

Summers, L. H. 1989. Some Simple Economics of Mandated Benefits. *American Economic Review* 79 (2): 177–183.

Swartz, K. 2006. *Reinstating Health: Why More Middle-Class People Are Uninsured and What Government Can Do.* New York: Russell Sage Foundation.

Turcotte, L., J. Robst, and S. Polachek. 2006. Medical Interventions among Pregnant Women in Fee-For-Service and Managed Care Insurance: A Propensity Score Analysis. *Applied Economics* 38:1513–1525.

Ware, J. E., R. H. Brook, W. H. Rogers, et al. 1986. Comparison of Health Outcomes at a Health Maintenance Organization with Those of Fee-For-Service Care. *Lancet* 1 (8488): 1017–1022.

Winter, R. A. 1991. The Liability Insurance Market. *Journal of Economic Perspectives* 5 (3): 115–136.

Woolhandler, S., T. Campbell, and D. U. Himmelstein. 2003. Costs of Health Care Administration in the United States and Canada. *New England Journal of Medicine* 349 (8): 768–775.

Woolhandler, S., and D. U. Himmelstein. 1991. The Deteriorating Administrative Efficiency of the United States Health Care System. *New England Journal of Medicine* 324 (18): 1253–1258.

Woolhandler, S., and D. U. Himmelstein. 1997. Costs of Care and Administration at For-Profit and Other Hospitals in the United States. *New England Journal of Medicine* 336 (11): 769–774.

Xu, A., and A. Jensen. 2007. Managed Care and the Near-Elderly: Effects of Plan Enrollment on Functionality. *Applied Economics* 39: 2027–2037.

Zweifel, P., and F. Breyer. 1997. *Health Economics.* Oxford: Oxford University Press.

Market Structure in the Health Care Sector

CHAPTER 11

PRIVATE FINANCING OF HEALTH CARE SERVICES

Up to now, this book has discussed decision making at the individual and firm levels, either individuals as patients or individuals—physicians and nurses—as suppliers of health services, and hospitals, pharmaceutical manufacturers, and health insurers as firms. Part I (chapters 2–4) focused on the demand side of the health care market, while Part II (chapters 5–10) focused on the supply side of this market. In Part III, comprising chapters 11 through 13, we analyze resource allocation at the level of the market and consider interactions among various parties in the health care market, including patients as the demand side, providers as the supply side, and third-party payers, both private and public, which stand in the middle.

In this chapter's first section, we explain the difference between analysis at the individual and firm levels (Parts I and II) and analysis at the market (system) level (Part III), which serves the purpose of providing a rationale for analysis of health systems.[1] We then explain the economic rationale for using shares of public financing and public supply as criteria for classifying health care globally. Based on the share of revenue from government sources and the share of hospitals operated by the public sector, we classify health care markets at a national level into four categories: (1) cash system, (2) private system, (3) quasi-public (or social insurance) system, and (4) public system.

In section 3, we discuss how health care resources are allocated in a cash system using India and China as examples. In section 4, we discuss similar issues in a private system, using managed care in the United States as an example. (We discuss quasi-public systems in chapter 12 and public systems in chapter 13, respectively.) Section 5 describes managed competition, a concept that elicited widespread policy interest in the United States during the 1990s and among

1. In the following three chapters, we use "system" and "market" interchangeably. Since the components of health care markets are more complicated than the components of markets in most other sectors, we use the term "system" to capture a broader concept that includes consumers, producers, third-party payers, and regulators, in contrast to the more standard concept of "market," which includes only consumers and producers.

students of health care delivery worldwide. Managed care represents a general class of approaches for managing care for individual patients. By contrast, managed competition applies to an entire health care system. In section 6, we compare multiple-payer systems, the largest of which is in the United States, with single-payer systems, common to many countries. Section 7 presents a summary and conclusions.

11.1 Rationale for Health Systems Analysis

In previous chapters, we used *partial equilibrium analysis*, which involves analysis of the behavior of one decision maker, assuming the behavior of other market participants remains constant. For example, we assumed that the behavior of suppliers—physicians or hospitals—remained unchanged when we analyzed demand for health care services. Similarly, we assumed that consumer behavior as captured by the demand curve was fixed or exogenously determined when we analyzed physicians' decisions. In reality, the behaviors of other parties in a market do not typically remain unchanged. For example, government subsidies of vaccines increase demand for vaccines, and at the same time, increased market size stimulates R&D on vaccines and entry of vaccine manufacturers. Thus, analysis at the system (market) level is needed in order to take the behaviors of all parties in the market into account. Economists refer to this approach as *general equilibrium analysis*.

The difference between partial equilibrium (individual-level) and general equilibrium (market-level) analysis in the health care sector arises for three reasons. First, partial equilibrium analysis only considers the responses of one market participant to changes in its circumstances. By contrast, general equilibrium analysis considers the responses of all market participants simultaneously. Second, partial equilibrium analysis is static in assuming that medical technology is given. However, in an environment in which medical technology changes rapidly, general equilibrium analysis, being dynamic, takes the impacts of technological change into account. Third, partial equilibrium analysis generally does not consider externalities, such as the spillover of treatment quality from one health care plan to another plan. General equilibrium analysis does incorporate these effects.

Whether or not one uses partial or general equilibrium analysis potentially has important implications for the analysis of the effects of health policies. Two examples serve to illustrate this point (table 11.1).

The first example concerns the effectiveness of imposing demand-side cost sharing to control rising health care costs. Based on the results of the RAND Health Insurance Experiment (HIE), the implication is that demand-side cost sharing would be effective in health care cost control (see chapter 3). Figure 11.1 shows

TABLE 11.1
Effect of Selected Health Policies under Alternative Analytic Frameworks

Policy	Policy Impact Under	
	Partial Equilibrium Framework	General Equilibrium Framework
Using demand-side cost sharing to control health care costs	Moderate	Small or null
Effect of introducing health insurance on the growth of health expenditure	Moderate	Larger

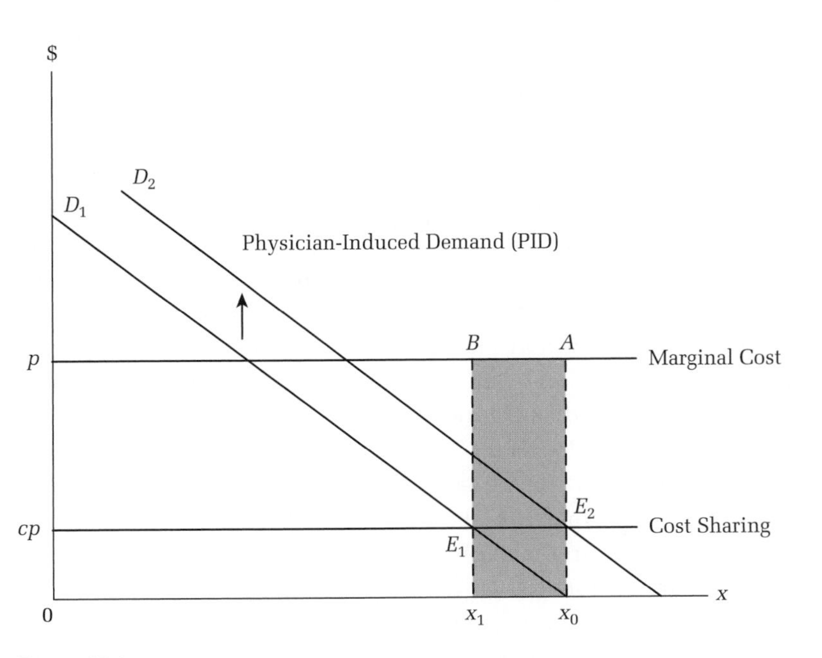

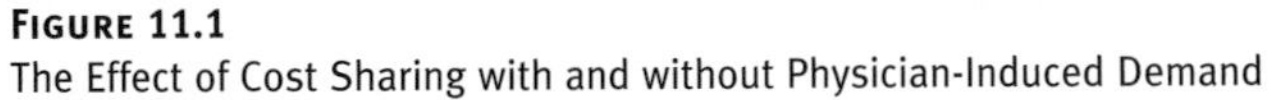

FIGURE 11.1
The Effect of Cost Sharing with and without Physician-Induced Demand

that the quantity of demand for health care is x_0 when demand for personal health care services is represented by D_1 and the country provides "free care" through health insurance, that is, it does not impose co-payments on the users of such services.

However, such care is not really "free." In the figure, marginal cost is p. Thus, the country spends $0pAx_0$ on health care. Now, suppose the country, seeking to reduce its outlays on these services, introduces demand-side cost sharing, as represented by cp. The quantity of health care services demanded consequently declines to x_1 under a partial equilibrium analysis that ignores suppliers' reactions. This leads to a saving in spending, represented by the shaded area ABx_1x_0. That imposing cost sharing would result in such a saving is supported by the evidence from the HIE (see chapter 3).

However, although the HIE has many important strengths and has been highly influential in both public policy and academic arenas, a criticism of the HIE is that it studied only consumer responses to changes in cost sharing and assumed that provider behavior would be unchanged if insurers introduced cost sharing. In chapter 5, we discussed the possibility that physicians may use their informational advantage to induce demand in order to offset the reduction in their demand. As seen in figure 11.1, the effect of demand-side cost sharing would be completely offset by physician-induced demand if such induced demand were to shift the demand curve to D_2. This suggests that the effect of demand-side cost sharing may be small or even nonexistent in a general equilibrium framework that considers both demand and supply sides simultaneously. Thus, in the real world, whether or not the effect of demand-side cost sharing could be as effective as the HIE suggests it would be is an empirical question. The answer partly depends on provider responses to the policy change on the demand side.

A second example concerns the effect of introducing health insurance on spending on personal health care service via its effect on technological change. The implementation of health insurance can markedly increase market size, which in turn can lead to important changes in incentives to innovate and for health care suppliers to adopt these innovations. For example, Finkelstein (2007) found that the introduction of the US Medicare program led to substantial new hospital entry and new technology adoption. Finkelstein performed a comparison between partial equilibrium and general equilibrium effects of health insurance. According to the results from the HIE, she concluded that just in terms of the additional people covered by introducing Medicare in the United States, the static HIE findings would imply an increase in hospital spending of 5.6 percent. This result is consistent with a statement in Newhouse (1992) that the implementation of health insurance in the United States should not have led to substantial growth in national health expenditures in that country. However, in fact, the implementation of Medicare in 1966 was associated with a 37 percent increase in real (adjusted for general inflation) hospital expenditures between 1965 and 1970. This change is more than six times larger than what the evidence from the HIE would have predicted.

The distinction between partial equilibrium and general equilibrium effects of health insurance is illustrated in figure 11.2. Suppose a country's demand for health care is represented by D_1 and the equilibrium market price of health care in this country is p_1. Thus, this country spends $0p_1Ax_1$ on health care if there is no health insurance, and it spends $0p_1Bx_2$ on health care if it implements a health insurance system providing "free care" to all its citizens. The introduction of such

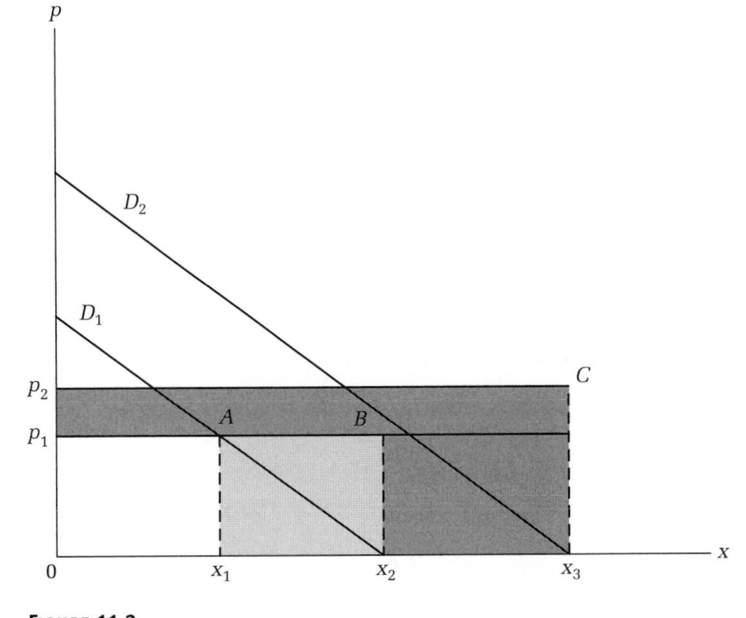

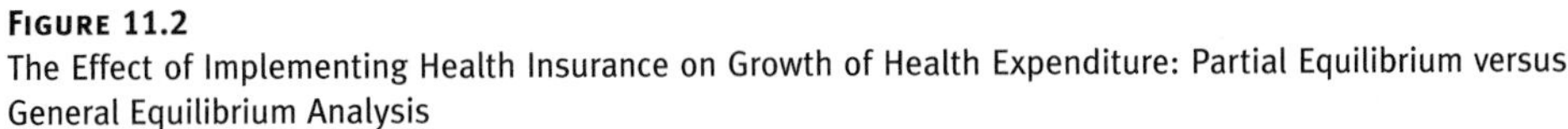
FIGURE 11.2
The Effect of Implementing Health Insurance on Growth of Health Expenditure: Partial Equilibrium versus General Equilibrium Analysis

a health insurance plan would lead to an increase in health expenditure in the amount indicated by the lightly shaded area, Ax_1x_2B, under a static (partial equilibrium) framework that assumes "other things remain constant."

However, as Finkelstein (2007) notes, a major expansion in health insurance coverage, which occurred when Medicare was introduced, would lead to market-wide changes. The substantial increases in demand for care that lead to corresponding increases in revenue are likely to be sufficient to more than offset the fixed cost of entry (e.g., building a new facility, obtaining regulatory approval for entry). Thus, because a major demand stimulus occurred, one could expect many providers to enter the market. Further, rates of return on medical research and development are likely to increase, leading to a substantial amount of technological change, which in health care has tended to lead to increased spending on services.

This effect is depicted by a shift in demand from D_1 to D_2. New medical technology may increase the quality of hospital care and hence increase the demand for such care. In addition, the equilibrium market price of hospital care may increase (from p_1 to p_2) as hospitals adopt new medical technology and new practice styles.

National health expenditures would increase from the area $0p_1Ax_1$ to the area $0p_2Cx_3$ following the introduction of a "free care" plan. The effect of introducing health insurance on the growth of health expenditures is represented by the dark shaded area ($p_2Cx_3x_2Bp_1$) plus the lightly shaded area (Ax_1x_2B), an amount substantially larger than the policy impact predicted by the partial equilibrium analysis (light shaded area alone).

As figure 11.2 illustrates, the introduction of health insurance is not a major factor in accounting for the long-run growth of health expenditures if we use a partial equilibrium approach that does not consider the responses of the supply side of the market. By contrast, health insurance could be a major source of growth in health expenditures if the policy change is evaluated with a general equilibrium framework. Using the latter approach, Finkelstein (2007) estimated the impact of implementing Medicare in the United States and concluded that the overall spread of health insurance between 1950 and 1990 could explain about half of the increase in US real health care expenditures over this time period.

The details of a general equilibrium impact are country-specific and depend on the characteristics of the country's health care system. In the next section, we describe a method for classifying national health care systems.

11.2 Classification of Health Care Systems

Health care systems around the globe are very diverse. Thus, the task of classifying health care systems worldwide is not a straightforward exercise. Some previous attempts at classifying health care systems based their classifications on a single attribute, while others used two or more dimensions to achieve this goal. Table 11.2 shows examples of various classification criteria.

An advantage of a single-attribute classification criterion is that countries are assigned binary (1–0) categories that are relatively easy to compare. Table 11.2 lists seven single-dimensional criteria widely used for comparing differences in health care systems internationally.

The first is whether or not countries use primary care physicians as gatekeepers to influence the use of specialty and hospital inpatient care. Some countries allow patients to freely choose their own providers, while others impose various restrictions on provider choice through gatekeeper mechanisms. This type of mechanism requires a referral by a general practitioner or other primary care physician before other personal health care services, such as physician specialist services, can be covered by health insurance.

The second is whether or not a country's government imposes a pre-set budget ceiling on its health care spending. Systems with budget ceilings, such as global budgeting, are often referred to as closed-ended financing systems, while systems without budget ceilings, such as in the United States, are often referred to as open-ended financing systems.

A third criterion pertains to how hospitals pay their physicians. In some countries, physicians who practice in hospitals are employees of those hospitals, and physicians practicing in clinics do not have hospital admitting privileges. This is characterized as a closed-staff system (see chapter 6). By contrast, in other

TABLE 11.2
Criteria for Classification of Health Care Systems around the World

Criteria	Categories of Health Care System
Single dimension	
Gatekeepers for inpatient care	With gatekeepers vs. without gatekeepers
Budget ceiling	Open-ended finance vs. close-ended finance
Physician staff in the hospital	Open-staff system vs. closed-staff system
Access	Universal coverage vs. partial coverage
Public financing	Higher public financing vs. lower public financing
Public supply	Public hospital vs. private hospital
Physician dispensing	Separation vs. integration of dispensing and prescribing
Multiple dimensions	Five control knobs (financing, payment, organization, regulation and behavior) to reform the health care system
Two dimensions	
Public financing and public supply shares	Use 2 × 2 matrix to classify health care system into four categories: (1) cash, (2) private, (3) quasi-public, (4) public

countries, physicians practicing in clinics have admitting privileges at hospitals, an open-staff system.

The fourth distinction is based on citizens' financial access to personal health care services. Some countries provide universal health insurance coverage to all their citizens, while others provide coverage only to selected groups of their population.

Next, some countries finance most of their health expenditures through public funds, while others rely predominantly on private funds. In some countries, public hospitals are the major providers. By contrast, other countries rely on private hospitals to deliver most personal health care services.

A final attribute relates to the style of physician practice. For example, some countries, such as Japan, have an integrated health care system in which physicians both prescribe and dispense drugs. By contrast, physician dispensing is prohibited in countries where there is a separation between prescribing and dispensing for prescription drugs.

Using a single attribute to classify a health care system is too simple. A health care system reflects its several components, including financing, payment, organization, regulation, and behavior—the five control knobs (fig. 11.3) for reforming a health care system (Roberts, Hsiao, Berman, et al. 2004). Thus, on balance, it is more appropriate to use multiple-dimensional criteria, provided the classification system does not become unwieldy.

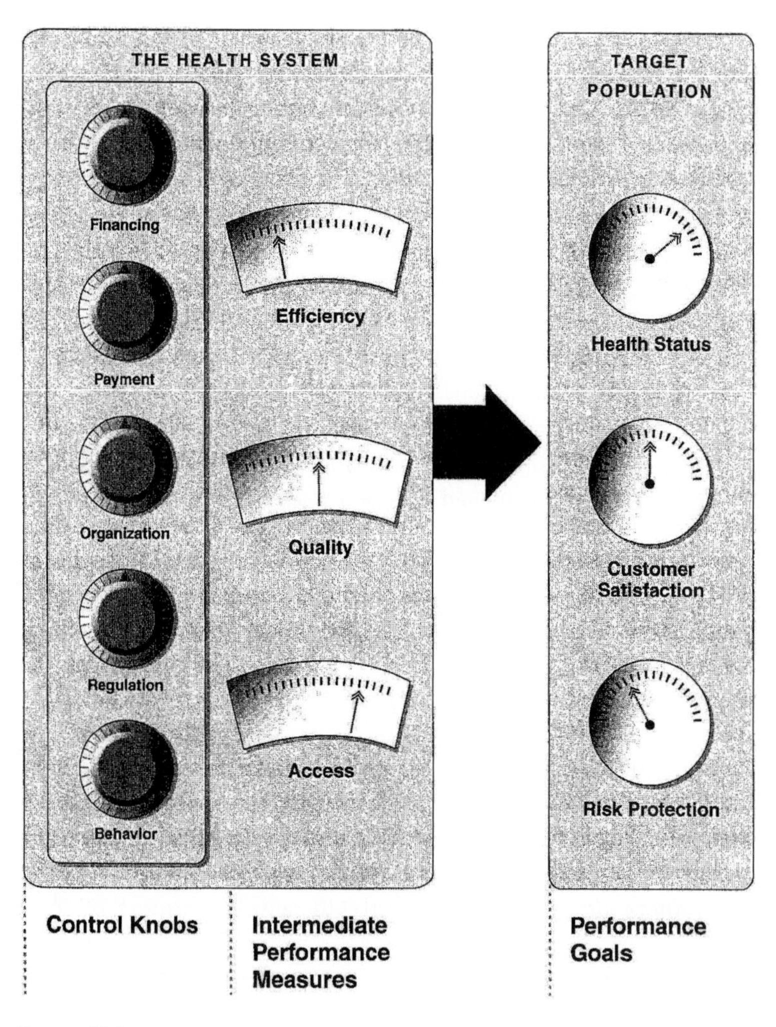

FIGURE 11.3
The Five Control Knobs for Health Sector Reform
Source: Roberts, Hsiao, Berman, et al. (2004), p. 27. Reproduced by permission of Oxford University Press.

A change in the position of any one of the five control knobs would immediately affect health care system performance, as measured by various indicators such as efficiency (cost), quality, and access to services. These changes in turn affect long-term outcomes of the health care system, including population health. For example, an increase in public funds to finance personal health care services, such as implementing a national health insurance program, would immediately affect access to personal health care services among the target population, which in turn would affect the level of expenditure risk protection of the target population. This framework is useful for evaluating the impact of reform policy on the intermediate and final performance of the health care system. But it is too complex for classifying health care systems because the five-dimensional criteria would lead to many possible combinations.

Therefore, we use the two dimensions of government activity in health care financing and in delivery to describe the gamut of options for a country's health care system. A two-dimension criterion represents a compromise between being "too simple" or "too complex" when single-and multiple-dimensional criteria are utilized, respectively. The two-dimensional criterion forms a two-by-two matrix yielding four categories (table 11.2).

The first dimension describes the extent to which the system relies on public financing. Sources of funds for financing personal health care services fall into four major categories: (1) out-of-pocket payments, (2) private health insurance premiums, (3) general tax revenue, and (4) earmarked tax revenue specifically tied to spending on personal health care services, including social health insurance premiums, payroll taxes, and social security taxes specifically earmarked for health care services. The first two sources come from private sources, while the latter two are mandatory assessments based on public law. In effect, we measure the extent of government involvement in health care financing by the share of public funds in a country's total funds allocated to personal health care services, hereafter referred to as the public financing share.

Data from 166 countries (fig. 11.4) show the relationship between national income (as measured by gross domestic product [GDP] per capita population) and share of public financing. With a few exceptions, the share of public financing is positively related to a country's level of national income. A regression with the dependent variable the country's public financing share and the explanatory variable the country's GDP per capita population, both expressed in natural logarithm form, indicates that a 10 percent increase in GDP per capita leads on average to an increase in the public financing share of 1.2 percent. The major outlier is the United States, which relies more extensively on private health insurance for financing personal health care services than is predicted by its GDP per capita population.

Table 11.3 shows the global distribution of national public financing shares. The mode of this distribution is in the range of 40–50 percent. At one extreme, there are three countries with public sector percentages below 20 percent,

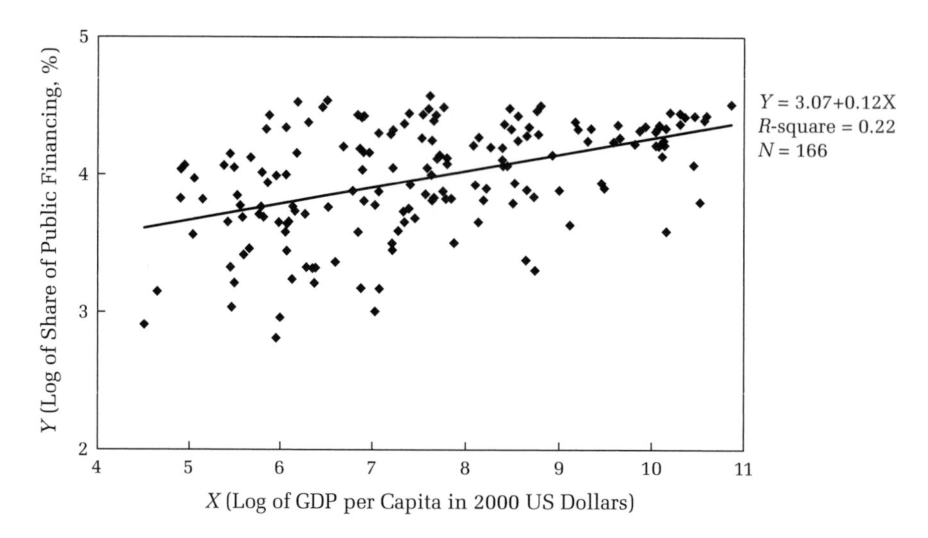

FIGURE 11.4
The Relationship between GDP Per Capita and the Public Financing Share
Source: Public financing share is from World Health Organization, World Health Report (2006);GDP per capita is from World Bank Group, World Development Indicators (2007) (sample size = 166). The regression line was calculated by the authors.

including Cambodia, Congo and Guinea. At the other extreme, twenty-six countries have public sector percentages exceeding 80 percent. Most of the latter are high-income countries, such as Denmark, the UK, and Japan.

The second dimension we use for classifying health care systems is the extent to which the government is involved in the provision of personal health care services. In many countries, governments play a direct role in providing personal health care services; most hospitals in these countries are public. By contrast, private hospitals are predominant in some other countries, with public hospitals limited to providing services for selected population groups, such as veterans and low-income individuals. We measured the extent of government involvement in health care delivery by the share of public hospitals in a country's hospital sector, hereafter referred to the public supply share.

Data from twenty-one high-income countries show the relationship between national income, measured by GDP per capita of population, and public supply shares (fig. 11.5). In contrast to the public financing share, there is no clear pattern between countries' public supply shares and their national per capita incomes. Rather than being related to national income, the choice of public supply share seems to reflect such factors as historical context, culture, and social values.

Table 11.4 shows national public financing and public supply shares. Since data on the latter are unavailable for many countries, the number of countries reported is limited to some high-income countries. Data on public financing and supply shares are plotted in figure 11.6, where the extent of public financing from

TABLE 11.3
The Distribution of the Public Financing Share in Countries Globally

Share of Public Financing (%)	Number of Countries	Mean Income within the Group (in 2000 US$)	Represented Countries
<20	3	292.79	Cambodia, Congo, Guinea
20–30	15	1301.09	India, Pakistan, Vietnam
30–40	21	2525.18	China, Singapore, South Africa
40–50	30	3571.01	United States, Mexico, Korea
50–60	21	3707.98	Russian Federation, Greece, Malaysia
60–70	25	8334.98	Australia, Canada, Netherlands
70–80	25	10307.14	France, Germany, Spain
>80	26	11796.28	Denmark, UK, Japan
All countries	166	6211.91	

Source: Public financing share is from World Health Organization, World Health Report (2006); GDP per capita is from World Bank Group, World Development Indicators (2007). The authors calculated mean income within the group.

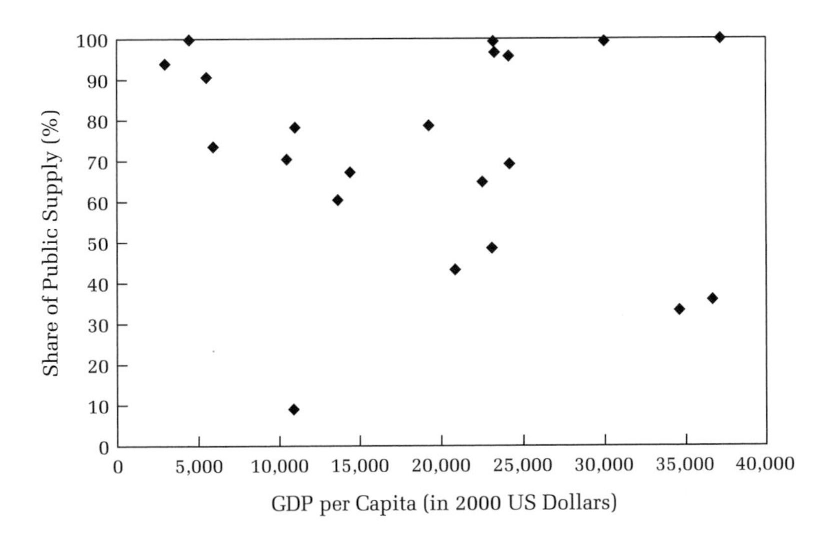

FIGURE 11.5
The Relationship between GDP Per Capita and the Public Supply Share
Source: OECD, Health Data (2000) (sample size = 21).

TABLE 11.4
Public Financing Share versus Public Supply Share in Selected OECD Countries and Taiwan

Countries	Share of Public Financing, 1998	Share of Public Supply, 1998
Australia[a]	69.3	43.2
Austria	70.5	69.2
Canada[a]	69.6	99.3
Czech Republic	91.9	90.6
Denmark[a]	81.9	99.3
Finland	76.3	96.6
France	76.4	64.8
Germany[a]	74.6	48.5
Greece[b]	56.8	70.4
Italy[a]	68.0	78.6
Japan	78.3	35.8
Korea	45.8	9.0
Mexico	46.0	73.5
New Zealand	77.1	60.4
Norway[a]	82.8	99.9
Poland	73.3	99.8
Portugal	66.9	78.2
Spain[b]	76.9	67.2
Taiwan	63.0	32.0
Turkey	71.9	93.9
United Kingdom	83.7	95.7
United States[b]	44.7	33.2

Notes: Belgium, Hungary, Iceland, Ireland, Luxembourg, Netherlands, Slovak Republic, Sweden, and Switzerland are excluded because of missing data. a. Data from 1997. b. Data from 1996.
Source: OECD, Health Data (2000).

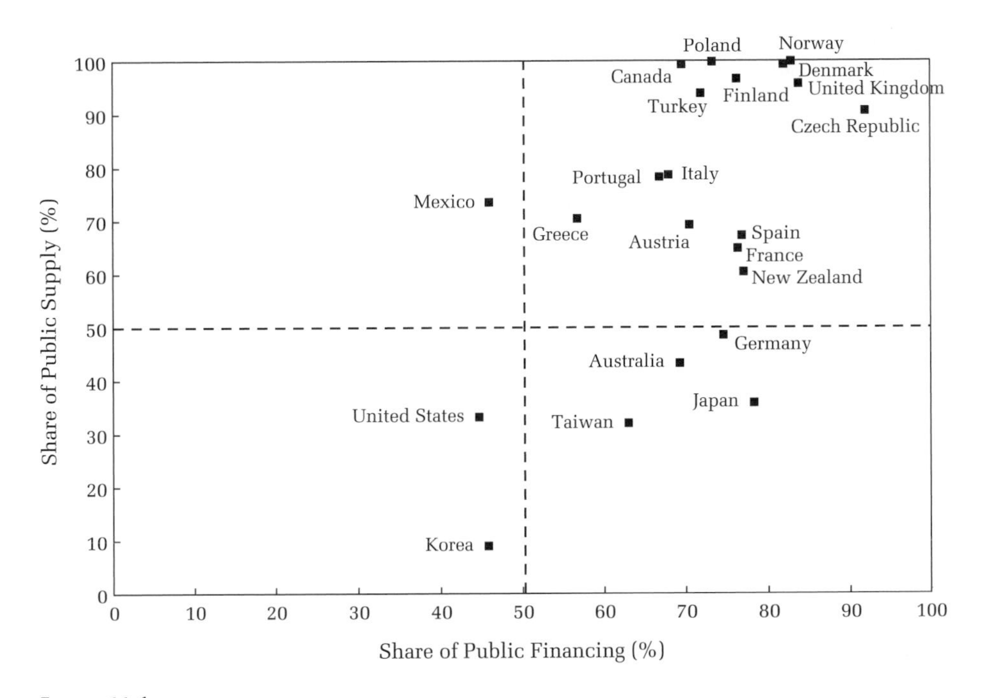

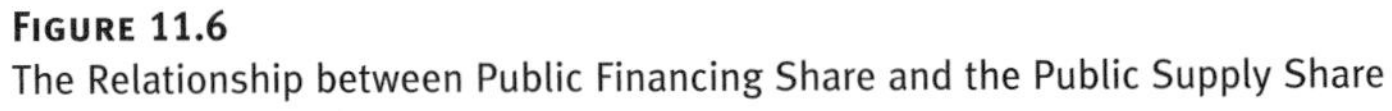
FIGURE 11.6
The Relationship between Public Financing Share and the Public Supply Share

low to high is on the horizontal axis and the extent of direct public provision is on the vertical axis. Using 50 percent cutoffs to categorize countries as "high" or "low" in public versus private financing and "high" or "low" in direct public provision of care, there are four quadrants, corresponding to our four health system categories.

The upper right quadrant in figure 11.6 contains systems relatively high in public financing from general tax revenue and earmarked payroll taxes *and* relatively high in public (hospital) provision; they include Great Britain, Canada, and the Scandinavian countries. For simplicity, we call these "public systems" (table 11.5).

The upper left quadrant includes countries in which the government operates hospitals as public institutions but primarily relies on private financing, for example, China, India, and many low-income countries. Since data on shares of public supply for many low-income countries are lacking, we cannot be precise about this in figure 11.6. But these countries tend to have a low share of public financing (table 11.3) and a high share of public supply, placing them in this quadrant. We term these "cash systems" because of the importance of out-of-pocket payments in these countries.

The lower left quadrant includes countries in which the private sector plays a dominant role in financing in the form of private health insurance and in the delivery of personal health care services, for example, the United States, where

TABLE 11.5
Classification of Health Care Systems

		Public Financing Share	
		Lower	*Higher*
Public Supply Share	*Higher*	**Cash System** India China	**Public System** UK Canada Italy France
	Lower	**Private System** USA	**Quasi-Public System** Germany Japan South Korea Taiwan USA China

Note: The United States and China are multiple-system countries. Thus, they are classified in more than one system.

more than half of the population has private employer-provided health insurance and more than 70 percent of hospitals are privately owned and operated. We term this a "private system."

In the lower right quadrant, the public sector finances health care through compulsory social insurance and the private sector is primarily responsible for the provision of services. Some countries provide social insurance for the entire population, while others limit such insurance coverage to certain population groups, such as civil servants, wage sector employees, and those with monthly earnings below a specific threshold. Countries in this category include Germany, Japan, South Korea, and Taiwan. Also, the Medicare and Medicaid programs in the United States and the new social insurance program in China belong in this category. We term this system a "quasi-public" or a "social insurance system."

The coexistence of alternative models of health care systems, even for countries at comparable levels of economic development, suggests that there is no consensus on the optimal mix of public financing and public supply. For example, Hong Kong, Singapore, South Korea, and Taiwan shared a similar experience in terms of economic growth during 1960–2010, but their health care systems evolved very differently during this period (Wagstaff 2007).

The choice of health system affects a country's distribution of income. Income distribution is affected both by the relative burden a country's method of health care financing imposes on households with varying incomes and by patterns of use of services by income. Costs incurred and benefits received are measured in terms of "progressivity/regressivity." If the system leads to a more equal distribution of income, it is considered to be progressive. Conversely, if less affluent households bear a relatively high share of payments or receive fewer benefits, the system is regressive. Research on European and Asian health care systems indicates that cash systems in low-income countries tend to be progressive in that the relatively affluent pay more but also receive more health care services. Systems in high-income countries that rely substantially on private health insurance, such as the United States and Switzerland, tend to be regressive. Systems we term "public" tend to be the most progressive, and quasi-public systems tend to be somewhat regressive. The main reason why quasi-public systems impose less redistribution from higher- to lower-income families than the public systems do is that general tax revenues tend to impose a higher relative burden on the relatively affluent than do social insurance premiums, which are more likely to be set in direct proportion to income (Wagstaff and van Doorslaer 1992; O'Donnell, van Doorslaer, Rannan-Eliya, et al. 2008).

Based on the two-dimensional criterion, our analysis of health care systems is focused on four systems represented by the four quadrants (table 11.5). In this chapter, we start our discussion of health system classification with descriptions of cash and private systems (upper left and lower left quadrants). However, the major source of private financing differs between these two systems: the cash system mainly relies on out-of-pocket payments, while the private system relies substantially on private health insurance. In addition, relatively speaking, the cash system relies on public provision to deliver personal health care services, while the insured private system relies on private provision for service delivery. Systems described by the lower right quadrant, private provision and public insurers, and the upper right quadrant, public provision *and* financing, are discussed in chapters 12 and 13, respectively.

Countries differ in having single-payer versus multiple-payer systems. For example, in the United States, private health insurance accounts for much health care financing, but about half of the financing is from public sources, specifically from Medicare and Medicaid. Thus, we split the health care system in the United States into two parts, an insured private system and a quasi-public system.

Similarly, China (like some other countries) does not fit neatly into a single category. China currently relies substantially on out-of-pocket costs payments and in this respect fits the cash category, but this country has also begun to expand the coverage of social insurance programs. Thus, we also split the health care system into two parts, a cash system and a quasi-public system.

Our analysis treats a country's system as exogenous. We do not analyze how national health care systems are shaped and why they have evolved in the ways that they have. Since we take health systems as given, we do not provide detailed accounts of the history of individual countries' health systems. Once in place, health systems develop important constituencies that benefit from maintaining the status quo. Changes have occurred, for example, as a consequence of major changes in political systems such as in countries that belonged to the former Soviet Union and China. Yet even when major political upheavals have occurred, as in Germany between 1933 and 1945, when National Socialists controlled the government, and were succeeded by a communist regime in East Germany, a reunified Germany created after the fall of the communist regimes returned to the basic health system structure that had prevailed before 1933.

We employ the paradigm of structure-conduct-performance used in the industrial organization literature (the branch of economics that studies the effects of market structure on firms' performance) to assess how each type of health care system affects choices, which in turn affect price, quantity, quality, health expenditures, and innovation.[2]

11.3 CASH SYSTEMS

OVERVIEW

Many countries, especially low- and some middle-income countries, rely extensively on direct out-of-pocket payments as the principal source of health services' financing. In some countries, official user fees have been adopted, in large part to mitigate the risk of high health expenditure risk to citizens of those countries. But there is evidence that providers often obtain fees far in excess of the officially sanctioned fees.

Perkins, Brazier, Themmen, et al. (2009) presented evidence on fees for labor and delivery in three African countries, Kenya, Burkina Faso, and Tanzania, showing that direct out-of-pocket costs to families were substantial. A survey of out-of-pocket cost of care in fourteen Asian countries and territories accounting for 81 percent of the Asian population likewise showed that users of health care services incur substantial out-of-pocket obligations (van Doorslaer, O'Donnell, Rannan-Eliya, et al. 2007) even when they receive care from public facilities. Of the countries the authors considered, out-of-pocket payments as a percentage of household non-food consumption was relatively high in Bangladesh (10.7 percent), India (10.7 percent), and Vietnam (12.6 percent), and relatively low in Hong Kong (3.4 percent, a high-income territory), Malaysia (2.1 percent), and Thailand (2.9 percent). China was in between (5.3 percent).

Although exposure to high levels of out-of-pocket health expenditure risk clearly exacts a toll on risk-averse populations, and there is a risk that people will invest too little in preventive care in such countries, there is a silver lining. When people pay for care out of pocket, the welfare loss from moral hazard is averted; also, individuals who pay out of pocket may be more prone to monitor quality and insist that care delivery be efficient.

2. Although with few exceptions, we do not describe the system in a specific country in substantial detail, grouping countries by health system type offers several advantages. First, we can make generalizations about a common set of issues facing specific types of health care systems without getting mired in details of the specific attributes of each countries health system. Second, health care systems can change rapidly in terms of particulars, but the general orientation of particular health system types generally changes more slowly.

However, as the case studies reveal, the actual performance of cash systems is quite mixed. While there are examples of high-quality and efficient provision of care, there is much evidence of the opposite as well.

THE INDIAN HEALTH CARE SYSTEM

India substantially relies on direct payments from patients to providers for services rendered. In 1999, total spending on personal health care services in India was 6.0 percent of GDP, of which 75 percent, or 4.5 percent of GDP, was for health expenditures from private, out-of-pocket sources (Bhat 1999). Another estimate, for 2001, is that public health expenditure accounted for 17.9 percent of total health expenditure in India (Rahman 2008). This compares to 17.8 percent in Myanmar, 25.1 percent in Indonesia, and 29.7 percent in Nepal, but to 90.6 percent in Bhutan, 83.5 percent in the Maldives, and 73.4 percent in North Korea (Rahman 2008). Overall, India is an outlier in terms of the low share of total personal health care expenditures from public sources (Singh 2008). Its health indicators are somewhat better than for low-income countries overall, but they are lower than China's and middle-income countries' health indicators overall (table 11.6).

Funding by Indian states is more than twice that by the central government. Local governments contribute very little to public spending (much less than 10 percent; Singh 2008). Per capita public spending by Indian states during 1971, 1981, and 1991 rose with state per capita GDP, but the associated elasticity was far

TABLE 11.6
Comparative Health Indicators in Average Low- and Middle-Income Countries, India, and China, 2003

Health Indicator	Low-Income Countries	India	China	Middle-Income Countries
Births attended by skilled health staff (% of total)	—[a]	42.5[b]	96	—[a]
Immunization, measles (% of children ages 12–23 months)	61.5	56	84	86.4
Life expectancy at birth, total (years)	58.6	63.42	71.05	69.7
Mortality rate, infant (per 1,000 live births)	83.9[b]	64	33[b]	35.4
Mortality rate, children under 5 years (per 1,000)	127.7[b]	94	42[b]	45.2
Gross national income per capita, Atlas method (current US$)	438.5	530	1,270	1,938.0

Notes: a. Not available. b. 2000.
Source: Copyrighted and published by Project HOPE/*Health Affairs* as Exhibit 1 in Singh (2008). The published article is archived and available online at www.healthaffairs.org.

less than one; that is, a 10 percent increase in per capita GDP led to a far less than 10 percent increase in public expenditures on personal health care services. States with higher rates of literacy also allocated more public funds to personal health care services (Rahman 2008).

One estimate is that only 3–5 percent of Indians are covered by any form of health insurance (Bloom, Kanjilal, and Peters 2008). Other estimates are that 11–15 percent of the population has insurance coverage. The higher estimates do not change the essential conclusion that the vast majority of Indians lack health insurance of any kind (Bhattacharya and Sapra 2008; Yip and Hslao 2008). India's health insurers do not question the appropriateness of fees charged by hospitals, laboratories, or physicians (Chandra 2010); unlike in the United States, their collective market share is so low that tough payment policies would not influence the price and quantity of care in India even if insurers were to become more aggressive in cost containment. More than half of India's hospitals were private in 2004 (58 percent in rural areas and 62 percent in urban areas). Four-fifths of outpatient utilization in the same year was in private clinics (Bloom, Kanjilal, and Peters 2008). Several major systems of medicine coexist in India, including allopathic medicine (Western medicine), ayurveda, unani, siddha, and homeopathy (Berman 1998).

Public oversight of health care in India is the responsibility of the states and territories rather than the central government. Central government efforts at influencing public health have focused on the five-year plans, coordinated planning with the states, and sponsoring major health programs.

Interestingly, while the existence of a cash market has adverse consequences—it is not good for population health and serves to perpetuate health disparities within the population—a positive feature is that the lack of regulation of price and entry has probably facilitated the entry of some facilities that offer excellent quality of care at a low cost. Some examples are the two heart hospitals described in box 11.1. Care from facilities of this type is inaccessible to a large portion of the Indian population; such facilities are primarily used by Indians with relatively high incomes and by foreigners. The majority of the Indian population is unable to access high-quality health care provided by private providers as a result of high prices and widespread lack of health insurance. Low quality of care is a major problem in India (see, e.g., Das and Hammer 2006).

The Chinese Health Care System

While most of China's population lacks health insurance and high rates of out-of-pocket payment prevail in China as in India, although to a lesser extent, this was not the case in China several decades ago (Blomquist and Qian 2008). The Chinese health care system has experienced several fundamental changes during the past six decades, during which the health system in China at one time or another resembled almost all major health system options (table 11.7). After the communist

Box 11.1
Two Heart Hospitals in India

Richman, Udayakumar, Mitchell, et al. (2008) describe two heart hospitals in India that offer open heart surgery for about $6,000 a case, compared to $100,000 per case in the United States. The authors assert that the quality of care in the Indian facilities is comparable to that in the United States. How do the Indian hospitals achieve high quality of care at such a low cost?

The simplest answer would be low input prices in India. While this may be so for labor inputs, the difference in input prices cannot explain the entire difference in prices between the two countries. For one, the differences are likely to be greatest in labor inputs. The Indian hospitals have to obtain at least some of their equipment on world markets.

There are other plausible reasons for the price difference. Most important, patients in Indian hospitals pay cash for surgery, whereas in the United States, the surgery is largely paid by private or public insurers. In the end, the demand response of out-of-pocket consumers is greater than for insured consumers—much greater, in fact—and also greater than for insurers acting in the role of purchasers for patients. When patients are paying the bill, health care providers are likely to be much more cautious about supplying services for which marginal benefit is low relative to marginal cost. Patients at risk of overruns are likely to be much more insistent that such overruns do not occur. Not surprisingly, the hospitals offered open heart surgery for a fixed price per operation as a means of assuring patients that overruns would not occur. In a piece rate system, which applies to some hospital inpatient care in the United States, more pieces (e.g., billing for each diagnostic [e.g., x-rays, MRIs] and therapeutic service [e.g., pills, respiratory therapy]) mean more revenue for the institution. Not surprisingly, then, a higher than expected number of pieces is a frequent occurrence.

Does the efficiency-enhancing feature of a cash system imply that it is preferable from the standpoint of social welfare? We leave the analysis of this question to our readers.

revolution in 1949 and before economic reforms were instituted in 1978, rural residents mostly belonged to agricultural communes and had access to basic primary care and, on referral to hospitals, care at a low out-of-pocket cost to the individual, which was known as the Cooperative Medical Scheme (CMS). Residents of urban areas had access to subsidized care through their employers, which were either the government or a state-owned enterprise (Labor Insurance Scheme [LIS] and Government Insurance Scheme [GIS]). During this central planning era, China adopted a public health systems model. Out-of-pocket payments were minimal. Equal access to health care contributed substantially to improved population health. During the 1950s to the 1970s, China experienced better performance in improving population health than did other countries with the same income (table 11.6).

TABLE 11.7
Evolution of China's Health Care System

Years	Central Planning Era (1949–1978)	Market-Based Era (1978–2002)	Health Care Reform Era (Post-2002 Period)
Classification of the health system	Public system (public provision of near free care)	Cash system (a personal responsibility system)	Quasi-public system (increased public financing)
Major programs in the system	• Cooperative Medical Scheme (CMS) • Labor Insurance Scheme (LIS) • Government Insurance Scheme (GIS)	Basic Medical Insurance (BMI)	• New Cooperative Medical Scheme (NCMS) • Urban Resident Basic Medical Insurance Scheme (URBMI) • Medical Assistance
Features of the system	• Health institutions (e.g., hospitals and clinics) were owned and operated by various level of the government. • Health care providers were paid a fixed salary.	• The central government gradually decentralized its power over the health care system. • Collapse of the CMS • Decline of government financing • Government privatize public providers or make them financially autonomous	• Government expanded insurance coverage with a target of achieving universal coverage by 2011. • Increased government spending on health services
Percentage of population by insured public program (%)	90%	Decreasing over time: 56% (urban population); 21% (rural population)	Increasing over time: 79% (rural population)
Share of out-of-pocket payment	Minimal (less than 20%)	Increased from 20% in 1978 to 60% in 2000	Increasing trend turns to decreasing, but remains at a high level

However, government insurance financing of personal health care services was substantially reduced with the market-oriented reforms that began in 1978. These reforms, which affected the general Chinese economy, led to a dismantling of the rural commune system and the conversion of many state-owned enterprises to private businesses. Public subsidies of government hospitals decreased. The government changed its financing and payment method to block grants, but with the size of the block grants generally much less than the grant recipient's operating costs (Ma, Lu, and Quan 2008). Privatization had adverse consequences for population health as well, increasing health disparities well beyond what they otherwise would have been (Blumenthal and Hsiao 2005).

The CMS collapsed during this market-oriented era, and many residents of rural areas lost the safety net for medical expense available earlier. Similarly, the coverage afforded by the two other public insurance programs, the LIS and GIS, declined as a result of cutbacks in public financing. In response to the decline in public coverage, in 1995 the government launched a new public program, known as Basic Medical Insurance (BMI), which aims to cover all urban formal sector workers.

Nevertheless, at the beginning of the twenty-first century, the percentage of the population with access to some form of health insurance coverage was appreciably lower than during the central planning era. In 2003, 44 percent of urban residents and 79 percent of rural residents lacked health insurance (Blomquist and Qian 2008, 8). Even so, on several measures the health of urban residents was substantially worse in urban areas than in rural areas of China during 1997–2006 (Fang, Chen, and Rizzo 2009).

As a result of the collapse of the CMS and the decline in insurance coverage by the two other public insurance programs, households increasingly had to rely on out-of-pocket payments to finance health care expenditures. The share of out-of-pocket payments in total expenditures increased from 20.4 percent in 1978 to about 60 percent in 2000 (fig. 11.7). Although the out-of-pocket payment share began to decline after 2000, it remained at a very high level throughout the

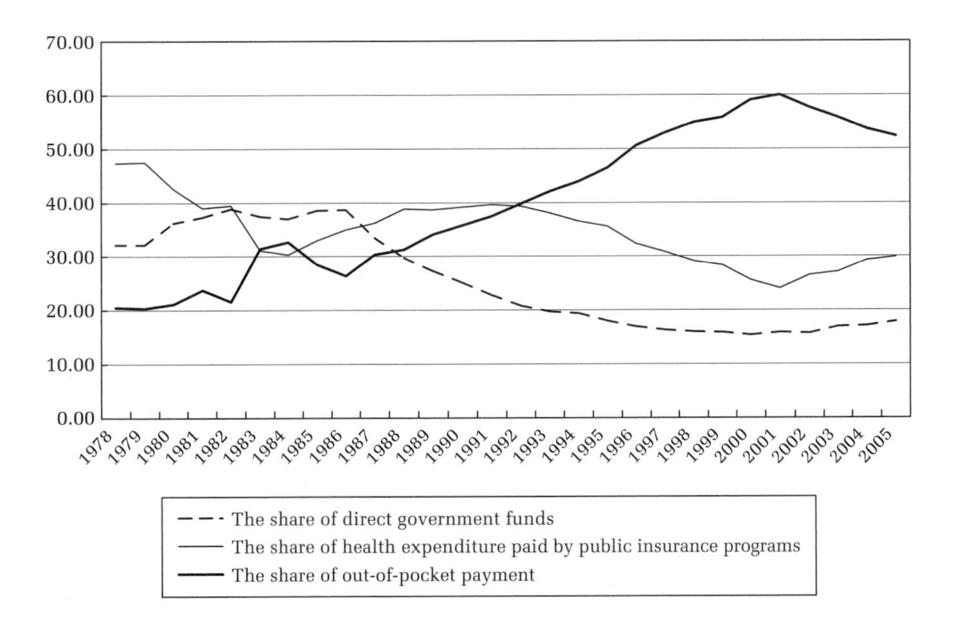

FIGURE 11.7
Sources of Health Care Financing in China, 1978–2005
Source: Huang and Yang (2009). Courtesy Yanfen Huang, Yiyong Yang, Karen Eggleston, and the Walter H. Shorenstein Asia-Pacific Research Center, Stanford University, Palo Alto, CA.

following decade, at over half of personal health care expenditures. The economic reform that began in 1978 led to a shift from a public system to a cash system, where it remained at the turn of the twenty-first century. Yet although China has a high out-of-pocket share, in India, the share paid out of pocket remains considerably higher, around 80 percent (Bhattacharya and Sapra 2008, 1006).

Reliance on a cash system in China (a high out-of-pocket share) has had several adverse consequences. First, the lack of coverage is reflected in high probabilities of families incurring catastrophic medical expense in a year. In 2003, an estimated 14 percent of urban households and 16 percent of rural households incurred such catastrophic expense, defined in a study by Liu, Rao, Wu, et al. (2008) as an out-of-pocket medical expense in the year exceeding 30 percent of the family's annual nonsubsistence spending—equal to total household spending minus subsistence food expenditure.

Second, the transition from the public system to a cash system created inequalities in health and health care utilization. For example, recent evidence has suggested that the difference in insurance coverage between the urban and rural populations has led to a widening gap in health status and utilization between urban and rural residents (Wagstaff, Yip, Lindelow, et al. 2009).

Third, the reduction in insurance coverage and the increase in out-of-pocket payments have led to a slowdown in health improvement. Wagstaff and colleagues (2009) documented that during the central planning era, China experienced a major improvement in population health, as measured by a dramatic reduction in mortality. However, this reduction did not continue after the introduction of market reforms.

Based on evidence from a cross-country regression relating a country's under-age-five mortality rate to its lagged mortality rate and per capita income, China was an overperformer; its rate of reduction exceeded its expected rate during the 1960s and 1970s. By contrast, China became an underperformer in the 1980s and 1990s.

In sum, market economic reforms in China have had several adverse impacts on health care and health in that country, including a slowdown in health improvements, high rates of catastrophic out-of-pocket spending, and increased inequalities in health and health care utilization (Wagstaff, Yip, Lindelow, et al. 2009). Responding to these multiple challenges, the Chinese government initiated health care reform plans starting in 2003. The major thrust of these reforms has been to move China's health care system from essentially a cash system to a quasi-public system. Specifically, the government plans to allocate additional funds to the health sector to expand insurance coverage, with a target of achieving universal coverage by 2011. Universal insurance coverage is to be achieved through three new insurance programs: (1) the New Cooperative Medical Scheme (NCMS) for the rural population, (2) the Urban Resident Basic Medical Insurance Scheme (URBMI) for the urban uninsured, and (3) Medical Assistance for the poorest and most vulnerable population in rural and urban areas (table 11.7). We discuss the NCMS and analyze its effects in chapter 12.

11.4 THE PRIVATE SYSTEM: THE US EXPERIENCE

BASE CASE: PRIVATE PROVISION AND NO INSURANCE COVERAGE

In the early twentieth century and before, the US population lacked health insurance of any kind and paid for personal health care services out of pocket. Health services provision was overwhelmingly private. The disadvantages and advantages of this approach are those of a cash system.

EVOLUTION OF PRIVATE HEALTH INSURANCE IN THE 1930S AND 1940S

Private health insurance was first introduced in the United States in the 1930s and 1940s. The major impetus for expanding coverage during the 1930s was the Great Depression. When personal incomes fell during the Great Depression, physicians and hospitals found it increasingly difficult to collect fees from patients, many of whom were unemployed. As a result, partly or largely out of self-interest, hospitals joined forces in forming Blue Cross plans, nonprofit insurance plans for hospital services. And physicians helped form Blue Shield plans, which provided coverage for physicians' services. Blue Cross reimbursed hospitals on a retrospective cost or charge basis (see chapter 6). Blue Shield paid physicians on a fixed-fee basis. In some states, Blue Shield was able to require that its fixed-fee payment be accepted by physicians participating in the Blue Shield program as payment in full. As with US Medicaid (see chapter 5), a physician who accepted Blue Shield payment could not "balance bill" patients with such insurance for the difference between the physician's usual fee and the amount that Blue Shield paid.

During the early 1940s, a major impetus for the growth of private health insurance plans was the wage and price controls implemented during World War II, which limited the wage increases that could be offered to employees. Health insurance and other fringe benefits were not considered to be part of wage compensation. Nonwage compensation was not subject to personal income taxation. Thus, from the outset, such compensation was subsidized under the US tax code.

The nature of private health insurance in the United States has changed markedly since the 1940s. Traditional plans with no elements of managed care are now rare.[3] Yet some aspects of managed care with the most promise in achieving cost containment met widespread opposition, particularly in the 1990s (see chapter 10).

11.5 THE MANAGED COMPETITION MODEL

Another casualty of the mid-1990s in the United States was the *managed competition* model, a concept originally developed in the 1970s. This model is worth discussing, however, since it is down (in popularity) but not out as a policy option for the future.

3. See chapter 10 for a detailed description of managed care in the United States.

The overall goal of managed competition is to obtain quantity and quality of care at the point at which marginal benefit equals marginal cost, where marginal cost does not embody the inefficiencies inherent in the current system. Managed competition has several key features.

First, following Alain Enthoven (1993), who conceptualized managed competition, is the notion of the sponsor, which may be an employer, government agency, labor/management health welfare trust, or other organization representing individuals who do not have access to another sponsor. A sponsor establishes rules for the equitable treatment of all persons eligible for insurance under its jurisdiction, selects and contracts with health plans, manages the enrollment process, creates a market in which demand facing individual providers is elastic, and manages risk selection.

Equitable treatment is achieved by implementing the following types of rules: no exclusion from coverage because of preexisting health conditions and guaranteed renewal of coverage. The sponsor pays a fixed dollar subsidy per insured individual roughly equivalent to per enrollee cost in the lowest-cost plan. If the individual selects a more expensive plan, he or she bears the additional premium as an out-of-pocket expense. No one pays an additional premium on account of adverse health.

Sponsors can select which health plans will be offered to the individuals they sponsor. As Enthoven (1993) noted, a private employer may have a greater choice of plan—that is, may be able to exclude more plans—than a public employer. An insurance purchasing cooperative, organized specifically to offer health insurance in a locality, is likely to have even less choice of plan since it is likely to be tied to a specific geographic area.

A sponsor manages the enrollment process; individual subscribers notify the sponsor of their choice of plan, and this information is conveyed to the specific health plan the subscriber selects. The sponsor defines enrollment procedures and oversees the enrollment process to ensure that equitable enrollment practices are maintained. The sponsor has responsibility for communicating pertinent features of each plan, including out-of-pocket premiums and cost sharing at the point of service to potential subscribers.

Sponsors create price-elastic demand. They accomplish this by making a fixed dollar contribution to the purchase of each plan. Thus, if a plan has a higher quality (coverage)-adjusted premium, individuals will select another plan. The price sensitivity of consumers puts pressure on the plan to negotiate tough bargains with providers who become part of their networks. To allow individuals to make "apples-to-apples" comparisons, plan features should be standardized. When there are differentiating features, these should be explicitly identified so that direct comparisons of features and premium differences can be made. Health outcomes from each plan should be reported in a standardized way so that any differences in outcomes are clear to individuals who make choices among the sponsored health plans. As managed care is conceptualized, premiums paid out of pocket by individuals should be fully taxable, avoiding the tax subsidy of generous coverage that exists in the United States currently (see chapter 10). Some empirical evidence indicates that the choice of health plan is premium-elastic (see Buchmueller and Feldstein 1997 for the United States and Tamm, Tauchmann, Wasem, et al. 2007 for Germany).

Sponsors manage risk selection to ensure that some plans do not obtain disproportionate shares of the healthiest individuals, thereby leaving less healthy individuals to other health plans.[4] Achieving this objective requires some form of risk adjustment. That is, the sponsor pays plans additional amounts on behalf of less healthy individuals so that the amounts in premiums paid by individuals do not vary by health risk and health plans have an incentive to improve quality, patient satisfaction, and efficiency rather than to profit by selecting the favorable health risks.

Large employers, those with 10,000+ employees, are of sufficient size to be effective sponsors. However, smaller employers and other groups may be insufficiently large to serve as sponsors. To deal with this issue, the managed care model employs health insurance purchasing cooperatives (HIPCs). HIPCs would contract with employers and other groups to perform the functions of a sponsor. They are likely to be organized as private not-for-profit organizations. HIPCs, like other sponsors, would not bear risk. Under managed competition, health plans bear risk. Managed competition was seriously considered in 1994 by the Clinton administration. The proposal died in the US Congress for various political reasons. In part, the Clinton proposal was unsuccessful because in the interest of creating a level playing field, the proposal became so complex that it resembled the complex regulatory systems that it was not supposed to be. It is difficult to know whether managed competition failed the political test in general or whether it was particular features of the proposal and the way it was marketed that failed.

Robinson (2003) and others have taken the view that managed competition itself failed the test. In Robinson's words, "managed competition demanded too much individual restraint and too much joint collaboration on the part of both the public and private sectors" (ibid., 343). As a specific example, he noted that employers were to offer several health plans under managed competition. However, employers have not generally shown an inclination to do this. They not only continue to offer few plans but often subsidize expensive plans more than less expensive ones, thus giving plans little incentive to cut their costs and ultimately their premiums.

Another type of criticism of managed competition is that payers and providers would have unequal bargaining power. In Germany, for example, providers and payers conduct collective bargaining at the state level. In the United States, by contrast, such collective bargaining is illegal. It is illegal for providers to form groups for the sole purpose of negotiating terms of contracts with health plans.

4. The empirical evidence on whether or not managed care plans in general and HMOs in particular obtain a favorable mix of enrollees from the standpoint of health status is mixed, although views on this point are strongly held by various stakeholders. Mello, Stearns, Norton, et al. (2003), for example, in studying the issue of biased selection in US Medicare HMOs, found some evidence of favorable selection on some but not all measures. Controlling for risk selection into Medicare HMOs, Mello, Stearns, and Norton (2002) found that Medicare HMOs significantly reduced the probability of hospitalization and the number of days in the hospital conditional on a hospital admission. But they found no effect on the use of physicians' services. Using data from the 2000 Medical Expenditure Panel Survey to study selection into private HMO plans in the United States, Shin and Moon (2007) found empirical evidence of favorable selection into HMO plans.

11.6 COMPARISONS BETWEEN SINGLE- AND MULTIPLE-PAYER SYSTEMS

In many countries, a single health insurance plan is responsible for financing health care, while in other countries, especially some of the more populous ones, such as the United States and China, there are many health insurance plans. With multiple insurance plans, health care providers receive payment from various sources, private, public, or a combination of the two. Single-payer systems tend to have an advantage on various dimensions of the cost of care. By contrast, multi-payer systems can better satisfy heterogeneous preferences within a country's population. Although this an advantage, and there may be others—for example, multipayer systems are probably less likely to stifle innovation in health care—the multipayer system may generate some negative and positive externalities that would not occur under a single-payer system. Three types of externalities are (1) cost shifting from some payers to others, (2) the shifting of patients from some payers to others, and (3) other spillover effects. The first two involve negative externalities and the third (briefly discussed above) involves a positive externality.

COST SHIFTING

In a competitive market as under managed competition, payers compete for customers by offering insurance at low quality-adjusted prices. However, insurers may differ in market power. A large insurer is likely to be in a better position to negotiate lower prices of services with providers than is a small insurer or, even more so, an uninsured individual who pays for care out of pocket. Cost shifting occurs when a reduction in service price to one payer results in a higher service price to others. At first glance, it might appear that this is one of competition's strong points. Competitive forces eliminate the inefficient competitors, in this context health insurers that fail to negotiate low prices with providers. But this may be highly undesirable if the individual "competitor" is an individual patient or a small group of insured persons, such as the employees of a small business. Furthermore, eliminating the small participants in a health insurance market may leave the market to one or a few large insurers, who then possess market power to set premiums at a high level.

Cost shifting as defined here differs from price discrimination as described in chapter 5. In price discrimination, a reduction in one seller's price results in a reduction in other sellers' prices, not price increases.

In the model of cost-shifting behavior described by Dranove, Simon, and White (1998), a nonprofit hospital that maximizes utility with output and profits as arguments of the utility function, there are two payers, a public payer and a private payer. A reduction in the price the public payer pays to the hospital results in an increase in price to the private payer under two conditions. First, the hospital must have market power in its private sector product market. Second, the market power must not have been fully exploited before the public payer reduced the price it paid hospitals. That is, the hospital did not set price at the profit-maximizing price before the public payer decreased price. The intuition is that the hospital raises its price toward the profit-maximizing price to make up for the shortfall caused by the fall in the price paid for hospital care by the public payer.

In Dranove, Simon, and White's empirical analysis, the public payer is the US state of Illinois' Medicaid program. This program substantially reduced its payments to hospitals in the early 1980s. Dranove, Simon, and White found that for each $1 *decrease* in hospital profits (which can be negative) from serving Medicaid recipients per private admission there was a 51 cent *increase* in hospital price per private admission. This implies that about half of the revenue loss from the Medicaid cutback was recovered through cost shifting.

As a result of the growth in managed care plans, hospital markets in the United States have become more competitive since the early 1980s. Consequently, to the extent that cost shifting existed in the past, it is likely to be decreasing since it is becoming much more difficult for hospitals to recoup losses from public payers by raising prices to private payers. The private payers face tough product markets of their own and are likely to resist upward price pressures from hospitals. However, to the extent that competition among hospitals and physicians is lacking in a market, it may be difficult to restrain health care cost growth or at least more difficult with multiple payers to do so than under a single-payer system.

PATIENT SELECTION

In a multiple-payer system, some insurers may earn higher profits by selecting favorable risks, leaving unhealthy risks to other insurers, including the government plans. Insurers covering relatively healthy persons may, at first glance, appear to be efficient, but this efficiency difference may be partially or even totally due to favorable patient selection.

There are differences between managed care and traditional insurance plans (plans relying on fee-for-service payment and not limiting insureds' choice of provider) in the illness severity of persons they cover. Managed care plans more frequently enroll disproportionately higher numbers of young families and persons without long-standing ties to physicians, those with fewer chronic illnesses, and persons with lower rates of prior personal health care services utilization. Based on a review of several studies of patient selection by insurers, Glied (2000) concluded that managed care plans in the private sector tend to enjoy a 20–30 percent prior utilization advantage over traditional insurance plans. Differential patient selection by managed care and traditional plans can be a confounder in studies that estimate the effect of managed care plans on health care cost growth relative to that of traditional plans. While most studies have found that increased managed care activity is associated with a reduced growth rate in health care costs, some studies have concluded that managed care raises or has no overall effect on health care costs (Glied 2000). This conflicting evidence may be partly a consequence of how the studies have accounted for temporal changes in the case mix of insured persons in the two types of health plans. In sum, patient selection is another reason why multiple-payer systems may have limited potential in health care cost containment. It may be easier for insurers to compete on the basis of attracting low-cost individuals than by realizing actual efficiencies.

SPILLOVER EFFECTS

While cost shifting and favorable patient selection involve negative externalities, spillover effects involve a positive externality. An efficiency gain by one insurer may result in efficiency gains accruing to other insurers in the same market. Suppose that utilization monitoring by one insurer results in a reduced length of stay among patients hospitalized for heart attacks. This may change the practice patterns of physicians practicing in the area. The physicians begin by reducing the length of stay of patients covered by the one insurer that has become aggressive in utilization monitoring, but rather than reduce stays just for persons covered by this insurer, physicians change their practice for all of their heart attack patients, not just those covered by the one insurer. Here the action of one insurer has a much larger effect on patient care and health care cost than on expenditures incurred by the insurer that initiated the action. In this respect, a multiple-payer system has a favorable impact on health care cost containment.

In fact, several studies have reported that the growth of managed care plan enrollments is associated with reductions in hospital beds, reductions in the supply of physicians, mergers of providers, and reductions in technology adoption (Baker and McClellan 2001).

There is empirical evidence of spillovers affecting the quality of care and physician prescribing patterns. There is evidence that the treatment of heart attacks tends to be better in areas with high managed care penetration, pointing to a spillover effect of higher-quality care to patients enrolled in the traditional insurance plans (Baker and McClellan 2001). In addition, physicians tend to prescribe similar drugs to non-managed-care patients, although these patients are not restricted by the drug formulary imposed by the managed care plans. This aspect, too, is a positive attribute of a multiple-payer system in general and of managed care plans in particular. With the important caveat that the empirical evidence comes only from the United States, the evidence does suggest that countries with a multiple-payer system can realize higher quality and a higher rate of innovation than countries with a single-payer system.

11.7 SUMMARY AND CONCLUSIONS

This chapter has described a typology to be used in this and the next two chapters. This chapter has focused on systems with substantial financing from private sources. No country, including the United States, has adopted a completely private health care system of the type described in this chapter. Yet particularly in the United States, a major part of health expenditure is privately financed, and the vast majority of health care providers are private as well. For the elderly in the United States who are covered by social insurance, Medicare, the model more closely resembles social insurance with the private provision of services. This program is described in the next chapter, which focuses on social insurance and private provision.

For various reasons, managed care is now under attack from stakeholders, both physicians and members of the public alike. While we as economists typically honor private preferences, we need to be somewhat careful in this context since there are important distortions in the marketplace, especially in the United States, within the tax subsidy of private insurance purchases. Also, many of those who are most critical of managed care are health care providers who would presumably prefer not to negotiate over fees and other terms of work. The empirical evidence on managed care, overall, is much more favorable.

One way of structuring a health care system of the future is to build one based on managed competition. In an important sense, managed competition remains to be subjected to a true market test. To have a true market test, certain preconditions must be satisfied, including neutral tax and employer treatment of the alternatives among which consumers are to choose. Another precondition is transparency in prices, what is covered, as well as in the quality of the health care providers include in health plan's network. These preconditions have proved to be very difficult to establish in the United States, although various building blocks are currently in place.

Having a multiple-payer system in which payers compete for business has both advantages, possibly in terms of quality and the rate of innovation, as well as disadvantages in terms of cost shifting and patient selection, sometimes termed "patient cream skimming." The choice of multiple- versus single-payer systems involves important trade-offs. Strong arguments can be made for either system. Competition in health care lacks an organized political constituency, which at least some forms of public regulation have. For example, health care providers often argue for entry regulation since they stand to benefit from it. Providers do not argue for managed competition since it promises low profit margins and exit for those who cannot meet the terms of a competitive marketplace. By contrast, citizen consumers are not well organized. Efficient health care is only one of many issues that occupy their concerns.

The typology includes a category in which out-of-pocket payment by patients predominates. Out-of-pocket payment may rank high in terms of economic efficiency, but it is poor in protecting households against health expenditure risk. Moreover, individual patients are poorly positioned to negotiate with providers over the price of care. Yet in many countries throughout the world, out-of-pocket payment is the main source of health care financing. We have summarized systems in China and India; health systems in both countries, especially in China, are in transition, and economic growth may lead to major changes in these systems in these countries.

Key Concepts

- health care system
- financing of personal health care services
- public financing
- private financing
- private system
- public system
- delivery of personal health care services
- public provision
- private provision
- cash system
- quasi-public system

Review and Discussion Questions

11.1 Explain the distinction between patient-driven competition and payer-driven competition. Give examples of how these two types of competition would lead to different outcomes in a hospital market.

11.2 What are the elements of the managed competition model? What do you see as the advantages and disadvantages of the managed competition model?

11.3 Distinguish between the "cash system" and the "private system" described in this chapter. Which system provides better protection against health expenditure risk? Which system is in a better position to avoid a welfare loss arising from moral hazard?

Exercises

11.1 Use the concepts of cost of capital (COC) and marginal efficiency of investment (MEI) that you have learned in chapters 2 and 9 to analyze the effect of managed care on the diffusion of new and expensive medical technology in a hospital market. Present a graph to show how the growth of managed care affects COC and MEI for hospital investment in new technology. Justify your answer.

11.2 Collect time-series data on the share of public financing and the share of public supply in your country or any other single country you prefer and plot these data in a figure that has a similar format as figure 11.6. Does the health care system in the country you selected remain stable over time or change from one system to another system? Explain the reason why the system remains constant or change over time.

11.3 In China, the share of national health expenditure paid through out-of-pocket payment increased from about 20 percent in 1980 to about 60 percent in 2000 (see fig. 11.7). During the same period, real GDP per capita (in 2000 US dollars) increased from US$186 to US$949 (see World Bank Group 2007). Explain why the share of out-of-pocket payment increases as national income rises. Does this relationship imply that health insurance is an inferior good? Is it valid to generalize from the experience of China to predict the effect of economic growth in the share of out-of-pocket payments in other countries, such as India?

11.4 The following is a summary statistics table for China and India in 2003.

	China	India
GDP per capita (in 2000 US$)	1,209	511
Out-of-pocket payment as percent of total health expenditure (%)	56	73
Health care spending as percent of GDP (%)	5.6	4.8
General government expenditures on health as percent of total government expenditures (%)	9.7	3.9

Sources: World Health Organization, World Health Report (2006); World Bank Group, World Development Indicators (2009).

Using information from this table, why is the share of out-of-pocket payment higher in India than in China? If you were hired by the Indian government as a consultant, which policy options would you recommend to solve the problem of a high out-of-pocket share in India? Is promoting economic growth on your list of policy options? Why or why not?

11.5 Recall the discussion in chapter 5 about a long-run decision involving practice location. Suppose that the World Trade Organization (WTO) signed a treaty among all member countries guaranteeing no legal impediments to physician movement among countries. Physicians trained in one country could choose to practice location in any country in the world. Suppose you were a physician. Would the country's health care system be an important consideration in your choice of country in which to practice? If your choice were limited to cash versus private systems, which system you prefer for your practice location, other things being equal? Explain the rationale for your choice.

11.6 Based on the time-series observations on China (see exercise 11.3 and fig. 11.7) and the cross-sectional comparisons between China and India (see question 4), it seems difficult to draw a clear conclusion on the relationship between the share of out-of-pocket payments and national income. The share of out-of-pocket payment is positively associated with national income in time-series data, but this relationship is reversed in cross-sectional data. Can you develop a theory (or a story) to explain the relationship between the share of out-of-pocket payment and national income for most of the countries in the world? Based on your theory (or story), which relationship between share of out-of-pocket payment and national income (positive or negative) is the general case (i.e., applies to many other countries) and which relationship is a special case (i.e., applicable to a single country)?

ONLINE SUPPLEMENTAL READINGS

HEALTH MAINTENANCE ORGANIZATIONS

http://www.rand.org/pubs/research_briefs/RB4540/index1.html

http://www.cbsnews.com/stories/2001/05/01/national/main288749.shtml

HEALTH CARE LEGISLATION

http://www.cbo.gov/publications/collections/collections.cfm?collect=10

SUPPLEMENTAL READINGS

Glied, S. 2000. Managed Care. In *Handbook of Health Economics*, ed. J. P. Newhouse and A. J. Culyer, 1A:707–745. Amsterdam: Elsevier Science.

Perkins, M., E. Brazier, E. Themmen, et al. 2009. Out-of-Pocket Costs for Facility-Based Maternity Care in Three African Countries. *Health Policy and Planning* 24 (4): 289–300.

Wagstaff, A., W. Yip, M. Lindelow, et al. 2009. China's Health System and Its Reform: A Review of Recent Studies. *Health Economics* 18 (S2): S7–S23.

van Doorslaer, E. V., O. O'Donnell, R. P. Rannan-Eliya, et al. 2007. Catastrophic Payments for Health Care in Asia. *Health Economics* 16 (11): 1159–1184.

References

Baker, L. C., and M. B. McClellan. 2001. Managed Care, Health Care Quality, and Regulation. *Journal of Legal Studies* 30 (2): 715–741.

Berman, P. A. 1998. Rethinking the Health Care Systems: Private Health Care Provisions in India. *World Development* 26 (8): 1462–1479.

Bhat, R. 1999. Characteristics of Private Medical Practices in India: A Provider Perspective. *Health Policy and Planning* 14 (1): 26–37.

Bhattacharya, A. S., and P. K. Sapra. 2008. Health Insurance in China and India: Segmented Roles for Public and Private Financing. *Health Affairs* 27 (4): 1005–1015.

Blomquist, A., and J. Qian. 2008. Health System Reform in China: An Assessment of Recent Trends. *Singapore Economic Review* 53 (1): 5–26.

Bloom, G., B. Kanjilal, and D. H. Peters. 2008. Regulating Health Care Markets in China and India. *Health Affairs* 27 (4): 952–963.

Blumenthal, D., and W. Hsiao. 2005. Privatization and Its Discontents: The Evolving Chinese Health Care System. *New England Journal of Medicine* 353 (11): 1165–1170.

Buchmueller, T. C., and P. J. Feldstein. 1997. The Effect of Price on Switching among Health Plans. *Journal of Health Economics* 16 (2): 231–247.

Chandra, M. K. 2010. Inclusive Growth in Neoliberal India: A Façade? *Economic and Political Weekly* 45 (8): 43–56.

Das, J., and J. Hammer. 2006. Money for Nothing: The Dire Straits of Medical Practice in Delhi, India. *Journal of Development Economics* 83:1–36.

Dranove, D., C. Simon, and W. D. White. 1998. The Determinants of Managed Care Penetration. *Journal of Health Economics* 17 (6): 729–745.

Enthoven, A. C. 1993. The History and Principles of Managed Competition. *Health Affairs* 12 (Suppl.): 24–48.

Fang, H., J. Chen, and J. A. Rizzo. 2009. Explaining Urban-Rural Health Disparities in China. *Medical Care* 47 (12): 1209–1216.

Finkelstein, A. 2007. The Aggregate Effects of Health Insurance: Evidence from the Introduction of Medicare. *Quarterly Journal of Economics* 122 (1): 1–37.

Glied, S. 2000. Managed Care. In *Handbook of Health Economics*, ed. J. P. Newhouse and A. J. Culyer, 1A:707–745. Amsterdam: Elsevier Science.

Huang, Y., and Y. Yang. 2009. Pharmaceutical Pricing in China. In *Prescribing Cultures and Pharmaceutical Policy in the Asia-Pacific*, ed. K. Eggleston. Washington, DC: Brookings Institution Press.

Liu, Y., K. Rao, J. Wu, et al. 2008. Health System Reform in China: China's Health System Performance. *Lancet* 372:1914–1923.

Ma, J., M. S. Lu, and H. Quan. 2008. From a National, Centrally Planned Health System to a System Based on the Market: Lessons from China. *Health Affairs* 27 (4): 937–948.

Mello, M. M., S. C. Stearns, and E. C. Norton. 2002. Do Medicare HMOs Still Reduce Health Services Use after Controlling for Selection Bias? *Health Economics* 11 (4): 323–340.

Mello, M. M., S. C. Stearns, E. C. Norton, et al. 2003. Understanding Biased Selection in Medicare HMOs. *Health Services Research* 38 (3): 961–992.

Newhouse, J. P. 1992. Medical Care Costs: How Much Welfare Loss? *Journal of Economic Perspectives* 6 (3): 3–21.

O'Donnell, O., E. van Doorslaer, R. P. Rannan-Eliya, et al. 2008. Who Pays for Health Care in Asia? *Journal of Health Economics* 27 (2): 460–475.

Organisation for Economic Co-operation and Development. 2000. OECD Health Data 2000.

Perkins, M., E. Brazier, E. Themmen, et al. 2009. Out-of-Pocket Costs for Facility-Based Maternity Care in Three African Countries. *Health Policy and Planning* 24 (4): 289–300.

Rahman, T. 2008. Determinants of Public Health Expenditure: Some Evidence from Indian States. *Applied Economics Letters* 15:853–857.

Richman, B. D., K. Udayakumar, W. Mitchell, et al. 2008. Lessons from India in Organizational Innovation: A Tale of Two Heart Hospitals. *Health Affairs* 27 (5): 1260.

Roberts, M. J., W. Hsiao, P. A. Berman, et al. 2004. *Getting Health Reform Right.* New York: Oxford University Press.

Robinson, J. C. 2003. The Politics of Managed Competition: Public Abuse of the Private Interest. *Journal of Health Politics, Policy and Law* 28 (2–3): 341–353.

Shin, J., and S. Moon. 2007. HMO Plans, Self-Selection and Utilization of Health Care Services. *Applied Economics* 39:2769–2784.

Singh, N. 2008. Decentralization and Public Delivery of Health Care Services in India. *Health Affairs* 27 (4): 991–1001.

Tamm, M., H. Tauchmann, J. Wasem, et al. 2007. Elasticities of Market Shares and Social Health Insurance Choice in Germany: A Dynamic Panel Data Approach. *Health Economics* 16 (3): 243–256.

van Doorslaer, E. V., O. O'Donnell, R. P. Rannan-Eliya, et al. 2007. Catastrophic Payments for Health Care in Asia. *Health Economics* 16 (11): 1159–1184.

Wagstaff, A. 2007. Health Systems in East Asia: What Can Developing Countries Learn from Japan and the Asian Tigers? *Health Economics* 16 (5): 441–456.

Wagstaff, A., and E. van Doorslaer. 1992. Equity in the Finance of Health Care: Some International Comparisons. *Journal of Health Economics* 11 (4): 361–387.

Wagstaff, A., W. Yip, M. Lindelow, et al. 2009. China's Health System and Its Reform: A Review of Recent Studies. *Health Economics* 18 (S2): S7–S23.

World Bank Group. 2007. World Development Indicators.. http://data.worldbank.org/indicator.

World Bank Group. 2009. World Development Indicators. http://data.worldbank.org/indicator.

World Health Organzation (WHO). 2006. World Health Report 2006. www.who.int/whr/2006/en.

Yip, W., and W. Hslao. 2008. The Chinese Health System at a Crossroads. *Health Affairs* 27 (2): 460–468.

CHAPTER 12

GOVERNMENT FINANCING AND PRIVATE SUPPLY

Many countries have single-payer government financing or private financing under strict government oversight, combined with the private provision of personal health care services. Health insurance in such situations is often provided as social insurance. This means that insurance coverage is universal and provided without regard to a person's ability to pay. Benefits are provided uniformly to the entire covered population. If differences are allowed—for example, if supplementation with a private insurance plan is allowed—these differences are above a high minimum level of benefits. Taxation or premiums may be progressive or, more frequently, may be proportional to individuals' earnings, the latter in systems that obtain program revenue from a payroll tax.

The major underlying premise in most high-income countries is that coverage be universal. This can be achieved by the direct public provision of health insurance or by laws requiring that individuals have health insurance coverage, which may be provided through groups, such as through employment, or as individual health insurance.

Nevertheless, even though the above broad principles are widely shared, there is much variation among countries in how the concept of social insurance is implemented. There are choices about how such insurance is to be financed. First, should special taxes be levied, and if so, which ones? Second, should the program be financed on a pay-as-you-go basis or should reserves for future (and uncertain) payments be maintained? If the latter, at what level should the reserves be maintained? How can the revenue system be structured so as to protect it from raids for use by other public programs? If the system is to be operated as a private mandate, how should the solvency of the private funds be ensured, and which specific conditions should be imposed on the private plans (e.g., provisions regarding the insurability of persons with prior health conditions and the premiums such persons are expected to pay)?

On the expenditure side, first, how should payments be structured? What is the appropriate unit of payment, such as for hospitals, the patient day, stay, or fixed total budget? There is empirical evidence on this issue for some countries. Second, once the unit of payment is selected, how should the price per unit of service be determined? Third, should payment be payment in full, or is there a role for patient supplementation of fees, including co-payments and reference pricing for drugs? Governments in effect set separate prices for providers and patients. Fourth, which services should be covered (e.g., brand-name pharmaceuticals versus generics, medical devices such as implantable cardiac defibrillators)? And how should the process of making coverage decisions about new products and services be designed and implemented? Private health insurers must make similar decisions, but their decisions are private. When there is public financing, these matters become public choices.

12.1 The Role of Government as a Payer: Rationale for the Public Provision of Health Insurance

Universal Coverage, Social Insurance, and Means-Tested Insurance

A direct approach to achieving universal coverage is the direct public provision of health insurance. Payment can be public while health care providers are private entities as in the fully private system (see chapter 11). The rationale for universal coverage is that personal health services are a merit want. People are presumed to have the right to be able to use personal health care services regardless of their financial status. According to the merit want concept, personal health services are not to be allocated according to ability and willingness to pay as are the vast majority of goods and services. Milk for young children and school lunches for elementary and secondary school children are other examples of merit wants. People regard it as only fair that children have access to these goods, not only if parents have the ability or willingness to pay.

Another justification for universal coverage is that it avoids adverse selection in health insurance patients. Under universal coverage, everyone is insured and under the same terms. Universal coverage is generally seen as equitable in that in systems without universal coverage, when services are provided to uninsured persons, the insured end up paying the bill. Advocates for the public provision of health insurance often argue that public insurers are more efficient than private insurers. Insurers that pick and choose among persons they want to insure incur appreciable underwriting expense. Under universal coverage, enrollment is almost automatic.

When a government is the health insurer, it assumes the roles of (1) determining eligibility for coverage and actually enrolling individuals in the plan, (2) ensuring the continued actuarial soundness of the program by collecting revenue sufficient to cover anticipated program outlays, (3) setting coverage and payment policies, (4) processing health insurance claims and actually paying health care providers for covered services rendered, and (5) serving as a health care regulator, monitoring fraud and abuse and increasingly monitoring the quality of care provided.

An alternative and often used social insurance model leaves much of the provision of health insurance in private hands. The role of the government is to specify the terms of the relationship between the insurer and the health care provider, as well as the terms of the "contract" between the insurer and the beneficiary, including patient cost-sharing obligations, if any, the types of services covered, and the extent to which the beneficiary is free to choose his or her own health care provider, as well as the insurer's allowable underwriting and premium-setting practices. *Underwriting* refers to practices of insurers related to the types of risks the insurer covers (e.g., whether or not persons with certain preexisting conditions are covered). Under this model, perhaps only the regulatory role is housed in the government. The remaining functions are the responsibility of private organizational entities.

Another alternative to social insurance is government-supplied means-tested insurance. Under the latter, only a subset of persons is eligible for public coverage. Means testing employs income and asset tests for program eligibility. Persons with income or assets above a maximum threshold are no longer eligible. In some cases, rather than employ a fixed income or income-plus-assets threshold as the criterion for eligibility, persons may earn a higher income than the threshold, but the income is partly or entirely confiscated by requiring that income above the threshold be used to defray the government's cost of providing the service to the individual. An example of a means-tested health insurance program is the US Medicaid program (see chapter 5).

The underlying rationale for social insurance is that access to the covered goods and services is a right of all individuals. With means-tested insurance, such access is a right to individuals with especially low ability to pay for such goods and services. Since means-tested programs apply only to a fraction of the population, some of the efficiencies in administration that accrue under social insurance are lost. Further, means-tested programs lack the purchasing power of single public insurers.

Arguments of Advocates for the Public Provision of Health Insurance

Advocates for the public provision of insurance or the alternative, in which there is private insurance but under the strict supervision of public law, make the following arguments. First and foremost, they argue that public provision is needed to ensure universal health insurance coverage. Under a private health insurance system not subject to strict public scrutiny, it is almost inevitable that some persons will remain uncovered by health insurance plans even if universal coverage is the public goal. The essential feature of a private system is choice, including the choice not to purchase the good or service. Under a private system, even if personal health insurance is viewed as a merit want, the main policy instrument to achieve high levels of coverage is the "carrot" of financial incentives, generally tax incentives that accrue to persons who purchase health insurance. Under a public system, people are compelled to be insured.

There is another argument for the direct public provision of health insurance or for statutes compelling individuals to be insured. Many people may not be sufficiently forward-looking or may be forward-looking but discount costs in future periods substantially so that the cost of possible of future out-of-pocket health care expenditures receives little weight in current consumption decisions. If so, such persons may need a government's help so that they act in their long-run self-interest.

Compulsion offers two related advantages. By compelling healthy people to enroll in insurance plans and pay premiums or taxes, there is a cross subsidy from healthy to sick individuals. Without the participation of the healthy individuals, who may be tempted to eschew coverage under a voluntary system, this type of cross subsidy would not occur. Also, some of the healthy individuals will eventually become sick. When sick and lacking health insurance, these healthy-turned-sick individuals may not be willing or able to pay for the care they receive. When people are sick, it goes against social norms to refuse to care for them simply because they do not pay. Thus, since these individuals consume scarce resources when they are sick, these costs must be covered by someone. It is often argued that those with health insurance end up paying the bill. In the jargon of the health field, hospitals in particular "cost shift" shortfalls from their nonpaying customers to the bills of those who pay—those patients with health insurance (see chapter 11).[1]

Third, in some respects, the public model is more efficient than the private one. Private insurers need to market their products and incur costs in enrolling people in their plans. Under the public model, it is likely to be necessary to prove one's personal identity, but there is no need for marketing, and enrollment is almost automatic. Since the benefit structure and the fees are the same for all covered individuals, as are the terms of coverage, health care providers in a country with a public health insurance system do not need to check the patient's eligibility, whether or not the patient's plan covers a particular service, which may vary according to the patient's specific health condition, and how much the insurance plan pays for a particular service. For all of these reasons, it is argued that public insurance is less costly administratively both to insurers and to health care providers, who do not need to investigate the terms of a patient's coverage on a

1. See chapter 11 for a discussion of some of the empirical evidence on cost shifting. To the extent that the hospital market in the United States has become more competitive in recent years, there should be a reduction in hospitals' ability to cost shift.

patient-specific basis. A patient merely shows his or her health insurance card, and this is the only checking that the provider has to do.

Fourth, given the purchasing power and other powers of government, a public insurer can obtain services at lower prices than a private insurer can. Greater bargaining power accrues to the benefit of the public, if not to the collective benefit of health care providers, who may prefer a private health insurance system for this reason.

Fifth, government may be more efficient in providing regulatory oversight of a public than a private entity. For example, for purposes of evaluating insurer solvency risk, access to accounting records may be more easily obtained by regulators from public enterprises. In any case, the regulation of private health insurers in particular and of health care costs in general may be more effective when government controls the health insurance apparatus.

Although these five alleged advantages of the public provision of health insurance are supported by a large community of health policy experts, government officials, and politicians, there are counterarguments as well.

First, it is one thing to require that all individuals have health insurance but quite another to ascertain that all individuals actually comply with this statutory requirement. Physicians are unlikely to want to be in the position of verifying the insurance status of their patients as long as they are paid. In the United States, physician reporting of patients who lack health insurance may violate privacy laws.

This is less of an issue when the government provides insurance coverage directly rather than when the government compels individuals to obtain specific types of coverage from any source. As long as the statute requiring coverage is not enforced, universal coverage is not likely to be achieved. A related problem is what to do about a violation of the compulsory insurance law in cases in which a violation is detected. Would a fine be levied? How would this work if at the same time the violator is critically ill or dead?

Mandatory cross subsidies do not necessarily enhance social welfare. The argument for cross subsidies relies on an equity argument that the healthy have an obligation to subsidize the sick. Cross subsidies are inefficient to the extent that they require some individuals to forgo more consumption of other goods and services than they would absent compulsion. In other words, for some individuals, the amount paid for health insurance exceeds their marginal valuation of the benefit of coverage, in particular risk-neutral persons and risk lovers, and those with "good" genes. The compulsion aspect involves a trade-off between the loss in individual welfare and the social gains from having what is judged to be a fairer distribution of societal resources. Although government compulsion may offset bad personal decisions made by myopic individuals, the downside is that forward-looking and rational individuals are likely to be made worse off by compulsion.

There is no dispute that public health insurers incur fewer costs in enrolling persons in their programs; there are savings in the cost of marketing their plans to potential consumers. Savings accrue to health care providers from being able to bill a single insurer rather than multiple insurers. However, multiple insurers with varying characteristics may provide a better match with consumers that have heterogeneous preferences. When Henry Ford marketed the first Model T Ford, which was painted a black color, some individual wants were likely to have been satisfied. But it is likely that some consumers preferred a car in a color other than black. (All Model T's were painted black.) Advocates for single public health insurers implicitly argue that the benefits of heterogeneity are more than offset by the savings in overhead expense of having multiple insurers with varying attributes competing for health insurance business.

Granting a single insurer or government agency the exclusive right to negotiate fees and other conditions with providers may indeed give them monopsony power in purchasing health care services. The exercise of monopsony power may lead to (1) too little quantity of the service being produced, (2) reductions in the quality of care, and (3) because of lower prices, less incentive for innovation (i.e., monopsony power may lead to dynamic inefficiency; see chapter 9). Undoubtedly, suppliers of health care goods and services are made worse off, but even though monopsony power may relieve pressure on public budgets and achieve cost containment, it is not self-evident that the public at large is better off with monopsony.

Finally, the public provision of health insurance plausibly facilitates the regulation of health services. Such regulation includes entry regulation—that is, the regulation of entry of hospitals and other health care facilities—and regulation of prices and hospital budgets. However, whether or not such regulation serves the public interest and whether or not the results are superior to those seen with private health insurance that relies on competition to achieve socially desirable outcomes are unresolved issues.

Choices in the Design of Public Payment Systems

Health care includes a complex array of services, including physician visits, inpatient admissions, prescription drugs, and diagnostic and therapeutic procedures, including surgical procedures. As medical technology has changed over time, many new drugs, devices, and treatment procedures have emerged, expanding the feasible set of health services. Given limited resources, policy makers in any health insurance system, public or private, face a choice of what kind of services the health insurance program should cover. In private systems, a decision facing the public sector is the benefit structure of private plans that qualify for favorable tax treatment; or when there is policy form regulation, as in some US states, there is government oversight of the content of private insurance policies and how provisions of companies' offerings are presented to potential customers. Here we focus on public insurance, drawing on insights from economic analysis.

At least five criteria have been proposed in the literature for designing a public health insurance program, which indirectly answers the question of what

TABLE 12.1
Criteria for Designing a Public Health Insurance Program

Criterion	Implications: Services Preferred for Coverage
1. Minimize efficiency loss	Health services with lower price elasticities
2. Maximize risk protection	Health services with higher variance of loss and larger magnitude of potential loss
3. Budget impacts not too large	Health services that would not consume a substantial share of the national health care budget
4. Maximize health benefits	Treatments for which the benefit-cost ratio is greater or equal to 1 or that have cost-effectiveness rates below the criterion threshold
5. Maximize social welfare	Services for which the marginal benefit is greater than or equal to the marginal cost

services health insurance should cover (table 12.1). The first criterion is to minimize the efficiency loss resulting from the implementation of health insurance. The introduction of health insurance results in a "moral hazard" problem in the sense that individuals increase consumption of health care as health insurance reduces the money price of health care at the point at which services are received (see chapter 3). The moral hazard problem in turn leads to a welfare loss because the social cost of increased consumption in health care exceeds the corresponding social benefit. The magnitude of welfare loss resulting from moral hazard depends on the price elasticity of demand for personal health care services (see chapter 3, fig. 3.5b). A higher price elasticity, that is, a higher responsiveness of health care demand to price change, leads to a larger welfare loss. This suggests that health services with relatively low price elasticities should be given higher priority as candidates for inclusion in the public health program than health services with higher price elasticities.

The price elasticity of inpatient care is smaller than is the price elasticity of outpatient care (Newhouse and the Insurance Experiment Group 1993). Thus, almost all health insurance programs provide coverage for hospital care because of its lower price elasticity. In contrast, some insurance programs may exclude coverage of outpatient services because the utilization of such services is often more responsive to price changes. Similarly, such personal health services as dental care and physical examinations have higher price elasticities. For this reason, many public insurance programs also exclude coverage for dental care and well care. Excluding preventive care may be foolish in the long run to the extent that insured persons may demand more care later when they become sick from conditions that might have been prevented with some preventive care earlier (see Ellis and Manning 2007 and Newhouse and Sinaiko 2008).

If inpatient care and outpatient care are substitutes rather than complements, then providing insurance coverage for inpatient care only encourages the consumer to use inpatient care as a substitute for outpatient care. Consequently, the welfare loss may be higher than that incurred by providing health insurance coverage for both inpatient and outpatient care. The empirical findings obtained by the RAND Health Insurance Experiment (HIE) do not support this concern. Rather, the HIE found that hospital inpatient and outpatient care are complements. The group with the high deductible plan in the HIE did not increase its utilization of inpatient care compared to the group with the free care plan (see chapter 3). Recall that the deductible applied only to outpatient care.

A second criterion for determining the scope of a public payment system focuses on maximizing the benefit of risk protection. The value of health insurance reflects the welfare gain from reduced risk bearing (see chapter 4). The benefit of risk protection through health insurance depends on the variance of loss and the size of the loss when people become sick. Events with a probability of loss near 1, such as a common cold and obtaining a regular physical examination, or near 0, such as getting tuberculosis in high-income countries, have a low variance. Decision makers should therefore give lower priority to including such events in the health insurance program. By contrast, this criterion suggests that high-cost health services should be given higher priority as candidates for inclusion in a public health program than low-cost health services. Compared to physician visits in an outpatient setting, hospital care is relatively more expensive. This helps to explain why almost all public health insurance programs globally provide more comprehensive insurance coverage for inpatient hospital care than for outpatient care.

The criterion of maximizing the benefit of risk protection can also explain why the scope of coverage of public health insurance plans has changed over time. For example, in the 1960s and 1970s, few health insurance programs, either public or private, provided coverage for prescription drugs because expenditures on prescription drugs accounted for only a small share of health costs at that time (Berndt 2002). With population aging and advances in pharmaceutical technology, spending on prescription drugs for chronic diseases has increased. As a result, more and more health insurance programs began to provide coverage for such expenses. For example, in the United States, Medicare began to provide insurance coverage for prescription drugs in 2006.

The third criterion relates to budgetary impacts on the public insurance program. Holding other factors constant, governments will be more resistant to covering new products or services that have relatively expensive budgetary impacts.

With advances in medical technology, many new diagnostic and therapeutic procedures and drugs have been introduced. The new technologies in turn affect the cost of health care through two channels: a treatment substitution effect and a treatment expansion effect (Cutler, McClellan, and Newhouse 2000). A *treatment substitution effect* describes the substitution of new treatments for older ones for treating established patients. This effect may result in an increased or decreased cost of health care, depending on whether the new therapies are cost-saving or cost-increasing. The *treatment expansion effect* refers to the phenomenon of more people being treated for disease when new drugs or treatment procedures are introduced. Hence, the treatment expansion effect *always* leads to increased health care expenditures. In most cases, the treatment expansion effect dominates the treatment substitution effect (Glied 2000). This suggests that a predictable consequence of adopting new technology is an increase in health care costs. As a result, many policy makers in public insurance program use the budgetary impact of adopting a new technology as a criterion for deciding whether or not a new technology should be covered by health insurance. Under this criterion, new technology that would potentially consume a major share of a country's health care budget is less likely to be included in the public insurance program.

The fourth criterion is to maximize the net health benefits of health care resources. Although new technologies are costly to society, they often yield major health benefits. Thus, focusing on the budget impact only may not allocate scare resources efficiently. Cost-effectiveness analysis and cost-benefit analysis provide guidance for optimal resource allocation (see chapters 14 and 15). Under the optimal resource allocation criterion, the decision about which new technologies should be covered by public health insurance is made by evaluating new products and services according to their benefits relative to their costs. This criterion suggests that public health insurance should cover all products or services whose benefit is greater than or equal to their cost, a benefit-cost criterion; or, using cost-effectiveness analysis, products and services are ranked in inverse order to their cost-effectiveness ratios, and a larger or smaller number of items are covered as a function of the size of health budget (Hoel 2007).

Since Australia led the way in 1992, several countries have adopted such approaches for deciding whether their public insurance programs should provide coverage for a new technology, especially new prescription drugs (Drummond 2007).

The fifth criterion is to maximize social welfare. This criterion differs from the above criterion that maximizes health benefits if there exists an opportunity for consumers to access a private market. If so, consumers either pay out of pocket or use private health insurance to finance care not covered by public insurance. Hoel (2007) argues that the criterion of maximizing health benefits explicitly or implicitly assumes there is no private market for services not covered by the public insurance program. In other words, these services would not be offered at all if they were not covered by the public insurance program. An example of this type of service is biologics, which are costly and have small market sizes because of the specialized nature of these therapies.

Treatments using specific biologics may not be available in a country when the public insurance program does not provide coverage for these products. This is because the fixed costs of these products, including the costs of marketing and educating physicians about the products and their use, may be high relative to the small population served. Hence, introducing such products in a country may be unprofitable to sellers of these products. In such a case, the value of health insurance would include not only the gain of risk protection but also the gain of access to health care that would otherwise be unavailable or unaffordable—a value derived from the value of health care that insurance makes accessible (Nyman 1999).

However, in most cases, there is an option of paying out of pocket if a particular treatment is not covered by public insurance. When the option of paying for treatment out of pocket is available, the criterion of maximizing health benefits is not necessarily the best one for health care budget allocation (Hoel 2007). This is because the availability of other choices (paying out of pocket) alters the value of public health insurance. On the one hand, the health benefit of public health insurance cannot be measured by total health gains of treatment. Rather, it can only be measured by the marginal health gain of treatment because individuals can obtain treatment in the private sector if the coverage in the public sector is not available. On the other hand, public health insurance does not create added value because the treatment is already available through another payment option. In this case, public health insurance only offers the public the benefit of risk protection.

Given the availability of financing care out of pocket, Hoel (2007) suggests that an efficiency criterion be used for deciding which types of care should be covered by the public health insurance, namely, to maximize social welfare—the sum of the individual utilities of persons through being covered by the public health insurance program. Based on this criterion, he offers the following three propositions as a guide to decision making. First, given the same ratio of health benefits to costs, services with no private market should be assigned a higher priority for inclusion in the public health insurance program than services with private markets. This proposition suggests that policy makers can increase the value of public health insurance through offering improved access to services that would have been unavailable otherwise.

Second, even if a private market for a treatment (or diagnostic procedure) is available, some patients may choose to be untreated (or undiagnosed) if the treatment (diagnostic procedure) is not covered by public health insurance. In this case, private care is available, but some individuals judge it to be "unaffordable." Based on the criterion of maximizing social welfare, services with greater health benefits should be given higher priority for inclusion in the public health insurance program, so long as the costs of the various treatments are the same. This indicates that public health insurance can increase its value by making care with substantial health benefits affordable—care that, absent government intervention, would often be unaffordable.

Third, a priority for public insurance coverage should be given to those services with higher costs among various services that have the same benefit-to-cost ratios. This proposition also highlights the fact that public insurance can increase social welfare by making unaffordable health care more accessible.

In sum, diverse criteria exist for making decisions about the scope of public coverage, and the choices depend on the relative weights assigned to each criterion. For example, if the value of public health insurance is limited to expenditure risk protection, then the criterion of minimizing the efficiency loss (moral hazard) yields the same conclusion as the criterion of maximizing the benefits of risk protection. Both criteria suggest that hospital care should be given a higher priority for inclusion in public coverage than outpatient care. By contrast, the criterion of maximizing social welfare expands the value of public health insurance by considering the possibility of private care. Hence, this criterion yields a different ranking of public coverage priorities than does a criterion solely based on the results of cost-effectiveness analysis.

The next sections provide country case studies of publicly supplied insurance with private provision of personal health services. These case studies are interesting in their own right, but they also suggest approaches that might be adopted by low- and middle-income countries that currently lack universal health insurance coverage.

Table 12.2 presents health and economic indicators in countries selected for country case studies in chapters 11–13. In some countries the public insurance

TABLE 12.2
Health and Economic Indicators: Case Study Countries

Country	GDP Per Capita, 2005 (in 2000 US $)	Share of GDP Spent on Health Care, 2005 (%)	Public Financing Share, 2005 (%)	Public Supply Share, 1998 (%)	Life Expectancy at Birth, 2005 (years)
Canada	25,064	9.9	70.2	99.3	80.2
China	1,449	5.6[a]	36.2[a]	—	71.8
Germany	23,905	10.7	77.0	48.5	78.9
India	588	4.8[a]	24.8[a]	—	63.5
Japan	39,075	8.2	82.7	35.8	82.1
South Korea	13,210	6.0	53.1	9.0	77.6
Taiwan	12,016	6.0	62.5	32.0	77.4
United Kingdom	26,890	8.2	86.9	95.7	78.9
United States	37,267	15.2	45.1	33.2	77.7

Note: a. Data for 2003.
Sources: Data for Taiwan are from the Department of Health, the Statistics of General Health (2008). Data for other countries are from the following three sources: (1) World Bank Group, World Development Indicators (2009); (2) OECD, Health Data (2008); and (3) World Health Organization, World Health Report (2006).

system has a monopoly. In others, such as China, the system has a monopoly, but a large share of national health expenditures is financed by out-of-pocket payments for care. In still a third category are the US public insurance programs, which coexist with private health insurance plans. We shall return to a discussion of the issues just described after we present the country case studies. In reality, no country actually uses the above criteria in making choices about its health care system. Rather, the criteria provide a useful guide for evaluating health system performance.

12.2 EVOLUTION AND STRUCTURE OF THE PAYMENT SYSTEM: GERMAN STATUTORY HEALTH INSURANCE

The German experience provides an excellent case study for two reasons. First, the country has an unusually long history of health insurance provision. The system was established in 1888 as the country was industrializing, and socialism represented a threat to the government in power and to industrial interests. Second, the German model has been adopted by several other high-income countries, such as Japan and other East Asian countries. Unlike in many other countries, such as Canada, the federal government Germany has no role in financing health services. However, in Germany, there is a federal mandate requiring employers to provide health insurance to their employees, and certain important health policies, such as those related to the pricing of pharmaceuticals, are federal (Swami 2002).

The German health insurance system is largely employment-based. Most care is delivered by self-employed, office-based physicians in the ambulatory sector and by salaried physicians in the hospital sector. The vast majority of institutions in the hospital sector are public or church-affiliated not-for profit organizations.

Individuals with monthly earnings below a fixed money threshold, set to apply to about 90 percent of the population, must be covered by statutory health insurance (SHI). Persons with earnings above this threshold may opt out of SHI but must then enroll in a private health insurance plan. The remainder, about two percent of the population, consists of government civil servants who are enrolled in their own plan—most of the two percent, with a very small proportion of population covered by a means-tested health insurance program, *Sozialhilfe*, similar to Medicaid in the United States. In 2002, 57 percent of funding for health care came through the SHI system in the form of employer and employee contributions, assessed as a percentage of the employee's pay (Altenstetter and Busse 2005, 124), and 8 percent came from private health insurance premiums. Only 8 percent of funding came from general tax revenue.

Health insurers under SHI are sickness funds (*gesetzliche Krankenkassen*). These are private nonprofit organizations that qualify as health insurers under the federal statute. The largest single sickness fund is a geographically based fund with membership determined by where the individual lives. Other sickness funds are specific to the company at which a person is employed or to an occupation, such as farming, maritime occupations, mining, and white-collar work. Employer and employee contributions are proportional to the employee's earnings. Thus, more highly paid employees (and their employers) pay more. However, sickness funds are not allowed to base contributions on employee age, gender, marital status, numbers of dependents, or the individual's health status. Private health insurance plans may base their premiums on such factors, but even the most highly paid employee has access to SHI.

Historically, an individual employee had no choice of sickness fund. If the factory, for example, had a sickness fund, the employee enrolled in this fund (Wörz and Busse 2005). However, in recent years, individuals have had a choice of sickness fund. We describe this development more fully below.

Throughout most of its 120-year history, the basic ground rules for health insurance have been established by the central government, but much decision making is vested in *private* organizations at the state (*Land*) level. These private organizations are subject to strict legal requirements. Much policy is the result of negotiations between associations of sickness funds, consisting of the various types of sickness funds, and associations of sickness fund health care providers, hospitals, and physicians. Claims management, processing bills, and paying providers are tasks performed by associations of providers in each state. Exceptions to this pattern occurred during the period in which the National Socialists were in power (1933–1945) and in the German Democratic Republic (East Germany, 1949–1989), when health care providers in all or part of what is Germany today were employed by the state.

Physicians and hospitals are private entities in Germany. However, their fees are set through bilateral negotiations between the association of sickness funds and the association of providers at the state level. Individual providers are price takers. When SHI insureds show their *Versichertenkarten*, credit card–like insurance cards, they are entitled to unlimited ambulatory and hospital care (Schulenburg 1994). Since the prices and conditions of payment do not vary by sickness fund, the only relevant factor to the physician is whether or not the patient presents a card. Privately insured patients may pay higher prices than do those insured through SHI sickness funds, but the vast majority of patients are enrolled in SHI.

Much German health policy attention during the latter part of the twentieth century was devoted to health care cost containment. Nearly complete health insurance coverage has been a factor in expenditure growth. Further, although the system placed reliance on bilateral negotiations between associations of sickness funds and providers, such reliance may have been misplaced. Associations of providers may be expected to promote the interests of their members, even when, as under SHI, membership is compulsory. Since higher expenditures translate into higher provider incomes, these associations cannot be expected to promote cost containment. The parties on the other side of the table, the associations of sickness funds, did not have a real incentive to promote cost containment because its consumer base was assured (see Zweifel and Breyer 1997, 257–264, for a discussion of professional associations in health care).

Higher costs translated into higher payroll contribution rates. Dissatisfied consumers did not have an exit option but rather were compelled to pay the higher rates. The fact that health care providers were and continue to be able to negotiate collectively, which is not allowed in countries such as the United States, has had the effect of offsetting the monopsony power of insurers if insurers choose to exercise it.

In 1996, Germany began to allow individuals free choice of sickness fund under its SHI system. An objective of the change was to increase efficiency by improving competition discipline on insurers. This approach can succeed only if people are willing to switch insurers in return for a lower premium. Tamm, Tauchmann, Wasem, et al. (2007) examined the repercussions of differences in required contribution percentages (payroll contribution percentages as imposed by the insurer) on individual choice of statutory health plan. The short-run price elasticities in a sickness fund they obtained were lower than in previous studies, including those conducted with data from other countries, but they found substantial long-run price elasticities, implying that the price of insurance had important effects on individuals' choice of statutory health plan. In recent years, especially since reunification of the two parts of Germany, health care reform has been a persistent public policy issue (Pfaff and Kern 2005; Carrera, Siemens, and Bridges 2008). The major impetus for the reform initiatives has been the rise in the fraction of gross domestic product devoted to personal health care services. Because the statutory health insurance is financed through a payroll tax, increases in the contribution percentages of employees and employers are transparent to all. The increase in the share of GDP devoted to health care reflects both growth in such expenditures and a sluggish growth of the German economy. Even with twelve major health care reforms between 1992 and 2007, what is perceived as a problem of a rising health care share remains.

12.3 Evolution and Structure of the Payment System: The US Medicare Program

Background

Because of the United States' population size and high levels of expenditure on personal health care services per capita population, viewed in absolute terms, both private and public health care financing are sizable in the United States. As

Reinhardt (2005, 83) has noted, "The U.S. health system arguably represents the most complex intersection between the private and public sector to be found anywhere in the world." Reinhardt attributed reliance on public and private systems in the United States to two mutually contradictory strands in US culture and politics. On the one hand, there is a widespread belief in the United States that the private sector is inherently more efficient than the public sector can ever be. On the other, government seems to be the sector that the US public ultimately trusts, especially when confronted with disasters, such as hurricanes or terrorist attacks.

An alternative interpretation is that the US public has an unmistakable preference for private provision but recognizes that governments can accomplish some objectives that the private sector cannot. For example, achieving society's distributional objectives is likely to require government intervention. The altruism of private individuals only goes so far. Furthermore, there are limits to the extent to which private organizations can diversify away risk. In the United States, public financing is principally done for the elderly and work-disabled through the Medicare program (table 12.3).

Medicare is a social insurance program with eligibility determined on the basis of age (for persons aged 65 and older) and disability status (for persons younger than age 65 with major disabilities). Since the early 1970s, persons with end-stage renal disease have also been covered by Medicare.

For most of the program's history, premium assessments have been independent of a person's income. By contrast, Medicaid has strict income and

Table 12.3
Sources of Health Insurance Coverage for the US Population

Source	Groups Insured	Share of Total Population (%)	Share of Total Payments (%)
Public			
Medicare	Elderly; disabled; end-stage renal disease patients	13	22
Medicaid	Elderly; blind and disabled; poor women and children	10	15
Other	Military personnel and their dependents	1	8
Private			
Employer-sponsored	Workers and dependents	56	53
Nongroup	Families	6	<1
Uninsured		*16*	*2*

Note: Other public spending includes expenditures on public hospitals, theVeteransAdministration, etc.
Source: Cutler and Zeckhauser (2000, table 1).

asset eligibility standards. In this sense, given means-tested eligibility standards, Medicaid, though publicly financed, should not be considered a social insurance program. In 2005, nearly 14 percent of Americans were covered by Medicare (US Census Bureau 2011) and 13 percent were covered by Medicaid (US Census Bureau 2011). Although Medicare and Medicaid, taken together, cover only about one-quarter of the US population, these two public programs account for nearly 40 percent of total health care expenditure in the United States (table 12.3). Some Medicare beneficiaries have Medicaid coverage for the part of personal health care expenditure that Medicare does not cover.

Medicare and Medicaid were implemented in the mid-1960s. When initially implemented, Medicare primarily covered hospital and physician expenses, and it provided generous reimbursement to both hospitals and physicians. Finkelstein (2007) has estimated that in 1963, only 25 percent of the elderly in the United States had meaningful coverage. After implementation, the coverage of persons aged 65 and older in the United States rose to virtually 100 percent. If, counterfactually, Medicare had not been implemented, it is highly likely that the percentage of elderly persons in the United States with insurance coverage would have been much higher than 25 percent 40–50 years hence. However, it seems likely that the percentage would have been far less than universal. And the increase in the share of the elderly population covered would have been far less than it was in the latter decades of the twentieth century. Extending coverage is only one indicator, however. As discussed below, the implementation of Medicare had several other important effects as well.

Using a body count to compute the percentage of elderly persons with health insurance coverage is misleading in one important sense. Only slightly more than half of payments for personal health care services made on behalf of Medicare beneficiaries come from Medicare (Reinhardt 2005, 89). The other half consists of payments from Medicaid (for those beneficiaries with dual Medicare and Medicaid coverage), private ("Medigap") insurance, out-of-pocket payments by Medicare beneficiaries, and other programs such as the Veterans Administration. The vast majority of Medicare beneficiaries have supplemental coverage of some type.

Why would Medicare cover such a small percentage of expenditures on personal health care services? The answer is complex. At the risk of oversimplification, a major reason reflects the way that the Medicare program is financed. Medicare has several parts, of which the two largest and oldest are Part A and Part B. Part A, which mainly covers hospital care, is financed by a payroll tax, with equal percentages from employer and employee as its revenue source, as in the German system. A payroll tax dedicated to a single use is highly transparent to taxpayers. This is in contrast to employer-provided health benefits as in the United States, the major cost of which is only irregularly and voluntarily reported to employees. Part B is financed by a combination of general tax revenue, including the federal personal income and corporate income taxes, and beneficiary-paid premiums. In recent years the premiums have become means tested, that is, dependent on the beneficiary's income. The existence of supplementary coverage provides a safety valve that lessens the pressure on politicians to raise Medicare benefits and provider reimbursement.

The two major forms of supplementary insurance are quite different and must be considered separately. Medigap policies serve two functions. First, they cover expenses associated with covered inpatient and outpatient benefits that are unpaid by Medicare. For example, as explained more fully below, Medicare currently pays physicians based on a Resource-Based Relative Value Scale (RBRVS). Most of the payment to hospitals by Medicare is on a prospective basis through the Medicare prospective payment system (PPS). A fixed price is paid according to the diagnosis-related group (DRG), which characterizes the diagnosis or principal procedure that the beneficiary received while in the hospital. Physicians who accept Medicare payment can bill up to 15 percent above this fee schedule. Medigap can pay this 15 percent. In addition, Medicare imposes deductibles and coinsurance. Medigap policies can pay the cost-sharing obligations for hospital and physicians' services. While Medigap coverage provides Medicare beneficiaries with additional out-of-pocket health expenditure risk protection, the downside is that it increases moral hazard. Second, Medigap policies provide some coverage for services not included in the Medicare benefit package, such as lengthy nursing home stays.

Since the mid-1980s, Medicare has permitted beneficiaries to opt out of the government-run Medicare program to join a Medicare-qualified HMO (Medicare Part C). The HMO must provide a benefit package that is at least as generous as that offered by Medicare. In exchange, the HMO is paid a fixed capitation payment plus, depending on the plan's benefits, a direct payment from the beneficiary.

In 2006, Medicare introduced prescription drug coverage (Medicare Part D). Previously, drugs were not covered by Medicare, but drugs were covered by Medigap plans and by Medicaid.

HOSPITAL PAYMENT UNDER MEDICARE: THE MEDICARE PROSPECTIVE PAYMENT SYSTEM

Although the public is mainly concerned about the benefit structure of its insurance plans and is generally unaware of how the plan pays providers for services covered by the plan, payment methods have a major influence on the cost of, access to, and quality of services. At the time Medicare was initially designed and implemented, comparatively little discussion was devoted to how providers, mainly hospitals and physicians, would be paid. The decision was made to adopt the payment system used by many Blue Cross plans at the time. Blue Cross plans are private insurance plans, at the time all private, not-for-profit organizations. Blue Cross paid hospitals on a retrospective cost-based reimbursement basis. In a retrospective cost-based reimbursement system, hospitals are paid for costs incurred in caring for persons covered by the plan after the costs are incurred.

Hospital incentives were substantially altered when in 1983, Medicare began to transition to a PPS. Medicare PPS has had an enormous influence on hospitals in the United States; on methods of payment used by other US programs, such as Medicaid; and in other countries, including Australia, Germany, and South Korea. A diagnosis-related group is a grouping based on diagnoses and procedures provided that is associated with a payment weight. Initially, the payment weights were derived from hospital prices on bills submitted to Medicare reduced by the ratio of hospital revenue to cost. Thus, for example, if the mean revenue per case for a particular DRG was $10,000 and the revenue-to-cost ratio was 1.2, then the $10,000 price was reduced to $8,333. The weights are recalculated annually as the ratio of the mean charges reported by hospitals to Medicare within the DRG to the mean reported charges for all admissions, adjusted for various geographic and hospital-specific factors (McClellan 1997, 96).

A general problem with regulation of prices is that the regulator does not know the regulated firm's cost function. A PPS-type program offers a remarkable approach for cost finding. The government announces to regulated firms, in this context hospitals, that it will pay the firms an amount adequate to cover the unit cost incurred by an efficient firm. Each firm reasons that other firms will reduce cost to the efficient level and that if it does not do the same, it will receive a payment that does not cover its cost. Thus, reasoning that other firms will do the same, each hospital cuts its costs and becomes efficient. In this way, the regulator discovers the efficient level of cost. This process of cost finding is called "yardstick competition" (Shleifer 1985).

Paying a fixed amount per admission provides a number of incentives to hospitals. First, PPS replaced a system in which hospitals were paid on a retrospective cost basis. Under retrospective cost reimbursement, a dollar increase in allowable (by the insurer) cost leads to a dollar increase in revenue. By contrast, under prospective payment per admission, payment does not increase with increases in hospital costliness. Thus, hospitals have a direct incentive to be efficient. Under retrospective cost reimbursement, a dollar saved by the hospital translates into a dollar of revenue lost. Under PPS, when a hospital incurs a dollar less per case, this dollar accrues to the hospital as increased profit.

Second, PPS gives hospitals an incentive to reduce patient length of stay since payment does not increase when duration of stay is lengthened. Similarly, there is an incentive to perform procedures before and after the hospital stay since procedures not performed during a stay are not included in the prospectively determined price paid for the hospital inpatient stay.

The PPS has potential adverse side effects as well. For example, hospitals have an incentive to upcode diagnoses since this may cause the patient to be classified into a higher-priced DRG (Silverman and Skinner 2004). And while from one perspective, saving on diagnostic and therapeutic procedures is a favorable development, from another, there may be adverse effects on beneficiary health.

Box 12.1
Specific Incentives to Hospitals under the Prospective Payment System

The Medicare prospective payment system (PPS) provides several important incentives to hospitals. The basic structure of the PPS is described in the text. This box describes two studies that investigated specific features of the PPS.

Dafny (2005) explains that *average* payment incentives remain under the PPS, although the implementation of the PPS regime has eliminated *marginal* reimbursement incentives for services rendered. (More care for inpatients with a given diagnosis does not normally result in higher levels of payment from Medicare to the hospital.) Average payment matters because the fixed amount of payment that hospitals receive per hospitalized patients under the PPS varies among the approximately 500 diagnosis-related groups (DRGs). For various reasons, hospitals earn more "profit" (fixed payment received from Medicare program minus cost incurred by the hospital) from treating patients in some DRGs than from treating patients in other DRGs.

These differences occur for at least two reasons. First, hospitals have an incentive to code existing patients into DRGs with higher profit margins (upcoding). Second, hospitals also can potentially attract more patients into that diagnosis by offering quality or intensity improvements. Dafny (2005) termed the former "nominal responses" because they operate only through accounting changes, and termed the latter "real responses" because they relate to changes in resource use for specific treatments.

In 1988, there was a simple change in the DRG classification system for the Medicare program, which in turn generated large and exogenous price changes for 40 percent of DRG codes, accounting for 43 percent of Medicare admissions. Based on a data set containing nearly seven million Medicare admissions covering 186 DRGs and 5,352 hospitals nationwide, Dafny (2005) found empirical evidence for nominal responses but no evidence of real responses. That is, hospitals responded to these price changes by upcoding patients to DRG codes with the largest price increases from the retrospective cost reimbursement system to PPS. This nominal response was particularly strong among for-profit hospitals. By contrast, hospitals did not increase admissions differentially for those patients with diagnoses with the largest price increases, nor did they increase the intensity or quality of care provided to patients with these diagnoses. The lack of evidence on real responses suggests that hospitals do not compete for patients at the diagnosis level. This inference should be considered more suggestive than conclusive, pending further empirical support from other studies.

In another study of the effects of the PPS, Acemoglu and Finkelstein (2008) characterized the implementation of a PPS as a reform from full-cost to partial-cost reimbursement. One reason for maintaining this distinction is that until 2001, hospital expenditures on plant and equipment continued to be reimbursed on a retrospective cost basis. The program covered other expenses with the fixed price paid per unit of output. Thus, the effective price to the hospital of inputs other than for plant and equipment (labor, supplies, etc.) increased as a result of the change, but the effective

Box 12.1
(continued)

price of plant and equipment was left unchanged. In effect, then, implementation of the PPS altered the prices of plant and equipment relative to other inputs in the production of hospital care. Using a simple neoclassical economic model, Acemoglu and Finkelstein argued that the increase in factor prices for inputs other than plant and equipment should have led to a decline in demand for these inputs but stimulated demand for new medical technologies that are embodied in new plant and equipment. This should have decreased demand for labor and encouraged the adoption of new medical technologies.

Using panel data from US hospitals for the period 1980–1986, Acemoglu and Finkelstein found empirical support for their hypothesis. Specifically, they found there was a statistically significant and sizable increase in the capital-labor ratio in hospitals with a relatively high Medicare patient share after implementation of the PPS. They also found evidence that after the introduction of the PPS, there was an increase in the rate of adoption of several new medical technologies. Their empirical findings imply there is a relatively high degree of substitution between technology and labor in the production of hospital care. Therefore, the empirical finding from several studies is that the introduction of the Medicare PPS was associated with a decline in length of stay that may have represented a substitution of high-technology capital equipment for relatively labor-intensive hospital stays.

However, a substantial body of empirical research indicates that although Medicare PPS did reduce length of stay and the use of diagnostic procedures after admission to the hospital (Sloan, Morrisey, and Valvona 1988a, 1988b), overall, PPS did not have adverse effects on patient outcomes (see, e.g., Kahn, Keeler, Sherwood, et al. 1990).

Physician Payment under Medicare: Fixed Fees Based on a Resource-Based Relative Value Scale

When Medicare was first implemented, a flexible payment system was used for reimbursing physicians. The physician submitted a bill to Medicare for a service rendered to a Medicare beneficiary. The company that administered Medicare Part B for a particular geographic area (called a "carrier," in Medicare jargon) applied a set of fee screens to determine how much the physician would be paid for the service.

The carrier first ascertained whether or not the physician's fee was the fee the physician usually charged for the service. This was done out of a concern that a physician might charge more just because the patient was covered by Medicare. If the fee was higher than the usual fee, it was reduced to the usual fee. A second screen determined how the physician's usual fee compared to the usual fees of other physicians in the same area. If the fee was in the top 25th percentile of the frequency distribution of usual fees, Medicare reduced the fee to the 75th percentile. Finally, under certain circumstances, a higher fee might be justified, for example, if a physician spent an unusually long amount of time with a particular patient. If sufficient justification was provided, Medicare would pay a higher fee than would result from a strict application of the first two screens.

The rationale for this approach to paying physicians was to ensure that Medicare beneficiaries had access to physicians in the areas where they lived. If fees were higher in a particular area, the system was presumably sufficiently flexible to reflect this difference. On the other hand, this system could seriously distort the fee structure. For example, a young physician setting up practice, realizing that Medicare's first screen was the physician's usual fee, would want to set his or her fee as close to the top 75th percentile as possible.

The alternative to this type of flexible fee arrangement is a fixed fee. In the German system, fees are negotiated between an association representing the sickness funds in the state (*Land*) and an association representing sickness fund physicians in the same state. The alternative, which applies in the United States, is for the insurer to unilaterally set the fees it pays physicians. In the United States, collective action in the form of direct negotiations by physicians to influence their fees would violate antitrust law, although physicians' groups can lobby the government as political organizations to make changes in public programs, including the way that fees are paid. For example, the American Medical Association (AMA) makes recommendations to the government about annual updates of the fees Medicare pays physicians. In 2010, for example, the AMA recommended to the US Congress that Medicare not cut physicians' fees by 21 percent.

Medicare adopted a system of fixed fees based on the Resource-Based Relative Value Scale in 1992 (Hsiao, Braun, Dunn, et al. 1992), and the RBRVS approach has been adopted as well by many other non-Medicare insurers (McCormack and Burge 1994). The "relative values" of the RBRVS are designed to reflect the input costs of providing specific services. These costs are for physician work, practice expense, and medical malpractice insurance premiums. The mean values of these costs are translated into relative value units (RVUs), and payments to physicians are calculated by multiplying the combined RVUs of a service by a conversion factor—a monetary amount that is determined by the Medicare program. Payments are also adjusted for geographic differences in input costs.

A key goal of using the RBRVS has been to pay physicians on the basis of the cost of doing business. However, for the economy as a whole, prices reflect both demand and cost factors. One could imagine pricing a buggy (of horse and buggy) using the RBRVS approach. The buggy might be expensive since manufacturing a high-quality buggy may be resource-intensive. But in a market, the price of buggies reflects individuals' willingness to pay for this type of transportation, which in the last few decades may be low. Thus, the RBRVS for a buggy might be high, but the value to consumers may be low. If so, using RBRVS, buggies would be overpriced, and if the market for buggies were similar to that of the market for personal health care services, we would have to worry that buggy output would exceed the socially optimal amount. Similarly, Medicare may pay a lot for an old technology using the RBRVS approach.

Traditionally, fees for diagnostic (e.g., interpreting a CT scan) and certain therapeutic procedures (e.g., surgical procedures) have been high relative to fees for primary care physician visits. One original goal of the RBRVS was to increase fees paid for physician visits relative to those paid for diagnostic and therapeutic procedures. In practice, implementing this change in relative fees has proved to be difficult because of potential pressure from those physician stakeholders who would tend to lose from this policy change.

Starting in the late 1980s, US federal and state governments restricted the ability of physicians to "balance bill" for charges in excess of Medicare's co-payment and reimbursement amounts approved by Medicare, most recently the amounts being determined by the RBRVS system. McKnight (2007) found that this policy change resulted in a 9 percent reduction in out-of-pocket medical expenditures incurred by elderly families. However, she found no evidence that this restriction adversely affected patterns of care. Thus, this restriction of prices paid to physicians amounted to a transfer from physicians to elderly persons covered by Medicare. We cannot be sure that under different circumstances, such as lower physician-to-population ratios and greater restrictions on balance billing, insured persons would not experience an increase in barriers to care.

Effects of Medicare

There is a voluminous empirical literature on the effects of the Medicare program in general and of particular features of the program on behavior. We provide a brief overview of this literature here.

The introduction of Medicare in the 1960s represented the largest single change in health insurance coverage in US history. Finkelstein and McKnight (2008) estimated that the introduction of Medicare was associated with a 40 percent decline in out-of-pocket spending for elderly persons with high health care expenditures.

Technological Change

Studies such as the RAND HIE (Newhouse and the Insurance Experiment Group 1993), which analyzed data for a relatively short time period (3–5 years in the case of the HIE), can examine only short-run changes from the expansion of health insurance coverage. In the short run, technology is fixed (see chapter 9). But technological change occurs over the longer run, and it may be influenced by the extent of health insurance coverage as well as by insurer payment practices. If we consider only the static effects, the spread of health insurance could explain only one-eighth to one-tenth of the increase in real per capita population spending on personal health care services in the United States that occurred between 1950 and 1990.

Based on her calculations, Finkelstein (2007) concluded that the introduction of Medicare can explain about half of the sixfold increase in real per capita health care spending that occurred between 1950 and 1990. She speculated that growth in health insurance coverage might explain the high rate of growth in real per capita health spending in other OECD countries as well. Many OECD countries implemented health insurance systems in the 1960s and 1970s (Cutler 2002). In contrast to Finkelstein's (2007) finding, Acemoglu, Cutler, Finkelstein, et al. (2006) looked for evidence that Medicare induced pharmaceutical innovation. They failed to find an effect, but until 2006, Medicare did not cover prescription drugs.

Population Subgroups

A major policy issue in the United States as pertains to Medicare relates to variation in use of services and health outcomes among Medicare beneficiaries. In a frequently cited article published in the *New England Journal of Medicine,* Gornick, Eggers, Reilly, et al. (1996) documented differences in use and outcomes among Medicare beneficiaries by income and race. They reported black-white differences in mortality of 1.19 for men (i.e., 19 percent higher for black males than for white males) and 1.16 for women. These differences are among Medicare beneficiaries and do not reflect differences in the probability of reaching age eligibility for Medicare between blacks and whites. For every 100 female Medicare beneficiaries, there were 26.0 mammograms for whites and 17.1 for blacks. The black-white ratio was 3.64 for amputation of all or part of the lower limb. For every 1,000 beneficiaries there were 515 influenza immunizations among whites and 313 among blacks. Adjusting mortality and utilization rates for differences in income (measured for a small area [zip code area] in which the beneficiary resided) reduced the black-white differences, but not by a large amount.

Two economic studies focused on the distributional impacts of Medicare (Bhattacharya and Lakdawalla 2006; McClellan and Skinner 2006). However, the economic studies measured individuals' payroll contributions to Medicare as well as the benefits from Medicare accruing to the same individuals. In addition, they viewed the flow of contributions and benefits as processes occurring over the life cycle, unlike previous studies, which used cross-sectional data. Medicare benefits increase with the personal income of households, but so do payroll taxes flowing to the Medicare program. On an accounting basis, McClellan and Skinner found that benefits increased with Medicare beneficiary income more than payroll taxes did. However, they acknowledged that concentrating on dollar flows alone ignores the insurance value of the Medicare program. Medicare provides health insurance to many low-income elderly persons. Because the expenditure risk for such persons was reduced after they were covered by Medicare (see chapter 4 for a discussion of utility gains from reductions in expenditure risk), previously uninsured persons experienced a utility gain that is not reflected in the dollar flow estimates. Bhattacharya and Lakdawalla (2006), using a somewhat different methodology, reached the opposite conclusion. They concluded that the distributional impact of Medicare is highly progressive, that is, Medicare benefits the poor more than the non-poor.

To explain the differences in conclusions would require a detailed discussion of the empirical methodologies of the studies, which would take us far afield. It is sufficient to note that to measure the progressivity of a social insurance program such as Medicare, it is necessary to examine the income gradient for both program benefits and contributions. Taking both studies together, it appears that at a minimum, this type of social insurance program is mildly redistributional, that is, progressive. However, we cannot be sure whether or not the same conclusion would apply to other countries that have implemented social insurance systems for personal health care services. In fact, O'Donnell, van Doorslaer, Rannan-Eliya, et al. (2008), who studied social insurance program incidence in thirteen Asian countries, including both affluent countries such as Japan and lower-income countries such as Sri Lanka and Nepal, concluded that in high-income countries, social insurance is proportional to regressive. This means that higher-income persons in such countries derive as much (proportional) or more (regressive) from social insurance than do less affluent individuals in these countries.

Population Health

Philipson and Becker (1998) developed the idea that longevity depends in part on the availability of mortality-contingent subsidies such as pension programs; "mortality-contingent" means that the subsidy is paid only if the person is alive, or is paid in lesser amount if the covered person is deceased. Philipson and Becker argued that the availability of such income payments increases health investments, leading to a longer life.

Bethencourt and Galasso (2008) studied interactions among social insurance programs. They argued that there are important political complementaries between social insurance programs. For example, to the extent that a social insurance program such as Medicare increases longevity, this increases the length of the retirement period, which affects the amount of pension benefits accruing to retirees from a mortality-contingent pension benefit program. The higher expected pension benefit in turn increases political support for government pension programs, even among young persons with low incomes. Technological improvements in health care strengthen this complementarity and lead to higher levels of welfare spending.

Box 12.2
Does the Provision of Public Health Insurance Lead to Improvements in Population Health?

Many countries have implemented health insurance programs financed by the public sector. One of the important goals of public health insurance programs, as described in various government documents, is to increase individual and population health, although the major benefit of health insurance is "risk protection." However, the empirical evidence on whether public health insurance programs really succeed in health improvement is very limited.

There are two plausible explanations for the lack of such empirical evidence. First, most high-income countries implemented public health insurance programs to achieve the goal of universal coverage before the 1980s. Thus, the lack of data generated from these "natural experiments" prevents researchers from investigating this issue. Second, even when newly industrialized countries (e.g., South Korea, Taiwan) implemented public health insurance programs in more recent years, researchers may not have sufficient information to control for the effect of other variables on health when the evaluation of public health insurance program relies on comparisons between pre and post periods of these policy interventions.

Although the United States implemented its Medicare program almost a half century ago (in 1966), this program has a unique feature that enables the researcher to evaluate the effect of this program by using the more recent complete data without having to rely on analysis of old data before 1966. Compared to the public health insurance programs adopted in other countries, eligibility for the US Medicare program is not completely dependent on the timing of policy implementation; it also depends on the individual's age. The vast majority of persons in the United States become eligible for Medicare at age 65. Card, Dobkin, and Maestas (2009) took advantage of this eligibility requirement to investigate the effect of the Medicare program on individual health by comparing differences in mortality for severely ill people who were admitted to hospitals just before (not eligible for Medicare) and just after their 65th birthdays (when eligible for Medicare).

Card, Dobkin, and Maestas (2009) focused on unplanned admissions through the emergency department (ED) for patients with diagnoses such as obstructive chronic bronchitis, acute myocardial infarction (AMI), and stroke. These diagnoses are "non-deferrable" conditions, which means that the decision to seek care at an ED for these conditions is unlikely to depend on whether or not the person with symptoms of potentially serious disease has health insurance; furthermore, admission rates on weekdays and weekends are very similar.

Their investigation yielded two important findings. First, there was a modest but statistically significant increase in the number of procedures performed in the hospital and a 3 percent rise in total charges for patients at age 65, implying that becoming eligible for Medicare leads to an increase in treatment intensity. Second, compared to patients who were just under 65, patients who were just over 65 experienced about a one percentage point drop in seven-day mortality, which is equivalent to a 20 percent reduction in deaths within a week of admission. This result suggests that Medicare coverage has had an important impact on patient survival.

12.4 Evolution of Payment Systems: The US Medicaid Program

Background

When Medicare was implemented, the Medicaid program was implemented at the same time. In contrast to Medicare, Medicaid is a means-tested program that focuses on the providing public insurance coverage to the poor. Medicare is a single federal program; Medicaid is a federal-state program. The US government subsidizes the cost of the states' Medicaid program. The fifty US states design and operate their own Medicaid plan, which must conform to federal guidelines. Although persons of all ages are eligible for Medicaid, because of the Medicaid program's eligibility criteria, enrollees are predominantly infants, young children, pregnant women, and the elderly who use long-term care services, particularly nursing homes. Many low-income elderly persons are covered by both Medicaid and Medicare. While Medicare provides the basic benefit for physician and hospital services and recently for prescription drugs, Medicare has a very limited nursing home benefit. This coverage gap is plugged by Medicaid for elderly with low income and wealth. Originally, Medicaid programs were linked to receipt of public assistance. This link has been severed at various dates, depending on changes in federal and states' laws since the 1980s.

As a means-tested program, Medicaid's economic issues differ substantially from those for a non-means-tested program such as Medicare and a practically non-means-tested program such as the German SHI plan. First, in all states, Medicaid covers only a minority of the population, often around 10 percent or less. Second, people can affect their eligibility for Medicaid benefits by altering their income and wealth. Thus, market work and saving are potentially affected by the availability of Medicaid benefits. Third, Medicaid payments for hospital care and physicians' services are low relative to those of private insurers and Medicare. While virtually all US hospitals accept Medicaid payment, many physicians do not. Fourth, since Medicaid pays for nursing home care, there are concerns about the effect of Medicaid payment policies on nursing home decisions, including the quality of care provided to nursing home residents. There is concern for both Medicaid-sponsored and as well as other persons since Medicaid requires that a nursing home provide the same level of care for both Medicaid and non-Medicaid recipients who reside in the same nursing home.

Choice of Medicaid Benefits versus Self-Insurance versus Private Insurance

An insight of microeconomic theory is that people make choices about their income, savings, hours devoted to market and household production, and personal health based in part on prices and other constraints they face. Personal health care services

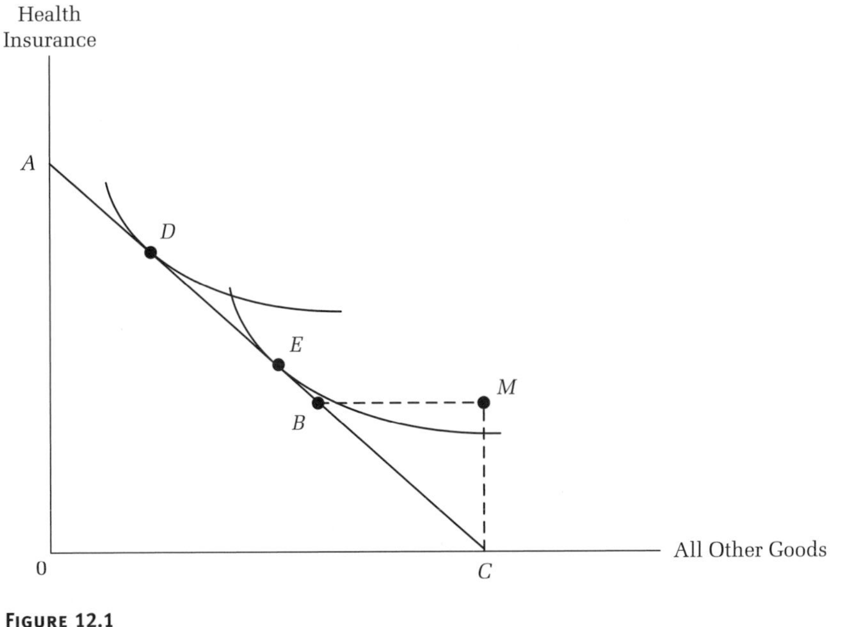

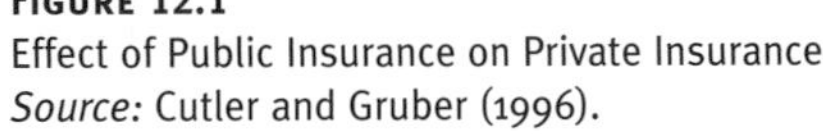
Figure 12.1
Effect of Public Insurance on Private Insurance
Source: Cutler and Gruber (1996).

can be financed by a combination of public and private insurance and self-insurance. When an individual self insures, he or she finances personal health care services from personal income and wealth. People can affect their eligibility for means-tested insurance, such as Medicaid, by altering their incomes and wealth (Hubbard, Skinner, and Zeldes 1995). However, given what some persons see as the stigma of receiving means-tested benefits and other factors, some persons, even if eligible, may not apply for the benefit (see, e.g., Moffitt and Galloway 1992; Currie and Gruber 1996).

Consider the relationship between purchasing private insurance when a public insurance program is not available or, alternatively, available (fig. 12.1). The choice is between paying a premium to purchase private insurance and consuming other goods. If the individual purchases a more comprehensive insurance policy, there is less income available for the purchase of other goods. More insurance requires paying a higher premium. Without a means-tested public insurance program, the household budget constraint is *AC*.

Figure 12.1 shows two tangencies between indifference curves showing the individual's trade-off between insurance and other goods and the budget constraint *AC*. More risk-averse individuals are at *D*; less risk-averse persons are at *E*.

Now suppose that a means-tested public insurance program offering a fixed amount of insurance—*CM* units of health insurance—at no premium cost to the individual. Now the choice is between consuming *CM* units of insurance and *OC* units of other goods or more health insurance than *CM* and fewer units of other goods. The budget constraint becomes *ABMC*. If the individual wants more health insurance than is offered by the public plan, *CM*, the person rejects the public plan and buys a private policy offering more generous coverage. This is precisely the option faced by Germans with incomes over a certain threshold amount; they can reject statutory health insurance and select a private alternative.

The individual's choice in figure 12.1 when public health insurance is offered involves a comparison of utility at point *M* with utility at a point on the original budget constraint to the northwest of point *B*. If the indifference curve is relatively steep, which suggests that the marginal utility of having health insurance relative to the marginal utility of other goods is comparatively high, the person is likely to select a combination of health insurance and other goods on the original budget constraint to the northwest of *B*. In this case, the provision of public health insurance will have no effect on the person's demand for private health insurance. However, if the indifference curve is relatively flat, the person may well select the combination of health insurance and other goods at point *M*; in this case, the person does not buy private health insurance, and the availability of public health insurance can be said to have "crowded out" the demand for private health insurance.

The introduction of public insurance "crowds out" private insurance demand in one case but not in the other. Realistically, people have different preferences. Thus, although not every individual's demand for private health insurance is crowded out, private demand on the part of some individuals is crowded out when public health insurance is made available.

One may ask, why do we care? We care because the goal of providing public health insurance coverage is largely to increase the proportion of the population with health insurance coverage. To the extent that there is crowding out, this public policy objective is not met.

Figure 12.1 is drawn for a person with a fixed income. In practice, the introduction of public insurance may also crowd out private savings since less money is needed for precautionary savings for use in the event of a health shock (Hubbard, Skinner, and Zeldes 1995; Chou, Liu, and Hammitt 2003). Precautionary savings are savings for use following an adverse event, such as an accident or illness. If the family has public health insurance, there is less reason to save for this reason. The household may still have precautionary savings for other reasons, such as in the event of property damage due to fire or an earthquake, hazards not covered by health insurance.

Market work may be reduced by the availability of means-tested public health insurance to the extent that working reduces the probability of eligibility for the public insurance plan. Hubbard, Skinner, and Zeldes (1995) argued that lower-income individuals and those with less human capital tend to accumulate less private wealth in part because of the availability of public safety nets, including public health insurance.

Several empirical studies have assessed the extent to which the availability of Medicaid has crowded out private health insurance. The study by Cutler and Gruber (1996) took advantage of the exogenous (to individuals) Medicaid expansions in eligibility for benefits to pregnant women and children that occurred during 1987–1992. They estimated that about 50 percent of the increase in Medicaid coverage was associated with a reduction in private health insurance coverage—a substantial amount of crowding out. This reduction mainly occurred because employees took up employer-based health insurance less often, thereby saving the monthly payroll deductions for their share of health insurance premiums. Hamm and Shore-Sheppard (2005) attempted to replicate Cutler and Gruber's findings using another database. They found substantially less crowding out of private health insurance than Cutler and Gruber reported. More recently, Gruber and Simon (2007) used the same database as Hamm and Shore-Shepard but incorporated some recent changes in public insurance program policy. They concluded that public insurance has a substantial crowding-out effect on private health insurance plan enrollments. Clearly, the results are sensitive to how the empirical analysis is conducted, which data sources are used, and which time periods are analyzed.

Yelowitz (1995) examined the effects of a change in eligibility requirements that allowed women with infants and young children to earn more without losing eligibility for Medicaid benefits. He found that the change in eligibility standards that allowed a mother's earnings to increase without losing eligibility for Medicaid resulted in a decrease in receipt of public assistance benefits and an increase in labor force participation among these women. The effects were large for ever married women but negligible for never married women. Overall, these results provide at least partial support of another form of crowding out, namely, the availability of means-tested government health insurance may crowd out market work.

Gruber and Yelowitz (1999) analyzed the effect of means-tested public insurance, more specifically Medicaid, on the savings behavior of households. They too relied on Medicaid eligibility expansions to assess the impact of Medicaid eligibility on personal wealth accumulation. They found that eligibility for Medicaid benefits had a sizable negative effect on both personal wealth and personal consumption. Increased consumption coincided with lower amounts of saving.

Thus far, we have stressed distortions caused from the introduction of a public health insurance plan such as Medicaid. However, while these distortions exact welfare costs on society, it is also important to consider these programs' social benefits. Currie and Thomas (1995) found that relative to no insurance, Medicaid coverage increased the probability that a child had a routine checkup in the past year by 15 percent. Currie and Gruber (1996) examined the effects of Medicaid eligibility expansions on the utilization of medical care and on child health, finding substantial increases in use of care that were broadly consistent with the findings of Currie and Thomas, as well as reductions in child mortality.

The astute reader may attribute the increase in utilization to moral hazard and recall the discussion in chapter 3 about the welfare loss from excess health insurance. However, the reduction in child mortality that Currie and Gruber documented shows the increase in coverage brought about by the expansions in Medicaid availability also had benefits.

Empirical Evidence on Medicaid Fee Schedules

Research on Medicaid using the price discrimination model was described in chapter 5. This research focused on physician office practices.

More recent research has focused on shifts of Medicaid-covered patients from hospital outpatient settings to physicians' offices. The presumption is that continuity of care is better and care is more personal in physicians' offices. For example, Gruber, Adams, and Newhouse (1997) investigated whether or not a shift from hospital outpatient clinics to physicians' offices occurred after the Medicaid program in Tennessee increased its fee schedules. The control group was the US state of Georgia, which did not raise its Medicaid fees. The authors found that care shifted from clinics (other than hospital outpatient clinics) to offices, but not from hospital outpatient clinics or emergency rooms to offices. They did find that inpatient admissions of Medicaid enrollees fell after the fee increase in Tennessee. Thus, overall, the evidence was mixed.

An expansion of Medicaid eligibility may mean a higher number of persons in the Medicaid market and fewer persons in the market in which physicians set prices. An inward shift in the private market demand curve should make physicians more willing to accept Medicaid patients. Baker and Royalty (2000) found that the increased Medicaid enrollees following eligibility expansions went to public clinics and hospital clinics rather than to private physicians' offices.

Medicaid fee policy may also affect the mix of services provided to Medicaid recipients. Gruber, Kim, and Mayzlin (1999) evaluated whether or not an increase in the relative Medicaid fee for a normal obstetric delivery versus a cesarean section delivery affects choice of delivery method. They found that larger Medicaid fee differentials between cesarean and normal deliveries tend to lead to higher rates of C-sections.

The price-discriminating monopoly model of physician behavior described in chapter 5 assumes that Medicaid fee schedules do not affect quality of care, only physicians' decisions about output. Gray (2001) investigated the relationship between Medicaid payment levels and quality of care empirically, finding that a

10 percent higher than average relative Medicaid fee was independently associated with a 7.4 percent lower absolute risk of low birth weight and a 3.5 percent lower risk of very low birth weight, both outcome-based measures of quality of care. Both estimates applied to women covered by Medicaid. Since premature births and low birth weight led to a higher health care cost of caring for infants, there were cost offsets from avoiding low and very low birth weight, as well as benefits to families and other from delivering healthier children.

Medicaid and Nursing Home Care

In contrast to the other major types of personal health care services, the primary sources of revenue for the US nursing home industry are out-of-pocket payments by residents and their families ("self-pay") and Medicaid. In many cases, nursing home residents are admitted as self-pay patients. However, after long stays and considerable out-of-pocket expense, these patients deplete assets to the point that they become Medicaid-eligible. The process of depleting assets while living in a nursing home is called "spending down." Because Medicaid is such an important revenue source for nursing homes, its policies have important impacts on these facilities. There is empirical evidence that specific incentives that might be implemented by Medicaid plans affect both the cost and quality of nursing home care (see, e.g., Norton 1992).

Given that private prices tend to be much higher than prices paid to nursing homes by Medicaid, variants of the two-market price discrimination model (see chapter 5) have been used to study US nursing home behavior in general and the effects of Medicaid policies on such behavior in particular (e.g., Dusansky 1989; Gertler 1989; Cohen and Spector 1996; Nyman 1999). In the nursing home models, authors stress the requirement that the quality of care be the same in caring for non-Medicaid and Medicaid nursing home residents. In contrast to US physicians, nursing homes in the United States are often subject to certificate of need entry regulation (see chapter 6) and to moratoria on nursing home bed construction in particular.

Economic models of nursing home behavior typically assume that given the large number of elderly persons who are either eligible for Medicaid or could become eligible, there is very high Medicaid demand for nursing home care. In the presence of a binding nursing home bed constraint, nursing homes compete for non-Medicaid residents on the basis of the quality of care they offer (presumably as well as on price). Since there are so many Medicaid residents, however, nursing homes are able to fill their facilities with such residents even if they do not offer high quality. But if they want to be able to admit non-Medicaid residents, nursing homes must offer high quality of care to residents; furthermore, Medicaid requires that the same level of quality be provided to Medicaid residents at the same facility as is provided to self-pay and privately insured residents. When Medicaid raises its level of reimbursement, nursing homes become less interested in attracting non-Medicaid residents (self-payers and the privately insured). Thus, since there are so many potential Medicaid residents, especially when there is a binding bed constraint resulting from certificate of need laws, nursing homes can lower quality and fill their facilities with such persons. For this reason, there is a negative relationship between Medicaid payment levels and nursing home quality.

David Grabowski (2001), using national data and an outcomes-based measure of quality of nursing home care, in contrast to earlier studies found a positive but small relationship between Medicaid payment levels and quality of care—evidence that is contrary to earlier economic studies, which reported a negative relationship. Grabowski attributed part of the reason for the difference between his findings and the findings of the earlier studies to a general decline in nursing home utilization in the United States toward the end of the twentieth century.

12.5 EVOLUTION OF PAYMENT SYSTEMS: CANADA'S MEDICARE

BACKGROUND

Canada's Medicare program is unique among major industrialized countries' public insurance programs in not allowing private health insurance plans or private out-of-pocket payment to supplement amounts paid by the public health insurance plan for covered services. Private supplementary insurance for services not covered by Medicare is permitted. In this sense, Canada does not have a two- or a multi-tiered health care system. Although Canadian Medicare is partly financed by the national government, constitutionally, the provinces have primary responsibility for the financing and delivery of personal health care services. Provincial health ministries negotiate physician fee schedules with provincial medical associations and the level of capital expenditures and annual global operating budgets of hospitals (Hoffmeyer and McCarthy 1994, 274–275).

Patients pay a zero money price for physicians' services at the point of service delivery. However, to control expenditures on physicians' services, some provinces have imposed ceilings on the amount that general practitioners can bill the provincial plan for their services. By employing hospital-specific global operating budgets (fixed amounts paid by Medicare to the hospital that do not increase as spending by the hospital increases) and controlling the capital expenditures of hospitals, provincial governments determine the diffusion of new medical technology. Provincial governments control which facilities are to receive capital and operating funds for particular technologies.

Patients have a complete choice of physician. Medicare imposes no restrictions on such choices, in contrast to many managed care plans in the United States. Almost all physicians practice on a fee-for-service basis and are in private practice.

Individual physicians are price takers and do not face the variety of fee schedules offered by various payers as in the United States. The only way to increase physician practice revenue is by increasing volume of service, which the ceilings just described seek to counteract.

Each provincial Medicare program has substantial market power vis-à-vis physician and hospital providers. In principle, physician fees are negotiated bilaterally, as in Germany, at the provincial level between the Ministry of Health and the medical association. In practice, several provinces have reduced their fee schedules unilaterally, and some provinces have imposed limits on quarterly gross billings allowed for individual physicians.

Global budgets for hospital operating cost provide a powerful incentive for cost control, but they can also have adverse side effects. For example, a hospital with a revenue cap from Medicare specified by the global budget can reduce its cost by increasing length of stay. Since per diem cost typically declines as length of stay increases, hospitals can keep patient "bed blockers" in the hospital (a bed filled by one patient is not available for another) and prevent other, more costly persons (at least during the first days of their admission) from being admitted. Another type of bed blocker is a patient who requires only low-intensity care.

Bed blockers introduce two types of inefficiency. First, the marginal benefit from an increased length of stay may be below the marginal cost of extending the stay. Second, patients requiring low-intensity care may be treated as well in less costly settings than a hospital, such as on an outpatient basis.

EFFECTS OF THE CANADIAN MEDICARE PROGRAM

Since Medicare relies on control of supply to achieve cost containment rather than such demand-side cost containment mechanisms as cost sharing, studies have examined indicators of non-price rationing and, to the extent that such rationing exists, the effects of such rationing on health services use and health outcomes.

PATIENT WAITING TIME TO RECEIPT OF CARE

One frequently heard complaint about the Canadian system, especially among opponents of single-payer systems in the United States, is that there are long waiting lists for receipt of care. Such complaints are largely based on anecdotes. However, there is some empirical evidence on this issue. Coyte, Wright, Hawker, et al. (1994) compared waiting times for receipt of knee replacement surgery in the United States and in Ontario, Canada. Most knee replacements are to relieve pain and are not medical emergencies. The median waiting time for an initial orthopedic consultation was two weeks in the United States and four weeks in Ontario. Median waiting time for knee replacement after the operation had been planned was three weeks in the United States and eight weeks in Ontario.

Hamilton, Ho, and Goldman (2000) compared waiting times for hip fracture surgery, often not an elective procedure, and the impacts of delays to surgery on length of stay in the hospital after the operation and on hospital inpatient mortality in the United States and Canada. Waiting times for such surgery were longer in Canada than in the United States, and longer waiting times led to longer lengths of hospital stays. However, there were no differences between the two countries in inpatient mortality rates among persons who had this type of surgery.

Even when procedures can be postponed without medical consequences, waiting longer may lead to more pain and discomfort and worry about the impending surgery. These are very real societal costs,though not frequently quantified.

Use of Costly Procedures

Several studies indicated that heart attack victims in the United States had higher rates of use of invasive cardiac procedures than in Canada. For example, Rouleau, Moye, Pfeffer, et al. (1993) found that a higher percentage of patients admitted to hospital coronary care units in Canada had had heart attacks than in the United States, implying a higher severity of illness threshold for provision of intensive care in Canada than in the United States (but with no difference in mortality or rates of repeated heart attacks between the two countries, though more Canadians had activity-limiting chest pain afterward). However, Ko, Krumholz, Wang, et al. (2007), who compared rates of use of such procedures in the northeastern United States and in in nearby Ontario, found similar rates of use. This finding implies that the differentials documented in the previous studies were likely due to regional differences in practice patterns within the two countries rather than to differences in capacity in between the two countries.

Disparities in Health and in the Use of Services

Canada has made an unusual effort to create a one-tier health system. Thus, it is of some interest whether the disparities in use and in health outcomes evident in other countries, particularly the United States, also exist in Canada. In a review of the literature on this issue, Birch and Gafni (2005) concluded that Canadian Medicare has reduced disparities in health care use and health outcomes by income. However, income-based differences in use still exist (Roos and Mustard 1997; Alter, Naylor, Austin, et al. 1999; Dunlop, Coyte, and McIsaac 2000), as do disparities in the use of non-Medicare-covered services, such as dental care.

12.6 Evolution of Payment Systems in Asian Countries on the Pacific Rim

Background

Japan, South Korea, and Taiwan all have social insurance systems for health care and mainly rely on the private provision of personal health care services. All three countries rely on social insurance for half of health care spending, with South

Korea slightly less than half. Appreciable shares of spending in 2001–2002 came from out-of-pocket outlays in all three countries, most in South Korea (about 40 percent) and least in Japan (about 20 percent). The high share of out-of-pocket payments in Korea reflects that the lack of insurance coverage for many services continues, and people pay for these services out of pocket (Kwon 2003). Private health insurance accounts for a small share of revenue in Taiwan and a negligible share in the other two countries.

JAPAN

Japan is the most populous and affluent of the three countries. Japan's health system, implemented in the late 1950s (Ramseyer 2009), adopted the German system as it existed well before World War II. Insurance is provided by a patchwork of private-employment-based plans and government plans. As in the United States and Germany, most persons in Japan obtain their health insurance through their place of employment. A separate insurance plan is available for persons who are not eligible for health insurance through employment, such as retirees.

Enrollment in an insurance plan has been mandatory for all persons since 1961. There are five major sources of funding for personal health care services in Japan: participants' premiums paid to various insurers, with premiums being proportional to income; employer-employee matching contributions to employment-based health insurance plans; patient co-payments to hospitals, clinics (physicians), and pharmacies; national government subsidies; and local government subsidies (Rapp and Shibuya 1994, 594; Ikegami and Campbell 1995). There are over 5,000 employer-based plans, each with its own contribution rate (Wagstaff 2007). Tax revenue includes revenue from personal income, corporate income, and consumption taxes (Ogura, Kadoda, and Kawamura 2006, 87).

Compared to Canada and even to the US public health insurance programs, patient cost sharing is high in Japan. The coinsurance rate (share of expense borne out of pocket by the patient) is 30 percent except among the elderly, for whom the coinsurance rate is 10 percent (Yashiro, Suzuki, and Suzuki 2006, 22). Private insurers are only allowed to offer coverage for expenses not covered by the universal health insurance program.

Despite the existence of multiple insurers, payments to providers all flow from a single source, as in the German system, where payments to physicians are funneled though the state's (*Land*'s) association of sickness fund physicians' organizations. There is a uniform fee schedule that applies to all health plans. As is usually the case, the United States being the major exception, the fee schedule is negotiated between the Japan Medical Association and the Ministry of Health and Welfare. When these bilateral negotiations first began, the negotiation process was acrimonious. Since then, the parties have recognized that they need each other, and the negotiations have gone more smoothly. In contrast to the German system, where negotiations take place at the state level, in Japan, negotiation is on a national basis. Unlike in the United States and other countries, such as Germany, hospital and physicians' fees are not separated in Japan (Yajima and Takayanagi 2002, 466).

The fee schedule lists all procedures and products that can be paid by the universal health insurance program as well as the prices associated with each code. As in the other systems discussed thus far in this chapter, with the exception of US Medicare, balance billing over the official fee schedule is prohibited. While most providers are wholly reliant on revenue from services provided as the single source of revenue, public sector and academic hospitals also receive direct subsidies from governments (mostly local governments) or university budgets for capital and even some operating expenses (Ikegami and Campbell 1995). In practice, the prices of procedures that show large increases in volume are frequently reduced, as has happened with magnetic resonance imaging (MRI) of the head. In this way, the financial impact of introducing new technologies can be negated (Ikegami and Campbell 2004). In Japan, government authorities undertake a biannual review of each of more than 3,000 items, rather than making across-the-board proportionate changes to all fees (Wagstaff 2007), as is the practice of US Medicare. While Japan has achieved cost containment by limiting fees, capping prices on complex procedures has reduced the incentive physicians would otherwise have had to invest in specialized expertise and technologies (Ramseyer 2009).

Patients have almost complete freedom of choice of physician. Unlike in the United States, where group practice predominates, almost all physicians in Japan are in solo practice, and most hospitals are small organizations linked to physicians' offices. Most large hospitals are government-owned or are private not-for-profit, either linked to universities or free-standing. Unlike in the United States, for-profit investor-owned hospitals are prohibited in Japan.

There is some control of entry of health care providers. Japan began to control the number of hospital beds in 1985. The government has specified the number of beds needed in several hundred areas of the country. Physicians are prohibited from increasing the number of beds in areas in which bed supply is deemed to be adequate. The government has also frozen the number of places in medical schools in the country (Yashiro, Suzuki, and Suzuki 2006, 30).

As in Germany, but unlike in the United States, office-based physicians cannot care for their patients while they are in the hospital. Instead, physicians' services in the hospital are delivered by hospital-based physicians, who are paid on a salaried basis and hence are not rewarded financially for providing a greater volume of service. Hospitalization rates in Japan are extremely low by international standards, but rates of use of physicians' services and prescription drugs are relatively high.

Prescription drugs in Japan and in other East Asian countries have followed the Chinese tradition in which there is no formal separation between pharmacists and physicians. Physicians and hospitals derive a special fee from dispensing prescription drugs. The provider buys drugs at wholesale prices and sells them at retail prices. In 1995, the difference between wholesale and retail prices was 26 percent on average (Ikegami and Campbell 1995, 1296). Japanese physicians often sell higher-priced drugs because expensive drugs result in higher profit margins (Yoshikawa and Bhattacharya 2002, 257).

Japan ranks highest in the world in terms of life expectancy at birth, and it ranks high on other dimensions of health as well (e.g., infant mortality, percentage of infants born who are low birth weight or very low birth weight). However, this long life expectancy may have as much or even more to do with health behaviors and the relative equality of the income distribution in Japan than with access to care and the quality of the health care delivery (Tsuda, Aoyama, and Froom 1994; Bezruchka, Namekata, and Sistrom 2008).

SOUTH KOREA

As in Taiwan, the process of implementing universal coverage in South Korea occurred in two major steps. First, South Korea extended national health insurance in 1989 to almost all of its population (97 percent). The remaining three percent are covered by a public insurance program focusing on the poor, a program also established in 1977. Second, up to the year 2000, insurance was provided by multiple social insurers. In that year, more than 350 health insurance societies were merged into a single National Health Insurance (NHI) Corporation (Lee, Chun, Lee, et al. 2008). Insurance remains tied to place of employment; insurance coverage is mandatory. The government has key roles in regulating insurance and in setting benefit levels and fee levels to be paid to health care providers (see, e.g., Gauld, Ikegami, Barr, et al. 2006).

A notable characteristic of the South Korean system is the high level of patient cost sharing. In addition, many common but expensive high-technology services, such as MRI, fall outside the NHI benefit package. Mandatory health insurance coverage was first established in 1977 for firms with more than 500 employees. This suggests that South Korea achieved the goal of universal coverage through a strategy of a combination of a low benefit level but wide coverage. As a result, about 45 percent of health expenditures are financed from private sources—37 percent from out-of-pocket payments and 8 percent from private insurance and other private sources (Gauld, Ikegami, Barr, et al. 2006).

In South Korea, following implementation of the first phase of mandatory coverage, the mean number of ambulatory visits rose from 1.3 per year in 1977 to 6.9 in 1985 (Peabody, Lee, and Bickel 1995). A common strategy employed by the insurance societies, in effect until 2000, was to increase co-payments. Although there appears to be no rigorous empirical evaluation of this, the perception is that increased co-payments did not decrease utilization rates. Physicians could increase the volume of services provided in two ways, by providing more frequent, shorter visits and by unbundling or relabeling services to reflect additional or more complex services. Peabody, Lee, and Bickel (1995) cited evidence that physician office visits average three minutes per patient, versus 10–15 minutes in other developed countries.

Physicians are paid on a fee-for-service basis. In the late 1990s, a DRG payment system was introduced on a pilot basis. An RBRVS fee schedule for physicians was introduced in 2001 (Kwon 2003). The private sector plays a dominant role in providing health care services. A substantial share of South Korean hospitals are organized on a for-profit basis, which physicians own and manage. Fewer than 10 percent of hospitals are public.

As in many East Asian countries, in South Korea physicians both prescribe and dispense drugs. This practice, in combination with direct government price controls on pharmaceutical products, puts physicians and hospitals in a position to earn profits directly from the sales of prescription drugs. Given the profit margin for prescription drugs, providers have financial incentives to substitute prescription drugs for other inputs, such as time spent on diagnosis or on surgical treatment. Spending on pharmaceuticals consequently accounts for a larger share of health care expenditures in South Korea. In 2004, the share of health care expenditures spent on drugs ranged from 10 to 20 percent among most high-income countries. However, like Taiwan, South Korea allocates more than a quarter of its health care expenditures to drugs.

In response to the rapidly rising share of pharmaceutical expenditures, South Korea adopted two major pharmaceutical reforms in recent years. First, in July 2000, the Korean government adopted a mandated separation policy between drug prescribing and dispensing. This reform stimulated significant opposition from physicians, including strikes, which in turn forced the government to substantially increase physician fees to compensate for the income loss from the separation of drug prescribing and dispensing (Kwon 2003). At the same time, South Korea increased coverage of prescription drugs, which has led to a substantial increase in the use of prescription drugs, including high-priced drugs (Jeong 2005; Kim and Ruger 2008). Second, in 2008, South Korea became the first Asian country to adopt economic evaluation in the reimbursement decision of new drugs (Yang, Bae, and Kim 2008).

TAIWAN

Taiwan began to adopt the social insurance approach in 1950. The program was first made available to industrial workers and covered only about two percent of the total population in that year. In 1995, Taiwan achieved universal health coverage by integrating the three existing programs into a single system and expanding coverage to the uninsured population. This development process suggests that universal health insurance was not created in one day. Instead, health insurance was adopted piecemeal over a 45-year period, and expansion of coverage was slow, proceeding sector by sector. The percentage of the population covered by public insurance programs reached 49 percent in 1991, with the public sector contributing about half of health care financing. After the implementation of universal coverage, the share of public financing increased to about 63 percent.

Following the expansion in insurance coverage and economic growth, real health expenditure per capita increased rapidly and exceeded the mean real economic growth rate between 1991 and 2006. As a result, the share of GDP spent on health care increased from 4.4 percent in 1991 to 6.1 percent in 2006.

The universal health insurance program is known as national health insurance (NHI) in Taiwan (see chapter 3, box 3.4). After NHI was implemented, the government introduced new payment systems to control rising health care expenditures. Most noteworthy are the single-payer system and global budgets. The single-payer system employs a uniform fee schedule to reimburse providers in all geographic regions. A single-payer system achieves cost containment in part by being administratively simple, thus substantially reducing administrative overhead as compared to other systems, and by conferring monopsony power on the purchaser of services in setting fee schedules. Lower prices in turn lower public expenditures under NHI (Chiang 1997; Reinhardt 2007).

In addition, the government has had the advantage of being able to learn from the experiences of Canada, Germany, and France, which adopted global budgets earlier as a cost-containment strategy. The global budgets were divided into subbudgets by type of services, and implementation was incremental. This system was first applied to dental services in July 1998. Then, based on the experiences gained from implementing this initial pilot experiment, global budgets were subsequently applied to Chinese traditional medicine in July 2000, to outpatient clinic services in July 2001, and to the hospital sector in July 2002.

Taiwan's health care delivery system has changed over time. After World War II, Taiwan relied on public provision. Public hospitals accounted for more than 90 percent of the market share in terms of the number of hospital beds. However, after years of economic growth, many large, private, not-for-profit hospitals entered the market. The market share of public hospitals consequently declined steadily and the health care system in Taiwan rapidly became one in which the private sector dominated the supply of personal health care services. By 2000 the market share of private hospitals had increased to about 70 percent. In addition, almost all physician clinics are now owned by the private sector.

Like those in many Asian countries such as China, Japan, and South Korea, the hospitals in Taiwan employ a closed-staff system, under which almost all physicians who practice in hospitals are employees of those hospitals and physicians who practice in clinics do not have admitting privileges at hospitals. Patients are free to choose their own providers; that is, there is no gatekeeper mechanism. Under a closed-staff system, except in emergency cases, patients who receive inpatient services mainly come from the outpatient department of the same hospital. Thus, to increase the flow of inpatients, hospitals in Taiwan have a strong incentive

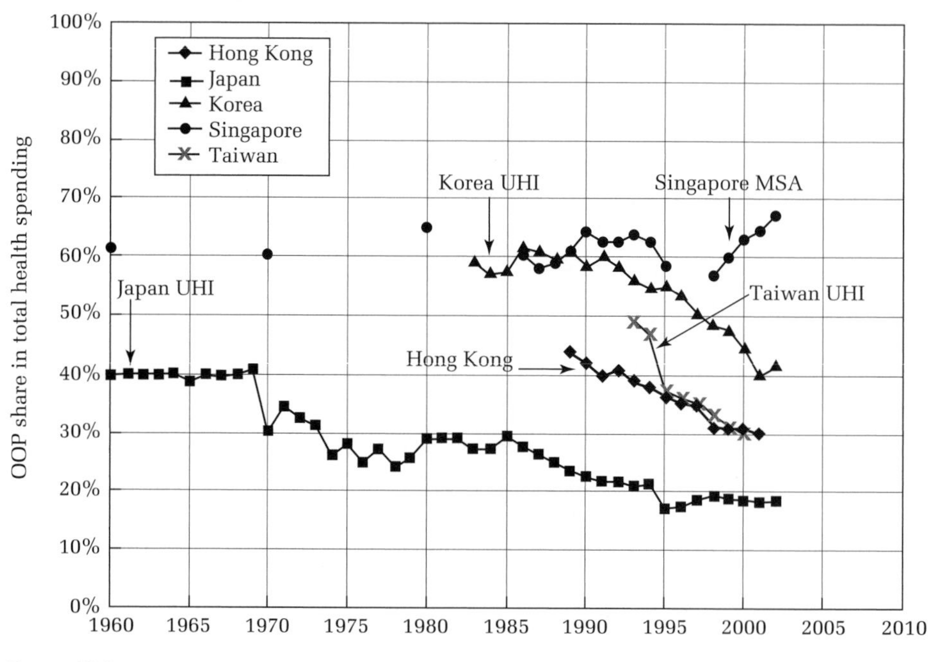

FIGURE 12.2
Trends in the Out-of-Pocket (OOP) Share in Japan and Other East Asian Countries
Source: Wagstaff (2007).

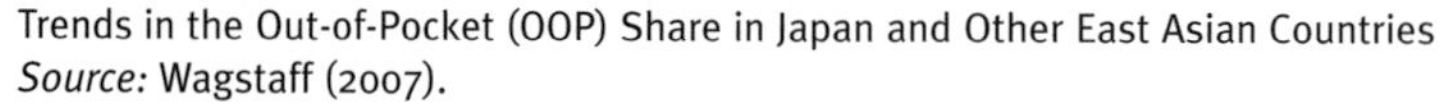

to operate a large outpatient department. As a result, local clinics and hospitals compete for outpatient services, and the referral system is almost nonexistent.

EFFECTS OF UNIVERSAL HEALTH INSURANCE

In all three East Asian countries, the out-of-pocket share declined appreciably after the implementation of universal health insurance, which occurred in 1961 in Japan, in 1989 in South Korea, and in 1995 in Taiwan (fig. 12.2). In 1993, before Taiwan implemented its universal health insurance program, out-of-pocket payments for health care amounted to 48 percent of the total. By 2000, out-of-pocket payments had declined to 30 percent (Lu and Hsiao 2003). Interestingly, in Singapore, which introduced medical savings accounts in 1984, a form of cost sharing which imposes a substantial deductible before insurance coverage takes effect, there was no decrease in the out-of-pocket share following implementation of this policy (see fig. 12.2).

Social insurance contributions are regressive in all three countries, which is attributable to income-based ceilings placed on such contributions (Wagstaff 2007). Such ceilings are not imposed on payroll contributions to US Medicare. In South Korea and Taiwan, but not in Japan, there are exemptions or reduced contribution rates for the poorest individuals, as well as some government subsidies for coverage of such persons.

The World Health Organization has developed an index to measure inequality in the share of households' income spent on personal health care services. The value of the index ranges from 0 to 1, with 1 representing the most equitable distribution of health care financing. In 1998, Taiwan had a value of 0.992 versus 0.881 in 1994, the year before universal coverage was implemented in that country. By comparison, Japan had a value of 0.977, Canada 0.974, Germany 0.978, and the United States 0.954. The implementation of universal coverage in Taiwan clearly increased equality in the share of household income devoted to health care, but it also brought the country up to the level of other countries with social health insurance systems.

The single-payer system in Taiwan has achieved cost containment not achieved by similar programs, such as Medicare in the United States. Lu and Hsiao (2003) attributed the fact that Taiwan could cover a large number of previously uninsured persons at basically no incremental cost to several factors, including the implementation of higher cost sharing for some previously insured persons, the introduction of a DRG-type payment system for high-volume hospital services, and the use of global budgets for several types of services. To know whether or not these policies truly achieved cost containment would require a more rigorous evaluation than has been conducted. Further, even if cost containment is achieved, it is not at all clear that the use of these various non-price rationing devices really increases social welfare. This too remains to be demonstrated.

The use of personal health care services in Taiwan has risen following implementation of universal health insurance coverage. Chen, Yip, Chang, et al. (2007) reported that among previously uninsured elderly persons, the proportion of such persons receiving outpatient care increased by nearly 28 percent as compared with a much smaller increase, 13 percent, for elderly persons who were previously insured. They attributed the 15 percent difference to the effect of implementing universal health insurance coverage. Even three years later, the difference in utilization between the two groups remained at 11 percent. Similar patterns were observed for the utilization of hospital inpatient care. In addition, they found that utilization increased in relative terms for lower-income persons, suggesting that implementation of universal coverage had the effect of redistributing services to lower-income families. By contrast, the authors did not find an effect of universal coverage in Taiwan on health status as measured by either the one-year mortality rate or self-reported health status.

In addition to the demand side, the implementation of universal coverage has had an important effect on the supply side. As Finkelstein (2007) observed for the United States, the introduction of NHI in Taiwan increased the entry of large hospitals and the exit of small hospitals, with the result that mean hospital size has increased over time. Furthermore, implementation of NHI encouraged hospitals to invest in new advanced medical technologies, such as CT scanners, radiation isotope therapeutic equipment, and linear accelerators. Chou, Liu, and Hammitt (2004) found that implementation of NHI in Taiwan significantly increased the probability of technology adoption, ownership, and the use of technologies by private hospitals, after controlling for hospital characteristics and market competition.

Taiwan was the first Asian country to adopt global budgets as a tool for cost containment. Using a panel data on outpatient dental care, Lee and Jones (2004) reported that the implementation of global budgets in Taiwan had three major effects. First, the introduction of global budgets decreased dental care utilization and hence reduced the growth rate of outpatient dental care expenditures. Second, by providing relatively favorable funding for dental care in deprived areas, global budgets had a weak effect on improving the distribution of dental care and dentist supply. Third, global budgets changed the labor supply of dentists. Overall, dentists' labor supply decreases following the implementation of global budgets. However, the dentists altered the mix of their services toward high-charge services.

As noted above, there is a risk that the public provision of health insurance coverage may crowd out private saving. One motivation for personal saving is precautionary, which is to reserve funds for a "rainy day," which the occurrence of an illness represents.

Chou, Liu, and Hammitt (2003) studied the effect of introducing universal health insurance coverage in Taiwan in 1995 on precautionary saving. In conducting this study, the authors took advantage of (1) the major exogenous change to households in health insurance coverage, (2) the fact that many Taiwanese had government-provided health insurance coverage before the introduction of universal health insurance coverage in 1995, and (3) the availability of household consumption data for a sufficiently long time period. The authors found that compared to the preceding government insurance program, the introduction of universal health insurance coverage in Taiwan resulted in a decrease in personal savings by 8.6–13.7 percent, with the largest effects being seen among households with the least personal saving. Recall that Hubbard, Skinner, and Zeldes (1995) concluded that a means-tested public insurance program reduced savings rates. In Taiwan, the program is not means tested. Nevertheless, the impact has been larger for households at the bottom than for those at the top of the wealth distribution.

Should we regard reductions in personal saving as a positive or negative development? Certainly for risk-averse individuals, reductions in out-of-pocket expenditure risk are welfare-enhancing. People would clearly prefer a situation in which public insurance is provided and they have less motivation to engage in precautionary saving. They may even prefer this if made to pay higher taxes for the risk reduction.

But there is another concern. Pay-as-you-go (PAYGO) financing typically accompanies public financing. With PAYGO financing, current taxpayers pay for current benefits. To the extent that real program benefits are increasing, there is an intergenerational transfer from younger persons, who tend to be low utilizers of personal health care services, to older persons, who tend to be relatively high utilizers. An alternative is a fully funded insurance system. Under the latter, when a person is added to the insurance rolls, the insurer computes the present value of benefit flows and develops a schedule of premiums that has a present value equal to the present value of benefit flows. Full funding eliminates intergenerational transfers. While income-based transfers may reflect a country's social welfare function, intergenerational transfers may take place for reasons of political expediency rather than reflect underlying societal preferences.

12.7 The Public Health Insurance Program in Rural China

Background

Beginning in 2003, China introduced a new health insurance program, the New Cooperative Medical Scheme (NCMS), in rural areas. By 2007 this program had a total of 730 million participants. Thus, NCMS is the world's largest public insurance program, gauged in terms of number of enrollees. The NCMS has three major characteristics.

First, participation in the NCMS is voluntary—the opposite of the compulsory universal programs adopted in other countries. The government uses a subsidized flat-rate contribution to encourage informal sector workers and their families to enroll. In 2006, the mean premium (budget) per insured population was about 52 RMB; insured members paid only 28 percent of the premium, and central and local governments paid the rest. On average, central government bore 30 percent of the government subsidy while local governments bore the rest (Lei and Lin 2009).

Second, the focus of the NCMS is on coverage for catastrophic illness. Thus, the system has been designed to provide lower coverage and higher cost sharing—the opposite of the comprehensive benefit plans adopted in high-income countries. Most coverage is for hospital inpatient care. Outpatient care is not covered or is covered only partially, with high deductibles and high coinsurance rates.

Third, the NCMS operates at the county level, and local governments have considerable discretion in the design of their NCMS programs. Hence, there is considerable heterogeneity in benefit packages among counties. Specifically, reimbursement in the NCMS is of four types (table 12.4).

The first only provides public coverage for inpatient care, with a very high coinsurance rate, ranging from 59 to 66 percent (Wagstaff, Lindelow, Jun, et al.

TABLE 12.4
China's NCMS Benefit Package

NCMS Model	Market Share (%)	Reimbursements and Benefits
1. Inpatient expenses only	16.87	The NCMS reimburses inpatient services only. Outpatient services are not covered.
2. Inpatient expenses and catastrophic outpatient expenses	11.17	The NCMS reimburses inpatient services and outpatient services for catastrophic diseases, with separate deductibles and reimbursement caps.
3. Inpatient expenses and pooling account for outpatient expenses	6.70	The NCMS reimburses inpatient services, outpatient services are paid from collective funds.
4. Inpatient expenses and household account for outpatient expenses	65.26	The NCMS covers inpatient care, while outpatient care is covered by a household account, an MSA. There is a deductible and a reimbursement cap for the MSA.

Note: NCMS is the abbreviation of the New Cooperative Medical Scheme in rural China.
Source: Wagstaff, Lindelow, Jun, et al. (2009) and Lei and Lin (2009).

2009). Outpatient services are not covered. Only 16.9 percent of counties with the NCMS fit in this category.

The second type covers inpatient and outpatient expenses for catastrophic diseases with high deductibles and coinsurance rates, a model in use by 11.2 percent of counties with the NCMS. The third covers inpatient expenses as well as outpatient expenses on a pooled basis, an approach used by 6.7 percent of counties.

The fourth and most popular model, used in nearly two-thirds of counties, provides hospital inpatient coverage through insurance funds and coverage for outpatient services through a medical savings account (MSA), an approach adopted from Singapore. Each household has its own MSA accounts that accumulate funds from household members' contributions. Such MSA accounts are earmarked for outpatient services only.

In sum, all NCMS models cover hospital inpatient services. The bulk of NCMS reimbursement, from about 66 percent to 100 percent, is for such expense (Wagstaff, Lindelow, Jun, et al. 2009).

EFFECTS OF THE NCMS

As in other countries, the major policy objectives of the NCMS are to reduce financial burdens on individual patients, increase access to personal health care services, and improve population health. Given that the NCMS is the newest health plan discussed in this chapter, empirical evidence on the effects of the NCMS is very limited. However, the following three studies reveal a clear picture of the effectiveness of the NCMS.

Lei and Lin (2009) used longitudinal survey data to assess the impact of the NCMS with several state-of-the-art econometric methods. Based on their empirical research, they concluded that implementation of the NCMS did not reduce out-of-pocket expenditure. Similarly, the NCMS did not increase utilization of formal medical services and did not improve health outcomes, as measured by self-reported health status and by sickness and injury reports for the four weeks before the interviews were conducted. By contrast, they found that NCMS enrollees were less likely to visit traditional Chinese folk physicians and were more likely to use preventive care than were others. Using a similar econometric method but different data, Wagstaff, Lindelow, and Jun (2009) found that implementation of the NCMS led to increased outpatient and inpatient utilization, results inconsistent with Lei and Lin's (2009) results. However, Wagstaff, Lindelow, and Jun (2009) confirmed Lei and Lin's (2009) finding that NCMS did not reduce out-of-pocket expenses for both outpatient and inpatient services. In another study, Wagstaff and Lindelow (2008) used data including both the urban and the rural population. They found that the implementation of NCMS increased the risk of incurring high and catastrophic health expenditures.[2]

A common finding of these three studies is that the implementation of NCMS and other public health insurance programs in China did not significantly reduce out-of-pocket payments by individual patients. This result is counter to the usual theory that insurance should reduce households' financial risk (see chapter 4).

There are two plausible explanations for this paradox. First, an explanation from the demand side is that the program's per capita budget has been too small for there to be a substantial reduction in households' out-of-pocket payments. The NCMS paid only 52 RMB per insured individuals in 2006—only 20 percent of total rural health care spending per capita population. Given the low level of per capita payments, the NCMS must impose high rates of patient cost sharing, and low payment ceilings for providers. In addition, many services, especially outpatient services, are not covered by this public program. In implementing the NCMS with a low budget, the Chinese government faced a tough trade-off between the amount it could spend per insured person and the number of persons who were covered.

This trade-off is illustrated by the budget line shown in figure 12.3. Given the fixed budget, the government can implement a public insurance program to cover the entire population but with very low benefits per covered person, such as at point *B*. Or the government could implement a program with relatively generous benefits, one with zero cost sharing and broad coverage of services, for a very small population group, such as at point *A*. Besides these two extreme cases, there are many possible combinations of number of insured persons (quantity) and the generosity of insurance coverage (price). Thus, line *AB* represents the public health

2. In this study, Wagstaff and Lindelow (2008) defined annual health spending as "high" if it exceeded a threshold of local average income and as "catastrophic" if it exceeded a threshold of the household's own per capita income.

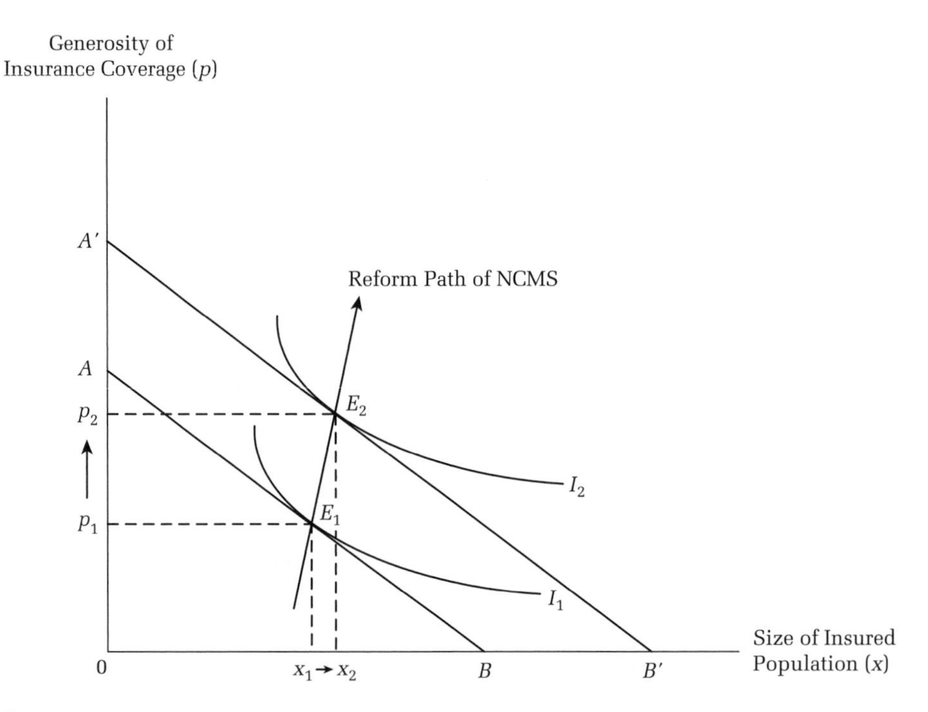

FIGURE 12.3
Choice of the Optimal Reform Path for China's NCMS

insurance program's budget line, depicting the public policy maker's trade-off between quantity (number of insured persons) and price (generosity of insurance coverage).

The program design actually selected by the policy makers is at the point of tangency of the budget line and the policy maker's indifference curve, such as at point E_1. The indifference curve shows combinations of quantity and price that yield the same utility level to the policy maker, such as I_1 and I_2. Apparently, policy makers in China value quantity more than price.[3] Thus, the indifference curve is rather flat. Given that the marginal utility of covering more persons tends to be high relative to the marginal utility of adding to payments per capita of covered persons, government payments per capita are low. If the government increases the health budget, reflected in a shift of the budget line from *AB* to *A′B′*, the new tangency is at E_2. Then price (the public insurer's payment per insured) increases from p_1 to p_2. As a result, the out-of-pocket payment declines. This is the plan announced by the Chinese government in April 2009, to the effect that it will spend an additional 850 billion RMB (about equivalent to US$125 billion) in the next three years, indicating that line E_1E_2 is the future reform path of the NCMS.

3. The term "price" here refers to benefits per insured person. Ordinarily, a decision maker would not place a positive valuation on price. But here, price stands for generosity of the health insurance benefit.

The second explanation for the lack of effect of the NCMS in reducing out-of-pocket spending is from the supply side. More than 70 percent of counties implementing the NCMS have adopted fee-for-service payment (Wagstaff, Lindelow, Jun, et al. 2009). The government has set fee schedules in a way that gives basic services a low price-cost margin and higher price-cost margin on prescription drugs and high-technology services. The NCMS and other public health insurance programs in China thus give physicians an incentive to prescribe more drugs and use more high-tech services. Implementation of the NCMS has increased ownership of expensive equipment in central township health centers (Wagstaff, Lindelow, Jun, et al. 2009). In addition, between 1990 and 2005, 45–50 percent of the national health expenditure in China was allocated to drugs, compared with an OECD average of 15 percent (Huang and Yang 2009).

All these supply-side responses imply that the NCMS and other public health insurance programs in China may encourage people to seek more expensive care when sick than they otherwise would, such as seeking care from higher-level providers (Wagstaff and Lindelow 2008). The increase in unit prices of care, in combination with the increase in the quantity of services induced by insurance, may account for the increased levels of out-of-pocket payments. This result is consistent with the conceptual framework illustrated in figure 11.2 and Finkelstein's (2007) evidence to the effect that the expansion of health insurance can lead to a substantial increase in health expenditures, especially in view of suppliers' responses to the expansion of coverage.

12.8 DISCUSSION AND CONCLUSIONS

This chapter has analyzed the economic rationale for the public provision of health insurance and the evolution of such systems in several countries, including Germany, the United States, Canada, Japan, South Korea, Taiwan, and China. We first discussed the advantages of the public provision of health insurance, including benefits from achieving universal coverage, efficiency gains from lower administrative costs and lower enforcement cost of regulation, enhanced bargaining power of public payers, and cross subsidies from healthy to sick individuals. However, countries that gain these advantages also incur an opportunity cost in the sense that they must give up several advantages of the private provision of health insurance. For example, the public provision of health insurance is less efficient than private provision in satisfying the wants of consumers with heterogeneous preferences. In addition, public payers may exercise monopsony power, with one adverse consequence being reduced incentives for innovation. In sum, neither public provision nor private provision of health insurance is clearly preferable.

We then analyzed the evolution of health care systems in several countries that have adopted the public provision of health insurance. In the United States, the public provision of health insurance has primarily focused on elderly persons and the poor. In Germany, the system is not mandatory for the relatively affluent, but applies to 90 percent of the population whose income is less than a statutory threshold. In other countries, including Canada, Japan, South Korea, and Taiwan, the coverage of public health insurance reaches the entire population. The services that are covered by public health insurance vary among countries. Some countries provide comprehensive insurance coverage, such as Canada, Japan, and Taiwan, while others provide more limited coverage, such as South Korea and China. Almost every country faced a rapid increase in health care costs after achieving the goal of "universal coverage" (Cutler 2002). In response, countries adopting government financing and private supply have substantially relied on public cost-containment policies to control the growth of their health expenditures. On the demand side, all seven countries discussed in this chapter have implemented various forms of cost sharing to control moral hazard. On the supply side, countries have adopted several payment system reforms to change the incentives of health care providers.

We have reviewed many studies investigating the effect of universal coverage and payment system reforms. Overall, universal coverage has had large impacts not only on demand, as reflected in increased health care utilization and expenditures, but also on supply, as reflected in the entry of new hospitals and technological change in health care, especially in larger countries, for which the increase in coverage has had a major effect on the pharmaceutical medical device market as well as the equipment (e.g., imaging) market size. In addition, empirical studies of payment system reforms consistently find that incentive matters in guiding providers' choices on quantity and quality. For example, the US Medicare's PPS substantially reduced lengths of hospital inpatient stays but did not adversely affect patient outcomes. Similarly, the introduction of global budgets in Taiwan substantially reduced the quantity of services provided by the dentists, thus lowering the growth rate of health care expenditures overall.

Although countries differ in their evolution and in the structure of their payment systems, the experiences of individual payment system reforms may offer valuable lessons for other countries. For example, as a pioneer, the United States experienced a high growth in health care expenditures following the implementation of Medicare in 1966. By contrast, as an imitator, Taiwan faced only a moderate increase in health care expenditures after the establishment of universal coverage in 1995. This suggests that imitator countries enjoy an advantage in being able to learn from the experiences of their predecessors. Similarly, South Korea and Taiwan learned lessons from the US PPS for the design of their own payment systems.

The recent experience in China—the adoption of a major public health insurance program may not substantially reduce out-of-pocket payments by individuals—highlights the importance of doing more than just assuming that this type of intervention will transform the system, making it both more efficient and more effective. Governments in China and several other middle-income countries have committed to increasing public funds for personal health care services. Whether or not such additional resources injected into health care can be effective in transforming the system by improving financial access to health care, or alternatively might just be captured by providers in the form higher fees, incomes, and profits, depends on payment system design. How this will play out is an open question.

Key Concepts

- social insurance
- means-tested public insurance
- Medicare program
- payment system
- Resource-Based Relative Value Scale
- balance billing
- universal coverage
- sickness funds
- Medicaid program
- prospective payment system
- diagnosis-related groups
- national health insurance

Review and Discussion Questions

12.1 What is meant by the term "social insurance"? How does it compare with other forms of public insurance?

12.2 Suppose you were asked by a policy maker in a low-income country to list the pros and cons of public provision of health insurance. The policy maker is busy and would like to see a short summary with no more than three points on each side. Which three advantages and disadvantages of the public provision of health insurance would you list? Justify each point you list.

12.3 Distinguish between treatment substitution effects and treatment expansion effects of new medical technologies. Give examples of new technologies that in important ways provide each.

12.4 What are key differences between Medicare and Medicaid in the United States?

12.5 What does it mean to say that public health insurance "crowds out" private health insurance? If this is so, why does the government still want to provide health insurance on its own?

12.6 Explain the term "means-tested public insurance" in your own words. If the government expands the eligibility of this public program, do you expect this policy to have any effect on labor force participation in a country? Is there any evidence to support your expectation?

12.7 Which criteria can be used to determine the benefit structure of public health insurance plans? By benefit structure, we mean the preventive, diagnostic, and therapeutic procedures covered by the health insurance plan.

12.8 What is meant by a "contribution percentage," as in the German statutory health insurance system? Does a fixed contribution percentage (one not dependent on earnings) mean that the plan is regressive? Why or why not? How would you determine whether the plan is regressive? Be sure to indicate what is meant by the term "regressive."

12.9 The US Medicare program offers an HMO option for its beneficiaries. What are the characteristics of beneficiaries who would be likely to select the HMO versus fee-for-service Medicare? Justify your answer.

12.10 Conceptually, how does paying hospitals a fixed prospective amount per patient admission affect hospital behavior? How does prospective payment differ from retrospective payment of hospitals?

12.11 Describe the Resource-Based Relative Value Scale (RBRVS). What are alternative methods that a public insurer could use to set the fees it pays? Evaluate the pros and cons of each alternative that you list.

12.12 Describe the concept of "spending down" to Medicaid. What is the likely effect of offering a means-tested health insurance program such as Medicaid on the private precautionary saving of individuals? What is meant by "precautionary" saving?

12.13 Canada employs global operating budgets and controls over capital expenditures. What is a global operating budget? How is the use of a global operating budget likely to affect the behavior of individual hospitals?

12.14 Public health insurance programs often require eligible individuals to enroll in such plans. What is the rationale for mandating public insurance coverage?

12.15 Economists distinguish between price and non-price rationing. What is meant by non-price rationing? Economists have often argued that non-price rationing entails a "deadweight loss." What is meant by this term? Are there valid economic arguments for non-price rationing?

12.16 In Japan and some other East Asian countries, physicians dispense drugs directly to their patients. What do you see as the advantages and disadvantages of this arrangement?

12.17 What is meant by pay-as-you-go (PAYGO) financing? What is the alternative to PAYGO? What are some disadvantages of PAYGO? What then explains its popularity? Identify a public program in your country that is funded on a PAYGO basis.

12.18 Based on the empirical evidence reviewed in this chapter, list the social benefits and costs of the US Medicaid program.

12.19 Explain the distinction between social insurance and means-tested public insurance. Do these two types of health insurance programs affect saving behavior in the same way? Is there any evidence to support your answer?

12.20 Explain the distinction between "compulsory" social insurance and "voluntary" social insurance. Do these two types of health insurance program affect health expenditure in the same way? Why have most countries included in this chapter adopted compulsory social insurance while only a few countries, such as China, have adopted voluntary social insurance?

Exercises

12.1 Define "retrospective cost-based reimbursement system" and "prospective payment system." Suppose you were asked by a policy maker to design the payment system for a public insurance program. If the policy maker would like to use the payment system to achieve the goal of cost containment, which payment system you would recommend? If the policy maker changes the goal of policy and would like to focus on increasing the quality of health care, would you change your recommendation for the design of the payment system? Justify your recommendation.

12.2 In the United States, the real treatment cost (in 2000 dollars) per case for depression decreased from US$2,012 in 1987 to US$1,073 in 1996. However, total real costs for treating depression increased from US$4.83 billion to US$9.22 billion during the same period. Use the concept of treatment substitution and treatment expansion to explain why the mean treatment cost decreased but the total treatment cost increased.

12.3 Suppose country A traditionally relies on out-of-pocket costs to finance personal health care services. Assume this country receives a substantial amount of foreign aid for its many infrastructure investments, hence the government can release public funds to finance personal health care services. Suppose the government decides to introduce an additional system of universal coverage through a single-payer program. Conceptually, what effect do you expect the introduction of universal coverage to have on the demand and supply sides of the country's health care market? List at least two impacts on both sides of the health care market in country A. Justify each effect you list.

12.4 In the early 1970s, only a few health insurance plans provided coverage for prescription drugs. Many health insurance programs have added coverage for prescription drugs in more recent years. For example, in the United States, less than 20 percent of spending on prescription drugs was covered by health insurance in 1970. This share increased to near three-quarters by 1998. What factors account for this?

12.5 Finkelstein (2007) reported that implementation of the Medicare program in the United States led to a 37 percent increase in real hospital expenditures between 1965 and 1970. However, based on estimates from the RAND HIE study (see chapter 3), the implementation of Medicare increased real hospital expenditures by only 5.6 percent. Explain the differences between these two estimates.

12.6 Use the concept of cost of capital (COC) and marginal efficiency of investment (MEI) introduced in chapters 2 and 9 to analyze the effect of implementing the Medicare program on hospitals' investment in new technology. Will the implementation of Medicare program affect COC or MEI for hospital investment in new technology? Justify your answer.

12.7 Use three graphs to show the effect of Medicaid fees on the physician's incentive to accept Medicaid patients. Graph A is a horizontal line that represents the demand curve for Medicaid patients. Graph B is a downward-sloping curve that represents the demand curve for non-Medicaid patients. Graph C represents the sum of demand from the two separate markets. Assume that the physician's marginal cost curve has a positive slope. Show:

a. How will the physician set the price for non-Medicaid patient if the physician pursues maximum profit?

b. Under what conditions will the physician not accept Medicaid patients? Show graphically.

c. Will the physician be more likely to accept Medicaid patients if the government increases the Medicaid fees paid to the physician? Show the effect of an increased Medicaid fee graphically.

12.8 Prepare a table to compare social insurance programs in Canada, China, Germany, Japan, South Korea, Taiwan, and the United States for the following dimensions:

a. beneficiary eligibility;

b. sources of public financing;

c. payment methods;

d. type and extent of cost sharing.

12.9 Assume a country's health care expenditures (HCE) are financed from two sources: (1) public expenditures (PE) and (2) out-of-pocket payments (OOP). Thus, HCE = PE + OOP. Given the following relationships: (PE/HCE) + (OOP/HCE) = 1 and HCE/GDP = PE/GDP + OOP/GDP, where GDP represents the gross domestic product. Suppose this country currently spends 5 percent of GDP on personal health care and services, and out-of-pocket payments account for 60 percent of the country's total health care expenditures. Use the above-mentioned information and relationships to answer the following questions:

a. If the government increases funding for personal health care services by adding 1 percent of GDP to health care, and assuming that other things remain constant, that is, the share of GDP spent on health care (HCE/GDP) remains unchanged, will this policy reduce the share of out-of-pocket payments on health care expenditure (OOP/HCE)? Calculate the new values of OOP/HCE under this scenario.

b. If the new funds injected into the health care sector lead providers to raise fees, with the result that HCE/GDP increases from 5 percent to 6 percent, will this policy reduce the share of out-of-pocket payments in the health care expenditure? Calculate the new value of OOP/HCE under this scenario.

c. If the new funds injected into a health care system induce a high rate of health care inflation caused by increased wasteful health care spending, with the result that HCE/GDP increases from five percent to 10 percent, will this policy reduce the share of out-of-pocket payments in total health care expenditures? Calculate the new value of OOP/HCE under this scenario.

d. Based on the scenarios in parts (a) to (c) of this question, explain how a government could use the new funds to promote effective and efficient health care provision so that the new public sector funds lead to a reduction in the share of out-of-pocket payments in total health care expenditures. Under what conditions would the government fail to achieve this policy goal, with the new funds being captured by providers in the form of higher income and profits?

12.10 In 2005, China spent about half its health care expenditures on pharmaceutical products, while this share was only about 12 percent in the United States. What factors account for this large difference?

Online Supplemental Material

US Medicare Program: General Description

http://www.medicare.gov

http://www.cms.gov/home/medicare.asp

US Medicaid Program: General Description

http://www.cms.hhs.gov/home/medicaid.asp

German Health Care System

http://www.civitas.org.uk/pubs/bb3Germany.php

Kamke, Kerstin. 1998. The German Health Care System and Health Care Reform. *Health Policy* 43(2):171–194.

http://www.codebluenow.org/vital-signs/Germany.pdf

http://content.healthaffairs.org/content/13/4/22.full.pdf

http://www.med-kolleg.de/german-health-system_e.html

http://lcweb2.loc.gov/frd/cs/detoc.html

Canada's Medicare and Health Care System:

http://www.cihi.ca/CIHI-ext-portal/internet/EN/Home/home/cihi000001

Japan's Health Care System:

http://www.npr.org/templates/story/story.php?storyId=89626309

http://www.niph.go.jp/English/index.html

South Korea's Health Care System:

http://lcweb2.loc.gov/cgi-bin/query/r?frd/cstdy:@field(DOCID+kr0084)

http://lcweb2.loc.gov/frd/cs/krtoc.html

Taiwan's Health Care System:

http://www.npr.org/templates/story/story.php?storyId=89651916

http://www.westga.edu/~bquest/1999/hmo.html

SUPPLEMENTAL READINGS

Bhattacharya, J., and D. Lakdawalla. 2006. Does Medicare Benefit the Poor? *Journal of Public Economics* 90 (1–2): 277–292.

Chou, S. Y., J. T. Liu, and J. K. Hammitt. 2003. National Health Insurance and Precautionary Saving: Evidence from Taiwan. *Journal of Public Economics* 87 (9–10): 1873–1894.

Drummond, M. 2007. Using Economic Evaluation in Reimbursement Decisions for Health Technologies: Lessons from International Experience. In *Pharmaceutical Innovation: Incentives, Competition, and Cost-Benefit Analysis in International Perspective*, ed. F. A. Sloan and C.-R. Hsieh, 215–225. New York: Cambridge University Press.

Hoel, M. 2007. What Should (Public) Health Insurance Cover? *Journal of Health Economics* 26 (2): 251–262.

Lei, X., and W. Lin. 2009. The New Cooperative Medical Scheme in Rural China: Does More Coverage Mean More Service and Better Health? *Health Economics* 18:s25–s46.

McClellan, M., and J. Skinner. 2006. The Incidence of Medicare. *Journal of Public Economics* 90 (1–2): 257–276.

REFERENCES

Acemoglu, D., D. Cutler, A. Finkelstein, et al. 2006. Did Medicare Induce Pharmaceutical Innovation? *American Economic Review* 96 (2): 103–107.

Acemoglu, D., and A. Finkelstein. 2008. Input and Technology Choices in Regulated Industries: Evidence from the Health Care Sector. *Journal of Political Economy* 116 (5): 837–880.

Altenstetter, C., and R. Busse. 2005. Health Care Reform in Germany: Patchwork Change within Established Governance Structures. *Journal of Health Politics, Policy and Law* 30 (1–2): 121–142.

Alter, D. A., C. D. Naylor, P. Austin, et al. 1999. Effects of Socioeconomic Status on Access to Invasive Cardiac Procedures and on Mortality after Acute Myocardial Infarction. *New England Journal of Medicine* 341 (18): 1359–1367.

Baker, L. C., and A. B. Royalty. 2000. Medicaid Policy, Physician Behavior, and Health Care for the Low-Income Population. *Journal of Human Resources* 35 (3): 480–502.

Berndt, E. R. 2002. Pharmaceuticals in U.S. Health Care: Determinants of Quantity and Price. *Journal of Economic Perspectives* 16 (4): 45–66.

Bethencourt, C., and V. Galasso. 2008. Political Complements in the Welfare State: Health Care and Social Security. *Journal of Public Economics* 92 (3–4): 609–632.

Bezruchka, S., T. Namekata, and M. G. Sistrom. 2008. Improving Economic Equality and Health: The Case of Postwar Japan. *American Journal of Public Health* 98 (4): 589–594.

Bhattacharya, J., and D. Lakdawalla. 2006. Does Medicare Benefit the Poor? *Journal of Public Economics* 90 (1–2): 277–292.

Birch, S., and A. Gafni. 2005. Achievements and Challenges of Medicare in Canada: Are We There Yet? Are We on Course? *International Journal of Health Services* 35 (3): 443–463.

Card, D., C. Dobkin, and N. Maestas. 2009. Does Medicare Save Lives? *Quarterly Journal of Economics* 124 (2): 597–636.

Carrera, P. M., K. K. Siemens, and J. Bridges. 2008. Health Care Financing Reforms in Germany: The Case for Rethinking the Evolutionary Approach to Reforms. *Journal of Health Politics, Policy and Law* 33 (5): 979–1005.

Chen, L., W. Yip, M.-C. Chang, et al. 2007. The Effects of Taiwan's National Health Insurance on Access and Health Status of the Elderly. *Health Economics* 16 (3): 223–242.

Chiang, T. L. 1997. Taiwan's 1995 Health Care Reform. *Health Policy (Amsterdam)* 39 (3): 225–239.

Chou, S.-Y., J.-T. Liu, and J. K. Hammitt. 2003. National Health Insurance and Precautionary Saving: Evidence from Taiwan. *Journal of Public Economics* 87 (9–10): 1873–1894.

Chou, S. Y., J. T. Liu, and J. K. Hammitt. 2004. National Health Insurance and Technology Adoption: Evidence from Taiwan. *Contemporary Economic Policy* 22 (1): 26–38.

Cohen, J. W., and W. D. Spector. 1996. The Effect of Medicaid Reimbursement on Quality of Care in Nursing Homes. *Journal of Health Economics* 15 (1): 23–48.

Coyte, P. C., J. G. Wright, G. A. Hawker, et al. 1994. Waiting Times for Knee-Replacement Surgery in the United States and Ontario. *New England Journal of Medicine* 331 (16): 1068–1071.

Currie, J., and J. Gruber. 1996. Health Insurance Eligibility, Utilization of Medical Care, and Child Health. *Quarterly Journal of Economics* 111 (2): 431–466.

Currie, J., and D. Thomas. 1995. Does Head Start Make a Difference? *American Economic Review* 85 (3): 341–364.

Cutler, D. 2002. Health Care and the Public Sector. In *Handbook of Public Economics*, ed. M. Feldstein and A. J. Auerbach, 4. Amsterdam: Elsevier Science.

Cutler, D., and J. Gruber. 1996. The Effect of Medicaid Expansions on Public Insurance, Private Insurance, and Redistribution. *American Economic Review* 86 (2): 378–383.

Cutler, D. M., M. McClellan, and J. P. Newhouse. 2000. How Does Managed Care Do It? *RAND Journal of Economics* 31 (3): 526–548.

Cutler, D. M., and R. J. Zeckhauser. 2000. The Anatomy of Health Insurance. In *Handbook of Health Economics*, ed. A. J. Culyer and J. P. Newhouse, **1A**:617–621. Amsterdam: Elsevier Science.

Dafny, L. S. 2005. How Do Hospitals Respond to Price Changes? *American Economic Review* 95 (5): 1525–1547.

Drummond, M. 2007. Using Economic Evaluation in Reimbursement Decisions for Health Technologies: Lessons from International Experience. In *Pharmaceutical Innovation: Incentives, Competition, and Cost-Benefit Analysis in International Perspective*, ed. F. A. Sloan and C.-R. Hsieh, 215–225. New York: Cambridge University Press.

Dunlop, S., P. C. Coyte, and W. McIsaac. 2000. Socio-economic Status and the Utilisation of Physicians' Services: Results from the Canadian National Population Health Survey. *Social Science & Medicine* 51 (1): 123–133.

Dusansky, R. 1989. The Demand for Money and Goods in the Theory of Consumer Choice with Money. *American Economic Review* 79 (4): 895–901.

Ellis, R. P., and W. G. Manning. 2007. Optimal Health Insurance for Prevention and Treatment. *Journal of Health Economics* 26 (6): 1128–1150.

Finkelstein, A. 2007. The Aggregate Effects of Health Insurance: Evidence from the Introduction of Medicare. *Quarterly Journal of Economics* 122 (1): 1–37.

Finkelstein, A., and R. McKnight. 2008. What Did Medicare Do? The Initial Impact of Medicare on Mortality and Out of Pocket Medical Spending. *Journal of Public Economics* 92 (7): 1644–1668.

Gauld, R., N. Ikegami, M. D. Barr, et al. 2006. Advanced Asia's Health System in Comparison. *Health Policy (Amsterdam)* 79 (2–3): 325–336.

Gertler, P. 1989. Subsidies, Quality, and the Regulation of Nursing Homes. *Journal of Public Economics* 38 (1): 33–52.

Glied, S. 2000. Managed Care. In *Handbook of Health Economics*, ed. J. P. Newhouse and A. J. Culyer, 1A:707–745. Amsterdam: Elsevier Science.

Gornick, M. E., P. W. Eggers, T. W. Reilly, et al. 1996. Effects of Race and Income on Mortality and Use of Services among Medicare Beneficiaries. *New England Journal of Medicine* 335 (11): 791–799.

Grabowski, D. C. 2001. Medicaid Reimbursement and the Quality of Nursing Home Care. *Journal of Health Economics* 20 (4): 549–569.

Gray, B. 2001. Do Medicaid Physician Fees for Prenatal Services Affect Birth Outcomes? *Journal of Health Economics* 20 (4): 571–590.

Gruber, J., K. Adams, and J. P. Newhouse. 1997. Physician Fee Policy and Medicaid Program Costs. *Journal of Human Resources* 32 (4): 611–634.

Gruber, J., J. Kim, and D. Mayzlin. 1999. Physician Fees and Procedure Intensity: The Case of Cesarean Delivery. *Journal of Health Economics* 18 (4): 473–490.

Gruber, J., and K. Simon. 2007. Crowd-Out 10 Years Later: Have Recent Public Insurance Expansions Crowded Out Private Health Insurance? National Bureau of Economics Research Working Paper, 201–217. Cambridge, MA: National Bureau of Economic Research.

Gruber, J., and A. Yelowitz. 1999. Public Health Insurance and Private Savings. *Journal of Political Economy* 107 (6): 1249–1274.

Hamilton, B. H., V. Ho, and D. P. Goldman. 2000. Queuing for Surgery: Is the U.S. or Canada Worse Off? *Review of Economics and Statistics* 82 (2): 297–308.

Hamm, J. C., and L. Shore-Sheppard. 2005. The Effect of Medicaid Expansions for Low-Income Children on Medicaid Participation and Private Insurance Coverage: Evidence from the SIPP. *Journal of Public Economics* 89 (1): 57–83.

Hoel, M. 2007. What Should (Public) Health Insurance Cover? *Journal of Health Economics* 26 (2): 251–262.

Hoffmeyer, U., and T. R. McCarthy. 1994. The Health Care System in Germany. In *Financing Health care*, ed. U. Hoffmeyer and T. R. McCarthy, 1:419–512. Dordrecht: Kluwer Academic..

Hsiao, W., P. Braun, D. L. Dunn, et al. 1992. An Overview of the Development and Refinement of the Resource-Based Relative Value Scale. *Medical Care Research and Review* 30 (11): NS1–NS12.

Huang, Y., and Y. Yang. 2009. Pharmaceutical Pricing in China. In *Prescribing Cultures and Pharmaceutical Policy in the Asia-Pacific*, ed. K. Eggleston. Washington, DC: Brookings Institution Press.

Hubbard, R. G., J. Skinner, and S. P. Zeldes. 1995. Precautionary Saving and Social Insurance. *Journal of Political Economy* 103 (2): 360–399.

Ikegami, N., and J. C. Campbell. 1995. Medical Care in Japan. *New England Journal of Medicine* 333 (19): 1295–1299.

Ikegami, N., and J. C. Campbell. 2004. Japan's Health Care System: Containing Costs and Attempting Reform. *Health Affairs* 23 (3): 26–37.

Jeong, H.-S. 2005. Health Care Reform and Change in Public-Private Mix of Financing: A Korean Case. *Health Policy (Amsterdam)* 74 (2): 133–145.

Kahn, K. L., E. B. Keeler, M. J. Sherwood, et al. 1990. Comparing Outcomes of Care Before and After Implementation of the DRG-Based Prospective Payment System. *Journal of the American Medical Association* 264 (15): 1984–1988.

Kim, H.-J., and J. P. Ruger. 2008. Pharmaceutical Reform in South Korea and the Lessons It Provides. *Health Affairs* 27 (4): w260–w269.

Ko, D. T., H. M. Krumholz, Y. Wang, et al. 2007. Regional Differences in Process of Care and Outcomes for Older Acute Myocardial Infarction Patients in the United States and Ontario, Canada. *Journal of the American Heart Association* 115 (2): 196–203.

Kwon, S. 2003. Payment System Reform for Health Care Providers in Korea. *Health Policy and Planning* 18 (1): 84–92.

Lee, M. C., and A. M. Jones. 2004. How Did Dentists Respond to the Introduction of Global Budgets in Taiwan? An Evaluation Using Individual Panel Data. *International Journal of Health Care Finance and Economics* 4 (4): 307–326.

Lee, S.-Y., C.-B. Chun, Y.-G. Lee, et al. 2008. The National Health Insurance System as One Type of New Typology: The Case of South Korea and Taiwan. *Health Policy (Amsterdam)* 85 (1): 105–113.

Lei, X., and W. Lin. 2009. The New Cooperative Medical Scheme in Rural China: Does More Coverage Mean More Service and Better Health? *Health Economics* 18:s25–s46.

Lu, J. R., and W. Hsiao. 2003. Does Universal Health Insurance Make Health Care Unaffordable? Lessons from Taiwan. *Health Affairs* 22 (3): 77–88.

McClellan, M. 1997. Hospital Reimbursement Incentives: An Empirical Analysis. *Journal of Economics & Management Strategy* 6 (1): 91–128.

McClellan, M., and J. Skinner. 2006. The Incidence of Medicare. *Journal of Public Economics* 90 (1–2): 257–276.

McCormack, L. A., and R. T. Burge. 1994. Diffusion of Medicare RBRVS and Related Physician-Payment Policies. *Health Care Financing Review* 16 (2): 159–173.

McKnight, R. 2007. Medicare Balance Billing Restrictions: Impacts on Physicians and Beneficiaries. *Journal of Health Economics* 26 (2): 326–341.

Moffitt, G. K., and M. Galloway. 1992. Patient Focused Care and Total Quality Management: A Marriage Made in Heaven. *Review (Patient Focused Care Association)* (Summer 1992): 2–6.

Newhouse, J. P., and A. D. Sinaiko. 2008. What We Know and Don't Know about the Effects of Cost Sharing on the Demand for Medical Care—And So What? In *Incentives and Choice in Health Care*, ed. F. A. Sloan and H. Kasper, 85–102. Cambridge, MA: MIT Press.

Newhouse, J. P., and the Insurance Experiment Group. 1993. *Free for All? Lessons from the RAND Health Insurance Experiment.* Cambridge, MA: Harvard University Press.

Norton, E. C. 1992. Incentive Regulation of Nursing Homes. *Journal of Health Economics* 11 (2): 105–128.

Nyman, J. A. 1999. The Value of Health Insurance: The Access Motive. *Journal of Health Economics* 18 (2): 141–152.

O'Donnell, O., E. van Doorslaer, R. P. Rannan-Eliya, et al. 2008. Who Pays for Health Care in Asia? *Journal of Health Economics* 27 (2): 460–475.

Ogura, S., T. Kadoda, and M. Kawamura. 2006. Removing the Instability and Inequality in the Japanese Health Insurance System. In *Health Care Issues in the United States and Japan*, ed. D. A. Wise and N. Yashiro, 83–112. Chicago: University of Chicago Press.

Organisation for Economic Co-operation and Development (OECD). 2008. OECD Health Data. http://www.who.int/whr/2008/en.

Peabody, J. W., S.-W. Lee, and S. R. Bickel. 1995. Health for All in the Republic of Korea: One Country's Experience with Implementing Universal Health Care. *Health Policy (Amsterdam)* 31 (1): 29–42.

Pfaff, M., and A. O. Kern. 2005. Public-Private Mix for Healthcare in Germany. In *The Public-Private Mix for Health*, ed. A. Maynard, 191–218. Oxford: Radcliffe Publishing.

Philipson, T. J., and G. S. Becker. 1998. Old-Age Longevity and Mortality-Contingent Claims. *Journal of Political Economy* 106 (3): 551–573.

Ramseyer, J. M. 2009. Universal Health Insurance and the Effect of Cost Containment on Mortality Rates: Strokes and Heart Attacks in Japan. *Journal of Empirical Legal Studies* 6 (2): 309–342.

Rapp, R. T., and K. Shibuya. 1994. The Health Care System in Japan. In *Financing Health Care*, ed. U. Hoffmeyer and T. R. McCarthy, 1:585–696. Dordrecht: Kluwer Academic..

Reinhardt, U. 2005. The Mix of Public and Private Payers in the US Health System. In *The Public-Private Mix for Health*, ed. A. Maynard, 83–116. Oxford: Radcliffe Publishing.

Reinhardt, U. E. 2007. Why Single-Payer Health Systems Spark Endless Debate. *British Medical Journal* 334 (7599): 881.

Roos, N. P., and C. A. Mustard. 1997. Variation in Health and Health Care Use by Socioeconomic Status in Winnipeg, Canada: Does the System Work? Yes and No. *Milbank Memorial Fund Quarterly: Health and Society* 75 (1): 89–111.

Rouleau, J. L., L. A. Moye, M. A. Pfeffer, et al. 1993. A Comparison of Management Patterns after Acute Myocardial Infarction in Canada and the United States. *New England Journal of Medicine* 328 (11): 779–784.

Schulenburg, J. M. 1994. The German Health-Care System at the Crossroads. *Health Economics* 3 (5): 301–303.

Shleifer, A. 1985. A Theory of Yardstick Competition. *RAND Journal of Economics* 16 (3): 319–327.

Silverman, E., and J. Skinner. 2004. Medicare Upcoding and Hospital Ownership. *Health Economics* 23 (2): 369–389.

Sloan, F. A., M. A. Morrisey, and J. Valvona. 1988a. Effects of the Medicare Prospective Payment System on Hospital Cost Containment: An Early Appraisal. *Milbank Quarterly* 66 (2): 191–220.

Sloan, F. A., M. A. Morrisey, and J. Valvona. 1988b. Medicare Prospective Payment and the Use of Medical Technologies in Hospitals. *Medical Care* 26 (9): 837–853.

Swami, B. 2002. The German Health Care System. In *Handbook of International Health Care Systems*, ed. K. V. Thai, E. T. Wimberley, and S. M. McManus, 333–358. New York: Marcel Dekker.

Taiwan Department of Health. 2008. Statistics of General Health. http://www.doh.tw.

Tamm, M., H. Tauchmann, J. Wasem, et al. 2007. Elasticities of Market Shares and Social Health Insurance Choice in Germany: A Dynamic Panel Data Approach. *Health Economics* 16 (3): 243–256.

Tsuda, T., H. Aoyama, and J. Froom. 1994. Primary Health Care in Japan and the United States. *Social Science & Medicine* 38 (4): 489–495.

US Census Bureau. 2011. The 2011 Statistical Abstract: Tables 142 and 147. http://www.census.gov/prod/2011pubs/11statab/health.pdf.

Wagstaff, A. 2007. Health Systems in East Asia: What Can Developing Countries Learn from Japan and the Asian Tigers? *Health Economics* 16 (5): 441–456.

Wagstaff, A., and M. Lindelow. 2008. Can Insurance Increase Financial Risk? The Curious Case of Health Insurance in China. *Journal of Health Economics* 27:990–1005.

Wagstaff, A., M. Lindelow, G. Jun, et al. 2009. Extending Health Insurance to the Rural Population: An Impact Evaluation of China's New Cooperative Medical Scheme. *Journal of Health Economics* 28:1–19.

World Bank Group. 2009. World Development Indicators. http://data.worldbank.org/indicator.

World Health Organzation (WHO). 2006. World Health Report 2006.

Wörz, M., and R. Busse. 2005. Analysing the Impact of Health-Care System Change in the EU Member States: Germany. *Health Economics* 14 (S1): 133–149.

Yajima, R., and K. Takayanagi. 2002. The Japanese Health Care System: Citizen Complaints and Citizen Possibilities. In *Handbook of International Health Care Systems*, ed. K. V. Thai, E. T. Wimberley and S. M. McManus, 457–486. New York: Marcel Dekker.

Yang, B., E.-Y. Bae, and J. Kim. 2008. Economic Evaluation and Pharmaceutical Reimbursement Reform in South Korea's National Health Insurace. *Health Affairs* 27 (1): 179–187.

Yashiro, N., R. Suzuki, and W. Suzuki. 2006. Evaluating Japan's Health Care Reform of the 1990s and Its Efforts to Cope with Population Aging. In *Health Care Issues in the United States and Japan*, ed. D. A. Wise and N. Yashiro, 17–42. Chicago: University of Chicago Press.

Yelowitz, A. 1995. The Medicaid Notch, Labor Supply, and Welfare Participation: Evidence from Eligibility Expansions. *Quarterly Journal of Economics* 110 (4): 909–939.

Yoshikawa, A., and J. Bhattacharya. 2002. Japan. In *World Health Systems: Challenges and Perspectives*, ed. B. Fried and L. Gaydos. Chicago: Health Administration Press.

Zweifel, P., and F. Breyer. 1997. *Health Economics*. Oxford: Oxford University Press.

CHAPTER 13

PUBLIC SUPPLY AND FINANCING

Many countries have neither private financing nor social insurance. Rather, there is direct provision of health care services through public clinics and hospitals. This system is found in some high-income countries, including the United Kingdom, Denmark, Norway, Australia, and New Zealand, and it predominates (or has predominated) in some developing countries, such as China in the period immediately following the communist revolution (see chapter 11).

An overriding question concerns the rationale for such systems. Since our subject is health economics, our particular focus is on the economic rationale for such systems. Further, we want to know how direct provision and financing compares with the other systems described in the two previous chapters, in terms of both efficiency and equity.

In these public delivery systems, governments play particularly important roles in resource allocation in the health sector, and face certain issues. First, how much money should be allocated to health care in the aggregate? Second, how should these resources be allocated geographically—by demographic group, such as provision for children or the elderly, or by type of care, such as preventive, curative, or palliative care? (Palliative care is designed to relieve pain and suffering among persons with a low life expectancy.) Third, how should providers, such as physicians, be paid? This becomes an issue when care is provided by public organizations. Otherwise, such decisions are left to the private sector. Fourth, should private supplementation of government payment for personal health care services be permitted, and if so, under what circumstances should such supplementation be permitted or encouraged?

This chapter first discusses the rationale for public provision. We then investigate public provision in practice, including the National Health Service in the United Kingdom and Australia. We also present the theoretical rationale and empirical evidence on rationing of health care services by queues, or non-price rationing, rather than rationing by price. Since many low-income countries rely on the public provision of personal health care services, we provide an overview of the evidence on the performance of public provision of these services in such countries. Finally, we evaluate and compare health systems with different supply and financing arrangements as a conclusion to Part III.

13.1 The Rationale for Public Provision of Health Care

The Role of Transaction Costs

Under public provision, major providers of health care, such as hospitals, are owned and operated by the government. Governments worldwide face a choice that they make actively or passively just as a matter of historical fact: when should a government provide health care services directly or "in-house," and when should health care services be provided privately by contract or some other arrangement? Even if the system is public by accident of history, the question of whether or not historical arrangements should be retained or an alternative system selected is a highly relevant and important one. Further, an alternative is to retain public provision but allow private provision as well, or institute cost sharing as a financing mechanism to supplement tax-based financing.

A lesson from economics is that a country's choice of ownership form should reflect the relative transaction costs of different forms of ownership. Transaction costs are administrative costs incurred to achieve societal objectives. For example, if the objective is to avoid corruption and ensure that funds are used for their intended purposes, what is the relative cost of achieving this objective when health facilities are under different forms of ownership? Transaction costs are also involved when governments institute various forms of regulatory oversight to ensure that protections are consistent in the societal objectives, such as the provision of care to disadvantaged populations.

In some areas, market size is insufficient to support more than one firm. Governments often regulate the prices of such "natural monopolists" (Breyer 1982; Joskow 2007). However, it may be more costly for a government to regulate a private seller than to own the firm and provide output directly. If the objective is to promote innovation, what is the administrative cost of structuring adequate incentives under different ownership forms? For example, by owning the firm, the government would gain insider knowledge about company operations.

If an important social objective is to promote access to care, how do the alternative ownership forms compare in terms of the resources needed to accomplish this objective? Perhaps it is easier to be sure that the facilities actually are located in geographically remote areas of a country if they are publicly owned and operated. In countries with a high proportion of illiterate or otherwise not well-educated persons, direct public provision may be more efficient than private provision financed by private or public insurance, in part because public provision of care tends to eliminate the paperwork required for obtaining reimbursement.

By contrast, providing incentives to promote innovation may be more difficult under public than under private ownership. There may be important trade-offs, with some ownership forms being more efficient in achieving some objectives and other forms being more efficient in achieving other objectives. In the end, public policy makers need to weigh the relative important of various, sometimes conflicting, objectives.

Further, some forms may be more efficient than others when there are noncontractible outputs. Achieving socially desirable outcomes when there are noncontractible outputs may require greater resource allocations for monitoring with some ownership forms than with others. When consumers are unable to adequately gauge some aspects of quality of care, there is concern that for-profit hospitals may require greater external scrutiny than other organizational forms. Achieving an adequate supply of facilities in geographically remote areas of a country may be easier if the facilities are government-owned and can be placed in such areas by the government than if the government must provide incentives for private organizations to locate there.

NONCONTRACTIBLE OUTCOMES REVISITED

The choice of public versus private provision is an old question in economics, but the answers economists give, as well as the rationale for their answers, have changed somewhat over time. Traditionally, economists and many others have often favored the for-profit organizational form over government-owned and government-operated facilities on the grounds of relative efficiency. Because for-profit organizations have well-defined residual claimants, the shareholders, a dollar realized in savings from greater efficiency is an added dollar that goes to shareholders.

By contrast, when government is the owner of an enterprise, the residual claimant is not as well defined. Millions of citizens are taxpayers, and the return from savings from efficiency gains to individual taxpayers is so small as to go unnoticed and insufficient to activate the individual citizen/voter/taxpayer to devote personal resources to ferret out inefficiency.

Or the enterprise may serve the objectives of politicians rather than maximize efficiency, which would yield higher returns to shareholders if the enterprise were privately owned. One key objective of politicians is employment since employed persons represent major voting blocks (see, e.g., Boycko, Shleifer, and Vishny 1996). One reason why public enterprises may be inefficient is that they often institute work rules and protect seniority to a greater extent than can be justified on efficiency grounds. Happy and content workers may be more industrious, but only up to a point. The notion that for-profit enterprises are more efficient than public enterprises has had a broad following among economists and others more generally. There is some empirical support for this view (see, e.g., Peltzman 1971; Megginson and Netter 2001).

The fall of communism in the Soviet Union and Eastern European countries, which led to large-scale privatization of public enterprises, has provided many natural experiments for empirical assessments of the relative efficiency of private and public enterprises. These natural experiments have the advantage of offering the possibility of pre- versus post-conversion to for-profit status comparisons of efficiency changes. The evidence from these studies is nuanced. There is no overall conclusion. Rather, relative efficiency depends on important details.

Frydman, Gray, Hessel, et al. (1999), who studied the privatization of enterprises in the Czech Republic, Hungary, and Poland, found that privatization to outsider owners but not to insiders led to improvements in the enterprises' performance—more so in terms of revenue enhancement than in terms of cost reduction. Insiders, as owners, are likely to pursue other objectives, such as employment maintenance, which does not generally lead to higher efficiency and profitability. Frydman and coauthors' finding of no effect of privatization on efficiency but an improvement in revenue generation is supported by a comparison of private not-for-profit and public hospitals in Uganda. Ssengooba, Atuyambe, McPake, et al. (2002) found no clear differences in efficiency between the two ownership types, but private not-for-profit hospitals were more successful in generating revenue.

In addition, legal protections for investors in enterprises are important factors in ensuring that company managers have a clear incentive to serve outside owners, and the strength of such legal protections varies appreciably among countries (Shleifer and Vishny 1997). The impact of privatization on efficiency seems to be greater when the product market in which the establishment is being privatized is competitive.

The case for privatization is less compelling in markets for public goods and when natural monopolies are involved (Megginson and Netter 2001, 329–330). Proponents of government ownership point to imperfections in markets and argue that in some sectors, firms should seek other objectives than to maximize profit.

Advances in the theories of ownership and contracting have shed new light on the question of public versus private supply. From the perspective of contracting, there is, at least in principle, no difference between public and private provision of goods and services if a public official can sign a complete contract with public employees or a private supplier. Such a complete contract specifies key attributes of the quality of services to be delivered by the public agency or private supplier. However, in the context of health care, it is likely to be impossible to specify all pertinent attributes in a contract with a private supplier. The government agency cannot fully anticipate, describe, stipulate, regulate, and enforce exactly what it wants in advance (Shleifer 1998). Health care quality is difficult to specify in advance because so many contingencies are involved. For example, given heterogeneity among patients, such as differences in illness severity, providers should optimally devote varying amounts of time and effort to their care. Yet as a practical matter, it is impossible to develop a sufficiently detailed payment formula that could adequately account for such variation in time and effort. As a result, a profit-seeking organization may not be inclined to care for complex cases for which payment is judged to be inadequate.

When contracts are incomplete in that important attributes of output cannot be fully specified by contract, the provider's ownership form matters a great deal because private ownership and public ownership are fundamentally different in the allocation of residual control rights, which in turn affects suppliers' incentives for cost reduction and quality improvement (Hart, Shleifer, and Vishny 1997). We employ Hart and coauthors' framework to explain how ownership form affects incentives for innovation and under which conditions public provision is superior to private supply.

At the risk of oversimplication, but to highlight some analytic points, assume that a provider of services can engage in two types of innovation: one is innovation to improve quality of care, the other is innovation to reduce cost. Neither type of innovation is contractible ex ante. Although the government and the provider can specify some attributes of output in advance, many contingencies are difficult to anticipate and cast in sufficiently detailed contract terms. In particular, a cost reduction may increase profit but may not be easily monitored by consumers or public policy makers.

Specifically, private suppliers, especially when organized as for-profit organizations, have residual control rights over the asset, and hence have an incentive to adopt innovations that cut cost. Also, their incentive to engage in cost reduction is strong because they ignore the adverse effects of cost reductions on noncontractible quality. In contrast, the suppliers' incentive to engage in quality improvement is not as strong as is the incentive for cost reduction because they must renegotiate with the government for a higher price if they want to improve quality. As a consequence, compared to the efficient outcome of complete contracting, cost reduction is inefficiently high and quality improvement efforts are inefficiently low under private ownership.

By contrast, a manager of a public enterprise must obtain approval from a government agency for both quality and cost innovation because he or she does not have the residual control rights over the asset. In addition, other public employees can replace the person to whom the public supplier reports. On the one hand, both of the above two factors weaken incentives for cost reduction and quality improvement. On the other hand, public managers have no reason to favor cost cutting by reducing quality.

Hart, Shleifer, and Vishny (1997) argue that public provision is most likely to be superior to private provision under two circumstances. The first circumstance arises when the adverse effect of cost reduction on noncontractible quality is sufficiently large as to fully offset the value of cost savings achievable under private ownership. If so, public provision is socially efficient because it provides weak incentives for cost reduction. In the second circumstance, ongoing innovation is not a major contributor to quality improvement or public employees do not have weaker incentives to make innovations that improve quality. In either case, public provision may be preferred.

The above conclusion is based on a framework in which incomplete contracts predominate, and whether or not incomplete contracts have the consequences predicted by the Hart, Shleifer, and Vishny framework in a health care context is ultimately an empirical question. In health care, gains from quality innovation are large (see chapters 9 and 16), but quality can deteriorate if cost is reduced.

Therefore, neither public nor private provision can be said to be generally preferred. This depends on whether or not the government can prevent quality deterioration from cost cutting through various efforts, such as by writing sufficiently detailed contracts and/or by effectively regulating and monitoring quality of private firms (Cutler 2002). If the government can write a contract that gives the private supplier appropriate incentives or penalizes the firm for shirking on quality of care, and if the results can be adequately monitored, private provision may be superior to public provision. In contrast, if the noncontractible deterioration of quality results in substantial welfare loss, public provision may be superior to private provision. Whether or not countries are motivated by the reasoning of Hart, Shleifer, and Vishny (1997), in fact, in many countries, public provision is the dominant delivery approach in the health care sector.

The Medicaid program in the US state of California provides an example of a public program switching from public control over financing to contracting public services out to the private sector. Under the old system, the state Medicaid program paid physicians directly on a fee-for-service basis. Although most of the physicians practiced in the private sector, the issue we focus on here is the contracting-out feature. The advocates of contracting out argued that private firms are more efficient, both in their operations and in offering services that Medicaid recipients prefer. Opponents of contracting out contended that private firms lower noncontractible quality and avoid unprofitable patients—undesirable behavior that is hard to monitor through contracting. Duggan's (2004) empirical analysis of this change revealed that the switch from fee-for-service to managed care resulted in higher government spending but no corresponding improvement in infant health outcomes. Presumably the cause was not so much the incentives of managed care but rather the difficulty Medicaid had in monitoring the decisions of private parties.

Redistributive Concerns

While pure efficiency concerns, that is, that quality-adjusted price will be higher under private provision, given noncontractible quality, provide one rationale for public provision, redistributive concerns also play an important role in the choice between private and public provision. One reason why efficiency and equity are related is that some organizational forms may be more efficient in achieving a country's equity goals.

Because personal health care services are one of the important inputs into the production of good health, access to health care, like access to education, has been mostly if not universally regarded as a basic right (Besley and Gouveia 1994; Poterba 1996; Hurley 2000). The norm of universal access emphasizes that everyone in society should have the same opportunity to receive at least a certain minimal level of health care. This norm is rooted in the concept of "specific egalitarianism," which holds that societies attach special importance to limiting the domain of inequality in certain areas, such as health care (Tobin 1970). This view implies that access to health care should not be conditioned on the basis of ability to pay (e.g., on a person's income).

Although equal access to personal health care services is widely regarded as an important social objective, there is little agreement among countries as to how best to achieve it. However, there is a general consensus that some form of government intervention in health care is inevitable because market forces, absent some government intervention, are likely to fail to provide even minimally adequate levels of care to the poor. Some have argued that altruistic affluent persons can voluntarily give to less affluent persons, but this argument is not widely shared globally and certainly falls far short of constituting a consensus.

Among the possibilities for government interventions are price subsidies, public mandates for private provision, and direct government provision. Compared to price subsidies and mandates, public provision has the advantage that it gives government greater control over the nature of the services individuals receive (Poterba 1996).

Usher (1977) developed the notion of "socialization of commodities" to explain why public provision is chosen as an instrument to achieve the norm of universal access. He defined socialization as a process in which the government appropriates the entire supply of a commodity, such as health care services, and then redistributes that commodity among all of its citizens, equally or according to nonpecuniary criteria. His model assumes the following: (1) the principal motive for socialization is to reduce income inequality; (2) whether or not a commodity is socialized or not is made by majority rule; and (3) the government uses proportional or progressive income taxation to finance the socialization of a commodity. In this framework, the poorer half of the community receives a net gain from socialization because it pays less in taxes than the per capita cost of government acquisition of the socialized commodity. In contrast, affluent individuals are the losers because they pay more in taxes than they benefit from socialization. However, the gainers can outvote the losers in a society in which the distribution of income is highly unequal in favor of the rich.

Usher's model yields the prediction that a commodity is more likely to be socialized in a community with a greater degree of income inequality and less diversity in individuals' tastes for the commodity. The level of public provision is set at the level favored by the median voter. Furthermore, the level of public provision depends on the structure of the tax system because the structure affects the tax price of public provision. Countries with a more progressive tax structure, such as a personal income tax, will be more reliant on public provision.

The socialization of commodities through public provision imposes a redistribution of welfare from higher- to lower-income persons because tax payments increase with personal income but the benefit received from public provision is independent of such income.

The public provision of personal health care services redistributes income in two ways (Besley and Gouveia 1994). First, there is an implicit income transfer from the healthy to the sick. This is because the tax payments used to finance the public provision of health care do not depend on the individual's health status, except to the extent that poor health reduces earnings, which in turn reduces tax payments. By contrast, private health insurance premiums may be experience-rated in the sense that higher-morbidity individuals pay more for the same insurance policy (see chapter 10).

Second, there is an implicit income transfer from affluent to indigent individuals. Under public provision, the government typically provides personal health care services uniformly to all individuals and finances its purchases out of general tax revenues. Income is redistributed if tax payments increase with income. Under a flat tax regime, the tax rate does not change with income; the rate is set as a fixed proportion of earnings or income. But tax payments do vary with earnings or income.

Although the public provision of health care has several potential advantages, including a potential advantage in achieving equal access through income redistribution, one important disadvantage is that it tends to be less responsive than private provision in recognizing heterogeneity among individuals. Countries with public provision tend to provide relatively uniform personal health care services to their citizens.

Two types of heterogeneity among individuals may result in a difference between public supply and private demand for care. First, people are heterogeneous in their personal incomes. More affluent individuals are likely to demand a higher quality of care than the poor do. Thus, the quality level of government-supplied personal health care services determined by the median voter may fall short of the level of quality demanded by more affluent persons. Second, individuals may differ in their risk preferences (see chapter 4). For example, risk-averse persons are likely to prefer complete coverage with little or no cost sharing. More risk-tolerant individuals would probably rather have more cost sharing for health care services and have more resources available for the consumption of other goods and services.

Individuals with wants that are unmet by the public system may opt out of this system if they are unable to consume services simultaneously in both the public and the private sectors. The timing of treatment is an important dimension of quality of health care. Public systems tend to use waiting time, such as waiting time to undergo a surgical procedure, and waiting time in the physician's office or clinic before being seen by a physician, as instruments for rationing personal health care services (see the discussion of waiting periods in Canada in chapter 12).

In contrast, the private sector can provide treatment more quickly, but at a higher out-of-pocket price. Thus, individuals seeking to reduce waiting time may choose to opt out the public system and receive care from private sources. In such cases, private supply is substituted for public provision.

Rather than private supply substituting for public provision, individuals may use privately supplied care to complement care received from public sources. In this type of situation, individuals increase the quantity of health care they consume through purchases from private suppliers. For example, individuals may purchase supplemental health insurance to pay for services not covered by the public health system (see chapter 12), such as dental care, or to pay the difference between fees charged to patients and the regulated price paid by the public sector when providers can balance a bill.

There are pros and cons to allowing private supply to coexist with a system of public provision (Besley and Gouveia 1994; Propper and Green 2001). On the one hand, opting out of public services that are available at low or no out-of-pocket cost in favor of privately provided services that the user must purchase while at the same time losing the publicly subsidized service, and supplementation (i.e., the use of privately provided services in addition to services available from the public sector) may result in a more efficient outcome because individuals who opt out or purchase supplemental health insurance are better off and others who do not make such choices are not made worse off. This is not a preferred outcome, however, if disparities in the use of services themselves generate negative externalities. Some persons may view a two-tier health care option, public provision for some and public-private or purely private for others, as inherently unfair.

From another perspective, under public provision with a fixed budget (a budget that does not strictly depend on the number of persons served), individuals remaining in the public sector tend to benefit from the opting out of others because opting out increases the per capita resources for those who remain in the public system, which in turn helps improve such their access to care in the public sector. A less congested system may lead to improvements in quality of care as well.

However, the combination of private supply and public provision can have several adverse consequences on access and quality of care. First, allowing individuals to opt out of the public system or to purchase supplemental health insurance creates a multi-tiered health system, which may be widely viewed as inequitable. Second, a private sector coexisting with the public one can create several negative externalities in respect to the quantity and quality of personal health care services provided by the public sector. Physicians employed by the public sector may be able to moonlight. They may work for the public clinic in the morning and see private patients in the afternoon. Some physicians may refer public patients during the hours they work for the public sector to their private practices or shirk on quality of care provided to their public patients (Chaudhury, Hammer, Kremer, et al. 2006; Biglaiser and Ma 2007). In addition, the private and public sectors may compete for scarce resources of health personnel. The public sector may be at a disadvantage in such competition, which in turn may lead to deterioration in patient access to high-quality personal health care services provided by a public system.

13.2 Public Provision in High-Income Countries in Practice

The United Kingdom's National Health Service

Overview

Probably the best-known example of the public provision of personal health care services is the National Health Services (NHS) of the United Kingdom, which was established in 1948. The principal source of finance for the NHS is general tax revenues, which accounts for near three-fourths of NHS funds (Aaron and Schwartz 2005). Earmarked compulsory contributions by individuals and their employers are a secondary source of revenue, accounting for 20 percent of NHS funds. User charges apply to a limited number of services, such as prescription drugs and dental care. Various population groups, such as children, the elderly and disabled, and people with low incomes, are exempted from these user charges. User charges represent only 2 percent of NHS revenues. The money price of personal health care is generally zero at the point of service.

Although the NHS provides free care or nearly free care to UK citizens, individuals are not free to choose their providers. Rather, the government uses the general practitioner (GP) as a gatekeeper to direct the flow of patients in accessing health care.

The first decision individuals make is to choose a GP through patient registration (Scott and Vick 1999). The GP provides all primary care at no charge to the patient. Patients cannot switch to other GPs unless they formally switch their registrations. Nor can they visit a physician for free specialty care unless they obtain a referral from their GP. Patients cannot self-refer to an NHS surgeon or hospital. Rather, they must be referred by their GP. On seeing a patient, a hospital surgeon or consultant may recommend surgery or inpatient treatment, and if such care is recommended, the patient is placed on the NHS waiting list. At this stage, the patient makes his or her second decision; whether to join the NHS waiting list or to opt out the public system and purchase care from a private source (Martin and Smith 1999).

The NHS is organized by region. Regional health authorities receive funds and administer the provision of health services through three distinct government channels: (1) primary care physicians (GPs); (2) hospital and other institutional care; and (3) nonhospital community care. GPs are government employees and are paid on a capitation basis—that is, based on the number of persons enrolled in their practices—a fee that covers only the cost of primary care. Most hospitals in the UK are public. All specialists are employed on a salaried basis.

Rationing by Queues Rather Than by Prices

Economics teaches that resources are scarce but wants are unlimited. Thus, some form of rationing needed and inevitable for allocating scarce resources. The pejorative term "rationing" when used in the context of health care has no meaning in economics. Rationing will inevitably take place. The only question is how it is to be done.

Rationing is generally accomplished through the price mechanism. However, when price is controlled or there is no market price, non-price rationing devices allocate scarce resources.

The waiting line and the waiting list constitute two common non-price rationing mechanisms (Martin and Smith 1999). However, the two mechanisms affect waiting cost differently. When waiting in line, individuals join a physical queue and wait for receipt of a good (e.g., bread, as in wartime) or service (e.g., students waiting in tents for tickets to sports events, medical care). With this form of rationing, the time price is the opportunity cost of waiting in line (see chapter 3). Although some persons may derive pleasure from waiting in line, in analyzing such queuing, economists typically assume that waiting is not pleasurable and involves an opportunity cost of time. In contrast, being on a waiting list does not require that individuals queue in person. Rather, individuals are placed on a list to wait to receive a good or service.

Such waiting imposes three types of costs. First, there is a loss of the utility of consumption if the value of a good or service to be received declines with time (Lindsay and Feigenbaum 1984). A surgical procedure may be less effective if postponed. Second, since being on a waiting list may prolong time in poorer health and may lessen the likelihood of a full recovery, there is a loss in utility for this reason as well (Propper 1995). Third, there is the cost of not being as productive for a period because of the delay in receipt of care.

Waiting in line, or more realistically in this context, waiting in a chair in a physician's office or clinic to see a physician, wastes a scarce resource—an individual's time. Since there is no social benefit from waiting in line (again assuming people do not enjoy being in a queue), only a cost, there is a welfare loss from waiting in line.

Yet from the standpoint of equity, such rationing by the queue may be advantageous. People with low time prices bear a lower cost of waiting and are less likely to drop out of the queue than are more affluent persons. This results in a redistribution of goods and services to the poor. There may be more efficient mechanisms for accomplishing this objective, and from society's standpoint, waiting lines impose a welfare cost.

Nevertheless, the (somewhat) silver lining is that the queue, especially waiting time in the physician's office or clinic, tends to redistribute health care use by income. Queues reduce relative utilization by the affluent.

Waiting lists for appointments or for procedures are probably a more important form of non-price rationing than is physical waiting in a physician's office or clinic. Specifically, patients with chronic or nonemergency conditions cannot obtain inpatient or surgical treatment immediately. Rather, they must join a waiting list for hospital admission or elective surgery. Cases in which people wait to be seen by an NHS health care provider are well documented. In some cases, people either eventually give up waiting or obtain services from private sources. There are consequently savings in public budgets. However, despite such savings, whether or not the public is better off is questionable because the other costs of waiting must be considered. Other countries in which waiting lists are also widely used include the Scandinavian countries.

Non-price Rationing: Pros and Cons

Before examining the empirical evidence from the NHS on waiting lists, we discuss some conceptual issues related to such lists. Using waiting lists as a mechanism for resource allocation imposes both social costs and benefits. On the one hand, increasing waiting time can reduce pressures on budgets to expand the capacity of public health systems. Also, lower-priority services presumably are assigned a lower priority in the queue. While patient waits in hospital emergency rooms are well publicized, presumably the real emergencies are given highest priority. On the other hand, increasing waiting time may reduce the benefits from treatment as the value of medical treatment often decreases with delay to treatment. Therefore, governments with publicly financed and operated health systems face a trade-off between increasing treatment benefits for their citizens and controlling the size of government health care budgets and being able to prioritize persons with respect to their potential benefits from treatment. Of course, prioritization has a value only if it is done accurately. In the real world, there may be a tendency to overstate the need for treatment as a way to gain a higher position in the queue.

In economics, the standard solution to a policy trade-off, such as the length of waiting lists, is to seek an optimal balance between marginal social cost and marginal social benefit. Thus, the waiting list issue can be viewed as a decision about the optimal timing of medical treatment (Cullis, Jones, and Propper 2000). Figure 13.1 illustrates how a social planner who seeks to maximize societal well-being decides on the socially optimal length of the waiting list. When we speak of social welfare losses from queuing, more precisely only queuing in excess of the socially optimal queue length generates a social welfare loss. Some queuing may be efficient.

The horizontal line represents the length of the waiting list, the number of persons on the list. For simplicity, we assume there is a linear relationship between the length of time that a person needs to wait to obtain nonemergency care and the length of waiting list. The upper part of figure 13.1 shows the relationship between the length of the waiting list and total health care cost and benefit, both expressed in terms of per capita population. The total cost (TC) curve is downward sloping and the slope diminishes (in absolute terms) with time to service, suggesting that the total cost of providing health care to the representative patient decreases with waiting time, and the change in total cost as waiting time increases also decreases with waiting time. The total cost of public provision under a regime of no waiting time (the intersection of TC and the vertical line) exceeds TC with some waiting time. This is so because the government must expand the capacity of government health care system, such as increasing the number of hospital beds, physicians, nurses, and other health personnel employed and other operating costs, such as electricity, if the public system is to accommodate all demand immediately. If the government does not accommodate all demand, the total cost of public provision may be expected to be proportionately lower.

Thus, the benefit of increasing waiting time is the reduction in total cost of public provision as the length of the waiting list increases. Geometrically, marginal benefit is the slope of the TC curve. Since the slope of the TC curve decreases with the number of persons on the waiting list, the marginal benefit of using the waiting list as a rationing device also decreases with the length of the list, as seen in the lower part of figure 13.1.

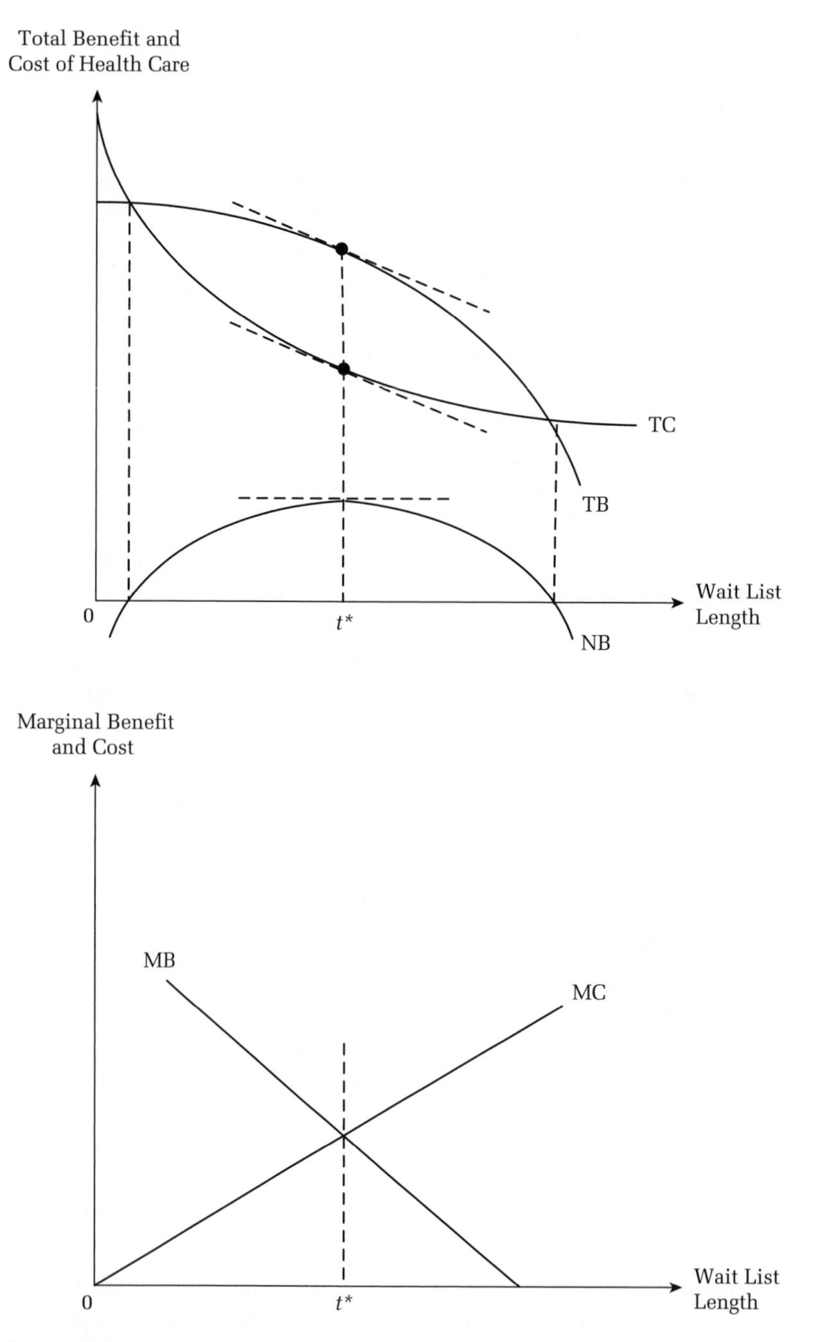

Figure 13.1
Determination of Optimal Waiting List Length

Similarly, the total benefit (TB) curve shows the relationship between the total benefit received from treatment and waiting list length. The slope of the TB curve is also negative, suggesting that treatment benefit is higher if delay to treatment is shorter. The change in treatment benefit with respect to waiting time to treatment is a rate of decay, which indicates a loss in treatment benefit as people wait longer for such care. This rate of decay measures the cost of using the waiting list as a rationing device. Also, the slope of the TB curve increases as time to treatment lengthens.

The net benefit (NB) curve is the difference between TB and TC. Suppose that the government is a perfect agent for its citizens. Government officials do not pursue their self-interests or their self-interests perfectly coincide with the country's citizens. Then they would pick the socially optimal length of the waiting list by maximizing net benefit. This is equivalent to determining optimal waiting time by equating marginal cost and marginal benefit, t^* in figure 13.1.

Using the analytic framework depicted by figure 13.1, one can see how the optimal waiting list length varies by type of disease. Suppose that the total cost does not vary by disease type. But there is considerable variation among diseases in total benefit of treatment and the decay rate of benefit. For some diseases, treatment benefit is high as is the decay rate of benefit; that is, the benefit of treatment falls and disappears rapidly if there is a delay in treatment, TB_1 in figure 13.2. Then a short time to treatment is socially optimal (t_S). For other diseases, the total benefit of treatment is not much affected by how long patients wait for the procedure, TB_2 in figure 13.2. In the latter case, a long wait (t_L) is likely to be optimal. Thus, the socially optimal waiting time for each disease depends on the decay rate in treatment benefit. A higher decay rate in treatment benefit implies a shorter waiting time to treatment.

The theory is useful for thinking about optimal waiting list lengths and recognizing that the socially optimal waiting list length is unlikely to be zero. But what does the empirical evidence say? Siciliani, Stanciole, and Jacobs (2009) estimated the elasticity of hospital cost with respect to the length of waiting lists using NHS hospital data for 1998–2002. They obtained mixed results on this relationship. If there is a negative relationship, it mainly occurs at a low level of waiting list length, below 10 days. This research is important but not necessarily definitive, being based on a sample of 137 hospitals observed over a relatively short time period.

While economists like to think in terms of socially optimal values, more realistically, government officials act, at least in part, in their own self-interest, which leads to an agency problem in setting the optimal length of time to treatment. To the extent that such officials do not fully internalize the marginal cost of waiting time for the representative patient and instead pursue bragging rights of having cut public budgets or other strategies that serve their own interests, these officials may select waiting times greater than socially optimal waiting times. For example,

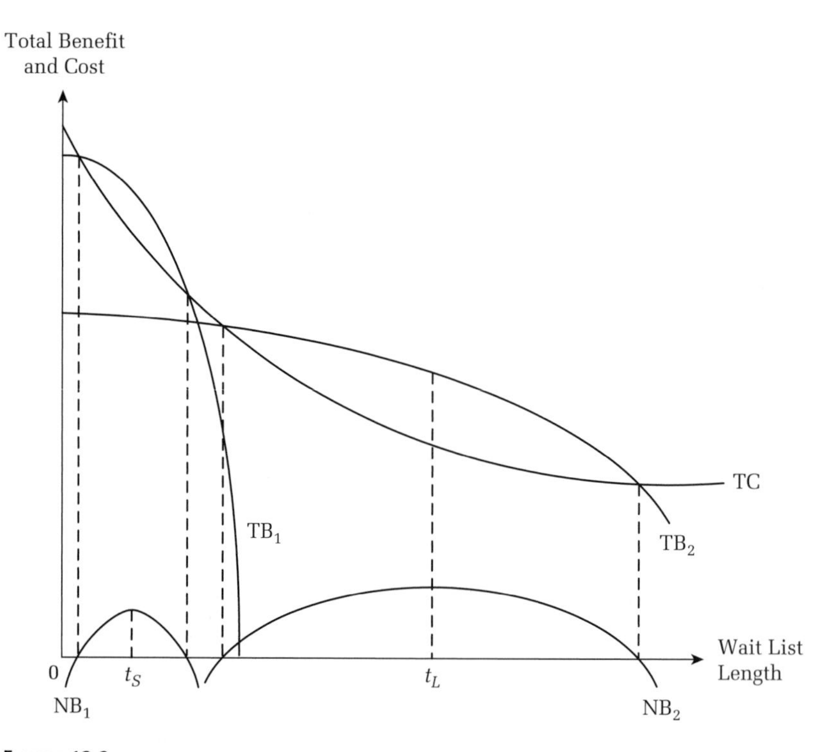

FIGURE 13.2
Short Optimal Waiting List versus Long Optimal Waiting List Length

hospital administrators may prefer to maintain a long waiting list to increase their bargaining power for a higher hospital budget in the next period. Similarly, physicians may receive monetary and nonmonetary benefits from maintaining a long waiting list. Such delays may increase their income by increasing demand for their services in their private practices, or may enable them to select patients with more medically interesting diagnoses (Iversen 1993, 1997; Cullis, Jones, and Propper 2000). In the imperfect agent case, the behavior of various public decision makers and suppliers of care, as well as the availability of private supply, becomes an important determinant of waiting time to care.

Iversen (1993) used a political bargaining process framework to show that how the government and the hospital interact in the budget allocation process affects the length of time to treatment. In his model, data on waiting times to treatment form an important part of the information base used by government to allocate public budgets for health care. In a variant of the model in which the budget decision is sequential, the hospital chooses a wait that maximizes its utility and is compatible with the government's reaction function; the government's reaction function is based on the hospital's choice of waiting time. When the hospital acts as the leader and the government acts as the follower, the hospital has an incentive to maintain long waiting times if the government's willingness to pay the hospital increases with increases in waiting times to treatment. This conclusion holds for treatments for which the decay rate in treatment benefit is relatively small. Then the hospital is incentivized to maintain long waiting lists to maintain an optimal budget because waiting time has a positive influence on the hospital's budget. Iversen (1997) showed that a higher capacity of the private health care sector results in a longer waiting time to treatment in the public sector if physicians who work in the public sector also work part-time in the private sector.

EMPIRICAL EVIDENCE ON THE COSTS OF WAITING LISTS

Using the waiting list as non-price rationing device imposes several costs on individual patients who seek care, as well as on society as a whole. Several empirical studies have estimated the costs of waiting lists. Since there is no market for the transaction of waiting times among individuals who are on waiting lists, revealed preference measures of willingness to pay for shorter waits are not available. Researchers, however, have used two indirect approaches to measure the cost of waiting lists. The first method estimates the cost of waiting lists from observed behavior in the private health care market. The second method uses contingent valuation ("stated preference" approach; see chapter 15) to elicit the cost of waiting lists (Cullis, Jones, and Propper 2000). As explained in chapter 15, the contingent valuation method relies on survey data that elicit individuals' maximum willingness to pay for a particular good or service.

Cullis and Jones (1986) employed the first approach to estimate the costs of waiting by assuming that the only cost to waiting arises because health care received later is worth less. They ignored the cost to waiting arising from the disutility of waiting per se. In the UK health care system, individuals desiring care choose between two alternatives: wait on a list for treatment in the public sector or "opt out" of the public sector and use the private sector, where the waiting time is about zero. The authors argued that the maximum cost of waiting is equal to the price of seeking treatment in the private sector (p) because the individual will select the private sector if the cost of waiting exceeds the price of private health care. If the cost of waiting is less than the private price, the individual will eschew private care and will wait for care at an NHS facility. The minimum cost of waiting is zero if the decay rate of delay in treatment is zero.

The above analysis implies that the cost of waiting ranges between p and 0, which in turn implies that the average value of the waiting cost for a representative patient is $p/2$, assuming a random distribution of patients. Cullis and Jones (1986) calculated the aggregate cost of waiting lists in the NHS by multiplying the annual number of patients waiting for admission to hospitals by the mean value of waiting cost per patient ($p/2$). They estimated that the cost of waiting ranged from 9 percent to 16 percent of UK government expenditure on the NHS, which was equivalent to 0.5–0.8 percent of GDP in the year to which their analysis applied.

In addition to the costs of waiting arising from the decline in treatment benefits over time, the individual on a waiting list for treatment is generally in less good health than he or she would be after treatment, even when there is a zero decay rate in treatment benefit.

More realistically, time spent waiting per se exacts a cost in terms of disutility. Propper (1995) used estimates from a survey to estimate the monetary value of this disutility. She found that on average, a reduction of a month spent on a waiting list for a nonurgent medical treatment was worth about £50 (in 1991 UK prices). In addition, she estimated the monetary value of the disutility arising from uncertainty in the date individuals are actually admitted to a hospital, approximately £30 (in 1991 UK prices). Combining these two estimates, the implication is that individuals were willing to pay £80 (in 1991 UK prices) per month for reduced time to treatment.

Using a similar approach with data from Sweden, Johannesson, Johannesson, and Söderqvist (1998) estimated willingness to pay for a reduction of a month on a waiting list to be £95 to £110 per month (in 1991 prices). That these two studies produced similar results adds strength to the notion that there is a disutility associated with time spent on waiting lists.

Not only do waiting lists exact a cost from those individuals on the waiting lists, they also affect the supply of health care in both public and private sectors. Besley, Hall, and Preston (1999) studied the impact of waiting lists on the supply of private care. Waiting lists are associated with a reduction in quality of services and inflexibility in the public sector. Thus, those individuals who demand a higher quality of health care opt out of the public sector and purchase private health insurance to finance their care in the private sector. Besley, Hall and Preston (1999) used survey data from the UK to test the hypothesis that demand for private health insurance is a function of the quality of care in the public sector and other characteristics, such as personal income. They used long-term waiting lists, measured by the number of individuals who were on waiting lists for twelve months or more, as a proxy for quality of care in the NHS.

The authors found that increases in NHS waiting lists are associated with increases in private health insurance purchases in the long term. The probability of purchasing private health insurance increases by 2 percent when the long-term waiting list rises by one person per 1,000 population. Moreover, they found that higher-income persons are more likely to purchase private health insurance than are those with low incomes. These findings suggest that public provision limits the quality of health care owing to waiting lists, and the quality of health care is a normal good. A lower quality level in the public sector, gauged in terms of long waiting lists, encourages the growth of private insurance coverage.

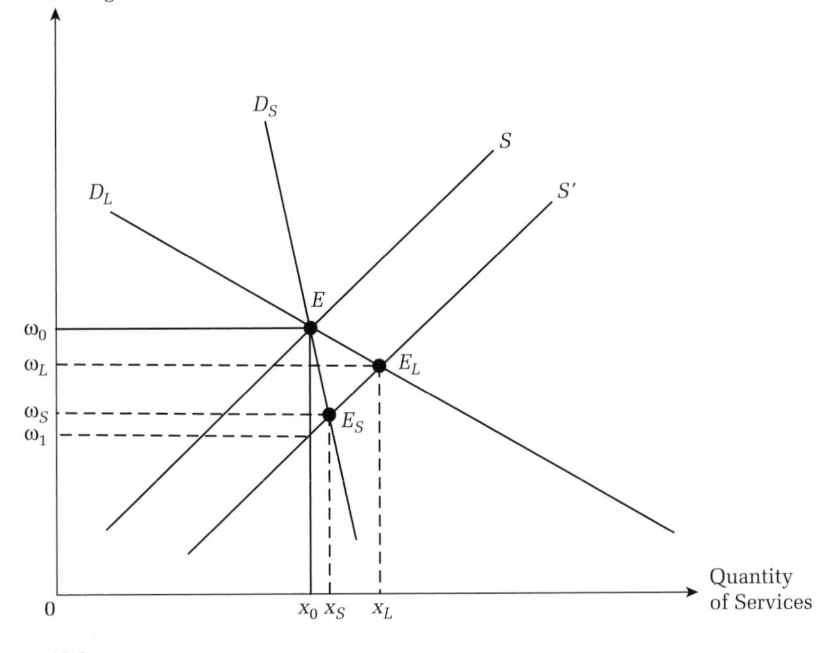

FIGURE 13.3
Using Waiting List Length as the Rationing Device for Elective Surgery

Martin and Smith (1999) investigated the effect of waiting times on the supply of public care. They developed a simultaneous equation model in which demand for and supply of elective surgery depend on waiting times. In their model, waiting times act as prices to determine the equilibrium quantity of elective surgery. In figure 13.3, the horizontal axis represents quantity and the vertical axis represents length of time to treatment. Martin and Smith's (1999) theoretical analysis shows that the demand for elective surgery is negatively associated with increases in length of waits. Thus, the demand curve for elective surgery is a downward sloping in figure 13.3. Time to treatment acts as a price to ration demand. Individual demand for elective surgery in the public sector declines as waiting times increase. The individual tends to opt out of the public sector and use private care when waiting times become long.

In contrast, the supply of elective surgery curve is upward sloping. There are two plausible reasons for the positive relationship between supply of elective surgery and waits. First, as mentioned previously, an increase in waiting time leads to additional resources being allocated to care and hence increases in-service capacity. Second, an increase in waiting time may increase political pressure on public providers and force them to improve efficiency.

The simultaneous equation model of demand and supply in figure 13.3 shows that the equilibrium time waiting for treatment is determined at the intersection of the demand and supply curves. ω_0 is the equilibrium wait, and x_0 is the equilibrium quantity of elective surgery. This model provides a useful framework for analyzing the effectiveness of government policies targeted at reducing waiting time.

Since the major cause of lengthy waits is high demand for health care, a potential solution for such waits is to increase the supply capacity of the public sector, such as by increasing public funds for the number of public hospital beds. However, the effort of reducing waiting times through increasing the capacity of the public sector may be offset by an increase in demand because the demand for elective surgery is responsive to a reduction in waiting time. Thus, whether or not increasing public budgets can effectively reduce waiting times for care depends on the slope of the demand curve, or the responsiveness of demand with respect to a change in waiting times.

As shown in figure 13.3, an increase in public budgets causes a shift of the supply curve from S to S', indicating a reduction in waiting times if the quantity of services provided remains constant. If demand for elective surgery does not increase with decreased waiting time (a vertical demand curve with respect to waits), an increase in public funds results in a decrease in the equilibrium waiting time from ω_0 to ω_1. However, the decrease in waiting time in turn increases demand (as suggested by Martin and Smith 1999). If the demand increase is small, as with D_S, then the equilibrium waiting time decreases from ω_0 to ω_S, and the equilibrium quantity increases from x_0 to x_S as the supply curve shifts to the right. In this case, the reduction in waiting time to care resulting from higher levels of public funding is offset by only a small increase in demand. Under these circumstances, increasing public funding is an effective policy for reducing waiting time to care.

By contrast, if the demand increase is large, as with D_L, then equilibrium waiting time decreases from ω_0 to ω_L, and equilibrium quantity increases from x_0 to x_L as the supply curve shifts to right. In this case, the reduction in waiting time resulting from higher levels of public funding is mostly offset by the demand response caused by the decline in waiting times. Then, adding more funds may not substantially reduce waiting time.

Whether this demand response is small or large is an empirical question. Martin and Smith (1999) estimated parameters of the simultaneous equation model of demand and supply using data from elective surgery in the UK. They found that waiting time had the expected negative impact on demand, but the marginal effect was small. The long-run elasticity estimate was –0.09, indicating that a 1 percent decrease in waiting times is associated with a 0.09 percent increase in demand for elective surgery. The association between waiting times and the supply of elective surgery was relatively large: the elasticity of supply with respect to waiting time was 0.35, indicating that a 1 percent increase in waiting times would lead to a

0.35 percent increase in supply of elective surgery. These results suggest that the increased demand effect following any reduction in waits is relatively small. Thus, increased public funds can be an effective policy to bring about reductions in waiting times.

The NHS Internal Market

An important NHS reform implemented in 1991 and ending in 1997 involved the creation of an internal market. The stated purpose of this reform was to use competition to improve the efficiency of the NHS. Under the reform, funds from general taxation were transferred to public agents or "purchasers," who were given the responsibility of purchasing personal health care services for designated populations. One type of purchaser was the district health authority, which purchased all hospital services for persons in a given geographic area. The second type was primary care physician groups, General Practice Fundholders, who decided to purchase a subset of elective services for their patients. The reform transformed GP groups into Fundholders; capitation payments were increased to cover not only primary care but also prescriptions and nonemergency hospital care (Martin and Smith 1999; Aaron and Schwartz 2005). As Fundholders, GP groups were both (1) providers of primary care and (2) physician case managers who assumed responsibility for allocating resources among primary care, elective procedures, and outpatient prescription drugs. This dual role in turn affected GPs' incentive to refer, which may have reduced their rates of referrals to specialists or hospitals.

From the vantage point of hospitals, the effect of the reform was to tighten hospitals' budget constraints and increase their uncertainty, especially about revenue. If hospitals did not successfully compete on both price and waiting lists (time until patients were admitted by the hospital), they lost operating revenue. Propper, Burgess, and Gossage (2008) assessed the impact of this experiment with competition on mortality rates following heart attacks. They found that increased competition from this reform led to decreased quality as measured by 30-day (post-admission) heart attack mortality outcomes.

The authors argued that such hospital-specific mortality rates are poorly observed by the public, and hence quality, which affects such rates, can be cut without there being an adverse effect on demand for the hospital's services (box 13.1). However, competition also reduced time spent on hospital waiting lists, and elective admissions rose. In contrast to mortality rates, the authors contended that the length of a hospital's waiting list is easily observed by the public. Hence, demand for care at a hospital is highly waiting list length elastic. This way, hospitals in a competitive environment could cut cost and shift their demand curves outward, thus being able to operate within their tight budget constraints.

Box 13.1

Does a Pro-Competitive NHS Reform Save Lives?

Whether or not increased competition leads to a higher or lower quality of health care is still unsettled empirically. Most empirical estimates in this line of research rely on studies that use nonexperimental data obtained from the US Medicare program. Here we present a study that exploits a policy change in the UK's NHS program to identify the effect of competition on health care quality.

In 2006, the UK government adopted a new round of market-oriented reforms to promote competition between hospitals. Compared to the previous reform on the NHS internal market discussed in this chapter, the 2006 NHS reforms introduced two major changes. First, the reform provided patients with a choice of five providers for their hospital care. To help patients make more informed choices, the government also introduced a new information system that provided information on quality and allowed patients to book hospital appointments online. Second, the reform changed the hospital payment system from negotiated (between buyer and seller) to ex ante fixed prices, which are a case-based payment system known as "payment by results." This new payment system is similar to the Medicare hospital payment system in the United States.

A potential effect of increasing patient choice is to increase the (quality) elasticity of demand faced by hospitals, which in turn leads to more intense competition. In addition, the shift of payment system from negotiated prices to fixed prices should encourage firms to compete for consumers on non-price dimensions—that is, quality—if the regulated price is set above marginal cost.

Gaynor, Morena-Serra, and Propper (2010) used the context of this NHS reform to implement a difference-in-differences research design to test the hypothesis that the pro-competitive policy improved hospital quality. Specifically, they identified the impact of competition from the interaction of market concentration index (as measured by the Herfindahl-Hirschman Index) with a binary variable for the post-reform year. This is because the intensity of the competition induced by the reforms may be expected to vary according to market structure: a hospital in an unconcentrated market would face more exposure to the policy change than would a hospital in a highly concentrated market. By using data from 2003 to capture the period before the policy change and data from 2007 for the period after the policy change, the authors tested their hypothesis on market concentration. Their database contained information on approximately 68,000 discharges per year per hospital from 162 hospitals.

The empirical estimates show that the introduction of competition significantly reduced heart attack and all-cause death rates in markets with lower levels of market concentration, without changing total expenditures. This result suggests that the introduction of competition led to an increase in quality of hospital care without a commensurate increase in expenditures on care.

The authors further calculated the benefits in monetary terms from the observed change in market structure following the reforms. First, between 2003 and 2007, the reform led to a decrease in market concentration index by 118. Second, the estimated

Box 13.1
(continued)

coefficient suggests that the average hospital experienced a 0.2 percent fall in its overall mortality rate from this decrease in the market concentration index. Third, a 0.2 percent drop in mortality led to an estimated 3,354 life years saved, given that the average age at death of patients in hospital was 77 years, and a 77-year-old patient had an additional life expectancy of 9.5 years for a male and 11 years for a female, respectively. Fourth, the monetary benefit of the life years saved was equal to US$335.4 million, assuming US$100,000 for the value of a year of life.

Overall, this study suggests that the effect of the pro-competitive NHS reform was to save lives without raising costs.

AUSTRALIA

OVERVIEW

Implemented in 1984, Australia's universal health insurance program, which is also known as Medicare, covers Australian citizens, New Zealand citizens, and holders of permanent visas. Some visitors and temporary residents from countries with which Australia has made reciprocal health care agreements are also eligible for Medicare, with some restrictions. Australia's Medicare is funded through general revenue, which in turn is largely income tax–based and progressive (Hall 1999).

An interesting feature of Australia's Medicare program involves the integration of public financing and public provision of care during a covered person's hospital stay. Although this feature is similar to the NHS in the UK, there are two differences between Australia's Medicare and the UK's NHS. First, there is a larger private health sector in Australia than in the UK. In 2005, private funds, including those from private health insurance and individuals' out-of-pocket costs, contributed 33 percent of total health expenditure in Australia, compared with 13 percent in the UK. Similarly, the private hospital sector in Australia accounts for 30 percent of admissions and 25 percent of all hospital bed days (Hall 1999). Second, in contrast to the UK, there is no patient registration and there are no restrictions on where GPs may establish their practice. Consequently, patients enjoy free choice of providers. That is, patients can choose whether to be treated in public or private hospitals, and can attend whichever public hospital they like (Scott, Schurer, Jensen, et al. 2009).

On admission to public hospitals, patients may choose to be public (Medicare) patients or private patients. If they choose to be public patients, they receive free medical and allied health or paramedical care from physicians selected by the hospitals, accommodation at no out-of-pocket expense, meals, and other health services while hospitalized. Medicare-eligible patients who choose to be private patients in public hospitals are charged fees by doctors, and are charged by the hospital for hospital care, usually at a price less than the full cost of providing these services.

If the patient is eligible for private insurance, such insurance usually covers all or nearly all of the charges by a public hospital. Medicare subsidizes part of physicians' fees and private insurance pays an additional amount toward such fees. An advantage of patients of using private sources for payment in a public hospital is that they can choose their own physicians. Private insurance benefits can also pay part of the amounts charged the patient for allied health or paramedical care and other costs (e.g., surgically implanted prostheses) incurred during the hospital stay.

People may choose care in a private hospital. Private patients in private hospitals are charged fees by doctors and some allied health/paramedical staff, and are billed by the hospital for accommodation, nursing care, and other hospital services, such as the use of operating rooms for surgery.

Charges incurred by patients receiving private doctors' services or surgery, whether in or out of hospital, are generally reimbursed at least in part by Medicare. For out-of-hospital services, private insurers are prohibited from insuring all or part of the cost of the difference between the Medicare benefit and the fee charged by the doctor. This provision aims to avoid incentives for unnecessary increases in fees.

The purchase of private insurance is encouraged by imposing a financial penalty on persons above a certain income threshold who do not purchase such insurance. Private insurance is purchased by individuals and families, in contrast to the United States, where most private insurance is provided through a person's place of employment. The coexistence of private health insurance and a universal public insurance program allows some individuals to opt out of the restrictions of the public health sector. Overall, the benefits of purchasing private health insurance in Australia include more choice of physicians, shorter waiting lists for some procedures, and greater access to new (and expensive) treatment and equipment (Jensen, Webster, and Witt 2009).

EMPIRICAL EVIDENCE

In 1989–1990, 44 percent of households had private hospital insurance and 35 percent of hospital users used a private facility (Savage and Wright 2003). Length of stay in private hospitals has been shown to be increased, at least for some demographic groups, when the patient is covered by private insurance (Savage and Wright 2003).

Jensen, Webster, and Witt (2009) studied the health outcomes of persons admitted to public and private hospitals with a primary diagnosis of a heart attack. Outcome measures were readmission to a hospital for a heart attack and mortality. In terms of these outcomes, the authors found that private hospitals persistently outperformed public hospitals. Private hospitals in their analysis sample were both for-profit and not-for-profit hospitals. They attributed the better performance of private hospitals to budget constraints, which were more binding on input use in public than in private hospitals. They argued that the difference in outcomes was unlikely to be due to differences in physician quality since the same physicians generally cared for patients in public and private hospitals.

13.3 Public Provision of Personal Health Care Services in Other Countries

High-Income Countries

Pedersen (2005, 164) characterized Scandinavian health care systems "as a decentralized NHS." None of these systems is operated by the central government; they are operated and financed by either counties—in Denmark and Sweden, municipalities—in Finland and to some extent in Norway, or the state is the sole owner and shareholder of regional corporations that run the country's hospitals, as in Norway. In Finland and Sweden, GPs are generally employed by counties. In Denmark and Norway, GPs are private but are regulated by counties and municipalities, respectively (Pedersen 2005, 165). Although there is a trend toward more private involvement in each of these countries, the Scandinavian welfare model for health care basically remains intact. In 2005, public expenditure on health as a percentage of total expenditures on health in these four countries remained high compared to other OECD countries, ranging from 75 percent in Finland to 83.5 percent in Norway. Public provision may have reduced but has not completely eliminated differences by income in the burden of disease (see, e.g., Ljung, Peterson, Hallqvist, et al. 2005).

Middle- and Low-Income Countries

Dominance of Public Ownership Form

Public provision is dominant in numerous middle- and low-income countries. For example, in Asia, in about the year 2000, among selected Asian countries, public provision was dominant in Bangladesh, Indonesia, the Kyrgyz Republic, Nepal, the Philippines, Punjab, Sri Lanka, and Thailand. Despite public provision, consumers paid for more than half of expenditures in the form of out-of-pocket payments in well over half of these countries (O'Donnell, van Doorslaer, Rannan-Eliya, et al. 2008; see also chapter 11, this book). In the Kyrgyz Republic and other Central Asian countries, public provision is a legacy of the Soviet era. While these countries offer universal access to at least basic health care services, they have often suffered from years of underinvestment in facilities, and in rural areas even basic amenities such as running water or sewage are lacking (McKee and Healy 2002, 7). In at least one of these countries, Kazakhstan, the situation has improved in recent years because of its oil resources and increases in the price of oil.

In Central America, Costa Rica relies on the public provision of personal health care services (Dow and Sáenz 2002) and overall has excellent health outcomes. Two-thirds of physicians are public employees, although most also have private offices. Although health indicators of the country's population are favorable, there are frequent complaints about the quality of publicly provided health care services. There are long queues, and there have been complaints about lack of motivation among civil service workers, which have led some users to opt for private physicians' services. Workers employed by the state are not incentivized to be productive. For one, there is no threat of unemployment for poor performance.

Nigeria, like Bangladesh, is among the countries with the lowest level of per capita income in the world. Health care systems in very poor countries tend to be publicly operated and financed. Such systems are plagued by problems of understaffing, lack of equipment, inadequate logistics for delivering even essential drugs, and poor incentives for government workers (see, e.g., Lacey 2002). It is difficult, however, to disentangle the effects of system ownership from pervasive lack of resources in such countries. Even in low-income countries there is not complete reliance on public finance and provision. For example, in several low-income countries—Côte d'Ivoire, Indonesia, Kenya, Madagascar, Mali, and Zimbabwe—more than five percent of total expenditures on personal health care services came from private health insurance in 2001 (Sekhri and Savedoff 2005).

EVIDENCE ON QUALITY OF CARE

A persistent finding from many low-income countries in particular is that quality of care is low. This conclusion is based on evidence from vignettes that present hypothetical cases to physicians and elicit how these physicians would respond in these situations, and from direct observation of how physicians respond in treating actual patients (see, e.g., Banerjee, Deaton, and Duflo 2004; Das and Gertler 2007). In the majority of these situations, the physician is a public sector employee.

Why is quality of care as low as it is reported to be? There are several possibilities. First, the physicians could lack the quality of medical education that physicians in more affluent countries receive. Second, because of the relative poverty of their countries, hospitals and clinics could lack the facilities and equipment that physicians in high-income countries typically have. Third, physicians in low-income countries could be competent on average but lack incentives to exert effort in patient care. Incentives could be lacking because of inadequate monitoring of physician performance by system managers or because pay is based on factors other than actual performance. These factors could be political or personal favoritism, years of schooling completed, or seniority. Another possibility is that physician compensation is so low in low-income countries with public systems that physicians feel compelled to moonlight in the private sector. For all of these reasons, quality may be low because of inadequate clinician effort rather than because of low competence or lack of facilities and equipment.

Empirical analysis of these issues has been conducted in only a few countries, and in only a few communities within these countries. Thus, generalizability is an issue. Nevertheless, studies to date have revealed some interesting and important findings. First, high rates of absenteeism have been documented for schoolteachers and medical personnel (Chaudhury, Hammer, Kremer, et al. 2006). Absenteeism rates tend to be higher for the latter. Medical personnel presumably have better opportunities than teachers to work in the private sector. Often, when health care providers are absent, the facility is closed. A patient (frequently accompanied by family members) may travel a long distance to visit a facility, only to find it closed. High rates of absenteeism have been attributed to inadequate monitoring and civil service systems. Civil service systems in many countries were established to protect government employees from being discharged because of their political views or affiliations. This is an advantage of such systems. However, such systems often base compensation on educational attainment and tenure rather than on performance on the job. Clearly, educational attainment and tenure can be objectively measured, while measures of performance can contain a subjective component. Thus, a poor performance evaluation can be used as the basis for discharging an employee who is objectionable on political grounds. But a poor performance evaluation may also mean actual poor performance, and civil service systems often prevent appropriate as well as inappropriate use of performance measures. If promotion and pay are not to be based on performance, there is understandably a lesser incentive to perform well. Regular attendance at work is one attribute of good performance. Aside from civil service regulation, public employment decision making in at least some low-income countries is highly centralized—in India, for example, at the level of the Indian state.

Second, studies have used essentially two approaches to measure quality of care. In one approach, a person acts as if he or she were a patient and presents a reason for the visit, and the clinician acts on what he or she hears from the patient. Quality of care is based on the clinician's response to the scenario as presented by this actor-patient. The clinician is told that this is not a real patient. In the second approach, the clinician's response to an actual patient is monitored by an independent observer. Quality of care is judged to be inadequate if the clinician does not provide care that is appropriate to the specific situation. With both approaches, quality of care has been judged to be often inadequate in low-income countries in which such studies have been conducted.

Third, there is an issue of whether low-quality of care is mainly attributable to low levels of provider competence or to the amount of effort exerted in the provision of low quality of care, conditional on a given level of competence. The evidence seems to favor the latter explanation. The study researchers directly measured clinical competence, which seemed to be adequate. The main source of low-quality care seemed to be in providers not applying what they knew (Leonard, Masatu, and Vialou 2007).

Fourth, patients seem to be aware of quality-of-care differences among providers. Patients do not always visit the nearest facility but select from among alternative facilities those offering relatively higher quality. Facilities judged to be inferior based on independent evaluations of quality are sometimes bypassed by patients, presumably because patients also judge them to be inferior (Leonard 2007; Klemick, Leonard, and Masatu 2009). Patient choice of facility is systematically influenced by variation in process quality (Mariko 2003).

Fifth, visit rates in the communities included in the studies are not that different from visit rates in more affluent countries. The problem seems to be with the quality, not quantity, of care.

Sixth, although health status is lower in low-income than in middle- or high-income countries, a causal effect of the provision of low-quality services on poor population health has not been established. There is a positive correlation between quality of care and population health; a causal relationship may be presumed but has not been rigorously demonstrated by research. Even if there is a causal effect, its importance relative to other factors leading to poor health is currently unknown.

Seventh, the quality-of-care indicators reported in the studies represent averages. Quality of care varies cross-sectionally in these as in other countries.

PUBLIC POLICY OPTIONS FOR IMPROVING QUALITY OF CARE

Diagnosing a problem, in this context, low quality of care, is one thing. Doing something about it is another. There are several possible types of public policies that might be implemented to address this issue.

First, since most of the facilities are publicly owned and most employment is public, one approach would be privatization of health care delivery in low-income countries. Although some studies have found that quality is higher in private facilities (see, e.g., Lien, Chou, and Liu 2008; see also chapter 6, this book), there is no consensus that private facilities are better even in high-income countries. And there is no consistent empirical evidence that quality of care is higher in private facilities in low-income countries either. Further, if the issue is inadequate monitoring and inadequate incentives to provide high quality of care, the solution involves improving monitoring and incentives rather than making changes in ownership per se. For example, decentralizing public decision making (Pandey, Sehgal, Riboud, et al. 2007; Singh 2008) and giving these decision makers power to promote and grant pay increases based in part on performance would represent more direct approaches than the more general strategy of changing ownership form.

A second approach involves expansion of facilities for medical education in low-income countries, coupled with policies to promote the retention of physicians. Such policies may have merit in their own right, but, as noted above, there does not seem to be a deficiency in the quantity of care residents of low-income countries receive as much as there is inadequate quality.

Third, improved public regulation of health care quality is often proposed as a solution to the widespread provision of low-quality care. Such regulation can take the form of barring entry to low-quality facilities or to health professionals with inadequate training. Such barriers to entry generally take the form of facility and professional licensure. But for such entry limitations to be effective, they must be enforced. Furthermore, economists have long been suspicious of such regulation since entry regulation serves to grant existing providers a de facto franchise, which in turn gives them market power. Another disadvantage is that, barring an egregious act, licensure is forever. As a practical matter, delicensure is rare.

Fourth, policies that empower health care consumers to monitor the quality of care they receive may enhance the quality of care that is provided. The presumption underlying this set of public policies is that quality of care is poor when consumers are insufficiently empowered to do anything about it.

EMPIRICAL EVIDENCE ON EFFECTS OF INTERVENTIONS TO IMPROVE QUALITY OF CARE

Two recent studies have assessed the success of interventions in low-income countries specifically designed to empower consumers in this way. Pandey, Sehgal, Riboud, et al. (2007) report the results of a randomized controlled trial conducted in Uttar Pradesh, a very populous (180+ million residents) in northern India, designed to determine the impact of provision of information to consumers on the provision of health and social services. The underlying hypothesis was that once consumers were informed about quality and other attributes of services, they would be better able to monitor the performance of providers in their local market areas.

Sites for the experiment were randomly selected. By randomly selecting sites, confirming that sites in the intervention group were similar to those in the control group at baseline, and conducting a follow-up one year after information was provided at the intervention sites, the authors could validly attribute changes in the use of health services following implementation of the intervention to the intervention itself. Randomizing the intervention among individuals in a given site (village), that is, providing information to some residents of a community and not to others, would likely have been viewed as unethical. Not providing the information to residents of all communities in the state could easily be justified on the basis of budget constraints.

At baseline and follow-up, households were asked questions about access to health care and social services. For example, one health care question was whether or not a nurse midwife had visited the adult female household member of child-bearing age when she was pregnant. On social services, people were asked whether or not their school-aged children attended school, and if so, the school fees charged; whether or not there had been a village council meeting in the last six months; and whether or not development work had been or was being performed in the village.

With a couple of exceptions, post intervention, the use of personal health care services was significantly higher in the intervention group than in the control group. Prenatal examinations were 30 percent higher, tetanus vaccinations were 27 percent higher, and the use of prenatal supplements and infant vaccinations were 24 and 25 percent higher, respectively, in the intervention group than in the control group.

There were also differences in the social services domain. For example, the probability of having had a village council meeting in the last six months was significantly higher in the intervention group than in the control group. Overcharging of tuition declined in the intervention group relative to the control group. Overall, the authors concluded that their findings highlighted the importance of empowering communities to facilitate individual and collective action.

A similar field experiment was conducted in sub-Saharan Africa and described by Björkman and Svensson (2009). This study was conducted in fifty communities in nine districts in Uganda. The intervention consisted of village and staff meetings facilitated by local nongovernmental organizations and designed to encourage development of a plan to improve and facilitate implementation of a plan to improve quality of service provision. As in the previous study, there was randomization by community.

The study began with surveys of fifty health care providers and a survey of households. Following collection of these data, a series of meetings was held in those communities randomly selected for the intervention. No meetings were held in the control communities.

In the intervention villages, there were meetings with community members. These meetings included a discussion of concerns that residents of the communities had about the local provision of health care services. Common concerns were the high rates of absenteeism, long patient waits at the facilities, inattention of the medical staff to patients, and differential treatment depending on the patient's status in the community. In addition, there were meetings at a health facility in each intervention community and interface meetings between community members and health workers.

A main study outcome involved whether or not the intervention increased the quantity and quality of health services provision and whether or not the intervention improved health outcomes. The researchers also paid attention to changes at all steps in the accountability chain. Did the intervention communities become more involved in monitoring health workers in their areas? As a result of the intervention, did health worker behavior change?

The study documented improvements in the use of available equipment during health examinations and reductions in patient waiting times at the clinics. On average, following the intervention, the absentee rate was thirteen percentage points lower at intervention facilities than at control facilities versus no difference before the intervention. Vaccinations of children increased in intervention communities. Persons in intervention communities appeared to be more involved in monitoring the providers after the intervention.

That both studies showed that empowering consumers led to improvements in health services provision and outcomes is interesting and important. The intervention did not involve implementing major organizational changes from the top down.

Nevertheless, this approach to empowering consumers should not be viewed as a panacea. Rather, it represents one approach, if a promising one, to quality improvement. Further studies of this type should have a high priority.

13.4 EVALUATION AND COMPARISON OF HEALTH CARE SYSTEMS

One very knowledgeable commentator on health care systems has remarked, "Choices of financing and provision of healthcare are determined by ethics and ideology" (Maynard 2005, 4). The choice is never made on the basis of economic analysis. We are reluctant to go this far in rejecting the role of economics in shaping health care systems. But we acknowledge that much, if not most, of the variation in health care systems in countries around the world cannot be explained by economic reasoning.

Even conceding this, economists have important roles to play in improving decision making conditional on a choice of health care financing and provision having been made and even helping inform decision makers about the trade-offs involved in choosing among types of health systems.

As in classifying health care systems, the evaluation and comparison of health care systems is not a straightforward exercise. In this section, we employ two methods for assessing the performance of different health systems. The first uses a set of intermediate performance measures that has been widely used and described in terms of indicators of access, cost, and quality. The second uses two performance goals that measure the overall performance of a system, efficiency and equity. Clearly, neither approach alone captures all aspects of system performance. Rather, the combination of the two methods provides insights useful for understanding overall performance among different health care systems.

COMPARISONS BASED ON INTERMEDIATE PERFORMANCE MEASURES

ACCESS

Access refers to individuals' ease of consuming personal health services. Since personal health care services are an important input in the production of good health, access to health care has long been widely perceived as a right, not a good to be consumed by only some members of society. Thus, access is a frequently used measure of intermediate performance. Although access is multidimensional, encompassing financial (e.g., the out-of-pocket cost to individual consumers of health care services), geographic (e.g., distance to health care providers), and cultural (e.g., ability to communicate with providers because of language similarities or differences) factors, most studies and statistical indicators focus on the financial dimension. The question is whether the poor have the same access to health care as the non-poor. There are at least two major indicators that can be used to measure financial accessibility to health care.

One is the percentage of the population covered by health insurance. In a system with public provision and financing, all citizens have free or nearly free access to health care, at least in terms of facing zero or nearly zero money prices. In a system with private supply, access to health care depends on whether insurance coverage is compulsory or not. With public provision of health insurance, insurance is compulsory, so coverage extends to the entire population (universal coverage) or to certain groups of population based on region, occupation, and economic activity ("corporatism"). By contrast, in a system of private provision of health insurance, individuals may be uninsured under the guise of "free choice" or "lower ability to pay." In this respect, countries with private provision of health insurance tend to be at a disadvantage in achieving equal access to personal health care services. The percentage of the population covered by health insurance provides only a rough measure of access to personal health care services because health insurance program benefits vary among countries and even among health insurance plans within a country. Some countries provide health insurance with comprehensive coverage while others provide health insurance with only limited coverage.

A second indicator for measuring access is the degree of generosity of insurance coverage. While an average coinsurance rate—the percentage of personal health care expenditures not covered by public and private health insurance—is such a measure, there is a practical issue of which services to include for the purposes of computing the percentage. For example, should expenditures on nursing home care be included or not? The answer is likely to vary among countries. In a country in which elderly, disabled persons are primarily cared for by other family members, having access to nursing home care is likely to be less critical than in countries in which there is substantial reliance on purchased services for the care of such persons.

There are three ways of moving toward increasing financial accessibility to health care: (1) by increasing breadth (who is insured?), (2) by increasing depth (which benefits are covered?), and (3) by increasing height (what proportion of the costs is covered?) (fig. 13.4). Increasing insurance coverage to more of a country's population leads to universal coverage through added breadth. Adding more services, such as new medical technologies and nursing home care, to the list of

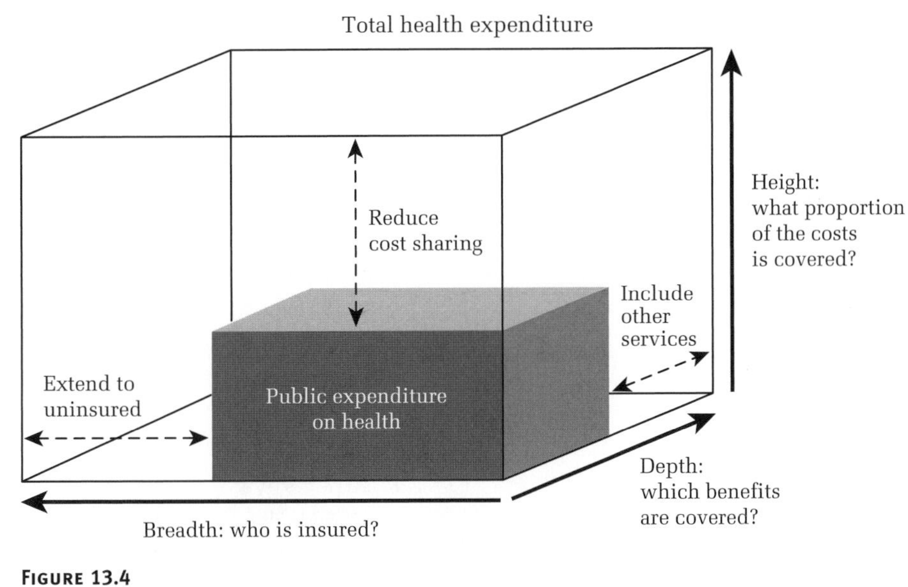

FIGURE 13.4
Three Ways of Moving toward Universal Coverage
Source: World Health Organization, World Health Report (2008).

services covered by public insurance increases the depth toward universal coverage. Reducing cost sharing increases the height toward universal coverage. These three directions, working together, increase the share of public expenditure on health (and reduce the share of out-of-pocket cost) and hence increase financial accessibility to personal health care services.

A higher out-of-pocket share leads to lower equality in access because such access is more likely to depend on ability to pay in systems with higher out-of-pocket share. The out-of-pocket share ranges from 6 percent to 51 percent in OECD countries (fig. 13.5). Countries with public financing and supply tend to have a lower out-of-pocket share. However, some countries with universal coverage, such as South Korea, do not have a lower out-of-pocket share than some countries relying on the private provision of health insurance, in particular the United States. These exceptions occur because universal coverage may provide health insurance with limited benefits. Overall, countries with a higher share of public financing have a lower share of out-of-pocket payments, except the United States. Thus, the choice of health care system per se does not provide a precondition for ensuring equal access to health care.

COST

Although countries in the world make various efforts to provide their citizens with full or easy access to health care, "affordability" is another major consideration.

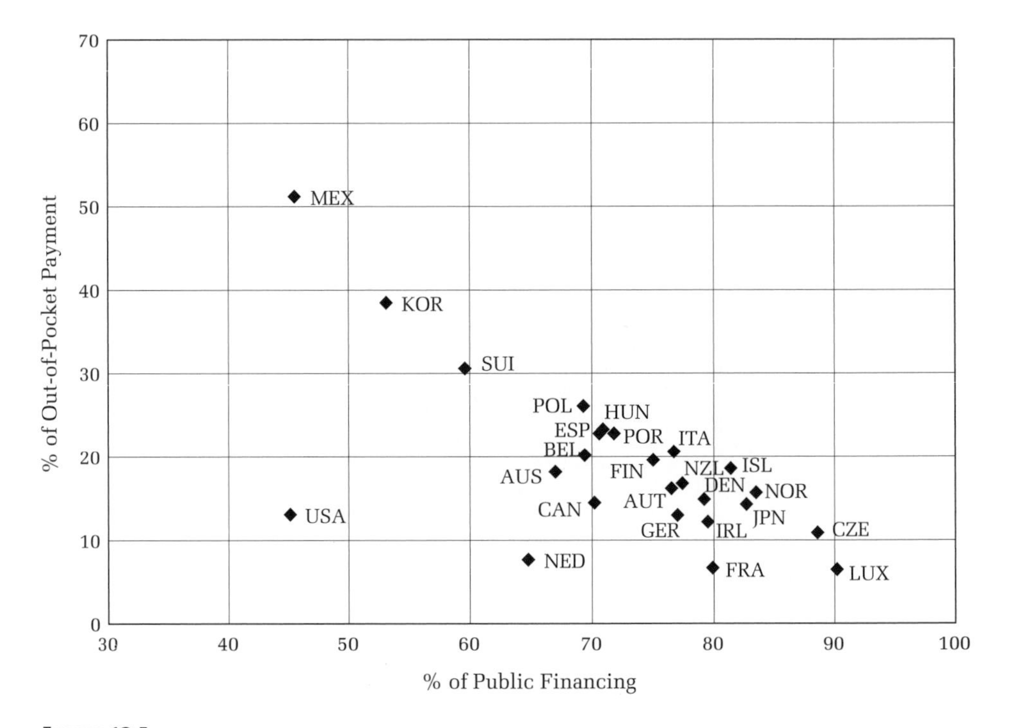

FIGURE 13.5
The Relationship between Share of Public Financing and Share of Health Expenditures of Out-of-Pocket Payments
Source: OECD, Health Data (2008).

Scarce resources, labor and capital inputs, are used in the production of personal health services. If other factors, including service quality, are held equal, from society's vantage point (but not necessarily from the vantage point of the private interest of suppliers of health care services), lower resource use is to be preferred to higher levels of resource use. Thus, cost is the second indicator in measuring the intermediate performance of health care system.[1] We use total health expenditures within a country as a measure of cost for purposes of comparing intermediate performance using countries' health care systems.

Following Newhouse's (1977) pioneering work, international comparisons of health expenditure have become a well-developed research area. A stylized fact evident from these comparisons is that there is substantial variation in per capita health expenditures among countries, ranging from spending US$16 to US$5,274 (in 2002 purchasing power party) a year. Among the factors accounting for such differences, the relationship between health expenditures and per capita GDP is the one that is best documented. National income is the most important factor in explaining international differences in health care expenditures. There is a positive relationship between health expenditure per capita and GDP per capita, the

1. In chapter 14, we provide a detailed analysis of how to measure costs in the health care sector at the disease or program level.

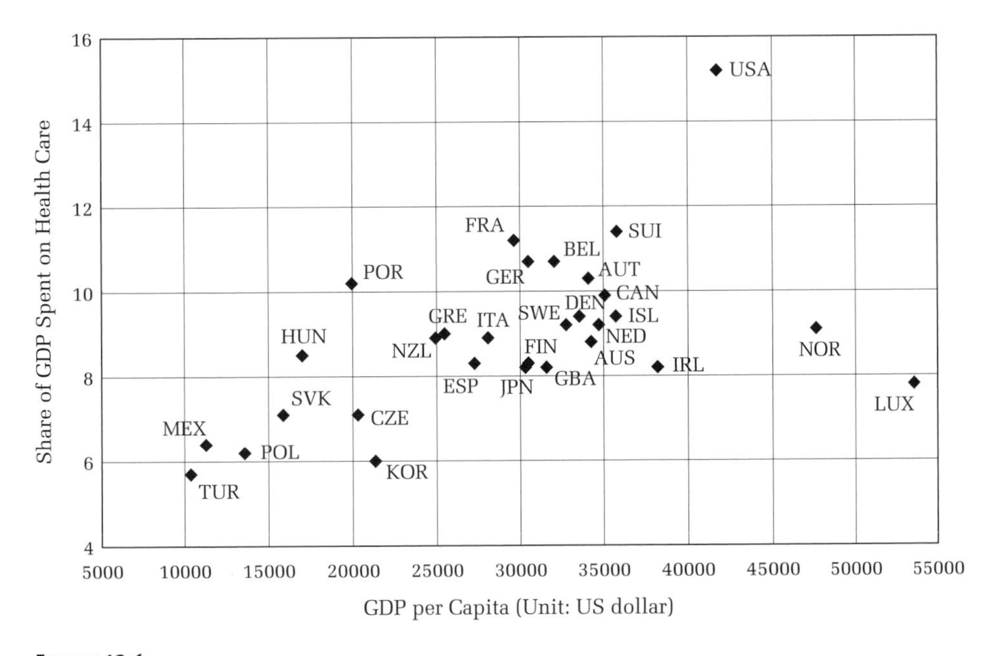

FIGURE 13.6

The Relationship between Share of GDP Spent on Health Care and GDP per Capita
Source: OECD, Health Data (2008).

estimated income elasticity is greater than one (Gerdtham and Jönsson 2000). A 10 percent increase in GDP is associated with an even higher rate of increase in health care spending. Thus, there is also a positive relationship between share of GDP spent on health care and GDP per capita (fig. 13.6). High-income countries tend to spend a larger portion of their GDP on health care than low-income countries. Economic growth and the growth of health care spending are simultaneously determined. Higher economic growth spurs increases in health care spending, but such spending is also productive in terms of stimulating economic growth (see chapter 16).

Although income is the most important variable accounting for the substantial differences in health expenditures among countries, other non-income variables, including institutional features of health systems, also are quantitatively important in determining the level of health expenditures. Several studies have found that countries with primary care physicians as gatekeepers for inpatient and specialist care or countries that pay their physicians on a capitation basis have lower health expenditures (see chapter 11). The introduction of a gatekeeper mechanism reduces health expenditure by 18 percent on average compared to systems without gatekeepers. Similarly, capitation systems lead to lower health expenditures by around 17–21 percent compared to fee-for-service systems (Gerdtham and

Jönsson 2000). Since gatekeepers and capitation have been widely used in systems with public provision of health services, most notably in the UK, the above-mentioned empirical findings suggest that countries with public provision of health services are in a better position to control spending on personal health care services. However, as mentioned above, this goal has been achieved by using waiting lists as rationing devices. There is a trade-off between controlling health care costs and improving timely access to health care.

In addition to public provision, public financing also an important factor to explain the variations in health expenditure across countries. For example, Gerdtham, Søgaard, Andersson, et al. (1992) assessed determinants of spending on personal health services in nineteen OECD countries. These researchers did not find that countries with a higher share of public financing had higher health expenditure as would be consistent with the efficiency argument, namely, that public systems are less efficient. In fact, the opposite was true. When the share of public health expenditure increased by 10 percent, total health care expenditures fell by about 5 percent, but total spending on inpatient care was less responsive to the public-private financing mix. A 10 percent increase in the share of public health expenditure reduced such expenditure by only 2.2 percent on average. Although both public financing and public supply are advantageous in containing costs as measured by total health expenditures, this type of measure excludes costs arising from rationing access to personal health care services.

The United States is an outlier in terms of the GDP share spent on health care (see fig. 13.6). In 2005, health care spending accounted for nine percent of GDP on average in thirty OECD countries. By contrast, the United States allocated 15.2 percent of its GDP to health care. The substantial deviation in health spending from the average level of OECD countries raises an important question as to why the United States spends so much on health care compared to other high-income countries.

Woolhandler, Campbell, Himmelstein, et al. (2003) attributed this deviation to differences in health administrative costs among countries. They found that administrative costs accounted for 31 percent of total health expenditures in the United States but only 17 percent of such expenditures in Canada. More recently, Spithoven (2009) confirmed that variations in health administrative costs matter. He concluded that differences in administrative costs between the United States and Canada accounted for 15–50 percent of the five percentage point difference in GDP share spent on health care between these two countries. A widely accepted explanation for higher administrative costs in the United States is that this country has a pluralistic health care financing system. Systems with private provision of health insurance may pay a price for satisfying the wants of consumers with heterogeneous preferences.

In addition to the higher administrative cost, there are other arguments as well. Anderson, Reinhardt, Hussey, et al. (2003) concluded that the higher prices of personal health care services in the United States are the major factor accounting for the higher health expenditures in the United States compared to other high-income countries. They based this conclusion on a finding that the utilization of health care services in the United States by various measures is consistently below the median level in OECD countries, although the United States spends much more on health care than any other country. Spithoven (2009) agreed with this argument. By comparing determinants of health expenditures in the United States and Canada, Spithoven found that pharmaceutical price differences alone accounted for 4–20 percent of the five percentage point difference in GDP share allocated to health care between these two countries. Such evidence suggests that a system dominated by public payer(s) or a single payer may have an advantage in controlling health care costs compared to systems in which private payers or multiple payers predominate. However, cost containment may come at the expense of decreasing health care innovation (Grabowski and Wang 2006).

Quality

Based on relative cost alone, it is not possible to draw definitive conclusions about the relative efficiency of public versus private health care systems. A health system with lower costs may be achieved at the expense of lower quality because higher quality is costly to produce. For example, providers or payers may compromise service quality (may adversely affect health care outcomes) under a strict cost-containment policy or in an environment of tight health care budgets. That is, there is a trade-off between cost and quality. Quality is another important indicator to measure the intermediate performance of different health care systems.

Like access, quality is multidimensional (see chapter 7). The most common outcome comparison across countries is that of the United States and Canada because of similarities in history (both were British colonies), demographic characteristics, and medical education, and their geographic proximity. Based on the data of patients hospitalized with a primary diagnosis of heart attack (AMI for acute myocardial infarction), several studies have reached almost the same conclusion, namely, that mortality rates of AMI patients are very similar in the United States and Canada. The US-to-Canada one-year mortality ratio ranges from 0.96 to 1, indicating that the outcomes of AMI patients are a few percentage points better in the United States or are equal in the two countries (Cutler 2002).

In addition, there is only limited evidence on outcome comparisons between the United States and other countries. Noguchi, Masuda, Kuzuya, et al. (2006) compared treatments and outcomes for heart attack patients in the United States and Japan. They measured short-term quality by 30-day mortality and readmission to a hospital within 30 days, and long-term quality by one-year mortality and one-year readmission. For patients undergoing intensive procedures such as cardiac catheterization within seven days of the first hospital admission for an AMI, they found that short-term quality was similar in the United States and Japan but long-term quality was very different in these two countries. After accounting for other factors, long-term quality, as measured by mortality and hospital readmission rates, tended to be much better in the United States than in Japan. However, for patients not undergoing intensive procedures such as cardiac catheterization, both short- and long-term quality were better in Japan than in the United States. Given these conflicting findings, it is difficult to draw definitive conclusions about quality in the United States versus Japan.

Comparisons Based on Two Performance Goals

Efficiency

In economics, *efficiency* bundles two key concepts, how services are produced and what services are produced. The former is defined as *technical efficiency*—a good or service is produced at minimum cost, which in turn is described by any point on the production possibility frontier. Technical inefficiency is reduced by lowering the unit cost of producing a given service. The latter is *allocative efficiency*—the optimal mix of outputs that achieves the goal of maximizing social welfare or health gain, which in turn is described by the right (optimal) point on the production possibility frontier. Allocative inefficiency is reduced by altering the mix of services that the health system produces so that more health gains or higher social welfare is achieved from a given resource endowment.

With regard to technical efficiency, there are two prevailing views of alternative health systems. First, countries with a single-payer system have an efficiency advantage over the countries with multipayer systems because of lower administrative costs (Woolhandler, Campbell, and Himmelstein 2003; see also chapter 11, this book). However, based on cost alone, and without comparing health outcomes across countries, one should not draw definitive conclusions about the relative efficiency of single-payer versus multiple-payer systems. Second, countries with a public health care provision often seem to be at an efficiency disadvantage compared to countries with a private supply because it is assumed that public provision is less efficient. However, even if this assumption were supportable empirically, evidence obtained from micro studies, such as comparative studies of hospitals with different ownership forms, does not necessarily apply to the whole system. At the country level, there is certainly no widely accepted evidence showing that the direct public provision of health care is any less efficient.

With regard to allocative efficiency, the evidence is more convincing than for technical efficiency. Compared to a system with private financing, countries with public sector financing tend to restrict services using new medical technologies. For example, the public financing system in Canada restricts the use of high-tech care for patients with AMI relative to US practice (Cutler 2002).

In addition, a system of direct public provision may use primary care physicians as gatekeepers for the use of medical specialists and hospitals. By contrast, private supply systems often give patients an unrestricted choice of providers. In such systems, with the exception of some managed care plans, patients can make appointments with whichever physicians they wish to see. Further, they can go to the hospital emergency room and, depending on their condition, be admitted to the hospital as an inpatient without consulting a primary care physician.

The lack of a gatekeeper mechanism may lead to high use rates of medical specialists and a low use rate of primary care physicians, an inefficient allocation of resources. The social marginal cost of specialty care exceeds its social marginal benefit, while the social marginal benefit of primary care exceeds its social marginal cost (box 13.2).

EQUITY

In health care, the concept of equity has been widely used in two dimensions: financing and delivery. In measuring equity, researchers and policy makers commonly accept the principle that health care ought to be financed according to ability to pay and distributed according to health needs (Wagstaff and Van Doorslaer 1992). In practice, equity in the financing of health care is measured in terms of vertical equity; that is, individuals or families with unequal ability to pay make different contributions. An empirical indicator of equity in health care financing is an index of progressivity to measure the extent to which the more affluent pay a larger proportion of their incomes on personal health care services than the poor do.

Wagstaff and van Doorslaer (1992) conducted a ten-country study of health care financing systems and compared these countries on the basis of the relative burdens borne by persons of different income levels in each country. They compared countries with predominantly tax-financed systems—Denmark, Ireland, Portugal, and the UK; social insurance systems—France, Italy, the Netherlands, and Spain; and predominantly private systems—Switzerland and the United States. They found that health care financing was progressive in only three of the ten countries, all with tax-financed systems—the UK, Ireland, and Portugal. The two countries with the most regressive financing structures were the two private ones, the United States and Switzerland. Overall, they concluded that tax-financed systems tend to be proportional or mildly progressive, social insurance systems are regressive, and private systems are the most regressive of all. A study of Asian countries found that health care financing was slightly regressive in the three high-income Asian countries they studied (Japan, South Korea, and Taiwan), each of which has universal social insurance (O'Donnell, Van Doorslaer, Rannan-Eliya, et al. 2008), and similar to European countries with similar systems. The same was true of Hong Kong, which was similar to high-income countries in Europe. Among

Box 13.2
Is American Health Care Uniquely Inefficient?

This chapter described two concepts of efficiency, technical efficiency and allocative efficiency. In addition, we mentioned that the United States has spent more on personal health care services than any country in the world during the past four decades. This raises two concerns about the efficiency of US health care expenditures: (1) Does US health care display inferior technical efficiency? (2) Is US health care spending allocatively efficient compared to other countries' health care spending? Garber and Skinner (2008) undertook a comprehensive evaluation to address these two questions.

With regard to the first concept, Garber and Skinner (2008) identified "heterogeneous demand" as an important factor accounting for the technical inefficiency in the US health care system. Heterogeneous demand is the consequence of differences in preferences or income but may also reflect the presence of racial or ethnic disparities or from regional differences in health care spending. Fragmentation of care arising from diversity in the sources of health care financing and insurance coverage in the United States leads to lower technical efficiency than would be realized in an egalitarian health care system.

There are at least three lines of evidence to support this argument. First, the United States lags behind most other developed countries in the diffusion of information technology. Just 28 percent of primary care physicians in the United States use electronic health records, compared to 98 percent in the Netherlands and 89 percent in the UK. Second, there are a higher percentage of chronically ill persons who experience access barriers to health care than in other developed countries. About 42 percent of chronically ill persons failed to adhere to recommended treatments or did not take full medication doses because of costs, compared to just five percent in the Netherlands and nine percent in the UK. Third, the US health care system also exhibits a more pronounced regional variation in per capita Medicare expenditures or in highly effective low-cost care (e.g., the use of beta blockers for heart attacks) than other developed countries. This suggests that the technical efficiency of health production function in the United States would more closely resemble that of other developed countries if care were provided more uniformly for people with similar clinical characteristics.

With regard to allocative efficiency, Garber and Skinner (2008) point out the following three factors that contribute to the allocative inefficiency in the US health care system: (1) high prices for inputs, (2) lack of incentives for restraining overutilization, and (3) a tendency to adopt expensive medical innovations rapidly. One aspect of the high prices of health care inputs is that US physicians earn more than physicians in most other countries. In addition, the US health care system tends to offer the most expensive treatments, such as newer drugs with accompanying higher prices. Furthermore, compared to other developed countries, the United States typically does not consider effectiveness relative to its costs in the provision of new health care technologies.

poorer countries, more affluent persons paid more relative to other persons in their countries with lower incomes, but they also received more services.

Another concept of equity is horizontal equity, which is based on the principle of equal treatment for equal need. Van Doorslaer, Wagstaff, van der Burg, et al. (2000) applied this concept in measuring equity in health care utilization in ten European countries and the United States. They found that in all countries, the lower-income groups were more intensive users of health care services, including outpatient visits to general practitioners, medical specialists, and inpatient care. However, after controlling for differences in health needs, there was little or no evidence of an appreciable inequity in the overall health care utilization. This result may have arisen from combining offsetting inequalities in utilization among various components of health care. On the one hand, they found that in half of the countries sampled, there was a substantial bias toward more affluent persons since high-income persons used more physician visits than would be expected on the basis of need alone. On the other hand, hospital utilization was much higher among low-income persons, even after accounting for differences in needs. Overall, their results suggest that in the aggregate, health care systems of ten European countries and the United States performed reasonably well in terms of horizontal equity measured as equal treatment for equal need, although there were some exceptions for some specific components of health care.

13.5 SUMMARY

This chapter has analyzed major economic issues surrounding the health system with public supply and financing. We first explained the rationale for public financing *and* provision based on the argument that health care outcomes are noncontractible. Under such circumstances, public provision may be more efficient than private supply if the adverse effect of cost reduction on noncontractible quality under the latter is sufficiently large and innovation in health care is not a major contributor to quality improvement. We then explained the rationale for this system from the vantage point of redistribution. In this respect, public provision of health care is advantageous in achieving equal access through income redistribution.

We then analyzed the effects of public provision using the UK's NHS as an example. The NHS rations health care resources by queues rather than by prices. For this reason, our discussion focused on the role of waiting lists. Optimal waiting list length depends on the marginal cost and the marginal benefit of waiting, the latter of which in turn varies by disease type. We also reviewed several empirical studies on estimating the cost of waiting lists. The cost of waiting ranged from 0.5 percent to 0.8 percent of GDP in the UK. Increases in NHS waiting lists are associated with increases in private health insurance purchases.

Public provision is especially common in low-income countries. While certainly not the only causal determinant of low quality of care, public systems in these contexts often have not provided sufficient oversight or monitoring of service provision. Furthermore, incentives to encourage clinicians to provide adequate quality of care have often been lacking. We documented the evidence from empirical studies of the issue that have been conducted to date and discussed policy options that might be implemented for improving the quality of care provision. Only one of the options involves privatizing the delivery of health care services.

There is a paucity of empirical evidence on the effects of policy interventions to improve the quality of care in low-income countries. We reviewed two recent interesting randomized controlled trials of interventions to help consumers as individuals and collectively demand improvements in quality. The results of both studies are encouraging.

Finally, we evaluated different health care systems in terms of intermediate performance measures and performance goals. Intermediate performance measures, such as access, cost, and quality, do not always, or even generally, move in the same direction. Rather, there are many trade-offs between intermediate performance measures. Specifically, there is a trade-off between access and cost because achieving better access to care requires more resources and hence increases the cost burden to society. There is also a trade-off between cost and quality. There is no perfect system that has an advantage in achieving all of the intermediate performance measures. Without comparing costs and outcomes, it is not possible to draw definitive conclusions on the relative efficiency of alternative health care systems. Although cost-effectiveness or cost-benefit analysis has been widely used for comparisons at the disease level or program level, empirical evidence on the efficiency of alternative health care systems at a national level is nonexistent. Hence we are unable to draw definitive conclusions about the overall performance of different health care systems.

Nevertheless, there are some consistent patterns. First, systems with public financing are in a better position to achieve the goal of equity in the health care financing, especially when tax financing plays the dominant role. Second, a system with a larger share of public financing appears to be better at controlling growth in overall expenditure on personal health care services. Thus, a system with public financing has a comparative advantage in obtaining an optimal balance among different policy goals.

By contrast, the case for the public supply of health care seems weaker because there is no consistent evidence showing that this system is in a better position to achieve a good balance among competing goals. Quality has been judged to be low in some public systems. Incentives provided by market forces to innovate may be lacking in public systems. While queuing may redistribute services to low-income persons, there is a deadweight loss from queuing.

Health systems characterized by the combination of public financing and private supply of health care are thus likely to become the most common model as a result of worldwide health care reform, although such a system must wrestle with the trade-off among different measures of performance, such as cost containment, quality, and innovation in health care.

KEY CONCEPTS

- public provision of health care
- non-price rationing
- noncontractible outcomes
- rationing by queues
- access
- quality
- allocative efficiency
- vertical equity
- National Health Service
- transaction cost
- socialization of commodities
- waiting list
- cost
- technical efficiency
- horizontal equity

REVIEW AND DISCUSSION QUESTIONS

13.1 What are the major advantages and disadvantages of the public provision of personal health care services? Under what conditions is public provision likely to be the preferred mode of delivery?

13.2 What are some of the disadvantages of the public provision of personal health care services? Identify the most important trade-offs in a country's decision between public versus private provision.

13.3 Describe the concept of an optimal waiting list. Why would this vary by disease? What are the key costs of waiting?

13.4 Distinguish between the concepts of horizontal and vertical equity. Describe specific indicators that can be used to evaluate horizontal and vertical equity of a health system.

13.5 One rationale for the public provision of health care is that the public sector is better at achieving society's redistributive concerns. How does a government redistribute income by providing health care directly?

13.6 What is meant by the term "heterogeneity among individuals"? Give three examples in which heterogeneity among individuals creates a gap between the public supply of and the private demand for health care (i.e., some individuals may have an unmet want in the public health system).

13.7 Explain the term "noncontractible outcomes" in your own words. Noncontractible outcomes do not only pertain to health care. Explain how noncontractible outcomes may operate in markets for long-term care and in the government procurement of defense weapons.

13.8 Based on the theory of noncontractible outcomes, what are two preconditions that must be met for public provision to be superior to private provision?

13.9 What is meant by the term "opt out of the public system"? Give two examples of opting out the public system in markets other than for health care, and explain the rationale for each choice

13.10 Why is a waiting list for receiving health services very common in systems where the government provides health care directly but not so common in other health care systems?

13.11 The long waiting list has been the major issue in public health systems for decades. Can the government solve this issue solely by increasing health care budgets? If so, please explain under what conditions raising public funds can become an effective policy to ease the problem of waiting lists.

13.12 Define "equity" in health care financing. Based on the existing evidence, which type of health care system is in a better position to achieve equity in health care financing? Justify your answer.

Exercises

13.1 For which of the following services is public supply likely to be superior to private supply? Discuss each service and justify your answers.

a. prison;

b. schooling;

c. vaccination;

d. housing.

13.2 In chapter 12, we introduced social insurance programs in many countries. All these countries have incorporated various forms of demand-side cost sharing, such as coinsurance or co-payments, into their health systems. But in the public health systems discussed in this chapter, it is rare to see countries adopting demand-side cost sharing. What is the reason for this difference?

13.3 Collect data on GDP per capita and percentage of out-of-pocket payment in total health expenditures for at least twenty countries from any data set you can access (e.g., OECD Health Data or the World Health Organization's World Health Report for 2006). If you cannot access any data set, you may use the data on these two variables from figures 13.5 and 13.6 to answer the questions. Plot the data, with GDP per capita on the horizontal axis and percentage of out-of-pocket payment on the vertical axis, and answer the following questions:

a. Based on your figure, is there any clear relationship between GDP per capita and percentage of out-of-pocket payment? If so, does the relationship have a negative or a positive slope? How do you interpret such a relationship?

b. Did any country become an outlier in your figure? How do you explain this exception?

13.4 According to a study conducted by the World Bank, around 50 percent of health care financing in sub-Saharan Africa comes from out-of-pocket payments paid by largely impoverished populations. Assume that the World Bank calls for a proposal to solve this problem and receives two policy recommendations: one suggests a "public solution" through the direct public provision that requires the governments in these countries to allocate more funds to public hospitals; the other suggests a "private solution" through private health insurance that requires the governments in African countries to encourage the development of the private health insurance market. The World Bank hires you as an expert to review these two proposals. What are your main comments on these two proposals from the vantage points of efficiency and equity?

13.5 In recent years, government revenues from taxing tobacco and selling lottery tickets have been widely used to finance health care provision and services. Suppose both China and India were to adopt a major health care reform to reduce their citizens' share of out-of-pocket payment in total health expenditure, but each country decides to use a different funding source. China uses a tobacco tax and the net revenue from selling lottery tickets as the source of public funds; India uses the personal income tax as its source of public funds. Assume that other aspects remain constant. Compare the equity in health care financing between these two countries.

13.6 In chapters 11–13, we have provided reviews of the evolution of health care systems in more than ten countries. Among them, which country has had a relatively "stable" health system that has not changed appreciably for a very long time, and which country has had a relatively "unstable" health care system that has changed frequently during a short time period? Why is the health system in some countries more stable than in other countries? List at least two factors contributing to the stability of a health care system and at least two factors contributing to the instability of a health care system.

13.7 Many countries have a "mixed" health care system, that is, a private health care sector exists alongside a larger public health care sector. Under such a system, individuals may choose to "opt out" of the public system and receive care from private sources. Does this opting-out behavior occur more frequently in low-income countries than in high-income countries? Why or why not? Do the major drivers that induce people to opt out the public system differ between high-income and low-income countries?

ONLINE SUPPLEMENTAL MATERIAL

NATIONAL HEALTH SERVICE: UK

http://www.nhs.uk/Pages/homepage.aspx

http://news.bbc.co.uk/1/shared/spl/hi/guides/456900/456959/html/nn1page1.stm

http://www.gresham.ac.uk/event.asp?PageId=45&EventId=664

AUSTRALIA

http://www.health.gov.au/internet/main/publishing.nsf/Content/healthsystem-overview-contents

SCANDINAVIAN HEALTH CARE SYSTEMS

http://www.ub.uib.no/elpub/rokkan/N/N05-04.pdf

DENMARK

http://www.civitas.org.uk/pdf/Denmark.pdf

http://www.im.dk/publikationer/healthcare_in_dk/all.htm#c1

SWEDEN

http://www.sweden.se/templates/cs/FactSheet____15865.aspx

http://www.fraserinstitute.org/commerce.web/product_files/SwedishHealthcareSystem.pdf

Finland

http://countrystudies.us/finland/72.htm

http://lcweb2.loc.gov/frd/cs/fitoc.html

Norway

http://www.helsetilsynet.no/templates/ArticleWithLinks____5520.aspx

Middle- and Low-Income Countries

Costa Rica

http://www.costarica.com/Retirement/Cost-of-Living/Health-Care/

http://www.internationalliving.com/Countries/Costa-Rica/Health-Care

http://www.cehat.org/rthc/paper5.htm

Nigeria

http://countrystudies.us/nigeria/50.htm

http://lcweb2.loc.gov/frd/cs/ngtoc.html

Thailand

http://www.amazing-thailand.com/Health.html

Supplemental Readings

Björkman, M., and J. Svensson. 2009. Power to the People: Evidence from a Randomized Field Experiment on Community-Based Monitoring in Uganda. *Quarterly Journal of Economics* 124 (2): 735–769.

Das, J., J. Hammer, and K. Leonard. 2008. The Quality of Medical Advice in Low-Income Countries. *Journal of Economic Perspectives* 22 (2): 93–114.

Jensen, P. H., E. Webster, and J. Witt. 2009. Hospital Type and Patient Outcomes: An Empirical Examination Using AMI Readmission and Mortality Records. *Health Economics* 18 (12): 1440–1460.

O'Donnell, O., E. van Doorslaer, R. P. Rannan-Eliya, et al. 2008. Who Pays for Health Care in Asia? *Journal of Health Economics* 27 (2): 460–475.

Pandey, P., A. R. Sehgal, M. Riboud, et al. 2007. Informing Resource-Poor Populations and the Delivery of Entitled Health and Social Services in Rural India: A Cluster Randomized Controlled Trial. *Journal of the American Medical Association* 298 (16): 1867–1875.

Propper, C., S. Burgess, and D. Gossage. 2008. Competition and Quality: Evidence from the NHS Internal Market 1991–1999. *Economic Journal* 118 (525): 138–170.

REFERENCES

Aaron, H. J., and W. B. Schwartz. 2005. *Can We Say No?* Washington, DC: Brookings Institution Press.

Anderson, G. F., U. E. Reinhardt, P. S. Hussey, et al. 2003. It's the Prices, Stupid: Why the United States Is So Different from Other Countries. *Health Affairs* 22 (3): 89.

Banerjee, A., A. Deaton, and E. Duflo. 2004. Wealth, Health, and Health Services in Rural Rajasthan. *American Economic Review* 94 (2): 326–330.

Besley, T., and M. Gouveia. 1994. Alternative Systems of Health Care Provision. *Economic Policy* 19 (2): 199–258.

Besley, T., J. Hall, and I. Preston. 1999. The Demand for Private Health Insurance: Do Waiting Lists Matter? *Journal of Public Economics* 72 (2): 155–181.

Biglaiser, G., and C. T. A. Ma. 2007. Moonlighting: Public Service and Private Practice. *Rand Journal of Economics* 38 (4): 1113–1133.

Björkman, M., and J. Svensson. 2009. Power to the People: Evidence from a Randomized Field Experiment on Community-Based Monitoring in Uganda. *Quarterly Journal of Economics* 124 (2): 735–769.

Boycko, M., A. Shleifer, and R. W. Vishny. 1996. A Theory of Privatisation. *Economic Journal* 106 (435): 309–319.

Breyer, F. 1982. Rational Purchase of Medical Care and Differential Insurance Coverage for Diagnostic Services. *Journal of Health Economics* 1 (2): 147–156.

Chaudhury, N., J. Hammer, M. Kremer, et al. 2006. Missing in Action: Teacher and Health Worker Absence in Developing Countries. *Journal of Economic Perspectives* 20 (1): 91–116.

Cullis, J. G., and P. R. Jones. 1986. Rationing by Waiting Lists: An Implication. *American Economic Review* 76 (1): 250–256.

Cullis, J. G., P. R. Jones, and C. Propper. 2000. Waiting Lists and Medical Treatment: Analysis and Policies. In *Handbook of Health Economics*, ed. J. P. Newhouse and A. J. Culyer, 1B:1201–1245. Amsterdam: Elsevier Science.

Cutler, D. M. 2002. Equality, Efficiency, and Market Fundamentals: The Dynamics of International Medical-Care Reform. *Journal of Economic Literature* 40 (3): 881–906.

Das, J., and P. J. Gertler. 2007. Variations in Practice Quality in Five Low-Income Countries: A Conceptual Overview. *Health Affairs* (special issue), w296–w309.

Dow, W. H., and L. B. Sáenz. 2002. Costa Rica. In *World Health Systems*, ed. B. J. Fried and L. M. Gaydos, 463–474. Chicago: Health Administration Press.

Duggan, M. 2004. Does Contracting Out Increase the Efficiency of Government Programs? Evidence from Medicaid HMOs. *Journal of Public Economics* 88 (12): 2549–2572.

Frydman, R., C. Gray, M. Hessel, et al. 1999. When Does Privatization Work? The Impact of Private Ownership on Corporate Performance in the Transition Economies. *Quarterly Journal of Economics* 114 (4): 1153–1191.

Garber, A. M., and J. Skinner. 2008. Is American Health Care Uniquely Inefficient? *Journal of Economic Perspectives* 22 (4): 27–50.

Gaynor, M., R. Moreno-Serra, and C. Propper. 2010. Death by Market Power: Reform, Competition and Patient Outcomes in the National Health Service. National Bureau of Economic Research Working Paper 16164. Cambridge, MA: National Bureau of Economic Research.

Gerdtham, U.-G., and B. Jönsson. 2000. International Comparisons on Health Expenditure: Theory, Data, and Econometric Analysis. In *Handbook of Health Economics*, ed. J. P. Newhouse and A. J. Culyer, 1A:11–49. Amsterdam: Elsevier Science.

Gerdtham, U.-G., J. Søgaard, F. Andersson, et al. 1992. An Econometric Analysis of Health Care Expenditure: A Cross-Section Study of the OECD Countries. *Journal of Health Economics* 11 (1): 63–84.

Grabowski, H. G., and Y. R. Wang. 2006. The Quantity and Quality of Worldwide New Drug Introductions, 1982–2003. *Health Affairs* 25 (2): 452–460.

Hall, J. 1999. Incremental Change in the Australian Health Care System. *Health Affairs* 18 (3): 95–110.

Hart, O., A. Shleifer, and R. W. Vishny. 1997. The Proper Scope of Government: Theory and an Application to Prisons. *Quarterly Journal of Economics* 112 (4): 1127–1161.

Hurley, J. 2000. An Overview of the Normative Economics of the Health Sector. In *Handbook of Health Economics*, ed. J. P. Newhouse and A. J. Culyer, 1A:55–110. Amsterdam: Elsevier Science.

Iversen, T. 1993. A Theory of Hospital Waiting Lists. *Journal of Health Economics* 12 (1): 55–71.

Iversen, T. 1997. The Effect of a Private Sector on the Waiting Time in a National Health Service. *Journal of Health Economics* 16 (4): 381–396.

Jensen, P. H., E. Webster, and J. Witt. 2009. Hospital Type and Patient Outcomes: An Empirical Examination Using AMI Readmission and Mortality Records. *Health Economics* 18 (12): 1440–1460.

Johannesson, M., P. Johannesson, and T. Söderqvist. 1998. Time Spent on Waiting Lists for Medical Care: An Insurance Approach. *Journal of Health Economics* 17 (5): 627–644.

Joskow, P. L. 2007. Regulation of Natural Monopoly. In *Handbook of Law and Economics*, ed. A. M. Polinsky and S. Shavell, 2:1227–1348. Amsterdam: Elsevier Science.

Klemick, H., K. L. Leonard, and M. C. Masatu. 2009. Defining Access to Health Care: Evidence on the Importance of Quality and Distance in Rural Tanzania (2008–2010). *American Journal of Agricultural Economics* 91 (2): 347–358.

Lacey, L. 2002. Nigeria. In *World Health Systems: Challenges and Perspectives*, ed. B. J. Fried and L. M. Gaydos, 507–520. Chicago: Health Administration Press.

Leonard, K. 2007. Learning in Health Care: Evidence of Learning about Clinician Quality in Tanzania. *Economic Development and Cultural Change* 55 (3): 531–555.

Leonard, K., M. C. Masatu, and A. Vialou. 2007. Getting Doctors to Do Their Best: The Role of Ability and Motivation in Health Care Quality. *Journal of Human Resources* 42 (3): 682–700.

Lien, H. M., S. Y. Chou, and J. T. Liu. 2008. Hospital Ownership and Performance: Evidence from Stroke and Cardiac Treatment in Taiwan. *Journal of Health Economics* 27:1208–1223.

Lindsay, C. M., and B. Feigenbaum. 1984. Rationing by Waiting Lists. *American Economic Review* 74 (3): 404–417.

Ljung, R., S. Peterson, J. Hallqvist, et al. 2005. Socioeconomic Differences in the Burden of Disease in Sweden. *World Health Organization* 83 (2): 92–99.

Mariko, M. 2003. Quality of Care and the Demand for Health Services in Barmako, Mali: The Specific Roles of Structural, Process, and Outcome Components. *Social Science & Medicine* 56:1183–1196.

Martin, S., and P. C. Smith. 1999. Rationing by Waiting Lists: An Empirical Investigation. *Journal of Health Economics* 71 (1): 141–164.

Maynard, A. 2005. International Healthcare Reform: What Goes Around, Comes Around. In *The Public-Private Mix for Health*, ed. A. Maynard, 1–6. Oxford: Radcliffe Publishing.

McKee, M., and J. Healy. 2002. Health Care Systems in the Central Asia Republics: An Introduction. In *Health Care in Central Asia*, ed. J. Faulkinham. Buckingham, UK: Open University Press.

Megginson, W. L., and J. M. Netter. 2001. From State to Market: A Survey of Empirical Studies on Privatization. *Journal of Economic Literature* 39 (2): 321–389.

Newhouse, J. P. 1977. Medical-Care Expenditure: A Cross-National Survey. *Journal of Human Resources* 12 (1): 115–125.

Noguchi, H., Y. Masuda, M. Kuzuya, et al. 2006. A Comparison of Quality of Health Care in the United States and Japan: Treatment and Outcomes for Heart Attack Patients. In *Health Care Issues in the United States and Japan*, ed. D. A. Wise and N. Yashiro, 165–194. Chicago: University of Chicago Press.

O'Donnell, O., E. van Doorslaer, R. P. Rannan-Eliya, et al. 2008. Who Pays for Health Care in Asia? *Journal of Health Economics* 27 (2): 460–475.

Organisation for Economic Co-operation and Development. 2008. OECD Health Data. http://www.oecd.org/document/56.

Pandey, P., A. R. Sehgal, M. Riboud, et al. 2007. Informing Resource-Poor Populations and the Delivery of Entitled Health and Social Services in Rural India: A Cluster Randomized Controlled Trial. *Journal of the American Medical Association* 298 (16): 1867–1875.

Pedersen, K. M. 2005. The Public-Private Mix in Scandinavia. In *The Public-Private Mix for Health*, ed. A. Maynard, 161–190. Oxford: Radcliffe Publishing.

Peltzman, S. 1971. Pricing in Public and Private Enterprises: Electric Utilities in the United States. *Journal of Law & Economics* 14 (1): 109–147.

Poterba, J. M. 1996. Government Intervention in the Markets for Education and Health Care: How and Why? In *Individual and Social Responsibility: Child Care, Education, Medical Care, and Long-Term Care in America*, ed. V. R. Fuchs. Chicago: University of Chicago Press.

Propper, C. 1995. The Disutility of Time Spend on the United Kingdom's Nation Health Service Waiting Lists. *Journal of Human Resources* 30 (4): 677–700.

Propper, C., S. Burgess, and D. Gossage. 2008. Competition and Quality: Evidence from the NHS Internal Market 1991–1999. *Economic Journal* 118 (525): 138–170.

Propper, C., and K. Green. 2001. A Larger Role for the Private Sector in Financing UK Health Care: The Arguments and the Evidence. *Journal of Social Policy* 30 (4): 685–704.

Savage, E., and D. J. Wright. 2003. Moral Hazard and Adverse Selection in Australian Private Hospitals: 1989–1990. *Journal of Health Economics* 22 (3): 331–359.

Scott, A., S. Schurer, P. H. Jensen, et al. 2009. The Effects of an Incentive Program on Quality of Care in Diabetes Management. *Health Economics* 18:1091–1108.

Scott, A., and S. Vick. 1999. Patients, Doctors & Contracts: An Application of Principal-Agent Theory to the Doctor-Patient Relationship. *Scottish Journal of Political Economy* 46 (2): 111–134.

Sekhri, N., and W. Savedoff. 2005. Private Health Insurance: Implications for Developing Countries. *World Health Organization* 83:127–134.

Shleifer, A. 1998. State versus Private Ownership. *Journal of Economic Perspectives* 12 (4): 133–150.

Shleifer, A., and R. W. Vishny. 1997. A Survey of Corporate Governance. *Journal of Finance* 52 (2): 737–783.

Siciliani, L., A. Stanciole, and R. Jacobs. 2009. Do Waiting Times Reduce Hospital Costs. *Journal of Health Economics* 28 (4): 771–780.

Singh, N. 2008. Decentralization and Public Delivery of Health Care Services in India. *Health Affairs* 27 (4): 991–1001.

Spithoven, A. H. G. M. 2009. Why U.S. Health Care Expenditure and Ranking on Health Care Indicators Are So Different from Canada's. *International Journal of Health Care Finance and Economics* 9 (1): 1–24.

Ssengooba, F., L. Atuyambe, B. McPake, et al. 2002. What Could Be Achieved with Greater Public Hospital Autonomy? Comparison of Public and PNFP Hospitals in Uganda. *Public Administration and Development* 22 (5):415–428.

Tobin, J. 1970. On Limiting the Domain of Inequality. *Journal of Law & Economics* 13 (2): 263–277.

Usher, D. 1977. The Welfare Economics of the Socialization of Commodities. *Journal of Public Economics* 8 (2): 151–168.

van Doorslaer, E., A. Wagstaff, H. van der Burg, et al. 2000. Equity in the Delivery of Health Care in Europe and the U.S. *Journal of Health Economics* 19 (5): 553–583.

Wagstaff, A., and E. van Doorslaer. 1992. Equity in the Finance of Health Care: Some International Comparisons. *Journal of Health Economics* 11 (4): 361–387.

Woolhandler, S., T. Campbell, and D. U. Himmelstein. 2003. Costs of Health Care Administration in the United States and Canada. *New England Journal of Medicine* 349 (8): 768–775.

World Health Organzation (WHO). 2006. World Health Report, 2006. www.who.int/whr/2006/en.

World Health Organization (WHO). 2008. World Health Report, 2008. www.who.int/whr/2008/en.

Performance of the Health Care Sector: Positive and Normative Aspects

CHAPTER 14

COST AND COST-EFFECTIVENESS ANALYSIS

Up to now, this book has largely dealt with positive economics—explaining why behaviors are observed, including the role of incentives in the decisions made in a health care context. In the next two chapters we focus on normative economic questions. Answers to normative questions involve recommendations about policies that should be adopted. There are many normative questions in the health care sphere. Here we deal with recommendations about the allocation of health care resources. Which personal health care services should be provided, and under what circumstances? If resources were unlimited, it would be unnecessary to have methods for determining the best way to allocate resources.

Decision makers—governments, insurers, individuals, physicians, and others—make choices about resource allocation on some basis. Some decision makers may rely on their past professional and personal experiences or on material they learned in school. Physicians and other health professionals may follow rules and guidelines developed by others. On the other hand, they may follow the advice of drug sales personnel who visit them in their offices. Government decision makers may be influenced by precedent or by budget constraints, even if the budget constraints are "soft" (see chapter 6), as well as by political pressures from self-interested stakeholders, in making resource allocation decisions.

Although the economist's prescription for optimal resource allocation involves comparisons of benefits and costs, decisions often focus almost exclusively on either costs or benefits or on neither costs nor benefits. In the end, public decisions are political. This does not mean, however, that there is no role for the economic analysis of resource allocation decisions. Even if the decision is eventually guided by political considerations, decision makers often want to know the results of quantitative analyses of the costs and benefits of a particular choice. The task of the analyst is to provide unbiased advice based on the best evidence available. The public official then can weigh the evidence provided along with other considerations in reaching a final decision.

Unfortunately, the advice sought or obtained is often incomplete, which inevitably leads to poor resource allocation decisions. For example, because costs are highly visible and often immediate while benefits are less visible, more diffuse, and often accrue over a long period of time, decisions to cover the cost of a specific drug may be largely based on the cost of the drug, even if the drug has important benefits. Sometimes the use of a drug reduces other costs, such as from hospitalizations, which have favorable effects on the decision maker's budget. However, without analysis, these favorable impacts may not be identified.

At the other extreme, some public policy makers and manufacturers of medical products focus exclusively on the benefits of a technology; an example here is government agencies with responsibility for regulating the safety and efficacy of prescription drugs. In some cases, public agencies are not allowed to consider cost in their decision making. Some private insurers are not much different. They cover drugs if the drugs are deemed to be safe and effective, sometimes imposing a higher co-payment rate on branded versus generic drugs, with no explicit consideration given to the quantitative benefits of the drug.

This chapter and the following one describe analytic techniques to guide decisions that reflect not only costs or benefits, each taken independently, but costs and benefits of specific technologies evaluated jointly. While it would be naive to presume that decision makers will use these analytic techniques to the total exclusion of other considerations in decision making, use of these techniques can add both consistency and rigor to the decision-making process, which can lead to a better allocation of scarce resources.

The methodologies we describe assume a social perspective. Both social benefits and costs are considered. Social benefits include not only benefits to the user of a particular technology but any benefits accruing to others from its use. Similarly, social costs include costs accruing to all parties, not just the user and the user's family. An individual family member or an insurer may adopt a narrower perspective on benefit and cost. An insurer may not be concerned about the cost burdens on families, and conversely.

14.1 Overview of Cost-Effectiveness and Cost-Benefit Analysis

Cost-effectiveness analysis (CEA) assesses cost per unit of outcome, such as cost per life years saved, cost per quality-adjusted life year saved (QALY) (see chapter 7), or cost per accident averted. A QALY is a measure of the quality as well as the quantity of life. It measures the number of life years, but with the life years adjusted downward to the extent that people are limited in terms of mental health, pain, and physical or cognitive functioning during these years. Thus, for example, a technology might extend life by five years, but because persons suffer severe disability during these years, the technology may raise QALYs by only one or two units.

Costs are calculated in monetary units. Outcomes in CEA are not expressed in monetary terms but rather in such units as life years, QALYs, and nonfatal accidents averted. In comparing different alternatives for achieving the same type of outcome, the task is to select that alternative with the lowest cost per unit of outcome. When comparing alternative preventive, diagnostic, or therapeutic approaches with different outcomes, such as lives saved versus days of work lost versus improvements in the physical functioning of elderly persons who are not employed in the workforce, the decision maker needs to weigh the relative importance of each outcome type in some way for a comparison to be made. QALYs offer an explicit approach for making comparisons when the units of output for various technologies differ. For example, QALYs permit comparisons of benefits from a drug designed to reduce migraine headaches with a vaccine aimed at preventing HIV/AIDS.

In cost-benefit analysis (CBA), both costs and benefits are expressed in monetary units. Thus, the ratio of costs to benefits or the difference in benefits and costs is compared. Such analysis is often used in some public policy areas, such as in resource and environmental decision making. In the health area, CEA is far more commonly used than CBA.

The advantages of CEA, described in this chapter, and CBA, described in chapter 15, are that such analyses provide (1) a framework for making underlying assumptions explicit, (2) a common methodology that facilitates making benefit versus cost comparisons among various technologies, and (3) an approach for assessing the far-reaching consequences of adopting a technology or implementing a health program. Many technologies and programs have impacts on personal health that persist for years if not decades.

For example, a knee replacement may improve a person's physical functioning for several years, but eventually a reoperation may be necessary. A through assessment involves calculating cost and benefit streams over a number of years. These intertemporal calculations are likely to be difficult for decision makers to make in their heads, but to date, the intuitive approach has been the more common one.

As will become more apparent later, CBA and CEA have important deficiencies as well. The quality of the empirical evidence that goes into the models used in such analyses varies. For example, a drug may be more effective in some populations than in others, or adverse side effects may differ. Thus, even if a new drug is cost-effective on average, its cost-effectiveness may vary appreciably among individuals.

Although in principle, both long- and short-run costs and benefits should be considered, in practice, long-run costs and benefits often are not known. The randomized controlled trials (RCTs) used to assess drug or medical device safety and efficacy for regulatory purposes do not typically measure long-term effects. Then, even if the studies are well conducted, decision makers may not have adequate technical knowledge to assess the studies' quality. And even though the study has a social perspective, the decision may be based on narrower criteria that are more relevant to the decision maker.

CEA measures benefits in terms of a change in a clinical outcome, such as mortality, blood pressure, time to recurrence of a type of cancer, or QALYs. In a CEA, the cost may be only that of the technology itself, such as the cost of a drug. In CBA, benefits are measured in pecuniary terms, such as the value of additional years of life. In both CEA and CBA, the costs of the intervention are in the numerator of the ratio. The outcomes (CEA) or benefits (CBA) are in the denominator.

Economists generally prefer CBA to CEA. Ultimately, resource allocation involves comparisons in monetary terms (Pauly 1996). Even a family deciding on gifts to purchase for holidays or birthdays has to allocate resources based on costs and benefits in monetary terms or some other common unit of measure. How else can one compare an expenditure on a scarf versus a toy? Expenditure per gift will probably not do. Keeping warm and being entertained need to be expressed explicitly or at least implicitly in some common metric, such as money. For reasons that are difficult to explain, resource allocation decisions for environmental protection generally rely on CBA, even though health effects are among the most important targets of environmental policy.

Others, including many physicians, prefer CEA. Health professionals are often reluctant to place a pecuniary value on good health, a life year, or a life. Also, there is a concern that valuing outcomes in pecuniary terms will result in resource allocation that favors the affluent over less affluent individuals. Suppose, for example, affluent people have high relative willingness to pay for beauty-enhancing plastic surgery. There is perhaps a risk that a society that bases decisions about the allocation of its resources completely on CBA would allocate too many resources to such procedures. This is so since benefit may be measured as the sum of maximum willingness to pay for the service by all members of society; maximum willingness to pay on the part of relatively affluent persons may represent a disproportionate part of total willingness to pay and hence of total benefit. On the other hand, decision makers could examine an allocation priority list developed from CBA and cull those projects that seem disproportionately influenced by preferences of the country's most affluent citizens.

To further illustrate the concern that the use of CBA may discriminate against the poor, suppose there are two types of care, a prenatal visit and a surgical procedure to remove facial hair, and the decision is whether or not a public insurer should include these services as benefits. To determine social benefit, we add the maximum willingness of each individual to pay for coverage of each service. Person A, who has a low income, is willing to pay up to $15 for coverage for a prenatal visit and $5 for coverage of facial hair removal. Person B, who is affluent, is willing to pay up to $20 for coverage of a prenatal visit and up to $800 for facial hair removal. In this two-person economy, the aggregate benefit of the prenatal visit is $35, and coverage for facial hair removal is worth $805. Hence, based on aggregate benefit, covering facial hair removal merits a higher priority, even though person A would have preferred to have coverage for a prenatal visit.

Benefits in CBA can be measured in several alternative ways: (1) revealed preference data, which provide evidence on choices people actually make, for example, revealed choices such as wage premiums when employees take riskier jobs or the amount people pay for safety devices such as radon detectors, which offer specific reductions in the probability of getting lung cancer from radon located in or under one's home; (2) surveys of willingness to pay for reductions in specific risks, sometimes called contingent valuation (CV) surveys (because the surveys elicit maximum willingness to pay for goods or services contingent on those goods or services being offered); or (3) the costs averted by use of the technology, such as reductions in spending on hospitalizations.

Maximum willingness to pay (WTP) for a year of additional life or for an additional QALY, or for coverage of prenatal care or removal of facial hair, is likely to be positively related to the individual's income and wealth. And the benefit from a good or service being evaluated reflects the sum of all members of society's WTP. Advocates for CBA argue that it is possible to reweigh benefits by income category or on other basis to reflect society's values regarding the appropriate distribution of income (Pauly 1996). Even if we accept the arguments for CBA as valid, CEA is so much more common that it has become the standard method used in health care technology evaluation.

CBA or CEA is not needed for the vast majority of decisions we make in daily life. The consumer decides how much ice cream to purchase without performing a formal analysis of benefits versus cost and the time stream over which such benefits and cost accrue. For example, ice cream may be tasty now but lead to obesity later, and to diabetes even later. In this sense, a CBA or CEA prior to the ice cream consumption decision may be good to have, but most people would think they could decide such matters without employing CBA or CEA as a decision-making tool.

But consider a decision by a public agency about whether or not to cover an oral medication for glycemic (blood sugar) control of diabetes. The adoption decision involves a collective choice, not an individual decision. The public decision maker should consider the benefits and costs that individual decision makers would not. Much of the cost of future diabetes complications will be financed by the public insurer, not by the individual with the diabetic complication. Long-run effects or multiple effects are often difficult for one patient or even one physician, based on his or her practice experience, to evaluate, especially when the effects occur only very rarely. An individual physician may have prescribed the drugs for years and never observed a patient with a particular adverse effect. However, such rarely occurring adverse effects can be incorporated into formal analysis of the technology's costs and benefits using larger samples than a single physician's practice would be likely to yield.

14.2 Cost-Effectiveness Analysis: Measuring Cost

Overview

The objective of cost measurement in CEA is to estimate the cost of the intervention net of savings if there are cost offsets accruing from the intervention. Cost offsets represent savings attributable to reductions in the use of some services attributable to the intervention other than the intervention itself. For example, the intervention might be a new drug and the cost offset might be reduced hospital stays among persons taking the drug.

At first glance, measuring cost might seem quite straightforward. However, a number of complexities are involved, starting with the concept of opportunity cost and its measurement. Some costs can be measured from market values, such as the wage of a hospital employee. For other types of cost for which no market value is available, we must find some method for imputing the cost, such as the cost of patient waiting time, particularly when the patient is not employed. And, as we shall see, not all costs are relevant for computing a cost-effectiveness ratio.

Concept of Opportunity Cost

Essential to the economic concept of cost is *opportunity cost.* Deploying a good or a service in one activity usually means reducing its use in some other activity. If there is no reduction in input use because, for example, some units of the input would not be utilized in any case, the input use has a zero opportunity cost. Thus, for example, if a hospital has unutilized beds, allocating some of these unutilized beds to a new activity does not involve an opportunity cost. The beds must have alternative uses that generate value. If the hospital operates at full capacity, raising admissions of persons with one health condition must mean a decrease in admissions of another type. In the latter case, treating one type of patient has an opportunity cost in not being able to treat another type of patient because of bed capacity constraints.

Many CEAs in health care are done to inform decisions about drugs and medical devices. The meaning of the opportunity cost in each application depends on the decision being made. If the decision is whether or not to make a public investment in research and development for a drug for a particular disease, the relevant opportunity cost includes the cost of R&D, as well as the additional cost of manufacturing and distributing the drug. R&D requires the work of scientists, technicians, materials, and attorneys (e.g., to obtain patents), which if used for one drug is not available for other uses. Manufacturing and distribution requires these labor inputs, but in different combinations, such as storage facilities, transport, and other inputs. The costs of administering the drug are also relevant opportunity costs. However, when R&D is involved, the main cost is likely to be for R&D (see chapter 9).

By contrast, if the public decision maker in a country is considering inclusion of a drug on the country's health insurance plan's formulary (a list of drugs covered by the insurance plan), a drug that already has been invented and marketed elsewhere, then the relevant opportunity cost includes the cost of the drug to its health insurance plan. This will depend on the price the plan can negotiate, as well as the number of units the plan expects to purchase in a time period, such as a year.

Direct and Indirect Costs

In much of the literature on the economic evaluation of drugs and other medical technology, a distinction is made between *direct* and *indirect* costs. Direct costs include the value of all goods and services consumed in the provision of the technology, both the resources used in the program and those used in treating the adverse side effects of the technology or program, present and future. An example of a program's adverse effects is the cost of relocating people displaced from a contaminated site. Included in direct costs are all health care costs, as well as such non-health care costs as child care utilized when parents visit a doctor, the cost of transportation to clinics (presumably not on buses with empty seats), and the value of the patient's time lost from work while receiving the technology, such as a physician visit.

Not all direct costs need be positive. For example, although the direct cost of a drug is plausibly positive, if use of the drug results in savings in physician visits or in hospital stays, these cost offsets would enter the cost calculation (the numerator of the cost-effectiveness ratio) as negative values.

Indirect costs include lost output due to illness, either in terms of missed work or lower productivity on the job or in terms of inability to perform household tasks. Indirect costs are legitimate costs; in fact, they are as legitimate as the direct ones. Thus, the distinction is not really very meaningful, although the distinction is often made. They are all costs.

In CBA, reductions in indirect costs are likely to be considered part of benefits. Other costs such as those attributable to pain and suffering and mortality are generally not included as indirect costs, but they too affect consumer welfare and merit inclusion in cost-benefit calculations. Since such costs are nonpecuniary, they present unique measurement issues, to be described in the next chapter.

OTHER COST CONCEPTS

TRANSFER COSTS

A transfer payment, such as the payment of a fixed amount per unit of time (e.g., a day) to a person suffering from an illness or disability, is not a cost from society's perspective. It is a cost to the party making the transfer and a benefit to the party receiving it. However, except for the administrative cost of determining eligibility and making the transfer (e.g., writing and recording the check and sending it), the transfer per se involves no use of scarce resources and hence is not a social cost and not a cost considered in CEA. Transfer of money places purchasing power in different hands, but increases in the recipient's purchasing power are offset by reductions in the donor's/taxpayer's purchasing power. By contrast, the public provision of goods and services does involve the use of scarce resources, and hence the cost of such public provision is counted in CEA.

FUTURE COSTS

Future costs associated with the use of a technology are as legitimate as current ones. Many technologies involve future costs. For example, artificial knees wear out and need to be replaced. Cardiac pacemakers require regular monitoring; batteries wear out and must be replaced periodically. Many drugs require regular monitoring by physicians to check for adverse health effects.

Future costs are worth less than currently occurring costs in that future costs are discounted to present value (discussed in chapter 2). The effect discounting has on the present value of future costs depends on the discount rate used. If the social rate of time preference is high—that is, if consumption today is worth much more to people than the same amount of consumption at a later time—society is relatively present-oriented, and conversely for a low time preference. When time preference is high, future benefits and costs receive low weight relative to ones accruing closer to the present.

Determining the appropriate social rate of time preference or the *discount rate* is not straightforward. If the rate selected is too low, future costs will be overstated, and conversely if the rate selected is too high. The social discount rate should be a real rate; the social rate is the nominal social discount rate less annual rates of inflation. For example, if the anticipated inflation rate is 4 percent annually, then a nominal discount rate of 6 percent corresponds to a real rate of 2 percent. Unless deflation (price declines) is anticipated, real discount rates must be positive values.

Real social discount rates should generally be less than or equal to real market interest rates. There are several reasons for this. First, market rates reflect credit and market risk. Governments' central banks that issue their own currency face no credit risk, although market risk, which applies to all securities, remains. Second, societies have a longer time horizon than do consumers or other private parties. For example, an individual may attach less weight to outcomes accruing in future decades than societies do. Of course, public officials may be worried about the next election and have high rates of time preference (high discount rates) for this reason. The long-run real return on US government long-term fixed income securities, measured from 1870 to 2004, was 2.96 percent (Girola 2005). For a shorter period, 1961–2004, the yield on such securities was 3.44 percent, compared with 3.20 percent on the US Social Security Trust Fund (Girola 2005). It seems unlikely that the social discount rate is higher than a weighted average of these two long-run rates, if that high.

Some analysts add a factor to discount rates to reflect the uncertainty of their calculations. This approach may represent a conservative method for accounting for uncertainty when the costs are incurred initially and the benefits accrue later, since the conservative approach would reduce benefits relative to costs. But in CEA, costs are in the numerator of the cost-effectiveness ratio.[1] Unless substantial cost offsets occur downstream, introducing a "fudge factor" into the discount rate to reflect uncertainty is not a conservative approach, particularly when costs are incurred downstream. Particularly for chronic diseases, for example, it may be necessary to take the drug on an ongoing basis. Then using the fudge factor would understate the present value of costs accruing downstream. Other methods for taking account of uncertainty are described below.

Future costs present some additional conceptual issues. For example, suppose a drug raises the probability that a person will survive a heart attack. Should one include the future costs of food, housing, and medicine as a future cost? Or do measures of willingness to pay for an additional life year, discussed below, account for the benefit of living longer net of the cost of maintaining the person during that life year?

SUNK VERSUS INCREMENTAL COSTS

A sunk cost is a cost incurred irrespective of whether the good or service is consumed or not. For example, after a drug has been invented and marketed, whether or not the drug is used, there is the sunk cost of the investment in R&D that led to availability of the drug. The cost of a hospital plant and equipment is sunk if there are no alternative uses for the facility.

Incremental cost, by contrast, depends on the level of output. If another unit is produced, distributed, and consumed, additional cost is incurred. Whether or not a cost is sunk or incremental depends on the decision being made. If the decision is made to invest in drug R&D, the cost of R&D is incremental. If a decision is made whether or not to cover a drug for an additional medical condition, the R&D investment on that drug is likely to be a sunk cost. Sunk costs are not appropriate for inclusion in CEA (or CBA) calculations.

JOINT COSTS/JOINT PRODUCTION

Joint production occurs everywhere. In a company producing several products, much labor and capital are frequently devoted to manufacturing and distributing

1. In CEA, the denominator represents some measure of health outcome, such as number of life years saved. Discounting these values at a higher rate would increase the cost-effectiveness ratio, making the activity being evaluated appear to be less worth while.

more than one product. Suppose a company produces cameras and film. How should the salary of the company's president be allocated? There is an almost infinite number of ways in which the president's salary could be allocated to the various company products, including cameras and film. One approach would be to base the allocation on the square feet allocated to the production of each good. Another would be to allocate the CEO's salary based on relative sales of the different products. Or the company could perform a time-and-motion study (direct observation of how time is spent on various activities) to determine how the president's time is allocated. But this approach will not result in an accurate allocation either since the president's time may often involve more than a single product, for example, time spent deciding whether or not to market several of the company's products in a particular part of a country or to particular countries.

The economist's solution (to continue this example) is that the company should consider only the value of the *additional* time spent by the president if the company were to increase its output for one product by a unit. Economists' focus is on marginal cost, not on allocating total or average cost by some measure of product share. If raising output by a unit does not increase the president's use of time, there is no additional such cost to count. But any additional cost arising from output increases *should* be counted. In practice, it is often difficult to estimate marginal cost, even for those who have access to information inside the company.

Cost from Alternative Perspectives

The societal perspective, the perspective from which cost for the purposes of conducting CEAs should be measured, is only one of several alternative perspectives. Others include those of the patient and patient's family, the self-insured employer, the public or private insurer, the managed care plan, or the hospital, physician, or pharmaceutical manufacturer. Perspective makes a substantial difference to which costs are considered. A societal perspective incorporates all costs and benefits to whomever they accrue.

However, in making personal decisions about health care use and other personal resource allocation decisions, the patient would have a different perspective —a valid one from the patient's vantage point. The individual patient is likely to consider only his or her opportunity cost of time and the costs he or she incurs out of pocket. The employer that provides health insurance to its employees on a self-insured basis is likely to consider patient time only if it adversely affects time away from the workplace for physician visits, paid sick time, and associated administrative costs, such as finding substitutes for the worker's lost work time. A private health insurer might not consider the value of sick time at all. Of course, a private insurer might become interested if it was clear that demand for its insurance product was affected by the success of the health plan in reducing employee sick days. While in principle, a public insurer's decisions would be guided by a consideration of social costs and benefits, in practice, public insurers may have a more limited perspective. For example, public insurers may be subject to pressure from politicians most directly and from taxpayers indirectly through their pressure on politicians to constrain the program's expenditure growth. Thus, even if a new technology were to reduce sick time, since public insurers do not compensate for sick time or otherwise bear the cost of sick time, such cost may not seem germane to the insurer's decision-making process. While we would argue that such cost should be germane, more realistically, even public decision makers often have more narrowly defined perspectives.

Having discussed the numerator of the cost-effectiveness ratio, we now describe its denominator.

14.3 COST-EFFECTIVENESS ANALYSIS: MEASURING EFFECTIVENESS

EFFECTIVENESS VERSUS EFFICACY

Health care analysts distinguish between *effectiveness* and *efficacy*. *Efficacy* refers to the input's marginal product under ideal circumstances. Circumstances are ideal when the technology is used exactly as it is designed to be used, for example, by patients in an RCT, or by physicians after the technology is introduced into the market. In practice, technologies are not used exactly as prescribed; they are often prescribed to persons who do not have the same condition for which the technology was designed. Patients often do not adhere to physicians' recommendations. Or patients have other conditions in addition to the condition for which the technology was designed. Efficacy refers to the relationship between inputs and outputs in an idealized laboratory setting, or under idealized conditions, which prevail in an RCT.

By contrast, *effectiveness* refers to the input's (technology's) marginal product in *actual* use. For example, a drug may be ideally suited for patients with a specified set of characteristics, and the RCT may be limited to samples of patients with these same characteristics. In practice, the drug may be used more widely, for a broader set of indications or for patients with other characteristics, such as patients with other diagnoses or patients who fall outside the age range included in the RCT. Therefore, effectiveness may fall short of the drug's efficacy or conversely if the drug is used for more indications than for which it is officially approved. Since in the real world, drugs and other technologies are used in ways physicians and their patients want to use them, effectiveness is the relevant concept for CEA (and CBA) calculations.

The first step in measuring effectiveness is to select the appropriate measure or measures of output or outcome. In CEA, these outputs or outcomes are often called *endpoints*. The next step is to actually measure the marginal product of the technology.

Endpoints

The most objective endpoint or outcome measure is survival (mortality). Drugs, diagnostic tests, devices, surgical procedures, and hospitalizations all may affect the probability of surviving to certain dates in the future. For technologies that are largely designed to be life-saving, such as an emergency response system or an implantable cardiac defibrillator, survival is a very appropriate endpoint.

A defibrillator is a device that sends shocks to the heart to return heartbeats to normal rhythm. Serious abnormal rhythm can lead to death. The value one attaches to a life saved depends in part on how long the person would live if he or she did not die from an abnormal heart rhythm. For this reason, the number of life years saved may be a better metric than the number of lives saved. Such devices sometimes fire when a person's rhythm is not that abnormal or fail to fire when they should. Regardless of its accuracy, firing is painful to the wearer. Such intangible costs are generally not incorporated into a CEA calculation, although they would generally be included in a CBA.

A second global endpoint measure is the QALY. A QALY is assigned a weight between 0 and 1 to each time period, where 1 signifies perfect health and 0, death. Since QALYs or disability-adjusted life years (DALYs) are in widespread use, especially in applications of CEA, we describe them in some detail.

The psychological approach to measuring QALYs involves the use of rating scales and magnitude estimation. One rating scale method starts with the description of a case involving illness or disability. People are asked to rate the severity of the condition on a 0–10 scale where 0 is for death and 10 is for optimal function (Kaplan 1995, 37).

Magnitude estimation is a psychometric method. An interviewer or interview instrument describes a case in terms of a person's health, functioning, and quality of life, and assigns a specific value to the case, say 6. Then survey respondents are asked to rate other cases relative to the standard case—higher or lower than 6. If, for example, survey respondents regard a case as half as desirable as the comparator, it is assigned a value of 3 (Kaplan 1995, 39). After the data have been collected, the researcher can rescale responses to a 0–1 interval or to any other interval the researcher desires.

A deficiency of these types of methods is that they do not force the respondent to perform explicit trade-offs in rating. There is no cost to consistently assigning high or low values when rating. Without a cost of doing so, respondents can say that all the options are good or bad or highly valued or of low value.

An alternative approach that does require the evaluator to make a trade-off is the *standard gamble* (see chapter 2). The concept of a standard gamble is based on the theory of decision making under uncertainty (fig. 14.1). The interview gives the respondent two options. The first is to do nothing, which implies that circumstances will play out a certain way in the future. The alternative is to make a decision to undertake a certain action that, if successful, leads to an improvement over

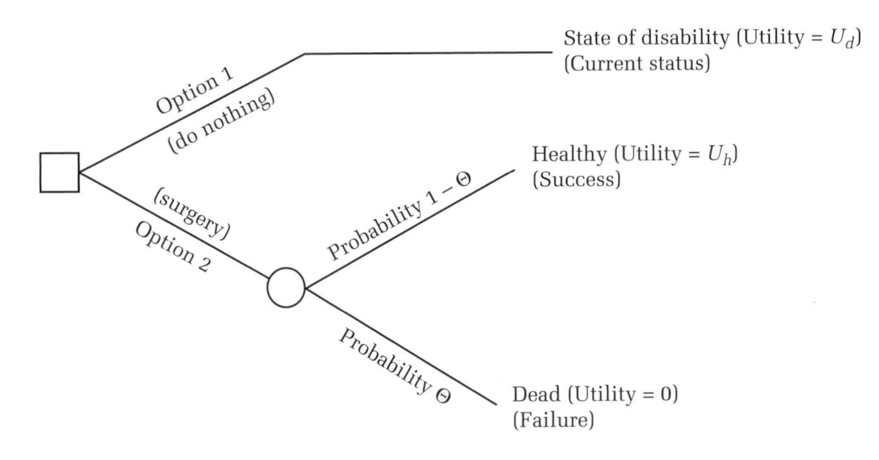

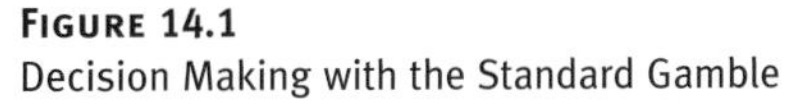
FIGURE 14.1
Decision Making with the Standard Gamble

the projected trajectory from the "do nothing" option. However, there is a non-zero probability that the action, if undertaken, will not be successful, in which case the person is worse off than if he or she did nothing.

For example, after experiencing pain when walking, suppose a physician told you that you have an injury to your spinal cord, which will lead to an inability to walk. The benefit of the operation is that you will be able to walk normally and painlessly. However, the operation itself entails risks, and a certain percentage of people who undergo this operation die during surgery. The choice then is between two unpleasant alternatives, living a life of immobility or making a decision that may result in a cure or in a sudden, if painless, death.

Define U_d as utility in the state of disability and U_h as utility in the healthy state, that is, without the disability. Assume that utility in the dead state is 0. Let Θ be the probability that the person does not survive the operation.

Then for $U_d = (1 - \Theta)U_h$, the decision maker is indifferent between having and not having the operation since $1 - \Theta$ is the probability of surviving the operation, being cured, and realizing utility U_h. The object of the standard gamble approach is to find the Θ, Θ^*, the probability of dying during surgery, that makes the person indifferent between undergoing and not undergoing the operation. Once Θ^* has been elicited, and given that $U_h = 1.0$ by assumption, we have an estimate of the value of U_d. The ratio U_d/U_h provides an estimate of a QALY for a person with this illness type and extent of disability.

The underlying logic is that when U_d is relatively low, one is likely to be willing to bear a greater mortality risk to achieve a cure. This kind of reasoning may well seem morbid at first glance, but in effect, this is the kind of trade-off that a person with a disability or other serious health condition may face. The physician may explain the risk of surgery to the patient or a member of the patient's family, and it is eventually up to the patient or family to determine whether or not the operative risk is worth it.

Values of Θ are not generally obtained from patients making actual decisions but rather are obtained from surveys in which hypothetical disease states and associated adverse effects of the disease are described and the respondent is asked for the Θ value that would make him or her indifferent between undergoing the procedure or not. A Θ^* value yielding indifference is obtaining by varying Θ and eliciting which choice the person makes.

For example, to elicit Θ^*, an interviewer might randomly start a series of questions with an assumed probability of 0.10. If the respondent selects the operation at $\Theta = 0.10$, the probability is increased to, for example, 0.20. If the respondent still accepts the operation, the probability is raised still higher. The probability is raised until the respondent refuses the operation. Then Θ^* is located between the final question's Θ and the Θ in the immediately previous question.

However, if the operation is refused on the first question, the next question might be whether or not the person would undergo the operation if the probability of death were 0.15. If the operation is still refused, the person is asked about his or her response if the probability were 0.125. If the answer is that the person would refuse the operation at $\Theta = 0.125$, the person is asked about his or her choice if the probability were 0.1125. If the answer is affirmative, the probability is increased to the midpoint of 0.1125 and 0.125. The process continues until a Θ value is found within this small interval at which the person states that he or she would refuse the operation.

This survey approach works well if the disease in question is sufficiently well characterized and the respondent is able to assess the trade-off as if it were real. This technique has the advantage of eliciting utilities from an explicit trade-off, but, as with the psychological measures, there is a question of whether or not persons who have not experienced the illness can know what their utility in the sick state would be if they actually had the illness described in the scenario.

While the standard gamble is based on von Neumann and Morgenstern's (1944) framework for decision making under uncertainty (discussed in chapter 2), and in this sense has a sound theoretical basis, there is a question of whether or not people who have not personally experienced the hypothetical situation can truly grasp the nuances and provide sufficiently accurate estimates of Θ. Also, some people may have difficulty working with the concept of a probability. Rating scales and magnitude estimation do not require survey respondents to think about probabilities.

Another, somewhat simpler trade-off approach uses a trade-off in terms of time. The *time trade-off* approach has the advantage of being clearer to respondents who do not understand the concept of probability. In a time trade-off, a person is offered a choice of living for a certain amount of time in perfect health, such as X

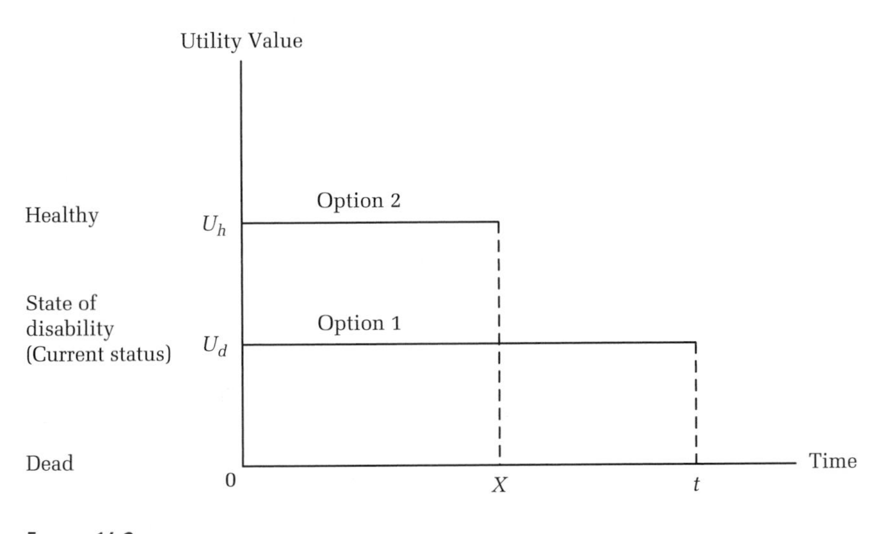

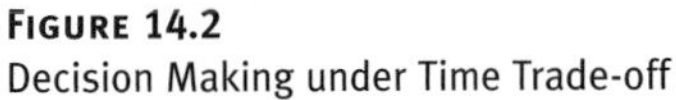
FIGURE 14.2
Decision Making under Time Trade-off

in figure 14.2, or a variable amount of time in a health state that is less than perfect health (corresponding to an illness or disability), such as t in figure 14.2. Any respondent would prefer being in perfect health (option 2) to the alternative (option 1). However, keeping time (t) with the illness constant, the interviewer reduces time in perfect health (X) until the respondent is indifferent between being in perfect health and the alternative, or $U_d t = U_h X$. This approach, like the standard gamble, can be used to derive QALY weights. In this case, U_d is given by X/t when $U_h = 1$.

Another outcome measure is the disability-adjusted life year. DALYs are used to calculate the global burden of disease.. One DALY can be interpreted as one year of "healthy" life lost. Summing DALYs for a given population yields an estimate of the difference between current health status and an ideal health situation in which the entire population lives to an advanced age, free of disease and disability. DALYs for a disease or health condition are calculated as the sum of the years of life lost (YLL) due to premature mortality in the population and the years lost due to disability (YLD) for incident cases of the health condition: DALY = YLL + YLD, where YLL equals the number of deaths multiplied by the standard life expectancy at the age at which death occurs and YLD equals the product of (1) the number of incident cases, (2) a disability weight for each disease, and (3) the mean duration of the case until remission or death in years, whichever occurs first.

Because YLL measures the incident stream of lost years of life due to deaths, an incidence perspective is also taken for the calculation of YLD. To estimate YLD for a particular cause in a particular time period, the number of incident cases in that period is multiplied by the average duration of the disease and a weight factor that reflects the severity of the disease on a scale from 0 (perfect health) to 1 (dead).

Some outcome measures used in CEA calculations, such as lives saved, life years saved, and DALYs, abandon the concept of utility entirely. Other such measures quantify changes in the incidence of specific illnesses or days lost due to illness or disability or days lost from work.

Still other measures focus on physical functioning, especially the functioning of elderly persons. Important among these are limitations of activities of daily living (ADL), limitations in instrumental activities of daily living (IADL), and Nagi disability measures (see, e.g., George, Ruiz, and Sloan 2008). ADL limitations refer to whether or not the person needs or receives assistance with basic routine activities such as bathing, toileting, getting out of bed, eating, dressing, and crossing a room. IADL limitations refer to limitations with other activities that, although important, are not performed by everyone who is not impaired in physical functioning: shopping, cooking, doing the laundry, doing personal finances, and using the telephone. Nagi disability measures gauge the person's ability to perform four basic lower- and upper-body functions: pushing large objects, kneeling, stooping, reaching above one's shoulders, and writing or handling small objects. This group of measures is useful in evaluating therapies for such potentially debilitating conditions as arthritis and stroke. These outcome measures are applicable to CEA calculations of total hip or total knee replacement surgery, and the cost-effectiveness ratios are estimates of cost per procedure per reduction in ADL or IADL limitations.

Another dimension of disability is cognitive impairment. Various instruments for evaluating cognitive status are available. One, the Short Portable Mental Status Questionnaire, asks such questions as "What is the date today?" "What day of the week is it?" "What is your telephone number?" "What is your age?" and asks the patient to perform cognitive tasks such as "Subtract 3 from 20 and keep subtracting 3 from each new number, all the way down" (Pfeiffer 1975). Measures of change in cognitive function would be appropriate for use in a cost-effectiveness analysis of a new drug for treating Alzheimer's disease.

The Center for Epidemiologic Studies Depression Scale CES-D asks a series of questions about mood in the recent past (Andresen, Malmgren, Carter, et al. 1994). Such a scale might be used for a CEA of a new drug for treating depression. For a CEA of a new drug designed to regulate blood pressure, blood pressure readings may be the outcome measure of choice.

Evaluating the Marginal Effect of Specific Technologies

Goal of Evaluation

A basic component of any cost-effectiveness (or cost-benefit) analysis is translating input use into outputs. In economics, this is the role of the production function. In health care, the production function is often expressed as a conditional

TABLE 14.1
Two-by-Three Transition Matrix

Health Status in Year $t + 1$	Health Status in Year t		Probability in Year $t + 1$
	Good	Poor	
Good	Θ_{GG}	Θ_{PG}	$\Theta_{.G}$
Poor	Θ_{GP}	Θ_{PP}	$\Theta_{.P}$
Dead	Θ_{GD}	Θ_{PD}	$\Theta_{.D}$
Probability in year t	$\Theta_{G.}$	$\Theta_{P.}$	

probability of observing particular outcomes—conditional on a given level of input use. Inputs may be nurse staffing per patient in the hospital, a drug, a diagnostic test that leads to a more timely therapeutic intervention, or a medical device, such as knee or hip prosthesis or a lens implanted in the eye of a patient with cataracts.

TRANSITION PROBABILITIES

In the simplest form, the relationship between inputs and outputs can be expressed as a transition probability, or the probability that in a given time period, the person remains in the same health state as at the beginning of the period, or alternatively transitions to another state. Suppose, for example, that there are three health states: good health (G), poor health (P), and dead (D).

Table 14.1 is a two-by-three matrix displaying transition probabilities from year t to year $t + 1$. The matrix is two by three because death is an "absorbing state" (there are no transitions in a nonbiblical context from death back to life). By contrast, a person's health can improve or deteriorate. The bottom row gives the probabilities that a person is in good or poor health in year t; the rightmost column gives the probabilities that the person is in good or poor health or dead in year $t + 1$.

Suppose that a new drug has been shown in an RCT to be effective in treating people with a specific health condition who are initially in poor health. Let Θ_{PG} be the probability that a person initially in poor health is in good health in the next period. Thus, if the drug is effective, Θ_{PG} is expected to rise for drug users relative to Θ_{PG} for nonusers of the drug. Further, $\Theta_{PG} + \Theta_{PP} + \Theta_{PD} = 1$. Thus, the sum of Θ_{PP} and Θ_{PD} falls by the same amount that Θ_{PG} rises.

MARKOV CHAINS

Data on long-term outcomes from the use of diagnostic and therapeutic procedures are rarely available. Waiting for data on long-term outcomes before approving a procedure for use would substantially and often unacceptably delay the introduction of new procedures. Thus, long-term outcomes are inferred from repeated application of transition probabilities of the type shown in table 14.1. In its simplest form, the transition probabilities are constant among periods. Such probabilities can be used to form a Markov chain (see, e.g., Keeler 1995, 195–201). The transition probabilities are constant in the sense that a transition probability between two adjacent periods t and $t + 1$ depends only on state the individual is in t, not only states prior to t. For example, all persons in the good (G) health state in a year are assumed to be the same, regardless of their health histories before the year. Using this assumption, one can project health states far into the future. Persons who die (D) in a year are dropped from the sample from this point forward.

For example, suppose that 1,000 individuals are in the poor (P) health state in t and Θ_{PG} is 0.45, Θ_{PP} is 0.40, and Θ_{PD} is 0.15, the probability of being in poor health in period 1 and dead in period 2, without the drug. With the drug, the probabilities are 0.65, 0.30, and 0.05, respectively. Then one can compute the number of persons in the each health state over a number of years if the drug is not taken or is taken on a continuous basis. Populations in each health state change in each period, as does the number of persons involved in health state transitions. We leave it for an exercise for students to compute populations in good and poor health after several years, given that people take or do not take the drug.[2]

Obtaining Transition Probabilities from Observational Data

In the above example, the transition probabilities with and without the drug are known. The transition probabilities would ideally be determined from an RCT. But while trials have the advantage of dealing with the endogeneity problem discussed earlier in chapter 3 and immediately below, they measure effects when procedures are applied under medical protocols, which reflect ideal conditions, not necessarily how they are applied in the world of actual medical practice. Further, for some procedures, RCTs are not ethical. For example, surgical procedures are not subject to regulatory review prior to their introduction. It is likely to be unethical to withhold a specific therapy already being used by some physicians with reports of success specifically for purposes of research. Thus, researchers often rely on observational data.[3]

An example of the production function approach using observational data is an evaluation of the impact of intensive treatment on the mortality rates of elderly persons following admission to the hospital for heart attacks (McClellan, McNeil, and Newhouse 1994). The treatment of heart attacks can be solely medical, which involves monitoring the patient in the hospital and use of medications. More intensive treatment involves coronary artery bypass surgery or a procedure called angioplasty, in which a catheter with a balloon is inserted into the patient's coronary arteries to remove the obstruction that caused the heart attack and to widen the blood vessels to allow blood to flow more freely. The main outcome measure in the above-mentioned study was the probability that an elderly person survived four years following a heart attack.

2. Also, see Keeler (1995) for useful applications of Markov processes.

3. See chapter 3 for a discussion of observational data versus data from RCTs for evidence on the marginal product of particular procedures.

The authors did not have data from an RCT. Rather, they had administrative data—claims data and demographic data from the US Medicare program on persons who were hospitalized with a heart attack. With observational data, there is the possibility that patients with a disease that is more severe in ways not documented in the data could have influenced the choice of intensive or nonintensive care following the heart attack.

A production function measures the effect of inputs on outputs—not the effect of outputs—in this case, the effect of outcomes on input use. Outcomes may be highly correlated with the patient's severity of illness and other clinical factors, which often are not well measured in administrative data, such as claims submitted to an insurer such as Medicare. Since severity of illness (observable to the patient's physician but not to researchers using the administrative data) and other clinical factors affect the choice of inputs, input choice is endogenous, and the parameter estimates relating inputs to outcomes are biased. For example, if otherwise healthy heart attack victims are more likely to undergo open heart surgery, it may appear that survival is better among heart attack victims who receive surgery than those who do not. But the better outcomes would actually be due to unmeasured severity of illness and not at all reflect the effectiveness of such surgery. In an RCT, patients are randomly assigned to treatment and control groups. So the choice of inputs is not related to unmeasured factors. Because of randomization, unmeasured factors in treatment and control groups should be the same.

The authors' solution for avoiding biased parameter estimates with the use of observational data was to find a variable that is uncorrelated with patient severity of illness or other clinical factors not explicitly included in their analysis but was highly correlated with the use or non-use of intensive treatment for a patient's heart attack, cardiac catherization and open heart surgery. In technical terms, such a variable is called an instrumental variable. The authors determined the distance from the patient's residence to each hospital in the area in which the patient lived. If, for example, there were three hospitals in the patient's area, the authors computed the distance to each of the facilities. Only some of the hospitals offered intensive therapies to patients with heart attacks. The others just offered less intensive, medical therapies. If the patient lived relatively near a hospital with intensive and medical therapies, the hypothesis was that the probability of being admitted to a hospital with intensive therapy would be higher.

In fact, relative distance from the alternative hospitals was an important determinant of hospital choice. Relative distance was a good instrumental variable since it seems unlikely that people chose where they live based on the type of heart attack care hospitals in the area offered. Rather, location of residence may reflect location of job or relatives. In this way, differential distances approximately randomized patients to different probabilities of receiving intensive treatments. Comparisons of patient groups that differed only in differential distances showed that intensive treatment increased the survival probability of Medicare patients admitted to hospitals with a diagnosis of heart attack by up to five percentage points. Given their analytic approach, the authors could argue that this was a true measure of treatment effectiveness, not just a reflection of some unmeasured factor associated with poor health outcomes.

DISCOUNTING

RATIONALE FOR DISCOUNTING

Many decisions involve costs or benefits accruing over several years. The principle of discounting is that costs and benefits accruing later should receive less weight than those occurring earlier. The process of discounting applies to all economic decisions—decisions involving the allocation of scarce resources—of which medical decisions are a subset. Pharmaceutical products for treating various diseases such as high blood pressure and cancer, diet therapies, and smoking cession and exercise regimens, and as we have just seen, treatments for heart attacks can have long-run effects on health spanning several years and, in some cases, decades. Likewise, incurring costs later is preferable to incurring costs earlier. The issue is not whether or not to discount but which discount rate to use.

In an idealized risk-free, tax-free, competitive world in which outputs could be perfectly traded among time periods, there would be only one interest rate. That rate would reflect (1) the marginal rate of time preference—the rate that equalizes a given amount of consumption in two adjacent periods (the same amount of consumption is worth less to consumers if consumed later than earlier), and (2) the marginal rate of return on investment—the time trade-off in production. The interest rate is that rate that equates the time trade-off in consumption with the time trade-off in production.

If there were absolutely no risk, the real rate of interest (the rate that takes inflation into account) might be about 1 percent (Lind 1982) rather than one to three times larger. Market risk occurs because the value of an interest- bearing security varies inversely to the rate of interest paid on that security. Thus, if there is market risk, the holder of the security bears a risk that interest rates will increase and the market value of the security will fall. Credit risk refers to the probability that the issuer of the security will default on its payments to the holder of the security. Suppliers of capital face risk and therefore demand an additional return for risk bearing.

Economists distinguish between social and private discount rates. In the case of private decision makers, the appropriate rate of discount reflects the individual's own willingness to trade present for future consumption or, in the case of a firm's decision to borrow or invest, its marginal cost of funds. Because the government as the agent for society faces fewer intertemporal borrowing constraints, the social discount rate may be less than its private counterpart. Further, national governments' debt obligations are not subject to credit risk.[4]

4. We assume here that the government is affiliated with a central bank, which controls the money supply. Other governments may become bankrupt, and hence the securities they issue are subject to credit as well as market risk.

On the other hand, it is possible to underestimate the social discount rate for purposes of project evaluation. For example, in the former Soviet Union, where interest was seen as a capitalist concept, capital projects with very low rates of return were undertaken on the presumption that the social discount rate in a socialist society was zero or nearly so. Using such extremely low discount rates can result in too few resources being devoted to projects with not-too-distant investment returns.

The social discount rate is the relevant one for public decisions, including decisions about investments in health care infrastructure, biomedical research, and even social insurance programs with a deferred benefit. In practice, the social rate may not be that much lower than its public counterpart. Too much of a discrepancy if applied to evaluations of net benefits of public investments could divert too many resources from the private sector to the public sector.

Determining the Appropriate Discount Rate: Financial versus Health Discount Rates

There are many market rates of interest in financial markets. These are private rates reflecting the demand and supply of capital funds, the former reflecting rates of return on investment projects and the latter reflecting a combination of rates of time preference of suppliers of capital and their own investment opportunities. At a point in time, interest rates reflect monetary policy, expectations about future prices, and other factors.

Among health care experts who think about discounting, there has been some discussion about whether or not financial rates should be used in decisions about health. The alternative is to use health discount rates, which involve trade-offs in time in health rather than in money terms (see, e.g., Viscusi 1996). Health and financial discount rates would differ if people have different time trade-offs when making intertemporal health decisions as opposed to financial decisions.

There are several arguments for using financial discount rates. First, in CBA, all costs and benefits are expressed in monetary terms. Second, as seen in chapter 2, health flows (e.g., healthy days) can enter as an argument in the individual's utility function in the same way that the consumption of other goods and services can enter. It makes sense to discount consumption from the person's health stock and consumption of other goods and services in the same way. Third, not discounting at the same rate could introduce biases in resource allocation, for example, if the health rate were set lower than for other goods and services or conversely.

The main argument against using a financial discount rate to compute the present value of health benefits is that unlike other commodities, health cannot always be traded across time. For example, one can undergo the agony (for some persons) of long-distance running now, a health investment, for the benefit of improved cardiovascular fitness later. Or one can disinvest now, by enjoying a smoke, with the consequence of a higher probably of getting a smoking-related disease a decade or several decades later. But some adverse health conditions, such as stage IV cancer and congestive heart failure, both of which often lead to death, are irreversible.

In the end, the argument favors those who would use financial rates. Empirical studies tend to find no systematic difference in financial and health discount rates (see, e.g., Chapman, Freiberg, Quiggin, et al. 2003).

There are several sources of information on discount rates. Surveys have been employed to elicit rates of time preference (see, e.g., Harrison, Lau, and Williams 2002; Khwaja, Silverman, and Sloan 2007). These studies show considerable individual variation in discount rates and often implausibly high rates, especially for decisions with a short time span. Harrison and co-authors reported that persons with more education, those with higher skills, and homeowners in their survey had lower discount rates, while retired persons had higher rates. These differences in discount rates suggest that the poor, less educated, unskilled, and retired persons are relatively worse off when policy makers select projects with more delayed returns.

A second approach infers discount rates from decisions people make about labor market choices or product choices (Moore and Viscusi 1990a, 1990b). For example, suppose that an energy-saving refrigerator saves $100 a year in energy bills and is usable for 20 years, but the refrigerator costs $400 more than otherwise identical refrigerators. Then it is possible to solve for the discount rate that makes buyers indifferent between the two types of refrigerators. This type of calculation has yielded implicit discount rates of well over 20 percent (Viscusi 1996). This high rate reflects data indicating that people are not willing to pay a much higher price for a refrigerator now to save money on energy bills later.

There are many reasons why purchasers may be willing to pay so little extra for an energy-saving refrigerator. One reason may be that the person does not have a time horizon of 20 years but a much shorter time horizon. For example, perhaps the person expects to move in a few years. Or the purchaser may expect energy prices to fall, and for this reason, the annual savings in energy bills may be less than $100. Readers may be able to think of other reasons for why some people may not be willing to pay much more for an energy-saving refrigerator.

A third approach is simply to use a real interest rate, such as 3 percent, as the real social rate of discount. Between 1965 and 2005, real interest rates on US three-month Treasury bills have varied from about minus 3 percent to slightly over 5 percent, with 2 to 3 percent being a common value (see, e.g., Mankiw 2007, 541–542), and as already noted, real interest rates have been around 3 percent on long-term US government bonds. The US Panel on Cost Effectiveness suggested using a 3 percent discount rate in cost-effectiveness calculations, but it noted that many studies have used a 5 percent rate (Gold, Siegel, Russell, et al. 1996). The panel suggested that 0 to 7 percent rates be used in sensitivity analysis to gauge the sensitivity of the recommendations obtained from the CEA to changes in the assumed discount rate.

COMPUTING A COST-EFFECTIVENESS RATIO

The results of CEA are typically presented as a ratio (CER) of the net costs to the net health outcomes of alternative intervention strategies (or health programs or products):

$$CER = (C_1 - C_2)/(O_1 - O_2), \quad (14.1)$$

where C represents costs, O represents the outcomes of an intervention, and the subscripts 1 and 2 refer to alternative interventions 1 and 2. One of the "interventions" can be doing nothing other than continue current practice. Costs include (1) those directly (e.g., additional physician visits for monitoring for complications following the intervention) associated with the intervention and (2) cost increases attributable to the intervention (e.g., work losses during the recovery period), minus (3) the costs saved by the intervention (e.g., reductions in work losses and in medical expenditures after the recovery period has been completed).

For example, suppose patients are being treated with a generic drug to lower blood pressure, product 2. A new branded drug, product 1, is being evaluated with CEA. The new drug is more expensive than the old drug, and the new drug requires an additional physician visit for monitoring potential adverse side effects. But on average, the new drug, product 1, reduces hospitalizations for stroke. All additional cost net of cost offsets should be included in the numerator of equation 14.1. Since the reduced hospitalizations may occur years after the new drug is initially taken, the cost offsets (savings) should be discounted.

The outcomes, represented by the O's in the denominator of equation 14.1, can be any of the output measures discussed above (or others).

Health policy makers and private insurers are confronted with many new technologies that are proposed to be covered by insurance during a year. Suppose one CER measures a cost of $\$x$ per reduced hospitalization for stroke. A problem with CEA is that another technology under consideration might reduce children's days lost from school. Although the numerators are in monetary terms, the denominators are not in the same units.

Comparing apples to oranges is difficult. Many CEAs use life years or QALYs gained for the O's. Then multiple projects can be compared in the same units.

Even if the numerators and the denominators of the technologies being compared are in the same units, the question remains as to where the line is between those technologies to adopt and those to reject. There is no natural cut point.

Arbitrary cutoffs are CERs, such as cost per life year saved, where the value of a year life saved equals the country's GDP per capita population or some multiple of the country's per capita GDP, such as three times per capita GDP. If analysts assume that the value of life saved equals the value of a life year saved, a cutoff could be figured this way: the mean per capita GDP from 163 countries in 2005 was US$10,200, with a range of over US$66,000 for Luxembourg to US$556 for

Malawi. The US per capita GDP was slightly over US$39,000. Using the all-country average as the value of a life year, and assuming the technology saves half a life year per unit, the technology would be considered "cost-effective" if the cost were US$5,100 or less. Using a criterion of three times per capita GDP, the procedure would be cost-effective if it cost US$15,300 or less. Using per capita GDP as the value of a life year amounts to assigning a value of life year well over 100 times higher in Luxembourg than in Malawi.

Many health experts are reluctant to place a monetary value on life for ethical reasons. Indeed, valuing a life year in Luxembourg at over 100 or even 300 times more valuable than in Malawi is troublesome and seems arbitrary. However, since public budgets are not limited to health, it is also necessary for policy makers to be able to compare health with non-health investments. Private insurers must also make choices about what to cover. Comparing life years/QALYs gained with a mile of highway paved is a difficult task unless benefits can be characterized in units common to all projects. The common denominator is likely to be money (Pauly 1996).

14.4 APPLICATIONS OF COST-EFFECTIVENESS ANALYSIS

DISEASE PREVENTION

CEA has been used to assess the costs and health benefits of screening strategies for colorectal cancer, including fecal occult blood testing, or FOBT (testing for blood in the stool), sigmoidoscopy (examination of the lower third of the intestine with a scope), barium enema studies, and colonoscopy (examination of the entire intestine with a scope). CEA can also be used to determine the optimal age at which screening should be done, and how often it should be done.

THE EXPERIENCE OF A US STATE, OREGON

In the above applications, CEA is applied to individual technologies to determine if and under which circumstances a particular diagnostic or therapeutic procedure should be implemented. At the other end of the spectrum are decisions about the overall allocation of health care resources. CEA has been applied to overall resource allocation, with mixed success.

A well-publicized lack of success occurred in the US state of Oregon (Kaplan 1995; Saha, Hoerger, Pignone, et al. 2001). The broad objective was to improve the allocation of health care resources in the state, especially those resources used by low-income persons—in other words, to "get more bang for the health care buck."

In pursuit of this objective, the Oregon Health Services Commission ranked health care services according to their CERs in order to expand health services to the poor in that state. While there was an expansion in some services, coverage of services with high CERs (unfavorable) was reduced or eliminated. This reallocation process was highly criticized as tantamount to unethical "rationing." Patients and health professionals objected to withholding services with high CERs to save money to reallocate public budgets to services with lower CERs. In the end, the US federal government ended this interesting state experiment.

Oregon tried to use CEA to allocate health services across the board to a segment of its population. In practice, CEA seems to be less objectionable if used to decide the net benefit of a particular program rather than to determine overall health resource allocation. The latter is a far more complex undertaking that, in the end, requires many assumptions to complete the comparisons. To illustrate the use of CEA, we describe three successful applications in some depth.

COST-EFFECTIVENESS OF THROMBOLYTIC THERAPY FOR ACUTE MYOCARDIAL INFARCTION

Hospital pharmacy budgets are rising all over the world because many of the drugs introduced in recent years have been much more expensive than the older ones. Thus, in the interest of optimal resource allocation at the hospital level, it is important to compare the cost-effectiveness of new versus older drugs, which are designed to treat a given patient type.

A relatively new idea is to treat patients with a heart attack, in technical jargon known as acute myocardial infarction, or AMI, with a blood thinner to break up clots that block the coronary arteries. If done in a timely manner, within a certain time period after the onset of symptoms (within 1.5–3 hours), clearing the arteries in this way can reduce the damage to the heart muscle that otherwise is likely to result from an AMI. Mark, Hlatky, Califf, et al. (1995) undertook a comparative study of streptokinase and a newer drug called tissue plasminogen activator, or t-PA. Both are clot-busting drugs for use in the early phase of an AMI, but t-PA is a more expensive than streptokinaise.

Mark and co-authors evaluated four treatment regimens: (1) t-PA, (2) streptokinase with intravenous heparin, (3) streptokinase with subcutaneous heparin, and (4) a combination of t-PA and streptokinase. Heparin is a blood thinner, an older drug. *Intravenous* means that the drug is injected directly into a vein. *Subcutaneous* means that the drug is injected under the skin. The authors were able to use empirical evidence on the comparative effectiveness of t-PA and streptokinase from a randomized clinical trial, GUSTO. From GUSTO, it is known that t-PA improves the probability of surviving after an AMI more than streptokinase does, yet t-PA is more expensive, and the question for Mark and colleagues was whether or not t-PA's extra cost is worth it.

Data from the GUSTO trial provided information on the one-year survival probabilities following AMI. The authors had information from medical records regarding the services provided to over 23,000 patients hospitalized for AMI. In addition, 2,600 of these patients were surveyed at 30 days, six months, and one year following the AMI on their use of services since hospital discharge and their quality of life. The authors used a social perceptive, although they did not include such costs as patient time lost from work and nonmedical costs, such as paid help in the home following hospital discharge and the cost of travel to physicians. The primary outcome measure was survival. Quality-of-life information obtained from the patient surveys was used in sensitivity analysis—analysis that seeks to determine whether varying the parameters, outcome measures, and so forth alters a study's conclusions. Cost-effectiveness was measured as the additional lifetime cost required to add a year of life using t-PA compared with streptokinase therapy.

To determine therapy cost, the authors gathered data from the hospital accounting system at Duke University Hospital in the US state of North Carolina on costs per unit of service (e.g., a hospital day), including the cost of drug administration. Only costs for the year following the AMI were included in the analysis. Thus, the authors assumed that there was no cost difference between t-PA and streptokinase after the first year following the AMI.

Survival probabilities were computed for 15 years following the AMI, but the authors assumed no difference between t-PA and streptokinase after the first year following the AMI. GUSTO provided survival data only up to a year. It seems plausible that the effects of the two drugs would not extend more than the first year.

To measure quality of life at the survey dates, the authors asked patients time trade-off questions. Patients were asked a series of questions, including how much of their current life expectancy (which the interviews postulated was 10 years from the interview date) the patients would be willing to give up to be in excellent health for the rest of their lives.

The results from the study were enlightening. First, other than for the added cost of t-PA, resource consumption within the first year following the AMI was similar for the t-PA- and streptokinase-treated patients. With drug costs included, the *added* cost of t-PA during year 1 was $2,845 (1993 US$). On average, patients who received t-PA lived an extra 0.14 years. The cost per extra life year saved was $32,678, with a 95 percent confidence interval of $18,781–$71,039; the $32,678 estimate is less than the $50,000 threshold that is sometimes used in the United States to separate cost-effective from non-cost-effective technologies. Hence, while t-PA cost more, it was worth it in terms of life extension. Using an alternative estimate of the price of t-PA, the relative cost was $27,115 per life year saved.

In an alternative calculation, the authors adjusted for the quality of life of both groups. The mean utility weight or QALY one year post AMI for both groups was 0.9 (implying that quality of life was the same). Dividing the $32,678 estimate by 0.9 yields a CER of $36,402 per life year saved. But in addition, GUSTO revealed that in the first 30 days post AMI, t-PA produced one extra stroke per 1,000 patients relative to streptokinase. The higher stroke rate would be expected to decrease the survival differential for patients receiving t-PA from 0.14, which was actually observed in GUSTO, to 0.13. Adjusting for the higher stroke probability and its possible impact on survival at one year increased the CER of using t-PA over streptokinase by about $7,000. Still, relative to the $50,000 threshold, t-PA was seen to be cost-effective.

The authors concluded that providing t-PA to persons who experience heart attacks in the United States and are eligible for such therapy would add $500 million to annual health spending in the United States, but providing t-PA would also result in 3.5 million additional life years. In a country as populous as the United States (over 300 million persons) and for a common condition, such as AMI, even small changes in survival probabilities yield substantial changes in life years saved.

Cost-Effectiveness of HIV Treatment in Low-Income Settings

Human immunodeficiency virus (HIV) and acquired immunodeficiency syndrome (AIDS) are major sources of morbidity and mortality worldwide but particularly in low-income countries, such as those on the African continent. Effective antiretroviral therapies have been developed in recent years, but these therapies are costly. Different treatment strategies may be appropriate for low-resource countries than for more affluent countries where new technologies are typically developed.

Goldie, Yazdanpanah, Losina, et al. (2006) used cost-effectiveness analysis to determine optimal treatment strategies for HIV/AIDS in a resource-poor country in Africa, the Ivory Coast. The study evaluated combinations of antiretroviral therapy (ART) and a regimen called trimethoprim-sulfamethoxazole prophylaxis (TSP). Antiretovial drugs inhibit the spread of the HIV virus. TSP acts on the opportunistic infections that are caused by the virus (e.g., pneumonias). In other contexts, TSP is prescribed for urinary tract infections, frequently occurring bronchitis, and travelers' diarrhea in adults and severe middle ear infections in children.

The authors used first-order Monte Carlo simulation to model disease progression of each individual patient from month to month. The key feature of this approach is that transitions from one health state to another are probabilistic. Transitions are only a function of the person's health state in the previous month, not on the person's entire health history. A key task for the research is to define the health states. In this study, health states were defined in terms of the person's current (period t) and maximum HIV RNA levels, current and lowest ever CD4 counts, and current and prior opportunistic diseases (e.g., pneumonia). RNA and CD4 counts measure the amount of the person's infection with the HIV virus. The use of past maximum or minimum values of RNA and CD4 counts might seem to violate the first-order assumption, but in practice, the authors updated these maximum and minimum values each month. Thus, transitions to period $t + 1$ were based entirely on information on the individual recorded at t.

The authors had data on the probabilities of persons with HIV/AIDS in the various health states at baseline from an RCT conducted on persons with this disease in the Ivory Coast. This was fortunate, since the baseline probabilities are likely to differ among countries. They obtained data on the efficacy of TSP (probabilities of reduction in specific types of infections, e.g., acute unexplained fever, severe bacterial infection), the efficacy of ART (percent HIV RNA suppression attributable to use of TSP at 52 weeks), and drug toxicity (adverse side effects due to TSP use) from other studies. They also obtained data on relevant costs, such the costs of TSP and ART and costs for treating drug toxicity, testing, treating opportunistic diseases, long-term care (stratified by CD4 count), and terminal care (care rendered after it is determined that death is imminent), as well as the direct costs of HIV-related care other than for TSP and ART (such as for a clinic visit, hospital day, and day care).

The information on efficacy of therapies came from countries other than the Ivory Coast. Thus, there was a question as to how well the model based on information from other sources fitted the Ivory Coast. For this reason, a analytic first step was to determine how well predicted values from the model fitted actual changes over time from the trial conducted in Ivory Coast, a process that is called "model validation." Projected model outcomes were generally within 10–15 percent of reported trial results, which is a good result. Model parameters were based on averages, often drawn from data from other countries. Yet the predictions fit the Ivory Coast–specific data well.

The next step was to evaluate the cost-effectiveness of alternative treatment strategies. Figure 14.3 shows main results of this analysis for specific treatment approaches between cost (horizontal axis) and life expectancy in months (vertical axis). The symbols in black represent strategies using both ART and TSP. The open symbols show the results with the use of ART only.

There are separate points for "no treatment" and for the use of TSP alone, both of which ae associated with very low life expectancy.

A key element in a treatment strategy is the duration of treatment. Points in the figure are specific to the circumstances under which ART is initiated and stopped. For example, "Start ART: 2 ODs" and "Stop ART: 1 OD" mean that ART was initiated after the occurrence of a second opportunistic infection and stopped after the next opportunistic infection occurred. Thus, a strategy that initiates therapy at 1 OD and stops after 5 ODs following initiation of therapy involves a longer duration of ART than does a 2 OD–1 OD strategy. Longer duration is associated with higher cost but longer life expectancy. If ART were ineffective, the cost would be higher but there would be little or no gain in life expectancy. CD4 cell counts represent additional or alternative clinical criteria for the initiation and cessation of therapy in some of the strategies depicted in the figure.

The solid line or *frontier* in figure 14.3 identifies efficient treatment strategies. Points below the frontier represent inefficient treatment strategies in that a lower gain in life expectancy is achieved for a given cost. In this application, the strategies employing ART alone are inefficient and some of those using both ART and

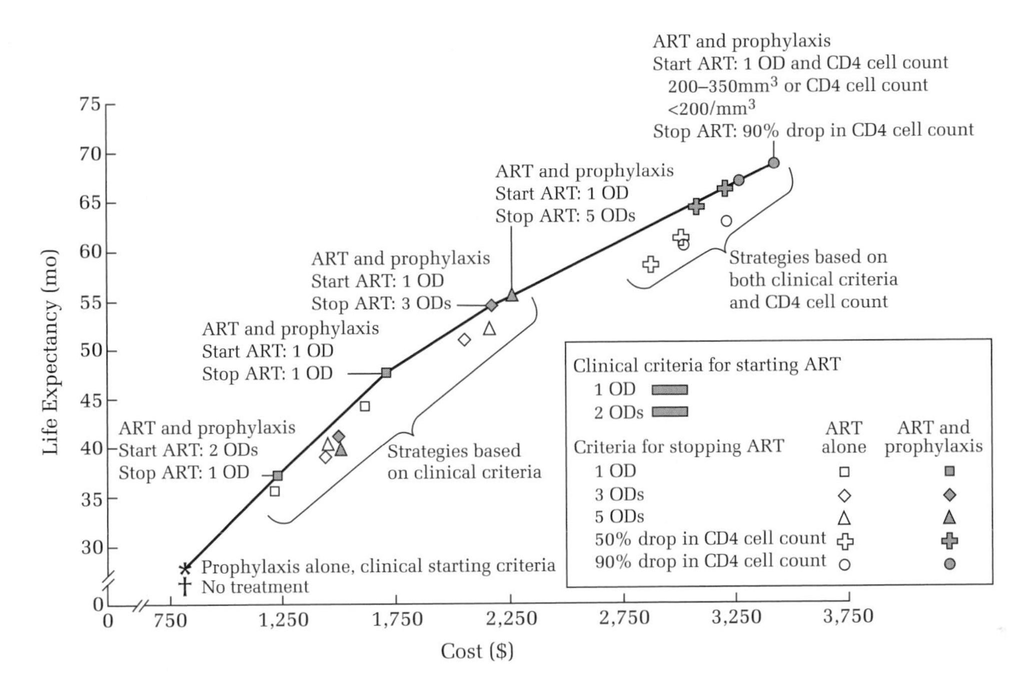

Figure 14.3
Cost-Effectiveness of Treatment Strategies
Strategies lying on the curve were more efficient than those lying to the right of the curve because they were more effective and either cost less or had a lower cost-effectiveness ratio, as compared with the next least expensive strategy. Strategies that relied on clinical criteria alone for starting and stopping antiretroviral therapy (ART), which are clustered in the lower left portion of the curve, were always less effective than strategies that included CD4 testing (clustered in the upper right portion of the curve). Strategies that involved ART alone (open symbols) were always more costly and less cost-effective than those that involved both ART and trimethoprim-sulfamethoxazole prophylaxis (solid symbols). All costs are in 2002 US dollars. OD, opportunistic disease.
Source: S. J. Goldie, Y. Yazdanpanah, E. Losina, et al., "Cost-Effectiveness of HIV Treatment in Resource-Poor Settings: The Case of Côte d'Ivoire," *New England Journal of Medicine* 355, no. 11 (2006): 1141–2253. Copyright © Massachusetts Medical Society. Used with permission.

TSP are efficient. In general, the recommendation from this type of analysis is to employ strategies on the frontier.

The frontier depicts the total cost of achieving specific levels of life expectancy. The frontier's slope depicts the marginal cost of achieving a month's increase in life expectancy. As the figure is drawn (with cost on the horizontal axis rather than on the vertical axis as cost curves are typically drawn), a higher slope represents a lower marginal cost. Thus, marginal cost increases as cost increases (although in stepwise fashion). Said another way, incremental cost effectiveness, the additional cost to obtain additional life years, rises with the amount of treatment given. The figure gives a menu of strategies that are socially optimal (those strategies with points on the frontier), but which specific strategy should the policy maker select?

CEA offers no ideal answer to this question. The authors took a fairly common approach, which is to define the boundary between therapies that are cost-effective and those that are not cost-effective by the country's per capita GDP, which was 708 US$. Using this criterion, one would increase program cost per life year saved up to the point that it equaled the country's per capita GDP. Thus, wealthier countries would have higher thresholds for the dividing line between cost-effective and non-cost-effective technologies and hence would generally employ more costly treatment strategies than poorer ones. Another possible threshold for cost-effectiveness is three times per capita GDP. If the latter threshold is utilized, more costly treatment strategies would be employed.

Box 14.1
A Procedure Yielding $1,374,246 per Life Year Saved

In a high-income country such as the United States, a cost per life year saved of $100,000 is often considered the maximum amount for which a technology is considered to be cost-effective. By contrast, in low- and middle-income countries, the threshold is considerably lower. From this perspective, how should we view a procedure that costs more than $1.3 million per life year saved? And why do people demand such technologies, even if they have to pay for the entire cost out of pocket? And should such technologies be made available to the public, and should some restrictions be imposed? Generally, economists promote choice and consumer sovereignty.

Kaimal, Smith, Laros, et al. (2009) used standard methods for evaluating the cost-effectiveness of private umbilical cord blood banking versus no umbilical cord blood banking. Umbilical cord blood yields stem cells, which may be used as stem cell transplants by the child or a relative in the future. Alternatively, bone marrow transplants from a matched but often unrelated donor may be performed. According to the authors, currently, bone marrow transplants and stem cell transplants are equally effective.

Cost-effectiveness reflects the cost of the technology, the probabilities of the technology being used, its effectiveness, and the probabilities and costs of treating adverse events from the use of the technology. Kaimal and colleagues assumed a cost of $3,620 for umbilical cord blood banking and storage for 20 years, a 0.0004 probability of the child subsequently requiring an autologous stem cell transplant, a 0.0007 probability of a sibling requiring the same, and a 50 percent reduction in the probability of graft-versus-host disease if a sibling used banked umbilical cord blood. The probability of the child acquiring such a disease from his or her own blood is 0.

Using these parameters, the cost of private umbilical cost blood banking per life year saved was estimated to be $1,374,246. The procedure becomes cost-effective at conventional levels only if the cost of such blood banking is less than $262 or the probability of a child needing a stem cell transplant is 0.0091, rather than the 0.0004 estimate used in the baseline calculations. The $262 value assumes substantial

Box 14.1
(continued)

technological change in the cost of the technology. Very few children would be estimated to have a nearly 0.01 probability of receiving a stem cell transplant.

If the cost-effectiveness of umbilical cord banking is so poor, why is the technology demanded as much as it is? There are several possibilities. One is that many households value a life year at more than $1 million. This seems unlikely and runs counter to estimates published in the literature. Kaimal and colleagues mention two other possibilities. One is that people cannot accurately gauge the very low probabilities; cognitively, probabilities such as 0.0004 are too low for people to accurately comprehend them. If they plug in a higher probability in their mental calculations, even implicitly, demand for the technology will be higher than it otherwise would be. Advertising by private blood banking firms may have increased demand, possibly by making people think that the probability of such blood being needed in the future is higher than it is objectively. Another possibility, not mutually exclusive of the others, is that people believe there will be technological change in the future—in the technology of storing blood, for example, which would reduce the future cost of blood banking, or in the uses for umbilical cord blood. Such beliefs should increase demand for the technology currently. Basing calculations of cost-effectiveness on assumptions that are appropriate currently is often a weakness of CEA.

The authors conducted various sensitivity analyses to gauge the robustness of their results to changes in assumptions about treatment efficacy and cost. This analysis showed that the results were quite sensitive to alternative assumptions about treatment cost.

Sensitivity analysis is very useful in policy analysis. The analyst should inform policy makers about the robustness of findings. Doing so avoids some unpleasant surprises later on.

What did CEA accomplish in this application? First, it identified a set of preferred strategies. Those that are dominant are clearly inferior to those on the frontier. Second, it ranked strategies in terms of their incremental cost-effectiveness. Third, through the internal validation process, it helped ensure that the model parameters were sufficiently applicable to the country's situation. Fourth, with the use of sensitivity analysis, the authors could learn which of their underlying assumptions had most effect on their results and hence on their recommendations to policy makers.

In their conclusion, the authors emphasized that cost-effectiveness is only one consideration in the allocation of a country's scarce resources. One can expect that there may be variation in the availability of strategies, such as the availability of particular drugs. Also, there are considerations of infrastructure, equity, non-pecuniary factors, and interactions with other public programs. However, the presence of these other considerations should not be an acceptable pretext for not undertaking CEA or CBA.

Cost-Effectiveness of Screening for Cervical Cancer in Low-Income Settings

Cervical cancer is a leading cause of death among women in countries throughout the world. In low-income countries, up to 80 percent of women with cervical cancer first appear at a health care provider with an advanced stage of the disease. In high-income countries, routine screening of women for cervical cancer is common where the Papanicolaou (Pap) smear is widely used to screen for cervical cancer. However, in low-income countries and in parts of middle-income countries in which low-income families predominate, screening for this cancer is much less common. Also, the facilities for interpreting Pap smears, such as laboratories with properly trained cytotechnologists, are lacking. And given the distances from the testing site and the lack of availability of good transportation, asking women with positive screening results to return for treatment is often burdensome. For this reason, simple visual screening methods and approaches that allow for screening and treatment to be performed on the same visit have been proposed.

Our third application of CEA is also about optimal strategies in low-income settings where the resources for screening and other forms of care are very limited. In essence, this is the polar opposite case of the t-PA versus streptokinase example. Ratios of cost to life years saved in this application are far different than in the case of t-PA versus streptokinase, although the methods are similar.

Goldie, Kuhn, Denny, et al. (2001) performed a CEA of alternative cervical cancer screening strategies in low-resource settings. The analysis focused on the screening of previously unscreened 30-year-old black South African women. Several strategies were considered, which differed in the number of clinic visits required, frequency of screening, and actions taken based on a positive test finding. The outcome measures were years of life saved, lifetime cost (in US dollars), and incremental CERs expressed in incremental cost per life year saved.

A diagram showing the transitions of cervical disease status, substantially simplified from Goldie and colleagues' article, is given in figure 14.4. In general, for our purposes, we do not need to know many of the technical medical details of the cervical cancer disease process. However, a few details are needed to interpret the figure.

Cervical cancer is caused by the human papillomavirus (HPV). HIV can add to the effect of HPV, increasing the rate of progression to cervical cancer. HIV infection can also progress on its own. Disease severity is measured by the CD4 cell count, with a low cell count worse than a high one (e.g., "count 1" worse than "count 2"). SIL stands for squamous intraepithelial lesions, which occur with cervical cancer. High values of SIL indicate worse health than low values. Once cancer has developed, it can spread to other parts of the body (metastasis 1–3). In contrast

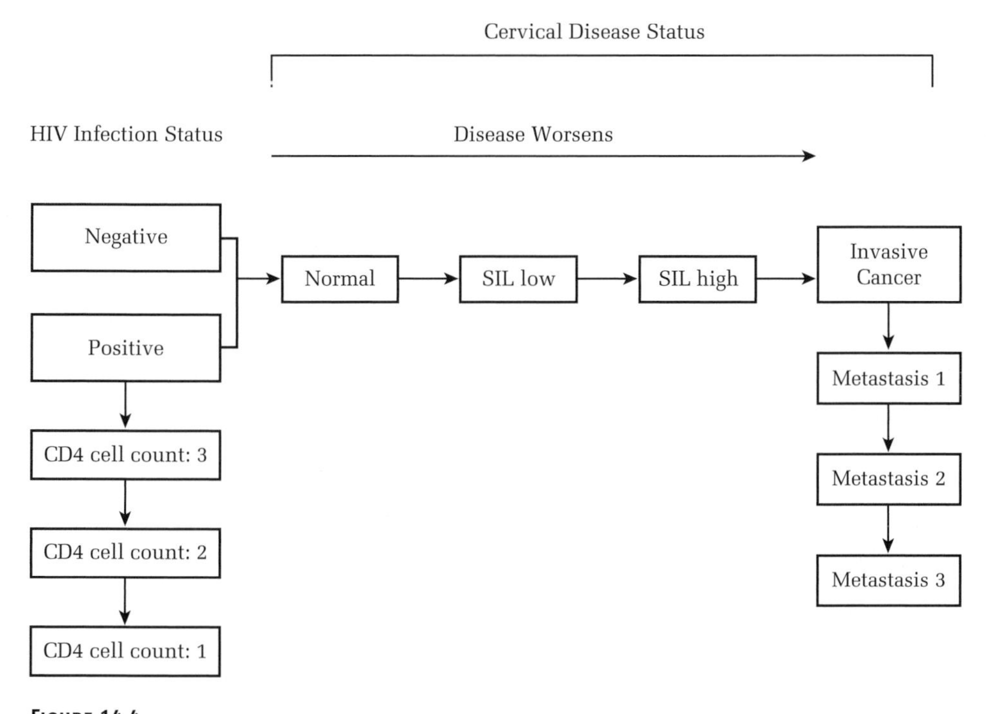

FIGURE 14.4
Cervical Disease Progression
Source: Adapted from Goldie, Kuhn, Denny et al. (2001).

to the previous examples, cervical disease status can both progress and regress. To keep the figure simple, only disease progression is shown in the chart.

Like the other studies, this application of CEA adopted a societal perspective, which means that all costs and benefits were counted, irrespective of to whom they accrued. However, unlike in the previous examples, the authors did account for the patient cost of travel time. They discounted costs/benefits (this is a CEA, not a CBA) at a 3 percent real rate. Transition probabilities came from the published literature. The authors accounted for heterogeneity in transition probabilities, which varied according to the woman's DNA. The transition probabilities also differed by screening approach, which differed according to the number of clinical visits, the use of one or two screening tests, screening frequency, and the ages at which the women were screened.

The authors considered three-, two-, and one-visit strategies, the first of these being most common in high-income countries, with testing occurring on the first two visits (the second depending on the test result from the first visit) and treatment occurring on the third visit. In the two-visit strategy, the diagnostic visits are compressed into one. In the one-visit strategy, diagnosis and treatment occur on a single visit. Given the distance that many women in low-income countries live from diagnosis and treatment facilities and the lack of adequate modes of transportation, it is important to consider streamlined approaches that reduce the number of times the patient must visit the facility.

To estimate visit costs, the authors first identified the specific services associated with each screening strategy and then applied unit prices from a South African fee schedule to arrive at costs per visit. In addition, they conducted surveys of patients to estimate time spent traveling, waiting, and receiving health care and the cost of transportation to facilities. Time spent was multiplied by estimated hourly wage rates of low-income women.

The authors presented a graph similar to that in figure 14.3 but with values from their analysis. As in the previous example, discounted lifetime total costs were on the horizontal axis and discounted life expectancy was on the vertical *y*axis.

Relative to the other examples, judged in terms of cost-effectiveness, the strategies on the curve were great bargains. For example, HPV testing followed by treatment of screened positive women at a second visit cost $39 per life years saved, not tens of thousands of dollars as in the previous examples. Clearly, there is much to be done to improve the health of populations in low-resource settings, and cervical cancer screening is among the most promising strategies.

14.5 Use of Economic Evaluation in Practice: Conclusions and Implications

The techniques described in this chapter and the next one are often called *economic evaluation*, a term in widespread use in the health field but one we are less than thrilled about since virtually all of the topics in health economics as well as in general economics could fall under this heading. In CBA, all costs and consequences are valued in monetary terms. However, in health care, cost-effectiveness is much more commonly used, where the difference in cost between alternatives is compared with the difference in outcomes measured in units such as life years gained or QALYs gained.

The first country to formally adopt economic evaluation as a method for making health care reimbursement decisions was Australia in 1992. Since then, economic evaluation has been adopted as a method for making reimbursement decisions or the development of national guidance for health technologies in more than ten other countries, including eight EU countries—Belgium, Finland, Hungary, Ireland, the Netherlands, Portugal, Sweden, and the United Kingdom—plus Canada, New Zealand, and Norway (Drummond 2007).

How economic evaluation is conducted varies among these countries. Generally, it has been confined to pharmaceuticals. The National Institute for Health and Clinical Excellence (NICE) in the UK assesses medical devices, medical procedures, and public health interventions in addition to pharmaceuticals. Even among countries that limit economic evaluation to pharmaceuticals, there are variations in policy, with some countries evaluating only new pharmaceutical products, while others limit evaluation to high-priced drugs, or those likely to have a large effect on the health care system in the country. The extent of regulatory control also varies. Some countries use the process of economic evaluation to make a formal decision to list or not list the drug for reimbursement on a national or a provincial formulary. Others use economic evaluation to issue evidence-based guidelines for appropriate use of the technologies. The same analytic techniques have been used by private medical organizations for guidelines, which are advisory but carry no enforcement teeth.

While CEA represents an advance over not doing CEA, it is not perfect by any means. For example, Pauly (2007) is critical of how drug cost is typically measured in CEA. Given the markup over the marginal cost of a drug, the drug's wholesale price tends to be far above marginal cost. From a social cost perspective, the resource use required to produce an extra unit of the product is relevant. The wholesale price includes the return to the manufacturer of its R&D cost, but the cost of R&D is a sunk cost once the drug has been developed. If CEA or CBA is used to decide whether to invest in R&D in developing a new drug, then the R&D cost is no longer sunk and should be included.

Although these techniques are not perfect, much of the opposition to formal evaluations of medical technologies probably reflects the business interests of enterprises that seek to avoid scrutiny, rather than an in-depth analysis of the methodological approaches that are being used. One legitimate concern is that the methods used in economic evaluation are not sufficiently transparent. In the applications we discussed and the articles we summarized, methods are described in capsule form, which is understandable, given tight journal space. Yet particularly since decisions based on economic evaluation can have important implications for a new product's success, firms with a new product should be able to understand and critique the assessment methodologies that are used (see Reinhardt 2007).

Governments in countries that have adopted economic evaluation techniques as a tool in the decision-making process do have a conflict of interest in that they are both payers and assessors, raising a suspicion that CEA or, much less commonly, CBA methods are skewed by the assessors to save public funds. There is indeed a potential conflict of interest. When new products are approved for payment, the immediate impact is on public budgets. The health gains, such as reductions in mortality from AMI, HIV/AIDS, and cervical cancer, are often realized later. Although using a social discount rate, these deferred benefits should be considered, the length of time that decision makers spend in their jobs is limited. Thus, being in a position of responsibility during a period of budget increases may be penalized, even if from a resource allocation standpoint the increased expenditures prove eventually to have been warranted.

Largely for this reason, Reinhardt (2007) suggests establishing nonprofit pharmacoeconomic research institutes (PERIs), as opposed to government-run organizations, to produce systematic information on the relative cost-effectiveness of rival pharmaceutical products. PERIs presumably would not be subject to the same budgetary pressures as politicians are and therefore could assess particular technologies more objectively.

Finally, individual countries may benefit from information, whether or not they contribute to the information dissemination process. For this reason, the feasibility of multicountry efforts is worth exploring.

Key Concepts

- cost-effectiveness ratio
- value of life year
- DALY
- Markov model
- time trade-off
- discount rate
- incremental cost-effectiveness ratio
- transition probability
- standard gamble

Review and Discussion Questions

14.1 What is meant by "opportunity cost," and how does opportunity cost relate to cost as economists measure it?

14.2 If you were setting up a program for the prevention, diagnosis, and treatment of breast cancer in a low-income country, which types of costs would you include in the cost-effectiveness analysis (CEA)? For each type of cost you mention, how would you measure it?

14.3 What is meant by "sunk cost?" Describe when the cost of R&D of a new therapy is a sunk cost.

14.4 Distinguish between direct and indirect costs, and give examples of each.

14.5 What is meant by a "cost offset"? Is it possible with cost offsets for the cost of an intervention to be negative? Explain your answer.

14.6 Describe different perspectives in cost analysis: society's, the payer's (insurer's), the patient's.

14.7 Why are costs discounted? What are the consequences of assuming a too high or too low discount rate? Why might social discount rates differ from private market discount rates?

14.8 What is meant by a QALY? Describe different approaches to measuring QALYs.

14.9 What are transition probabilities? How are they measured? Why are they used in a CEA? Use an example from an application described in the chapter.

14.10 Explain the concept of a cost-effectiveness ratio (CER). How are CERs used in practice? That is, once one has a CER, what does one do with it?

EXERCISES

14.1 Given the information listed in table 14.1, suppose that 1,000 individuals are in the poor health state in period *t* and Θ_{PG} is 0.45, Θ_{PP} is 0.40, and Θ_{PD} is 0.15 without the drug. With the drug, the probabilities are 0.65, 0.30, and 0.05, respectively. Compute the numbers of persons in the each health state over three years if people do not take drug. Similarly, compute the numbers of persons in the each health state over three years if people take drug.

14.2 Suppose the health department in a small country has been given a budget of $10 million to spend on new drugs. Its objective is to maximize health gains per dollar. The department's analysts have developed a list of drugs that could be covered by the insurance program, together with estimates of their costs and benefits (in QALYs gained):

Drugs	Benefit (QALYs)	Cost ($)
A	500	1,000,000
B	500	2,000,000
C	250	2,000,000
D	200	1,200,000
E	150	4,500,000
F	100	1,200,000
G	100	1,800,000
H	100	2,000,000
I	100	5,000,000
J	50	800,000

a. Calculate the CER for each drug.

b. List the drug that could be reimbursed by the insurance plan, and the threshold value of your reimbursement decision.

c. If the budget of health department is cut and only $3 million can be allocated to spending for new drugs, which drugs will be included in the reimbursement list, and what is the threshold value of your reimbursement decision?

14.3 Referring to chapter 2, suppose you were asked the following trade-off question. Assume you had a particular disease (you need to pick a specific disease) and there was a surgical operation that would (1) either cure you of the disease completely, and you would be in perfect health, *or* (2) possibly kill you during the operation, painlessly and quickly. Would you choose to have the operation if the chance of dying was 15 percent?

14.4 Suppose you were asked by a policy maker to measure cost for a new drug. Here is the information you receive about this drug (per daily dose):

Market price: US$25

Average wholesale price: US$18

Insurer acquisition price: US$15

Marginal cost: US$3

a. What kind of measurement will you choose to measure the cost of new drug if you like to conduct CEA from a social perspective? Explain your answer.

b. Will you change the measurement of cost if the policy maker asks you to conduct CEA from the perspective of the payer? Explain the measurement of cost you choose and justify your answer.

ONLINE SUPPLEMENTAL MATERIAL

NATIONAL INSTITUTE FOR HEALTH AND CLINICAL EXCELLENCE

http://www.nice.org.uk/

TECHNOLOGY ASSESSMENTS

http://www.ahrq.gov/clinic/techix.htm

COST-EFFECTIVENESS ANALYSIS

http://www.cdc.gov/owcd/eet/CostEffect2/fixed/1.html

http://hspm.sph.sc.edu/courses/Econ/Classes/cbacea/ce.html

http://www.who.int/choice/publications/p_2003_generalised_cea.pdf

http://www.nejm.org/doi/full/10.1056/NEJMsb050564

http://www.nice.org.uk/newsroom/features/measuringeffectivenessandcosteffectivenesstheqaly.jsp

Supplemental Readings

Drummond, M. 2007. Using Economic Evaluation in Reimbursement Decisions for Health Technologies: Lessons from International Experience. In *Pharmaceutical Innovation: Incentives, Competition, and Cost-Benefit Analysis in International Perspective*, ed. F. A. Sloan and C.-R. Hsieh, 215–225. New York: Cambridge University Press.

Goldie, S. J., Y. Yazdanpanah, E. Losina, et al. 2006. Cost-Effectiveness of HIV Treatment in Resource-Poor Settings: The Case of Côte d'Ivoire. *New England Journal of Medicine* 355 (11): 1141–1153.

Goldie, S. J., J. J. Kim, K. Kobus, et al. 2007. Cost-Effectiveness of HPV 16, 18 Vaccination in Brazil. *Vaccine* 25 (33): 6257–6270.

Kahn, J., E. Marseille, and B. Auvert. 2006. Cost-Effectiveness of Male Circumcision for HIV Prevention in a South African Setting. *PLoS Medicine* 3 (12): 2349–2358.

Pauly, M. V. 2007. Risks and Benefits in Health Care: The View from Economics. *Health Affairs* 26 (3): 653–662.

References

Andresen, E. M., J. A. Malmgren, W. B. Carter, et al. 1994. Screening for Depression in Well Older Adults: Evaluation of a Short Form of the CES-D (Center for Epidemiologic Studies Depression Scale). *American Journal of Preventive Medicine* 10 (2): 77–84.

Chapman, B., A. Freiberg, J. Quiggin, et al. 2003. Rejuvenating Financial Penalties: Using the Tax System to Collect Fines. Centre for Economic Policy Research, Research School of Scoail Sciences, Discussion Paper 461. Canberra: Australian National University.

Drummond, M. 2007. Using Economic Evaluation in Reimbursement Decisions for Health Technologies: Lessons from International Experience. In *Pharmaceutical Innovation: Incentives, Competition, and Cost-Benefit Analysis in International Perspective*, ed. F. A. Sloan and C.-R. Hsieh, 215–225. New York: Cambridge University Press.

George, L. K., D. Ruiz, Jr., and F. A. Sloan. 2008. The Effects of Total Hip Arthroplasty on Physical Functioning in the Older Population. *Journal of the American Geriatrics Society* 56 (6): 1057–1062.

Girola, J. 2005. *The Long-Term Real Interest Rate for Social Security*. Washington, DC: United States Department of the Treasury.

Gold, M., J. E. Siegel, L. B. Russell, et al., eds. 1996. *Cost Effectiveness in Health and Medicine*. New York: Oxford University Press.

Goldie, S. J., L. Kuhn, L. Denny, et al. 2001. Policy Analysis of Cervical Cancer Screening Strategies in Low-Resource Settings: Clinical Benefits and Cost-Effectiveness. *Journal of the American Medical Association* 285 (24): 3107–3115.

Goldie, S. J., Y. Yazdanpanah, E. Losina, et al. 2006. Cost-Effectiveness of HIV Treatment in Resource-Poor Settings: The Case of Côte d'Ivoire. *New England Journal of Medicine* 355 (11): 1141–2253.

Harrison, G., M. I. Lau, and M. B. Williams. 2002. Estimating Individual Discount Rates in Denmark: A Field Experiment. *American Economic Review* 92 (5): 1606–1617.

Kaimal, A. J., C. C. Smith, R. K. Laros, et al. 2009. Cost-Effectiveness of Private Umbilical Cord Blood Banking. *Obstetrics and Gynecology* 114 (4): 848–855.

Kaplan, R. M. 1995. Utility Assessment for Estimating Quality-Adjusted Life Years. In *Valuing Health Care*, ed. F. A. Sloan, 31–60. New York: Cambridge University Press.

Keeler, E. B. 1995. *Decision Trees and Markov Models in Cost-Effectiveness Research: Valuing Health Care*, ed. F. A. Sloan, 185–206. New York: Cambridge University Press.

Khwaja, A., D. Silverman, and F. Sloan. 2007. Time Preference, Time Discounting, and Smoking Decisions. *Journal of Health Economics* 26 (5): 927–949.

Lind, R. C. 1982. *A Primer on the Major Issues Relating to the Discount Rate for Evaluating National Energy Options: Discounting for Time and Risk in Energy Policy*. Baltimore, MD: Johns Hopkins University Press.

Mankiw, N. G. 2007. *Essentials of Economics*. Orlando, FL: Harcourt College Publishing.

Mark, D. B., M. A. Hlatky, R. M. Califf, et al. 1995. Cost Effectiveness of Thrombolytic Therapy with Tissue Plasminogen Activator as Compared with Streptokinase for Acute Myocardial Infarction. *New England Journal of Medicine* 332 (21): 1418–1424.

McClellan, M., B. J. McNeil, and J. P. Newhouse. 1994. Does More Intensive Treatment of Acute Myocardial Infarction in the Elderly Reduce Mortality? Analysis Using Instrumental Variables. *Journal of the American Medical Association* 272 (11):859–866.

Moore, M. J., and W. K. Viscusi. 1990a. Discounting Environmental Health Risks: New Evidence and Policy Implications. *Journal of Environmental Economics and Management* 18 (2): S51–S62.

Moore, M. J., and W. K. Viscusi. 1990b. Models for Estimating Discount Rates for Long-Term Health Risks Using Labor Market Data. *Journal of Risk and Uncertainty* 3 (4): 381–401.

Neumann, J. von, and O. Morgenstern. 1944. *Theory of Games and Economic Behavior*. Princeton, NJ: Princeton University Press.

Pauly, M. V. 2007. Risks and Benefits in Health Care: The View from Economics. *Health Affairs* 26 (3): 653–662.

Pauly, R. 1996. Convergence of Economic Variables in EC Member Countries: A Statistical and Economic Analysis. *Jahrbucher für Nationalökonomie und Statistik* 215 (1): 33–49.

Pfeiffer, E. 1975. Short Portable Mental Status Questionnaire. *Journal of the American Geriatrics Society* 23 (10): 433–441.

Reinhardt, U. 2007. The Pharmaceutical Sector in Health Care. In *Pharmaceutical Innovation: Incentives, Competition, and Cost-Benefit Analysis in International Perspective*, ed. F. A. Sloan and C.-R. Hsieh, 25–53. New York: Cambridge University Press.

Saha, S., T. J. Hoerger, M. P. Pignone, et al. 2001. The Art and Science of Incorporating Cost Effectiveness into Evidence-Based Recommendations for Clinical Preventive Services. *American Journal of Preventive Medicine* 20 (3S): 36–43.

Viscusi, W. K. 1996. Alternative Institutional Responses to Asbestos. *Journal of Risk and Uncertainty* 12 (2–3): 147–170.

Chapter 15

Measuring Benefits and Cost-Benefit Analysis

Until now, we have discussed benefits in terms of units of health outcomes. Cost-benefit analysis (CBA) measures benefits and costs in monetary terms, which allows benefits from health care programs to be compared not only with each other but also with those of programs in other areas. Cost-effectiveness analysis (CEA) is much more widely used in health policy applications.

CBA is more widely used in other areas, such as in appraising the value of environment programs, than it is in health. It is difficult to explain this difference. Environmental hazards cause damage to personal health and loss of longevity, too.

Proponents of CBA respond that in the final analysis, overall resource allocation requires the use of a common denominator such as money. Also, it is possible to adjust for the higher valuations of more affluent persons by weighing benefits accruing to less affluent individuals more highly (see, e.g., Pauly 1996). While we are persuaded by these arguments, we recognize that direct comparisons between projects across areas are not generally made; for example, a vaccine program is generally not directly compared with a highway construction program. Also, although it makes sense as a purely conceptual matter, reweighing benefits to adjust for the distributional effects of programs is hardly ever done in practice—at least as part of formal analysis. Decision makers may reject a project with benefits exceeding costs because of undesirable effects on one or more segments of the population.

The purpose of this chapter is to describe CBA and how it is implemented in particular. Since cost measurement has been discussed in the previous chapter, the emphasis here is on benefit measurement in theory and in application.

15.1 MEASURING BENEFITS IN COST-BENEFIT ANALYSIS: A REVIEW

Using a cost-benefit decision rule, the set of programs that is preferred is one that maximizes the excess of benefits over costs (Mishan 1976). If the decision maker faces no budget constraint, all projects for which the benefit is greater than or equal to the cost should be undertaken. The difference between benefit and cost is then the relevant metric, not some other metric such as the ratio of benefit to cost. A ratio is a relevant measure comparison if the budget is fixed, lest the relatively small projects for which the difference between benefit and cost is necessarily relatively small and hence not be selected, even though the return per dollar is higher for some relatively small projects.

When we use the metric that the benefit exceed or be equal to cost as the criterion for project adoption, it is not necessary that the benefit exceed the cost for each and every member of society. People differ in how much they benefit from a particular program. And for some persons, cost, for example, taxes paid for the project, is likely to exceed benefit even if in the aggregate, benefit exceeds cost. In principle, according to the Pareto criterion for a social optimum (see, e.g., Frank 2006, 591–594), when benefits exceed costs, it should be possible for winners from the project to compensate the losers. However, this is rarely done in practice. Pareto optimality, that is, a situation in which the winners could compensate the losers and still be better off than without the program, does not require that the losers actually be compensated.

Underlying the appropriate measure of benefit is the concept of individuals' maximum willingness to pay (WTP) for a given quantity of a good or service. Under ideal circumstances, maximum WTP is given by the demand curve for that good or service. For each quantity, there is a price that represents the person's maximum willingness to pay for the last unit of quantity. Of course, if the person could get the good for a lower price, he or she would prefer this. The aggregate demand for that good or service is the sum of each market participant's demand curve. In this sense, the aggregate demand curve for a private good, such as video games, represents the societal benefit of video games.

Several issues arise in benefit valuation of the types of goods and services considered in this book. The first concerns external benefits. When person A is vaccinated, person B potentially benefits. Further, there are financial externalities. Thus, if the good or service is covered by health insurance, the failure of person A to undergo screening potentially affects person B financially, in addition to affecting person A in terms of his or her health as well as financially. There are financial implications both in terms of person A's and person B's own spending on personal health care services and because each person is a taxpayer who will pay higher taxes if the burden of disease is higher. External benefits are not reflected in market demand curves.

Second, not all health goods and services are marketable or marketed. Many public health programs fall into this category. For example, there is no market for a reduced probability of getting an infectious disease. In some cases, there is no existing prevention method, such as an effective vaccine to prevent the disease. Yet decision makers may want to know what the benefit of investing in research and development of the vaccine would be. Or a vaccine or drug for preventing or treating a certain disease may exist, but it is not available in the country in question, and decision makers in the country may want to know if they should make the vaccine available to its citizens, which it might do if benefits exceed costs. When the market provides no metric, it is necessary to find another metric to measure benefit.

Third, for a private good such as a video game, there is little and probably no concern about distributional effects. If the rich buy more video games, perhaps because they consistently purchase the newest editions, this is fine with most people (with the notable exception of many children and video game–playing adults with low incomes). However, for personal health care services, the distributional effects of programs may be a matter of public, and hence public decision maker, concern.

CBA is mainly about public programs. A private decision maker, such as a for-profit firm, naturally views benefits in terms of revenue and costs in terms of the costs it incurs. With CBA, by contrast, the benefit should encompass various externalities as well as society's distributional norms.

In a CBA, benefits are measured in essentially two ways. In one, the *revealed preference* approach, benefits are based on the values implicit in choices people actually make. An example could be the additional wages people demand to work at jobs with greater personal health risks or the amount people pay for safety devices, such as in their automobiles or in their homes (e.g., radon detectors).

The other major method is based on surveys of individuals' willingness to pay for a good or service, the *stated preference* approach. These surveys most often use the method of *contingent valuation* to derive a valuation from choices made within a hypothetical context. A good or service is described, and the survey elicits the person's maximum WTP for the good or service if it were provided. The good or service could be a personal health service, such as a screening test. Or it could be an environmental program or outcome, such as air of a certain quality or the provision of a park in the vicinity of the person being interviewed. The choices made by the respondents are used as measures of preference, and hence this methodology often is referred to as the stated preference approach. This is in contrast to the revealed preference approach, in which evaluation of the individual's maximum WTP is based on the observed actions within a market, for instance from purchases of radon detectors to reduce the personal risk of getting cancer.

Benefits can be viewed as negative costs. Thus, costs averted by programs can be considered beneficial. For example, if taking a particular drug can reduce hospitalizations, such as aspirin to reduce subsequent heart attacks, the savings in expenditure on hospitalization is a potential benefit of adopting the drug. A potential benefit of smoking cessation program is the reduction in life years lost from continued smoking.

15.2 THE REVEALED PREFERENCE APPROACH

OBJECTIVE

Most studies that use the revealed preference approach stipulate changes in longevity as the outcome measure. The objective of the revealed preference approach is thus to derive the value of a statistical life (VSL) or a year of life. The most important word in this expression is *statistical*, which means that in this context, the value of a life is an abstraction, rather than the value of the life of a specific individual. As newspaper reporters often remind us, the public tends not to be as interested in such abstract concepts as statistical lives; rather, the experiences of specific individuals are much more salient. Yet from the standpoint of public decision making, statistical lives are much more relevant. The use of VSL here is not in allocating resources to particular individuals. No one is suggesting that physicians allocate their resources on the basis of the monetary and nonmonetary value of the lives of their patients, allowing those with a high value to live and terminating the lives of others. To do so would be highly illegal and inequitable, and most of us would judge such allocations immoral, apart from special cases such as providing high levels of medical care to very high-level executives and public officials.

Yet resource allocations are unavoidable at the policy level. Resources are scarce, and the traditional view held by many in the health care sector that all technologies that offer *some* benefit should be adopted is also very wrong in our view and clearly unrealistic, especially in low-resource countries. The principle in some high-income countries that every type of care that yields positive benefits with regard to cost should be adopted inevitably leads to overspending on health care services.

The methods described below offer help to policy makers in making better public policy decisions. Many persons in and out of government are involved in performing the types of studies we describe.

Economists prefer to infer individuals' underlying preferences from their actual choices, not from what people say they would do in hypothetical situations. Economists place a great deal of confidence in information obtained from individuals' actual choices, not their intended choices. The colloquial expression "put your money where your mouth is" is the essence of the revealed preference approach. Literally, revealed preference means preferences as revealed by actual choices people make.

Given the value of a life year, the analyst can multiply this value by an estimate of life years gained by a project, or, alternatively, quality of additional life years (QALYs) gained, which is a method for scaling life years to roughly account for the quality of life of the added years of life. The result is a benefit measure usable in CBA.

Underlying Assumptions

Several key assumptions underlie the revealed preference approach. First, people routinely make decisions that reflect the value they place on health and on mortality risks versus the value they place on other goods and services and on nonhealth outcomes. Such valuing is implicit in the act of operating a motor vehicle, smoking, or eating high-caloric food. Second, empirical evidence from choices that people make in the marketplace that involve trade-offs between risk and money reveal individuals' valuations or maximum WTP for an extra life year or QALY. Third, these values represent ex ante maximum WTP, not an ex post value. In other words, the values embedded in peoples' decisions reflect preferences before a decision is actually made. In revealed preference analysis, a decision is made before outcomes stemming from the decision are known. "Crying over spilled milk," or ex post regret, is understandable but has no role in this approach.

Evidence from Labor Markets

Most literature on the VSL calculated using the revealed preference approach comes from labor market studies. Associated with each job is a specific accident risk, including the risk of getting involved in a fatal accident. Conceptually, accident risk differentials among jobs are reflected in compensation differentials among jobs.

The firm's demand for labor is a function of how much it must pay for a unit of labor.[1] Such compensation reflects wage payments, fringe benefits, training provided through employment (especially training that raises a worker's productivity on several jobs), and investments the firm makes in providing a safer work environment for its employees. If, for example, workers are provided with helmets, this is as much a labor cost to the employer as are wage payments. Expenditures on fringe and other worker benefits and protections (e.g., helmets) appear as a cost on the firm's income statement. Firms make investments in making the workplace safer for their employees. However, safer jobs tend to pay lower wages, which offsets the additional cost of investments in job safety, at least in part.

In this framework, workers are assumed to be expected utility maximizers (see chapter 4 for a discussion of expected utility). They maximize utility over wage

1. Our description here draws on Viscusi and Aldy (2003).

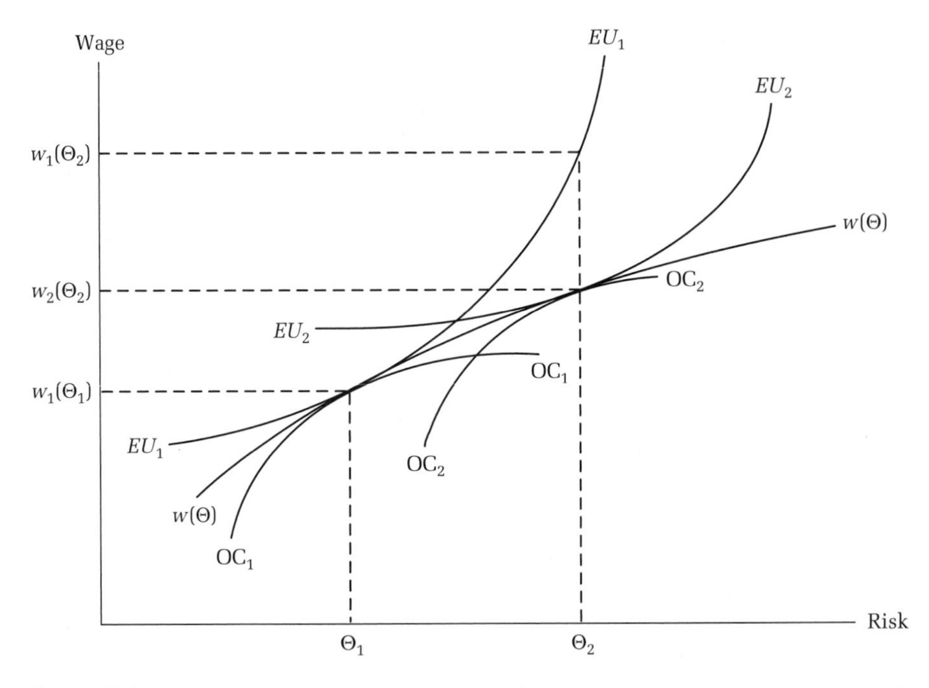

FIGURE 15.1
Choice of Wage and Job-Related Risk
Source: W. K. Viscusi and J. E. Aldy, "The Value of a Statistical Life: A Critical Review of Market Estimates Throughout the World," *Journal of Risk and Uncertainty* 27, no. 1 (2003): 5–76, figure 1. Reprinted with permission from Springer Science+Business Media B.V.

and fringe benefit compensation *and* job-related risk. Since wages and fringe benefits are a function of such risk, a worker need only pick a probability Θ that maximizes his or her expected utility. If he or she selects a higher probability of experiencing an adverse outcome on the job, he or she receives a higher wage, all other factors held constant, and conversely if the worker picks a lower probability.

In figure 15.1, the relationship between wages (disregarding fringe benefits, the inclusion of which would yield no additional insights) and risk for the firm is shown as two offer curves (OC curves). Their slopes and positions reflect the technology of risk reduction as well as the price of such risk reduction technology. Think of the cost of making a coal mine safer. Such costs will depend on both the personnel employed in making the mine safer and the price of the technologies used, as well as on the marginal product of such technology measures in terms of the difference in the probability of an accident before and after implementation of the mine safety measures.

Since less investment in such technology is needed if there is to be higher job-related risk, the firm is able to offer higher wages when the work environment is less safe. The relative expense of risk reduction technology is likely to differ among and even within industries, such as for different kinds of mines. While the slopes of the offer curves are positive, the curves are flatter at high levels of risk, implying that investments in reducing risk are relatively productive at high levels of risk. However, as risk levels are reduced, further investments in risk reduction technology eventually become relatively unproductive.

Risk reduction technology is reflected in the firm's offer curves. By contrast, the preferences of employees are reflected in the indifference curves. Figure 15.1 shows two indifference curves. The indifference curves also have positive slopes, but in contrast to offer curves, the wage-risk gradient becomes very steep as the risk is increased beyond some level. This means that at relatively high levels of risk, workers require a highly increased wage differential to compensate them for bearing an additional unit of risk (e.g., an additional 0.01 probability of being the victim of a fatal on-the-job accident). The optimal points are at wage-risk levels at which the marginal rate of substitution between goods (wages) and risk is equal to the marginal rate at which reduced risk is translated into lower wages, that is, where the slopes of the two types of curves are the same.

More formally,[2] the worker maximizes expected utility through the following:

$$Z = (1 - \Theta)U(w) + \Theta V(w), \qquad (15.1)$$

where U(w) is the utility of consumption (wages) in the healthy state, V(w) is the utility of consumption in the sick state—the health state after an accident occurs—and Θ is the probability of the accident occurring. For a given amount of wage compensation, total utility U is definitely higher than total utility V. However, the marginal utility of a unit of wage compensation in the healthy versus the marginal utility of a unit of such compensation in the sick state cannot be determined from theory alone. Both marginal utilities are plausibly positive. The slope of the worker's indifference curve is given by equation 15.2, which is a first-order condition:

$$\frac{dw}{d\Theta} = -\frac{Z_\Theta}{Zw} = \frac{U(w) - V(w)}{(1-\Theta)U'(w) + \Theta V'(w)} > 0 \qquad (15.2)$$

The change in wage rate per unit change in the probability of an accident, $dw/d\Theta$, is larger when the difference in total utility between the healthy and the sick states is larger—the numerator of equation 15.2 is larger, other factors being equal. The worker demands a higher wage for a given level of risk when the utility loss from having the accident is greater, which is plausible. For a given difference between *U* and *V*, $dw/d\Theta$ is larger when the marginal utilities of *w* are lower. These marginal utilities are in the denominator of equation 15.2. When the worker derives

2. The reader who has not had courses in microeconomics beyond the principles level or has not had differential calculus may skip the discussion of equations 15.1 and 15.2 and go directly to the discussion of how willingness to pay to avoid job risk is reflected in wage differentials, as reflected in equation 15.3.

less added enjoyment from consuming additional goods, the worker in essence places a higher weight on having a relatively safe job at a lower wage, and conversely for a higher marginal utility of consumption. The level of Θ also matters. If Θ increases and $V'(w)$ is high relative to $U'(w)$, the unit increase in Θ will result in a lower $dw/d\Theta$ compared to a situation in which $V'(w)$ is low relative to $U'(w)$.

The estimated wage-risk trade-off $w(\Theta)$ does not indicate how a *particular* worker must be compensated for nonmarginal changes in risk. The two indifference curves in figure 15.1 are for two different workers with different preferences. The points of tangency are at different marginal rates of substitution between wage compensation and job-related risk.

What *is* observed in the data are points of tangency of the two types of curves. We observe, after worker-job matching, firm- or establishment-level observations on wage rates and job risk. The parameters of an equation such as 15.3 are estimated.

$$\ln w_t = \alpha + H_i'\beta_2 + \gamma_1\Theta_i + \gamma_2\Omega_i + \gamma_3\Omega_i WC_i + \gamma_4 X + \Theta_i H_i'\beta_3 + \varepsilon_i \qquad (15.3)$$

where

w = worker's wage rate;

H = human capital measures of worker (e.g., education, job experience, age, gender, union status);

X = vector of job characteristic variables for worker;

Θ = fatality risk of worker i's job;

Ω = nonfatal injury risk of worker i's job;

WC = workers' compensation benefits payable to the worker if injured on the job;

ε_i = random error reflecting unmeasured factors affecting w.

The relationship depicted by equation 15.3 represents an average of marginal rates of substitution of workers (the rate at which workers are willing to trade off wage compensation for reductions in the probability of a job-related accident or injury) who select different combinations of wages and risk.

The use of the natural logarithm (ln) of the wage is commonplace in empirical research on wages. Other things being equal, higher levels of human capital should result in higher wages. The variable X includes various job characteristics, such as health and life insurance benefits and vacation days offered by the employer. If the employer provides generous workers compensation benefits that are payable in the event that a job-related injury or fatality occurs, the wage should be lower. Measures of risk (Θ, Ω) include rates of injury and fatalities or workers' subjective beliefs about this risk if subjective beliefs differ from their objective counterparts.

There are several econometric problems that arise in estimating the parameters of equations like equation 15.3 using regression analysis. Since our focus is not on econometrics but rather on conceptual issues in the revealed preference approach, we will mention only the problems and not go into detail about solution methods.

One problem is that job-related risks are endogenous to wages. Both wages and risks are jointly determined, that is, determined at the same time. Rather than having the worker's wage on the left side of the equation, it would be as reasonable to put a job-related risk variable on the left side of the equation and regress it on wages and other factors as it is to estimate equation 15.3. This violates an important assumption of regression analysis, namely, that causation unambiguously runs from the variable on the right side of the equation to the variable on the left side. While causation runs in this direction, wages affect job risk as well. This issue arises in many other empirical applications discussed in this book as well.

Another and perhaps more serious problem in this application is that workers differ in ways not measured in the data, which is called *omitted heterogeneity*. For this reason, researchers may not observe a trade-off between wages and job-related risk. Rather than a positive relationship being observed between these variables (i.e., wages rise when risk rises), a negative relationship may be observed. Particularly capable, industrious, or well-connected workers in ways unobservable to the researcher and therefore not accounted for in the statistical analysis may obtain jobs with *both* high wages and low risk. Even if a positive relationship is observed, the estimated parameter may be biased. Economists deal with this issue by using longitudinal data on the same individuals. With such data, one can specify a variable to capture differences among individuals that do not vary for an individual over time (e.g., manual dexterity) in the sample, and hopefully capture factors that are unmeasured in the data sets but are important wage determinants and may be correlated with the risk at the job the worker selected.

VALUE OF A STATISTICAL LIFE

Researchers have used parameter estimates for γ_1 and γ_2 in equation 15.3 to derive VSL and life year values. If wages rise by a dollar per increase of 0.0001 per year in the probability of dying from a job-related accident or illness, then one can readily compute the implied value of life and of a life year (divide 0.0001 into 1). This has been done in numerous studies.

An alternative is to compute the VSL from other decisions, such as the effect of safety equipment on automobile prices. According to Viscusi and Aldy (2003), estimates of the value of a life from US market data range from US$5 to US$12 million per statistical life (2000 US$). There are considerably fewer studies of value of a statistical life outside the United States. Canada ranks next in terms of number of studies. In general, the estimated value of a life varies with income. Viscusi and Aldy (2003) estimated that the VSL has an income elasticity of about 0.5 to 0.6, implying that a 10 percent increase in a country's per capita income increases the valuation of a life by 5 to 6 percent. Not surprisingly, individuals who live in more affluent countries are the ones to emphasize the value of risk reduction from all sources.

While this is what the data show, the normative implications of this finding may be somewhat disconcerting. The finding implies that a life is more valuable in a high-income country than in a middle- or low-income country. Decision makers charged with the responsibility for allocating funds for international aid may not want to place full or partial reliance on this finding in many allocation decisions.

An Application of the Revealed Preference Approach: Cigarette Smokers as Job Risk Takers

Viscusi and Hersch (2001) focused on the preferences of cigarette smokers, the risks of the jobs in which they are employed, and why smokers are paid lower compensating wage differentials for assuming additional job-related risk when compared to others. Smokers select jobs in industries in which the risk of an accident or illness is greater, but given the lower wage-risk trade-off faced by smokers, their total compensation is lower nevertheless. The standard approach outlined above assumes that worker preferences affect workers' choice of job from the offer curve (the OC curves in fig. 15.1), but that differences in preferences do not affect the offer curve itself. If the wage premium for assuming higher job-related risk is lower for smokers than for nonsmokers, using the method for calculating the value of life described above, the estimated value of a statistical life for smokers will be lower for smokers than for nonsmokers.

It is not at all surprising that smokers have different preferences from nonsmokers. One reason why smokers continue to smoke (at least ex ante, before the health loss is actually experienced) is that nonsmokers believe they will have less utility in the sick than in the healthy state, but the loss they expect to experience is lower for smokers than for nonsmokers. In fact, there is some empirical evidence that adult smokers are willing to pay less to avoid poor health than are adult nonsmokers (Khwaja, Sloan, and Wang 2009). If so, it is not at all surprising that smokers would locate themselves on an offer curve at a higher wage-risk combination than others.

As seen in figure 15.1, the positive slope of the offer curve becomes flatter at higher levels of job risk, and if the tangency between a worker's indifference curve and the firm's offer curve occurs there, the slope at the point of tangency will be flatter. This is case 1 in figure 15.2. But this does not explain the anomaly

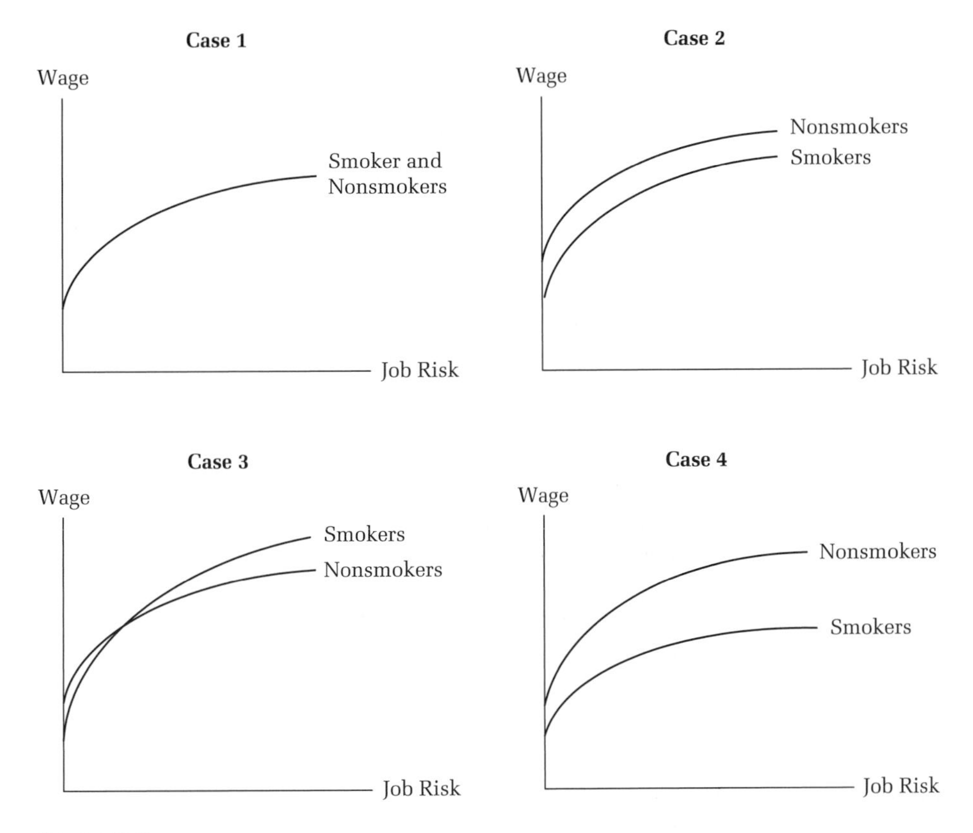

FIGURE 15.2
Summary of Smoker and Nonsmoker Wage-Risk Cases

Source: W. K. Viscusi and J. Hersch, "Cigarette Smokers as Job Risk Takers," *Review of Economics and Statistics* 83, no. 2 (2001): 269–280, figure 1. © 2001 by the President and Fellows of Harvard College and the Massachusetts Institute of Technology.

that smokers do not get paid as much for assuming the same level of risk as nonsmokers.

A second possibility is that the offer curve is lower for smokers than for nonsmokers but the two curves are parallel, as shown in case 2 in figure 15.2. Smokers may be paid less because their marginal productivity is lower on average, even after controlling for several worker characteristics, such as in equation 15.3. Empirical evidence based on US Social Security earnings history data suggests that this is true (Sloan, Ostermann, Picone, et al. 2004). With a number of other earnings determinants held constant, smokers earned less on average.

A third possibility is that although the offer curve faced by smokers is lower at low levels of job risk, at some point the offer curve for smokers becomes higher than the offer curve for smokers, as in case 3. Although a conceptual possibility, this pattern of offer curves, however, is inconsistent with the empirical evidence on smokers' versus nonsmokers' wage-job risks.

Fourth, the offer curve facing smokers may be everywhere below the offer curve facing nonsmokers, but unlike in case 2, it becomes relatively flatter at higher levels of job risk, which is case 4. Like case 2, case 4 is consistent with empirical evidence.

Using a national sample of persons in the United States in 1987, found in the National Medical Expenditure Survey (NMES), Viscusi and Hersch (2001) documented that smokers in their sample had lower mean wages, tended be slightly older (though less than a year older on average), had lower educational attainment (more than a year less on average), had longer job-related experience but lower tenure at their current jobs, were more likely to have a physical condition that limited work, were much less likely to be in a white-collar job, experienced a higher number of lost workdays, had a higher job-related injury rate, and were more likely to have experienced an injury off the job than were nonsmokers. Thus, smokers not only assumed a higher risk by smoking but were more accident-prone on and off the job. One can see why employers might offer smokers lower wages, given their higher rate of work absences, for one, and why they might be less willing to offer a wage premium to smokers than to nonsmokers.

Viscusi and Hersch (2001) regressed the natural logarithm of the wage rate on job risk and others factors, using a specification similar to equation 15.3, separately for smokers and nonsmokers. The results showed that the wage premium nonsmokers received for taking a riskier job was much higher than for the wage premium received by smokers. Further, the wages of nonsmokers were not affected by whether or not the worker had been injured on the job in the preceding year. However, in the analysis of smokers' wages, persons who had experienced an injury during the preceding year were paid less in the year after the injury occurred. This result is consistent with the view that employers regarded smokers as being more careless for a given risk level in a particular industry.

However, the authors conceded that the pattern of results is open to other interpretations as well. Perhaps, for example, smokers were employed in settings in which injuries, when they occurred, tended to be more disabling. The authors lacked the data to distinguish among these alternative interpretations.

Another finding was that smokers earned less in jobs in which the risk of injury was zero. This result, in combination with the results for the higher wages obtained by nonsmokers versus smokers for risk bearing, suggests that the valid case is case 4—an offer curve with a lower intercept and slope for smokers than for nonsmokers.

This study's findings are interesting in their own right, but the findings also offer important implications for the use of the revealed preference approach as the basis for assessing the VSL. Clearly, there is heterogeneity in tastes among individuals. Thus, even if the offer curves were the same, the points of tangency imply differences in the VSL. In some applications, applying the same value to all people should not result in misleading inferences. However, in others—say, in assessing the benefits of a smoking cessation program versus a program to provide colorectal screening to adults—using the same VSL is likely to result in misleading comparisons. The fact that the offer curves are likely to vary adds another important complication. If people differ in their compensation opportunities, the above analytic framework for obtaining VSL estimates breaks down. For example, if smokers had the same job opportunities as nonsmokers did, they may have made different choices and hence been located at different wage-risk combinations in the data. Next, we consider an alternative approach to valuing health benefits of programs. Yet in the end, no single approach is perfect.

15.3 THE STATED PREFERENCE APPROACH

The stated preference approach often uses questioning methods such as "Would you pay $X for . . . ?" and "Which of the following alternatives do you prefer?" to elicit WTP for life extension, a higher quality of life, or the cure of a specific disease, although these particular example questions are in a simplified form. There are three broad categories of stated preference questions: contingent valuation (CV) questions, stated choice of attribute-based questions, and contingent behavior or contingent activity questions.[3]

Stated preference approaches are highly controversial,[4] in part because they have been used to measure damages in litigation and to set a regulatory standard, which persons employed by sectors negatively affected by the regulations often oppose for reasons of self interest. But even when used purely for academic purposes, stated preference has encountered substantial criticism, mainly because of its hypothetical questioning rather than reliance on actual decisions made, as in the revealed preference approach. In response to various specific criticisms, researchers have substantially improved methods used to elicit values from surveys. In reviewing the criticisms, Freeman (2003, 183) states, "My own assessment of SP (stated preference) methods is cautiously optimistic. . . . It is hard to do a SP study well. There is no substitute for a careful reading in the now substantial and rapidly growing literature."

CONTINGENT VALUATION

In the CV approach, respondents are asked about monetary values for a specific nonmarket good, such as a type of personal health or a specific improved environmental outcome or the maximum amount the person would be willing to pay for a specific change to occur, such as a reduction in waiting time of one month. Some

3. For a more in-depth description and assessment of the alternative stated preference approaches discussed here, see Freeman (2003).

4. There is a large literature on issues related to eliciting WTP from surveys. See, e.g., Arrow, Solow, Portney, et al. (1993), Portney (1994), Hanemann (1994), Diamond and Hausman (1994), Hirth, Chernew, Miller, et al. (2000), Carson, Flores, and Meade (2001), and Venkatachalam (2004) for excellent reviews.

CV-type surveys have open-ended questions about maximum WTP rather than precoded monetary values from among which the respondent chooses. Open-ended questions allow respondents to give responses other those prespecified. On the other hand, some respondents may give wild and implausible answers to open-ended questions.

Another CV approach asks the respondent whether or not he or she would be willing to pay $X for an outcome. With this approach, one obtains only an upper or lower bound on maximum WTP—an upper bound if the person says no and a lower bound if the person says yes. In more sophisticated variants of this approach, people who say no to the first question are asked a second question with a lower value. The value is lowered in successive questions until the person finally says yes. After a yes is obtained, the next question is for a value between the last and second-to-last questions. Questions about values in increasingly small intervals are asked until successive yes answers or no answers are obtained that the midpoint between the two values yields a sufficiently precise estimate of maximum WTP.

A potential problem in CV studies is starting point bias. Such bias occurs to the extent that the value at which the questioning starts influences the final result. The reason is that respondents often anchor their answers on the first value mentioned in a series of questions. This problem may be reduced by randomizing starting values. Thus, even if each final value is influenced by the starting value, by randomizing starting values and having many survey respondents, this problem should be of minimal importance.

Using a series of yes-no questions and iterating to a final value should yield more valid and reliable estimates of maximum WTP than using open-ended questions, partially because people are used to making choices on a take-it-or-leave-it basis. Additionally, it is easier to answer yes or no than to give a monetary value for a good that one rarely or never purchases. The line of questioning with yes-no answers is incentive compatible. It is easiest to give a truthful answer. With an open-ended maximum WTP question, there is more room for respondent strategizing.

Nevertheless, two major concerns with the CV method remain. First, people may be cognitively unable to deal with complex trade-offs such as those embodied in surveys eliciting WTP, and individuals are likely to vary substantially in terms of their ability to evaluate trade-offs. For these reasons, it is a good idea to measure the individual's cognitive ability during the survey and adjust the responses in some manner based on measured cognitive ability. Widely accepted and used survey questions for assessing cognition exist.

A second concern with CV, as well as the other stated preference approaches, is the hypothetical nature of questions used to elicit WTP in lieu of inferring WTP from actual transactions; hypothetical questions can often provide incredibly inflated values of maximum WTP. To assess the credibility of the responses, it is useful to compute WTP based on different types of CV questions. We describe below an actual application of the CV approach that did this. In some cases, it may be possible to compare results from a revealed preference with values obtained from the CV approach.

STATED CHOICE OR ATTRIBUTE-BASED METHODS

An alternative to CV is to give respondents a set of hypothetical alternatives and ask them to select the most preferred alternative or to rate the alternatives on some scale according to the extent to which an alternative is preferred or not. Based on the responses, the researcher can infer the marginal rate of substitution between any pair of attributes that are different for the two alternatives. If one of the alternatives is money, it is possible to compute the respondent's maximum WTP for the attribute based on the responses. These methods are used extensively in environmental economics applications but much less frequently by health economists.

CONTINGENT BEHAVIOR OR CONTINGENT ACTIVITY QUESTIONS

In a third approach, individuals are asked how they would change the level of some activity in response to a change in the level of a nonmarket good, such as fishing if the quality of the water in a lake were improved. If the activity can be valued in monetary terms, such as the cost of travel to the lake, the method can be used to obtain an estimate of maximum WTP. If, for example, the respondent would fish once a year with water as it is but would fish three days annually if the water quality were improved, and if the person lives an hour away from the lake, one can infer a value from the amount the person is willing to pay to get to and spend time at the lake and fish, as well as the fees for fishing once there.

This approach may be used in health applications, but to date it has been mainly used in environmental economics applications. The approach has the advantage of explicitly considering the role of prices and in this sense is nearest to revealed preference; however, the situations posed are hypothetical, whereas revealed preference is based on actual choices.

ASSESSING THE VALIDITY OF STATED PREFERENCE MEASURES

The quality of any survey may be gauged in terms of its validity and reliability. Validity refers to the extent to which a question or set of questions accurately measures what it is designed to measure, in this context, maximum WTP. For example, how do the survey findings compare with results of an actual randomized controlled experiment (that is, if comparable results from such an experiment are available)? There is some evidence that CV-based values are often too high. If there is a case in which an apples-to-apples comparison between a CV-based and an experiment-based value can be made, then the differential could be used to adjust CV-based values in other applications. Or if an experiment is not available, a

CV-generated value could be compared with a result based on the revealed preference approach.

Another way to judge validity is to compare results based on a variable for which economic theory can provide some guidance. For example, if the value of life year is a normal good, we would expect maximum WTP for an extra life year to rise with increases in personal income. If a particular CV survey yields this result, this can be taken as some indication that the survey results are valid. Finally, one can compare how a particular survey was done with best survey practices, such as how scenarios on which WTP questions were based were specified, how values were elicited, incentives respondents had to reveal their true underlying preferences, and how the analysis was conducted.

Survey reliability concerns the ability of a well-designed survey to yield accurate estimates of the underlying value of the population being interviewed. If, for example, the sample size is small, mean values and standard deviations of such values may vary substantially, depending on the persons selected for the interviews.

To illustrate how stated preference analysis is conducted in practice, we describe three actual studies in some detail.

Stated Preference Method Application 1

Krupnick, Alberini, Cropper, et al. (2002) reported the results of a CV survey of 930 persons in Hamilton, Ontario, Canada, aged 40–74, who were surveyed to elicit WTP for mortality risk reductions. The authors accounted for potential deficiencies of past CV studies in designing their survey. One concern was that respondents might not have understood the risk changes they were being asked to value. To help individuals understand risk changes, the authors showed respondents graphs with 1,000 cells, the cells corresponding to persons who died shaded as shown in figure 15.3. Risk changes were displayed to respondents by changing the number of shaded cells in the grid. Tests of respondents' ability to deal with probabilities when shown the grid showed that for the vast majority of respondents, comprehension of probabilities was good.

Another potential problem is that survey respondents may not have believed that the risk changes or baseline risks applied to them. Like parents who believe that their children are all above average (called the Lake Wobegon phenomenon in the United States), people may think that while others are subject to specific risks, for one reason or another (e.g., "my grandfather smoked cigars and drank a liter of beer every evening but lived to be 90," at the same time forgetting that the other grandfather died suddenly of a heart attack at age 48), people may reason that the risks do not really apply to them. To deal with this issue, respondents were explicitly asked to assume that the risks in the survey questions applied to them.

A third issue is that respondents may have lacked experience in trading money for quantitative risk changes or failed to have engaged in the particular

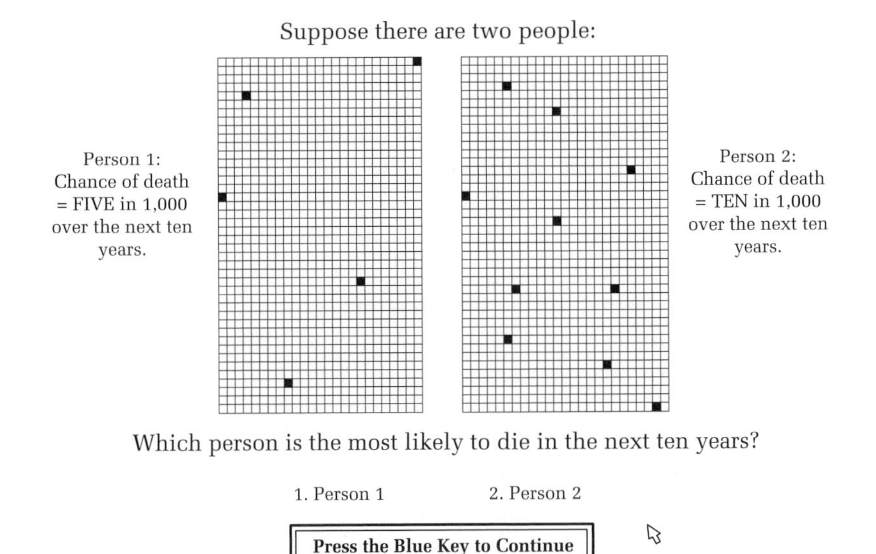

FIGURE 15.3
Use of Grids to Represent Probabilities in Mortality Risk Questionnaire
Source: A. Krupnick, A. Alberini, M. Cropper, et al., "Age, Health and the Willingness to Pay for Mortality Risk Reductions: A Contingent Valuation Survey of Ontario Residents," *Journal of Risk and Uncertainty* 24, no. (2002): 161–186, figure 1. Reprinted with permission from Springer Science+Business Media B.V.

activity. To help respondents make such trade-offs, respondents were told about risk reductions for common diagnostic tests, such as for mammograms and drugs to reduce high blood pressure. To deal with the issue that people might not be able to deal with changes in very small probabilities of an adverse outcome, respondents were asked to value changes in probabilities of risk over a 10-year time frame. The advantage of a 10-year period is that probabilities in the questions were ten times larger than they would have been had the questions applied to the probability of an adverse outcome occurring in a single year. Since the sequence of questions could affect the answers, the order of risk scenarios was varied. Some persons were asked if they were willing to pay for a product that, when used and paid for over 10 years, would reduce baseline risk by five in 10,000 annually or by five in 1,000 in 10 years. In a second set of WTP questions, the risks were reduced by a factor of five. Other persons were asked these questions in reverse order.

The survey revealed that WTP for mortality risk reduction is constant up to age 70 with reductions of about 30 percent in WTP for persons above this age. This is undoubtedly due to the fact that older persons face a much higher probability of dying in a specific time period than younger individuals do. Likewise, the WTP did not vary much according to the respondent's physical health status. A given reduction in risk is much lower as a percentage of an older person's or a sicker person's mortality risk than for a younger or healthy person. That age and physical health did not have a greater impact on WTP is surprising.

The authors concluded that it is inappropriate to compute the value of a life year from a value of life, or to use life year values to compute program benefit. Since older persons have fewer expected life years, holding other factors constant, the program benefit would be lower when applied to older persons. While the authors' argument logically follows from their finding on WTP and age, it seems extreme to assign the same benefit of a program that cures disease *X* for person A, who has disease *X* and is expected to live for many years even with the disease, and person B, who also has disease *Y*, which is expected to kill person B within two weeks unless he or she receives a (rapid) cure. For this reason, it makes more sense to use life years than a value of life in calculating benefit.

Mean WTP for a reduction of risk of five in 10,000 per annum was only 1.6 times the WTP for an annual risk reduction of one in 10,000. Thus, WTP seems to be highly sensitive to the magnitude of the risk reduction under consideration.

Stated Preference Method Application 2

Multiple sclerosis is a serious neurological disease that often first affects people in early adulthood. Depending on its severity, multiple sclerosis can cause substantial pain and immobility. Furthermore, for many persons with the disease, the symptoms are intermittent, making it hard for them to predict how well they will feel on a given day. There is currently no cure, and medical care for the disease is expensive. Also, many persons incur expenditures for special equipment, including specially equipped motor vehicles for their transportation, and sometimes there are expenditures for alterations of the home. Additional costs may occur because many patients are dependent on help from paid and unpaid caregivers. Financial outlays for multiple sclerosis have been estimated by Whetten-Goldstein, Sloan, Goldstein, et al. (1998). However, nonfinancial or intangible loss (loss attributable to pain and suffering) is also likely to be substantial. Sloan, Viscusi, Chesson, et al. (1998) used stated preference approaches to estimate the value of such loss.

The authors used two alternative methods for eliciting estimates of intangible loss: risk-dollar and risk-risk, the latter being the standard gamble approach that was briefly described in chapter 14.

Theory: Risk-Dollar Trade-offs

Let $U(Y)$ be the utility of a healthy individual, where Y represents consumption or income (with a zero rate of savings). Let $V(Y)$ be the utility of a sick individual. For any level of Y, total utility when healthy exceeds total utility when sick, $U(Y) > V(Y)$. Assume that there are two communities, a and b, each with a different probability of acquiring a specific disease. Let Θ_a and Θ_b indicate the probability of getting sick in each of the two communities. Let c_a be the cost of living in community a and c_b be cost of living in community b. To simplify the analysis, set c_a to zero; then let c_b vary, so that equation 15.4 is satisfied:

$$\Theta_b V(Y - c_b) + (1 - \Theta_b)U(Y - c_b) = \Theta_a V(Y) + (1 - \Theta_a)U(Y). \tag{15.4}$$

THEORY: RISK-RISK TRADE-OFFS

Risk-risk trade-offs were explained as the standard gamble in chapter 14. With this approach, the researcher finds the probability of dying instantly and painlessly from a surgical procedure that, if successful, completely cures a person of a disease. When the person is cured, he or she has the utility function for the health state. Once we know the value of the probability of death that makes the person indifferent between having the operation and not having the operation, we can compute total utility in the sick state from the product of $(1 - \Theta)$ and total utility in the healthy state.

In some applications, if we have an estimate of the value of life that reflects utility in the healthy state and one minus the probability of dying during the operation painlessly, we can compute utility in the sick state as the product of the value of life and one minus the probability of dying during the operation. People who have a relatively low utility in the sick state compared to their utility in the healthy state will be willing to bear a higher risk of surgery. That is, for diseases that cause a lot of pain, suffering, and disability, people can be expected to be willing to expose themselves to greater mortality risk from the surgical procedure in order to obtain a cure.

SURVEYS OF WTP TO AVOID INTANGIBLE LOSS OF MULTIPLE SCLEROSIS

Surveys were conducted of 292 persons at a shopping center in Greensboro, North Carolina, USA. None of these persons had multiple sclerosis. In addition, interviews were conducted with forty-three patients who had multiple sclerosis in two North Carolina counties. Since the interviews were conducted in person, sicker individuals were less likely to have been willing to participate.

Each survey respondent was randomly assigned to one of four videotapes describing the life of person with multiple sclerosis. Since there is so much heterogeneity in the severity of this disease, it was important that all sample persons have the scenario on the videotape in mind in responding to the survey questions. People were asked to focus on the disease scenarios, not on their personal health in responding to the WTP questions. Respondents were asked to assume that all monetary loss associated with the type of multiple sclerosis depicted in the scenario the respondent was shown was covered in full by a health insurance policy.

Table 15.1 shows the risk-dollar and risk-risk questions as presented to respondents. For the risk-dollar set of questions, respondents were asked to assume that the cost of living in the first area was the same as in the respondent's own area. The second area had a higher cost of living but a lower risk of getting multiple

TABLE 15.1
Risk-Dollar and Risk-Risk Questions

Part A. Risk-Dollar		
Choose which area you like better		
	Area A	Area B
Cost of living (per year)	same as your area	US$100 higher
Risk of getting MS(per year)	40 out of a million	30 out of a million
Which area would you rather live in?		
1. Area A		
2. Area B		
(Press the number that goes with your answer.)		
Part B. Risk-Risk		
Would you choose to have the operation if the chance of dying was 15%?		
1. YES, I would have the operation.		
2. NO, I would not have the operation.		
(Press the number that goes with your answer.)		

Note: The information in this table was provided piece by piece on the computer screen at a pace determined by the subject. That is, the cost of living in area A was presented, and, when the subject indicated readiness to proceed, the cost of living in area B was presented, and so on.
Source: Sloan, Viscusi, Chesson, et al. (1998).

sclerosis. The probabilities of getting multiple sclerosis were stated to be 40 out of a million and 30 out of a million in the two communities, respectively. These are very low probabilities, but realistic in terms of the actual probability of getting multiple sclerosis.

The table shows the first round of questions. The cost of living differential was randomly assigned to each individual, not a set amount as in the table. If the higher cost of living community was initially selected, the cost of living differential was raised until the person stated that he or she would select the other community. The cost of living differential in the question was varied until the survey was able to determine with considerable accuracy what the cost of living difference was that made the respondent indifferent between living in each of the two communities. The cost of living difference for that person was taken at the midpoint of a cost of living differential that caused the person to prefer each of the two communities. If the respondent placed a higher value on the intangible loss from multiple sclerosis of the type the respondent viewed, the monetary value of the difference in cost of living between the two communities that made the person indifferent was deemed to be higher, and conversely for those who placed a lower value on the intangible loss.

For the risk-risk questions, to avoid starting point bias, respondents were initially given a probability of dying during surgery selected at random (e.g., 0.15 as in table 15.1). The probability of dying was varied until the probability yielding a yes, willing to undergo the operation, and the probability yielding a no to this question was very small. The midpoint of this interval was taken as the probability of death that the person was willing to accept that made him or her indifferent between having the surgery and facing the prospect of a healthy life versus refusing surgery and living the rest of life in the sick state.

RESULTS

There was substantial variation in the risk-dollar analysis in the implied WTP to avoid a case of multiple sclerosis. Overall, respondents who actually had multiple sclerosis had a much higher WTP to avoid getting multiple sclerosis than did persons who did not have the disease. The implied WTPs to not get multiple sclerosis were $10.5 million for persons without the disease and $22.0 million for those with the disease. Both values exceeded most VSL estimates. While it is possible that some people regard having multiple sclerosis as worse than being dead, this is not the assumption that health services researchers and economists make when using QALY or when analyzing utility change based on a standard gamble question. A QALY of 0 is dead. If the subject is alive, the QALY is constrained to be above 0 and less than or equal to 1. Another possibility, discussed below, is that the high values placed on avoiding multiple sclerosis reflected survey respondents' risk misperceptions. If respondents considered the difference in risk between the two communities as larger than was stated by the probabilities in the question, then the final cost-of-living difference should be too high. Although most people know what a million is, thinking about what 30 out of a million really means may be very demanding cognitively.

As with the responses to the risk-dollar questions, there was considerable variation in responses to the risk-risk questions as well. Here respondents with multiple sclerosis were much more reluctant to undergo the operation, which implies that such persons attach a much lower utility loss to having the disease than others do. The median value of Θ^* for persons with multiple sclerosis was 0.18, while for the general population the median value was more than twice this value, 0.45. Multiplying either estimate by VSL values from the literature yielded values of maximum WTP to avoiding getting multiple sclerosis that were far lower than those obtained from responses to the risk-dollar questions.

Two of the findings indicated that respondents misperceived the risk of getting multiple sclerosis from the risk-dollar questions. First, the estimates of maximum WTP were implausibly high. The second was the different relative values obtained on the risk-dollar and the risk-risk questions.

The authors used nonlinear regression to recover a parameter representing the factor by which respondents overestimated the probability of getting multiple sclerosis. (The analytic approach used is beyond the scope of this discussion.) For persons without multiple sclerosis, the authors estimated that the probability of getting multiple sclerosis in the risk-dollar analysis was overestimated by a factor of 30 to 39. That is, the probability of getting multiple sclerosis, 0.000030 in one community, was treated as if it was 0.0009 (if the misperception factor is 30). For persons with multiple sclerosis, the factor ranged from 47 to 71, far higher than for persons without the disease. It is quite possible that because they actually had the disease, persons with multiple sclerosis tended to overestimate the probability in their own thought processes by even more than respondents from the general population did.

Correcting for misperception of risk, the estimates of intangible loss using responses from both the risk-dollar and the risk-risk questions ranged from US$346,000 to US $510,000 for the general population and from US $375,000 to US$881,000 for persons with multiple sclerosis. These values are far below VSLs reported in the literature and are plausible in this respect.

The authors conducted several tests of consistency of responses. For one, the correlation between responses from the risk-dollar and risk-risk questions was 0.72, which is fairly high. The survey asked respondents to rate various symptoms of multiple sclerosis on a scale. Persons with the disease were able to discriminate among the symptoms in terms of their relative severity much better than the other respondents were.

Implications

Benefits and costs in CBA take a societal perspective. In decisions on how much to allocate to research and development for disease prevention, diagnosis, and treatment, analysts must consider potential benefits as accruing to every member of society, not just to those with the disease. Such analysis is inherently future-oriented, and thus includes benefits to those who do not currently have the disease but may get it in the future. By contrast, in decisions about whether or not a particular patient should receive a diagnostic or therapeutic procedure, the benefit is the benefit to that particular patient. For the type of study just described, the relevant preferences are those of the general population. Yet, as just acknowledged, those with the disease are likely to know more about the disease in question than others do. If their knowledge were superior in all respects and there were no gaming in the responses—in the sense that persons with multiple sclerosis may reason that if they state the losses are high, they will garner more support for public investment in treating the disease—perhaps the analyst should base the benefit calculation on these persons' responses to WTP questions.

In this application, the multiple sclerosis patients were not uniformly more knowledgeable. In fact, they overestimated the probability of getting multiple sclerosis by an even larger factor than did respondents from the general population.

Another issue relates to Viscusi and Aldy's (2003) conclusion that VSL estimates vary positively with personal income. Might reliance on WTP studies not bias the allocation of public expenditures in favor of the rich? In the multiple sclerosis study, higher-income persons had higher estimates of intangible loss in one regression but not in the other two. To the extent that the estimated loss is higher for persons with higher income, it is possible to adjust for income to eliminate the effect of income on the loss estimates. Also, any bias toward allocating public funds in favor of the rich can be offset in large part by progressive taxation of personal income.

Stated Preference Application 3: Benefits and Costs of Cholera Vaccination

Background and Study Rationale

Cholera has a high incidence in some low-income countries and is the source of much morbidity. Cholera is transmitted through contaminated water. It causes dehydration, but with proper treatment, death rates are low (around one percent) A new generation of cholera vaccines provides an alternative approach to improving water supplies in areas with unsafe water. Beira, Mozambique, a city of about 550,000 on the coast of southern East Africa, has experienced a number of cholera epidemics. In general, the life expectancy at birth in Mozambique is 31 years. Jeuland, Lucas, Clemens, et al. (2009) conducted a CBA to determine whether or not a two-dose oral cholera vaccination technology should be adopted, and if so, how the vaccination program should be designed.

The authors evaluated three options. Option 1 was a school-based vaccination program for schoolchildren aged 5 to 14. Option 2 involved school-based vaccination of all eligible children aged 1 to 14, and option 3 was a community-based vaccination of all eligible people more than one year old. For medical reasons, the vaccine cannot be administered to persons younger than one. Children have the highest incidence of cholera and face the highest probability of death, conditional on having the disease. Option 3 was the most expensive option, and it also potentially involved the most implementation problems in that the schools are likely to be an efficient venue for administered the vaccine. Yet limiting the vaccinated population to children would exclude adults with a relatively high WTP for the cholera vaccine.

Program Benefit and Cost

The authors specified three types of benefit of a vaccination program. The first is the private benefit from being vaccinated among persons who actually receive the vaccine. The second is the benefit that unvaccinated persons derive from the fact that some persons in the community get vaccinated. There is an externality in that persons who are vaccinated reduce the probability that an unvaccinated person will contract this infectious disease. There is an epidemiological concept termed *herd immunity*. Herd immunity describes a type of immunity that occurs when the vaccination of a portion of the population (or herd) provides protection to unprotected individuals. Herd immunity theory proposes that in diseases passed from person to person, it is more difficult to maintain a chain of infection when large numbers of a population are immune. As the proportion of individuals who are immune rises, the likelihood that a susceptible person will come into contact with an infected individual falls.

The third benefit was specified as the discounted cost of illness incurred by government per case of illness. The vaccination program potentially reduces this burden on the public sector.

The cost in this benefit-cost analysis was the total monetary cost of vaccination per person (including production, shipping, delivery, and the additional private cost of vaccination per person incurred from travel and waiting for vaccine). These costs per person vaccinated were multiplied by the number of persons vaccinated.

Measuring Private Benefit to the Vaccinated

The private benefit to persons receiving the vaccination conceptually can be estimated from a private demand curve for vaccinations. Then the total private benefit to all persons who are vaccinated is the sum of their out-of-pocket expenditure on vaccinations (area A in fig. 15.4), the magnitude of which itself is a policy variable, and the consumer surplus accruing to persons who get vaccinated (area B). Total private benefit can be expressed in per vaccinated person terms by dividing total private benefit by the total number of persons who are vaccinated (the sum of areas A and B).

Why would some persons be willing to pay more to be vaccinated than others? One reason might be that they are more affluent, and health and longevity are normal goods. Second, some people may believe that the probability of getting cholera is higher for themselves than for others and are willing to pay more for the vaccine for this reason. Conceptually, it seems likely that individual demand for the vaccine should depend on the percentage of persons in the area with immunity to cholera. In practice, the study on which Jeuland and co-authors relied for information on private vaccine WTP did not measure the effect of the probability of contracting cholera on private demand for the vaccine. Third, there is likely to be variation in how much loss of utility having cholera causes. Persons who experience more utility loss from having the disease should be willing to pay more for the vaccine, other factors being equal. Using the above notation, persons for whom $U(Y) - V(Y)$ is large should be willing to pay more. Of course, consumption (a function of Y) could fall as a result of the disease as well, depressing utility in the sick state V even more.

Use of Stated Preference Method to Measure Vaccine Demand

Demand curves are often estimated from observational data on market transactions. Price is varied across space or time (or both), and changes in quantity demanded are observed. Regression analysis is used to estimate the parameter relating

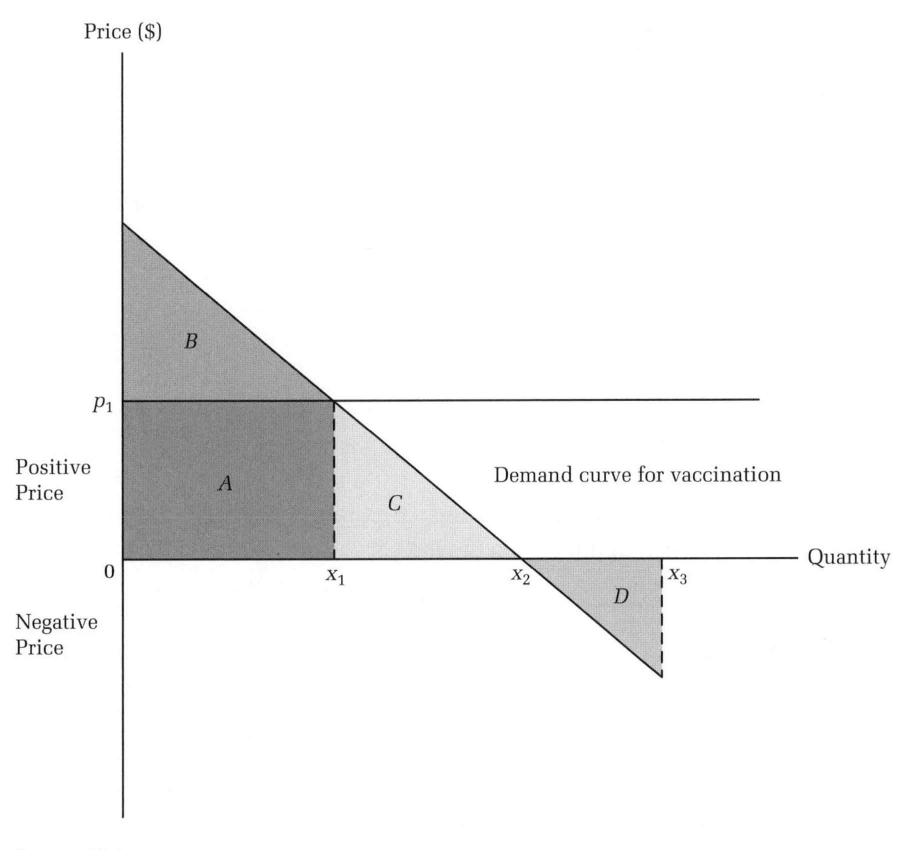

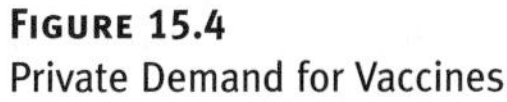
FIGURE 15.4
Private Demand for Vaccines

quantity demanded to price. These are applications of the revealed preference method.

Due to lack of market transactions data, one reason being that vaccines are often administered at a zero price to the person being vaccinated, Jeuland and co-authors used evidence from a stated preference study of demand from another country. In such a study, one elicits WTP from respondents, an approach that is subject to the limitations described above.

MEASURING PRIVATE BENEFIT TO THE UNVACCINATED

The second component of program benefit is the benefit to the unvaccinated. As seen in figure 15.4, area C represents the maximum aggregate amount of benefit to those who chose not to be vaccinated at a price p_1.

Area C, however, overstates the benefit to the unvaccinated, for two reasons. First, the health benefit to the direct recipient of the vaccine must be greater than or at least equal to the benefit to the unvaccinated. Thus, the triangle's area may exceed the true aggregate benefit to the unvaccinated. Second, a point not made by the authors, some persons would demand the vaccine only at a negative price, that is, they would require a bribe to be vaccinated. Some reasons are concern about the adverse side effects of the vaccine, the time and inconvenience of getting vaccinated, and so on. Thus, unless the segment $0x_2$ represents the entire population in the area, rather than $0x_3$ as figure 15.4 is drawn, it seems likely that some persons would demand the vaccine only at a negative price. Then the negative triangle (area D) would have to be subtracted from area C, and the benefit would then be only some proportion ρ of area C – area D, or ρ(area C – area D), where $0 < \rho \leq 1$.

MEASURING SAVINGS IN PUBLIC HEALTH EXPENDITURES ATTRIBUTABLE TO THE VACCINE PROGRAM

The third component of demand is the savings in public health expenditure attributable to the vaccination program. Such savings are negatively related to the percentage of the area population that receives the cholera vaccine.

SOME KEY FINDINGS

Total benefit is then the sum of the three components, and cost is the full cost of the vaccination program under the various options the authors evaluated. In general, the vaccination programs proved to have benefit – cost > 0 and benefit/cost > 1. However, the differences and ratios depended critically on the present of herd immunity; without this externality, the differences and ratios were sometimes unfavorable to program adoption. (A negative difference mechanically translates into a benefit/cost ratio of <1). Second, although countries often distribute vaccines at zero money prices, the differences (ratios) critically depend on the level at which the administered (out-of-pocket) price p_1 is set. In the study by Jeuland and colleagues, net benefit ($B - C$) was higher for $p_1 > 0$.

Setting the price at a positive value ensures that the vaccine recipients will have higher WTP for the vaccine than the unvaccinated do. This results in a better allocation of scarce resources and is economically efficient for this reason. However, allocation by money price raises some equity concerns since persons with scant personal resources may predominate among the unvaccinated, although they benefit somewhat from herd immunity. Another advantage of charging a positive price is to obtain revenue to defray some of the cost of vaccine purchase and administration.

Although this is an excellent study overall, it clearly suffers from data limitations, in particular in assessing benefits to the unvaccinated and in having to ignore the effect of infection probabilities on demand. Also, most economists would feel more comfortable with empirical evidence from revealed preference than stated preference on demand.

15.4 USE OF COST-BENEFIT AND COST-EFFECTIVENESS ANALYSIS IN PUBLIC DECISION MAKING

The techniques described in this chapter and in chapter 14 are used in some countries as an aid to public policy decision making. Calculations of benefits versus the costs of regulation, including VSL as part of the benefit calculation, are used at various levels by the US government for assessing whether or not specific regulations should be adopted at the federal level (box 15.1).

The Department of Environment, Transport, and Regulation in the UK has also used VSL estimates in its benefit calculations. However, in contrast to the United States, where the revealed preference method is generally preferred for generating estimates of VSL, particularly outside the health field, there is greater reliance on contingent valuation in the UK, again outside the health field. Transport Canada also uses VSLs in the decision-making process, but it uses a range of values rather than a point estimate.

Various issues regarding the use of VSLs in designing public policy remain unresolved. For example, should the type of death (e.g., from cancer, from a motor vehicle accident) affect the VSL? In one sense, a death is a death. In another sense, some types of deaths may involve more pain and suffering or seem more unjust, or for some other reason society may place a relatively high value on preventing them. Do revealed preference estimates based on labor market data generalize to groups that are unlikely to be employed, such as the elderly? Several public agencies use age-adjusted VSLs, but the use of age adjustment is controversial. Likewise, how should analysts adjust for the effect of income on VSL?

There are few public agencies with a focus on health that perform CEA or CBA analyses, and even then the emphasis is on cost-effectiveness rather than on costs versus benefits. The most notable example is the National Institute for Clinical Excellence (NICE) in the UK. NICE was established to provide guidance in decisions on the use of new and existing technologies. NICE's conclusions are advisory to the British National Health Service (NHS) for NHS decisions about allocations of its resources. NICE operates independently of the NHS. In contrast to similar units in Australia and in Ontario, Canada, NICE is not a regulatory agency but rather provides guidance, which the recipients of the guidance can accept or reject. At the same time, NICE operates independently of manufacturers, but private money is used to sponsor NICE evaluations. NICE evaluates about thirty technologies annually from a pool of thousands of new and existing technologies.[5]

NICE does not conduct original research but rather relies on empirical evidence from existing studies. Evidence on the long-term effects of technologies is frequently unavailable, but, as described in chapter 14, methods for inferring long-term effects from short-term transitions between health states exist and are widely

5. See, e.g., Birch and Gafni (2002) for additional detail on NICE.

Box 15.1
Value of Life Estimates and Their Importance to Business

For the academic community, placing a value on human life is largely an intellectual matter, but for business, such calculations can have important financial implications. For example, a higher value of life may translate into a higher benefit from improving the quality of air. An article appeared on the front page of the *New York Times* on this topic on February 16, 2011 (Appelbaum 2011). The article describes how various US government agencies differ in the value they place on a life: $9.1 million—the US Environmental Protection Agency (EPA); $7.9 million—the US Food and Drug Administration (FDA); $6 million—the US Transportation Department. These values not only differ by agency, which is somewhat inexplicable, but they have risen appreciably in recent years. The EPA used values as low as $6.8 million under the previous US president. The FDA's value was $5 million three years previously. The US Department of Homeland Security has argued that the value of life lost to terrorism may be 100 percent higher than for deaths from other causes.

Others have raised the possibility that the value of life may be higher for persons undergoing a slow death from cancer than a quick death in a motor vehicle accident. Then there is the idea that people are altruistic, placing a higher value on the common good than on their own survival. Of course, some experts may argue the opposite, that the value should be higher for risks to which the person is personally exposed rather than to abstract others. According to one economist cited in the article, the previous values used by US government agencies were too low.

Businesses have complained about the increases in values of life. Higher values on life saved translate into higher benefits from regulatory programs, such as regulations requiring cleaner air or stronger roofs on automobiles sold in the United States. Businesses have instead stressed the negative consequences of increased regulation that would result from these increased values of life rather than focusing on the validity of the values themselves. However, historically businesses have advocated use of CBA as a basis for deciding whether or not regulations should be adopted. The alternative is not no regulation or the imposition of regulatory standards without any specific consideration of monetary benefits versus costs, but rather the adoption of regulation simply because it is likely to do some good, irrespective of what regulation costs.

While supporting the increased values of life, some consumer groups maintain that CBA fails to reflect some considerations. For example, one consumer advocate asked how one could put a price on global warming. The answer is that one could compute the benefits of damage averted by reducing global warming. Admittedly, since damage would only occur many years from now, the discounted present value of the benefit may be low—probably too low for some environmental advocates.

As an alternative to using a value-of-life estimate common to several types of regulatory decisions, such as air and water pollution, most US government agencies have relied on findings from surveys that asked respondents how much they would spend to avoid a specific risk. According to the *New York Times* article, this willingness-to-pay technique tends to yield substantially lower values than those based on wages lost when a worker dies.

used. Often, head-to-head comparisons of technologies designed for the same medical condition are unavailable. Thus, for example, it may not be possible to directly compare the benefits and costs of a new drug versus an established drug for treating a given condition. NICE has been criticized for placing undue emphasis on program cost, and in any case, NICE does not perform CBA.

Since 1993, the Australian Pharmaceutical Benefits Advisory Committee (PBAC) has reviewed every new drug on the basis of the drug's cost-effectiveness before it can be added to the country's national drug formulary. This agency uses a broad definition of costs, including medical, home health care, day care, special food, nursing, and physiotherapy costs, but it excludes indirect costs such as earnings lost due to illness. New drugs are compared with the most commonly utilized existing drug, which provides the basis for computing the incremental cost-effectiveness of the new drug. When appropriate, the comparator therapy may be a nonpharmaceutical treatment (e.g., surgery). The agency uses a discount rate of 5 percent in its calculations. While cost-effectiveness is an important consideration in the decision to adopt a new drug, sometimes other considerations intrude, reflecting, among other things, strong lobbying on the part of special interest groups such as pharmaceutical manufacturers or on the part of patient groups who are potential users of the new technology.

Incremental cost-effectiveness is highly dependent on drug price, and the Australian government negotiates drug prices with manufacturers. Nevertheless, as discussed in chapter 14, the use of product prices has been criticized on the grounds that such prices may greatly exceed marginal cost. On the other hand, a small country like Australia is a drug importer, and the drug's price represents an opportunity cost to the public sector. What the government pays for a drug is money that cannot be used for another public purpose. In this sense, use of drug prices is appropriate. While the main emphasis is on pharmaceutical technologies, the PBAC has assessed some non-drug technologies as well.

The most ambitious attempt to use these technologies was by the US state of Oregon (see Kaplan 1995). For a while, Oregon attempted to allocate all of its Medicaid program resources on the basis of comparative cost-effectiveness. Medicaid is a federal-state program, and the federal government ultimately prevented Medicaid from allocating resources on the basis of relative cost-effectiveness. Among the major objections to the Oregon program was that it discriminated against persons with disabilities.

For example, suppose that a person is wheelchair-bound. Then the quality of the person's life year is less than one. As a result, any program that targets such people will get a lower score than a program that targets young and healthy people. We leave it to our readers to judge whether or not this is a fundamental flaw of CEA or CBA. At a practical level, allocating *all* resources on the basis of such analysis is a virtual nightmare. The requisite information on many, if not most, technologies is simply not available, necessitating the use of many "fudge" factors.

15.5 Conclusion

In contrast to other chapters, chapters 14 and 15 have considered how societies allocate their scarce resources. If societies' health sectors are to maximize the value obtained from scarce resources, some method must be found to assess the value of technologies. Years ago, when societies relied on professional norms, such as physicians' assessments were based on such factors as practice experience; to determine whether or not a service was effective, there was a reliance on the individual decisions of physicians and other health professionals to do what was best to achieve socially optimal outcomes from expenditures on personal health services. Insofar as patients pay only a small part of the health care bill in many countries, and because it is recognized that physicians should rely on evidence-based medicine, not just on their own experiences in clinical decision making, it is no longer appropriate to rely solely on private decisions made in the examining room based on the professional experiences of individual practitioners. Instead, methods for assessing the productivity and value of specific technologies are needed.

That a methodology will be used to make collective decisions about resource allocation is not in question. The only issue is how these assessments will be done. Clearly, the techniques described in these two chapters represent work in progress. Yet in the end, although they are imperfect, it is important to ask, what is the alternative? Refinements in techniques are constantly being made, and much progress has been realized.

Key Concepts

- Pareto optimality
- revealed preference and revealed preference approach
- contingent valuation
- offer curve
- marginal rate of substitution
- omitted heterogeneity
- contingent behavior
- risk-dollar trade-off
- intangible loss
- maximum willingness to pay
- stated preference and stated preference approach
- value of a statistical life
- marginal utility of wealth (or income)
- subjective beliefs
- wage premium
- contingent activity
- risk-risk trade-off
- National Institute for Clinical Excellence

REVIEW AND DISCUSSION QUESTIONS

15.1 When is it appropriate to use $B - C$ (the difference between benefit and cost) as a criterion for project adoption? When is it appropriate to use B/C (the ratio of benefit to cost)?

15.2 Suppose you are asked to evaluate the desirability of public investment in a vaccine to prevent HIV/AIDS. Which benefits and which costs will you include? How will you measure the benefits of an HIV/AIDS vaccine?

15.3 Some object to benefit-cost analysis on the grounds that it favors the wealthy. Explain the argument, being sure to discuss why benefit-cost analysis might favor the wealthy.

15.4 What is meant by the value of a statistical life (VSL)? Is a life worth more in a high-income country, such as the United States, than in a low-income country, such as Haiti? Why or why not?

15.5 Why do smokers on average have a lower VSL than nonsmokers?

15.6 What is meant by the "revealed preference" approach to benefit valuation?

15.7 What is meant by the "stated preference" approach to benefit valuation? Explain how it has been implemented empirically. Describe the pros and cons of this approach.

15.8 What does it mean that VSL has an income elasticity of about 0.5–0.6? Based on this finding, what are the implications of using VSL as a measurement of benefit in allocating health care resources?

15.9 The literature review conducted by Viscusi and Aldy (2003) indicates that VSL decreases with age. How should this result be interpreted? Based on this finding, draw the offer curve (as shown in fig. 15.2) for young and elderly individuals. Is your comparison between the young and the elderly similar to the comparison between nonsmokers and smokers?

15.10 Why do respondents who actually have a disease (e.g., multiple sclerosis) have a much higher willingness to pay (WTP) to avoid getting the disease than persons who do not have the disease?

15.11 Describe the use of benefit-cost analysis and cost-effectiveness analysis in public decision making.

EXERCISES

15.1 Lichtenberg (2001) estimated the benefits and costs of newer drugs. Their results are summarized as follow:

Expenditure Type Mean Effect of Switching from 15 Year-Old Drugs to 5.5-Year-Old Drugs on Expenditures for Entire Population (in US$)

	Mean
Prescription drugs	18
Hospital	–80
Home health care	–12
Office visits	–24
Outpatient	–10
Emergency room	–3

a. Based on the above findings, identify the benefits of using newer drugs.

b. Given the above information, do you have enough information to conduct a CBA for using newer drugs? Justify your answer.

15.2 Given the following information, compute the value of a statistical life.

	Industry Fatality Rate Per 100,000 Workers	Mean Hourly Wage
Construction	13.4	25
Manufacturing	3.8	15

15.3 Bishai and Lang (2000) used the stated preference approach to estimate the WTP for a one-month reduction in a waiting time for cataract surgery. They found that an average cataract patient in Barcelona, Spain, would be willing to pay US$107 (in 1992 prices) for a reduction in waiting time of one month. But the same WTP estimate for an average cataract patient in Denmark is only US$24. Their study also reports that 40 percent of cataract surgeries in Barcelona are performed in the private sector to avoid the waiting time in the public sector. By contrast, only 15 percent of the cataract surgeries in Denmark are performed in the private sector. How would you use the information on the ratio of cataract surgeries performed in the private sector across countries to judge the validity of this study?

15.4 A recent study found that drugs that offer therapeutic advantages over existing drugs are associated with a greater number of serious adverse drug reactions (ADRs), including those that result in hospitalization and death. Suppose one pharmaceutical manufactures develops a genetic test that can substantially reduce the probability of ADRs, and this firm hires you as consultant to estimate patients' WTP for this genetic test.

a. Which approach will you take to estimate the WTP for a reduction in the risk of ADRs? Will you use the revealed preference approach or the stated preference approach? Justify your answer.

b. Suppose your boss (the pharmaceutical firm) asks you to use the contingent valuation method to elicit the WTP for reducing the risk of ADRs. How would you design your questionnaire form? Describe your overall strategy.

c. Use a questionnaire from part b or another source to conduct a "pre-test" by interviewing ten persons individually, and analyze your results. Show minimum, maximum, and mean value of the WTP. Does the WTP vary with age and income? Explain your findings.

ONLINE SUPPLEMENTAL MATERIAL

COST-BENEFIT ANALYSES

http://www.who.int/indoorair/publications/guidelines/en/index.html

http://ec.europa.eu/regional_policy/sources/docgener/guides/cost/guide2008_en.pdf

http://www.springerlink.com/content/xg422145n9535818/fulltext.pdf

WHITE HOUSE OFFICE OF MANAGEMENT AND BUDGET

http://www.whitehouse.gov/omb/

VALUE OF LIFE YEAR

http://www.rff.org/documents/rff-dp-07-05.pdf

http://www.nytimes.com/2007/06/11/business/businessspecial3/11life.html?pagewanted=all

STATED PREFERENCE

http://www.communities.gov.uk/publications/corporate/402113

SUPPLEMENTAL READINGS

Diamond, P. A., and J. A. Hausman. 1994. Contingent Valuation: Is Some Number Better Than No Number? *Journal of Economic Perspectives* 8 (4): 45–64.

Hirth, R. A., M. E. Chernew, E. Miller, et al. 2000. Willingness to Pay for a Quality-Adjusted Life Year: In Search of a Standard. *Medical Decision Making* 20 (3): 332–342.

Jeuland, M., M. Lucas, J. Clemens, et al. 2009. A Cost-Benefit Analysis of Cholera Vaccination Programs in Beira, Mozambique. *World Bank Economic Review* 23 (2): 235–267.

Venkatachalam, L. 2004. The Contingent Valuation Method: A Review. *Environmental Impact Assessment Review* 24 (1): 89–124.

Viscusi, W. K., and J. E. Aldy. 2003. The Value of a Statistical Life: A Critical Review of Market Estimates throughout the World. *Journal of Risk and Uncertainty* 27 (1): 5–76.

REFERENCES

Appelbaum, B. 2011. As U.S. Agencies Put More Value on a Life, Businesses Fret. *New York Times*, February 17, 2011, A1.

Arrow, K. J., R. Solow, P. R. Portney, et al. 1993. Report of the NOAA Panel on Contingent Valuation. *Federal Register* 58:4601–4614.

Birch, S., and A. Gafni. 2002. On Being NICE in the UK: Guidelines for Technology Appraisal for the NHS in England and Wales. *Health Economics* 11 (3): 185–191.

Bishai, D. M., and H. C. Lang. 2000. The Willingness to Pay for Wait Reduction: The Disutility for Cataract Surgery in Canada, Denmark, and Spain. *Journal of Health Economics* 19: 219–230.

Carson, R. T., N. E. Flores, and N. F. Meade. 2001. Contingent Valuation: Controversies and Evidence. *Environmental and Resource Economics* 19 (2): 173–210.

Diamond, P. A., and J. A. Hausman. 1994. Contingent Valuation: Is Some Number Better Than No Number? *Journal of Economic Perspectives* 8 (4): 45–64.

Frank, R. H. 2006. *Microeconomics and Behavior.* Boston: McGraw-Hill Irwin.

Freeman, M. 2003. *Measurement of Enviornmental Resources Values.* Washington, DC: Resources for the Future.

Hanemann, W. M. 1994. Valuing the Enviornment through Contingent Valuation. *Journal of Economic Perspectives* 8 (4): 19–43.

Hirth, R. A., M. E. Chernew, E. Miller, et al. 2000. Willingness to Pay for a Quality-Adjusted Life Year: In Search of a Standard. *Medical Decision Making* 20 (3): 332–342.

Jeuland, M., M. Lucas, J. Clemens, et al. 2009. A Cost-Benefit Analysis of Cholera Vaccination Programs in Beira, Mozambique. *World Bank Economic Review* 23 (2): 235–267.

Kaplan, R. M. 1995. Utility Assessment for Estimating Quality: Adjusted Life Years. In *Valuing Health Care*, ed. F. A. Sloan, 31–60. New York: Cambridge University Press.

Khwaja, A., F. A. Sloan, and Y. Wang. 2009. Do Smokers Value Their Health and Longevity Less? *Journal of Law & Economics* 51 (1): 171–196.

Krupnick, A., A. Alberini, M. Cropper, et al. 2002. Age, Health, and the Willingness to Pay for Mortality Risk Reductions: A Contingent Valuation Survey of Ontario Residents. *Journal of Risk and Uncertainty* 24 (2): 161–186.

Lichtenberg, F. 2001. Are the Benefits of Newer Drugs Worth Their Cost? Evidence from the 1996 MEPS. *Health Affairs* 20: 241–251.

Mishan, E. J. 1976. Use of Compensating and Equivalent Variations in Cost-Benefit-Analysis. *Economica* 43 (170): 185–197.

Pauly, R. 1996. Convergence of Economic Variables in EC Member Countries: A Statistical and Economic Analysis. *Jahrbucher fur Nationalokonomie und Statistik* 215 (1): 33–49.

Portney, P. R. 1994. The Contingent Valuation Debate: Why Should Economists Care? *Journal of Economic Perspectives* 8 (4): 3–18.

Sloan, F. A., J. Ostermann, G. Picone, et al. 2004. *The Price of Smoking*. Cambridge, MA: MIT Press.

Sloan, F. A., W. K. Viscusi, H. W. Chesson, et al. 1998. Alternative Approaches to Valuing Intangible Health Losses: The Evidence for Multiple Sclerosis. *Journal of Health Economics* 17 (4): 475–497.

Venkatachalam, L. 2004. The Contingent Valuation Method: A Review. *Environmental Impact Assessment Review* 24 (1): 89–124.

Viscusi, W. K., and J. E. Aldy. 2003. The Value of a Statistical Life: A Critical Review of Market Estimates throughout the World. *Journal of Risk and Uncertainty* 27 (1): 5–76.

Viscusi, W. K., and J. Hersch. 2001. Cigarette Smokers as Job Risk Takers. *Review of Economics and Statistics* 83 (2): 269–280.

Whetten-Goldstein, K., F. A. Sloan, L. B. Goldstein, et al. 1998. A Comprehensive Assessment of the Cost of Multiple Sclerosis in the United States. *Multiple Sclerosis* 4 (5): 419–425.

CHAPTER 16

The Contribution of Personal Health Services to Longevity, Population Health, and Economic Growth

In many countries, population health and longevity have increased substantially over the previous century. By contrast, in others, trends in health indicators are far less favorable (Becker, Philipson, and Soares 2005). Improved health may have important benefits in improving market and nonmarket (e.g., in such activities as parenting) productivity, as well as having value in its own right. This raises an important concern about the extent to which the improvement in population health can be attributed to the use of personal health care services and to the technological change in these services realized over the past century.

This chapter addresses this issue by investigating the interaction between the health and economic sectors. Resources allocated from the economic sector to the health sector are inputs and improvement in population health is the output. On the one hand, how the health care system is structured in financing personal health care services has important implications for other macroeconomic outcomes, such as precautionary saving, labor market outcomes, and deadweight losses associated with higher rates of taxation, which may in turn discourage entry of business enterprises in a country. On the other hand, the health sector's output, gain in population health, has several important potential impacts on the overall performance of the economic sector, including increased productivity, higher educational attainment and saving rates, and substantial changes in demographic structure.

This chapter begins with an overview of the link between health and economic sectors. There are many comparisons among countries on various health indicators, often contrasting amounts spent on personal health care services per capita population with a single health indicator, such as infant mortality or life expectancy at birth. We discuss the shortcomings of such simple comparisons. More rigorous studies, also reviewed here, quantify the effects of personal health care services in the aggregate and of particular health services on national output or health and longevity. Four feedback connections between the economic and health sectors are discussed: (1) how various forms of health care financing create incentives that affect macroeconomic outcomes, (2) major pathways through which health gains boost economic performance, (3) the role of the health sector as a major employer in the national economy, and (4) how development of the economic sector changes disease patterns in the health sector.

16.1 THE LINK BETWEEN HEALTH AND ECONOMIC SECTORS

OVERVIEW

Economists often depict links between different sectors in terms of (1) the flow of funds and (2) the flow of goods and services, for example between the "economic sector," which includes other goods and services, and the health sector (fig. 16.1). From the perspective of funds flow, in the economic sector there are resource allocation issues—how much and which kinds of resources to commit to the country's health sector. These choices in turn affect the amount and sources of funds for financing personal health care services.

At the individual level, people decide how much and what type of health insurance to purchase and how much to spend on such services out of pocket. On a national level, policy makers decide on the amounts and types of resources to be allocated to the health sector, including the share of and methods of public financing. In some countries, such as the UK and Denmark, the public sector devotes a substantial share of its resources to financing health care (see chapter 13). Public financing consequently accounts for more than 80 percent of total health expenditures in these countries. By contrast, in other countries, such as the United States and Mexico, the government spends a smaller share on personal health care services. In these countries, public financing accounts for less than half of total health expenditure (see chapter 11). Although public sectors in high-income countries tend to allocate a larger share of resources to personal health care services, there is appreciable variation in methods of financing. Some countries rely on general tax revenue as the major source of financing health care, while other countries use a tax specifically earmarked for health care, such as a payroll tax; examples of the latter funding are Medicare in the United States and the statutory sickness funds in Germany (see chapter 12).

Combining resource allocation decisions at the individual and national levels, flows of funds from the economic sector to the health sector can be subdivided into four major components: (1) out-of-pocket spending by individuals, (2) private

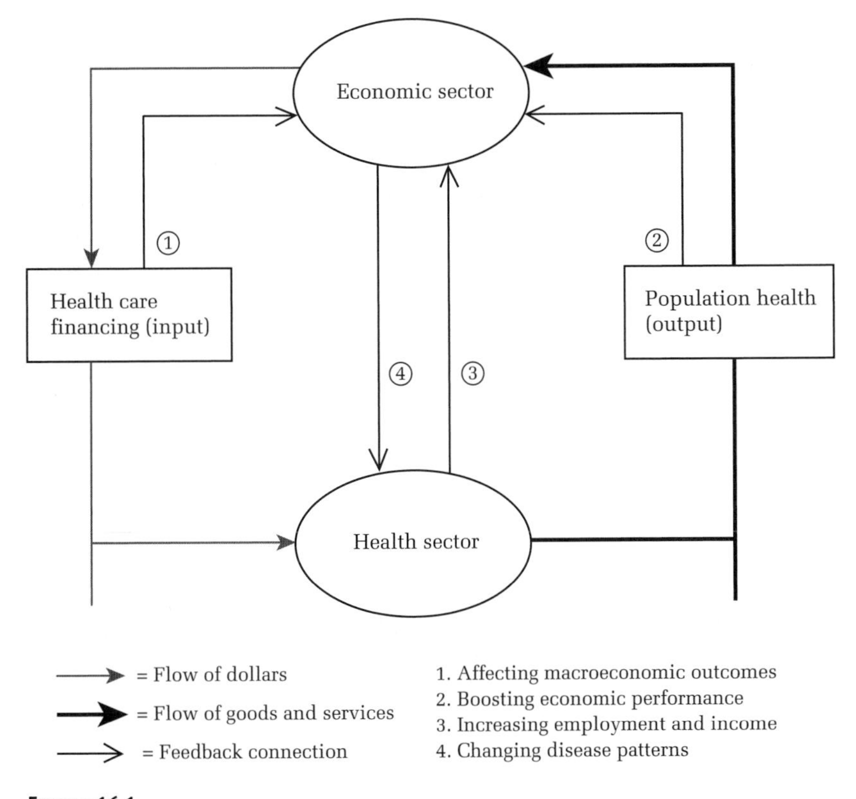

Figure 16.1
Links between the Health and Economic Sectors

health insurance, (3) general tax revenues, and (4) earmarked tax revenues. The relative importance of alternative sources of funds varies among countries. Also, the source of financing of employed persons affects the incentives of decision makers in each sector, and hence the choices they make about resource allocation may affect various macroeconomic outcomes, as described below.

First, many individuals are at a high risk of impoverishment from high and unanticipated health expenditures if the country relies on out-of-pocket spending as a major source of health care financing (see chapter 11). As emphasized earlier (see chapter 4), individuals face uncertainties about their future health.

Second, individuals' saving decisions may be affected by the extent to which they are protected from catastrophic health expenditures. One motivation for saving, identified by John Maynard Keynes (1936), is precautionary saving. Many people save today to avoid some uncertain situations that may occur in the future, including the possibility that they will suffer a major illness and consequently incur a large out-of-pocket health expenditure. Being covered by health insurance, private or public, reduces such expenditure risk, which in turn decreases demand for precautionary saving and increases current consumption (Chou, Liu, and Hammitt 2003). Thus, whether or not health insurance coverage is widespread may have a major impact on a country's saving rate, other factors being equal.

Third, in some countries, health insurance provision is linked to employment. Since many workers value having health insurance coverage, the provision of health insurance should affect job choices and labor supply more generally. Also, employment-based health insurance may reduce labor mobility since employers differ in the amounts and types of health insurance they offer, as well as in waiting periods before new employees can receive full insurance benefits (discussed in chapter 10).

Fourth, favorable tax treatment of employer-provided health insurance reduces the price of employer-provided health insurance relative to wage income (discussed in chapters 4 and 10). Not surprisingly, according to the law of demand, if the relative price of a good is reduced, more of it will be demanded. Although the tax subsidy may be justified as a means of encouraging employment-based coverage and hence risk protection, changes in the relative price between wages and health insurance premiums introduce a distortion, which leads to an inefficient outcome in that people tend to purchase more health insurance than they would absent the public subsidy. Thus, viewed from the standpoint of society as a whole, there is trade-off between the social benefits of risk sharing and the social cost of moral hazard when people purchase excessive amounts of health care (see chapters 3 and 4).

The health sector transforms resources allocated to the health sector into personal health care services. Thus, from the vantage point of the flow of goods and services, the health sector furnishes goods and services, which, when combined with patient inputs in health production, yield an output in the form of improved health (see chapter 2). In the second stage, the higher level of health, at both individual and national levels, improves the overall performance of the economic sector, measured in terms of higher personal income and other metrics of economic well-being. In addition, the health sector is a major employer in all high-income and to a lesser extent middle- and low-income countries. These employment opportunities and capital investments in the health sector contribute to income growth in the general economic sector.

In addition to the feedback connections from the health sector to the economic sector, there is an additional set of causal relationships that operates in the opposite direction, from the economic sector to the health sector. Both economic growth (increases in national output) and business cycles (fluctuations in national output) affect disease patterns in the health sector, which in turn affect the allocation of health care resources for treating diseases. In low-income countries, morbidity and mortality are predominantly connected to infectious diseases. By contrast, in high-income countries, most morbidity and mortality are associated with chronic diseases.

The Relationship between Improved Health and Longevity and Economic Growth

Two important questions arise from linkages in flows of goods and services between health and economic sectors. First, how much of the long-term gains in population health can be attributed to the provision of personal health care services and goods, such as physicians' services, prescription drugs, and medical devices? Second, what are the major pathways through which health gains boost economic performance?

With regard to the first question, early studies based on cross-sectional data found that higher health expenditures did not improve health outcomes. For example, the RAND Health Insurance Experiment, with a few exceptions, failed to find that higher consumption of health services leads to improved health (see chapter 3). However, that study monitored health changes for a period of only three to five years, which may be too short a period over which to detect health gains. Additionally, the sample was limited to persons aged 62 and younger, yet many chronic diseases appear only after this age.

In addition, international comparisons show that variation in health expenditures per capita population or as a share of the gross domestic product (GDP) among high-income countries is substantially larger than is variation in measured health status on a few widely used indicators, such as life expectancy and infant mortality.[1] An important implication of these studies is that spending on personal health care services is fairly unproductive in improving health, but such a conclusion is premature for several reasons.

First, since there are many dimensions of health, comparisons on only one or two indicators can be highly misleading. Second, with some exceptions, such as infant mortality, there are important lags between health inputs and health outcomes, often spanning decades. For example, plaque in one's arteries accumulates over decades; sports injuries in one's youth may lead to subsequent pain and disability of the knee in one's fifties and sixties; and malignant tumors are often years in the making. Thus, the health effects of a healthy diet, treatment by a sports injury physician, or having regular mammograms may not yield important health benefits for decades. Third, other factors than purchased health inputs affect health outcomes; if the analyst does not account for these other factors (e.g., health behaviors and environmental factors), estimates of the effect of health sector spending on health are likely to be biased, perhaps overstated if, for example, people who visit a physician regularly also engage in healthy behaviors.

By contrast, several recent studies based on long aggregate time-series or longitudinal data on individuals reach the opposite conclusion, namely, that allocating more resources to personal health care services is highly productive in terms

1. We leave it to the interested reader to find such studies. They are numerous in popular discussions of health policy.

of improved health outcomes. The difference in findings is not at all surprising. Over time, one can observe the effects of technological change. At a single point in time or even over a period of three to five years, technology is fixed.

Bloom and Canning (2000) decomposed the relationship between improved health and income growth into (1) productivity gains, (2) higher educational attainment, (3) increased saving rates (not because of the precautionary motive but because people expect to live longer), and (4) a demographic dividend. By *demographic dividend*, the authors referred to the effects of improved health on the demographic structure of the population, which in turn leads to higher rates of economic growth.

Health, like education, is a form of human capital that potentially affects one's productivity in both market and nonmarket work. Healthier individuals tend to devote more hours to market work and tend to be more productive per work hour. In addition, healthier youth not only are likely to remain in school but learn more while there. Several studies have emphasized that accumulation of knowledge capital is a major engine of economic growth (see in particular Romer 1990; Warsh 2006).

An important model in economics is the life-cycle model of consumption (Modigliani and Brumberg 1954). According to the life-cycle model, people accumulate wealth during their early years and spend their wealth in their later years. To the extent that longevity is increased, people are led to save more in their early years.

In low-income countries, the increase in life expectancy mainly comes from reduced infant (deaths in the first year of life) and child mortality (deaths between years one and six) rates. Mortality declines among infants and children induce subsequent declines in fertility rates (see, e.g., Soares 2005). The demographic structure changes substantially when a country moves from a state of high mortality and fertility rates to one of low mortality and fertility rates. This demographic change increases the proportion of the working-age population, thus increasing the labor supply, which in turn increases the national product. Also, lower mortality and lower fertility increase parents' incentives to invest in their children's human capital. Combining these two effects, there is a clear relationship between demographic change and higher economic growth.

16.2 Effects of Health Care Financing on National Economies

Savings Behavior

Other things being equal, the financial risk of unanticipated medical expenses, measured as the ratio of a household's spending on personal health care services to income, plausibly declines with income. Therefore, high-income individuals should be exposed to lower out-of-pocket health expenditure risk following health shocks. For this reason, the precautionary saving motive should be stronger for low-income households than for the affluent.

Given the precautionary motive for saving, which is greater when households lack health insurance, one would expect that expanding health insurance, either through public provision or the private market, would reduce saving rates, health insurance being a substitute for self-insurance accomplished by precautionary saving. Using data from Taiwan, Chou, Liu, and Hammitt (2003) obtained empirical evidence in support of this prediction.

Some countries provide health insurance to low-income individuals or households for persons with incomes and assets below specific thresholds. An example of this type of means-tested program is the Medicaid program in the United States (discussed in chapter 12). Medicaid in effect imposes a 100 percent tax on income and assets above the program's income and asset thresholds. This 100 percent tax creates a financial disincentive for households with assets near the threshold to accumulate wealth (Hubbard, Skinner, and Zeldes 1995).

Even though providing a safety net is welfare-enhancing in that it reduces the expenditure risk of low-income households, which presumably are risk averse, at the same time, it may increase wealth inequality among households. We use the term "may" since the overall effect on wealth distribution depends on how the public program is financed.

While having a lower saving rate may have deleterious effects on a country's economic growth, precautionary saving is an inefficient method for insuring against the risk of a large medical expense because of the lack of risk pooling (see chapter 10), which both private and public health insurance accomplish.

Labor Market Outcomes

Efficiencies in marketing and claims processing are realized when health insurance is furnished through large employers rather than sold on an individual basis (see chapter 10). Yet at the same time, employer-based insurance introduces an inefficiency in labor markets, namely, job immobility or "job lock" (see also chapter 10). Workers may be reluctant to switch jobs out of fear of losing their current health insurance or because they may face limitations on insurance coverage at new jobs, even though they would be more productive in other jobs.

Researchers have implemented two different approaches to empirically investigate the impact of health insurance on mobility decisions. One approach uses a difference-in-differences research design. Using this approach, Madrian (1994) found that the availability of health insurance substantially reduces job mobility, by 30–67 percent.

The second approach uses variation in state laws in the United States that require employers to offer health insurance for a specific time after the employee leaves the employer, with the premiums paid by the employer. Such mandates would presumably reduce the job-lock effect (Gruber 2000). Based on this approach, Gruber and Madrian (1994) found that laws requiring employers to continue health insurance coverage indeed increased job mobility. More specifically, requiring employers to offer coverage for one year following an employee's termination boosted job mobility rates by 12–15 percent. Summarizing this and other evidence on job lock and health insurance, Gruber (2000) concluded that employer-based health insurance in the United States reduces job mobility substantially, by roughly 25–30 percent.

The lack of universal health insurance coverage in the United States also has had implications for retirement decisions. Medicare coverage generally becomes available only at age 65. The availability of health insurance from sources other than Medicare has been an important consideration for persons contemplating retiring before this age. Some employers in the United States offer health insurance to persons who retire before age 65. There is empirical evidence that the availability of such health insurance increases the odds of early retirement by 20–50 percent (Gruber 2000).

Another effect of employer-provided health insurance, at least in the United States, is that such insurance is generally offered to the employee's entire family. This practice reduces the incentive for persons other than the highest earner in the family to work. This type of "wife lock" reduces the labor force participation of wives by about 11–20 percent (Gruber 2000).

Another potential impact of employer-provided health insurance is on the level of wage compensation. There is empirical evidence that the cost of health insurance to employees is fully offset by reductions in wage compensation (see chapter 10). Gruber (1994) examined whether or not the substantial increase in the cost of health insurance arising from laws requiring US employers to provide comprehensive health insurance coverage for prenatal care and obstetric delivery reduced the earnings of married women. Using a difference-in-difference approach, he compared differences in wages between an affected group (women of child-bearing age) and an unaffected group (such as older workers and single men), in states with and without such mandates. Gruber found a statistically significant relative decline in the wages of married women between the ages of 20 and 40, and the magnitude of wage reduction was almost identical to the increased insurance cost of this insurance mandate to employers.

Overall, empirical studies indicate that non-universal employment-based health insurance reduces job mobility, discourages early retirement, and reduces the labor force participation of female spouses with lower earning potential than the male wage earner in the family. In addition, the cost of employer-provided health insurance appears to be largely offset by reductions in wage compensation.

These findings have two important implications. First, introducing universal health insurance should increase job mobility, thus increasing worker productivity by improving matching between workers and jobs. Some empirical support for this implication comes from a study of Canadian data. Using monthly data on employment and wages in eight industries and ten provinces over 1961–1975, Gruber and Hanratty (1995) found that the introduction of universal health insurance in Canada raised employment by 2 percent and wages by 3 to 4 percent.

Second, there may be a change in employment and work hours. The direction of the effect is hard to predict a priori because of the effects of providing universal health insurance coverage, which move in opposite directions. In Taiwan, there was a substantial reduction in the size of the labor force after an expansion of eligibility for health insurance by the government. In 1982, the health plan for government employees expanded health insurance coverage to the spouses of government employees. At the time, these spouses were the only nonemployed persons who could obtain health insurance.

Chou and Staiger (2001) treated this reform as a natural experiment to investigate whether or not the availability of health insurance to the nonworking population affects the labor force participation (LFP) rate of married women. They compared the LFP rate of government employees' wives to that of non-government employees' wives. They found that the availability of health insurance to nonworkers reduced the LFP rate among married women by about four percentage points.

Taiwan's implementation of universal health insurance in 1995 provided a "reverse test" of the test Chou and Staiger conducted. Given the Chou-Staiger findings, the LFP of non-government employees' wives should have been affected by the universal health insurance, while government employees' wives should have been unaffected by this change in insurance coverage. The results were substantively consistent with those obtained for the 1982 reform.

Welfare Loss of Taxation

While in the political sphere, one hears a lot about the benefits of health insurance coverage, health services use scarce resources, and health insurance for such services must be financed in some way. Further, despite political promises that only others will pay for the extra benefits, not the "we who are deserving," in the end, we all pay.

Financing from general tax revenues, and by dedicated revenue sources such as a payroll tax, for social health insurance are two common approaches to raising revenue. In addition, in countries relying on private financing of personal health care services, governments may provide tax subsidies to employer-provided health insurance. How public funds are obtained potentially affects resource allocation choices people and firms make. Such altered choices in effect represent distortions, with associated welfare losses for society. The economic rationale for these distortions is that they account for externalities that, absent these taxes and subsidies, would not be accounted for in private decision making. Whether or not this is so is an important and complex question.

Two sources of general tax revenue are (1) direct taxes, such as personal and corporate income taxes, and (2) indirect taxes, such as excise taxes. Direct taxes on personal income generate deadweight losses or excess burden mainly through the distortion of the labor supply decision. Excise taxes also affect individuals' consumption choices.

Several studies have evaluated the effect of taxation on labor supply by treating a tax on personal income as a reduction in the net, after-tax wage (e.g., Hausman 1985). Imposing the tax changes the supply of labor (or hours of work) through the substitution effect and the income effect (see chapter 5). Through the substitution effect, the tax reduces the price (or opportunity cost) of leisure, and hence the worker increases his or her demand for leisure and decreases the number of work hours by a corresponding amount. Through the income effect, the tax reduces net income, and the individual "purchases" fewer hours of leisure as a consequence. In theory, the net effect of these offsetting substitution and income effects is indeterminate. If the substitution effect is sufficiently large that it offsets the income effect, an increase in the tax rate on personal income causes a decrease in labor supply, thus providing a disincentive for people to engage in market work.

If tax financing comes from indirect taxes, the deadweight losses occur from a distortion in the relative prices of goods and services. Figure 16.2 illustrates the conceptual framework for the definition of excess burden of an indirect tax. The downward-sloping curve represents the market demand for a good (D) and the upward-sloping curve represents the market supply of the good (S). In a perfectly competitive market with zero taxes, the intersection of demand and supply curves determines the equilibrium price and quantity at p_0 and x_0, respectively. The supply curve shifts upward when an indirect tax (τ) is imposed on the good. In this case, the new equilibrium price increases to $p_1 + \tau$, and the new equilibrium quantity decreases to x_1.

As a result of taxation, the consumers' surplus, defined as the maximum amount consumers are willing to pay in excess of the amount they actually pay ($p_0 \times x_0$), decreases by the area $A + B$. Similarly, the producers' surplus, defined as the level of profits received in supplying the quantity sold (represented by ($p_0 -$ MC) $\times x_0$, assuming that marginal cost (MC) coincides with the supply schedule S), declines by the area $C + D$. Since the sum of the losses in consumers' surplus and producers' surplus ($A + B + C + D$) exceeds the amount of revenue collected ($\tau \times x_1$, represented by the area $A + C$), there is a deadweight loss in the amount of $B + D$ (Auerbach 1985). An empirical estimate of the marginal deadweight loss is that a $1 increase in taxes leads to a deadweight loss ranging from $1.07 to $1.33 (Summers 1989).

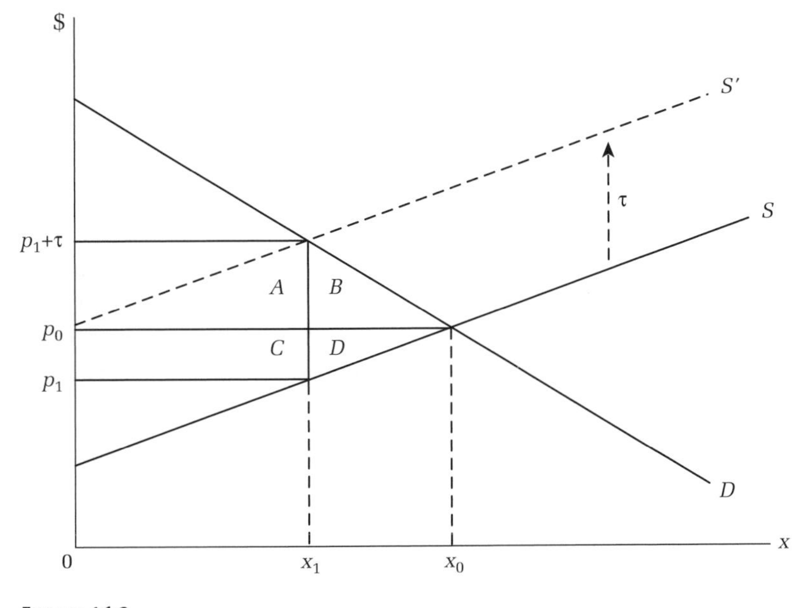

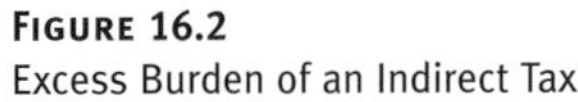
Figure 16.2
Excess Burden of an Indirect Tax

Most countries collect revenues for social health insurance from a payroll tax; there are mandatory contributions based on employees' wages, with the employer and employee sharing the cost. In addition to the excess burden of such taxes, payroll financing has a number of potential impacts on the performance of a country's economy, such as on the employment level and economic growth. The impact of payroll tax on economic activity depends on tax incidence—on who bears the taxes.

Conceptually, consumers, employers, and employees can bear the burden of payroll taxes. Employers may shift the cost of payroll taxes to consumers in the form of higher product prices (forward shifting). When forward shifting occurs, using payroll taxes to finance health care would potentially lower the country's competitiveness globally, thereby reducing the economy's growth rate. If employers bear the burden of a payroll tax, then a payroll increases the cost of hiring labor, which in turn reduces employment and increases the country's unemployment rate. Alternatively, employers may pass the cost of payroll taxes on to workers in the form of lower wages (backward shifting).

The ambiguity in theoretical predictions suggests that empirically investigating the incidence of payroll taxation is critical for assessing the efficiency implications of financing personal health care services through a payroll tax. Most of the empirical evidence on the incidence of payroll taxation shows that the major part of the burden of such cost is typically shifted onto workers; that is, employees bear the full costs of payroll taxation in the form of reduced wage compensation (Gruber 1994, 1997), which is analogous to the effect of employer-provided health insurance coverage on employees' wages in countries with a private employer-based health insurance. An added important implication of this finding is that payroll taxes per se have minor impacts on employment levels (Nickell 1997).

The tax subsidy from the favorable treatment of employer-provided health insurance in the United States substantially reduces government revenues and reduces the net price of such insurance by about 30 percent (Gruber and Poterba 1996). The reduction in the price of employer-provided health insurance in turn distorts the employee's decision to purchase such insurance, as well as the generosity of such insurance coverage. In the end, this distortion generates deadweight losses since the loss of government tax revenues arising from the tax subsidy exceeds the gains in consumers' and producers' surpluses.

16.3 SECULAR TRENDS IN DETERMINANTS OF HEALTH INPUTS AND OUTPUTS

SECULAR TRENDS IN EXPENDITURES ON PERSONAL HEALTH CARE SERVICES

A major justification for public intervention is that something in addition to the better health of persons directly advantaged by the public program is involved. In part, the something is the externalities from reductions in infectious disease rates, as well as consumption externalities (see chapter 1). But it is becoming increasingly apparent that a healthy population also yields dividends in terms of improved performance of a country's economy.

Health expenditures measure a country's final consumption of health care goods and services plus capital investments in health care infrastructure. Table 16.1 provides a summary of personal health care expenditures as a percentage of GDP in thirty OECD countries for the period 1970–2005.

This international comparison of health expenditures reveals two stylized facts. First, at a single point in time, or cross-sectionally, there is substantial variation in health expenditure among OECD countries, not only in terms of the health expenditure but also as a share of GDP allocated to personal health care services. For example, in the year 2005, the share of GDP spent on health care ranged from 5.7 percent in Turkey to 15.2 percent in the United States. Second, over time, all countries, irrespective of whether their health expenditure levels were initially high or low, have experienced a very similar trend in the growth of health care spending. The growth rate of health expenditures has consistently exceeded the growth rate of GDP. For example, in Australia, the share of GDP spent on health care increased from 4.6 percent in 1970 to 8.8 percent in 2005, an increase of 4.2

TABLE 16.1
Share of GDP Spent on Personal Health Care Services in 30 OECD Countries, 1970–2005

Country	1970	1980	1990	2000	2005	Change in GDP Share between 1970 and 2005 (percentage points)
Australia	4.6	6.3[d]	6.9[d]	8.3[d]	8.8[d]	4.2
Austria	5.2	7.5	8.4[b]	9.9	10.3	5.1
Belgium	3.9	6.3	7.2	8.6	10.7	6.8
Canada	6.9	7.0	8.9	8.8	9.9	3.0
Czech Republic	—	—	4.7	6.5[b]	7.1	—
Denmark	8.0	8.9	8.3	8.3	9.4	1.4
Finland	5.5	6.3	7.7	7.0	8.3	2.8
France	5.4	7.0	8.4	9.6	11.2	5.8
Germany	6.0	8.4	8.3	10.3	10.7	4.7
Greece	5.4	5.9	6.6	7.8[b]	9.0	3.6
Hungary	—	—	7.0	6.9	8.5	—
Iceland	4.7	6.3	7.8	9.5	9.4	4.7
Ireland	5.1	8.3	6.1[b]	6.3	8.2	3.1
Italy	—	—	7.7	8.1	8.9	—
Japan	4.6	6.5	6.0	7.7	8.2	3.6
Korea	—	3.4	4.0	4.6	6.0	—
Luxembourg	3.1	5.2	5.4	5.8	7.8	4.7
Mexico	—	—	4.8	5.6	6.4	—
Netherlands	6.9	7.4	8.0	8.0	9.2	2.3
New Zealand	5.2	5.9	6.9	7.7	8.9	3.7
Norway	4.4	7.0	7.6	8.4	9.1	4.7
Poland	—	—	4.8	5.5	6.2	—
Portugal	2.5	5.6	5.9	8.8[b]	10.2	7.7
Slovak Republic	—	—	—	5.5	7.1	—
Spain	3.5	5.3	6.5	7.2	8.3	4.8
Sweden	6.8	8.9	8.2	8.2	9.2	2.4
Switzerland	5.4	7.3	8.2	10.3	11.4	6.0
Turkey	—	3.3	3.6	4.9	5.7	—
United Kingdom	4.5	5.6	6.0	7.2	8.2[d]	3.7
United States	7.0	8.7	11.9	13.2	15.2	8.2

Note: b represents a break in the series; d represents differences in methodology.
Source: OECD, Health Data (2008).

percentage points during a thirty-five-year period. Similarly, in the United States, this share increased from 7.0 percent in 1970 to 15.2 percent in 2005, an increase of 8.2 percentage points. Among the twenty-two OECD countries with complete data on health expenditures for 1970–2005, in twenty-one countries the share of GDP devoted to personal health care services rose by more than two percentage points.

DETERMINANTS OF PERSONAL HEALTH CARE EXPENDITURES

These stylized facts have provided an impetus for research on the causes of these increases. Empirical studies have yielded consistent findings on the determinants of personal health care expenditures. National income (such as GDP per capita) is the most important single determinant of cross-sectional variation in health care expenditures, with an associated income elasticity of about one; a 10 percent increase in national income leads to an increase in health expenditures of about 10 percent, holding other factors constant (Gerdtham and Jönsson 2000).

Other factors affect health expenditures as well, including institutional arrangements. For example, compared to countries in which consumers have free choice of providers, countries using primary care physicians as gatekeepers for inpatient care consistently have lower health expenditures. Also, countries in which physicians are paid on a capitated basis tend to have lower health care expenditures (Gerdtham and Jönsson 2000).

While differences in income alone can explain most of the cross-sectional variation in health expenditures, growth in income cannot explain why health expenditures have risen so substantially over time. Such other factors as population aging, the increased coverage of health insurance, growth in the number of health professionals and hospital capacity, and lower productivity growth in the service sector than in other sectors of countries' economies may partly explain health care expenditure growth.

However, Newhouse (1992) argued that the above-mentioned factors taken together account for less than half of the long-run growth in health care expenditures. Instead, Newhouse proposed that the major part of the increase in health expenditures stems from technological change in health care. Included in technological change are newly developed types of equipment, pharmaceuticals, and medical devices, as well as new surgical technologies and the development and diffusion of such technological tools as renal dialysis.

This view is widely accepted by health economists. In a survey of US health economists, 81 percent of respondents agreed with the statement that the primary reason for the increase in the health sector's share of GDP is technological change in medicine (Fuchs 1996), a view supported by other empirical evidence (Okunade and Murthy 2002).

Hall and Jones (2007) developed a conceptual framework for explaining why health expenditures are commanding a rising share of national income in many high-income countries. In their framework, as people become more affluent and the consumption of goods and services other than personal health care services rises, the marginal utility per dollar of non-health-care consumption declines. It is, after all, possible to drive only one car or to take one vacation at a time. Even if, as economists assume, consumers do not reach the point of satiation, even increasing the quality of the car and the vacation has its limits and can yield only so much extra satisfaction. But health care spending extends longevity and improves quality of life per year of life, thus adding years during which a person can consume. In contrast to other consumption goods, the marginal utility of life extension does not fall as longevity increases, at least as long as health status is maintained. Because the marginal utility of non-health-care consumption declines but the utility of spending on health care does not, nations spend an increasing share of their income on health care as their national incomes rise.

The authors predicted that by the mid-twenty-first century, spending on health care will be 30 percent of GDP in the United States, more than double the percentage in the year 2000. This growth in share is approximately what one would calculate from simple extrapolation of the differential in growth in national income and in national health care spending during 1970–2000. Hall and Jones argued on the basis of empirical evidence from one published and one unpublished study that the value of life increases twice as fast as income, a result consistent with the growing secular trend in personal spending on health care services as a share of GNP in the United States and other high-income countries.

This line of argument raises more questions than it answers. First, it is not clear how much of the improvement in longevity is really traceable to health care. Second, it is not clear that the current absolute level of US spending or the projected level of spending is optimal. The United States spends twice as much per capita as the other ten richest countries, but it has a slightly shorter average longevity than other affluent countries have (see tables 16.1 and 16.2). Should one infer that other countries spend too little or that the United States spends too much? More to the point, one should conclude that correlations do not establish optimality with respect to consumption of a good, the cost of which is drastically reduced by insurance at the time of use.

Of course, the astute reader will remind us about our warning earlier in this chapter that comparisons of spending and health are subject to omitted variables bias. Factors other than personal health care services affect health and longevity. These other factors may be positively correlated with trends in the use of personal health care services. To not explicitly incorporate these other factors in analysis of trends in health outcomes will almost certainly lead to an overestimate of the effectiveness of personal health care services in contributing to the health improvements that have occurred. On the other hand, the differences are so large that the other factors would have to have substantial explanatory power for the gaps to be closed.

TABLE 16.2
Life Expectancy at Birth in 30 OECD Countries, 1960–2005

Country	1960	1970	1980	1990	2000	2005	Longevity Gains between 1960 and 2005 (years)
Australia	70.9	70.8	74.6	77.0	79.3	80.9	10.0
Austria	68.7	70.0	72.6	75.5	78.1	79.5	10.8
Belgium	70.6	71.0	73.3	76.1	77.8	79.1	8.5
Canada	71.3	72.9	75.3	77.6	79.3	80.4	9.1
Czech Republic	70.7	69.6	70.3	71.6	75.1	76.1	5.4
Denmark	72.4	73.3	74.3	74.9	76.9	78.3	5.9
Finland	69.1	70.8	73.4	75.0	77.7	79.1	10.0
France	70.3	72.2	74.3	76.9	79.2	80.2	9.9
Germany	69.6	70.6	72.9	75.3	78.2	79.4	9.8
Greece	69.9	72.0	74.5	77.1	78.0	79.3	9.4
Hungary	68.0	69.2	69.1	69.4	71.7	72.8	4.8
Iceland	72.9	74.3	76.7	78.0	80.1	81.2	8.3
Ireland	70.0	71.2	72.9	74.9	76.6	79.5	9.5
Italy	69.8	72.0	74.0	77.2	80.0	80.9	11.1
Japan	67.8	72.0	76.1	78.9	81.2	82.0	14.2
Korea	52.4	62.2	65.9	71.4	76.0	78.5	26.1
Luxembourg	69.4	70.3	72.5	75.6	78.0	79.5	10.1
Mexico	57.5	60.9	67.2	71.2	74.1	75.5	18.0
Netherlands	73.5	73.7	75.9	77.0	78.0	79.4	5.9
New Zealand	71.3	71.5	73.2	75.4	78.7	79.9	8.6
Norway	73.8	74.4	75.9	76.7	78.8	80.3	6.5
Poland	67.8	70.0	70.2	70.7	73.9	75.1	7.3
Portugal	63.8	66.6	71.4	74.1	76.7	78.1	14.3
Slovak Republic	70.6	69.8	70.6	71.0	73.3	74.0	3.4
Spain	69.8	72.0	75.4	77.0	79.4	80.4	10.6
Sweden	73.1	74.7	75.8	77.6	79.7	80.6	7.5
Switzerland	71.4	73.1	75.7	77.5	79.9	81.4	10.0
Turkey	48.3	54.2	58.1	66.1	70.5	71.4	23.1
UK	70.8	71.9	73.2	75.7	77.9	79.1	8.3
US	69.9	70.9	73.7	75.3	76.8	77.8	7.9

Source: OECD, Health Data (2008).

Secular Trends in Health Outcomes

Table 16.2 summarizes data on life expectancy at birth for the total population of thirty OECD countries for 1960–2005. Again, there are two stylized facts. First, at a single point in time, there are substantial differences in life expectancy among countries. For example, in 1960, life expectancy at birth ranged from 48.3 years in Turkey to 73.8 years in Norway—a longevity differential between these two countries of 25.5 years. Although differences among countries in longevity declined over time, international differences in life expectancy remained in 2005. In that year, the life expectancy at birth ranged from 71.4 years in Turkey to 82 years in Japan, a gap of 10.6 years.

Second, there is a secular trend toward increased life expectancy in all OECD countries. The longevity gains between 1960 and 2005 ranged from 3.4 years in the Slovak Republic to 26.1 years in South Korea. Countries with a lower life expectancy in 1960 tended to experience greater subsequent improvements in life expectancy. Except for the Slovak Republic, longevity gains between 1960 and 2005 were more than 4.5 years—a growth in life expectancy at birth of at least one year per decade in high-income countries.

In addition, there is another stylized fact concerning life expectancy within countries. There are substantial differences in life expectancy among population subgroups, such as race/ethnicity and socioeconomic status groups, within countries. For example, in England and Wales in 1997–2001, male manual workers had a life expectancy that was 8.4 years less than that of white-collar workers. Similarly, in 2002, blacks in the United States could expect to live 5.4 years fewer years than whites in that country (Cutler, Deaton, and Lleras-Muney 2006).

Determinants of Mortality

Compared to health care expenditures, the determinants of mortality and life expectancy are more complex. The determinants of mortality may depend on the stage of economic development. Also, a general theory of mortality should explain all of the above-mentioned stylized facts: cross-sectional differences in life expectancy across countries and across groups within countries, as well as the rise in life expectancy over time. This section provides a brief review of the explanations of the stylized facts as they pertain to life expectancy.

Between 1840 and 2000, the longevity gains in countries with the highest longevity documents were nearly 40 years (Oeppen and Vaupel 2002; also see chapter 1). About three-quarters of these longevity gains occurred before 1950, with the remaining quarter occurring since then.

Cutler, Deaton, and Lleras-Muney (2006) attributed the longevity gains over this long time period to three factors, improvements in nutrition and economic growth, in public health, and in vaccinations and medical treatment. The factors were relatively important in different periods. Before the mid-nineteenth century, improved nutrition and economic growth were the most important contributors to mortality reductions. However, during the late nineteenth century, improvements in public health accounted for a greater share of longevity gains. After the 1930s, beginning with the introduction of vaccines and antibiotics, as well as the development of expensive and intensive treatments, technological change in medicine became the dominant factor in accounting for longevity gains.

Although the availability of medical technology is an important factor in explaining the longevity gains realized in the most recent decades, it is not a key factor accounting for the substantial differences in life expectancy among countries and among groups within countries. By contrast, educational attainment, social factors, and health-related behavior play more important roles than personal health care services in accounting for cross-sectional differences in life expectancy.

After examining various factors accounting for longevity gains over time and cross-sectional differences in life expectancy, Cutler, Deaton, and Lleras-Muney (2006) concluded that the determinants of mortality may be summed up in three words: knowledge, science, and technology. They emphasized that the application of new knowledge arising from advances in the science and technology of health is key to reducing mortality. To buttress their argument, they point out that knowledge of the germ theory of disease and knowledge of the health effects of smoking have had profound effects on public health policies by, among other things, stimulating the enactment of laws to limit smoking and the levying of higher excise taxes on cigarettes, and through effects on on personal behavior. In addition, recent advances in medical technologies, such as new treatment procedures and new pharmaceuticals, have had substantial effects on health.

Having summarized the qualitative evidence on the determinants of health and longevity gains, we now turn to quantitative assessments of the effects of the use of personal health services on population health.

16.4 Contributions of Personal Health Care Services to Improved Population Health

Conceptual Framework

The relationship between health inputs and outcomes may be described by a health production function (see chapter 2). While a production function expresses the relationship between the employment of several inputs and an output, when we measure the marginal product of an input, other input levels are held constant. Figure 16.3 describes the relationship between health inputs and output. At a point in time, input level M_0 yields health output at H_0 at point A. The input's marginal product at point A is the slope of the total output curve at this point. Holding other input levels constant, as the health input increases, its marginal product declines.

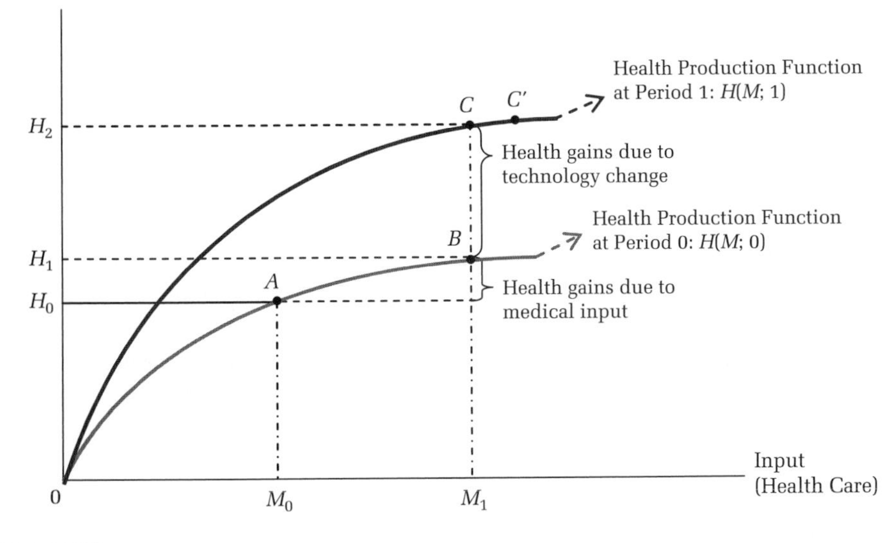

FIGURE 16.3
Health Production Function in a Static and Dynamic Context

However, the lower curve in figure 16.3 is for a constant health technology. Over time, technological change in health care occurs, resulting in an upward shift in the total output curve and corresponding changes in the marginal product of health inputs. For example, at point C, the marginal product of health care exceeds its marginal product at point B, which applies to technology of an older vintage. Each output curve exhibits diminishing returns on the use of health care inputs. The way around diminishing returns is either to increase the levels of the other inputs or to have technological change, which potentially boosts the marginal product of all health inputs, perhaps to differing degrees.

Thus, at any given point in time, the causal relationship between a change in health care expenditures and a change in health outcomes is a movement along a given health production function (e.g., from point A to point B in fig. 16.3). As Fuchs (1996) explained, at any given point in time, the health production function, especially in high-income countries, may be near the flat curve part of the total output curve (e.g., near point B). This implies, in a static context, that a large increase in personal health expenditures would not produce a major overall improvement in overall health.

Economists describe technological progress as the implementation of new knowledge leading to higher output per unit of input. Often a distinction is made between *process* and *product* innovations. With a process innovation, the characteristics of the output are unchanged, but the output is produced with the use of fewer resources. An example is the introduction of the cotton gin, which allowed seeds to be removed from cotton by machine, which was much more efficient than removing the seeds by hand.

A product innovation involves the introduction of a new product, such as the personal computer. There are many product innovations in health care, such as new drugs and new surgical procedures, and new ways to image the body. However, as the concept of technological change is being used here, the output is improved health and the health inputs are types of labor and capital. In this context, the distinction between process and product innovation is unimportant. If, for example, a new imaging machine enables a diagnosis to be made more accurately and quickly, fewer resources are required to produce a given health outcome. Patients spend fewer days in the hospital than previously or perhaps may avoid the hospital entirely. In sum, the distinction between the static context (movements along a given health production function) and the dynamic context (a shift in the health production function) provides a useful framework for examining the causal relationship between health care and health outcomes. Whether health care has contributed to improved health and longevity in any important way depends in large part on the extent of technological change in medicine that has occurred. We use this conceptual framework to synthesize the empirical studies reviewed below.

Empirical Evidence from Cross-Sectional Studies

To our knowledge, the study by Auster, Leveson, and Sarachek (1969) is the earliest published study to employ regression analysis to examine the relationship of mortality to both health care and environmental variables, such as income and education. Based on an analysis of data on US states in 1960, the authors found that health care makes a positive contribution to improved health, but the effect was not statistically significant, and the magnitude of marginal impact was quite small—a 1 percent increase in health expenditure was associated with a reduction in mortality of about 0.1 percent. "Environmental variables," such as educational attainment and income, had more important influences on health than health care inputs did.

The RAND Health Insurance Experiment investigated the impact of cost sharing on both the use of services and health outcomes (see chapter 3). Although reduced cost sharing led to increased spending on personal health care services, with a few exceptions, reduced cost sharing did not lead to improvements in health. Free care did improve blood pressure control and vision for some population subgroups (Brook, Ware, Rogers, et al. 1983). These findings are consistent with the argument that the production of health in high-income countries is near a flat part of the curve, and hence the variation in health care utilization across individuals did not lead to a significant difference in health outcomes.

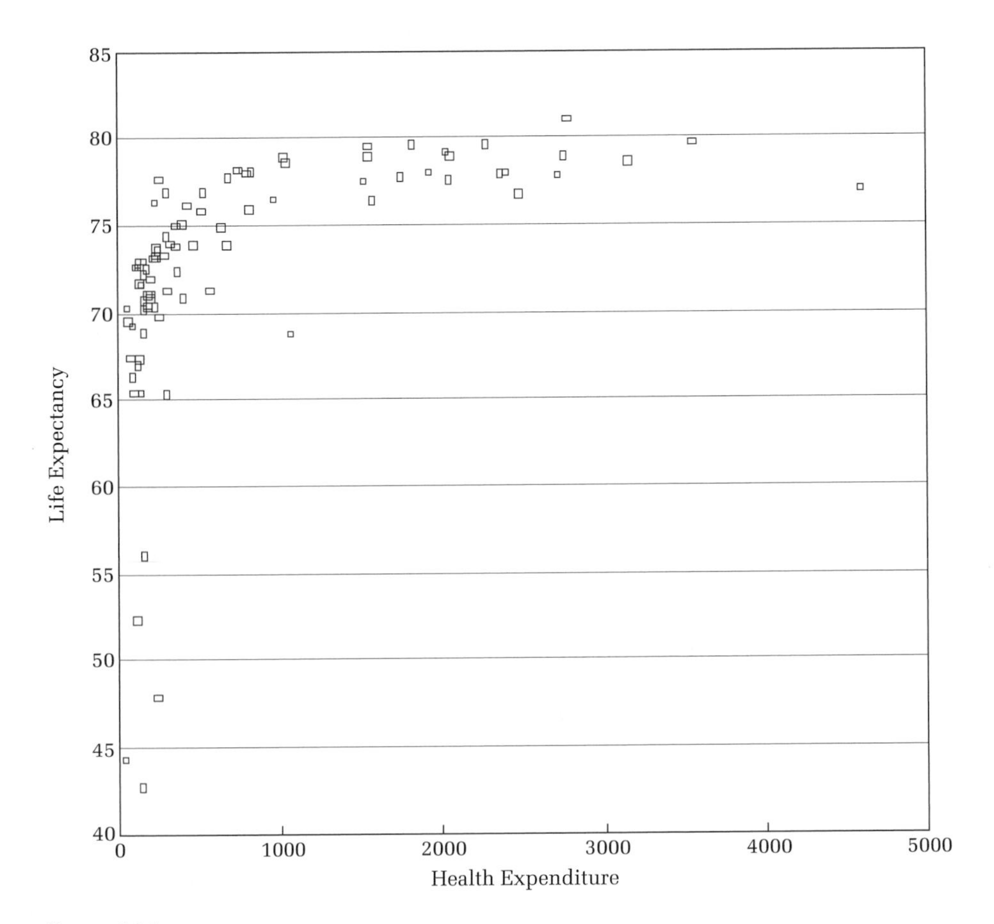

FIGURE 16.4
Relationship between Annual Health Expenditures Per Capita Population and Health Outcomes in High-Income Countries
Note: High-income countries are countries with a GDP per capita above the 50th percentile of world income distribution.
Source: Data for annual health expenditures and life expectancy are from World Bank Group, World Bank Development Indicators (2009). Both health expenditures and life expectancy at birth are for the year 2000, and health expenditures are measured in constant 2000 US dollars.

These empirical findings are consistent with the statistical relationship between health expenditure and life expectancy at birth seen among high-income countries. Figure 16.4 shows the relationship between health expenditures (horizontal axis) and life expectancy at birth (vertical axis) for high-income countries, defined as countries with income levels above the 50th percentile of world income distribution among 175 countries, in 2000. Meanwhile, figure 16.5 shows the same relationship for low-income countries, those with income levels under the 50th percentile of the world income distribution, in 2000.

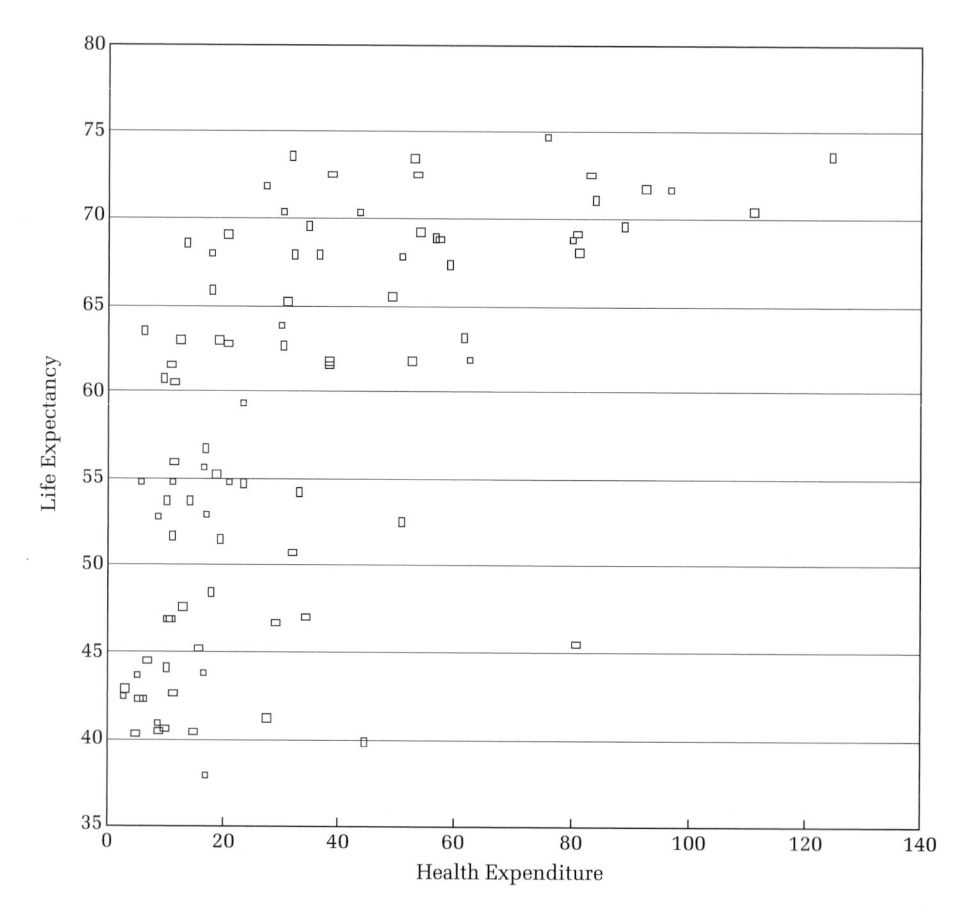

FIGURE 16.5
Relationship between Health Expenditures Per Capita Population and Health Outcomes in Low-Income Countries
Note: Low-income countries are countries whose GDP per capita is below the 50th percentile of world income distribution.
Source: Data for health expenditures and life expectancy are from World Bank Group, World Bank Development Indicators (2009). Both health expenditures and life expectancy at birth are for the year 2000, and health expenditures are measured in constant 2000 US dollars.

These two figures reveal a very different pattern in the shape of health production function. For high-income countries, the shape of the health production function is near the flat part of the curve, indicating that an increase in expenditures on personal health care services does not lead to much change in population health as measured by life expectancy at birth. By contrast, the shape of the health production function is upward sloping for low-income countries, indicating that an increase in such expenditures leads to substantial improvements in health outcomes. These cross-sectional comparisons suggest there is a diminishing marginal return to health care inputs where medical technology is fixed and health inputs are employed at high levels.

Overview of Analytic Approaches

A technical problem in attributing gains in health and longevity to technological change is that although individual technological changes are observable, there is no aggregate measure that adequately captures this phenomenon. In addition, over a long time period, improvement in health outcomes also depends on various other factors, such as economic growth, public health, better access to personal health care services, and better public information about the new medical knowledge and behavioral changes, in addition to new medical knowledge and its implementation. Hence, quantifying the influence of technological change on health and longevity is a challenging task. Researchers have approached this challenge in several ways.

Some researchers have used data at the level of the individual to quantify the relationship between technological change and health outcomes, focusing on a specific disease or therapeutic procedure. Using data on individual patients with a single disease has the advantage of allowing investigators to control for other factors, including other diseases (comorbidities), demographic characteristics, and characteristics of the disease the person has that may also influence health outcomes, which is more difficult in a study using aggregate data. For example, as practitioners gain proficiency with a specific new procedure, they may accept patients at higher risk for an adverse outcome for treatment. To the extent that this is so, and lacking adequate controls, researchers may understate the contribution of the technological change to population health.

Other researchers have attempted to find a proxy variable to capture the effect of technological change, such as using the increase in personal health expenditures over time or the cumulative number of new drugs available in the market (box 16.1). However, there is a risk that other important factors systematically related to technological change are excluded from the analysis, which can lead to biased estimates of the effects of technological change.

A third approach has used an accounting method to calculate the contribution of technological change to better health outcomes. This approach uses available evidence from clinical studies, where individual patients are the observational unit, to identify all factors that potentially contribute to improved health outcomes. Based on this information, researchers have constructed estimates for a country as a whole of the proximate effect of technology change on better health.

The Disease Approach

Treatment for a heart attack (acute myocardial infarction, AMI) is the best-known example of employing the disease approach to quantify marginal benefits of technological change. Using a sample of Medicare beneficiaries, Cutler and McClellan (2001) presented evidence that the life expectancy for the average person experiencing a heart attack in the United States increased by about one year between 1984 and 1998. Based on their empirical analysis, they concluded that about 70 percent of this longevity gain resulted from technological change in heart attack

Box 16.1
How to Measure Technological Change in Medicine

Technological change in medicine has been a major cause of rising health expenditures in many countries. Meanwhile, there is a growing body of empirical evidence indicating that technological change in medicine has made a substantial contribution to increased longevity and an improved quality of life. A common issue in these empirical studies is how to measure technological change in medicine empirically.

Some studies focus on technological change in medicine in general, while others focus pharmaceutical innovation in particular. The former literature typically uses total R&D spending in the whole economy or R&D spending specific to health care as proxies for technological change (e.g., Okunade and Murthy 2002).

In addition, there is international medical technology diffusion. The rest of world may benefit from medical technological change occurring in countries at the frontier of medical technology. Thus, the diffusion of technological change in medicine can be measured by medical imports and by diffusion in the forms of ideas, such as the number of foreign-trained medical students (Papageorgiou, Savvides, and Zachariadis 2007).

Studies of pharmaceutical innovation rely on three different types of proxies to measure technological change: (1) the cumulative number of drugs approved with new molecular entities, (2) newer drugs as a proportion of total prescriptions, (3) and the average vintage of drugs. For example, Lichtenberg (2005) used the first approach. He emphasized that approval of new molecular entities represents the most important form of innovation. Using the cumulative number of new molecular entities available in the market by year, Lichtenberg found a significantly positive relationship between his measure of pharmaceutical innovation and life expectancy in the United States and in a sample containing data from fifty-two countries.

A second approach used by Lichtenberg (2003) measured innovation in pharmaceuticals by both the development *and* diffusion of new drugs. This approach implicitly assumes that the rate of market penetration of new drugs is an appropriate measure of the rate of technological change. He reported that diseases with relatively high rates of technological change in drug therapy experienced relatively greater reductions in disease-specific mortality. He estimated that increases in the market share of new drugs explained more than 45 percent of the variation among diseases in mortality reduction during 1971–1990 in the United States.

A third approach, used by Lichtenberg and Virabhak (2002), measured the vintage of the drugs by the year in which the US Food and Drug Administration first approved the drug's active ingredients. This approach implicitly assumes that newer vintage drugs represent technological improvements in medical care. Using data from the US Medical Expenditure Panel Survey in 1997, Lichtenberg and Virabhak found that patients who used newer vintage drugs had a higher probability of survival, better self-evaluated health status, and fewer limitations in physical function.

care. During the same period, mean expenditures per heart attack increased by about $10,000 (1993 US$), of which about half reflected technological change. Comparing costs and benefits, they concluded that the benefit exceed the cost growth of treating AMI in a ratio of 14 to 1, if the health benefit of an additional year of life is valued at $100,000.

Substantial health benefits attributable to technological change also apply to several other conditions. For example, Cutler and Meara (2000) found that technological change in treating low-birth-weight infants increased the life expectancy of such infants by about 12 years. By contrast, innovations in the therapeutic treatment of breast cancer have increased life expectancy by only about four months (Cutler and McClellan 2001; Luce, Mauskopf, Sloan, et al. 2006).

The heterogeneity of health benefits attributable to technological change among diseases can be explained by differences in the ways that technological change operates. There are basically two channels through which technological change affects treatment and hence health outcomes: treatment substitution and treatment expansion (Cutler and McClellan 2001). The *treatment substitution* effect describes the substitution of a new for an old technology for treating a person with a given health condition. This effect represents a shift in the health production function, such as from point A to point C in figure 16.3, which signifies improvement in health outcomes from the technological change. In the case of the *treatment expansion* effect, introducing the new technology increases the number of persons who receive treatment for the condition. The treatment expansion effect refers to the movement along the new health production function, such as from point C to point C' in figure 16.3; marginal health benefits may decline as the new technology is applied to more patients.

The overall effect of technological change as captured by empirical analysis of the effects of technological change on health encompasses a combination of treatment substitution and treatment expansion effects. The health benefits of treatment substitution are significantly positive as long as innovations in medical technology are productive. However, the health benefits of treatment expansion are not always positive; rather, both the sign and magnitude of the effects depend on how valuable the treatment is in the marginal patients.

Skinner, Staiger, and Fisher (2006) provided empirical evidence in support of the view that the health benefits of treatment expansion may decrease over time as more patients receive the treatment of new technology. Using AMI as an example, they noted that the adjusted one-year survival for the US Medicare beneficiaries remained almost constant during between 1995 and 2002, although the survival rate had increased appreciably between 1984 and 1994.

THE PROXY VARIABLE APPROACH

Another analytic approach uses observational data to establish the causal relationship between technological change and improvements in health outcomes by multivariate regression analysis. This approach faces two challenges in measuring dependent and key independent variables. First, better health outcomes are multidimensional, including at least the following three components: (1) reductions in mortality; (2) reductions in disability and morbidity; and (3) improved quality of life, such as reduced pain and suffering. Partly reflecting lack of data on other outcomes, most studies have focused on better health outcomes from reduced mortality.

Second, researchers need to search for a proxy for technological change to assess how much medical technology has contributed to better health. Some analysts use the change in personal health expenditures or pharmaceutical expenditures to capture the effect of technological change. These studies have empirically estimated the relationship between health expenditures and health outcomes using variation among countries (or states or provinces within a country) and over time within individual countries (or states or provinces). This group of studies generally found that higher health expenditures in general and pharmaceutical expenditure in particular are associated with better health outcomes, as measured by such health indicators as increased life expectancy or lower infant mortality rates.

For example, using data on Canadian provinces for 1978–1992, a period during which there was universal coverage in that country, Cremieux, Ouellette, and Pilon (1999) reported that an increase in health expenditures led to a statistically significant effect on the improvement of health outcomes: a 10 percent change in health expenditures led to an change in infant mortality rates of 0.4–0.5 percent and a change in life expectancy by three to six months.

A limitation of this approach is that using change in health expenditures or pharmaceutical expenditures as a proxy for technological change may be confounded by other changes in expenditures influenced by other factors, among them increases in the price, quality, or quantity of personal health care services. To the extent that these other factors are not explicitly accounted for, estimates of the effects of technological change on health may be misstated.

Others studies have investigated the effect of technological change on better health outcomes by focusing specifically on the role of pharmaceutical innovation. This type of study uses the cumulative number of new molecular entities available in the market or the average vintage of drug to measure pharmaceutical innovation and empirically estimate their impact on population health. These studies generally find a significant positive relationship between pharmaceutical innovation and life expectancy. For example, in a number of studies, Frank Lichtenberg has assessed the health benefits of new drugs (Lichtenberg 2003, 2004, 2005). He evaluated the effects of a broad range of drugs, including older and newer drugs, and found that the introduction of new drugs does have benefits in terms of decreased mortality. An econometric issue with observational data is that other factors, such as health behaviors, may not be held constant, and parameter estimates may be biased as a result (see chapter 3).

Most studies investigating the effect of technological change on health outcomes have used data obtained from high-income, technologically advanced countries. Whether technological change in medicine occurring in high-income countries has a similar impact on health outcomes in the rest of the world is an interesting question to explore.

Papageorgiou, Savvides, and Zachariadis (2007) found that the global diffusion of medical technology is an important contributor to improved population health, as measured by life expectancy and mortality rates. They argued that medical technology generated in the technologically advanced countries diffuses across the world through two major channels: (1) imports of medical goods, such as pharmaceutical products and medical equipment; and (2) the direct flow of medical knowledge from countries at the technological frontier to other countries.

Using cross-sectional data from sixty-three technology-importing countries, Papageorgiou and coauthors measured imports of medical goods as the sum of a country's medical imports, including all pharmaceuticals, medical, and health-related products. They measured the flow of medical knowledge by the number of foreign-trained medical students and distance-weighted foreign R&D. They found that both imports of medical goods and flow of ideas are positively correlated with health status in nontechnological frontier countries (i.e., those countries that import technology rather than develop it). Specifically, they reported that an increase in medical technology diffusion from the bottom 25th to the top 75th percentile of countries led to longevity gains of seven to ten years. In addition, they found that medical technology diffusion in the form of tangible goods (i.e., medical goods) was a more important contributor to improved health status than in the form of intangible goods (e.g., transfers of ideas).

Although the proxy variable approach is subject to potential bias as a result of measurement errors or omitted variables, studies with different empirical methodologies have yielded consistent empirical findings. Taken as a whole, the evidence suggests that the increase in personal health care expenditures in general and the adoption of new medical technology in particular, such as the introduction of new drugs, have contributed to improved health outcomes, especially with regard to longevity.

The Accounting Method

In addition to econometric analysis, other studies have employed an accounting approach to quantify the importance of the role of health care as a determinant of the long-run gains in health that have been observed. For example, in the United States, life expectancy at birth was 69.9 years in 1960 and 76.9 years in 2000, an increase of seven years. Cutler, Rosen, and Vijan (2006) estimated that 70 percent of the seven-year increase in life expectancy could be attributed to reductions in mortality from cardiovascular disease. Reductions in infant mortality accounted for another 19 percent of the increase in life expectancy between 1960 and 2000

TABLE 16.3
Causes of Increases in Life Expectancy among Newborns in the United States, 1960–2000

Causes: Reductions in Deaths from	Increase in Life Expectancy (years)	Relative Contribution (%)
Cardiovascular disease	4.88	70
Infancy	1.35	19
Reduction in rate of death from external causes	0.36	5
Pneumonia or influenza	0.28	4
Cancer	0.19	3
Total	6.97	100

Note: The data do not sum to the total because of slight increases in the rates of death from other causes (not listed) and because of rounding.
Source: D. M. Cutler, A. B. Rosen, and S. Vijan, "The Value of Medical Spending in the United States, 1960–2000," *New England Journal of Medicine* 355, no. 9 (2006): 920–927, table 2.

(table 16.3). Although causes of mortality reductions from cardiovascular disease and infant deaths are multifactorial, some research has concluded that at least half of the reductions in these types of mortality have resulted from medical advances (Cutler, Rosen, and Vijan 2006). Taken together, these two estimates imply that over 40 percent ((70 + 19)/2) of the longevity gains in the United States is attributable to medical advances.

16.5 CONTRIBUTION OF IMPROVED HEALTH TO ECONOMIC GROWTH

DIRECT EFFECT ON PRODUCTIVITY

The notion of that health contributes to an individual's human capital and the importance of human capital to productivity in market work have been widely recognized for decades (see, e.g., the seminal work of Becker 1965). In short, healthier populations are more productive.

In recent years, many researchers have attempted to quantify the impact of health improvement on labor productivity using aggregate data on countries. For example, Bhargava, Jamison, Lau, et al. (2001) used data on adult survival rates (ASRs) to measure health and estimate the impact of changes in ASR on economic growth. The ASR was defined as the probability of surviving to age 60, conditional on having reached age 15, or past the age at which children are at elevated risk of death, especially at age 60 or younger. In low-income countries, improvements in mortality are concentrated in the 0 to 6 years age range (Deaton 2006). By contrast, in higher-income countries, most deaths occur to persons over age 65.

Using data grouped in five-year intervals from ninety-two countries for the years 1965–1990, Bhargava and coauthors found that improvements in health (as measured by the ASR) resulted in higher growth rate in GDP. However, the improvements did not occur consistently. Past a level of GDP, further increases in ASR did not have much of an effect on GDP. The effect was much more important for low-income countries than for other countries.

Bloom, Canning, and Sevilla (2004) constructed data from a panel of countries observed every 10 years over 1960–1990 to estimate the parameters of a model of aggregate economic growth. They used life expectancy as a proxy of health, finding that health has a positive and statistically significant effect on economic growth. After accounting for the effect of physical and other forms of human capital, the parameter estimate on life expectancy indicates that each extra year of life expectancy leads to an increase in output of 4 percent. This result reinforces the findings of previous studies that an improvement in health raises the productivity of workers.

Jamison, Lau, and Wang (2005) employed a similar approach. While they found that improved health is an important determinant of economic growth, other factors had a greater influence. More specifically, although better health accounted for about 11 percent of the total growth rate, growth in the stock of physical capital and educational attainment had still larger effects, 67 percent and 14 percent, respectively.

Weil (2007) used available microeconomic estimates to quantitatively assess the role that health differences play in accounting for the gap in income between rich and poor countries. He found that differences in health, measured by the ASR, accounted for about 10 percent of income differences between rich and poor countries. Eliminating health gaps among countries would reduce the differential by about 10 percent.

Despite the range of statistical methods and data sources, the studies overall provide fairly consistent evidence that improved health boosts labor productivity.

Indirect Effects Operating through Fertility, Education, and Saving

In addition to the direct effects of improved health, there are several indirect channels through which health can affect national income. The reduction in infant and child mortality has reduced fertility rates. Especially in low-income countries, children are an important source of income support in old age. Parents know they will need to depend on children, and alternative support from social insurance programs is not widely available. Thus, if they expect a high proportion of their children to die before reaching adulthood, they will overshoot in having more children than they would if the probability of a child dying was very low, as it is in high-income countries. In low-income countries, reductions in mortality mainly stem from reduced deaths from infectious, respiratory, and digestive diseases, which are often causes of mortality in young children, as well as congenital and perinatal conditions (Becker, Philipson, and Soares 2005).

When children are more likely to reach adulthood, there is an added incentive for parents to invest in their children's education (Soares 2005). Reductions in mortality increase the returns from investment in human capital because longer life increases the time horizon over which the benefits of investment in human capital accrue. Increases in educational attainment in turn lead to higher productivity in both market and nonmarket work. Both lower fertility and higher investment in human capital have a positive effect on economic growth.

Thomas Malthus is known for his pessimistic prediction that population would expand and output per worker would fall until national output per capita reached the level at which mere population subsistence was attained (Malthus 1798). However, he did not consider that higher levels of human capital, achieved in part by reductions in mortality, could allow a country to grow and achieve income far in excess of the subsistence level. In the Malthusian model, population grows until a point is reached at which further population growth cannot be sustained, which is the subsistence level. The alternative just described offers a diametrically opposed prediction. Mortality falls, which leads to increased human capital and reduced fertility. This process provides an engine for a country's sustained economic growth.

The reduction in fertility rates caused by reduced mortality, especially for infants and children, also creates a "demographic dividend," which promotes economic growth (Bloom and Canning 2000). Following a decline in fertility, the number of young dependents gradually decreases and the proportion of the working-age population increases. These trends, in combination with other development policies that create increased demand for the working-age population, create a favorable environment for economic growth. Bloom, Canning, and Malaney (2000) provided strong empirical evidence to support this argument. They found that demographic changes of the sort just described have contributed in important ways to the economic success in East Asian countries.

In addition, increased longevity leads to higher saving rates. With a longer life span, people accumulate more assets during their working years to finance a longer anticipated period of retirement (Bloom, Canning, and Graham 2003). This prediction is consistent with evidence from several Asian countries. For example, both Taiwan and Thailand have experienced rapid increases in life expectancy since the 1960s. The consequent changes in demographic structure led to a boom in national savings.

Empirical analysis conducted by Bloom, Canning, and Graham (2003) indicates that a 10-year increase in life expectancy is associated with a rise in saving rates of about 4.5 percentage points. Higher rates of saving permit higher rates of investment without producing inflationary pressures. With a larger capital stock and one of a more recent vintage, labor becomes more productive (Bloom and Canning 2000).

Other Indirect Effects

Improved health also has potentially important, but less tangible benefits (Howitt 2005). First, good health, especially during childhood, may lead people to be more creative adults, which in turn increases a country's rate of innovation. But increased creativity in the arts also yields consumption benefits. Thus, just like healthier populations tend to have higher labor productivity, healthy people are also more efficient in producing new ideas. Knowledge capital plays an important role in generating technological change, which in turn increases productivity for the economy as a whole (Warsh 2006). Second, improved child and maternal health can improve individuals' ability to cope with stress and to adapt to new technology as adults. The expected return on investment in R&D is higher when workers are more likely to adapt to product and process innovations. Third, countries with healthier populations tend to have less income inequality (Deaton 2003). This finding implies that an improvement in population health may lead to a decrease in income inequality. When the income distribution becomes more equal, lower-income families are better able to finance the education of their children, in turn increasing years of educational attainment, an important form of human capital.

Contested Issues

Although empirical evidence that improved health raises economic growth is strong, as is the theoretical case for this relationship, several issues remain hotly debated in the literature. Two of the more important issues are discussed here.

First, in this chapter, we have emphasized the causal link from good health to high levels of economic activity, but does causation go the other way, from high levels of economic activity to better health (Pritchett and Summers 1996)? If so, an important implication is that several health problems in low-income countries, such as high infant and child mortality rates, can be solved as a byproduct of high economic growth.

There is evidence that runs contrary to this view (Deaton 2006). The rapid economic growth in China and India in recent years has not been associated with a major improvement in health. In fact, in China, almost all of the improvements in health were realized before the economic reform of 1978 that subsequently led to a rapid economic growth in that country. For example, the longevity gain (at birth) in China between 1960 and 1980 was more than 30 years, from 36.3 to 66.8. In contrast, during the period between 1980 and 2005, the longevity gain was five years only (World Health Organization 2008). A similar pattern exists in India (Deaton 2006). A plausible explanation for this finding is that the relationship between health (as measured by life expectancy) and income (as measured by per capita GDP) is not positive and linear but positive and concave, indicating diminishing returns.

Consequently, rapid economic growth after attainment of a certain threshold income level did not lead to further improvements in health. Another plausible explanation is that there are important lags before substantial impacts of economic growth on health are realized.

In addition, if the lags are not too great, and if causation runs from the level of economic activity to improved health, one would expect to observe a significant relationship between the *change* in income and the *change* in health (e.g., in the country's infant mortality rate). However, no statistically significant relationship between these two changes has been observed (Deaton 2006). Rather, a lower *level* of infant mortality is associated with a higher growth rate of income.

Based on this observation, Deaton (2006) proposed an alternative interpretation of the link between health and income. He suggested that there are common third factors that are important determinants of both economic growth and health, such as education and the ability of the government to deliver public health services. This implies that the positive relationship between income and health is not causal but rather is just a *correlation*. The quality of several social institutions, such as regulatory agencies and organizations that deliver personal health care services, is correlated with both national income and the health status of the country's people.

Another unresolved issue regarding the relationship between health and income pertains to the secular trend in global inequality. More specifically, is variation in levels of health among countries becoming more or less equal? While there has been some increase in life expectancy in low-income countries since the mid-twentieth century, higher-income countries have experienced improvements in longevity as well. If there were a single metric of health, the comparisons would be easy; however, health is multidimensional, making intertemporal and intercountry comparisons difficult to make.

Becker, Philipson, and Soares (2005) obtained a common metric, converting health gains into money. Often, measures such as GDP are taken as measures of the overall well-being of a country's population. However, a country's GDP does not include a value for the longevity of its population. Becker and coauthors quantified the value of the longevity gains in dollar terms and added this to the change in GDP to obtain a more comprehensive measure of social well-being.

Based on a data for ninety-six countries for 1960–2000 and using the comprehensive measure, Becker and coauthors found that low-income countries (the poorest 50 percent of countries in 1960) tended to grow faster than the higher-income countries (the most affluent 50 percent of countries in 1960). Specifically, the mean annual growth rate was 4.1 percent for the low-income countries, of which 1.7 percentage points could be attributed to longevity gains. By contrast, the mean annual growth rate for the more affluent countries was 2.6 percent, of which only 0.4 percentage points reflected longevity gains. Viewed another way, the gain in longevity accounted for about 40 percent (1.7/4.1) of the growth in low-income countries but for only 15 percent (0.4/2.6) of growth in the other countries.

An important implication is that once longevity gains are considered, the growth rate in low-income countries has been relatively high. This result is not obtained from standard GDP accounts, which exclude the value of health gains.

However, this important finding is not universally accepted. Deaton (2006) argued that health inequality across countries is not necessarily narrowing even with substantial improvements in life expectancy in low-income countries. Specifically, he emphasized that mortality patterns differ between rich and poor countries. In low-income countries, most deaths involve children, and hence the reduction in mortality mainly reflects reductions in infant and child mortality rates. By contrast, in high-income countries, most deaths are among persons over age 50. Thus, Deaton argued, life expectancy is not necessarily a good indicator for comparing changes in health among countries, especially between high- and low-income countries.

16.6 THE HEALTH SECTOR AS A JOB MACHINE

Most countries in the world spend about 5–10 percent of their GDP on health care. Thus, the health sector accounts for a substantial share of employment in the national economy. As in other industries, the major inputs of the health care industry are labor and capital. Earnings from labor and returns on capital investment are the major components of GDP. In this sense, the growth of the health care industry makes an important direct contribution to national economic growth, as measured by the growth in GDP.

The health sector acts as a "job machine" (a major source of employment) through the following two channels. First, an increase in the demand for personal health care services increases demand for health professionals, including nurses, physicians, physicians' assistants, and dentists. The demand for labor in the health sector is a derived demand arising from the demand for personal health care services. Moreover, health is a labor-intensive industry relative to other industries, such as electronics and even agriculture in high-income countries. As a result, the use of capital as a substitute for labor is less likely to occur in the health sector than in other high-tech industries. This suggests that the increase in demand for health care has a greater impact on demand for labor than on demand for capital in the health sector. As discussed elsewhere in this book, various factors, including expansion of insurance coverage, income growth, and population aging, have contributed to an increase in demand for personal health care services, which in turn has increased employment in national economies as the suppliers of such services (and goods, e.g., pharmaceuticals and medical devices) have responded to changes in demand for health care products.

Second, governments globally often seek to promote economic growth by developing new industries that have the potential of increasing national employment and developing new technology. As the growth of life expectancy globally increases demand for personal health care services, two new health sector industries have emerged and matured: the biopharmaceutical industry and the long-term care industry.

For example, facing wage competition in the manufacturing sector from less well-developed countries, many newly industrialized countries, such as South Korea, Taiwan, and Singapore, seeking to promote economic growth, are encouraging growth of the biopharmaceutical industry as a means toward this end. Major technological advances such as those occurring in genomics have made this path to economic growth even more attractive (Sloan and Eesley 2007). Similarly, the global trend in population aging has created the increased demand for long-term care provided by the formal sector, which in turn has led to the growth of long-term care industries in many countries (Norton 2000). These two new industries, in combination with the existing industries in health sector (e.g., the hospital industry), enhance the capability of the health sector to promote employment and income growth for the whole economy.

16.7 ECONOMIC GROWTH AND DISEASE PATTERNS

Throughout this chapter, we have focused on the contribution of personal health care services to improved population health and the feedback connections from the health sector to the economic sector. Here we focus on a reverse feedback connection, from the economic to the health sector. Economic growth may fundamentally affect the health sector in terms of changed disease patterns.

As mentioned above, several studies have documented a link between economic development and morbidity and mortality patterns. For example, between 1965 and 1995, about two-thirds of longevity gains in Middle Eastern and North African countries came from reductions in deaths caused by respiratory and digestive diseases. By contrast, over half of the longevity gains in North America have come from reductions in mortality caused by diseases of the nervous system and sense organs and cardiac and circulatory conditions (Becker, Philipson, and Soares 2005).

In addition to economic growth per se, the business cycle (economic sector) affects morbidity and mortality patterns. Ruhm (2000) provides an interesting test, the results of which lend support for a relationship between the business cycle and health. Based on US longitudinal data for the 1972–1991 period, Ruhm found

Figure 16.6
Total Mortality and Unemployment Rates in the United States
Source: Christopher J. Ruhm, "Are Recessions Good for Your Health?," *Quarterly Journal of Economics* 115, no. 2 (2000): 617–650, figure 1.

strong evidence that unemployment rates in US states are negatively and significantly associated with total mortality rates and eight of ten specific causes of fatalities. Hence, health *improved* when the output of the economy temporarily fell, as reflected in rising state unemployment rates. An important exception is the suicide rate. Suicide rates rose during recessions.

An important result from this study is reproduced in figure 16.6, which shows the relationship between national total mortality and unemployment rates over time. There is a strong inverse relationship between level of economic activity and mortality. In particular, as seen in figure 16.6, there was a substantial reduction in mortality during two major recessions, both of which were attributable to an oil crisis, 1975 and 1982–1983. During those periods, unemployment rates reached record highs in the United States for the period after the World War II but less than the United States has experienced recently (the effects of which cannot yet be reflected in a figure).

Ruhm (2000) provides several plausible mechanisms to explain why recessions are good for your health. First, time is the major input in the production of good health (see chapter 2). Thus, the time prices of several health-augmenting activities, including making physician office visits and engaging in vigorous activity, rise during economic upturns. This mechanism is supported by other empirical findings obtained in this study that smoking and obesity increase, physical activity is reduced, and diet becomes less healthy during periods of relative prosperity.

Second, work-related accidents may increase during economic upturns. For example, when home construction activity is at a relatively high level, employment is also high, leading to more on-the-job accidents. Similarly, the rates of other causes of death, such as motor vehicle accident, rise in prosperous periods because people drive more.

16.8 SUMMARY AND CONCLUSIONS

This chapter has used a macroeconomic perspective for investigating interactions between the health sector and economic sector. We first examined the link between the health sector and the economic sector based on dollar flows. Each country faces decisions about how much to allocate to the health sector and about sources of financing. Policy choices about sources of health care financing are influenced by several feedback effects on the performance of macroeconomies, including saving rates, labor market outcomes, and welfare losses. Specifically, the implementation of universal coverage reduces saving rates and female labor force participation. Similarly, the expansion of public means- and asset-tested insurance program reduces household saving rates.

We then examined the link between the health sector and the economic sector for the flow of goods and services. Health care services may be viewed as inputs in the production of health outputs. There are two stylized facts about trends in health inputs and outputs. First, at a single point in time, there is substantial variation in personal health expenditures and health outcomes, such as life expectancy at birth, among countries. Second, over time, all countries have experienced a very similar trend in growth of health expenditures and in longevity gains. An interesting follow-up question explored in this chapter is to what extent the improvement in population health in general and longevity gain in particular are attributable to the growth in health inputs as measured by personal health expenditures. Although the analytic approaches used to explore this question have varied, the existing studies overall provide fairly consistent evidence that the increase in personal health expenditures in general and the adoption of new medical technology in particular have made substantial contributions to the improvements in health outcomes.

We also explored how the improvement in population health affects economic sector. We identified several important channels through which better health may make a positive contribution to economic growth: (1) by a direct effect, in that healthier populations are more productive, and (2) by indirect effects, in that better health has a significant impact on education, saving, and demographic structure. Specifically, our analysis suggests that better health accounted for about 11 percent of the total growth rate. In addition, an increase in longevity leads to several effects that have a positive impact on economic growth, including an increase in formal education, higher saving rates, and an increase in the share of the working-age population in the total population.

Economic growth in turn may have feedback impacts on the health sector. However, whether the relationship between income growth and the improvement in health is causal or just a correlation is a debated issue. This is an avenue for future research.

KEY CONCEPTS

- health sector
- job lock
- labor force participation
- direct tax
- welfare loss of taxation
- life-cycle model of consumption
- life expectancy at birth
- economic growth
- health production function
- process innovation
- demographic dividend
- labor productivity
- economic sector
- precautionary saving
- payroll tax
- indirect tax
- knowledge capital
- health care expenditure
- longevity gains
- difference-in-difference approach
- product innovation
- treatment expansion effect
- diminishing returns

REVIEW AND DISCUSSION QUESTIONS

16.1 What is "precautionary saving"? What is the effect of purchasing health insurance on precautionary saving? Does this effect vary by income level?

16.2 If a country currently provides health insurance only to its employees, what effect on female labor force participation would you expect if the country decides to implement a national health insurance (NHI) program that expands the insurance coverage to all its citizens? Explain your answer.

16.3 Assume the country in 16.2 decides to use a personal income tax as the source of funds to finance the implementation of the NHI program. Specifically, the government announces it is raising the income tax rate by 5 percent. Explain the potential effects of such a policy on labor supply.

16.4 What is a payroll tax? List three potential parties who bear the payroll tax if the government uses a payroll tax as the major source of health care financing. Discuss the impact of the payroll tax on the whole economy if the incidence of the payroll tax falls on alternative parties.

16.5 Based on the statistical data reported in table 16.1, the share of GDP spent on health care in every country increases over time. Do you expect this share to continue to rise in the future? Is it possible that a country such as the United States will spend more than 30 percent of its GDP on personal health care services in 2030? Explain why this would happen if you think so.

16.6 Which two stylized facts do international comparisons of health expenditures show? Use two words to describe these stylized facts. Justify your answer.

16.7 What are three stylized facts about international comparisons of health outcomes? Use three words to describe these stylized facts. Justify your answer.

16.8 What do "causation" and "correlation" mean? Using the relationship between economic growth and health outcome as an example, show the importance of the distinction between causation and correlation. Then discuss the differences in policy implications in the following two cases:

a. Economic growth *causes* an improvement in health outcome.

b. Economic growth is positively *correlated with* an improvement in health outcome.

16.9 Why is the health sector a "job machine"? In chapters 11–13, we described four different types of health care systems. Which type is most likely to be a job machine for a nation's economy?

16.10 Why may economic recessions be good for health? Can you find some other evidence to support this argument? Why are suicides an exception?

16.11 Distinguish between "precautionary saving behavior" and "life-cycle saving behavior." Suppose, following implementation of universal health insurance, there is a substantial increase in life expectancy at birth. Use these two theories of saving behavior to explain the effect of implementing universal health insurance on saving behavior in the short and the long run.

16.12 Use the framework in figure 16.1 to explain the effect of population aging on the economic and health sectors, and feedbacks between the two.

EXERCISES

16.1 Collect data on health expenditures per capita (HE) and life expectancy at birth (LE) for at least fifteen countries in a given year, and run a simple regression in which LE is the dependent variable and HE is the independent variable. You can obtain data for these two variables from World Development Indicators published by the World Bank. What is the sign of your estimated coefficient? Is the parameter estimate statistically significant at the 5 percent level? How do you interpret your result? What kind of "bias" might you have from this simple regression?

16.2 In recent years, many countries have begun to use a tobacco tax as a source of health care financing. In most cases, the tobacco tax is imposed in the form of excise tax, that is, the consumer pays a fixed amount of tax per pack of cigarettes. Does a tobacco tax create any deadweight loss to the society? If there is a deadweight loss associated with a tobacco tax, does the magnitude of the deadweight loss depend on the price elasticity of demand for cigarettes?

16.3 Use the concept of marginal efficiency of investment (MEI) and cost of capital (COC) described in chapters 2 and 9, and extend this framework to consider how parents decide the optimal year of educational investment for their children. Draw the MEI and COC lines on a graph, with the amount of educational investment (which could be measured by the number of years in school) on the x-axis and the rate on the y-axis. What are the shapes of the MEI and COC schedules? Explain intuitively why they look as they do. Based on this framework, can you predict the effect of reduction in child mortality on the parents' optimal investment in education for their children? Justify your answer.

16.4 Economists often use the following functional form (Cobb-Douglas production function) to describe the aggregate production function of a country:

$$Y = AK^{\alpha} H^{1-\alpha}$$

$$H = h \times s \times L,$$

where Y is output, A is a country-specific productivity term, K is physical capital, and H is a labor composite, which in turn is determined by human capital in the form of health (h), human capital in the form of education (s), and the number of persons in the labor force (L). Use this functional form to show the direct effect of health on output and the indirect effect of health on output through education and saving behavior.

ONLINE SUPPLEMENTAL MATERIAL

DATA

http://data.worldbank.org

http://www.oecd.org/statsportal/0,3352,en_2825_293564_1_1_1_1_1,00.html

http://www.who.int/research/en

WORLD DEVELOPMENT INDICATORS

http://data.worldbank.org/indicator

RANKING OF LIFE EXPECTANCY AT BIRTH

https://www.cia.gov/library/publications/the-world-factbook/rankorder/2102rank.html

ECONOMIC GROWTH

http://www.stanford.edu/~promer/EconomicGrowth.pdf

SUPPLEMENTAL READINGS

Becker, G. S., T. J. Philipson, and R. R. Soares. 2005. The Quantity and Quality of Life and the Evolution of World Inequality. *American Economic Review* 95 (1): 277–291.

Cutler, D., A. Deaton, and A. Lleras-Muney. 2006. The Determinants of Mortality. *Journal of Economic Perspectives* 20 (3): 97–120.

Hall, R. E., and C. I. Jones. 2007. The Value of Life and the Rise in Health Spending. *Quarterly Journal of Economics* 122 (1): 39–72.

REFERENCES

Auerbach, A. J. 1985. The Theory of Excess Burden and Optimal Taxation. In *Handbook of Public Economics*, ed. A. J. Auerbach and M. S. Feldstein. Amsterdam: North-Holland.

Auster, R. D., I. Leveson, and D. Sarachek. 1969. The Production of Health: An Exploratory Study. *Journal of Human Resources* 4 (4): 411–436.

Becker, Gary S. 1965. Human Capital; a Theoretical and Empirical Analysis, with Special Reference to Education. *The American Economic Review* 55 (4): 958–960.

Becker, G. S., T. J. Philipson, and R. R. Soares. 2005. The Quantity and Quality of Life and the Evolution of World Inequality. *American Economic Review* 95 (1): 277–291.

Bhargava, A., D. T. Jamison, L. J. Lau, et al. 2001. Modeling the Effects of Health on Economic Growth. *Journal of Health Economics* 20 (3): 423–440.

Bloom, D. E., and D. Canning. 2000. The Health and Wealth of Nations. *Science* 287 (5456): 1207–1209.

Bloom, D. E., D. Canning, and B. Graham. 2003. Longevity and Life-cycle Savings. *Scandinavian Journal of Economics* 105 (3): 319–338.

Bloom, D. E., D. Canning, and P. N. Malaney. 2000. Population Dynamics and Economic Growth in Asia. *Population and Development Review* 26 (suppl.): 257–290.

Bloom, D. E., D. Canning, and J. Sevilla. 2004. The Effect of Health on Economic Growth: A Production Function Approach. *World Development* 32 (1): 1–13.

Brook, R. H., J. E. Ware, W. H. Rogers, et al. 1983. Does Free Care Improve Adults Health? Results from a Randomized Controlled Trial. *New England Journal of Medicine* 309 (23): 1426–1434.

Chou, S.-Y., J.-T. Liu, and J. K. Hammitt. 2003. National Health Insurance and Precautionary Saving: Evidence from Taiwan. *Journal of Public Economics* 87 (9–10): 1873–1894.

Chou, Y. J., and D. Staiger. 2001. Health Insurance and Female Labor Supply in Taiwan. *Journal of Health Economics* 20 (2): 187–211.

Cremieux, P.-Y., P. Ouellette, and C. Pilon. 1999. Health Care Spending as Determinants of Health Outcomes. *Health Economics* 8 (7): 627–639.

Cutler, D., A. Deaton, and A. Lleras-Muney. 2006. The Determinants of Mortality. *Journal of Economic Perspectives* 20 (3): 97–120.

Cutler, D., and M. B. McClellan. 2001. Is Technological Change in Medicine Worth It? *Health Affairs* 20 (5): 11–28.

Cutler, D., and E. Meara 2000. The Technology of Birth: Is It Worth It? *Forum for Health Economics & Policy* 3 (1).

Cutler, D. M., A. B. Rosen, and S. Vijan. 2006. The Value of Medical Spending in the United States, 1960–2000. *New England Journal of Medicine* 355 (9): 920–927.

Deaton, A. 2003. Health, Inequality, and Economic Development. *Journal of Economic Literature* 41 (1): 113–158.

Deaton, A. (2006). Global Patterns of Income and Health: Facts, Interpretations, and Policies. National Bureau of Economic Research Working Paper No. 12735. Cambridge, MA: National Bureau of Economic Research.

Fuchs, V. R. 1996. Economics, Values, and Health Care Reform. *American Economic Review* 86 (1): 1–24.

Gerdtham, U.-G., and B. Jönsson. 2000. International Comparisons on Health Expenditure: Theory, Data, and Econometric Analysis. In *Handbook of Health Economics*, ed. J. P. Newhouse and A. J. Culyer, 1A:11–49. Amsterdam: Elsevier Science.

Gruber, J. 1994. The Incidence of Mandated Maternity Benefits. *American Economic Review* 84 (3): 622–641.

Gruber, J. 1997. The Incidence of Payroll Taxation. *Journal of Labor Economics* 15 (3): s72–s101.

Gruber, J. 2000. Health Insurance and the Labor Market. In *Handbook of Health Economics*, ed. J. P. Newhouse and A. J. Culyer, 1A:645–700. Amsterdam: Elsevier Science.

Gruber, J., and M. Hanratty. 1995. The Labor Market Effects on Introducing National Health Insurance: Evidence from Canada. *Journal of Business & Economic Statistics* 13:163–173.

Gruber, J., and B. C. Madrian. 1994. Health-Insurance and Job Mobility: The Effects of Public-Policy on Job-Lock. *Industrial & Labor Relations Review* 48 (1): 86–102.

Gruber, J., and J. M. Poterba. 1996. Tax Subsidies to Employer-Provided Health Insurance. In *Empirical Foundations of Household Taxation*, ed. J. M. Poterba and M. F. Poterba. Chicago: University of Chicago Press.

Hall, R. E., and C. I. Jones. 2007. The Value of Life and the Rise in Health Spending. *Quarterly Journal of Economics* 122 (1): 39–72.

Hausman, J. A. 1985. *Taxes and Labor Supply: Handbook of Public Economics*, ed. A. J. Auerbach and M. S. Feldstein. Amsterdam: North-Holland.

Howitt, P. 2005. Health, Human Capital, and Economic Growth: A Schumpeterian Perspective. In *Health and Economic Growth*, ed. G. Lopez-Casanovas, B. Rivera, and L. Currais. Cambridge, MA: MIT Press.

Hubbard, R. G., J. Skinner, and S. P. Zeldes. 1995. Precautionary Saving and Social Insurance. *Journal of Political Economy* 103 (2): 360–399.

Jamison, D. T., L. J. Lau, and J. Wang. 2005. Health's Contribution to Economic Growth in an Environment of Partially Endogenous Technical Programs. In *Health and Economic Growth*, ed. G. Lopez-Casanovas, B. Rivera, and L. Currais. Cambridge, MA: MIT Press.

Keynes, J. M. 1936. *General Theory of Employment, Interest, and Money*. London: Macmillan.

Lichtenberg, F. R. 2003. Pharmaceutical Innovations, Mortality Reduction, and Economic Growth, in *Measuring the Gains from Medical Research: An Economic Approach*, ed. K. M. Murphy and R. H. Topel. Chicago: University of Chicago Press.

Lichtenberg, F. R. 2004. Source of U.S. Longevity Increase, 1960–2001. *Quarterly Review of Economics and Finance* 44 (3): 369–389.

Lichtenberg, F. R. 2005. The Impact of New Drug Launches on Longevity: Evidence from Longitudinal, Disease-Level Data from 52 Countries, 1982–2001. *International Journal of Health Care Finance and Economics* 5 (1): 47–73.

Lichtenberg, F. R., and R. Virabhak. 2002. *Pharmaceutical Embodied Technical Progress, Longevity, and Quality of Life: Drugs as "Equipment" for your Health.* Cambridge, MA: National Bureau of Economic Research.

Luce, B. R., J. Mauskopf, F. A. Sloan, et al. 2006. The Return on Investment in Health Care: From 1980 to 2000. *Value in Health* 9 (3): 146–156.

Madrian, B. C. 1994. Employment-Based Health-Insurance and Job Mobility: Is There Evidence of Job-Lock? *Quarterly Journal of Economics* 109 (1): 27–54.

Malthus, T. R. 1798. *An Eassay on the Principle of Populations.* New York: W. W. Norton.

Modigliani, F., and R. E. Brumberg. 1954. Utility Analysis and the Consumption Function. In *Post Keynesian Economics*, ed. K. K. Kurihara, 388–436. New Brunswick, NJ: Rutgers University Press.

Newhouse, J. P. 1992. Medical Care Costs: How Much Welfare Loss? *Journal of Economic Perspectives* 6 (3): 3–21.

Nickell, S. 1997. Unemployment and Labor Market Rigidities: Europe versus North America. *Journal of Economic Perspectives* 11 (3): 55–74.

Norton, E. C. 2000. Long-Term Care. In *Handbook of Health Economics*, ed. A. J. Culyer and J. P. Newhouse, 1B:955–994. Amsterdam: Elsevier Science.

Oeppen, J., and J. W. Vaupel. 2002. Broken Limits to Life Expectancy. *Science* 296 (5570): 1029–1031.

Okunade, A. A., and V. N. R. Murthy. 2002. Technology as a "Major Driver" of Health Care Costs: A Cointegration Analysis of the Newhouse Conjecture. *Journal of Health Economics* 21 (1): 147–159.

Organisation for Economic Co-operation and Development. 2008. OECD Health Data. http://www.oecd.org/document/56.

Papageorgiou, C., A. Savvides, and M. Zachariadis. 2007. International Medical Technology Diffusion. *Journal of International Economics* 72:409–427.

Pritchett, L., and L. H. Summers. 1996. Wealthier Is Healthier. *Journal of Human Resources* 31 (4): 841–868.

Romer, P. M. 1990. Endogenous Technological Change. *Journal of Political Economy* 98 (S5): S71–S102.

Ruhm, C. J. 2000. Are Recessions Good for Your Health? *Quarterly Journal of Economics* 115 (2): 617–650.

Skinner, J. S., D. O. Staiger, and E. S. Fisher. 2006. Is Technological Change in Medicine Always Worth It? The Case of Acute Myocardial Infarction. *Health Affairs* 25:w34–w47.

Sloan, F. A., and C. Eesley. 2007. Implementing a Public Subsidy for Vaccines. In *Pharmaceutical Innovation: Incentives, Competition, and Cost-Benefit Analysis in International Perspective*, ed. F. A. Sloan and C.-R. Hsieh, 107–126. New York: Cambridge University Press.

Soares, R. R. 2005. Mortality Reductions, Educational Attainment, and Fertility Choice. *American Economic Review* 95 (3): 580–601.

Summers, L. H. 1989. Some Simple Economics of Mandated Benefits. *American Economic Review* 79 (2): 177–183.

Warsh, D. 2006. *Knowledge and the Wealth of Nations: A Story of Economic Discovery*. New York: W. W. Norton.

Weil, D. N. 2007. Accounting for the Effect of Health on Economic Growth. *Quarterly Journal of Economics* 122 (3): 1265–1306.

World Bank Group. 2009. World Development Indicators. http://data.worldbank.org/indicator.

World Health Organzation (WHO). 2008. World Health Report, 2008.

FRONTIERS OF HEALTH ECONOMICS

This book concludes with a discussion of five ongoing controversies in health economics and in some cases in economics more generally. (1) Are people and institutions really rational and forward-looking in decision making, as economists generally assume? (2) How do people and institutions obtain information relevant to their decisions? To what extent does asymmetric information really affect the performance of health care markets, including markets for private health insurance? (3) How do the way health care providers are paid and how they compete affect the performance of providers and social welfare more generally? (4) How does the regulatory process affect the behavior of regulated health care firms? (5) How do physicians really make clinical decisions, and how do these clinical decisions affect the substantial geographic variation in expenditures within and among countries?

17.1 RATIONAL VERSUS IRRATIONAL DECISION MAKING IN HEALTH CARE

A key assumption in economic analysis is that people, as individual and household decision makers and as decision makers for organizations, are rational and forward-looking optimizers. By rational, economists mean that decision makers use all information available to them when making choices, recognizing that information can be costly to obtain. For this reason, decisions are often based on incomplete information about the options. As optimizers, individuals make choices that yield the highest level of utility subject to the constraints they face.

Assumptions are not an end in themselves in economic analysis. Rather, they are part of the modeling process. Economists recognize that few of the assumptions they make are "realistic." Models are judged by the accuracy of the predictions they offer rather than on how plausible the assumptions appear to be.

Some health and health care decisions are readily understood within a standard economic framework. For example, more medical care is demanded when there is complete insurance coverage for such services or when physicians are more willing to accept an insurer's payment as payment in full at higher payment levels.

However, some decisions, while not necessarily inconsistent with standard economic models, at a minimum raise questions about whether or not they accurately describe behavior. For example, why would people engage in behaviors that clearly impair personal health, such as smoking? Easy answers are "they are addicted" or "they simply enjoy the activity so much that they do it" without recognizing the long-term consequences of present actions. But another possibility is that the framework itself is not up to the task of adequately describing behavior.

Similarly, why do persons diagnosed with diabetes not follow health care regimens that have been documented in randomized controlled trials to reduce the onset of complications of the disease and about which there is no dispute among clinicians as to their efficacy? Personal health care decisions can be very major ones, especially after an individual has experienced a major adverse health event, such as being informed that he or she has been diagnosed with cancer.

The question of whether or not the assumption of rational and forward-looking behavior is appropriate has been asked by economists in a number of decision-making contexts. Descriptions of alternative frameworks are now being taught in undergraduate courses in microeconomics. For example, Frank (2006), in a textbook on microeconomics but one that has a behavioral economics perspective, devotes an entire chapter to cognitive limitations and consumer behavior. The chapter discusses Herbert Simon's concept of "bounded rationality," which led to Simon being awarded a Nobel Prize in Economics. Simon stressed the complexity of many decision problems. Consumers take shortcuts. Often they are "satisfiers" rather than "maximizers." Economists typically maintain that more choice is better than less choice. However, this may not be true for a boundedly rational individual.

Amos Tversky and Daniel Kahneman (1981), the latter a Nobel Laureate in Economics and the former a scholar who died before he could receive the Nobel Prize, argued that people use shortcuts in solving problems even when the problems are not all that complex. Accordingly, few individuals are the rational teenager contemplating whether or not to initiate the smoking habit whom we described in chapter 2. Richard Thaler (1980) argued that individuals treat gains and losses asymmetrically, not symmetrically, as in cost-benefit analysis. Tversky and Kahneman (1974) have argued that the von Neumann–Morgenstern expected utility model (chapter 2) is violated in many decisions people make under uncertainty.

Tversky and Kahneman described several types of biases they regarded as empirically relevant. Some events seem to stand out in people's minds much more than do others, the *availability heuristic*. For example, when asked whether homicides or suicides are more common, people are likely to answer the former although the latter is true. Murders are more widely publicized and more easily recalled, especially if the victim was not personally known by the individual. People make inferences about attributes based on prior experience. For example, if a medical institution is famous, people might think that the quality of care is good for every type of case, even if this is not a valid assumption. Further, such "representativeness bias" may substitute for effort to obtain information about quality in the specific case relevant to the individual's decision. *Anchoring bias* occurs when individuals start with a preliminary estimate that could be virtually drawn at random, and then update from this value. The starting value has an important effect on the final value selected for the estimate. We discussed anchoring or starting-point bias in chapter 15 in the context of eliciting estimates of maximum willingness to pay for a service.

Underlying the assumption that people are rational and forward-looking is the assumption that people exercise self-control over their decisions. Once a decision is reached, there will be no problem in executing it. For example, if a person decides to save a given amount per month, she will do this, and not stop after a few months (Ameriks, Caplin, and Leahy 2003; Thaler and Benartzi 2004). Or, in a health context, a person who decides to quit smoking will not restart (Schelling 1984). More realistically, however, people may lack such self-control. Individuals may postpone executing certain decisions, saying, "I'll call the doctor tomorrow" or "I'll start dieting next week." This type of postponing of decisions may reflect hyperbolic discounting (O'Donoghue and Rabin 1999; Gruber and Köszegi 2001).

Even within the framework of rational forward-looking behavior, differences in time preference (e.g., Bickel, Odum, and Madden 1999; Khwaja, Silverman, and Sloan 2007), risk preference (e.g., Barsky, Juster, Kimball, et al. 1997), and willingness to pay for good health (Khwaja, Sloan, and Wang 2009) can potentially account for differences in consumer behavior. That this can be so is well understood conceptually by economists, but empirical evidence on these differences in preferences is incomplete. A further complication is that the differences in preferences we are able to observe may be context- or decision-specific.

Given the importance of decisions people make about their personal health and health care, health economics can provide a useful laboratory for studying consumer decision making. In the end, it may be that whether or not the assumption of rational and forward-looking behavior is empirically relevant depends on the specific decision being made. The assumption of rational and forward-looking decision making may be valid in some contexts and not in others.

17.2 INFORMATION, ASYMMETRIC INFORMATION, AND ITS EFFECTS

HOW PEOPLE OBTAIN INFORMATION

In an idealized perfectly competitive market, market participants possess perfect knowledge about the alternatives. A more nuanced insight is that information is not free, but rather comes at a cost. To the extent that information becomes more costly, people choose to be partially ignorant. Critical to the operation of competitive health care markets is that obtaining information about cost and quality and other attributes of various options is not too costly. There was a time, thankfully mostly in the past, when physicians were assumed to know everything and patients were assumed to know practically nothing. Societies relied on professional ethics to prevent patients from being duped.

In sharp contrast to the situation three or four decades ago, there is now widespread recognition that health care providers are not omniscient and patients are capable of learning. For a competitive market or even one that is not perfectly competitive to exist, consumers as patients must know quite a bit about their options, including the pros and cons of various options open to them. These options include choice of health plan (in countries with a choice) and providers, as well as choices made conditional on these choices being made. Since a lot of health is produced by the individual him- or herself, knowledge extends beyond health care to decisions about health behaviors that are not directly observable by health care providers.

We know comparatively little about the cost to consumers of obtaining health care information, how consumers process the information they obtain, and what the potential of programs aimed at improving consumer information about health and health care really is. Although they have much more basic information than consumers do, the same could be said of physicians and other health care providers. How do providers learn about the range of outcomes from various therapies and how the marginal products of specific therapies vary according to the characteristics of the individual patient, such as educational attainment and age?

Lack of adequate information and asymmetric information between patients and providers underlie many of the market failures in health care. Not surprisingly, economists and others have tended to view public policies that involve dissemination of information as necessarily welfare-improving. As a practical matter, however, the extent to which welfare is actually improved depends on the quality of the information and the process by which it is disseminated.

One approach in the United States has been to encourage dissemination of information on the performance of hospitals in the form of report cards (Gowrisankaran 2008). Report cards provide measures of the process of care or outcomes for a common set of conditions diagnosed and treated in hospitals. The problem is not with the concept but possibly with the details of implementation. When report cards are based on a few indicators, as is inevitable to a certain extent, providers have an incentive to game the system, that is, to perform well on the indicators that are measured, possibly at the cost of poorer performance on indicators that are not measured. When report cards are based on outcome measures, there is an incentive for hospitals to accept less severely ill patients for treatment, thus creating access barriers for more severely ill patients. Further, some hospitals are very small, so that sample sizes with respect to outcomes are too small to generate reliable measures of performance in the outcome domain.

For better or worse, patients may not rely much on report cards. They may not be sufficiently empowered to choose hospitals, given the important role of physicians in the referral decision, and consumers may also have information on dimensions of quality that are not monitored and hence are unreported. Moreover, the empirical evidence to date does not make a clear case that consumer welfare has been improved by report cards. In countries that place less reliance than the United States does on consumer decision making in health care, the role of information dissemination of any sort is quite limited.

When the choice of the hospital is left to the physician, there is a question of the information base used by physicians when making the hospital admission decision on behalf of patients. Until very recently, physicians were unlikely to have had access to any source of information even resembling report cards. The decision was made on the basis of impressions about quality of care or perhaps convenience to the patient and the patient's family, and in some cases, simply the convenience of the doctor him-or herself.

Similarly, when health plans, such as those in the United States, form networks of providers (see chapter 11), what is the information base on which they rely? And how do health plans update their beliefs about the quality of care offered by individual providers in their networks?

Very little is known about how health care decision makers update their beliefs in the health care context or in other contexts (see, e.g., Sacerdote 2001; Hanushek, Kain, Markman, et al. 2003; Argys and Rees 2008). Peers are a likely source of information on attributes of health care providers, the effects of various health behaviors, and choice of health plans, among other decisions. Currently we have insufficient information on peer networks, how they operate, and how information obtained through peer networks influences decisions about health care and health. Interesting studies have been conducted, such as a recent study of learning about the effects of deworming programs in Kenya (Kremer and Miguel 2007), but at present, lacking more direct information, researchers must make specific assumptions about how information is transmitted.

Lack of information is a reason why moral hazard and adverse selection exist. All insurers face exceptional hurdles in monitoring the benefits of use of covered services, given the patient-provider relationship, the importance of maintaining confidentiality, heterogeneity of patients and patients' illnesses, and professional norms. If health were perfectly observable and hence care regimens conditional on health changes perfectly contractible, moral hazard could not exist (see, e.g., Vera-Hernandez 2003). The insurer would have an exact measure of the insured individual's health and could determine whether or not a particular service was justified. Moral hazard exists because such precise information is unavailable. This gives the patient and provider some room in which to maneuver. With improvements in information technology, one should expect corresponding improvements in characterizing patient health and at the same time in measuring care that is provided in the health states thus characterized.

Adverse selection in health insurance markets arises because consumers possess private information that health insurers do not have. Based on his review of the evidence, Pauly (2008) concluded that concerns about adverse selection in health insurance markets have been overemphasized. He argued that when adverse selection occurs to any considerable extent, it is due to some type of regulation that requires insurers to ignore information that they have or could have obtained.

In other words, adverse selection arises not so much because insurers lack knowledge but because they are unable to obtain relevant information owing to regulations or social prohibitions against such information gathering. An example of adverse selection in employer groups was provided in chapter 10 in the example of Harvard University switching to a fixed contribution on behalf of employees. Empirical evidence on the relative importance of asymmetric information and limits on information acquisition by insurers is currently lacking.

Adverse selection in a variety of insurance markets has piqued the interest of economists who focus on microeconomics. One line of research has questioned whether or not the selection process is necessarily in the direction of adverse selection. Rather, sometimes the selection process may be reversed in the direction of "advantageous selection." For example, suppose that drivers who purchase more comprehensive automobile liability policies are risk averse not only when it comes to buying insurance but also in their driving behavior. Then persons who demand relatively complete coverage may be more careful, not less careful, drivers. That is, the selection of high-option insurance plans may be advantageous rather than adverse. Cohen and Einav (2007) examined whether risk aversion can serve as a source of advantageous selection counteracting the adverse selection based on ex post risk and found that the result goes in the opposite direction: more risk-averse drivers seem to have higher, not lower, accident risks.

Previous work on asymmetric information in automobile insurance markets, such as that by Chiappori and Salanie (2000), which treats private information as unidimensional—that is, people know they are risk averse while insurers do not know an individual's risk preferences—found no correlation between ex post risk (e.g., whether or not a person had an accident at some time after the insurance policy was purchased) and the nature of the contract (as measured by the completeness of insurance coverage), suggesting that there is no asymmetric information in such markets. However, others (e.g., Finkelstein and McGarry 2006) have speculated that private information may potentially occur in multiple dimensions, such as risk aversion, in the context of long-term care insurance purchasing decisions and a distaste for nursing home stays in the case of insurance coverage for nursing home care. People who really hate the thought of living in a nursing home may be both less likely to purchase comprehensive insurance coverage for nursing home care *and*, conditional on being insured for such care, less likely to enter a nursing home, which can be observed ex post by insurers after the person dies following an end-of-life illness that would have caused many of them to enter a nursing home.

17.3 INDUSTRIAL ORGANIZATION OF THE HEALTH CARE SECTOR

PRINCIPAL-AGENT ISSUES: PHYSICIANS

In health care as in many other sectors, health care, consumers, the principals, rely on others, the agents, for advice on consumption decisions. Often the agent stands to gain when there is a transaction. Car salespersons and mechanics and real estate agents are cases in point. An auto mechanic diagnoses a car problem and provides recommendation for action, where action typically involves the mechanic himself. Department store salespersons have a role in advising consumers about their options. In these cases, the agent has a self-interest that may run counter to the self-interest of the principal. These arrangements persist, perhaps because of widespread faith in the notion that market pressures from competition among agents will in the end force agents to act in the principals' interest. At least in the long run, if an agent mainly acts in his or her own interest without sufficient regard to the principal's interest, the agent will lose business to competitors who act in the principal's interest.

In the case of cars, there are alternative sources of information. Consumers can read publications that rate cars. And real estate offerings can be found in newspapers and on the Internet.

There are situations in which the relationship between the principal and the agent may be even more asymmetric than in the above examples. For example, if a person is charged with a felony and retains a lawyer, he or she can only hope that the lawyer is a good one and represents his or her interests. While the client can appeal to the state bar or perhaps ask for a retrial, the transactions cost of addressing failed representation can be substantial. Further, if a person is diagnosed with cancer, given the trauma of the diagnosis and often the immediate need for treatment, the principal can only hope that the agent will take his or her best interests to heart. Some but not all medical care falls into this category. Even if physician decision making is not fully motivated by financial self-interest, it may depend on adherence to practices learned from mentors or some other factor, with the result that care may not be fully in the patient's interest.

The method according to which physicians are paid is particularly important in situations in which the physician is empowered relative to patients. Countries have faced different choices in how physicians are paid. One method is a fixed salary per unit of time; another is fee-for-service practice. Still another is a combination of salary and fee-for-service (McGuire 2008). One common approach is to employ the physician in a clinic on a salaried basis but allow the physician to practice on a fee-for-service basis on the physician's own time. Still another approach is to pay physicians on a capitated (per patient) basis, as general practitioners in the UK are paid. With asymmetric information, the risk is that the physician will put forth too little effort when compensated on straight salary or on a capitated basis. And when paid on a piece rate basis, that is, fee for service, there is the risk of overprovision of services.

With some exceptions (e.g., Hickson, Altemeier, and Perrin 1987), carefully controlled studies of the effects of physician compensation on physicians' decisions about care are lacking. Given the importance of physician compensation policy in all countries, such studies merit a high priority.

Pay for Performance

Pay is only one type of reward for services provided. Other rewards take the form of professional pride, recognition, opportunities to do challenging work, regular hours of work, and supportive colleagues. In fact, the theory of compensating wage differentials argues that people are willing to be paid less for attributes of jobs that they value, such as vacation time or a pleasant work atmosphere, or require to be paid more for attributes they dislike, such as jobs with a high risk of injury on the job. In this sense, high nonfinancial rewards should substitute for pay. There is an argument that increased extrinsic rewards, such as higher financial rewards, may devalue intrinsic awards, such as the warm glow from doing good for others while on the job. This implies that physicians and other professionals may be willing to provide some services for altruistic reasons, but once an explicit price is attached to these services, their value is diminished to some extent.

A proposed alternative to attaching prices to units of service, as has been common practice for physician and hospital services, is to pay for performance, that is, to pay higher prices to reward better outcomes (see Golden and Sloan 2008 for a review of this literature). This raises the question of whether performance should be based on certain care processes being performed (e.g., whether certain medications are prescribed after a heart attack) or on outcomes of care (e.g., rates of survival or health indicators at a certain period after a heart attack. Physicians and hospitals may prefer to be paid for following a process rather than on outcome results on the grounds that they are risk averse and outcomes also depend in important ways on factors outside the provider's control. Moreover, there are questions about the validity and reliability of specific outcome indicators as measures of performance. In the end, health care is heterogeneous. Pay for performance may provide a better fit for some types of services than for others, such as for services for which health outcomes are easily monitored.

There is some empirical research on pay-for-performance systems (see, e.g., Rosenthal and Frank 2006 for health care and Jensen and Murphy 1990 and Hall and Liebman 1998 for evidence from other industries). This important research is still in its infancy.

Competition among Hospitals

Likewise, there is still much to be learned about how hospitals compete when they are able to compete. Important issues about hospital competition include the impact of such competition on quality of care and on prices. That greater competition in a market leads to higher quality or a greater variety of goods or services in general cannot be deduced from economic theory alone. Rather, this is an issue to be settled empirically. A case can be made that competition among hospitals raises or lowers the quality of care. If competition does not take place on price, hospitals may boost quality in order to attract patients. However, if consumers or physicians acting in their role of agents are unable to assess the quality of a hospital accurately, hospitals may cut corners so that they can offer care at a lower price and still remain profitable.

Not only do we not know that competition raises the quality of hospital care, if in fact it does, but also we do not know how these changes compare to the normative benchmark of socially optimal care. In other words, it is possible that competition among sellers of health care services raises quality, but quality may be increased to a level above that at which marginal social benefit equals marginal social cost.

A major insight of economics is that higher quality is not always better from the standpoint of social welfare. It can be too high as well as too low. Hospitals often justify mergers with other hospitals on the basis of efficiencies, including the consolidation of services that may be realized as a result of the merger. Yet these efficiencies remain to be documented empirically.

Empirical studies of industrial organization of health care have been largely confined to the United States. Studies are needed in other countries, including middle-income and low-income countries. We have discussed public and private provision of services in chapters 11–13. Head-to-head cross-country comparisons of performance in various countries that organize health services differently are difficult to make; these comparisons have been done mainly between the United States and Canada (e.g., Mark, Naylor, Hlatky, et al. 1994).

17.4 Competition versus Public Regulation versus Public Ownership in Health Care

Countries face choices about public versus private ownership and, within private ownership, between for-profit and private not-for-profit organizational forms (see chapters 6 and 11–13). When ownership is private, there is a policy question about both the types of public regulation that are appropriate and the allocation of resources to regulatory oversight and enforcement of the regulated private entities. Most often regulatory rules are implemented with the implicit assumption that the rules themselves will automatically fix the problem that regulation addresses, be it pricing, the solvency of the regulated organization, or the quantity or quality of services provided.

In countries that rely on private financing or the private provision of services, there has been a substantial amount of regulation in health care markets, in the United States beginning in the twentieth century, with a rapid acceleration in such regulation following World War II. Regulations cover market entry (e.g., physician licensure, hospital health planning, certificate of need), pricing (regulation of hospital and pharmaceutical prices, regulation of insurance premiums), product offerings (e.g., requirements that private insurers cover certain types of health care services, including parity for mental and physical health), and activities of not-for-profit providers (e.g., requirements that not-for-profit hospitals offer certain unprofitable services as a payback for the tax exemptions that they have). In various chapters of this book, we have stressed the potential importance of regulations on choices that are made, such as the effect of price controls on pharmaceutical manufacturers' decisions to invest in R&D on a new product.

The pendulum against regulation may well swing in the opposite direction in the future. This appears to be happening in financial markets, and this trend may well spread to health care. Especially to the extent that these changes occur, it will be important to model the regulatory decision-making process and document empirically how regulatory decisions affect outcomes. Further, there is substantial heterogeneity among countries in the contexts in which specific regulatory policies are adopted, the specific features of the regulatory process, and the effects of such policies on outcomes. There is more, for example, for experts in the United States to learn about how hospital entry regulation operates in practice in countries that view capital budgeting as a collective choice (i.e., the state has a capital budget) versus a system like that in the United States, where the state health planning authorities do not have a budget but rather view each certificate-of-need application largely on an individual basis.

In addition, although the correlation is not perfect, in general, health care provision becomes more private as countries attain higher levels of per capita income. While there are some benefits to privatization, there are likely to be some costs as well. Important research on outcomes before and after privatization of health care providers remains to be conducted.

17.5 Clinical Decision Making

There is an important distinction between positive and normative economics. Positive economics studies the behavioral responses of various actors in a market. Rather than focus on what is, normative economics prescribes what should be. Most of this book has been devoted to positive economics. For example, the emphasis has been on how the market for physicians' services operates in practice rather than on how it should work. In this sense, we have focused on gaining a better understanding of physician decision making rather than recommending how physicians might make better decisions. Important exceptions to this generality are chapters 14 and 15, which discuss cost-effectiveness and cost-benefit analysis.

Many health economists are employed in a subfield called *pharmacoeconomics*. Practitioners in this field conduct cost-effectiveness analysis of pharmaceuticals and other health care technologies.

While there are some important methodological innovations, most cost-effectiveness analysis applies existing techniques. There remain important unresolved issues. First, cost-effectiveness analysis remains dominant because of a general reluctance to quantify health care benefits in monetary terms. Yet in deciding how much to allocate to a particular product, quantifying in monetary terms is implicit. For example, even if a technology is described in terms of dollars per life years saved, in deciding how much to spend on the technology, someone must decide what a life year saved is actually worth.

In an important sense, physicians' and public policy makers' reluctance to place a dollar value on a life year saved, a QALY (see chapter 14), or other types of health outcomes is understandable, given the limits of existing methodologies for quantifying health benefits in monetary terms. This is especially true in light of the types of cognitive biases described in chapter 2 and earlier in this chapter. Refinement of techniques for eliciting individuals' maximum willingness to pay for particular health benefits should be a high priority. Given cognitive biases, there is also a question about whose preferences to quantify. Suppose the issue is willingness to pay for a treatment for a specific disease. Can people who have never experienced the disease accurately assign a value of the utility gain from treatment?

Another set of issues relates to how physicians made decisions about patient care. There is substantial variation in treatment patterns in a country like the United States (see, e.g., Fowler, Gallagher, Anthony, et al. 2008; Zuckerman, Waidmann, Berenson, et al. 2010), and in other countries as well (see, e.g., Magan, Otero, Alberquilla, et al. 2008). But except for describing such variation, there is currently a lack of understanding about why such variation exists. For example, why do cesarean section rates differ so markedly within countries and across countries? Certainly, biological factors alone cannot explain this difference. Presumably the preferences of pregnant women affect the choice of mode of obstetric delivery in part, but it seems likely that a major part of the decision reflects what the physician recommends. What is needed is more empirical analysis of the physician decision-making process. While health economists have something to contribute to this area of inquiry, experts in many other fields have an important role to play as well.

17.6 FINAL WORD

This book has covered a lot of territory. Before you began this journey, you may have thought that health economics is a narrow topic, and many scholars with postgraduate degrees share this opinion. In reality, the field is incredibly broad, spanning many parts of the health sector as well as drawing on many other disciplines—medicine, law, corporate finance—and many subfields of economics, such as industrial organization, public economics, labor economics, econometrics, and risk, uncertainty, and insurance. Further, although health economics is seen as a field in applied microeconomics, as discussed in chapter 16, health economics also relates to the macroeconomy, and to economic development and growth.

For some readers, this will be the last course in health economics specifically, but you may take courses in other economic fields that relate to topics in health economics or use similar analytic methods. Some readers will graduate and enter a health profession. Others will graduate and enter some other field, but as individual household members or citizen voters will face decisions involving the allocation of resources to health care. Hopefully, a few readers will decide to become health economists. Whatever your future, we hope that this book has provided relevant and useful material, and that you will regard this experience as a beginning in a lifelong interest in some aspect of what this book has discussed.

KEY CONCEPTS

- rationality
- cognitive limitations
- self-control
- asymmetric information
- principal-agent issue
- extrinsic rewards
- public ownership
- positive economics
- pharmacoeconomics
- forward-looking behavior
- bounded rationality
- hyperbolic discounting
- advantageous selection
- pay for performance
- intrinsic rewards
- public regulation
- normative economics
- variation in treatment patterns

REVIEW AND DISCUSSION QUESTIONS

17.1 What is "bounded rationality"? Using smoking behavior as example, explain how the concept of the bounded rationality answers the question of "why people continue to smoke although they have full information on the adverse consequence of cigarette smoking on health."

17.2 What do we mean when we say that "people may lack self control"? Is this argument consistent with the assumption of rational choice? Governments around the world have adopted public policies to control tobacco consumption, including information provision, restricting smoking in public places, and imposing exercise taxes on tobacco products. If people lack self-control, what is the most effective policy for tobacco control?

17.3 What is advantageous selection? List three examples of advantageous selection in the real world.

17.4 Explain the distinction between fee for service and pay for performance in health care markets. Which payment system is in a better position to incentivize the provision of higher-quality health care? Justify your answer.

17.5 Distinguish between positive economics and normative economics. Using inequality in health (as measured by life expectancy at birth) within a country as an example, list three research questions that can be answered by positive economics and another three research questions that can be answered by normative economics.

17.6 Compare the approaches of "market competition" and "public regulation" to promote quality of hospital care in a health system in which private hospitals dominate the market. Is there any precondition under which market competition is in a better position to achieve a higher quality of hospital care level than public regulation does? Explain your answer

17.7 What are "principal-agent issues" in health care markets? Give three examples from health care markets. Principal-agent issues prevail not only in health care markets; they exist in other markets, too. List three examples of principal-agent issues in other markets.

Supplemental Readings

Fowler, F. J., P. M. Gallagher, D. L. Anthony, et al. 2008. Relationship between Regional Per Capita Medicare Expenditures and Patient Perceptions of Quality of Care. *Journal of the American Medical Association* 299 (20): 2406–2412.

Gowrisankaran, G. 2008. Competition, Information Provision, and Hospital Quality. In *Incentives and Choice in Health Care*, ed. F. A. Sloan and H. Kasper, 319–352. Cambridge, MA: MIT Press.

Kremer, M., and E. Miguel. 2007. The Illusion of Sustainability. *Quarterly Journal of Economics* 112 (3): 1007–1065.

Magan, P., A. Otero, A. Alberquilla, et al. 2008. Geographic Variations in Avoidable Hospitalizations in the Elderly, in a Health System with Universal Coverage. *BMC Health Services Research* 8 (42): 48–52.

McGuire, T. G. 2008. Physician Fees and Behavior: Implications for Structuring a Fee Schedule. In *Incentives and Choice in Health Care*, ed. F. A. Sloan and H. Kasper, 263–288. Cambridge, MA: MIT Press.

Zuckerman, S., T. Waidmann, R. Berenson, et al. 2010. Clarifying Sources of Geographic Differences in Medicare Spending. *New England Journal of Medicine* 363 (1): 54–62.

References

Ameriks, J., A. Caplin, and J. Leahy. 2003. Wealth Accumulation and the Propensity to Plan. *Quarterly Journal of Economics* 118 (3): 1007–1047.

Argys, L. M., and D. I. Rees. 2008. Searching for Peer Group Effects: A Test of the Contagion Hypothesis. *Review of Economics and Statistics* 90 (3): 442–458.

Barsky, R. B., F. T. Juster, M. S. Kimball, et al. 1997. Preference Parameters and Behavioral Heterogeneity: An Experimental Approach in the Health and Retirement Study. *Quarterly Journal of Economics* 112 (2): 537–579.

Bickel, W. K., A. L. Odum, and G. J. Madden. 1999. Impulsivity and Cigarette Smoking: Delay Discounting in Current, Never, and Ex-Smokers. *Psychopharmacology* 146 (4): 447–454.

Chiappori, P. A., and B. Salanie. 2000. Testing for Asymmetric Information in Insurance Markets. *Journal of Political Economy* 108 (1): 56–78.

Cohen, A., and L. Einav. 2007. Estimating Risk Preferences from Deductible Choice. *American Economic Review* 97 (3): 745–788.

Finkelstein, A., and K. McGarry. 2006. Multiple Dimensions of Private Information: Evidence from the Long-Term Care Insurance Market. *American Economic Review* 96 (4):9 38–958.

Fowler, F. J., P. M. Gallagher, D. L. Anthony, et al. 2008. Relationship between Regional Per Capita Medicare Expenditures and Patient Perceptions of Quality of Care. *Journal of the American Medical Association* 299 (20): 2406–2412.

Frank, R. G. 2006. Behavioral Economics and Health Economics. In *Economic Institutions and Behavioral Economics*, ed. P. A. Diamond and H. Vartianinen. Princeton, NJ: Princeton University Press.

Golden, B. R., and F. A. Sloan. 2008. Physician Pay for Performance: Alternative Perspectives. In *Incentives and Choice in Health Care*, ed. F. A. Sloan and H. Kasper, 289–317. Cambridge, MA: MIT Press.

Gowrisankaran, G. 2008. Competition, Information Provision, and Hospital Quality. In *Incentives and Choice in Health Care*, ed. F. A. Sloan and H. Kasper, 319–352. Cambridge, MA: MIT Press.

Gruber, J., and B. Köszegi. 2001. Is Addiction "Rational"? Theory and Evidence. *Quarterly Journal of Economics* 116 (4): 1261–1303.

Hall, R. E., and J. B. Liebman. 1998. Are CEOs Really Paid Like Bureaucrats? *Quarterly Journal of Economics* 113 (3): 653–691.

Hanushek, E. A., J. F. Kain, J. M. Markman, et al. 2003. Does Peer Ability Affect Student Achievement? *Journal of Applied Econometrics* 18 (5): 527–544.

Hickson, G. B., W. A. Altemeier, and J. M. Perrin. 1987. Physician Reimbursement by Salary or Fee-for-Service: Effect on Physician Practice Behavior in a Randomized Prospective Study. *Pediatrics* 80 (3): 344–350.

Jensen, M. C., and K. M. Murphy. 1990. Performance Pay and Top-Management Incentives. *Journal of Political Economy* 98 (2): 225–264.

Khwaja, A., D. Silverman, and F. Sloan. 2007. Time Preference, Time Discounting, and Smoking Decisions. *Journal of Health Economics* 26 (5): 927–949.

Khwaja, A., F. A. Sloan, and Y. Wang. 2009. Do Smokers Value their Health and Longevity Less? *Journal of Law & Economics* 51 (1): 171–196.

Kremer, M., and E. Miguel. 2007. The Illusion of Sustainability. *Quarterly Journal of Economics* 112 (3): 1007–1065.

Magan, P., A. Otero, A. Alberquilla, et al. 2008. Geographic Variations in Avoidable Hospitalizations in the Elderly, in a Health System with Universal Coverage. *BMC Health Services Research* 8 (42): 48–52.

Mark, D. B., C. D. Naylor, M. A. Hlatky, et al. 1994. Use of Medical Resources and Quality of Life after Acute Myocardial Infarction in Canada and the United States. *New England Journal of Medicine* 331 (17): 1130–1135.

McGuire, T. G. 2008. Physician Fees and Behavior: Implications for Structuring a Fee Schedule. In *Incentives and Choice in Health Care*, ed. F. A. Sloan and H. Kasper, 263–288. Cambridge, MA: MIT Press.

O'Donoghue, T., and M. Rabin. 1999. Doing It Now or Later. *American Economic Review* 89 (1): 194–199.

Pauly, M. 2008. On the Role of Language in Social Choice Theory. *Synthese* 163 (2): 227–243.

Rosenthal, M. B., and R. G. Frank. 2006. What Is the Empirical Basis for Paying for Quality in Health Care? *Medical Care Research and Review* 63 (2): 135–157.

Sacerdote, B. 2001. Peer Effects with Random Assignment: Results for Dartmouth Roommates. *Quarterly Journal of Economics* 116 (2): 681–704.

Schelling, T. C. 1984. Self-Command in Practice, in Policy, and in a Theory of Rational Choice. *American Economic Review* 74 (2): 1–11.

Thaler, R. H. 1980. Toward a Positive Theory of Consumer Choice. *Journal of Economic Behavior & Organization* 1 (1):39–60.

Thaler, R. H., and S. Benartzi. 2004. Save More Tomorrow (TM): Using Behavioral Economics to Increase Employee Saving. *Journal of Political Economy* 112 (S1): S164–S187.

Tversky, A., and D. Kahneman. 1974. Judgment under Uncertainty: Heuristics and Biases. *Science* 185 (4157): 1124–1131.

Tversky, A., and D. Kahneman. 1981. The Framing of Decisions and the Psychology of Choice. *Science* 211 (4481): 453–458.

Vera-Hernandez, M. 2003. Structural Estimation of a Principal-Agent Model: Moral Hazard in Medical Insurance. *Rand Journal of Economics* 34 (4): 670–693.

Zuckerman, S., T. Waidmann, R. Berenson, et al. 2010. Clarifying Sources of Geographic Differences in Medicare Spending. *New England Journal of Medicine* 363 (1): 54–62.

INDEX